HANDBOOK OF
MULTICULTURAL
COUNSELING

THIRD EDITION

The editors and contributing authors of this third edition of the *Handbook of Multicultural Counseling* dedicate their efforts to the 12 pioneers and elders whose respective life stories open Part I of this volume.

Eduardo Duran

Carolyn G. Barcus

Rosie Phillips Bingham

Joseph L. White

Patricia Arredondo

Amado M. Padilla

Richard M. Suinn

Mary A. Fukuyama

Susan L. Morrow

Rhoda Olkin

Allen E. Ivey

Michelle Fine

You have devoted a significant portion of your professional and personal lives to serving others—to healing, teaching, mentoring, and caring in some way for culturally diverse people. You have courage, vision, and strength, and because of your career-long contributions, you have helped shape the status of counseling and psychology worldwide; you have helped push the profession to its ethical imperative of serving all people and advocating for those with less. You are our wisdom bearers and role models. We, the 100+ contributors to this *Handbook,* are honored that your voices, your life stories, open this volume. As noted by Eduardo Duran in Chapter 1, we are all connected by seven generations passed on, and seven generations yet to come. Through your life work, you have honored your personal and professional ancestors, and your voices will guide seven generations of counselors and psychologists yet to come. Thank you!

HANDBOOK OF
MULTICULTURAL
COUNSELING
THIRD EDITION

EDITORS

JOSEPH G. PONTEROTTO
Fordham University

J. MANUEL CASAS
University of California, Santa Barbara

LISA A. SUZUKI
New York University

CHARLENE M. ALEXANDER
Ball State University

Los Angeles | London | New Delhi
Singapore | Washington DC

For information:

SAGE Publications, Inc.
2455 Teller Road
Thousand Oaks, California 91320
E-mail: order@sagepub.com

SAGE Publications Ltd.
1 Oliver's Yard
55 City Road
London EC1Y 1SP
United Kingdom

SAGE Publications India Pvt. Ltd.
B 1/I 1 Mohan Cooperative Industrial Area
Mathura Road, New Delhi 110 044
India

SAGE Publications Asia-Pacific Pte. Ltd.
33 Pekin Street #02-01
Far East Square
Singapore 048763

Printed in the United States of America

Library of Congress Cataloging-in-Publication Data

Handbook of multicultural counseling / editors, Joseph G. Ponterotto ... [et al.]. — 3rd ed.
    p. cm.
Includes bibliographical references and index.
ISBN 978-1-4129-6431-9 (cloth)
ISBN 978-1-4129-6432-6 (pbk.)
   1. Cross-cultural counseling. 2. Multiculturalism—United States. 3. Minorities—Counseling of—United States.
I. Ponterotto, Joseph G.
BF636.7.C76H36 2010
158′.3—dc22   2009017679

This book is printed on acid-free paper.

10 11 12 13   10 9 8 7 6 5 4 3 2

Acquisitions Editor:	Kassie Graves
Editorial Assistant:	Veronica K. Novak
Production Editor:	Astrid Virding
Copy Editors:	Liann Lech and Gillian Dickens
Typesetter:	C&M Digitals (P) Ltd.
Proofreader:	Joyce Li
Indexer:	William Ragsdale
Cover Designer:	Janet Kiesel
Marketing Manager:	Stephanie Adams

Contents

II. ETHICS IN MULTICULTURAL COUNSELING   125

III. EMERGING AND INTERNATIONAL ISSUES IN MULTICULTURAL COUNSELING   163

IV. RACIAL, ETHNIC, AND GAY/LESBIAN/BISEXUAL IDENTITY DEVELOPMENT: UPDATES ON THEORY, MEASUREMENT, AND COUNSELING IMPLICATIONS   213

Preface

We feel pleased and honored to present this third edition of the *Handbook of Multicultural Counseling*. The field of multicultural counseling is growing rapidly, and to keep pace with these changes, we have completely revised and expanded this newest edition. The previous editions of this *Handbook* have been highly praised and often cited, and we believe this new edition presents an up-to-date and comprehensive overview of the field. Our goal in this third edition parallels the goals of the first two editions, and that is to provide a thorough summary of the field's latest developments while also providing a vision as to the future of the field.

Significant changes in this third edition are as follows:

1. We have expanded the book from 40 chapters in the second edition to 57 chapters in this new edition. The expanded coverage was necessary given the rapid development and growth of the field of multicultural counseling.

2. More than 100 chapter co-authors, representing both seasoned, world-renowned scholars and practitioners as well as new, cutting-edge minds, have contributed their thoughts, ideas, and experiences to the contents of this new edition. Without question, this *Handbook* is the world's most comprehensive singular resource on multicultural counseling theory, ethics, research, and practice.

3. This new edition presents either totally new or markedly expanded coverage in the following topical areas: ethics in multicultural practice and research; the growth of international issues in multicultural counseling; theories, research, and measures of racial and ethnic identity and acculturation; research methods and procedures for multicultural counseling, including qualitative and mixed methods designs; spiritual and religious issues in counseling; multicultural health counseling; social justice issues and exemplars for the profession; multicultural assessment practices across the lifespan; and career development and counseling across the lifespan.

4. In fact, the only section of this new *Handbook* that resembles the second edition is Part I on life stories of eminent, visionary pioneers in the field. In this edition, 12 new pioneers or elders have honored us with their very personal life stories. The pioneers were nominated by professionals in the field, including many of the authors of the three editions of this *Handbook*.

As with the first two editions of the *Handbook*, the contributing authors represent a broad spectrum of the profession in terms of national origin and geographic locale, race, ethnicity, age, sexual orientation, religion, gender, current ability-disability status, body size and type, and employment emphasis. Represented among the authors are visionary, trend-setting scholars; master practitioners in a variety of clinical and counseling settings; experienced supervisors; administrators; and social justice advocates and change agents.

Furthermore, as with the first two editions, all royalties from the sale of this new edition will be alternately donated to the organizing committees of the Winter Roundtable on Multicultural Psychology and Education held annually at Teachers College, Columbia University on the East Coast, and the American Psychological Association–sponsored biannual Multicultural Conference and Summit, usually held in the western part of the United States. The intent of the royalty distribution is to support student involvement in the conferences in whatever way deemed most appropriate by the conference organizers.

BOOK CONTENTS

This edition of the *Handbook of Multicultural Counseling* is organized into 11 parts. Part I presents brief life stories of 12 pioneers who have had a significant impact on the development of the multicultural counseling field. As in the second edition, the pioneers are diverse in terms of gender, race, ethnicity, sexual orientation, religion, and other personal variables, including the experience of having a physical disability. The 12 pioneers honored in this edition are Eduardo Duran, Carolyn G. Barcus, Rosie Phillips Bingham, Joseph L. White, Patricia Arredondo, Amado M. Padilla, Richard M. Suinn, Mary A. Fukuyama, Susan L. Morrow, Rhoda Olkin, Allen E. Ivey, and Michelle Fine. Rosie Bingham's life story includes an added poem of appreciation by a graduate student, Gloria Wong, that was read aloud at a recent APA Multicultural Summit (Seattle, 2007). Finally, Joseph G. Ponterotto summarizes the life stories in this section's final chapter.

Part II contains two lengthy and comprehensive chapters focused on ethical issues in multicultural counseling practice and research. Two pioneers and giants in the field, so honored in the second edition of this *Handbook*, Melba J. T. Vasquez and Joseph E. Trimble, provide the material for this critical section of the *Handbook*. Drawing on their combined 60+ years of experience in the field of multicultural counseling and psychology, Drs. Vasquez and Trimble provide state-of-the-art commentary and guidelines on ethically vigilant practice and research.

In recent years, increased attention has been paid to the intersection of counseling psychology with positive psychology, as well as to the interface of multicultural counseling in North America and counseling issues internationally. Part III consists of four chapters addressing salient and emerging issues in this area. Leading multicultural and positive psychologists Jennifer Teramoto Pedrotti and Lisa M. Edwards discuss the intersection of positive psychology and multicultural counseling, while two teams of authors, Stefanía Ægisdóttir and Lawrence H. Gerstein, and J. Manuel Casas, Yong S. Park, and Brian Cho, discuss the relationship between multicultural and international

counseling. Finally, Ellen Short and colleagues address the latest practical and research developments in counseling immigrants and refugees.

Part IV of the *Handbook* revisits a critical section of the first edition on updates in theory, research, and measurement of racial and ethnic identity development. This section contains eight chapters summarizing recent developments in the area of Native American and Alaska Native identity development (Andrea L. Dixon and Tarrell Awe Agahe Portman); African and Afro-Caribbean identity development (Tina Q. Richardson and colleagues); Latina/o identity development (Marie L. Miville); Asian American identity development (Mark H. Chae and Christopher Larres); Native Hawaiian identity development (Laurie D. McCubbin and Thu A. Dang); White racial identity development (Lisa B. Spanierman and Jason R. Soble); multiracial identity development (SooJean Choi-Misailidis); and counseling and identity issues relevant to lesbian, gay, bisexual, and transgender individuals (Leo Wilton).

The construct of acculturation has always been a central focus in multicultural counseling with many theoretical variations and measurement/assessment tools. Part V of the *Handbook* consists of two substantive chapters summarizing theory, research, and the measurement of acculturation (Lourdes M. Rivera), as well as how issues and levels of acculturation are actually realized in day-to-day counseling practice (Eric L. Kohatsu and colleagues).

Part VI of this new edition presents six chapters on research issues in multicultural counseling. This section opens with an archival qualitative study of the rewards and challenges that go hand-in-hand with a career in multicultural counseling research (Joseph G. Ponterotto). Subsequent chapters address designing quantitative research (Germine H. Awad and Kevin O. Cokley), issues of language and translation in psychological tests (Kwong-Liem Karl Kwan and colleagues), the design and interpretation of qualitative research (Heather Z. Lyons and Denise H. Bike), the use of mixed methods research (Vicki L. Plano Clark and Sherry C. Wang), and the empirical assessment of culturally congruent practices in multicultural counseling and psychotherapy (Timothy B. Smith).

Part VII of the *Handbook* encompasses four chapters on spiritual and religious issues in counseling. Lewis Z. Schlosser and colleagues open the section with a comprehensive content analysis evaluating the inclusion of religion in counseling psychology research. Next, Muninder K. Ahluwalia and Noreen K. Zaman discuss counseling issues related to working with Muslims and Sikhs in a post-9/11 society. John J. Cecero discusses practical spiritual exercises in counseling and therapy, and John Huang's chapter closes this section by discussing counseling approaches consonant with clients practicing Eastern religions and spiritualities.

In Part VIII, authors examine the interface of physical health and mental health across diverse populations. Carolyn M. Tucker and her colleagues present innovative and integrative work on customized multicultural health counseling focused on racial and ethnic diversity. Merle A. Keitel and colleagues focus their work on women's issues in health counseling, with a particular focus on issues around fertility. Finally, Eric C. Chen and his colleagues present a developmental-contextual minority stress model to guide work with lesbian, gay, and bisexual clients.

In recent years, an important emphasis in the counseling profession has been its commitment to issues of social justice and advocacy for disempowered and oppressed groups. In Part IX of the *Handbook,* five teams of social justice specialists present innovative positions, programs, and strategies for addressing social justice in the field. Alan W. Burkard and colleagues open the section by highlighting the social justice imperative of ensuring educational achievement for diverse racial and ethnic minority students. Roger L. Worthington and colleagues extend this focus to young adults on college campuses, highlighting how counselors can work as diversity change agents. Staying with a focus on the college campus, Charlene Alexander and her team of colleagues and students describe two innovative programs and consultations on their campus in the Midwest. Two renowned scholars whose names historically go hand-in-hand with topics of social justice are Michael D'Andrea and Judy Daniels, and they present a case study and theoretical model for social justice originating in their university advocacy. Finally, Rebecca L. Toporek and colleagues share their experiences in a valuable university-community collaborative engagement project.

Part X of the *Handbook* focuses on recent developments in assessment and counseling across the lifespan. Jennie Park-Taylor and colleagues open the section with a discussion on diagnostic and assessment considerations in working with ethnic-racial minority children.

Christine J. Yeh and Kwong-Liem Karl Kwan highlight the latest advances in multicultural assessment with adolescents, and they examine the topic in depth within an ecological and social justice perspective. Focusing on adults, Alex L. Pieterse and Matthew J. Miller review major developments in multicultural assessment with a focus on issues of acculturation, racial/cultural stressors, and the multicultural personality. Moving to older adults, Luis A. Vázquez and colleagues present a poignant look at psychological challenges and assessment strategies for counseling this underserved and growing population. Finally, George V. Gushue and colleagues introduce the reader to cutting-edge, postmodern models of multicultural family counseling.

This third edition *Handbook* closes with a five-chapter section on multicultural career counseling and development. Robert W. Lent and Hung-Bin Sheu open the section with a look at the utility and validity of applying social cognitive career theory across cultures. Next, Nadya A. Fouad and Neeta Kantamneni look at the validity of John Holland's popular career theory for multicultural populations. Focusing on proven practical applications, Margo A. Jackson and colleagues take a close look at salient career counseling interventions for adolescents vulnerable to discrimination. Mark Pope looks at practical issues of career counseling with culturally diverse adults, and V. Scott Solberg and Judith M. Ettinger end the section, and close out the *Handbook,* with a critical discussion of career development interventions for culturally diverse older adults without the option of retiring.

This new *Handbook* is by far our most comprehensive edition, covering in great depth and breadth multicultural ethics, history, theory, research, and practical assessment and counseling. This text provides a thorough snapshot of the field as it is today, and also presents a vision as to how the field of multicultural counseling is evolving and developing. We feel honored to present this new edition to you, and we are proud of the work of all of the contributing authors who made this cutting-edge edition possible.

Joseph G. Ponterotto

J. Manuel Casas

Lisa A. Suzuki

Charlene M. Alexander

New York City

Acknowledgments

This third edition of the *Handbook of Multicultural Counseling* represents the culmination of three years of collaborative work among 115 scholars dispersed throughout the United States (and internationally). The editors acknowledge and sincerely thank these contributing authors who worked diligently to produce 57 state-of-the-art chapters that, we believe, set a world standard for multicultural counseling scholarship. These authors contributed their efforts and donated their valuable and limited time without any financial remuneration; they contributed because of their commitment to the profession, to their mentees and students, and to the cause of social justice and improved mental health services for all people. Thank you!

We want to thank the highly professional Sage Publications team that has worked with us throughout the multiple editions of this classic text. Among the Sage visionary editors who, over time, have contributed to *Handbook* development and production are Marquita Flemming (1993–1995), Jim Nageotte (1995–1999), Nancy Hale (1999–2001), and Kassie Graves (2006–2009). Loyal and always friendly Sage staff who worked on this new edition along with Kassie are Veronica Novak, Astrid Virding, Carmel Schrire, Helen Salmon, Candice Harman, Janet Kiesel, and copy editors Liann Lech and Gillian Dickens. Thank you! It is always such a pleasure to work with the Sage team.

We are each deeply indebted to our families and friends, whose love, emotional support, guidance, and laughter provide a springboard for our professional work. With gratitude, we also acknowledge the collegial support emanating from our home institutions, Fordham University, the University of California at Santa Barbara, New York University, and Ball State University. The enthusiasm and anticipation that our work colleagues have for the *Handbook* is a motivating force to produce our best editing work.

Finally, the *Handbook* editors gratefully acknowledge permission to quote or reprint material from the following sources:

American Counseling Association
Journal of Vocational Behavior

PART I

Honoring Our Elders: Life Stories of Pioneers in Multicultural Counseling and Psychology

This *Handbook* opens with the voices of 12 historic figures in multicultural counseling and psychology. The life stories you are about to read are poignant and deeply personal. The 12 pioneers honored in this section are diverse of life experiences, professional focus, religion, race, ethnicity, sexual orientation, and physical abilities, among other demographic and personal variables. Yet all of these individuals also have an important life task in common: a commitment to diversity, justice, fighting oppression in its many forms, political advocacy, teaching and mentoring students and young professionals, and helping others through counseling and psychotherapy and through culturally indigenous healing ways. Furthermore, each is an internationally renowned scholar whose writing and research has raised the status of counseling and psychology to new heights.

We learned in the second edition of this *Handbook*, where we first presented life stories of eminent multicultural psychologists, that the personal stories deeply affected thousands of readers worldwide—it was as if readers were being indirectly mentored by the voices of our wisdom-bearers, our elders. Readers of all ages and professional experience levels, and of all racial and ethnic backgrounds, resonated with parts of the stories. Through some level of identification with the struggles and/or rewards of the life work of these pioneers, readers felt empowered, validated, and motivated to continue their training and work in multicultural counseling. So, too, will the current set of distinguished life stories affect readers of this new edition.

The 12 pioneers honored in this third edition of the *Handbook* are Eduardo Duran, Carolyn G. Barcus, Rosie Phillips Bingham, Joseph L. White, Patricia Arredondo, Amado M. Padilla, Richard M. Suinn, Mary A. Fukuyama, Susan L. Morrow, Rhoda Olkin, Allen E. Ivey, and Michelle Fine. Each life story is rather unique in its contents and mode of presentation. Most of the mini-autobiographies are told in first-person, vivid, self-revealing prose. Qualitative researchers use the term *thick description* (Ponterotto, 2006) to describe writing that is so fluid, vivid, and contextualized that the reader is transported back in time as if he or she were present and witnessing the life story as it unfolded (verisimilitude). And so, you will witness, through the life stories of our elders, roughly half a century of the history of the multicultural counseling field. Some pioneers' life stories will resonate with you more

1

than others, depending on your own life experiences and professional goals. Hopefully, the collective set of stories will stimulate self-reflection among readers and can be used as stimulus for discussion in counseling education and supervision.

In addition to the 12 life stories, a graduate student, Gloria Wong, presents a poem in honor of Dr. Rosie Bingham. Gloria's voice provides an example of the profound personal and professional impact that our pioneers have on younger generations of counselors.

Part I ends with a chapter by Joseph G. Ponterotto that attempts to provide some integration of the multiple life stories.

REFERENCE

Ponterotto, J. G. (2006). Brief note on the origins, evolution, and meaning of the qualitative research concept "thick description." *Qualitative Report, 11,* 538–549.

1

Psychology as the Study of Soul's Dream

EDUARDO DURAN

There is always a dream dreaming us.

—Kalahari saying

It came as a surprise when the editors of this book approached me and asked me to write as a "pioneer" in the field of psychology. There were a couple of associations that arose as thoughts. One was that this implied being an elder, which, in Native life worlds, one is not an elder until about age 80. The other thought had to do with the word *pioneer,* which is a very loaded word in Indian country because pioneers were instrumental in the removal of the Native life world. Fortunately, after speaking with the chief editor and reading some of the stories that the other pioneers of psychology wrote in previous editions, I began to feel as if perhaps my life narrative may be of help to some of the people who read this.

Dreams have always had an important part in my life, and even as a youngster, dreams had a way of materializing and actually being a bit frightening.

Growing up in the mountains of northern New Mexico as a "mixed blood" made it necessary to live in at least two cultures simultaneously. Perhaps the mixed DNA would contribute to my later and present work, in which the meaning of culture has held a key place in the work that I do. Not being part of the mainstream of any stream provided me with the frustration that has provided the seeds that have grown into the theoretical and clinical work that I do and write about.

CHAOS AND DREAM

Growing up in a chaotic and dysfunctional family system where alcohol and violence were common both in the nuclear family as well as in the community provided fertile ground for transformation. I was fortunate to have spent extended periods of time with my grandparents, where the transformation had already occurred. During these times, I would listen to my grandfather, who had virtually no education, discuss deep subjects with other elders. These subjects had deep philosophical and spiritual meaning, and I would sit in the corner and be fascinated by their discussions on the nature of the universe, God, Devil, and other light topics.

I returned to my family of six siblings after these visits and felt as if I didn't belong in the chaos that surrounded me; I found myself fascinated as to the meaning of this and other realities. Dreams were always there, although a system for understanding the dreams was not available except through some understanding from a fundamentalist Christian group that had become part of the extended family. Most of their interpretations of my realities were judgmental and guilt based, which discouraged me from discussing much with anyone.

During the time that high school was to begin in my life, my family decided to move to California in search of a better life. The better life quickly turned into a nightmare because the whole family ended up working in migrant-type field work in the heat of the San Joaquin Valley. The sadness of what was already going on in the family system, compounded by the extreme poverty and the incredible difficulty of the work, was a millstone that took my soul and ground it into pieces that were not distinguishable even to me. At this time, I decided to immerse myself in school work and was on my way to becoming an engineer, or so I thought.

College was out of the question because of money, or rather, the lack of it. This was also the time of severe collective chaos in our country as the Vietnam War cut deeply into the soul of the United States. Not being able to go to college and not wanting to work in the hellish heat of the San Joaquin Valley, I opted for the military. At 17, I joined the U.S. Navy for 6 years because they offered extensive training in electronics, which I saw as an avenue toward a better life. The chaotic rigor of the military was not difficult for me because my upbringing in difficult situations prepared me well for this experience. After finishing the electronics training, I volunteered for submarine duty and served in the western Pacific and Southeast Asian theatre (I still don't know why they call it a theatre).

Serving on submarines during the cold war was an amazing experience because my job entailed gathering and analyzing intelligence. I quickly became aware that things are not what they appear in the mainstream news, and there is a lot going on that most folks will never be remotely aware of. It was at this time that I realized I was not following the dictates of my inner self, which turned the confused energy into anger and depression. Later in life, I realized that anger and depression were closely related, but I'm getting ahead of this story.

During this time, I also started taking college courses on naval vessels, where local professors did intensive, 6-week courses in order to help us advance in our education. Philosophy and psychology grabbed my attention because of the earlier eavesdropping on Grandpa's talks and the inner quest of trying to figure out what was going on internally and also collectively. After all, it was the 1960s, and it was all about the journey and meaning. Amazingly enough, I was never pulled by the spirit of alcohol or substance use to find meaning, although many around me in the military were continuously stoned or at least recovering from being stoned or drunk.

THE ROAD TAKEN

I was getting close to the end of my military commitment when I made a trip to visit my ailing grandfather. It was a feeling of being disconnected as well as connected seeing my grandparents in their old adobe home. My grandfather was ill with respiratory problems that he acquired while working at the Los Alamos laboratory as a laborer. It was a talk that he gave me during this visit that cracked my cosmic egg and set me on a different path. He talked to me about symbols that can help one change or transform one's life in a profound way. While he talked, I wondered why he was telling me all this and at this time in my life, when I thought that I was on my career track toward becoming a psychologist.

After the visit, I returned to San Diego where I was stationed. A couple of weeks after returning to my regular life, I happened to be in a bookstore where I picked up Jung's *Symbols of Transformation* (Volume 6 of the collected works). In leafing through the book at the store, I saw that some of what I was reading sounded amazingly similar to my grandfather's last words to me. I bought the book and read it. I knew then that there was some other energy guiding my thinking and life process, and my dreams intensified.

I left the military and enrolled in a university while at the same time working for the Department of Defense in the area of engineering psychology. I completed a bachelor's degree in psychology even though some of my professors were trying to make me into a social worker because they felt that I did not have what it takes to be a psychologist. I enrolled in a master's program and still my professors were not encouraging me, even though I was getting excellent grades. One professor was bold enough to tell me that he did not feel I should be a psychologist because I was questioning some of the basic assumptions of psychological measurement with what were then known as "minority populations." I was even threatened with being released from the program unless I stopped expressing my views on this topic (I'll never forget my last interaction with this professor as he closed the door in my face and said, "and you want to be a psychologist . . . huh!"). I went undercover with my thoughts and got the master's degree.

I wanted to do something meaningful and have the authority to do so. In our society, this can be done by having a doctoral degree. I signed up. Well, it wasn't that easy, as you all know. I was in a doctoral program a few weeks when one of the Native American tribes requested to see me. I resisted this because I had no idea who the Native people of that area were and I was up to my ears in homework in the area of assessment. The tribe was insistent, so I went to see what this was about, and they offered me a paying job to start a mental health program for their community. I took the job not having any idea what to do or how to do it.

Shortly after doing the usual literature review, I realized that there was close to nothing in the area of Indigenous psychology, although the need appeared to be great. Through the internship process, I was able to work under supervision and began to develop a program. Early on, I found out that the Western approach of working with Native communities was not sufficient

and was told so in a very straightforward manner by some of the elders in the community. They related to me that they felt I had not learned anything from my grandparents and was pretty useless to them as long as I persisted in this vein. This was my first and most painful lesson in cultural incompetence, and I almost changed careers because of this.

WHEN THE STUDENT IS READY, THE TEACHER WILL APPEAR

During my time of studying religions of the world, the teachings of Zen masters had a peculiar appeal. Their teaching on the appearance of the teacher was one that became real in my process. I was asked to go see an aging gentleman who happened to be a quadriplegic. I had some preliminary questions about him, as is the custom in our field. I was told that once or twice a year, he was taken to the mountains and left there to sit for 4 days. When I inquired into this, I was told that he was there to see. Of course, I inquired further about what he sees, thinking there may be a thought disorder or some other serious mental problem. The response I got from the community health worker was that he "would just see." By now, I was wondering not just about the old man but also about the community health worker.

The health worker took me to his place shortly after our conversations about the elder whom she wanted me to visit. He lived in a shack that was simple and very bare as far as structure. I went into his room, and when I saw what appeared to be a live skeleton on the bed, I had a deep internal anxiety and fear reaction. He smiled and said, "Don't think that way, there are other realities." When he related these words to me, I became more anxious, although I wasn't sure why. He then asked me if I had ever seen the colors. Again, my anxiety increased, and all I could do was to tell him that I had not seen colors. His next question elevated my anxiety to panic. He asked if I wanted him to show me the colors. I had no doubt that if I had said yes, that I was not ready to see what he was going to show me, and I responded by saying, "No, sir, I do not want to see the colors." My internal process was in a literal panic, and I ended the interaction in the most polite way I could muster and left the house. I remained anxious and did not know how to process this brief cultural encounter with the tools that I had gained so far in my doctoral studies. (I urge the reader to look deeply into yourself and ask yourself what you would do in this situation.)

I decided to go back after a few days and started to relate to this elder, and over the months I became familiar with him. During the 3 years that I knew him, he always spoke in riddles and was quite aggravating to my up-and-coming empirical mind. He thought that my understanding of the life-world was quite funny, and he gave me feedback only through riddles that meant little or nothing to me at the time. I still continued my visits in order to give him company, or so I thought. He never asked me for anything and wanted only to visit.

Two days before the summer solstice, I went to see him. He was sitting on his chair on his porch. He proceeded to give me an eloquent linear lecture that tied many of the pieces together from the past 3 years. I was amazed at his ability and wondered at the same time why he had such a radical shift in approach. On June 21st, he had his altar brought to him. As he prayed, he expelled his consciousness into the next realm known as death. It was at this point that I realized that I had been in the presence of a holy man who had been teaching me as part of my preparation for the work that was ahead of me. It is ironic or synchronistic that his teaching started and ended at the same time that my doctoral program started and ended.

THE AMALGAMATION PROCESS

In keeping with my root teacher's method, I will purposely not be linear in this discussion. So, back to where the internship and work with the tribe started and to the needs assessment that changed my way of working with the Native community. The initial step toward starting a program requires an assessment, whether it's a single patient or a whole community. During my empirical needs assessment, I found that the community was suffering from a variety of problems that can be described through a clinical paradigm. The needs assessment that I reported was rejected by the community, although my methodology was precise and in keeping with research methodology.

A deep feeling of mistrust was developing between me and the community because it appeared as if all that I was doing was correct from the Western perspective, but the Indigenous perspective discarded my approach. This was also occurring in the clinical work that I was doing with patients who sought mental health services that I had implemented. So, there I was, full of information and method and feeling as if all I was accomplishing was to further insult the community. I approached some of the leaders and pitifully asked for help.

There was a consensus that the elders in the community did not feel that alcoholism, depression, anxiety, and so on were the problems of the community, although these were quite obvious to my up-and-coming highly trained clinical mind. When I enquired as to what they thought was the problem, they told me that the root of the problems was a "wounded soul and wounded spirit." I went right to the literature to see what our literature has to say about wounded souls and such. To my disappointment, there were no references to soul or spirit. At this point, I felt pretty hopeless as far as being able to do anything useful for the people who had asked me to help them. At the same time, the patients I was seeing clinically were pressing me to talk about dreams, and I had no training in dream interpretation (again, I ask the reader to look deeply and see what you would do).

Fortunately, I had started the relationship with the elder mentioned earlier (who became my root teacher without me knowing it). When I approached him with my dilemma, he laughed and thought that my dilemma was quite funny. Of course, I was duly insulted and quite resentful at this, but I had nowhere else to go as far as tracing this soul stuff. I had a supervisor at the time who offered some relief through Jungian amplification, which helped, and in this manner, I was able to begin the interpretation of Native epistemology through Jungian metaphor. At last, it seemed as if I had found a bridge that also helped me to get through the dissertation process. In essence, this was the beginning of taking "Indian talk" and translating it into "White talk," which is how I refer to this process presently in the clinical work that I do. This process of translating has become the quintessence of the work. Simple but not easy, as we're finding out in this story.

When asked about the soul-wounding stuff, my teacher talked about intent and how, when someone hurts or wounds someone, this is at all levels of the whole person (i.e., body, mind, and soul). Because it is an assault also on mind and soul, this makes the wounding process one in which sorcery is involved. The elder's rationale is clear: The body knows how and heals itself. We can assist in healing the mind, although, because of its close ties to the soul, we need to use soul-healing strategies as well. If the soul is not healed, the wounding is passed on to the next generation for at least seven generations. Therefore, the issue being dealt with involves seven past generations as well as seven generations into the future. This idea endows the present moment with a tremendous amount of potential for healing the ancestors and the unborn descendants.

In other discussions with my teacher, he gave me the root metaphors for much of the theoretical work that I have done. It is important to note that the clinical work has driven the theoretical formulations from the beginning. I believe that having theory drive clinical practice is backwards and may not bring the effectiveness that our communities need. The process has also involved intensive formulations from Indigenous practitioners in order to make the work culturally effective and meaningful.

For the work to have evolved in the usual manner—where theory and existing ideas and material are implemented into communities that are culturally different from the core philosophies of the theories being implemented—is not only culturally incompetent but also oppressive. Many communities of color have had to suffer the indignities of being "therapized" by ideologies that aren't congruent to how they live and see the life-world. I was fortunate early on in my training that my life-world was shattered by my root teacher, and through this, I was able to step into another way of seeing how psychology needed to be reinterpreted for use with the communities with which I have been working.

During my early training in clinical work, I had a lot of difficulty making sense of the world in which my teacher was immersing me and the world of being a graduate student in Western-based psychology. I had the sense that "never the twain shall meet," and my personal situation became one in which I simply wanted to stop graduate school and do something else. During this time, I had a discussion with my root

teacher and he basically vetoed my decision, which was very surprising to me. I really thought that he would encourage me to drop out of the clinical program because he himself had no formal education. When I asked him why he wouldn't allow this, he simply said, "Because then you will have twice the power." At the time, I didn't understand this statement, but history has proved him correct. I have been able to have a say in both worlds, and this would not have been possible if I had dropped out of the doctorate program.

In one of the talks I had with my teacher, he was able to illustrate to me how critical it is to make the cultural life-world of one culture available to another culture in a way that helps both cultures to experience the life-world that they are in. Customarily, cross-cultural work has entailed intellectual understanding that is second to actually being able to experience the life-world of another group. When one is able to move into a different cultural reality, it then becomes possible to start a new narrative that enriches both groups.

The way that he was able to show me how to bridge life-worlds was not obvious at the time, and I must say that most of what he said was not obvious to me at that time. I felt as if our conversations were a series of Zen Koans that had little meaning to me and, for the most part, sounded unreal. One critical tool that he gave me through this type of teaching was that we can immerse another person in culture through a process in which we shift cognitive root metaphors. This method gives us a twofold result in that the metaphor shifts and, at the same time, creates ego confusion. As most of you know, it is this very ego confusion that is the fertile ground for change in the work that we do, and without it, our work is merely "stinkin' thinkin'," as they say in Alcoholics Anonymous. The shape shifting that he taught me in the theoretical realm became the vehicle that has influenced my writings as well as my day-to-day work with communities and individuals.

BEFORE COMPLETION

My evolution as the human being and psychologist that I am today has had a curious development, as you have seen from what you have read so far. I need to get into the actual development of my ideas as they emerged through a process that was fierce at times because of the profound differences in the cognitive dissonance that my work provided for my brothers and sisters in the profession. It is interesting and even a bit humorous that it did not start in this manner. The subtitle of this section is from the last hexagram found in the I' Ching, and it advises that even though things may be completed, they are also already in the process of disintegrating, thus creating the space for future changes. The work is never perfect and is in constant movement as part of natural law.

Early on in my training, I was a staunch or perhaps a fundamentalist behaviorist. I literally walked around with Skinner's *Human and Science Behavior* in my hand and felt that I had found ultimate truth. I was so immersed in this world that I truly believed that unless you added the cognitive piece to the equation, you were no longer on the right path. In essence, I thought that all could be explained, changed, and made better through this system of thought—especially after working for the military as an engineering psychologist who was part of a team that worked on weapons systems development.

Anyway, my psyche came under fierce attack the very day I met my root teacher. I had no idea why he produced such a profound anxiety in me during our first meeting, but I'm sure it's obvious to you at this point as to what was going on. The notion of soul wounding and all that it entails is a total shifting of ideas and world-view. Behaviorism got only to the gate of the path I was traveling and could not go any further. Realizing the limits of behavior paradigms became apparent during this time because this was the time that I also started working with patients in a clinical setting. I attempted behavioral interventions, and patients insisted on telling me dreams. They were polite enough to hear my behavioral machinations, and then they would want to know what the dream meant. Of course, I was not able to make behaviorism cross into the dream-time realm.

I am glad that I was able to at least listen to the people who came in to see me and at least hear their dreams. Much of the time, I had little to offer, and when dreams became most of what people wanted to talk about, I went to my teacher and got acquainted with symbols that were relevant to the tribe with which I was working. I also began to read Jung's works so that I could have some clue as to the world in which the patients were interested. It is worth noting that Native people dropped out of therapy before three visits according to the literature (of that time, circa 1980), and I found that Native people would drive long distances in serious storms to be able to make their appointments; this persisted for months and, at times, years.

The main reason that they came to therapy was to discuss dreams and the meaning in their lives. It was interesting to me that the patients with whom I was working were making significant life changes through the process, and it was mostly because I listened to and discussed their dreams. Needless to say, I became deeply interested in dreams and studied relentlessly in this area. This became the vehicle for the work that was to come and became the topic of my dissertation, in which I was able to use Jung's system to act as an intermediary vehicle between the Western and the traditional Native life-world. This phase can be characterized by theoretical explanations within the historical trauma paradigm.

Historical trauma and internalized oppression have been a much-needed explanation for some of the issues that have created much suffering in Native and other communities. Many treatment strategies have emerged out of this line of thinking and shifting of therapeutic metaphor. Dealing with clinical issues from this perspective has taken me to remote Native communities all over the hemisphere and Africa, and the ideas have resonated with young and old people in those communities as well as with people from other groups in and out of the Native community. A new narrative has emerged that clearly embraces the ideas stipulated in historical trauma theory and praxis. It is remarkable that very few healing conferences held in Indian country have, as part of the main presentations, discussions in the area of historical trauma and internalized or lateral oppression.

Now what? This is the question that must always be a part of the work that we do in healing communities. The process unfolds and evolves, and it can never become static. If we allow the process to become static, we become complicit in the ongoing problems that need fresh interpretations and healing on a daily basis. In my latest writings, I have attempted to bring new ideas to the forefront and move the narrative from historical trauma to a liberation psychology discourse.

Liberation discourse entails taking a crucial eye to the processes of colonization that have had a deep impact on the identity of Original Peoples. By doing this, I am merely bearing witness and bringing awareness to this process, and by simply observing the process, it changes. By turning a critical eye on activities of healing, we liberate ourselves as well.

Liberation psychology requires that we examine our root metaphors of being in a cultural life-world and being able to understand how cultural hybridity may offer understanding for liberation of all peoples. The challenge will be to move beyond cultural competency and toward an understanding of epistemological hybridity, which will get us closer to the life-world experience of being a human being with infinite possibilities rather than a personal or familial screenplay that governs our lives in the world. The new narrative of understanding our essence of humanity will liberate us to become all things yet not be one thing.

Liberation psychology also allows the field to move into new paradigms of research and exploration. It no longer suffices to be stuck on Newtonian models of explanation, which are outdated in all scientific endeavors, and liberation psychology presses us to explore models in which random linearity and chaos theory may bring better understanding to the problems that we face as human beings subject to natural law. I can see the evolution of my work already, moving from liberation psychology to a psychology that is in balance theoretically and practically with natural law. In order to do this, we must begin to explore our ancient mythological roots as they complete the circle toward the future.

Future work must be accepted with an open heart. Understanding of the heart's wisdom and knowledge will be one of the challenges to us as human beings. Realizing that the brain is a secondary organ will require courage because this is one of the most critical Koans to be realized if we are to keep this secondary organ from not only self-destructing but also destroying all that is in process in our awareness. This will not be easy, but it will be simple once the realizations are made within a heart/mind understanding of life, the world, and the universe as being part of an integrated totality in which there is no separateness. All of this is an ongoing process for me, and I want to end this story by quoting from my root teacher and clearly illustrating the ongoing process and constant change, impermanence, and emptiness in all things:

> There has always been a dream. Everything is still the dream. All that we call creation and Creator is the dream. The dream continues to dream us and to dream itself. Before anyone or anything was, there was a dream, and this dream continued to dream itself until the chaos within the dream became aware of itself. Once the awareness knew that it was, there was a perspective for other aspects of the dream to comprehend itself. One of the emerging dream energies, or "complexes," that came from the chaos of the dream and still remains in the dream as a way for the dream to recognize itself, is called "human beings." Human beings required a way to have perspective and reference, and because of this, another energy emerged from the dream, and this is known today as "time." It is from the two energies of dream and time that the third was given birth to, and that third one is known as the "dream time." Dream time is also known as "mind," which is by nature luminescent and pure. And the dream time mind is reflected by the emptiness of awareness.

Aho! All my relations!

RECOMMENDED READINGS

Butz, M. R., Duran, E., & Tong, B. (1995). Cross-cultural chaos. In R. Robertson & A. Combs (Eds.), *Chaos theory in psychology and the life sciences* (pp. 319–329). Mahwah, NJ: Lawrence Erlbaum.

Duran, E. (2001). *Buddha in redface*. Lincoln, NB: Universe Press.

Duran, E. (2006). *Healing the soul wound: Counseling with American Indians and other native peoples*. New York: Teachers College Press.

Duran, E. F. (1990). Underserved peoples: An introduction. In G. Stricker, E. Duran, E. Bourg, W. R. Hammond, & E. Davis-Russell (Eds.), *Toward ethnic diversification in psychology education and training*. Washington, DC: American Psychological Association.

Duran, E., & Duran, B. (1995). *Native American postcolonial psychology*. Albany: State University of New York Press.

Duran, E., Duran, B., Yellow Horse Brave Heart, M., & Yellow Horse-Davis, S. (1998). Healing the American Indian soul wound. In Y. Danieli (Ed.), *International handbook of multigenerational legacies of trauma* (pp. 341–354). New York: Plenum.

Duran, E., Firehammer, J., & Gonzalez, J. (2008). Liberation psychology as the path towards healing cultural soul wounds. *Journal of Counseling and Development, 86*, 288–295.

Lewis, E. W., Duran, E., & Woodis, W. (1999). Psychotherapy in the American Indian population. *Psychiatric Annals, 29*(8), 477–479.

2

A Personal History

CAROLYN G. BARCUS

I am honored to have been asked to share my personal history. I am a member of the Blackfeet Tribe of northern Montana. My Blackfeet name is Bear Woman. I was born in 1939, the third child and oldest daughter to Rome Elisabeth Samples and Isaac Emery Barcus in Cardston, Alberta, Canada (because it was the closest hospital to our Montana ranch). My older brother, Steve, is 10 years older; his twin brother, Clinton, died shortly after birth. My sister, Saralee, was born 3 years after me, and Acel, the youngest son, was born 9 years later.

We grew up on a small cattle ranch on the north side of the Blackfeet Reservation, with our north pasture fence being the Canadian-U.S. border. The land was allotted to my mother as a girl in 1907 or 1908 as an infant member of the Blackfeet Tribe. Her land and that of her father, Jessie Samples, and sisters Melba and May adjoined along Willow Creek. The Rocky Mountains and Glacier National Park stand to the west about 25 miles away. The family land stretched down the valley about 10 miles, but by Montana standards, we were considered small-time ranchers. "Our" valley is bordered by high ridges on each side that run to the

mountains and is about 6 or 7 miles across north to south. Old Chief Who Sits By Himself, the sacred mountain of the Blackfeet, is directly west of the valley, and a picture of Old Chief Mountain hangs on my office wall and in my heart.

My mother's nickname was Gypsy. Her Blackfeet name was Sweet Pine Woman, after her great-grandmother. She was proud of her Blackfeet heritage. When someone would say to her, "My ancestors came over on the *Mayflower*!" she would say, "Mine were here to meet the boat!" The story passed down in our family is that a French trapper named Augustine Armelle (Hamel) came into Canada and took three Blackfeet wives, Pine Woman, her sister Iron Woman, and Hawk Woman, who was later stolen in a raid. By the time the first Catholic priests came into Montana, he and Pine Woman had six children. Pine Woman was baptized Helena, and they were married on the same day, December 27, 1846, in Helena, Montana, by Father Nicholas Point. Our family lore says that theirs was the first marriage certificate issued in the territory of Montana.

As a girl, my mother rode across the north ridge to go to school in Canada. She graduated from the eighth grade along with two other girls. That was the last year of formal schooling for my mother, but certainly not the end of her education. She was an avid reader, had many hobbies and interests, loved to travel, and had a better memory the day she died at 91 than I do today. The greatest gift my mother ever gave me was when she taught me "Carolyn, you can do anything that you put your mind to!" and she believed it. Before she died, she told me that if she were starting over, she would want to live as I have lived, learning and doing. Her place and time in history limited her in what she did, but not in her vision of what was possible.

My father was of Swedish and English heritage and came into Montana with the Fry Cattle Company. He never went past the third grade and was a jack-of-all-trades. When my parents divorced, he left the ranch and became a carpenter, working for the National Park Service at Glacier National Park for many years. I appreciate my dad for teaching me to do things and then trusting me to do them. I was his right-hand man after my brother left for the Navy, and Dad never said to me, "No, you can't do that because you are a girl." I also appreciate him for teaching me to fish. Sometimes, when the day's tasks were done or when we just quit early, we would drive over to the North Fork of the Milk River to go fishing. I have fished all of my life, and I still carry my fishing pack when we go on pack trips into the wilderness.

Our ranch is 40 miles north of Browning, Montana, hub of the Blackfeet Reservation. When I was in first grade, there were enough children in the valley to qualify us to have a school, located about 5 miles from our ranch. A teacher was assigned, a one-room building was moved in, and we all rode our horses to the school each day, including the teacher. We did not have a horse suitable for a first grader to ride, so I rode behind my cousin, Kathryn, who is a year older, for the first half of first grade. When the teacher quit that winter, Dorrie Harrison, who lived on the south side of the valley, taught us. Next came a difficult transition time for a country kid. We had to move to Browning to go to school for my second-grade year. With only a few exceptions, for the next 10 years, we would move to town in the fall to go to school and back to the ranch in the summer. I lived for the weekends when the roads were clear enough that we could go home.

Living on the ranch was about work, but because I loved it, it did not count as work to me. We raised our own food—beef, chickens, pigs, turkeys, rabbits, duck, geese, and a garden. My dad plowed the garden with one horse on a hand plow. We put up hay with horses until we finally got a tractor when I was about nine. I learned to drive a two-ton truck and a tractor by the time I was 12. Tending our animals, we would ride to check the cattle, find strays, or round up a herd of unbroken horses. I remember running the "wild bunch" of horses west of Grandma's ranch with my sister. We were both teenagers and riding hard to stay with them and not let them get away. Her horse hit a hole and fell, throwing her off, and by the time she quit rolling, I had her horse caught and her back on it, and we were running again. We corralled the horse herd at Grandma's about the time my sister regained consciousness. She had no memory of getting back on or the last part of the ride. Perspective taking and empathy were not part of our culture. Getting the job done was.

As I write this history, I am aware that if the reader is not from a rural culture, there is no way for you to understand the joy of living that I had. I think that my mother's belief that she was one of the world's lucky people stemmed from the same love of life as I have, an appreciation of being your own person, having a healthy body, and being able to make things happen. You depended on yourself to handle things as they came, and you came to believe that you could truly "do anything that you put your mind to," as my mother taught me. I, too, came to believe that I was, and am, one of the world's lucky people. The connection to the land; the importance of the places and the animals, tame and wild; and the changing seasons were all part of me. My psychologist friend, Robert, who grew up in rural Louisiana, refers to it as "growing up wild." I have long been aware that I was more undersocialized than most people that I know, but I had never thought of myself as "wild." But it does help explain to me the distress that I felt when I was confined to a town to go to school. It was strange, and it was like being caged.

Compared to my life on the ranch, work is what I did in 1957 when I stayed in Browning for the summer after graduating from high school. I had to earn money so I could go to college in the fall. I learned to wait tables from a pro, a woman who had waited tables her whole life, including in the Chicago train station during World War II with thousands of soldiers coming and going. I became good at it, and I can tell you that it motivated me to go to college and would motivate me every time I thought of it thereafter.

When I left for college at Montana State College (University now), I had no idea what I wanted to study, or even what the options were. At the freshman orientation, I was exposed to the great variety of departments on campus and was invited to become part of the physical education (PE) department. Given that PE was not offered by Browning High School when I was there, nor were there extramural sports of any kind for girls, I came without any background other than I could throw a softball farther than any other girl in the high school. It was the interest and encouragement of one of the faculty that brought me in, and her interest, mentoring, and support persisted throughout my 4 years there. My mother had arranged for Bureau of Indian Affairs funding for college, but by spring quarter, I was out of money and very homesick. I returned to the ranch for spring quarter and helped my dad take care of the cattle. That same faculty member found me a board and room arrangement with a family in the community so that I would come back, and I spent my sophomore year working for my keep by ironing clothes, tending kids and helping in any way I was needed, and going to school. I had no expertise in any sport, so in my spare time, I participated in sports, practicing and soaking in how it all worked. I had no idea who I was or what I was good at and spent a great deal of time trying to figure it out.

I graduated in 1961, the first member of my family to earn a college degree, with a B.S. in physical education and minors in biology and general science. I took a teaching job in Conrad, Montana, not very far from home. I taught two classes of PE, a health class, a spelling class, a math class, and a biology class in the junior high. In Conrad, I learned to pheasant hunt. Having grown up with guns, hunting had always been part of my life, but there were no pheasants on the reservation, so pheasant hunting was new to me. I smile when I think about being invited to go trap shooting with another teacher and a group of high school boys and outshooting all of them. It puzzled me then, the dilemma that I faced then and women still face today. I had experienced times as a PE major when a man would refuse to play a sport with me because "If I win, it won't mean anything, but if I lose, it will mean a lot!" Growing up on the ranch, there was no competing; everyone pitched in to get the work done. Today, having taught diversity classes for many years, I now have the language to better describe rural and Native cultures as interdependent cultures, and the survival of the group is what is valued, not individual achievement and competition.

I was close enough to go home to help at the ranch on the weekends. By this time, my parents were divorced and my mother summered cattle for other ranchers and lived in town during the winter. She depended upon her grandkids and me to help her keep track of the cattle that had been brought in for the summer and to keep the fences repaired. I called her a week before school was out and the cattle were already there, and I asked how she was doing. She said, "Oh, all right. I have only lost 200 head." Trying to find 200 yearlings, which are the adolescents of the bovine species, takes a lot of riding! We usually sent as many back as we brought in, except when one of the purebred Angus bulls strayed south and was killed by the neighbor's bulls. That was a sad day. Ranchers take pride in caring for their animals, and to see that healthy young bull lying in the coulee dying was very distressing to me. I experienced a similar feeling many years later on a ranch in South Dakota. One of my students wanted me to visit his family's ranch, so I went. I was there for branding time, and they were castrating a young stallion that belonged to a 12-year-old girl. No tranquilizers were used, and the horse fought the ropes fiercely! In his fight, he broke his leg and had to be shot. Out of all of the people there, only two of us cried for that young horse whose life was over, the 12-year-old girl and me. Her mother told her, "Stop crying. We will get you another horse!" They did not know what to do with me. I was now an outsider! It was not that they did not feel badly about what had happened. It was that they were not allowed to cry or talk about their feelings. I recognized the cultural constraints and realized that their feelings would be acted out, rather than talked out. I had become bicultural, walking in both worlds, the rough-and-tough world of ranch life and a more psychologically attuned world that teaches different ways of coping with distressing emotions.

After 2 years of teaching, I decided that I did not like it. As I think back to teaching in Conrad, it was not teaching that I disliked; it was what I was teaching. I left that job and went to work for my brother, who owned a bowling alley in Browning. After a year, I knew I needed to move on with my life, so I put in to go on Indian Relocation and was sent to Denver. Never again did I live at home on the reservation. For 6 months, I worked in low-paying jobs in Denver until I was called about an opening to teach PE halfway though the school year in Windsor, between Greeley and Fort Collins in northern Colorado. I took the job, lived in Greeley, and taught junior and senior high PE and junior high science for 5½ years. I started a girls' gymnastic team in the high school, which was my first experience in coaching.

Life in Colorado was hard. It was my first time to be far from home, I did not know anyone, and it was a different culture. As a 24-year-old woman from rural Indian culture, I could not use the same coping skills I did in rural Montana. I know now that I was experiencing acculturation stress, but then it was just confusing, painful, and lonely. I met some people from a Baptist church in Greeley, and they were kind and friendly, inviting me to come to church with them, so I did. I have mentioned nothing about religion or spirituality up to this point because it was not a significant part of my upbringing. Our ranch is on the northern side of the Blackfeet Reservation, which is not a traditional Blackfeet area. Browning is predominantly Catholic, and my mother's mother was Mormon. The Mormon Church sent her family from Clarkston, Utah (across the valley from where I live now), to Canada. Her father helped to build the Mormon temple in Cardston, Alberta, the town where I was born. My mother attended the Methodist Church when she was in town. So I had exposure to many Christian denominations and to my mother's Native spiritual beliefs, but there was no requirement that I adhere to any one of them. Attending the Baptist Church in Greeley provided the most in-depth formal religious training of my life. During the difficult times, I would talk to the God that I had never doubted was there but had little previous experience in seeking. It was the beginning of what has been a lifetime of seeking.

One of the most significant, life-changing experiences for me that last summer in Colorado was when I attended the University of Colorado. I was talking to one of my professors about her degree and what it took to get a graduate degree. It was the first time that it had occurred to me that I could go to graduate school. That fall, I applied to master's programs in physical education, seeking a program that would not require me to do a research thesis, because I knew nothing about research nor how to do it. I was accepted at Utah State University (USU), and in the fall of 1968, I moved to

Logan, Utah, to go to graduate school. It was in graduate school that I learned about building community. I did not call it that, but as I look back, I had spent 10 years as a sojourner, gathering no moss, never looking back, a mover, so to speak. In contrast, in graduate training, I learned to make connections with people and to provide support. I still have people that I learned to love in graduate school in my life today. It is amazing to me how love endures time and distance if you value relationships and work at staying connected.

I spent three years getting a MS degree in physical education. I ended up doing a master's research thesis, and I coached the women's tennis team and the women's bowling team. I also competed in local tournament tennis and in bowling tournaments for many years. It was my coaching experience as a graduate student that led me to psychology. As a coach traveling all over the western United States, I spent a lot of time with those women, and they talked to me. One was having difficulty in her marriage; another was depressed and confused about what she wanted to do with her life; and still another, who came from central Utah, finally came to talk to me about me. I was the first non-Mormon person that she had ever known, and I was not at all like what she had been taught nor what she expected, and what did that mean? But my ignorance and desire to be able to help did motivate me to find out. I went to the psychology department and talked to the professor who was teaching the graduate-level Introduction to Counseling class, Elwin Nielsen, and he allowed me to take the class, even though I was in PE. What a gift that turned out to be for me! I went on from there, finishing my MS in physical education and then on to get an EdD in psychology.

For a Montana ranch woman, graduate training in counseling, clinical, and school psychology was a reach. I was 31 years old before I knew that if you felt like hitting a wall, it meant you were angry. Thus, I have a lot of empathy for most men, who are frequently socialized as I was socialized in my rural, cowboy/Indian culture. But it also meant that I had a lot to learn. I learned the book and head knowledge in classes, but because I learn best from experience, I sought out a wide variety of experiences, including group and Gestalt therapies, to help me catch up with my more sophisticated classmates. During my graduate student career, I worked in public schools as a certified school psychologist; at Wyoming State Hospital in Evanston, Wyoming; at Head Start; and at four different elementary schools as part of an affective education program for my dissertation. I also worked at the Center for Persons with Disabilities, its most recent name, on an assessment and consulting team. One of my mentors, Reed Morrill, teased me that I was like a badger. Once I got hold of something, I never let go of it until I understood it, and I always wanted to know how things worked. I told him I was Indian, and we Indians always say "How." Something else that Reed taught me was about calluses, being tough without blocking out your feelings. Having grown up cowboy/ Indian, I had no idea how to recognize feelings, label feelings, sit with feelings, modulate feelings (to be able to put feelings away and then go back to them), and disengage in a situation and manage your feelings. I teach my clients these skills today, but I do not claim to have mastered them myself. I still have to make myself talk when I am angry or upset, and I need time to sort it all before I can talk about it.

This learning went on for 5 years in graduate school, and I loved every minute of it. I am not saying it was easy, because sometimes it was very painful, but it was immensely rewarding. When I graduated, I did not want to leave. I had bought a home in 1971 for $10,000, and I borrowed the $500 down payment to do it! I lived in that home in Providence for 29 years. I also bought my first horse in this valley in 1971, for $150. I regret that I never kept a log of all of the horses that I have bought and sold since then. It has been many.

After I graduated, I accepted contract work until I received a call that there was an opening at Intermountain Indian School, an off-reservation boarding high school operated by the Bureau of Indian Affairs, which was over the mountain in Brigham City. I started working for Indian Health Service (IHS) as a mental health specialist, which I did for 2½ years. We served more than 1,000 Native students from more than 100 tribes across the nation when I first started. Later, the school was downsized to fewer than 500 students until it closed. I went on to serve as the Service Unit Director for the health clinic until, due to politics, the school was closed in 1984. There were several firsts for me in my work at Intermountain School: my first time to work for the government; my first time to do mental health work with Native people; my first experience with being an administrator; and my first experience of being called a "f— Honky!," which took some getting

used to because I considered myself to be Blackfeet, even though my genetics made me look more Swedish than Blackfeet. An African American teacher told me not to feel badly about it. They said that to her, too, when they were angry. And many of them were angry and hurt and confused. Many others were kids for whom Intermountain was their school because there was no school close to their homes on the rez. The other first was to be part of developing a mental health dorm, which served as a more restrictive environment for those students with severe disorders and provided an alternative to sending them home, where there were no options. The schoolwide token economy, called the demerit system, kept track of each student's behavior, and an IHS mental health worker provided treatment in the dorm. With enough demerits because of their destructive behavior, and with the support of the therapist, students could be placed in the therapeutic dorm, where they could earn their way back to a regular dorm by changing their behavior. At the time, it was the only mental health facility of its kind in an off-reservation boarding school. And that was the school that was closed! Ten years later, I received an invitation to travel to Washington, DC, to meet with ongoing off-reservation boarding school personnel about the program that we had at Intermountain School. I was amazed at how angry I was still, 10 years later, by the blind political decision that closed Intermountain School, and then the thinking that said it would be possible to drop a program that took years to develop into an unprepared environment with an already taxed mental health service.

When Intermountain School closed, I again relied on my contract work so I did not have to leave my home. I had maintained my work with the halfway houses run by the Utah State Department of Corrections in Ogden during my years at Intermountain School. Overall, I worked for Corrections for eight years, serving people who were incarcerated for substance abuse offenses. In January 1985, I was contacted by one of my professors at USU about helping the psychology department with a project that they had started to train graduate-level Navajo school psychologists. Twenty students had started the reservation-based program, but no one had graduated after 4 years. Their coursework was completed, but not their theses. I contracted to work with these students and have been at USU since that time.

The American Indian Support Project was formalized in June 1986 with a grant from the U.S. Office of Education to train Native school psychologists, and 2 years later, a grant from the National Institute of Mental Health expanded the Support Project to include recruiting Native PhD students into our Combined program. We were able to help 7 of the original 20 Navajo students to complete their MS degrees, but only by having them come to USU to receive help in writing their theses. Writing a thesis and/or dissertation has continued to be the thorn that inflicts the most pain for each of the 35 Native MS and PhD students who have completed degrees in psychology at USU under the American Indian Support Project. This is equally true of most majority students as well. In the introductory seminar that is part of my teaching load, I say, "Have your dissertation completed before you go on internship because it is much more difficult to do when you leave here." Some students actually do stay to complete their dissertation, but it is seldom true of Native students, or any of our minority students, for that matter. Being far from home, family, and community is extremely difficult for Native students, and they are usually in a hurry to get back. Those of us who train graduate students are always grateful for supportive families who say to the student, "You stay there and get your training. Our tribe needs you here educated to help us." Family support is such important support! The pull from home is so strong! I had one student who came to me in the middle of the semester and asked if he could get more financial help. I said, "I thought that we had you squared away financially?" He replied, "My family did not have money for heating oil, so I sent them my money." Ceremonies, deaths, illnesses, special occasions, and difficult times—they all pull at the heart of a student from an interdependent culture. One of our Native students told me that she had never before had to be the sole provider of child care for her daughter and how hard that was for her with no family around.

I have struggled with how to share 23 years of building and maintaining the American Indian Support Project in the psychology department at Utah State University. USU is a Research 1 University, a competitive, mainstream, white man's school. Some Native people would say that I had no business bringing Native students into such an environment. I argue that Native people who are going to have the sophistication to get a PhD and be a competent psychologist who can serve Native people and Native tribes must be bicultural and must be *better* trained than mainstream psychologists. Their job is much more complicated with many unknowns. Watered down "Indian programs" are pet peeves of mine. It is insulting to offer them less that what is offered mainstream students. Hold them to high standards and they will achieve those standards! The battles that must be fought to recruit and support minority students are many and are at multiple levels of the university. Our time in history has helped us, and I say *us* because I certainly have not done this by myself. The issue of diversity is in the forefront today, as well it should be, so selling administrators on the need to enhance the diversity of the student body and the faculty was not the problem. Being able to build in enough flexibility and understanding of the needs of these students in order to retain students from different cultures in a rigid, independent cultural system was a problem. Students from interdependent cultures have many obligations to their families and communities, and these obligations are not put on hold for graduate training. They must be accommodated. I continually challenge majority students from independent cultures who want to be therapists to work at understanding an interdependent construct of self and what that would mean in treatment. We worked for many years to educate a system to understand these same issues related to the retention and training of minority students.

The advantage that I had in starting and maintaining the American Indian Support Project at USU was caring and supportive administrators in psychology with whom I had long-standing relationships. Over the years, we built a faculty culture that valued diversity. Each new faculty member hired knew that this is what we do at USU: We train American Indian psychologists. One of the most influential new faculty members was Sue Crowley. How a white woman from suburbia born with a silver spoon came to understand poor, rural, and minority culture as she does remains a mystery to me, but she has proven herself to be a valuable ally and friend. She has helped in the past 10 years to expand the diversity mission of the department to include all ethnic minority groups, particularly Latino students. She has been instrumental and influential in the development of the Rural/Minority emphasis in the Combined program and in the hiring of wonderful and competent rural and minority faculty. The community that is healthy, cooperative, supportive, open, and genuine at the faculty level fosters the same community at the student level. This healthy environment works for both minority and majority students, as well as faculty. When we hire another Native psychologist to take my position, that person will fit right into the culture as a team player, I will cut my role back, and everything will go on as it does now, only better!

From being a Montana ranch woman to being a rural, Native psychologist in a Research 1 University that is predominantly white is a journey. There were no women faculty in the psychology department when I was a graduate student, nor when I returned 10 years later. There were no Native mental health workers at Intermountain School. I worked for 7 years in my faculty position at USU on soft money before the provost gave the psychology department a permanent position for me. I was given the option of a tenure-track position or a clinical position, and I chose a clinical position. I was encouraged to participate in the University promotion process, and I tried. Of all of the painful things that I have done in my career, that was certainly one of them. I had the world's most supportive promotion committee. All I had to do was "toot my own horn." How many times have I heard that? I left the meeting in tears and never went back. I have great admiration for minority faculty who can survive the promotion and tenure process. It contradicts everything that is taught in interdependent culture! Native psychologists must walk a bicultural path and understand how to operate in both worlds. I imagine every Native student to go through the USU program has heard the words "You need to speak up more," or "You need to be more assertive." Yet when they return to Indian country, they need to know when and how to speak up and do it carefully so as not to offend. In white culture, they may get criticized for not having a line of research when they actually adhere to a culturally appropriate, community-based research approach that is not understood in independent culture. One of our Native students was asked why he did not query an older gentleman client when he failed to answer a question, and the student said, "If he had wanted me to know, he would have told me in the first place." It is indeed a complex and difficult journey for minority graduate students.

One of my interests over the past 20 years has been in the question, "Is there such a thing as American Indian psychology, and if so, what makes American Indian psychology different from mainstream psychology, and even more complex, what makes American Indian psychology different from the psychology of other ethnic minority people in this country or other indigenous people of the world?" Margaret Mead, in 1959, wrote *An Anthropologist at Work: Writings of Ruth Benedict,* and says on page 16, "Never look for a psychological explanation unless every effort to find a cultural one has been exhausted." If we understand a Native person's culture and history, do we then understand that Native person? I think not. But I do not claim to be a deep thinker. I just watch and wonder about how things work, and I have not tried to articulate a psychological explanation.

Not being a researcher, one of the ways that I "study" this question is through the Annual Convention of American Indian Psychologists and Psychology Graduate Students. June 2008 marked the 21st convention, which is held at Utah State University. The Bear Lake retreat held in conjunction with the convention is the community/spiritual part, and the convention is the scientific/programs/philosophical part. The business meeting of the Society of Indian Psychologists (SIP) is held during the convention. The retreat/convention and the SIP listserv help to keep Native psychologists and Native graduate students from across the nation connected with each other.

I am a past president of SIP. For 2 years, I presided over the business meeting, handled the business of SIP, and represented SIP nationally by traveling to the Council of Presidents meeting twice a year, hosted by the American Psychological Association's (APA's) Office of Ethnic Minority Affairs. I came to appreciate the importance of the ethnic minority psychologist organizations during the time I spent serving SIP. This experience and exposure led to my being nominated for Member at Large for the Executive Committee for Division 45, The Society for the Psychological Study of Ethnic Minority Issues, of APA. I came to believe that serving on national committees and doing national committee work is a very important task for a psychologist to do, although I never liked it, nor was I very good at it.

I understand, however, that we as Indian psychologists need to be at the table when important decisions are being made at these national meetings, and we each need to take our turn representing Native psychology. When I talk to Native applicants to the PhD program, I ask them what they want to do with a PhD, and the answer is almost always "to help my Indian people," which for them means direct care. Being the president of SIP, serving on ethnic minority committees of APA and Division 45, are also ways of serving our people. These contributions are not as direct nor as concrete as direct care, but they are equally important, and they require a different knowledge and skill base, as does research. A role that I am adjusting to is that of being an elder. Several years ago, when I looked around at a Retreat dinner to find the oldest person to invite to go through the line first, and I discovered that person to be me, I was a bit jolted. I did not think of myself as old or as an elder. I still do not think of myself as old, but the years have brought some wisdom and a commitment to leaving things better than I found them. I am willing to speak out and to lead if there is a need. I read on the SIP listserv, "Ask Carolyn. She is the heart of SIP," and I know what is meant, but that cannot continue forever. Others will step up. Those of us in my generation need to mentor up-and-coming Native psychologists to take on this commitment, and as I write this, I can think of many of them by name. It brings joy to my heart!

I like teaching and psychotherapy. I have been working at one or the other for more than 40 years. I cannot think of a year in the past 37 that I have not been involved in a therapy group, as a member or as a facilitator. When I returned to USU as a faculty member, I shifted my contract work from the corrections system to a sexual abuse treatment center, working first with perpetrators and then with victims as well. I left contract work to open a part-time private practice, primarily with women who were severely sexually abused as children. That work continues today. I have had no greater teachers in my lifetime than my clients. I consider it a privilege to walk with them. I share their pain as they endure the pain of getting better; struggle with them as they struggle to learn who they are; and finally, I walk with them as they learn to make their lives work. I rejoice when they are finally free of the pain and can have a life. What could be more rewarding! And what amazing women they are! There is a natural selection process that occurs in situations of severe abuse: the bright, creative, strong, and talented children survive; overwhelming abuse is too much for some children, and they die or become hopelessly

insane. Therefore, the adult clients who present for therapy because they can no longer tolerate the lifelong pain they have endured are very bright and creative, very strong and talented women. Being very strong, however, can frequently translate into being very stubborn in therapy. Fortunately, I am equally stubborn. My mother called it "Barcus bullheadedness," but I see it as tenacity, persistence, and commitment to the stated goal of the client to achieve a healthier and happier state of being. These women have my love and admiration, and I am indebted to them, for I am better off for having known them.

To come full circle, I am still a rural ranch woman, only now it is on 60 acres in northern Utah, a place called Bear River Ranch. Bear River Ranch is a horse ranch, and the goal is to raise Tennessee Walking Horses. The first foal will be born in 2009, if all goes well. In the early 1980s, I began packing into the wilderness with my horses. The first year that we went, three friends and I packed into the Uintah Mountains in eastern Utah. Since that time, I have done two or three pack trips per year, every year. Now four of us take three pack horses and travel across country. Sue Crowley and I have ridden from Cache Valley to the south boundary of Yellowstone Park. We have explored much of the wilderness south of Yellowstone, and now we have set our goal to ride to the ranch where I grew up in Montana. Four of us put in our application to ride halfway across Yellowstone Park in 2008, and hopefully, we will reach the north boundary in 2009, and then on to the Canadian border.

I retired from Utah State University in the summer of 2008, and I then contracted to do my job for another year because we did not fill my position during the first search. I have mixed feelings about retirement; I have a hard time keeping up with everything on the ranch while working full time, and I love my work at the university. How could you not love working with bright young people, both students and faculty, who are interesting, interested, and energetic? I am committed to having a young Native psychologist on the faculty in a tenure-track position. Having two would be better, so check on me in 10 years. I still have some things that I want to accomplish, and as long as I can, I will serve Native people and my clients.

3

My Life Is a Balance Between . . .

ROSIE PHILLIPS BINGHAM

LOVE AND CHAOS

She was the first born, but not the oldest, child of Jake and Savanah Phillips, who lived their first 5 years of marriage on hot Fallback Plantation in the Mississippi Delta. Although she honestly does not know how many children her father had, the family story is that at the time of her parents' marriage, her father had two sons and her mother had two daughters. They would go on to have nine more children, including two sets of twins. She never got to know her first younger brother because he died as an infant when she was not quite 2 years old; so, conveniently, she was able to say that she had six brothers and five sisters, and that's all she has ever known—although from time to time, she still feels a small pain for that small child who never really quite was. On the plantation, her parents were sharecroppers who grew most of the vegetables for the family (she especially remembers sweet potatoes, peanuts, spinach, and butter beans); pumped water from a well; used an outhouse; drank red soda pop with peanuts; chopped and picked cotton for the plantation owners; and were always in debt to the company store.

When her life was full of love, it was funny and she was confident. Her parents named her Rosie Mae to match her older sister's name, Georgia Mae. They had wanted twins and later got them—Willie Lee and Lillie B—later still Carrie and Larry. Funny and unfortunate for the last child, his name is Harry. Rosie thought she could do anything, even beat her brothers in a contest to see who could pee farthest off the porch. To this day, she thinks she won! Love made her confident and determined. Her first memory of love outside the family was a boy who must have been a teenager and he was beautiful, tall with "good" slightly curly Black hair, and very light skinned, perhaps Black, or Mexican or Native American. But the chaos in her life told her that she could never have the boy, not because of the difference in their ages that she never thought about, but because she was too Black and her hair was too nappy. How does a 4-year-old begin to know that, even though she is loved, she is not good enough?

Rosie, and later Willie, became very ill with typhoid fever from drinking the water in the barrels delivered by the men who had that cute boy that she loved with them. Because she became ill first, she was the one who came very near death. But because of his love, her father gave her a life-saving direct blood transfusion. Her mother stayed with the children in the hospital day and night, often with no place to sleep in the colored section of the hospital, so she stood and slept on her feet. When they let Rosie out of that hospital to go home, her mother told her that she had to stay in bed, but Rosie had had enough of being in the bed. The love in her life made her very confident that she could get up, put her shoes on, and go outside. She got out of bed, sat in a chair, leaned to get her shoe, and fell right on the wood-burning stove. She sustained a serious burn on her left wrist where the scar can still be seen today. Back to bed she had to go.

The chaos in her life arrived with the insolent voice of the White sheriff deputy, who came to their home and talked in such a mean and demeaning way to her mother. Rosie did not understand what was going on, but she did know that she hated the man because after he left, she saw her mother lean on the icebox with her head held high as she stared out the window and cried. Rosie had never seen her mother cry and even now rarely sees tears in her mother's eyes. Shortly after this incident, the family moved to Memphis to join her father. Years later, Rosie would learn that her father had been accused of rape. Sometimes, the story went that it was a White girl; other times that it was a Black girl . . . chaos in either case.

INFERIORITY AND ACCOMPLISHMENT

The move to Memphis brought two very significant events into Rosie's life. First, she learned to read before she went to first grade, in part as a result of sometimes going to the one-room schoolhouse in Mississippi attended by her sister. Second, her father descended into alcoholism and spousal abuse.

Reading allowed Rosie an escape from her day-to-day world and an entrée into worlds she otherwise would never have discovered. One world was that of imagination. Skin color was and is a major psyche phenomenon in the lives of African Americans. If one is too dark, he or she is not good enough. If one is too light, he or she could be accused of unearned privilege.

When Rosie was in junior high school, on her walks to and from her segregated school, other children would taunt her by yelling out that she was "Black and ugly." But reading books had shown Rosie that there was another world out there that was not as poor as the one in which she currently lived. People actually had shoes without holes that required a piece of cardboard inserted to keep their feet off the ground. Some children had telephones and cute dresses. So Rosie decided to play a game with herself when she heard the "Black and ugly" chant. Each time a child said that she was Black or ugly, she would pretend that she got one dollar. At the end of the day or 2 days, she could buy whatever she wanted. Amazing how those chants turned to positives. Still, the walk to the segregated schools and the knowing that she was too Black helped to fuel a sense of inferiority that lingered with Rosie.

But reading also let her know that there was work beyond cleaning the homes of White women like her mother did. She could be a nurse like Cherry Ames, the fictional character who lived in a residence hall and got in adorable trouble. Rosie secretly began to dream about going away to college. She could live in a dorm and sleep in a bed all by herself. She could become a psychiatrist, a secret agent, a counselor, but probably not a dancer. Rosie never read anything about dancers, didn't know anybody who was a dancer, but she imagined herself one when she danced on her toes in her living room as she pretended that she didn't know others were watching her. No, dancing was not an option, but maybe moving to New York City or somewhere with tall buildings like those she read about was a possibility. She would go somewhere. Reading made that dream a reality as Rosie became a very good student, got scholarships to numerous colleges and universities, and did go off to school.

Her father's alcoholism and spousal abuse was another motivator to run away to college. Rosie's father worked two jobs. By day, he dumped garbage as a sanitation worker for the city of Memphis. That job allowed him to bring his lunch from home and sit on or near the truck to eat it. Until after the sanitation strike during which Dr. Martin Luther King, Jr., was killed, Black sanitation workers had to stay out with the maggot-infested trucks even during the rain, sleet, and snow. An upside of being a sanitation worker is that one person's garbage is another person's gold. Rosie's dad brought home the gold to her when one day, because he knew his little daughter of 10 loved to read, he brought an entire box of books all with their covers wrapped in brown paper. Rosie read every single book from cover to cover with her mouth hanging open. She enjoyed the books and never told her father what was in those books. Because he had only completed third grade, he was not a reader. Of course, she didn't talk to him much anyway because he usually went directly from the sanitation job to his cleaning job at one of the local hospitals. On weekends, he was usually drunk and often mean and abusive at those times. Rosie always wondered when the other shoe would drop, although she tried hard to be a good girl.

When her mother would run away from her father, she would take her two older daughters because he was not their father. Rosie was left to be responsible for all of the others. When her mother and father were not speaking, it was that little girl who had to walk downtown to pay the bills. Rosie felt miserable about her parents, but quite competent about being able to effectively pay the bills and never letting anyone cheat her with the money. Still, she played seesaw with feelings of fear, competence, bravery, shame, and inferiority. At home, she felt the fear of her father's episodes. At school, she felt the pressure to achieve because her teachers told her she had to do well so that White people would not see how ignorant Black people were. But she knew she was competent and could do it. She felt brave when she stood up for what she believed in. At home, she felt shame because her dad was a garbage man and got drunk, and they were poor. At school, she was tracked into classes with friends who seemed middle class. At home, she was around friends pretty much like her. Her worlds were divided yet connected because they were all Black. The combination left her feeling inferior even as she won scholarships and went off to college. When she came home with her scholarships, Rosie saw her mother cry for the second time. Confused, Rosie asked her why. She said, "You always wanted to go to college, and I didn't know how we would pay for it." Funny—Rosie had never thought about her parents paying. She knew her parents didn't have any money. What was her mother thinking?

MY LIFE IS A BALANCE BETWEEN THEN AND NOW

As I wondered about what might be important for students and young professionals to hear from a "pioneer," I thought it might be worthwhile to note that my life as a child was pretty much like any other little Black kid of that era. And the things that laid the foundation for my life are the things with which I still struggle today. I am constantly finding myself looking for balance yet getting out of balance one way or the other. Race is a big issue in my life and might be until I die. Race is always a double-edged sword whether I am talking about what happens to the psyche as a result of intragroup interactions or whether I am talking about what happens to the psyche in intergroup relationships. African Americans have helped me to feel inferior and powerful, loved and betrayed, nurtured and loved. I have felt many of the same things about Caucasians in the United States, but I don't know that I have ever felt diminished by Black people, and I have with White people. So I have wondered how in the world I gave White people that power, and how do I take it back? Well, I suspect that I had lots of help handing it over, and I get lots of help taking it back. My help comes from family, friends, and faith. If we let friends stand as a moniker for community, then we can begin to look at what I think might be important to consider if one is going to study multicultural psychology.

FAMILY

Culture begins at home. Most individuals are born into families that are part of a community of people who define themselves in some ways that could be thought of as a shared worldview. They have customs and beliefs that help to shape behavior. The family begins to tell the individual who he or she is. In my early life, hopefully, you began to see some of the messages that I may have gotten. One was that I was always responsible, no matter how young or old. I have no idea how Black people came to be viewed with that "lazy" stereotype. In order for my family to survive on that plantation, we all had to work whether it was our turn to sweep the dirt-filled yard, chop cotton, or wash dishes. Later, everyone had to work because both parents worked. But somehow, the issue of race and inferiority began early, and the negative messages began to take root. Right alongside the negative messages were the positive ones of competence, ability, love, and possibility. The family often holds and transmits these messages.

Strong family messages can help return a sense of power to the individual. In my own life, the messages of strength and the nurturance from my sisters in particular continue to help me migrate through the minefields of sexism and racism.

COMMUNITY

When individuals step outside the family, they begin to witness the behavior of those surrounding them. The behavioral messages can reinforce or contradict those from the family. In my case, there was too much reinforcement of the negative skin color messages. And certainly, children are cruel enough to find any child's vulnerabilities and exploit them. No reason is necessary and perhaps not even understood by those children. In my case, the church and the school provided relief. In each instance, I got a chance to achieve. At church, I had an opportunity to hear that no matter how awful or ugly I may have been, God loved me. That's a pretty powerful message for a little girl who feels fear and shame. The community can also provide a look into the world of possibilities or lack thereof. It is important for multicultural researchers to get a firm understanding of community if they want to understand the dynamics of an individual life.

Furthermore, it is important to understand that the family and the community may extend beyond the boundaries as defined by sociologists, psychologists, demographers, and others. As I grew older, I began to hear more positive messages from my friends in my geographical community as well as from my enlarged family and community. My family and friends/community began to include the professional colleagues I met in my journey from graduate student to licensed professional.

One of my early daydreams as a young child was to have a family of children from many races and ethnicities. My dream from then reflects my life today in that my circle of friends, my community, now includes a mix of Mexican, Chinese, Indian, African, European, and more—better than a rainbow. This circle surrounds me

in a nurturing way that helps me find the balance between insecurity and confidence, shyness and boldness; balance between who I try to be and who I am; balance between holding back and reaching out; balance between crying softly and laughing out loud; balance between giving up power and taking it back.

FAITH

In many African American communities, the church continues to be a salient part of life. What is sometimes difficult for many to understand is that the church is far more than the family. I attended churches that were Baptist, African Methodist Episcopal (AME), and AME Zion; visited Church of Christ, Church of God and Christ, United Methodist, and so on. In almost all, I was taught to have a personal relationship with God. For me, that meant self-discovery no matter what the minister said. I believe that is part of the difficulty people have with Barack Obama's attending his church. My pastor's beliefs are not always mine. I am taught to think for myself. I believe that this message allows me to develop a deeper spiritual side and to hear that to which I am called. So, for me, psychology is a "calling." You won't find "calling" as a part of most vocational inventories. In order to be an effective vocational multicultural practitioner, it may be important to know that some of your clientele may not fit the client profile because their spiritual beliefs have influenced the outcome, or that no matter the outcome, their spiritual beliefs will dictate their career choice.

My life is a balance between fear and faith. Faith has allowed me to step up and step out, even when fear whispers, "Remember, you are not good enough." Faith shouts, "Yes, you are!" So I ran for president of the American Psychological Association. I keynoted at the National Multicultural Conference and Summit. I want students and young professionals to hear that if the garbage man's daughter can do it, you can, too.

BEGINNINGS AND ENDINGS

This chapter began with a brief peek into my early life, and now I want to end with where I am now. First, it is important to acknowledge the inspiration for the title of the chapter. In November 2007, I saw my son, Akil, perform a song titled "Balance Between" with the band Ippazzi, in which he free styles or raps. I was deeply moved by the wisdom of the words flowing from my then 23-year-old child and was surprised when I woke up one morning recently and realized the concept was how I wanted to frame my discussion for this chapter.

Next, I want to leave some concluding thoughts for graduate students and young professionals. So here is the ending.

1. I want to keep on claiming my power. I have no interest in being a victim of sexism and racism. That is not to say that these two societal problems do not and will not affect my life. It is to say that in my fight with them, I want to use them to become stronger.

2. I always want to be a giving person. Sometimes, we hear people say "I want to give back." Giving back sometimes sounds hierarchical to me, so I think about enlarging circles. I want more and more people in. I want to be a part of empowering the lives of as many

people as I can. And I depend on my family, friends, and faith to keep me doing it and to hold me to it.

3. I want to keep on increasing my faith because my faith conquers my fear. I am whole and at my best when I am in the spirit.

4. I wish you an interesting and balanced life.

RELEVANT PUBLICATIONS

Bingham, R. P. (2003). Fostering human strength through diversity and public policy: A counseling psychologist's perspective. In W. B. Walsh (Ed.), *Counseling psychology and optimal human functioning* (pp. 279–295). Mahwah, NJ: Erlbaum.

Bingham, R. P. (1999, August). *Lessons learned at the half-century mark*. Presidential address at the annual meeting of the American Psychological Association (Division 17), Boston.

Sue, D. W., Bingham, R. P., Porche-Burcke, L., & Vasquez, M. (1999). The diversification of psychology: A multicultural revolution. *American Psychologist, 54*, 1061–1069.

Head up . . . back straight

As she walks up to the stage

One can see the battles across her face

And today . . .

She is called to open the doors into her space

Giving us a peek through her lens

Her lived experience

Where the battles never end

She's called to share a glimpse of her pain once again

But just a glimpse . . . cuz they're asking for academic solutions

Clarify the white confusion

That racism is an integral part of the institution

"let's as a people move forward"

and some time ago . . . she was called to dedicate her life to ascertaining the answers

to inspire

to touch

the struggle . . . the love

has she fought hard enough?

Tomorrow . . .

Will things stay the same?

After endless hours of preparation

Will any thing change?

So to end . . .

This little Asian girl will like to say

Your talk hit my core

Thanks for focusing my lens

"to the blood on the floor"

in the same struggle.

© Gloria Wong

EDITORS' NOTE: Gloria Wong, a graduate student in counseling, read this poem to a large audience assembled to hear Dr. Rosie Bingham's keynote speech at the APA Bi-Annual Multicultural Summit in Seattle in 2007. Gloria approached the microphone to read this poem and thus honor Dr. Bingham at the end of Dr. Bingham's speech.

4

Transformative Adaptations to Linear Pathways

JOSEPH L. WHITE, AS INTERVIEWED BY THOMAS A. PARHAM

Change is the inexorable law of life.[1]

—John Fitzgerald Kennedy

His stature is small, but his presence is powerful. His voice awakens a room with the sound of cheerful acquaintance. His eyes survey any environment with a keen ability to decipher both pockets of support and affirmation as well as pockets of resistance. His hair is completely gray, as are the bushy eyebrows that frame the face that defined an entire discipline of Black Psychology. His lips protrude with the words that calm excitable declarations, consolidate massive amounts of information into clearly identifiable themes, and provide affirmation and validation to one's spirit and personhood that just makes you feel better about yourself. The lines on his face mark the decades of both challenge and triumph from which his wisdom and inner strength were born. And yet, the twinkle in his eyes signals that he is still excited about life and the lessons it has taught him, and grateful for the ways he has been blessed to emerge from life's journey relatively unscathed. This is the face of Dr. Joseph L. White, a master teacher, mentor, psychologist, and author, and I sat down with him in interview style to allow him to express his thoughts on being labeled a pioneer in multicultural psychology.

In writing the text for two mentoring citations he has received, and related recommendation letters that supported the nominations, I had my own chance to reflect on Joe's life and what he has meant to me in my life. I remarked that it is often said that "the measure of a man is not where he stands in times of comfort and convenience, but where he stands in times of challenge and controversy." Throughout his life, Dr. Joseph White has stood on the side of social justice and directed the activities of his clinical and academic ministry with visions of hope and possibility for transforming dark yesterdays into brighter tomorrows.

He was born in Lincoln, Nebraska, in 1932 and retired from the University of California, Irvine as a Professor of Psychology, Psychiatry, and Comparative Culture in 1994, after 27 years. In between those years, he managed to help raise a family, write several books, contribute to the anchoring of Head Start and educational opportunity programs throughout California, taught thousands of students, counseled scores of patients, lectured throughout the country, and reframed the discourse on an academic discipline that is well over 100 years old. Not surprisingly, he is still going strong, traversing the landscape of this nation speaking and training on a host of topics and issues.

During his life, Dr. White has walked the adult corridors of the world, being able to converse equally well with "paupers and kings." He has talked with Malcolm X; conversed with Eldridge Cleaver; taught students such as Stokeley Carmichael, Wade Nobles, and Thomas and William Parham; and walked with political leaders such as Bobby Kennedy and Willie Brown. Indeed, his career has spanned many activities and cut across many disciplines, reflecting a destiny that has been shaped by a passion for equality.

Throughout his career in the academy, Dr. White has been the consummate mentor, helping young people and professionals alike to first fashion out a dream, develop a belief that the goal can be achieved, and then create a plan to take them from where they are to where they need to be. His wisdom has also helped numerous mentees to navigate the murky waters of life, where progress and opportunity are influenced by factors beyond one's talent and ability. While incorporating the elements of creativity, improvisation, resourcefulness, spirituality, and a belief in the value of direct experience into his style, his track record for producing and guiding brilliant students and professionals is unparalleled. He has taught others how to identify and nurture young talent, and his legacy will continue to grow through their work. I can personally attest to the authenticity of his mentoring as my life has benefited from his guidance and support.

Indeed, a lifetime of self-determination, advocacy, human connection, and sensitive guidance and nurturance have earned him the titles of "Mzee" (respected elder) and "Jegna" (warrior and master teacher). But beyond the mentoring and guidance he has provided, Dr. White's contributions extend to other areas as well.

During his career, he has been a pioneer in the contemporary field of Black Psychology and has been affectionately referred to as the "Godfather" of the Black Psychology movement by his students, mentees, and colleagues. His seminal article in *Ebony* in 1970, "Toward a Black Psychology," was instrumental in beginning the modern era of African American and ethnic psychology. He has also authored or coauthored several papers and seven additional books: *The Psychology of Blacks* (three editions); *The Troubled Adolescent; Black Man Emerging: Facing the Past and Seizing a Future in America; Black Fathers: An Invisible Presence in America;* and *Building Multicultural Competency: Development, Training, and Practice.* Indeed, his contributions to the literature have been intellectually stimulating, penetrating, and profound, and these materials, I believe, have had a profound effect on the lives of all who read them.

In addition to his mentoring, teaching, and research, he has been a practicing psychologist and a consultant throughout his career. He has served as a supervising psychologist and staff affiliate psychologist in five hospitals and three clinical practices in the southern California area. Dr. White has also worked as a consultant to school districts, universities, private organizations, drug prevention programs, and government agencies. He has been a friend and consultant to many political leaders, including governors, speakers of the state assembly in California, and members of Congress. And yet, the genius of his career is not simply in the writings and books he has produced, the clients he has treated, the causes for which he has advocated, the leaders with whom he has rubbed shoulders, or the students he considers himself blessed to have taught. The genius of his work is in the lives he has touched and in the souls he has inspired to actualize their God-given talents, dreams, and aspirations.

In beginning the interview, I asked Dr. White if there was a quote from his past or present that seemed to capture the essence of his life. Rearing back in his chair, he paused reflectively and then replied:

WHITE: I think what comes to mind was what John Kennedy said in 1960 about the inevitability of change. Change is the inexorable law of life. And that is the story of my life. I set out to move in an established direction and ended up encountering change both in the process and in the content of psychology, and in my interactions with American society.

As you know, I am being inducted this year (May 2008) into the Hall of Fame at San Francisco State, but when I came to live in San Francisco, I wanted to get a job as a waiter at one of the big hotels, because that is what I had done in high school. I worked as a waiter in a good hotel in Minneapolis. But they wouldn't let Black waiters into the union, so there was no way I could get a job. So, I was demoted from a waiter to a busboy. And I remember complaining to my aunt, who was living in San Francisco, and she had just graduated from UCLA. She told me, "Well, maybe that is not what you are meant to do."

She talked to me for about an hour, saying, "You know, maybe rather than beating your head against the stone wall because you can't get a job out at Fisherman's Wharf or the Fairmont Hotel, I think you ought to think about going to college." So, again, that was the first direction of change. Then I went to college and thought about going to graduate school, and it took me a couple of tries, but I got through graduate school, and then I encountered a set of circumstances that would change what I had been taught. I had been well schooled in the Euro-American model, but I began to confront and encounter Black America and Chicano America. I was one of the very few Black psychologists in America, and what I had been taught wasn't fitting right in terms of the deficit efficiency model or just the invisibility of it all. Also, the community was pushing me to be a social activist, so then again I encountered another set of changes. Then I intended, as you know, to be in the classroom, to be a child psychologist, but people began to push me to represent an ethnic force in diversity and

bring students into colleges and universities like UC Irvine and Long Beach State. They also asked and expected me to redo certain parts of the curriculum, not only in psychology, but in our first Black Studies program at San Francisco State, the theme being that American higher education, with its rich process and content, should reflect the lives of people in America. When I came into higher education, Blacks were invisible, Chicanos were invisible, Asians were invisible in terms of the process and the content of instruction, not only in psychology, but in the other disciplines. So, that was the whole battle of Black Studies (which, back then, also meant Ethnic Studies), deciding if we should include these disciplines fully in the curriculum. So now that is another change.

I would say that for my generation, we were sort of the pathfinders without role models in our disciplines. So our parents and the people in the community who were the elders taught us as best that they could. But we were the ones that began to face these new situations in higher education in the 1960s, and so on, trying to make higher education and our professions more representative of the Black and African communities. My education prepared me for a static and linear model, and I found myself as a young adult, trying to figure out on my own a change model.

One more thing I had to learn is that if you are trying to change society and institutions of higher learning, you have to use a variety of tools and that you cannot always use confrontation. That's one model; but there are other models that you have to use at given times, like political models, administrative dialogue models, and timing. There are varieties of tools and skills that you have to learn, and then consider what combination of those, at any given juncture, will produce the outcome you are seeking.

You can't always use confrontation; you have to build alliances, you have to use the political process. You have to sense when the time is right for an opening. For an example, when I worked to change the medical school here at the University of California, Irvine, from an osteopathic college to a medical school, the money was controlled by Willie Brown, then Speaker of the California State Assembly. And I had been trying for 2 years to increase the number of Black and Chicano students in the medical school. However, when Willie controlled that money that the university needed, and I had a relationship with him, then we had a foundation from which to now present our lists of requests.

I had been in dialogue with the medical school for 2 years, without much movement, but when the power people fell into place, and their position was backed up with resources, then the whole thing (demands to increase underrepresented students in the medical school) moved more in 2 weeks than it had in 2 years. Then, say, fast forward to 5 or 6 years ago, I have been in the change process 40 years, so by the time I started working as a consultant for the University of Nebraska, they said let's increase the African American faculty, we were able to line up the legislature, the regents, put the resources in place, set out targets, and control the money. So when you got the regents, legislature, you have the systemwide president, you got the stars all lined up, so it is just not me going up there, saying "you ought to do this." All the pieces were lined up and the initiative closed.

My generation had to learn that through experience, trial and error, and creativity. There was no handbook that somebody handed to me out of graduate school, saying OK, put all these pieces together, then make change in content and process.

PARHAM: **Looking at your career in retrospect, what has been your biggest surprise?**

WHITE: The biggest surprise was the range of opportunities that I would have. Never in my wildest dreams did I think I would vote for a African American presidential candidate, that I would be involved in writing several books, that I would mentor over 100 PhDs and other professionals in other fields, that I would become a voice in psychology, or that I would have two children follow me in higher education. In fact, I have had more opportunities than I could handle. For example, I was a 35-year-old dean at San Francisco State University, however, for a fact, maybe I had skipped a couple of steps along the way, where I had not really learned the inner workings of university administration. So, I was fast tracked, but I had opportunities, and I had more opportunities than most folks, given where I started in life.

PARHAM: **Sounds like you believe that you were one of the "inspired seeds of possibility" I talk about when I teach my youth programs.**

WHITE: Yes, I took off, and that is what I couldn't figure out that day when I was thinking about coming out of retirement. You sat down with me at that time, and wrote that brochure marketing my background and availability to speak and train throughout the country. Interestingly, I hadn't fully internalized the lessons, which was when I stepped back out there after retirement, then a whole other set of opportunities emerged, just like it had in the previous 35 years. It surprised me, but when I look back, if you do one thing well, and you've got people skills, something is going to happen. I gave two speeches, and all of a sudden, all kinds of requests started to come. I hadn't fully learned it, but now, looking back, that's what happened. And at times when I was just shucking and jiving, and coasting along, then nothing happened. But when I started to produce some excellence in any area, no matter what it was, doors of opportunity opened.

PARHAM: **What was one big surprise in your life about the range of opportunities that were available?**

WHITE: Well, there was a negative surprise in my life. I really didn't believe in my heart and soul that racism was as deep as it was in America. Because if I had believed that, I never would have spent my first 28 years climbing the mountain. But I truly believed that once I got that PhD, my military service, got married, that I would be an American citizen with full privilege. And not only did that not come to pass, , but it made me open up my eyes to how Blacks were treated in America, and I began to see the poverty, restriction on jobs, and all the problems that 360 years of racism had bred. Back then, there was no Thomas Parham or Bill Cross conducting research in racial identity development, and I didn't understand these stages of identity that I would go through. I thought that I had already crystallized my identity. But I had to go through the encounter of racial shock and immersion, kind of wade through that darkness of "who am I" really, and what am I all about relative to American society, to find myself.

PARHAM: **Your belief was that you would be a full participant in American citizenship.**

WHITE: That's right. If I paid the dues in my first 28 years, or however long you were supposed to take to get those things that you were asked to do, from being a little boy, and the script was real clear to me, what you were asked to do. You were asked to try your best to get along with others, have good people skills, and if you were from a low-income family, have a part-time job. I was taught and believed that if you kept doing these things, then the future would open up to you, one would gradually build a foundation, and then whatever your future career was would open up to you. The other half of that lesson was that for people that the future closed down on, I was taught that was because they didn't do any of these things I had done. I believed that was White society talking to me, and telling you if you do these things, you will be all right.

PARHAM: **Your comments raise an interesting question about how parents should socialize their children. Should parents insulate their children to this reality you talk about, or rather should they, in fact, expose them in a way to toughen them up?**

WHITE: Well, there is a third possibility, they [parents] have to show them, to the extent that they can, somebody who has followed the script and then gone on to become a change agent. What I didn't anticipate was that after I got the skills and so on, I didn't know there was another step. The societal contract said, you get these skills, and you are going to go out and meet the world, but now you will be able to deal with it and have some responsibility for your people. And I thought that getting into the game was when I got all my tickets punched [degrees, certifications, etc.]. So in a way, being protected was good, but if somebody could have given me just another piece, and told me the realities, I would have understood the journey much better. Whereas for your generation, the message was, all right, the man employs this phenomenon called racism, and there is all that bad stuff out there, but we're going to get you these tools, and then we're gonna see what we can do to help you succeed. It took me a while to kind of go through an identity which allowed me to recognize that, all right, I do have the education, the white man sometimes acts like the devil, now I have to figure out a way to deal with this in terms of social change. That it is not impossible.

PARHAM: **Are there any more negative surprises?**

WHITE: One more I can think of is the importance of spirituality. Along the way, I somehow forgot the need for a spiritual foundation. I mistakenly believed that science could take you where you needed to go. I have since learned, fortunately, that having a strong spiritual foundation is a key asset in making it in this world.

PARHAM: **Let's shift lanes a bit. As you look back on your life and career, of what are you the proudest?**

WHITE: What I am proudest of, and what my soul feels, is that life was worthwhile. I believe that life and my career have been a beautiful ride, and that I now understand, for whatever reason, setbacks, a little trauma, heartbreak, is part of the ride. If you are trying to go to the next level, you might have to fight Goliath four or five times before you win, because Goliath is going to expect you to come and take it, so that when you step out there, you have to understand to get to the victory, you have to move through some heartbreak. There is no way I know of to get around that. But I also know that adversity makes you a full human being, because all this is part of life.

The goal in Black Psychology is to come out of the distant past, to use your resilience to become stronger by playing the role you are playing. And so, the beauty of it all is that I landed on my feet, with all these wonderful things. Between healthy children, all the young people I have met, the beautiful students I have met and been a part of mentoring and training, that's something. And then to see the people like the Obamas coming along, who

are going to take it to the next level, whatever that might be. Each generation fashions the struggle anew. It takes off from the old, and then lifts it up.

I am proud that I had the opportunity to be a teacher, mentor, and elder. Since I am from the community, I know that young people have talent (and many have much more talent than me), but they didn't have the breaks I did. So I knew that talent was there; and the fact then that I had a chance to be a mentor, a teacher and facilitator, a developer of the talent of so many young people who are now going on to productive lives has just been fascinating. It has affirmed my belief that (no matter their origins or ethnicity) there are young people with talent who, with some mentoring and guidance, can develop.

There are a couple of fantastic lecturers [in this new generation], and teachers connected with our Black Psychology network. . . . I am not going to mention names . . . but they can't seem to produce that effect or it hasn't seemed to happen, because I can't see the next generation excelling them and then them learning from it. It may be happening, but I don't see it.

But as I look at my own life, I am just totally blown away by the fact that I have had a voice in America. And my mother, as you know, was a nurse. And someone asked my aunt when I got the honorary Doctor of Laws degree [from the University of Minnesota] what my mother would say. If asked what was she proudest of, what would she say? And the answer was she would say, she knew it from day one that this was going to happen to this boy. So she wouldn't be a bit surprised at all.

PARHAM: **Most of us, as we think back across our lives, have been influenced by a number of social leaders, academic scholars, etc. In looking at your career, who have been the most profound thinkers or writers to influence you?**

WHITE: Well, I would say there are five people who have been heroes to me, who have made an impact on life: Ed Barnes; Martin Luther King, Jr.; Nelson Mandela; Bobby Kennedy; and John Kennedy.

Ed Barnes and I were contemporaries at San Francisco State, but we were 3 years apart in age. So he had done his military service before college; I did mine after college. He was the first brother I met that had a 3.5 or above grade point average. He ended up graduating summa cum laude from SF State. At the time I met him, I thought a good student was a C+ student (I was 17 years old). We started talking about becoming psychologists, he told me I had to consider graduate school, and I didn't know what that was; but the fact that this brother was knocking down A's in statistics, abnormal psyche, experimental, you know, he kind of took me under his wing. We both ended up going to Michigan State together. Eventually, there was a role reversal, and I became the mentor. He didn't have the good fortune to live a long life, he died at age 45, of a heart attack, caused by stress. Right before he died, we were going to bring him here to UC Irvine, in the social ecology program. But he (inspired) me, just by his behavior. I watched him study, organize his notes, and model how to be an A student.

When I came out of graduate school, there was no one in psychology [who really caught my attention], so from a distance, I attached myself to **Martin Luther King**. I only met him on one occasion; Bob Green was the psychologist for Martin Luther King. But King impressed me. Once I saw him standing up to the sheriffs and going to jail, and fire hoses, I said something is going on with this brother. He may not be a clinical psychologist, but this brother is saying something. What impressed me was his inner strength, his ability and willingness to stand up for a belief system for the rights of others, and equality in this so-called American democracy.

Then there was **John Kennedy**. What impressed me about President Kennedy was he seemed to have a vision for a future in America, which to use today's term, would be more inclusive. We were going to change, and create a new day. And with this theme, the old order is dying. The old ways are not working; change is coming, let us begin anew. I admire him because he had that intellectual depth, but he had physical courage. He was a man who had a boat shot out from under him, pulled another man 3 miles, with a rope in his mouth; so, he had that physical toughness. Of course, I had the good fortune to get into that network, I never met John, but I met **Bobby Kennedy.**

What I admired about him (Bobby) was his ability to come through the darkness. Here he was at the pinnacle of power, his brother is the most powerful man in the world, and he was his brother's right-hand man, and they took his brother the president out, just like that. That boy [Bobby Kennedy] went into a big depression, and then he developed a different sense of spirituality. He tried to read the Greek philosophers. But what happened to him was that when he was down in Mississippi, went to the black churches, and saw all that suffering. But he also saw the joy in the people, something got resurrected, no, discovered in him, and he got some soul. And I said, we are going to go with this one. The Kennedys, for whatever reason, decided that they were going to develop a younger cast of so-called Black leaders. Willie Brown was in the state legislature at the time, so they got Willie up on the radar screen, and asked him about some different people, and Willie told them about me. So they interviewed me, and what they were looking for were people they thought had the right stuff. I had worked my way through college, I was from a single-parent home, the Korean war, and so they figured by accomplishing a PhD and becoming the third or fourth Black clinical psychologist in America at that time, that was something they could work with. They thought I was an intellectual; they liked that, and I was also tough, so I met their criteria. So we were in the lowest echelon when we started, that is when they would come to town, or into L.A., I would get to chauffeur, or drive them around, but that didn't bother me, because I was learning. So that cadre of Willie Brown, Bob Green, Joe White, we became their folks. They never said it, but they didn't have a great deal of respect for some of the older Black leaders. They wanted people like them, that's what they wanted; individuals with strength and vision for the future.

Then into my 40s and early 50s, there was **Nelson Mandela**. I just had to admire a man who said I'm not leaving jail unless I'm a free man. Keep me in or let me go free with no conditions. And even his jailers came to admire him. Of course, he has that depth of his convictions, a whole person, he had been through the stages of racial identity development. He had integrity and wisdom, and that just gave me strength, and I had a tremendous amount of admiration; and I said, well, look, if he can deal with this, then this stuff I have to deal with is small (in comparison).

PARHAM: **In my own work and mentoring, I encounter students and professionals alike who comment on being challenged by life's adversities. In my responses to them, I often talk about the notion of "conceptualizing struggle," which sounds like what you've done in relating to the life of Nelson Mandela. In fact, as a psychologist, you, too, have said**

many times that struggle is part of the process that made you grow, and that you can't have major growth without struggle. That is just part of it, and once you internalize that, then struggle is not struggle in the sense that it's bad for you, or too difficult to overcome.

WHITE: Yeah.

PARHAM: **Beyond these heroes and personalities you admired, who were the most important people in your life?**

WHITE: There were three men in my life, two of them were uncles, and one was the director of the college center. The two uncles were 9 years apart in age; my uncle Dave was only 9 years older than me. And his mom died when he was 12, so when he was a teenager, he lived with us. He went to the military during World War II when he was only 18. After his discharge from the military, he was the only Black person to pass the bar in California in 1952. The summer he was taking the bar exam, I stayed with him in Los Angeles. I watched him study and saw his determination. It convinced me that if you really want something, and you want to excel at it, that is what you have to do. I saw him do that. Here was a boy who lost his mom when he was 12, was in the military at a young age, and just kept going. That had a profound influence on me. I saw that and said if this is the way it's done, then that is what I have to do.

Uncle Robert was an inner-city real estate man, a speculator, a hustler, an operator, but managed to keep the real estate piece together. He was very innovative and resourceful; he could look at a situation and immediately see three, four, or five possibilities, and he was sort of a crisis manager of the family, and patriarch. So, watching him in operation showed me there are more ways to "skin a cat" than one. If you run up against an obstacle, just back off it and try to think of two or three other ways to come around.

Mr. Curry was a white man, a director of the community center, which was three blocks from our house. They used to call the community center a neighborhood house, back in the day. They had programs from childhood up to old age. At 11 years old, I was the runner-up for the camper of the year. I made up my mind that I was going to be the winner next year. When we got there, I did all the things I thought you should do. But, as fate would have it, I didn't win the award and they gave it to another child at camp. I really thought I deserved it, had worked hard for it, and so I was very angry, disappointed, and hurt. Consequently, I decided to boycott the center. After some time, the director sent word that he wanted to see me, and subsequently held a meeting with my mother and I. He told me that yes, I deserved the award, but the other boy who won it "needed" the award. He explained that I had everything: a mother who loved and cared about me, good looks, a good personality, was popular, and intelligent. The other boy had very little of that, and that's why he needed something in his life to help him feel better about himself and his situation. From that moment on, I understood, and that was a profound lesson that really helped me appreciate how I had been blessed.

PARHAM: **As you think about your career, and the status as a "pioneer" in the multicultural field, I wonder if you can talk about what you believe are the fundamental principles you want to convey?**

WHITE: The fundamental principle that I want to convey after 47 years is that Black people and other ethnic minorities in America have psychological strengths. And in recognizing those potential psychological strengths in culturally diverse people, be they Black, White, men, women, the professional's role as a teacher, therapist, counselor, or mentor is to help people get in touch with those strengths. It gives these young people a better chance to move toward wellness and optimal living. Given that, the trouble with the pathology models, whether you are using them to characterize Blacks or Whites, is that if you never get to the person's strengths, then it is very hard for a person to live a productive life, and move toward wellness and optimal living, if they are not in touch with their strengths. And without realizing it, White psychology ironically is now moving towards a strength-based set of models that we laid out decades ago. Not only are we the fourth force, but we offer a fifth force, too. And I am not denying that people get mixed up or get under stress, or get confused, and have delusions, or whatever. But I am saying that ultimately, whatever you are doing as a teacher, a therapist, or a mentor, you should get to the strengths of an individual.

The second dimension of that fundamental principle is, having said that, what are those strengths? So saying that these folks have strengths, they've come through 400 years of whatever we've been through in America, and to land on their feet, they must have something going for them. Now, can we identify what those strengths were psychologically that allowed them to survive, and then for the next generation of psychologists, after we've identified that, can we package this, and teach it to children?

Barack Obama has six of the strengths, and this week he developed seven. Improvisation, resilience, spirituality, connected to others, emotional vitality, gallows humor, and a healthy suspicion of White folks.

And one more life lesson that I got from my mother that is a fundamental principle of my life: No matter how poor you are, you will always have to be prepared to give to others.

And she didn't see that as a deficit, she saw that as something that makes you feel better. So by the time I started school, I would always bring some child over to the house that was hungry, and my mama would give them something, and send them back home. That was in the Depression of the 1930s when people didn't have jobs or the means for self-sufficiency. There were hobos that would come to the back door of our house, and my mother would pack them a meal and give them a bowl of hot soup. It didn't matter how little we had, my mother always shared it with others. I have tried, in my life and career, to do the same and have mentored my students to do likewise.

PARHAM: **You have been blessed to receive numerous recognitions and many accolades in your career. Among those awards, which of them stands out for you and why?**

WHITE: There are two awards that stand out for me, maybe three. The one that stands out is one of the more recent awards, where I received an honorary PhD from the University of Minnesota. Why that award was important is because I grew up five blocks away from that school, I could have walked to school, and I had a good part-time job, and I could have worked in the community center and worked as a coach, working with the younger children, it wouldn't have cost them any money, and they had a community college built right into the university for children like me, but nobody encouraged me to become a student there, because Black boys of my generation were raised to be shoeshine boys, or to shovel coal. So 57 years after I graduated high school, here they come with this honorary PhD. Now, some white

folks love complications; you can't do anything simple. You ask them how much two and two is at the Math Department, and they will give you a complex answer, but they can't just say "four." I don't know what it is about them sometimes. Now 57 years ago, when I graduated high school, all some admissions dean had to do was sign an admissions slip and I would have been in school right there. Now that we have come through this whole honorary degree process, they have got a dossier on me, this thick. They have checked me out since the time I was born. So now they have given me this honorary degree, when 57 years ago they could have admitted me right out of high school. So, now I have come full circle, and that is why this particular award is so meaningful, if not ironic.

The second award that stands out in my memory was bestowed by Michigan State University, who gave me an award because of my experience of being with the School of Social Science some 30-plus years before. The Psych Department called me out there. Interestingly, the Psychology Department and I had a falling out, because they said that while they trained me to be a leader in psychology, after I left graduate school, I'm jumped off into this "Black thing." So they felt that I was the one who brought the racism into psychology, and they were very disappointed in me. Because when I left there, I was one of the nicest people you wanted to meet. I was a Black Anglo-Saxon. I had a Black face but I had a white identity. Now when I came to California, according to their version of events, I had changed my career path and identity as a psychologist in a way that violated their expectations of what they thought I was supposed to be doing.

But then in 1996, they had the 50th anniversary of the PhD program there at MSU, and called everyone back who started in 1946 up to 1996. They had a big reception. They gave out awards, one in every area—-clinical, social, experimental. They gave me an award saying I was the best in clinical psychology. Then the professors got up to speak and said they were the ones who put the idea of Black Psychology into my head. My wife, who is normally very quiet, was so shocked and surprised that she jumped up intending to protest. But I said "no," if they want to believe that, let them. But in that moment, I felt good based upon the fact that I had defined what was excellent, and what was Black in my own terms, rather than their terms. When I left graduate school, I tried to seek affirmation on their terms and it didn't work. So now I have come around after 47 years after graduate school and have been part of this whole Black and multicultural movement in psychology, which makes me feel pretty good.

I think the awards from the Association of Black Psychologists are very important as well because they represent the recognition from my peers. The awards say, in essence, that this brother is OK, he paid his dues, and he stood up for us. The Janet Helms award for mentoring was the same thing, it said, this brother was a pioneer and he opened up the door for the rest of us, and we appreciate that. You may not agree with everything he says, but this brother broke the barrier. And finally, I received that outstanding teaching award here at UC Irvine. I am smiling, because I was suppose to have received it 25 years ago, when you guys were still here as students, but they said no. Now, all these many years later, I am awarded the Lauds and Laurels Award, which is one of the highest distinctions you can receive from this university.

PARHAM COMMENTARY: In considering all of the awards Dr. White has received, I had occasion to be present when he received the 2008 San Francisco State University Distinguished Alumnus of the Year Award. In ceremonies at the university one evening and a private celebration for Joe the following night, the university president, family and friends, former classmates from 50 years ago, and many of his mentees gathered to congratulate him and celebrate his achievement. This was a very moving and auspicious occasion, as the former student, who returned home once to join the faculty and administration in the late 1960s, had now returned home again some 40 years later, a celebrated son of San Francisco's legendary academia. In recalling his exploits as a student, his challenges as a young faculty member and Dean of Undergraduate Studies in the turbulent 1960s, his battles with the discipline of psychology to claim a presence for persons of African descent, his mastery of teaching and mentoring, his contributions to the literature, and his long list of students he has mentored, all were clear that his status as a "pioneer" was solidified through years of struggle, perseverance, excellence, and faith.

PARHAM: **As we close this interview, I wonder if you can sum up for all those who will read this manuscript and transcript, a parting word about Dr. Joseph L. White, a pioneer in this thing we call Black Psychology, multiculturalism, and diversity.**

WHITE: At the core of my being, the healthy side of me is fascinated with life. The healthy side of me just came later as I got older and wiser and was able to push through life's adversities. I am just fascinated with the process of social change, and in my life, that's what I've tried to instigate and achieve. Of course, I brought somebody with me to the promised land in the spirit of Dr. King, but then I finally figured out that Martin Luther King wouldn't make it there to finish his journey. That final step of the journey I would have to figure out on my own, with others looking to me for the blueprint.

What I want to leave behind is that I experienced it all; that I tried to give it my best shot. It was a good ride!

NOTE

1. Schlesinger, A. (1965). *A thousand days: John F. Kennedy in the White House.* New York: Houghton Mifflin.

5

Living the Contradictions of a Mexican American Feminist

PATRICIA ARREDONDO

¿Estoy complicando la cosa? Am I being too complicated?

There are many ways I have thought about to weave together the many threads, pathways, and *fronteras* (borderlands) of my life thus far. As has often been remarked, the professional is personal, and for me, this cliché is quite accurate. So, I thought about a chronological order by decades of my life. A career evolution review also lends itself to capturing benchmarks of my self-empowerment through professional adventures. Then, of course, there is the geographical locus, where integration of the personal and professional themes emerged from rich cultural landscapes of Lorain, Ohio; Boston; Phoenix; and now Milwaukee. So many options, somewhat symbolic of the windy and self-charted roads I have traveled on this psychohistorical journey.

Two recent interviews of a biographical nature were easier to participate in than this self-directed commentary, which is so dependent on my retrieval of memories. In the final analysis, this is an imperfect accounting. It is a *mezcla* (mixture) of themes, highlights, and constructs that have been continuous threads between the personal and professional. Undoubtedly, constructs of identity, worldview, feminism, empowerment, and multidimensionality will become apparent, as will the anthropological lens I have applied to countless situations, all out of curiosity and a desire to learn more about the "other."

This is an extensive, yet necessary, preamble to other reflections on my journey as a Mexican American

This chapter is dedicated to *mi abuela*, María Estefana Morales de Zaldívar, and my parents, Eva Manuela Zaldívar and Apolinar Arredondo

37

feminist. Although I tried to organize this chronologically, there will be passages that mix the past and the present. I hope this will not be too confusing and that the readers are not bored with this process of thinking out loud as I begin to share personally meaningful experiences. May they be relevant and, perhaps, even inspiring. This entry is dedicated to my parents and my *abuela*, who wrote the screenplay for Patricia. Enacting their expectations and hopes has been a great responsibility and I do not want to disappoint them. *Adelante con ganas*/I move along (this commentary) with desire.

AN ANTHROPOLOGIST'S NIRVANA

Lorain, Ohio, likely does not evoke associations to people of Mexican heritage. On the shores of Lake Erie, 15 miles west of Cleveland, bordered by farmland, a union city with U.S. Steel, the Gypsum Plant, the Lorain Shipyards on the old Black River, and the Thew Shovel heavy machinery manufacturer, Lorain was a destination for immigrants. Yes, it was blue collar, except for the east side, which had homes for professionals like physicians, lawyers, and school administrators. Like many industrial cities, Lorain's neighborhoods were ethnic based with the Catholic or Protestant ethnic, bilingual churches within walking distance for parishioners. We, and other Mexican families, lived in South Lorain among Hungarians, Croatians, Serbians, Greeks, and Slovenians.

The African Americans I knew growing up lived in public housing, a couple of blocks from my *abuela*. One of their churches was across the street from her home. On Sundays, my siblings and I sat on her porch swing, fascinated by the rhythmic gospel music, so upbeat compared to the stoic Latin music at our Slovenian parish, SS. Cyril and Methodius. Newcomers in the 1950s were Puerto Ricans and Southern Whites, primarily from West Virginia. The little anthropologist in me was continuously making observations about all these different families, their traditions and lifestyles.

In the mid-1950s, Puerto Rican families moved into the houses across the street. I was curious about my new neighbors. They spoke primarily Spanish, but a different-sounding Spanish; wore summer clothes almost year-round; and sometimes used two last names. I guess we were Americanized Mexicans; my parents had the same last name. My early contact with Puerto Ricans provided rich cross-cultural lessons.

I think I was in about the seventh or eighth grade when I was given permission to go with my *abuela* to the *capilla*/chapel, the Spanish-speaking, Catholic Church established for the Puerto Rican families. There I learned about the missionary nuns who did not teach school, but seemed to be more like social workers. Yes, I wanted to volunteer, but I also went to the *capilla* in my private anthropologist role. I was bilingual and therefore allowed to get involved by registering families, serving meals, providing interpretation of the English paper, and so forth. Admittedly, I wanted to be helpful, but I also wanted to know the people and how they were or were not like the Mexicans. There were many differences, similarities, and ambiguities.

Multicultural diversity was the by-word for Lorain. There were extended families under the same roof, grandparents who spoke little to no English (or "broken" English like my *abuela* and *tios*), private ethnic clubs, and even two ethnic-branded bowling alleys—the Croatian Club and the Slovak Home. Religion was pronounced as well. There were ethnic Protestant and Catholic churches; one synagogue downtown near St. Mary's school; and Black Protestant churches, primarily Baptist and Methodist AME. This was all so fascinating to me. Ethnic enclaves or barrios were also about class. We lived in South Lorain, south of the tracks, two blocks from the steel mill that spewed dirty soot several times a day. *Mi familia* and our non-Mexican neighbors had equal access to the pollution that rained down on the clothesline.

EARLY FASCINATION WITH IMMIGRANT EXPERIENCES

The multicultural milieu and aura of Lorain was more than incidental for me, and I could not ignore it. Yes, my early years were in a city of immigrants, traditional, class-bound, ethnically defined, working class, and with highly visible religious practices. In this multicultural milieu, the seeds for my professional interests were planted. With a Mexican immigrant father, a mother of Mexican heritage, and Mexican grandparents, I wanted to know how we fit into this story of immigrants and immigration. As Handlin (1951) noted, "The immigrants lived in crisis because they were uprooted. In transplantation while their roots were sundered, before the new were established, the immigrants existed in an extreme situation" (p. 6).

The dream of immigrants was to own their own home and our *familia* was no different. Ours was the second house from the corner, a duplex, co-purchased by my parents and my *tios,* my father's eldest brother and his wife. Both men worked for U.S. Steel. Six of the seven Arredondo children spent our early years on 29th Street in South Lorain. Our home had two bedrooms, one bath, and a large basement for doing the wash and for the coal furnace that bellowed during the cold winter nights. We had front and back porches, and sitting on the front porch glider, watching people walk by, was a favorite summer activity.

The neighbors with the corner home were White Protestants; their ethnicity was not known to me at the time, but I think they were of English or Scottish heritage. I learned that owning a corner home was a sign of affluence; owners had more yard space and were unencumbered at least on one side. Our neighbors to the left were Greek immigrants, a couple, two children, and a paternal grandfather who tended his garden with great love. My classmates in Grades 1–8 were primarily children of immigrants—blonde, blue-eyed, and fair-skinned. Our teachers were the Sisters of Notre Dame from Germany and Yugoslavia, often speaking with strong accents. We were the only Mexican Americans in the Slovenian Catholic school, and here emerged my self-consciousness about color and my intentionality to bring attention to myself through academic achievement. The nuns made this easy for me because they, too, valued the female students, especially ones who were smart and/or wanted to go to the convent to become nuns. However, the latter was an option I turned down.

Going to public school for Grades 9–12, my choice to leave the rigidity of Catholic school, but also aware that tuition was going to be a problem for my parents, brought me into more contact with students of African, Mexican, and Puerto Rican heritage. The other students of European heritage came from throughout the city, not just South Lorain. Now I encountered more socioeconomic differences. This change opened my worldview and raised further awareness about ethnic

color lines and cliques. This was understandable and also obvious. There was no bilingual education, so the new students from Puerto Rico were often relegated to a corner of the classroom, unable to participate. I made an effort to get to know them, but obviously could not admonish my teachers for not encouraging them.

Public school was a type of borderland for me. Socially, I wanted to fit in with the White girls who were part of clubs like sororities. I got in, but it seemed empty; as Julia de Burgos would say, an attempt at being something others thought I should be. I easily reverted to my oasis of comfort—academic achievement.

Learning About Being a Woman and Always Trying Harder

Gloria Anzaldúa, Chicana feminist poet and essayist, has written eloquently about the psychic struggles of Latinas, particularly women of Mexican heritage. In her classic book, *Borderlands/La Frontera* (1987), she discusses the topic of mestiza consciousness. Her entry titled *"Una lucha de fronetas/A struggle of borders"* is one with which I strongly identify.

> Because I, a *mestiza,*
> Continually walk out of one culture
> And into another, because I am in all cultures at the same time,
> *alma entre dos mundos, tres, cuatro,*
> *Me zumba la cabeza con lo contradictorio.*
> *Estoy norteada por todas las voces que me hablan*
> *Simultáneamente*
> (Anzaldúa, 1987, p. 77)

Over the years, the eloquent prose and poetry of feminist writers such as Gloria Anzaldúa, bell hooks, Sandra Cisneros, and Simone de Beauvoir engaged and validated my tendencies for independent thinking and challenging the status quo, through actions more than words. My roots for feminism, in different forms and expressions, were intimately influenced by my parents and maternal grandmother. In the midst of a highly structured, Mexican family-centered milieu and a city with its "isms," they taught me that, as a girl and a woman, I could think for myself and make sound decisions. Little did I know then the powerful effects of their examples on my adult development.

I had the privilege of having a feminist father and grandmother, as well as a "traditional" mother. *Mi abuela,* affectionately referred to as *Mamá* (my grandmother), was the consummate pioneer woman. She ran away from her home in Oaxaca, Mexico at age 13 so she would not have to marry an older man. Her resilient, stoic nature and her faith in God and *La Vírgen de Guadalupe* served as her bedrock. After my grandfather died at the age of 46, she was emancipated again. She went to work at the steel mill and eventually bought her first of two homes. When I think I am having a tough time, I have often thought about *Mamá.* She was a woman who led by her quiet and caring yet impactful behavior.

My parents also influenced my cultural and gender worldviews through their examples and individual relationships with me. From each, I learned different experiences about struggles with covert and overt racism, the art of biculturalism in a culturally segregated community, civic engagement, and how they had to put off their young lives to give to their parents in troubling economic circumstances. For my mother, it was quitting school after ninth grade to contribute to the household income because of my grandfather's alcoholism. For my father, it was working the land in the midst of the Mexican revolution and the Catholic Church's collusion with the powerful landowners. However, they always inspired in me a "can do" attitude. My father was always the optimist, looking at the glass as ¾ full, and my mother reminded us to never take anything for granted. From *Mamá* and my parents, I learned that *sí se puede* (yes, we can) is about women.

My mother's (Eva's) structured approach toward child rearing had its own feminist worldview. She wanted her four daughters to learn the responsibilities and rules as daughters, but also to know how to be in the world of White middle-class women. She taught us social etiquette, the necessity of (good) appearances, and the importance of caring parenting. With my older brothers (last child was a male, 20 years younger than my older sister), she expected exemplary behavior at school. Her constant admonishment was that they had

to be *bien educados*/well-mannered and reflecting positively on the family. I know that today, my parents would be very proud of their achievements. My oldest brother Joel is president of the Lorain City Council and the Mexican Mutual Society, following my father's civic-minded, servant leadership.

With seven children, my mother was the consummate mother and wife, harsh at times, prideful of our accomplishments, and very protective of our well-being. My mother was riddled with contradictions—she was strong-willed and goal-oriented, but also preoccupied with what became of her children. Her perfectionism was a means to cope in a world full of oppression toward women and Mexicans. No doubt, there were many times I resented her strictness and expectations of me as her right-hand helper. When I was in grade school, I used to think, "When I am 13, I'm just going to run away from home." These "poor me" feelings lingered until I went to college, but my appreciation for my mother increased. She had a tremendous responsibility and, even today, I am amazed at how she managed. Although her standards of perfection were a weight to drag through at least four decades of my life, I now know that the motto of *doing more than* and *working twice as hard* have served me well.

Learning About Being Different

As a Mexican American woman, I quietly struggled with cognitive dissonance for being of dark complexion in a White society, smarter than most boys in my U.S. history and English classes, and always trying to overachieve. My mother always reminded us that very few Mexican students graduated from high school. She would lament this every June when the pictures of high school graduates were posted in the local newspaper, *The Lorain Journal.* In many ways, I think her sadness was associated with her lost opportunity to go to high school. She wanted us, her children, to fulfill her dreams and be full participants in U.S. society. Having our pictures among those of other Lorain high school graduates was evidence of success.

I took my mother's spoken and unspoken expectations to heart. By then, I was well aware of the negative portrayals of Mexicans on television. They were always the bad guys or the singing *señoritas* in bars frequented by bad *hombres*/men. I recall watching Disney's version of the Alamo and feeling confused about where my sympathies should lie—with the Tejanos or the Mexicanos? *West Side Story* came out when I was in high school. This Romeo-and-Juliet tale set in the Bronx captivated my attention because Puerto Ricans were featured and not in entirely negative ways. Although there were stereotypes in the production, I appreciated the platform this gave to all Latinos. I guess one could say that this musical was one of the first cross-over productions in mainstream theater, introducing Americans to Latinas/os.

INFILTRATING AND PUSHING INSTITUTIONAL BOUNDARIES

Compensating behavior because of my sense of "inferiority" or second-class status had its upside. I was tenacious and learned that, through relationship building, I could be mentored by others. My counselors and teachers helped to nurture my goals and overproductivity. I recall deliberate mental calculations about how I was going to infiltrate the mainstream activities in school and college, and make my mark. Yes, I did get in and excel. When I graduated from high school, I received the top service award. It made my mother proud. In college, I was the only Latina in student government, a situation that I repeated many times.

As I moved into workplaces and professional associations, I learned that I still had to persist to fit in and make a difference. Trying harder was not sufficient; I had to learn how to work the system as well. Similar to my approach to high school activities, I moved into professional organizations such as the American Counseling Association (ACA) and the American Psychological Association (APA) with an action orientation. Initially, I knew that this overachieving demeanor with professional groups was about proving that Latinas and women could have a seat at the table. As will be discussed in a later section, I continue to be professionally active, but it is about the next generations, not about me.

MY MULTIDIMENSIONAL IDENTITY

In workforce diversity consultation, I have always reminded participants that employees take their personal identity to work. For ethnic minorities, this is even more pronounced; we cannot leave our "color" or other manifestations of our ethnicity outside the office door. My Mexican American heritage is a great source of personal pride. As I learned when I applied to the doctoral program, and later, when I accepted my first university appointment at the University of New Hampshire, I facilitated institutional affirmative action goals. The "twofer" attribution was not meant to be insulting, but it was. Furthermore, because of the institutional focus on my ethnic and gender identity, it seemed as though my professional competencies were being overlooked. How others saw me was limited to these two identity factors, and it did not make me feel good. However, I decided that as long as I was a Mexican American woman, I needed to know the depth of this personhood and enact it.

Beginning in the late 1970s, with my discovery of *Toward a New Psychology of Women* by Jean Baker Miller (1975), I immersed myself in literature by feminists such as Simone de Beauvoir, Sor Juana Inés de la Cruz, and others. Their voices of self-discovery and struggles for self-respect and self-determination engaged my long-standing self-consciousness about the role of women in professional settings. I learned that women are taught to fear and avoid power and often not to support other women. It did not take long for me to apply the inspiration of these writings. I instigated the creation of women's professional networks and a Latina/o organization, as well as set up my first business. I found my power.

My ethnic minority identity status also gave rise to academic creativity, linking the personal with the professional again. It is quite obvious that I have special affection for newcomers, more typically immigrants and refugees. Postdissertation, I developed a conceptual figure to capture the multiple dimensions of immigrants' identity. My concern was that these hopeful, hard-working individuals, students and adults alike, were so often minimized and their personhood reduced to their immigrant status. Being an immigrant meant you did not speak English, wanted to marry an American to stay in the United States, and had different customs and lifestyles. Deficit associations were generally attributed to immigrants, and if you were of African heritage or another visible cultural group, perceptions were even more negative. In the early 1990s, with the assistance of a colleague, Tom Workman, my conceptual figure emerged as the "Dimensions of Personal Identity" model (see Arredondo, 1996, p. 8). In retrospect, my model was also about me and my wish not to be known only as a Mexican American woman. There is more to me, even though I may not look the part.

CAREER SELF-DETERMINATION THROUGH RISK TAKING

It is probably quite apparent that I am a very driven person. I have had the good fortune of climbing on big waves and riding them with pleasure and a sense of accomplishment. My career process has not been linear or very predictable until lately. Being an educator has been a consistent theme in my career life, from teacher to trainer in corporate settings. I believe that education, particularly higher education, is key to inclusion in a society that easily marginalizes those who are not of privilege. For now, I am in the "right" place, although this was not always the case. I will now share a couple of other scenes from my life to discuss self-determination.

There were times that being an academic was a bitter pill. I left Boston University in 1985, untenured and cynical about institutional leadership. The rules changed, and as a junior professor, my peers and I were caught in the crossfire of faculty-administrator battles. I had to selectively trust my senior peers and be the mentor to disenfranchised students. However, the 7 years of my term of service were productive and life altering. I became licensed as a psychologist, went through a divorce, changed to a single-woman lifestyle, and engaged in serious career exploration. The latter paid off and paved the way for the next chapter of my career.

With the establishment of Empowerment Workshops, Inc., in Boston in 1985, I launched a new career identity. Although I could not sufficiently explain to my parents what I was doing as a consultant, I felt very alive and passionate about promoting my values for organizational change through a focus on diversity in a range of workplace settings. During these 15 years, I learned to wear different hats simultaneously. I was an entrepreneur, consultant, psychologist in private practice, adjunct professor, nonprofit board member, and contributor to professional counseling and psychology.

"Being true to my values" and "transferability of skills" were my touchstone thoughts as I moved into the private sector, being the responsible agent for my own paycheck and benefits. As might be expected, Empowerment Workshops was not an overnight success; it took 5 years before I had my first big corporate client, the Gillette Company. This multiyear relationship was a springboard to many more rich engagements in the corporate and nonprofit business worlds. In 1996, *Successful Diversity Management Initiatives* was published, a valuable credential for consulting on organizational diversity goals.

Moving back into higher education was not a casual decision. I was fortunate to have choices. Joining Arizona State University (ASU) in 1999 was more than a career redirection, it was also my first major relocation in 30 years. From the predominantly Irish, Italian, and WASP multicultural milieu of Boston, I stepped into the cowboy conservative politics of Arizona, where persons of Mexican heritage used the term *Hispanic* as an identity referent. So many concepts taught in our multicultural psychology literature were palpable in Arizona, from White privilege to indigenous models of healing and living. For the first time, I had a real-life introduction to American Indian tribes and their complicated histories, and the resentment of Mexican Americans who asserted that the "border had moved," thereby disenfranchising their families. In the midst of Arizona pink skies, beautiful mountains, gated communities, and glitzy lifestyles are the profound pain and misery of oppressed American Indian and Mexican peoples. I felt guilty and powerless about this, recognizing my fate had been different and privileged.

Now, as a senior administrator at the University of Wisconsin–Milwaukee, I assess why I am doing this and what it means. My answer is the same as the one I have stated for stepping into professional association leadership roles. I want to be a role model for other Latinas and women in general. Perhaps in the next 10 to 20 years, there will be more than a handful of Latina tenured full professors in senior administrative positions.

Points of Pride and Responsibility

My scholarship in four areas—immigrants' transitions and change, Latina/o psychology, cultural competency development, and organizational diversity—has privileged me in different professional sectors. I leveraged my passion in these areas to professional engagements that led to an increasing foothold in the counseling and psychology professions and brought notice to me.

In 1998, I was awarded an honorary doctorate by the University of San Diego for my leadership in the multicultural arena. This was quite unexpected, but a source of *orgullo*/pride for me. Of greatest importance was that my mother was able to attend the award ceremony, where I also delivered the commencement address. In 2005, I was recognized as a Living Legend by the ACA for my pioneering work in the multicultural counseling competency field. Although I truly appreciate these two recognitions, I have told my colleagues that "I never aspired to these achievements." Rather, out of a sense of responsibility, these are doors I have tried to open for Latinas/os, women, and other underrepresented groups.

In the past 8 years, I have been president of several national associations. In so doing, I am trying to be a role model, an example to others that our servant leadership matters. I believe other professionals from underrepresented groups can become president of ACA, Division 45, and someday APA.

SOME OF MY "HIDDEN" DIMENSIONS

Not unlike other professional psychologists, I have outlets besides my career and involvement in professional associations. My hidden dimensions are known to friends who may have shared in my experiences over the years. I doubt that these revelations will have any shock value; rather, they illuminate other characteristics I articulated in the Dimensions of Personal Identity model (Arredondo, 1996).

As a child, I was introduced to sports, particularly baseball and football. I grew up in Ohio, home to football championship high school and college teams. As a child and adolescent, I sampled ice skating, tennis, swimming, diving, softball, and bowling. I again have to thank my father for promoting sports gender equity. He would always include my older sister and me in all sporting activities, not just my brothers.

Some of my favorite earliest memories were going to baseball games at the Cleveland stadium. Even better, my father would buy us big balloons that cost 3/10¢. I learned how to keep score and cheer for my favorite players. I was, and continue to be, very interested in baseball. Today, I belong to the Red Sox Nation—and cheer for the team shamelessly—thanks to my 30 years in Boston.

My second favorite early sports activity, because it also involved my father and siblings, was bowling. On Sundays, my father's day off from the mill, we would drive over to the Croatian Club with the boys who set the pins, or to the modern Redman lanes with automatic pin setters. Bowling alleys were more than about recreation for me, they were also about watching others interact. Lorain's immigrant families frequented the lanes, and conversations in Hungarian, Croatian, and Polish were commonplace. My dad was a bowling maverick, playing at times on three different teams (no wonder I overdo!). My siblings and I have introduced our children to this sport, continuing the family tradition.

When I was first married, I realized that to have more time with my husband, I would have to learn to play golf. Little did I realize that I would become so consumed with this activity. Golf gives me the freedom to be by myself if I choose, to enjoy nature, and to compete against myself. I have won my share of local club tournaments, and, although I have not done so lately, I do enjoy playing with men and beating them. Quirky but true.

Another release is yoga. Again, it is an individual activity I can do alone at home or at the yoga studio. I enjoy the time to focus on breathing, to experience my body stretching, and to rest my racing mind. Yoga is a lifelong activity, and, like golf, I intend to practice these as long as possible. Here again, my father is a role model. We played nine holes when he was 90.

FAMILISMO Y PERSONALISMO

In a close-knit nuclear family of seven children, I learned about caring, sharing, and giving. There are many ties that bind us together, but more than anything, it is our parents' legacy of loving interdependence and striving for excellence. My 10 nieces and nephews have learned to have pride in being Mexican and have also accepted the higher education expectation. Of the 10, 6 will be in or have graduated from college by the time this book goes to press. The new twist is that they are cracking the public education ceiling by attending private and Ivy League schools. I only dreamed of doing this, but they are living my dream.

When I married the father of six children, I became part of another family. He was much older and, thus, I was in the same generation as four of his five daughters. Fast-forward 35 years, and I find myself in deepening connections with my "daughters," their children, and now the first Dowd great-grandchild. With the grandchildren, there is easy conversation about college and career plans. When my grandson Ryan went on a trip through the vineyards of Spain and France, he tripped into the town of Arredondo in northern Spain and brought me Arredondo memorabilia. Not too long ago, it was a little embarrassing to refer to my "daughters'" children as my grandchildren. They, too, found it awkward, because I was not the grandmother type, nor the mother of their moms. Because we are on a first-name basis, it really does not matter; we all know how we are related. More recently, I had the dubious distinction of becoming a great-grandmother. Our oldest granddaughter, Jubilee, gave birth to Kelea Darling DeCaro on Maui in December 2007. The family circle widens and deepens.

MIS ESPERANZAS/MY HOPES

Many opportunities have come my way, and many others I have created with encouragement from friends, colleagues, and mentors. I want to continue to give to others by example and through a legacy. Like an immigrant, I want the next generation of Latinas/os to do better; have greater success; become the second, third,

and fourth presidents of the American Counseling Association; swell the number of doctoral graduates and tenured professors; be counseling center and agency directors; and have a consciousness of *raza* (identity).

My nonlinear life journey has introduced many wonderful colleagues and friends into my life. I would be remiss to not mention that these include the following: my ASU graduate students, faculty peers at ASU and UWM, colleagues and friends from the National Latina/o Psychological Association, lifelong relationships with individuals I met through ACA and APA, and friends in my prime locations—Lorain, Boston, Phoenix, and now Milwaukee. I continue to evolve and enjoy life in relation to and with them. I am extremely grateful for the good fortune of well-being, others' caring and support, and the continuing new experiences I am encountering at this time in my life.

This brief accounting suggests that the *personal is professional* for me.

My life has been full of contradictions because the data are stacked against a Mexican American woman of my generation. There are no scientific explanations for why I became a mestiza feminist, but certainly there is abundant qualitative evidence. I inherited my parents' and *Mamá*'s legacy for self-determination and for living out the poetry of Julia de Burgos. The poem, *Yo misma fui my ruta* (I was (created) my own pathway), continues to serve me as a mantra and a connection to a powerful Puerto Rican woman. It is my inspiration as I enter uncharted spaces and hopefully create visions and aspirations for others.

REFERENCES

Anzaldúa, G. (1987). *Borderlands/La frontera.* San Francisco: Spinsters/Aunt LuteBook.

Arredondo, P. (1996). *Successful diversity management initiatives.* Thousand Oaks, CA: Sage.

Handlin, O. (1951). *The uprooted.* Boston: Little, Brown.

Miller, J. B. (1975). *Toward a new psychology of women.* Boston: Beacon.

6

My Life in Fast Forward

Reflections on the Making of a Latino Psychologist

AMADO M. PADILLA

What follows is a glimpse of my life story. It is not a complete story, but it contains most of the essential details about my development as a psychologist and my work. The story is linear because this is mostly how I think about things. I thank the editors of this volume for asking me to contribute to this volume, and I am honored to be able to share my story with readers. I will begin by saying that I am a very fortunate man. You will learn why as you read through the following pages.

MY FAMILY BACKGROUND

I am the oldest son of Manuel and Esperanza Padilla. I was born at home surrounded by four grandparents and several uncles and aunts during World War II. My parents named me after my father's best friend and first cousin. My father worked for the Santa Fe railroad as a blacksmith during World War II and continued to do so for the next 30 years. My mother did her part for the war effort by working as a parachute packer and later was a stay-at-home mother. Together, my parents, my four younger brothers, and my large extended family provided a supportive home environment until I left at 17 to begin my university studies. Our home was filled with a rich linguistic mix of Spanish and English. All of my uncles and aunts conversed with ease as they switched between languages. When the adults gathered, there was loud conversation about politics, religion, local news, and what the neighbors did or should have done. The Padillas and Lopezes (my mother's family) were avid consumers of the news, strongly opinionated, and always ready to debate some issue. My mother was the best educated of the family with a high school diploma, but as she would sometimes mumble under her breath, "Ignorance doesn't stop a Padilla from having an opinion."

Our house was filled with the aroma of beans boiling in a pot, fresh flour tortillas, spicy red or green chilis, Spanish rice, sopapillas, and on weekends, our favorite tamales bought at a local tamale factory. My mother also enjoyed baking for her boys, and we frequently had homemade apple pie, German chocolate cake, and upside-down pineapple cake.

In those days, people proudly referred to New Mexico as tricultural, referring to the Hispanic, American Indian, and Anglo cultures. The Anglos were the dominant group, but there were some Hispanics in visible positions in government and business. Pride in triculturalism, however, was mostly without substance. American Indians were mostly excluded from any discourse of power, and Hispanics were pressured to speak only English and acculturate to Anglo culture. Most of my childhood friends were other Latinos, and this was to remain the case until I entered college.

MY CATHOLIC UPBRINGING

Catholicism was an important part of my upbringing. Although I did not start out in a Catholic school, I switched to one very early. Initially, my mother enrolled me in first grade at a local public school. Several weeks into the school year, my mother began to ask what we did at school, and I reported that we took naps twice a day. After a time, my mother grew suspicious and decided to make a surprise visit to the school. When she arrived, she found the classroom lights off and all of the students curled up on the floor or at their desks napping, including the teacher, who was sitting at her desk sleeping. My mother's advocacy on my behalf began right then and there. I still remember my mother yelling at the teacher that she wasn't sending me to school to nap, but to learn to read and write. My mother withdrew me from public school that same day and enrolled me at Sacred Heart Elementary School, which was our parish parochial school. I remained in Catholic schools until I graduated from St. Mary High School. After that first grade incident, I was forever wary about reporting my school activities to my mother.

I was a good student, but never at the top of my class. However, I always liked school, even though I had few memorable teachers. In high school, I was something of a jock—I played football, ran the mile on the track team, threw the javelin, played tennis, and tried my hand at baseball. My high school had three academic lanes: business (considered to be the low track), classics (which required 4 years of Latin), and science (requiring 3 years of math and 4 years of science). I was in the science track and also took 2 years of Latin and 2 years of German. Of all my classes, chemistry was my favorite.

Like any other adolescent boy in my Catholic high school, I spent considerable time fantasizing about girls, especially after Father Curtain delivered the only sex education class to a boys-only filled ninth-grade classroom. In this single hour of Catholic "sexuality" instruction in my 4 years of high school, Father Curtain's take-home message was that we could lose our souls if we allowed the devil to get the best of us with girls. Father Curtain was a young Jesuit priest who was probably coerced by the nuns at the school to talk to the boys about sex. I still remember Father Curtain's sex hour, because it was by far the most incompetent lesson I had in 12 years of Catholic education.

There were only 60 students in my graduating high school class; about half the class consisted of Italian and Irish Catholics, and, with the exception of one American Indian student, all the rest were Latinos. Most of my classmates came from lower-middle-class families. This was also at a time when there was no discussion of culture or race in the curriculum, and scarcely little about helping the poor through charity and community service. I did not leave high school with a deep sense of religiosity, but I did leave with the conviction that I could do anything if I persevered and worked hard. These values have served me well throughout my life.

MOVING ON TO COLLEGE

Graduating from high school was always a certainty; however, I received no guidance in the transition to college. I knew I wanted to go to college, but I wasn't sure what the process was for going to college or what to study. In my youthful way, I also entertained fantasies of traveling to Alaska, for reasons that I don't remember, or joining the navy to see the world. By working as a gardener during the summers, I saved enough money to enroll at a now nonexistent Catholic college in Albuquerque. None of my close friends went to college. Some joined the military, others found jobs, and most were married within a few years after graduating from high school.

College was a life-transforming experience for me and one that began to set the course of my life in ways that I had not expected. When I enrolled in college, I hit upon the idea of pursuing a career in medicine, so I enrolled in the usual mix of prerequisite classes and chemistry. To help pay for my education, I also secured a job at a local hospital in a new department called Inhalation Therapy. I never understood why I was hired, because I was 18 years old and had absolutely no experience beyond gardening. I also discovered at this time that I really enjoyed learning, but more importantly, I realized that I was good at school. Learning was easy, and I was motivated to study everything I could get my hands on. This had certainly not been my high school experience.

After working in a hospital for about 9 months, I knew that medicine was not a career option for me, nor was chemistry. I wasn't comfortable with sick people, and I didn't really enjoy chemistry much. By coincidence, I took an introduction to psychology course three times from different instructors, each of whom taught the course very differently. My first course was a summer class offered by Henry Ellis at the University of New Mexico. The class was very stimulating because Professor Ellis focused on human memory and cognition, which were entirely new to me. The second course was very different. The instructor was a Scottish professor, Stuart Boyd, who, with a great deal of humor, spent the quarter on Freud and personality dynamics. The sequel to Boyd's class was a course taught by Professor Joel Greene, who was a behaviorist who approached psychology from a stimulus-response and physiological perspective. His lectures relied heavily on D. O. Hebb's unifying neurophysiological theory of behavior. Incidentally, if any reader is asking why I took introductory psychology three times, it wasn't because I needed to repeat the course. Remember, I said I enjoyed learning and found I was good at it. Well, I had heard good things about Stuart Boyd and Joel Greene's courses and decided to see for myself. Thus, when I decided to declare psychology as my major, I had a thorough grounding of the broad range of specialty fields in psychology.

MY BEGINNING IN PSYCHOLOGY

My interest in psychology was partially due to the fact that my mother had a nervous breakdown when I was in elementary school and spent roughly a year institutionalized in a state hospital. I remember accompanying my father to visit my mother in the hospital, and still remember our visits with my mother after she had received electroconvulsive shock treatments. On reflection, my interest in psychology probably had to do with trying to understand my mother's illness and how it subsequently affected her and our family. As an undergraduate student and a member of the Psi Chi Honorary Society, I and other Psi Chi students visited the same hospital where my mother had been institutionalized. The idea was to give students exposure to mental illness and to "cheer up" the patients. I remember that I never told any of my friends or professors that I had visited my mother at that same hospital years before. The stigma of mental illness weighed heavily on me at the time.

I completed all requirements for my degree by December 1963, but didn't have a clue what I was going to do next. I thought about the military and, on a whim, went to the Marine recruiting office and expressed my interest in the officer training program in marine aviation. In what now seems like just a few minutes, I passed both the written and the physical examination. The recruiter said that I would be receiving a letter with information about when to report for duty. So, it seemed I had a plan for the future.

Because I didn't have a job, I decided to return to school in mid-January and finish a second major in sociology and a minor in philosophy. I thought this would be a good way to fill my time while I waited to hear from the Marines. Also, I had received a National Science Foundation undergraduate fellowship for my work with Joel Greene in his laboratory and had support until June. A few days after the start of classes, one of my instructors, Harry Saslow, asked what I was going to do after I graduated. I casually mentioned that I planned to join the Marines and go to officer training school. I remember the look of shock on Harry's face. He told me I was making a huge mistake and I should go to graduate school. His arguments included the fact that the United States was becoming entangled in Vietnam and that the military was not a good career option. Harry was right, of course, and I knew it.

With Harry's encouragement, I applied to three graduate programs—the University of New Mexico, Oklahoma State University, and the College of William and Mary. These were the only programs I could find that still had February 15th deadlines. This was way before any type of electronic data retrieval, and the only way to search for programs was to examine the flyers that graduate programs sent out to departments of psychology. I was accepted to all three programs, but the offer to Oklahoma State University came with a National Institute of Health research fellowship in child experimental psychology. Goodbye Marines, hello Oklahoma. Incidentally, this was a time before affirmative action and special programs for minority students. I still recall having to include a photograph with my application materials to OSU. I soon lost track of my friend Harry Saslow, but until the Vietnam War ended nearly 12 years later, I often thanked Harry Saslow for guiding me to graduate school.

Before moving on to graduate school, though, I need to mention a couple of things about my undergraduate years. At no time as an undergraduate student did I ever meet a Latino professor. There might have been a Latino professor in the Spanish department, but I am not even certain of this. In high school, I had studied Latin for 2 years and German for another 2 years; and in college, I again took German for 2 years because I heard that to get a doctoral degree in psychology, I needed a foreign language, and German was recommended in psychology. This was back in the day when a reading knowledge of at least one foreign language was required for the PhD in psychology. How things have changed in higher education. I also recall that there was absolutely no discussion of culture or ethnicity in any of my psychology classes, and I don't remember any discussions of social class except in sociology. At best, these were considered extraneous variables and of little consequence in the science of psychology.

I did have the opportunity, however, to take two courses that would lay the foundation for some of my later work in Latino psychology. The first was a course in rural sociology taught by Professor Clark Knowlton, who was researching the loss of land grants by the native Hispano population in New Mexico after 1848, when Mexico lost its northern territory to the United States. Professor Knowlton's class was a mind-opening experience because my maternal grandmother often told stories about the large ranch that was part of her family's land in northern New Mexico that was lost to

the *Americanos,* as my grandmother would say. I also had the opportunity to take a course on Southwest history from Professor Lynn Perrigo, who authored our textbook that told the story of conquest and colonization first by the Spanish and then by the Americans. These two courses stimulated my interest in history, but more importantly, on the psychological effects of colonization on people who had lost their homeland.

MY GRADUATE SCHOOL YEARS

Graduate school was not a breeze, but neither was it particularly difficult. I struggled with numerous existential questions, coupled with identity issues, and of course there was the Vietnam War and the civil rights movement. I got married after my first year of graduate school to a Latina also from New Mexico. I decided to leave Oklahoma after I completed my master's degree. The major reason for my decision was that my interests changed from child experimental to a more behavioristic program in learning theory. Strangely, this shift in interest led me back to the University of New Mexico. I decided that I wanted to study with Frank Logan, whose papers and books on learning and motivation I found inspiring. I discussed my interest with Robert Beecroft, who was teaching learning theory at OSU and who said he would call Professor Logan at Yale University and ask if he was taking new graduate students. Much to my surprise, Professor Beecroft reported back to me that he had managed to reach Professor Logan and that he was no longer at Yale, but had moved to the University of New Mexico as chair of the psychology department. As it turned out, Logan was in the initial stage of building an experimental psychology program and invited me to work for him as his research assistant.

Returning to New Mexico was an important decision because it brought me and my wife back to our families and our cultural roots. The civil rights protests and anti-Vietnam War activities were everywhere, and in New Mexico, the Chicano movement added to the drama for social justice and equality. Although raised in New Mexico and always aware of my status as a Chicano, I had never had any contact with Chicano intellectuals or with the pressing issues of land reform that were beginning to take hold in New Mexico because of the Chicano movement. With a master's degree in psychology, I was now part of the Chicano intellectual elite. However, I didn't feel prepared with much substantive knowledge about my people or culture other than that acquired from my family and my classes with Professors Knowlton and Perrigo.

As a doctoral student, I was deeply involved in my coursework and research in an experimental program and trying, when time permitted, to be active in Chicano issues. Here I was, a doctoral candidate in psychology in my home state, and still I had never had a Latino faculty member in any of my university coursework or a Latino mentor. I was intimately aware that I had become a very self-reliant graduate student who was still seeking to reconcile my cultural roots with my development as a psychologist. I was only 24 years old and still searching to define myself in the context of the social and political activism that was permeating daily life. Although I had an excellent relationship with Frank Logan, my dissertation advisor, he was not a mentor. He was an outstanding teacher of learning theory and research methodology, but he couldn't help me with the existential crisis I was experiencing on a daily basis because of the social upheaval going on in America at the time.

My first involvement in Latino issues as a budding psychologist was as a consultant with the Albuquerque public schools on special education placement of Latino children. Because I had done psychometric assessments while working on my master's degree, I was familiar with the administration of the Stanford Binet and the Wechsler Intelligence Scale for Children. So I tested Latino children, many of whom spoke little or no English, and made many modifications to the administration of these tests, trying to bolster the scores of my children. This experience gave me a deep appreciation for high-stakes tests with children who were in the process of learning English and with instruments that were not normed with such children in mind. By administering the tests in Spanish and being more flexible on the timed parts of the tests, I did my best to enable children to shine, but often it was not enough to save them from a special education class. This experience has stayed with me, and to this day, I

contribute papers and chapters on culturally appropriate assessment whenever possible.

MY FIRST FACULTY POSITION

I completed my dissertation when I was 25 years old; however, because I was still of draft age, my dissertation chair and I decided that I would hold off on submitting my dissertation until after I turned 26 and was no longer of draft age. It was a good plan, but excruciatingly long because I had nothing particularly interesting to do other than wait. During this period, I occupied myself by trying to work up some publications while also trying to absorb all the social turmoil among people my age because of the Vietnam War and the struggle for civil rights. I applied for teaching positions, but there were few jobs and lots of competition. My wife and I wanted to go someplace different, and I landed a job at the State University of New York College at Potsdam. We were both excited about this change and looked forward to living in upstate New York. Little did I know this was going to be a life-transforming experience for me.

There was some culture shock in moving to the "north country" of New York State, and the cold and seemingly endless winter did not help. But the move did have a good outcome because it brought me into closer contact with my own cultural roots; in addition, I had several experiences that broadened my thinking about culture and language in ways that my training had not done. For example, I had the opportunity to work with students from the Mohawk Indian Reservation, and from them, I was able to draw parallels between their stories and what I knew about the Pueblo Indians I was accustomed to in the Southwest. I also made friends with a handful of Puerto Rican and African American undergraduates from New York City. Together, we commiserated about the rural and largely white community that was upstate New York and about the bitterly cold winter days. Importantly, I was an outsider in this community just like the students, but I was also on the faculty, and the students looked to me for guidance and support; however, I was only 26 at the time and not much older than my students. Little did they know that I, too, was in need of a mentor.

Because of my proximity to Montréal, Canada, I made many trips to Montréal, which was a hotbed of activity for the Québec separatist movement. What I experienced in Montréal reminded me of the Chicano movement in my home state of New Mexico and in the Southwest. At this time, I became acquainted with the research and writing of Wallace Lambert and his students at the University of Montréal. Lambert was writing important papers on Francophone and Anglophone intergroup relations, bilingualism, and biculturalism. I was enamored with Lambert's research because I could draw parallels with what he was doing and what could be an important research program for me with Latinos. Thus, I began to think seriously for the first time of researching Spanish-English bilingualism. However, in order to do this, I needed to relocate to an area with a large Latino population. I went on the job hunt during my second year in New York. The search was successful, and I was invited for job interviews at the University of Utah and at the University of California, Santa Barbara. I had a good reception on both job interviews, but fell in love with Santa Barbara and California. After leaving Santa Barbara, I returned to upstate New York with my mind set on moving to California whether I had a job or not. Fortunately, I did get a job offer at Santa Barbara and I accepted immediately.

FINDING A MENTOR AT LAST

Another set of events occurred at this time that also changed my direction as a psychologist. The first was an acquaintance that I began with Rene (Art) Ruiz, who was the chair of clinical training at the University of Missouri in Kansas City. Art Ruiz had single-handedly begun an effort to identify other Latino PhD psychologists. In the early 1970s, there weren't many of us around. Art and I began a correspondence that culminated in me traveling to Kansas City to meet him in the spring of 1971. He was the first Latino psychologist I knew, and he would soon take on the role of mentor to me. Also in the spring of 1971, I received a call from Dr. Juan Ramos from the National Institute of Mental Health (NIMH), who had been referred to me by my new friend Art Ruiz. Juan explained that he was looking for a psychologist to come to Washington, DC, in the summer to work on a special project to assess the

mental health needs of the Spanish-speaking peoples in the United States. I met Juan at NIMH in April of 1971. Juan knew that I was an experimental psychologist and had no background in mental health or clinical psychology, but he hired me as a consultant anyway.

The 3 months I spent at NIMH were challenging because there were few guideposts along the way to know what the needs of the Latino population were in the area of mental health. During the day, I worked largely alone in gathering as much information as possible about Latinos and mental health through library searches (this was back in the day before computerized searches), NIMH grant applications and final reports of funded projects, and community mental health center statistical reports. When not occupied with mental health literature, I also began my self-study on the psychology of bilingualism and the social psychological literature on intergroup relations. All of this began to shape my thinking about my new research agenda. In addition, my stay at NIMH brought me into contact with other Latino mental health researchers from around the country and with the American Psychological Association (APA). I communicated frequently with Art Ruiz, who assumed the role of mentor, giving me advice about one matter or another. I also participated in what I believe was the first symposium on the Mexican American experience at an annual meeting of the APA in Washington, DC. Ed Casavantes organized the symposium on "The Effects of Cultural Variables on Mexican Americans," and the panelists included Casavantes, Manuel Ramirez, Albert Ramirez, Art Ruiz, Ernest Bernal, and me. This was a historic symposium because it was the first time that Chicano psychologists had organized a symposium on Chicano psychology at an APA meeting. This was also a memorable event for me because it was the first APA convention I attended, it was my first conference presentation on Latinos, and I had the opportunity to be among Latino colleagues for the first time.

MOVING TO CALIFORNIA AND FINDING MY PROFESSIONAL IDENTITY

After 3 months in Washington, DC, I moved to UC Santa Barbara and took up my post as assistant professor of psychology. I taught large Introduction to Psychology classes with my colleague Howard Kendler, a well-known behaviorist and introductory psychology textbook author, and I taught a course on the psychology of learning. I extended my teaching by co-teaching a course on Introduction to Chicano Studies. There were no established ethnic studies courses at this time, and I didn't know how a psychologist could contribute to such a course. However, the course proved to be an incredibly stimulating experience that contributed to my emerging identity as an ethnic psychologist. The instructors were Pedro Castillo, a Chicano historian; Carlos Zamora, a professor of Spanish literature; and me. My task in the course was to bring in the psychological perspective. Frankly, I can't remember how I contributed to the course, but I do remember what I learned from my colleagues. Pedro Castillo focused on the theme of Chicano resistance to the invading Americans whose philosophy of manifest destiny resulted in the war with Mexico and the colonization of what was Mexican territory north of the Rio Grande River. Pedro argued that Mexican Americans had never been a passive people who stood by and watched their land taken by conquest; rather, they had countered conquest and oppression in many different ways, from armed insurgency to legal action in the courts. Carlos Zamora enriched the discourse with his literary interpretations of the "masks of identity" embedded in the works of writers such as Frantz Fanon and Octavio Paz. This was also a time when Chicano literature was going public, and we used the themes of resistance, pride, and cultural identity in this literature to enliven our lectures and class discussions.

I also initiated a seminar with a few interested undergraduate students on the topic of bilingualism. Together, we read the literature on the psychology of bilingualism and developed an annotated bibliography on which I relied frequently for the next 10 years. In addition, I offered a course on the Psychology of the Chicano Child. I was surprised by student interest in the course and by my ability to stay one small step ahead of my class in the readings—we were all learning about Chicano children together.

On the research side, I extended my summer work by persuading NIMH to give me a contract to compile the literature on Latino mental health and to prepare a monograph summarizing the literature. The contract was substantial enough for me to bring my colleague Art Ruiz to Santa Barbara to work with me on this project. I also applied for and received a grant from the National Science Foundation to conduct a cross-sectional study of 2- to 5-year-old children who were learning Spanish and English simultaneously. These two funded projects began a long series of grants and contracts that I have had during my career to support my research and writing projects.

My work with Art Ruiz culminated in a monograph titled *Latino Mental Health* (1973), which was the first of numerous papers that Art and I would co-author. The work on child bilingualism also resulted in several published papers, which began a long line of studies and papers that I continue to work on that fall in the area of second-language learning and teaching. While at UC Santa Barbara, I began a project with Professor Manuel Carlos of the Anthropology Department and a graduate student, Susan Keefe, to conduct a three-community survey of mental health utilization by Mexican Americans. We were fortunate to receive a 4-year NIMH grant to support this project.

Although UC Santa Barbara was a stimulating environment for me and the place where I began to really form my professional identity, I found myself restless. Following a divorce, I decided that a move was in order. I had started to work with researchers at nearby UCLA, most notably Rodolfo Alvarez, who was in the Department of Sociology. One thing led to another, and I applied for a position in psychology. In the spring of 1974, I was offered a tenured position as an associate professor of psychology at UCLA, and without hesitation accepted the offer.

MY YEARS AT UCLA

The move to UCLA was exciting because my research opportunities seemed limitless. Once at UCLA, I organized my research agenda around two major strands with the idea of maximizing my productivity, and this would allow me to interact with different professional communities. One research strand focused on the psychology of acculturation and ethnic identity, and the other fit more broadly into applied linguistics with a focus on second-language learning.

I concluded my work with Carlos and Keefe on the three-community study of mental health utilization. One of the main features embedded in this community survey was the idea of ethnic identification and the measurement of acculturation among Mexican American adults who differed by generation and length of residence in the United States. Until this time, research on acculturation was the domain of anthropologists, but with Susan Keefe, we conceptualized ways in which acculturation could be viewed as a psychological construct and measured as such. This work resulted in several publications, including two books: an edited volume, *Acculturation: Theory, Research and Some New Findings,* published by the American Association for the Advancement of Science, and a book with Susan Keefe, *Chicano Ethnicity.* These works have been cited widely, and they laid the foundation for much of the early work on psychological acculturation that was to follow not only with my research group, but with many other researchers.

I remained at UCLA from 1974 through 1988. These were incredibly productive years. I continued my collaboration with Art Ruiz and also worked with Martha Bernal, who was then at the University of Denver, and the noted Latino sociologist Lloyd Rogler from Fordham University in New York. I also co-taught a graduate course in learning theory with Professor John Garcia, the only Chicano psychologist elected to the National Academy of Sciences. In 1975, I became the director of the Spanish Speaking Mental Health Research Center (SSMHRC), which was funded by a grant from the National Institute of Mental Health and housed in the Department of Psychology at UCLA. I directed the SSMHRC until 1989. During this period, I had the good fortune of working with Esteban Olmedo, Gerardo Marin, Barbara Marin, Nelly Salgado de Snyder, Manuel Miranda, Manuel Casas, Hortensia Amaro, Arturo Romero, Robert Perez, Steve Lopez, and Richard Cervantes. These were heady times because we were the major research engine driving Latino mental health research in the country.

In 1977, I received a Fulbright-Hays Senior Lecturer appointment and spent 7 months as a visiting professor at the Pontifica Universidad Catolica del Peru in Lima. This was a much-needed sabbatical leave for me, and even though I taught a research methods and statistics class in Spanish at the Catholic University, I enjoyed living in Peru and having the opportunity to reflect on my research. This was my first opportunity to be completely self-reliant as a university professor in Spanish.

Although Spanish was my mother tongue, I had never had any formal instruction in it, so teaching research methods and statistics was challenging. In Lima, I also had the opportunity to lecture on Pavlov and behaviorism on Saturdays at a free university without walls run by a group of leftist students, who fondly called me their Yanqui-Latino profé.

I returned to UCLA in the spring of 1978 renewed, and also with the news that I had been promoted to full professor. That summer, with the encouragement and assistance of Gerardo Marin and Esteban Olmedo, we launched the *Hispanic Journal of Behavioral Sciences* as part of the dissemination effort of the SSMHRC. We decided that there was a need for an interdisciplinary scientific journal that would publish articles of importance to Hispanics. One consideration that entered into this decision was the growing resentment that Latino researchers were expressing about being locked out of APA and other mainstream, guild-oriented journals because their work focused on nontraditional, ethnocultural topics that often challenged contemporary theories and interpretations of Latinos. We decided on launching the journal as an interdisciplinary quarterly in 1979. I was the editor of the journal and had no idea whether we could sustain a quarterly journal; nonetheless, the first issue of Volume 1 appeared in the spring of 1979. It has continued to this day, and we are now in Volume 31. The journal was more work than I ever imagined it would be, but at the same time, it has had a major influence in Hispanic behavioral science research. Articles from the journal are cited widely, and a broad cross-section of authors has published in the journal. In 1989, the *Hispanic Journal of Behavioral Sciences* became a part of Sage Publications, and my burden was lightened by no longer worrying about printers, subscriptions, or mailings.

I also found time to co-author with Elaine Levine a book, *Crossing Cultures in Therapy: Pluralistic Counseling for Hispanics,* which was certainly one of the earliest cross-cultural counseling texts in the field at the time. This book was ahead of the multicultural counseling curve, and although it sold well for a few years, the large number of books on multicultural counseling today has long since overshadowed it.

During the 1980s, I continued to be very engaged in language research. From 1982 to 1985, I directed the

National Center for Bilingual Research located at the Southwest Regional Laboratory in southern California. The National Institute of Education funded the work of the bilingual research center. I took a half-time leave from UCLA and served as the director of both the SSMHRC and the National Center for Bilingual Research. I was busy, but enjoyed the two research enterprises by which I had set my compass. When the contract for the bilingual research center came to an end, I campaigned to win a new contract for language research. The goal was to broaden the base to include foreign language education and to bring the center to UCLA. We won a national competition for a new language research center at UCLA and named it the Center for Language Education and Research (CLEAR). My collaborators at UCLA included Russell Campbell and Ann Snow in applied linguistics, Concepcion Valadez in education, and Kathryn Lindholm and Hal Fairchild in psychology. We also collaborated with Richard Tucker from the Center for Applied Linguistics in Washington, DC, Kenji Hakuta from Yale University, and Richard Duran from UC Santa Barbara. I was familiar with Richard Tucker and his bilingual work with Wallace Lambert in Canada. Kenji Hakuta, a developmental psychologist, provided empirical support for the idea that Spanish-English bilingualism contributed to both intellectual and linguistic development, which had been another idea put forth by Wallace Lambert in his work with French-English bilingual children in Canada. I served as the director of CLEAR until my departure to the School of Education at Stanford University in 1988.

By 1985, I began to be disillusioned with the direction that mental health funding was taking at NIHM under the Reagan administration. Funding for social problem-focused mental health research was losing ground to biomedical research. By this time, too, I was convinced that education was the best mental health intervention for Latino youth. However, the Reagan administration, and Secretary of Education William Bennett in particular, were attacking bilingual education from every direction, and xenophobia was very much in the air as the English Only Movement gained momentum across the country. In this atmosphere, I found myself drawn to educational research and Latino concerns for educational equity. Some of this interest began to be reflected in my growing interest in research on educational resilience and highly successful students who come from challenging home and community backgrounds.

In this research, I saw my own roots as a child who entered school speaking Spanish and from a working-class background. In my private moments, I wondered how I had managed to move from a small working-class barrio community in Albuquerque to being a full professor at one of the country's premier public universities. I wondered, too, about my younger brothers, who, like me, also had advanced degrees while our friends remained in the barrio. I decided to make a career shift to education and reinvent myself as an educational psychologist. I also decided to shed the administrative burdens of running research centers and traveling constantly and to focus my attention on my family, which now included my son Diego.

MOVING AGAIN—CHANGING INSTITUTIONS AND RESEARCH DIRECTIONS

In 1988, I received an offer to join the Stanford University School of Education as a full professor in psychological studies. I went through the usual motions of requesting a counteroffer from UCLA, but in my heart, I knew that I had made the decision to leave for Stanford. I left UCLA in good spirits, knowing that I was about to reinvent myself again, just as I had when I first went to UC Santa Barbara and later when I moved to UCLA.

The move to Stanford was a good one because it has given me the opportunity to work on issues that I could not have done as easily had I remained in a department of psychology. I have had many good students who, like me, see the importance of education as crucial to the well-being and upward social mobility of minority youth. Yet the dream of a first-class education for so many disenfranchised Latino youth and their families remains only a dream. Because of my interest in language research and education, I chaired the graduate program in language learning and policy (1991–1998), and more recently, I have been chairing the program in psychological studies in education (2005 to the present). I have taught courses on second-language acquisition research, adolescent development and schooling, educational and psychological resilience in children and adolescents, and the education of immigrant students. I have also teamed with Duarte Silva to run the California Foreign Language Project, which provides me with the opportunity to work with talented language teachers.

My research has not varied too much from what I have been doing for the past 3 decades—psychology of acculturation, second-language teaching and learning, strategies for developing biculturalism, and education. I still edit the *Hispanic Journal of Behavioral Sciences,* and I still experience the same anxiety I did as an assistant professor if I wasn't writing and publishing. Sometimes, I wake up in the middle of the night in a panic, thinking that I am going to lose my tenure because I am enjoying life too much. Then I realize that these are just the mad rumblings of a person who loves his work and wouldn't have it any other way.

WHAT HAVE I LEARNED?

What have I learned through my travels as a psychologist? What knowledge have I gained through my reflections that might be useful to students? Would I do things differently if I could start over? First of all, I have had a fantastic journey as a psychologist, and I am so thankful that I switched interests from chemistry to psychology. I am by nature a risk taker and an optimist, and I am very focused once I set a course. I have taken many professional risks over the years by shifting my research and teaching interests to focus on Latinos, changing academic positions, and following multiple tracks in my research and writing. I never worried about the downside of the risks; after all, I started as the son of a railroad worker and a mother whose early years were spent as a migrant worker in Colorado. I knew that a few bumps along the way weren't going to hurt. Fortunately, I have found more roses than thorns in my wonderings.

When I say that I am a risk taker, I do not mean that I am a gambler. All of my risks were calculated, and I had a pretty good sense that I could achieve my goal. In the process, I have had great fun in my work and in the relationships I have formed along the way. I have surpassed most of my own dreams and lived and traveled in places I only dreamed about as a brown-skinned boy growing up in Albuquerque. My advice to any young person

seeking a career in psychology—do what interests you and do it with passion by cutting your own path; don't worry about the trees falling behind you; and above all else, stay focused on the forest ahead.

RELEVANT PUBLICATIONS (IN CHRONOLOGICAL ORDER)

Padilla, A. M., & Ruiz, R. A. (1973). *Latino mental health: A review of the literature.* Washington, DC: Government Printing Office. (Reprinted 1974, 1976).

Padilla, A. M., Ruiz, R. A., & Alvarez, R. (1975). Community mental health services for the Spanish speaking/surnamed population. *American Psychologist, 30,* 892–905.

LeVine, E. S., & Padilla, A. M. (1980). *Crossing cultures in therapy: Pluralistic counseling for the Hispanic.* Monterey, CA: Brooks/Cole.

Padilla, A. M. (Ed.). (1980). *Acculturation: Theory, models and some new findings.* Boulder, CO: Westview.

Keefe, S. E., & Padilla, A. M. (1987). *Chicano ethnicity.* Albuquerque: University of New Mexico Press. (5th printing 1998)

Cervantes, R. C., Padilla, A. M., & Salgado de Snyder, V. N. (1991). The Hispanic Stress Inventory: A culturally relevant approach toward psychosocial assessment. *Psychological Assessment: Journal of Consulting and Clinical Psychology, 3,* 438–447.

Padilla, A. M., Lindholm, K. J., et al. (1991). The English-only movement: Myths, reality, and implications for psychology. *American Psychologist, 46,* 120–130.

Padilla, A. M. (1994). Ethnic minority scholars, research and mentoring: Current and future issues. *Educational Researcher, 23*(4), 24–27.

Arellano, A., & Padilla, A. M. (1996). Academic invulnerability among a select group of Latino university students. *Hispanic Journal of Behavioral Sciences, 18,* 485–507.

Padilla, A. M. (2006). Second language learning: Issues in research and teaching. In P. Alexander (Ed.), *Handbook of educational psychology* (2nd ed., pp. 571–591). Washington, DC: American Psychological Association.

Padilla, A. M. (2008). The need to be ethnic: The role of perceived discrimination in ethnic identity. In C. Willis Esqueda (Ed.), *Motivational aspects of prejudice and racism. Nebraska Series on Motivation, Volume 53* (pp. 7–42). New York: Springer.

Padilla, A. M., & Borsato, G. (2008). Issues in culturally appropriate psychoeducational assessment. In L. A. Suzuki & J. Ponterotto (Eds.), *Handbook of multicultural assessment: Clinical, psychological, and educational applications* (3rd ed., pp. 5–21). New York: Wiley.

7

Life Messages, Messages for Life

RICHARD M. SUINN

Across life, we hear messages. Some are people-voices that are direct, others are messages whispered to our subconscious from experiences surrounding us. All are instrumental in shaping us. Here are messages from my life, and messages I offer you.

Early messages, Asian parental voices: Hawaii is a melting pot of races with people blending seamlessly together. Friends have diverse names like Hashimoto, Cadiz, Wong, O'Sullivan, and Hanohano, but with no differences in how each is viewed or treated. The message: Race is not a salient personal quality; we are too similar for race to matter.

Yet alongside surges another message. Mother's instructional voice: "You are pure Chinese." Mother's actions also provide messages, such as being taken for treatment by Chinese traditional herb doctors. Mother's own characteristics are also revealing: mystical premonitions, viewed by some as a healer, respectful of dead spirits. Ancestors are remembered as including a traditional fortune teller in the Buddhist temple.

But there was the paradox that parents are traditional and are fluent in Chinese, but we children of pure Chinese ancestry know only English. The words "you are pure Chinese" are thus spoken often, but carry no meaning and no impact. Instead, their blocking our learning of our native language and their emphasis that we fit into the Western culture conveys the opposite message: You shall achieve a better life through being thoroughly American, better educated than your parents (mother third grade, father high school), and different from us . . . and we will be proud of this difference.

Comment: Despite the seeming contradiction to ethnic identity development, I experienced little conflict. Being Chinese was not a defining element, having no more influence than a rarely used middle name. More influential were the values instilled by other messages: obedience to parental authority, striving/achieving but always muted by modesty. Mother's own behaviors implied major values; as I observed her offering the same respect and kindness toward beggar or banker, being nonjudgmental to strangers pending information from their actions, declaring that "actions speak louder than words." And from a laconic father, other communications from his persona: that a quiet person can earn as much respect as the person who stands out in the crowd, and that inner peace is a major life achievement deserving of the highest recognition.

Compelling messages, from my body: From age one to late adolescence, the most powerful sound is that of a single labored breath . . . as I struggle to capture that one gasp that means survival, over the asthma disease that strangles my lungs . . . nightly . . . and shapes my frail body that is prevented from the normal play of children. The joy that comes from pure physical activity is denied, as is the pleasure of favorite foods, such as ice cream; foods that are instead enemies of simple breathing because of allergies. Without the release of physical activity, I become engaged in studies. The tasks of the classroom become familiar, and the work behaviors are easily acquired. Simply stated, studies were easy, living was difficult. So, demanding messages were instilled: You are limited and must be disciplined enough to avoid normal activities—such activities will only precipitate suffering. Self-discipline is mastered from the hardest master possible.

Comment: Learning to cope with being different was not so bad, even peers were understanding and often supportive. Still, there lurked a desire to overcome, to control my health, and thereby to be personally in control of my own life. Meanwhile, adversity was building skill in being disciplined and being focused on intellectual tasks, which will be important for my future. I learned patience as well, because medication requires time for absorption needed to provide release from breathing spasms.

Messages from mentors: The hierarchy of the Chinese family means that the voice of the child is seldom heard when adults are around. So, spontaneous speaking remained an unused ability until fostered in high school. Teachers assumed that I would participate in speech competitions, the premise being that intelligence came with verbal skills and comfort in public settings. Thus, speaking to an audience seemed a natural activity. Although I tend to feel anxious before public addresses, I simply prepare for a fluid start, knowing that once I begin, I will be fine. But I know preparation matters.

Perhaps the first important turning point resulted from action from a teacher noting my shy nonengagement. "Come and visit the camera club." This short visit turned into a long love affair with all things photographic. The new talent produced an abundance of creativity, selection as the school photographer, and a newfound popularity. Classmates' voices, from the popular football players to the class elected leaders, whose voices had once been silent, now shout "Hey, little guy lugging that big camera . . . take my picture!"

Almost simultaneous with these developments was my incidental decision to try the game of tennis. Another breakthrough occurs: Midway through the physical exercise, breathing spasms began, but persistence won out over pain and I was startled to discover that it was possible to play through the spasms and regain relatively normal breathing. From that day onward, the potential for living a normal life seemed possible, and the seeds of confidence, optimism, hope, patience, and persistence were planted.

Comment: Optimism about what one can achieve starts with hope, and hope arrives when risky decisions prove out to be wonderfully rewarding. I do not try to explain this health breakthrough because direct tests proved how the asthmatic condition was caused by the allergy to molds, foods, pollen, and volcanic dust. As a turning point, however, this one event has a place alongside the camera club event—conveying the message to me that single, possibly chance circumstances can dramatically shape one's life. My camera work became my identity and access to social acceptance; my moment of conquering my self-perception of being physically limited opened up an optimism about dealing with obstacles that seem insurmountable.

The APA presidential election: Let me digress ahead some 40 or so years to the campaign for the APA presidency, and the loss in my first attempt. It is questionable how much support could be gained by a candidate known to actively promote ethnic minority issues. However, I had hope based upon my achievements. I lost by 36 of 15,000 votes.

I am digressing because of the prior reference to confronting obstacles. The role of optimism when facing obstacles requires another element to encourage action, the quality of persistence. I am uncertain about the source of this trait in my life. I am reasonably competitive, and persistence may be an offshoot of seeing an obstacle as a challenge. But my competitiveness is situation-specific, and I can as easily turn it off. Perhaps it is fueled by that early maternal voice, "Strive to be the best . . . don't lose face." But I think a key comes from the belief that there is a time to give it up, and a time to continue. Is the end goal worth the energies needed to continue to strive? Is the evidence from reality communicating that the obstacle cannot be overcome no matter the effort? But we must add patience to the mix, because persistence without patience can end in impulsiveness.

So, even while settling my emotions, I knew I would run again. The 36-vote difference was too close to be convincing evidence that the goal was unreachable. I lost again, to a candidate whose name appears in every introductory psychology textbook, who is among the who's who of psychologists, and who also worked hard to reach out to the electorate—a more than deserving candidate. So, I was 0 for 2, but in my reasoning, the jury was still out; persistence had me try one last time . . . and the third time was indeed a charm. I won!

Comment: Sometimes, life seems a series of obstacles, some real, some perceived, but all testing one's optimism, self-confidence, persistence, and patience, and leaving one feeling alone. The first time I ran was because I was asked by APA's Division 45 during a goal-setting meeting. Crucial was the heart-warming offer of support from members of that executive committee—especially Dr. Gordon Nagayama Hall— and other professional friends who believed in acting upon their promises. Many obstacles might be overcome through individual action, but some are group projects. In some cases, the group is there to provide emotional support and strength to move forward. Sometimes, the group provides the hands and minds as active participants. Sometimes, the group is a essential sounding board as you test your reasoning/assessment of the situation you face. The message is, you need never be alone; people are blessings as they were for my election.

Messages from college: Heading for college was inevitable after high school; not only was my identity firmly anchored to studies, but the parental message solidified it through expectations. They displayed no interest in course contents but predictable interest in grades; yet no comments about "A's" were given—these were expected, and I always met those expectations. Because all of my close friends headed for universities in the mainland United States, the only question was, where would I choose to enroll?

I always perceived my parents as poor, possibly based on the frugal lifestyle—no trips, recreation, extra or fancy clothes, or entertaining, and even birthday celebrations were soon eliminated. Hence, my choice for college was at home, the University of Hawaii (UH), to save travel, tuition, and housing expenses. I also continued to be a summer laborer in the pineapple factory, becoming known among the full-timers as "the most educated employee" in this nonskilled position. This low-paying job was perhaps my attempt to reduce the stress of family finances. But there was another, private message: proof that I had control over my asthmatic condition and I could toil hard next to normal working people.

The first weeks of UH life were a chaos of decisions about a major; a decision I felt essential to avoid wasting time and money. My parents were no help, being content to tell their friends I was at the university. Possibly influenced by the implicit value "My son, the doctor," but resisting this full commitment, my first declared major was medical technology . . . then the science field of physics . . . then chemistry, until my lab partner, who copied my lab report, received an "A" to my "B," leading to my losing my taste for science instructors. A near-jump to Speech as a major was based on my admiration for the only ethnic faculty and only Chinese faculty there. But sound mentoring prevailed as this same teacher advised that this was a dead-end career, and soon after, I discovered the beginning psychology class—and found my niche. Here was a perfect blend of science and helping people, along with information I intuitively grasped.

Despite the continuing lure of a mainland education, a few UH opportunities were attractive. Air Force ROTC was commissioning graduates of the program, and I earned a third-place medal in the annual wing field competition—with the feedback that one officer would have ranked me first had I only had a haircut that day! However, poor eyesight—common to Asian heritage—led to rejection. Simultaneously, a more emotional rejection came from a university Chinese fraternity, which befriended me as a recruit but was not interested enough to accept me as a "brother." With nothing to hold me back, and a firm major in focus, off I went to Ohio State University (OSU).

The decision in favor of OSU was entirely a reasoned one: Not knowing which specialty, I picked a program that offered a full schedule of diverse courses, ranging from aeronautical psychology to personnel psychology to clinical and counseling psychology. But not everyone approved. The Catholic teachers at my high school did their best to turn me toward the "excellent Catholic universities" instead of "that secular school."

Reason for me won out over faith, establishing a pattern that reason, empirical data, scientific methods, and logic take precedence in my life when I'm faced with conflicting messages, although I do admit that I listen to my intuitive signals, because these may be, in the rationale of science, responding to implicit cues and connections.

The trip to Ohio was physically and psychologically a trip into a new world. Physically, it started on an Army C-47 cargo plane, our luggage strapped to the floor, our seats being medical stretchers (a year later, still flying military transport as the dependent of a Pearl Harbor employee, the conditions were better in a Navy MARS seaplane). Then came the transfer to a cross-country train sleeping on hard seats, and a trolley bus from the Columbus train station finally to the entrance of the university. With dormitory reservation clutched tightly in hand, and with eager anticipation that fought against fatigue, I asked at the student union for directions to my sleeping quarters. I heard the discouraging reply, "It's Sunday, nothing is open, your dorm is closed, but I can let you spend the night in the Ohio State stadium dorm." So began my new life in the new world, alone on a cot literally in the OSU horseshoe football stadium!

With the new environment also came an entry into the freedoms and responsibilities of adulthood. All decisions—from what to eat, clothes to buy and wear, courses to take, finances to manage, and friends to make—were solely mine; no protective parents to make the decision, no good friends to offer advice, no mentor to provide guidance. Somehow, this all seemed not only easy but as though an open door beckoned me to a wonderful world for which my whole life had been

breathlessly awaiting. Through a fraternity that did want me, good friends were quickly available as well as leadership opportunities. Knowing that any progress in daily living skills, money management abilities, and achievements in studies were truly through personal effort contributed greatly to self-esteem. Only one minor puzzle remained unsolved. Overall, I earned acceptance for the qualities I demonstrated, except when introduced as being from Hawaii. No one grasped my explanation that I lived in Hawaii but was Chinese, not Hawaiian. This did not seem to be Asian-oriented racism—Asians were a nearly nonexistent group in Columbus and OSU—as much as the exotic fantasy associations held by fellow students. However, even with such encounters, the issue of my core ethnic identity was still dormant, and I went through college life fitting in as an "American" person.

Comment: Sometimes, life seems to hit a downturn or, at the least, enter a period where the future is uncertain. Sometimes, well-meaning advisors seek to force their values and goals and direct your choices. And sometimes, disappointments threaten to dominate one's mood and shake one's confidence. Some days at UH were truly hard times, facing the message of not being wanted by the fraternity after being courted. But life has a way of testing your resilience, the strength of your grip on your self-esteem, and your ability to pursue equally important alternate paths. These disappointments were not easily pushed aside; they remain sad memories, but hindsight now provides a more tolerable perspective on this past, which is balanced by memory of the Ohio State adventures.

At OSU, there were surely opportunities for my personal decisions to be improper ones. But I was never fully free of the internal voices reminding me of core values. I enjoyed Big 10 football weekends, the social life, club membership, and tennis workouts, and I could be seen in my "white-bucks" shoes and fashionable gray flannels sporting the latest flat-top hairstyle. But these were balanced by focus on studies and work as a student librarian. After all, earning the degree was my primary goal, guaranteed to please my parents!

Ethnic message surfaces: The "me" that existed beyond graduation was the image of an American westerner, with the vital yet quiescent voice from Asian heritage yet to speak. Then came a letter of invitation to the National Conference on Asian American Psychology. Arriving at this conference, I entered a room as I have at dozens of other research conferences, and once more walked from one familiar world into a startling new place. Faces abound . . . faces that mirror mine . . . hair, eyes, features alike, and the temptation is to recall the weak joke "all Asians look alike." But it is not false humor that is triggered; instead, it is sudden awareness of identity. How does one put into words the emotion of "arriving," of the unfolding of one's core self, of the parental voices speaking again with the message, "Here is who you are, who you have always been, and who you will always be!" And so, I was born again in 1976. To this day, I remain unable to speak or understand the language of my ancestors and my parents, yet from that day forward, I hear this important message—of who I am in my core where it counts most.

It is impossible to overstate the enormous impact of the single epiphany and its source. In the era of my educational and early professional life, ethnic minority issues simply did not exist. I had not been surrounded by curriculum, writings, discussions, or public or personal concentration on being ethnic. Yet the existential experience aroused these amazing insights and emotions with volcanic explosiveness.

Comment: Up to that fateful day, I was content with who I was, a person whose ethnic heritage remained in the shadows. But ethnic traits were suddenly spotlighted when I encountered those many individuals, all sharing the Asian background and all psychologists! Therapists often refer to the corrective emotional experience, and perhaps this was one. I was also awakened to knowing at that moment that I shared in every ethnic person's sense of isolation by reason of being different, every ethnic person's awareness that racism exists and can appear in unpredictable ways, and every ethnic person's knowledge that he or she possesses two personas: the true inner one, and the one perceived by others based upon your ethnic appearance. It does not require living through such experiences to have this understanding. In fact, my early surroundings in Hawaii provided protective blinders. However, in the instant of acknowledging and accepting my ethnic nature came the comprehension of what comes with being an ethnic person. I also recall that such understanding did not bring a feeling of anger at injustices. Instead, an instant sense of positive bonding was released, as an orphan who identifies and meets his biological family for the first time and feels no regret at having been abandoned.

Developing an ethnic identity brings up the often-debated issue of the conflict assumed to emerge when an ethnic-identified person is faced with adopting the values or behaviors of the dominant culture. This is often labeled "selling out." Elsewhere, I have written more extensively about possible end-states of acculturation (http://www.awong.com/~randy/dad/index.html). Briefly, I first believe in the distinction between identity (or self-concept) and behaviors. There is no conflict when an ethnic person decides to learn the skills that will enable making a contribution or earning advancement in the dominant society, even if such skills meet the standard defined by the dominant group. We think nothing of acquiring computer skills to better our chances of entering a position in a valued employment setting. Because the ethnic person has developed the skills to move fluidly in the Euro-American environment, does not preclude a strong core ethnic identity existing as well. In my acculturation scale, I propose items that permit the following identity: "Although I fit very well in a Western environment, deep down I am an Asian." Furthermore, I believe that the influence that one's ethnic identity has on actions is situationally determined. For instance, possessing a strong Asian identity with its corresponding Asian values may influence the decision about whom to marry. Similarly, an Asian-identified client may prefer to be matched with an ethnic counselor in discussing a personal-emotional conflict involving parental expectations. But this same client might have no preference were the issue one of acquiring improved study skills for better comprehension. My point is that an ethnic person can retain a core ethnic identity while still exhibiting non-Asian behavioral decisions depending upon the situation. This is not "selling out" or rejecting ethnic values. Although I possess a strong awareness of my Asian identity, which includes being modest and quiet, I can also choose to engage in self-promotion—during elections—and speaking my opinion—as a member of a work group. The latter are skills I have acquired over time and upon which I rely as appropriate.

Giving voice to anger: The absence of anger does not mean an absence of passion. The presence of anger does not guarantee meaningful action. An incident occurred after settling in to Colorado. We selected a home for its access to a nearby primary school for our children's education. Not long after, it was revealed that the boundaries were being changed, moving our children to a different school that needed more numbers. I organized a presentation documenting safety and other salient issues and even an alternate solution to the numbers issue. With the favorable superintendent's response, I confidently presented my case to the school board—to be met with silence. With no questions of me, with no discussion among themselves, with no attempt at explanations, the board routinely voted the change, as if their minds had been made up and the "hearing" was a farce. I was so angry and ready to release my bile to all who might listen, until I recognized that my angry voice would carry no more weight than it did that night unless it came as an inside policymaker. So I became a candidate for the school board—a young academic versus a four-term board member. The election was not even close; still, I felt satisfied that I acted on my values, making sure that I was not a single-topic candidate fueled by anger alone. Soon afterward, my candidacy bore unexpected fruit as those who liked my values and vision asked me to be their candidate for the city council; and eventually, my voice grew into a new role as mayor of our city.

Comment: Campaigning required persistence, being willing to engage strangers door to door, studying the issues, and displaying my strengths not shown by other candidates. It also involved finding ways to shake off the stereotype of knowing only the impractical life of the ivory tower. However, as an academic, I knew how to tease out the issues by reading documents, and, serving as department head, I knew how to formulate plans. As a psychologist, I was a people-oriented mayor: responsive to needs, understanding the importance of listening to messages from all aspects of the community, being respectful to diverse viewpoints. I will always cherish that experience and especially remember the student who thanked me for doing what "faculty refuse to do . . . take the risk of exposing oneself to the community and being willing to be evaluated." As faculty that felt special.

Risk-taking endeavors: I am not by nature a risk taker. Too many years of living with the painful and immediate consequences of straying beyond my physical or food limitations taught me too well. But I also faced a series of other experiences: one that demonstrated the stupidity of ignorant cautiousness and another that enabled discovering that opportunity may be reached through alternative, nonrisky pathways by putting fear aside.

Question: Should one be brutally honest? Answer: Only if you are being factually honest rather than ignorant. The application to graduate work at Stanford University required a self-statement. Not knowing anything about research but fearing the unknown, I firmly stated my intention to become a practitioner and never a researcher. Fortunately, the department chairperson recognized my ignorance and wrote a letter of admittance, warning that Stanford students did engage in research as well as clinical activities. Once there, I became a research assistant, and any fears about research were quickly put to rest. Henceforth, I knew that research was simply asking questions about things that capture our interest and call for answers. Interestingly, my first published study was to disprove a colleague's scoffing at my use of a brief vocabulary test to assess a patient's IQ. I selected this test because it had common acceptance by other colleagues. Correlating the estimates against Wechsler full-scale results, I validated my actions to my critic and had my first publication. The change in my attitude about research was so complete that I later turned down promotion and tenure and left a comfortable faculty position because research activities were not considered important at that institution.

Second incident: Years and experiences later, I was certain I would never seek to be an administrator despite my senior rank. Again, fear and ignorance were the basis: fear that I could not confront a faculty member with direct feedback about poor performance (derived from Asian politeness habits) and fear of being unable to cope with budgets. Both fears were founded on ignorance because neither doubt had ever been tested directly. Instead, these fears came from a self-image of deficiency. Then, I filled in as acting head of the department with the opportunity to test my skills on a safer, temporary appointment, and I discovered I was competent when given the chance. I served as head of the department for 20 years, being reelected for four continuous terms, a national record at that time.

Comment: Fears based on ignorance are bad yet influential forces. Twice I was ready to avoid an opportunity without any data but steered by self-doubt and anxiety. I now see the value of risk taking, where the situation may be an opportunity to test one's abilities and perhaps discover the talent exists, or finding that the path is not the right one, but at least acquiring clear confirming evidence. My attitude toward such decisions has now transformed from avoiding all risks, to careful evaluation of the risk/reward ratio and reward/negative impact ratio, before making any rash approach or avoidance choices. This has extended outside my professional life into my personal. Despite my lack of swimming ability, I do snorkel and have scuba dived, learning to remain calm and to trust that the equipment will enable me to breathe normally. What was initially a scary risk has been replaced by the gratifying exposure to the unique undersea world.

The APA presidency and my message to students: There are many memorable images from the presidency, but the strongest came from my commitment to meet ethnic minority graduate students at their institutions. There were many messages they needed to hear: "You are our future. You are needed. You are valuable." "Persevere. You were admitted because you have the capability to earn the doctorate." "Remember to believe in yourself . . . and your future." These visits had as much impact on me as it had on these students. It was initially uncomfortable to be *the* role model; I felt as though I were in someone else's shell pretending to be what I was not. I soon recognized this as the "imposter syndrome," so often experienced by ethnic minorities. With an Asian American valuing of modesty, it was even stronger. In addition, because life often seems not under our own control, then accepting responsibility for achievements seems false. I have become better over time and can be more objective and write this type of autobiography as a "pioneer" without embarrassment or apologies. I think we must all, as ethnic peoples, learn how to take action to move ahead and to value ourselves, what we have accomplished, and who we have become.

Messages in retirement: I've always heard the advice voiced, "Don't just retire, retire *to* something!" Before retiring, I fantasized the something to be aikido classes—better for the aging body—or renewal of photography interests. What I have found instead is that you need to retire to something about which you have a *passion.* My passion has always been being with students. I am now in a new role as mentor. Previously, I avoided actively directing students, preferring to encourage them, hoping they perceived the direction. Now I see that clearly sharing my opinion still permits students the final decision because I hold no formal faculty position, have no authority, and—dare I say this?—therefore, I can be trusted. Students perceive that I have more time because I am not writing another manuscript, refining my lecture notes, or evaluating a thesis. I can interact with a student for as long as that student is willing, and this may be uncommon in today's multitasking environment. I even host an annual ski weekend to expand their horizons. So, I have retired to my passion: being faculty.

Comment: Various messages have been valuable guides in my life and I would share these:

Act upon your values. *Many of my actions can be understood as coming from value, such as running for school board instead of bitterly complaining. In planning the ethnic emphasis of my APA presidential opening ceremonies, many warned that my ethnic values would bring hardship. Yet this ethnic focus brought unbelievably positive responses (and yes, a few disgruntled ones).*

Identify your goals and dreams and do your best to reach them *. . . persist and believe!*

Know that happiness and peace derive from congruence between what you are and what you choose to do. *Earning tenure or promotion has never been associated with tension or discomfort for me. My values have matched the values of my work environment. My advice to new faculty candidates: If you select a position that matches your values, earning tenure will arrive painlessly as a natural course of events, a value-added benefit to the ongoing happiness you have already been experiencing in your job.*

Extend yourself. *It seems that I continue to integrate activities from one realm that extend to another. Questions raised in classroom discussions led to collection of data and then publications with my undergraduates. Work with a client recovering from surgery on his vocal* *cords led to my experimenting with positive imagery, then to being appointed as the first team psychologist for U.S. Olympians and a place in sport psychology history books. The common message is to avoid limiting your range of activities. Apply your talents and skills to other horizons; this provides balance. Stretch yourself!*

Know thyself. Understand both your strengths and your weaknesses. Seek conditions to maximize using your strengths as well as opportunities to develop new strengths. Acknowledge your weaknesses and take steps to overcome them. If you have self-doubts, review your strengths realistically; do not fear reaching for dreams. If you are overcome by what you perceive as a huge task, set subgoals to reach a step at a time and enjoy your progress. Are you feeling burdened? Regain your equilibrium through your social support system. Always remember to value yourself!

BIBLIOGRAPHY

American Psychological Association. (1999). *APA opening ceremonies, 1999 APA convention* [Video]. Washington, DC: Author.

Deffenbacher, J. (1999). Travels of a shy youngster to the presidency of the American Psychological Association: An interview with Richard M. Suinn. *Counseling Psychologist, 27,* 408–434.

Suinn, R. (1990). *Anxiety management training: A behavior therapy.* New York: Plenum.

Suinn, R. (2006). Teaching culturally diverse students. In W. McKeachie & M. Svinicki (Eds.), *McKeachie's teaching tips* (pp. 151–171). New York: Houghton Mifflin.

Suinn, R. (2009). Acculturation: Measurements and review of findings. In N. Trinh, Y. Rho, F. Lu., & K. Sanders. (Eds.). *Handbook of mental health and acculturation in Asian American families* (pp. 3-23). Totowa, NJ: Humana Press.

8

Seeds of Consciousness

MARY A. FUKUYAMA

My parents told me the story of how they met at "camp." It sounded like fun, but I didn't grasp the significance until well into adulthood. The camps were the prisoner camps set up to detain more than 110,000 Japanese Americans (most of whom were U.S. citizens) from the west coast during World War II. My father had been attending Berkeley Baptist Divinity School in California just prior to the outbreak of the war. He was called home to be forcibly moved with his mother and sister and her family to a relocation center, the Puyallup Fairgrounds, where they slept in horse stalls until they were sent by train to Minidoka, Idaho, a veritable desert where they spent the remainder of the war years. Because of my father's divinity school background, he was recruited into being a youth minister at the camp.

My mother, who had been raised in the Willamette Valley near Eugene, Oregon, volunteered to go as a college student on a Methodist mission trip to work with youth at the camps during the summer of 1944. This is where my parents met, and they married a year later, August 10, 1945, at the close of World War II—a difficult time for an interracial couple to marry. They traveled east to avoid hostility against the Japanese Americans who were returning from camps.

Such is the beginning of my life story as a pioneer in multicultural counseling. I observed my 60th birthday this year. It is a timely opportunity to review the chapters of my life that have been framed within the multicultural movement in counseling and psychology. I appreciate this opportunity to reflect and share some memories and thoughts with you, the reader of the third edition of the *Handbook of Multicultural Counseling*. The theme of being a *pioneer* is also a part of my family history. I have titled this contribution "Seeds of Consciousness" because in hindsight, I can see that I consider my experience of multiculturalism as informed by a process of consciousness raising that began in childhood and continues to this day. These seeds, or "moments of awakening," are like planting and cultivating a forest, a long-term project characterized by growth and stagnation, floods and droughts, successes and failures. My multicultural journey might also be described as "going full circle" in that it is more circular than linear, and I marvel at how it feels ever more like "returning home."

MY ANCESTRY

Where did my multicultural journey begin? Let me begin with my ancestry. My father's parents were emigrants from Japan at the turn of the 20th century, landing in the Seattle, Washington, area. Family stories alluded to "grandpa who jumped ship," a gambler who settled on Bainbridge Island to work the rocky soil as a farmer. One day, he sent home for a "picture bride," and my grandmother (known for her stubborn personality) immigrated to a foreign land at age 30 to marry a man whom she had never met. My father and his sister worked the strawberry fields and acquired a strong work ethic. A lesson learned and passed along to us kids was "Don't ever waste anything!" Quite literally, my Japanese grandparents were pioneers in the Pacific Northwest.

My mother's ancestors also were pioneers to the Pacific Northwest but by a different passage. The Adkins lineage can be traced back to a tobacco farmer who settled in Virginia in the 1700s. I believe my mother's ethnicity is captured by the acronym WASP (White-Anglo-Saxon-Protestant), and these great-great-grandparents ventured across the country on the Oregon Trail to settle in eastern Oregon, where my mother was born. My mother was proud of her English-French-Scottish ancestry, although it was problematic when she married my father.

They eventually started a family in Denver, Colorado, and raised five kids in northeastern Iowa, where my father served as a minister for a Congregational church. Issues of racism were salient for my father, who told me that he had helped to desegregate the Denver YMCA pool and was featured as a "brown-skinned pastor of a white congregation" when accepting a call to serve in Iowa.

My childhood experiences of growing up biracial taught me about racism and differences based on physical appearances. I didn't feel like I belonged fully to either group (white or nonwhite) and felt the pain of being an outsider. Later in life, I would become a bridge between them. The movie South Pacific and the song "You've Got to Be Carefully Taught" helped name prejudice that I had felt but not understood. I also learned about cultural adaptation from an early age, visiting Oba-san, who never learned to speak English, and "Grandma A," whose soft-spoken voice communicated both frailty and forbearance. I can attribute my lifelong pursuit of understanding multiculturalism to my mixed heritage.

These were some of the sociopolitical circumstances of my birth: an interracially married couple, raising children in the Midwest in a mostly white community where the biggest social divide seemed to be between Catholics and Protestants. As it is with many hyphenated Americans, my cultural and ethnic identity has been constructed and deconstructed over time through the various stages of personal and sociopolitical consciousness raising in the United States. In addition, my faith development and spiritual growth went through various transformations. What follows are some selected highlights of my personal and professional development, organized by decades, which closely parallel significant events during my lifespan.

THE 1950s—THE CHURCH IS HOME

During my childhood, I felt different for any number of reasons . . . the color of hair and shape of eyes, gender roles being a tomboy, as a Preacher's Kid (P.K.), or my own personal social struggles to fit in. I think it was academic success that saved me, that and feeling somehow protected by my father's role and affiliation with a small-town church. Living next door to the church was like having an extended family that provided extra care when my mother was sick or when there was a new arrival. Background noise to the family focus in the 1950s included the cold war and Sputnik, the first Russian satellite in space. Otherwise, black-and-white TV shows like Leave It to Beaver defined my consciousness.

I recently wrote the following creative writing exercise as a reflection on gender roles:

Me and the boys on the block, we were a gang that lived to be outdoors. Our turf ranged from the backside of the county courthouse lawn, across the street from my house, which served as a football field in summer and sledding hill in winter, down to the creek, which by today's standards probably was a drainage culvert, where we'd catch minnows and search out crawdads. The year was 1956 and I was 8 years old.

It was a hot Iowa summer night and several of us were hanging out on the Methodist church steps. Being a Preacher's Kid and playing with the Methodist preacher's boy Bobbie, we felt pretty entitled to do whatever we wanted on church property. We were having a spitting contest, seeing who could spit the farthest. Sometimes if you curled your tongue just right, you could project a blob of spit like it was shot out of a blow gun. Standing on the top steps we had a clear view of our spitting range onto the church lawn, both height and depth made it more impressive. Until along came an older boy, maybe all of 12 years old, who knows. In a low tone, he leaned over and said to me "girls don't spit."

I had an immediate reaction of disbelief, but his tone sounded so authoritative, so morally right. I could feel my spit-blowing ego deflate immediately. How was it that these three words, this gender based rule had such weight with me? Was it before or after I had been told "girls don't play football," which seemed totally ridiculous since I was the best passer on the block. Was it before or after I was told, "girls play the flute," and here I had admired the trombone ever since going to the premiere of the movie *The Music Man* in Mason City, totally smitten with "76 trombones led the big parade." Was it before or after I came home brandishing my new cowboy 6-shooter pistol, only to feel shame in front of the church ladies, because somehow I knew this was not a girly thing to do? How come the boys got to do all the cool things, like spit and play football and wave brassy instruments and shoot guns? The year was 1956 and I was 8 years old. It was the year that I learned that "girls don't spit."

Later in life, I asked my parents why they didn't talk to us about our ethnic backgrounds. They said that they were too busy trying to survive . . . taking care of five kids, one with special needs, barely making it economically (my dad would say that "we were as poor as church mice"). In terms of Fowler's faith development model, my childhood spirituality was defined primarily by my family. Somehow, I believed there was some virtue in living a modest lifestyle, and that living next to the church somehow gave me added status and resources.

THE 1960s—EDUCATION COMES FIRST

My parents moved back to Washington State when I was about to enter high school. There was never any doubt that I would go to college as both of my parents had a liberal arts education. When I moved to Portland, Oregon, to attend Lewis and Clark College, I had no idea that I would eventually study to become a psychologist. Nevertheless, a series of fortuitous events at LCC laid a foundation for my educational directions in the future.

As a sophomore in college, I went to Japan on a study-abroad group program. I began to sort out my ethnic identity there. When I arrived, I attended a recognition ceremony for 20-year-olds through my host family that conveyed the message, "Welcome to adulthood." For the first time, it was an advantage to have the last name Fukuyama, which was loosely translated by my peers as "happy mountain." I began to develop a positive ethnic identity, whereas before, I had regretted being a "person of color" when everyone else seemed white. I was intrigued by seeing Shinto shrines and Buddhist temples and realized that Christianity was not universal. It gave me pause to think about my religious beliefs, even if my dad was a minister.

Some of my early exposures to psychology were through humanistic influences. I recall being profoundly affected by Carl Rogers's book *On Becoming a Person,* and I was exposed to humanistic values through a gestalt therapist, Don Nickerson, who conducted weekend encounter groups (T-groups) with students. My statistics professor taught us self-hypnosis techniques to help us decrease our math anxiety. I still value a liberal arts education, which espoused values such as personal balance and social consciousness. Reading books such as Alvin Toffler's *Future Shock* and Paul Ehrlich's *Zero Population Growth* was a precursor for social shifts that are relevant today.

I married my high school sweetheart during my senior year of college. Being adventurers, we immediately left for Detroit to study at an urban institute on the family. This was my first introduction to inner-city urban poverty, and the memories of the Detroit riots of 1968 were still fresh. As I think about my undergraduate education, these two off-campus experiences had a profound effect on my consciousness. In Japan, I was totally enthralled with cultural learning, especially through the enthusiasm and trust of our professor, Dr. Robin Drews, a cultural anthropologist, and later I decided to major in sociology. Having traveled in Asia and been raised by pacifist parents, I felt troubled by the Vietnam War and joined in student protests. Witnessing firsthand the effects of inner-city poverty and effects of mob violence in Detroit, I became aware of severe social ills at home.

THE 1970s—SEARCH AND STRUGGLE

The 20-something years can be challenging for many, and I was no exception. The beginning of the 1970s was marked by a continuation of the Vietnam War, inflation and recession, and difficult times for many families. My first professional job was working for the welfare system as a caseworker for single mothers needing to go to work. I lasted on this job for about 2½ years. What good could I do after becoming disillusioned with "the system" that seemed to hurt the people it was designed to help? We quit our jobs and went traveling around the world for a year. My education has come through travel. My favorite subject as a kid was social studies, to study culture and the many cultures of the world. I connect in our common humanity through diversity (a theme song in my multicultural work).

Upon return from travels that took us to Europe, the Middle East, Africa, India, and parts of East Asia, I had to deal with more personal development issues: questions about career, divorce, and sexual orientation. My first exposure to consciousness raising through feminism began to have an impact. Here is part 2 of the creative writing exercise on gender roles to illustrate:

> I would not seriously question gender roles again until 1973. I was 25 years old and had successfully dodged emerging feminist consciousness-raising of the 60's, feeling that it was something that privileged white women did in their spare time. Questioning gender roles was just not on my radar screen, as I tried to fit into traditional marriage roles and do my twenty-something-see-the-world-thing. This was the year that Jim and I quit our welfare caseworker jobs, sold our Mazda station wagon, and took off to travel around the world for a year. This seemed like the perfectly logical choice for two young adults who had not yet figured out their career goals.
>
> It was while we were traveling in a group tour through Europe that I experienced my first feminist "aha" or moment, an awakening of consciousness. We

were on a 6 week camping tour into Russia, setting up tents every night, washing out clothes by hand, when I overheard a woman from New England say loudly to her husband, "I'm not going to wash your snotty handkerchiefs for you, you can do it yourself!" Now, I asked myself, "Why hadn't I thought of that before?"

> The concept that men could wash their own clothes seemed so radical at the time. Now I don't personally object to washing clothes, and it's one of my favorite chores. But to question the larger schema of gender role was the beginning. Just like you can't put the genie back into the bottle, once this liberating thought was out, it couldn't be contained. I had started out on our worldwide tour as a conventional wife and returned with troubling questions.
>
> Within the next year, I attended a Gloria Steinem lecture at the local community college and asked her afterwards, "Why was I angry all of the time?" I don't recall that she had an answer, but I can say in hindsight that it was just the beginning of many life changes that would unfold throughout the remaining decade. The year was 1973, and I was 25 years old. It was the year that I learned that "women don't *have* to do laundry."

During this time, I had stopped attending church, not so much out of disillusionment than apathy. I began graduate studies at Washington State University (WSU) in counselor education, with a focus on women's career development. Dr. Jim Shoemaker, my advisor, had a vision to start a counseling psychology program. I fell into it, not knowing really what it meant to become a psychologist. Sorry, but I came in the back door. I just wanted a job when I graduated and I knew that I loved learning. My first practicum teacher was Dr. Janet Helms. I learned basic counseling microskills and assessment, and more importantly, I learned from her about being patient and about watching emotions pass over like clouds, learning that I can't push them to go faster than they will naturally.

During graduate school, I left my husband and identified more with the women's movement. I was strongly influenced by humanistic psychology and feminism through my professors and clinical supervisors. I also became involved in Asian American consciousness raising and advocated for the establishment of an Asian American Studies Program at WSU. My dissertation research was on assertiveness and Asian Americans. As I approached 30 years of age, I explored re-engagement with religion by joining a Unitarian Universalist Fellowship, feeling that I needed to have broader, more inclusive boundaries after having traveled the world and visiting sacred sites from many religions.

Identity development was a key theme throughout graduate school, related to gender roles, marital status, ethnicity, and sexual orientation. As with multiple social identities and oppressions, this process was uneven, and I compartmentalized parts of self to ease the pain and stress. Even though these were early coming-out years for me, I did not fully embrace becoming a lesbian until years later.

THE 1980s—PROFESSIONAL IMMERSION

My predoctoral internship at the University of California, Irvine had a profound effect on my understanding of multiculturalism, and key figures from that era continue to influence my thinking. I attended my first cross-cultural counseling workshops with Dr. Derald W. Sue and Dr. Chalsa Loo, respectively. In those days, multiculturalism meant being part of the big four ethnic groups: Asian, Black, Hispanic, and Native American. The combination of confronting feminism and racism both were important with my colleagues and trainers in the California ethos. My first job after internship took me back to WSU for a joint position at the counseling center and in Asian American studies. I benefited from that immersion in Asian American consciousness immeasurably.

In 1982, I moved to Gainesville to work at the University of Florida Counseling Center, at the encouragement of Dr. Greg Niemeyer. It has been an excellent site for me to grow professionally and personally, a place to cultivate a forest of multicultural trees. In the 1980s, I collaborated with Dr. Max Parker in co-teaching a cross-cultural counseling course, and we developed ways to apply theory to practice. Our work culminated in publishing a book together on developing multicultural counseling competencies last year. I began attending the Teachers College Winter Roundtable in New York City and found a place where multicultural issues were valued and discussed.

I committed myself to a broader understanding of multiculturalism.

In 1988, my father died after a 2-year bout with cancer. His death precipitated a midlife and spiritual crisis, as I felt like I needed to answer some of my own spiritual questions rather than depend upon his presence to get me through. I discovered that spiritual awakening, as with consciousness raising, involves a process that begins with resistance, perhaps because the ego wants to remain in control and change is difficult. My resistances were dissolved by death and grief work. Also, my father's illness and death were the impetus to pursue writing a book on spiritual issues, which would come to fruition with co-author Todd Sevig nearly a decade later.

THE 1990s—LOVE AND LIFE LESSONS

If the 1980s was a time of establishing myself professionally, the 1990s was a time of getting my personal life together. I was blessed to meet my life partner, Jackie, who shares my passion for travel. In addition to raising teenage boys and emptying the nest, we have gone on many cross-cultural travels and adventures together. The most significant and most difficult was the year we took a sabbatical leave and went to work in Latin America. As described in my journal entries in "El Otro Lado" (2004), I learned that cultural immersion is not easy, but it provides valuable lessons about experiencing "the other" and truly understanding another worldview. I returned from Guatemala with greater humility and awareness of privilege, and lessons beyond anything that I could have learned in the classroom.

Spiritually speaking, over several years I went through a period of "new age" searching and experimentation, which opened me to respect even more diverse expressions of spirituality: Yoga, Spiritualism, Goddess worship, Zen Buddhism, and Sufism, just to name a few. Personally during this time, I also coped with my mother's death and felt like an adult orphan.

One of my spiritual teachers cautioned me not to dig so many shallow wells, but to stay with one form and reap the benefits of deeper spiritual practice. It was at this time that I deepened my spirituality through spiritual direction. I had found a church home in Gainesville that has ties to my childhood church denomination (United Church of Christ). My home congregation incorporates diverse spiritualities into the services, so now I don't have to leave home to have diverse spiritual experiences anymore. Another significant shift was when the church voted to become "open and affirming" for lesbians, gays, and bisexuals. I began to experience the edges of the compartments of my life softening. I most comfortably identify with being a Universalist when it comes to religion, honoring the traditions of all world religions.

A synthesis of these life lessons was explored in the book I wrote with Todd Sevig (Fukuyama & Sevig, 1999). We described the interaction of spirit and matter, suggesting that "the dance of ego development and ego surrender in life's journeys ultimately enhances the process of spiritual awakening" and that "multiculturalism and spirituality are intimately interlocked" (p. 158). We advocated that spiritual and religious issues could be addressed in counseling by incorporating multicultural guidelines and respect for differences. In addition, I was fortunate to find interdisciplinary colleagues at the University of Florida who formed a Center for Spirituality and Health that continues to support my teaching in this area (see http://spiritualityandhealth.ufl.edu/).

THE NEW MILLENNIUM— EMBRACING WISDOM

If I were to summarize in one page how my professional life evolved, I'd begin with my first volunteer job. As a teenager, I was a "Volunteen" at the local mental hospital; I wore a pink candy stripe dress. It was at this stage of life that curiosity was my best friend. As previously mentioned, I worked as an entry-level caseworker in the state welfare system. Entry-level work for me was a rite of passage for the helping professions. I learned about student personnel roles through a part-time job at a community college as a student activities advisor, which led me to pursue a master's degree in counseling with a focus on career development. I was a residence hall director during graduate school, which furthered my understanding of student development. My multicultural studies began conjointly with studying Asian American issues and working as an ethnically identified counselor. I learned that I am more naturally inclined toward a breadth of interests when I moved to a generalist position

as a psychologist at the University of Florida. My career as practitioner and faculty has evolved further with various emphases: career development, multicultural teaching, intern training, writing, and integrating spirituality into multicultural counseling.

The current decade has brought postmodernism to the forefront. No longer do I live in dichotomies. Living with multiple social identities and dealing with multiple oppressions are now essential for understanding the whole person. Living in a post-9/11 era, where fears of "the other" have once again become headline news, I am reminded of my family story and the importance of preserving human rights and freedoms. I am troubled that, as a country, we are once again at war and wish that, as a nation, we could seek understanding of differences rather than the need to dominate.

I am surprised and encouraged by recent developments in multicultural counseling and psychology. It is gratifying to see the emergence of a social justice ethic in the field. What is the status of multiculturalism today? Is it so powerful that it has achieved an "-ism" status? I have spent so much of my life energies as a pioneer, pushing the edges, the frontiers of multicultural counseling, as my pioneer ancestors did, that I am not sure that I will know what to do if multiculturalism is defined as a mainstream paradigm. It has always been more familiar for me to live on the edges of groups.

Nevertheless, I continue to hone my multicultural skills and to nurture the seeds of consciousness that are growing into full-sized multicultural trees. I am integrating more theory and literature from the intercultural communications field and expanding my consciousness to include international perspectives whenever possible. I've had the opportunity to teach in a University of Florida Study Abroad Program with American students in Florence, Italy, on the subject of "psychology of intercultural diversity." Global concerns ranging from ecological crises to global economic restructuring dominate the news. The "world is flat" thanks to the Internet and high-speed technology. I ask myself now, "What is global consciousness?"

The multicultural journey has been about returning home. I now embrace lost parts of self from childhood as I mature, another way of saying, "Life is a journey toward wholeness." Recently, I took trombone lessons just so I could address that childhood desire. I have taken up flute again, and I play in a klezmer band and jazz ensemble, just for fun. I continue to enjoy travel and cultural learning. In addition, creative expressions such as art help me to keep balance and nourish me spiritually.

My life has been enriched and challenged by multiculturalism, and my spiritual life is deeply intertwined with these processes. The multicultural mix has made the journey all the more interesting. Now, with love, I do my partner's laundry. I enjoy playing the flute, and I don't spit.

ACKNOWLEDGMENTS

Many thanks to the people who have touched my life: clients, students, trainees, friends, family, and colleagues, both named and unnamed. You made the telling of my career life story possible.

BIBLIOGRAPHY

Fukuyama, M. (1999). Personal narrative: Growing up biracial. *Journal of Counseling and Development, 77,* 12–14.

Fukuyama, M. A. (2004). El otro lado. In G. S. Howard & E. A. Delgado-Romero (Eds.), *When things begin to go bad: Narrative explorations of difficult issues* (pp. 19–32). Lanham, MD: Hamilton Books.

Fukuyama, M. A. (2007). Weaving sacred threads into multicultural counseling. In O. J. Morgan (Ed.), *Counseling and spirituality: Views from the profession* (pp. 93–109). Boston: Lahaska.

Fukuyama, M. A., & Sevig, T. D. (1999). *Integrating spirituality into multicultural counseling.* Thousand Oaks, CA: Sage.

Parker, W. M., & Fukuyama, M. A. (2007). *Consciousness raising: A primer for multicultural counseling* (3rd ed.). Springfield, IL: Charles C Thomas.

9

Roots of Activism and My Evolution as a Social Justice Advocate in Academe

SUSAN L. MORROW

It is a bit of a contradiction when I ponder how I, a white, middle-class girl from the South, raised in a conservative Lutheran Republican family, came to be asked to write a "multicultural pioneer" chapter for the *Handbook of Multicultural Counseling*. I am humbled to be in the company of current and former multicultural pioneers. I wonder if they were as surprised as I when they were honored in this way by an invitation to write for the *Handbook*. As I worked to integrate my insights and experiences as an activist, academic, practitioner, and psychologist, I found roots of my multicultural passions throughout my life. Thus, this story is a journey back in time for me as I make sense of my own evolution. Through this journey, I share with you some of my earliest memories of my awareness of injustice, identify the critical events and mentors who helped me find my way, and reflect on what I have learned and have yet to learn. Throughout this journey, the personal has always been political.

LIFE'S NOT FAIR!

I would never stop fighting, and I had to point out what was wrong and what was unfair, and I would never, ever let anything slide. 'Cause I had, you know, meticulous notes on exactly what was unfair in the world and made sure everybody was aware. . . . As a kid, I was told, "Life's not fair," . . . and I said, "But I got proof! I've got some important details to share with you here!" . . . [Now] I've discovered this feminist side of me that is so wonderful! (Velvia, interview transcript)

Velvia was a co-researcher/research participant in my dissertation research on the ways that women who had been sexually abused as children had survived and coped, and her words resonated with me very personally. As a child from a home characterized by both love and abuse, I developed optimism about the world as well as a passion for justice. My early years as a white girl in an upwardly mobile, lower-middle-class family in Louisiana were characterized by confusion about racial and social inequities. When I was in high school, my mother hired a young Black woman close to my age to iron our clothes, but when I became close to her, I was reprimanded. I don't remember my parents ever saying anything derogatory about people different from us, yet their message to me was consistent—associate with people who were "like us." When we visited my parents' friends in El Paso, Texas, on our move to Los Angeles, I became "too friendly" with a Mexican girl (also hired help) and was told once again that I was being inappropriate. When I asked why, my mother just said, "Mexican people here are like Negroes (this was, after all, the 1950s) in Louisiana—we don't mix with them." Little by little, I was learning the rules of being white and middle class, yet not to my parents' satisfaction. To their consternation, I hung out with "poor white" and lower-middle-class Italian kids through much of high school as my parents rapidly embraced an upper-middle-class lifestyle.

When we returned to Baton Rouge in the middle of my sophomore year in high school, I had lost my Southern accent, had neither "old family" nor "old money," and found myself on the margins—white and middle class, to be sure, but unable to fit in with my former friends who were now the country club set. In the late 1950s, when talk began of integrating Baton Rouge High School, I was an outcast, eating my lunch alone on the front steps of the school and wondering if, when we integrated, the Black kids would be my friends.

Over the next several years, my family returned to California, I finished high school and started college, and those early contradictions and awarenesses went dormant as I became more popular and related exclusively to people like me. It would be many years before I questioned inequities and a social system that reinforced my white, middle-class privilege. It was not until early in my senior year in college, in 1965, that my first multicultural mentor, a white faculty member, urged me to join the newly forming Human Rights Club (HRC) at my predominantly white Lutheran college. I remember that there were two African American women students in our entire college and that they were not members of the HRC. I also remember my confusion when someone wrote on the HRC flyer on the bulletin board, "HRC is racist!" Looking back, of course, I understand the dynamics of unconscious

racism that were at work in the white faculty sponsor and students of HRC; despite our good intentions, we had not created a safe or inclusive space in HRC for the two students of color who attended our school.

Nonetheless, HRC provided an opportunity for my early experiences to bear fruit, and I began reading works that came out of the civil rights movement. Jonathan Kozol's book, *The Night Is Dark and I Am Far From Home,* was a turning point for me as I realized not only that "life wasn't fair" but that I could do something about it. My first position as a new elementary school teacher was in a fifth- and sixth-grade classroom in an inner-city Lutheran school in St. Louis. I shudder to remember my naïveté as I walked into that classroom, yet I hope I made up for my lack of knowledge by my dedication to do the right thing. I threw out the *Dick and Jane* readers, created culturally relevant reading materials, and found books with Black characters. I challenged the notion of a blonde, blue-eyed Jesus in my religion classes and asked the children to draw pictures of how Jesus would look if He were Black. Not all of the Black parents of my students were overjoyed when they came to parent-teacher conferences and saw Black Jesuses on the bulletin boards, but it was a beginning for me of taking risks, even naïve risks, in order to do what I believed was right. It was also the start of finding mentors who were people of color to guide me in my evolution as an activist.

My second multicultural mentor (after my HRC faculty sponsor) was a Black woman who was the kindergarten teacher in my school. She told me stories of her own life, and I began to understand the realities and horrors of racism in a way that I had never grasped before. I could not understand how she could think of me, a white woman, as a friend after the violence she had experienced at the hands of white people. I felt deeply ashamed of being white; yet at the same time, I embraced both the acceptance that I received from my friend and my students' parents as well as my responsibility to create change. Somewhere around this time, I heard Eldridge Cleaver, a Black activist, leader, and author of *Soul on Ice,* say, "If you're not part of the solution, you're part of the problem." I sidestepped the temptation to live in white guilt by adding to his challenge in my own mind: "If I am part of the solution, I don't need to feel guilty. Just get busy." Thus began my career as an activist.

ACTIVISM

I was a political activist long before I heard the terms *multiculturalism* or *social justice*. If I were to create a white activism identity development scale, the second stage (right after "Do it because it's the law") would be "Do it because it's the right thing to do." Long before I knew how I would change and grow, before I understood what kind of human being I would become, I was enraged at injustice and determined to fight it with all that I had in me. Black and white members of the church that sponsored my inner-city school formed a Black-white consciousness-raising group. It was there that I encountered two more mentors—one white, one Black—who helped to guide me along this path of activism. The white man, whose name I cannot remember, modeled activism without guilt.

The Black man, Willie Smith, was the father of two girls in our school, one in my fifth-grade class. Following the assassination of the Reverend Dr. Martin Luther King, Jr., Willie asked my then-husband and me if we would like to join him for the Poor People's March on Washington, DC, in 1968. We drove all day and spent the night in Willie's car, waking to a brilliant May morning and a hostile police officer pounding on the windows telling us we could not camp in our car. I don't know what I had expected as we gathered at the Washington Monument, but I was overcome by the sea of Black and white faces and supremely aware that we were breaking the rules I had been taught since birth. Led by Ralph Abernathy, Coretta Scott King, Jesse Jackson, and others, the sea became a river as we marched up both sides of the Reflecting Pool to the foot of the Lincoln Memorial. Of all the memories I treasure from that day, the most precious is marching, singing "We Shall Overcome," and having a young Black man about my age (I was 25) hold my hand and call me "Sister."

From St. Louis, I moved on to another inner-city Lutheran school in Detroit. My class of first and second graders was racially mixed, about half Black, half white. My students were profoundly affected by racial tensions in Detroit, and on the morning after the Detroit riots began, one of my white students ran into

the class yelling, "All the Blacks are rioting!" I gently asked the student to check out this perception with his classmates; and, as the students, Black and white, responded one by one, it became clear that the Black students—who were not rioting, nor were their parents—had far greater reason to be afraid than the white students. The students as a whole came together in support of those who were living closest to the riots. Later that year, during recess, I found that silky blonde-haired white boy and a nappy black-haired Black classmate sitting under a tree, stroking one another's hair.

The Poor People's March was as much about class as about race, and race and class were intertwined in my inner-city experiences. These experiences began to prepare me for looking at other intersections of privilege, power, powerlessness, and oppression. Over the next decade, I was to continue to expand my activism into the peace, women's liberation, environmental, and lesbian/gay/bisexual (LGB) movements. In addition, I grappled with the intersections, contradictions, and points of connection across these various movements.

In my early work in the civil rights movement, I fought for justice for people whose race and social class were different from mine. As a young mother of a boy during the Vietnam War, the peace movement spoke to me directly. I was active in Another Mother for Peace, met presidential peace candidate George McGovern at the airport rally with my 6-week-old son in my arms, but was ignorant that Black mothers' sons were much more likely to go to war than my own. (Later, when he did go to Desert Storm, he had a choice, unlike many of his fellow soldiers of color.) At the time, I failed to understand that wheeling my child from door to door for peace intersected with my civil rights efforts; today, I understand the intersections of war, class, and race much better.

Then, one day, I received an advertisement in the mail for a charter subscription to a new "women's lib" magazine called *Ms.* I had not previously had any feminist yearnings or consciousness, but something—perhaps the front cover with Wonder Woman in full regalia—called to me; and I said yes, knowing I could cancel the subscription after the first issue if I didn't like it. When my first issue came, I devoured the magazine, cover to cover. About midway through, I noticed an ad down the left side of the page that read, "What will you say when your granddaughter asks, 'What did you do in the women's movement?'—Join NOW!" And so I did.

In my late 20s, in the summer of 1972, I was a Missouri Synod Lutheran minister's wife in Long Beach, California, with a toddler and another baby on the way, when I attended my first feminist consciousness-raising (CR) group. There, with other women, I began to understand that all of my personal life experiences were imbued with issues of power—"the personal is political"—and I began to make sense of my life in a way that would change me forever. Not only was I fighting for justice for other people, I was fighting for myself. (I had been fighting for myself all along, but it would be decades before I understood this.)

I find it impossible to articulate what the women's liberation movement and feminism meant and still means to me. It has given me sisters I never had in my own family, strong female role models, a philosophy, a politic, and love that I had never known. In that "Aha!" moment that feminists call "The Click," I suddenly understood things that had not been quite right in my world. I understood why my mother could stay with a man who abused her children, why my husband still believed in the "obey" part of the wedding ceremony, and why fear was my companion when I went out alone at night. I also understood my own complicity as I sought male approval, turned to men as the experts, and denied my own power. For the first time in my life, I became a leader. My spirituality took on a new form: In the words of Ntozake Shange, "I found god in myself and I loved her/I loved her fiercely" (Shange, 1977).

From 1972 to the present, my feminism has guided my life, my activism, and my evolution. As I look back, I understand how embryonic was my understanding then of women's oppression. To me, reproductive freedom meant the right to birth control and abortion, until I learned that Black and young poor white women in the South were being sterilized against their will and without their knowledge. I fought for women's right to work outside the home until a Black feminist said, "Honey, Black women have always worked!" With the mentorship, challenge, and love of feminist/womanist women of color, I began to grasp and still grapple with the complexities of the intersections of gender, race, and class—and later disability, sexual orientation, religion, age, body size, and all the other human variations

that should just be interesting differences but instead are a source of stereotyping, privilege, power, and oppression. Today, I consider these intersections to be one of my primary "growing edges" as a multicultural and social justice-oriented psychologist.

Yet another major change would affect my life profoundly. As I fought for not only my own liberation but that of other women, I met, for the first time in my conscious awareness, women who identified as lesbians. Somewhere back in college in the early 1960s, I had first heard the word "lesbian" and asked a classmate what a lesbian was. She responded that lesbians were "just like homosexuals, only women." I found this interesting, but nothing more. Later, listening to two of my college roommates making homophobic remarks, I had that old gnawing sense of something wrong but was unable to pinpoint or act on my feelings of discomfort. The feminist movement led me to advocacy for lesbian and later bisexual women, starting with a major challenge to my own religious beliefs. I used my intensive theological training to examine my church's teachings about homosexuality, coming to a critical interpretation that integrated my personal faith and politics. With this backdrop, I embraced my lesbian sisters while still identifying as heterosexual, ultimately falling in love with a woman.

The 1970s were a time when many heterosexually identified women "came out" as lesbians as a result of their close relationships with lesbian women, admiration for lesbians' strengths, and a glimpse of freedom and equality in relationships. For many, the feminist sisterhood that was so powerful moved naturally into passionate friendships and love relationships, giving birth to the words attributed to activist Ti-Grace Atkinson, "Feminism is the theory; lesbianism is the practice" (Koedt, 1973, p. 246). Coming out as a lesbian initiated me into a culture that is rich with music, art, spirituality, humor (yes, feminists *do* have a sense of humor!), and political activism; it is for both personal and political reasons that I identify as a lesbian. However joyful, though, coming out as a lesbian was also accompanied by personal tragedy as my husband won legal custody of my children based on my lesbian status. Once again, my experience of personal injustice led me to political action; and over the past 33 years, I have worked fiercely to challenge that injustice in academic, mental health, and civil arenas. Not surprisingly, this work has led me once again to the many facets of oppression as I have worked to explore the intersections of gender, race, sexual orientation, and religion.

Thus, it was as a long-time civil rights activist, seasoned feminist, and emerging lesbian that I met my partner of now more than 34 years, Donna Hawxhurst. As lesbian feminist activists in Phoenix, Arizona, we were at the center of feminist and lesbian consciousness raising, community building, and civil rights. As part of our community-building work, we were active in the Lesbian Rights Task Force of Phoenix National Organization for Women (NOW) (later transformed to the Feminist Lesbian Activist Coalition when we did not adhere to NOW's agenda for us) and were central organizers for the lesbian feminist community in Phoenix. An important creation and contribution that we coauthored was our book *Living Our Visions: Building Feminist Community,* which built on radical principles of community organizing and addressed feminist process in communities and organizations. We continue to work individually and together to create change, now in the university setting, where I am a professor in the University of Utah's Counseling Psychology Program and Donna is the training coordinator of a feminist multicultural therapy training program at the university's Women's Resource Center.

AN ACTIVIST IN ACADEME

It was also as a civil rights activist and lesbian feminist that I embarked upon my academic career. First in my Master of Counseling program, and then in my PhD program at Arizona State University, my politics were the filter through which I critically assessed my education. With the mentorship of multiculturalists Miguel Arciniega, Teresa Branch, Marvalene Hughes, and Elsie Moore, and feminists Jean Parsons, Gerry Thompson, Gail Hackett, Arlene Metha, Judith Homer, Ruth Fassinger, and most importantly, my partner Donna, I found the courage to speak out when I believed my professors and other students were missing the bigger picture. When I began my PhD program, I remember believing that if I wanted to "make it" in counseling psychology as an academic, I would need to choose a research area that was part of counseling psychology's

traditional domain. Because I was interested in vocational counseling, I toyed with the idea of going that route. However, I was not enthralled with any of the ideas I could imagine, and I felt somewhat disgruntled over my options.

Fortunately, about the time I was starting to think seriously about my dissertation research, I attended an Association for Women in Psychology conference. There I saw and heard feminist psychologists who had built their careers on issues important to women. I began to believe that if I followed my passions, my career would unfold in a direction that would be meaningful and enriching to me. Up until this time, I had worked as a master's-level feminist counselor with women who were dealing with a number of issues, including career decision making, sexual orientation and identity, and trauma. The topic closest to my heart was trauma, and this led me to conduct a feminist qualitative study on women who had been sexually abused as children.

Although I had intended to pursue trauma research after I obtained my first academic position at the University of Utah, I soon became aware of a pressing need to be more political in my research endeavors. I initiated a feminist research group in my program that met for several years, thus providing feminist students a forum for their own feminist consciousness raising and all of us a challenging environment in which to think more critically about feminist issues in our field. During my first year as an assistant professor, I led a discussion in my practicum class about counseling LGB clients. Following that class, one of my practicum students gave me an article that was a first-person account by a young man who had struggled with being gay and Mormon. I privately asked my student, "Are you gay?" to which he responded in a whispered, "Yes." I was stunned that a doctoral student in his second year of a counseling psychology program had not felt comfortable to come out to anyone before this, and I knew I had my work cut out for me at the University of Utah. Fortunately, our program and department were and are LGB-affirmative (the late Richard Rodriguez was a graduate of our program and had been an openly gay man who conducted his dissertation research on Mexican American gay men's identity development). However, the absence of openly LGB faculty or a critical mass of LGB students had, until this time, created an environment, embedded in the larger conservative religious culture, that contributed to silence. I made a decision to increase my own visibility as a lesbian by conducting research and scholarship on LGB issues; this scholarship has pervaded my academic career.

My activism has taken me in many directions since I entered academe. My scholarship has focused on LGB issues, feminist therapy, academic climate for graduate women of color, feminist/multicultural/qualitative research methods, and violence against women. My feminist perspective undergirds it all. I have coordinated two conferences for the Association for Women in Psychology and am currently the organization's treasurer. I have served as chair and now newsletter editor of the American Psychological Association's Society of Counseling Psychology (Division 17) Section for the Advancement of Women. On my campus, I have served on Women's/Gender Studies committees and the President's Commission on the Status of Women, and I am currently on the College of Education Diversity Action Task Force and chair of the Educational Psychology Department's Diversity Committee. My grassroots activism provides both strengths and challenges for me as an activist in academe. I often long for the time and energy to move back into community-based activism. I hope, before the end of my professorial life, to conduct a radical feminist participatory action research project. I'm looking for suggestions!

My feminist and multicultural mentors in my academic career have been too numerous to mention, and many do not even know the gifts they have given me. Ruth Fassinger and Donna Hawxhurst continue to be catalysts to my evolution and provide shelter when times are difficult. Melba Vasquez, Laura Brown, Rosie Bingham, Linda Forrest, and Joe Ponterotto have all been mentors and role models in this work. Many have opened doors that have placed me in the right places at the right time, thus providing me the opportunities to follow my passions for social justice.

LOOSE ENDS, CHALLENGES, AND GROWTH EDGES

As I look back over my life experiences as a multicultural being, a civil rights activist, a lesbian feminist, and an academic, I am aware of so many loose ends. Like perhaps most of us who are committed to social justice, I often feel I am not doing enough. The blessings and curse of academe are that it offers the potential for real freedom of thought if we don't cave in to the pressures we encounter to become domesticated. I have dreams for contributing to a stronger multicultural, social justice orientation in my program and my discipline; but competing forces, such as the rapidly emerging business model for higher education, often dull my vision and sap my energy.

Despite my ongoing commitments to multiculturalism and social justice, along with a herstory of activism, I am acutely aware of my challenges and growth edges as a multiculturally competent human being, teacher, scholar, and advocate for social justice. Because of my privilege as a white, middle-class, United States-born and -raised, well-educated individual, I continue to centralize my own experience as the norm and assume the experiences of others are the same as mine until my assumptions are mirrored back to me. In doing this, I continue to engage "other" people who come from different cultures, classes, countries, and educational statuses from my own. I suspect that reversing this tendency is a lifelong project for all of us with privilege. Another area in which I am challenged is adequately dealing with the intersections of privilege, power, and oppression across various statuses and groups. I believe that effectively addressing these intersections is the next important step in my own—and possibly our collective—progress as multicultural counselors, psychologists, and educators. Finally, a lifelong challenge that has been with me since my earliest days as an activist is to deeply respect people where they are—even if what they are saying is prejudiced or uninformed—and finding effective ways to share my journey with them in order to help them on their own path. I suspect I will need to live a very long time to make a dent in these challenges. I celebrate being born in the 1940s, raised in the security of the 1950s, and given the opportunity to come of age and activism in the 1960s and 1970s. In the 21st century, I see hints of a new activism, and I embrace the opportunity to continue to fight for justice.

EXEMPLARS OF MY LIFE AND CAREER

Hawxhurst, D., & Morrow, S. (1984). *Living our visions: Building feminist community*. Tempe, AZ: Fourth World.

Morrow, S. L. (2000). First do no harm: Therapist issues in psychotherapy with lesbian, gay, and bisexual clients. In R. M. Perez, K. A. DeBord, & K. J. Bieschke (Eds.), *Handbook of counseling and psychotherapy with lesbian, gay, and bisexual clients* (pp. 137–156). Washington, DC: American Psychological Association.

Morrow, S. L. (2004). Finding the "yes" within ourselves: Counseling lesbian and bisexual women. In D. R. Atkinson & G. Hackett (Eds.), *Counseling diverse populations* (3rd ed., pp. 366–387). Boston: McGraw-Hill.

Morrow, S. L., Hawxhurst, D. M., Montes de Vegas, A. Y., Abousleman, T. M., & Castañeda, C. L. (2006). Toward a radical feminist multicultural therapy: Renewing a commitment to activism. In R. L. Toporek, L. Gerstein, N. Fouad, G. Roysircar, & T. Israel (Eds.), *Handbook for social justice in counseling psychology:* *Leadership, vision, and action* (pp. 231–247). Thousand Oaks, CA: Sage.

Morrow, S. L., Rakhsha, G., & Castañeda, C. L. (2001). Qualitative research methods for multicultural counseling. In J. G. Ponterotto, J. M. Casas, L. A. Suzuki, & C. M. Alexander (Eds.), *Handbook of multicultural counseling* (2nd ed., pp. 575–603). Thousand Oaks, CA: Sage.

REFERENCES

Koedt, A. (1973). Lesbianism and feminism. In A. Koedt, E. Levine, & A. Rapone (Eds.), *Radical feminism* (pp. 246–258). New York: Quadrangle.

Shange, N. (1977). *For colored girls who have committed suicide/when the rainbow is enuf.* New York: Macmillan.

10

Limping Towards Bethlehem

A Personal History

RHODA OLKIN

> The darkness drops again; but now I know
> That twenty centuries of stony sleep
> were vexed to nightmare by a rocking cradle,
> And what rough beast, its hour come round at last,
> Slouches towards Bethlehem to be born?
>
> —From *The Second Coming*, W. B. Yeats, 1920

It is hard for me to write the story of my life because, frankly, it's a bit depressing. Not many life stories have an iron lung in the first paragraph. But ultimately, this is the story of going from point *A* to point, say, *N* (just over the halfway mark). And at point *N*, I am happy. So now that you know the ending (to date), bear with me for the story of the journey over a long and slippery road.

My story is of a female, a Jew, a professor's daughter, a middle child, and, oh yeah, polio. If it were up to me, I might have selected the first four, and there are times I imagine I would have chosen polio because of the life lessons it has imparted. But one isn't given a menu in life with the freedom to choose the combination of ingredients. Although if one were, sometimes I imagine the scene would go something like this:

God: "Hi, I'm God, I'll be your waiter today."

Me: "Hi, God."

God: "I need to tell you we're out of a few items: Long-legged blondes, green eyes, and anything that looks remotely like Tyra Banks."

Me: "Are there any specials today?"

God: "Yes, we do have some lovely disabilities, just in. The birth defects, you could have your pick, cerebral palsy, spina bifida. And we really have a surplus of polio now—it's been 2 years since the last big epidemic, so the kitchen is pushing polio."

Me: "Does that come with any sides?"

God: "We could make you short, nearsighted, just so-so looking, give you mousy brown hair. That plus the polio would really make a complete package."

Me: "I was leaning more toward an Albert-Einstein-meets-Beyoncé-meets-Ellen-DeGeneres kind of package."

God: "Oh, honey, I'm God, but even I can't do that. Take the polio; you'll like it."

Me: "Okay, but I'm going to need a sense of humor with that."

HAVING POLIO

I learned to talk before I could walk. My walking was delayed by contracting polio at age 15 months. Thus, learning to stand was a proud accomplishment that I announced to my parents—"*standing!*"—that they might come and clap for me. I sometimes wonder what I would be like if I hadn't had parents who clapped for me; if, like so many of my clients, I did not have "good-enough" parents.

I do not have any memory of having polio, for which I'm grateful. In 1954, a year before the Salk vaccine was first available, I was 15 months old, and my older sister was 4. My parents were to drive us from East Lansing, Michigan, where my father, age 29, was an assistant professor at Michigan State University, to New Hampshire, where he had a summer research job. Shortly after our arrival in Hanover, I became ill. There was suspicion of polio, but the definitive test was a spinal tap, and doing that procedure on an infant was risky. My mother, age 28,

left to attend the wedding of her cousin in New York City, and my father, a family man through and through, stayed with us two girls. One night, he was feeding me in my high chair, and I started to choke. Somehow, my father recognized this as more than just the response of an infant learning to feed, for what it was—paralysis of throat muscles. He scooped up his two children and dashed to the hospital, where a spinal tap confirmed the diagnosis of polio. I was put into an iron lung, which breathes for you when lungs can't function independently. In the short time it took my frantic mother to return, I wasn't in the iron lung anymore. My sister was not allowed at the hospital, nor would my parents have wanted her near me, because polio is highly contagious, and it was not uncommon for more than one child in a family to contract it. The question of the first few days was whether I would die, as many children did. Then recovery began, and many of the previously paralyzed muscles started to return. The question became what functions would remain intact, which partially intact, and which would experience complete paralysis. After months of therapy, hot packs (the Sister Kenny treatment), and exercises, it seemed that the lasting effects would be complete paralysis below the thigh in my right leg, some slight deformity in my left foot, leg length differential, and mild scoliosis.

Those were the physical effects; the emotional effects ran deeper. My mother flew back with me to East Lansing while my father and sister went by car. Because I had to lie perfectly flat, my father built a wooden box in which I lay on the plane. His best friend came to pick us up from the airport, and as my mother emerged from the plane down the steps to the tarmac, holding this wooden box, his friend thought it was a coffin and couldn't speak. The serious illness and potential for death of an infant affected not just my immediate family, but their close friends as well. And my parents had important decisions to make. Who could do the exercises with me? (My mother; my father had to leave the house; to this day my pain is his pain.) How would they raise me? (As *normal* as possible.) Should they delay having a third child? (They did; she is 6 years younger than I.)

I seemed to weather the polio and hospitalization rather well, perhaps because I was too young to remember it. I relearned to stand and to walk, making my mother come clap for me. But I did have separation anxiety. My first day of nursery school, in a classroom observed by graduate students in child development at Michigan State University, I clung to my mother, sobbing. After an hour of this, she announced to the teachers that she was leaving, and she did. (I imagine a slew of dissertation students taking careful notes.) And I survived. But a second hospitalization at age three (for adenoids) cemented my separation fears. That same year I saw *The Wizard of Oz* (it haunted me for years), and my older sister introduced me to the concept of kidnapping, a fear that dogged me through adolescence. I was afraid to walk home from school, sure that every passing car contained a person who would snatch me away. That was it, the entire fear—nothing beyond the snatching, and the fact that I would never get home, and I would cease to exist. My grown-up version of this is my need to hold the car keys when I go places with people, so that when they disappear off the face of the earth, I can still get home.

I think of my childhood in sections bracketed by hospitalizations: at ages 1, 3, 7, 15, and 16. My early years were marked by resiliency and good-enough parenting, coupled with a crippling (sorry, bad pun) fear of separation and kidnapping. Surgery at age 7 marked the beginning of my dysthymia. My mother told me about the surgery the day before, very matter-of-factly, and I don't remember being afraid in advance, but I do vividly remember the ether mask coming down, and my tiny hand trying to push the doctor's hand back, certain that the mask would kill me. I woke up from surgery in a full body cast from chest down across my torso and down my right leg. My left leg was held in one position by a pin attaching it to my right leg. My genital area was open, and it took a while for me to realize I had to cover it, or the boys would look and point. The cast was a surprise, but even more disturbing was that no one seemed inclined to remove it. It remained for several months, then was replaced with a series of ever smaller casts. The metal wheel used to cut off casts was loud and made sparks, and I was always afraid it would cut me. I bragged to the nurses that when the final cast was off I was going to jump up and run around. No one warned me about muscle atrophy after being in a cast for so long.

There were weekly blood tests on Thursdays. Children over a certain age got blood withdrawn from the inner elbow, and the younger children got finger pricks. I didn't know that decision rule, of course, and thus was anxious each week. But it also was the time my favorite orderly came to help me get weighed. He stepped on the scale, then hoisted me up and stepped on it again, making jokes and chatter the whole time. For Thanksgiving, I got to go home for a few days (imagine going home from the hospital on vacation!) and was still in the hospital at Chanukah; my grandmother sent me a small menorah that used birthday candles. When I went home, I entered second grade midyear, and felt then what I still feel now sometimes—that I am entering a room of people who are already friends with each other, and there is no place for me. This feeling was compounded by the fact that every recess when it wasn't snowing, kids ran to the far field to play running games. It would take me the whole recess just to walk to the field and back, so I stayed near the building, and if anyone was to be with me, it meant not being with any of the other kids, and not playing with them. I was a choice for them—quiet talk on the stoop, or running with a gaggle of kids. This essential nature of being outside the group, apart, separate because of difference, was repeated throughout my childhood and adolescence, and has never left me.

"Would you like to dance?"

"Sorry, I can't dance."

"Aw, come on, everyone can dance."

"I can't. I had polio."

"Oh." He looks uncomfortable, then walks away without another word.

This scene, or one nearly like it, plays out many times over the course of my life. My polio makes other people uncomfortable. I can be in the checkout line at a grocery store, buying stamps, lowering the wheelchair lift in my car, and someone asks, "What happened to you?" "I had polio," I reply. Such a simple sentence: *I had polio*. Why does it make people so uncomfortable? And why is it my job to make them feel better?

A COED WITH A DISABILITY

So in college, I started to lie. "A football injury!" "A skiing accident; never ski in fog!" "I had a head transplant and they are trying a new approach!" It doesn't take much therapy to see that this was a tad hostile.

Not coincidentally, the friends I made over the years were those with whom my disability was able to be discussed openly, joked about, and made a part of me but not the definition of me. One friend married a man in a wheelchair. Another had a brother who died of polio. Another has a husband with a liver transplant. Another is a man with polio. I don't have to teach them.

One of the hard things about being a person with a disability is having to teach the whole world about disability, everywhere I go. The University of Oregon gave me my own parking space with my name on it, but didn't do anything about the stairs to classrooms. Stanford University told me to park wherever I could find a spot, but couldn't do anything about buildings with no parking. (Both of these experiences were prior to the Rehabilitation Act of 1973, which required institutions receiving federal monies—virtually every university—to be accessible.) The University of California, Santa Barbara, had me park my scooter in the bike rack, but didn't think disability was a topic worthy of study in a doctoral program in psychology, until my advisor contracted ALS (amyotrophic lateral sclerosis, also known as Lou Gehrig's disease). Reading my dissertation on attitudes toward disability, he looked up at me briefly, said "I'm sorry, I understand now" and returned to reading so I could graduate before he died. I taught UC San Diego (predoctoral internship) and the VA in San Francisco (postdoc) that the person with the disability wasn't necessarily the client. I taught California State University (my first teaching job) that disability should be taught as part of the diversity requirements, and the California School of Professional Psychology (my current job) a little bit at a time, year by year, until I got tired of teaching about it altogether.

A PSYCHOLOGIST WITH A DISABILITY

When I started writing about disability, I showed my work to a colleague, who said it had "a tone"—an undercurrent of anger. Imagine that. So I wrote empirical pieces, ones that relied on data for their punch, and did my best to leave my personal tone out of them. But still now, after writing about disability for many years, both empirical and opinion pieces, an undercurrent sometimes comes through more than I know. My ability to alienate an entire group, even a whole Division of the American Psychological Association (APA), still surprises me, although it shouldn't. My rage—a hallmark of living as a stigmatized person—lies like a crimson tulip under the winter ground, able to be released with the right conditions.

Let's talk about rage. Anger, which is not the same thing, comes from situations and the thoughts we have about them (I'm a good cognitive behaviorist). But rage comes from the core of our being. It's a visceral response that feels inevitable, like a sneeze.

Here is one example. My fellow faculty were embarking on a series of retreats in which we were talking about race and ethnicity. During one such retreat, the two leaders suggested we go on a "trust walk" in which one person would be blindfolded and led by the other person. As the leaders explained the activity, I found my mouth opening and words of protest pouring out: "Oh no, we are not going to use pretending to be blind as a way to demonstrate trust!" The leader told me I didn't have to participate, and I said *that wasn't the point.* Some faculty said they didn't want to do the activity if it upset me, so all the faculty sat down and discussed this turn of events while I sat there with a metaphorical neon arrow pointing to my head, afraid to speak lest I cry. Some of the faculty of color were angry that I made the day about disability; some white faculty were perhaps a little too eager to change the topic.

This example illustrates not only the rage that erupts like Old Faithful, only less predictably, but of the uneasy alliance of different types of minorities. Disability has been a topic that takes time away from ethnicity—if you have three units in a curriculum to devote to diversity, every class period spent on one topic is a class period not spent on something else. So to get my class on disability accepted as part of the diversity requirements, I renamed and reconceptualized it as Disability, Ethnicity, and Culture. And it is a much better class because it puts disability where it should be, in the context of gender, ethnicity, social class, sexual orientation, religion, and age. And I find that it is the community of professionals most devoted to diversity that are those who invite me aboard. When APA formed a task force to examine diversity content in undergraduate texts, it was the participants who looked around the table and noticed disability was missing, and invited me. When I teach about how people with disabilities have separate stalls in bathrooms and separate entrances to buildings and separate drinking fountains, it is the students of color who nod with knowing about the toll of segregation. This paradox of being pitted against one another for meager resources yet being the most open to disability studies' concepts has played out in myriad ways in my professional life.

A student who uses a wheelchair was working on a dissertation about disability-specific daily hassles. She asked many of the people with disabilities in our dissertation group to keep a record of disability hassles for 2 weeks. This was necessary because some of the hassles are so ubiquitous that to survive, we have learned to tune them out. Here are some of the notations from my log:

Friday: I am to meet the faculty at a restaurant, but a flight of stairs prevents entry. The waitress offers to help me down the stairs, an offer I refuse (because I'm an adult). She then suggests I park in the bus stop, assuring me that because I have a handicapped placard, the ticket is bound to get thrown out (when I take the time to fight it). I respond that I live in another city, and she says, "This is getting complicated!" I send a message to the faculty via this waitress, but later learn that all they heard was that I couldn't find parking.

Saturday: At a pizza restaurant, a young waiter tries to orchestrate where I sit until I say "I'll handle it!" Service is slow and surly thereafter.

Sunday: I back out of a parking space with the scooter lift still down, having forgotten to raise it before driving. Horrible sound of scraping. Few days later notice scooter lift seems pulled out, I drive 22 miles home from work worrying that lift and scooter will fall off car.

Monday: Lower water fountain in my office building is still not working.

Tuesday: Go to stationery store. Car next to handicapped spot too far over the line, rendering handicapped spot unusable.

Wednesday: Elevator installed at work, and I am able to go to 2nd floor for the first time, having worked there for over seventeen months. Some of the staff applaud my arrival; none of the faculty notice.

Thursday: At medical supply store, delivery truck blocking ramp. There are other spots to park, but they are useless because the only ramp is blocked by truck.

Friday: Checkout at drug store has inaccessible ATM slider. I have to give the checkout person my pin. She asks, "Can you sign your name?" as if I might not know how to do this.

Saturday: At shopping center there is a car parked in front of sole curb cut, despite room elsewhere to park. There are two young kids in car, so I wait, expecting parent to return shortly. Fifteen minutes later no sign of parent, so I go about ¼ mile to next nearest curb cut.

Sunday: Drug store aisles blocked by merchandise. Will not be able to go to certain stores until after Christmas inventory cleared out, about two months away. Mercedes with Christian fish bumper sticker parked illegally in handicapped spot.

And so it goes. When we share our logs in class, many of us find it very depressing, noticing how much we have to ignore just to get through the days. I am older than my students, possibly a role model, and wonder if they are looking to me to see that I, too, am affected, and thus feel comforted by this, or whether they need to see me rise above it, to hold out hope that one gets more impervious over time. I find myself getting quieter. Finally, I tell the woman who is doing the dissertation on disability hassles that I think her work will be a significant contribution. It has been about 14 years since she graduated, and I still have the log book.

A THERAPIST WITH A DISABILITY

I find that clients attribute certain characteristics to me that help foster a therapeutic alliance. My readily visible disability seems to convey that I have been an underdog, that I have suffered, that I have been left out, and clients who believe that no one can understand them unless that person has also suffered slings and arrows give me the benefit of ready trust. Parents of children with disabilities want to know facts about me, that I was married, had children, hold a full-time job, as a picture of the future for their children, who grow up with an absence of role models. Some clients with disabilities get annoyed that I'm not as empathetic as they think I should be when I insist they get on with their lives. And when one adolescent client with cerebral palsy told an outrageous lie about his disability being caused by a bus accident on the way to school in which the bus driver and 20 kids died, I am able to think, "Ah, yes, point *B,* I remember it well," and empathize as I hold out hope for point *N.* I wish I had some magic words that would move people—clients and students with disabilities alike—to later points in their development, that they could bypass some of the painful and hard-learned lessons. But I can't.

A MOTHER WITH A DISABILITY

I have raised two children, much of the time as a single mom. It is in my role as a mother that I have thought most deeply and critically about disability. I can find meaning and purpose in disability as a therapist and a professor; what is the meaning and purpose to disability as a mother? I believed, as do other parents with disabilities I've talked to, that my children would become more sensitive, aware, and tolerant of differences. Then I conducted research on parents with and without disabilities and found that all parents, not just those with disabilities, believe they are raising children who are especially sensitive, aware, and tolerant. So much for that illusion! So, if my disability didn't make my children better people, is it possible that it made me a better mother? What would my kids say?

My kids have remarkably little to say about my disability. They complain about my bad cooking, my tendency toward overprotective anxiety (separation anxiety from the other side! Who knew?), my passion for mail-order catalogues (shopping without leaving the house—a disability dream come true!). Disability greatly affected the early years of carrying, diapering, transitioning, lifting. But once they could climb by themselves into the car

seat, the main disability issue was my fatigue. So my bed became a playground on which we did projects, corrected homework, ate pizza, read books, and watched TV. And now, as they turn into young adults, they are remarkably unsympathetic to my disability issues. I try to play the trump card (to justify why my daughter and not I should go get us ice cream from the freezer), but it fails to work. And that is as it should be.

There are lessons I learned from having a disability that I took into the role of mothering. One was the importance of humor about even dark subjects ("Come, limp with me," I used to say to my daughter as we walked down the hall together; now she says this to me). I learned priorities, that homemade cookies weren't vital to a happy home. I managed to impart a fundamental belief in social justice without ever lecturing about it. But most importantly, I learned that disability is irrelevant to the essential aspects of mothering—caring, nurturing, soothing, encouraging, and fostering development and independence. After having disability affect so many aspects of my life, it is nice to have this one area where it is mostly irrelevant.

A PERSON WITH A DISABILITY

Yesterday, I fell and hurt my bad leg. Let us parse this sentence. *Yesterday, I fell.* An unfortunate event, could happen to anyone, but happens to me more often due to leg weakness, and the level of injury is usually more severe than it would be for someone without a disability. It is a reminder that in an instant, my life can become once again about disability. I feel fragile after a fall, more inclined to stick with crutches, scooter, or wheelchair, to put in more grab bars around the house, to sit and drink tea and use a hot pad, as if to comfort myself. *And hurt my bad leg.* I have a "good" and a "bad" leg. This is the language I've heard and used all my life. Only when I began thinking and writing about disability professionally did the full impact of those terms become clear to me. The disabled part of my body is labeled as bad and becomes disavowed. Well, now, that just can't be psychologically healthy! So let's reframe it: *I hurt the leg most affected by polio.* Now, isn't that better? But it still hurts like anything—paralysis, despite the misconception most people have, does not mean loss of feeling. In fact, that leg has hypersensitive feeling. I still remember the great splinter incident of '02!

This example of falling and of disability becoming a feature of daily life is the way things go now. As I age (not at all gracefully!), disability has become more salient once again. It waxes and wanes like the stages of the moon, sometimes illuminating the path ahead, sometimes leaving it in darkness. As I limp towards Bethlehem, not to be born, but to be at peace, I am amazed at the very idea that anything here that I have written might help someone else.

SELECTED BIBLIOGRAPHY

Olkin, R. (1999). *What psychotherapists should know about disability*. New York: Guilford.

Olkin, R. (2004). Making research accessible to participants with disabilities. *Journal of Multicultural Counseling & Development, 32*(extra), 332–343.

Olkin, R. (2005). Why I changed my mind about physician-assisted suicide: How Stanford University made a radical out of me. *Journal of Disability Policy Studies, 16*(1), 68–71.

Olkin, R. (2006). Persons of color with disabilities. In M. Constantine (Ed.), *Clinical practice with people of color: A guide to becoming culturally competent.* New York: Teachers College Press.

Olkin, R. (2008). Disability-affirmative therapy and case formulation: A template for understanding disability in a clinical context. *Counseling & Human Development, 39*(8), 1–20.

Olkin, R., Abrams, K., Preston, P., & Kirshbaum, M. (2006). Comparison of parents with and without disabilities raising teens: Information from the NHIS and two national surveys. *Rehabilitation Psychology, 51*(1), 43–49.

Olkin, R., & Pledger, C. (2003). Can disability studies and psychology join hands? *American Psychologist, 58*(4), 296–304.

11

50 Years in the Counseling Field

From Baba Ram Dass to Neuroscience[1]

ALLEN E. IVEY

EARLY RECOLLECTIONS: HOW I BECAME COMMITTED TO A MULTICULTURAL APPROACH

Immigration and Poverty. Both my parents were born in poverty or near poverty in a time when there was no social safety net. My father's parents had emigrated from Kernow/Cornwall, Great Britain, at the turn of the century. Cornwall was then and remains now under the thumb of the English crown, whose "majesty" is founded on Cornish tin. My grandfather died when my father was 9, leaving my grandmother as sole support of the family. She literally took in washing to support the family and made Cornish butter from her few cows to sell to homes near a local mill. One day, when she went to sell butter, the people refused to buy any more. She eventually found out that the mill owners required them to buy everything at the company store. At one point, the situation was so desperate that my father and his older brother were almost sent to a foundling home.

Compulsive Gambling. On my mother's side, my grandfather inherited the local paper, founded by my great-grandfather, but he soon lost the paper playing cards. Therefore, my mother had no money for shoes for school or for the required books. From my parents' painful experiences in childhood, I gained some sense of economic oppression and injustice.

The Great Depression. Bad times were in full force when my mother and father were to be married in 1930 and Dad lost his rather good job with Standard Oil the week before the wedding. They still got married and rented a very small gas station in rural Mt. Vernon, Washington State. I grew up in a small house attached to the store and slept in a closet as a small child. A quarter-mile south was my mother's family farm, and a quarter-mile west was my dad's family farm (my grandmother had married my grandfather's brother—a common practice at that time).

It's a Small, Small World. All this makes for a very small world, oriented to family relationships and the need to work together for mere survival. A mile away was a two-room school, which was to be my learning base until finally I was the only person in the eighth grade. The teaching practice at that time was for each class to go to the teacher's desk and read the assignment aloud. This was true whether it was language, reading, social studies, or math. I recall reading all the books I was to read in the next several years early in the second grade. I anticipated a boring time ahead and I was right!

An Early Lesson in Racism. One of the school lessons focused on capitalization, and the teacher taught us that the names of all people were to be capitalized. A few days later, presenting the history of the Civil War, she wrote the word "negro" on the board. Being the type of child a teacher hates, I immediately raised my hand and pointed out that she had just taught us to capitalize the names of peoples. She was flustered and angry. I don't recall her exact response, but it was something like "Well . . . I guess they are not that important and are not really a people." I was not satisfied with her answer, but have always capitalized Negro and Black ever since.

Multicultural Encounters as a Child. My hero during early childhood days was Tandy Wilbur, manager of the Swinomish Nation, eight miles down the road. He always made a fuss over me. I was very impressed that he was a "manager" and he always dressed in a suit and tie. In high school, his son, Tandy, Jr., was an outstanding basketball player for nearby LaConner High, and he became a hero as well. Later, I played my accordion for dances at the Swinomish Hall and got to know Tandy in a new way.

In the 1960s, the Bolt decision in the Washington state court validated fishing treaties signed in the previous century, which had been ignored to this point. The decision returned 50% of salmon rights to Washington nations and tribes. Needless to say, this caused quite a conservative outcry, which has not died down fully even today. Tandy, Jr. became quite active as a spokesperson for Native American Indians. He was found murdered in a bathroom in SeaTac Airport at the high point of resistance to the decision. No murderer has ever been found.

In the summers, Native Canadian Indians (Dene) came to our area to pick strawberries and do other farm work. Dad used to take our pickup truck to camps around the area and sold groceries off the truck. One day, he came home looking sad. I asked what had happened, and he said, "The farmers want a kickback from me. If I sell groceries there, I'd have to raise the price to the Indians." Dad wouldn't pay the farmer the kickback, even though the economic loss was important to our family.

At school, I endured frequent teasing and was called many anti-Semitic names that I'd rather not repeat in print. As a Baptist in a rural, provincial community, I did not even know what a Jew was, but the names certainly were not fun. I suspected that my "friends" did this because they learned those words at home from their parents, who likely were referring to my merchant father running a small store in a farm community. The stereotype of the Jew exploiting the gentile seems to have taken hold in this small corner of America. Nonetheless, it was necessary to smile at those parents when they came into the store as customers. I never shared this story with my own parents. Later, when teaching Jewish students at Boston University, I found that several of them had had experiences similar to my own in school. They also did not share such stories of oppression with their parents.

Out of this rural childhood, I learned to hate oppression in all forms. And fortunately, my parents' value system of standing up alone for right gave me a foundation for understanding and supporting multicultural issues. A few years after I went to college, a Swinomish child was named "Miriam" after my mother, and my parents were invited to participate in community pow-wows, including exchange of gifts.

EARLY ACADEMIC INFLUENCES

Tradition and Culture Collide. Richard Alpert, the son of a railroad CEO, was a dashing young teaching assistant to Ernest Hilgard in my Stanford introduction to psychology class. He went on to fame at Harvard with Timothy Leary as they introduced LSD to popular culture and became American idols of the 1960s. After being fired, Leary continued his LSD salesmanship while Alpert journeyed to India, where he was introduced to his guru, Neem Karoli Baba. He changed his name to Baba Ram Dass and has become one of the leading figures of modern approaches to meditation and spirituality. His *Be Here Now* (1978) has become an American classic and is still available in most bookstores.

Baba Ram Dass's life and legend are a metaphor for those of my generation. Hilgard was one of the foremost presidents of the American Psychological Association and has the most solid of traditional credentials. Yet in our intro class, he spoke of strange things such as meditation and lying on nails, suggesting that American psychology had a lot to learn from other cultures. Safe in retirement, Hilgard was the psychologist who did the research that made hypnosis understandable and respectable. Ram Dass took another approach and perhaps accomplished even more than his mentor.

Encountering Racism, Classism, and Anti-Semitism. Stanford in 1955 was virtually all White and certainly a bastion of the privileged and entitled. My fundamentalist Baptist background left me so naïve that I thought that one bottle of beer would make the individual literally "falling down drunk." My wealthy roomies saw it differently, spent the term drinking and harassing my naïveté, and they flunked out in 3 very long (to me) months. It is not easy dealing with the wealthy and privileged! The only people of color on our campus were a few Chinese and Japanese, well liked, but you would not want to date them, and the comments behind their backs were not all that pleasant.

I recall no African Americans at all except one very popular older gentleman, Sam MacDonald, who was key to the success of the Stanford Convalescent Home for Children (http://histsoc.stanford.edu/pdfST/ST7n02. pdf). Anti-Semitism was rife. A friend, considering medical school, sought counsel with the Dean of Students, who told him, "You're lucky to be here. We take very few Jews, and I suggest you consider a different medical school from Stanford." I worked in the dining hall to cover my meals and part of my room, but in my last term, I decided to work on campus. My friends found a place for me in Stern Hall, but three of them came to me to discuss "a problem." Would I be willing to room with a Jewish student? No problem for me! At that time, I was merely puzzled by the idea that they thought that it

would make a difference to me, but in retrospect, I am disappointed that I was not sophisticated enough to respond more appropriately and use this as an opportunity to educate them.

Before I go further, I need to comment on my ambivalence toward Stanford—the excellent education and high standards, but also my frustration with what I now see as Stanford's naïveté and, in many ways, support of unfair and elite systems. Now, Stanford, at times, has been a leader in multiculturalism, but they still sell and profit from the Stanford-Binet, a test that has had a negative impact on many lives. The psychology department still needs consciousness raising, although it is much more aware than it was years ago.

Get Out and Learn Something. I received a very strong and traditional training at Stanford. Yet Robert R. Sears, another APA president, told me that most of what I was learning would soon be irrelevant, and "Get out and get that doctorate so that you can learn something." I learned from him how to read psychological research and literature. Sears was one of Lewis Terman's gifted children and was committed to heredity as key to human development (perhaps because he was a gifted child?). A frequent focus of his seminar presentations were attacks on the environmental orientation at the University of Iowa Child Study Center.

Heredity Versus Environment and Fundamentalism Versus Biology. I came to Stanford imbued with the conservative Baptist outlook. But my introductory biology class changed my mind over two quarters. It was taught by Graham DuShane and David Regnery (how many of you remember the names of your intro bio profs?). Five hundred of us sat spellbound listening to the finest lectures I would ever hear. From them, I learned that it is difficult and nearly impossible to separate environment from heredity and genetics. Later, Sears's position on the genetic base of IQ puzzled me, as he was a hero otherwise. Over the years, it has amazed and troubled me many times as I see that many still argue for one "cause" over the other. How much we lose over this silly argument, when we are truly products of interactions of heredity and environment. Recently, I listened to a series of lectures by Robert Sapolsky of Stanford, now a famous neuroscientist

(Sapolsky, 2005). Sapolsky's presentations now virtually duplicate the content and values of the lectures of DuShane and Regnery given 50 years ago. I highly recommend the Sapolsky lectures as the ideal entry into neuroscience today.

Culture Shock—The Community Makes a Significant Difference for the Client. I was fortunate to study for a Fulbright year at the University of Copenhagen, Denmark, with Poul Perch, chief social adviser to the government. Perch was likely the first person in the world to advocate for psychological education rather than an exclusive focus on therapy. In 1955, Denmark was far ahead of the United States in social programs. (It still is.) Deinstitutionalization and the return of psychiatric patients to the community had just been completed. But instead of homelessness, I saw a variety of programs to integrate the patients into the community via well-managed group homes and a variety of alternatives for those who needed special care. Many other social programs that we are only now beginning to consider were keeping costs down, and of course, the health needs of all were met. A mixed capitalist/socialist economy works and provides safety and wellness for the total population. Would this work here in our excessively individualistic nation? At the moment, no, as the United States has failed in developing a communitarian and caring view in our population.

But the main learning for me was that my elite Stanford education was very incomplete. Sears was right—"Get out and learn something." What I learned in Denmark was that the individualistic, heredity-oriented Stanford psychology department was in many ways rather naïve and potentially damaging not only to the field, but to the nation as well.

Learning Humbleness in the Doctoral Program and Further Cultural Awakening. Harvard was an incredible challenge for me and I struggled—I really struggled. But persistence and motivation are what it takes to complete a degree. After my first year, I was married and thus took a position as Instructor at Boston University ($4,300). But I continued my doctoral work and finished my degree in 2 more years while working full time. This is not something that I recommend, but finally I was ready to go out in the world and learn something!

BU and Multiculturalism. I was 23 when I obtained my first university position as Instructor and Director of Student Activities. Boston University represented my first real contact with Jews. And as I counseled them on their issues, I was amazed to find how many had life experiences similar to my own. I heard my own life story repeated to me—harassment, keeping childhood anti-Semitism to themselves rather than troubling their parents, and a feeling of alienation and loneliness, sometimes wondering if the fault was in them. At that point, I simply empathized and understood. Counseling was not seen as a force for social change. We had no idea of oppression, multicultural awareness, and helping clients build social awareness of systemic causes of their issues. I know that you will do better.

PROFESSIONAL CHALLENGES

Too Young, but I Survived. At the ripe age of 25, fresh with a new doctorate, I became Director of the Counseling Service at Bucknell University in Lewisburg, Pennsylvania. No one should take such a job at that age! I needed mentoring, and I found that in Donald Ford, Director of Counseling, at nearby Penn State. Don was doing some wonderful community campus change interventions, and, because of my Denmark experience, I immediately bought into this model and later implemented similar interventions in full detail with our own variations at Colorado State University.

Bucknell has a gorgeous campus and represents the best of the small-college tradition. There were only a few African American students on campus and one came to me for counseling—the issue was his uncomfortableness on this nearly all-White campus. Needless to say, multicultural issues were not taught in my school years. I fear that he taught and helped me more than I helped him, although he returned for several visits, so perhaps I did something. Years later, I was excited to read in the papers that he had considerable success on the national scene. I also worked with my first gay client with approximately the same result. He came back, but I think I developed far more than he did. I wish that I knew then what I know now.

Colorado State University, a Fountain of Excellence. At 29, I became founder and director of what was to become a major college counseling center. The smartest thing that I did was always try to hire someone smarter and more capable than I was—or, at least to bring in staff who knew areas where I was weak and needed to learn. Our young staff with the guidance of a great man and dean (Burns Crookston) rapidly became a solid working unit. We were the first student development center in the nation and we were written up in the *Journal of Counseling & Development* for our innovative programs. I'd particularly mention Eugene Oetting, Charlie Cole, Dean Miller, Wes Morrill, Jim Hurst, and Ursula Delworth as prime movers of our program. Three presidents of the Society of Counseling Psychology came out of that group, and more were deserving of that honor. Our colleague, Dick Suinn, became president of the American Psychological Association.

In addition to counseling services, our focus was on outreach, campus research, and community programs. At this point, the typical counseling center staff sat in their office and waited for clients. We believed in education and prevention, ran groups in the dorms, developed what may have been the first family counseling campus program in student housing, and published like crazy so that we could share our ideas. An important part of this initiative was the Mental Health and Manpower program, where we worked with a psychiatric hospital in Denver to place patients in the community, often using principles that I learned in Denmark. Although I wrote the original grant, Eugene Oetting turned out to be the major force, and he went on to generate nearly $10 million in research and development grants, beyond our original $350,000.

CSU and Microcounseling. My interest in the interview led to a small grant from the Kettering Foundation, where I was interested in demystifying the counseling interview via videotaped recordings of the session. Videorecording was totally new at this point, and no one knew its many possibilities. What are the *specific skills* that make an interview successful? The team of this grant included staff members, Cheryl Normingon, Wes Morrill, Dean Miller, and graduate students Richard Haase and Max Uhlemann (who went on to be president of the Canadian Counseling Association).

All of us visited Dwight Allen and Albert Bandura at Stanford to learn more about social skills and observational learning. Bandura at that point had just completed his classic Bobo doll study, which clearly indicated that watching a model of someone hitting the doll led to increased hitting and aggression in children as compared to a control group. For me, the study was definitive—TV affects aggression. But years later, despite endless supportive research, the corporate interest to TV continues to encourage violence in our children, while parents sit passively and wonder why their children act as they do.

The first 6 months of the grant were a series of failed tries—we had real difficulty in identifying concrete skills of the interview. Giving up on reading and discussion, we decided to videotape our center secretary, Judy (not her real name). Judy was wonderful. She did everything wrong. Her body language was tense, she only asked questions, and she obviously was not listening to the answers. After 5 minutes of trauma for her, we brought her out of the interview and on-the-spot, generated the now-obvious concepts of attending behavior—visuals (appropriate eye contact), vocal qualities, verbal following, and appropriate body language (3 Vs + B). We communicated these new (to us and her) concepts and she returned to another short session and *looked like* a counselor. I say "looked like" as Judy obviously had much more to learn. Particularly fascinating was the fact that Judy returned to work the following Monday glowing, "I paid attention and listened to my husband, he listened to me, and we had a wonderful weekend." Clearly, the learning had generalized to the real world.

We moved on from that to other key skills of the interview such as reflection of feeling, paraphrasing, and summarization. The influence of Carl Rogers at that time is apparent in this list. Very soon, questioning and other skills began to enrich the model.

CSU and Multiculturalism. My first really deep encounter with multiculturalism was teaching the psychology course Individual Differences. I used a book by Leona Tyler, a hero in graduate school and an even larger hero today. Tyler was one of the first female presidents of the American Psychological Association. Although she did not use the word *multiculturalism*, her book opened my eyes to issues of class, race, and gender after my closed Stanford experience. Opening this book randomly just now, I find that 50 years ago, she was very much in tune with modern ideas. Consider the following on intelligence testing and her early identification of the ideas of privilege.

> Our present intelligence tests are not fair to lower-class children . . . because the questions asked them do not give their ability a chance to show up (as) they are consistently underestimated and discriminated against. . . . The second explanation, fitting in with Hebb's and Piaget's emphasis on the importance of early learning in intellectual growth, holds that by the time they reach school age lower-class children have not, on the average, developed mentally to the level that more privileged groups have reached, and that the differences widen as the years pass. (Tyler, 1956, p. 325)

Journals, publishers, and professors (and you students as well) want and demand articles and books written after the year 2000 used as references. I've been corrected on this issue more than once. Apparently, we prefer to bury the past rather than learn from it. Tyler's comments, made 50 years ago, are still clear and cogent today. It is hard to believe that key figures at Harvard, Stanford, and UC Berkeley still hold naïvely to the belief in inheritance as the key dimension of human growth.

Why is that? Could it be that elite institutions (where I was lucky enough to struggle through) have a bias toward their own privilege? Do they think that they are inherently worthy of being the "cream at the top"? Although I treasure my Stanford/Harvard background, I worry about elite institutions, their self-centeredness, and their missionary attitude toward the rest of society and the world. I rather doubt that they have as many answers as they claim.

Tyler's thinking led me to read the original journals in which Terman published his work on gifted children and intelligence. There are many who still endorse this ancient and racist point of view. Here are some items from his highly influential book *The Measurement of Intelligence* (Terman, 1916):

1. The median IQ for children of the superior social class is about 7 points above, and that of the inferior social class about 7 points below the median IQ of the average social group. . . .

2. That the children of the superior class make a better showing in the tests is probably due, for the most part, to superiority in original endowment. Five supplementary lines of evidence support this conclusion:

   a) the teachers' rankings of the children according to intelligence;

   b) the age-grade progress of the children;

   c) the quality of the schoolwork;

   d) the comparison of older and younger children as regards the influence of social environment; and

   e) the study of bright and dull children in the same family. (pp. 72–73)

After going back to the original literature, I found myself troubled at both Robert R. Sears and my elite Stanford education. Fortunately, Sears and his other highly qualified colleagues had taught me to go to the source and check out the findings for myself. This is a very different demand and scholarly standard that we seldom find in our graduate schools, our journals, and professional books. It is much easier to go to the Internet; get some informal, uninformed information; and rush to publication—or complete yet another paper for grad school that purports to be scholarship or worse, one's less-than-original work.

In short, we have produced a profession where we no longer can trust what we read. You can see my ambivalent feelings toward Robert R. Sears. He taught me what scholarship is about, and yet he and his colleagues frankly did not measure up. Expertise and scholarship are clearly not enough; there is need for openness of mind. But this leaves me with some insecurity as well. Have I measured up to those lofty standards? Frankly, sometimes yes, sometimes no. But simply writing this reminds me of my history and the need to go back to the original work.

Shortly after these discoveries, the Kettering Foundation gave me another very small grant. Here I developed a behavioral objectives curriculum for human relations. This behavioral-outcome orientation curriculum includes the social skills of microcounseling, but it also dealt with issues of racism and gender discrimination. Later, I was to teach this curriculum at the University of Massachusetts, Amherst. This was the first time that I put my thinking together in writing about social issues. They had been perking throughout my life, but I only really began to understand these issues in 1967 (long before many of you were born).

Although multiculturalism and diversity have made immense gains in the ensuing 40 years, each time we reach what we think of as Martin Luther King, Jr.'s "mountain top," we see another mountain of racism, sexism, or other form of oppression that needs study and climbing.

On to UMass and a Fuller Commitment to Multiculturalism. Thirty years were spent at the University of Massachusetts, Amherst, during which I taught a variety of multicultural courses from the very beginning. The human relations and antiracism course mentioned above was one of them. But most influential to me was working with Dean Norma Jean Anderson in an encounter group course titled "Black and White in Helping." The course was always about half White and half African American and resulted in powerful learning experiences for us all.

My central discovery came during the second year of the course. I had prided myself for several years on being "nonracist" and "color blind." The discovery of institutional racism was an important marker for me. Banks, car dealerships, employers, and all the institutions of our predominantly White society tend to discriminate against people of color. I had sensed this type of discrimination in my rural background. I recall how liberating it was for me to leave Mt. Vernon, Washington and the baggage of oppression I felt there. But if I were a person of color, I could not have left that oppression behind as I would have encountered new issues. I'll admit the class prejudice I experienced in my freshman year is perhaps a variety of oppression that is not easily left behind. But being White in a predominantly White society keeps me safe from the most damaging oppression of all—racism.

I began to sense my White privilege, although we did not have that language at that time. In one of the groups, I came to the discovery that as a White person, I could never get rid of the privileges and benefits that I received from simply being a European-American White person. Thus, I came to know and acknowledge that a form of almost inborn racism will also be in me. Admitting that I am a racist was not a pleasant task. But as I see so many people say, "I'm not racist" or worse, "I'm not racist, but . . ." I find myself discouraged and

sometimes angry. All majority people need to learn and acknowledge the constant benefits that come to them from being White. Privilege and power extend to many other dimensions such as gender; social and economic class; sexual identity; physical and mental ability; area of the country; religion/spirituality; and life experience with trauma (war, rape, cancer). Each of the many multicultural constellations comes with a certain dimension of power and entitlement. Where do you stand on these dimensions of privilege?

There are many things that I could share from these years. But as I do, I must say that I am not perfect. I've made many mistakes, but I tend to learn from my errors and keep plugging. Don't use me as a model. Take some of these ideas and move far beyond me as a person and professional.

Some experiences during my time at UMass:

- *Mary and Other Joys.* The best thing at UMass was meeting Mary Kathryn Bradford, now my spouse, lover, co-author, and joy of my life. Somehow, we were destined for each other. Several years before we even spoke to each other, we had eye contact across a crowded room. We did not meet and talk, but both of us recall that magical moment. She was definitely not the "other woman," but was I ever delighted to find that she was available after a relatively amicable divorce from my first wife. All that I have done since that time has been with Mary. We say that we are "joined at the hip" with very permeable boundaries.

Beyond writing and lecturing, we have many fun and important activities. First of all is our blended family—four children (all still married to the same person and working with benefits) and nine grandchildren (obviously all "above average" as in Lake Wobegon, Minnesota). And the blended family seems to get along quite well—we have them visit us in Florida for about 5 to 6 weeks each year. Needless to say, we can take only one family at a time!

Mary and I have had some really fun and intellectually challenging travel. Our visit to Israel is a real standout. There, we lectured to all the counseling supervisors in Jerusalem and talked with them about how to handle the threat of gas attacks and bombings. We've been to Australia and Japan multiple times, where we enjoy special colleagues. David Rothmans, CEO of Aboriginal Affairs in South Australia, made it possible for us to meet with all the judges in the state where we discussed multicultural issues and the law. Machiko Fukuhara in Japan has established the Japanese Microcounseling Association, a scientific organization with its own journal, approved by the Japanese government.

• *The Multicultural Course and Faculty Challenges.* It was late in my years at UMass that I finally got the multicultural course required in our program. Then I went on sabbatical and they cancelled the requirement. Fortunately, by that time, the Massachusetts Psychological Association included the course as a requirement for licensure. The faculty discovered that and returned the course to the curriculum. From this, you learn that faculty are often not enthused about the changes that multicultural awareness requires in their teaching.

At this point, I give special thanks to my two best friends at UMass—Norma Jean Anderson and Ernest Washington, two superb co-teachers, scholars, friends, and innovators. They are with me always!

Multicultural issues should be a part or centerpiece of every course. We work in a culture-centered profession, for every session we have and every concept we learn is influenced in some way by many multicultural dimensions. We ought to thank Paul Pedersen for his emphasis on the words *culture-centered counseling,* for this is the only reasonable way to consider our complex profession.

• *The Vail Conference and Multicultural Ethics.* In 1970, I was invited as a delegate to the APA conference on the status of clinical work in our field. This turned out to be a radical group, highly influenced by the 1960s. The conference summary (Korman, 1974) was full of great ideas, but so far ahead of the psychology field that the conference had very little impact. I particularly recall working and writing with two giants—George Albee and Joe White (read Joe White's life story in Chapter 4)—on the ethics of multicultural counseling. We stated that counseling or therapy with a client who is culturally different from the therapist is unethical if proper training and supervision are not in place. Needless to say, this statement

was ignored and continues to be considerably distant from the mainstream.

• *Discovering White Privilege.* In my early teaching and writing on multicultural issues, I was proudly nonracist. But through Black/White encounter group experience and reading about systemic racism, I learned that my inner and unconscious self could never fully cleanse myself from racism and that, inevitably, I would always benefit from racism in some way. This was ultimately clarified when Peggy McIntosh named White privilege. Just being White in this society benefits me greatly and protects me from most oppression and harassment. As I continued to understand privilege, I learned that I also benefit from male privilege, English-speaking privilege, socioeconomic privilege, heterosexual privilege, and many others. I need to think of myself as a person of privilege, even though my beginnings are such that this is hard for me. I still see myself as the harassed minority—childhood experience is hard to forget.

• *My Failure to Implement the Nantucket Statement.* Early in my time at UMass, a faculty group visited Nantucket Island and wrote a culture-centered manifesto for our School of Education. Faculties don't like manifestos, especially when that manifesto asks them to change their teaching style and, even worse to some, to include new ideas with which they are unfamiliar. The Nantucket statement was dead in the water.

A few years later, I thought things had improved, and with another faculty member, I wanted to return to discussion and implementation of that statement. We were politically naïve and got little farther than the original group. As I look back on it now, I needed more community organizational training. We needed a larger group. We needed to find people who would actually implement the ideas as a starting point. Social action requires solid community understanding and the willingness to persist and work toward worthwhile goals. Frankly, I did not plan well and gave up too easily.

With greater knowledge now, I'd handle this situation very differently. I hope that you will take up this cause and do a far better job than I did. Very few of us really challenge the systems within which we work—racism and other forms of oppression still form much of the foundation of our programs. What are you doing about that?

• *The Multicultural Competencies.* I was president of the Society for Counseling Psychology in 1980–1981 and did one important thing. I was wise enough to appoint Derald Wing Sue as head of the Professional Affairs Committee with the charge to look at multicultural issues in the counseling and therapy field. Out of his committee came an important report on competencies for effective multicultural counseling. Unfortunately, the Counseling Psychology Executive Committee refused to endorse this report, thus delaying real action on implementation for at least 10 or more years. Gerald Stone is to be recognized as the leader who broke through the Counseling Psychology Executive Committee resistance and restarted the process. Under Gerry, I was lucky enough to head the committee that led to the next stage of implementation. As you know, Sue has been the originator and leader of the multicultural competency movement, and Patricia Arredondo and Nadya Fouad have been the leaders to take this home to American Counseling Association and American Psychological Association approval. I've been lucky and proud to be associated with this movement since its inception. I'd point out that it took almost 25 years to win endorsement of the original Sue report. *If you really want to produce change in the profession, you have to be persistent and stand up for what you believe in over a very long time.*

• *Writing, Writing, Writing.* During my time at UMass, I focused on writing articles and books, almost all with some type of multicultural emphasis. Depending on how you count, I have more than 40 books published to date and translations in 20 languages. I've burned through a lot of trees with an additional 200 articles and chapters. When people ask how I do it, I say—"get old and continue writing, you'll get there."

In 1974, I introduced multicultural differences and variations in the skills training model. Unfortunately, there are still derivative skill textbooks on the market that continue to resist placing multicultural issues at the center—or even at the periphery. In 1980, I wrote the first theories of counseling text that referenced the word *culture,* and as I moved more to a culture-centered approach over the years, the sales went down.

I'm particularly pleased with my *Developmental Counseling and Therapy,* a revisioning of information processing and Piagetian theory that I wrote in a frenzied week, but then spent two years rewriting and reworking. Here you will find one of the more complex integrative theories of counseling and therapy available (Ivey, 1986/2000). The applied version is more accessible and provides a clear way to integrate and use multicultural theory in practice as well as many other ways to integrate varying theories in an effective and strategic case conception and treatment plan (Ivey, Ivey, Myers, & Sweeney, 2006). Take a look at it—a bit different and challenging, but it works.

Re-wards and A-wards. I've received quite a few. As a friend once said, "It's nice to be noticed." There are three, however, that really pleased me. The first was being named a Fellow of the Society for the Study of Ethnic Minority Issues, the second was a Presidential Citation and Fellow Status in the Association of Asian American Psychologists, and especially gratifying was being named an Elder of the Multicultural Movement at a recent Multicultural Summit and Conference. All of these motivate me to continue the path.

Running Through the Theories of a Lifetime. A big issue when I started counseling was, "Are you directive (Thorne) or nondirective (Rogers)?" There were very few who were psychoanalytically oriented. Fortunately, I had Leona Tyler as a model, and I bought into both theories, but I added the positive orientation to Tyler, which now expresses itself in the wellness movement and positive psychology (with, of course, little reference, if any, to Tyler's pioneering work). So I described myself as a "directive, nondirective counselor."

Shortly after my degree, along came the famous Rogers, Perls, and Ellis films. This only reinforced my Rogerian leanings, but Perls intrigued me and I started looking into Gestalt. This was followed by transactional analysis, and 5 years in psychoanalytic therapy (everything that Freud said is true, but it strikes mainly as good creativity training). I have taught the psychodynamic course for years and still consider it a fine framework for understanding client history and its influence on present behavior and thinking.

My behavioral and cognitive-behavioral phase was very strong. I rejected everything from my past. I recall my board certification exam in which I said to the psychoanalytically oriented examiners—"Motivation? I've never seen one of those."

Then came encounter groups and weekend marathon encounters. The hot tubs at Esalen were great fun, and I became an encounter groupie.

Nonetheless, throughout much of these multicultural issues, campus outreach and prevention, and social justice thoughts were active—although I often did not have the words and concepts that you enjoy today.

But somewhere in there, I noted that I had been totally committed to at least six or seven theories—and I had to admit that each one had something important to say to me. As you might anticipate, this led to more reading and writing and led me to my own integrative theory, developmental counseling and therapy, which has allowed me in its most recent versions to integrate multicultural theory and practice as well. Now, I can intentionally engage in an interview and move from theory to theory, anticipating and even predicting which strategy from which theory will be most effective at a particular time. I guess this is one of the joys of lasting a long time in the profession.

HOW NICE IT WOULD BE TO RETIRE— OR WOULD IT?

Discerning the Meaning of Retirement. Mary and I moved out of academic work in 1999, taught once again in Australia, and then moved to our intellectual and social home here in Sarasota, Florida. At first, I fought retirement and felt that I should be doing something different from the past. Retirement is a major life transition, and we all need to give that area of life change much more attention. Much of a retiree's difficulties center around meaning, spirituality, and values.

St. Boniface Church has been an inspiration for both Mary and me. We went through a 2-year discernment program that helped us both through the trauma of retirement. Discerning one's life goal and vision is critical to happiness and purpose. Through systematic discernment, I found that what I wanted to do was what I always have been doing—counseling and therapy

with a multicultural focus. But, please—just a bit more balance and a bit more fun.

Yet More Writing. Computers and writing obviously have continued for both of us. We have a courtesy appointment at the University of South Florida, Tampa, and have close faculty relationships there. In fact, we have invited Carlos Zalaquett, an incredible scholar and person, to join us with our most important book in its next edition (Ivey, Ivey, & Zalaquett, in press). We attend about four conventions a year, among them ACA, APA, Association for Counselor Education and Supervision, the Multicultural Summit, the Columbia Roundtable, and the Janet E. Helms Conference at Boston College. Needless to say, we can't make it to all of those every year, particularly as I want to start attending the national conference on neuroscience.

Neuroscience and the Future. For the past several years, I've been studying neuroscience and its relationship to counseling and therapy. To my delight and surprise, neuroscience supports most of our present research and therapy practices. Furthermore, it offers the promise of helping us become more planful and precise in our interventions. As far as I can tell, I made the first practical, applied neuroscience presentation on interviewing, counseling, and therapy to the American Counseling Association (and I know of no such presentation at APA either). On the other hand, each time I've presented on neuroscience, I find that students in the audience are well aware that effective counseling can change client brain networks. What is needed are more specifics that we can use to apply in the interview. The seventh edition of our basic book, *Intentional Interviewing and Counseling,* explores this matter with my specifics for practice. I'll just mention two or three items that fascinate me, even though you may be familiar with them already.

- *Brain Plasticity.* The brain has an infinite capacity for change and growth. Although we may lose neurons as we age, new neurons are developed with new learning (neurogenesis). This is true whether you are 9 or 90—we all have the possibility for brain development regardless of age. Evidence is that successful counseling and therapy can change neural networks in the client, but let us recall that each person we encounter in the interview changes us as well.

• *Mirror Neurons and Empathy.* The foundation of empathy is hardwired into the brain through mirror neurons "that respond and await development through interaction with others. . . . Empathy (is) an intentional capacity" (Decety & Jackson, 2004, pp. 71, 93). In counseling, our brains and our bodies literally mirror what our clients are telling us—*if* we are empathic. The idea of a neurological base for one of our most important constructs is both amazing and critical to becoming ever more empathic and understanding. And let us recall that the antisocial personality's mirror neurons do not fire when another person is in pain. This may provide a clearer direction for us in therapy with this group.

• *Social Justice and Neuroscience.* Brain science strongly indicates that counselors and therapists have a duty and obligation to move out of the office and work toward social goals and health for our clients.

"Poverty in early childhood poisons the brain." That was the opening of an article in the Financial Times, summarizing research presented . . . at the American Association for the Advancement of Science.

As the article explained, neuroscientists have found that "many children growing up in very poor families with low social status experience unhealthy levels of stress hormones, which impair their neural development." The effect is to impair language development and memory—and hence the ability to escape poverty—for the rest of the child's life. (Krugman, 2008, p. 15A)

SOME FINAL THOUGHTS

You are entering an alive and exciting profession, one that will make a difference in our society. I'm really pleased to look back and see how our field has grown. The changes are amazing. As an elder, I'll summarize just a few thoughts on change and the future of our field.

• In 1959, my dissertation was completed on a manual typewriter. Each page had to be redone if there was even one error.

• I knew virtually *all* of the literature in both counseling and psychology. It was possible then. Later, I knew just counseling and counseling psychology, but

that became too much. In 1980, I knew all the literature in multiculturalism, and that is impossible now for anyone. You are entering a huge field and will have to make many choices.

• I recall being strongly criticized in the 1960s by other counseling center directors for reaching out to the campus and the Denver community, 60 miles distant. This is an argument that still rages—should counseling prevent problems or just treat them? I obviously argue strongly for prevention, social action, and social justice. This is still a very live issue—where do you stand?

• Theory-of-the-week courses need to be carefully studied and, I think, changed radically. Integrative methods with selective teaching of key strategies from important theories need to become central. But in this, we also need to focus on the client/counselor relationship as central. Unless there is a connection, change is much less likely to happen and to endure after the session. How are your social skills? How well do you relate to others? Can you listen? Can you deal with and respect multicultural difference? If you can't meet these basic criteria, I suggest that you move on to another profession.

• More recently, I have come to the realization that counselors and therapists need to learn community organizing skills. These can be used within to change and move our profession. They also need to be used to develop more of a communitarian vision in our schools, institutions, and communities.

As I look back to 1952 and Dr. Hilgard and Baba Ram Dass, it takes my breath away. Our field has changed so much and grown so fast. I do deeply respect the learning and opportunities that the counseling and psychological fields have offered me. But I also get very impatient with the pace of change. When I think of Poul Perch and psychoeducation in 1955–1956 and the success of the Danish model, why are we still not there? Why is our country so slow to realize that caring for others will make a difference not only for them, but also for ourselves?

I pray that the counseling and psychotherapy professions will grow faster and stronger, with a greater realization of our responsibility to the downtrodden and the oppressed. I recall reading in the journal *Christian Counseling* that the author had discovered that rich people had as many problems as the poor. He used this to justify his work as a "Christian coach." Probably he is right, but the poor have very different issues from the rich. Where does our responsibility lie?

Here are two final comments for you students seeking your degrees in counseling and clinical work:

Robert R. Sears said, "Get that degree and get out and learn something."

Baba Ram Dass said, "Be here now."

NOTE

1. This chapter is based partially on work in Ivey, Allen E. (2005). Living with change. In Conyne, R., & Bemak, F. (Eds.), *Journeys toward professional excellence*. Alexandria, VA, American Counseling Association. Reprinted with permission. No further reproduction authorized without permission of the American Counseling Association.

REFERENCES

Decety, J., & Jackson, P. (2004). The functional architecture of human empathy. *Behavioral and Cognitive Neuroscience Reviews, 3,* 71–100.

Ivey, A. (2000). *Developmental therapy.* Hanover, MA: Microtraining Associates. (Originally published in 1986 by Jossey-Bass)

Ivey, A., Ivey, M., Myers, J., & Sweeney, T. (2006). *Developmental counseling and therapy.* Boston: Lahaska.

Ivey, A., Ivey, M., & Zalaquett, C. (in press). *Intentional interviewing and counseling* (7th ed.). Belmont, CA: Brooks/Cole/Cengage.

Korman, M. (1974). National Conference on Levels of Performance and Patterns of Professional Training in Psychology. *American Psychologist, 29,* 441–449.

Krugman, P. (2008, Feb. 18). Poverty is poison. Available: http://www.nytimes.com/2008/02/18/opinion/18krugman.html?_r=1&ex=1204174800&en=0fe16bf6d26ac6cc&ei=5070&emc=eta1

Sapolsky, R. (2005). *Biology and human behavior: The neurological origins of individuality* (2nd ed.) [Audiotapes]. Chantilly, VA: The Teaching Company.

Terman, L. (1916). *The measurement of intelligence.* Boston: Houghton Mifflin.

Tyler, L. (1956). *The psychology of human differences.* New York: Appleton-Century-Crofts.

12

Loss and Desire in New Jersey

MICHELLE FINE

Suburbia, circa 1955.

"You walk into the house and first thing you see is a toilet?"

The bathroom sat directly inside the doorway of 510 Summit Street; more evidence of our failure to exit the working class. My mother would prefer you not look at the bathroom. No, turn right please. Glide down

    four

        steps

            into

                the

                    sunken living room;
                    a grand entrance,
                    signaling mobility.

My memory pulls back to the door. I don't remember if it was heavy or not; metal or wood. Probably metal with a cursive F tucked into a circle, smack in the middle of the door.

The door was my childhood transitional object; connecting and separating me from the world; progress from depression; us from the *Goyim* (Yiddish: non-Jews).

Each morning, before I was old enough to attend school, my 3- and 4- and 5-year-old eyes followed as Daddy, Sherry, and Richard left for America. From my TV perch with a bowl of sugary cereal in my lap, I watched, as I cared for and was cared for by my mother, in bed often, riddled with headaches. The wet *shmate* (Yiddish: rag) on her head carried the secrets of generations of women—their desires and losses.

My mother called our home *"the cemetery."*

I often wondered how many of us were buried there. At least until 6:00 p.m.

Then, most nights, when we heard his key in the door, we ran to greet my father. Sweaty with an acrid aroma of pipes, trucks, copper nipples, and elbows, his body carried traces of the plumbing supply shop, seeping through the flannel. As these seductive new smells of America—money, working-class masculinity, and possibility—swept in, we lined up like ducks waiting for our pecks. Standing tall and smiling, we were the evidence; his receipt for the voyage to America.

If my father didn't exist, capitalism would have had to invent him. Poor immigrant Jew sells junk in a horse and buggy on the Lower East Side, goes to war and makes good.

A few nights a month/year, Dad would drive home in his truck. The words *Rockland Plumbing Supply* were spray-painted on the side. And every time he drove it home, the police would arrive. That is, Mrs. Steinberg would call the police. Dad would answer the door, and Mom would hide behind him and ask (in a stand-by-your-man kinda way), "What's wrong with the plumbing truck?" She'd always pronounce the B, *plumBing*, much to our collective shame. "No commercial vehicles in the neighborhood." My father knew that and drove it home anyway.

We hated the Steinbergs. They hated us.

And they were the only other Jews in the area.

They were rich.

We were "*traif*" (Yiddish: trash), ghetto, greenhorn.

We didn't mow the lawn very often. In fact, Richard, my older brother, wanted to cement over the grass and rent out parking spaces.

Cousin Bobby would arrive at our house well after midnight, driving in from Brooklyn with a car on its last legs. He'd sleep in there 'til morning.

Sundays we had the "*gantseh meshpokah*" (Yiddish: entire clan) for barbecues.

Lots of large-breasted women and short men. All loud.

We were just the wrong kind of Jews.

Living within 10 miles of Palisades Amusement Park and within 10 years since the end of the Holocaust, we, too, rode the roller coaster of assimilation strapped in with ambivalence, shame, and pride.

My sister put adhesive tape on her nose at night so it wouldn't grow.

Our family name was Yankelovich, but it got mangled at Ellis Island and came out as Fine.

Richard got TB in high school. The only kid who did. They told me it was a broken leg. Just one of a million family secrets. "*Who needs to know?*"

Dad refused to join a synagogue even though Mom yearned for a community, longing for the melodies of her orthodox childhood. And of course, he remained fluent in all the prayers up until his death.

The living room sofa was covered in plastic. No mess you can't wipe away.

My mother baked *tzimes* (carrot pudding) with marshmallows dripping off the sides.

And we proudly celebrated Christmas: tree, tinsel, and balls.

* * *

Mom never ate dinner with us; that is, she never sat. "*Who can sit?*" (Much to my embarrassment, I didn't notice this until well into my 20s, when David, my partner, said, "I'm not eating this food until she sits and eats it first.")

Dinner was served in the dining room.

I mean to say, Mom served us dinner in the dining room, once Dad came home.

Never trust the passive voice; it hides her labor and his privilege.

The warm glow of sunset blanketed us, surrounded by floral wallpaper. I loved that wallpaper, stained with the grease of marrow bones and chicken necks and feet and Minute Steaks, circling my tongue and my memory. The grease slid up into the middle class with us. To this day, I still love marrow bones. I've been known to sneak into a Thanksgiving kitchen to rip off and devour the juicy, killer turkey butt.

The fat of childhood keeps me connected to and repulsed by that home.

Connected and repulsed. Like the Steinbergs.

The not-so-silent B, the unruly lawn, cousin Bobby, the wet rag, her migraines and depressions, our days marinating in the working class, skipping into the solid middle class, White skin privilege, the truck, the loss and pain of what was left behind, all surface in my work.

I have been bequeathed, then, to ask over and over in my research, my teaching, and my activism, in schools, communities, prisons, and youth social movements:

Where in the body, the family, the culture, the nation and the globe do bodies of sadness swell and grow limp in the shadow of progress? What buried knowledges do they hold?

And then, where lies the missing discourse of desire?

* * *

The double helix of my DNA twists at the neck. One line stretches from a Polish *shtetl* (Yiddish: Jewish ghetto).

In 1921, my parents sailed as children on separate disease-infected and dream-infused boats, from Poland to the "green lady" in New York harbor; with and without parts of their families who knew too well the price of living through a pogrom.

Seven-year-old Rose Hoffer, my mother, was the baby of an orthodox Jewish family of 18, or 16, or 15 births—depending on who was counting, and who was counted. She came to Ellis Island accompanied by two brothers, a sister, and her 60-year-old mother. "*Who knows how old she was? No one from Europe knows how old they are!*"

As family folklore tells it, triplets may have died before age one and the "hermaphrodite" was "allowed" to die, possibly smothered, at birth. Sometimes, they all lived in Poland, sometimes in Austria, sometimes Germany. Not that they had relocated. The moves of war ruthlessly yanked and distorted the borders of nations and emotions, carving out ghettos of trauma and blood.

At age 7, Jack Fine also traveled to the United States—Harlem, in fact—with his grandmother. This was 4 years after he was "given up" by his young widowed mother whose second husband "didn't want a child who wasn't his own."

"How did you feel about that, Dad?" asks the aspiring psychologist baby daughter of Rose and Jack, circa 1975, just entering graduate school. "Never thought about it, honey."

This amazing, proud man had a laser-like focus on the future. And no rearview mirror.

Years later, my father learned that his mother, stepfather, and stepbrothers were eventually killed, left behind in the Polish ghettos to be crushed under Nazi boots.

Referencing life in the United States, "Anything is possible in this country, baby, best country in the world."

My father never spoke pain or sadness. Directed and passionate, he was thoroughly dedicated to a better life for us. Narrating a life of blissful mobility, his capillaries quietly filled with joys and denial, eventually, at age 85, stealing his last breath. His final words were classic: "I'm feeling better today, Mommy."

In most households, we find a social psychological diaspora of emotional bodies. Some carry and speak the unbearable weight of loss; others bury, deny, and silence. The youngest chubby child, lucky to be born when the family financial profile was approaching a middle-class smile, always a watcher and a performer, I tracked my mother's migraines that moved deeper and deeper into her body as our family "made it." Only she could embody what the rest of us were forbidden to speak.

***

Back to my neck: Braided with this genetic line of matzoh ball soup, broken Yiddish-English, 36 first cousins, and the Ellis Island "makeover" of my father's surname, the other line of inheritance stems from my academic lineage. The DNA that I crafted, that I stitched together across college and graduate school, that is my psychological researcher/activist genes, come from Kurt Lewin by way of Morton Deutsch, with wonderful contributions from existential philosopher Maxine Greene. Trained in experimental social psychology, with deep roots in the lab, I was well schooled in the theory and practice of action research, work groups, force field theory, and the mid-century version of social psychology designed for social change.

From Rose and Jack and Kurt and Mort, and then later existential philosopher Maxine Greene and human rights activist Thea Jackson, I have come to recognize that my project—across methods and topics—has been/is to bear witness to injustice; to expose *shanda*—Yiddish for the deep scar tissue of shame that blankets us all as we participate in, collude with, are privileged by, and are victimized by injustice—and to find the "*missing discourse of desire.*"

My stance as critical psychologist has matured in the soil of a thoroughly immigrant Jewish family; a working-class home filled with love but not books; deep involvement in feminist, antiwar, and antiracism struggles; eventual privilege; mother of a very diverse group of boys/young men—Demetrius, Sam, and Caleb (two by C-section and one by foster care); a 30-year love affair with David (we never married, refusing yet another institution that legitimates "some"—couples and children—while casting a long shadow of illegitimacy on others); teacher and learner with scores of graduate students and colleagues from the University of

Pennsylvania and the Graduate Center at the City University of New York.

My dual genetic lines endowed me with the *chutzpa* (Yiddish: nerve) to theorize and study the visible and cellophane lines of power and (in)justice that stretch from the political to the psychic, by way of the social psychological. Situated in prisons, schools, and communities; using participatory methods, feminist, social psychological, and critical race theory, the work tracks empirically the capillaries of racial, sexual, classed, and gendered injustice, documenting the rage, despair, and migraines, and tracing too the ripples of resistance and flames of desire. Although my work maps a geography of shame and appetite, each project holds my little autobiographic secret—that those *persons and affects most viciously evacuated are the soul of our moral community.*

From the "psych lab" at Teachers College in 1979 to the Participatory Action Research Collective at the Graduate Center in 2008, from street surveys to ethnography, over the past 29 years, in thrilling collaborations (see Acknowledgments), our research has been designed to trouble the common sense about unjust arrangements that seem so natural or deserved, to destabilize what we think of as "normal," and to reveal where resistance gathers.

Using qualitative and quantitative methods, we aim to document, across our varied projects, what Nell Painter has called *soul murder;* we cultivate evidence of activism and challenge as well as what James Scott has called the *hidden transcripts of resistance* and we return a critical analytic gaze to the *social arrangements, institutions, distributions, ideologies, and social relations that reproduce and legitimate everyday injustice.* Our "research camps" include activist elders, youth, women in prison, students in over- and underresourced schools, Muslim American adolescents. . . . Together, we write and perform scholarly and popular re-presentations of individuals and groups that have long been demonized in the culture, held responsible for their own struggles and blamed for larger social problems. Some scenes . . .

June 2001: A collective of feminist participatory action researchers gathered to reflect on our work. We were asked to bring an artifact that represented our biography, research, and activism, our struggles.

Hiking past all the crosses, saints, and Catholic *chatchkas* (Yiddish: stuff), I arrived at the Education Building, Boston College, yearning to break into Yiddish, bags heavy with the presence of an absence. Maria Torre and I spoke that night for/with/despite those who were "otherwise detained"—our friends, co-researchers, Kathy, Iris, Judith, Donna, Migdalia, Missy, Pam. Still behind bars. I brought a plaid, flannel pillowcase, a symbol of movement and comfort, threads of many colors, patterned as if they fit. And we spoke about the project at Bedford Hills Correctional Facility, a maximum security prison for women, where our research team of seven women in prison and five of us not, came together to study the impact of college in prison, or the meanings of freedom inside hell, or the collusion of racism and sexism in the lives of women of color in prison, or how their babies sleep at night in the Bronx without their moms.

Participatory action research behind bars; under surveillance; in the warm, fictional comfort of a space of women; in a college in a prison in a nation with 2,000,000 behind bars. At 10:57 a.m. on Tuesdays, some of us rushed to leave; some had to stay. We all flinched. Critical research among women, in a tense little collusive corner, behind bars, in prison, "interrogating" and "theorizing" college, T-tests, analyses of variance, Spanish, sex, stories, voices, danger and pleasure, guilt and redemption. Only some of us are allowed to hold the tape recorder. Others had their cells searched last night . . . poetry journals confiscated. We dare not speak of our hatreds or outrage; we may go nuts, slowly or as a collective.

Deep into our work, probably 3 years in, we were writing up our final report and talking about how to write about our participatory research team. Neither wanting to flatten power issues nor reify the differences between insiders and outsiders, we struggled to craft the section on who is the "we" of the research collective. I naively offered,

"What if we write something like, 'We are all women concerned with violence against women; some of us have experienced, most of us have witnessed, and all are outraged.'"

To which Donna said,

"Michelle, please don't romanticize us. Your writing is eloquent, but you seem to have left out the part that some of us are here for murder."

Another woman extended the point, "And some of us for murder of our children."

The argument was growing clear: "When we're not here, in the college, and we're alone in our cells, we have to think about the people affected by our crimes. We take responsibility and we need you to represent that as well as our common concerns as women, as feminists, as political . . ."

There, I did it again—writing to make the pain disappear.

Why did I bring the pillowcase? Plaid—threads stream together, bleeding, blending, braiding. Warm lines of difference swim in a pool of color. Pillowcases smother the screams. And they create a safe space to release them.

***

Academic year 2006–2007, I was on sabbatical and invited to spend time at the Institute for Jewish and Arab Studies at Haifa University. I had never been to Israel; held deeply critical views of the Israeli government's annexation of occupied territories and treatment of Palestinians; worried that the radical/progressive edge of Judaism in the United States was eroding, only to be replaced by a right-wing, anti-Palestinian, pro-Israel-at-all-costs ideology; and that leftist Jews were fading away. . . . Once I decided to spend some of my sabbatical time in Israel, I asked friends to arrange visits to the occupied territories, the "wall," the women's prison, and the Bedouin communities; to set up dinners with Palestinian activists and scholars . . . and so we did.

December 2006: He was playing with his grandson, trying to distract the young boy from the stares of the soldiers, the humiliation of the long hot lines, when he caught my eye. "You're American, no? Jewish? Please tell them what we have to go through just to get home." We had been driving along the contours of the Separation Barrier designed to prevent the "uncontrolled entry of Palestinians into Israel." Our guide works at B'T Selem: The Israel Information Center for Human Rights in the Occupied Palestinian Territories (OPT) (see www.btselem.org). B'T Selem documents and litigates human rights violations in the OPT. We were joined by a woman who has long been a member of Checkpoint

Watch (CPW), a group of Israeli Jewish women who monitor the checkpoints for human rights violations.

He was an older man, on a long line of men, women, and children, waiting simply to go home, at the Qalandiya checkpoint in Palestine. I stood there, obviously Jewish, for we could move through unencumbered. I remembered a Palestinian scholar who had spoken only the week before, at CUNY, reported dozens and dozens of births at checkpoints, with many infant mortalities and some dead mothers. As we drove to/through these varied checkpoints, I saw the faces of the young soldiers, Jewish men and women, probably no more than 19, waving through the Jews and stopping, checking, holding gun to car, to face, to future of Palestinians who wait, without recourse, as children and grandchildren watch.

Time doesn't seem to matter. At another checkpoint, a friend tells me, a soldier denies two women, traveling together, entry into Israel. A CPW member inquired and learned that the older woman, the aunt, was accompanying her niece who was supposed to sit for qualifying examinations that afternoon, in order to attend university. The soldier insisted that they lacked the proper papers to be permitted entry. Women from CPW tried to intervene, to no avail. Suddenly, the soldier turned away and the two women ran through.

We'll never know if he turned by intent, if she made it to the exams, if they made it home. All we know is that the young woman, her aunt, the soldier, and those who watched were captured and gravely damaged. Obviously and painfully, some pay a greater price for injustice. But no one is simply a witness, a bystander. Incidents of intimate-State violence ensnare us all; at once joined, we also separate. Together traumatized, we split. And some could drive home.

***

As we bear witness, in our homes and in our research, in our nation and across the globe, where/how do we situate our ethical obligation to speak back?

I write. Maybe if I write, then you—policymakers, readers, students, friends, colleagues, strangers—may catch the contagion of outrage; you/we will be electrified to action, no longer petrified to passivity or despair. You will see the complex dialectical relation of migraines and mobility, my father's optimism and my mother's despair, your freedom and the lockdown of women and men in prison, the well-funded schools of the suburbs and the devastated institutions called schools in our cities, the trauma of the Holocaust and the injustice of the occupation of Palestine.

These scenes of work represent a commitment borne early in my biography—to retell and trouble already settled stories, from a critical perspective of those who have paid the greatest price for "normalized" injustice; to seek out those spaces where the light doesn't shine; to document the long shadow of exclusion and humiliation cast by national policies designed to protect "us," and to ask who is (and is not) "us"?

Indeed, I write to echo and answer, in part, the question posed by the late Carolyn Payton (1984) when she asked, in the pages of the *American Psychologist,* "Who Must Do the Hard Things?" I assume, as she did, that the answer is us; we must do the hard things. That all said . . .

I am, simply, honored (and appalled) to be invited to write as an elder for the *Handbook of Multicultural Counseling.* It is important to remember, however, that the elders still write, have sex, laugh, drink, swim, and engage in radical social struggles . . . elder is an opportunity to reflect, not stop.

***

My advice as you go forward in your projects of teaching, research, and social justice activism is to always ask:

Who is not in the room? And thereby, who and what emotions have been exiled?

Where do shame and loss live?

What knowledge lies buried in bodies of betrayal?

Who must sacrifice for "success" or "progress" to be achieved?

How does privilege hide its pathologies?

How can we hear, and make public, the whispered voices of resistance?

Where are the sounds of the missing discourse of desire?

How can psychologists engage with social movements for social justice?

As the girl child who learned intimately to be repulsed by any mention of pain or loss or sadness as a stain on our family's narrative of prosperity and mobility, I want to press on the weight of our work as psychologists. My plea is that you place your body, your work, your teaching, and your activism squarely inside the opening of the door on Summit Street, at the checkpoint in Palestine, on the barbed wire around Bedford Hills prison, understanding that these hyphenated spaces separate and connect, repulse and ignite, signify oppression and potentiate possibilities unseen.

My Work in a Bouillon Cube

In low-income schools among those youth called "dropouts": In the early 1990s, long before I was involved with participatory work, my ethnography of Comprehensive High School looked critically at how schools produce failure; how underresourced public schools, serving primarily youth of color, create massive rates of dropout and miseducation. For the first few months of this work, I searched, with no success, trying to find the bastard who was throwing these kids out. Instead, I found a school where almost everyone was doing his or her job very well, well, or adequately—but few saw it as their responsibility to interrupt the flow of youth out the door. The book *Framing Dropouts* tells the story of urban school failure from the perspective of those young people who had been pushed out/encouraged to leave prior to graduation, recognizing that if this were a White, middle-class school, it would have been shut down long before.

In elite educational settings among students of color and White women: A few years later, Lani Guinier, Jane Balin, and I studied the same phenomenon of academic alienation and the production of failure—this time in an elite setting where no one drops out but many fade. We studied micro-practices by which White women, and women and men of color at the University of Pennsylvania Law School, come to be marginalized, to academically underachieve despite extremely impressive incoming credentials. In the book *Becoming Gentlemen,* we were able to examine critically how elite law school policies and practices systematically disadvantage White women and men and women of color who refused to "become gentlemen" in their professional socialization and paid a price for their dignity.

In deindustrialized urban communities: In the volume *The Unknown City,* Lois Weis and I craft a counternarrative about urban communities, told from the perspective of White, African American, and Latina working-class women and men who live their lives in the shadows of deindustrialization and the defunding of the urban public sphere.

In prison: A rich research collective of women in prison and graduate center students—Kathy Boudin, Iris Bowen, Judith Clark, Donna Hylton, Migdalia Martinez, "Missy," Melissa Rivera, Rosemarie Roberts, Pamela Smart, Maria Torre, and Debora Upegui—we were able to study the impact of college in prison on women, their children, and the prison environment; but more broadly, we published a variety of scholarly and organizing documents that could re-present the women in prison with a deep sense of their humanity, capacity to transform, and desire to give back.

Retelling American history through the lives of elderly Black lesbians: Ruth Hall and I had the amazing opportunity to analyze life interviews with two vibrant elderly African American lesbians—a couple joined by politics and love. We saw this as a chance to rewrite 20th-century American history from the perspective of critical race, feminist, and queer theory, relying upon Clara Mayo's notion of radical marginality, DuBois's understanding of double consciousness, and Anzaldúa's writings on mestiza consciousness to appreciate the depth of these women's critical consciousness—and pleasures—at a historic moment of incredible oppression, and seemingly very good sex.

With Muslim American youth contending with the war on terror: More recently, with an advisory group of Muslim American youth, Selcuk Sirin and I have been able to produce a book, *Muslim American Youth: Understanding Hyphenated Identities Through Multiple Methods* (2008), filled with maps, focus groups, interviews, and life stories of young Muslim youth living on a precarious political hyphen; turned suddenly, on 9/12/01, into "potential" terrorists or profoundly "oppressed" women. With these young people, we come to understand their desire for citizenship; their hyphenated selves; and the devastating impact of "homeland security" on communities of poverty, communities of color, and Muslim communities—and on the rest of us.

ACKNOWLEDGMENTS

My work has involved deep and intimate collaborations with David Surrey, Lois Weis, Lani Guinier, Kathy Boudin, Maria Torre, Sara McClelland, Susan Opotow, Bill Cross, AJ Franklin, Yasser Payne, Debora Upegui, Michelle Billies, Maddy Fox, Mayida Zaal, Katie Cumiskey, Bernadette Anand, Selcuk Sirin, Suzanne Ouellette, Donnie Cook, Perry Gilmore, Julio Cammarota, Pearl Rosenberg, Julie Blackman, Adrienne Asch, Rosemarie Roberts, Anne Galletta, Jen Ayala, Eve Tuck, Brett Stoudt, Tracey Revenson, Colette Daiute, Kay Deaux, Lori Chajet, Anita Harris, Sarah Carney, Sandy Silverman, Jane Balin, Janice Bloom, Kersha Payne, Monique Guishard, Ruth Hall, Linda Powell Pruitt, Ethel Tobach, Valerie Futch . . . and many more. See our Participatory Action Research Collective Web site for more information on these projects: www.web.gc.cuny.edu/che/start.htm

REFERENCES

Payton, C. (1984). Who must do the hard things? *American Psychologist, 39,* 391–397.

Sirin, S. C., & Fine, M. (2008). *Muslim American youth: Understanding hyphenated identities through multiple methods.* New York: New York University Press.

13

Learning From Voices of Wisdom

Reflections on Multicultural Life Stories

JOSEPH G. PONTEROTTO

I feel deeply honored to respond to and integrate the wonderful life stories you read in Chapters 1 through 12. Life stories of luminary figures in multicultural psychology have emerged as a unique and essential feature of Sage's *Handbooks of Multicultural Counseling.* We first presented life stories in the second edition of this *Handbook* (Ponterotto, Casas, Suzuki, & Alexander, 2001), and they were remarkably well received by our readers in North America and worldwide. In fact, as the four editors have traveled over the past decade promoting and speaking about the 2001 second edition, it was the life story section that individuals most frequently wanted to talk about. These first-person, very personal life stories resonated with readers. In a way, the pioneers who presented their stories served as indirect role models and mentors for thousands of readers, particularly graduate students and new professionals.

The pioneers or elders in multicultural psychology honored in this new edition of the *Handbook of Multicultural Counseling* were nominated by their peers as having had a profound, almost immeasurable impact on the status of multiculturalism in psychology. These 12 visionary researchers, practitioners, and healers, along with those honored in our second edition, have helped to transform the profession to the point where culture, multiculturalism, and the acknowledgment of injustice and oppression in the lives of many are situated at the core of psychology rather than on the periphery of the field.

This chapter is organized along three sections. First, I briefly review the place of, and rationale for, the "study of lives" (life story analyses) in psychology generally, and in multicultural counseling particularly. Next, I reflect on the individual elders who have penned their stories for us. I present select quotes from each pioneer that, in part, capture important components of their lived experience. Finally, I cull common threads or themes from the life stories in the hopes of capturing, in part, a common essence of seasoned multiculturalists.

A PLACE FOR LIFE STORY ANALYSIS IN PSYCHOLOGY AND DIVERSITY

As highlighted in our parallel chapter in the second edition of this *Handbook* (Ponterotto, Jackson, & Nutini, 2001), biographical tools such as oral histories, life stories, life histories, personal narratives, and mini-autobiographies have a long history in psychology. Erikson's (1958, 1969) studies of Luthar and Gandhi, as well as Freud's (1910/1957) treatise on Leonardo da Vinci, are often cited as forerunners of psychological biographies and life stories. In reality, narrative means of self- and other-understanding likely can be traced back to the origins of the disciplined study of the human mind and behavior—to the roots of psychology in Kemet (now Egypt), and the philosopher Imhotep around 2700 BC (see Asante, 2000), known by some as the "father of psychology" (e.g., Ponterotto, Utsey, & Pedersen, 2006, p. 139).

Contemplating, revealing, and/or writing one's life story is a challenging yet rewarding process. For academic, research-oriented scholars, like many of our pioneers, first-person, revealing expression may be particularly difficult. These scholars were trained as "scientists" in their graduate programs, with a goal of investigator neutrality and distancing one's self from the research process in the name of scientific objectivity. In fact, while they were writing their life stories, a number of the pioneers honored in this edition shared with me the challenge they were having in presenting their life story in such a written form.

Notwithstanding the challenge, the emotion, and the sense of vulnerability that often accompanies very personal writing, the process is invariably growth producing for the storyteller. As summarized well by Robert Atkinson, the Director for the Study of Lives at the University of Southern Maine,

> We become fully aware, fully conscious, of our own lives through the process of putting them together in story form. It is through story that we gain context and recognize meaning. Reclaiming story is part of our birthright. Telling our story enables us to be heard, recognized, and acknowledged by others. Story makes the implicit explicit, the hidden seen, the unformed formed, and the confusing clear. (Atkinson, 1998, p. 7)

In addition to the self-benefit in life story telling, the stories themselves serve as guides for the many who might read them. Most of this *Handbook*'s readers will never know personally the healing visionaries whose life stories appear in this volume. Yet by reading their very personal stories, students and professionals are often deeply affected—and, in a way, mentored—through reflecting on, and perhaps connecting with, part of the stories.

Finally, life stories are particularly important to the study of diverse lives, in that many people live within the historical and contemporary context of oppression based on differences due to race, religion, income, gender, sexual orientation, body shape and size, and ability status, among other variables. These diverse voices so often have been belittled, minimized, diminished, or altogether silenced; and so, it is essential to hear and acknowledge these first-person life stories.

REFLECTIONS ON THE LIFE STORIES OF INDIVIDUAL ELDERS AND PIONEERS

In this section, I revisit the life story of each pioneer by presenting quotes that particularly affected me as their student, mentee, and colleague. I apologize up front as there is always the danger of "context" in presenting just a couple of quotes from a lengthy life story. It is important that the full life story of our elders is read before digesting my reflections below.

Eduardo Duran

What immediately struck me when beginning to read Eduardo Duran's life story was my own ignorance and culture-bound ways in how I use language. More specifically, we (the *Handbook* editors) had invited Dr. Duran to share part of his life story with our readers because of his stature as a "pioneer" in psychology and a respected "elder" in our professional community. We can read Dr. Duran's initial reaction to this invitation as he opens his life story:

> It came as a surprise when the editors of this book approached me and asked me to write as a "pioneer" in the field of psychology. There were a couple of associations that arose as thoughts. One was that this implied being an elder which in Native life worlds one

is not an elder till about 80. The other thought had to do with the word "pioneer," which is a very loaded word in Indian country since pioneers were instrumental in the removal of the native life world. (p. 3)

Dr. Duran's life story is rich with vivid images. He noted the challenges and transformative impact of growing up "in a chaotic and dysfunctional family system where alcohol and violence were common both in the nuclear family as well as in the community" (p. 3). During this time, Dr. Duran found refuge through extended periods of time spent with his grandparents. Time spent with his grandparents appeared to provide both a source of support and anchoring and a mechanism for processing events and experiences around him. He noted:

> I was fortunate to have spent extended periods of time with my grandparents where the transformations had already occurred. It was during these times that I would listen to my grandfather, who had virtually no education, discuss deep subjects with other elders. Subjects that were discussed were of deep philosophical and spiritual meaning, and I would sit in the corner and be fascinated by their discussions on the nature of the universe, God, Devil and other light topics. . . . I would return to my family of six siblings after these visits and would feel as if I didn't belong in the chaos that surrounded me and would find myself fascinated as to the meaning of this and other realities. (pp. 3–4)

Around the time of high school, Dr. Duran and his family moved from northern New Mexico to California, searching for a better life. However, life in the San Joaquin Valley was difficult indeed as the whole family worked in the hot agricultural fields. The strain of these years is poignantly captured in Dr. Duran's words, as follows:

> The sadness of what was already going on in the family system, compounded by the extreme poverty and the incredible difficulty of the work, was a millstone that took my soul and ground it into pieces that were not distinguishable even to me. (p. 4)

A transformative point for Dr. Duran appeared to come in reading Jung's (1962) *Symbols of Transformation,* where he began to make connections with this

form of psychology and the stories and ways of his grandfather. From this point, Dr. Duran began to pursue undergraduate and graduate degrees in psychology. Soon after entering a doctoral program, he was approached by a local Native American tribe, whereupon he was offered a job to start a mental health program for their community. In his work starting this mental health program, Dr. Duran witnessed firsthand the clash between his Western-trained psychological perspectives and those of the native people. For example,

> There was a consensus that the elders in the community did not feel that alcoholism, depression, anxiety, and so on were the problems of the community, although these were quite obvious to my up-and-coming, highly trained clinical mind. When I enquired as to what they thought was the problem, they told me that the root of the problems was a "wounded soul and wounded spirit." (p. 6)

Not finding any explanation for "soul wounds" in the Western psychological literature, Dr. Duran consulted his root teacher, a holy man:

> My teacher talked about intent and how someone hurts or wounds someone this is at all levels of the whole person, i.e., body, mind, and soul. Because it is an assault also on mind and soul, this makes the wounding process one in which sorcery is involved. The elder's rationale is clear: the body knows how and heals itself. We can assist in healing the mind, although because of its close ties to the soul, we need to use soul healing strategies as well. If the soul is not healed, the wounding is passed on to the next generation for at least seven generations. Therefore, the issue being dealt with involves seven past generations as well as seven generations into the future. This idea endows the present moment with a tremendous amount of potential for healing the ancestors and unborn descendants. (p. 7)

An important message from Dr. Duran's life story is the need to anchor our theory and research in our professional and personal experiences interacting with the communities we serve. As he notes,

> It is important to note that the clinical work has driven the theoretical formulations from the beginning.

I believe that having theory drive clinical practice is backwards and may not bring the effectiveness that our communities need. The process has also involved intensive formulations from Indigenous practitioners in order to make the work culturally effective and meaningful. (p. 7)

Carolyn G. Barcus

The second elder honored in Part I of this *Handbook* is Carolyn Barcus, a member of the Blackfeet Tribe of northern Montana. Early in her life story, Dr. Barcus noted the profound influence of her parents. In discussing her mother, she noted,

She was an avid reader, had many hobbies and interests, loved to travel, and had a better memory the day she died at 91 than I do today. The greatest gift my mother ever gave me was when she taught me "Carolyn, you can do anything that you put your mind to!" and she believed it. (p. 12)

Then speaking of her father, she reflected,

He never went past the third grade and was a jack-of-all-trades. I appreciate my dad for teaching me to do things and then trusting me to do them. I was his right-hand man after my brother left for the Navy, and Dad never said to me, "No, you can't do that because you are a girl." (p. 12)

An important aspect of Dr. Barcus's life story is her strong attachment to the land and nature. She talked about her life on the ranch and noted,

Living on the ranch was about work, but because I loved it, it did not count as work to me. . . . As I write this history, I am aware that if the reader is not from a rural culture, there is no way for you to understand the joy of living that I had. . . . The connection to the land, the importance of the places and the animals, tame and wild, and the changing seasons were all part of me. (p. 12)

Another theme reflected in Dr. Barcus's life story is her learning to navigate two worldviews with regard to processing and expressing emotions. In the following excerpt, she talked about visiting the family ranch of one of her students.

One of my students wanted me to visit his family's ranch, so I went. I was there for branding time, and they were castrating a young stallion that belonged to a 12-year-old girl. No tranquilizers were used, and the horse fought the ropes fiercely! In his fight, he broke his leg and had to be shot. Out of all of the people there, only two of us cried for that young horse whose life was over, the 12-year-old girl and me. Her mother told her, "Stop crying. We will get you another horse!" They did not know what to do with me. I was now an outsider! It was not that they did not feel badly about what had happened. It was that they were not allowed to cry or talk about their feelings. I recognized the cultural constraints and realized that their feelings would be acted out, rather than talked out. I had become bicultural, walking in both worlds, the rough and tough world of ranch life and a more psychologically attuned world that teaches different ways of coping with distressing emotions. (p. 13)

She talked more about emotive expression in describing her transition from ranch life to academe.

For a Montana ranch woman, graduate training in counseling, clinical, and school psychology was a reach. I was 31 years old before I knew that if you felt like hitting a wall, it meant you were angry. Thus, I have a lot of empathy for most men, who are frequently socialized as I was socialized in my rural, cowboy/Indian culture. But it also meant that I had a lot to learn. . . . Having grown up cowboy/Indian, I had no idea how to recognize feelings, label feelings, sit with feelings, modulate feelings (to be able to put feelings away and then go back to them), and to disengage in a situation and manage your feelings. I teach my clients these skills today, but I do not claim to have mastered them myself. I still have to make myself talk when I am angry or upset, and I need time to sort it all before I can talk about it. (pp. 14–15)

Through her life story, we see Dr. Barcus's deep commitment to assisting Native and other minority students in their efforts to obtain graduate degrees. She highlights the deep challenges for collectivist and interdependent-oriented students who train as psychologists in independent and individual-oriented training programs.

Some students actually do stay to complete their dissertation, but it is seldom true of Native students, or any of our minority students, for that matter. Being far from home, family, and community is extremely difficult for Native students, and they are usually in a hurry to get back. Those of us who train graduate students are always grateful for supportive families who say to the student, "You stay there and get your training. Our tribe needs you here educated to help us"; family support is such important support! The pull from home is so strong! . . . I continually challenge majority students from independent cultures who want to be therapists to work at understanding an interdependent construct of self and what that would mean in treatment. (p. 16)

Finally, a poignant segment of Dr. Barcus's story highlights her commitment and dedication to her clients. In the following quote, Dr. Barcus discussed her private practice work, which focuses on helping women who were severely sexually abused in childhood.

I have had no greater teachers in my lifetime than my clients. I consider it a privilege to walk with them. I share their pain as they endure the pain of getting better, struggle with them as they struggle to learn who they are, and finally, I walk with them as they learn to make their lives work. I rejoice when they are finally free of the pain and can have a life. What could be more rewarding! And what amazing women they are! There is a natural selection process that occurs in situations of severe abuse: the bright, creative, strong, and talented children survive; overwhelming abuse is too much for some children and they die or become hopelessly insane. Therefore, the adult clients who present for therapy because they can no longer tolerate the lifelong pain they have endured are very bright and creative, very strong and talented women. Being very strong, however, can frequently translate into being very stubborn in therapy. Fortunately, I am equally stubborn. My mother called it "Barcus bullheadedness," but I see it as tenacity, persistence, and commitment to the stated goal of the client to achieve a healthier and happier state of being. These women have my love and admiration, and I am indebted to them, for I am better off for having known them. (p. 18)

Rosie Phillips Bingham

Dr. Rosie P. Bingham is the third pioneer honored in the *Handbook*. Interestingly, Dr. Bingham opens her life story in the third person, as an observer of herself.

Then, roughly midway, she shifts her prose to her first-person voice. In the following quote, she described both the racism that "Rosie" experienced as a child, as well as coping mechanisms and cognitive schemas that helped her survive and thrive in racist surroundings.

When Rosie was in junior high school, on her walks to and from her segregated school, other children would taunt her by yelling out that she was "Black and ugly." But reading books had shown Rosie that there was another world out there that was not as poor as the one where she currently lived. People actually had shoes without holes that required a piece of cardboard inserted to keep their feet off the ground. Some children had telephones and cute dresses. So Rosie decided to play a game with herself when she heard the "Black and ugly" chant. Each time a child said that she was Black or ugly, she would pretend that she got one dollar. At the end of the day or two days, she could buy whatever she wanted. Amazing how those chants turned to positives. Still, the walk to the segregated schools and the knowing that she was too Black helped to fuel a sense of inferiority that lingered with Rosie. (p. 20)

Switching now to first-person voice, Dr. Bingham continued her reflection on race, community, and nurturance.

Race is always a double-edged sword whether I am talking about what happens to the psyche as a result of intragroup interactions or whether I am talking about what happens to the psyche in intergroup relationships. African Americans have helped me to feel inferior and powerful; loved and betrayed; nurtured and loved. I have felt many of the same things about Caucasians in the United States, but I don't know that I have ever felt diminished by Black people, and I have with White people. So I have wondered how in the world I gave White people that power and how do I take it back. Well, I suspect that I had lots of help handing it over, and I get lots of help taking it back. My help comes from family, friends, and faith. . . . (p. 21)

One of my early daydreams as a young child was to have a family of children from many races and ethnicities. My dream from then reflects my life today in that my circle of friends, my community, now includes a mix of Mexican, Chinese, Indian, African, European, and more—better than a rainbow. This circle surrounds me in a nurturing way that helps me find the balance between insecurity and confidence; shyness and boldness; balance between who I try to be and who I am; balance between holding back and reaching out; balance between crying softly and laughing out loud; balance between giving up power and taking it back. (p. 22)

An important theme in Dr. Bingham's story is her reliance on faith. In the following quote, she discussed faith as a means to a personal relationship with God.

In many African American communities, the church continues to be a salient part of life. What is sometimes difficult for many to understand is that the church is far more than the family. I attended churches that were Baptist, African Methodist Episcopal (AME), and AME Zion; visited Church of Christ, Church of God and Christ, United Methodist, and so on. In almost all, I was taught to have a personal relationship with God. For me, that meant self-discovery no matter what the minister said. I believe that is part of the difficulty people have with Barack Obama's attending his church. My pastor's beliefs are not always mine. I am taught to think for myself. I believe that this message allows me to develop a deeper spiritual side and to hear that to which I am called. So, for me, psychology is a "calling." You won't find "calling" as a part of most vocational inventories. So, in order to be an effective vocational multicultural practitioner, it may be important to know that some of your clientele may not fit the client profile because their spiritual beliefs have influenced the outcome or that no matter what the outcome, their spiritual beliefs will dictate their career choice. . . . My life is a balance between fear and faith. Faith has allowed me to step up and step out even when fear whispers, "Remember, you are not good enough." Faith shouts, "Yes, you are!" (p. 22)

In this final quote from Dr. Bingham's life story, she leaves concluding thoughts intended for graduate students and new professionals.

1. I want to keep on claiming my power. I have no interest in being a victim of sexism and racism. That is not to say that these two societal problems do not and will not affect my life. It is to say that in my fight with them, I want to use them to become stronger. 2. I always want to be a giving person. Sometimes, we hear people say, "I want to give back." Giving back

sometimes sounds hierarchical to me, so I think about enlarging circles. I want more and more people in. I want to be a part of empowering the lives of as many people as I can. And I depend on my family, friends, and faith to keep me doing it and to hold me to it. 3. I want to keep on increasing my faith because my faith conquers my fear. I am whole and at my best when I am in the spirit. 4. I wish you an interesting and balanced life. (p. 23)

Joseph L. White

A historic figure in American psychology is Dr. Joseph L. White. Dr. White shares part of his life story with us by way of a one-on-one interview with one of his close mentees, Dr. Thomas A. Parham, a pioneer and legend in his own right. Below is Dr. Parham's opening description of Dr. White.

His stature is small, but his presence is powerful. His voice awakens a room with the sound of cheerful acquaintance. His eyes survey any environment with a keen ability to decipher both pockets of support and affirmation as well as pockets of resistance. His hair is completely gray, as are the bushy eyebrows that frame the face that defined an entire discipline of Black psychology. His lips protrude with the words that calm excitable declarations, consolidate massive amounts of information into clearly identifiable themes, and provide affirmation and validation to one's spirit and personhood that just make you feel better about yourself. The lines on his face mark the decades of both challenge and triumph from which his wisdom and inner strength were born. And yet, the twinkle in his eyes signals that he is still excited about life and the lessons it has taught him, and grateful for the ways he has been blessed to emerge through life's journey relatively unscathed. This is the face of Dr. Joseph L. White, a master teacher, mentor, psychologist, and author. (p. 25)

Below are three successive quotes from Dr. White in response to Dr. Parham's query about career and life surprises. The reader will note positive, negative, and existentially based surprises.

The biggest surprise was the range of opportunities that I would have. Never in my wildest dreams did I think I would vote for an African American presidential candidate, that I would be involved in writing several books, that I would mentor more than 100 PhDs and other professionals in other fields, that I would become a voice in psychology, or that I would have two children follow me in higher education. (p. 28)

Well, there was a negative surprise in my life. I really didn't believe in my heart and soul that racism was as deep as it was in America. Because if I had believed that, I never would have spent my first 28 years climbing the mountain. But I truly believed that once I got that PhD, my military service, and got married, that I would be an American citizen with full privilege. And not only did that not come to pass, when I did think about trying to run for office, but it made me open up my eyes to how Blacks were treated in America, and I began to see the poverty, restriction on jobs, and all the problems that 360 years of racism had bred. Back then, there was no Thomas Parham or Bill Cross conducting research in racial identity development, and I didn't understand these stages of identity that I would go through. I thought that I had already crystallized my identity. But I had to reencounter that immersion, kind of wade through that darkness of "who am I" really, and what am I all about relative to American society, to find myself. (p. 29)

One more I can think of is the importance of spirituality. Along the way, I somehow forgot the need for a spiritual foundation. I mistakenly believed that science could take you where you needed to go. I have since learned, fortunately, that having a strong spiritual foundation is a key asset in making it in this world. (p. 30)

Dr. Parham then asks Dr. White to ponder and reflect on "fundamental principles" he wants to leave with *Handbook* readers. His response follows:

The fundamental principle that I want to convey after 47 years is that Black people and other ethnic minorities in America have psychological strengths. And in recognizing those potential psychological strengths in culturally diverse people, be they Black, White, men, women, the professional's role as a teacher, therapist, counselor, or mentor is to help people get in touch with those strengths. It gives these young people a better chance to move toward wellness and optimal living. . . . And I am not denying that people get mixed up or get under stress, or get confused, and have delusions, or whatever. But I am saying that ultimately, whatever you are doing as a teacher, a therapist, or a mentor, you should get to the strengths of an individual. The second dimension of that fundamental principle is having said that, what are those strengths? . . . Now, can we identify what those strengths were psychologically that allowed them to survive, and then for the next generation of psychologists, after we've identified that, can we package this, and teach it to children? Barack Obama has [seven] of the strengths, improvisation, resilience, spirituality, connected to others, emotional vitality, gallows humor, and a healthy suspicion of White folks. (p. 33)

Finally, Dr. White ends his life story interview by highlighting a critical lesson he learned from his mother regarding giving to others.

And one more life lesson that I got from my mother that is a fundamental principle of my life: No matter how poor you are, you will always have to be prepared to give to others. And she didn't see that as a deficit, she saw that as something that makes you feel better. So by the time I started school, I would always bring some child over to the house that was hungry, and my mama would give them something, and send them back home. That was in the Depression of the 1930s, when people didn't have jobs or the means for self-sufficiency. There were hobos that would come to the back door of our house, and my mother would pack them a meal and give them a bowl of hot soup. It didn't matter how little we had, my mother always shared it with others. I have tried, in my life and career, to do the same and have mentored my students to do likewise. (pp. 33–34)

Patricia Arredondo

Strengthened through the wisdom of her *abuela* (grandmother), Patricia Arredondo engages and advances her life story with desire (*Adelante con ganas*). She recalls with vivid detail her childhood in Lorain, Ohio, and the influential impact her family had on her developing worldview:

My roots for feminism, in different forms and expressions, were intimately influenced by my parents and maternal grandmother. In the midst of a highly structured, Mexican family-centered milieu and a city with its "isms," they taught me that, as a girl and woman, I could think for myself and make sound decisions. Little did I know then the powerful effects of their examples on my adult development. . . . My parents also influenced my cultural and gender worldview through their examples and individual relationships with me. From each I learned different experiences about struggles with covert and overt racism, the art of biculturalism in a culturally segregated community, civic engagement, and how they had to put off their young lives to give to their parents in troubling economic circumstances. For my mother, it was quitting school after ninth grade to contribute to the household income because of my grandfather's alcoholism. For my father, it was working the land in the midst of the Mexican revolution and the Catholic Church's collusion with the powerful landowners. However, they always inspired in me a "can do" attitude. My father was always the optimist, looking at the glass as ¾ full, and my mother reminded us to never take anything for granted. From *Mamá* and my parents, I learned that *sí se puede* (Yes, we can) is about women. (pp. 39–40)

Dr. Arredondo's life story highlights that we never stop growing professionally and culturally. At one point in her story, she reflects on her move back into academia after a highly successful career in multicultural consultation:

Moving back into higher education was not a casual decision. I was fortunate to have choices. Joining Arizona State University (ASU) in 1999 was more than a career re-direction, it was also my first major relocation in 30 years. From the Boston predominant Irish, Italian, and WASP multicultural milieu, I stepped into the cowboy conservative politics of Arizona, where persons of Mexican heritage used the term "Hispanic" as an identity referent. So many concepts taught in our multicultural psychology literature were palpable in Arizona, from white privilege to indigenous models of healing and living. For the first time, I had a real-life introduction to American Indian tribes and their complicated histories and the resentment of Mexican Americans who asserted that the "border had moved," thereby disenfranchising their families. In the midst of Arizona pink skies, beautiful mountains, gated communities, and glitzy lifestyles is the profound pain and misery of oppressed American Indian and Mexican peoples. I felt guilty and powerless about this, recognizing my fate had been different and privileged. (p. 42)

As Dr. Arredondo's story began with family reflections, so too does it end. Once again, we see the impact of her family on her life and her emphasis on the continuation of the family legacy as she discusses with great pride her nieces and nephews:

In a close-knit nuclear family of seven children, I learned about caring, sharing, and giving. There are many ties that bind us together, but more than anything, it is our parents' legacy of loving interdependence and striving for excellence. My 10 nieces and nephews have learned to have pride in being Mexican and have also accepted the higher education expectation. Of the 10, six will be in or have graduated from college by the time this book goes to press. The new twist is that they are cracking the public education ceiling by attending private and Ivy League schools. I only dreamed of doing this; they are living my dream. (pp. 43–44)

Amado M. Padilla

School, education, and teaching have always been central to the life of pioneer Amado Padilla. He recalls both the "quality" of his early childhood education as well as the influential role of his "aware" and diligent mother. For example, he notes,

Several weeks into the school year, my mother began to ask what we did at school, and I reported that we took naps twice a day. After a time, my mother grew suspicious and decided to make a surprise visit to the school, and when she arrived, she found the classroom lights off and all of the students curled up on the floor or at their desks napping, including the teacher, who was sitting at her desk sleeping. My mother's advocacy on my behalf began right then and there. I still remember my mother yelling at the teacher that she wasn't sending me to school to nap, but to learn to read and write. My mother withdrew me from public school that same day and enrolled me at Sacred Heart Elementary School, which was our parish parochial school. I remained in Catholic schools until I graduated from

St. Mary High School. After that first-grade incident, I was forever wary about reporting my school activities to my mother. (p. 46)

As an adolescent student, Amado Padilla already could tell a good lesson plan from a poor one:

> Like any other adolescent boy in my Catholic high school, I spent considerable time fantasizing about girls, especially after Father Curtain delivered the only sex education class to a boys-only filled ninth-grade classroom. In this single hour of Catholic "sexuality" instruction in my 4 years of high school, Father Curtain's take-home message was that we could lose our souls if we allowed the devil to get the best of us with girls. Father Curtain was a young Jesuit priest who was probably coerced by the nuns at the school to talk to the boys about sex. I still remember Father Curtain's sex hour, because it was by far the most incompetent lesson I had in 12 years of Catholic education. (p. 46)

More poignantly, Dr. Padilla's lifelong commitment and dedication to education and psychology was fueled not just by his own multicultural and educational experiences, but also by family challenges and illness. Below, he recalls his mom's illness during critical periods in his own childhood development.

> My interest in psychology was partially due to the fact that my mother had a nervous breakdown when I was in elementary school and spent roughly a year institutionalized in a state hospital. I remember accompanying my father to visit my mother in the hospital, and still remember our visits with my mother after she had received electroconvulsive shock treatments. On reflection, my interest in psychology probably had to do with trying to understand my mother's illness and how it subsequently affected her and our family. As an undergraduate student and a member of the Psi Chi Honorary Society, I along with other Psi Chi students visited the same hospital where my mother had been institutionalized. The idea was to give students exposure to mental illness and to "cheer up" the patients. I remember that I never told any of my friends or professors that I had visited my mother at that same hospital years before. The stigma of mental illness weighed heavily on me at the time. (p. 47)

Finally, like other pioneers of his time, Dr. Padilla had few "same-culture" professional role models, and he blazed his own trail to career achievements and personal development. For instance, he notes,

> Before moving on to graduate school, though, I need to mention a couple of things about my undergraduate years. At no time as an undergraduate student did I ever meet a Latino professor. . . . I also recall that there was absolutely no discussion of culture or ethnicity in any of my psychology classes, and I don't remember any discussions of social class except in sociology. At best, these were considered extraneous variables and of little consequence in the science of psychology. . . . As a doctoral student, I was deeply involved in my coursework and research in an experimental program, and trying when time permitted to be active in Chicano issues. Here I was a doctoral candidate in psychology in my home state and still had never had a Latino faculty member in any of my university coursework or a Latino mentor. I was intimately aware that I had become a very self-reliant graduate student who was still seeking to reconcile my cultural roots with my development as a psychologist. I was only 24 years old and still searching to define myself in the context of the social and political activism that was permeating daily life. (pp. 48–49)

Richard M. Suinn

Dr. Richard Suinn conceptualizes his life story as a series of unspoken "messages"—messages from his own body, from his family and community, and from his explorations of his own racial identity. From a processing and synthesis of these "messages," Dr. Suinn "gifts us" with messages and lessons we can take to heart. Let's begin with messages from his own body:

> From age 1 to late adolescence, the most powerful sound is that of a single labored breath . . . as I struggle to capture that one gasp that means survival, over the asthma disease that strangles my lungs . . . nightly . . . and shapes my frail body that is prevented from the normal play of children. The joy that comes from pure physical activity is denied, as is the pleasure of favorite foods, such as ice cream; foods that are instead enemies of simple breathing due to allergies. Without the release of physical activity, I become

engaged in studies. The tasks of the classroom become familiar and the work behaviors are easily acquired. Simply stated: studies were easy, living was difficult. So demanding messages were instilled: you are limited and must be disciplined enough to avoid normal activities—such activities will only precipitate suffering. Self-discipline is mastered from the hardest master possible. (p. 56)

Next, Dr. Suinn processes unspoken messages he perceived regarding family struggle and responsibility:

I always perceived my parents as poor, possibly based on the frugal lifestyle—no trips, recreation, extra or fancy clothes, or entertaining, and even birthday celebrations were soon eliminated. Hence my choice for college was at home, the University of Hawaii (UH), to save travel, tuition, housing expenses. I also continued to be a summer laborer in the pineapple factory, becoming known among the full-timers as "the most educated employee" in this nonskilled position. This low-paying job was perhaps my attempt to reduce the stress of family finances. But there was another, private message: proof I had control over my asthmatic condition and I could toil hard next to normal working people. (p. 57)

Finally, Dr. Suinn talks about his own rebirth in 1976, as he deeply connects with his own Asian American identity:

The "me" that existed beyond graduation was the image of an American westerner, with the vital yet quiescent voice from Asian heritage yet to speak. Then came a letter of invitation to the "National Conference on Asian American Psychology." Arriving at this conference, I entered a room as I have at dozens of other research conferences, and once more walked from one familiar world into a startling new place. Faces abound . . . faces that mirror mine . . . hair, eyes, features alike, and the temptation is to recall the weak joke "all Asians look alike." But it is not false humor that is triggered; instead, it is sudden awareness of identity. How does one put into words the emotion of "arriving," of the unfolding of one's core self, of the parental voices speaking again with the message, "Here is who you are and who you have always been, and who you will always be!" And so I was born again in 1976. To this day, I remain

unable to speak or understand the language of my ancestors and my parents, yet from that day forward I hear this important message—of who I am in my core where it counts most.

It is impossible to overstate the enormous impact of the single epiphany and its source. In the era of my educational and early professional life, ethnic minority issues simply did not exist. I had not been surrounded by curriculum, writings, discussions, public or personal concentration on being ethnic. Yet the existential experience aroused these amazing insights and emotions with volcanic explosiveness. (pp. 58–59)

Mary A. Fukuyama

Being identified as a "pioneer" by her colleagues had resonance for Dr. Mary Fukuyama as she reflects on her family's history:

The theme of being a *pioneer* is also a part of my family history. I have titled this contribution the "Seeds of Consciousness" because in hindsight, I can see that I consider my experience of multiculturalism as informed by a process of consciousness-raising that began in childhood and continues to this day. These seeds or "moments of awakening" are like planting and cultivating a forest, a long-term project characterized by growth and stagnation, floods and droughts, successes and failures. My multicultural journey might also be described as "going full circle" in that it is more circular than linear, and I marvel at how it feels ever more like "returning home." (p. 63)

Dr. Fukuyama reflects poignantly on her parents' first meeting and their early life together as an interracial couple:

My parents told me the story of how they met at "camp." It sounded like fun, but I didn't grasp the significance until well into adulthood. The camps were the prisoner camps set up to detain more than 110,000 Japanese Americans (most of whom were U.S. citizens) from the West Coast during World War II. . . . This is where my parents met and they married a year later, August 10, 1945, at the close of World War II—a difficult time for an interracial couple to marry. They traveled east to avoid hostility against the Japanese Americans who were returning from camps. (p. 63)

Dr. Fukuyama reflects on her early awareness of her identity and the existence of racism:

My childhood experiences of growing up biracial taught me about racism and differences based on physical appearances. I didn't feel like I belonged fully to either group (white or nonwhite) and felt the pain of being an "outsider." Later in life, I would become a bridge between them. The movie *South Pacific* and the song "You've Got to Be Carefully Taught" helped name prejudice that I had felt but not understood. I also learned about cultural adaptation from an early age, visiting *Oba-san* who never learned to speak English, and "Grandma A" whose soft-spoken voice communicated both frailty and forbearance. I can attribute my lifelong pursuit of understanding multiculturalism to my mixed heritage. . . .

During my childhood, I felt different for any number of reasons . . . the color of hair and shape of eyes, gender roles being a tomboy, as a Preacher's Kid (P.K.), or my own personal social struggles to fit in. I think it was academic success that saved me, that and feeling somehow protected by my father's role and affiliation with a small-town church. Living next door to the church was like having an extended family that provided extra care when my mother was sick or when there was a new arrival. (p. 64)

Dr. Fukuyama has always been a gifted storyteller and poet, as we see in an excerpt from one of her creative writing exercises:

I recently wrote the following creative writing exercise as a reflection on gender roles:

Me and the boys on the block, we were a gang that lived to be outdoors. Our turf ranged from the backside of the county courthouse lawn, across the street from my house, which served as a football field in summer and sledding hill in winter, down to the creek, which by today's standards probably was a drainage culvert, where we'd catch minnows and search out crawdads. The year was 1956 and I was 8 years old.

It was a hot Iowa summer night and several of us were hanging out on the Methodist church steps. Being a Preacher's Kid and playing with the Methodist preacher's boy Bobbie, we felt pretty entitled to do whatever we wanted on church property. We were having a spitting contest, seeing who could spit the farthest. Sometimes if you curled your tongue just right, you could project a blob of spit like it was shot out of a blow gun. Standing on the top steps we had a clear view of our spitting range onto the church lawn, both height and depth made it more impressive. Until along came an older boy, maybe all of 12 years old, who knows. In a low tone, he leaned over and said to me "girls don't spit."

I had an immediate reaction of disbelief, but his tone sounded so authoritative, so morally right. I could feel my spit-blowing ego deflate immediately. How was it that these three words, this gender based rule had such weight with me? Was it before or after I had been told "girls don't play football," which seemed totally ridiculous since I was the best passer on the block. Was it before or after I was told, "girls play the flute," and here I had admired the trombone ever since going to the premiere of the movie *The Music Man* in Mason City, totally smitten with "76 trombones led the big parade." Was it before or after I came home brandishing my new cowboy 6-shooter pistol, only to feel shame in front of the church ladies, because somehow I knew this was not a girly thing to do. How come the boys got to do all the cool things, like spit and play football and wave brassy instruments and shoot guns? The year was 1956 and I was 8 years old. It was the year that I learned that "girls don't spit." (pp. 64–65)

Finally, Dr. Fukuyama highlights her identity during young adulthood:

As a sophomore in college, I went to Japan on a study-abroad group program. I began to sort out my ethnic identity there. When I arrived, I attended a recognition ceremony for 20-year-olds through my host family that conveyed the message, "Welcome to adulthood." For the first time, it was an advantage to have the last name Fukuyama, which was loosely translated by my peers as "happy mountain." I began to develop a positive ethnic identity, whereas before, I had regretted being a "person of color" when everyone else seemed white. I was intrigued by seeing Shinto shrines and Buddhist temples and realized that Christianity was not universal. It gave me pause to think about my religious beliefs, even if my Dad was a minister. . . . (p. 65) The current decade has brought postmodernism to the forefront. No longer do I live in dichotomies. Living with multiple social identities and dealing with multiple oppressions are now essential for understanding the whole person. Living in a post-9/11 era, where fears of "the other" have once again become headline news, I am reminded of my family story and the importance of preserving human rights and freedoms. I am troubled that as a country we are once again at war and wish that as a nation we could seek understanding of differences rather than need to dominate. (p. 68)

Susan L. Morrow

Dr. Susan Morrow talks about the lessons learned throughout her life—from early family lessons about the "proper" role of race relations, to lessons learned from being embraced and welcomed by colleagues and mentors of color. Let's begin with a window into Dr. Morrow's early socialization about race relations:

As a child from a home characterized by both love and abuse, I developed optimism about the world as well as a passion for justice. My early years as a white girl in an upwardly mobile lower-middle-class family in Louisiana were characterized by confusion about racial and social inequities. When I was in high school, my mother hired a Black young woman close to my age to iron our clothes, but when I became close to her, I was reprimanded. I don't remember my parents ever saying anything derogatory about people different from us, yet their message to me was consistent—associate with people who were "like us." When we visited my parents' friends in El Paso, Texas, on our move to Los Angeles, I became "too friendly" with a Mexican girl (also hired help) and was told once again that I was being inappropriate. When I asked why, my mother just said, "Mexican people here are like Negroes (this was, after all, the 1950s) in Louisiana—we don't mix with them." Little by little, I was learning the rules of being white and middle class, yet not to my parents' satisfaction. To their consternation, I hung out with "poor white" and lower middle-class Italian kids through much of high school as my parents rapidly embraced an upper-middle-class lifestyle. (pp. 71–72)

Dr. Morrow has been deeply affected by colleagues of color who shared their life experiences with her. She discusses a colleague, an African American woman, who taught with Dr. Morrow in elementary school:

My second multicultural mentor . . . was a Black woman who was the kindergarten teacher in my school. She told me stories of her own life, and I began to understand the realities and horrors of racism in a way that I had never grasped before. I could not understand how she could think of me, a white woman, as a friend after the violence she had experienced at the hands of white people. I felt deeply ashamed of being white; yet at the same time, I embraced both the acceptance that I received from my friend and my students' parents as well as my responsibility to create change. Somewhere around this time, I heard Eldridge Cleaver, a Black activist, leader, and author of *Soul on Ice*, say, "If you're not part of the solution, you're part of the problem." I sidestepped the temptation to live in white guilt by adding to his challenge in my own mind: "If I am part of the solution, I don't need to feel guilty. Just get busy." Thus began my career as an activist. (pp. 72–73)

In the next quote, Dr. Morrow discusses a trip to Washington, DC, arranged by Willie Smith, a Black father of two girls in Dr. Morrow's elementary school. Reading this quote, which was written months before Barack Obama's presidential election, I wonder what Dr. Morrow must have been thinking and feeling as she watched the new president's inauguration on January 20, 2009!

The Black man, Willie Smith, was the father of two girls in our school, one in my fifth-grade class. Following the assassination of the Reverend Dr. Martin Luther King, Jr., Willie asked my then-husband and me if we would like to join him for the Poor People's March on Washington, DC, in 1968. We drove all day and spent the night in Willie's car, waking to a brilliant May morning and a hostile police officer pounding on the windows telling us we could not camp in our car. I don't know what I had expected as we gathered at the Washington Monument, but I was overcome by the sea of Black and white faces and supremely aware that we were breaking the rules I had been taught since birth. Led by Ralph Abernathy, Coretta Scott King, Jesse Jackson, and others, the sea became a river as we marched up both sides of the Reflecting Pool to the foot of the Lincoln Memorial. Of all the memories I treasure from that day, the most precious is marching, singing "We Shall Overcome," and having a young Black man about my age (I was 25) hold my hand and call me "Sister." (p. 73)

Finally, Dr. Morrow ends her story with reflection on where she is now and where she feels she needs to go personally and professionally.

As I look back over my life experiences as a multicultural being, a civil rights activist, a lesbian feminist, and an academic, I am aware of so many loose ends. Like perhaps most of us who are committed to social justice, I often feel I am not doing enough. . . . Despite my ongoing commitments to multiculturalism and social justice, along with a herstory of activism, I am acutely aware of my challenges and growth edges as a multiculturally competent human being, teacher, scholar, and advocate for social justice. Because of my privilege as a white, middle-class, United States-born and -raised, well-educated individual, I continue to centralize my own experience as the norm and assume the experiences of others are the same as mine until my assumptions are mirrored back to me. In doing this, I continue to engage "other" people who come from different cultures, classes, countries, and educational statuses from my own. I suspect that reversing this tendency is a life-long project for all of us with privilege. Another area in which I am challenged is adequately dealing with the intersections of privilege, power, and oppression across various statuses and groups. I believe that effectively addressing these intersections are the next important step in my own—and possibly our collective—progress as multicultural counselors, psychologists, and educators. (p. 76)

Rhoda Olkin

Dr. Rhoda Olkin's life story is poignantly presented. Her cognitive and affective experiences as a person with a disability are vivid in beautiful writing. She opens her story as follows:

It is hard for me to write the story of my life, because frankly, it's a bit depressing. Not many life stories have an iron lung in the first paragraph. But ultimately this is the story of going from point *A* to point, say, *N* (just over the halfway mark). And at point *N*, I am happy. So now that you know the ending (to date), bear with me for the story of the journey over a long and slippery road. . . . My story is of a female, a Jew, a professor's daughter, a middle child, and, oh yea, polio. If it were up to me, I might

have selected the first four, and there are times I imagine I would have chosen polio, because of the life lessons it has imparted. But one isn't given a menu in life with the freedom to choose the combination of ingredients. Although if one were, sometimes I imagine the scene would go something like this:

God: "Hi, I'm God, I'll be your waiter today."

Me: "Hi, God."

God: "I need to tell you we're out of a few items: Long-legged blondes, green eyes, and anything that looks remotely like Tyra Banks."

Me: "Are there any specials today?"

God: "Yes, we do have some lovely disabilities, just in. The birth defects, you could have your pick, cerebral palsy, spina bifida. And we really have a surplus of polio now—it's been two years since the last big epidemic, so the kitchen is pushing polio."

Me: "Does that come with any sides?"

God: "We could make you short, nearsighted, just so-so looking, give you mousy brown hair. That plus the polio would really make a complete package."

Me: "I was leaning more towards an Albert-Einstein-meets-Beyoncé-meets-Ellen-DeGeneres kind of package."

God: "Oh, honey, I'm God, but even I can't do that. Take the polio; you'll like it."

Me: "Okay, but I'm going to need a sense of humor with that." (pp. 79–80)

Throughout her story, Dr. Olkin captures the feelings of differentness, disconnectedness, and aloneness that her illness sometimes fostered:

For Thanksgiving, I got to go home for a few days (imagine going home from the hospital on vacation!) and was still in the hospital at Chanukah; my grandmother sent me a small menorah that used birthday candles. When I went home, I entered second grade midyear, and felt then what I still feel now sometimes—that I am entering a room of people who are already friends with each other, and there is no place for me. . . . This essential nature of being outside the group, apart, separate because of difference, was repeated throughout my childhood and adolescence, and has never left me. (p. 81)

Dr. Olkin talks about the intersection of her disability with the multiple life roles she plays day to day. Here, she discusses how her "readily visible disability" affects clients in different ways in terms of both forming a therapeutic alliance and in expectations they have regarding her role as a therapist:

> I find that clients attribute certain characteristics to me that help foster a therapeutic alliance. My readily visible disability seems to convey that I have been an underdog, that I have suffered, that I have been left out, and clients who believe that no one can understand them unless that person too has suffered slings and arrows give me the benefit of ready trust. Parents of children with disabilities want to know facts about me, that I was married, had children, hold a full-time job, as a picture of the future for their children who grow up with an absence of role models. Some clients with disabilities get annoyed that I'm not as empathetic as they think I should be when I insist they get on with their lives. And when one adolescent client with cerebral palsy told an outrageous lie about his disability being caused by a bus accident on the way to school in which the bus driver and 20 kids died, I am able to think, "Ah, yes, point *B*, I remember it well," and empathize as I hold out hope for point *N*. I wish I had some magic words that would move people—clients and students with disabilities alike—to later points in their development, that they could bypass some of the painful and hard-learned lessons. But I can't. (pp. 83–84)

In a final quote from Dr. Olkin, she talks about her role as a mother:

> There are lessons I learned from having a disability that I took into the role of mothering. One was the importance of humor about even dark subjects ("Come, limp with me," I used to say to my daughter as we walked down the hall together; now she says this to me). I learned priorities, that homemade cookies weren't vital to a happy home. I managed to impart a fundamental belief in social justice without ever lecturing about it. But most importantly, I learned that disability is irrelevant to the essential aspects of mothering—caring, nurturing, soothing, encouraging, and fostering development and independence. After having disability affect so many aspects

of my life, it is nice to have this one area where it is mostly irrelevant. (p. 84)

Allen E. Ivey

The next pioneer acknowledged in this *Handbook* is Allen E. Ivey. Dr. Ivey was one of the first White European Americans to focus his counseling career on issues of cultural diversity, the psychology of liberation, and on understanding racism and privilege. In these first quotes from his life story, we get a glimpse into some of the origins of his justice orientation and activism. First is a recollection of his father:

> In the summers, Native Canadian Indians (Dene) came to our area to pick strawberries and do other farm work. Dad used to take our pickup truck to camps around the area and sold groceries off the truck. One day, he came home looking sad. I asked what had happened and he said, "The farmers want a kickback from me. If I sell groceries there, I'd have to raise the price to the Indians." Dad wouldn't pay the farmer the kickback, even though the economic loss was important to our family. (p. 88)

As a child, Dr. Ivey experienced firsthand the sting of anti-Semitism. He also implies that these painful early experiences helped him to understand some aspects of his Jewish students' lived experiences, as he noted:

> At school, I endured frequent teasing and was called many anti-Semitic names that I'd rather not repeat in print. As a Baptist in a rural, provincial community, I did not even know what a Jew was, but the names certainly were not fun. I suspected that my "friends" did this because they learned those words at home from their parents, who likely were referring to my merchant father running a small store in a farm community. The stereotype of the Jew exploiting the gentile seems to have taken hold in this small corner of America. Nonetheless, it was necessary to smile at those parents when they came into the store as customers. I never shared this story with my own parents. Later, when teaching Jewish students at Boston University, I found that several of them had had experiences similar to my own in school. They also did not share such stories of oppression with their parents. (p. 88)

Dr. Ivey progresses into his early work as a college counselor as he talks about his first cross-cultural counseling relationships with an African American student and a gay student:

> Bucknell has a gorgeous campus and represents the best of the small college tradition. There were only a very few African American students on campus, and one came to me for counseling—the issue was his uncomfortableness on this nearly all-White campus. Needless to say, multicultural issues were not taught in my school years. I fear that he taught and helped me more than I helped him, although he returned for several visits, so perhaps I did something. Years later, I was excited to read in the papers that he had considerable success on the national scene. I also worked with my first gay client with approximately the same result. He came back, but I think I developed far more than he did. I wish that I knew then what I know now. (p. 90)

An experience that had a big impact on the personal and professional development of Dr. Ivey was working with colleague Dean Norma Jean Anderson in an encounter group titled "Black and White in Helping." In the following quote, he reflects on this experience and then describes his developing awareness of his own privilege as a White person in America:

> My central discovery came during the second year of the course. I had prided myself for several years on being "nonracist" and "color blind." The discovery of institutional racism was an important marker for me. Banks, car dealerships, employers, and all the institutions of our predominantly White society tend to discriminate against people of color. I had sensed this type of discrimination in my rural background. I recall how liberating it was for me to leave Mt. Vernon, Washington, and the baggage of oppression I felt there behind me. But if I were a person of color, I could not have left that oppression behind as I would have encountered new issues. I'll admit the class prejudice I experienced in my freshman year is perhaps a variety of oppression that is not easily left behind. But being White in a predominantly White society keeps me safe from the most damaging oppression of all—racism.

> I began to sense my White privilege, although we did not have that language at that time. In one of the groups, I came to the discovery that as a White person, I could never get rid of the privileges and benefits that I received from simply being a European American White person. Thus, I came to know and acknowledge that a form of almost inborn racism will also be in me. Admitting that I am a racist was not a pleasant task. But as I see so many people say "I'm not racist," or worse, "I'm not racist, but . . . ," I find myself discouraged and sometimes angry. All majority people need to learn and acknowledge the constant benefits that come to them from being White. Privilege and power extend to many other dimensions such as gender; social and economic class; sexual identity; physical and mental ability area of the country; religion/spirituality; and life experience with trauma (war, rape, cancer). Each of the many multicultural constellations come with a certain dimension of power and entitlement. Where do you stand on these dimensions of privilege? (p. 93)

Michelle Fine

The final pioneer honored in this third edition of the *Handbook of Multicultural Counseling* is Michelle Fine. She notes that her professional life has been guided by two fundamental questions:

> I have been bequeathed, then, to ask two questions, over and over in my research, my teaching and my activism, in schools, communities, prisons, and youth social movements:
>
> Where in the body, the family, the culture, the nation, and the globe do bodies of sadness swell and fester in the shadow of progress?
>
> And, then, where lies the missing discourse of desire? (p. 100)

In part, the origins of Dr. Fine's professional commitment and focus can be found in her recollections of childhood, where she notes,

> In most households, we find a social psychological diaspora of emotional bodies. Some carry and speak the unbearable weight of loss; others bury, deny, and silence. The youngest chubby child, lucky to be born when the family financial profile was approaching a middle-class smile, always a watcher and a performer,

I tracked my mother's migraines that moved deeper and deeper into her body as our family "made it." Only she could embody what the rest of us were forbidden to speak. (p. 101)

In our final quotes from Dr. Fine, she vividly summarizes the critical focus of her research, service, and activism, on behalf of those most neglected in their communities, and she closes with questions for us to consider as we pursue our professions of mental health service and research:

My dual genetic lines endowed me with the "*chutzpa*" (Yiddish: *nerve*) to theorize and study the visible and cellophane lines of power and (in)justice that stretch from the political to the psychic, by way of the social psychological. Situated in prisons, schools, and communities, using participatory methods, feminist, social psychological and critical race theory, the work tracks empirically the capillaries of racial, sexual, classed, and gendered injustice, documenting the rage, despair, and migraines, tracing too the ripples of resistance and flames of desire. While my work maps a geography of shame and desire, each project holds my little autobiographic secret—that those *persons and affects most viciously evacuated are the soul of our moral community.* (p. 102)

Dr. Fine advises us that as we go forward with our careers as counselors and psychologists, we should always keep in mind the following:

My advice as you go forward in your projects of teaching, research and social justice activism is to always ask:
　Who is not in the room? And thereby, who and what emotions have been exiled?
　Where do shame and loss live?
　What knowledge lie buried in bodies of betrayal?
　Who must sacrifice for "success" or "progress" to be achieved?
　How does privilege hide its pathologies?
　How can we hear, and make public, the whispered voices of resistance?
　Where are the sounds of the missing discourse of desire?
　How can psychologists engage with social movements for social justice? (p. 104)

INTEGRATION OF LIFE STORIES

I found the 12 life stories presented in Part I of this *Handbook* moving, poignant, and inspiring. I thank these 12 healers and psychologists for providing us with a window into their hearts, minds, and souls. You have provided us with a lens into your life experiences, allowing us some understanding of your worldview centered on deep personal awareness, a marked appreciation for those who paved your own paths, and a sense of the origins of your career-long contributions to serving others, particularly those whose voices have been silenced. Each of the 12 life stories was very unique. Yet I see some common threads that transcend the stories of our individual pioneers and elders. I now close this chapter by presenting 10 themes that emerged for me across multiple life stories.

1. Various pioneers appeared to channel hurtful and sometimes chaotic early lives into a lifelong empathy for others in need. Experiencing and/or witnessing struggles and pain early in life affected our pioneers' developing personalities, their rate of maturation, and their early vocational "callings."

2. Common to the life stories is a sense of commitment to others, particularly those who have been neglected in some way; those on the margins or borders of society. There is a sense of "giving back" to the community, and honoring one's own role models through service to, and the empowerment of, others.

3. Many of the pioneers emphasized the impact of family members, particularly parents and grandparents, on their personal and professional development. Many of these early childhood memories of parents were positive and empowering, but some were difficult and even hurtful. Yet collectively, these experiences were processed and positively integrated into our pioneers' ongoing personality development and worldview toward serving others.

4. Interestingly, school work and academic studies provided a refuge and safe haven for some of our pioneers who experienced varying degrees of trauma in early and adolescent (even adult) life. In a way, academic success provided nourishment of both the mind and soul, built high degrees of self-confidence and

self-efficacy, and instilled a sense that "I can achieve a lot in this life." Marked success in educational pursuits also helped our pioneers develop cognitive schemas, coping skills, and a life optimism that could generalize to life outside of school.

5. By and large, our group of pioneers is spiritual, though not necessarily very religious. The "spiritness" is manifested as a deep connectedness with others: those who came before, those present in our pioneers' lives, and those yet to be born. Furthermore, this sense of spirituality is also reflected in a connectedness to the land, nature, and animals, not just other humans. The sense of spirituality also appears to extend into day-to-day work with students, clients, patients, research participants, and communities. One pioneer noted that her work in serving others and advocating for those with less power is not accurately captured by the words "career" or "work," but by the term "a calling."

6. The pioneers express a deep appreciation and admiration for those they serve—clients, patients, students, and participant "co-researchers." They highlight the strengths, resiliency, adaptability, and survivorability of those who have endured extreme hardship as a result of various identity-based oppressions, poverty, and early child abuse. The pioneers seem honored to work with those who have endured, and they in turn are strengthened and bettered by their service to those with fewer resources and less power.

7. Interestingly, the pioneers, though professionally established and world renowned, still appear to be in the midst of their professional and personal journey. Many account for what they have yet to accomplish, where their next stages of life, work, and service will go. They feel they have more to contribute, more work to do for others, and more unfinished personal and professional business.

8. Our pioneers demonstrate that their own multiple identities are constantly evolving. Some had a deep pride and sense of their ethnic, racial, and/or other identities early in life. However, for others, connectedness to oneself as "Asian" or "White" or "female," and so on, happened later in life. Identity development does not follow a linear path beginning in childhood and extending into late adolescence; identity

development, in its many forms, is a living, changing, and evolving process.

9. A number of the pioneers noted the absence of culturally similar professional role models growing up and throughout school, and they highlighted the significant impact that finally meeting culturally similar mentors had on their personal and professional development. In turn, these pioneers feel a strong allegiance to students and young psychologists from their own racial/ethnic/cultural background, and they are committed to serving as professional and personal mentors to others.

10. The European American scholars among our pioneers addressed the development of their own "White" identity, their socialization into a racist society, and the growing awareness and processing of their own "White privilege." These individuals discuss the tremendous impact that colleagues and mentors, particularly those of color, had on their own developing racial identity and personal and professional development.

CONCLUSION

This chapter has presented quotes from the life stories of a select group of psychologists who had been nominated by their professional peers as "pioneers" or "elders" in multicultural counseling and psychology. These scholars, along with the 12 presented in the second edition of this *Handbook,* are among a group of visionary and courageous thinkers who have helped move the study and integration of "culture" to the core of the psychology profession. The 24 pioneers, along with others honored in other forums (e.g., "elder"-type ceremonies at the biannual APA National Multicultural Conference and Summit, and the annual Teachers College, Columbia University Winter Roundtable on Multicultural Psychology and Education), have led a paradigm shift in the fields of counseling and psychology.

In closing Part I of this *Handbook,* I thank the pioneers for sharing part of their life stories with us. I have no doubt your words, experiences, and reflections will be inspirational to us, and we will learn from your wisdom. It is my hope that the select quotes from each of your life stories that I have presented in this chapter are good representations of your experiences and reflections. Finally, I call on readers to process and comment on the 10 themes that I culled from the set of stories, and I invite you to find other commonalities across the diverse lives.

REFERENCES

Asante, M. K. (2000). *The Egyptian philosophers: Ancient African voices from Imhotep to Akhenaten.* Chicago: African American Images.

Atkinson, R. (1998). *The life story interview.* Thousand Oaks, CA: Sage.

Erikson, E. (1958). *Young man Luthar: A study in psychoanalysis and history.* New York: Norton.

Erikson, E. (1969). *Gandhi's truth: On the origins of militant nonviolence.* New York: Norton.

Freud, S. (1957). Leonardo da Vinci and a memory of his childhood. In J. Strachey (Ed.), *The standard edition of the complete psychological works of Sigmund Freud* (Vol. 12, pp. 3–82). London: Hogarth. (Original work published 1910)

Jung, C. G. (1962). *Symbols of transformation: An analysis of the prelude to a case of schizophrenia.* London: Harper Torchbooks.

Ponterotto, J. G., Casas, J. M., Suzuki, L. A., & Alexander, C. A. (Eds.). (2001). *Handbook of multicultural counseling* (2nd ed.). Thousand Oaks, CA: Sage.

Ponterotto, J. G., Jackson, M. A., & Nutini, C. D. (2001). Reflections on the life stories of pioneers in multicultural counseling. In J. G. Ponterotto, J. M. Casas, L. A. Suzuki, & C. M. Alexander (Eds.), *Handbook of multicultural counseling* (2nd ed., pp. 138–161). Thousand Oaks, CA: Sage.

Ponterotto, J. G., Utsey, S. O., & Pedersen, P. B. (2006). *Preventing prejudice: A guide for counselors, educators, and parents* (2nd ed.). Thousand Oaks, CA: Sage.

PART II

Ethics in Multicultural Counseling

Part II of the *Handbook* contains two substantive chapters on ethics in multicultural counseling. Melba J. T. Vasquez, who was honored as a pioneer in the second edition of our text (see Vasquez, 2001), presents a state-of-the-art treatise on competent counseling practice within a multicultural context. In addition to an up-to-date review of ethical mandates for multicultural practice, Dr. Vasquez captures the essence of what constitutes "cultural competence" in counseling services. She highlights the importance of the therapeutic alliance in counseling diverse others, reviews key variables in therapeutic effectiveness, and discusses barriers hindering effective service to racial/ethnic minority clients. Dr. Vasquez also discusses the latest research on contemporary racism, racial microaggressions, privilege, perceptions of bias and stereotype threat, and the role of neurobiology in understanding client and counselor perceptions in cross-cultural encounters. Furthermore, she highlights the importance of incorporating a strength- and resilience-based focus in multicultural counseling. A riveting and inspiring component of this chapter is Dr. Vasquez's open and revealing discussion of her own clinical work with culturally diverse clients. This is a classic chapter on effective, ethically guided multicultural counseling practice.

The second chapter in this section is on ethical perspectives of multicultural counseling research. The chapter is written by the visionary and forceful scholar Joseph E. Trimble, who was also identified as a pioneer in multicultural counseling in our second edition of the *Handbook* (Trimble, 2001). Dr. Trimble anchors his discussion of ethical research on the investigator's task of carefully balancing moral judgment and scientific inquiry. Specifically, he guides the reader in applying a culturally resonant perspective in evaluating research risks and benefits, and he highlights the importance on community engagement and participation throughout the research endeavor. Dr. Trimble has a wealth of experience and knowledge in research with diverse cultural communities, and he reminds readers of the legacy of our past unethical contact with diverse ethnocultural communities. He reviews the more well-known Tuskegee syphilis study, along with a number of more recent examples of ethical misconduct that readers are likely less aware of, such as university-sponsored research on Havasupai tribal members in the Southwest. Importantly, Dr. Trimble provides readers with a review of exemplar conceptualizations and models for principled culturally sensitive research, including the goodness-of-fit model, community-based participatory research, and the tribal participatory research model. We consider this a classic chapter on culturally sensitive, ethical research. Taken together, the Vasquez and Trimble chapters in Part II provide a continuing education course on competent, ethically anchored multicultural counseling practice and research.

REFERENCES

Trimble, J. E. (2001). A quest for discovering ethnocultural themes in psychology. In J. G. Ponterotto, J. M. Casas, L. A. Suzuki, & C. M. Alexander (Eds.), *Handbook of multicultural counseling* (2nd ed., pp. 3–13). Thousand Oaks, CA: Sage.

Vasquez, M. J. T. (2001). Reflections on unearned advantages, unearned disadvantages, and empowering experiences. In J. G. Ponterotto, J. M. Casas, L. A. Suzuki, & C. M. Alexander (Eds.), *Handbook of multicultural counseling* (2nd ed., pp. 64–77). Thousand Oaks, CA: Sage.

14

Ethics in Multicultural Counseling Practice

MELBA J. T. VASQUEZ

The U.S. population is more diverse than ever before. The demographic changes have significant implications for our profession. The U.S. Census Bureau (2008) announced that racial/ethnic minorities who consist of one third of the U.S. population will make up the majority of the U.S. population by the year 2042, 8 years sooner than previously thought.

These changing demographics may serve to widen the existing gaps in the ability of psychologists to provide culturally competent services, because many, if not most, providers of psychological services may not have developed culturally competent skills. According to data compiled by the American Psychological Association (APA) Center for Psychology Workforce Analysis and Research (APA, 2008), 86% of APA members and 92% of early career professionals who practice reported that they practice with racial/ethnic minorities. Understanding the cultural context of behavior is critical to competent and ethical interventions in all areas of psychological work. The ethical imperatives that underlie the importance of competence in psychotherapy with members of various diverse groups will thus be described here.

Cultural competence includes awareness of the role of counseling professionals in their work with those different from them. This awareness is a key issue in the ethical provision of services and will be one of the foci of this chapter. Because the client/patient's sense of the alliance is one of the most important of the common factors in the success of all psychotherapies (Frank & Frank, 1991; Wampold, 2000), the quality of the alliance between psychotherapist and the client of color should be a key area of examination. Potential obstacles in developing a therapeutic alliance as well as positive strategies for overcoming obstacles will be identified for those wishing to provide competent, ethical services to racial/ethnic minority, international, and immigrant populations. Racial and ethnic diversity among clients/patients presents challenges for all psychotherapists and counselors, without exception, and these challenges are often subconscious (Greenwald & Banaji, 1995; Vasquez, 2007a, 2007b).

Cultural competence is no longer a marginal topic of interest; cultural competence in our modern mental health care environment requires far more knowledge and sophistication on the part of the professional, and it is becoming part of the mainstream fundamental knowledge and skill set required for effective practice. Therefore, there are several reasons why multicultural competency, and diversity training in general, should be more incorporated into the fabric of training programs, continuing education, and lifelong learning for mental health professionals.

MULTICULTURAL COMPETENCE AS AN ETHICAL IMPERATIVE

As human beings, we tend to relate most easily to, and have more knowledge and understanding of, those most similar to us, in our lives, as well as in our work, including in regard to the major variables of gender, race, ethnicity, and social class. Therefore, our professions in psychology and counseling have developed ethical imperatives that underlie the importance of multicultural competence in psychotherapy with members of racial/ethnic minority groups, including immigrant and international groups, as well as with members of other diverse groups whose identities vary according to factors such as gender, religion, sexual orientation, social class, and others. To practice ethically requires awareness, sensitivity, and empathy for the client as an individual, including knowledge of and attention to the client's cultural values, beliefs, norms, and behaviors.

All mental health organizations provide various principles and standards to inform us of professional expectations, including about work with diverse populations. The American Psychological Association's Ethical Principles of Psychologists and Code of Conduct (APA, 2002) and the American Counseling Association's Code of Ethics (ACA, 2005) include such standards. The standards include the notion that we be aware enough not to engage in unfair, discriminatory, and harassing or demeaning behaviors, and that we maintain evidence-based knowledge about the groups with whom we work.

The specific standards relevant to competence are the APA Ethics Code (2002) Standard 2.01 Boundaries of Competence, and the American Counseling Association Code of Ethics (2005) standard C.2.a. Boundaries of Competence.

In the APA, a number of special guidelines have been developed in order to provide more specific guidance for providers who work with members of diverse populations, including the Guidelines on Multicultural Education, Training, Research, Practice and Organizational Change for Psychologists (APA, 2003b); Guidelines for Psychological Practice With Girls and Women (APA, 2007); Guidelines for Psychotherapy With Lesbian, Gay, and Bisexual Clients (APA, 2000); and Guidelines for Psychological Practice With Older Adults (APA, 2003a).

The explosion of evidence-based and theoretical multicultural literature in the past couple of decades has enhanced the possibility for mental health providers to meet the ethical requirements to attain competency in provision of services to members of diverse groups. Whaley and Davis (2007) discuss the development of culturally adapted interventions of effectiveness studies and provide a variety of models of adaptations for both treatment of and research with clients of color. The next section will begin the description of cultural competencies in more detail.

CULTURAL COMPETENCY

Knowledge of and sensitivity to cultural issues are important features of professional behavior and practice. Among the various definitions of cultural competence, Tseng and Streltzer's (2004) is comprehensive in its scope and particularly appropriate for the mental health setting because of its attention to the impact of cultural issues in psychotherapy and other psychological applications. According to this definition, cultural competence is demonstrated by the attainment of three qualities and their use in the service of therapeutic goals. The first quality is *cultural sensitivity*, an awareness and appreciation of human cultural diversity. The second quality is *cultural knowledge*, the factual understanding of basic anthropological knowledge about cultural variation. Cultural knowledge can be obtained through courses, workshops, reading, consultation with experts, and/or meaningful interactions with individuals of diverse backgrounds. The third quality is *cultural empathy*, the ability to connect emotionally with the patient's cultural perspective.

The culturally competent clinician is also able to provide what Tseng and Streltzer (2004) term *cultural guidance,* by assessing whether and how a patient's problems are related to cultural factors and experiences and suggesting therapeutic interventions that are based on cultural insight. Increased insights and understanding about working with those different from us leads to increased competence.

Whaley and Davis (2007) reviewed several definitions of cultural competence and concluded that all definitions agree that knowledge and skills germane to the cultural background of the help seeker are fundamental to a definition of cultural competence, and that perspective taking is also a defining characteristic. This perspective taking requires cognitive flexibility. In addition, a definition of cultural competence should include organizational and system-level activities. Their definition included the following:

> a) the ability to recognize and understand the dynamic interplay between the heritage and adaptation dimensions of culture in shaping human behavior; b) the ability to use the knowledge acquired about an individual's heritage and adaptational challenges to maximize the effectiveness of assessment, diagnosis, and treatment; and c) internalization (i.e. incorporation into one's clinical problem-solving repertoire) of this process of recognition, acquisition, and use of cultural dynamics so that it can be routinely applied to diverse groups. (p. 565)

This definition is congruent with that of Tseng and Streltzer (2004) in that a process model of cultural competence has the advantage of being less prone to cultural stereotypes than a content model, which emphasizes the aspects of culture that matter for culturally different groups (Whaley & Davis, 2007).

VARIABLES THAT CONTRIBUTE TO THERAPEUTIC EFFECTIVENESS

In order to better understand barriers to multicultural competence in psychotherapy practice, it is helpful to understand the factors that contribute to therapeutic effectiveness. Psychotherapy is a change process designed to provide symptom relief; personality change; prevention

of future symptomatic episodes; and an increase in the quality of life, including the promotion of adaptive functioning in work and relationships, the ability to make healthy and satisfying life choices, and other goals arrived at in the collaboration between client/patient and psychotherapist (APA Task Force on Evidence-Based Practice, 2006). Evidence-based practice in psychology is "the integration of the best available research with clinical expertise in the context of patient characteristics, culture and preferences" (APA Task Force, 2006, p. 273). Psychologists must attend to a range of outcomes that may sometimes suggest one strategy and sometimes another, and they must also attend to the strengths and limitations of available research regarding these different ways of measuring success.

PSYCHOTHERAPY OUTCOME STUDIES

The empirical evidence on the outcomes of counseling and psychotherapy informs us that generally, treatment is effective. That is, in most control group studies in counseling and psychotherapy, treated persons are found to be more functional and less distressed than untreated persons as a result of treatment (Wampold, 2000). Various psychotherapy treatments intended to be therapeutic are equivalent in terms of the benefits produced; generally, no one treatment seems to be more effective than another, in most meta-analyses of different types of psychotherapy. For example, Cuijpers, van Straten, Andersson, and van Oppen (2008) conducted seven meta-analyses of seven major types of psychological treatment for mild to moderate adult depression. All were effective to some degree, but they found that interpersonal psychotherapy may be somewhat more efficacious and nondirective supportive therapy somewhat less efficacious. Their conclusion was that there are few significant differences in efficacy between most major types of treatments of mild to moderate depression and that "they all should have prizes, but not all should have the same prize" (p. 919).

Most effects of psychological treatments are caused by common, nonspecific factors and not by particular techniques (Cuijpers et al., 2008). The common factors include the therapeutic alliance between therapist and client, belief in the treatment, and a clear rationale explaining why the client has developed the problems (Lambert, 2004). In a review of studies examining outcomes of individual counseling and psychotherapy, Frank and Frank (1991) believed, and the evidence demonstrates, that the success of all techniques depends especially on the patient's sense of alliance with the healer. Frank and Frank (1991) believed that therapists should learn as many approaches as they found "congenial and convincing," and then select for each patient the therapy that accords, or can be brought to accord, with the patient's personal characteristics and view of the problem.

To do this, we have to quickly assess what our clients might want and need. That means knowing and understanding as much as possible about our clientele. Stark (1999) described how the

> optimal therapeutic stance is one that is continuously changing. . . . Moment by moment, the therapist's position shifts. How the therapist decides to intervene, depends on both what she has come to understand about the patient by virtue of the listening position she has assumed and what she believes the patient most needs—whether enhancement of knowledge, a corrective experience, or interactive engagement in relationship. (p. 5)

In work with members of racial/ethnic minority groups, an additional overlay in this ongoing stance with clients/patients includes what Tseng and Streltzer (2004) term *cultural guidance,* including therapeutic interventions based on cultural insight and the assessment of whether and how a patient's problems are related to cultural and/or environmental factors.

The therapeutic alliance has thus been identified as one of the most important of the common factors in therapeutic effectiveness. It is the quality of involvement between therapist and client or patient, as reflected in their task teamwork and personal rapport, and the therapist's contribution to the alliance is an important element of that involvement. The ability of the practitioner to tune into the client/patient of color, with cultural sensitivity, cultural knowledge, and cultural empathy, as well as to provide cultural guidance when appropriate, are factors that promote the therapeutic alliance with clients/patients of color (Tseng & Streltzer, 2004; Vasquez, 2007a, 2007b).

BARRIERS TO EFFECTIVE TREATMENT OF MULTICULTURAL CLIENTS/PATIENTS

Although there is mixed evidence, most clients of color are more comfortably matched with therapists similar to them (Casas, Vasquez, & Ruiz de Esparza, 2002; Pedersen, Draguns, Lonner, & Trimble, 2002; Sue & Sue, 2003). More specifically, clients working with clinicians of similar ethnic backgrounds and languages tend to remain in treatment longer than do clients whose therapists are neither ethnically nor linguistically matched (Sue & Sue, 2003). However, such matches are not always possible. Dingfelder (2008) reported that although there have been increases among those with recent psychology doctorates from multiethnic backgrounds, they are still underrepresented among psychologists in general. For example, in the U.S. population estimates for 2005, the population consisted of 14.4% Hispanic, 4.3% Asian, 12.8% Black, 1.5% Two or more races, 1.0% American Indian, and 66.9% White/Non-Hispanic. Dingfelder (2008) cited the Center for Psychology Workforce Analysis and Research 2005 Doctorate Employment Survey, which reported that recent psychology doctorates consisted of 6.2% Hispanic, 6.0% Asian, 4.4% Black, 2.7% Two or more races, 0.4% American Indian, and 80.4% White/Non-Hispanic (Dingfelder, 2008). Blacks and Hispanics are particularly less well represented among new psychology doctorates.

In addition, matches do not guarantee a healthy therapeutic alliance. As indicated previously, 86% of American Psychological Association members and 92% of early career professionals who practice reported that they practice with racial/ethnic minorities (APA, 2008). Thus, the vast majority of people of color who enter treatment most likely enter therapy with a person not from their racial/ethnic background.

Given the sociopolitical context in which we all exist, we are all influenced by racism, ethnocentrism, sexism, heterosexism, and other "isms," whether we are conscious of them or not (APA, 2003b; Vasquez, 2007a, 2007b). The APA Guidelines on Multicultural Education, Training, Research, Practice and Organizational Change for Psychologists (2003b) include various assumptions and guidelines that address this reality. Referred to here as the "Multicultural Guidelines" (APA, 2003b), they were endorsed as policy of the American Psychological Association by the Council of Representatives and were developed over nearly a 40-year period (Constantine & Sue, 2005). The first two of the six multicultural guidelines inform the other four guidelines and encourage psychotherapists to recognize that they may hold attitudes and beliefs that can detrimentally influence their perceptions of and interactions with individuals different from themselves, and to recognize the importance of knowledge and understanding about ethnically and racially different individuals.

The first guideline states, "Psychologists are encouraged to recognize that, as cultural beings, they may hold attitudes and beliefs that can detrimentally influence their perceptions of and interactions with individuals who are ethnically and racially different from themselves" (APA, 2003b, p. 382). Our worldviews, including the way we perceive our lives, our experiences, and those of others, are shaped in large part by our cultural experiences. Each of us has a set of cultural experiences and backgrounds, both conscious and subconscious, that influences our interactions with others, including in our professional work.

We all possess unconscious bias, and the social psychological literature provides evidence that even those with egalitarian values act in negatively biased ways to those different from them (Allport, 1954; Dovidio, Gaertner, Kawakami, & Hodson, 2002; Greenwald & Banaji, 1995; Opotow, 1990; Sue & Sue, 2003). More specifically, our societal structures have compounding effects on our cognitive structures, and ultimately our social attitudes and our beliefs about people. The way society constructs societal representations of groups affects the social order and has tremendous impact on the identities of individuals in various groups, both ethnic minority and White majority. These representations have an impact on judgments, decisions, choices, and behaviors in various implicit ways (Greenwald & Banaji, 1995). We could thus unwittingly compromise the cultural sensitivity and cultural empathy that Tseng and Streltzer (2004) describe as essential to be a culturally competent clinician.

The American Counseling Association (ACA) Code of Ethics includes a standard (C.5. Nondiscrimination) that addresses these concerns:

Counselors do not condone or engage in discrimination based on age, culture, disability, ethnicity, race, religion/spirituality, gender, gender identity, sexual orientation, marital status/partnership, language preference, socioeconomic status, or any basis proscribed by law. Counselors do not discriminate against clients, students, employees, supervisees, or research participants in a manner that has a negative impact on those persons. (p. 10)

APA Ethical Standard 3.01 Unfair Discrimination states, "In their work-related activities, psychologists do not engage in unfair discrimination based on age, gender, gender identity, race, ethnicity, culture, national origin, religion, sexual orientation, disability, socioeconomic status, or any bias proscribed by law" (APA, 2002, p. 1064). Also, 3.03 Other Harassment clearly states that

psychologists do not knowingly engage in behavior that is harassing or demeaning to persons with whom they interact in their work based on factors such as those persons' age, gender, gender identity, race, ethnicity, culture, national origin, religion, sexual orientation, disability, language, or socioeconomic status. (p. 1064)

Although the latter standard seems to imply that if one does not "knowingly" engage in harassing or demeaning behavior, one is not held accountable, the spirit of the standard certainly implies that we must make an effort to be cognizant of the potential to treat people unfairly. The standard is designed to prevent a situation in which a client/patient may perceive offense without the psychotherapist's awareness that it was perceived as offensive.

Indeed, many stereotypes and generalizations, and the ensuing behaviors, are often, if not usually, *subconscious*. Typically, others have to bring those to our attention. *No one* is immune to these processes, including ethnic minority psychologists and our own ethnic group members. "Internalized racism" is a dynamic that we all work against, but that can be subtle, unconscious, and powerfully destructive. It is thus important for providers of services to maintain knowledge of the evidence-based information about language and behaviors considered demeaning to those from different groups, as well as to continuously develop awareness of one's biases about groups of people that are systematically devalued in society. Subconsciously, we may be influenced negatively by the fact that a client's identity group is outside of our personal experience, or may treat people on the basis of their identity with lower quality of care without full awareness.

For example, I saw a new client with a heavy accent. Because of the accent, I realized later, I assumed that her employment by one of the local school districts was as a teacher aide or as clerical staff. In the first session, I learned that not only was she a teacher, she was a "lead teacher," and she was involved in training other teachers by the regional service center. I was aware of the increase in respect and regard I felt for her, and simultaneously embarrassed by the status and prestige variables associated with achievement that affect me. After all, are we not to value all of our clients as worthy of regard and respect? We probably do to some extent or another, and the fact is that we are influenced by multiple variables. The issue is to try to be as aware as possible when some of those influences come from unfair biases.

Categorization: Constructive and Destructive Strategy

One of the things we do when we perceive others is to place them in category. This is a helpful psychological process that helps to organize the often overwhelming amount of information and reduce it into manageable chunks of information that go together (Allport, 1954). This normal process leads to associating various traits and behaviors with particular groups, even if they are inaccurate for most individuals from those groups. Stereotyping and generalizing are consequences of this process.

Opotow (1990) described how we tend to further form groups in a we/they dichotomy. This leads to a subconscious and automatic categorization of people into our "in-groups," those with whom we identify, and our "out-groups," those whom we see as being outside our realm of identification. People in our in-groups are more highly valued, are more trusted, and engender greater cooperation as opposed to competition. We have more compassion for those in our in-group than for those in our out-group and are more likely to endorse and support those in this category.

On the other hand, people in our out-groups are implicitly conceptualized as "they," and these categorizations affect behavior. We tend to treat out-group members as objects, in insensitive ways. At minimum, people in our out-groups are ignored or neglected; behaviors can extend to the point of engaging in abusive and genocidal activities. Examples include hate crimes, Japanese internments, concentration camps, Holocaust activities, and lynching. Specific horrific examples include the murder of gay student Matthew Shepard in Wyoming in 1998, whose death from severe head injuries brought national and international attention to hate crime legislation at the state and federal levels, and the dragging death of African American James Byrd, Jr. in Jasper, Texas, in 1998, described in the book *Hate Crime* by Joyce King (2002). Recent hate crimes have targeted members of Latino/a immigrant groups. According to FBI statistics, 62% of victims of hate crimes in 2007 were Latinos (Reyes, 2008), making Latino immigrants in particular the number one victims of hate crimes.

In the context of psychotherapy, application of the "in-group, out-group" phenomenon would perhaps result in the following scenarios. A White male therapist would have a tendency to have more compassion for a White male client who perceived that he did not get a promotion due to affirmative action policies. A Latina therapist may have a tendency to have more compassion for a Latina client who perceived that she did not get a promotion because of biased evaluations. One of the basic assumptions in much of the multicultural counseling literature is that ethnic similarity between counselor and client increases the probability of a positive outcome (Pedersen et al., 2002). What happens when a White male therapist has an African American woman professing discrimination? It is quite common to have automatic biases, stereotypic attitudes, and negative attributions and interpretations about people in the out-group. Unfortunately, for most psychologists and other mainstream health providers, individuals in racial/ethnic minority groups are in an out-group, simply by virtue of being different.

Furthermore, when a person of color or a woman in the public eye does something wrong or makes a major mistake, those negative stereotypes are often reinforced. Selective perception of racial/ethnic minorities in key positions causes many of us to notice the negative exception and generalize, as opposed to when European White men make major mistakes. These reinforced negative stereotypes unfortunately encourage us to keep people in the out-group in our categorization schema (Opotow, 1990).

CONTEMPORARY/AVERSIVE RACISM

Various studies have indicated that it is very difficult, if not impossible, to be color blind; as much as we perceive ourselves to be egalitarian, we are not *subconsciously* color blind. Dovidio et al. (2002) have demonstrated in a series of studies that contemporary racism among Whites is subtle, often unintentional, and unconscious, but that its effects are systematically damaging and foster miscommunication and distrust. They demonstrated that people (employers, admissions counselors) give off negative body language (less eye contact, voice tone not as warm or natural) in response to those different from themselves. In the studies, although the White interviewers were not aware of the negative body language, the African American interviewees were aware of it. Employee selection and promotion studies continuously indicate bias, especially when those behaviors can be based on some factor other than race (Dovidio et al., 2002; Jones, 1998).

As challenging as the idea may be, practitioners may wish to examine to what degree they may demonstrate unconscious bias to ethnic minority clients or potential clients who are different from them. It is possible that we do not accept new clients whose differences evoke anxiety in us, but rationalize that our practices are "almost full." It is also possible that we do not make extra effort to follow up with a visible minority client who does not return to psychotherapy. As practitioners, we must also challenge ourselves to question the possibility that we demonstrate negative body language to those different from ourselves (less eye contact, voice tone cooler than usual, etc.). Based on Dovidio et al.'s (2002) studies that indicate that ethnic minorities are aware of the distance projected by interviewers, it may be important to realize that some, if not most, minority group members may be particularly sensitive to signs of rejection, dislike, or discrimination (Dovidio et al., 2002; Vasquez, 2007a, 2007b).

MICROAGGRESSIONS AND PRIVILEGE

Microaggression is a term coined to convey power dynamics in interactions in cross-cultural encounters that convey attitudes of dominance superiority and denigration; that a person with privilege is better than the person of color, who "is less than" according to Fouad and Arredondo (2007) and Sue (2003). Microaggressions are often perpetrated by well-meaning people who hold egalitarian beliefs, but who have not become aware of their negative attitudes and stereotypes about people of color and/or who have not had sufficient contact with people different from them (Fouad & Arredondo, 2007).

We must examine to what degree these microaggressions occur in psychotherapy between White clinicians and clients of color. We must examine to what degree they occur for any psychotherapist with those different from them by virtue of differences based on any factor that is negatively socially constructed without privilege in society. The nature of the role of psychotherapist confers power that can be beneficial in facilitating constructive change (Sue & Sue, 2003). Historically, power has been a factor in cross-cultural encounters (Fouad & Arredondo, 2007; Sue & Sue, 2003). Practitioners must be careful to understand and remember this power, and take care to not abuse it. The privilege that is conferred upon us by virtue of possessing credentials such as a master's degree or a doctorate is often unspoken, but it is a central dynamic in the psychotherapeutic relationship. According to the U.S. Census Bureau (2003), only 6.5% of the U.S. population holds master's degrees and only 1.17% holds doctorate degrees. The infrequency of contact of most clients/patients with those who hold such credentials can contribute to the power dynamic in the relationship, and we may unwittingly contribute to microaggressions.

MISSED EMPATHETIC OPPORTUNITIES

Some, if not most, ethnic minority clients have experiences of discrimination to address in psychotherapy, usually in addition to other issues. What happens in psychotherapy when an ethnic minority conveys the perception of an unfair evaluation, or that a lack of promotion has to do with prejudice and discrimination? What if the facial expression of the therapist reflects disbelief? What if the client may be struggling with a failure experience/event, *without* perceiving the possibility of discrimination, when discrimination is, in fact, a part of the process? What happens for that individual client when the therapist fails to suggest bias/discrimination as a possible factor?

Nelson and Baumgarte (2004) demonstrated that individuals experience less emotional and cognitive empathy for a target experiencing distress stemming from an incident reflecting unfamiliar cultural norms and that this reduction of empathy is mediated by a lack of perspective taking on the part of the observer. These findings suggest that representations of prior experience and lack of similarity between self and other can have a negative impact on the ability to mediate perspective taking or empathy on the part of the observer (Opotow, 1990). A consequence may be that the White therapist who has negative stereotypes about the competency of marginalized group members may have a difficult time staying present and empathic with the person of color who is struggling with a painful discriminatory event or a cultural experience foreign to the psychotherapist (Vasquez, 2007a, 2007b).

Comas-Díaz (2006) discussed how cross-cultural encounters often include a variety of "missed empathetic opportunities." These include those moments when a client reports emotional issues, and the clinician changes the topic without addressing or reflecting the client's feelings. Comas-Díaz contends that these missed empathetic opportunities may be more frequent when clinicians work with those different from themselves based on a variety of cultural identities. A very good suggestion is to learn the client's uses of words to facilitate and guide learning of a new common language, as well as to teach the client concepts in the therapeutic dialogue.

PERCEPTION OF BIAS AND STEREOTYPED THREAT

Steele's (1997) "stereotyped threat" research indicates that when ethnic minorities are asked to perform a task on which ethnic minorities stereotypically underperform, they end up underperforming because of the threat/fear/anxiety of underperforming, regardless of

actual ability to perform. Ethnic minority clients may experience negative judgment, rejection, and criticalness on the part of White therapists without the White therapists being aware of this. Because of a history of oppressive and rejecting experiences, many, if not most, ethnic minorities are easily shamed. A psychotherapist may not always know when he or she conveys negative judgments in body language, including facial expressions, voice tone, and eye contact.

It is likely that because of stereotyped threat, many people of color respond to the perception of mistakes or failures or rejections or biased treatment with humiliation and shame. It is critical that individuals be supported to respond with healthy coping skills to those normal but painful life events that everyone unfortunately experiences. The application of cognitive reframing and perspective taking can help one through this process, especially if they are suggested in the context of the client/patient's cultural context. Self-disclosure of the practitioner's similar experiences of failures or mistakes may also convey the normalcy of this aspect of life, as well as convey that one does survive painful mistakes, failures, or rejections.

As a case example, I would like to describe a situation when a Latina client came in for an initial session, referred as a crisis situation from a faculty member. Her presenting concern was that she was overwhelmed by a failure on a major review of a project that, if she had passed, would have advanced her to candidacy in her doctoral program. She was filled with humiliation, shame, and confusion. As I explored her perceptions, she was very aware that her failure had little to do with her competency. Two of her three examiners made very racist and derogatory remarks about the cultural aspects of her project throughout the exam. Other members of her department were outraged; she had been caught in a political struggle about emphasis of cultural issues in the department. She had already initiated an appeal, and other students and faculty were very supportive of her and her work. Yet she still felt at fault, as if she should have been able to somehow avoid such a situation and experience. She expressed deep feelings of failure. I led with questions and statements that indicated that I believed and assumed that discriminatory practices in her department existed, and that she had suffered as a result. I was able to be present as we talked through the pain, hurt, frustration, and anger of yet another situation of discrimination that so affected her life. It became important to explore other traumatic experiences of discrimination that had become the source of posttraumatic stress reactions.

The client seemed to hear me as I expressed sorrow for her experience. In the next few sessions, we moved on to strategies of managing her acute posttraumatic stress disorder symptoms (panic, anxiety at thought of retaking exam, or even entering the hall where her exam was held); as well as validating her need to not define herself by this experience. She was not a failure; she had experienced an unfortunate, painful event that she simply had to get through.

We began to explore the various choices she had for her future (to retake the test and stay in the program, retake the test and leave or transfer to another university, not take the test, etc.). With this client, and others who have experienced oppression, it was important to her for me to (a) believe and help identify the oppressive aspects of her experience, (b) focus on the client's resourcefulness and survivability, and (c) convey how lucky and honored I felt to share her process of recovery from this trauma. We also explored how she could have presented material that was less provocative to biased individuals.

One of the important values in most of our models of psychotherapy is for the client to take responsibility for his or her actions and behaviors. I reconceptualize this value as the importance of helping the client become empowered to control as many aspects of his or her situation as possible, and to learn from mistakes. However, it would be potentially damaging if, with this client, for example, I led with that line of questioning or intervention too early in the intervention process. "What part of this problem is yours?" "What was your role in the circumstances that you experienced?" Although these questions, or versions of them, may be appropriate at some stage in the therapeutic process, the timing and how these issues are addressed can be shaming and humiliating with clients who have had difficult, shaming, and biased experiences of oppression throughout their life. It can be very validating for a person from a diverse background to have a psychotherapist take on the burden of identifying the issues of oppression.

RESEARCH ON NEUROBIOLOGY

Siegel (2003) described how our experiences shape brain structure, which shapes brain function, which creates the mind. Both implicit and explicit memory results in the creation of particular circuits of the brain responsible for generating emotions, behavioral responses, perception, and the encoding of bodily sensations. Implicit memory is present at birth and continues through the life span. Mental models create generalizations of repeated experiences. A feature of implicit memory is that when it is retrieved, it lacks an internal sensation that something is being "recalled" and we are not even aware that this internal experience is being generated from something from the past. Thus, emotions, behaviors, bodily sensations, perceptual interpretations, and the bias of particular nonconscious mental models may influence our present experience (both perception and behavior) without our having any realization that we are being shaped by the past. Siegel (2003) believes that conscious awareness and continued reflection of unresolved issues can change emotions, behaviors, bodily sensations, perceptual interpretations, and the bias of those mental models. This is an important aspect of the change process.

There are two ways in which I think this information is helpful in understanding problematic alliances between racial/ethnic minority clients and White therapists, and other pairings of differences. First, I believe that many racial/ethnic minority clients may have developed brain structures to easily perceive biased behaviors. Second, I think that practitioners (not just White therapists) may have developed brain structures resulting in biases obtained from the society in which we grew, developed, and live.

Neuroscience is further confirming social psychological responses associated with race. The use of functional magnetic resonance imaging is a noninvasive means of examining the functioning of healthy brains. In an article titled "Imaging Race," Eberhardt (2005) demonstrated the process by which ideas about racial groups produce physical changes in the brains of individuals and thus come to shape who those individuals are. As Siegel (1999) explained, social variables can influence biological brain development. Studies reviewed by Eberhardt (2005) indicated that White participants exhibit more positive (greater amygdala response habituation) response to in-group White faces than to out-group Black faces. Black participants exhibit a more positive evaluation bias to Blacks than Whites do.

This is further demonstration of the possibility that even psychotherapists may exhibit unintentional bias in their work with clients or patients who are culturally different from them. The White therapist who becomes immersed in an implicit memory bias about how ethnic minorities have chips on their shoulders, and/or who has negative stereotypes about the competency of marginalized group members, may have a difficult time staying present and empathic with the person of color who is struggling with a painful discriminatory event. Siegel (1999) believes that implicit recollections without explicit processing may be the source of the experience of flashbacks or serve as the origin of rigid implicit mental models that may, for example, block a therapist's ability to remain flexible and attuned to the minority client. Eberhardt (2005) is optimistic in believing that awareness, such as that resulting from seeing pictures of the brain, may lead people to understand their own race-based perceptions and have the capacity to change and shape who they are themselves in ways never before thought possible.

REDUCTION OF BIAS

One develops a nonracist identity by first acknowledging that one's racism exists; this requires the tolerance of the unpleasant association with an honest appraisal of one's biases and prejudices (Sue, 2003). As long as one denies racism, the more difficult it is to understand oneself as a racial/cultural being and to develop an authentic and positive identity. In addition, we must not continue to view racial/ethnic minority groups as "disloyal aliens in their own country" (Sue, 2003, p. xiii). Finally, most multicultural experts recommend that every individual is responsible for combating racism, not only in oneself but also in society at large (Sue, 2003).

Green (2007) suggested that most people do not want to be considered racist or biased in any way, but they spend more of their time seeking to avoid those labels rather than exploring their behavior and the ways that they benefit from or have participated in systems of interrelated privilege and oppression, intended or not. We are all responsible for acknowledging the presence of social privileges in our own lives and the ways we benefit from them. Although we are not personally responsible for the existence of these systems of privilege and disadvantage, we do move within them all the time in some role or roles (Green, 2007).

Fowers and Davidov (2006) described how the social, intellectual, and moral aspects of the multicultural movement, with its values of inclusion, social justice, and mutual respect, have the ability to reshape psychology because of its ethical force. More specifically, they

> place the cultural competence literature in dialogue with virtue ethics (a contemporary ethical theory derived from Aristotle) to develop a rich and illuminating way for psychologists to understand and embody the personal self-examination, commitment and transformation required for learning and practicing in a culturally competent manner. (p. 581)

Indeed, the "virtue of multiculturalism" implies an openness to the other (Fowers & Davidov, 2006).

DEVELOPING THE THERAPEUTIC ALLIANCE WITH ETHNIC MINORITY CLIENTS/PATIENTS

Ackerman and Hilsenroth (2003) identified therapists' personal attributes and in-session activities that positively influenced the therapeutic alliance from a broad range of psychotherapy orientations. Personal attributes found to contribute positively to the alliance included being flexible, honest, respectful, trustworthy, confident, warm, interested, and open. Techniques such as exploration, reflection, noting past therapy success, accurate interpretation, facilitating the expression of affect, and attending to the patient's experience were also found to contribute positively to the alliance.

Although these attributes and techniques may very well work with clients of color, Comas-Díaz (2006) suggests the careful application of any evidence-based findings, given the dearth of research with populations of color. Individuals of one cultural group may require a form of psychotherapy and a stance by the therapist different from others. For example, cognitive behavior therapists may need to assess the role of racism and oppression in their client's ability to achieve mastery and agency. Racial stress management may be an additional empowering technique for clients who have experienced oppression systemically. The therapeutic relationship may be even more important with immigrants who feel distrustful of authority figures in this country. Some culturally diverse clients may be unsettled with the egalitarian and nondirective interaction styles of some therapists. Others may be put off by an authoritarian stance. These are factors and issues that must be continuously assessed, as cultural groups vary, and as individuals within those groups are heterogeneous based on acculturation, language, generational status, and other related factors (APA, 2003b).

The Multicultural Guidelines (APA, 2003b) suggest a variety of strategies, gleaned from the social psychological literature, to reduce bias. The first and most critical is *awareness* of those attitudes. The second and third strategies are *effort* and *practice* in changing the automatically favorable perceptions of in-group members and negative perceptions of out-group members. How this change occurs has been the subject of many years of empirical effort, with varying degrees of support (Hewstone, Rubin, & Willis, 2002). The social psychological literature further describes how *increased contact* with other groups (Pettigrew, 1998) is helpful, particularly if, in this contact, the individuals are of equal status and the majority group person is able to take the other's perspective (Galinsky & Moskowitz, 2000) and has empathy for him or her (Finlay & Stephan, 2000).

The psychotherapeutic situation potentially can be an ideal place for us to develop multicultural competence. Although the relationship is not equal, and there is a power differential, it is a mutually engaging endeavor. The relationship is one based on respect and care, and the responsibility of the psychotherapist is to take the client's perspective with compassion and empathy. The combination of awareness of our attitudes and biases, with effort and practice and contact with clients from diverse racial/ethnic groups, will promote multicultural competence *if* one is willing to challenge one's negative socialized biases.

Another strategy is to change the perception of "us versus them" to "we," or recategorizing the out-group as members of the in-group (Gaertner & Dovidio, 2000). This model has been shown to be effective, particularly under low-prejudice conditions and when the focus is on interpersonal communication (Hewstone et al., 2002). In addition, psychologists may want to actively increase their tolerance and trust of those different from themselves (Kramer, 1999). The psychotherapeutic encounter can provide a way to recategorize the out-group individual as a member of one's in-group when one accepts a client into treatment in one's independent practice. Continuous consciousness to one's reactions to clients would be important. Attention should be paid, for example, to tendencies to not try as hard to begin on time, to the temptation to make just one more call, to a failure to make sure that all is ready before the session (e.g., reviewing notes).

We all have clients who evoke respect in us, as well as clients who do not. Sometimes, these reactions are client personality variables, which are grist for the mill. Other times, our failure to feel respect for clients may be a result of biases, which a client has to really work hard to overcome unless they are incredibly special. The review of the literature above implies that an important constructive strategy is to assume the individual is worthy of the category of in-group. The therapeutic stance involves tuning into the individual, listening to their narratives, stories, and connecting with them as human beings. The goal of empathy means suspending and managing our negative judgments, triggers, and reactions. If we do react to negative aspects of the client, and judge those reactions to be legitimate and important therapeutic material (as opposed to bias), we must find ways to reflect that information in a way that they can hear and incorporate helpful feedback.

"Cultural mutuality," as defined by the APA Guidelines for Providers of Psychological Services to Ethnic, Linguistic, and Culturally Diverse Populations (1990) describes, in part, the importance of relating to clients of color, women, and other oppressed groups in a respectful, connecting manner based on our knowledge of clients' culture and also tuning in to aspects of the clients' needs that our therapeutic processes may help. This is an important value for psychotherapists who wish to promote alliances with persons of color and others who have been historically disenfranchised.

De las Fuentes (2007) and Hardy and Laszloffy (1995) promoted the use of a cultural genogram for clinicians to learn about their own unique values, transmitted through their families and experiences, as well as learn better how to assess those values for their clients, especially clients who are different from them. This tool is a didactic-experiential training tool to promote awareness of how the family is the principal mode by which people learn and develop an understanding about their cultures and ethnicities. Helms (1990) and Sue (2003) talk about the importance of becoming aware of and developing a "White identity" as part of the process of overcoming one's racism, and the cultural genogram can facilitate that process.

Identify Areas of Strength and Resilience

One of the most important strategies in working with persons of color is to identify strengths and resilience of the client. Fortunately, the psychotherapeutic process generally provides the opportunity, if the psychotherapist is open to it, to become intimately acquainted with the strengths and resilience of their clients. Feminist and multicultural approaches in particular, but also others, emphasize the empowerment of individuals and work toward the increased quality of life for all people.

Future research will hopefully shed light on the strengths and survivorship of various ethnic groups, despite various challenges (Vasquez & de las Fuentes, 1999). A variety of cultural factors may provide powerful sources of emotional resilience. A 1992 report, for example, indicated that despite enduring poverty-level income, Latinos exhibit values and behaviors that include a strong belief in marriage and family, a vigorous work ethic, and a desire for education (Hayes-Bautista, 1992). California's fast-growing Hispanic population also had a historically low rate of welfare dependency, a high rate of participation in the labor force, good life expectancy rates, and a high percentage of healthy babies. In Texas, according to the Texas Department of Health's Bureau of Vital Statistics

("Hispanic Girls' Life Expectancy Longest," 1996, p. B4), Hispanic baby girls born in 1995 will have the highest life expectancy of any racial or gender group; they are expected to live an average 80.3 years. The hypotheses for this finding include that because extended families provide emotional support, Hispanic women are less likely to live alone and less likely to be smokers or drinkers, they may have a better diet, and their infant mortality rate is lower than that of other groups.

In a meta-analysis of various studies of depression and racial/ethnic minorities, Plant and Sachs-Ericsson (2004) found that interpersonal functioning protected against depressive symptoms for Latinos and other minorities to a greater extent than for non-Latino Whites. The Latino cultural value of *familismo*, which implies an emphasis on strong family relationships, may foster positive social support that protects individuals against depression, even in the face of substantial environmental risk. The Hispanic/Latino/a Paradox (Palloni & Morenoff, 2001) is a phenomenon termed to describe unique resilience to the usual negative health outcomes of poverty and other psychosocial challenges, such as infant mortality and low birth weight, in contrast with non-Latino Whites and other groups. The specific "pathways" or protective factors that may buffer Latinos and enhance mental health have not yet been identified, but are hypothesized to include family networks and perhaps spirituality. More study is needed.

We are encouraged to be aware of barriers, obstacles, and experiences of oppression for clients of color, but it is also important to remain open to strengths and positive aspects of identity.

MULTICULTURAL KNOWLEDGE

The second of the APA Multicultural Guidelines (2003b) states, "Psychologists are encouraged to recognize the importance of multicultural sensitivity/responsiveness to, knowledge of, and understanding about ethnically and racially different individuals" (p. 385). The more we understand about those with whom we work, including understanding their worldview and perspective, the more likely we are to promote a psychotherapeutic alliance. This implies learning as much as possible about the various histories, values, norms, and expectations of various ethnic and racial group members with whom one works. Attaining cultural knowledge, the factual understanding of basic anthropological knowledge about cultural variation (Tseng & Streltzer, 2004), is one step in the process. The challenge in learning about cultural groups is to avoid stereotyping; rather, the practitioner must develop the knowledge to be used to assess the degree of application of various cultural values, behaviors, and expectations with each individual. The more knowledge we have about cultural groups, the more able we may be to transform interventions into culturally congruent adaptations.

Psychologists and counselors are encouraged to learn how cultures differ in basic premises that shape the worldview of individuals from those cultures. One of the risks in not being aware of one's own worldview as well as that of a racial/ethnic minority client is that one may unconsciously and automatically judge the client negatively, and perhaps in a pathological manner. Examples of values in White culture that could lead to inappropriate negative pathological conceptualizations include strict adherence to time schedules, the prioritization of achievement and success over personal relationships, and valuing of independence.

In addition, a culturally sensitive psychotherapist would employ a variety of interventions that take into account the needs of clients. This assessment process is complex and is informed by self-awareness, cultural knowledge, and familiarity with the evidence base of treatments, preferably those that include ethnic minority populations in the research samples. Not only must we possess sophisticated and ongoing self-awareness, we must continuously evaluate our theories, assumptions, practices, and clinical skills to correctly apply culturally resonant interventions to accommodate the needs of the wide variety of clients with whom we work.

Ponterotto, Fuertes, and Chen (2000) summarized several models of multicultural counseling. All are helpful in potentially providing knowledge, skills, and awareness in improving effectiveness in counseling and psychotherapy with ethnic minority populations. Constantine (2007), Constantine and Sue (2005), de las Fuentes (2007), Fouad and Arredondo (2007), Sue (2003), Vasquez (2005), and many others have applied the Multicultural Guidelines (2003b) to psychotherapy in particular.

CULTURAL ADAPTATIONS OF EVIDENCE-BASED PRACTICE

Miranda et al. (2005) provided a comprehensive review of the research on psychosocial interventions with racial/ethnic minority populations. They concluded that both traditional, empirically supported treatments and adapted interventions are effective with racial/ethnic minorities. Whaley and Davis (2007) suggested that the impact of culture may be most important during the process of therapeutic engagement, rather than the outcome; that is, a change in the approach to service, whether in content, language, or approach, may be necessary to engage and retain the client in treatment. Miranda et al. (2006), for example, developed a culturally adapted treatment of depression. They modified service delivery by providing child care and transportation to enable low-income minority women to take part in their empirically supported treatment intervention. They also had providers give the participants several educational sessions about depression and its treatment prior to delivering the intervention. They used a manualized version of culturally adapted cognitive behavior therapy developed by Munoz and Mendelson (2005) that included culturally relevant examples in techniques. These examples helped to validate the values and experiences particular to the participants' racial/ethnic group. For example, the culturally relevant example from Latino/a culture was applied by using the saying *la gota de aqua labra la piedra* (a drop of water carves a rock) to illustrate how thoughts, although transient, can gradually influence one's view of life and cause and maintain depression (Whaley & Davis, 2007). Cultural adaptation of evidence-based treatments may indeed be a method of making mental health services more culturally competent, and may enhance the probability of therapeutic engagement and treatment retention.

KNOWLEDGE OF THE EVIDENCE BASE ABOUT RACIAL/ETHNIC MINORITY POPULATIONS

What do we know about the mental health needs of people of color? We do know that marginalized groups continue to face formidable economic and social barriers in this country (Mendelson, Rehkopf, & Kubzansky, 2008).

As an example, 8% of non-Latino Whites live in poverty, but 14% of Cuban Americans, 27% of Mexican Americans, and 31% of Puerto Ricans live in poverty. Although it is important to not assume homogeneity within cultural groups, these figures are indicative of lack of opportunity for significant numbers from each group described. Only 56% of Latinos/as have graduated from high school, compared with 83% of the total population (U.S. Department of Health & Human Services, 2001).

Individuals of low socioeconomic status are more likely than individuals of high socioeconomic status to become depressed and experience persistent depressive symptoms (Lorant et al., 2003). Lack of access to critical economic and social resources is stressful, and depression often develops in the context of psychosocial stress. Stress arises not only from material deprivation but also from perceptions/experiences of relative inequality (Wilkinson, 1997). Racism and discrimination, unfair treatment, and negative external judgments about one's worth have deleterious effects on both physical and psychological health (Clark, Anderson, Clark, & Williams, 1999). Indeed, stress-based theories of health have argued that minority race or ethnicity may confer population-level risk for poor health and mental heath outcomes as a result of racism and discrimination, lack of access to economic and social resources, and other sources of stress exposure due to social disadvantage (Mendelson et al., 2008).

However, Plant and Sachs-Ericsson (2004) found that interpersonal functioning protected against depressive symptoms for Latinos and other minorities to a greater extent than for non-Latino Whites. It is important to note that this resilience may decrease as individuals acculturate in the United States. Acculturation is apparently bad for one's health, in some ways. In addition, the burdens of poverty and discrimination result in effects that are not always mediated by resilience.

INTERSECTION OF OPPRESSIVE FACTORS

It is helpful to recognize, according to one of the assumptions of the Multicultural Guidelines (APA, 2003b), the ways in which the intersection of racial and ethnic group membership with other dimensions of identity is important. Gender, age, sexual orientation, disability, religious/spiritual orientation, educational attainment and experiences, and socioeconomic factors are examples of other dimensions of identity that enhance or detract from one's identity and influence the way we relate to our clients.

Green (2007) indicated that when individuals have multiple identities, some of those identities or characteristics may place them in privileged groups, whereas, simultaneously, others may place them in disparaged groups. Many people of color have additional aspects of identity that intersect with racial/ethnic identity to form "multiple oppressions." It behooves the practitioner to be aware of how those out-group multiple dimensions of a person's identity affect one. Green (2007) suggested that being disadvantaged may evoke empathy and concern, whereas being privileged may evoke anger, resentment, and a lack of empathy for those struggles a person encounters that are not protected by privilege.

The commitment to provide services to those with whom we experience differences requires cognitive complexity, increased attention, and management of anxiety. It is also important to know when to refer, because we will not be likely to provide services without ill effects of bias and the ensuing distance, anxiety, empathic failures, and so on. I would also recommend that we need to work to not only tolerate differences, but also value and appreciate them. One strategy from the social psychological literature is to approach diversity and different experiences with curiosity and openness rather than with distance, skepticism, and criticalness.

ATTENDING TO THE CLIENT'S EXPERIENCE OF OPPRESSION IN THE PSYCHOTHERAPEUTIC PROCESS

One of the major issues that presents an overlay to the general problems presented is that most racial/ethnic minority clients will have a historical and/or personal experience of oppression and biases. Historical experiences for various populations differ. This may be manifested in the expression of different belief systems and value sets among clients and across age cohorts. For example, therapists are strongly encouraged to be aware of the ways that enslavement has shaped the worldviews of African Americans (Cross, 1991). At the same time, the within-group differences among African Americans and others of African descent also suggest the importance of not assuming that all persons of African descent will share this perspective. Thus, knowledge about sociopolitical viewpoints and ethnic/racial identity literature would be important and extremely helpful when working with individuals of racial/ethnic minority descent (see McGoldrick, Giordano, & Garcia-Preto, 2005, for a comprehensive resource for understanding families and histories in relation to ethnic heritage).

Culturally centered practitioners assist clients in determining whether a problem stems from institutional or societal racism (or other prejudice) or individual bias in others so that the client does not inappropriately personalize problems (Helms & Cook, 1999). Consistent with the discussion in Multicultural Guideline #2, psychologists are urged to help clients recognize the cognitive and affective motivational processes involved in determining whether they are targets of prejudice.

Unique Issues of Assessment

Multiculturally sensitive practitioners are encouraged to be knowledgeable of the limitations of assessment practices, from intakes to the use of standardized assessment instruments (APA, 2002; Constantine, 1998). The APA Ethics Code (2002) urges psychologists to "use assessment instruments whose validity and reliability have been established for use with members of the population test. When such validity or reliability has not been established, psychologists describe the strengths and limitations of test results and interpretation" (p. 1071). In addition, psychologists are urged to attend to the issue of an individual's language preference. Other ongoing areas of research focus on identifying issues around translation of instruments, the appropriate or inappropriate use of instruments, identifying different scores that may be more accurate for various groups, and so on. Other key issues of assessment are addressed elsewhere in this volume (see Part X).

Understanding Boundary Crossings Versus Boundary Violations

It is helpful to distinguish between the terms *boundary crossings* and *boundary violations*. Boundary crossings refer to any activity that moves therapists away from a strictly neutral position with their patients. This activity may be helpful or harmful. A boundary violation is a harmful boundary crossing. The notion of boundaries has evolved as an important strategy to "do no harm" because the needs of the psychologist could potentially obstruct therapy. It is the therapist's responsibility to know which behaviors harm and which help clients.

Practitioners are encouraged to recognize the importance of multicultural sensitivity/responsiveness, knowledge, and understanding about ethnically and racially different individuals to the area of professional boundaries, such as receiving/giving gifts, attending clients' transitional life events, answering clients' questions and self-disclosure, and nonsexual touch. Sometimes maintaining strict boundaries does more harm than engaging in a humane, genuine, authentic manner that is culturally congruent. Many, if not most, multicultural ethicists construe boundary maintenance in therapy as a continuous rather than a dichotomous issue. Exceptions to boundaries must be compatible with one's theoretical conceptualization, and I encourage consultation with knowledgeable colleagues as well as articulation of the exception in treatment process notes (Barnett, Lazarus, Vasquez, Moorehead-Slaughter, & Johnson, 2007).

SPECIAL ISSUES FOR PRACTITIONERS OF COLOR

I am aware that as a Latina psychotherapist, many of my clients of color choose to come to see me because of my ethnic identity. Other people of color, with internalized racism, might choose to avoid seeing someone like me. I am also aware that many of my White clients have to go through some process of cognitive dissonance to assume my competency, because if they grew up in this society, people from my ethnic background are not assumed to be competent. So what happens when I, as a Latina therapist, have a White male client who is angry at affirmative action policies and makes derogatory statements of other racial/ethnic minorities, or perhaps even about members of my ethnic group?

A basic task for ethical practice is to remember the humanity of those with whom we work (Pope & Vasquez, 1998). Therefore, my primary task with the angry client is to attend to his pain, anxiety, and fears in the context of his own experience. It may be that at some point, later in the session or later in the therapy, issues regarding transference and countertransference and/or dealing with the impact of his insensitive methods of dealing with his pain can be processed. But the primary responsibility is to attend to his core issues, and to later address his biases as I perceive them. Green (2007) suggested that "keeping track of your humanity" involves being aware of someone else's vulnerability to injury or harm as a result of our actions. We must especially do this when what we are doing involves using the power at our disposal.

Comas-Díaz and Jacobsen (1995) address the interracial dyad involving a therapist of color and a White patient, and they provide a dynamic analysis of the contradictions, such as significance of power reversal and transferential and countertransferential reactions. They conceptualize this dyad as an opportunity for therapists of color to acquire a perspective from White patients and witness the reality experienced by their majority group patients. Alternatively, White patients can benefit from the contributions of the therapist of color, who has experience in overcoming the odds of achieving success. Both clients and therapists can thus heal and become more empowered.

Let me provide an example from my perspective of dealing with differences that evoke negative reactions in me. An older White male called by phone to explore the possibility of entering psychotherapy, and he asked an extensive number of questions about my background, training, years of experience, and approach to treatment. He had a medical degree and a law degree. My automatic reaction was to deal with the anxiety he evoked in me by pathologizing him as paranoid and obsessive compulsive; the healthier alternative was to compassionately acknowledge that this was his first time to consider psychotherapy, and that it was very difficult for him to be vulnerable and ask for help. I was able to conceptualize

his "interrogation" as simply strategies he used to feel safer in embarking on a vulnerable endeavor with a person of color. These strategies eventually can be explored in the psychotherapeutic process, and their relative merits and consequences can help the client make more informed choices about the behaviors.

Most importantly, the Multicultural Guidelines ask us to acknowledge differences and, even if they make us uncomfortable, to be respectful about the differences. We have all had experiences in which our critical, negative judgments and perceptions were misplaced, inappropriate, and unfounded. We must be cautious as to whether such stances are ever legitimate in the psychotherapy room. If so, I suggest that we must refer.

CONCLUSION

The social construction of race and ethnicity in this country means that we all suffer from unintentional biases, resulting in discriminatory, oppressive behaviors that lead to microaggressions and other offenses. It is highly likely that these attitudes and behaviors extend to the process of psychotherapy. Change involves awareness of biases, and the ability of professionals to promote knowledge, attitudes, and skills important to the cultures of those with whom they work. The therapeutic alliance, of significant importance in positive therapeutic outcome, may be positively or negatively affected by the choices that psychotherapists make in overcoming those "isms." Various activities and experiences are suggested in the literature, and all practitioners have a responsibility to engage in those endeavors to reduce bias and enhance the probability of a strong and positive psychotherapeutic alliance. Continuing lifelong learning in order to keep up with the explosion of evidence-based research, especially about the various groups with whom we work, will be key in maintaining cultural competence.

In the words of Dan Siegel (1999), we can "rewire our circuitry" through explicit processing of our biases, immersion with different groups and individuals, readings, training, and practice in behaving in ways to change our subconscious perceptions in the psychotherapeutic process (staying attuned to clients, demonstrating cultural empathy, being respectful and open to worldviews). We can change our "neural pathways" developed through negative biases and stereotypes in society (Eberhardt, 2005; Siegel, 1999). I recommend approaching those different from us with curiosity, interest, and openness.

More research is recommended to assess the quality of the therapeutic alliance and how that affects the outcome for clients of color. This would be a complicated endeavor, because results of studies investigating the therapeutic alliance often consider different treatment modalities, with mostly heterogeneous groups of patients with various disorders. However, it is an important goal, both to determine the degree to which it is a problem in the psychotherapeutic underutilization of services for clients of color, as well as to identify unique factors related to the promotion of the therapeutic alliance in cross-cultural dyads.

REFERENCES

Ackerman, S., & Hilsenroth, M. (2003). A review of therapist characteristics and techniques positively impacting the therapeutic alliance. *Clinical Psychology Review, 23*, 1–33.

American Counseling Association. (2005). *ACA code of ethics.* Obtained from http://www.counseling.org/Resources/CodeOfEthics/TP/Home/CT2.aspx

Allport, G. W. (1954). *The nature of prejudice.* Cambridge, MA: Addison-Wesley.

American Psychological Association. (1990). *Guidelines for providers of psychological services to ethnic, linguistic, and culturally diverse populations.* Washington, DC: Author.

American Psychological Association. (2000). Guidelines for psychotherapy with lesbian, gay and bisexual clients. *American Psychologist, 55,* 1440–1451.

American Psychological Association. (2002). Ethical principles of psychologists and code of conduct. *American Psychologist, 57,* 1060–1073.

American Psychological Association. (2003a). *Guidelines for psychological practice with older adults.* Retrieved from PsychNet Website: http://www.apa.org/practice/Guidelines_for_Psychological_Practice_with_Older_Adults.pdf

American Psychological Association. (2003b). Guidelines on multicultural education, training, research, practice, and organizational change for psychologists. *American Psychologist, 58,* 377–402.

American Psychological Association. (2007). *Guidelines for psychological practice with girls and women: A Joint Task Force of APA Divisions 17 and 35.* Retrieved on November 2, 2008, from http://www.apa.org/about/division/girlsandwomen.pdf

American Psychological Association Center for Psychology Workforce Analysis and Research. (2008). *APA members practicing with underserved populations by state, 2007.* Retrieved September 9, 2008, from UNDERSERVED PRACT 07_HTM.htm

American Psychological Association Task Force on Evidence-Based Practice. (2006). Evidence-based practice in psychology. *American Psychologist, 61,* 271–285.

Barnett, J. E., Lazarus, A. A., Vasquez, M. J. T., Moorehead-Slaughter, O., & Johnson, W. B. (2007). Boundary issues and multiple relationships: Fantasy and reality. *Professional Psychology: Research and Practice, 38,* 401–410.

Casas, J. M., Vasquez, M. J. T., & Ruiz de Esparza, C. A. (2002). Counseling the Latina/o: A guiding framework for a diverse population. In P. B. Pederson, J. G. Draguns, W. J. Lonner, & J. E. Trimble (Eds.), *Counseling across cultures* (5th ed., pp. 133–160). Thousand Oaks, CA: Sage.

Clark, R., Anderson, N. B., Clark, V. R., & Williams, D. R. (1999). Racism as a stressor for African Americans: A biopsychosocial model. *American Psychologist, 54,* 805–816.

Comas-Díaz, L. (2006). Cultural variation in the therapeutic relationship. In C. D. Goodheart, A. E. Kazdin, & R. J. Sternberg (Eds.), *Evidence-based psychotherapy: Where practice and research meet* (pp. 81–105). Washington, DC: American Psychological Association.

Comas-Díaz, L., & Jacobsen, F. M. (1995). The therapist of color and the White patient dyad: Contradictions and recognitions. *Cultural Diversity and Mental Health, 1,* 93–106.

Constantine, M. G. (1998). Developing competence in multicultural assessment: Implications for counseling psychology training and practice. *Counseling Psychologist, 26,* 922–929.

Constantine, M. G. (Ed.). (2007). *Clinical practice with people of color: A guide to becoming culturally competent.* New York: Teachers College Press.

Constantine, M. G., & Sue, D. W. (Eds.). (2005). *Strategies for building multicultural competence in mental health and educational settings.* Hoboken, NJ: Wiley.

Cross, W. E., Jr. (1991). *Shades of Black: Diversity in African American identity.* Philadelphia: Temple University Press.

Cuijpers, P., van Straten, A., Andersson, G., & van Oppen, P. (2008). Psychotherapy for depression in adults: A meta-analysis of comparative outcome studies. *Journal of Consulting & Clinical Psychology, 76,* 909–922.

de las Fuentes, C. (2007). Latina/o American populations. In M. G. Constantine (Ed.), *Clinical practice with people of* color: A guide to becoming culturally competent (pp. 46–60). New York: Teachers College Press.

Dingfelder, S. (2008). How representative are new psychologists? *Monitor on Psychology, 39*, 11.

Dovidio, J. F., Gaertner, S. L., Kawakami, K., & Hodson, G. (2002). Why can't we just get along? Interpersonal biases and interracial distrust. *Cultural Diversity & Ethnic Minority Psychology, 8*, 88–102.

Eberhardt, J. L. (2005). Imaging race. *American Psychologist, 60*, 181–190.

Finlay, K. A., & Stephan, W. G. (2000). Improving intergroup relations: The effects of empathy on racial attitudes. *Journal of Applied Social Psychology, 30*, 1720–1737.

Fouad, N. A., & Arredondo, P. (2007). *Becoming culturally oriented: Practical advice for psychologists and educators.* Washington, DC: American Psychological Association.

Fowers, B. J., & Davidov, B. J. (2006). The virtue of multiculturalism: Personal transformation, character, and openness to the other. *American Psychologist, 61*, 581–594.

Frank, J. D., & Frank, J. B. (1991). *Persuasion and healing: A comparative study of psychotherapy* (3rd ed.). Baltimore: Johns Hopkins University Press.

Gaertner, S. L., & Dovidio, J. F. (2000). *Reducing intergroup bias: The common ingroup identity model.* Philadelphia: Brunner/Mazel.

Galinsky, A. D., & Moskowitz, G. B. (2000). Perspective-taking: Decreasing stereotype expression, stereotype accessibility, and in-group favoritism. *Journal of Personality and Social Psychology, 78*, 708–724.

Green, B. (2007). *The complexity of diversity: Multiple identities and the denial of privilege (within marginalized groups).* Keynote address presented at the National Multicultural Conference and Summit, Seattle, Washington.

Greenwald, A. G., & Banaji, M. R. (1995). Implicit social cognition: Attitudes, self-esteem, and stereotypes. *Psychological Review, 102*, 4–27.

Hardy, K. V., & Laszloffy, T. A. (1995). The cultural genogram: Key to training culturally competent family therapists. *Journal of Marital and Family Therapy, 21*, 227–237.

Hayes-Bautista, D. (1992). *No longer a minority: Latinos and social policy in California.* Los Angeles: University of California, Los Angeles, Chicano Studies Research Center.

Helms, J. E. (1990). *Black and White racial identity: Theory, research, and practice.* Westport, CT: Greenwood.

Helms, J. E., & Cook, D. E. (1999). *Using race and culture in counseling and psychotherapy: Theory and process.* Boston: Allyn & Bacon.

Hewstone, M., Rubin, M., & Willis, H. (2002). Intergroup bias. *Annual Review of Psychology, 57*, 575–604.

Hispanic Girls' Life Expectancy Longest. (1996, Dec. 11). *Austin American Statesman,* pp. B4–B5.

Jones, J. M. (1998). Psychological knowledge and the new American dilemma of race. *Journal of Social Issues, 54*, 638–652.

King, J. (2002). *Hate crime: The story of a dragging in Jasper, Texas.* New York: Pantheon/Random Books.

Kramer, R. M. (1999). Trust and distrust in organizations: Emerging perspectives, enduring questions. *Annual Review of Psychology, 50*, 569–598.

Lambert, M. J. (Ed.). (2004). *Bergin and Garfield's handbook of psychotherapy and behavior change* (4th ed.). New York: Wiley.

Lorant, V., Deliege, D., Eaton, W., Robert, A., Philippot, P., & Ansseau, M. (2003). Socioeconomic inequalities in depression: A meta-analysis. *American Journal of Epidemiology, 157*, 98–112.

McGoldrick, M., Giordano, J., & Garcia-Preto, N. (Eds.). (2005). *Ethnicity & family therapy* (3rd ed.). New York: Guilford.

Mendelson, T., Rehkopf, D. H., & Kubzansky, L. D. (2008). Depression among Latinos in the United States: A meta-analytic review. *Journal of Consulting & Clinical Psychology, 76*, 355–366.

Miranda, J., Bernal, G., Lau, A., Kohn, L., Hwang, W. C., & LaFromboise, T. (2005). State of the science of psychosocial interventions for ethnic minorities. *Annual Review of Clinical Psychology, 1*, 113–142.

Miranda, J., Green, B. L., Krupnick, J. L., Chung, J., Siddique, J., Beslin, T., & Revicki, D. (2006). One-year outcome of a randomized clinical trial treating depression in low-income minority women. *Journal of Consulting and Clinical Psychology, 74*, 99–111.

Munoz, R. F., & Mendelson, T. (2005). Toward evidence-based intervention for diverse populations: The San Francisco General Hospital prevention and treatment manuals. *Journal of Consulting and Clinical Psychology, 73*, 790–799.

Nelson, D. W., & Baumgarte, R. (2004). Cross cultural misunderstandings reduce empathic responding. *Journal of Applied Social Psychology, 34*, 391–401.

Opotow, S. (1990). Moral exclusion and injustice: An introduction. *Journal of Social Issues, 46*, 1–20.

Palloni, A., & Morenoff, J. D. (2001). Interpreting the paradoxical in the Hispanic paradox: Demographic and epidemiologic approaches. *Annals of the New York Academy of Sciences, 964*, 140–174.

Pedersen, P. B., Draguns, J. G., Lonner, W. J., & Trimble, J. E. (Eds.). (2002). Introduction: Multicultural awareness as a generic competence for counseling. In *Counseling across cultures* (5th ed., pp. xii–xix). Thousand Oaks, CA: Sage.

Pettigrew, T. F. (1998). Applying social psychology to international social issues. *Journal of Social Issues, 54,* 663–675.

Plant, E. A., & Sachs-Ericsson, N. (2004). Racial and ethnic differences in depression: The roles of social support and meeting basic needs. *Journal of Consulting and Clinical Psychology, 72,* 41–52.

Ponterotto, J. G., Fuertes, J. N., & Chen, E. C. (2000). Models of multicultural counseling. In S. D. Brown & R. W. Lent (Eds.), *Handbook of counseling psychology* (3rd ed., pp. 639–669). New York: Wiley.

Pope, K. S., & Vasquez, M. J. T. (1998). *Ethics in psychotherapy and counseling: A practical guide.* San Francisco: Jossey-Bass.

Reyes, R. (2008). Hot rhetoric fuels Latino hate crimes. Retrieved December 21, 2008, from http://blogs.usatoday.com/oped/2008/12/hot-rhetoric-fu.html

Siegel, D. J. (1999). *The developing mind: How relationships and the brain interact to shape who we are.* New York: Guilford.

Siegel, D. J. (2003). *The developing mind: Toward a neurobiology of interpersonal experience.* New York: Guilford.

Stark, M. (1999). *Modes of therapeutic action: Enhancement of knowledge, provision of experience, and engagement in relationship.* Northvale, NJ: Aronson.

Steele, C. M. (1997). A threat in the air: How stereotypes shape the intellectual identities and performance of women and African-Americans. *American Psychologist, 52,* 613-629.

Sue, D. W. (2003). *Overcoming our racism: The journey to liberation.* San Francisco: Jossey-Bass.

Sue, D. W., & Sue, S. (2003). *Counseling the culturally diverse* (4th ed.). Hoboken, NJ: Wiley.

Tseng, W. S., & Streltzer, J. (Eds.). (2004). *Cultural competence in clinical psychiatry.* Washington, DC: American Psychiatric Publishing.

U.S. Census Bureau. (2003). *PCT034. Educational attainment for the population 25 years and over, masters, professional and doctorate degrees.* Retrieved May 20, 2005, from joanna.r.gonzalez@census.gov.

U.S. Census Bureau. (2008). *An older and more diverse nation by midcentury.* Retrieved August 14, 2008, from http://www.census.gov/Press-Release/www/releases/archives/population/012496.html

U.S. Department of Health and Human Services. (2001). *Mental health: Culture, race and ethnicity—A supplement to Mental Health: A Report of the Surgeon General.* Rockville, MD: U.S. Department of Health and Human Services, Public Health Office, Office of the Surgeon General.

Vasquez, M. J. T. (2005). Independent practice settings and the multicultural guidelines. In M. G. Constantine & D. W. Sue (Eds.). *Strategies for building multicultural competence in mental health and educational settings* (pp. 91–108). Hoboken, NJ: Wiley.

Vasquez, M. J. T. (2007a). Cultural difference and the therapeutic alliance: An evidence-based analysis. *American Psychologist, 62,* 878–886.

Vasquez, M. J. T. (2007b). Ethics for a diverse world. In J. Frew & M. D. Spiegler (Eds.), *Contemporary psychotherapies for a diverse world* (pp. 20–40). New York: Houghton Mifflin/Lahaska Press.

Vasquez, M. J. T., & de las Fuentes, C. (1999). American-born Asian, African, Latina, and American Indian adolescent girls: Challenges and strengths. In N. G. Johnson, M. C. Roberts, & J. Worell (Eds.), *Beyond appearance: A new look at adolescent girls.* Washington, DC: American Psychological Association.

Wampold, B. E. (2000). Outcomes of individual counseling and psychotherapy: Empirical evidence addressing two fundamental questions. In S. D. Brown & R. W. Lent (Eds.), *Handbook of counseling psychology* (3rd ed., pp. 571–600). New York: Wiley.

Whaley, A. L., & Davis, K. E. (2007). Cultural competence and evidence-based practice in mental health services: A complementary perspective. *American Psychologist, 62,* 563–574.

Wilkinson, R. G. (1997). Socioeconomic determinants of health: Health inequalities: Relative or absolute material standards? *British Medical Journal, 314,* 591–595.

15

The Principled Conduct of Counseling Research With Ethnocultural Populations

The Influence of Moral Judgments on Scientific Reasoning

JOSEPH E. TRIMBLE

Most social scientific research involves direct, intimate, and more or less disturbing encounters with the immediate details of contemporary life, encounters of a sort which can hardly but affect the sensibilities of the persons who practice it. An assessment of the moral implications of the scientific study of human life which is going to consist of more than elegant sneers or mindless celebrations must begin with an inspection of social scientific research as a variety of moral experience.

—Clifford Geertz (2001, pp. 22–23)

The words of the distinguished cultural anthropologist Clifford Geertz set the tone and context for the primary theme of this chapter. His poignant and well-expressed observation points to the need for field-based researchers to balance moral experiences with scientific inquiry and is in keeping with the fundamental ethical principle that one "should do no harm" when it comes to the conduct of research regardless of its level of analysis and method of investigation. Framing ethical principles and guidelines to include "moral considerations" is an indispensable condition for guiding research endeavors. Geertz's clarion call to researchers comes none too soon as community voices are challenging the way research has been conducted and the way that respondents were treated during the research process.

In the past few decades, there has been a remarkable increase in mental health research conducted among ethnocultural communities and populations—in this chapter, *ethnocultural* refers to a group or groups in a larger society with distinctive cultural traits who share and identify with a common national, racial, linguistic, or religious heritage and whose shared beliefs and practices identify a particular place, class, or time to which they belong.

As the research ventures increased, so have the concerns of many ethnic and cultural communities about research in general and the presence of researchers in their communities. The mounting community concerns accompanied by the emergence of community-based research review committees present unplanned and unusual challenges for researchers—challenges that are only beginning to be fully and seriously acknowledged at methodological and conceptual levels. The most important challenge is the responsible conduct of researchers while they are in the field and the relationship they establish with their respondents; a relationship that should be included as part of the research method (Trimble & Mohatt, 2006). Equally important are researchers' virtuous and moral principles and the extent to which they are closely aligned with professional ethical standards.

The purpose of this chapter is to raise considerations and essentials to encourage ethical decision making for mental health research with ethnocultural populations that reflect the unique historical and sociocultural realities of ethnic and racial people and their communities. A secondary objective is to highlight the untoward consequences of irresponsible research and cultural incompetence and the effects they generate for the researchers and respondents. The end result of cultural and ethical insensitivities of field-based research has often been harmful to the participants, leaving many with indelible emotional scars and memories. As a result, many communities are now taking steps to protect themselves against future abuses of research practices and the insensitivities of the researchers.

The chapter follows three ethical dimensions of culturally meaningful research: applying a culturally resonant perspective to the evaluation of research risk and benefits, evaluating and implementing culturally respectful moral beliefs and value orientations, and engaging in community and participant consultation with a standard of *principled cultural sensitivity*.

MORAL ORDER AND VALUE PERCEPTIONS

Although professional normative ethical principles and standards serve as comprehensive guidelines for the conduct of research, the personal moral persuasion and value orientations of researchers should take precedence. Ethical principles and standards require researchers and practitioners to be vigilant and self-reflective about the consequences of their actions and the corresponding behavioral-cognitive-emotional influence on their respondents; ignorance of professional ethical principles and standards is not acceptable. Moreover, for one to be successful in a research field setting, there must be concurrence with professional normative standards and personal moral persuasions. As Geertz (2001) reminds us, "An assessment of the moral implications of the scientific study of human life . . . must begin with an inspection of social scientific research as a variety of moral experience" (p. 23).

"Moral assessment," argues Smith (2005), "is not that we have voluntarily chosen it or that we have voluntary control over it, but that it reflects our own evaluative judgments and standards" (p. 237). The assessment of morality can be construed as a rational process, and thus the assessment of whether or not one's research approach will do no harm should lead to a logical decision in favor of protecting the rights of study participants. Unfortunately and regrettably, some researchers take a more self-serving approach where their needs, aspirations, desire, and wants overshadow those of their host communities, and that approach—likely judged rational by the researcher—is the foremost reason for the problems ethnocultural communities have and continue to experience with outside researchers. Self-serving researchers may believe they can mask their selfish intentions, but they may be deceiving themselves to believe they will go unnoticed. The prominent cultural anthropologist Ward Goodenough (1980) reminds us,

> The principle that underlies problems of ethics is respecting the humanity of others as one would have others respect one's own. If field [researchers] genuinely feel such respect for others, they are not likely to get into serious trouble. But if they do not feel such respect, then no matter how scrupulously they follow the letter of the written codes of professional ethics, or

follow the recommended procedures of field [research] manuals, they will betray themselves all along the line in the little things. (p. 52)

Virtues and Personal Ethics

What are the personal qualities of people, and how do they influence their conduct of research with ethnocultural communities? ask Trimble and Mohatt (2006). Does it mean that one must be a morally decent person who closely adheres to a precise set of values that will not be compromised? Does one consider ethical standards in the context of viewing community-based dilemmas from a principled perspective guided by the fixed rules of objectivity, reason, and impartiality? Is that approach likely to be acceptable to the community's research partners? Is it possible that one's character and thus moral and ethical standards are incompatible with those likely to exist in the host research community? (p. 327). In addition to the personal challenges, the questions prompt communities to learn more about the kind of person with whom they will be working in the course of the relationship.

As Goodenough reminds us, if researchers don't show respect for their hosts, then no matter what they do, they will betray themselves. Similarly, if researchers don't closely follow and live by a set of *principled virtuous ethics* such as prudence, integrity, respectfulness, benevolence, and reverence, then at some point, they will gradually alienate their hosts; if the distrust and perceived lack of respect increases, researchers may be asked to cease their study and leave the community (Trimble & Mohatt, 2006).

Ibrahim (1996) and Vasquez (1996) prompt us to consider the possibility that most, if not all, ethnocultural groups have their own set of well-framed ethical standards often grounded in legends, traditions, and customs. In effect, a community's culturally specific standards may not resonate with those of the researcher's cultural orientation. For example, there may be different lexicons for what constitutes trust, respect, reverence, and honesty. If there are differences in the meaning of these values, how does one earn trust and respect within the context of another culture? And most important, how does one know that he or she has earned and established trust and respect? The questions

are not merely academic exercises but ones that require careful self-reflection. "To facilitate character and moral development in a multicultural system," maintains Ibrahim (1996), "we have to identify all the moral ideals that each [cultural] system subscribes to and find common ground" (p. 83). Learning the deep cultural meaning of what constitutes trust and respect therefore requires the researcher to spend time with the community. One will soon discover that community members will put researchers through a series of subtle and not-so-subtle tests and trials to assess their level of commitment to working closely with them as well as their commitment to learn about their cultural ways (Trickett & Espino, 2004).

Do No Harm and Doing Harm to Others

The maxim that *one should do no harm* has become the fundamental ethical principle underlying all research relationships. Using Haidt and Graham's (2007) five psychological foundations for morality and applying them to research arrangements, one can ask the following questions:

> 1). Whether or not someone was harmed; 2). Whether or not someone acted unfairly; 3). Whether or not someone betrayed his or her own group; 4). Whether or not the people involved were of the same rank; and 5). Whether or not someone did something disgusting. (pp. 104–106)

Viewed from Haidt and Graham's perspective, harm means much more than physical damage as it can include impairments, destruction, mischief, insult, disobedience, offensiveness, unfaithfulness, impertinence, and an assortment of like-minded words.

Doing harm to others indicates that one is engaging in unethical, derelict, and possibly unlawful behavior where a variety of perspectives serve to describe and characterize unethical and unprincipled actions. Using a variety of descriptors, Paul and Elder (2006) provide seven major categories to describe unethical behavior:

> 1). Using unethical skills to get others to act against their own best interest (e.g., defraud, betray, deceive, mislead, misrepresent, swindle, dupe); 2). Ignoring the rights and needs of others to get what you want

(e.g., covetous, egoistic, greedy, selfishness); 3). Rigidity of mind which keeps people from being ethical (e.g., prejudice, fanatic, intolerant, unfair); 4). Causing emotional discomfort (e.g., rude, disrespectful, uncivil, heartless, contentious, callous, dishonor, ill-mannered); 5). Causing pain and suffering (e.g., unkind, oppress, malicious, inconsiderate, cruel, dominate); 6). Refusing to tell the truth due to self-interest (e.g., dishonest, deceitful, disloyal, disingenuous, insincere); and 7). Unethical behavior that results from a perceived grievance (e.g., vengeful, spiteful, vindictive). (p. 22)

It doesn't take much speculation to come to the conclusion that the source for the growing concerns of numerous ethnocultural communities about outside researchers rests with the insensitive character and motives of those who abused their invitations and a community's trust. Community members who at one time have had negative and troublesome experiences with research teams will be quick to use many of the descriptors provided by Paul and Elder (2006) to describe them. Words like *insincere, dishonest, inconsiderate, ill-mannered, unfair, racist,* and *misleading* appear to have occurred with great frequency by those embittered by the seeming lack of a researcher's cultural sensitivity. Consider the startling words of a former research participant from a Northern Plains American Indian community:

> I had this feeling of being violated and betrayed, then I went into shock, and then I got angry . . . and then I went into denial. I thought, "oh well they don't know who I am. I was just a research subject." After I participated in the study, I had no idea or didn't even realize what all it was going to entail in the future. And then I come to find out that all the results have been "shared" through journal articles and publications. The realization for me was "Oh my god, I've been abused and violated because I had no idea that they would talk about us like that. Now we've been labeled like we're just a bunch of people walking around with diseases on reservations." (Casillas, 2006, p. 73)

If one gets close enough to community members who have had negative experiences with outside researchers, one will eventually hear similar comments and thoughts. Additionally, one may learn that many community members are angry, intolerant, embittered, wary, and distrustful along with related emotional expressions, so much so that they no longer trust outside researchers and thus refuse to endorse or sanction any outside sponsored research endeavors. Unfortunately, the self-serving motives, needs, and pressures of some researchers overshadow the fundamental principles of ethical and responsible thoughts and actions embodied in professional codes of conduct; their selfish actions and attitudes set anti-research community precedents that get passed along from one generation to the next. Fortunately, within the past decade or so, scholars, academicians, and researchers have been devoting considerable attention to the *principled conduct of research* by drawing attention to the viewpoint emphasized by Geertz (2001), and that is that one begin an "inspection of social scientific research as a variety of moral experience" (p. 23).

COMPLAINTS FROM ETHNOCULTURAL COMMUNITIES ABOUT INCONSIDERATE RESEARCHERS

The growing concerns and complaints from ethnocultural communities about the presence and conduct of research are justified not only because of the cultural insensitivities and personal abuse of certain rogue researchers but also because more and more community-based research is occurring that involves or plans to involve members of various ethnocultural groups. Evidence for the rapid growth and interest can be found in a brief inspection of the scholarly literature. For example, the citations in PsycINFO for all of the principal ethnocultural groups in the United States suggest that the numbers are increasing rapidly. Examinations of the database citations for the major ethnocultural groups from 2003 to the present indicate that African Americans have 10,657 citations, Latina/o populations have 7,848 citations, Asian Americans have 3,863 listings, and American Indians and Alaska Natives have 3,209 citations. The number of citations from 2003 to the present represents an average of close to a 60% increase over all of the citations for the four groups for all years available in the PsycINFO database. The increase in citations referencing research related to the groups is a reflection of a maturing of psychology as a science discipline for all members of society. But the rapid growth of interest and levels of research activity must be tempered by an awareness of the ethical implications of research efforts and relationships involving groups with whom most investigators have little familiarity.

Continuing changes in North American demographic distributions and patterns call into question the relevance of a psychology field that historically has not been inclusive of underrepresented and diverse populations. During the past 40 years, the study of racial and ethnic minority issues in psychology has evolved into what can now be considered a significant and rapidly growing field or subfield of study.

Culture and ethnicity matter, but they did not seem to matter enough in the history of the development of psychology. Culture and ethnicity are so pervasive and significant in the enculturation process that they beg for more attention and recognition. It is this very attention that the field of racial and ethnic minority is giving to the cultural and ethnic constructs. Culture and ethnicity matter so much that it behooves the investigator to spend considerable time with an ethnocultural group of interest to learn about the deep cultural elements of one's lifeways and thoughtways and how they contribute to social and psychological character. Once that is understood, then the investigator may be in a position to explore and apply conventional and traditional psychological principles to understanding; the collection of the information will undoubtedly influence the nature of the research and data collection procedures and measures, and that introduces a whole new set of methodological and ethical considerations (Fisher, Hoagwood et al., 2002; Harris, Gorelick, Samuels, & Bempong, 1996; Israel & Hay, 2006; Trimble & Fisher, 2006). But it's the presence of the investigator and the nature of the research questions and methodological approaches that have been problematic for many communities.

Examples of Research Misconduct

Numerous scholars from many academic disciplines are keenly aware of the iniquitous Tuskegee Syphilis Experiment conducted in Macon County, Alabama, from 1932 to 1972. Originally titled the "Tuskegee Study of Untreated Syphilis in the Negro Male," by every ethical standard and principle, it was a shocking and scandalous example of medical research gone awry. The U.S. Public Health Service, in attempting to learn more about syphilis and justify treatment programs for Blacks, withheld treatment from a sample of 399 Southern Black males; the experiment cost the federal government millions of dollars in research funds when it was eventually terminated. Researchers told the men they were being treated for "bad blood," a local term used to describe several ailments, including syphilis, anemia, and fatigue (Caplan, Edgar, & King, 1992; Jones, 1993). In fact, they did not receive the proper treatment needed to cure the disease. In exchange for taking part in the study, the men received free medical exams, free meals, and burial insurance. Although originally projected to last 6 months, the study actually went on for 40 years.

Public knowledge of the study appeared in a news story written by Jean Heller on July 25, 1972, and ran in the *Washington Evening Star* and the *New York Times;* the next day, the story was carried in numerous newspapers worldwide and aired in radio and television newscasts (Jones, 1993). The shocking story gripped the attention of millions of readers and listeners and subsequently led to an immediate call for action and explanation from the U.S. Public Health Service. In response to the allegations, the U.S. government convened an ad hoc review committee to carefully investigate the charges and allegations. At the end of the investigation, the committee unanimously concluded that the study was unethical and that it must be terminated.

In a February 2004 Arizona newspaper article titled "Havasupai File $25M Suit vs. ASU," the journalist summarizes the research circumstances that prompted Havasupai tribal members and the tribe to file a combined lawsuit and status report on the suit's developments (Hendricks, 2004). Between 1990 and 1994, researchers from Arizona State University (ASU) collected blood samples from tribal members that were to be used to study diabetes. Tribal members eventually learned that the blood samples had been used for purposes other than those to which they agreed when the respondents signed the human subject consent forms. The ASU researchers apparently used the samples to study schizophrenia, inbreeding, and factors that could explain human migration patterns. In May 2007, a Maricopa Arizona County Superior Court judge dismissed the tribe's case because of a legal technicality;

tribal officials said they plan to resubmit the suit and take the case to the Arizona Court of Appeals.

In 1979, a team of researchers led by Edward R. Foulks from the University of Pennsylvania's Center for Research on the Acts of Man conducted a survey of alcohol use patterns among 88 Inupiat Eskimo villagers from Barrow, Alaska. The survey results

> indicated that 41% of the population considered themselves to be excessive drinkers and 60% felt badly about the consequences of their drinking. More than 50% reported that drinking ultimately created severe problems with family and spouse. Sixty-two percent regularly got into fights when they drank, and 67% experienced frequent blackouts and amnesia from the episodes. (Foulks, 1989, p. 8)

Considerable discussion occurred with members from the Inupiat community, the non-Native residents of Barrow, representatives from Alaska's Department of Health, and regional consultants; much of the discussion was heated, especially about identifying the indigenous population in the reports and publications.

A news item titled "Alcohol Plagues Eskimos" published in the *New York Times* on January 22, 1980, subsequently led to an Associated Press story that

> "alcoholism and violence had overtaken Eskimo society after the sudden development of Alaska's North Slope oil field." The United Press International Wire service wrote its story under the headline, "Sudden Wealth Sparks Epidemic of Alcoholism," with the subhead, "What We Have Here Is a Society of Alcoholics." (Foulks, 1989, p. 13)

Community members, countless Alaska Natives, some knowledgeable researchers, and concerned citizens were shocked by the press headlines. Foulks (1989) stated that, "the press confirmed the stereotype of the drunken Alaska Native, whose traditional culture had been plundered. The public exposure brought shame on the community, and the people were now angry and defensive" (p. 13).

The fallout from the press coverage, the ire of the Barrow community and a few incensed research ethicists, and the alarm and concern of some research sponsors and sensitive researchers fueled considerable controversy and contentiousness. In 1989, the editor-in-chief of the

Journal of the National Center for American Indian and Native Alaska Mental Health Research, Spero Manson, dedicated a special issue to the 1979 Barrow, Alaska alcohol study in which Foulks contributed the lead article, titled "Misalliance in the Barrow Alcohol Study"; the other contributors in the edition provided various perspectives and recommendations with the principal emphasis on ethical and principled research conduct. In closing out his lead article, Faulks (1989) emphasizes that

> we hope that our experience will provide a valuable lesson demonstrating the degree to which the questions and methods of science are rooted in ethical, social, and ethnical political issues of the times, and of how scientists must self-consciously include these sometimes value-laden factors into their research design and planning. (p. 17)

Writing about the publication of field-based research findings, Goodenough (1980) cautions us that, "One must always ask oneself whether publication of such information is necessary or really serves any useful purpose" (p. 49). Indeed, if such self-reflection occurred before, in the course of, and after the Barrow, Alaska research activities, perhaps the outcomes would have been much more productive and beneficial, and less contentious.

The Tuskegee syphilis study, along with the studies described in this section, are examples of instances where scientists have exploited historically oppressed groups presumably to advance an understanding of the human condition (Ibrahim & Cameron, 2005). The outcomes of the three studies and many others should serve as a warning to those who would abuse participants and deny them their rights; that does not appear to be the case.

Increasing Complaints About Scientific Misconduct

The three examples of research improprieties are part of a growing and alarming list of instances and examples of scientific misconduct. According to Langlais (2006), the U.S. Office of Scientific Integrity reported that the "allegations of misconduct by scientific researchers hit an all-time high in 2004" (p. B11) and that there is reason to believe that instances of misconduct are likely higher because researchers are unwilling to report or own up to ethical and moral transgressions. In a survey of 3,247 mid-career scientists, Martinson, Anderson, and de Vries (2005) report that "US scientists engage in a range of behaviours extending far beyond falsification, fabrication, and plagiarism" (p. 737). The range of the top 10 reported forms of misconduct extended from "falsifying or 'cooking' research data" to "changing the design, methodology or results of a study in response to pressure from a funding source" (p. 737); 15.5% of all of the respondents reported that they had engaged in the latter form of behavior. In closing out their report, Martinson et al. (2005) strongly uphold that

> It is now time for the scientific community to consider what aspects of this environment are most salient to research integrity, which aspects are most amenable to change, and what changes are likely to be the most fruitful in ensuring integrity in science. (p. 738)

What has not been factored in the allegations of research dishonesty and misconduct are the personal and psychological costs to the research participants as they strive to deal with anger, frustration, disbelief, trauma, and related hardships created by outside researchers who seemingly were more concerned about their professional welfare than they were about their participants. Although many community leaders have been forthcoming in their complaints about the conduct of certain researchers, there has been little attention to the aftereffects of the researcher's course of action. Darou, Hum, and Kurtness (1993), for example, point out that prior to 1993, there had been eight psychological studies conducted among Cree bands in northern Quebec, and all but one of the researchers had been ejected from the communities; the authors claim that the principal reason for the dismissal had to do with the researchers' lack of respect for the decisions made by local tribal leaders. Do the troublesome experiences continue to affect community members in harmful and depressing ways? What are the personal costs for those who continue to cope and deal with their objectionable memories and experiences, and the influences they have on their daily lives? What effect will the negative and objectionable experiences have on future generations as the stories are passed on from one

generation to another? What is the likelihood that future outside researchers will gain entry to those communities that have been negatively affected by previous research endeavors? No doubt there are other questions that flow from the sentiments and experiences of participants to whom harm was done. Some attention must be given to the fallout from negative and untoward research experiences and the likely enduring effect they have had on participants.

Consider the impact that the Tuskegee syphilis experiment had on the 400 or so participants and their descendants. No one has extensively documented the opinions and experiences of the original participants in large part because many of them passed away before the study was terminated in 1972. Indeed, considerable scholarly research and commentary have been written about the experiment representing numerous academic disciplines; a scan of the literature on the experiment in the PsycINFO electronic database, for example, generates more than 140 citations; also, a search through the Google Scholar Internet electronic database yielded 3,510 article citations.

There is evidence that the troublesome effects of the experiment linger on in thoughts and memories of the descendants. Writing in the *New York Times,* Yoon (1997) claims that

> The pain of Tuskegee is still very real even among grandchildren of the study participants, some of whom had not even been born when the study was officially ended after its existence was widely reported in the press in 1972. (p. 1)

Yoon interviewed several descendants of some of the participants in the Tuskegee syphilis experiment, and this is what they told her:

"I'm angry about it, very, very angry about it," said Carmen Head, whose grandfather, Freddie Lee Tyson, participated in the study. "It's a painful issue in my family."

"It was something to be ashamed of, so it wasn't talked about," said Mrs. Lillie Head, whose father was one of the participants. She said that, "We were really very disturbed after we found out my father was a part of it."

"You get treated like lepers," said Albert Julkes, whose father was a participant. "People think it's the scourge of the earth to have it in your family." He goes on to say, "It was one of the worse atrocities ever reaped on people by the Government. You don't treat dogs that way" (Toon, 1997, p. 1).

To begin the conversation, attention should be given to assisting communities and those harmed by the research endeavors and outcomes; the conversation could examine ways to facilitate community healing from a *principled cultural sensitivity* approach where an emphasis is placed on respect for those whom research and interventions are intended and that would prohibit interventions that violate cultural norms (Trickett, Kelly, & Vincent, 1985; Trimble & Fisher, 2006). Moreover, the culturally resonant approach emphasizes the importance of culture as a historical and contemporary aspect of the framework within which individuals appraise their situation and their options.

According to Casillas (2006), community healing involves three basic goals. First, identify whether the community has been harmed by a research project or has unanswered questions at the conclusion of a research project (i.e., Where is all the information going? Who is really benefiting? Where are the solutions? Why are there so many research projects in tribal communities?). The approach may be difficult for some researchers to take on, especially those who are conducting or who have conducted research studies in ethnocultural communities. Some may find it difficult to accept that their work has caused harm, because often there is a detachment between the researcher and the research participants. Specifically, principal investigators who conduct their research from afar often do not take the extra time needed in developing strong relationships with the community members. In many instances, outside researchers rely on local project staff to establish and sustain the relationships and partnerships. If the relationship between the researcher and community members sours, then local research assistants often bear the brunt of the community criticisms.

The second goal is helping people to acknowledge the pain versus denying that any harm has occurred. As the awareness grows about the deeper levels of harm that have been done or are still currently being done and experienced, acknowledging the people's anger at an individual level as well as at a societal level is crucial.

The third goal is providing a process to learn from what has happened and to set aside the pain and bitterness to improve the circumstances. Once the recognition and acknowledgment of what has happened and what is happening to people before, during, and after a research project has been conducted in their community, there may be more anger and frustration.

CULTURALLY RESONANT PERSPECTIVES AND THE AVOIDANCE OF RESEARCH RISKS

About 40 years ago, several federal government agencies within the National Institutes of Health initiated a vigorous research agenda that focused on the health and well-being of specific ethnocultural groups. Research projects that emerged from the agenda aimed to describe, understand, and remedy the disproportionate impact of health and well-being on the groups. Along with the scientific, social, and personal benefits that can be obtained from these laudable initiatives come risks of group stigmatization and exploitation rooted in the centuries-old legacy of political oppression and scientific exploitation of racial and ethnic minority groups in North America (Caplan et al., 1992; Darou et al., 1993; Foulks, 1989; Harris et al., 1996; Jones, 1993; Laosa, 1984; Norton & Manson, 1996; Trimble, 1989). The stakes are especially high for children and youth from underserved populations who require culturally authorized health services, but who are also most vulnerable to harm that can arise when ethical procedures do not adequately protect their rights and welfare (Fisher, Hoagwood et al., 2002).

To engage in any form of research, investigators are obligated to follow the ethical principles and codes of their respective profession; ignorance of the codes of conduct are inexcusable, although as incredible as it may seem, a few researchers have claimed they were uninformed and not aware of the guidelines, particularly those that pertain to ethnocultural groups. In the past, professional ethical codes of conduct did not specify principles that apply to research with ethnocultural groups. Anthropologists were the first professional organization to set standards for ethical conduct that provided a strict set of principles. In the prologue to their 1967 ethics statement, the American Anthropological Association states,

The situations which jeopardize research differ from year to year, from country to country, and from discipline to discipline. We are concerned here with problems that affect all the fields of anthropology and which, in varying ways, are shared by the social and behavioral sciences. (American Anthropological Association, 1948)

Unfortunately, the carefully worded prologue, together with a set of well-framed principles, were overlooked, ignored, or considered inconsequential by many field-based researchers. If they had been acknowledged, internalized, and adhered to, perhaps the critical and heated contentions of ethnocultural communities might not be at the intensity they are today.

Other professional organizations also took on the responsibility of crafting ethnocultural specific guidelines and principles. Guidelines published by the American Psychological Association (APA), such as *Ethical Principles of Psychologists and Code of Conduct* (APA, 2002a) and the APA *Guidelines for Providers of Psychological Services to Ethnic, Linguistic, and Culturally Diverse Populations* (APA, 1990), mandate psychologists to conduct research ethically and competently. APA has also published the *Guidelines for Research in Ethnic Minority Communities* (Council of National Psychological Associations for the Advancement of Ethnic Minority Interests, 2000), which emphasizes the importance of involving community members in the design, conduct, analysis, and interpretation of all research. According to the APA's Guidelines on Multicultural Education, Training, Research, Practice, and Organizational Change for Psychologists, Guideline #4 states that "Culturally sensitive psychological researchers are encouraged to recognize the importance of conducting culture-centered and ethical psychological research among persons from ethnic, linguistic, and racial minority backgrounds" (American Psychological Association, 2002b, p. 40).

In 2002, the International Union of Psychological Science (IUPsyS) convened an ad hoc committee to identify, develop, and submit a universal declaration of ethical principles. The Ad Hoc Joint Committee representing five continents was directed to articulate principles and values that would provide a common moral framework for psychologists worldwide that could be

used as a moral justification and guide for developing different standards appropriate for different cultural groups and their settings. In 2005, in collaboration with the IUPsyS, the International Association of Applied Psychology and the International Association for Cross-Cultural Psychology developed a draft version in which the Ad Hoc Committee acknowledges an extremely important principle:

Respect for the dignity of persons and peoples is expressed in different ways in different communities and cultures. It is important to acknowledge and respect such differences. On the other hand, it also is important that all communities and cultures adhere to moral values that respect and protect their members both as individual persons and as collective peoples. (Gauthier, 2008, p. 6)

In Principle 1, the authors maintain that

The continuity of peoples and cultures over time connects the peoples of today with the peoples of past generations and the need to nurture future generations. As such, respect for the dignity of persons includes moral consideration of and respect for the dignity of peoples. (Gauthier, 2008, p. 6)

The international professional psychological associations' emphasis on morality is in keeping with the fundamental ethical principle that one "should do no harm" when it comes to the conduct of research. As indicated earlier in this chapter, framing ethical principles and guidelines to include "moral considerations" is an indispensable condition for guiding research ventures. Successful ventures must follow a set of procedures that is aligned with moral principles and ethical guidelines.

Principled Cultural Sensitivity

The ethical conduct of research begins with the principle that one's investigations and explorations are guided by an authentic respect for the unique cultural lifeways and thoughtways of ethnocultural communities. Part of the respect means that researchers must embrace the value that ventures are collaborations and partnerships. Trickett and Espino (2004) summarized the emerging literature on community-based partnerships and commented that

> It is time to place the collaboration concept in the center of inquiry and work out its importance for community research and intervention. Although some would see it as merely a tool or strategy to getting the "real" work of behavioral science done, our strong preference is to view the research relationship in community research and intervention as a critical part of the "real" work itself. (p. 62)

Without establishing and working through community partnerships, research ventures are doomed to failure at every stage of the process. The perspective and orientation also add new research challenges. Some of those challenges are best captured in the advice offered by Goodenough (1980) when he affirmed that

> Field workers have to honor the ethical principles of the host community in which they work as well as those of their home communities. They have to be honest about their research objectives and their sponsorship. They must not deceive the local people regarding the intent or intended uses of their research. They must consider the impact of the conduct of the research on the people under study and do all they can to insure against what the people will regard as significant negative effects. (p. 49)

The concept of *principled cultural sensitivity* was introduced to the field of community psychology as a core component of the Ecology of Lives approach to field-based research collaboration by Trickett et al. (1985) and Trickett and Birman (1989). As indicated earlier in this chapter, it is based on respect for whom research and interventions are intended and which would prohibit interventions that violate cultural norms. The principal goal of Ecology of Lives research and intervention is community development in which the project is constructed in such a way that it becomes a resource to the community. Unless one cares and is knowledgeable about how lives are led at the community level, such a goal would be difficult, if not impossible, to achieve. Furthermore, the approach emphasizes the importance of culture as a historical and contemporary aspect of the framework within which individuals appraise their situation and their

options. The research perspective emphasizes the community context as the stage within which individual behavior occurs.

Tribal Participatory Research Model

In the past few decades, there has been considerable interest in the role and value of community-based participatory research (CBPR) for use with ethnocultural populations. The approach and perspective has in common the principle that research equitably involves community members, organization representatives, and researchers in all phases of the research (Burhansstipanov, Christopher, & Schumacher, 2005; Fisher & Ball, 2003; Mohatt & Thomas, 2006). The Tribal Participatory Research (TPR) model developed and encouraged by Fisher and Ball (2003) is a model that endorses and makes use of fundamental CBPR principles. (Brydon-Miller, 1997; Fisher & Ball, 2003; McTaggart, 1991; Whyte, Greenwood, & Lazes, 1991).

TPR emphasizes participatory action research, or collaborative community research, as an ongoing process of interaction between the researcher and research participants. The research team and participants exchange ideas and thoughts about the research process and then modify them as they conduct the research (Brydon-Miller, 1997; McTaggart, 1991; Whyte et al., 1991). Scientific principles are the basis of the research approach; however, great care and attention are given to the values and beliefs of the community members in formulating and conducting the inquiry (Fisher & Ball, 2002, 2003; Greenwood & Levin, 1998; Greenwood, Whyte, & Harkavy, 1993; Park, 1999).

The TPR model is sensitive to tribal community needs and agendas where community representatives set the research agenda and select and prioritize the research topics (Fisher & Ball, 2002, 2003, 2005). Fisher and Ball (2002, 2003, 2005) recommend four mechanisms for TPR for use in the American Indian and Alaska Native communities, but elements of their mechanisms can be generalized for use with other ethnocultural populations. The mechanisms are as follows: (a) community oversight that consists of tribal council resolutions, tribal oversight committees, and the development and implementation of a tribal research code; (b) use of local community members as facilitators involving research staff and oversight committees; (c) training and employment of community members as project staff; and (d) the development of culturally specific intervention strategies and assessment methods. TPR emphasizes the use of culturally grounded intervention strategies that may be in contrast to evidence-based approaches. To accommodate balance for the use of evidence approaches, community focus groups can be convened to provide a reaction about the cultural appropriateness of an intervention (Fisher & Ball, 2003).

Use of a TPR protocol is not without its complications and shortcomings. Letiecq and Bailey (2004) identified five basic challenges to the evaluation research approach as "majority-culture researchers": (a) constant evaluation of power differentials and evaluation research approaches, (b) training of local project staff in the meaning and purpose of the research and evaluation procedures, (c) provision of resources that cover the basic research needs of the local project staff and avoid logistical constraints, (d) review of research measures and assessment tools with community members to assure their cultural fit and resonance with local lifeways and thoughtways, and (e) use of researchers and assistants from ethnic backgrounds similar to the host community that can introduce problems associated with confidentiality and unfamiliarity with local traditions and customs.

Doing Good Well

An emphasis on researchers' virtues and moral principles is closely aligned with the Goodness-of-Fit model developed and encouraged by Fisher and Ragsdale (2006). Along with several important considerations, the model and its prescriptions can create a circumstance where one can *do good well*. Doing good well means that the researcher and the team are virtuous and moral people and embody values and beliefs that community members and research participants find acceptable.

Based in part on Immanuel Kant's categorical imperative tenet that one's highest moral obligation is to do the right thing—to act in a good way that benefits the community in ways that promote the greatest good for citizens—Fisher and Ragsdale's approach emphasizes that harm can be minimized by aligning ethical principles to participant characteristics, the research context, and factors that can contribute to susceptibilities to personal and physical damage. Attention therefore should be given to the circumstances that potentially place participants at risk for harm in the components and features of the research method, implementation, and dissemination (Fisher, 2002; Fisher & Ragsdale, 2006). The Goodness-of-Fit model views scientists and participants as moral agents joined in a partnership where the researcher and the team are virtuous people who embody values and beliefs that the community finds acceptable. To establish and sustain a collaborative partnership, researchers should ask themselves the following three questions: What are the special life circumstances that render participants more susceptible to research risk? Which aspects of the design, implementation, or dissemination may create or exacerbate research risk? How can research and ethical procedures be aligned to participant characteristics to reduce vulnerability? By reflecting on these questions, Fisher and Ragsdale emphasize that the model can advance multicultural ethics further by posing the following value-based questions: Do the values embodied in current codes and regulations reflect the moral visions of different ethnocultural groups selected for a study? Do scientists and participants have different conceptions of research risks and benefits? In essence, Fisher and Ragsdale (2006) maintain that the purpose of the Goodness-of-Fit model and approach "is to provide models of ethical procedures reflective of specific participant group perspectives that can challenge current ways of thinking about ethics-in-science issues and point to new directions of moral awareness and scientific inquiry for multicultural research" (p. 21). Their position is closely tied to the observation offered by Meara and Day (2003) that in order "to be a virtuous researcher one must be self-regulatory and self-reflective and at the same time abide by 'normative' professional ethics" (p. 459).

ETHICAL PRINCIPLES AND COUNSELING PSYCHOLOGY RESEARCH THEMES

The conduct of psychological counseling and clinical studies with any population is riddled with potentially serious complications. The complications derive largely from the conduct of studies on people who may be experiencing complicated emotional and behavioral problems such as depression, historical trauma, abuse of psychoactive substances, physical abuse and molestation, as well as the effects of life-threatening diseases and economic hardships. Research on these and related topics present situation-specific hurdles and challenges for the counselor and clinician when the studies occur in natural group or field settings; in essence, the researcher gives up control of a rigid research design and thus runs the risk of external sources influencing the validity of the study. Moreover, in the course of selecting respondents, the researcher runs the risk of publicly identifying people at risk for emotional and behavioral problems that in turn can lead to public shame, humiliation, embarrassment, and ridicule.

The conduct of clinical and counseling research with ethnocultural populations adds to the problems and challenges researchers may encounter. Mio and Iwamasa (1993), for example, focus their findings and observations on the influence and impact of "white researchers" who investigate and study ethnic minority populations; they raise troubling questions about the "community outsider problem" and the likelihood that white researchers may not be successful. In effect, the cultural identities of the researcher and interviewees, claim Song and Parker (1995), should be closely evaluated and explored in research settings. Moreover, because most field-based, community-centered research draws on the use of qualitative procedures, the techniques and approaches may be viewed as intrusive, threatening, and invasive; they can, and often do, lead to unique ethical challenges and problems (Baeaernhielm & Ekblad, 2002). Indeed, as described earlier in this chapter, the mistreatment of ethnocultural groups by researchers has led to skepticism, mistrust, anger, wariness, frustration, and a multitude of similar concerns and expression. Ethical standards of conduct and principled moral perspectives can lead to unique ethical challenges that may require philosophical changes to render principles more responsive to the lifeways and thoughtways of ethnocultural communities (Alvidrez & Areán, 2002; Casas & Thompson, 1991). In turn, counseling and clinical psychology graduate programs must provide opportunities for students to critically examine research-related ethical principles in general and those specific for the needs of ethnocultural populations and how they influence service delivery and intervention and prevention research approaches (Fisher, Hoagwood et al., 2002; Harris, 2002; Ibrahim & Arredondo, 1986).

Considerable attention is being devoted to the ethnocultural ethical principles associated with specific mental health topics such as family violence, suicidal individuals, depression, psychoactive substance abuse, and immigrant health care (Fisher, Pearson, Kim, & Reynolds, 2002; Fontes, 1998; Marshall, Koenig, Grifhorst, & van Ewijk, 1998; Mohatt & Thomas, 2006; Trimble, Scharrón-del Río, & Bernal, in press). Fisher, Pearson et al. (2002) argue that clinical intervention and prevention research with suicidal individuals and their kin and friendship networks face complex ethical challenges that go beyond those for basic clinical research. They add that researchers should expect to deal with a respondent's capacity to comprehend confidentiality and informed consent, respondent safety, the validity and reliability of assessment, and community collaboration. Researchers must be aware of the fact that most ethnocultural communities are closely intact enclaves consisting of people who are related to one another through an elaborate and often complex extended family or clan network. In these settings, everyone knows everyone else and what they're all about on a daily basis—there are no secrets. Research with individuals who are different from community norms cannot occur without others knowing about it; protection of respondents' anonymity may be extremely difficult, if not impossible, in these settings, yet the research can occur as long as it conforms with the way the community deals with and acknowledges "people differences."

SUMMARY AND CONCLUSIONS

Part of the principles and codes carefully and thoughtfully described in the 1946 ethical standard-setting Nuremberg Code emphasizes the fundamental principle that research in every sense of the word should meaningfully benefit society (Nuremberg Code, 1949); the Code also overwhelmingly emphasizes the value of respect for all research participants. The core theme of this chapter extends the Nuremberg Code's emphasis on respect to include personal moral and value orientations that influence the nature of the relationship that researchers should establish and maintain with their host communities. As pointed out earlier in the chapter, moral assessment begins with self-reflection and the possibility that we do have control over our judgments and standards. Researchers must appraise community lexicons for morals and values to be certain they understand the similarities and differences that align or separate them for local customs and traditions.

A few rogue researchers took self-serving approaches to their research inquiries that eventually created strained and contentious relationships with their host communities. Ethnocultural communities no longer tolerate the "interloper" whose values and research goals are not resonant with local values, customs, beliefs, traditions, and needs. For research to resonate effectively with local lifeways and thoughtways, investigators are encouraged to embrace a principled cultural sensitivity approach that emphasizes prudence, integrity, respectfulness, benevolence, reverence, and community participation and involvement in the research venture. Additionally, research ventures can be proactive if they adopt the perspective of Doing Good Well that embraces the Goodness-of-Fit model and approach that provide models of ethical procedures reflective of specific participant group perspectives. Community-based participatory research, like all research, is conducted with the firm conviction that one should do no harm under any circumstances. The conviction is fundamental to proactive and conscientious value and moral persuasions. And, as Ward Goodenough (1980) insists, they

follow from the basic principle that investigators owe all of the people with whom they deal, both as scientists and as human beings, the kind of respect for them and their humanity that they would like others to show them. (p. 48)

REFERENCES

Alvidrez, J., & Areán, P. A. (2002). Ethical considerations in conducting clinical trials. *Ethics & Behavior, 12,* 103–116.

American Anthropological Association. (1948). *Statement of ethics: Principles of professional responsibility.* Retrieved November 12, 2008, from http://www.aaanet.org/stmts/ethstmnt.htm.

American Psychological Association. (1990). *Guidelines for providers of psychological services to ethnic, linguistic, and culturally diverse populations.* Washington, DC: Author.

American Psychological Association. (2002a). Ethical principles of psychologists and code of conduct. *American Psychologist, 57,* 1060–1073.

American Psychological Association. (2002b). *Guidelines on multicultural education, training, research, practice, and organizational change for psychologists.* Washington, DC: Author.

Baeaernhielm, S., & Ekblad, S. (2002). Qualitative research, culture and ethics: A case discussion. *Transcultural Psychiatry, 39,* 469–483.

Brydon-Miller, M. (1997). Participatory action research: Psychology and social change. *Journal of Social Issues, 53*(4), 657–666.

Burhansstipanov, L., Christopher, S., & Schumacher, A. (2005, Nov.). Lessons learned from community-based participatory research in Indian Country. *Cancer Control: Cancer, Culture, and Literacy Supplement,* pp. 70–76.

Caplan, A., Edgar, H., & King, P. (1992). Twenty years later: The legacy of the Tuskegee Syphilis Study. *Hastings Center Report, 22,* 29–38.

Casas, J. M., & Thompson, C. E. (1991). Ethical principles and standards: A racial-ethnic minority research perspective. *Counseling and Values, 35,* 186–195.

Casillas, D. M. (2006). *Evolving research approaches in tribal communities: A community empowerment training.* Unpublished master's thesis, University of South Dakota, Vermillion.

Council of National Psychological Associations for the Advancement of Ethnic Minority Interests. (2000). *The guidelines for research in ethnic minority communities.* Washington, DC: American Psychological Association.

Darou, W. G., Hum, A., & Kurtness, J. (1993). An investigation of the impact of psychosocial research on a Native population. *Professional Psychology: Research & Practice, 24,* 325–329.

Fisher, C. B. (2002). Participant consultation: Ethical insights into parental permission and confidentiality procedures for policy relevant research with youth. In R. M. Lerner, F. Jacobs, & D. Wertlieb (Eds.), *Handbook of applied developmental science* (Vol. 4, pp. 371–396). Thousand Oaks, CA: Sage.

Fisher, C. B., Hoagwood, K., Boyce, C., Duster, T., Frank, D. A., Grisso, T., Levine, R. J., Macklin, R., Spencer, M. B., Takanishi, R., Trimble, J. E., & Zayas, L. H. (2002). Research ethics for mental health science involving ethnic minority children and youths. *American Psychologist, 57*, 1024–1040.

Fisher, C. B., Pearson, J. L., Kim, S., & Reynolds, C. F. (2002). Ethical issues in including suicidal individuals in clinical research. *Ethics & Human Research, 24*, 9–14.

Fisher, C. B., & Ragsdale, K. (2006). A Goodness-of-Fit ethic for multicultural research. In J. E. Trimble & C. B. Fisher (Eds.), *Handbook of ethical and responsible research with ethnocultural populations and communities* (pp. 3–25). Thousand Oaks, CA: Sage.

Fisher, P. A., & Ball, T. J. (2002). The Indian Family Wellness Project: An application of the tribal participatory research model. *Prevention Science, 3*, 235–240.

Fisher, P. A., & Ball, T. J. (2003). Tribal participatory research: Mechanisms of a collaborative model. *American Journal of Community Psychology, 32*(3/4), 207–216.

Fisher, P. A., & Ball, T. J. (2005). Balancing empiricism and local cultural knowledge in the design of prevention research. *Journal of Urban Health, 82*(Suppl. 3), III44–III55.

Fontes, L. A. (1998). Ethics in family violence research: Cross-cultural issues. *Family Relations: Interdisciplinary Journal of Applied Family Studies, 47*, 53–56.

Foulks, E. F. (1989). Misalliances in the Barrow Alcohol Study. *American Indian and Alaskan Native Mental Health Research, 2*, 2–17.

Gauthier, J. (Chair). (2008). *The universal declaration of ethical principles for psychologists: Third draft.* Retrieved from: http://www.am.org/iupsys/ethics/2008-universal-decl-report.pdf

Geertz, C. (2001). *Available light: Anthropological reflections on philosophical topics.* Princeton, NJ: Princeton University Press.

Goodenough, W. H. (1980). Ethnographic field techniques. In H. C. Triandis & J. W. Berry (Eds.), *Handbook of cross-cultural psychology: Methodology* (Vol. 2, pp. 39–55). Boston: Allyn & Bacon.

Greenwood, D. J., & Levin, M. (1998). *Introduction to action research.* Thousand Oaks, CA: Sage.

Greenwood, D. J., Whyte, W. F., & Harkavy, I. (1993). Participatory action research as a process and as a goal. *Human Relations, 46*, 175–192.

Haidt, J., & Graham, J. (2007). When morality opposes justice: Conservatives have moral intuitions that liberals may not recognize. *Social Justice Research, 20*, 98–116.

Harris, J. L. (2002). Ethical decision making with individuals of diverse ethnic, cultural, and linguistic backgrounds. In S. S. Bush & M. L. Drexler (Eds.), *Ethical issues in clinical neuropsychology* (pp. 223–241). Lisse, Netherlands: Swets & Zeitlinger.

Harris, Y., Gorelick, P. B., Samuels, P., & Bempong, I. (1996). Why African Americans may not be participating in clinical trials. *Journal of the National Medical Association, 88*, 630–634.

Hendricks, L. (2004, February 28). Havasupai file $25M suit vs. ASU. *Arizona Daily Sun*, p. A1.

Ibrahim, F. A. (1996). A multicultural perspective on principle and virtue ethics. *Counseling Psychologist, 24*, 78–85.

Ibrahim, F. A., & Arredondo, P. M. (1986). Ethical standards for cross-cultural counseling: Counselor preparation, practice, assessment, and research. *Journal of Counseling and Development, 64*, 349–351.

Ibrahim, F. A., & Cameron, S. C. (2005). Racial-cultural ethical issues in research. In R. T. Carter (Ed.), *Racial-cultural psychology and counseling: Theory and research* (Vol. 1, pp. 391–414). New York: Wiley

Israel, M., & Hay, I. (2006). *Research ethics for social scientists: Between ethical conduct and regulatory compliance.* Thousand Oaks, CA: Sage.

Jones, J. H. (1993). *Bad blood: The Tuskegee syphilis experiment* (Rev. ed.). New York: Free Press.

Langlais, P. (2006, January 13). Ethics for the next generation. *Chronicle of Higher Education, 52*(16), B11–B11.

Laosa, L. M. (1984). Social policies toward children of diverse ethnic, racial, and language groups in the United States. In H. W. Stevenson & A. E. Siegel (Eds.), *Child development research and social policy* (Vol. 1, pp. 1–109). Chicago: University of Chicago Press.

Letiecq, B. L., & Bailey, S. J. (2004). Evaluating from outside the circle: Conducting cross-cultural evaluation research on a Native American reservation. *Evaluation Review, 28*, 342–357.

Marshall, P. A., Koenig, B. A., Grifhorst, P., & van Ewijk, M. (1998). Ethical issues in immigrant health care and clinical research. In S. Loue (Ed.), *Handbook of immigrant health* (pp. 203–226). New York: Plenum.

Martinson, B. C., Anderson, M. S., & de Vries, R. (2005). Scientists behaving badly. *Nature, 435*, 737–738.

McTaggart, R. (1991). Principles for participatory action research. *Adult Education Quarterly, 41*, 168–187.

Meara, N. M., & Day, J. D. (2003). Possibilities and challenges for academic psychology: Uncertain science, interpretative conversation, and virtuous community. *American Behavioral Scientist, 47*(4), 459–478.

Mio, J. S., & Iwamasa, G. (1993). To do, or not to do: That is the question for white cross-cultural researchers. *Counseling Psychologist, 21*, 197–212.

Mohatt, G. V., & Thomas, L. R. (2006). "I wonder, why would you do it that way?" Ethical dilemmas in doing participatory research with Alaska Native communities.

In J. E. Trimble & C. B. Fisher (Eds.), *Handbook of ethical and responsible research with ethnocultural populations and communities* (pp. 93–115). Thousand Oaks, CA: Sage.

Norton, I. M., & Manson, S. M. (1996). Research in American Indian and Alaska Native communities: Navigating the cultural universe of values and process. *Journal of Consulting and Clinical Psychology, 64*, 856–860.

Nuremberg Code. (1949). *Trials of war criminals before the Nuremberg military tribunals under Control Council Law No. 10* (Vol. 2, pp. 181–182). Washington, DC: Government Printing Office.

Park, P. (1999). People, knowledge, and change in participatory research. *Management Learning, 30*, 141–157.

Paul, R., & Elder, L. (2006). *Understanding the foundations of ethical reasoning.* Dillon Beach, CA: The Foundation for Critical Thinking.

Smith, A. M. (2005). Responsibility for attitudes: Activity and passivity in mental life. *Ethics, 155*, 236–271.

Song, M., & Parker, D. (1995). Commonality, difference and the dynamics of disclosure in in-depth interviewing. *Sociology, 29*, 241–256.

Trickett, E. J., & Birman, D. (1989). Taking ecology seriously: A community development approach to individually-based interventions. In L. Bond & B. Compas (Eds.), *Primary prevention and promotion in the schools* (pp. 361–390). Newbury Park, CA: Sage.

Trickett, E. J., & Espino, S. L. (2004). Collaboration and social inquiry: Multiple meanings of a construct and its role in creating useful and valid knowledge. *American Journal of Community Psychology, 34*, 1–71.

Trickett, E. J., Kelly, J. G., & Vincent, T. A. (1985). The spirit of ecological inquiry in community research. In E. Susskind & D. Klein (Eds.), *Community research: Methods, paradigms, and applications.* New York: Praeger.

Trimble, J. E. (1989). Malfeasance and foibles of the research sponsor. *American Indian and Alaska Native Mental Health Research, 2*, 58–63.

Trimble, J. E., & Fisher, C. B. (Eds.). (2006). *Handbook of ethical and responsible research with ethnocultural populations and communities.* Thousand Oaks, CA: Sage.

Trimble, J. E., & Mohatt, G. V. (2006). Coda: The virtuous and responsible researcher in another culture. In J. E. Trimble & C. B. Fisher (Eds.), *Handbook of ethical and responsible research with ethnocultural populations and communities* (pp. 325–334). Thousand Oaks, CA: Sage.

Trimble, J. E., Scharrón-del Río, M., & Bernal, G. (in press). The itinerant researcher: Ethical and methodological issues in conducting cross-cultural mental health research. In D. C. Jack & A. Ali (Eds.), *Cultural perspectives on women's depression: Self-silencing, psychological distress and recovery.* New York: Oxford.

Vasquez, M. L. (1996). Will virtue ethics improve ethical conduct in multicultural settings? *Counseling Psychologist, 24*, 98–104.

Whyte, W. F., Greenwood, D. J., & Lazes, P. (1991). Participatory action research: Through practice to science in social research. In W. F. Whyte (Ed.), *Participatory action research* (pp. 19–55). Newbury Park, CA: Sage.

Yoon, C. K. (1997, May 12). Families emerge as silent victims of Tuskegee Syphilis Experiment. *New York Times, Late Edition (East Coast)*, p. 1.

PART III

Emerging and International Issues in Multicultural Counseling

Part III of the *Handbook* contains four chapters on emerging and international issues in multicultural counseling. In recent years, multicultural counselors have devoted increasing attention to examining the field's relationship with sister disciplines, as well as its overlap with, and distinctiveness from, broader international counseling issues. Jennifer Teramoto Pedrotti and Lisa M. Edwards open Part III (Chapter 16) with a close look at the natural link between positive psychology and multicultural counseling. Positive psychology, with its emphasis on human strengths and optimal human potential, meshes well with multicultural counseling's recent emphasis on client strength and resilience rather than client deficiencies and faults (the outdated "cultural deficiency" or "cultural deprivation" models). Drs. Teramoto Pedrotti and Edwards review the history of the positive psychology-multicultural counseling link, review recent research regarding strengths within diverse cultures, discuss strength-anchored counseling approaches, and highlight suggestions for counseling training with a culturally informed, strengths-based perspective.

Chapter 17 and 18 both focus on broader international issues vis a vis counseling psychology. Stefanía Ægisdóttir and Lawrence H. Gerstein (Chapter 17) expand the traditional U.S.-based multicultural competency set (i.e., awareness, knowledge, and skills) for relevance in international counseling work. Domestic counseling training programs have all but ignored

counseling issues for trainees/professionals working abroad, or for those in North America working with international populations. This chapter, therefore, fills a major gap in current counseling practice and training. Specifically, Drs. Ægisdóttir and Gerstein highlight the value of learning about international cultures and increasing one's motivation and knowledge in this area, and they review specific methods for international work and collaboration within a social justice framework.

In Chapter 18, multicultural counseling pioneer J. Manuel Casas (see Casas, 2001) and his co-authors, Yong S. Park and Brian Cho, review "two revolutionary movements" in the counseling field: the multicultural movement and the international movement. Interestingly, over the past half-century, these two movements have developed as parallel forces, rarely intersecting. These authors convincingly propose that the profession is at a critical juncture with regard to the national versus international focus, and now is the time not for polarization, but for a coming together of the two movements for the common good of all who are involved.

The final chapter of Part III (Chapter 19), co-authored by Ellen Short, Lisa Suzuki, Maria Prendes-Lintel, Gina Prendes-Lintel Furr, Soumya Madabhushi, and Geraldine Mapel, focuses on counseling immigrants and refugees. The past two decades have witnessed exponential growth of immigrants and refugees from all over the world, and it is fair to say that their mental health needs are underserved and that counseling training programs are deficient in adequately preparing their students for the challenges of serving this very diverse group. This landmark chapter highlights critical issues facing immigrants and refugees and highlights treatment issues and strategies. The chapter ends with a poignant and detailed case study that effectively highlights treatment issues and counseling focus.

REFERENCE

Casas, J. M. (2001). I didn't know where I was going but I got here anyway: My life's journey through the labyrinth of solitude. In J. G. Ponterotto, J. M. Casas, L. A. Suzuki, & C. M. Alexander (Eds.), *Handbook of multicultural counseling* (2nd ed., pp. 78–95). Thousand Oaks, CA: Sage.

16

The Intersection of Positive Psychology and Multiculturalism in Counseling

JENNIFER TERAMOTO PEDROTTI AND LISA M. EDWARDS

Within the field of psychology, theorists, researchers, and practitioners have worked to understand and promote healthy functioning for years. From William James in the early 1900s, to Donald Super within counseling psychology, to humanistic psychologists in the 1960s such as Maslow and Rogers, many have discussed mental health and well-being (Day & Rottinghaus, 2003; Rich, 2001). The term *positive psychology* first appeared in Abraham Maslow's (1954) final chapter of *Motivation and Personality.* In this book, he used the term to describe a fully functioning person as well as the field of humanistic psychology as both poised to foster optimal human development (Lopez & Edwards, 2008).

Strengths-based perspectives also have been suggested by social workers for many years (Saleeby, 1992), and specific approaches such as solution-focused therapy have been developed that locate the process of change in the collaboration of client and therapist toward identifying strengths, solutions, and exceptions to distress (De Jong & Miller, 1995; de Shazer, 1985). The term *positive*

psychology resurfaced in 1998 when Martin Seligman, then president-elect of the American Psychological Association, described as his presidential theme a new initiative: prevention and the scientific pursuit of optimal human functioning (Seligman & Csikszentmihalyi, 2000). Soon after, the *American Psychologist* published a special issue devoted to positive psychology, which highlighted research about strengths and mental health and provided a framework for the scientific study of strengths (Seligman & Csikszentmihalyi, 2000). The general theme noted by these editors was that societal changes had caused professionals to work from a disease-based model that focused primarily on pathology, illness, and weakness. This focus on the negative needed to be augmented by a positive psychology initiative that would allow psychologists to study and apply research to prevention and the use of strengths and talents to promote well-being.

The lack of attention given to human strengths noted by Seligman and others (Seligman & Csikszentmihalyi, 2000) is paralleled by a historical neglect of attention given to issues of culture and diversity. People of color,

165

as well as other minorities, often have been patholo-gized as a result of their cultural background. Historically, individuals who did not assimilate to the "norm" (i.e., White majority culture) were thought to be "culturally deficient" (Sue & Sue, 2003, p. 55). When this view-point was challenged and research began to broaden to include people of nonmajority background, people of color were still often compared to a White standard, set-ting up what others have called *deficit models* (Sue & Sue, 2003). As such, people of color have been discussed in the field of psychology in relation to their weaknesses much more often than their strengths. Therefore, these minority groups are exposed to "double jeopardy"—branded as pathological in comparison to the majority group, and within a system that only acknowledges weakness and leaves no room for a balanced description of behavior (Lopez et al., 2006). Thus, in talking about multicultural and cross-cultural populations today, it becomes imperative to balance out these early ideas by discussing people of color in a more well-rounded way.

Multiculturalism has gained prominence in the field as a critical force as well (Fowers & Davidov, 2006; Pedersen, 1991). Within counseling psychology, the unifying theme of attention on the environment and context (Gelso & Fretz, 2001) has naturally empha-sized the importance of diverse approaches to theory, research, and practice. Counseling psychologists have emerged as leaders in psychology for their attention to multicultural issues (Gelso & Fretz, 2001; Lopez, Edwards, Magyar-Moe, Pedrotti, & Ryder, 2003), and many have provided useful perspectives on optimal human functioning in people of color (e.g., Boyd-Franklin, 1989; Hill, 1972; Myers, 1988; Sue & Constantine, 2003; White, 1984) and multiculturalism as a virtue (Fowers & Davidov, 2006). The intersection of strengths and multiculturalism is both logical and necessary. Although past research (particularly within the field of counseling psychology) exists on the inter-section of strengths and culture, research from within the scientific framework in contemporary discussions of positive psychology has been slow to develop (Lopez, Prosser et al., 2002).

In this chapter, we review salient issues that emerge in the intersection of multiculturalism and positive psy-chology, including definitional and methodological complexities. We provide examples of research about strengths among cultures, as well as therapeutic approaches that incorporate strengths and context. Finally, we provide suggestions for training and teaching about culture from a strengths perspective to encourage professionals to incorporate positive psy-chology and multiculturalism in all curricula.

WHAT IS A STRENGTH? CULTURE-FREE VERSUS CULTURALLY EMBEDDED VIEWPOINTS

Scholars have disagreed as to the importance or weight that cultural differences should be given in assessing, measuring, and making meaning of strengths (Pedrotti, 2007a). Some have the view that strengths and the empirical investigation of their nature can "transcend particular cultures and politics and approach univer-sality" (Seligman & Csikszentmihalyi, 2000, p. 5), whereas others argue that strengths must always be considered within a cultural context and framework (Sue & Constantine, 2003).

The scholars on the culture-free side of the debate argue that as psychologists, we are able to be objective in our measuring of various characteristics through the use of validated assessments and responsible research methods, and that this allows us to look at our research and practice separately from our own value systems (Snyder & Lopez, 2007). For example, Peterson and Seligman (2004) have conducted extensive research across many cultural groups and state that they have found 24 personal virtues that are present in all cul-tures. These researchers maintain that these virtues have positive designations in all cultures. Others have posited similar hypotheses, such as Myers's (1993) contention that all people want to be happy in their lives.

Other scholars, however, take the culturally embed-ded viewpoint that no psychological characteristic may be separated from culture and thus contextualization must occur when discussing strengths in research and practice (Snyder & Lopez, 2007). The American Psychological Association (2003) supports this per-spective in that they have provided specific guidelines and recommendations for developing multicultural competence, and for being culture-sensitive in research and practice in all areas of the field. Those on this side of the debate feel that it is impossible to completely divorce ourselves from our values, and that as such, our values will always influence decisions made in research and practice (Snyder & Lopez, 2007). Researchers state that our values affect us in making decisions regarding what topics to research, what measures we use, the development of our hypotheses, and then interpretations of our data (Sue & Constantine, 2003). In this sense, we are so fully embedded within our own cultures that we cannot keep these values outside our research labs or therapy rooms (Leong & Wong, 2003; Pedrotti, 2007b).

One area that scholars from a culturally embedded perspective have focused on has been the idea that although certain traits may be viewed as beneficial across cultures, "the most positive traits and processes manifest themselves in very different ways for different purposes in different cultures" (Snyder & Lopez, 2007, p. 89). Constantine and Sue (2006) have conducted empirical research and found that goals of attaining happiness may rank far below goals for achieving transcendence through suffering in some Eastern cultures. In addition, other scholars have found that although some traits may be valued across different cultures, the expression, practice, and rituals surrounding them may be very different (Christopher, 2005; Sandage, Hill, & Vang, 2003).

Multicultural perspectives on functioning emphasize that humans cannot be considered as separate from their culture and context. As such, many authors choose to operate from a culturally embedded framework (Lopez, Edwards et al., 2002; Sue & Constantine, 2003). It seems clear that cultural environment and the salience of cultural values in individuals' lives are major influences in determining what types of behaviors and characteristics are viewed as positive, and in making distinctions between beneficial and problematic behavior overall (Christopher, 2005; Constantine & Sue, 2006; Leong & Wong, 2003; Snyder & Lopez, 2007; Sue & Constantine, 2003).

METHODOLOGICAL AND CONCEPTUAL COMPLEXITIES

Several complexities emerge when trying to investigate, understand, and apply concepts of positive functioning and strengths within diverse populations. In addition to general concerns about criteria used to determine the nature of optimal functioning, there are additional issues to consider when working in this area. Primarily, issues of cultural equivalence are inherent in the process of identifying and defining cultural strengths. Closely related, value orientations inherently affect individual and community perceptions of strengths and positive functioning.

Cultural Equivalence Issues

One reason why discussing strengths and positive constructs while attending to multiculturalism can be difficult at times is due to the fact that cultural equivalence across groups has not been established with many positive constructs (Pedrotti, Edwards, & Lopez, 2009). Strengths may have different definitions in different cultures (conceptual equivalence); may not be measured as accurately by various instruments in different cultural groups (measurement equivalence); or may not be translated appropriately to ensure linguistic equivalence, or that the same meanings of terms and descriptions exist from group to group (Mio, Barker-Hackett, & Tumambing, 2006).

For example, a construct such as hope, as defined by Snyder and colleagues (1991), has been studied to some extent in non-White samples (Chang & Banks, 2007; Edwards, Ong, & Lopez, 2007); however, it is unclear whether hope has the same definition in all of these cultures. Without knowledge of this conceptual equivalence, issues arise as it is not clear if Snyder's definition of hope is the same for all groups. In terms of thinking style, for instance, the hope construct described by Snyder places the goal process in a linear pursuit, and yet some cultures, such as Eastern cultures, may not think of their lives in this same fashion (Pedrotti, 2007a). Thus, although assessments for many positive constructs are available, as are various interventions aimed at enhancing these constructs, it is unclear whether or not they would produce the same findings and results in racially or ethnically diverse samples.

Value Orientation Differences

In addition, value differences that exist between cultural groups such as time orientation (i.e., past, past-present, or future oriented) (Kluckhohn & Strodtbeck,

1961), and independent and interdependent self-construals (Markus & Kitayama, 1991), may also have an impact on the types of constructs that have the most value in a group (Leong & Wong, 2003; Pedrotti, 2007a; Sue & Constantine, 2003). Time orientation may determine whether or not a particular construct is valued differently in different cultures. Characteristics such as optimism, hope, and self-efficacy are grounded in more future-oriented thinking, and as such, it is possible that they hold different relevance for cultural groups that are not oriented to time in this way (Pedrotti, 2007a).

Self-construal theory (Markus & Kitayama, 1991) suggests that Western cultures share a belief in independence of the self from others, and an emphasis on internal abilities, thoughts, and feelings—an *independent* perception of one's relation to culture. In contrast, cultures that can be characterized as *interdependent* share a view of connectedness, meeting others' expectations, and facilitation of interpersonal harmony. Individuals with interdependent self-construals will have an enhanced ability to blend in with the group and will likely engage in self-criticism more than self-enhancement (Heine & Lehaman, 1995; Kitayama, Markus, & Kurokawa, 2000). Self-construal theory has served as the basis for research about well-being, cognition, and emotion among individuals from Western and non-Western backgrounds, and it has provided support for the influence of cultural perspectives on strengths and well-being (Pedrotti, Edwards, & Lopez, 2009).

Finally, the level of importance placed on a particular strength is dictated by culture, and this may be partially defined by the types of thought processes that are most comfortable to a particular culture (Pedrotti, 2007a). For example, an individual from an Eastern cultural background may think of life as occurring in a circular fashion (e.g., yin and yang) and as such may not place the attainment of happiness at the top in terms of level of importance. This individual may feel that in wishing for happiness, he or she will also receive great strife and sadness, as the world tends to balance itself. Thus, an individual with this more circular framework may value *balance,* as opposed to happiness, and thus strengths that reflect this, such as harmony, conformity, and lack of excess. This distinction between cultural mind-sets may manifest itself in such a way that will make the search for a characteristic such as happiness in these two examples look very different from one another (Pedrotti, 2007a).

Although the complexities described above illustrate the challenge of understanding strengths among culturally diverse groups, it is important to note that these issues do not mean that positive constructs are not applicable to nonmajority populations; however, adjustments may need to be made by clinicians to make them relevant to these different groups (Pedrotti et al., 2009). Thus, one can still talk about a positive construct such as hope, as defined by Snyder and colleagues (1991), but the end goals of the hope process may be different (e.g., goal of balance as opposed to happiness as described previously), as may be the pathways that are devised to attain it (e.g., a collectivistically oriented client may have more pathways involving soliciting help and advice from others) (Pedrotti, 2007a). Interventions may also take a different shape with different cultural groups. An example of this might be an intervention designed to increase well-being. Here, perhaps instead of focusing only on individual well-being, participants from collectivist backgrounds could be encouraged to think of ways to enhance well-being on a group level. Being mindful of the different conceptualizations of different groups of individuals may help us to tailor therapeutic interactions and interventions to a specific client.

EXAMPLES OF RESEARCH ABOUT STRENGTHS AND CULTURE

In this section, we will provide two examples of types of research being conducted about strengths and culturally diverse populations. First, we will discuss findings from positive psychology research about subjective well-being, which has been pioneered by Diener and colleagues (Diener, 2000; Diener & Diener, 1995; Diener, Diener, & Diener, 1995; Suh, Diener, Oishi, & Triandis, 1998). This extensive body of research has involved citizens from many nations who report their levels of life satisfaction affect based on standardized indexes such as the Satisfaction with Life Scale (Diener, Emmons, Larsen, & Griffin, 1985).

Our second example of research involves the investigation of culturally relevant strengths, or those that emerge directly from a cultural group. We will then briefly describe cultural resources that researchers are beginning to investigate and note others that can continue to be better understood. Although many examples of this type of research have emerged over the years, we chose to mention a few that might be used as illustrations of this work.

Subjective Well-Being Across Cultures

Diener and colleagues (Diener, Suh, Lucas, & Smith, 1999) have defined subjective well-being (SWB) as having a cognitive-judgmental component (life satisfaction) and affective components (positive affect and the absence of negative affect). Within this SWB framework, individuals are asked to provide a subjective appraisal of their lives, and the degree of well-being is determined from that subjective judgment. Over the past 25 years, researchers have investigated factors contributing to SWB at the individual and cultural levels, across many groups. SWB has been found to correlate with many factors, including good health, enough education, fit between personality and culture, personal growth, purpose in life, self-acceptance, sense of self-determination, having many acquaintances, and receiving social support from many close friends (Triandis, 2000, p. 32).

At the international level, a large body of research exists looking at differences in well-being (particularly life satisfaction) across citizens of a variety of nations (Diener & Diener, 1995; Diener et al., 1995; Suh et al., 1998). In their review of national differences in SWB, Diener and Suh (1999) reported that people living in individualistic cultures tend to have higher levels of life satisfaction than those in collectivist cultures. Individualist cultures, such as the United States, encourage autonomy, independence, and attention to personal feeling and opinions, whereas collectivist cultures give priority to the in-group and define the self in relational terms (Pedrotti et al., 2009). These distinctions suggest that SWB may be more salient to individualists, and that the characteristics traditionally associated with well-being may not be as relevant for members of collectivist cultures (Suh, 2002). It is important to note that this research has sought to compare levels of well-being across cultures and has shown support for linguistic equivalence of measures (e.g., translations to various languages) as well as measurement equivalence. Different conceptions of well-being (i.e., conceptual equivalence) across nations has not been investigated as thoroughly, however.

Culturally Specific Strengths

In addition to investigating the applicability of certain strengths to people from diverse backgrounds, researchers have noted the importance of identifying and promoting cultural values and strengths that may emerge directly from an individual's cultural background (Lopez, Prosser et al., 2002). Given the sociopolitical and historical context of discrimination and oppression that people of color have faced in society, understanding how these individuals flourish and experience well-being in spite of these challenges is critical (Sue & Constantine, 2003). For example, researchers have begun to investigate the role of cultural values and strengths as buffers against the negative effects of stress; these values and strengths include biculturalism (LaFromboise, Coleman, & Gerton, 1993; Romero & Roberts, 2003), ethnic identity (Phinney, 1992, 2003), religion and spirituality (Blaine & Crocker, 1995; Sue & Constantine, 2003), and familism (Edwards & Lopez, 2006). These constructs may help youth and adults navigate the challenges of multiple cultural contexts or discrimination stress, and they can be nurtured in order to promote positive change (Edwards, Holtz, & Green, 2007).

Hays (2001, p. 106) provides a useful list of culturally related strengths and supports that are relevant to individuals from diverse backgrounds. Some of the personal or individual strengths that Hays notes include bilingual or multilingual skills, religious faith, pride in one's culture, and wisdom. Interpersonal supports may be extended families, traditional celebrations and rituals, and cultural or group-specific networks. Finally, examples of environmental conditions that can serve as cultural strengths include having an altar to honor deceased ancestors, cultural foods, animals, or a space for prayer or meditation. Research focused on indigenous coping strategies and ethnic identity, for example, as well as these other individual and community-level resources, can provide more culturally relevant conceptions of well-being (Sue & Constantine, 2003).

PRACTICING FROM A STRENGTHS-BASED AND MULTICULTURAL PERSPECTIVE

Psychotherapy naturally involves the assessment and conceptualization of clients within a cultural context, which includes identifying challenges as well as strengths and resources. Understanding a client's unique cultural context of strengths can be complex; however, therapists' own cultural values will naturally influence the interpretation of what is a strength or a liability (Gelso & Woodhouse, 2003). In the following section, we describe several strategies that can be used in practice in order to better address strengths and multiculturalism in clients, including strengths conceptualizations in diagnostic processes (Lopez et al., 2006), the Four-Front Approach (Wright, 1991), and the Strengths-Based Counseling Model (Smith, 2006).

Strengths-Based Conceptualization in Diagnosis

As noted previously, the diagnostic system within the field of psychology emphasizes pathology and weakness over assets and strengths in all clients. This may be particularly damaging in clients of color due to the fact that their culturally related behaviors and practices have often been pathologized as well (Sue & Sue, 2003). Because of this, it is imperative for counselors today to consider conceptualizing their clients of color in ways that give a more balanced view (i.e., one that looks at both strengths and weaknesses). This may be difficult to do because of the *Diagnostic and Statistical Manual of Mental Disorders* (*DSM*) system, and as such, supplementary diagnostic aids might be considered. Lopez et al. (2006) discuss macro solutions such as adding on an Axis VI to the *DSM* system titled "Personal Strengths and Facilitators of Growth" (a complementary axis to Axis IV as it currently stands) (p. 265) or reanchoring the Global Assessment of Functioning (Axis V) so that scores 0 to 50 would categorize functional deficits and 51 to 100 would categorize functional assets in a person's life. At the more micro level, clinicians might consider using alternative diagnostic methods within their own conceptualizations of clients, including looking at disorders as lying on continua as opposed to a disorder being "present" or "absent" (see Oldham & Morris, 1995) or considering what criteria would be required for what Keyes and Lopez (2002) have called "flourishing in life" (Lopez et al., 2006, p. 264). This would increase accuracy in conceptualizations of clients of any cultural background, although it may be particularly beneficial for clients of color, whose culturally specific strengths may not be recognized within our current system.

The Four-Front Approach

The Four-Front Approach (Wright, 1991) provides a useful framework for identifying strengths and destructive factors in an individual's life (Lopez et al., 2006). By attending to both positive and negative aspects of an individual, as well as of his or her environment, the professional can have a more balanced and holistic conceptualization of client functioning (Pedrotti, Edwards, & Lopez, 2008). Specifically, clinicians using the Four-Front Approach gather information across four areas: (a) strengths and assets of the client (e.g., self-efficacy and hope), (b) deficiencies and undermining characteristics of the client (e.g., problems with frustration tolerance), (c) resources and opportunities in the environment (e.g., family and religious community support), and (d) deficiencies and destructive factors in the environment (e.g., poverty and discrimination). This information can be gathered using multiple methods, including observation, discussion with the client, and standardized assessments, and clinicians are encouraged to integrate the material into the therapeutic process (Edwards, Holtz, & Green, 2007). With this tool, the client and professional can be better attuned to strengths in both the individual and environment.

The Strengths-Based Counseling Model

A recent example of a strengths-based framework that can be used to conceptualize and work with individuals from diverse backgrounds is the Strengths-Based Counseling Model (SBCM) (Smith, 2006). Although developed as a model for counseling at-risk youth, the basic concepts and stages can be readily applied to other populations to help clients use strengths to overcome life challenges. SBCM provides a framework for the professional who "searches for what people have rather than what they do not have, what people can do rather than what they cannot do, and how they have been successful rather than how they have failed" (Smith, 2006, p. 38).

The SBCM acknowledges that culture has a major influence on individuals' views of human strengths, that all cultures have strengths, and that strengths exist in a cultural context (Smith, 2006). The model emphasizes the search for protective factors, strengths, and risk factors that are both internal and external in order to increase resiliency. The SBCM advances the field with a model of resiliency and strengths for at-risk youth, but Bowman (2006) notes that the model could be extended with even more attention to diversity, multilevel, and life span issues. She suggests using role strain and adaptation (RSA) theory to further clarify how culturally specific strengths might help youth cope with and adapt to the challenges inherent in their life roles. Using this theory, she encourages professionals to consider multilevel interventions that can address racial and class inequalities across individual, group, family, and community contexts, and which might require systemic change. Smith's SBCM, with the extension provided by Bowman, can be used to work with clients to promote positive change through the integration of strengths and culture.

The SBCM describes 10 stages of counseling that are based on counseling and psychotherapy literature and concepts, including common factors, resiliency, social work, prevention research, and positive psychology (Smith, 2006, pp. 39–48). Throughout the stages, the therapist is guided to help clients identify strengths within themselves and their environments, and to discover ways to build on these resources toward positive change. The stages and a brief description of the therapist's role at each stage are as follows:

Stage 1: Creating the Therapeutic Alliance—discussing client's strengths and conveying a respect for client's personal struggles.

Stage 2: Identifying Strengths—using narrative techniques to help clients clarify their strengths.

Stage 3: Assessing Presenting Problems—gaining information about client's perceptions of problems.

Stage 4: Encouraging and Instilling Hope—rekindling hope by identifying client's hopeful life experiences and circumstances.

Stage 5: Framing Solutions—using solution-focused strategies such as exception questions to formulate solutions to problems.

Stage 6: Building Strength and Competence—helping clients recognize their sense of autonomy by using internal and external strengths.

Stage 7: Empowering—collaborating with client to explore context and activate internal and external resources.

Stage 8: Changing—helping client become aware of goals and modifications that need to be made to improve circumstances, providing encouragement by noting client's efforts and success, and reframing the meaning of life events.

Stage 9: Building Resilience—developing coping skills to deal with problems should they recur.

Stage 10: Evaluating and Terminating—working with the client to identify resources that were most valuable to the change process and to honor progress that has been made.

Working through these 10 stages and understanding the basic assumptions of the SBCM can help professionals have a theoretically grounded framework for promoting well-being among clients. More details about the SBCM, including a case study, can be found in Smith's (2006) major contribution to *The Counseling Psychologist.* In addition, we encourage readers to consider Bowman's (2006) article, which extends the model, emphasizes cultural strengths, and highlights the possibility of multilevel intervention.

Teaching and Training About Culture From a Strengths Perspective

There are many reasons to integrate strengths in teaching and training of students in the area of multiculturalism. First, as may be obvious, this balanced view can assist students in conceptualization, assessment, and treatment with people who are culturally different from themselves by helping them to gain a more well-rounded view of others and by breaking down negative stereotypes about these groups as well (American Psychological Association [APA], 2003; Edwards, 2007; Pedrotti, 2007c). Some students may only be aware of negatives in thinking about people from cultures other than their own as a result of deficit perspectives in the field (Lopez, Prosser et al., 2002); this gives them a chance to see a broader viewpoint.

Being attuned to strengths in others also assists students in gaining self-knowledge (APA, 2003) and connecting with others across various cultural facets. As a starting place, students can be encouraged to identify their own culturally specific strengths (Hays, 2001) and can then share these with peers and others. Similarities are likely to be found across cultural groups in this type of exercise. For example, a White woman from a low socioeconomic status group who credits her success to her family's support may find that she has many similarities with an Asian American man with collectivist ideals who shows the same value for family support. Differences in strengths can also be highlighted, and in this way, all cultural groups can be seen as valuable and productive (Pedrotti, 2007c).

Discussions of strengths can also be used to help students deal with issues of racism, sexism, heterosexism, classism, and other issues in their lives (Pedrotti, 2007c) by assisting them in identifying coping strategies they have used in these situations. This can then be translated into a training experience by showing trainees how to look for these strengths in their clients as they tell their stories of discrimination and strife (Sue & Constantine, 2003). Thus, helping students and trainees become more aware of their own strengths and those of people from cultural backgrounds different from their own can be valuable teaching tools when training about multicultural issues.

CONCLUSION

Both culture and human strengths have been neglected over the years within the field of psychology. Overlooking strengths in any individual or cultural group is problematic; however, overlooking strengths in populations that have been overpathologized can be even more damaging. In this chapter. we have given some history of the emergence of each of these areas of the field and their integration in more current research today. By taking the balanced view posited by positive psychology in research and training, professionals can strive to better understand and apply this important intersection.

REFERENCES

American Psychological Association. (2003). Guidelines on multicultural education, training, research, practice, and organizational change for psychologists. *American Psychologist, 58,* 377–402.

Blaine, B., & Crocker, J. (1995). Religiousness, race, and psychological well-being: Exploring social psychological mediators. *Personality and Social Psychology Bulletin, 21,* 1031–1041.

Bowman, P. J. (2006). Role strain and adaptation issues in the strength-based model: Diversity, multilevel, and life span considerations. *Counseling Psychologist, 34,* 118–133.

Boyd-Franklin, N. (1989). *Black families: A multisystems approach to family therapy.* New York: Guilford.

Chang, E. C., & Banks, K. H. (2007). The color and texture of hope: Some preliminary findings and implications for hope theory and counseling among diverse racial/ethnic groups. *Cultural Diversity & Ethnic Minority Psychology, 13,* 94–103.

Christopher, J. C. (2005). Situating positive psychology. *Naming and Nurturing: The e-newsletter of the Positive Psychology Section of the American Psychological Association's Counseling Psychology Division 17, 2,* 3–4.

Constantine, M. G., & Sue, D. W. (2006). Factors contributing to optimal human functioning of people of color in the United States. *Counseling Psychologist, 34,* 228–244.

Day, S. X., & Rottinghaus, P. R. (2003). The healthy personality. In W. B. Walsh (Ed.), *Counseling psychology and optimal human functioning* (pp. 1–24). Mahwah, NJ: Lawrence Erlbaum.

De Jong, P., & Miller, S. D. (1995). Interviewing for client strengths. *Social Work, 40,* 729–736.

De Shazer, S. (1985). *Keys to solution in brief therapy.* New York: Norton.

Diener, E. (2000). Subjective well-being. *American Psychologist, 55,* 34–43.

Diener, E., & Diener, M. (1995). Cross-cultural correlates of life satisfaction and self-esteem. *Journal of Personality and Social Psychology, 68,* 653–663.

Diener, E., Diener, M., & Diener, C. (1995). Factors predicting the subjective well-being of nations. *Journal of Personality and Social Psychology, 69,* 851–864.

Diener, E., Emmons, R. A., Larsen, R. J., & Griffin, S. (1985). The Satisfaction with Life Scale. *Journal of Personality Assessment, 49,* 71–75.

Diener, E., & Suh, E. M. (1999). National differences in subjective well-being. In D. Kahneman, E. Diener, & N. Schwarz (Eds.), *Well-being: The foundations of hedonic psychology.* New York: Russell Sage Foundation.

Diener, E., Suh, E. M., Lucas, R., & Smith, H. (1999). Subjective well-being: Three decades of progress. *Psychological Bulletin, 125,* 276–302.

Edwards, L. M. (2007, August). Incorporating a strengths approach into graduate multicultural counseling courses. In J. Pedrotti (Chair), *Strengths in our heritage: Teaching multiculturalism from a strengths perspective.* Symposium presented at the annual meeting of the American Psychological Association, San Francisco.

Edwards, L. M., Holtz, C. A., & Green, M. B. (2007). Promoting strengths among culturally diverse youth in schools. *School Psychology Forum, 2,* 39–49.

Edwards, L. M., & Lopez, S. J. (2006). Perceived family support, acculturation, and life satisfaction in Mexican American youth: A mixed methods exploration. *Journal of Counseling Psychology, 53,* 279–287.

Edwards, L. M., Ong, A. D., & Lopez, S. J. (2007). Hope measurement in Mexican American youth. *Hispanic Journal of Behavioral Sciences, 29,* 225–241.

Fowers, B. J., & Davidov, B. J. (2006). The virtue of multiculturalism: Personal transformation, character, and openness to the other. *American Psychologist, 61,* 581–594.

Gelso, C., & Fretz, B. (2001). *Counseling psychology* (2nd ed.). Ft. Worth, TX: Harcourt.

Gelso, C. J., & Woodhouse, S. (2003). Toward a positive psychotherapy: Focus on human strength. In W. B. Walsh (Ed.), *Counseling psychology and optimal human functioning* (pp. 171–197). Mahwah, NJ: Lawrence Erlbaum.

Hays, P. A. (2001). *Addressing cultural complexities in practice: A framework for clinicians and counselors.* Washington, DC: American Psychological Association.

Heine, S. J., & Lehaman, D. R. (1995). Cultural variation in unrealistic optimism: Does the West feel more invulnerable than the East? *Journal of Personality and Social Psychology, 68,* 595–607.

Hill, R. B. (1972). A profile of Black aged. *Occasional Papers in Gerontology,* pp. 35–50.

Keyes, C. L. M., & Lopez, S. J. (2002). Toward a science of mental health: Positive directions in diagnosis and interventions. In C. R. Snyder & S. J. Lopez (Eds.), *Handbook of positive psychology* (pp. 45–59). New York: Oxford University Press.

Kitayama, S., Markus, H. R., & Kurokawa, M. (2000). Culture, emotion, and well-being: Good feelings in Japan and the United States. *Cognition and Emotion, 14,* 93–124.

Kluckhohn, R. R., & Strodtbeck, F. L. (1961). *Variations in value orientations.* Evanston, IL: Row Paterson.

LaFromboise, T., Coleman, H. L. K., & Gerton, J. (1993). Psychological impact of biculturalism: Evidence and theory. *Psychological Bulletin, 114,* 395–412.

Leong, F. T. L., & Wong, P. T. P. (2003). Optimal human functioning from cross-cultural perspectives: Cultural competence as an organizing framework. In W. B. Walsh (Ed.), *Counseling psychology and optimal human functioning* (pp. 123–150). Mahwah, NJ: Lawrence Erlbaum.

Lopez, S. J., & Edwards, L. M. (2008). The interface of counseling psychology and positive psychology: Assessing and promoting strengths. In S. D. Brown & R. W. Lent (Eds.), *Handbook of counseling psychology* (4th ed., pp. 86–99). Hoboken, NJ: Wiley.

Lopez, S. J., Edwards, L. M., Ito, A. S., Pedrotti, J. T., & Rasmussen, H. N. (2002). Culture counts: Examinations of recent applications of the Penn Resiliency Project. *Prevention and Treatment, 5,* Article 12. Available: http://journals.apa.org/prevention/volume5/pre0050012c.html

Lopez, S. J., Edwards, L. M., Magyar-Moe, J. L., Pedrotti, J. T., & Ryder, J. (2003). Fulfilling its promise: Counseling psychology's efforts to understand and promote optimal human functioning. In W. B. Walsh (Ed.), *Counseling psychology and optimal human functioning* (pp. 297–307). Mahwah, NJ: Lawrence Erlbaum.

Lopez, S. J., Edwards, L. M., Pedrotti, J. T., Prosser, E. C., Walton, S. L., Spalitto, S., & Ulven, J. C. (2006). Beyond the *DSM*: Assumptions, alternatives, and alterations. *Journal of Counseling and Development, 84,* 259–267.

Lopez, S. J., Prosser, E. C., Edwards, L. M., Magyar-Moe, J., Neufeld, J., & Rasmussen, H. (2002). Putting positive psychology in a multicultural context. In C. R. Snyder & S. J. Lopez (Eds.), *Handbook of positive psychology* (pp. 700–714). New York: Oxford University Press.

Markus, H. R., & Kitayama, S. (1991). Culture and the self: Implications for cognition, emotion, and motivation. *Psychological Review, 98,* 224–253.

Maslow, A. (1954). *Motivation and personality.* New York: Longman.

Mio, J. S., Barker-Hackett, L., & Tumambing, J. (2006). *Multicultural psychology.* Boston: McGraw-Hill.

Myers, D. (1993). *The pursuit of happiness.* New York: Avon.

Myers, L. J. (1988). *Understanding an Afrocentric world view: Introduction to an optimal psychology.* Dubuque, IA: Kendall/Hunt.

Oldham, J. M., & Morris, L. B. (1995). *New personality self-portrait: Why you think, work, love, and act the way you do.* New York: Bantam.

Pedersen, P. (1991). Multiculturalism as a generic approach to counseling. *Journal of Counseling and Development, 70,* 6–12.

Pedrotti, J. T. (2007a). Eastern perspectives on positive psychology. In C. R. Snyder & S. J. Lopez (Eds.), *Positive psychology: The scientific and practical explorations of human strengths.* Thousand Oaks, CA: Sage.

Pedrotti, J. T. (2007b, October). *Strategies for infusing multiculturalism into a positive psychology course.* Presentation given at the annual Global Well-Being Forum (formerly the Positive Psychology Summit), Washington, DC.

Pedrotti, J. T. (2007c, August). Teaching from a strengths perspective in an undergraduate multicultural psychology course. In J. Pedrotti (Chair), *Strengths in our heritage: Teaching multiculturalism from a strengths perspective.* Symposium presented at the annual meeting of the American Psychological Association, San Francisco.

Pedrotti, J. T., Edwards, L. M., & Lopez, S. J. (2008a). Promoting hope: Suggestions for school counselors. *Professional School Counseling, 12,* 100–107.

Pedrotti, J. T., Edwards, L. M., & Lopez, S. J. (2008b). Working with multiracial clients in therapy: Bridging theory, research and practice. *Professional Psychology: Research and Practice, 39,* 192–201.

Pedrotti, J. T., Edwards, L. M., & Lopez, S. J. (2009). Positive psychology within a cultural context. In C. R. Snyder & S. J. Lopez (Eds.), *The Oxford handbook of positive psychology* (pp. 49-57). New York: Oxford University Press.

Peterson, C., & Seligman, M. E. P. (2004). *Character strengths and virtues: A handbook and classification.* Washington, DC: American Psychological Association.

Phinney, J. S. (1992). The Multigroup Ethnic Identity Measure: A new scale for use with diverse groups. *Journal of Adolescent Research, 7,* 156–176.

Phinney, J. S. (2003). Ethnic identity and acculturation. In K. M. Chun, P. Organista, & G. Marin (Eds.), *Acculturation: Advances in theory, measurement, and applied research* (pp. 63–81). Washington, DC: American Psychological Association.

Rich, G. J. (2001). Positive psychology: An introduction. *Journal of Humanistic Psychology, 41,* 8–12.

Romero, A. J., & Roberts, R. E. (2003). Stress within a bicultural context for adolescents of Mexican descent.

Cultural Diversity and Ethnic Minority Psychology, 9(2), 171–184.

Saleeby, D. (1992). *The strengths perspective in social work practice.* New York: Longman.

Sandage, S., Hill, P. C., & Vang, H. C. (2003). Toward a multicultural positive psychology: Indigenous forgiveness and Hmong culture. *Counseling Psychologist, 31,* 564–592.

Seligman, M. E. P., & Csikszentmihalyi, M. (2000). Positive psychology: An introduction. *American Psychologist, 55,* 5–14.

Smith, E. J. (2006). The strength-based counseling model. *Counseling Psychologist, 34,* 13–79.

Snyder, C. R., Harris, C., Anderson, J. R., Holleran, S. A., Irving, L. M., Sigmon, S. T., Yoshinobu, L., Gibb, J., Langelle, C., & Harney, P. (1991). The will and the ways: Development and validation of an individual-differences measure of hope. *Journal of Personality and Social Psychology, 60,* 570–585.

Snyder, C. R., & Lopez, S. J. (2007) *Positive psychology: The scientific and practical explorations of human strengths.* Thousand Oaks, CA: Sage.

Sue, D. W., & Constantine, M. G. (2003). Optimal human functioning in people of color in the United States. In W. B. Walsh (Ed.), *Counseling psychology and optimal human functioning* (pp. 151–169). Mahwah, NJ: Lawrence Erlbaum.

Sue, D. W., & Sue, D. (2003). *Counseling the culturally diverse.* New York: Wiley.

Suh, E. (2002). Culture, identity consistency, and subjective well-being. *Journal of Personality and Social Psychology, 83,* 1378–1391.

Suh, E., Diener, E., Oishi, S., & Triandis, H. C. (1998). The shifting basis of life satisfaction judgments across cultures: Emotions versus norms. *Journal of Personality & Social Psychology, 74,* 482–493.

Triandis, H. C. (2000). Cultural syndromes and subjective well-being. In E. Diener & E. M. Suh (Eds.), *Culture and subjective well-being* (pp. 13–36). Cambridge: MIT Press.

White, J. L. (1984). *The psychology of Blacks: An Afro-American perspective.* Englewood Cliffs, NJ: Prentice Hall.

Wright, B. A. (1991). Labeling: The need for greater person-environment individuation. In C. R. Snyder & D. R. Forsyth (Eds.), *Handbook of social and clinical psychology* (pp. 469–487). New York: Pergamon.

17

International Counseling Competencies

A New Frontier in Multicultural Training

STEFANÍA ÆGISDÓTTIR AND LAWRENCE H. GERSTEIN

In this chapter, we discuss how counseling professionals can successfully address international issues, and we offer new strategies to strengthen and modify current multicultural training paradigms. In our discussion, we expand the dimensions of multicultural counseling competencies (awareness, knowledge, and skills) (Arredondo et al., 1996) when applying them to international settings, incorporate recent suggestions about international counseling competencies (Heppner, Leong, & Gerstein, 2008), highlight the importance of motivation as a fourth dimension, in recognizing the significance of international activities and enhancing one's international competencies, and integrate philosophies rooted in social justice to consider when working internationally. For the purposes of this chapter, unless otherwise specified, international work refers to U.S. mental health professionals and students who are performing services in an international setting or with an international population, and international professionals and students engaged in activities in the United States or in their home countries. More specifically, in this chapter, we discuss (a) the significance of learning about cultures around the world; (b) how to increase motivation, awareness, knowledge, and skills regarding international topics and work; (c) bias in international work and research; (d) the importance of identifying potential dangers of ethnocentric practices; (e) reward structures for students and professionals interested in international issues; and (f) methods, benefits, and risks of international work and collaboration. Our aim is to encourage counseling professionals to think and act outside of the U.S. "box" of psychology and counseling.

Internationalization of Counseling

In recent years, counseling professionals have demonstrated increased interest in international issues as evidenced, for instance, by the International Counseling Psychology Conference in Chicago, Illinois, in March

2008. Consistent with this growing interest is also a slight rise in publications on the role of counseling outside of the United States (Gerstein & Ægisdóttir, 2005a, 2005b, 2005c, 2007; Gerstein, Heppner, Ægisdóttir, Leung, & Norsworthy, in press; Heppner, 2006; Heppner & Gerstein, in press; Heppner et al., 2008; Kwan & Gerstein, 2008; Leong & Blustein, 2000; Leong & Ponterotto, 2003; Leong & Savickas, 2007; Ægisdóttir & Gerstein, 2005) and the greater attention paid to counseling international individuals living in the United States (e.g., Arthur & Pedersen, 2008; Fouad, 1991; Pedersen, 1991; Singaravelu & Pope, 2008).

Despite this exciting development within counseling, not much has been written about how to train students to address international issues successfully. Therefore, in this chapter, we briefly highlight some recommendations that have been offered (Gerstein & Ægisdóttir, 2007; Giorgis & Helms, 1978; Leong & Ponterotto, 2003; Leung, 2003; Takooshian, 2003), and we introduce new strategies to strengthen and modify multicultural training paradigms. The importance of training counseling graduate students to effectively serve the needs of international populations cannot be ignored as the U.S. population becomes increasingly diversified and the concerns of the people around the world become more apparent, immediate, and connected to our lives (Gerstein & Ægisdóttir, 2007).

MULTICULTURAL AND INTERNATIONAL COMPETENCIES

Jackson (1995) claimed that Murphy (1955) was one of the earliest scholars to publish a paper on the significance of culture in the context of counseling. The development of multicultural counseling competencies, however, really emerged from the social justice agenda (e.g., civil rights movement) sparked in the late 1950s and 1960s in the United States (Arredondo & Perez, 2003; Jackson, 1995). Publications in the 1970s further opened up the dialogue about cultural issues and counseling (e.g., Pedersen, Lonner, & Draguns, 1976; Sue & Sue, 1971; Vontress, 1971) and for the first time, the concepts of cross-cultural counseling and multicultural counseling could be found in the scholarly literature. In the 1980s, a committee within Division 17 (Society of Counseling Psychology) of the American Psychological Association

chaired by Professor D. W. Sue was formed to develop guidelines for multicultural competencies. A seminal publication by Sue and colleagues (1982) introduced the idea that specific competencies were required to perform multicultural counseling. Interestingly, during the 1980s and 1990s, a debate transpired in the multicultural counseling movement about whether international persons of color should be included along with domestic minorities in models of multicultural counseling (Jackson, 1995).

Additionally, in the 1990s, the American Association for Counseling and Development (currently called the American Counseling Association) and Divisions 17 (Society of Counseling Psychology) and 45 (Society for the Psychological Study of Ethnic Minority Issues) of the American Psychological Association (APA) endorsed guidelines for cultural competence (Ridley & Kleiner, 2003). It was not until 2002, or about 20 years after Division 17's formulation of multicultural competency guidelines, however, that the APA adopted such guidelines (Arredondo et al., 1996; Sue, Arredondo, & McDavis, 1992). The multicultural competency framework identifies three dimensions of competencies: awareness, knowledge, and skills. This framework for assisting diverse populations in the United States provides a useful paradigm for international work as well.

In addition to the tripartite model of multicultural competencies, Heppner et al. (2008) suggested a preliminary conceptual framework for international competencies in counseling psychology. Along with stressing the importance of counselor awareness, knowledge, and skills, Heppner et al. recommended that Bronfenbrenner's (1979) ecological systems model of child development be used as a guiding framework for counseling professionals working in international settings. According to Bronfenbrenner's model, a person's development is influenced by five different systems and the interactions between them: microsystem, mesosystem, exosystem, macrosystem, and chronosystem. These systems represent institutions (e.g., family, school) in direct contact with a person, and also systems that are not in direct contact with the individual, but influence an individual's life (e.g., environmental events and transitions). Heppner et al. (2008) recommended that counseling psychologists providing services or performing research in an international setting think of themselves and persons in the host country and culture in the context of the systems influencing their existence, values, beliefs, personality, and behavior.

Enhancing Awareness

The first step in understanding how individuals are influenced by their cultural context is recognizing and being aware of the role and impact of different systems (e.g., microsystem, macrosystem) on the person (self and others), and the fact that these systems may vary significantly by culture and country. As Arredondo et al. (1996) stated in regards to multicultural awareness, counseling professionals should be aware of their own and their clients' worldview; cultural values and biases; and how one's cultural background and experiences influence attitudes, values, and biases about psychological processes. Thus, culturally competent counseling professionals are willing to compare in a nonjudgmental fashion their own beliefs and attitudes with those of their culturally different clients (Arredondo et al., 1996). In terms of international work, self and other awareness is crucial, as is recognizing and confronting one's own cultural biases and behaviors. As we have said elsewhere (Gerstein & Ægisdóttir, 2007), self-awareness and open-mindedness are essential early steps to truly understanding and respecting the uniqueness of a culture and learning how to conceptualize and help others with issues and needs brought to one's attention.

Accomplishing this step effectively in an unfamiliar international context is not without challenges, though. One may be faced with a possible new language; a different social, cultural, political, religious, and economic system; different norms, values, and behaviors; a potentially unique or new psychological philosophy and worldview; and numerous other factors (e.g., operating outside one's own comfort zone). Often, one must cope with issues and experiences without any external support, input, feedback, or understandable stimuli. Essentially, one must exercise a high level of self-awareness, awareness of others, and awareness of the surrounding environment and context. It is also imperative to embrace the newness of the experience with open-mindedness, patience, and curiosity, and to accept one's anxiety and explore one's biases, expectations, and assumptions linked with the international setting (Gerstein & Ægisdóttir, 2007).

How can counseling professionals increase their awareness? A handful of recommendations have been offered. It has been suggested that they should embrace a multidisciplinary perspective of culture (Heppner, 1997; Leung, 2003; Pedersen, 2003; Varenne, 2003), be cautious about generalizing findings and constructs across cultures (Pedersen & Leong, 1997; Varenne, 2003; Ægisdóttir, Gerstein, & Çinarbas, 2008), be open-minded, and learn from different professionals around the world (Leong & Blustein, 2000). Furthermore, we argue that it is imperative that counseling professionals working in an international setting separate the observations they make from interpretations, as interpretations of one's surroundings are heavily influenced by one's values, biases, and experiences. Hofstede, Pedersen, and Hofstede (2002), in their book *Exploring Cultures: Exercises, Stories and Synthetic Cultures*, provided some excellent exercises to aid in heightening cultural awareness and to help persons separate observations from interpretations. For instance, they present ambiguous drawings of individuals in various situations, and they suggest that persons describe what they see in these pictures. Following these descriptions, Hofstede et al. encouraged people to analyze their descriptions based on their own values and cultural assumptions. Reading newspaper articles about events occurring in the United States and abroad and analyzing the content based on one's own and the target culture's values and norms may also increase one's cultural awareness.

Enhancing Knowledge

The multicultural counseling competencies framework also includes knowledge. This component refers to counselors' knowledge about their own cultural heritage and customs, and how such knowledge affects their definitions of normal and abnormal behavior and the process of counseling. This dimension also encompasses counseling professionals' specific knowledge and information about particular cultural groups. Knowledgeable professionals, therefore, appreciate that culture affects personality formation, career choices, signs and expressions of disorders, help-seeking behavior, and the suitability or lack of appropriateness of counseling approaches (Arredondo et al., 1996).

Knowledge about Bronfenbrenner's systemic approach to understanding a person's worldview is especially applicable here, as are the approaches of some other scholars (Ibrahim, 1985; Ibrahim, Roysircar-Sodowsky, & Ohnishi, 2001; Sue & Sue, 1999; Trevino, 1996) who have written extensively about worldview and multicultural competencies.

It can be argued that in the United States, knowledge about psychology and counseling outside of the United States is lacking. Some evidence exists to support this claim. For instance, Gerstein and Ægisdóttir (2007), in their review of publications between the years 2000 and 2004 in four select U.S. counseling journals (*Journal of Counseling Psychology, Journal of Counseling and Development, Journal of Multicultural Counseling and Development,* and *The Counseling Psychologist*) found that only 6% of the articles focused on an international topic. Furthermore, Arnett (2008), who conducted a content analysis of publications in six premier APA journals spanning the years 2003 to 2007 (*Developmental Psychology, Journal of Personality and Social Psychology, Journal of Abnormal Psychology, Journal of Family Psychology, Health Psychology,* and *Journal of Educational Psychology*), discovered that 68% of the samples studied were in the United States, 14% were in other English-speaking countries, and 13% were in Europe. Only 3% of the samples were in Asia, 1% in Latin America, and less than 1% in Africa or the Middle East. Based on these two studies, it is obvious and alarming how few articles published in the United States have gathered data from individuals living in countries outside of the United States. This lack of publications may contribute to limited knowledge about international issues among counseling professionals. In turn, counselors' limited knowledge may promote a cultural and professional encapsulation and an ethnocentric bias regarding psychological processes and the needs of individuals around the world.

How, then, can counseling scholars and students be exposed to more knowledge about psychology worldwide? Obviously, this may be a challenge when samples from outside of the United States are underrepresented. One way to increase knowledge, though, is for counselors to read the U.S. counseling publications on international issues. Furthermore, counseling professionals can expand their reading repertoire by examining publications in other fields (e.g., cultural anthropology, political science, linguistics) and, most importantly, by reviewing publications outside of the United States. Not everyone will be able to read documents published in languages other than English. However, in U.S.-based counseling training programs, we encourage bilingual and international students and faculty members to explore, for instance, the literature in psychology and anthropology written in other languages besides English and then share their findings with others in their program. Moreover, professionals and students can find articles relevant to counseling in noncounseling journals that publish papers from authors all over the world that are written in the English language (e.g., *Journal of Cross-Cultural Psychology, The European Psychologist, The European Journal of Psychological Assessment, International Journal of Psychology*).

To increase knowledge about international topics, we also encourage editors of U.S. journals to publish a greater number of studies on international subjects and samples. To this end, as the international forum editors for *The Counseling Psychologist,* Kwan and Gerstein (2008) have outlined a detailed list of international topics that need to be pursued and that would be relevant for publication in this particular journal.

Another strategy to further counseling professionals' knowledge of international issues and topics is for faculty members to encourage students to conduct research in this area and to secure training experiences relevant to the international arena. Mentoring students is critical to the acquisition of knowledge and competencies connected to working internationally.

To enrich students' knowledge about understanding the intricacies of culture and how to research diverse cultures, we highly recommend that students enroll in cultural anthropology and anthropological methodology courses. As others have stated (Gerstein, Rountree, & Ordonez, 2007), anthropology has much to offer the multicultural counseling movement in terms of philosophy, theory, practice, training, and research methodology.

A few other scholars also have offered recommendations about how to increase knowledge of psychology and counseling worldwide. Leong and Ponterotto (2003), for instance, outlined some specific suggestions for how counseling training programs might prepare students to become more internationally competent. They stressed that bilingualism be valued, that a modern language competence be encouraged, and that international publications be included in the curriculum. They also encouraged training programs to support students traveling to international conferences and countries outside of the United States for short periods of time and as exchange students. To date, there is no available research in the counseling literature indicating that traveling or studying abroad can enhance counseling students' international competencies. Such a study is definitely warranted. There is evidence, however, that social work (Boyle, Nackerud, & Kilpatrick, 1999; Krajewski-Jaime, Brown, Ziefert, & Kaufman, 1996; Lindsey, 2005) and nursing (Greatrex-White, 2007; Ruddock & Turner, 2007) students were culturally enriched and greatly benefited by studying abroad.

Giorgis and Helms (1978) also offered some recommendations concerning how to increase counseling professionals' knowledge about international issues. They suggested that international students in the United States be encouraged to secure psychology internships in settings that are similar (e.g., human and environmental factors) to those in their native countries, that faculty members urge international students to collect data and pursue research that is relevant to their home country, and that students be taught about the similarities and differences of educational systems throughout the world and be provided with firsthand experiences in some of them. Although these recommendations target international students, they are also relevant to counseling students planning to work internationally upon graduation. Additionally, we contend that it is essential for U.S. and international students as well as all counseling professionals to carefully evaluate the cross-cultural validity of psychological concepts, methods, and strategies of the profession (e.g., Ægisdóttir et al., 2008). Such an evaluation is necessary to select culturally appropriate and effective concepts and tools, and to avoid the potential of endangering or modifying the unique values, attitudes, and behaviors of a particular culture (Gerstein & Ægisdóttir, 2007).

Traveling to other countries is the optimal way to gain cultural knowledge, but this option is not always possible. There are other ways, however, that might also help

to enhance cultural knowledge. Classroom activities and assignments addressing international topics are probably the easiest to implement. Training programs can modify their courses to integrate material from cultures around the world. As Gerstein and Ægisdóttir (2007) suggested, students might be required to read literature and history, surf Web sites, and watch movies and television shows with an international theme. Students may also be exposed to the concerns and mental health issues of individuals and groups from different countries, and the contributions and uniqueness of different countries. The relativity of what is considered "normal" healthy functioning in different cultures and countries should be emphasized as well. Students might be encouraged to contrast and evaluate the cultural implications of different child-rearing practices. Additionally, they could be urged to assess the cultural implications of normal as compared to pathological signs in diagnostic systems and theories, such as ideas about boundaries between self and others versus enmeshment, and also hallucinations and delusions versus spiritual beliefs.

Moreover, training programs might draw on the knowledge and diverse perspectives gained from international students and students who have lived abroad. These students could be encouraged to discuss their experiences in the other country and how similarly or differently people from that country perceive and relate to the world (e.g., time, space, values, relationships, mental health). Likewise, international students could be encouraged, instead of silenced, when critically evaluating the validity and usefulness of the psychology/counseling theories they are exposed to in U.S. programs to their own country. Furthermore, international and U.S. students should be reminded that counseling and psychology theories they learn are culture specific, and their validity and utility in diverse cultures need to be examined (Gerstein & Ægisdóttir, 2007). Consistent with this recommendation, students and counseling professionals must be informed that the findings and observations published in the premier U.S. psychology journals are based on only about 5% of the population in the world (Arnett, 2008)! Therefore, a discussion about the personal, societal, and cultural dangers of simply implementing mental health delivery systems based on U.S. assumptions about human behavior should be emphasized (Gerstein & Ægisdóttir, 2007).

One other recommendation that can enhance students' cultural knowledge is important to mention. These days, Web-based conferencing is relatively easy to implement, making it possible for individuals affiliated with counseling training programs around the world to meet in real time and discuss a host of issues relevant to counseling and psychology, including those related to culture.

Enhancing Skills

To be competent in multicultural and international work, mental health professionals must not only acquire a sound base of knowledge, they must develop culturally sensitive, appropriate, and effective skills to serve diverse populations. In this regard, Arredondo et al. (1996) argued that skilled counselors should pursue educational, consultation, and training opportunities to enhance their understanding and effectiveness when working with culturally different populations. Competent counseling professionals should be familiar with the relevant research and findings on mental health and mental disorders for the cultural groups they serve, and they must seek consultation and make referrals if needed. Furthermore, we contend that competent counseling professionals must understand the limits of their knowledge about a foreign culture, and they should collaborate with native persons when working in international settings.

Currently, a couple of recommendations have been offered on how to increase counseling professionals' skill level when working internationally. Leong and Ponterotto (2003) suggested that students be encouraged to gain field internship experiences at local international-focused sites (e.g., community refugee or immigration centers) and abroad. Similarly, Giorgis and Helms (1978) recommended that students be supported in securing internships in settings that are similar to those in other countries where students want to work. Furthermore, Pedersen (2003) encouraged U.S. scholars to respond to the needs of international communities instead of simply describing and discussing the issues faced by such communities. He also stressed the importance of promoting the development of indigenous psychology outside of the United States. Many of the recommendations just mentioned can be accomplished,

in part, through effective multinational collaboration involving scholars, practitioners, and students.

Some basic skills to perform international work can also be taught in graduate-level counseling classes. For instance, faculty members teaching courses in counseling theory, research methods, ethics, appraisal, psychopathology, program evaluation, and other core classes might add an international section to their syllabi (Marsella & Pedersen, 2004). This suggestion is consistent with many who have suggested that multicultural topics should be incorporated into the counseling program curriculum (Collins & Pieterse, 2007; D'Andrea & Daniels, 1991; Reynolds, 1995). Students could be required, for example, to examine health care systems in different countries and/or research topics where international samples were used. This may be accomplished through gathering information on the Internet. Students might also be expected to interview mental health professionals from abroad about specific course-related topics. This could be done via email or Skype. As mentioned earlier, Internet-based teleconferences on targeted subjects could be arranged between classes held in the United States and in other countries. Furthermore, more emphasis in counseling training should be placed on students developing skills in interacting with clients in a different role from that of counselor or psychotherapist—roles that may not be applicable in non-Western countries. Atkinson, Thompson, and Grant's (1993) three-dimensional model of multicultural competence is highly applicable in this respect. In this model, the role of the helper is adjusted to clients' acculturation level to Western culture, locus of problem etiology, and whether the goals of helping are preventive or remedial. Therefore, based on the cultural context of the client, instead of acting in the role of a counselor or psychotherapist, the counselor may be more effective as an adviser, an advocate, a facilitator of indigenous support and/or healing systems, a consultant, or a change agent.

One other suggestion to increase students' skill level is for U.S.-based counseling training programs to establish exchange relationships with programs outside of the United States. Wang and Heppner (in press) have described one such innovative initiative. In alternate years, counseling graduate students and faculty members visit either National Taiwan Normal University

(Taipei, Taiwan, R.O.C.) or the University of Missouri–Columbia for a 2-week intensive immersion experience designed to foster the participants' greater understanding of and respect for each locale's culture, the acquisition of specific cross-cultural counseling knowledge and skills, and the development and maintenance of collaborative professional relationships. The two universities also have established a dual-degree master's program in counseling. The program is structured so that individuals from one university can study at the other institution for 1 year, and then earn a master's degree in 3 years from both universities.

To ensure that students have acquired the necessary knowledge and skills to engage in effective and appropriate international work based on a rich cultural appreciation and sensitivity, it is essential that some form of evaluation be conducted. Faculty members who implement any of the recommendations mentioned in the paragraphs above may assess students' international competencies by using traditional evaluation methods such as class papers, tests, journaling, and/or behavioral/experiential simulations.

Enhancing Motivation for International Issues

We firmly believe that if some of the aforementioned course and curricula recommendations were adopted to increase students' awareness, knowledge, and skills regarding international work, a reduction in the ethnocentric nature of the U.S. counseling profession would ensue. Regardless of the strategy employed to increase students' and scholars' international competence, we encourage those already involved in international work to model, reinforce, and shape students' and professionals' curiosity to seek out information and learning experiences linked with international settings, cultures, and individuals. We also challenge those not already involved in international work to do this as well. The time has come to look outside the U.S. box and expand the current repertoire of counseling paradigms.

To date, many individuals continue to minimize the interdependence of people and nations and ignore issues, developments, and problems outside of the United States. Yet direct and indirect contact between cultures has become more apparent and fraught with both positive and negative consequences. The connection between different cultures and their peoples confirms the importance of developing an understanding of and appreciation for international issues and populations (Gerstein & Ægisdóttir, 2007). Because of this and the fact that the current psychological knowledge in the United States is based on only a small proportion of the world population (Arnett, 2008), it is now essential that we include knowledge, challenges, and issues from around the world in our paradigms and that we also pursue international research and topics to advance the science and practice of counseling.

Embracing a philosophy of cultural interdependence may not be enough, though, to promote change. Awareness and knowledge about how humans are shaped by their cultural context also might not promote change. Possessing all this information might be futile without an interest and motivation to incorporate culture and context into the science and practice of psychology and counseling. Therefore, we contend that displaying the proper motivation is the driving force guiding the potential effective pursuit of international work for students, scholars, and practitioners.

How can one develop such a motivation? Gerstein and Ægisdóttir (2007) provided some suggestions about how faculty members can motivate students. They recommended, for instance, that faculty create informal (e.g., roundtable discussions, carry-in meals) and formal (e.g., poster and paper sessions, symposia) forums at conferences and in their departments and universities to introduce students to relevant issues around the world and to discuss topics related to international work and research. Additionally, they suggested that university administrators be encouraged to offer internal (e.g., department, university) grants to encourage faculty and student travel to international conferences and to pursue research and applied projects in another country. Gerstein and Ægisdóttir also recommended that professional organizations (e.g., Society of Counseling Psychology, American Counseling Association) offer external grants to accomplish the outcomes just mentioned. Moreover, they argued that students and faculty could be expected to network with students and faculty from around the world through the use of the Internet and e-mail in order to exchange ideas about issues and developments in psychology and counseling. Similarly, students and faculty members could be given additional credit for being involved in experiential courses devoted to international topics. Institutions might also be encouraged to give greater recognition to the importance of service performed outside of the United States (Gerstein & Ægisdóttir, 2007).

External rewards for scholars pursuing international work could be created as well. Professional awards could be made available, for example, to recognize a host of international accomplishments and/or contributions to the theory, science, practice, and teaching of psychology and counseling. Universities, departments, and professional organizations could dispense such awards (Gerstein & Ægisdóttir, 2007).

To potentially increase the motivation and likelihood that graduate training programs are uniquely designed to prepare students based on the C-CMAKS (cross-cultural motivation, awareness, knowledge, and skills) paradigm outlined in this chapter, educators might find it useful to adapt the multicultural counseling training program development model proposed by Ridley, Mendoza, and Kanitz (1994). This five-tiered (training philosophy, learning objectives, instructional strategies, program designs, and evaluation) pyramidal model offers a framework for how graduate programs can move through stages of integrating multicultural counseling training into the curriculum. In other words, this model offers educators some guidelines to design, structure, and implement a multicultural counseling training paradigm. We believe that many aspects of Ridley et al.'s model can be modified to help educators construct a training program to prepare students to engage in international work. For a review of specific models of multicultural counseling training that have the potential to be modified to train students for international work, we recommend Abreu, Chung, and Atkinson (2000) and LaFromboise and Foster (1992).

METHODOLOGICAL ISSUES FOR INTERNATIONAL SETTINGS

In addition to enhancing international competence through a multisystemic view and an awareness of and knowledge about how persons are shaped by culture, some specific skills are required to effectively solve the unique methodological and practical challenges when engaged in international research. Some of the practical challenges of this type of research are gaining accessibility to an international sample and motivating persons to participate in research conducted by a non-native (Gerstein & Ægisdóttir, 2007). Collaboration between an individual in the United States and a native scholar or professional in the country of interest would be of great help, as would involving native stakeholders in the process of developing and implementing the project, including encouraging the participation of the target sample. International research also can be time consuming and costly. Thus, increased funding may be necessary.

Numerous methodological issues need to be resolved as well. Issues of construct, method, and item equivalence need to be carefully considered, as do concerns about construct, method, and item bias (cf. Gerstein & Ægisdóttir, 2007; Ægisdóttir et al., 2008). The most fundamental issue involves functional equivalence and construct equivalence (e.g., Lonner, 1985; van de Vijver & Leung, 1997). One cannot, for instance, assume that a psychological construct exists in countries other than the one in which it was conceived. Pertinent examples for counseling professionals are culture-bound syndromes. Furthermore, one cannot assume that if a comparable construct does exist in the country of interest (e.g., friendship, life satisfaction), that individuals understand and/or attach the same meaning to it as individuals from the culture where the construct was originally developed. Therefore, careful preparatory work is needed in the target country. Collaborators who are native to the target country can be helpful in this regard.

Other issues that must be considered when conducting international research include carefully assessing the design validity of the intended procedures, and evaluating the cross-cultural validity and reliability of scales based on theory and research generated in the United States. It is possible that research methodologies (e.g., laboratory studies, paper-and-pencil instruments) employed in the United States may be less valid in other countries or cultures. Instead, qualitative strategies may be more fitting. This depends, however, on the potential cultural differences and cultural distance (e.g., language, cultural values, political structure, social norms) between the target country and the United States (Ægisdóttir et al., 2008). Qualitative strategies may, for instance, be construed as less contrived, more meaningful, and more consistent with the typical way of sharing personal information (Gerstein et al., 2007). Thus, the importance of communication systems, language, and meaning must be valued (Gerstein & Ægisdóttir, 2007).

If a quantitative methodology is considered appropriate in the international setting, issues of measurement and measurement equivalence and bias should be considered (e.g., Ægisdóttir et al., 2008). The researcher must discern if a new measure needs to be developed or if an existing instrument can be applied (literal translation) or adapted (changed to better fit the culture). For either of the two latter approaches (applied, adaptation), the researcher should be meticulous when translating, back translating, adapting (e.g., through decentering or adding emic items), and pretesting the measure before collecting the data for the study (Brislin, 1986; Brislin, Lonner, & Thorndike, 1973; Ægisdóttir et al., 2008).

Another methodological issue facing international researchers is potential bias when interpreting the data. Investigators may be tempted to base their interpretation on their own standards (Brislin, 1983; Gerstein & Ægisdóttir, 2007). This error underscores the importance of counseling professionals having the ability to separate observation from interpretation as a component of international competence. Using one's own standards when interpreting data collected in a foreign culture may result in researchers being judgmental or even paternalistic in their interpretation. Gerstein and Ægisdóttir (2007) provided a good example to illustrate these possibilities. Researchers studying counseling expectations in two countries might find that participants in one country have different counseling expectations from participants from the United States. The researcher may be tempted to recommend role induction as a counseling intervention in the "foreign" country, focusing on teaching clients to have appropriate expectations that are consistent with how counseling is practiced in the United States. Yet such expectations might not be suitable for persons from this "foreign" country. In order to interpret findings from a culture outside the United States, researchers need to acquaint themselves with the traditions of the culture they are studying, and they must incorporate this knowledge in their interpretations. Thus, the obtained difference in counseling expectations mentioned above might be better explained

in terms of how counseling or other types of indigenous mental health practices are commonly practiced in the country of interest (cf. Gerstein & Ægisdóttir, 2007, Ægisdóttir et al., 2008). Thus, changing the counseling strategy or adopting a different counseling role (i.e., Atkinson et al., 1993) might be more culturally appropriate than changing the expectations of the client.

Having discussed only a few of the methodological challenges when performing international research, we cannot help but wonder if such obstacles have discouraged counseling psychology investigators, resulting in their pursuit of more "politically" rewarding activities (i.e., more publishable material). We also cannot help but wonder how many papers with an international focus written by counseling psychology scholars from around the world are sitting in file cabinets or computer folders, collecting dust or taking up disc space instead of being embraced by consumers of counseling psychology? As we said earlier, it is alarming how few studies of an international focus or projects employing an international sample are published in U.S. counseling and psychology journals.

Counseling students are the future journal editors, convention chairs, researchers, and scholars (Gerstein & Ægisdóttir, 2007). Until they begin to understand the importance of conducting international research using emic (culture specific) and etic (transcending cultures) approaches (e.g., Ægisdóttir et al., 2008), we cannot expect any significant change in how members of our discipline value and incorporate international work into the science and practice of counseling.

THE ROLE OF SOCIAL CHANGE IN INTERNATIONAL WORK

As we discussed earlier, to become competent in performing international work, it is critical to operate from a multisystemic viewpoint and to be cross-culturally motivated, aware, knowledgeable, and skilled (C-C MAKS). Developing such competencies may help contribute to acquiring a broader and deeper understanding of the unique group norms, values, and behaviors of the culture of interest. Cross-cultural competencies also might help enhance rapport and positive relationships with the "local" community, and they increase the probability of designing and implementing interventions to address individual, group, and community problems that are appropriate and that might actually be employed by local stakeholders (Gerstein & Ægisdóttir, 2007).

As individuals involved in action research know, stakeholders connected to the targeted situation should have a voice in the conceptualization of the issue or problem at hand and the implementation of the solution. This means that counseling professionals engaged in international social action work should work closely with those affected by the problem. Obtaining the perspective of all stakeholders will help clarify the issue being considered, and it will reduce the possibility of misunderstanding or misrepresenting the presented concerns. It will also greatly enhance the validity and applicability of the eventual solution, increase the stakeholders' investment in and responsibility when implementing a solution, and make the solution more effective and long-lasting (Gerstein & Bennett, 1999; Gerstein & Sturmer, 1993; Gerstein & Ægisdóttir, 2007). Furthermore, an international social action approach can not only empower stakeholders to resolve the current situation, but also make them more confident in solving future challenges. There are a number of excellent examples of counseling professionals empowering stakeholders in different locations throughout the world (e.g., Horne & Mathews, 2006; McWhirter & McWhirter, 2006; Norsworthy, 2006).

Another critical factor to consider when designing an effective social justice intervention is how well it fits with what already is in place in the particular country (Gerstein & Ægisdóttir, 2007). Isomorphic solutions that are based on the current situation and that are designed to result in slight changes to the targeted system are ideal (deShazer, 1991; Gerstein & Bennett, 1999; Gerstein & Sturmer, 1993). An isomorphic solution is grounded in the assumption that people and systems do, sometimes, employ positive and effective solutions to their problems.

Various philosophies and strategies are available when conceptualizing and targeting a solution for an international setting. One can rely on solution-focused (deShazer, 1991; Gerstein & Bennett, 1999; Gerstein & Sturmer, 1993), action-oriented, anthropological (Gerstein et al., 2007), and/or social psychological (Triandis, 1972, 1994, 1995, 2001) models. Triandis

introduced a social psychological model to explain behaviors and attitudes of people affiliated with different cultures and countries. This model is frequently cited in the current multicultural counseling literature. The model describes the individualism-collectivism cultural syndromes. Triandis later added a horizontal-vertical continuum to his model. For example, he theorized that some cultures value equality (a horizontal feature), whereas other cultures value hierarchy (a vertical feature). Thus, Triandis (2001) proposed that there are four kinds of cultures:

> Horizontal Individualist (HI), where people want to be unique and do "their own thing"; Vertical Individualist (VI), where people want to do their own thing and also to be "the best"; Horizontal Collectivism (HC), where people merge their selves with their in-groups; and Vertical Collectivism (VC), where people submit to the authorities of the in-group and are willing to sacrifice themselves for their in-group. (p. 910)

Although it is dangerous to stereotype countries, as individual differences do exist within cultures and countries, it might be possible to identify countries in which these cultural syndromes are most prominent. For instance, the United States may be categorized as a VI country, Sweden as an HI country, India as a VC country, and an Israeli kibbutz as a HC (Triandis, 1995, 2001).

International counseling social change agents need to think and act differently when conceptualizing and intervening with each of these four types of cultures. One must learn to respect the need for freedom and independence of persons from an individualistic culture. Change agents should work closely with these people to design and implement solutions that reinforce their clients' individual goals and attitudes. In contrast, in a collectivist culture, change agents should honor the interdependence of persons in such a group and the communal nature of their transactions. Here, the solutions should emerge from the group, and they must be conceptualized and implemented in such a way that the group achieves its stated and implicit goals. Egalitarian perspectives versus respect for power differentials need to be taken into consideration as well. Given the basic assumptions of the individualism-collectivism continuum, it seems obvious that the most appropriate intervention is not always designed to encourage independence, self-awareness, and self-promotion. In some instances, practical, concrete solutions focused on communal challenges may be of greater value than interventions that facilitate internal change (Gerstein & Ægisdóttir, 2007).

BIASES AGAINST INTERNATIONAL WORK

One of the challenges for international counseling scholars is convincing journal editors and conference program chairs that their work is important and worthy of publication and/or presentation. This is particularly true if a scholar's effort involves studying international samples and the development of counseling in countries other than the United States. Although there has been a slight increase in U.S. publications on international topics, there is much room for improvement. As mentioned earlier, our review of articles published between the years 2000 and 2004 in four U.S. counseling journals revealed that only 6% focused on international samples and topics (Gerstein & Ægisdóttir, 2007). Furthermore, as stated earlier, the current knowledge in U.S. psychology is based on only 5% of the world population (Arnett, 2008), and most of this knowledge was derived from U.S. samples. It is obvious, then, that our current knowledge about counseling and psychology in the United States most probably does not apply worldwide.

Along with other counseling scholars, we have experienced challenges when trying to publish or present on international topics. Leung (2003), for instance, reported having a presentation at an APA convention rejected because his findings were considered to be irrelevant to practice in the United States. Likewise, we have received similar comments from reviewers and editors of U.S. counseling and psychology journals. Our work has been considered unworthy of publication. One reason we were given was that journal readers would probably never come across clients or individuals from the country we investigated. Interestingly, minority scholars also faced difficulties publishing their work in the 1950s, although for very different reasons, including racism, which restricted Black counseling professionals from publishing (Jackson, 1995).

Change is still needed in the counseling profession with regard to what is considered an important topic of study. Dissemination of research findings should not be controlled by popularity, but instead should be driven by the advancement of counseling as a science (Gerstein & Ægisdóttir, 2007). It is a journal editor's responsibility to educate his or her readers and to display leadership in acknowledging that cross-cultural and cultural research is imperative in theory development (see Brislin, 1976, 1983).

It seems ironic that international scholars in counseling are currently experiencing some of the same challenges that multicultural scholars were facing more than two decades ago. It took 20 years for the multicultural guidelines to be endorsed by APA (Arredondo & Perez, 2003). We certainly hope it will take less time for our discipline, professional organizations, and administrators to realize the importance of international work to enhancing the scientific foundation of our field.

CONCLUSION

As contact increases between people from various countries, the mission and philosophy of counseling must be adapted and expanded. Some scholars have even argued that international work represents "the next stage in the multicultural counseling movement" (Gerstein, 2006, p. 379). It is becoming more important and apparent that students and scholars want to acquire competencies in international work. Obviously, training opportunities must be created for this to occur. Uncritically relying on U.S. assumptions about emotions, cognitions, and behavior when working in an international setting or with persons of other countries should be questioned. To expand current theories of human behavior and social action, one must approach international issues with an open mind and an awareness of the power of culture in shaping behavior.

In this chapter, we discussed a modified framework of multicultural counseling competencies (C-C MAKS), and we offered numerous recommendations to help prepare counseling professionals to become more internationally competent. Future research is needed to explore the validity and applicability of the C-C MAKS and the relevance and significance of these recommendations. We also outlined some strategies to enhance the effectiveness of counseling practices outside of the United States, and we shared some suggestions about how to conduct cross-culturally valid and useful research. Hopefully, our recommendations will help aspiring and current students and scholars to think and act "outside of the box," particularly the U.S. box of psychology and counseling. Approaching international work based on the suggestions we have provided might result in affirming the culture, target country, and its members. In so doing, internationally competent counseling professionals will help to preserve and honor diverse cultures around the world while at the same time advancing the science and practice of counseling.

REFERENCES

Abreu, J. M., Chung, R. H., & Atkinson, D. R. (2000). Multicultural counseling training: Past, present, and future directions. *Counseling Psychologist, 28,* 641–656.

Arnett, J. J. (2008). The neglected 95%: Why American psychology needs to become less American. *American Psychologist, 63,* 602–614.

Arredondo, P., & Perez, P. (2003). Expanding multicultural competence through social justice leadership. *Counseling Psychologist, 31,* 282–289.

Arredondo, P., Toporek, R., Brown, S. B., Jones, J., Locke, D. C., Sanchez, J., & Stadler, H. (1996). Operationalization of the multicultural counseling competencies. *Journal of Multicultural Counseling and Development, 24,* 42–78.

Arthur, N., & Pedersen, P. B. (2008). *Case incidents in counseling for international transitions.* Alexandria, VA: American Counseling Association.

Atkinson, D. R., Thompson, C. E., & Grant, S. K. (1993). A three dimensional model for counseling racial/ethnic minorities. *Counseling Psychologist, 21,* 257–277.

Boyle, D. P., Nackerud, L., & Kilpatrick, A. (1999). The road less traveled: Cross-cultural, international experiential learning. *International Social Work, 42*(2), 201–214.

Brislin, R. W. (1976). Comparative research methodology: Cross cultural studies. *International Journal of Psychology, 11,* 213–229.

Brislin, R. W. (1983). Cross cultural research in psychology. *Annual Review of Psychology, 34,* 363–400.

Brislin, R. W. (1986). The wording and translation of research instruments. In W. J. Lonner & J. W. Berry (Eds.), *Field methods in cross-cultural research* (pp. 137–164). Beverly Hills, CA: Sage.

Brislin, R. W., Lonner, W. J., & Thorndike, R. M. (1973). *Cross-cultural research methods.* New York: Wiley.

Bronfenbrenner, U. (1979). *The ecology of human development: Experiments by nature and design.* Cambridge, MA: Harvard University Press.

Collins, N. M., & Pieterse, A. L. (2007). Critical incident analysis based learning: An approach to training for active racial and cultural awareness. *Journal of Counseling and Development, 85,* 14–23.

D'Andrea, M. D., & Daniels, J. (1991). Exploring the different levels of multicultural training in counselor education. *Journal of Counseling and Development, 70,* 78–85.

deShazer, S. (1991). *Putting difference to work.* New York: Norton.

Fouad, N. A. (1991). Training counselors to counsel international students. *Counseling Psychologist, 19,* 66–71.

Gerstein, L. H. (2006). Counseling psychologists as international social architects. In R. L. Toporek, L. H. Gerstein, N. A. Fouad, G. Roysircar-Sodowsky, & T. Israel (Eds.), *Handbook for social justice in counseling psychology: Leadership, vision, and action* (pp. 377–387). Thousand Oaks, CA: Sage.

Gerstein, L. H., & Ægisdóttir, S. (2005a). Counseling around the world. Guest editors for a special issue of the *Journal of Mental Health Counseling, 27,* 95–184.

Gerstein, L. H., & Ægisdóttir, S. (2005b). Counseling outside of the United States: Looking in and reaching out. Guest editors for a special section of the *Journal of Mental Health Counseling, 27,* 221–281.

Gerstein, L. H., & Ægisdóttir, S. (2005c). A trip around the world: A counseling travelogue! *Journal of Mental Health Counseling, 27,* 95–103.

Gerstein, L. H., & Ægisdóttir, S. (2007). Training international social change agents: Transcending a U.S. counseling paradigm. *Counselor Education and Supervision, 47,* 123–139.

Gerstein, L. H., & Bennett, M. (1999). Quantum physics and mental health counseling: The time is . . . ! *Journal of Mental Health Counseling, 21,* 255–269.

Gerstein, L. H., Heppner, P. P., Ægisdóttir, S., Leung, S. A., & Norsworthy, K. L. (Eds.). (in press). *International handbook of cross-cultural counseling: Cultural assumptions and practices worldwide.* Thousand Oaks, CA: Sage.

Gerstein, L. H., Rountree, C., & Ordonez, A. (2007). An anthropological perspective on multicultural counselling. *Counselling Psychology Quarterly, 20,* 375–400.

Gerstein, L., & Sturmer, P. (1993). A Taoist paradigm of EAP consultation. *Journal of Counseling and Development, 72,* 178–184.

Giorgis, T. W., & Helms, J. E. (1978). Training international students from developing nations as psychologists: A challenge for American psychology. *American Psychologist, 33,* 945–951.

Greatrex-White, S. (2007). A way of seeing study abroad: Narratives from nurse education. *Learning in Health and Social Care, 6*(3), 134–144.

Heppner, P. P. (1997). Building on strengths as we move into the next millennium. *Counseling Psychologist, 25,* 5–14.

Heppner, P. P. (2006). The benefits and challenges of becoming cross-culturally competent counseling psychologists. *Counseling Psychologist, 34,* 147–172.

Heppner, P. P., & Gerstein, L. H. (in press). International developments in counseling psychology. In E. Altmaier & B. D. Johnson (Eds.), *Encyclopedia of counseling: Changes and challenges for counseling in the 21st century* (Vol. 1). Thousand Oaks, CA: Sage.

Heppner, P. P, Leong, F. T. L., & Gerstein, L. H. (2008). Counseling within a changing world: Meeting the psychological needs of societies and the world. In W. B. Walsh (Ed.), *Biennial review of counseling psychology* (pp. 231–258). New York: Taylor & Francis.

Hofstede, G. J., Pedersen, P. B., & Hofstede, G. (2002). *Exploring culture: Exercises, stories and synthetic cultures.* Yarmouth, ME: Intercultural Press.

Horne, S. G., & Mathews, S. S. (2006). A social justice approach to international collaborative consultation. In R. L. Toporek, L. H. Gerstein, N. A. Fouad, G. Roysircar-Sodowsky, & T. Israel (Eds.), *Handbook for social justice in counseling psychology: Leadership, vision, and action* (pp. 388–405). Thousand Oaks, CA: Sage.

Ibrahim, F. A. (1985). Effective cross-cultural counseling and psychotherapy: A framework. *Counseling Psychologist, 13,* 625–638.

Ibrahim, F. A., Roysircar-Sodowsky, G., & Ohnishi, H. (2001). Worldview: Recent developments and needed directions. In J. G. Ponterotto, J. M. Casas, L. A. Suzuki, & C. M. Alexander (Eds.), *Handbook of multicultural counseling* (2nd ed., pp. 425–456). Thousand Oaks, CA: Sage.

Jackson, M. L. (1995). Multicultural counseling: Historical perspectives. In J. G. Ponterotto, J. M. Casas, L. A. Suzuki, & C. M. Alexander (Eds.), *Handbook of multicultural counseling* (pp. 3–16). Thousand Oaks, CA: Sage.

Krajewski-Jaime, E. R., Brown, K. S., Ziefert, M., & Kaufman, E. (1996). Utilizing international clinical practice to build inter-cultural sensitivity in social work students. *Journal of Multicultural Social Work, 4*(2), 15–30.

Kwan, K. L. K., & Gerstein, L. H. (2008). Envisioning a counseling psychology of the world: The mission of the International Forum. *Counseling Psychologist, 36,* 182–187.

LaFromboise, T. D., & Foster, S. L. (1992). Cross-cultural training: Scientist-practitioner model and methods. *Counseling Psychologist, 20,* 472–489.

Leong, F. T. L., & Blustein, D. L. (2000). Toward a global vision of counseling psychology. *Counseling Psychologist, 28,* 5–9.

Leong, F. T. L., & Ponterotto, J. G. (2003). A proposal for internationalizing counseling psychology in the United States: Rationale, recommendations, and challenges. *Counseling Psychologist, 31,* 381–395.

Leong, F. T. L., & Savickas, M. (2007). Introduction to special issue on international perspectives on counseling psychology. *Applied Psychology: An International Review, 56,* 1–6.

Leung, S. A. (2003). A journey worth traveling: Globalization of counseling psychology. *Counseling Psychology, 31,* 412–419.

Lindsey, E. W. (2005). Study abroad and values development in social work students. *Journal of Social Work Education, 41*(2), 229–249.

Lonner, W. J. (1985). Issues in testing and assessment in cross-cultural counseling. *Counseling Psychologist, 13,* 599–614.

Marsella, A. J., & Pedersen, P. (2004). Internationalizing the counseling psychology curriculum: Toward new values, competencies, and directions. *Counselling Psychology Quarterly, 17,* 413–423.

McWhirter, B. T., & McWhirter, E. H. (2006). Couples helping couples: Consultation and training in Penalolen, Chile. In R. L. Toporek, L. H. Gerstein, N. A. Fouad, G. Roysircar-Sodowsky, & T. Israel (Eds.), *Handbook for social justice in counseling psychology: Leadership, vision, and action* (pp. 406–420). Thousand Oaks, CA: Sage.

Murphy, G. (1955). The cultural context of guidance. *Personnel and Guidance Journal, 34*(1), 4–9.

Norsworthy, K. L. (2006). Bringing social justice to international practices of counseling psychology. In R. L. Toporek, L. H. Gerstein, N. A. Fouad, G. Roysircar-Sodowsky, & T. Israel (Eds.), *Handbook for social justice in counseling psychology: Leadership, vision, and action* (pp. 421–441). Thousand Oaks, CA: Sage.

Pedersen, P. B. (1991). Counseling international students. *Counseling Psychologist, 19,* 10–58.

Pedersen, P. B. (2003). Culturally biased assumptions in counseling psychology. *Counseling Psychologist, 31,* 396–403.

Pedersen, P., & Leong, F. (1997). Counseling in an international context. *Counseling Psychologist, 25,* 117–122.

Pedersen, P., Lonner, W. J., & Draguns, J. G. (1976). *Counseling across cultures.* Honolulu: University of Hawaii Press.

Reynolds, A. L. (1995). Challenges and strategies for teaching multicultural counseling courses. In J. G. Ponterotto, J. M. Casas, L. A. Suzuki, & C. M. Alexander (Eds.), *Handbook of multicultural counseling* (pp. 312–330). Thousand Oaks, CA: Sage.

Ridley, C. R., & Kleiner, A. (2003). Multicultural counseling competence: History, themes, and issues. In D. Pope Davis, H. L. Coleman, W. M. Lui, & R. L. Toporek (Eds.), *Handbook of multicultural counseling competencies* (pp. 3–20). Thousand Oaks, CA: Sage.

Ridley, C. R., Mendoza, D. W., & Kanitz, B. E. (1994). Multicultural training: Reexamination, operationalization, and integration. *Counseling Psychologist, 22,* 227–289.

Ruddock, H. C., & Turner, D. (2007). Developing cultural sensitivity: Nursing students' experiences of a study abroad programme. *Journal of Advanced Nursing, 59*(4), 361–369.

Singaravelu, H. D., & Pope, M. (2008). *A handbook for counseling international students in the U.S.* Alexandria, VA: American Counseling Association.

Sue, D. W., Arredondo, P., & McDavis, R. J. (1992). Multicultural counseling competencies and standards: A call to the profession. *Journal of Counseling and Development, 70,* 477–483.

Sue, D. W., Bernier, J., Durran, M., Feinberg, L., Pedersen, P., Smith, E., & Vasquez–Nuttall, E. (1982). Position paper: Multicultural counseling competencies. *Counseling Psychologist, 10,* 45–52.

Sue, D. W., & Sue, D. (1999). *Counseling the culturally different: Theory and practice* (3rd ed.). New York: Wiley.

Sue, S., & Sue, D. W. (1971). Chinese-American personality and mental health. *Amerasia Journal, 2,* 39–49.

Takooshian, H. (2003). Counseling psychology's wide new horizons. *Counseling Psychologist, 31,* 420–426.

Trevino, J. G. (1996). Worldview and change in cross-cultural counseling. *Counseling Psychologist, 24,* 198–215.

Triandis, H. C. (1972). *The analysis of subjective culture.* New York: Wiley.

Triandis, H. C. (1994). *Culture and social behavior.* New York: McGraw-Hill.

Triandis, H. C. (1995). *Individualism and collectivism: New directions in social psychology.* Boulder, CO: Westview.

Triandis, H. C. (2001). Individualism-collectivism and personality. *Journal of Personality, 69,* 907–924.

van de Vijver, F. J. R., & Leung, K. (1997). *Methods and data analysis for cross-cultural research.* Thousand Oaks, CA: Sage.

Varenne, H. (2003). On internationalizing counseling psychology: A view from cultural anthropology. *Counseling Psychologist, 31,* 404–411.

Vontress, C. E. (1971). *Counseling Negroes: Series 6. Minority groups and guidance.* Boston: Houghton Mifflin.

Wang, L., & Heppner, P. P. (in press). Cross-cultural collaboration: Developing cross-cultural competencies and yuanfen. In L. H. Gerstein, P. P. Heppner, S. Ægisdóttir, S. A. Leung, & K. L. Norsworthy (Eds.), *International handbook of cross-cultural counseling: Cultural assumptions and practices worldwide.* Thousand Oaks, CA: Sage.

Ægisdóttir, S., & Gerstein, L. H. (2005). Reaching out: Mental health delivery outside the box. *Journal of Mental Health Counseling, 27,* 221–224.

Ægisdóttir, S., Gerstein, L. H., & Çinarbas, D. (2008). Methodological issues in cross-cultural counseling research: Equivalence, bias and translations. *Counseling Psychologist, 36,* 188–219.

18

The Multicultural and Internationalization Counseling Psychology Movements

When All Is Said and Done, It's All Multicultural, Isn't It?

J. MANUEL CASAS, YONG S. PARK, AND BRIAN CHO

Like Gulliver who awoke to a world that had shrunken in size, counseling psychology is confronting a new dawn in which the world that we inhabit is, metaphorically speaking, shrinking. Concomitantly, as the world is shrinking, the variety and number of cultures and racial/ethnic groups with whom counseling psychologists are interacting, both within and outside the United States, is increasing largely as a result of two revolutionary movements. These two movements, which share much in common, especially in reference to their focus on culture, can be aptly called the internationalization and the multicultural movements. Given the importance of these two movements to the future of psychology in general, and counseling psychology in particular, we have opted to make the following the major goals of this chapter: (a) provide a historical and comparative overview of the two movements, (b) compare and contrast the commonalities and differences that exist between the movements, and (c) provoke thought and discussion regarding the logic and rationale for their continued separate and potentially unequal treatment. To reach these goals, we will address the following objectives:

- Identify and discuss the social, political, economic, and organizational forces that gave life to and nurtured the development of the internationalization and multicultural counseling psychology movements from a historical contextual perspective.

- Identify and/or clarify the goals and objectives that underlie the two respective movements.

- Direct attention to the barriers that both movements have had or will have as they work toward an equitable acceptance by psychology in general and counseling psychology in particular.

- Identify the professional and ethical challenges that the two movements have faced or will face as

189

they seek to deal with the major principles and guidelines that oversee all activities of the counseling psychology profession (e.g., training, research, and practice).

• Provide information that can help counseling psychology take steps to merge its international and multicultural interests and efforts into one force that will be of benefit to psychology as a whole.

In addressing these goals and objectives, we draw substantially from recent publications (e.g., Leong & Leach, 2007; Leong & Savickas, 2007; Savickas, 2007; Tikkanen, 2007) to make and/or illustrate the points and perspectives that are contained herein.

A HISTORICAL PERSPECTIVE OF THE INTERNATIONAL MOVEMENT

The internationalization movement is a reflection of the globalization movement, a force through which national boundaries are being "erased" to make room for a new integrated, international, multicultural, and global society (Daly, 1999). The elimination of such boundaries is the result of advances in global business relations, international travel, and computer networking technology (Friedman, 2005). These advances have essentially created an environment in which people are no longer restricted by geographic and national boundaries. Supporting this perspective, recent trends show an increase in international and multicultural interactions, including, but not limited to, increases in migration rates (Taylor, 2006), global traveling (Smith, 1994), acquisition of multiple languages (Walton, 2007), and international business collaborations (Chmielewski & Lee, 2007). A popular attribute of globalization is that, overall, it is a movement that follows economic and political trends and creations of sociopolitical and economic bodies such as the European Union and the North American Free Trade Agreement (Pawlik & d'Ydewalle, 1996).

Such internationalization trends are also evident at systemic levels. The past century witnessed the inauguration of international organizations whose primary purposes and responsibilities were to facilitate communication between and among nations that addresses shared political, economic, health, and sociocultural interests and concerns. Notable international organizations that were developed with such purposes in mind include the United Nations, to oversee international law and security; Amnesty International, to enforce human rights; the World Trade Organization, to facilitate international trading; and the World Health Organization, to oversee and address the health status of people across the globe.

In addition to these organizations, varied professions have enthusiastically joined the internationalization movement. One profession in particular that is the focus of this chapter is psychology, and more specifically, counseling psychology. Interestingly, with all the hoopla that is accompanying the so-called internationalization of psychology, one would think that this is the first time that psychology has gone abroad. Such is not the case. According to Pawlik and d'Ydewalle (1996), psychology's involvement in international affairs goes as far back as 1889, when 200 highly regarded psychologists from across the globe founded the first international psychology organization, the First International Congress of Physiological Psychology.

Starting at this time and continuing well into the latter part of the 20th century, such international forays consisted of interactions or exchanges (e.g., conferences, exchange of students, visiting professors, translations of books) between U.S. and European psychologists. A major reason for these interactions included efforts to strengthen the scientific and professional (i.e., applied) foundation of the emerging field of psychology in both the United States and Europe. This was done by providing forums and information outlets from which ideas could be promulgated and challenged. Reflecting the historical development of psychology, European psychologists took the lead in providing such forums; but early in the 1900s, as the field took hold and began to flourish in the United States, the focus shifted to the United States. An example of these interactions included, but were not limited to, G. Stanley Hall studying with Wilhelm Wundt (1879–1880) in Leipzig at the time when Wundt was establishing the first laboratory of experimental psychology in the world; the first International Conference of Psychiatrists interested in Freud's psychological theories that was organized by Jung in 1908; the "Clark Celebration" held in 1909, which included among its participants Sigmund Freud, Carl Jung, G. Stanley Hall, and William James (a highlight of this gathering was a series of five lectures on psychoanalysis that were delivered by Freud); the Watson-McDougal debate held in 1924; the 2002 International Congress on Applied Psychology held in Singapore; and the 2008 International Counseling Psychology Conference held in Chicago.

From an academic perspective, Wilhelm Wundt, considered to be one of the founding persons of psychology, produced a 10-volume work, *Cultural Psychology*, published between 1900 and 1920. In this work, he addresses psychology as a product of both internal and external phenomena, with both a national and an international basis (Schultz & Schultz, 2004). Acknowledging this and other complementary works, the American Psychological Association (APA) established the Wilhelm Wundt-William James Award for Exceptional Contributions to Trans-Atlantic Psychology, which recognizes a significant record of trans-Atlantic research collaboration (European Federation of Psychologists' Association, 2003).

Given these early beginnings, it is safe to say that psychology has developed and maintains an ongoing commitment to and involvement in the international arena. Such involvement was greatly facilitated by the fact that during the past 70 years, psychology in the United States, although borrowing many ideas from Europe, managed to become the leading force in the discipline of psychology from both an experimental and a clinical/counseling perspective. Concomitant with this fact was the belief that the international realm of psychology could greatly benefit from the work of U.S. psychologists (e.g., B. F. Skinner), while at the same time these psychologists could pick and use works that other parts of the world had to offer (e.g., Pavlov, Montessori). It should be noted that the term *world* in this context has a narrow application, as it largely continues to have today in psychology, to the "Western world"—Europe and the United States—or to other parts of the world (e.g., Australia, South Africa) that had been or were being colonized politically, socially, economically, and educationally by European countries or the United States. A note of interest is the fact that a recent international milestone on the European continent was the establishment of the European Federation of Psychologists' Associations (EFPA), which incorporates many of the APA principles and goals. For instance, two of the major aims of EFPA are to (a) further the development of psychology as a science and a profession with particular reference to training, qualification, and status; and (b) support the interests of psychology and its application in relation to any European or international organizations concerned with defining research or professional politics significant for psychology (Tikkanen, 2007).

Although today's internationalization movement in psychology (i.e., APA and Division 17) shares much in common with the early international psychological efforts, they are not identical. To this point, the globalizing force for going abroad may be similar across both past and present movements, but their goals and objectives are essentially not the same. More specifically, the early movement focused more on the establishment and/or strengthening of psychology as a discipline with special attention given to the identification and/or development of philosophical precepts that would underscore and guide the diverse activities associated with the discipline (e.g., research and practice) and the development of theoretical and positivistic-based research paradigms that would actually give impetus and provide direction to the work needed to affirm and validate psychology as an academic discipline (Schultz & Schultz, 2004).

The more recent internationalization movement, on the other hand, although continuing to give emphasis to the development and/or validation of applied and experimentally focused theories through the use of innovative research paradigms and models, is extending greater efforts and more time to the creation of formal structures and processes to institutionalize and facilitate the internationalization of psychology. Such efforts include, but are not limited to, the establishment of Division 17's International Section as well as the International Association of Applied Psychology (IAAP) Counseling Division (Division 16) in 2002.

According to several writers, the major underlying forces for the present internationalization movement in counseling psychology include, but are not limited to, formation of a global community, accessibility to cross-cultural research, and economic reasons.

Formation of a Global Community. Leong and Ponterotto (2003) contend that there is an apparent "need for American psychologists to be part of the global community of psychologists and healers and not act independently" (p. 383). Moreover, it is believed that an international body for counseling psychology can potentially improve the welfare and remediate distress for culturally distinct people across the globe (Leong & Ponterrotto, 2003).

Cross-Cultural Research. Pedersen and Leong (1997) also suggest that internationalization can improve our understanding of psychological phenomena through cross-cultural research. More specifically, they state that there is a need for psychologists to "continually assess the cultural validity and cross-cultural generalizability of our applied and research models and theories of counseling for clients in other cultures" (Pedersen & Leong, 1997, p. 118). According to Leong and Ponterotto (2003), theories that have not been investigated cross-culturally should be considered emic (i.e., culturally specific) as opposed to etic (i.e., culturally transcendent).

Economic Reasons. Outside psychology, the global movement has been largely motivated by economic forces. More specifically, some argue that globalization is essentially driven by economic forces to the benefit of multinational corporations. From this perspective, one must wonder if counseling psychology can also be considered a multinational corporation that is taking advantage of the global market through its profit-making consultative, publication, training, and overall educational efforts.

In line with the worldwide globalization trend, the recent APA internationalization movement has been quite methodical and forceful in its efforts to attain desired goals and objectives as witnessed by the passage of a resolution to increase visibility of psychology on a global level (Leong & Leach, 2007). Reflecting the essence of this resolution, APA partnered in many initiatives with such groups as the U.S. Fulbright Scholarship program, the Peace Corps, Head Start, and the World Health Organization (Pawlik & d'Ydewalle, 1996). Counseling psychology programs increased their international focus by expanding faculty research collaboration with colleagues from other countries, including international issues in coursework, hosting colleagues from other countries at their home institution, and increasing contracts with foreign universities to initiate exchange programs (Leong & Leach, 2007).

Exemplifying counseling psychology's organizational movement toward globalization, three recent Division 17 presidents emphasized or included globalization in their respective presidential themes. During his term as president in 2005, Heppner increased the Society of Counseling Psychology's international liaison representation, devised international lists of counseling organizations and individuals, moved toward greater incorporation of international information in coursework, and expanded the breadth of the field (Leong & Leach, 2007). Under the leadership of a group of counseling psychologists, IAAP Counseling Division (Division 16) was formed in 2002.

From the perspective of publications, Leong and Ponterotto (2003) report that recent special issues on internationalizing counseling psychology (e.g., *The Counseling Psychologist, Journal of Vocational Behavior*) have increased, whereas other applied journals related to counseling psychology (e.g., *Journal of Mental Health Counseling*) have directed attention to the application of much-studied U.S. constructs to the international domain. On an ongoing basis, *The Counseling Psychologist* has devoted a good portion of the journal, referred to as the "International Forum," to discuss international issues in counseling psychology (Pedersen & Leong, 1997). And last but not least, seeking to provide a friendly and receptive outlet for multicultural research, several racial/ethnic minority psychologists working with Lillian Comas-Díaz established a journal that eventually was subsumed by the APA as the official journal of Division 45 (The Society for the Study of Ethnic Minority Issues in Psychology) and is presently named *Cultural Diversity & Ethnic Minority Psychology.*

A HISTORICAL PERSPECTIVE OF THE MULTICULTURAL MOVEMENT

Broadly speaking, the multicultural movement is first and foremost a movement that directs its professional efforts and activities to the propagation of social justice. It is a movement that seeks to improve the living conditions (e.g., social, political, economic, health, educational) for all persons regardless of national boundaries, race, ethnicity, gender, sexual orientation, age, health status, and physical abilities. More specifically, with respect to multicultural counseling and therapy, it can be defined as encompassing both a helping role and a process that uses modalities and defines goals consistent with the life experiences and cultural values of clients; recognizes client identities to include individual, group, and universal dimensions; advocates the use of universal and culture-specific strategies and roles in the healing process; and balances the importance of individualism and collectivism in the assessment, diagnosis, and treatment of client and client systems (Sue & Sue, 2003).

Historically speaking, there were two major external and interacting sociohistorical forces that impelled counseling psychology to direct its attention to multiculturalism, and more specifically, to the issues associated with the unjust psychosocial treatment of racial/ethnic minority persons. The first is the social-political unrest and upheaval that has come to define the period between 1960 and 1980 (e.g., the Vietnam anti-war movement, the civil rights movement, the gay and lesbian movement, the farm workers' movement). Such unrest essentially served to increase the awareness of the social, political, and economic injustices that plagued and continue to plague persons of color in this country (e.g., poverty, lack of physical and mental health services, inequitable educational services, overrepresentation in the prison system).

The second is the tremendous increase, by either birth or immigration, of persons of color living in the United States (Casas, Raley, & Vasquez, 2008) who, for varied social and economic reasons, have a high probability of suffering from social, physical health, and mental health problems (U.S. Surgeon General, 1999). Making matters worse, according to the Special Populations Task Force of the President's Commission on Mental Health (1978), ethnic minorities are clearly underserved or inadequately served by the current mental health system in this country (Heppner, Casas, Carter, & Stone, 2000).

Although there are numerous reasons for the provision of inadequate services, the following have been identified time and again by a significant number of multicultural counseling psychologists (e.g., Sue & Zane, 1987): lack of bilingual therapists; therapists' stereotypes of ethnic clients; discriminatory practices; lack of familiarity with ethnic cultures and lifestyles;

and training limited to Western, non-Hispanic White forms of counseling.

Seeking to improve on this situation, researchers and practitioners advocated for changes in the mental health system, with the primary method being match or fit: treatment should match the cultural lifestyle or experiences of clients. Mental health services were urged to hire bilingual/bicultural personnel; provide continuing education of current staff members; establish parallel services in areas where large ethnic communities exist and nonparallel services for ethnic minority clients were necessary (e.g., due to the "issue" of stigma); and develop multiservice centers where mental health programs would be embedded in established services (e.g., legal, health, and social services) that are not directly provided per se (Sue & Zane, 1987).

As these requests and demands increased, the APA came to recognize the need to take action to rectify the situation. With respect to Division 17, although the early 1980s witnessed a somewhat wavering commitment to the development of multicultural counseling and diversity, the past 20 years have witnessed a more consistent increase in awareness and commitment to multicultural issues in the APA and the profession as a whole. From the onset, it is important to once more underscore that translating such commitment into actions, such as those that are selectively highlighted herein, did not come easily. To the contrary, the actions that came about frequently occurred in an atmosphere filled with tension (Heppner et al., 2000), resistance, and in some cases, outright hostility. In spite of such an atmosphere, the dedication and determination of concerned psychologists, and especially those from racial/ethnic minority groups, resulted in successful actions on the part of APA and Division 17 that included the establishment of new divisions (i.e., Divisions 44 and 45), standing committees, divisional sections (e.g., the International Section of Division 17), special publications (e.g., the position paper on multicultural competencies by Sue et al., 1982), conferences (e.g., the APA Multicultural Summit), and the revision of the ethical principles and accreditation guidelines (APA, 2002a, 2002b) to include the basic moral principle that centers on human diversity and nondiscrimination, curriculum guidelines, multicultural guidelines, and the acceptance of the multicultural competencies in 1982. For more details relative to such actions, see Heppner et al. (2000).

One of the early efforts by the APA to address racial/ethnic minority concerns was the establishment in 1963 of the Ad Hoc Committee on Equality of Opportunity in Psychology. This committee actually directed its attention to the following groups: Asian Americans, African Americans, Hispanics, and Native Americans. Although culture was not explicitly mentioned at this time, given the distinct cultures represented in each of the respective targeted groups, it was assumed to exist implicitly. This committee was given the task of formulating policy related to the education, training, employment, and status of minority groups in psychology. Subsequent committees have continued doing policy work in these areas. Wanting to increase the APA's efforts to address the needs of people of color, representatives from the major racial/ethnic minority groups eventually established their own respective associations within the APA: the Asian-American Psychological Association, the Association of Black Psychologists, the National Association of Latino Psychologists, and the Society for Indian Psychologists.

Largely through the leadership efforts of some of the APA and divisional leaders and the APA committees and boards, and the collaborative efforts of the membership of Divisions 45, 35, 44, and 17 and the respective racial/ethnic minority associations, significant steps have been taken toward reaching the following outcomes: (a) improving the status and treatment of individuals from oppressed groups; (b) increasing the number of racial/ethnic minority psychologists, and in particular, the number of graduate and undergraduate students preparing for the profession; (c) ensuring representation of persons from diverse groups in the APA organizational structure, especially at leadership levels; (d) ensuring that diversity issues and needs are addressed in the APA ethical principles and standards and taken into consideration in the accreditation process; and (e) developing a process to increase the representation of diversity issues in the curricula as well as in the educational/training experiences required of all psychologists (Heppner et al., 2000). The latest step taken toward improving the representation of racial/ethnic minority persons in the leadership structure of the APA has been the presentation of a resolution (yet to be approved) to give one voting seat on the APA Council of Representatives to each of the respective racial/ethnic minority associations.

THE PROFESSION'S RECEPTIVITY TO THE TWO MOVEMENTS: WELCOMING OR TOLERATING?

Having provided a historical perspective for both movements, attention is now directed to the organizational context and level of receptivity or acceptance in which the two movements came to be. Although one might assume that the context and receptivity in which they developed might be the same given the fact that they share much in common (e.g., reaching out into unfamiliar international and national territory, working with diverse cultural populations, and varying degrees of commitment to social justice), the fact of the matter is that if you put the two movements side by side, it quickly becomes apparent that their respective origins, commitments, and developmental paths are quite distinct.

To begin with, the internationalization movement can be characterized as having been openly received and nurtured by a significant number of the members of Division 17, or at least little or no opposition was voiced. In contrast, the multicultural movement can be characterized as having been imposed on the counseling profession, or at least it had to fight for its rightful place in the profession. The origin of multiculturalism is the product of sociopolitical pressures from without, whereas the origin of internationalism is the product of voluntary professional efforts from within. Internationalization has followed a top-down developmental path (i.e., from organizational leaders to members), whereas multiculturalism has followed a bottom-up path (i.e., from racial/ethnic minority members to organizational leaders—the majority of whom were non-Hispanic White). Multiculturalism has sought to change the heart and soul of the profession (i.e., the rationale for its existence) by working to change the core and focus of the profession toward social justice, whereas internationalization has mainly sought to "professionally colonize" new geographical locations where the traditional Western-based work of the profession, with less focus on social justice, can be conducted.

COUNTERACTING FORCES
TO THE TWO MOVEMENTS

According to Leong and Santiago-Rivera (1999), there have been six counteracting forces to the expansion of multiculturalism, and in addendum, internationalism (Leong & Leach, 2007), throughout the history of counseling psychology in the United States. Historically, the first counteracting force in the field of counseling psychology has been the tendency toward ethnocentrism and Anglocentricism, which, as a consequence, has (a) limited the generalizability and reliability of the field, (b) confined one's vision in the field of psychology, (c) distanced and separated cultural groups, and (d) increased cultural stereotypes.

The second counteracting force has been called the false-consensus effect and occurs when people designate or assume their own behavior to be characteristic of all people (Fiske & Taylor, 1991). Relative to this effect, people are inclined to seek out others who possess the same or similar attitudes, values, and behaviors. Doing so only serves to strengthen the idea that they are correct in their evaluations, analogous to the confirmation bias (Wason, 1960).

The third counteracting force is based on Schneider's (1987) Attraction-Selection-Attrition framework. From their onset, organizations are prone to attract individuals with the same or similar mind-sets while encouraging those who do not share the same mind-sets to leave. By so doing, such organizations become homogeneous and resistant to change.

The fourth counteracting force is that individuals have a tendency to offset threats that are seen as leading to a loss of freedoms (Brehm & Brehm, 1981). This force has been called psychological reactance. More specifically, it is synonymous with the difficulties that are encountered when efforts to change the conventional ways of doing business are considered.

According to Leong and Santiago-Rivera (1999), the fifth force takes the position that beliefs and values are not the same; beliefs are the conceptions of what one believes to be true and values are what one actually wants. At

times, these concepts (beliefs and values) become fused, creating a values-belief fallacy, that is to say, the idea that individuals function as if their values are indeed their beliefs. Because values tend to be hierarchical in nature, then by extension, beliefs also acquire this attribute. The final and sixth counteracting force, which is found in most, if not all, cultures (Leong & Leach, 2007), is the concept of conformity. According to this concept, individuals are driven to adhere to the prevailing majority attitudes (Devine, Hamilton, & Ostrom, 1994).

Because the six counteracting forces have had a long history of impact on U.S. psychology, they have become deeply imbedded in the profession's development. According to Leong and Leach (2007), "These six forces have a longstanding history within US psychology, and while many counseling psychologists have become more involved in multiculturalism and internationalism, old philosophies are difficult to change" (p. 172).

CHALLENGES FACING
THE TWO MOVEMENTS

Having addressed counteracting forces that both movements have encountered or will encounter, attention is now directed to the challenges and issues that these movements have or will eventually confront in their efforts to carry out the major responsibilities and tasks inherent in the profession. It goes without saying that the intensity of these challenges and issues is greatly determined by the profession's ethnocentric insistence to strictly apply the paradigms, theories, and models that were developed on and for the U.S.-based non-Hispanic White population to culturally diverse racial/ethnic groups. It is our contention that the challenges are similar for both movements, and as such, they are not addressed separately for each of the movements. However, it should be noted that the challenges and concomitant issues have been addressed disparately across the movements with some being addressed more successfully than others. Attention is also directed to the perspective that movement to successfully address many of the aspects of these challenges has been extremely slow as a result of the following: (a) the sociopolitical and institutional reality of the APA, which impedes timely movement on "controversial" issues; and (b) the barriers to movement detailed in the previous section and, as such, are not repeated here.

To exemplify these perspectives, in this section, the following selective challenges and issues are briefly addressed: ethics; curriculum; and training (i.e., practicum, internship).

Ethics. From the onset, major questions that have yet to be answered relative to ethics include the following: Are the principles and guidelines that govern and direct the work of psychologists etic (i.e., universally applicable and appropriate) or emic (i.e., culture bound) in nature? Are they situationally determined, or are they cast in stone? Is there room for cross-culturally sensitive interpretations and application? Are they equally valid and applicable across cultures/nations? These questions beg to be answered in light of the fact that both movements direct attention to working with persons from diverse racial, ethnic, and national groups. The work involved in addressing these questions can be exceedingly challenging, often requiring a redefining of terms and a reexamination of intent. For instance, when addressing the need to maintain confidentiality, does confidentiality and its maintenance mean the same for individually focused cultures as for collectivistic cultures? The multicultural counseling movement has been dealing with issues such as this for some time; in contrast, the U.S.-based international movement is only now beginning to grapple with issues such as these. For example, given the diversity of ethnic cultures and nationalities that comprise the European Union, the International Union of Psychological Science convened an ad hoc committee to identify, develop, and submit a universal declaration of ethical principles in 2002. Efforts such as this underscore the belief that there are basic universal moral principles toward which we all should strive, but researchers such as Trimble (this volume, Chapter 15) are quick to caution us that such principles may vary according to the lifeways and thoughtways of ethnocultural groups worldwide. Interestingly enough, internationally focused psychologists from the United States appear to be more sensitive to such caution by acknowledging the need for ethical flexibility in Europe and other parts of the world, but find themselves wearing blinders when it comes to such flexibility relative to the diverse populations and nations that exist within the boundaries of the United States.

Curriculum. For psychologists to carry out their internationally or nationally focused work with persons from diverse ethnic/cultural and/or national groups in the most culturally appropriate, effective, and ethical manner requires that they be provided with strong, multiculturally infused educational and training experiences. Although a variety of models (e.g., the one-course required model, the subspecialty model, the infusion model) have been used over the years (see Giannet, 2003), it would be safe to say that most fall short of training well-rounded multicultural psychologists who can work effectively across settings with a diversity of peoples who are confronted with a great number of psychosocial problems and issues. To improve on this situation may require that the process of accreditation be revisited with specific attention given to the development of evaluative criteria from which to better assess the multicultural content and focus of specified courses and, possibly more important, the qualifications and experiences required to teach such courses.

The challenge in the educational realm that is faced by both the multicultural and international movements is how to provide or obtain the best, most thorough, most up-to-date education/training that prepares students to work with diversity here and abroad. Needless to say, one required course is not enough. Providing more required courses is quite a challenge given that the number of APA licensing required courses is already exceedingly high. Infusing multicultural material into courses, not as an afterthought but as part of the goals and objectives of the course as a whole, is probably the best plan of action, the reason being that it illustrates how multiculturalism, whether international or national, is relevant to all aspects of psychology. After all, when all is said and done, counseling psychology, by its very nature, is multicultural. A major challenge to implementing the infusion model is the fact that to do so requires faculty and instructors who are knowledgeable about, or at least familiar with, the field of multiculturalism as it relates to psychology as a whole and to their own area of specialization in particular. The challenge lies in addressing questions such as the following: What does multiculturalism have to do with statistics? How do I infuse it into a course on research methodology? Are there certain research methods and models that are more appropriate for understanding and addressing the needs of differing racial/ethnic groups (e.g., quantitative and or qualitative— see Plano, Clark, & Wang, this volume, Chapter 35)? For more information relative to the training of multicultural counselors, refer to APA (2002b) and Pope-Davis and Coleman (1997). Questions such as these can be even more challenging in the context of a country other than the United States.

Training. Although many aspects of training are or could be challenging to both the multicultural and internationalization movements (e.g., providing sufficient experiences with a significant number of persons from diverse backgrounds and having supervisors who are capable of effectively working with clients and/or students from differing racial/ethnic groups and national backgrounds), attention is directed to a certain aspect of the internship requirement that (a) borders on the unethical and (b) has had and, unless revolutionary changes occur relative to this requirement, will continue to have what can be a very negative and stressful impact on a significant number of persons who fall outside the non-Hispanic White mainstream.

The aspect toward which attention is directed is the requirement/practice that students do their predoctoral internship at an APA-approved site. Given this requirement, students are instructed to apply to various APA sites in order to increase the probability of their being selected by one. Unfortunately, given the unavailability of APA-approved sites in various racial/ethic minority communities (e.g., there are only three APA-approved sites on the Native American reservations), students are often forced to choose less preferred sites that are not close to their communities and/or that do not or cannot provide them with the training, experiences, and supervision that they need to prepare them to return for work in and for their communities. The need to move far from home for so-called professional reasons can be extremely hard on individuals who are members of cultural groups that give emphasis to the family and the community. To a certain point, forcing these individuals to make such choices goes contrary to the ethical guidelines that underscore the need to understand, address, and respect the culture of the individuals with whom psychologists work, students included. It is analogous to requiring students to choose between their

ethnic culture and the profession's so-called cultural free perspective (Pedersen, 1987).

From an international perspective, if the profession is considering the exportation of the U.S. version of counseling and psychotherapy training to other nations, then it should be prepared to face other challenges that may make it quite difficult to do so (e.g., fewer university sites from which to choose, fewer psychologists trained to supervise using research-validated supervision models, the cultural practice of children living with their parents until they finish their education and/or get married). On the other hand, if alternate models are acceptable and international-focused psychologists help to develop them, then the following questions beg to be addressed from a U.S. multicultural perspective: Why not make the same kinds of exceptions, if the need exists, for racial/ethnic minority students in the United States? Why not make the internship experience more ethnically and culturally sensitive? For further information relative to the training challenges that might arise, refer to the Guidelines on Multicultural Education and Training (APA, 2002b) and Gerstein and Ægisdóttir, this volume (Chapter 17).

Another training issue brought forth by the international movement is the increasing scholarship of students (i.e., international students) coming to psychology programs to be trained in the United States (Leong & Leach, 2007). In theory, the exchange of scholars across countries can be mutually beneficial, giving students in the United States and abroad the opportunity to learn psychology from different cultural perspectives, but several issues need to be considered.

International students travel from far distances, taking a large risk and sacrificing much, to come learn from the experts in the field. However, past research indicates that the "American dream" of adjusting and finding success for international students is not often the case. According to Sodowsky and Lai (1997), international students often contend with the task of cultural adaptation, which includes the following struggles: culture shock, confusion about role expectations, homesickness, loss of social support, discrimination, and language barriers. Constantine, Okazaki, and Utsey (2004) added that these challenges may have mental health consequences; in particular, they may increase depression and anxiety in international students. More specific to the counseling profession, Adrian-Taylor, Noels, and Tischler (2007) recently investigated the quality of advisory and supervisory relationships among international graduate students and found that conflict is not uncommon. These authors indicate several reasons for conflict: lack of information, poor feedback, inadequate time, excessive control, discrimination, lack of close relationships, and lack of respect because of poor oral and/or written English skills.

In addition to issues concerning the psychosocial-emotional adjustment of international graduate students to their respective counseling programs and the United States in general, there is still the issue of how these training programs should train these individuals. Do they train with the goal that these individuals will eventually return to their countries of origin to engage in psychological work there? If so, it appears that the curriculum of programs would need to be flexible enough to accommodate training in the international students' home countries.

Related to this issue is whether or not an infrastructure is in place to assist these individuals with entering the job market in their country of origin or in the United States. Although no study was found in the literature review that investigated job placement of international graduate students after graduation, it appears that these individuals might face additional difficulties in the job market for various reasons, including, but not limited to, work visa status, lack of English proficiency, and financial reasons. Because these individuals sacrifice much to study in the United States, it would be unethical to enroll them without the benefit of a well-formed future employment plan. On a brighter note, APA Division 52 (International Psychology) offers a mentorship program for international students to help them publish in U.S.-based scientific journals. Needless to say, this is a step in the right direction (Leong & Leach, 2007).

The training of international graduate students, including curriculum issues mentioned previously, presents a dilemma relative to how accreditation bodies, such as the APA, evaluate the quality of training for U.S. students learning international psychology and/or international students studying in the United States.

Although, given limited space, only these three areas have been chosen to exemplify prevailing challenges,

others that merit careful study include, but are not limited to, research (see Ponterotto, this volume, Chapter 30), accreditation, supervision, and publication. It is our opinion that much work has yet to be done in these areas when it comes to racial/ethnic minority persons in the United States and even more work in reference to the exportation of ingrained U.S.-based counseling psychology's philosophies, theories, and practices to distant lands and cultures.

As such work is successfully undertaken abroad, the profession should take heed of the following cautionary remarks put forth by Arulmani (2007) and reported by Savickas (2007):

> Counseling psychology must not be "tied to the apron strings of the West," which would only serve to disconnect it from the social realities and specific needs in each country. It seems unlikely that empirical methods from North America can be easily adopted in cultures that have more intuitive and experiential practices. To flourish internationally, counseling psychology cannot be viewed primarily as a Western specialty rooted in logical positivism. To advance counseling psychology around the globe, Division 16 [IAAP] must formulate and implement strategies that facilitate development of indigenous psychological theory and research that are grounded in the specific cultural context where they are practiced. (p. 186)

If these remarks are heeded and acted upon in order to ensure the transplanting of counseling psychology across countries and cultures, the profession should also be prepared to act in a similar vein with respect to the racial/ethnic minority cultures and nations (e.g., the Sioux, the Navajo, the Pueblo) within the United States. What's good for the French goose is also good for the native gander.

A CRITICAL NATIONAL-INTERNATIONAL JUNCTURE: WHERE DO WE GO FROM HERE?

Given the above-noted internationally focused efforts and accomplishments, some authors have concluded that the field of counseling psychology may be heading toward a critical national-international juncture in its professional trajectory. More specifically, given limited resources (i.e., time and money); prevalence of health problems among racial/ethnic minority groups (e.g., AIDS, stress-related problems associated with race and living conditions) (see Tucker, Daly, & Herman, this volume, Chapter 41); social needs and problems (e.g., racism, violence, gangs) (Glazer, 2006; Guerra & Williams, 2006); and growing educational challenges (illiteracy, high dropout rates) (Castellanos & Jones, 2003), counseling psychology already may be at a juncture where it must decide how best to balance its international and national pursuits and commitments or, for the good of the profession as a whole, how to logically, responsibly, and cost-effectively combine these pursuits. To this point, some counseling psychologists, many of them persons of color who specialize in multicultural counseling, would argue that we still have much to do in our own "backyard," and as such, we should expeditiously limit our international treks into our neighbors' yards. In turn, others might argue that we have a lot to "earn" and learn from such treks, and as such, we should support and encourage them. Given the needs both at home and abroad, a happy medium must be found.

It is true that being at this juncture has the potential for polarizing the profession, but it also provides an excellent opportunity for self-examination. Such examination should not focus on differences but on the common issues and interests that both movements share, particularly their interest in culture and, to different degrees, social justice. In addition, attention should be directed toward the identification and merging of existing movements, interests, commitments, specializations, and organizational structures that already exist in the APA into *one* overarching, "culturally" sensitive and focused movement that would encompass both national and international interests, and that could become one of the major driving forces to help counseling psychology effectively navigate its way throughout our "shrinking world."

REFERENCES

Adrian-Taylor, S. R., Noels, K. A., & Tischler, K. (2007). Conflict between international graduate students and faculty supervisors: Toward effective conflict prevention and management strategies. *Journal of Studies in International Education, 11,* 90–117.

American Psychological Association. (2002a). *Guidelines and principles for accreditation.* Washington, DC: Author.

American Psychological Association. (2002b). *Guidelines on multicultural education, training, research, practice, and organizational change for psychologists.* Washington, DC: Author.

Arulmani, G. (2007). Counseling psychology in India: At the confluence of two traditions. *Applied Psychology: An International Review, 56,* 69–82.

Brehm, S. S., & Brehm, J. W. (1981). *Psychological reactance: A theory of freedom and control.* New York: Academic Press.

Casas, J. M., Raley, J. D., & Vasquez, M. J. T. (2008). Adelante! Counseling the Latina/o: From guiding theory to practice. In P. Pedersen, J. G. Draguns, W. J. Lonner, & J. E. Trimble (Eds.), *Counseling across cultures* (6th ed., pp. 129–146). Thousand Oaks, CA: Sage.

Castellanos, J., & Jones, L. (Eds.). (2003). *The minority in the majority: Expanding the representation of Latina/o faculty, administrators and students in higher education.* Sterling, VA: Stylus.

Chmielewski, D. C., & Lee, D. (2007, October 30). What's good for GM may be developed in China: The U.S. carmaker announces plans to build a facility there to study alternative fuels. *Los Angeles Times,* p. C3.

Constantine, M. G., Okazaki, S., & Utsey, S. O. (2004). Self-concealment, social self-efficacy, acculturative stress, and depression in African, Asian, and Latino international college students. *American Journal of Orthopsychiatry, 74,* 230–241.

Daly, H. E. (1999). Globalization versus internationalization—some implications. *Ecological Economics, 31,* 31–37.

Devine, P. G., Hamilton, D. L., & Ostrom, T. M. (Eds.). (1994). *Social cognition: Impact on social psychology.* San Diego, CA: Academic Press.

European Federation of Psychologists' Associations. (2003). Wilhelm Wundt-William James Prize presented for the first time. Retrieved September 2, 2008, from http://www.efpa.eu/news.php?ID=4

Fiske, S. T., & Taylor, S. F. (1991). *Social cognition* (2nd ed.). New York: McGraw-Hill.

Friedman, T. L. (2005). *The world is flat.* New York: Farrar, Straus, & Giroux.

Giannet, S. (2003). Cultural competence and professional psychology training: Creating the architecture for change. *Journal of Evolutionary Psychology, 24,* 117–127.

Glazer, A. (2006). Racism a factor in L.A. gang violence. Retrieved November 12, 2008, from http://www.amren.com/mtnews/archives/2006/08/racism_a_factor.php

Guerra, N. G., & Williams, K. R. (2006). *Preventing youth violence in a multicultural society*. Washington, DC: American Psychological Association.

Heppner, P., Casas, J. M., Carter, J., & Stone, G. (2000). The maturation of counseling psychology: Multifaceted perspectives from 1978–1998. In S. Brown & R. Lent (Eds.), *Handbook of counseling psychology* (3rd ed., pp. 3–49). New York: Wiley.

Leong, F. T. L., & Leach, M. M. (2007). Internationalizing counseling psychology in the United States: A SWOT analysis. *Applied Psychology: An International Review, 56*, 165–181.

Leong, F. T. L., & Ponterotto, J. G. (2003). A proposal for internationalizing counseling psychology in the United States: Rationale, recommendations, and challenges. *Counseling Psychologist, 31*, 381–395.

Leong, F. T. L., & Santiago-Rivera, L. (1999). Climbing the multicultural summit: Challenges and pitfalls. In P. Pedersen (Ed.), *Multiculturalism as a fourth force* (pp. 61–72). Philadelphia: Brunner/Mazell.

Leong, F. T. L., & Savickas, M. L. (2007). Introduction to special issue on international perspectives on counseling psychology. *Applied Psychology: An International Review, 56*, 1–6.

Pawlik, K., & d'Ydewalle, G. (1996). Psychology and the global commons: Perspectives of international psychology. *American Psychologist, 51*, 488–495.

Pedersen, P. B. (1987). Ten frequent assumptions of cultural bias in counseling. *Journal of Multicultural Counseling and Development, 15*, 16–24.

Pedersen, P., & Leong, F. (1997). Counseling in an international context. *Counseling Psychologist, 25*, 117–122.

Pope-Davis, D. B., & Coleman, H. L. K. (Eds.). (1997). *Multicultural counseling competencies: Assessment, education and training, and supervision*. Thousand Oaks, CA: Sage.

President's Commission on Mental Health. (1978). *Report to the president*. Washington, DC: U.S. Government Printing Office.

Savickas, M. L. (2007). Internationalization of counseling psychology: Constructing cross-national consensus and collaboration. *Applied Psychology: An International Review, 56*, 182–188.

Schneider, B. (1987). The people make the place. *Personnel Psychology, 40*, 437–453.

Schultz, D. P., & Schultz, S. E. (2004). *A history of modern psychology* (8th ed.). Belmont, CA: Wadsworth/Thomson.

Smith, C. (1994, December 15). Executive travel expect more travelers, more trips in '95. *Los Angeles Times* [Home Edition], p. D4.

Sodowsky, G. R., & Lai, E. M. W. (1997). Asian immigrant variables and structural models of cross-cultural distress. In A. Booth, A. C. Crouter, & N. Landale (Eds.), *Immigration and the family: Research and policy on U.S. immigrants* (pp. 211–234). Mahwah, NJ: Lawrence Erlbaum.

Sue, D. W., Bernier, J. E., Durran, A., Feinberg, L., Pedersen, P., Smith, E. J., & Vaszquez-Nuttall, E. (1982). Position paper: Cross-cultural counseling competencies. *Counseling Psychologist, 10*, 45–52.

Sue, D. W., & Sue, D. (2003). *Counseling the culturally diverse: Theory and practice* (4th ed.). New York: Wiley.

Sue, S., & Zane, N. (1987). The role of culture and cultural techniques in psychotherapy: A critique and reformulation. *American Psychologist, 42*, 37–45.

Taylor, E. J. (2006, June). International migration and economic development. *International Symposium on International Migration and Development*, pp. 1–28.

Tikkanen, T. (2007). 25 years of EFPA: From exchanging information to making policy. *European Psychologist, 12*, 156–160.

U.S. Surgeon General. (1999). *Mental health: A report of the Surgeon General*. Retrieved August 31, 2007, from http://www.surgeongeneral.gov/library/mentalhealth/home.html

Walton, B. (2007, January 9). More children learn more than one language. *USA Today*. Retrieved January 9, 2007, from http://www.usatoday.com/news/education/2007–01–09-language-children_x.htm?POE=click-refer

Wason, P. C. (1960). On the failure to eliminate hypotheses in a conceptual task. *Quarterly Journal of Experimental Psychology, 12*, 129–140.

19

Counseling Immigrants and Refugees

ELLEN L. SHORT, LISA SUZUKI, MARIA PRENDES-LINTEL,
GINA PRENDES-LINTEL FURR, SOUMYA MADABHUSHI,
AND GERALDINE MAPEL

Immigrants and refugees constitute a growing population throughout the world. The foreign-born population encompasses naturalized citizens, lawful permanent immigrants, refugees and asylees, legal nonimmigrants (e.g., student, work, or temporary visas), and undocumented persons. In the United States, the numbers have grown exponentially in the past two decades. The Migration Policy Institute (2008) indicates a 57.4% increase in number in the 1990s and a 20.7% increase in the past decade. Given these demographic changes, it is imperative that mental health professionals be aware of concerns and challenges relevant to the treatment of this diverse population. Our chapter begins with definitions and statistics regarding numbers of refugees and immigrants. We then highlight critical issues facing immigrants and refugees with respect to premigration, resettlement, and postmigration stressors. Brief highlights of treatment issues (i.e., manifestations of trauma, assessment, self-healing, and counseling) are provided. We conclude the chapter with an illustrative case study.

DEFINITIONS AND STATISTICS

Immigrants

Legally, immigrants are defined as those who are "lawfully admitted for permanent residence in the United States" (Batalova, 2006). The three general immigrant categories are family reunification, employment sponsorship, and humanitarian cases (refugee and asylum adjustments). Percentages by category indicate that in 2005, family reunification was the largest category at 58%, followed by employment at 22%, with 13% arriving as refugees or asylees. In 2005, more than 1 million people were granted lawful permanent residence status in the United States with more than 900,000 status adjustment applications pending (Batalova, 2006). An average of approximately 400,000 new arrivals were estimated yearly between 1986 and 2005. There are an estimated 35.2 million legal and illegal immigrants currently living in the United States, accounting for 11.5% of the total population (Camarota, 2005).

Refugees

The Office of Refugee Resettlement (n.d.-a) defines a refugee as,

> any person who is outside any country of such person's nationality or, in the case of a person having no nationality, is outside any country in which such person last habitually resided, and who is unable or unwilling to return to, and is unable or unwilling to avail himself or herself of the protection of, that country because of persecution or a well-founded fear of persecution on account of race, religion, nationality, membership in a particular social group, or political opinion.

The United States has a history of admitting refugees dating back to the Displaced Persons Act of 1948. Additional legislation made provisions for individuals fleeing Communist regimes from Hungary, Poland, Yugoslavia, Korea, China, and Cuba. In addition to existing government legislation, many of these refugee groups were supported by private American agencies, as well as ethnic and religious organizations (Office of Refugee Resettlement, n.d.-b).

According to an Office of Refugee Resettlement (n.d.-b) fact sheet, in the past quarter century, more than 1.8 million refugees have come to the United States. In 2004, the United Nations High Commissioner for Refugees reported the existence of 9.9 million refugees worldwide (cited in Ellis, MacDonald, Lincoln, & Cabral, 2008).

PREMIGRATION, RESETTLEMENT, AND POSTMIGRATION STRESSORS

A seminal review by Yakushko, Watson, and Thompson (2008) highlights the numerous sources of stress that recent immigrants and refugees face that are directly related to acculturative stress experienced during adjustment to their new environment. They emphasize that stress is a highly subjective experience and can be evidenced by many physiological and psychological symptoms. Prolonged exposure to high levels of stress can result in cognitive impairments, compromised immune systems, depression, arthritis, heart disease, diabetes, and posttraumatic stress disorder (PTSD) (Yakushko et al., 2008).

Premigration Stressors

Numerous stressors exist prior to refugee migration. Premigration stressors can include a loss of social supports (e.g., friends and family); economic, political, and/or cultural conflict in the homeland; witnessing of trauma (e.g., war, rape, torture, bombings, fighting); physical and/or emotional torture; unsanitary living conditions; poverty; imprisonment; loss of property (e.g., home); inhibited access to career choices; and discrimination (Yakushko et al., 2008). Because of a lack of epidemiological data, global estimates of torture prevalence remain crude. However, estimations suggest that up to 35% of the world's refugees are survivors of torture (Baker, 1992; Modvig & Jaranson, 2004), and a recent study of individuals seeking asylum in the United States found that 84% had experienced torture (Piwowarczyk, 2007) prior to arrival. Stress levels are also exacerbated by anticipation of devastation, worries for personal safety of friends and family, and tensions regarding secrecy in planning one's escape and avoiding capture. Obtaining exit visas can pose a number of difficulties for both immigrants and refugees. Premigration experiences, such as the nature and extent of exposure to war, torture, other human rights violations and traumas, and psychological conditions prior to migration, have an impact on positive adaptation of refugees after resettlement (Yakushko et al., 2008).

Arrival

Upon arrival, the recent immigrants or refugees may experience a number of health problems (e.g., malnutrition, parasites, hepatitis B, and dental caries) due to unsanitary conditions in their homeland or resettlement camp (Yakushko et al., 2008). In addition, as mentioned earlier, many may suffer from PTSD based upon experiences in their homeland. The early experiences that immigrants and refugees have upon arrival have been found to be critical in setting the stage for success and hardship, establishing both resiliency and risk factors for adjustment and economic development (Portes & Stepick, 1985; Stepick & Portes, 1986).

Postmigration and Resettlement: The Process of Acculturation

The process of resettlement and acculturation to a new country and culture poses many challenges for immigrants and refugees. According to Williams and Berry (1991), acculturation refers to changes that individuals and groups undergo when they come in contact with another culture. At the individual level, acculturation includes changes in behaviors, values, attitudes, and identity. At the group level, acculturation entails economic, cultural, technological, social, and political transformation.

Acculturative Stress. The stresses that immigrants and refugees face in resettlement are often tied to acculturation. Acculturative stress refers to reactions that can include depression, anxiety, feelings of marginality, and alienation. Psychological and behavioral symptoms of acculturative stress can include,

> disorientation, unusual fatigue, extreme mood swings, crying easily or laughing inappropriately, constant feelings of irritation and annoyance, general nervousness and restlessness, fearfulness, heightened anxiety, withdrawal, inappropriate levels of distress over small matters, and antagonism or suspicion toward members of the new culture. (Prendes-Lintel, 2001, p. 739)

Acculturative stress is composed of cultural, social, and psychological variables that are contextualized by interactions between two entities: the host and the refugee or immigrant.

Berry delineates several factors that influence the relationship between acculturation and stress:

> (1) Modes of acculturation: integration, assimilation, separation, marginalization; (2) Phase of acculturation: contact, conflict, crisis, adaptation; (3) Nature of larger society: prejudicial, discriminatory, multicultural vs. assimilationist; (4) Characteristics of acculturating group: age, status, social support; and (5) Characteristics of assimilating individual: appraisal, coping, attitudes, contact. The multitude of factors listed above interact in many different and complex ways influencing the level of adaptation for each individual. (Berry, 1991, as cited in Prendes-Lindel, 2001, p. 737)

For instance, levels of acculturative stress will be affected by race, ethnicity, culture, and racism. Acculturative stress is often highest when cultural and behavioral similarities and contact between the individual/group and host country is lowest. In these instances, tolerance for acceptance of minorities is low and pressure is placed by the host country on the refugee and/or immigrant population to adapt to the dominant culture (Organista, 2007).

Relational Stress. Many refugees and immigrants experience high levels of stress within their nuclear and extended families (Yakushko et al., 2008). Intergenerational conflicts may arise as family members acculturate to the host culture to varying degrees. Offspring may acculturate more quickly, given their exposure to the educational system. Their school experiences place pressure on them to learn the academic and social language of the host country in order for them to achieve and gain acceptance from peers. Familial stress is also evidenced in increasing levels of domestic violence (Yakushko et al., 2008).

As noted in the premigration section, refugees and immigrants face numerous losses as they have moved away from extended family and major community supports in their homeland. Refugees have experienced the demise of sources of social support in their homeland. Thus, immigrants and refugees may still be mourning and grieving these losses and experiencing loneliness and trauma postmigration (Yakushko et al., 2008).

Eisenbruch (1991) presents the concept of *cultural bereavement* to describe the grief that refugees may experience due to loss of home, social networks, cultural values, and self-identity. As Wilson (2004) states, "Torn away and uprooted from their soil, refugees seek in desperation and mercy a safe asylum in another place where strangers live in a foreign culture with different customs, language and histories" (p. 109). Birman and Tran (2008) note that a sense of belongingness and being comfortable in the new culture or country has been found to be an important measure of psychological adaptation for refugees. *Cultural alienation* is defined as the extent of estrangement or separation one feels from the surrounding culture. Among an adult Vietnamese refugee population, Birman and

Tran (2008) found positive correlations between depression and alienation, and between American acculturation and reduced alienation.

In addition, refugees and immigrants may experience a loss of self-esteem and concerns that they may not be able to function competently in the new culture (Yakushko et al., 2008). Resettlement brings with it pressures to establish a new social network and obtain employment. Refugees struggle with unemployment or legal limitations placed on seeking and maintaining employment. The need to survive economically in a new culture with the language of the host country also brings with it unique challenges. Because of lack of language proficiency or nontransferability of educational degrees, skilled workers or professionals are often unable to find equivalent employment (Gonsalves, 1992; Schweitzer, Melville, Steel, & Lacherez, 2006). The loss of status can then become a source of anger and anguish that affects their self-esteem. Obstacles to health care and other social welfare services may add further strain to an already difficult experience.

Oppression. Refugees and immigrants also face discrimination and social oppression in their new environment. Undocumented immigrants have no legal rights and are often subject to emotional harassment, and physical, emotional, and economic abuse at the hands of their employers (Yakushko et al., 2008). The past few years have seen an increase in the number of displaced individuals. Many Western nations have responded to this increase by tightening their borders and introducing deterrence policies, including detention. Prolonged or indefinite detention has adverse effects on the mental health and psychosocial adjustment of individuals and families (Ichikawa, Nakahara, & Wakai, 2006; Silove, Austin, & Steel, 2007)—effects that can extend well after their release (Silove et al., 2007). Moreover, detention can further reinforce feelings of helplessness and isolation (Silove, McIntosh, & Becker, 1993).

Fear of being repatriated is another common stressor among refugees (Sinnerbrink, Silove, Field, Steel, & Manicavasagar, 1997). The burden of proof lies with the asylum seeker to establish a well-founded fear of future persecution (Herlihy, Ferstman, & Turner, 2004). Prendes-Lintel (2001) suggests that living in a state of constant fear of being denied asylum and being sent back to the country the refugees have fled can lead to an increased risk for suicide and depression. Other related stressors include delays in processing refugee/asylum applications, forced separations from family members, and obstacles to visiting family even in emergency situations.

Since September 11, 2001, there has been a political shift in Western nations (Silove, 2004) that has manifested in a growing public fear of outsiders, particularly of those from different cultural and/or religious backgrounds. People from host communities may hold negative beliefs regarding refugees, including fears that these refugees might be dangerous or that they are putting undue stress on the economic conditions of the country or stealing jobs. Such negative attitudes can have a significant impact on the adaptation of refugees in their host communities by both limiting their access to opportunities and increasing their sense of alienation.

MANIFESTATIONS OF TRAUMA

Many refugees have experienced trauma in their homeland. In their review of the literature, Ellis et al. (2008) cite studies indicating that samples of refugee children who experienced trauma reported psychological disturbance that was more than three times the national average when compared to nonrefugee children sampled in the United Kingdom. In addition, Ellis et al. note rates of posttraumatic stress disorder ranging from 11.5% to 65% among samples of children and adolescents from Cambodia, Bosnia, Afghanistan, and Tibet.

A number of stress reactions have been documented in the literature based upon diagnostic categories of the International Classification of Diseases, 10th revision (Orley, 1994). These include acute stress reactions, posttraumatic stress disorder, adjustment disorders, and enduring personality changes.

War Trauma and Torture

The nature and extent of exposure to war trauma and torture have been found to be strong predictors of mental disturbance among refugees. Some of the most frequently reported mental health problems in refugee populations are PTSD, depression, and anxiety (Kinzie, 2006; Miller, Kulkarni, & Kushner, 2006). Latency of time and severity of trauma endured have an impact on the prevalence of posttraumatic stress symptoms, depression, and anxiety (Mollica, McInnes, Poole, & Tor, 1998). Based upon a survey of 993 Cambodian survivors of mass violence, Mollica et al. (1998) concluded that cumulative trauma continued to affect psychiatric symptom levels of these refugees a decade after the original traumatic events. The impact of trauma and torture is not isolated to the individual; rather, the effects can be seen in family members and transmitted across generations (Vesti & Kastrup, 1995).

Miller et al. (2006) note that cultural variations exist in the manifestations of PTSD. Friedman and Jaranson (1998) assert that,

> ethnocultural and religious traditions will certainly have a significant influence on the subjective experience and psychological appraisal of stressful events. Differences in language will determine how events are characterized and how such characterizations are communicated within each ethnocultural setting. Ethnocultural and religious traditions will modify the significance, interpretation, metaphor, and meaning that are attached to specific events. (p. 214)

Silove (1999) proposed an integrated model to understand the impact of torture and related mass abuses and suggested that these abuses disrupt five adaptive psychosocial systems (safety, attachment, justice, identity role, and existential meaning) that help in maintaining a sense of equilibrium in individuals and communities. Silove suggests that these systems may delineate the pathways through which traumatic experiences might affect a given individual and whether or not an individual develops psychiatric symptoms in the aftermath of traumatic and abusive experiences. Prolonged and repeated threats may put the psychobiological mechanisms of preservation (e.g., safety) in a constant state of arousal resulting in chronic symptoms of PTSD. The inexplicable cruelty inherent to torture and other forms of mass human rights abuses can shake the foundations of the survivor's sense of justice and faith in the beneficence of life and humankind. These extreme violations often leave survivors with existential preoccupations, struggling to find a coherent reason for the abuses they have suffered. Thus, the meaning of life and death, good and evil, and religious beliefs can all be challenged.

PROTECTIVE FACTORS

Protective factors are often linked with resiliency and can be defined as coping strategies and abilities that help individuals manage and adapt to ongoing traumatic and/or stressful situations and environments. Protective factors that are internal, such as self-esteem and self-efficacy; cultural, religious, and spiritual belief systems; and psychological preparedness, can all potentially enhance an individual's capacity to cope with stress and help him or her to develop a sense of coherence and perceived control. Social support systems—such as family; friends; community; and religious, service-oriented, and educational organizations—can be characterized as external protective factors that can provide support and valuable connections to individuals who may also be experiencing challenges related to acculturation and assimilation. Berry (1988) notes that although acculturation is often a very stressful process, it is not always negative. In fact, some experiences may serve to enhance the quality of individuals' lives and enhance mental and emotional health statuses.

ASSESSMENT OF REFUGEES AND IMMIGRANTS

The process of assessing immigrants and refugees presents a number of challenges for the evaluator. Okawa (2008) identified eight factors that affect the psychological evaluation of refugees: client's familiarity with the psychological evaluation process; body language, eye contact, and facial expressivity; grooming and attire; orientation to time; differing sets of experiences; culturally based beliefs; cognitive functioning; and language and nonverbal communication. Most of the potential challenges embedded in each of these areas may seem obvious, but Okawa is clear in mentioning the importance of clarity and understanding in the communication between clinicians and refugee clients. These same factors apply to the evaluation of immigrants as well.

It is critical in the process to explain the role of the evaluator, the purpose of the evaluation, what the evaluation will entail, and limits to confidentiality. The evaluator must maintain a stance of "learner" and be careful not to pass judgment based upon the client's body language, eye contact, dress, emotional presence, tardiness, and so on. Words must be "unpacked" to ensure equivalence of meaning between the evaluator and the client. Okawa (2008) notes that seemingly benign phrases may signify something very different to the client. For example, she shares that one client reported that the phrase "morning coffee" was used to identify the time when they were taken to be interrogated and tortured. In addition, although attention to the translation and equivalence of content is often made, she notes that response formats may be unfamiliar to refugees (e.g., speeded tests, multiple choice, and true-false). It is also important to note that many survivors of torture may be distrustful of professionals given that psychologists and physicians may have been part of the process of torture (Campbell, 2007). Additionally, it is common for survivors of torture to be inconsistent in reporting their history and experience (Campbell, 2007). This may be due to impaired memory, avoidance, numbing, and distrust. It is critical that they not be labeled as malingering unless there is clear evidence.

Given the lack of instruments normed and validated on refugee and immigrant populations, clinicians often rely upon translated measures. Fabri (2008) provides information regarding the complex process of interpreting and translating Western-based measures for refugees. She outlines the extensive process undertaken by Mollica et al. (1998) in translating the Harvard Trauma Questionnaire in Rwanda. Numerous focus groups and pilot-testing sessions were conducted with mental health workers in the community as well as torture survivors themselves. Suggestions were obtained throughout the process regarding linguistic and context changes to the scale.

Given the emphasis on understanding acculturative stress among immigrants, a number of scales have been developed to measure this construct empirically. Based upon our review of literature published in the past 5 years, a number of stress scales have been cited in the literature. Most of these scales have been developed on immigrant college student samples and may not be applicable to all immigrants.

More than 300 languages are spoken in the United States alone. Therefore, it is very likely that clinicians will be required to use interpreters when working with immigrant and refugee communities. As noted by Prendes-Lintel and Peterson (2008), "An interpreter is a person who translates orally, and a translator is a person who produces an interpretation from one language to another in a written format" (p. 222). Full bilingualism is required for the interpretive process. Prendes-Lintel and Peterson caution that "Languages are dynamic; they change over time and are affected by local culture" (p. 223). Thus, it is imperative that interpreters be skilled in the colloquial language as well as the cultural context of the refugee or immigrant being assessed, because they serve as cultural bridges to the community. In addition, interpreters must receive training to understand the process of interpreting in the mental health setting. In their work with interpreters, Prendes-Lintel and Peterson require an extensive application process to examine applicants' own healing (if they have experienced trauma) as well as personal politics that may interfere with treatment. Issues of ethics, confidentiality, and empowerment practices are also addressed. Additional characteristics of interpreters are self-awareness, trustworthiness, professionalism, and awareness of their own limitations.

INTERVENTIONS AND SELF-HEALING

Mollica (2006) cites the importance of self-healing among refugee and immigrant populations. He states that modern mental health practitioners often focus primarily on the treatment of survivors of violence, but rarely focus on the four elements of trauma: the facts, the cultural meaning of trauma, looking behind the curtain (i.e., "the survivor reaches deep insights when reflecting upon his or her situation" [p. 43]), and the listener-storyteller relationship. By focusing only on the violent and brutal aspects of the survivor's experience, the practitioner may unintentionally overemphasize or fetishize the experiences, based on the therapeutic assumption/belief that talking about the experiences will result in a decrease in the client's suffering. Mollica (2006) states that in addition to the therapeutic practices of applying theoretical frameworks to a client's case and the use of psychotropic drugs to alleviate symptoms, it is also important to individualize treatment by focusing on the "concrete realities" of the clients' "daily lives and their use of social instruments of healing" (p. 223).

Mollica (2006) states that self-healing among refugee and immigrant populations that embodies social activities such as altruism, work, and spirituality has been shown to have "a restorative impact on traumatized persons" (p. 165). Altruism, which is defined as "the practice of unselfish concern for the welfare of others" (p. 165), has often been associated with charity. Altruism "is not contingent upon the response of the recipient" (p. 165). It can enhance the process of healing for traumatized individuals because it allows them to feel useful and helpful toward others despite their own life challenges. Thus, by assisting someone else, the survivor can engage in self-healing. Altruistic behaviors, which, under traumatic circumstances, often involve risk taking and sacrifice, can also provide a foundation upon which individuals can find motivation to build on and enhance their new lives.

Although the research concerning the impact of work on healing is very limited, Mollica (2006) cites work as an important aspect of self-healing. Work, which includes conventional and unconventional forms of employment, refers to "any activity that enhances material well-being of a person, family, or community" (p. 172). Work functions as a mode of survival and serves to reassure individuals that they are not helpless, but productive and capable of supporting themselves and their families. Work also provides a sense of structure during the time of healing after traumatic experiences and may serve as a temporary method of escape from the psychological impact of the trauma. Conversely, after the experience of trauma has ended, work can also be a source of humiliation, despondency, and enforced dependency, particularly in instances in which there is joblessness and continued unemployment among, for example, paternal figures within the family (Mollica, 2006). Additionally, the quality of work that refugees and immigrants have available to them during the acculturative transition (regardless of their level of education, experience, or occupational interest) can include undesirable jobs, that are low paying and psychologically soul draining, and that embody dangerous or exploitive work conditions with very little opportunity for advancement. The host country may view

refugees and immigrants merely as workers who provide services, and they may be forced, in many instances, to take employment that is undesirable to other individuals within that country, in order to survive. A focus, therefore, on the psychological meaning of work for this population may be ignored. Thus, although work can provide a path to self-healing for refugee and immigrant populations, it is important for the practitioner to assess the host country's views of employment for individuals from these populations and how those systemic attitudes have an impact on the meaning of work for them.

Additionally, it is critical for practitioners to be mindful of the healing stage of the survivor. Herman's (1992) three-stage trauma healing process provides a broad conceptualization that is useful for working with survivors and setting appropriate goals. The three stages of healing are building trust, constructing the narrative of the trauma, and reconnecting socially. Vocational interventions are most appropriate for survivors who are comfortable in social settings and who are ready to build social relationships.

Recreating a link between the individual and the world of work is often a critical component in establishing a strong and reliable connection between the individual and society. Coates and Carr (2005) found that immigrants who were equally qualified for jobs compared to candidates born in the country were less likely to be offered the same position. This hiring bias was mediated by the degree of perceived difference between the immigrant's culture and the host culture, as well as the socioeconomic standing of the country of origin (Coates & Carr, 2005). In seeking employment, refugees and immigrants must not only be qualified, but also prove their qualifications with greater effort (Clayton, 2005). Immigrants and refugees experience a great deal of career-related discrimination. Research with various minority groups has shown that the mere anticipation of discrimination at a given job or by a given employer or co-worker has a stronger link to goals and performance than self-efficacy or outcome expectations (Barry & Grilo, 2003; Chartrand & Rose, 1996; Hackett & Byars, 1996; Morrow, Gore, & Campbell, 1996). In addition to the trauma survivors have already experienced, the racism they experience in their new society may be another source of trauma (Bryant-Davis & Ocampo, 2005).

Torture survivors are likely to benefit from receiving support concerning their experiences of discrimination. Mental health professionals may offer referrals to appropriate support sources, and may also address this topic in their vocational intervention.

Finally, Mollica (2006) states that the efficacy of spirituality for self-healing among refugees and immigrants has been studied empirically. He states that biological research and clinical experience have confirmed that unhealthy body changes associated with negative life experiences can be mitigated by spiritual and humanistic practices such as prayer, meditation, religious rituals, and groups that focus on self-care. Spiritual rituals and practices can provide survivors with the necessary structure that creates opportunities for expression of their feelings; participation in spiritual practices requires the development of control of one's feelings, as well as the commitment to comprehend them. In providing counseling to refugee and immigrant populations, it is important for practitioners to be aware of the challenges inherent in acknowledging and facilitating spirituality *and* psychologically oriented therapeutic treatment, because of traditional attitudes within the medical and psychiatric systems that view the healing power of spirituality with skepticism or "passive neglect" (p. 181).

As noted earlier, the counselor must be aware of the multiple losses that the client may be grieving, understand the process of using interpreters in the therapeutic relationship, and be aware of the importance of collaborative resources in aiding the immigrant and/or refugee client. Clinical boundaries may differ from traditional mental health guidelines. For example, at the For Immigrants and Refugees Surviving Torture Project (Prendes-Lintel & Peterson, 2008), picnics were held to familiarize members of the community with clinicians and staff members. The waiting room was equipped with a coffee bar and puzzles that the staff and clients worked on together when not in session. The staff was composed of psychologists, doctoral students, social workers, case workers, physicians, community members, and others who were specifically trained to work with members of the refugee and immigrant community.

In addition to psychological and health services, clients received help in finding employment and housing as well as political and legal advocacy. Counselors often wrote letters on behalf of clients and testified for them in refugee status court hearings.

CASE STUDY

The following scenario is provided to illustrate some of the issues that are described in this chapter. The reader is encouraged to think about premigration and postmigration stressors that are affecting this client.

A Survivor's Story

In his native country, prior to his immigration to the United States, L.A. experienced continuous episodes of torture because of political and cultural conflicts. In anticipation of his death at the hands of those who threatened him and his colleagues and friends, L.A. was forced to dig graves and eventually witnessed their deaths one by one. When his turn came, he stood near the firing squad waiting his turn for his body to fall back into the graves he had helped dig. But only those next to him died that day, and the next day, and the next. He was made to witness many unspeakable acts. He prayed it would soon be over, but the torture and trauma didn't stop for 3 years. During the day, he found himself continuously thinking about the atrocities that he had witnessed; visual and auditory images repeatedly interrupted his waking hours. There were also the nights when his whole body would go numb. At night was when soldiers came to where he slept side by side with the others, unable to move. Often, he waited with the others, wondering who would go next, thinking that perhaps that night it was his turn to be taken. He didn't know if he would be beaten unconscious, dismembered, or burned. Sometimes, he found the anxiety and fear of waiting to be unbearable, and he often wondered if it would be better to die. When he was released, he tried to hang himself because he could not bear to go on living. After his arrival and resettlement in his host country, he often had nightmares of wild animals tearing at his flesh and of dead bodies surrounding him.

L.A. still feels numb and finds it hard to breathe when those memories intrude upon him and feel so real. Although he is now able to talk about his traumatic experiences in counseling, it took 2 years before he could sit, be reflective and insightful, and trust anyone, yet he kept coming to see the counselor. Initially he could only tolerate 5 minutes of a session. He now stays through the entire session and continues to work on feeling better. On a good day he rides his bike and exercises. He is starting to meet and connect with other refugees from his native country. He has found that making these connections and assisting individuals who are experiencing similar challenges has been helpful for his own self-healing, but he limits these interactions because he becomes nervous and easily angered, and he prefers to be alone in his quiet house. He also experiences many medical problems from the torture sequelae.

L.A. misses his family; he and his relatives lived close together for generations. Now, the family is spread out and resettled in four different countries. Because of his challenged financial circumstances, he can't afford to go see them or to call them. He was working initially but found that he could not concentrate enough to follow directions, and he struggled to develop fluency in the language of his host country. He also found the work environment to be exploitive and the work itself to be meaningless and unrelated to the occupational skills and qualifications he earned in his native country. He wants the United States to know he appreciates being here, and he feels guilty not only because he is alive when many he knew are dead, but also because he would like to contribute by working. He worked successfully for many years in his home country, and he was proud of what he had accomplished, which all seems like a distant dream now. He often feels ashamed and embarrassed that he can't contribute here as he did at home. However, counseling has increased his ability to comprehend that his path to improved mental, emotional, and physical health and self-healing will take time and continued effort, as he struggles to build a new life in his host country.

This case serves to highlight the complex nature of the premigration (e.g., torture, political and cultural conflict) and postmigration stressors. Upon arrival in the United States, L.A. continued to experience nightmares and intrusive memories that affected his ability to adjust to his new environment. It was critical for the counseling process to be flexible and to make allowances for the psychological state of the client (e.g., initially having shorter sessions) in order to develop a trusting relationship. In addition, this case illustrates the necessity of measuring progress through a variety of behaviors (e.g., exercise, bike riding, limited reconnection, etc.) while also recognizing the importance of work and the need for vocational guidance.

The journey to a better life for refugees and immigrants in their new homeland is an arduous one with many obstacles. To provide appropriate mental health services to these diverse individuals and their unique circumstances is a challenge that must be met.

REFERENCES

Baker, R. (1992). Psychosocial consequences for tortured refugees seeking asylum and refugee status in Europe. In M. Basoglu (Ed.), *Torture and its consequences: Current treatment approaches* (pp. 83–106). New York: Cambridge University Press.

Barry, D. T., & Grilo, C. M. (2003). Cultural self-esteem and demographic correlates of perception of personal and group discrimination among East Asian immigrants. *American Journal of Orthopsychiatry, 73,* 223–229.

Batalova, J. (2006). Spotlight on legal immigration to the United States. Retrieved November 20, 2008, from http://www.migrationinformation.org/Feature/display.cfm?ID=414

Berry, J. W. (1988). *Understanding the process of acculturation for primary prevention* [Contract No. 278–85–0024 CH]. Minneapolis: University of Minnesota, National Institute of Mental Health Refugee Assistance Program.

Birman, D., & Tran, N. (2008). Psychological distress and adjustment of Vietnamese refugees in the United States: Association with pre- and postmigration factors. *American Journal of Orthopsychiatry, 78,* 109–120.

Bryant-Davis, T., & Ocampo, C. (2005). The trauma of racism: Implications for counseling, research, and education. *Counseling Psychologist, 33,* 574–578.

Camarota, S. A. (2005). Immigrants at mid-decade: A snapshot of America's foreign-born population. Retrieved December 22, 2008, from http://www.cis.org/articles/2005/back1405.html

Campbell, T. A. (2007). Psychological assessment, diagnosis, and treatment of torture survivors: A review. *Clinical Psychology Review, 27,* 628–641.

Chartrand, J. M., & Rose, M. L. (1996). Career interventions for at-risk populations: Incorporating social cognitive influences. *Career Development Quarterly, 44,* 341–354.

Clayton, P. (2005). Blank slates or hidden treasure: Assessing and building on the experiential learning of migrant and refugee women in European countries. *International Journal of Lifelong Education, 24,* 227–242.

Coates, K., & Carr, S. C. (2005). Skilled immigrants and selection bias: A theory-based field study from New Zealand. *International Journal of Intercultural Relations, 29,* 577–599.

Eisenbruch, M. (1991). From posttraumatic stress disorder to cultural bereavement: Diagnosis of Southeast Asian refugees. *Social Science Medicine, 33,* 673–680.

Ellis, B. H., MacDonald, H. Z., Lincoln, A. K., & Cabral, H. J. (2008). Mental health of Somali adolescent refugees: The role of trauma, stress, and perceived discrimination. *Journal of Consulting and Clinical Psychology, 2,* 184–193.

Fabri, M. (2008). Cultural adaptation and translation of assessment instruments for diverse populations: The use of the Harvard trauma questionnaire in Rwanda. In L. A. Suzuki & J. G. Ponterotto (Eds.), *Handbook of multicultural assessment: Clinical, psychological, and educational application* (3rd ed., pp. 195–219). San Francisco: Jossey-Bass.

Friedman, M., & Jaranson, J. (1998). The applicability of the posttraumatic stress disorder concept to refugees. In A. J. Marsella, T. Bornemann, S. Ekblad, & J. Orley (Eds.), *Amidst peril and pain: The mental health and well-being of the world's refugees* (pp. 207–227). Washington, DC: American Psychological Association.

Gonsalves, C. J. (1992). Psychological stages of the refugee process: A model for therapeutic interventions. *Professional Psychology: Research and Practice, 23,* 382–389.

Hackett, G., & Byars, A. M. (1996). Social cognitive theory and the career development of African American women. *Career Development Quarterly, 44,* 322–341.

Herlihy, J., Ferstman, C., & Turner, S. W. (2004). Legal issues in work with asylum seekers. In J. P. Wilson & B. Drož ek (Eds.), *Broken spirits: The treatment of traumatized asylum seekers, refugees, war and torture victims* (pp. 641–658). New York: Brunner-Routledge.

Herman, J. (1992). *Trauma and recovery.* New York: Basic Books.

Ichikawa, M., Nakahara, S., & Wakai, S. (2006). Effect of post-migration detention on mental health among Afghan asylum seekers in Japan. *Australian and New Zealand Journal of Psychiatry, 40,* 341–346.

Kinzie, J. D. (2006). Immigrants and refugees: The psychiatric perspective. *Transcultural Psychiatry, 43,* 577–591.

Modvig, J., & Jaranson, J. M. (2004). A global perspective of torture, political violence, and health. In J. P. Wilson & B. Drož ek (Eds.), *Broken spirits: The treatment of traumatized asylum seekers, refugees, war and torture victims* (pp. 33–52). New York: Brunner-Routledge.

Migration Policy Institute. (2008). MPI data hub: Migration facts, stats, and maps. Retrieved December 3, 2008, from http://wwwmigrationinformation.org/dataHub/state.cfm?ID=US

Miller, K. E., Kulkarni, M., & Kushner, H. (2006). Beyond trauma-focused psychiatric epidemiology: Bridging research and practice with war-affected populations. *American Journal of Orthopsychiatry, 76,* 409–422.

Mollica, R. F. (2006). *Healing invisible wounds: Paths to hope and recovery in a violent world.* Orlando, FL: Harcourt.

Mollica, R. F., McInnes, K., Poole, C., & Tor, S. (1998). Dose-effect relationships of trauma to symptoms of depression and post-traumatic stress disorder among Cambodian survivors of mass violence. *British Journal of Psychiatry, 173,* 482–488.

Morrow, S. L., Gore, P. A., Jr., & Campbell, B. W. (1996). The application of a sociocognitive framework to the career development of lesbian women and gay men. *Journal of Vocational Behavior, 48,* 136–148.

Office of Refugee Resettlement. (n.d.-a). Definition of refugees. Available: http://www.acf.hhs.gov/programs/orr/about/whoweserve.htm

Office of Refugee Resettlement. (n.d.-b). Fact sheet. Retrieved November 22, 2008, from http://www.acf.hhs.gov/programs/orr/press/office_refugee_factsheet.htm

Okawa, J. B. (2008). Considerations for the cross-cultural evaluation of refugees and asylum seekers. In L. A. Suzuki & J. G. Ponterotto (Eds.), *Handbook of multicultural assessment: Clinical, psychological, and educational applications* (3rd ed., pp. 165–194). San Francisco: Jossey-Bass.

Organista, K. C. (2007). *Solving Latino psychological and health problems: Theory, practice, and populations.* Hoboken, NJ: Wiley.

Orley, J. (1994). Psychological disorders among refugees: Some clinical and epidemiological considerations. In A. J. Marsella, T. Bornemann, S. Ekblad, & J. Orley (Eds.), *Amidst peril and pain: The mental health and well-being of the world's refugees* (pp. 193–206). Washington, DC: American Psychological Association.

Piwowarczyk, L. (2007). Asylum seekers seeking mental health services in the United States: Clinical and legal implications. *Journal of Nervous and Mental Disease, 195,* 715–722.

Portes, A., & Stepick, A. (1985). Unwelcome immigrants: The labor market experiences of 1980 (Mariel) Cuban and Haitian refugees in South Florida. *American Sociological Review, 50,* 493–514.

Prendes-Lintel, M. (2001). A working model of counseling recent refugees. In J. G. Ponterotto, J. M. Casas, L. A. Suzuki, & C. M. Alexander (Eds.), *Handbook of multicultural counseling* (2nd ed., pp. 729–752). Thousand Oaks, CA: Sage.

Prendes-Lintel, M., & Peterson, F. (2008). Delivering quality mental health services to immigrants and refugees through an interpreter. In L. A. Suzuki & J. G. Ponterotto (Eds.), *Handbook of multicultural assessment: Clinical, psychological, and educational applications* (3rd ed., pp. 220–244). Thousand Oaks, CA: Sage.

Schweitzer, R., Melville, F., Steel, Z., & Lacherez, P. (2006). Trauma, post-migration living difficulties, and social support as predictors of psychological adjustment in resettled Sudanese refugees. *Australian and New Zealand Journal of Psychiatry, 40,* 179–187.

Silove, D. (1999). The psychosocial effects of torture, mass human rights violations, and refugee trauma: Toward an integrated conceptual framework. *Journal of Nervous and Mental Disease, 187,* 200–207.

Silove, D. (2004). The challenges facing mental health programs for post-conflict and refugee communities. *Prehospital and Disaster Medicine, 19,* 90–96.

Silove, D., Austin, P., & Steel, Z. (2007). No refuge from terror: The impact of detention on the mental health of trauma-affected refugees seeking asylum in Australia. *Transcultural Psychiatry, 44,* 359–393.

Silove, D., McIntosh, P., & Becker, R. (1993). Risk of retraumatisation of asylum-seekers in Australia. *Australian and New Zealand Journal of Psychiatry, 27,* 606–612.

Sinnerbrink, I., Silove, D., Field, A., Steel, Z., & Manicavasagar, V. (1997). Compounding of preimmigration trauma and postimmigration stress in asylum seekers. *Journal of Psychology: Interdisciplinary and Applied, 131,* 463–470.

Stepick, A., & Portes, A. (1986). Flight into despair: A profile of recent Haitian refugees in South Florida. *International Migration Review, 20,* 329–350.

Vesti, P., & Kastrup, M. (1995). Refugee status, torture, and adjustment. In J. R. Freedy & S. E. Hobfoli (Eds.), *Traumatic stress: From theory to practice* (pp. 213–235). New York: Plenum.

Williams, C. L., & Berry, J. W. (1991). Primary prevention of acculturative stress among refugees. *American Psychologist, 46,* 632–641.

Wilson, J. P. (2004). The broken spirit: Posttraumatic damage to the self. In J. P. Wilson & B. Drožek (Eds.), *Broken spirits: The treatment of traumatized asylum seekers, refugees, war and torture victims* (pp. 109–157). New York: Brunner-Routledge.

Yakushko, O., Watson, M., & Thompson, S. (2008). Stress and coping in the lives of recent immigrants and refugees: Considerations for counseling. *International Journal for the Advancement of Counselling, 30,* 167–178.

PART IV

Racial, Ethnic, and Gay/Lesbian/Bisexual Identity Development: Updates on Theory, Measurement, and Counseling Implications

Models of racial and ethnic identity have served as theoretical anchors for hundreds of research studies over the past three decades. In the inaugural edition of the *Handbook* (1995), we summarized leading theories of racial identity. In the second edition of the *Handbook* (2001), we switched our focus to a critique of measurements and assessments used to operationalize theories of racial identity. Now, in this third edition, we felt it necessary to update the reader on both counts: developments in theory and in measurement of racial and ethnic identity. Part IV of the *Handbook* consists of eight in-depth chapters on racial, ethnic, and gay/lesbian identity.

Honoring our Native American and Alaska Native indigenous people, we begin this section, as we did Part I, with their story. Andrea L. Dixon and Tarrell Awe Agahe Portman (Chapter 20) present a clear and crisp overview of Native American and Alaska Native identity, review current measurement and diagnostic issues in working with Native clients, and provide culturally

informed counseling considerations for serving Native American and Alaska Native clients. In Chapter 21, Tina Q. Richardson, Angela R. Bethea, Charlayne Hayling, and Claudette Williamson-Taylor address identity development for African American and Afro-Caribbean Americans. The authors explore the intersection of ethnicity and race for African-descent Americans, review racial identity models relevant to the Black community, and highlight the implications of racial identity theory for research and practice.

Marie L. Miville (Chapter 22) provides a state-of-the-art discussion on Latina/o identity development. She opens the chapter with a helpful review of the history and diversity of the Latina/o people in the Americas. Next, Dr. Miville highlights the conceptual challenges in defining Latina/o identity and reviews important models of relevant ethnic identity. Also included in this chapter is a recent review of leading measures of identity development for the Latina/o population as well as a discussion on the application of identity assessment in the counseling process. Chapter 23, prepared by Mark H. Chae and Christopher Larres, focuses on Asian American identity development. Relative to research on Black and White racial identity development, Asian American focused research in this area is limited. The authors do a wonderful job of contextualizing Asian American identity theory and research in the context of broader and earlier models of identity. They then provide a comprehensive and scholarly review of assessment instruments used to measure Asian American racial and ethnic identity, and they close the chapter with insightful and pointed directions for much needed research on the topic.

Chapter 24 focuses on an often neglected indigenous population in the United States: Native Hawaiians. Authors Laurie D. McCubbin and Thu A. Dang review the history and colonization of Native Hawaiians; define the concepts of race, ethnicity, and culture relative to this group; and review extant models and assessments of Hawaiian identity. Importantly, the authors present a visionary, exceptionally well-thought-out ecological perspective for framing the Hawaiian identity experience and process. In Chapter 25, Lisa B. Spanierman and Jason R. Soble present a state-of-the-art review and discussion of "understanding Whiteness." Choosing their terms purposefully, the authors begin the chapter with a concise review of extant models of White racial identity/consciousness. Drs. Spanierman and Soble then review a new, cutting-edge construct (and related research) that helps us understand White persons' attitudinal responses to racism: psychosocial costs of racism to Whites. The chapter balances well a

concise, clear overview of theory with an integrated summary of empirical research.

A majority of theory and research on racial and ethnic identity has focused on a single racial or ethnic group (monoracial); yet demographic trends clearly point to a growing population of individuals who represent two or more racial heritages. In Chapter 26, SooJean Choi-Misailidis reviews writing and research on biracial and multiracial identity. The chapter presents a new model of multiracial identity developed and tested by the author. Dr. Choi-Misailidis introduces readers to her comprehensive theory of multiracial-heritage awareness and personal affiliation. This theory is based on a thoughtful integration of qualitative research on biracial identity development. The development and validation of the Multiracial-Heritage Awareness and Personal Affiliation Scale is also summarized.

Finally, Part IV of the *Handbook* closes with Chapter 27, authored by Leo Wilton and focusing on identity and counseling issues relative to lesbian, gay, bisexual, and transgendered (LGBT) communities. Dr. Wilton opens his chapter by placing the topic in historical and political context. He then reviews the origins and history of LGBT affirmative counseling and highlights the role of stigma and marginalization on the mental health of LGBT persons. Anchoring his positions in minority stress theory, Dr. Wilton provides clear insights and directions for mental health professionals working within the arena of LGBT affirmative counseling. Dr. Wilton's historical, political, and scholarly knowledge of the topic is deep and impressive, and he presents a thought-provoking, stimulating chapter.

20

The Beauty of Being Native

The Nature of Native American and Alaska Native Identity Development

ANDREA L. DIXON AND TARRELL AWE AGAHE PORTMAN

"Everything on the earth has a purpose, every disease an herb to cure it, and every person a mission. This is the Indian theory of existence."

—Mourning Dove, Salish Tribe, 1888–1936

It is projected that the United States will be a "nation of minorities" by 2050 (Chideya, 1999, p. 1; Lee, 2005; U.S. Bureau of the Census, 2001). The ever-increasing number of ethnic minorities living within the United States creates the continued need for understanding regarding diversity and culturally specific and responsive needs of minority clients seeking counseling services (Atkinson, 2003; Sue & Sue, 2008). In fact, throughout the past 30 years, the counseling and counseling psychology professions have been regularly called upon to adapt counseling services and counselor training in multicultural competence in order to meet the needs of our diverse population (Roysircar, Arredondo,

Fuertes, Ponterotto, & Toporek, 2003; Sue, Arredondo, & McDavis, 1992). As our nation of minorities manifests, it is important to continue our focus on the specialized needs and sociohistorical identity development of all of our minority groups; however, it appears timely to recognize Native American (NA) and Alaska Native (AN) individuals who represent two of the original *majority* groups that lived on this land long before they would be classified as U.S. minority groups.

Native American (natives of the land now known as the continental United States) and Alaska Native (natives of the land now known as the state of Alaska) persons represent the indigenous peoples of the Western

215

Hemisphere (Waldman, 2006). Scientists have documented that ancestors of Native Americans and Alaska Natives entered the Americas from Asia by way of the Bering Strait sometime during the late ice age, or more than 10,000 years ago (Waldman, 2006). These dates illustrate just how long the now-marginalized NAs/ANs have been living in the land within which counselors now offer mental health services.

In the 21st century, the U.S. Office of Management and Budget (OMB) defines Native American or Alaska Native persons as "having origins in any of the original peoples of North and South America (including Central America), and who maintain tribal affiliation or community attachment" (U.S. Office of Management and Budget, 2005, p. 1). Native persons are considered enrolled/registered members of federally recognized tribes or whose blood quantums are one fourth or more resulting from Native heritage (U.S. Bureau of Indian Affairs [U.S. BIA], 2001). However, many persons and organizations, including the U.S. Bureau of the Census, use *self-identification* to determine Native heritage. As of 2001, NAs/ANs formed about 1% of the total U.S. population (slightly more than 2.6 million self-identified persons), and population estimates for 2007 were slightly more than 2.9 million persons (U.S. Bureau of the Census, 2001). In addition, there are more than 561 federally and state-recognized tribes in the United States and a great number of tribes that reside together as unrecognized groups by the federal government (U.S. BIA, 2001).

Native Americans and Alaska Natives remain two of the least understood and, in terms of mental health, most underserved populations in the United States (Dixon Rayle, Chee, & Sand, 2006). The sociohistorical, cultural, and geographical adaptations that Native groups have endured throughout the past 300 years have created marginalized Native minority groups that have become *culturally dislocated* (the feeling as if one does not fit into the traditional Native culture or into the general U.S. culture) (Thomason, 1991; Waldman, 2006) over time. The well-being of Native persons has reportedly suffered throughout history, and this population appears to be at higher risk for mental health problems and substance abuse when compared to other ethnic groups (Thomason, 1991). Indeed, despite government reports of Native sovereignty (Garrett & Herring, 2001), the social and health issues facing

NAs/ANs appear to be more pressing than ever (Dixon Rayle et al., 2006). Poverty, school failure and dropout, unemployment, substance use and abuse, poor physical health, depression, feelings of hopelessness, and drastic transformations in NA/AN familial and cultural values contribute to these groups' declines in psychological and emotional well-being (Bischel & Mallinckrodt, 2001; Thomason, 1991). Because of these detrimental social and health issues, and the sociohistorical trauma of these ethnic groups, counselors and counselors-in-training equip themselves with the knowledge and skills to work with these unique and culturally diverse populations.

The purpose of this chapter is to present an overview of NA/AN identity development theory and measurement in counseling, and the resulting implications for offering culturally specific and responsive counseling interventions for these populations. The first section provides a complete overview of NA/AN identity development theories and experiences. The second section offers an overview of current measurement and diagnosis issues in counseling when working with NA/AN clients. The final section provides culturally specific and responsive counseling considerations focusing on the culturally specific needs of NA/AN clients.

NATIVE AMERICAN AND ALASKA NATIVE IDENTITY DEVELOPMENT: THE THEORY BEHIND IT ALL

Sociopolitical History of Being Native in America

An underlying premise of becoming culturally specific or responsive in providing counseling services to NA/AN individuals requires counselors and psychologists to acquire an overarching understanding of the unique sociopolitical histories of this population as a collective ethnic group, as individual familial groups, and as individuals. Historically, NA/AN peoples gathered in larger geographic groupings called Tribes or Nations and smaller familial groupings called Bands (Oswalt & Neely, 1998). A duality or parallel sociopolitical history appears to have existed for Alaskan Native and American Indian Nations based upon geographic location and governmental interventions. Colonization (as a governmental intervention) served as the conduit of oppression and "systemic genocide" that has devastated NA/AN peoples over the past 500 years (Duran & Duran, 1995, p. 6), thus constituting a sociopolitical history of military aggression, forced removal from sacred homelands, confiscation of familial property, banishment of cultural determinants (such as religion and language), and continuous efforts at cultural genocide through death and acculturation (Stone, 2002).

Indeed, an examination of historical documents provides evidence of a government Indian agent speaking coldly of extinguishing American Indian people:

> Many [Native Americans] are well educated, and the possessors of good, cultivated farms, and others managers of a prosperous business. A large number of those residing in Michigan and Kansas, as also the Winnebagoes in Minnesota, have become citizens, and the probabilities are that most of those remaining in Kansas and Nebraska will, in a few years, if not removed to the Indian country and brought under a territorial form of government, become merged into the citizen population and their tribal existence be extinguished. (*Annual Report*, 1871, p. 5)

The culmination of sociopolitical events for NAs/ANs resulted in federally mandated assimilation programs like the boarding schools for Native youth (Duran & Duran, 1995). Such interactions led to distrustful attitudes toward European Americans (LaFromboise, Trimble, & Mohatt, 1990).

NA/AN interactions with oppressors may have taken different paths, but the end result was a deliberate attempt at annihilation on the part of the U.S. government (Duran & Duran, 1995) and a rise to activism on the part of NA/AN groups. As Keohane (2006) stated,

> Native American activism rose quietly in parallel to other civil rights movements in the 1960s, reaching a crescendo in the early 1970s with the occupation of Alcatraz (1969), the Trail of Broken Treaties and takeover of the Bureau of Indian Affairs offices (1972), and the siege at Wounded Knee (1973). (p. 1)

Conceptually, the civil rights movement for NA/AN individuals and tribes may have brought to the forefront a sense of pride and political awareness to fight against the historical oppressor. This time period may have given birth to the articulation of NA/AN cultural identity from within the population as a necessary means to communicate with federal and state government agencies. NA/AN identity emerged in direct opposition to the stereotypical romanticized Indian (Portman, 2001).

Native American Indian and Alaska Native Identity Development

Native American and Alaskan Native Indian identity development have been examined through acculturation studies (Garrett, 1996; Garrett & Pichette, 2000). Garrett and Pichette examined acculturation as a counseling issue by comparing Native American cultural values to mainstream American cultural values. Government oversight does not separate NA/AN Nations into separate categories. NA/AN identities appear to be multifaceted, including worldviews, cultural values, and levels of acculturation. In the 21st century, Native Indian identity is externally dictated by federal recognition at the tribal level by the U.S. Office of Federal Acknowledgment (OFA):

> The Office of Federal Acknowledgment (OFA) within the Office of the Assistant Secretary–Indian Affairs of the Department of the Interior (DOI) implements Part 83 of Title 25 of the Code of Federal Regulations . . . , *Procedures for Establishing that an American Indian Group Exists as an Indian Tribe.* The acknowledgment process is the Department's administrative process by which petitioning groups that meet the criteria are "acknowledged" as Indian tribes and their members become eligible to receive services provided to members of federally recognized Indian tribes. (OFA, 2008a)

As of February 2007, there were approximately 385 tribes petitioning the federal government for recognition or reinstatement of recognition. Five of those tribes were in Alaska (OFA, 2008b). This process of gaining (or regaining) identity through a government entity may be foreign to many non-Indian individuals. Tribal recognition is important to Native American identity because tribal enrollment signifies that identity has been achieved *legally*. Individuals may apply for enrollment in a federally recognized tribe through the Bureau of Indian Affairs, which states the purpose for enrollment requirements as preservation of "the unique character and traditions of each tribe. The tribes establish membership criteria based on shared customs, traditions, language and tribal blood" (U.S. Department of the Interior, 2009).

Although NA/AN legal tribal identity may be oppressively dictated by federal guidelines, many individuals self-define as Native American or Alaskan Native (U.S. BIA, 2001). The spectrum of self-identified NAs/ANs appear to have a genealogical connection to historical tribes, but in some cases may be individuals who self-identify as NA/AN or who maintain an interest in Native American or Alaskan Native cultures (Oswalt & Neely, 1998). Identity development within sovereign tribal groups is more about growth and connection to the relationship of the Nation (which does entail blood quantum but can be fictive kinship through adoption) (Oswalt & Neely, 1998).

Culture and Native American/Alaska Native Identity Development

Tribal identity development occurs within NA/AN communities over the lifespan. Children are taught to embrace cultural determinants such as dance, religious ceremonies and beliefs, oral traditions, and cultural values (Garrett, 1996). Elders are respected and become primary mentors for cultural identity development among the children of the tribe, such as through teaching and passing on unwritten histories of the familial band or tribe (Garrett & Pichette, 2000). It is important for counselors to assess the involvement of their NA/AN clients with tribal groups (Attneave, 1987) by asking questions about connection and relationship to the tribal family or tribal administration centers. NA/AN identity may be assessed by other NA/AN individuals by the ability of an individual to respect tribal customs and traditions, adherence to cultural values, and relationship to known tribal members. It is important to note that no identity development models are available to assess NA/AN identity stages at this time. Many counseling professionals adapt existing identity development models to their NA/AN clients, which may or may not be problematic—thus, the importance of assessing NA/AN clients' geographic origins (reservation, rural, or urban-based) and levels of acculturation

(traditional to acculturated). At this time, research development of instruments to measure identity development among NAs/ANs is needed, because assessment and measurement instruments must be culturally appropriate for the NA/AN populations so that proper diagnosis can occur.

MEASUREMENT AND DIAGNOSIS ISSUES WITH NATIVE AMERICANS AND ALASKA NATIVES

Just as counselors are expected to display cultural awareness and competence when counseling (Sue, Ivey, & Pedersen, 1996), they also must strive to be culturally competent when implementing measurement and diagnosis with culturally diverse clients. Issues of prejudiced and biased assessment with minority groups in the United States (based on categories such as ethnicity, race, gender, sexual orientation, and socioeconomic class) have been in the forefront of the counseling profession for more than 35 years (Lonner & Ibrahim, 2002). However, one of the primary concerns in measurement and diagnosis of U.S. ethnic minority groups remains: that counselors be aware of and trained to conduct such assessments in fair and unbiased manners (Thomason, 1991).

Despite the advances in measurement and diagnosis in the counseling profession, there is a paucity of literature integrating culture and assessments and culture and the *Diagnostic and Statistical Manual of Mental Disorders, Fourth Edition, Text Revision* (*DSM-IV-TR*) (American Psychiatric Association, 2000). However, researchers continue to document the importance of the consideration of cultural issues in psychological measurement and diagnosis (Constantine, 1998; Lonner & Ibrahim, 2002). For example, the *DSM-IV-TR* provides counselors a cultural formulation for counselors to evaluate clients' cultural contexts. This cultural formulation helps counselors review (a) clients' cultural backgrounds; (b) possible cultural explanations of clients' issues; (c) possible cultural factors related to clients' psychosocial environments and functioning; (d) cultural components affecting the client/counselor relationship; and (e) an overall cultural assessment for proper measurement, diagnosis, and treatment (Lonner & Ibrahim, 2002; Tanaka-Matsumi, Higginbotham, & Chang, 2002).

Although this *DSM-IV-TR* effort provides evidence of advancement in the field of counseling measurement, research and literature on cross-cultural assessment, diagnosis, and treatment continue to expose the inaccuracy of the *DSM-IV-TR* and the ethnocentric errors that occur in test development, administration, and interpretation with underrepresented and marginalized groups, including Native Americans and Alaska Natives.

Overview of Measurement and Diagnosis with Natives

Native Americans and Alaska Natives represent two of the groups in counseling that may be dubious about traditional psychological measurement and diagnosis. Because of sociohistorical incidents and continued oppression of Native persons in the United States, traditional Natives are often skeptical of having mainstream culture and values forced upon them and may not accept results of measurements and psychological diagnoses that are not in line with their traditional beliefs and values. In fact, in many Native contexts, mental illness is viewed as a result of disharmony among the individual, family, or tribe/clan in relation to the natural order; thus, healing occurs when harmony and balance are restored (Herring, 1999; Thomason, 1991). This is in direct contrast to a traditional counseling diagnosis that has focused on individual psychology, which is not as helpful to NA/AN individuals, who focus more on the inseparable mind, body, and spirit.

It is also important for counselors to be aware that many Natives maintain considerable mistrust of Euro-American and ethnic minority counselors other than Native counselors (Dixon Rayle et al., 2006; LaFromboise et al., 1990). With this potential mistrust in mind, counselors should make themselves aware of their Native clients' beliefs and values by using the *DSM-IV-TR*'s formulation as well as spending significant amounts of time with clients before introducing psychological, educational, or vocational measurement and diagnosis and/or psychological terms that may cause feelings of isolation among their Native clients. In addition, it is critical that counselors use measurement instruments and strategies that are culturally specific and responsive for NA/AN clients.

Currently, various measurement methods can be used when assessing clients, including interviewing the client, family members, and acquaintances; reviewing client records; observing the client in real-life situations; and using norm-referenced or criterion-referenced tests (Thomason, 1991). In addition, psychological assessment may be based on an etic perspective, which emphasizes universal characteristics and experiences among all human beings, or an emic (culture-specific) perspective (Sue & Sue, 2008). However, counselors should be apprehensive of the use of nationally normed tests to assess various characteristics of NA/AN clients because these tests are typically based on the etic perspective and were normed with members of the U.S. majority population (Lee, 2005).

Historically, measurement and assessment with NA/AN clients has been culturally inappropriate and thus historically underutilized in counseling as a consequence. However, it is important for counselors to know that NA/AN clients can be assessed in counseling in unbiased ways if counselors take the time to understand their clients' concerns/issues, seek to be culturally specific and responsive, seek to be unbiased, and maintain their clients' best interests at all times. When considering measurement and diagnosis concerns with NA/AN clients, counselors should be aware of a few of the general issues in the assessment of these individuals, including language differences and reading levels, nonverbal communication styles, client beliefs and potential mistrust, counselor-client dissimilarity, client acculturation level, translation of tests, and potential bias in standardized tests (Thomason, 1991). In addition, when working with Native clients, the assessment of acculturation level to the general U.S. society is an important first step before using other assessment or diagnosis procedures.

The conflict in cultural values between traditional NA/AN values and mainstream American values represent the varying degrees of acculturation experienced by NA/AN individuals (Garrett & Garrett, 1994; Heinrich, Corbine, & Thomas, 1990; LaFromboise et al., 1990). Assessing Native clients' acculturation levels early on will allow counselors to have a greater understanding of the levels of clients' traditionalism with which they may be working in counseling. In addition, acculturation levels of NA/AN individuals cannot be assumed without creating the potential for misinterpretation and misunderstanding, potentially invalidating diagnosis and interventions in counseling, psychological testing, and the counseling relationship between counselors and their clients. Not all Native persons experience the same level of acculturation or traditionalism, as evidenced by following Pan-Indian (not tribal-specific) assessment of acculturation developed by Little Soldier (1985) and later adapted by LaFromboise et al. (1990): traditional, transitional, marginal, assimilated, and bicultural (it is critical to note that if tribal-specific acculturation assessments exist, counselors are urged to use these versus Pan-Indian versions). Results from acculturation assessments will allow counselors to gauge NA/AN clients' beliefs and values in relation to the larger U.S. society and thus be able to implement more culturally responsive assessment, diagnosis, and counseling interventions. Additional NA/AN acculturation assessments available to counselors are the *Native American* Interview of *Acculturation* (NAIA) (Smith, 2004); the Native American Acculturation Scale (NAAS) (Garrett & Pichette, 2000); the Native American Cultural Identity Scale (NACIS) (Ting & Bryant, 1997); and the Multigroup Ethnic Identity Measure Revised (MEIM-R) (Phinney & Ong, 2007), which has been found to be effective across racial/ethnic groups.

Although a variety of tools have been developed to assess acculturation levels of clients, the majority have not been normed with NA/AN individuals. Therefore, an additional appropriate suggestion would be to conduct acculturation assessments with Native clients through verbal checklist techniques versus written instruments. Acculturation information that counselors should collect from Native clients might include (a) personal and tribal definitions of traditional and nontraditional activities, beliefs, and values; (b) beliefs regarding family roles and religion; (c) level of traditionalism, acculturation, or assimilation; (d) clients' reactions to and experiences with mainstream society; (e) preferences for daily language use, meals, clothing, and music and reading selections; and (f) their overall cultural identity, which may include numerous identities—race/ethnicity, gender, spiritual/religious, and spiritual (Dixon Rayle et al., 2006).

Additional areas within which counselors may wish to assess NA/AN clients include personality assessments; psychological functioning assessments; assessments of interests, abilities, and attitudes; intellectual functioning assessments; needs assessments; vocational assessments;

and assessments of substance use and abuse, among many others used in counseling. However, it is critical for counselors to take heed of the suggestions above when conducting clinical assessment and diagnosis with *any* culturally diverse clients. Most importantly, counselors should place emphasis on verbal and nonverbal communications from NA/AN clients and may find verbal assessments to be the most effective when working with these particular individuals in counseling settings.

CULTURALLY RESPONSIVE COUNSELING FOR NATIVE AMERICANS AND ALASKA NATIVES

Even as professional counselors advance in their understanding of Native Americans' and Alaska Natives' sociohistorical backgrounds, current lifestyles, and potential needs in counseling, these groups remain two of the most underserved populations regarding the use of mental health services. Traditionally, NAs/ANs have not openly sought counseling services; however, more and more counselors are working in areas of the United States where they meet with Native clients (living both on and off traditional Indian reservations and whose levels of acculturation can vary greatly). Thus, when counselors are working with NAs/ANs, it is critical for them to understand clients' acculturation levels (traditional, transitional, marginal, assimilated, or bicultural), including their geographic origin/residence (reservation, rural, urban); tribal affiliation (tribal structure, customs, beliefs); as well as their gender identities; potential issues and concerns; and values orientations (Dixon Rayle et al., 2006; Garrett & Pichette, 2000; Kulis, Okamoto, Dixon Rayle, & Hawkins, 2006; Portman, 2001). This knowledge and awareness will aid counselors in being prepared to work collaboratively with their clients' needs and concerns through culturally appropriate and responsive counseling goals and interventions.

Awareness of Native Gender Identities

It is important to acknowledge that *awareness* of the above components *does not* make a counselor an "expert" in counseling Native clients; however, it does allow for a common understanding of how these individuals and their counseling needs may differ from other American minority clients. For Native individuals, there may be vast differences in the values and beliefs associated with being a female and a male. The American mainstream continuum of being female and male is not as stringently imposed on Natives, and it is not as rigidly designated as it is in mainstream society (Portman, 2001). Gender roles among Native individuals have evolved over the past few hundred years (Waldman, 2006); thus, it cannot be assumed that they live out well-known American female and male roles. Native individuals often view themselves psychologically and emotionally as more androgynous, taking on both feminine and masculine gender traits from their respective tribal and familial ideas of "female" and "male" (Dixon Rayle et al., 2006; Portman, 2001). Therefore, these clients may exhibit cross-gender behaviors in counseling, displaying both female and male characteristics. Counselors should be aware that these cross-gender verbal and nonverbal characteristics are viewed as strengths among most Native peoples, and because Native individuals consider themselves a combination of their respective tribes'/clans' gender roles, they are likely to reflect these cultural beliefs in counseling relationships and within everyday life issues and concerns (Dixon Rayle et al., 2006).

Awareness of Potential Native Issues and Concerns

As with any clients, there are numerous issues and concerns facing Native American and Alaska Native individuals in the 21st century, some of which are poverty and high unemployment, school failure and high dropout rates, substance abuse and alcoholism rates, depression, teenage pregnancy rates, reservation gang memberships, suicide rates, delinquency, diabetes, and other physical health concerns. However, when counseling NA/AN clients, no matter the issues/concerns, it is counselors' understanding and knowledge of, and respect for, cultural identity and Native values and beliefs that may enable the counseling relationship and outcomes to be most successful. Researchers consistently find that despite the between- and within-group diversity that exists among Native American and Alaska Native tribes/clans, there is a common core of traditional values that characterizes Native American traditional culture across tribal groups and geographic regions (DuBray, 1985; Heinrich et al., 1990; Herring, 1994; Sue & Sue, 2008; Thomason, 1991).

Awareness of Native Values

In general, it is important for counselors to be aware of NA/AN traditional values, some of which consist of the importance placed upon being versus doing, cooperation, community contribution, community and extended family, harmony with nature, sharing, non-interference, a living in the present time orientation, patience, humility, nonverbal communication, preference for explanation of natural phenomena according to the spiritual, and a deep respect for elders (Charleston, 1994; DuBray, 1985; Garrett & Garrett, 1994; Garrett & Pichette, 2000; Heinrich et al., 1990; Herring, 1994; Little Soldier, 1992; Locust, 1988; Marsiglia, Cross, & Mitchell, 1998; Sanders, 1987; Thomason, 1991; Trimble & Jumper-Thurman, 2002). At the same time, counselors should be aware of additional values studies that have revealed that NA/AN traditional values differ significantly from American mainstream values, which consist of importance placed on doing versus being, self-promotion, domination, competition, aggression, individualism and the nuclear family, verbal communication, mastery over nature, a futuristic time orientation, scientific explanations for everything, clock-watching, winning as much as possible, and reverence of youth (Charleston, 1994; DuBray, 1985; Little Soldier, 1992; Sanders, 1987; Sue & Sue, 2008). It is also critical that counselors remain aware that in the 21st century, they will meet with Native Americans and Alaska Natives who have traditional Native values, many that share both traditional and mainstream values, and numerous individuals who have acculturated into the mainstream and thus believe in America's mainstream values. Again, it is for these reasons that counselors should be trained and able to assess Native clients' acculturation levels in order to use culturally appropriate counseling goals and interventions.

Culturally Responsive Counseling Considerations

After understanding NA/AN clients' acculturation levels and beliefs and values stemming from sociohistorical events/circumstances and current life choices, counselors are encouraged to use focused counselor observational skills with Native clients' nonverbal and verbal communication patterns. For instance, Native clients will often speak softly and at slower rates versus other clients, who may often speak louder and faster. In addition, Native clients are not likely to address their counselors directly by name and may avoid direct eye contact with their counselors as they are speaking *or* listening in order to maintain privacy or show respect for their counselors. Native clients also use less obvious encouraging communication signs (i.e., uh-huh, head nods) and may desire their counselors to mirror this communication pattern to increase trust. NA/AN individuals are likely to place greater value on nonverbal communications versus counselors' tendency to place value on verbal communications. It is also likely that Native clients will interject less often verbally than other clients, who may be used to interrupting frequently in mainstream communication, and will likely exhibit delayed verbal responses to auditory messages received from their counselors. In fact, it is useful for counselors to use intentional silence whenever it seems appropriate in counseling (or even when it does not) to allow Native clients time and space to think and to feel. Counselors are encouraged to be patient and sensitive to Native clients' pauses and moments of processing information received versus expecting them to respond immediately when using verbal communications. The more amenable counselors are to allowing Native clients space to think and feel, and to articulate their stories, the more likely they will return for more counseling.

When using questions with Native clients, counselors should also work to pose them in respectful, unobtrusive manners because of potential mistrust from clients. In fact, counselors are encouraged to use probes and indirect leads versus questions when working with Native clients. Some of these general probes might include the following: "Tell me about where you come from"; "Tell me about your family and your tribe/clan"; "Tell me about you as a person, culturally and spiritually"; "Tell me about your culture"; "Tell me how your culture and spirituality play into how you live your life"; and/or "Tell me about your life and your concerns as you see them currently, as well as in the

past" (counselors should remember that Native clients may not be as future-focused as other clients depending on their acculturation levels).

Additionally, counselors should not assume that because a client appears Native, she or he follows traditional Native beliefs and values, or that because a client does not appear to be Native, she or he does not live by traditional Native beliefs and values. If, indeed, Native clients do live by more traditional beliefs and values, it may be helpful to suggest that extended family or other significant persons (e.g., a Medicine person or tribal elder) participate in the counseling process to support the client as she or he moves through important personal transitions and changes. In order to adapt culturally responsive counseling approaches, counselors are encouraged to interact and consult with family and elders from clients' respective communities for added dimensions of understanding to otherwise unfamiliar concepts, and should be aware of community outlets in consulting with other Native members in the urban community (Heinrich et al., 1990; LaFromboise et al., 1990). It is critical that counselors honor the sacred relationships that NA/AN clients may have as well as the counseling relationship by being open and respectful to all of NA/AN clients' family and tribal members as well as to their beliefs and values.

When counselors are focusing on verbal communications with Native clients, it is important for counselors to realize that it is not uncommon for NA/AN individuals to use humor and sarcasm in communicating about their issues and concerns, and often leave themselves open to being teased. Native clients believe that humor and sarcasm serve the purpose of keeping themselves and others (including their counselors) humble. Along with humor, Native clients are likely to use metaphors and imagery when expressing their issues and concerns, often integrating nature and animals as metaphoric symbols for themselves, their beliefs and/or values, and their concerns. In addition, counselors will find that Native clients most always ask permission whenever possible and always give thanks—even when counselors may not expect them to. Thus, counselors should attempt to verbally mirror asking permission and giving thanks to Native clients within counseling relationships. Native clients may also especially appreciate counselors' self-disclosure through personal anecdotes or short verbal stories, which Natives are quite fond of in verbal communications, and may use these as the way in which they verbally express themselves to counselors most efficiently in counseling.

In the past, counselors who are recognized as members of an indigenous group have been able to build trust and confidence with NA/AN clients (e.g., NA/AN clients feel free to speak freely and openly); however, those counselors who are not Native can build credibility with NA/AN clients by having the knowledge and awareness of NA/AN culture, values, and beliefs (Bischel & Mallinckrodt, 2001; LaFromboise et al., 1990). In order for counselors to integrate NA/AN cultural values and beliefs into a therapeutic framework for working with Native clients, it is important to weave Western-American counseling techniques with elements of Native cultures, beliefs, and philosophies (Bennett & BigFoot-Sipes, 1991; Bischel & Mallinckrodt, 2001). Well-known approaches such as bibliotherapy and narrative therapy are appropriate examples of "Westernized" counseling techniques that work well with Native clients (Frey, 2003). Traditional Native learning processes emphasize storytelling, narrative approaches; for example, using legends, stories, and metaphors to share themselves and their lives (Herring, 1999). In fact, Native clients' narratives and stories include symbolism, tribal histories, social relationships, and comical metaphors to convey complex issues, concerns, or relationships.

Because most Native clients consider the need for counseling to be indicative of their lack of balance and harmony in their personal and familial worlds, counselors may consider working from developmental holistic, wellness-based frameworks (examining all areas of systems and relationships within their lives) in order to allow Native clients to explore how they can personally redefine and/or rediscover their harmony and balance. This is a culturally responsive counseling approach that represents the collectivist nature by which many Native clients may live; this approach incorporates all areas and relationship systems in clients' lives and honors their values of holistic harmony and balance. This honorable approach from counselors with their NA/AN clients allows counselors to assess ceremonies and/or spiritual beliefs they may want to include in therapy; extended family or elders they may want to have involved in the healing process; their histories and presenting issues; their previous attempts at resolving dilemmas; the ways in which they define their identities; and their roles as individuals, immediate and extended family members, and members of their tribe/clan.

Finally, individual, group, and/or family counseling with NA/AN clients offers options to rebalance their relational, physical, emotional, psychological, and spiritual harmony and balance. If and when NA/AN individuals seek counseling (or are even mandated to counseling), they will assess counselors' trustworthiness early in the process. They will expect *all* counselors to honor their traditions, families, tribes, values and beliefs, sociohistories, needs for harmony and balance, and roles as Native and American citizens. Through holistic, intentional wellness-based collaboration, understanding, awareness, and knowledge, counselors can respect and honor Native clients' culturally specific needs in counselors through culturally responsive counseling goals and interventions. It is the ethical responsibility of all counselors to approach all clients in culturally responsive and respectful manners, to be capable and well trained in the area of multicultural competence and sensitivity, to be aware of personal prejudices and biases, and thus to be able to honor Native American and Alaska Native clients. These two groups of American minority clients are growing in population numbers and will seek out, and remain in, counseling if understood and respected by humble and knowledgeable U.S. counselors.

CONCLUSION

As traditional and assimilated NA/AN populations continue to grow and evolve, professional counselors are likely to meet with these individuals in a variety of counseling situations. As Native persons face various issues and concerns in the 21st century, it is likely that they may continue to be at higher risk for mental health problems and substance abuse when compared to other ethnic groups. This chapter presented an overview of Native American and Alaska Native identity development theory, measurement in counseling, and implications for offering culturally specific and responsive counseling interventions for these populations in order to advance counselors' understanding of Native Americans' and Alaska Natives' sociohistorical backgrounds, current lifestyles, and potential needs in counseling. As counselors, it is our ethical responsibility to approach *all* clients in culturally responsive and respectful manners, to be capable and well trained in the area of multicultural competence, to be aware of our own prejudices and biases, and thus to be able to honor racially and ethnically diverse clients.

For many Native clients, the goals in counseling may center on achieving unity of greater harmony and balance among their minds, bodies, spirits, relationships, and environments. If counselors meet Native clients as equals and set out to learn from them before teaching and helping them, they will find just how open NA/AN individuals are about their life stories. Almost always, Native Americans and Alaska Natives view the respected persons as those who act in friendly, generous, considerate, and modest manners (Lewis & Gingerich, 1980).

REFERENCES

Annual Report of the Commissioner of Indian Affairs to the Secretary for the Year 1871. (1871). Clum to Delano, 15 November 1871, in United States, Office of Indian Affairs, (Washington, DC: Government Printing Office, 1872), 1–8, NADP Document R871001.

Atkinson, D. R. (2003). *Counseling American minorities* (6th ed.). New York: McGraw-Hill.

Attneave, C. L. (1987). Practical counseling with American Indian and Alaska Native clients. In P. Pedersen (Ed.), *Handbook of cross-cultural counseling and therapy* (pp. 135–140). Westport, CT: Greenwood.

Bennett, S. K., & BigFoot-Sipes, D. S. (1991). American Indian and White college students' preferences for counselor characteristics. *Journal of Counseling Psychology, 38,* 440–445.

Bischel, R. J., & Mallinckrodt, B. (2001). Cultural commitment and the counseling preferences and counselor perceptions of American Indian women. *Counseling Psychologist, 29,* 858–881.

Charleston, G. M. (1994). Toward true Native education: A treaty of 1992 final report of the Indian Nations at Risk Task Force draft 3. *Journal of American Indian Education, 33,* 1–56.

Chideya, F. (1999, Fall). A nation of minorities: America in 2050. *Civil Rights Journal, 4.*

Constantine, M. G. (1998). Developing competence in multicultural assessment: Implications for counseling psychology training and practice. *Counseling Psychologist, 6,* 922–929.

Dixon Rayle, A. L., Chee, C., & Sand, J. K. (2006). Honoring their way: Counseling American Indian women. *Journal for Multicultural Counseling and Development, 34,* 66–79.

DuBray, W. H. (1985). American Indian values: Critical factor in casework. *Social Casework: The Journal of Contemporary Social Work, 66,* 30–37.

Duran, E., & Duran, B. (1995). *Native American postcolonial psychology.* Albany: State University of New York Press.

Frey, L. L. (2003). Use of narratives, metaphor, and relationship in the assessment and treatment of a sexually reactive American Indian youth. In G. Roysircar, D. S. Sandhu, & V. E. Bibbins (Eds.), *Multicultural competencies: A guidebook of practices* (pp. 119–128). Alexandria, VA: Association for Multicultural Counseling and Development.

Garrett, M. T. (1996). "Two people": An American Indian narrative of bicultural identity. *Journal of American Indian Education, 36,* 1–21.

Garrett, J. T., & Garrett, M. (1994). The path of good medicine: Understanding and counseling Native American Indians. *Journal of Multicultural Counseling and Development, 22,* 134–144.

Garrett, M. T., & Herring, R. D. (2001). Honoring the power of relation: Counseling Native adults. *Journal for Humanistic Counseling, Education, and Development, 40,* 139–151.

Garrett, M. T., & Pichette, E. F. (2000). Red as an apple: Native American acculturation and counseling with or without reservation. *Journal of Counseling & Development, 78,* 3–13.

Heinrich, R. K., Corbine, J. L., & Thomas, K. R. (1990). Counseling American Indians. *Journal of Counseling & Development, 69,* 128–133.

Herring, R. D. (1994). The clown or contrary figure as a counseling intervention strategy with Native American Indian clients. *Journal of Multicultural Counseling and Development, 22,* 153–164.

Herring, R. D. (1999). *Counseling with American Indians and Alaska Natives: Strategies for helping professionals.* Thousand Oaks, CA: Sage.

Keohane, J. R. (2006). The rise of tribal self-determination and economic development. *Journal of the Section of Individual Rights & Responsibilities, 33,* 9–11.

Kulis, S., Okamoto, S. K., Dixon Rayle, A. L., & Hawkins, S. (2006). Social contexts of drug offers among American Indian youth and their relationship to drug use: An exploratory study. *Cultural Diversity and Ethnic Minority Psychology, 12,* 30–44.

LaFromboise, T. D., Trimble, J. E., & Mohatt, G. V. (1990). Counseling intervention and American Indian tradition: An integrative approach. *Counseling Psychologist, 18,* 628–654.

Lee, C. C. (2005). *Multicultural issues in counseling: New approaches to diversity* (3rd ed.). Alexandria, VA: American Counseling Association.

Lewis, R. G., & Gingerich, W. (1980). Leadership characteristics: Views of Native American and non-Native American Indian students. *Social Casework, 61,* 494–497.

Little Soldier, L. (1985). To soar with the eagles: Enculturation and acculturation of Indian children. *Childhood Education, 61*(3), 185–191.

Little Soldier, L. (1992). Building optimum learning environments for Navajo students. *Childhood Education, 68,* 145–148.

Locust, C. (1988). Wounding the spirit: Discrimination and traditional American Indian belief systems. *Harvard Educational Review, 58,* 315–330.

Lonner, W. J., & Ibrahim, A. A. (2002). Appraisal and assessment in cross-cultural counseling. In P. B. Pedersen, J. G. Draguns, W. L. Lonner, & J. E. Trimble (Eds.), *Counseling across cultures* (5th ed., pp. 355–379). Thousand Oaks, CA: Sage.

Marsiglia, F. F., Cross, S., & Mitchell, V. (1998). Culturally grounded group work with adolescent American Indian students. *Social Work With Groups, 21,* 89–102.

Office of Federal Acknowledgment. (2008a). Brief overview. Retrieved on May 20, 2008, from http://www.doi.gov/bia/docs/ofa/admin_docs/ofa_overview_092208.pdf

Office of Federal Acknowledgment. (2008b). Number of Petitions by State as of September 22, 2008. Retrieved on May 20, 2008, from http://www.doi.gov/bia/docs/ofa/admin_docs/num_petitioners_state_092208.pdf

Oswalt, W. H., & Neely, S. (1998). *This land was theirs: A study of North American Indians.* Mountain View, CA: Mayfield.

Phinney, J. S., & Ong, A. D. (2007). Conceptualization and measurement of ethnic identity: Current status and future directions. *Journal of Counseling Psychology, 54,* 271–281.

Portman, T. A. (2001). Sex role attributions of American Indian women. *Journal of Mental Health Counseling, 23,* 72–84.

Roysircar, G., Arredondo, P., Fuertes, J., Ponterotto, J. G., & Toporek, R. (2003). *Multicultural counseling competencies 2003: Association for Multicultural Counseling and Development.* Alexandria, VA: ACA Press.

Sanders, D. (1987). Cultural conflicts: An important factor in the academic failures of American Indian students. *Journal of Multicultural Counseling and Development, 15,* 81–90.

Smith, D. S. (2004). A preliminary investigation of the value of the Native American Interview of Acculturation. *Dissertation Abstracts International, 64*(11-B), 5803.

Stone, J. B. (2002). Focus on cultural issues in research: Developing and implementing Native American postcolonial participatory action research. In J. D. Davis, J. S. Erickson, S. R. Johnson, C. A. Marshall, P. Running Wolf, & R. L. Santiago (Eds.), *Work group on American Indian research and program evaluation methodology (AIR-PEM): Symposium on research and evaluation methodology: Lifespan issues related to American Indians/Alaska Natives with disabilities* (pp. 98–121). Flagstaff: Northern Arizona University, Institute for Human Development, Arizona University Center on Disabilities, American Indian Rehabilitation Research and Training Center.

Sue, D. W., Arredondo, P., & McDavis, R. J. (1992). Multicultural counseling competencies and standards: A call to the profession. *Journal of Counseling & Development, 70,* 477–486.

Sue, D. W., Ivey, A. E., & Pederson, P. B. (Eds.). (1996). *A theory of multicultural counseling and therapy.* Pacific Grove, CA: Brooks/Cole.

Sue, D. W., & Sue, D. (2008). *Counseling the culturally diverse: Theory and practice* (5th ed.). New York: Wiley.

Tanaka-Matsumi, J., Higginbotham, H. N., & Chang, R. (2002). Cognitive-behavioral approaches to counseling across cultures. In P. B. Pedersen, J. G. Draguns, W. L. Lonner, & J. E. Trimble (Eds.), *Counseling across cultures* (5th ed., pp. 233–249). Thousand Oaks, CA: Sage.

Thomason, T. C. (1991). Counseling Native Americans: An introduction for non-Native American counselors. *Journal of Counseling & Development, 69,* 321–327.

Ting, S. R., & Bryant, A. (1997). *An analysis comparing Native American students' cultural identity and academic achievement: A preliminary report.* North Carolina State University, Department of Counselor Education.

Trimble, J. E., & Jumper-Thurman, P. (2002). Ethnocultural considerations and strategies for providing counseling services to Native American Indians. In P. Pedersen, J. G. Draguns, W. J. Lonner, & J. E. Trimble (Eds.), *Counseling across cultures* (5th ed., pp. 53–91). Thousand Oaks, CA: Sage.

U.S. Bureau of the Census. (2001). *2000 Census counts of American Indians, Eskimos, or Aleuts and American Indian and Alaska Native areas.* Washington, DC: Author.

U.S. Bureau of Indian Affairs. (2001). *American Indians today.* Washington, DC: Author.

U.S. Department of the Interior. (2009). Indian ancestry: Enrollment in a federally recognized tribe. Retrieved March 17, 2009, from http://www.doi.gov/enrollment.html

U.S. Office of Management and Budget. (2005). *Native Americans, Alaska natives, and Hawaiian natives.* Washington, DC: Author.

Waldman, C. (2006). *Encyclopedia of Native American tribes* (3rd ed.). New York: Checkmark Books.

21

African and Afro-Caribbean American Identity Development

Theory and Practice Implications

TINA Q. RICHARDSON, ANGELA R. BETHEA,
CHARLAYNE C. HAYLING, AND CLAUDETTE WILLIAMSON-TAYLOR

The social construct of race and related identities is significantly influenced by a number of factors that make the discussion of race as the primary identity characteristic for Black individuals a complex yet important dialogue. The dialogue must be grounded in the fact that the salience of race as an identity characteristic is profoundly influenced by one's own sociopolitical worldview regarding race. In the U.S. context, racial identity theorists assume that to a meaningful degree, the pan-ethnic collective of people who have been ascribed the racial designation *African American* embrace and share individual and group identities that are anchored in the Holocaust of Enslavement or Black Maafa (Cross, 1978, 1991; Cross, Parham, & Helms, 1991; Helms & Cook, 1999). These terms refer to a historical span that dates back more than 500 years during which Africans throughout the diaspora suffered

dehumanization through enslavement, imperialism, colonialism, and exploitation. It also includes the era of civil rights struggles (i.e., the movement to occupy full American citizenship) and the contemporary practices and legislative policies that invalidate and appropriate the contributions of people of African descent (see Smith & Palmisano, 2000 for a chronology). However, African Americans can belong to the same racial group, have different ethnic group membership, and consequently have very different race-based socialization experiences (American Psychological Association [APA], 2008, pp. 2–8).

Casas (1984) distinguishes ethnicity from race and defined ethnicity as a group classification of individuals who share a unique social and cultural heritage (customs, language, religion, and so on) passed on from one generation to the next (p. 787). The racial category

African American is composed of a vastly diverse group of people of African ethnic origins that include Caribbean, African, and the American Black experience. Thus, this reality has significant implications for work in the area of mental health with this population. The overall purpose of this chapter is to orient the reader to the multiplicative aspects of the Black collective, while also providing specific references to racial identity theory and practical application in the field of counseling psychology. Therefore, the three main goals of this chapter are to explore the extent to which ethnicity influences race-based identities for people of African descent, present information regarding the usefulness of the racial identity models within sects of the Black community, and discuss theoretical implications for research and practice.

THE CONCEPTS OF ETHNICITY AND RACIAL IDENTITY

Much of the mental health and social science literature that addresses Black or African American collectives does so without regard for ethnicity (Cokley & Helm, 2007). In the psychological literature, few analyses address how different categories of Blacks, such as descendants of free and freed people or slaves in the United States, differ from recent Black immigrants (in the 1960s–2000s) and their descendants. African and Afro-Caribbean groups have been described with regard to racial identification in spite of the fact that many of the ethnic communities within the Black population remain distinctively separate with regard to culture and racial socializations. As we reflect on racial identity in the U.S. context, two questions related to identity guide this chapter: Who constitutes the Black collective referred to as African Americans? and To what extent do existing models of racial identity apply to African Americans who have ethnic identities whose race-based socialization occurred outside the United States?

Race in the United States is intertwined with almost every aspect of the country's history and achievement. Race has been used as the primary system for classifying all people into groups and allocating resources based on the perception that people neatly fit ascribed phenotypic characteristics. Although it is widely known that race has no sound scientific foundation, a race-based classification system is persistently used to ascribe

identities to people in this country regardless of their national and continental origins. For people of African descent in the United States, societal references to race usually have been made in the context of perceived inferiority-superiority overlaid with racism. For many Black people, racism has been so pervasive that it is largely believed to shape the identity of Black people with such intensity that it outweighs most other possible identity characteristics. The basis for the assumption that race is more profoundly a defining identity characteristic than most, if not all, other characteristics is fundamentally grounded in the social and political founding principles of this country. The following excerpt from a speech delivered by Abraham Lincoln (1953) demonstrates the point quite clearly:

> There is a physical difference between the White and Black races which I believe will forever forbid the two races living together on terms of social and political equality. And inasmuch as they cannot so live, while they do remain together there must be the position of superior and inferior, and I as much as any other man am in favor of having the superior position assigned to the White race. (pp. 145–146)

Regardless of the individual characteristics of African people during the slavery era and immediately following it, the social and political landscape was entrenched with the reality that identity was solely one of an ascribed, deracinated nature, with unrelenting institutionalized disenfranchisement and discrimination as the standard reality. One of the responses to institutionalized oppression for African-descent people was to develop a psychological mechanism that enabled people to define their collective experience and cope with their physical realities. This response was both a profoundly appropriate survival strategy and a limited response to the much broader challenge of self-definition. It was a limited response because Black people have always known that there is a vast range of individuality and unique person characteristics within the collective group that was silenced through notions of race.

Diversity Within the Black Collective

According to the U.S. Census Bureau (2000), the African American population is approximately 12.3%

(34,658,190) of the U.S. population. The Black population in the Americas has always included Africans from various ethnic or tribal origins even though the enslavement experience and the deracination process stripped people of most of these identities. However, the Black community in the United States has become increasingly diverse with respect to ethnicity and the cultural values that its racial group members possess; 16% of the Black population growth since 1980 is attributed to immigration (Sue & Sue, 2003). In the year 2000, the number of Black immigrants who legally entered the country from Africa and the Caribbean islands were 345,000 and 1,285,000, respectively (U.S. Census Bureau, 2004). Significant numbers of West Indians immigrated to the United States around the turn of the century (Sowell, 1978); however, immigration trends among Africans have proliferated only since the 1980s (Brandon, 1997). In 2002, the highest numbers of U.S. immigrants born in sub-Saharan Africa were from the following countries: Ethiopia (7,574), Ghana (4,256), Kenya (3,207), Nigeria (8,129), and Sudan (2,924) (Bureau of Citizenship and Immigration Services, 2003). Additionally, the highest numbers of immigrants from the Caribbean, in 2002, were from the following countries: Haiti (20,268), Jamaica (14,898), and Trinidad and Tobago (5,771) (Bureau of Citizenship and Immigration Services, 2003). This continual influence of Black immigration to the United States has an inevitable impact on Blacks' collective identity development processes within the American context.

However, many scholars who study racial identity hold the fundamental assumption that the larger social context has dictated the content, shape, and form of Black identity in terms of racial identity models. The unavoidable system of racial classification and the extant reality of institutional racism that controls the extent to which groups gain access to resources and opportunities for social mobility are assumed to outweigh most other characteristics (i.e., culture, gender, religion, etc.) and provide the foundation for a collective racial identity regardless of when individuals entered American society.

Models of Collective Black Identity

Group identity, which is based on the life experiences, historical perspectives, and sociocultural experiences of a group, has been identified in the literature as an important psychological variable (Cross, 1991; Erikson, 1968; Operario & Fiske, 2001). Group identity with respect to racial classification has been described in racial identity literature as a salient defining character for people of African descent in the United States (Helms, 1995). Cross (1971, 1991, 1995) as well as Helms and Cook (1999) describe racial identity models as psychological frameworks that explain individuals' intrapsychic and interpersonal reactions to societal racism and how individuals overcome internalized racism to achieve a healthy racial group identity.

Research by Cross (1971, 1991, 1995) and Helms (1995) provides models of Black racial identity that are grounded in the political realities of racial oppression, the civil rights and racial pride movements, as well as contemporary dynamics of racism and discrimination. Initially, these models hypothesized that identity development is best characterized by movement across a series of sequential stages, and that changes were influenced by an individual's reaction to social/environmental pressures and situations (Parham, 1989).

The Cross Model. Cross (1971, 1978) developed a five-stage model describing Black identity development as "The Negro-to-Black conversion experience" or "Nigrescence," which was later revised to be a four-stage model with seven identities: (a) Pre-encounter, (b) Encounter, (c) Immersion-Emersion, and (d) Internalization-Commitment (Cross, 1991; Vandiver, Cross, Worrell, & Fhagen-Smith, 2002). The *Pre-encounter* stage is characterized by two identities: Assimilation and Anti-Black. Individuals with the Assimilation identity operate from a "pro-American" point of view and attach low salience to racial issues. Individuals with the anti-Black identity are characterized by miseducation (possess negative stereotypes of the African American community) and self-hatred (try to overcome their internalized societal stigma attached to being Black in order to gain approval from Whites). Individuals with these attitudes experience feelings of hatred toward their reference group, a perspective that comes extremely close to that of White racists (Cross, 1991; Vandiver et al., 2002).

A person may move to the *Encounter* stage as a result of experiencing and personalizing a single racial incident (e.g., witnessing police brutality) or a series of racial events. This process destroys the Pre-encounter identity and provides some direction for changes in worldview on race issues (Cross, 1991). The *Immersion-Emersion* stage is characterized by a state of cognitive dissonance, as the individual simultaneously adopts a new frame of reference while he or she attempts to destroy the old identity. This stage has two identities: Intense Black Involvement and Anti-White. Individuals who exhibit Intense Black Involvement glorify all things Black. Individuals who demonstrate an Anti-White identity are predisposed to denigrate White people and White culture. The *Internalization* stage consists of three separate identities: Black Nationalist, Biculturalist, and Multiculturalist. The Black Nationalist identity is reflected in a focus on Black community empowerment. The Biculturalist identity consists of two elements: self-acceptance and a pluralistic perspective that includes other cultural orientations (gender, sexual orientation). The Multiculturalist identity also includes a focus on two or more salient identities.

Parham (1989) added a lifespan perspective to the understanding of racial identity models. He challenged the assumption that identity development is resolved once a person has completed a single cycle through the stages. Parham extended Cross's model by describing Nigrescence as a lifelong process that begins in the late adolescence/early adulthood period (Parham, 1989). Unlike the Cross model of Nigrescence developed for adults, Parham's analysis of Nigrescence takes into account racial identity at three different phases of life: (a) late adolescence/early adulthood, (b) midlife, and (c) late adulthood. Parham reasons that the onset of Nigrescence varies with age and that a person's initial racial identity need not originate in the Pre-encounter stage. For example, if an African American adolescent adopts pro-Black parental and social messages, that adolescent's initial group reference orientation might be pro-Black as well (Cross et al., 1991; Parham, 1989).

In addition, unlike Cross's model, which allows only for linear progression, Parham proposes three ways in which a person can resolve an identity struggle: (a) stagnation, (b) stagewise linear progression, and (c) recycling. The concept of "recycling" is defined as "re-initiation into the racial identity struggle and resolution process after having gone through the identity process at an earlier stage in one's life" (Cross et al., 1991, p. 332). Parham (1989) suggests that racist events can trigger recycling. For example, as a result of having an added encounter experience (e.g., a racially motivated challenge or trauma), one becomes exposed to "small or giant gaps" in one's thinking about Blackness. Here, a person may regress to an earlier Nigrescence stage in order to address the incomplete thinking patterns. Parham's lifespan approach reflects variety in racial socialization and resolution in Black identity development.

The Helms Model. In contrast to the Cross model, Helms's model lends more attention to the subjective experience related to racial identity development. In addition, Helms (1995) conceptualizes the processes as statuses rather than stages in order to explain the capacity for an individual to exhibit attitudes, behaviors, and emotions reflective of more than one state (Helms, 1995). Helms's model is organized by "statuses," which regulate a person's interpretation of racial information and evolve into schemata or behavioral manifestations of the underlying statuses.

The *Pre-encounter* status is the least cognitively sophisticated in processing racial information (Helms & Cook, 1999). This status is characterized by attitudes that devalue the Black racial group and promote assimilation into White culture. The schema is reflected in one's obliviousness to racial issues in his or her environment. The *Encounter* status is reflected in an individual's confusion about perceived lack of fit with the White world, and ambivalence about identifying with one's own racial group. The individual struggles to replace idealization of Whites with positive information about one's own racial group. The *Immersion* status permits one to idealize one's racial group and denigrate White cultural standards. The Immersion schema evolves in the form of simplistic, dichotomous thinking about racial issues. The *Emersion* status is defined by a sense of solidarity and communalism when among other Blacks. Individuals feel grounded and connected as they revel in Blacks' accomplishments. The *Internalization* status entails a commitment to Blacks, self-defined racial attributes and perspectives, ability to objectively respond to the dominant racial group, and capacity to process complex racial information. The *Integrative Awareness* status allows for the most complex racial information processing, as an individual recognizes oppressive practices that disempower other racial and cultural groups without abandoning one's own Black identity.

The schemata of each status are critical for coping with racial information, as the schemata respond to protect the person's sense of well-being. Dominant schemata are used in situations when the ego perceives the situation as involving racial information. Each time a person believes that he or she is exposed to a racial event, the ego selects the dominant racial identity status to assist the person in interpreting the event. If a dominant schema does not work consistently, then the person relies on a secondary status schema that previously has been effective as a coping strategy. This process continues until the person finds a schema permitting him or her to survive the racial situation. Inability to resolve a situation results in discomfort that may act as a catalyst for strengthening existing statuses or developing new ones. Schemata are expressions of distinguishable information processing strategies (IPS) (Helms, 1995). For example, the Pre-encounter status is associated with the devaluing of one's own racial group based on the Pre-encounter status IPS, "selective perception an obviousness to social racial concerns" (Helms, 1995, p. 188). Theoretically, Helms's explanation of racial identity speaks to the racial identity process as an experience that all racial or ethnic groups share, however not necessarily in similar ways.

Like Helms, Robert Sellers and his colleagues (Sellers, 1993; Sellers et al., 1998) argue that racial identity provides a mechanism through which African Americans define themselves in comparison to other groups. Sellers and his co-authors (1998) propose the Multidimensional Model of Racial Identity (MMRI) to explain the diversity of racial identity profiles among African Americans. The model is based on four assumptions: (a) Like other aspects of self-concept, racial identity has properties that are both situationally dynamic and stable, and that interact to influence individuals' behavior in certain situations; (b) individuals have various identities that are ordered hierarchically within the self-concept; (c) the phenomenological approach to understanding racial identity is imperative to determine what constitutes a healthy racial identity versus an unhealthy racial identity; and (d) racial identity is multidimensional in nature because of various ways it manifests in behavioral and adaptational outcomes. Sellers and his colleagues propose independent but interrelated dimensions of racial identity in African Americans: racial salience, racial centrality, racial regard, and racial ideology. All of these except for racial salience are stable across situations.

Racial salience refers to the extent to which one's race is a relevant part of one's self-concept and functioning during ordinary, day-to-day interactions. Racial salience becomes evident in ambiguous situations. Based on the importance of race in an individual's self-concept, the individual determines whether race is likely to be salient during an ambiguous situation. *Racial centrality* refers to the significance of racial identity, as there is variability in the significance that individuals place on their racial and ethnic group membership. *Racial regard* refers to a person's affective and evaluative judgment of his or her race (e.g., the extent to which a person feels positively about his or her race). Sellers et al. (1998) distinguished between two types of racial regard: public and private. Private regard is defined as how individuals feel about being Black, analogous to racial self-esteem. Public regard refers to the extent to which individuals feel that others view African Americans positively or negatively. The final dimension, *racial ideology,* accounts for the individual's beliefs, opinions, and attitudes with respect to the way that he or she feels that African Americans should live and interact within society. Sellers and his co-authors propose four ideological philosophies within this dimension that vary across different life domains: (a) a *nationalist philosophy,* characterized by strong focus on experiences particular to being Black; (b) an *oppressed minority philosophy,* which refers to emphasis on commonalities among oppressed minority group experiences; (c) an *assimilationist philosophy,* which places emphasis on working within mainstream American structures to achieve life goals; and (d) a *humanist philosophy,* which endorses the idea that there are commonalities among all humans. These four ideologies manifest in four areas of individuals' attitudes with respect to political/economic development, cultural/social activities, intergroup relations, and interaction with the dominant group.

Nigrescence models have been useful because they explain a racinated and deracinated identity development process among African Americans (Constantine, Richardson, Benjamin, & Wilson, 1998). However, these models do not provide a framework for how ethnic culture, particularly for newly minted African Americans, serves as a means for healthy personality development. Racial identity models should not preclude an assessment of the full range of racial socialization experiences among African Americans. Given the changing demographics of the Black population in America due to immigration, intergenerational changes among Black ethnics, and diverse racial socialization experiences, solely focusing on racial identity models without a meaningful assessment of ethnic cultural variables potentially creates limitations and poses a significant challenge.

THE IMPACT OF ETHNIC DIVERSITY ON BLACK IDENTITY

The extent to which models of Black identity can be equally applied to people of African and Afro-Caribbean descent and other Black ethnic groups is an important discourse within the area of cultural psychology. Although African Americans and Black immigrants share a vulnerability to racial oppression (Rogers, 2006), it is likely that their racial identity development differs mainly because of problematic classifications of race as a measure of a collective sense of their identity. Studies show that racial identity and racial socialization vary between Black ethnic groups (Bagley & Copeland, 1994; Phelps, Taylor, & Gerard, 2001), which may lead group members to appraise racist events very differently (Waters, 1996) and perhaps have a less salient race-based identity compared to Blacks who have longer socialization experiences as members of the African American collective. A common practice in a majority of research on within-group differences of African and Afro-Caribbean Americans is the application of racial identity models to experiences of racism and discrimination in lived experiences in America. Hall and Carter (2005) examined the relationship between racial identity status attitudes, ethnic identity, and perceived discrimination in a sample of 82 Afro-Caribbeans and found that racial and ethnic identity

predicted perceptions of discrimination. In addition, the majority of studies use college students and thus lack generalizability. Phelps et al. (2001) examined cultural mistrust, ethnic identity, racial identity, and self-esteem in a total sample of 160 African, African American, and West Indian undergraduate and graduate students. Of the three ethnic groups, African Americans reported higher scores on the Encounter and Immersion/Emersion statuses, as well as the Internalization status, which indicated to some extent that they need to confront issues of race and racial identity given their racial minority group experience. Conversely, the West Indian and African respondents' scores suggest that they may hold race to be less salient given their socialization in majority-Black countries. To summarize, the length and type of racial socialization may differ significantly among U.S. Black ethnic groups, which may differentially affect racial identity events for these groups.

The sociopolitical realities of Black people from many African and Afro-Caribbean contexts involve racial dynamics in which Whites/Europeans numerically occupy minority status and therefore have disproportional access to power, privilege, and resources. Waters (1999) suggests that this difference may serve to make racism "endemic but not defining" as a primary identity characteristic. Comparatively, in relation to the U.S. context in which Whites occupy the numeric majority and disproportional privilege implemented through institutionalized racism, which is the direct outgrowth of slavery, race became a defining identity characteristic that is evident in the psychological literature. The majority of African and Afro-Caribbean immigrants are from countries where Blacks not only make up a "numerical majority" but also occupy positions of power despite experiencing European colonial oppression at the national level (Tormala & Deaux, 2006). Thus, the racial schemata that new immigrants and, in many cases, first-generation Africans and Afro-Caribbeans experience may differ significantly from that of African American descendants of U.S. slaves. These Black ethnic group differences are not adequately described in the psychological literature. Rather, Black identity development literature assumes that all African Americans experience and perceive race-related issues similarly and generalizes these patterns to explain identity development among other Black American subgroups (Cross, 1971, 1978, 1991; Helms, 1994; Sellers, 1993; Thomas, 1971). However, these models may not address some of the phenomenological racial identity experiences (i.e., the process of becoming, understanding of White privilege) of immigrant Blacks and their first- and second-generation descendants living in America.

An illustration of this point is observed in the process of identity among Black youth. In a study of African American adolescent females and young adults enrolled in a community college, Shorter-Gooden and Washington's (1996) qualitative study findings suggest that racial identity was the most salient aspect of their defined identities, making race a source of self-definition. In contrast, children of Caribbean immigrants often oscillate or struggle between identities of American culture and their family of origin, where perception of race will take on the varying meanings indicative of both cultures. Waters's (1996) qualitative study of second-generation West Indian adolescents yielded three identity pathways that reflect varying salience of race and ethnicity in identity: American identified, ethnic identified, and immigrant identified. Despite the documentation of race as a salient aspect of identity among Blacks in American psychological literature, research reveals that Black immigrants and their descendants living in the United States may not consider race to be a prominent aspect of their identity development (Phelps et al., 2001; Waters, 1994, 1996, 1999). This is not to suggest that race and racism do not provide a significant stimulus to which they must respond (Bethea, Richardson, Helms, Ladany, & DuPaul, 2006); however, it may have significant implications for racial/ethnic self-labeling, particularly regarding the initial use of the term *African American*.

In spite of a multitude of cultural, linguistic, regional, and religious differences due to their countries of origin, the transition to an American identity in terms of social mobility is often met with barriers due to societal racial constructions. For example, as Africans and Afro-Caribbeans become members of the African American collective, over time they begin to experience the impact of "Blackness" ascribed to them in American society. Foner (1998) suggests that these dynamics may contribute redefinition of some aspects of identity that, to some extent, may result in the emergence of new

racial and ethnic identities. In addition, the salience of skin color is another aspect of race that is likely to become more apparent, especially as immigrants experience residential segregation where "being Black" is more salient than other factors, including "socio-economic characteristics and ethnicity" (Hilaire, 2006). Anglin and Whaley (2006) explored how racial/ethnic labeling relates to group identity and socialization and found that the self-label "Black" did not significantly relate to socialization experiences, but ethnic-specific labels such as "West Indian" did. Thus, ethnic ties become another salient aspect of identity for Afro-Caribbean people living in America.

Robinson and Azibo (2003) have addressed the external validity of Black racial identity models. The authors indicate that Black racial identity models have inherent focus on Eurocentric concepts of Black personality: They describe Black identity as something that develops in reaction to living in a hostile, racially oppressive environment, and thus they ignore the natural development of African personality in a more nurturing environment. In most discussions about racial identity, race is isolated from other identity characteristics that may influence identity formation concurrently or more saliently. It seems reasonable to examine the appropriateness of various aspects of race-based identity models' ability to describe the identity formation for the complete range of African Americans, especially for ethnic Blacks who have not been socialized in America or who immigrate to America in later life. As an alternative to Nigrescence models, Kambon (1992) postulates that Black personality and collective behavior, not just identity, can be examined through an Africentric framework.

Kambon posits that Black personality consists of a biophysical structure made up of two components, the African self-extension orientation and African self-consciousness. African self-extension is the cardinal principle underlying Black personality that is an innate and unconscious process, otherwise operationally defined as spirituality. Spirituality exists as an interconnecting energy that allows people of African descent to transcend their individual existence and connect on a communal and psychological experience. African self-consciousness is central to Black personality and allows the conscious expression of the communal experience

(Baldwin & Bell, 1985; Kambon, 1992, 1998). When the African self-consciousness is nurtured both developmentally and situationally, the individual exudes basic traits, such as beliefs, attitudes, and behaviors, that affirm Black American life and African heritage. Four basic characteristics of African self-consciousness are (a) awareness of his or her Black identity and African cultural heritage, and value on the pursuit of self-knowledge (i.e., African history and culture throughout the world—encompassing the African American experience); (b) recognition of Black survival priorities and the true necessity for Africentric institutions to affirm Black life; (c) active participation in the proactive development of Black people; and (d) recognition of the detrimental nature of racial oppression (Baldwin & Bell, 1985).

One of the major contributions of Kambon's model is that it provides direction for a decrease in the focus on deracination and an emphasis on reconnection with African origins as a means to establishing a healthy Black identity (Constantine et al., 1998; Richardson, 1998). Although attention given to African personality and African identity has evolved from psychological literature for quite some time, little empirical research has been conducted on these constructs among varying Black groups in the past decade.

African personality and racial identity research with African American and other Black ethnic college students in the United States offers some information about these constructs in this population. For example, in a study of African self-consciousness (ASC) and racial identity conducted with different Black ethnic college students (e.g., African Americans, Caribbean American, etc.), participants scored high ASC scores and high Internalization scores, indicating strong value on racial and cultural awareness (Bethea et al., 2006). However, ASC and racial identity did not predict race-related stress. This finding suggests that even with the salience of racial and cultural awareness for these students, their identities may not be significantly associated with experiences of racism and/or a full understanding of racism. Further exploration of the concepts of race and identity are needed that will expand the theoretical framework of racial identity, be more inclusive of Black ethnic diversity, and ultimately update and clarify the identity process for all Black people.

Black Multiculturalism: Research, Theory, and Practice

The dialogue regarding diversity within the Black collective may be extended by discussing the necessity for meaningful mental health work within the various Black subcultures across country of origin, age, gender, sexual orientation, religion, and mental health disorder. Although the vastness of this topic spans far beyond the capacity of this single chapter, dialogues relevant for youth from a broad range of African and Caribbean social contexts are presented below along with vignettes to illustrate the implications for counseling. The idea is that researchers and practitioners will benefit from examining and enhancing the applicability of racial identity models in tandem with explorations of emotional, social, cognitive, and physical health and development of all clients who represent diversity within the "Black Collective."

Racial Identity and Adolescence

Black youth in the United States face significant challenges related to race and culture. African American adolescents endure the highest rates of poverty, single parenthood, violent acts, and special education placements (APA, 2008). The specific role of racial identity is yet to be fully discovered; nevertheless, scholars have found that racial identity can serve as a protective factor for adolescents of African descent (Caldwell, Kohn-Wood, Schmeelk-Cone, Chavous, & Zimmerman, 2004). Racial identity development/exploration is said to occur naturally during adolescence, with particular progress occurring during the transitory period between middle school and high school (Ponterotto & Park-Taylor, 2007). This is consistent with Erikson's (1968) work stating that critical development of a healthy ego identity occurs during adolescence. Furthermore, researchers purport that adolescents who focus on the positive aspects of their ethnic group report higher levels of both psychological and academic well-being (Ponterotto & Park-Taylor, 2007; Seaton, Scottham, & Sellers, 2006). Therefore, racial identity appears to be a critical component of the adolescent experience that must be explored further within the field of counseling psychology.

The Interplay Between Racial Identity and Racial Socialization. Scholars have found race to be a more salient factor in the lives of African American adolescents as compared to adolescents in other groups (Phinney, 1992; Phinney & Alipuria, 1996). Beyond the larger broader sociopolitical context, this phenomenon may be attributable to the *racial socialization* of African American adolescents (Stevenson, McNeil, Herrero-Taylor, & Davis, 2005). Racial socialization has been defined as a two-part concept consisting of *proactive racial socialization*—"beliefs about child-rearing practices that promote an appreciation of cultural empowerment in Black youth"—and *protective racial socialization*—"child-rearing practices or messages that promote in Black youth an awareness of societal oppression" (Stevenson, Cameron, Herrero-Taylor, & Davis, 2002, p. 87). Racial socialization has been linked repeatedly to racial identity development during adolescence in the literature (Hughes & Chen, 1999; Hughes & Johnson, 2001; Stevenson, 1995). What we know is that the racial socialization of African American youth informs concepts of the racial self and, in many cases, subsequent interactions with the world. What we do not know is the extent to which it is related to racial identity development; nevertheless, the literature suggests that there is a strong bond between the two, and this concept is likened to that of the bioecological model of development illustrated by Spencer's (1995) Phenomenological Variant of Ecological Systems Theory (PVEST) in that it identifies contextual factors (e.g., parental messages) and informs thoughts and behaviors.

IMPLICATIONS FOR RESEARCH AND PRACTICE

Black Adolescents. Although it has been noted that racial identity development is progressive, and that incidents of racism during adolescence prompt further development (Quintana, 2007), sufficient empirical research has not been done in this area (APA, 2008, p. 2). A deep understanding of racial identity development and significance in African American adolescence will inform training and practice in meaningful ways. The area of multiculturalism is clearly very complex; in fact, much of the literature speaks to the need for research to reflect the intersection of the many cultural facets of the individuals whom we serve. With regard to racial identity in adolescence, some studies have found that the role of racial identity differs across gender (Buckley & Carter, 2005; Stevenson et al., 2002). Yet much less is known about differences around level of material wealth, religion, sexual orientation, or disability. Practitioners would benefit from empirical evidence of the importance of racial identity as the field of counseling psychology leads the field in the training and practice of multicultural counseling competence. Additionally, research is lacking on the topic of culture/ethnic identity in relation to racial identity among African American adolescents. The history of forced slavery and ethnic dissonance in the United States has greatly stifled the ethnic identities of many African American youth (Seaton et al., 2006). Nevertheless, there are a number of cultural components yet to be explored for African American youth, and there are racial complexities that are of considerable relevance to research and therapeutic work (e.g., first-generation African Americans, Afro-Caribbeans, and Afro-Hispanics). Therapists working with African American adolescents would benefit greatly from empirical integrative research, training in racial identity theory and measurement, along with grounding in multicultural competence theory. The goal is for therapists to be able to recognize how racial identity theory may inform treatment.

The following vignette provides a case example to illustrate the practice implications:

Vignette #1. Jade is a 14-year-old African American female referred to therapy for aggression in school and depressive symptomology. She was assigned to a middle-aged Caucasian therapist in a community agency. Jade lives in an upper-middle-class African American neighborhood with both biological parents and one younger brother. Her parents have raised her to value her African ancestry (i.e., Ghanaian and Nigerian) by socializing her to appreciate the strength and brilliance of African people. Jade recently transferred to a predominantly Caucasian suburban school where she is one of only five African American students in her entire class. This is Jade's first experience being a minority in an academic setting. During her first week at the new school, Jade's classmates openly made fun of her natural hair, did not invite her to join them at lunch, and recited the lyrics to songs that included racial epithets. Subsequently, Jade was confronted with a more blatant incident of racism wherein one of her teachers stated that she was "not likely to do well on the first test" because she is African American. Jade did not verbally respond to her teacher, but began to show aggression at home (e.g., slamming doors, destroying personal property). Also, she began to show signs of social withdrawal and anhedonia. The therapist spent the first three sessions steering Jade toward appropriate anger management and using cognitive-behavioral techniques to reintegrate once-enjoyed activities. The roles of race, culture, racial socialization, and racial identity were not explored in therapy, causing Jade to withdraw further.

———————◆———————

This vignette includes several racial and cultural factors that are important to address. First, Jade seems to be experiencing race- and culture-related stress as she is struggling to function in a racially and culturally oppressive environment with her ascribed minority status. The racial and cultural origins of her family provide a context for examining how Jade's social environment will be perceived and responded to by her and her family. The therapist must also be sensitive to the vast range of racial socialization experiences and values that guide the responses of the family and how those may be expressed. In addition, the therapist's conceptual understanding of the problem (e.g., if it is an individualistic and countercultural approach to treatment) may reinforce oppressive dynamics that are maintaining Jade's presenting problem (i.e., aggression in response to a countercultural learning environment). Therefore, the therapist should first assess Jade's racial and ethnic identity in a substantive manner to identify culturally tailored interventions that normalize Jade's anger in response to oppressive practices, then integrate her cultural worldview with behavior modification interventions. In addition, the therapist may want to use a collective versus individualistic approach to therapy (e.g., family therapy sessions). The therapist's avoidance or ignorance of racial and cultural factors that have an impact on Jade's aggression may contribute to negative mental health outcomes.

The following vignette provides a second case example to further illustrate the practice implications:

———————◆———————

Vignette #2. Marshall is a 20-year-old student who just immigrated to the United States from Jamaica. He has recently enrolled as a freshman in a predominantly White institution in the South. Two months into the semester, he found out that his childhood friend died. As a result, his grades began to drop in his major classes. Because of his current status as an international student, he fears leaving to go home to Jamaica because he may not be able to return. At the request of his advisor, he makes an appointment to go to the counseling center at the university for an intake session. When he arrives at the center, he is greeted at the desk by a receptionist, who hands him some paperwork to complete. On the sheet, there is a demographic question that asks him to select his racial background. Marshall only sees a box for Black/African American. Reluctantly, he selects that box and returns the form to the receptionist. The counselor, a female Caucasian psychotherapist, takes the form from the receptionist and reviews it. She then greets Marshall with a warm smile and takes him to her office. She introduces herself and the process of counseling but does not inquire about Marshall's racial/ethnic or cultural background. Marshall shares with her his difficulties adjusting to school. At the end of the session, the counselor encourages him and normalizes his struggles in school. To offer support, she hands him a brochure of a support group at the center for African American men she is starting. Marshall takes the brochure and thanks her for meeting with him. Inside, he thinks, "How is this group going to help me?" Marshall fails to return for the following session.

———————◆———————

An influx of West Indians and Africans immigrating to the United States represents a challenge to counselors and mental health practitioners to adequately conceptualize "Black racial identity," especially those who work primarily with Western or European American ideals (Abreu, Chung, & Atkinson, 2000). In the previous vignette, the counselor attended to what she perceived as the racial needs of the client without inquiring about his group designation. In this scenario, she failed to see the intersection of race and ethnicity. One difficulty for counselors is to understand how ethnicity will affect the experience of race for individuals. As in the case of Marshall, the importance of being Black as well as its ascribed meaning is something to which he may have very limited exposure in the United States and thus is less prepared to handle (Hilaire, 2006; Kasinitz, 1992). As Helms (2007) states, "The nature of the racial identities of Americans and immigrants or other nationals differs if they have not experienced similar racial socialization during their lifetimes" (p. 236). Racial socialization becomes important as it gives rise to identity (Anglin & Whaley, 2006). Thus, earlier stages of identity models where there is assimilation or idealization of a dominant White culture may occur similarly for African and Afro-Caribbean Americans but because of different socialization experiences. Likewise, discrimination will affect both groups but be understood in different ways.

Comparisons of cultures of origin will help counselors understand varying values that play into racial socialization of Black immigrants and Americans living in the United States. Given generalizations and stereotypes that arise from phenotype, Black immigrants and African Americans are often erroneously perceived as African Americans devoid of their true ethnic and cultural identities (Tormala & Deaux, 2006), which has a negative impact on interactions between Whites as well as other people of color. An important question exists regarding racial identity models and that is whether the theories adequately and appropriately fit the needs of both Black immigrants, particularly first and second generation, and other Black American subgroups. This question stresses the importance of understanding racial and cultural identity needs of the diverse pan-ethnic groups (Rong & Fitchett, 2008).

SUMMARY AND CONCLUSIONS

African and Afro-Caribbean immigrants continue to increase the diversity of the African American population. Theories of Black racial identity must incorporate the range of racial socialization experiences that are associated with the members of the collective group. Counselors and mental health practitioners must be able to adequately conceptualize Black racial identity. The limitations of current models might make it difficult for some counselors to understand how ethnicity will affect the experience of race for African Americans.

REFERENCES

Abreu, J., Chung, R., & Atkinson, D. (2000). Multicultural counseling training: Past, present, and future directions. *Counseling Psychologist, 28,* 641–656.

American Psychological Association. (2008). *Resilience in African American children and adolescents: A vision for optimal development.* Washington, DC: Author.

Anglin, D., & Whaley, A. (2006). Racial ethnic self-labeling in relation to group: Socialization and identity in African-descended individuals. *Journal of Language and Social Psychology, 25,* 457–463.

Bagley, C. A., & Copeland, E. (1994). African and African American graduate students' racial identity and personal problem solving strategies. *Journal of Counseling & Development, 73,* 167–171.

Baldwin, J. A., & Bell, Y. R. (1985). The African Self-Consciousness Scale: An Africentric personality questionnaire. *Western Journal of Black Studies, 9,* 61–68.

Bethea, A. R. (2006). *An investigation of African identity, racial identity, and ethnicity among Black American college students.* Unpublished doctoral dissertation, Lehigh University, Bethlehem, PA.

Brandon, K. (1997). Policy and practical considerations in land-use strategies for biodiversity conservation. In R. Kramer, C. P. van Schaik, & J. Johnson (Eds.), *Last stand: Protected areas and the defense of tropical biodiversity* (pp. 90–114). New York: Oxford University Press.

Buckley, T. R., & Carter, R. T. (2005). Black adolescent girls: Do gender role and racial identity impact their self-esteem? *Sex Roles, 53*(9–10), 647–661.

Bureau of Citizenship and Immigration Services. (2003). *Immigrants admitted by region and country of birth: Fiscal year 1989–2002.* Retrieved July 27, 2003, from http://www.immigration.gov/graphics/shared/aboutus/statistics/IMM02yrbk/IMMExcel/table3.xls

Caldwell, H. C., Kohn-Wood, L. P., Schmeelk-Cone, K. H., Chavous, T. M., & Zimmerman, M. A. (2004). Racial discrimination and racial identity as risk or protective factors for violent behaviors in African American young adults. *American Journal of Community Psychology, 33,* 91–105.

Casas, J. M. (1984). Policy, training, and research in counseling psychology: The racial/ethnic minority perspective. In S. D. Brown & R. W. Lent (Eds.), *Handbook of counseling psychology* (pp. 785–831). New York: Wiley.

Cokley, K., & Helm, K. (2007). The relationship between African American enculturation and racial identity. *Journal of Multicultural Counseling and Development, 35*, 142–153.

Constantine, M. G., Richardson, T. Q., Benjamin, E. M., & Wilson, J. W. (1998). An overview of Black racial identity theories: Limitations and considerations for future theoretical conceptualizations. *Applied & Preventive Psychology, 7*, 95–99.

Cross, W. E. (1971). The Negro to Black conversion experience: Toward a psychology of Black liberation. *Black World, 20*, 13–27.

Cross, W. E. (1978). The Thomas and Cross models of psychological Nigrescence: A review. *Journal of Black Psychology, 5*, 13–31.

Cross, W. E. (1991). *Shades of Black: Diversity in African American identity.* Philadelphia: Temple University Press.

Cross, W. (1995). The psychology of Nigrescence: Revisiting the Cross model. In J. G. Ponterotto, J. M. Casas, L. A. Suzuki, & C. M. Alexander (Eds.), *Handbook of multicultural counseling* (pp. 93–122). Thousand Oaks, CA: Sage.

Cross, W. E., Parham, T. A., & Helms, J. E. (1991). The stages of Black identity development: Nigrescence models. In R. L. Jones (Ed.), *Black psychology* (3rd ed., pp. 319–338). Berkeley, CA: Cobb & Henry.

Erikson, E. H. (1968). *Identity youth and crisis.* New York: Norton.

Foner, N. (1998). West Indian identity in the diaspora: Comparative and historical perspectives. Latin American Perspectives, 25, 173–188.

Hall, S. P., & Carter, R. T. (2005). The relationship between racial identity, ethnic identity, and perceptions of racial discrimination in an Afro-Caribbean descent sample. *Journal of Black Psychology, 32*, 155–175.

Helms, J. E. (1994). Racial identity and career assessment. *Journal of Career Assessment, 2*(3), 199–209.

Helms, J. E. (1995). An update of Helms's White and people of color racial identity models. In J. G. Ponterotto, J. M. Casas, L. A. Suzuki, & C. M. Alexander (Eds.), *Handbook of multicultural counseling* (pp. 181–198). Thousand Oaks, CA: Sage.

Helms, J. E. (2007). Some better practices for measuring racial and ethnic identity constructs. *Journal of Counseling Psychology, 54*, 3, 235–246.

Helms, J. E., & Cook, D. A. (1999). *Using race and culture in counseling and psychotherapy: Theory and practice.* Needham Heights, MA: Allyn & Bacon.

Hilaire, D. (2006). Immigrant West Indian families and their struggles with racism in America. *Journal of Emotional Abuse, 6*(2–3), 47–60.

Hughes, D., & Chen, L. (1999). The nature of parents' race-related communications to children: A developmental perspective. In C. S. Tamis-LeMonda (Ed.), *Child psychology: A handbook of contemporary issues* (pp. 467–490). Philadelphia: Psychology Press.

Hughes, D., & Johnson, D. (2001). Correlates in children's experiences of parents' racial socialization behaviors. *Journal of Marriage and the Family, 63*, 981–995.

Kambon, K. K. (1992). *The African personality in America: An African-centered framework.* Tallahassee, FL: Nubian Nation Publications.

Kambon, K. K. (1998). *African/Black psychology in the American context: An African-centered approach.* Tallahassee, FL: Nubian Nation Publications.

Kasinitz, P. (1992). *Caribbean New York: Black immigrants and the politics of race.* New York: Cornell University Press.

Lincoln, A. (1953). The fourth debate with Stephen Douglas at Charleston, Illinois, on September 18, 1858. In R. P. Basler (Ed.), *The collected works of Abraham Lincoln* (Vol. 3). New Brunswick, NJ: Rutgers University Press.

Operario, D., & Fiske, S. T. (2001). Ethnic identity moderates perceptions of prejudice: Judgments of personal versus group discrimination and subtle versus blatant bias. *Personality and Social Psychology Bulletin, 27*, 550–561.

Parham, T. A. (1989). Cycles of psychological Nigrescence. *Counseling Psychologist, 17*, 187–226.

Phelps, R. E., Taylor, J. D., & Gerard, P. A. (2001). Cultural mistrust, ethnic identity, racial identity, and self-esteem among ethnically diverse Black university students. *Journal of Counseling and Development, 79*, 209–216.

Phinney, J. S. (1992). The Multigroup Ethnic Identity Measure: A new scale for use with diverse groups. *Journal of Adolescent Research, 7*, 156–176.

Phinney, J. S., & Alipuria, L. L. (1996). At the interface of cultures: Multiethnic/multiracial high school and college students. *Journal of Social Psychology, 136*, 139–158.

Ponterotto, J. G., & Park-Taylor, J. (2007). Racial and ethnic identity theory, measurement, and research in counseling psychology: Present status and future directions. *Journal of Counseling Psychology, 54*, 282–294.

Quintana, S. (2007). *Handbook of race, racism, and the developing child.* Hoboken, NJ: Wiley.

Richardson, T. (1998). Continuity in the identity development process for African Americans and Africans throughout the diaspora. In R. L. Jones (Ed.), *African American identity development* (pp. 73–83). Hampton, VA: Cobb & Henry.

Robinson, J. N., & Azibo, D. A. (2003). Are stages of African identity development consistent with the African personality construct? An empirical inquiry. In D. Azibo (Ed.), *African-centered psychology* (pp. 277–292). Durhan, NC: Carolina Academic Press.

Rogers, R. (2006). *Afro-Caribbean immigrants and the politics of incorporation: Ethnicity, exception, or exit.* New York: Cambridge University Press.

Rong, X. L., & Fitchett, P. (2008). Socialization and identity transformation of Black immigrant youth in the United States. *Theories Into Practice, 47,* 35–42.

Seaton, E. K., Scottham, K. M., & Sellers, R. M. (2006). The status model of racial identity development in African American adolescents: Evidence of structure, trajectories, and well-being. *Child Development, 77,* 1416–1426.

Sellers, R. M. (1993). A call to arms for researchers studying racial identity. *Journal of Black Psychology, 19,* 327–332.

Sellers, R. M., Shelton, J. N., Cooke, D. Y., Chavous, T. M., Johnson Rowley, S. A., & Smith, M. A. (1998). A multidimensional model of racial identity: Assumptions, findings, and future directions. In R. L. Jones (Ed.), *African American identity development* (pp. 275–302). Hampton, VA: Cobb & Henry.

Shorter-Gooden, K., & Washington, N. C. (1996). Young, Black, and female: The challenge of weaving an identity. *Journal of Adolescence, 19,* 465–475.

Smith, J. C., & Palmisano, J. M. (2000). *Reference library of Black America: Volume I.* Farmington Hills, MI: Gale Group

Sowell, T. (1978). Three black histories. In T. Sowell (Ed.), *Essays and data on American ethnic groups* (pp. 7–64). Washington, DC: The Urban Institute.

Spencer, M. B. (1995). Old issues and new theorizing about African American youth: A phenomenological variant of ecological systems theory. In R. L. Taylor (Ed.), *African American youth: Their social and economic status in the United States* (pp. 37–69). Westport, CT: Praeger.

Stevenson, H. C. (1995). The relationship of racial socialization and racial identity in African American adolescents. *Journal of Black Psychology, 21,* 49–70.

Stevenson, H. C., Cameron, R., Herrero-Taylor, T., & Davis, G. Y. (2002). Development of the Teenage Experience of Racial Socialization Scale: Correlates of race-related socialization from the perspective of Black youth. *Journal of Black Psychology, 28,* 84–106.

Stevenson, H. C., McNeil, J. D., Herrero-Taylor, T., & Davis, G. Y. (2005). Influence of perceived neighborhood diversity and racism experience on the racial socialization of black youth. *Journal of Black Psychology, 31*(3), 273–290.

Sue, D. W., & Sue, D. (2003). *Counseling the culturally diverse: Theory and practice.* New York: Wiley.

Thomas, C. S. (1971). *Boys no more.* Beverly Hills, CA: Glencoe.

Tormala, T. T., & Deaux, K. (2006). Black immigrants to the United States: Confronting and constructing ethnicity and race. In R. Mahalingam (Ed.), *Cultural psychology of immigrants* (pp. 131–150). Mahwah, NJ: Lawrence Erlbaum.

U.S. Census Bureau. (2000). *Profile of general demographic characteristics: 2000* [On-line]. Available: www.census .gov/census2000/states/us.html

U.S. Census Bureau. (2004). *Country or area of birth for the foreign population from Africa and Oceania: 2000.* Retrieved April 13, 2004, from http://www.census.gov/ population/socdemo/foreign/ppl-145/tab03-3.pdf

Vandiver, B. J., Cross, W. E., Worrell, F. C., & Fhagen-Smith, P. E. (2002). Validating the Cross Racial Identity Scale. *Journal of Counseling Psychology, 49,* 71–85.

Waters, M. (1994). *Modern sociological theory: A conceptual framework.* Thousand Oaks, CA: Sage.

Waters, M. (1996). The intersection of race, gender, and ethnicity in identity development of Caribbean American teens. In B. J. R. Leadbeater & N. Way (Eds.), *Urban girls: Resisting stereotypes, creating identities* (pp. 65–99). New York: New York University Press.

Waters, M. (1999). *Black identities: West Indian immigrant dreams and American realities.* Cambridge, MA: Harvard University Press.

22

Latina/o Identity Development

Updates on Theory, Measurement, and Counseling Implications

MARIE L. MIVILLE

This chapter will review theory and measurement regarding Latina/o identity development since the publication of Casas and Pytluk's (1995) chapter in the first edition of the *Handbook of Multicultural Counseling*. Some excellent work has occurred regarding theoretical models of identity, both new and revised, as well as empirical studies exploring predictors and outcomes associated with identity development among Latinos/as. A final section will discuss important counseling implications based on these findings.

WHO ARE LATINAS/OS?

Prior to discussing theory and measurement of identity, it is critical to discuss who is included in this racial-ethnic group and how Latinas/os today identify or describe themselves. Latinas/os refer to individuals whose ancestry is from Latin American backgrounds, such as Mexico, Puerto Rico, Cuba, the Dominican Republic, and other South and Central American countries, including Colombia, Nicaragua, and Costa Rica (Miville, 2006). Latinas/os represent the largest racial-ethnic minority group in the United States, numbering more than 44 million (including Puerto Rico) in 2004 and representing approximately 15% of the population (Hispanic Association of Colleges and Universities [HACU], n.d.). Although Latinas/os live in all parts of the United States, most reside in a specific number of regions and states, including the Southwest (e.g., California, Arizona); Texas; Florida; Illinois; and the Northeast (e.g., New York, New Jersey). More than half of all Latinas/os live in just two states, California and Texas (HACU, n.d.).

The 500-year history of Latinas/os in the Americas serves as an important basis of identity development (Santiago-Rivera, Arredondo, & Gallardo-Cooper, 2002). European settlers and indigenous people intermarried, producing what is known today as the *mestizo* culture among most Latina/o ethnic groups. The so-called

Conquest involved multiple oppressive forces of enslavement, persecution, religious conversion, and the overall disempowerment of indigenous people originally living in the Americas by the *conquistadores* of Europe (Gonzalez, 2000; Santiago-Rivera et al., 2002). Enslavement of more than 15 million people of African descent led to an intermingling of African cultures with European and indigenous groups, the resulting groups known as *criollos* and *mulattos* (Santiago-Rivera et al., 2002; Vaquera & Kao, 2006). Moreover, during the early 1800s, after many Latin American countries had established constitutional democracies, the United States began an expansionist policy (known as "Manifest Destiny") by annexing various portions of what became Florida, Texas, and the Southwest (Gonzalez, 2000). As a consequence, many Latinas/os were either forcibly reclassified as "aliens" (1848, Mexican Americans) or recolonized as noncitizens (1898, Puerto Ricans, although they were later made citizens in 1917). Issues of "circular migration" and immigration continue to play a major force today among Latinas/os, and many come to the United States for multiple purposes, including political asylum, better jobs, and education (Miville, 2006; Santiago-Rivera et al., 2002). For a variety of reasons, Latinas/os still tend to be overrepresented in the areas of poverty and unemployment, and underrepresented in the areas of education and high income.

In addition to long-standing historical considerations that may affect identity development of many Latinas/os living in the United States, there are other historical, economic, cultural and sociopolitical issues arising from the unique ethnic backgrounds of all Latinas/os. Due to space considerations, readers are referred to Gonzalez (2000) and Santiago-Rivera et al. (2002), who describe these important issues for several ethnic groups, including Mexicans/Mexican Americans, Puerto Ricans, Cubans, Dominicans, and Central and South Americans (see Miville, 2006, for a brief summary of these readings). In sum, Latinas/os are a very heterogeneous group of people in terms of race, ethnicity, region, socioeconomic status, and other significant variables, thus making the process of identity development an important challenge for researchers and practitioners alike to address effectively.

As might be imagined, there is some disagreement about the proper term by which Latinas/os are referred. As Comas-Díaz (2001) notes,

Encased within historical eras, ethnic self-designation reflects the dialectics between dominance and self-determination. Because the systematic negation and oppression of people of color result in pervasive identity conflicts . . . , Latinos' power to name themselves advances liberation by rejecting colonization. Searching for a name . . . can be a challenging and confusing ordeal. Because self- and other identification is a developmental process, naming evolves in response to psychosocial and geopolitical factors. (p. 115)

The period of the 1960s and 1970s was marked by a number of racial-ethnic groups striving for civil rights, including Latinas/os, and the self-selection of a group label became part of this process. For example, Pizarro and Vera (2001) describe how the Mexican American/Chicana/o community "began a process of redefinition. They developed a new, revolutionary ethnic identity that stood for community empowerment through affirmation rather than through the adoption of majority traits" (p. 95).

Comas-Díaz describes "a taxonomy of terms" by which Latinas/os have been or are currently designated by others and by themselves (pp. 115–116). For example, the term *Hispanic* was officially created by the U.S. Census Bureau for the 1970 Census for people of "Spanish origin." This term is based on historical and cultural origins arising from Spain and is seen as a source of pride by some. However, the term is considered controversial, even offensive, today because it is viewed as excluding individuals who do not trace their origins to Spain. As Santiago-Rivera et al. (2002) note, "Unfortunately, the term has led many to believe that Spanish-speaking individuals from these countries of origin have one common culture and that the term refers to a racial category" (p. 21).

Latina/o is instead considered a more inclusive term and is more commonly accepted: "the term *Latin* comes into use as the least common denominator for all peoples of Latin America in recognition of the fact that some romance language (Spanish, Portuguese, French) is the native tongue of the majority of Latin Americans" (Comas-Díaz, 2001, p. 116). Today, the term *Latina/o* represents the common languages, values, and history that Latinas/os living in the United States may share (Miville, 2006). Incidentally, because much of the Spanish language includes masculine and feminine connotations, the combined terms of *Latino/a* or *Latina/o* are used as inclusive terms to represent both genders (e.g., the National Latina/o Psychological Association, http://www.nlpa.ws/).

WHAT IS LATINA/O IDENTITY?— CONCEPTUAL CHALLENGES

As the previous section indicates, many complex variables affect identity development and makeup among Latinas/os, beginning with the type of collective identities that may be most psychologically important or salient to Latinas/os. Scholars continue to explore whether identifying as *Latina/o* refers to racial or ethnic backgrounds, or some combination of both. To be sure, multiple or complexly defined reference groups are essential to consider for identity development among Latinas/os. Moreover, as Casas and Pytluk (1995) noted more than a decade ago, "To understand accurately individuals from distinct racial/ethnic groups, one must understand both content and developmental variables and processes separately as well as interactively" (p. 157). Thus, in addition to exploring identity development, other psychological processes, including acculturation and assimilation, have been examined and included by several researchers as part of the definition of ethnic identity (Casas & Pytluk, 1995; Pizarro & Vera, 2001).

Psychologists and other scholars continue to engage in public discourse about the definition and meaning of race and ethnicity, particularly their distinguishing features and their respective psychological impact on identity development. For example, Cokley (2007) defined *ethnicity* as "a characterization of a group of people who see themselves and are seen by others as having a common ancestry, shared history, shared traditions, and shared cultural traits such as language, beliefs, values, music, dress, and food" (p. 225). Cokley identified the scope of definitions of ethnicity as varying from narrow to broad and argued that "unlike race, it is generally more mutable and involves comparatively more individual choice" (p. 225). Cokley defined *race* as "a characterization of a group of people believed to share physical characteristics such as skin color, facial features, and other hereditary traits" (p. 225). Many scholars today assert that "race as biology is fiction" (Smedley & Smedley, 2005, p. 16), although its impact remains

both socially and psychologically significant. In contrast to ethnicity, which may convey the social message of "You will become like us whether you want to or not," as in the process of assimilation (Smedley & Smedley, 2005, p. 19), race continues to evoke "the notion of differences that could not be transcended" (p. 19), regardless of individuals' desires.

Quintana (2007) noted that there are psychological complexities surrounding how Latinas/os have been classified, for example, by being differentiated by the federal government via ethnicity rather than race (the only such group for which this is the case). At the same time, Quintana described social distance between Latinas/os and non-Latinas/os, such as experiencing segregation in school systems and being targets of ethnic prejudice, as being more reflective of being perceived as racially, rather than ethnically, different. He referred to a 1997 statement of the American Anthropological Association, which declared that "by treating race and ethnicity as fundamentally different . . . the historical evolution of these category types is largely ignored. For example, today's ethnicities are yesterday's races" (p. 260). Because psychological research has not yet shown that the psychological impact of racial prejudice is empirically distinct from ethnic prejudice, Quintana contends that "the differentiation made between race and ethnicity in counseling psychology may be a distinction without a meaningful difference" (p. 260). He suggests a newly proposed hybrid classification by Cross and Cross (Quintana, 2007) of "racial-ethnic" that may more accurately capture features, in particular for Latinas/os, associated with each discrete type of collective experience but that may be dynamically additive in their psychological impact. Other scholars also have acknowledged the racial/ethnic experiences of Latinas/os as reflecting "hybrid" (Falicov, 1998, in Santiago-Rivera et al., 2002) and "multidimensional" components (Santiago-Rivera et al., 2002). Rodriguez (2005, in Vaquero & Kao, 2006) writes that "all Latinos, regardless of color may experience discrimination, for Hispanicity is based on more than skin color" (p. 377).

Trimble (2007) cautions that declassifying race

could obscure if not disclaim the racist experiences of millions of people who are subjected to them on a constant basis. . . . Hence, to forcefully confront racism headlong, race must be kept at the forefront of our vocabulary when discussing intergroup and interpersonal relations. (p. 250)

A declassification of race would likely affect Latinas/os for whom race is a multilayered yet much understudied topic. Forces of racial oppression, decimation, and subjugation clearly have played a role throughout most of Latin American history, yielding a multiracial population (Gonzalez, 2000; Santiago-Rivera et al., 2002). Moreover, Latinas/os may be differentially affected by the daily impact of racism, given their wide range of phenotypes, including skin color (Landale & Oropesa, 2002; López, 2008).

To better understand the intersections of race and ethnicity in self-labeling, Vaquero and Kao (2006) examined racial self-labels among a sample of 13,415 Latina/o adolescents, made up of Mexicans, Puerto Ricans, Cubans, and Central and South Americans (data were obtained from the National Longitudinal Study of Adolescent Health conducted during 1994–1995 for Grades 7–12). They found that 66% of the sample chose "no race" or "other" rather than the traditional categories of White, Black, Native American, and Asian. Interesting ethnic differences also were found, with Mexicans most likely choosing "no race" or "other," Cubans choosing White, Puerto Ricans choosing "other" and "no race," and Central/South Americans choosing "other" and White. The authors concluded that choosing "no race" or "other" "is the expression of the rejection of the current categories used in the United States" (p. 389) and that "race is ethnic to a certain degree" (p. 390). However, the intraethnic differences in racial self-labeling also indicate potentially meaningful differences that merit further exploration.

Landale and Oropesa (2002) explored racial self-labeling among 2,763 Puerto Rican women (data were based on the 1994–1995 Puerto Rican Maternal and Infant Health Study) and included participants from both Puerto Rico and the United States. Findings indicated that although the majority had been classified on their birth certificates as White, more than half today stated their race was "Puerto Rican"; participants chose from a list of labels also including White, Black, Trigueña (multiracial), Hispanic, Latina, Spanish, American, Hispanic American, and Other. Interesting

differences emerged between mainland and islander participants. For example, approximately 30% of mainland women chose a pan-ethnic label, such as Hispanic, Latina, or Spanish, whereas about 30% of islander women identified as White, Black, or Trigueña. The authors conclude that clearly, the common categories of race did not fit how Puerto Ricans racially self-labeled, particularly for islander participants. Jensen, Cohen, Toribio, De Jong, and Rodríguez (2006) similarly found a conflation of race and ethnicity for a sample of 65 Dominican immigrants living in Pennsylvania. The vast majority of participants (84%) used either an ethnic (Dominican) or pan-ethnic term to describe themselves racially. Thus, further research is needed to help disentangle how race and ethnicity may be defined and psychologically processed by Latinas/os, including the impact of variables such as phenotype and place of residence or social context.

Identity development based on both race and ethnicity has been a topic of psychological theory and research for several decades, most recently regarding their social constructions. As with the terms *race* and *ethnicity*, the relative importance and meaning of *ethnic identity* and *racial identity* continue to be topics of public discourse among psychologists. Ethnic identity has been defined as "an enduring, fundamental aspect of the self that includes a sense of membership in an ethnic group and the attitudes and feelings associated with that membership" (Phinney, 1996, p. 922). More recently, Phinney and Ong (2007) described ethnic identity as "dynamic; it changes over time and context and must therefore be considered with reference to its formation and variation" (p. 271). According to Phinney and Ong, ethnic identity is made up of several important components: self-categorization and labeling, commitment or sense of belonging and attachment, exploration, ethnic behaviors, evaluation and ingroup attitudes, values and beliefs, importance and salience, and relation to national identity.

Racial identity has been defined as "the collective identity of any group of people socialized to think of themselves as a racial group," as based on common physical traits, and is most appropriate to study when one is "interested in how individuals construct their identities in response to an oppressive and highly racialized society" (Cokley, 2007, p. 225). A number of models (Cross, 1991; Helms, 1995; Sue & Sue, 2007;

Vandiver, 2001) have been proposed to describe how racial identity evolves from an increasing awareness of the sociopolitical impact of race and racism on self, others, and society. Some scholars have explored the use of racial identity models with Latinas/os (e.g., Miville & Helms, 1996; Miville, Koonce, Darlington, & Whitlock, 2000), providing some evidence of the usefulness of these models for this group. However, Miville et al. (2000) used the term *cultural identity* for Latinas/os that acknowledged both the history of sociopolitical subordination of Latinas/os as well as the co-mingled impact of race and ethnicity in the social oppression of Latinas/os.

Ethnic identity clearly has been the most commonly researched type of identity among Latinas/os, and several excellent reviews summarize the varying definitions and conceptualizations of this construct (Casas & Pytluk, 1995; Pizarro & Vera, 2001; Umaña-Taylor, Diversi, & Fine, 2002). The models that have had the most impact in guiding research in the past decade have been proposed by Phinney (most recently in Phinney & Ong, 2007) and Martha Bernal, George Knight, and colleagues (Bernal, Knight, Ocampo, Garza, & Cota, 1993; Knight, Bernal, Cota, Garza, & Ocampo, 1993). Both models are multidimensional, though with somewhat different foci. Phinney's model is applicable for all ethnic groups, whereas the Bernal/Knight et al. model focuses on Mexican Americans or Chicanas/os, although it seems quite applicable to most Latinas/os. The Bernal/Knight et al. model also emphasizes socialization and ecological processes from family and community, along with acculturation and enculturation processes (learning language, cultural beliefs, norms, and customs from both majority and own backgrounds, respectively) in ethnic identity development, whereas Phinney's model derives from Eriksonian and social identity frameworks emphasizing "a subjective feeling of sameness and continuity that provides individuals with a stable sense of self" (Phinney & Ong, 2007, p. 274). Both have several components; the Bernal/Knight et al. model is made up of ethnic self-identification (self-categorizing as a group member), ethnic constancy (knowledge that membership is unchanging), ethnic role behaviors (reflecting cultural norms and customs), ethnic knowledge, and ethnic preferences and feelings (for own group members). Phinney acknowledged several

components that make up ethnic identity, such as self-categorization, commitment and attachment, exploration, behavioral involvement, in-group attitudes (private regard), ethnic values and beliefs, importance or salience of group membership, and ethnic identity in relation to national identity, but incorporates two components into her ethnic identity measure, exploration and commitment (Phinney & Ong, 2007).

An important aspect of Bernal/Knight et al.'s model is the incorporation of cognitive abilities in the development of ethnic identity. Other scholars have focused on cognitive abilities or skills critical for children's understanding of ethnic prejudice (Quintana & Vera, 1999) and ethnic perspective taking (Quintana, 1994). In the former study, the authors described cognitively distinct levels of children's understanding of ethnic prejudice, beginning from physicalistic and literal perspectives, and evolving into social and group-oriented perspectives. Results indicated that several components of Bernal/Knight et al.'s model were associated with cognitive aspects of understanding prejudice, including parental ethnic socialization about ethnic discrimination and ethnic knowledge.

Recently, Umaña-Taylor and Fine (2004) proposed and tested a model similar to that of Bernal/Knight et al. The newer model proposes that ecological factors influence ethnic socialization, which in turn influences ethnic identity. The latter relationship was proposed to be moderated by the development of adolescents' social and cognitive abilities. A sample of 343 Latino high school students in Texas completed measures of ecological factors, familial ethnic socialization, emotional autonomy, and ethnic identity achievement. Structural equation modeling demonstrated that, indeed, ecological factors "indirectly influence ethnic identity achievement through their influence on familial ethnic socialization" (p. 36). The newer model also has excellent potential for further empirical testing (Ponterotto & Park-Taylor, 2007).

MEASUREMENT OF LATINA/O IDENTITY

Thus far, we have reviewed models of identity for Latinas/os that have been empirically examined within the past decade. As noted earlier, one of the models in the empirical literature that has had the most impact has been Phinney's ethnic identity framework, primarily through the use of the Multigroup Ethnic Identity Measure (MEIM) (Phinney, 1992; Phinney & Ong, 2007). The MEIM was originally designed to assess ethnic identity across all groups and contained 14 items assessing three components: sense of belonging, identity achievement, and ethnic practices. Content-specific items related to values and norms were purposely left out because of their diversity across groups; the MEIM also does not include items related to awareness of sociopolitical oppression, racism or ethnocentrism, and discrimination (Phinney & Ong, 2007).

The MEIM has been used as an ethnic identity measure in most published studies of Latina/o adolescents and young adults, as both a predictor and an outcome variable. Variables that have been found to be significantly associated with ethnic identity include acculturation into Anglo or mainstream culture (Cuéllar, Nyberg, Maldonado, & Roberts, 1997); quality of life (Utsey, Chae, Brown, & Kelly, 2002); career decision self-efficacy (Gushue & Whitson, 2006); ethnocentrism (Negy, Shreve, Jensen, & Uddin, 2003); self-esteem (López, 2008; Lorenzo-Hernandez & Ouellette, 1998; Umaña-Taylor, 2003); proactive coping (Umaña-Taylor, Vargas-Chanes, Garcia, & Gonzales-Backen, 2008); academic grades and externalizing symptoms, as mediated by self-esteem (Schwartz, Zamboanga, & Jarvis, 2007); negative perceptions of the university environment (Castillo et al., 2006); traditional masculinity ideology (Abreu, Goodyear, Campos, & Newcomb, 2000); and family ethnic socialization (Umaña-Taylor, Bhanot, & Shin, 2006).

Increasingly complex models also have been a focus of recent ethnic identity research. For example, López (2008) found that ethnic identity was a significant moderator in relation to skin color (assessed in three ways: interviewer, self, and skin reflectance data) and self-esteem among 53 English-speaking Puerto Rican women. As hypothesized, both lighter skinned and darker skinned women with higher levels of ethnic identity had higher self-esteem than their respective counterparts with lower levels of ethnic identity. Castillo et al. (2006) explored whether the relationship between ethnic identity and academic persistence among Latina/o college students was mediated by university environment perceptions. No mediation effect

was found, leading the authors to conclude that perceived context, rather than ethnic identity, was predictive of persistence attitudes. Gushue and Whitson (2006) found that ethnic identity and gender role attitudes were fully mediated by career decision self-efficacy in the prediction of gender traditionality in career choice goals. Their findings highlighted the distal influence that ethnic identity can have on career decisions:

> To the extent to which a girl of color is successfully integrating race, ethnicity, and egalitarian gender role attitudes as part of her self-understanding, she may also demonstrate a stronger belief in her ability to negotiate the tasks associated with career decision-making. . . . A more fully integrated sense of self may serve as the basis for greater self-efficacy in general. (Gushue & Whitson, 2006, p. 383)

Syed, Azmitia, and Phinney (2007) conducted a longitudinal study of ethnic identity among Latina/o college students and found strength (endorsement of items) and membership changes during an academic year. Regarding the latter finding, cluster analyses revealed shifts from equivalent distribution across unexamined, moratorium, and achievement statuses in the fall term to most students falling either into moratorium or achievement statuses in the spring term. Social context differences were not found between students attending predominant majority versus minority university campuses. As a result, Syed et al. suggested the notion of *ethnic identity pathways* to acknowledge that "although these pathways arrive at the same result, the processes that lead [students] there as well as the actual meaning ascribed to their ethnic identities may be very different" (p. 173), a fruitful area of future research.

Umaña-Taylor and Fine (2001) examined the reliability of the MEIM across several Latina/o ethnic groups, including Colombian, Guatemalan, Honduran, Mexican, Nicaraguan, Puerto Rican, and Salvadoran adolescents. The MEIM showed adequate internal reliability across these samples, with the exception of Guatemalans (0.68) and Hondurans (0.59). Differential correlations also were found for the MEIM with measures of self-esteem and family ethnic socialization, indicating the importance of including intraethnic group variables in ethnic identity measurement. Most factor-analytic studies of the original MEIM have supported a single factor structure (e.g., Ponterotto, Gretchen, Utsey, Stracuzzi, & Saya, 2003, in Phinney & Ong, 2007). Roberts et al. (1999, in Phinney & Ong, 2007) and others found support for two or more factors, leading Phinney and Ong to develop a revised version, the MEIM-R. The new scale contains six items across two factors, Exploration and Commitment. Given the original scale's wide usage, research regarding the reliability and validity of the MEIM-R with Latinas/os will be of great value.

A newer measure, the Ethnic Identity Scale (EIS) (Umaña-Taylor, Yazedijian, & Bamaca-Gómez, 2004), also shows promise for future research (Ponterotto & Park-Taylor, 2007). Like the MEIM, it was based on Eriksonian and social identity theoretical frameworks. However, Umaña-Taylor et al. contend that ethnic identity is composed of three components: exploration, commitment, and affirmation (positive or negative). Thus, the EIS is distinct from the MEIM in that it separates items measuring affect from commitment, in contrast with the MEIM, which measures commitment (identity achievement) at the same time as positive affect (Phinney's theoretical conceptualization does not actually make this presumption). Initial reliability and factor analytic evidence supporting the three-factor structure of the EIS has been confirmed by later studies (Supple, Ghazarian, Frabutt, Plunkett, & Sands, 2006). Findings using the EIS (e.g., Supple et al., 2006; Umaña-Taylor & Updegraff, 2007) yielded predicted links of family ethnic socialization with exploration and commitment and resolution, and positive teacher reports with affirmation (Supple et al., 2006). However, Umaña-Taylor and Shin (2007) recently noted less than acceptable reliability coefficients for some racial-ethnic groups (Latinas/os and African Americans) but not others (European and Asian Americans). Interestingly, results have supported differential links of self-esteem with EIS components, being significantly linked with both identity exploration and resolution, but not affirmation (Umaña-Taylor et al., 2004), pointing to the usefulness of the three-factor approach.

As noted earlier, a limited number of studies have used racial identity-based measures with Latina/o samples. Both Miville and Helms (1996) and Miville et al. (2000) found that their 50-item racial-cultural identity measures (Helms & Carter, 1985, in Miville et al., 2000) were adequately reliable, with alphas ranging from 0.71 to 0.83, although Awareness in Miville et al. yielded an alpha of 0.65. Moreover, scale intercorrelations were in the generally predicted directions, providing some support for the construct validity of the scale. The two studies explored the relationships between cultural identity and ego identity for Latinas/os who were primarily of Cuban and Central or South American origin (Miville & Helms, 1996) and Mexican/Mexican Americans (Miville et al., 2000). Both studies found significant relations of parallel identity conflicts and resolutions for both cultural and ego identity. For example, Miville et al. (2000) found that

> Immersion attitudes predicted "foreclosed ego identity resolution." Foreclosure represents the adoption of parental values, and Immersion attitudes reflect the embracing of traditional Hispanic/Latino values. One critically important cultural value for Hispanics, including Mexican Americans, is *familismo*, a component of which might include the adoption of parental values. . . . These findings suggest that Foreclosure for Mexican Americans may represent a more healthy ego identity resolution through the adoption of parental cultural values. (p. 220)

Other research has used racial identity measures to explore links with cultural values. For example, Carter, Yeh, and Mazzula (2008) used the 43-item Visible Racial Ethnic Identity Attitude Scale (Helms & Carter, 1986, in Carter et al., 2008) to explore cultural values among Latinas/os; alpha coefficients ranged from 0.72 to 0.82. Results indicated that "racial identity status attitudes predict value orientation preferences of human nature as evil [Conformity], lineal and collateral social relationships [Dissonance], and a belief in harmony with nature [all statuses]" (p. 5). With the exception of belief and harmony and nature, results were somewhat inconsistent with previous findings with other racial-ethnic samples because differences in value orientations were not found for all identity statuses.

The findings of Miville et al. (Miville & Helms, 1996; Miville et al., 2000) and Carter et al. (2008) point to the potential usefulness of further research using scales based on racial-cultural identity models. A unique aspect of these scales is their inclusion of attitudinal items regarding awareness of racial and ethnic oppression and discrimination, a theme not found in other ethnic identity scales, but likely to affect Latinas/os' identities. Research exploring intraethnic differences regarding awareness and psychological impact, for example, might be one fruitful direction. Another is exploring how more recent racial identity measures (e.g., Cross & Vandiver, 2001) might fare among Latinas/os.

Other paper-and-pencil measures have involved operationalizing components of the Bernal/Knight et al. ethnic identity model. For example, Quintana and Vera (1999) developed measures of ethnic knowledge through interview questions. Children were asked to imagine Mexican and Anglo/White American towns and to rate a series of cultural practice items for each town (ratings consisted of circles with faces). At least two measures have been devised for another component of the model, parental/family ethnic socialization. Phinney and Chavira (1995, in Quintana & Vera, 1999) devised a series of five interview questions (e.g., "How important is it to you to teach your child about Mexican culture?") for parents; participants were encouraged to discuss their response as well as rate on a 5-point scale which response was most accurate. Umaña-Taylor and Fine (2001) developed the 9-item Likert-type Familial Ethnic Socialization Measure to assess adolescents' perceptions. Overt and covert aspects of socialization were included, overt referring to intentional events, and covert referring to unintentional events, such as the choice of family activity.

Qualitative methods also have been used successfully to describe identity themes among Latinas/os. For example, Hurtado (2003) interviewed Latinas in their 20s regarding their views on both racial-ethnic and gender identity, focusing specifically on the interplay of feminism and Chicana/o cultural beliefs. Rolón-Dow (2004, in Miville, 2008) interviewed Puerto Rican adolescents living in the United States regarding their construction of their ethnic and gender identities. Rolón-Dow used Black feminist critiques to frame the multiple means by which images are imposed on Latinas in the school setting. She found that both teachers and students viewed Puerto Rican girls in overly sexualized, restricted, either-or roles, and promoted the stereotyped image of low success in schools. Interestingly, although psychologists have used qualitative methods in their research with Latinas/os, few studies have used such methods to explore Latina/o identity development.

In sum, several instruments have been used quite successfully in operationalizing components of both ethnic and racial identity development. Future research may explore how these components interplay in their impact on psychological functioning (e.g., how does family ethnic socialization affect racial identity development). Future research also can explore the impact of intraethnic and racial differences (e.g., phenotypic features) on both ethnic and racial identity development. Qualitative methods can be used successfully to provide more nuanced understandings of the interplay of racial-ethnic and other critical contextual components in Latina/o identity development. In short, a variety of methods can be used to explore both the development and content of individuals' constructions of their identities as Latinas/os.

Counseling Implications

As the previous review indicates, it is imperative for practitioners to understand how Latina/o identity is important for their clients and themselves. A current theme—how is Latina/o identity defined?—might be applied effectively with clients by simply asking them about their racial-ethnic background. The Culture-Centered Clinical Interview (CCCI) (Santiago-Rivera et al., 2002) is an excellent place to begin a discussion about Latina/o identity. The CCCI includes items such as acculturation level, contacts with native culture, immigration history, language issues, sociopolitical concerns, ethnic identity, acculturative stress, and use of indigenous healers. Discussing these topics will help practitioners get a sense of how their clients identify, and which aspects of their identity may be sources of strength and stress.

Experiences of oppression, both racial and ethnic, also will be important to assess. Practitioners can attend to clients' choices of their labels. For example, are clients using a pan-ethnic term (Hispanic or Latina/o), and if so, which one? It is important not to presume what attitudes and feelings are associated with these labels for each individual, but to understand simply that the label choice likely is personally meaningful to clients in unique ways that need to be explored. The selection of an ethnic-specific label (e.g., Dominican, Cuban) may convey important connotations, such as ethnopolitical experiences, that may be clinically meaningful as well. As Comas-Díaz (2001) suggests, the choice of a racial-ethnic label, for both communities and individuals, reflect developmental processes that may be a part of therapeutic work. Furthermore, label choice can be an act of empowerment, a source of psychological strength and affirmation, that will be helpful for clients to articulate and acknowledge. The interplay of race and ethnicity might be explored, particularly because racial aspects of clients' identity (e.g., phenotype) may be a significant though potentially unacknowledged aspect of clients' presenting concerns.

Research also indicates that although Latina/o identity development is important for psychological functioning, it is not always the primary or unique focus of therapy. Indeed, as some findings indicate (Castillo et al., 2006; Gushue & Whitson, 2006), ethnic identity may be a distal or even unrelated aspect of clients' presenting concerns. Instead, focusing on variables more directly in line with the presenting problem, such as self-efficacy or perceptions of the environment, may be a more effective place to begin therapeutic work. Identity concerns eventually may become a focus and facilitate development in these more specific areas of concerns.

Social context will be a critical aspect to discern in working with Latinas/os. Contextual variables can include the family environment as well as the community and region where clients grew up and currently reside. An ecological perspective (Bernal et al., 1993; Umaña-Taylor et al., 2006) seems critical to best understanding identity development of Latina/o clients. Moreover, both process (development) and outcome (identity content) seem critical to explore with clients to develop a perspective that simultaneously recognizes individuals' unique constructions of their identity as well as its congruence with others in their communities.

Finally, a theoretical framework can help guide what is assessed about Latina/o identity. For example, the use of the MEIM/MEIM-R will provide information about individuals' stable sense of self, particularly the exploration and commitment that clients have engaged concerning their ethnic background. Bernal/Knight et al.'s approach will provide important information about the impact of clients' family and community

environment (e.g., languages spoken, prejudice acknowledged, etc.). Thus, depending on the nature of the presenting concern, each of these frameworks may provide helpful information to incorporate into therapy.

CONCLUSION

This chapter has presented theory and research concerning Latina/o identity development over the past decade. Models and measures of identity, several of which have been revised since their initial presentation, have been a focus of much research in this area. Although many of the studies have incorporated paper-and-pencil methods, these findings might be further illuminated with the use of qualitative or mixed methods.

REFERENCES

Abreu, J. M., Goodyear, R. K., Campos, A., & Newcomb, M. D. (2000). Ethnic belonging and traditional masculinity ideology among African Americans, European Americans, and Latinos. *Psychology of Men & Masculinity, 1*, 75–86.

Bernal, M. E., Knight, G. P., Ocampo, K. A., Garza, C. A., & Cota, M. K. (1993). Development of Mexican American identity. In M. B. Bernal & G. P. Knight (Eds.), *Ethnic identity: Formation and transmission among Hispanics and other minorities* (pp. 31–46). Albany: State University of New York Press.

Carter, R. T., Yeh, C. J., & Mazzula, S. L. (2008). Cultural values and racial identity statuses among Latino students. *Hispanic Journal of Behavioral Sciences, 30*, 5–23.

Casas, J. M., & Pytluk, S. D. (1995). Hispanic identity development: Implications for research and practice. In J. G. Ponterotto, J. M. Casas, L. A. Suzuki, & C. M. Alexander (Eds.), *Handbook of multicultural counseling* (pp. 155–180). Thousand Oaks, CA: Sage.

Castillo, L. G., Conoley, C. W., Choi-Pearson, C., Archuleta, D. J., Phoummarath, M. J., & Van Landingham, A. (2006). University environment as a mediator of Latino ethnic identity and persistent attitudes. *Journal of Counseling Psychology, 53*, 267–271.

Cokley, K. (2007). Critical issues in the measurement of ethnic and racial identity: A referendum on the state of the field. *Journal of Counseling Psychology, 54*, 224–234.

Comas-Díaz, L. (2001). Hispanics, Latinos or Americanos: The evolution of identity. *Cultural Diversity and Ethnic Minority Psychology, 7*, 115–120.

Cross, W. E. (1991). *Shades of Black: Diversity in African-American identity*. Philadelphia: Temple University Press.

Cross, W. E., & Vandiver, B. J. (2001). Nigrescence theory and measurement: Introducing the Cross Racial Identity Scale (CRIS). In J. G. Ponterotto, J. M. Casas, L. A. Suzuki, & C. M. Alexander (Eds.), *Handbook of multicultural counseling* (pp. 371–393). Thousand Oaks, CA: Sage.

Cuéllar, I., Nyberg, B., Maldonado, R. E., & Roberts, R. E. (1997). Ethnic identity and acculturation in a young adult Mexican-origin population. *Journal of Community Psychology, 25*, 535–549.

Gonzalez, A. G., Umaña-Taylor, A. J., & Hamaca, M. Y. (2006). Familial ethnic socialization among adolescents of Latino and European descent: Do Latina mothers exert the most influence? *Journal of Family Issues, 27*, 184–207.

Gonzalez, J. (2000). *A history of Latinos in America: Harvest of empire*. New York: Viking.

Gushue, G. V., & Whitson, M. L. (2006). The relationship of ethnic identity and gender role attitudes to the development of career choice goals among Black and Latina girls. *Journal of Counseling Psychology, 53*, 379–385.

Helms, J. E. (1995). An update on Helms' White and people of color racial identity models. In J. G. Ponterotto, J. M. Casas, L. A. Suzuki, & C. M. Alexander (Eds.), *Handbook of multicultural counseling* (pp. 181–198). Thousand Oaks, CA: Sage.

Hispanic Association of Colleges and Universities. (n.d.). Facts on Hispanic higher education. Retrieved August 25, 2008, from http://www.hacu.net/hacu/Data,_Statistics,_and_Research1_EN.asp?SnID=813591338

Hurtado, A. (2003). *Voicing Chicana feminisms: Young women speak out on sexuality and identity*. New York: New York University Press.

Jensen, L., Cohen, J. H., Toribio, A. J., De Jong, G. F., & Rodríguez, L. (2006). Ethnic identities, language, and economic outcomes among Dominicans in a new destination. *Social Science Quarterly, 87*, 1088–1099.

Knight, G. P., Bernal, M. E., Cota, M. K., Garza, C. A., & Ocampo, K. A. (1993). Family socialization and Mexican American identity and behavior. In M. B. Bernal & G. P. Knight (Eds.), *Ethnic identity: Formation and transmission among Hispanics and other minorities* (pp. 105–129). Albany: State University of New York Press.

Landale, N. S., & Oropesa, R. S. (2002). White, Black, or Puerto Rican? Racial self-identification among mainland and island Puerto Ricans. *Social Forces, 81*, 231–254.

López, I. (2008). "But you don't look Puerto Rican": The moderating effect of ethnic identity on the relations

between skin color and self-esteem among Puerto Rican women. *Cultural Diversity and Ethnic Minority Psychology, 14*, 102–108.

Lorenzo-Hernandez, J., & Ouellette, S. C. (1998). Ethnic identity, self-esteem, and values in Dominicans, Puerto Ricans, and African Americans. *Journal of Applied Social Psychology, 28*, 2007–2024.

Miville, M. L. (2006). Hispanic Americans. In Y. Jackson (Ed.), *Encyclopedia of multicultural psychology* (pp. 224–230). Thousand Oaks, CA: Sage.

Miville, M. L. (2008). Race and ethnicity in school counseling. In H. L. K. Coleman & C. J. Yeh (Eds.), *Handbook of school counseling* (pp. 177–194). Mahwah, NJ: Lawrence Erlbaum.

Miville, M. L., & Helms, J. E. (1996, August). *Exploring relationships of cultural, gender, and personal identity among Latinos/as*. Poster presentation at the annual meeting of the American Psychological Association, Toronto, Canada.

Miville, M. L., Koonce, D., Darlington, P., & Whitlock, B. (2000). Exploring the relationships between racial/cultural identity and ego identity among African Americans and Mexican Americans. *Journal of Multicultural Counseling and Development, 28*, 208–224.

Negy, C., Shreve, T. L., Jensen, B. J., & Uddin, N. (2003). Ethnic identity, self-esteem, and ethnocentrism: A student of social identity versus multicultural theory of development. *Cultural Diversity and Ethnic Minority Psychology, 9*, 333–344.

Phinney, J. (1992). The Multigroup Ethnic Identity Measure: A new scale for use with diverse groups. *Journal of Adolescent Research, 7*, 156–176.

Phinney, J. S. (1996). When we talk about American ethnic groups, what do we mean? *American Psychologist, 51*, 918–927.

Phinney, J. S., & Ong, A. D. (2007). Conceptualization and measurement of ethnic identity: Current status and future directions. *Journal of Counseling Psychology, 54*, 271–281.

Pizarro, M., & Vera, E. M. (2001). Chicana/o ethnic identity research: Lessons for researchers and counselors. *Counseling Psychologist, 29*, 91–117.

Ponterotto, J. G., & Park-Taylor, J. (2007). Racial and ethnic identity theory, measurement, and research in counseling psychology: Present status and future directions. *Journal of Counseling Psychology, 54*, 282–294.

Quintana, S. M. (1994). A model of ethnic perspective-taking ability applied to Mexican-American children and youth. *International Journal of Intercultural Relations, 18*, 419–448.

Quintana, S. M. (2007). Racial and ethnic identity: Developmental perspectives and identity. *Journal of Counseling Psychology, 54,* 259–270.

Quintana, S. M., & Vera, E. M. (1999). Mexican American children's ethnic identity, understanding of ethnic prejudice, and parental ethnic socialization. *Hispanic Journal of Behavioral Sciences, 21,* 387–404.

Rolón-Dow, R. (2004). Seduced by images: Identity and schooling in the lives of Puerto Rican girls. *Anthropology and Education Quarterly, 35,* 8–29.

Santiago-Rivera, A., Arredondo, P. & Gallardo-Cooper, M. (2002). *Counseling Latinos and la familia: A practical guide.* Thousand Oaks, CA: Sage.

Schwartz, S. J., Zamboanga, B. L., & Jarvis, L. H. (2007). Ethnic identity and acculturation in Hispanic early adolescents: Mediated relationships to academic grades, prosocial behaviors, and externalizing symptoms. *Cultural Diversity and Ethnic Minority Psychology, 13,* 364–373.

Smedley, A., & Smedley, B. D. (2005). Race as biology is fiction, racism as a social problem is real: Anthropological and historical perspectives on the social construction of race. *American Psychologist, 60,* 16–26.

Sue, D. W., & Sue, D. (2007). *Counseling the culturally diverse: Theory and practice* (5th ed.). New York: Wiley.

Supple, A. J., Ghazarian, S. R., Frabutt, J. M., Plunkett, S. W., & Sands, T. (2006). Contextual influences on Latino adolescent ethnic identity and academic outcomes. *Child Development, 77,* 1427–1433.

Syed, M., Azmitia, M., & Phinney, J. S. (2007). Stability and change in ethnic identity among Latino emerging adults in two contexts. *Identity: An International Journal of Theory and Research, 7,* 155–178.

Trimble, J. E. (2007). Prolegomena for the connotation of construct use in the measurement of ethnic and racial identity. *Journal of Counseling Psychology, 54,* 247–258.

Umaña-Taylor, A. J. (2003). Ethnic identity and self-esteem: Examining the role of social context. *Journal of Adolescence, 27,* 139–146.

Umaña-Taylor, A. J., Bhanot, R., & Shin, N. (2006). Ethnic identity formation during adolescence: The critical role of families. *Journal of Family Issues, 27,* 390–414.

Umaña-Taylor, A. J., Diversi, M., & Fine, M. A. (2002). Ethnic identity and self-esteem of Latino adolescents: Distinctions among the Latino populations. *Journal of Adolescent Research, 17,* 303–327.

Umaña-Taylor, A. J., & Fine, M. A. (2001). Methodological implications of grouping Latino adolescents into one collective ethnic group. *Hispanic Journal of Behavioral Sciences, 23,* 347–362.

Umaña-Taylor, A. J., & Fine, M. A. (2004). Examining ethnic identity among Mexican-origin adolescents living in the United States. *Hispanic Journal of Behavioral Sciences, 26,* 36–59.

Umaña-Taylor, A. J., & Shin, N. (2007). An examination of ethnic identity and self-esteem with diverse populations: Exploring variation by ethnicity and geography. *Cultural Diversity and Ethnic Minority Psychology, 13,* 178–186.

Umaña-Taylor, A. J., & Updegraff, K. A. (2007). Latino adolescents' mental health: Exploring the interrelations among discrimination, ethnic identity, cultural orientation, self-esteem, and depressive symptoms. *Journal of Adolescence, 30,* 549–567.

Umaña-Taylor, A. J., Vargas-Chanes, D., Garcia, C. D., & Gonzales-Backen, M. (2008). A longitudinal examination of Latino adolescents' ethnic identity, coping with discrimination, and self-esteem. *Journal of Early Adolescence, 28,* 16–50.

Umaña-Taylor, A. J., Yazedijian, A., & Bamaca-Gómez, M. (2004). Developing the Ethnic Identity Scale using Eriksonian and social identity perspectives. *Identity: An International Journal of Theory and Research, 4,* 9–38.

Utsey, S. O., Chae, M. H., Brown, C. F., & Kelly, D. (2002). Effect of ethnic group membership on ethnic identity, race-related stress, and quality of life. *Cultural Diversity and Ethnic Minority Psychology, 8,* 366–377.

Vandiver, B. J. (2001). Psychological nigrescence revisited: Introduction and overview. *Journal of Multicultural Counseling and Development, 29,* 165–173.

Vaquera, E., & Kao, G. (2006). The implications of choosing "no race" on the salience of Hispanic identity: How racial and ethnic backgrounds intersect among Hispanic adolescents. *The Sociological Quarterly, 47,* 375–396.

23

Asian American Racial and Ethnic Identity

Update on Theory and Measurement

MARK H. CHAE AND CHRISTOPHER LARRES

In the past three decades, there has been an influx of research devoted to racial and ethnic identity development (Cross, 1971; Helms, 1990; Phinney, 1992; Ponterotto & Park-Taylor, 2007). The majority of racial identity research has focused on White and Black racial identity formation (Helms & Cook, 1999; Sellers, Rowley, Chavous, Shelton, & Smith, 1997). This may be reflective of the historical and ongoing racial tensions between these two racial groups (Chen, LePhuoc, Guzman, Rude, & Dodd, 2006). As such, one consequence of this dichotomy has been the relative absence of psychological study of other racial groups, particularly Asian Americans. Indeed, with the exception of a handful of studies, Asian American racial identity has been virtually ignored.

In contrast, ethnic identity research has been applied more broadly to diverse ethnic groups. Consequently, there has been a substantial body of research on Asian American ethnic identity. A number of studies assessing ethnic identity have been conducted with this population as it relates to indexes of acculturation, self-construal, and psychological functioning. However, researchers have used different measures to assess the construct, which has resulted in inconsistent results.

The purpose of this chapter is to provide an overview of research related to the theory and measurement of racial and ethnic identity development among Asian Americans. First, we provide an overview of the constructs of racial and ethnic identity. Second, we review psychometric properties of measures that assess racial and ethnic identity for Asian Americans. Finally, directions for future research are discussed.

RACIAL IDENTITY

Theories of racial identity emerged out of the acknowledgment of the sociopolitical oppression that has negatively affected the lives of people of color (Helms, 1995; Ponterotto, Utsey, & Pedersen, 2006; Sue & Sue, 2008). A central theme in racial identity theory is recognizing and overcoming the internalized racism that has emerged from society's differential treatment of racial and ethnic minority groups. The extant literature on racial identity can be traced to the works of Cross (1971), Helms (1990), and Atkinson, Morten, and Sue (1989), whose collective refinement of the construct led to the recognition that the model could be applied to other marginalized groups in the United States (e.g., people of color).

In our attempt to examine the literature on Asian racial identity, we found a dearth of studies that examined this topic with this population. The small number of studies we did find used Helms's People of Color Racial Identity Attitude Scale (POCRIAS) to assess racial identity attitudes. Based on Helms's theory (Helms & Cook, 1999), Asian racial identity development is a two-fold process of transcending the negative worldview that Asians are devalued in society while concomitantly developing an identity grounded in one's cultural heritage and sociopolitical experiences. Because individuals respond differently to societal oppression, information-processing strategies employed to negotiate these conditions may differ based on the individual's psychological and cultural disposition. Racial identity statuses, then, reflect the different ways of perceiving and negotiating these racial-cultural experiences. Indeed, some individuals attempt to adjust and adapt to these conditions by conforming to societal norms; others develop new and more sophisticated ways of reacting and coping with social oppression (Atkinson, 2004; Helms & Cook, 1999).

Helms's People of Color Racial Identity Model

According to the People of Color (POC) racial identity model, there are five statuses of development (Chen et al., 2006; Helms, 1995; Helms & Cook, 1999; Ponterotto et al., 2006). Individuals operating from the first status, Conformity, believe that the customs and values of the dominant culture are superior and those of the minority culture are inferior or wrong. Often, individuals operating from this framework distort or minimize the effects of racism and may actively and unconsciously screen out information in order to preserve their belief in racial equality.

In the second status, Dissonance, the individual begins to acknowledge that he or she may not fit in the White world (Ponterotto et al., 2006). Additionally, the

individual may question the idea that all people can achieve the "American dream." At this point, the individual may feel ambivalent and confused about his or her earlier beliefs about race.

In the third status, Immersion-Emersion, the individual initially experiences hypersensitivity and divided thinking about his or her racial identity, which may be a remnant from the Dissonance stage. The Immersion status is characterized by a desire to replace a "White-imposed" definition of self with a racially affirming identity (Alvarez, 2002; Helms, 1995). The individual may have an emotionally jarring experience that influences him or her to identify with the minority culture and reject his or her former identification with White culture. This leads to the Emersion status of racial identity. Here, the individual may become excited and enthusiastic about his or her racial group and become engaged in learning about Asian culture, understanding its strengths, and developing an Asian perspective with a realistic view of its cultural roots (Alvarez & Helms, 2001).

In the fourth status, Internalization, the individual begins to question his or her total identification with the minority culture and negative view of the dominant culture. This status is marked by an ability to recognize the strengths and limitations of the minority culture. The individual may realize that he or she has over-idealized the minority culture and at the same time developed a view of White Americans based on generalizations and stereotypes (Alvarez, 2002).

In the final status, Integrative Awareness, the individual has worked through conflicts in earlier phases and has developed a sense of security in being able to acknowledge the strengths of his or her minority culture and of other cultures. The individual operating from this status espouses the view that each culture has strengths and weaknesses. This status is the most sophisticated and is characterized by a strong racial self-esteem, a firm sense of identity, and an appreciation for diversity (Chang & Kwan, 2009).

In summary, the five statuses of racial identity begin with the least sophisticated status, in which the individual is influenced by the dominant culture. In the most advanced status of racial identity, the individual is able to navigate the various forms of oppression and cope with a racially complex world (Carter, 1995; Helms & Cook, 1999).

Instrument Development

The POCRIAS is a 50-item measure that was created to assess the racial identity statuses of people belonging to marginalized racial/cultural groups (Helms & Cook, 1999), including African Americans, Asian Americans, Latinos, and Native Americans. Items are rated on a Likert-type scale, ranging from 1 (*strongly disagree*) to 5 (*strongly agree*). As noted above, the model describes five statuses. Although Helms's model includes all five statuses, the POCRIAS assesses four subscales, with the Integrative awareness status subsumed within the Internalization schema (Chen et al., 2006). The mean scores of these items determine the strength of each racial identity domain (i.e., Conformity, Dissonance, Immersion-Emersion, and Internalization/Integrative Awareness).

Psychometric Properties

Estimation of internal consistency of the POCRIAS with Asian American samples was assessed by calculating Cronbach's alpha. Cronbach's alpha is determined by a single administration method through calculating the mean of all split-half reliabilities (Nunnally & Bernstein, 1994; Ponterotto & Ruckdeschel, 2007). Ponterotto and Ruckdeschel (2007) contended that "Coefficient alpha can be considered an estimate of the expected correlation between an actual test and a hypothetical alternative form of the same length that may never have been constructed" (p. 998). This approach to assessing internal consistency has been considered one of the most precise ways to establish a reliability estimate (Nunnally & Bernstein, 1994). A number of researchers have suggested that a minimum alpha of .70 is acceptable for instruments used for research with large groups (Anastasi & Urbina, 1997; Ponterotto & Ruckdeschel, 2007).

A small number of studies using the POCRIAS with Asian Americans have been conducted (e.g., Alvarez & Helms, 2001; Alvarez, Juang, & Liang, 2006) (see Table 23.1). With a diverse sample of 323 Asian American men, Liu (2002) examined the relationship of racial identity, gender role conflict, and prejudicial

Table 23.1   Asian Ethnic Identity Development Using the MEIM

Author(s)	N	EI α	OGO α	Asian Ethnic Groups
Lee et al. (2001)	316	.90	.74	Korean
Juang et al. (2006)	261	.86	.74	Filipino, Japanese, Korean, Tai, Hmong, Vietnamese, Malaysian, and Burmese
Shrake and Rhee (2004)	217	.91	.77	Korean
Lee and Yoo (2004)	323	.78	.76	Chinese, Filipino, Vietnamese, Japanese, Korean, Indian, and Hmong
Lee et al. (2000)	186	.89	.76	Chinese, Vietnamese, Filipino, Korean, Japanese, and Indian
Avery et al. (2007)	201	.90	.81	Asian American (unspecified)
Lee (2005)	84	.76	.78	Korean
Lee (2003)	88	.87	.76	Asian American (unspecified)

Asian American Racial Identity Using the POCRIAS

Author(s)	N	Conformity α	Dissonance α	Immersion/ Emersion α	Internalization α	Asian Ethnic Groups
Alvarez and Helms (2001)	188	.75	.78	.83	.61	Chinese, Korean, and Indian
Alvarez et al. (2006)	254	.76	.79	.85	.71	Chinese, Filipino, and Vietnamese
Liu (2002)	323	.78	.72	.75	.86	Chinese, Korean, Japanese, and Filipino
Chen et al. (2006)	344	.69	.75	.82	.66	Chinese, Taiwanese, Korean, Japanese, and Vietnamese
Kohatsu et al. (2000)	160	.66	.65	.78	.67	Chinese, Korean, and Filipino

attitudes. He reported alpha coefficients that ranged from 0.72 to 0.86. Likewise, Chen et al. (2006) conducted a cluster analytic study using the POCRIAS with a sample of 344 self-identified Asian American men and women. The authors reported alpha coefficients that ranged from 0.66 to 0.82. In another study, Kohatsu et al. (2000) examined the relationship between racial identity and racial mistrust with a diverse sample of 160 Asian American male and female participants. The authors reported alpha coefficients that ranged from 0.65 to 0.78. In a study conducted with 254 Asian American college students, Alvarez et al. (2006) investigated the relationship between racial identity and perceived racism. The authors reported alpha coefficients that ranged from 0.71 to 0.85. Finally, Alvarez and Helms (2001) conducted a study with 188 Asian Americans, examining the relationship between racial identity, cultural mistrust, and racial adjustment. In their study, they reported alpha coefficients that ranged from 0.61 to 0.83.

Research on the construct validity of the POCRIAS has also been adequate. One way to assess construct validity is to examine the relationship of a measure to other instruments that purport to assess a related construct (Anastasi & Urbina, 1997). However, because we could not locate any other studies examining Asian American racial identity, the authors examined the degree to which each racial identity status was related to indexes for which the theory purports. As noted by Campbell (1957), when assessing construct validity, not only should a test or subscale positively correlate with other variables with which its theoretical premise purports, but there should be a small to no relationship with variables unrelated to the construct.

Research reports with Asian American samples have shown that subscales of the POCRIAS are related to indexes associated with each status. Alvarez and Helms (2001) found that the Immersion-Emersion status was positively associated with awareness of higher levels of White racism. Likewise, Alvarez et al. (2006) found that the Immersion-Emersion status was positively associated with greater perceived direct experiences related to racism as well as a significantly higher number of experiences of observing racism-related events that were directed toward other Asian Americans. Kohatsu et al. (2000) found that Asian Americans

operating from the Immersion-Emersion status developed a deep sense of ethnocentrism, whereby their Asian cultural background was perceived as the in-group and the standard by which to judge right from wrong. Moreover, in comparison to the other racial identity statuses, Immersion-Emersion participants were most likely to endorse the perception of high levels of racism. Finally, Liu (2002) found that Asian American participants operating from the Immersion-Emersion racial identity status defined their sense of masculinity based on Asian conceptualizations of self. He indicated that the "idealizing of Asian culture . . . translates to how the Asian American man relates to himself as a man" (p. 116). Hence, for individuals operating from this status, being male and Asian is inextricably intertwined.

Racial identity theory has suggested that those operating from less advanced identity statuses tend to report lower levels of psychological functioning, whereas those operating from more sophisticated racial identity schemas report higher levels of psychological functioning. The research with Asian Americans in this area has been mixed. Liu (2002) found that the Internalization status was related to low levels of gender role conflict and a general appreciation of the positive and negative aspects of traditional male norms. Similarly, Alvarez and Helms (2001) found that Asian American participants operating from the Internalization status reported high levels of collective self-esteem. In another study, Kohatsu et al. (2000) found that Asian American participants in the Conformity status showed a lack of awareness of sociopolitical issues and knowledge of their respective socioracial group. The study also indicated that participants operating from an Internalization status reported low levels of racial mistrust. This finding indicates that these participants showed more positive attitudes about engaging in interracial interactions.

In contrast, some studies using the POCRIAS have not rendered findings consistent with theory. Chen et al. (2006) contended that "evidence for the applicability of the model has not always been uniformly positive" (p. 464). In their study with Asian American participants, they found that individuals operating from the Internalization status reported elevated scores on the institutional racism and racial privilege subscales of the Color Blind Racial Attitudes Scale (CoBRAS) (Neville, Lilly, Duran, Lee, & Browne, 2000). High scores on the CoBRAS indicate a denial of prevalence of racism as well as its impact on people of color. Similarly, Alvarez and Helms (2001) found that Asian American participants operating from the Internalization status reported low levels of awareness of interpersonal racism. This result indicates that participants in this status did not recognize the significant impact of racial and cultural oppression on people of color. Both of these findings conflict with racial identity theory. In sum, it is evident that although there is research that supports the construct validity of the POCRIAS, other research does not fully support the tenets of the theory with Asian American participants.

Evaluation

The strength of the POCRIAS is that among the published studies we examined, the racial identity statuses rendered adequate to good reliability coefficients. Additionally, although some research findings have not been consistent with theory, the majority conducted with Asian samples have rendered findings in the expected direction. However, few studies have used the POCRIAS with Asian samples. As such, further investigation aimed at examining the factor structure of the measure is needed. We recommend that researchers conduct studies employing exploratory factor analysis (EFA) and confirmatory factor analysis (CFA) to determine if the POCRIAS is representative of the latent structure of racial identity.

ETHNIC IDENTITY

Ethnic identity is a set of self-conceptions whereby individuals derive a distinct group identity that is multidimensional. Ethnic identity should be differentiated from racial identity in that ethnic identity is not necessarily a response to racism. The formation of ethnic identity across individuals is variable because it is contingent upon the degree of value and emotional significance an individual attaches to his or her ethnic group (Bernal, Knight, Garza, Ocampo, & Cota, 1990; Phinney, 2003; Tsai & Curbow, 2001). This developmental process has been described as a complex progression of integrating the influences of one's ethnic group culture with society's perceptions of the ethnic group. It should

be noted that ethnic identity may not be limited to adherence to just ethnic minority culture, but often includes familiarity with one's cultural history, religious and spiritual influences, national origin, and the practice of customs and traditions associated with one's indigenous group (Chang & Kwan, 2009). Self-identification is a salient aspect of one's ethnic identity because it results from exposure to various sources of one's culture and heritage.

In this section, we provide an overview and description of three measures of ethnic identity that have been used with Asian American populations. In contrast to Asian racial identity, a number of studies have been conducted assessing Asian ethnic identity. The majority of studies that have examined this construct with Asian American samples have been conducted using the Multigroup Ethnic Identity Measure (MEIM) (Phinney, 1992). Other measures are the Internal and External Ethnic Identity Measure (Kwan & Sodowsky, 1997), and the more recently developed East Asian Ethnic Identity Scale (Barry, 2002). Theoretical and psychometric properties of these scales are presented.

Multigroup Ethnic Identity Measure

According to Phinney (1990, 1992), ethnic identity has been defined as the degree to which an individual has explored the meaning of his or her ethnic group membership and developed a sense of commitment to his or her ethnic heritage. Phinney's conception of ethnic identity development is based on the theory and research of ego identity theory (Bennion & Adams, 1986; Erikson, 1968; Marcia, 1966). According to Marcia (1966), ego identity development progresses developmentally from less sophisticated identity statuses to more cognitively complex ego identity statuses. In Marcia's model, there are four statuses: Diffusion, Foreclosure, Moratorium, and Achievement. Diffusion describes a person lacking direction. Foreclosure describes an individual who embraces a set of values, beliefs, and goals articulated by another rather than adopting self-attained values, beliefs, and goals. Moratorium characterizes a person experiencing an emotional or psychological crisis, seeking to form individual values, beliefs, and goals. Achievement describes an individual who has successfully passed through the Moratorium stage and now embraces self-derived values, beliefs, and goals (Marcia, 1966, 1980).

Bennion and Adams's (1986) Extended Objective Measure of Ego Identity Status (EOMEIS) emerged out of Marcia's research using an interview method. Accordingly, ego identity is related to two broad cognitive categories: a person's ideological perspectives and his or her interpersonal views. Ideological perspectives encompass a person's religion, political orientation, philosophical lifestyle, and occupation. Interpersonal views are based on friendship, dating, sex roles, and recreation (Erikson, 1968; Marcia, 1966; Phinney, 1993).

Early research on ego identity (Aries & Moorehead, 1989; Spencer & Markstrom-Adams, 1990) revealed that ethnic minority participants frequently scored higher in the Foreclosure identity status than White participants. As a result, researchers questioned whether ideas concerning the ego identity construct as espoused by Marcia were culturally appropriate for ethnic minorities. Interestingly, Waterman (1988) stated that few individuals from non-Western societies would be found to have an Achievement identity. He suggested that the measure is based on Eurocentric values and therefore may not be culturally appropriate for those adhering to an Eastern worldview. This assertion is noteworthy because data indicate that more than 60% of Asian Americans currently residing in the United States were born in Asia (Cheryan & Tsai, 2007).

Phinney (1992) pointed out that although the EOMEIS assessed many important aspects of identity (e.g., religious orientation, political worldview, philosophical lifestyle, and attitudes related to sex roles), ethnicity, which she viewed as an important component of identity for ethnic minorities, was conspicuously missing. Because of these concerns, Phinney (1990, 1992) developed the MEIM, which assesses ethnic identity exploration and commitment and attitudes toward individuals from other ethnic groups. The scale is consistent with Marcia's ego identity development process.

Instrument Development

Phinney assessed ethnic identity (EI) using the 20-item MEIM (Phinney, 1992). Participants are asked to respond to items on a 4-point Likert-type scale that ranges from *strongly disagree* to *strongly agree*. The measure consists of 14 items that assess three aspects of ethnic identity: positive attitudes and a sense of affirmation and belonging toward one's group, ethnic behaviors and practices, and a committed ethnic identity. Additionally, the instrument assesses participants' attitudes toward ethnic groups other than their own. This component of the MEIM, which consists of six items, has been regarded as other-group orientation (OGO). Among the 20 total items, 4 items are reverse keyed.

Psychometric Properties

In the developmental study, Phinney (1992) conducted a principal axis factor analysis with a multiethnic sample of 553 participants (417 high school students and 136 college students), using squared multiple correlations as the criterion for observed commonalities. The statistical procedure produced a two-factor solution. Phinney indicated that there was one factor for EI that accounted for 20% of the variance for the high school sample and 31% of the variance for the college sample. OGO, the second factor, accounted for 9.1% of the variance for the high school sample and 11.4% of the variance for the college sample.

Reliability estimates were calculated for this measure using a single administration method. Internal consistency was determined by the procedure Cronbach's alpha. Phinney (1992) calculated reliability for a multiethnic high school sample ($n = 417$) and a multiethnic college sample ($n = 136$). She reported a coefficient alpha of 0.81 for high school students and 0.90 for college students. In studies using Asian American participants, reliability of the MEIM ranged from satisfactory to strong (see Table 23.1). Lee, Falbo, Doh, and Park (2001) examined the effects of migration experiences and ethnic identity with 316 Korean and Chinese participants. They reported alpha coefficients ranging from 0.74 to 0.90. Using two samples of diverse Asian American participants, Juang, Nguyen, and Lin examined the relationship of ethnic identity and psychosocial functioning. Alpha coefficients ranged from 0.70 to 0.90. Lee (2005) examined the role of EI and OGO as protective factors against discrimination among 84 Korean Americans. Cronbach's alphas ranged from 0.76 to 0.78. Shrake and Rhee (2004) examined the relationship between ethnic identity and problem behaviors among 217 Korean Americans. They reported alpha coefficients ranging from 0.77 to 0.91. Lee and Yoo (2004), examining the structure of the MEIM with a heterogeneous sample of 316 Asian Americans drawn from previously collected data sets, reported Cronbach's alphas for the separate subscales that ranged from 0.76 to 0.81. In a study with 153 Asian Americans, Lee, Choe, Kim, and Ngo (2000) reported Cronbach's alpha coefficients ranging from 0.76 to 0.89. Finally, Avery, Tonidandel, Thomas, Johnson, and Mack (2007) examined the psychometric properties of the MEIM with 201 Asian American participants. They reported alpha coefficients ranging from 0.77 to 0.92.

Further evidence of the construct validity of the MEIM is based on research that supports the relationship of indexes with which the MEIM should theoretically correlate as well as measures from which it should differ (Kohatsu & Phinney, 1997). According to the literature on ethnic identity, individuals operating from more advanced statuses report higher levels of psychological functioning. In general, these assertions have been supported with Asian American samples. In a sample of 261 Asian American participants, Juang, Nguyen, and Lin (2006) found that ethnic identity was positively associated with self-esteem and a sense of connectedness with parents. Likewise, in a study with 100 Chinese participants, Yip and Cross (2004) examined the relationship between ethnic identity and several indexes of well-being. Their results showed that the MEIM was positively associated with self-esteem and the total score of the Collective Self-Esteem Scale. Yoo and Lee (2005) found that among 155 Asian American college students, a strong ethnic identity was positively associated with life satisfaction and positive affect. Ethnic identity was inversely related with negative affect. Lee and Yoo (2004) found that Asian American participants who scored high on ethnic identity reported a high level of social connectedness. Additionally, their research showed that two of the three subscales of the MEIM, achievement and affirmation and belonging, were positively associated with self-esteem. However, the ethnic behaviors subscale was not statistically significant.

Individuals with a strong ethnic identity have been theorized to be more aware of racial prejudice and show a high level of resilience when negotiating its effects. Research using the MEIM has not fully supported this assertion (Lee, 2003, 2005; Yoo & Lee, 2005). Yoo and Lee (2005) found that a strong ethnic identity was related to the employment of more active coping mechanisms and reliance of social support when presented with experiences of racial prejudice. However, results indicated that this buffering effect was evident only when there were low levels of perceived discrimination, but not when it was high. In another study with 158 Asian American students, Lee (2003) sought to examine if a strong ethnic identity served as a protective factor against discrimination on a university campus. The results indicated that contrary to theory, ethnic identity did not moderate the negative influence of a racially hostile campus environment. In another study with 82 Korean American college students, Lee (2005) sought to investigate if a strong ethnic identity would serve as a protective factor when confronted with racial prejudice. The results partially supported the hypothesis, as the subscale, racial pride, was the sole domain that facilitated resilience when exposed to perceived discrimination. These results further challenge the theory and research that suggests that ethnic identity serves as a buffer to the negative psychological effects of discrimination.

Lee and Yoo (2004) conducted the only published study we could find that examined the structure and measurement of the MEIM with an Asian American sample. They focused specifically on the EI component of the measure. With a sample of 323 Asian American college students, they performed a maximum likelihood factor analysis with an oblimin rotation, which produced a three-factor solution accounting for 60% of the common variance. According to Lee and Yoo, the three factors approximated three of Phinney's (1992) subscales that emerged in the developmental study: ethnic identity achievement, affirmation and belonging, and ethnic behaviors. Although these factors corresponded with those found by Phinney, they were not exact. As such, Lee and Yoo (2004) relabeled them as ethnic identity-clarity, ethnic identity-pride, and ethnic identity-engage. Correlational analyses indicated that the relationships between these factors were moderate ($rs = .51 - .54$). Lee and Yoo (2004) noted that it was not surprising that the structure of EI was somewhat different from Phinney's (1992) study because "it is likely that ethnic identity develops differently for various ethnic and racial groups" (Lee & Yoo, 2004, p. 267). It is evident based on these findings and other research that has examined the factor structure of the MEIM that further research is needed with Asian American participants.

To date, the majority of research examining the factor structure of the MEIM has been conducted with multiethnic samples. In one study with 275 college students from diverse backgrounds, Worrell (2000) investigated the factor structure of the MEIM employing a principal axis factor analysis with oblique rotation, considering eigenvalues of 1.0 and above. The factor analysis produced a two-factor solution that accounted for 44% of the variance. Similar to the results of Phinney's (1992) development study, Factor I consisted of the same 14 items (labeled EI), and Factor II consisted of six items (labeled OGO). The correlation between the two factors was low ($r = .006$), suggesting the factors are orthogonal.

Other studies employed both EFA and CFA to examine the construct validity of the MEIM. For example, with a sample of 219 high school students, Ponterotto, Gretchen, Utsey, Stracuzzi, and Saya (2003) conducted an EFA and CFA to test the goodness of fit of the MEIM as a one-factor model compared to Phinney's (1992) proposed two-factor model. Results indicated that a two-factor model was a better fit as compared to the global factor model, accounting for 41% of the variance. However, as noted by the fit indexes, the analysis rendered a less-than-satisfactory model fit ($\chi^2[169] = 2.37, p < .01$, TLI = .81, CFI = .83, RMSEA = .08). Given the poor fit, a principal axis factor analysis with varimax rotation and Kaiser normalization was performed. Results showed that Factor I (EI) accounted for 31% of the variance and Factor II (OGO) accounted for an additional 10% of the common variance. Additionally, results showed that the 14 items assessing ethnic identity had factor loadings of 0.45 or greater. With regard to OGO, five out of six items rendered factor loadings of 0.30 or greater. One item had a less-than-optimal loading of 0.21. This study was the first CFA conducted on the MEIM. Ponterotto et al. (2003) indicated that the results, in general, supported Phinney's (1992) two-factor model, but as indicated by the fit indexes, it was suboptimal.

This may have been the result of inconsistent responses on the OGO.

Avery et al. (2007) assessed the MEIM's measurement equivalence across 1,349 participants from four different ethnic groups. Also employing a CFA, Avery et al. sought to replicate Roberts, Phinney, Masse, and Chenet's (1999) results, which indicated that the EI component of the MEIM consisted of two factors: Affirmation/Belonging and Exploration. Avery et al.'s results indicated that Roberts et al.'s (1999) two-factor structure did not render a good model fit. Furthermore, a CFA indicated that when the EI was conceived as a global factor and certain items were modified, this rendered a good model fit ($\chi^2[200] = 716, p < .01$, TLI = .90, CFI = .92, RMSEA = .04). Further analysis with the OGO indicated that six items do fit the data ($\chi^2[36] = 174.8, p < .01$, TLI = .91, CFI = .95, RMSEA = .05).

Phinney and Ong (2007) sought to further refine the EI component of the MEIM, which resulted in the development of a two-factor, six-item measure (MEIM-R). A maximum likelihood factor analysis with oblimin rotation with 10 items from the MEIM-R was conducted with 192 college students from diverse backgrounds. The researchers did not include 2 items from the original 14 based on the research findings of Roberts et al. (1999), which indicated that these items were not a good fit to the overall model. Phinney and Ong (2007) dropped two additional items assessing ethnic behaviors and practices, reasoning that "although behaviors are typically correlated with ethnic identity, they are conceptually distinct from ethnic identity" (p. 275). The results produced a six-item scale with three items assessing EI exploration and three items assessing EI commitment. A CFA was performed to test the underlying structure of the six-item measure with a sample of 241 college students from diverse backgrounds. Results showed that a correlated two-factor model served as the best representation of the latent structure of ethnic identity ($\chi^2/df = 1.91, p < .001$, AGFI = .96, CFI = .98, RMSEA = .04). It is noteworthy to point out that although the correlated two-factor model rendered an excellent fit to the data, the hierarchical second-order model (i.e., single factor) also rendered very good fit to the model ($\chi^2/df = 1.88, p < .001$, AGFI = .95, CFI = .94, RMSEA = .05). Phinney and Ong (2007) contended that use of either of these models would be appropriate and that the decision to use one over the other should be contingent upon the research objective.

Evaluation

Since its development, the MEIM has undergone significant modifications as a result of ongoing research aimed at refining the psychometric properties of the instrument. These research results have rendered inconsistent findings that may be due to various factors (Cokley, 2007). First, it is evident that researchers have used different statistical procedures to examine the factor structure of the MEIM. Some have used different types of EFA (e.g., principal axis and maximum likelihood), whereas others have employed both EFA and CFA. Second, researchers have been inconsistent with regard to the number of items examined. In our review, studies varied with regard to the inclusion of 6, 12, 14, and 20 items. Third, studies have been conducted with samples from different demographic backgrounds. Future studies should continue to examine the structural invariance with samples from diverse groups. One major consequence of these factors is that examining comparisons of the MEIM's factor structure becomes difficult (Cokley, 2007). Perhaps one of the major strengths of the MEIM is the consistent reporting of good internal consistency. The most recent development of the MEIM-R (Phinney & Ong, 2007) appears to be promising. Indeed, Phinney and Ong (2007) administered the measure to 192 ethnically diverse college students and rendered the following alpha coefficients: 0.83 for exploration and 0.89 for commitment. However, the MEIM-R has yet to be tested with a sample of Asian Americans. Future studies employing the MEIM-R should be conducted with participants belonging to Asian ethnic groups.

Internal-External Ethnic Identity Measure (Int-Ext Measure)

Consistent with the early work of Isajiw (1990), Kwan and Sodowsky (1997) believed that ethnic identity formation consisted of internal and external aspects. Internal ethnic identity reflects cognitive, moral, and emotional aspects of identity. It consists of knowledge

and awareness of one's cultural heritage and background, as well as cultural beliefs, such as filial piety and saving face. External ethnic identity reflects observable social and cultural behaviors. It may include maintaining one's language, eating indigenous foods, and taking part in the customs of the Asian group (Chang & Kwan, 2009).

Instrument Development

The Int-Ext Measure was created to assess both internal and external aspects of ethnic identity among Asian Americans (Chang & Kwan, 2009; Kwan & Sodowsky, 1997). Items are rated on a Likert-type scale, ranging from 1 (*strongly disagree*) to 6 (*strongly agree*). Kwan and Sodowsky developed the Int-Ext Measure to improve upon what they perceived as limitations of other ethnic identity measures, contending that most models placed too much emphasis on cognitive and emotional aspects of ethnic identity and de-emphasized ethnic behaviors and practices. Inspired by the work of Breton, Isajiw, Kalbach, and Reitz (1990), they conceptualized ethnic identity as "how a person in a pluralistic society locates and expresses [oneself] socially and psychologically with reference to various ethnic groups, including [one's] own ethnic group" (cited in Kwan & Sodowsky, 1997, p. 57).

Psychometric Properties

Research on the construct validity of the Int-Ext measure has been adequate. Kwan (2000) conducted a principal components analysis with varimax rotation, considering eigenvalues higher than 1.0. A four-factor solution was found to be most interpretable, with 12 items being deleted because of low loadings (< .35) and low corrected item-total correlations (< .02) (Tabachnick & Fidell, 2007).

The principal components analysis produced four factors and reduced the item pool to 24 questions: 10 items for ethnic friendship and affiliation accounting for 25.5% of the variance (e.g., I trust and turn to individuals of my own ethnic group when I need help); 5 items for ethno-communal expression, accounting for 10% of the variance (e.g., I prefer my ethnic group's music, dances, and entertainment); 3 items for ethnic food orientation, accounting for 5.9% of the variance (e.g., I prefer to eat mostly my ethnic food); and 6 items for family collectivism, accounting for 4.8% of the variance (e.g., I adhere strictly to my ethnic values). Kwan (2000) indicated that 15 items assessed external ethnic identity, whereas 9 items reflected internal ethnic identity.

Based on the few studies in which the Int-Ext Id measure was used, estimation of internal consistency with Asian American samples was generally satisfactory. With a sample of 224 Asian American participants, Kwan and Sodowsky (1997) reported internal consistency for the following: 0.79 for Internal, 0.86 for External, and 0.90 for the entire scale. The correlation between the two domains was 0.78. Despite the high correlation, Kwan and Sodowsky (1997) decided to treat these factors as orthogonal. After conducting the principal components analysis, Kwan (2000) reported the following Cronbach's alphas for the four factors: 0.88 for ethnic friendship and affiliation, 0.80 for ethno-communal expression, 0.87 for ethnic food orientation, and 0.72 for family collectivism.

Convergent validity of the Int-Ext Id measure indicated that internal ethnic identity was positively related to measures assessing saliency of ethnicity and loss of face. External ethnic identity was unrelated to both indexes (Kwan & Sodowsky, 1997).

Evaluation

The Int-Ext measure appears to be a promising scale. The two studies above indicate that this is a reliable scale that shows good construct validity. However, it is evident that further research using EFA and CFA should be conducted. Second, future studies should include Asian ethnic groups other than Chinese American participants to determine whether it is appropriate for use with diverse Asian groups. One of the strengths of this measure is that because it was developed for Asian Americans, it may be better able to capture and assess the cultural nuances that a general measure of ethnic identity might fail to detect.

East Asian Ethnic Identity Scale

The East Asian Ethnic Identity Scale (EAEIS) (Barry, 2002) is a measure designed to assess the ethnic identity

development of Asian Americans from China, Japan, and Korea. Barry (2002) contended that many ethnic or cultural identity measures tend to be generic and do not assess the rich cultural variations among different ethnic groups. For example, East Asian culture is deeply influenced by the teachings and practices of Confucianism (Fairbank, Reischauer, & Craig, 1978). By using a generic measure, unique cultural values and beliefs could be overlooked. Additionally, Barry (2002) contends that an instrument such as the EAEIS would not only be more informative than a generic measure when conducting research with large samples, but also be very useful in clinical settings. Therapists may be better informed about their clients' adherence to East Asian culture, which in turn may reduce ethnocentrism and other barriers to effective treatment.

Instrument Development and Psychometric Properties

The development of the EAEIS was based on the input of Asian American professors and doctoral students at a midwestern university, Phinney's (1992) research using the MEIM, as well as Suinn, Richard-Figueroa, Lew, and Vigil's (1987) identity domain of the SL-ASIA. The EAEIS development study was conducted with a convenience sample of 150 Asian immigrants from China (25 male and 25 female), Japan (27 male and 23 female), and Korea (25 male and 25 female). A principal components analysis with varimax rotation, considering eigenvalues of greater than 1.0, rendering a three-factor solution. Items that reduced the overall internal consistency or rendered low loadings (< .40) were deleted. Furthermore, items with low item-total correlations were dropped, leaving an item bank of 41 questions. The three factors were family values (e.g., If my son or daughter was failing at school, I would handle it privately within the family); ethnic pride (e.g., Being Asian is an important part of who I am), and interpersonal distance (e.g., I don't like to stand out in a group).

Reliability of the EAEIS has been satisfactory. Barry (2002) reported the internal consistency for the three factors: 0.81 for family values, 0.85 for ethnic pride, and 0.80 for interpersonal distance. In a study that examined ethnic identity and sex role ideology among

170 Asian American male and female participants, Barry and Beitel (2006) reported a Cronbach's alpha of 0.80 for the full-scale EAEIS. In another study examining cultural identity, self-esteem, and perceptions of discrimination, Barry and Grilo (2003) reported an overall Cronbach's alpha of 0.82.

Research reports with Asian American samples have shown that the EAEIS has adequate convergent validity. Barry and Grilo (2003) found that participants scoring higher on ethnic identity also were more aware of discrimination. Additionally, Barry (2002) found that high ethnic identity scores were positively associated with an interdependent self-construal. In contrast, lower ethnic identity scores were associated with an independent self-construal. Finally, Barry and Beitel (2006) found that among Asian immigrants, higher ethnic identity scores were associated with adherence to traditional sex roles. Because East Asian cultures have traditionally been patriarchal, adhering to a more traditional sex role makes intuitive sense. The authors note that participants who had been in the United States for a longer period tended to score lower on ethnic identity, endorsed items consistent with an independent self-construal, and embraced a more egalitarian sex role.

Evaluation

The EAEIS is a measure that possesses some notable strong points. In particular, the reliability and construct validity are quite good. Additionally, in contrast to other measures that assess general ethnic identity, the EAEIS takes into account a more rich assessment of important ethnic and cultural factors unique to East Asians. However, as a relatively new measure, the EAEIS shows some limitations as well. For example, in the scale development study, Barry (2002) indicated that a three-factor solution was produced, but the amount of variance that was accounted for by each factor was not reported. In the same study, Barry (2002) noted that 41 items made up the EAEIS. However, there was no indication of how large the original item pool was and what statistical procedures or interpretations (e.g., corrected item correlations) were made to eliminate certain items. Another concern in the developmental study was that the sample of participants was small. One problem with a small sample size is that the

patterns of covariation may lack stability, potentially resulting in items that appear to increase internal consistency when, in fact, they may be rendered useless when administered to different samples (DeVellis, 1991). Ideally, when conducting a principal components analysis, a participant pool between 200 and 300 should be the target goal in order to decrease subject variance (DeVellis, 1991).

RECOMMENDATIONS AND DIRECTIONS FOR FUTURE RESEARCH

In the current review, we provided an overview of the POCRIAS, which was the only racial identity scale used with Asian American participants in the professional literature. We also examined the development and refinement of the MEIM, which has been renamed MEIM-R. Finally, we looked at two other ethnic identity measures that were designed to assess ethnic identity formation with Asian Americans. Based on the review of these constructs, several areas of concern have emerged. We provide recommendations and directions for future research in Asian American racial and ethnic identity.

In the counseling psychology literature, there has been a dearth of research focused on Asian American racial identity. As such, we believe that there is clearly a need to increase research productivity in this area. The POCRIAS has been shown to be a valid and reliable instrument with Asian American participants. We look forward to seeing more research using this measure. Additionally, development of other racial identity measures may help clinicians improve the effectiveness of clinical treatment with this population. One potential way to create new measures is to consider the use and adaptation of other racial identity scales, such as the Multidimensional Inventory of Black Identity (Sellers et al., 1997) or the Cross Racial Identity Scale (Cross & Vandiver, 2001). By refining and modifying these existing measures, new measures can be developed and tested. A second option is to consider the development and validation of measures based on prior qualitative and anecdotal research. For example, Kim's (1981) theoretical model of Asian American identity has been identified as clinically useful, but to date, there has been no development of instruments that assess her model. Researchers could extrapolate salient themes from the construct and develop an item pool that could be tested with Asian American samples. However, because Kim's theory of identity development is based on a sample of Japanese American women, one measurement concern is that it may not be applicable to Asian American males and other Asian American ethnic groups.

Another concern related to generic racial and ethnic identity measures is that they may not adequately assess the constructs with members from specific racial and ethnic minority groups. For example, measures such as the POCRIAS and MEIM were not developed for specific groups and therefore may fail to capture culture-specific information. Therefore, it is recommended that when using a generic measure (such as the MEIM), it should be accompanied with a culture-specific measure, such as the Asian Values Scale (Kim & Hong, 2004) or the Asian American Race-Related Stress Measure (Liang, Li, & Kim, 2004). Both of these measures have been developed and validated with Asian American samples and would better assess cultural and ethnic variables unique to Asian ethnic groups.

Additionally, researchers have differed in their conceptualizations and definitions of racial and ethnic identity (Trimble, 2007). Indeed, research indicates that there is little consensus regarding the meaning of these terms. In many cases, the reader is forced to assume the meaning of these constructs because authors have not clearly defined it. For example, Phinney and Ong's (2007) and Kwan and Sodowsky's (1997) conceptualizations of ethnic identity differ significantly. Phinney and Ong's (2007) MEIM-R places particular emphasis on the cognitive and emotional aspects of exploring and making a commitment to one's ethnic group, but do not view ethnic behaviors as part of ethnic identity. In contrast, Kwan and Sodowsky (1997) hold that ethnic identity embodies both internal (i.e., cognitive, emotional, and moral aspects) and external (i.e., engaging in ethnic customs, eating ethnic food, and speaking the ethnic language) aspects. They suggest that both components comprise ethnic identity. Discrepancies in defining constructs are problematic because they create confusion with regard to conceptualizing specific constructs. In this case, it is unclear as to why Phinney and Ong (2007) contended that ethnic behaviors should

not be regarded as a component of ethnic identity, particularly in light of Phinney's (1990) comprehensive review of ethnic identity literature, which indicated that one of the most useful indicators of ethnic identity is the degree of "involvement in the social life and cultural practices of one's ethnic group" (p. 505).

Disagreements such as these may, in part, be the reason why researchers believe that the "field of multicultural counseling lacks clearly defined constructs, which limit theory development, and seriously hampers empirical investigation" (Ponterotto & Park-Taylor, 2007, p. 283). Therefore, it is recommended that researchers provide clear and concise definitions of the constructs used in research studies. Additionally, researchers should provide the rationale for using specific scales. Why was one scale chosen over another? Use of a particular scale should be presented in the context of the psychological theory from which it emerged.

Our review showed that researchers used various statistical procedures to test the psychometric properties of various scales. However, in some cases, there has been disagreement about the appropriateness of employing certain statistical procedures. For example, Cokley (2007) exhorted that employing an EFA with heterogeneous groups can render different factor structures. Ponterotto and Park-Taylor (2007) add that when conducting analyses with heterogeneous groups, it is good general practice for researchers to conduct a CFA to examine the degree of fit to the model. We echo the recommendations of Cokley, who urged that researchers use discernment when determining which statistical approach to use in light of the sample that they are examining.

In closing, it is evident that the study of racial and ethnic identity development has become a cornerstone in the field of counseling psychology. In this chapter, we have provided an overview of Asian American racial and ethnic identity. Although there were a substantial number of studies on ethnic identity, there was very little research on Asian racial identity. Among the ethnic identity studies, there was little consensus regarding the construct. As noted earlier, there is clearly a need to establish concise definitions of racial and ethnic identity. Moreover, with the increasing number of Asian Americans in the United States, there is a need for researchers to increase research productivity on topics such as these in order that counselors and psychologists are better equipped to improve the overall delivery of health care services to this population.

REFERENCES

Alvarez, A. N. (2002). Racial identity and Asian Americans: Supports and challenges. In M. McEwen, C. M. Kodama, A. N. Alvarez, S. Lee, & C. T. H. Liang (Eds.), *Working with Asian American college students* (pp. 33–44). New York: Jossey-Bass.

Alvarez, A. N., & Helms, J. E. (2001). Racial identity and reflected appraisals as influences on Asian Americans' racial adjustment. *Cultural Diversity and Ethnic Minority Psychology, 7,* 217–231.

Alvarez, A. N., Juang, L., & Liang, C. (2006). Asian Americans and racism: When bad things happen to "model minorities." *Cultural Diversity and Ethnic Minority Psychology, 12,* 477–492.

Anastasi, A., & Urbina, S. (1997). *Psychological testing* (7th ed.). New York: Macmillan.

Aries, E., & Moorehead, K. (1989). The importance of ethnicity in the development of identity of Black adolescents. *Psychological Reports, 65,* 75–82.

Atkinson, D. (2004). *Counseling American minorities* (6th ed.). Boston: McGraw Hill.

Atkinson, D., Morten, G., & Sue, D. W. (1989). *Counseling American minorities: A cross-cultural perspective.* Madison, WI: Brown & Benchmark.

Avery, D., Tonidandel., S., Thomas, K., Johnson, C., & Mack, D. (2007). Assessing the Multigroup Ethnic Identity Measure for measurement equivalence across racial and ethnic groups. *Educational and Psychological Measurement, 67*(5), 877–888.

Barry, D. (2002). An ethnic identity scale for East Asian immigrants. *Journal of Immigrant Health, 4,* 87–94.

Barry, D., & Beitel, M. (2006). Sex role ideology among East Asian immigrants in the United States. *American Journal of Orthopsychiatry, 76,* 512–517.

Barry, D., & Grilo, C. (2003). Cultural, self-esteem, and demographic correlates of perception of personal and group discrimination among East Asian immigrants. *American Journal of Orthopsychiatry, 73,* 223–229.

Bennion, L. D., & Adams, G. R. (1986). A revision of the extended version of the objective measure of ego identity status: An identity instrument of use with late adolescents. *Journal of Adolescent Research, 1,* 183–198.

Bernal, M. E., Knight, G. P., Garza, G. A., Ocampo, K. A., & Cota, M. K. (1990). The development of ethnic identity in Mexican-American children. *Hispanic Journal of Behavioral Science, 12,* 3–24.

Breton, R., Isajiw, W. W., Kalbach, W. E., & Reitz, J. G. (1990). *Ethnic identity and equality.* Toronto: University of Toronto Press.

Campbell, D. (1957). Factors relevant to the validity of experiments in social settings. *Psychological Bulletin, 54,* 297–312.

Carter, R. T. (1995). *The influence of race and racial identity in psychotherapy: Toward a racially inclusive mode.* New York: Wiley.

Chang, T., & Kwan, K. K. (2009). Asian American racial and ethnic identity. In N. Tewari & A. Alvarez (Eds.), *Asian American psychology: Current perspectives* (pp. 113–135). New York: Taylor & Francis.

Chen, G., LePhuoc, P., Guzman, M., Rude, S., & Dodd, B. (2006). Exploring Asian American racial identity. *Cultural Diversity and Ethnic Minority Psychology, 12,* 461–476.

Cheryan, S., & Tsai, J. L. (2007). Ethnic identity. In F. Leong, A. Ebreo, L. Kinoshita, A. Inman, & L. Yang (Eds.), *Handbook of Asian American psychology* (2nd ed., pp. 125–139). Thousand Oaks, CA: Sage.

Cokley, K. O. (2007). Critical issues in the measurement of ethnic and racial identity: A referendum on the state of the field. *Journal of Counseling Psychology, 54,* 224–239.

Cross, W. E., Jr. (1971). The Negro-to-Black conversion experience: Toward a psychology of Black liberation. *Black World, 20,* 13–27.

Cross, W. E., Jr., & Vandiver, B. J. (2001). Nigrescence theory and measurement: Introducing the Cross Racial Identity Scale (CRIS). In J. G. Ponterotto, J. M. Casas, L. A. Suzuki, & C. M. Alexander (Eds.), *Handbook of multicultural counseling* (2nd ed., pp. 371–393). Thousand Oaks, CA: Sage.

DeVellis, R. F. (1991). *Scale development: Theory and applications.* Newbury Park, CA: Sage.

Erikson, E. H. (1968). *Identity: Youth and crisis.* New York: Norton.

Fairbank, J., Reischauer, E., & Craig, A. (1978). *East Asia: Tradition and transformation.* Boston: Houghton Mifflin.

Helms, J. E. (Ed.). (1990). *Black and White racial identity: Theory, research, and practice.* Westport, CT: Greenwood.

Helms, J. (1995). An update of Helms's White and people of color racial identity models. In J. G. Ponterotto, J. M. Casas, L. A. Suzuki, & C. M. Alexander (Eds.), *Handbook of multicultural counseling* (pp. 181–198). Thousand Oaks, CA: Sage.

Helms, J. E., & Cook, D. A. (1999). *Using race and culture in counseling and psychotherapy: Theory and process.* Needham Heights, MA: Allyn & Bacon.

Isajiw, W. W. (1990). Ethnic-identity retention. In R. Breton, W. Isajiw, W. E. Kalbach, & J. G. Reitz (Eds.), *Ethnic identity and equality* (pp. 34–91). Toronto: University of Toronto Press.

Juang, L., Nguyen, H., & Lin, Y. (2006). The ethnic identity, other-group attitudes, and psychosocial functioning of Asian American emerging adults from two contexts. *Journal of Adolescent Research, 21,* 542–568.

Kim, J. (1981). *Process of Asian-American identity development: A study of Japanese American women's perceptions of their struggle to achieve positive identities.* Unpublished doctoral dissertation, University of Massachusetts, Amherst.

Kim, B. S. K., & Hong, S. (2004). A psychometric revision of the Asian Values Scale using the Rasch model. *Measurement and Evaluation in Counseling and Development, 37,* 15–27.

Kohatsu, E., Dulay, M., Lam, C., Concepcion, W., Perez, P., Lopez, C., & Euler, J. (2000). Using racial identity theory to explore racial mistrust and interracial contact among Asian Americans. *Journal of Counseling and Development, 78,* 334–342.

Kohatsu, E., & Phinney, J. S. (1997). Ethnic and racial identity development and mental health. In J. Schulenberg, J. Maggs, & K. Hurrelmann (Eds.), *Health risks and developmental transitions during adolescence* (pp. 420–443). New York: Cambridge University Press.

Kwan, K. (2000). The Internal-External Ethnic Identity Measure: Factor-analytic structures based on a sample of Chinese Americans. *Educational and Psychological Measurement, 60,* 142–152.

Kwan, K., & Sodowsky, G. (1997). Internal and external ethnic identity and their correlates: A study of Chinese American immigrants. *Journal of Multicultural Counseling and Development, 25,* 51–67.

Lee, R. M. (2003). Do ethnic identity and other-group orientation protect against discrimination for Asian Americans? *Journal of Counseling Psychology, 50,* 133–141.

Lee, R. M. (2005). Resilience against discrimination: Ethnic identity and other-group orientation as protective factors for Korean Americans. *Journal of Counseling Psychology, 52,* 36–44.

Lee, R. M., Choe, J., Kim, G., & Ngo, V. (2000). Construction of the Asian American Family Conflict Scale. *Journal of Counseling Psychology, 47,* 211–222.

Lee, R. M., Falbo, T., Doh, H., & Park, S. (2001). The Korean diasporic experience: Measuring ethnic identity in the United States and China. *Cultural Diversity and Ethnic Minority Psychology, 3,* 207–216.

Lee, R., & Yoo, H. (2004). Structure and measurement of ethnic identity for Asian American college students. *Journal of Counseling Psychology, 51,* 263–269.

Liang, C. T. H., Li, L. C., & Kim, B. K. S. (2004). The Asian American Racism-Related Stress Inventory: Development, factor analysis, reliability, and validity. *Journal of Counseling Psychology, 51,* 103–114.

Liu, W. M. (2002). Exploring the lives of Asian American men: Racial identity, male role norms, gender role conflict, and prejudicial attitudes. *Psychology of Men and Masculinity, 3,* 107–118.

Marcia, J. (1966). Development and validation of ego-identity status. *Journal of Personality and Social Psychology, 3,* 551–558.

Marcia, J. (1980). Identity in adolescence. In J. Adelson (Ed.), *Handbook of adolescent psychology* (pp. 159–187). New York: Wiley.

Neville, H. A., Lilly, R. L., Duran, G., Lee, R. M., & Browne, L. (2000). Construction and initial validation of the Color-Blind Racial Attitudes Scale (CoBRAS). *Journal of Counseling Psychology, 47,* 59–70.

Nunnally, J. C., & Bernstein, I. H. (1994). *Psychometric theory* (3rd ed.). New York: McGraw-Hill.

Phinney, J. (1990). Ethnic identity in adolescents and adults: Review of research. *Psychological Bulletin, 108,* 499–514.

Phinney, J. (1992). The Multigroup Ethnic Identity Measure: A new scale for use with diverse groups. *Journal of Adolescent Research, 7,* 156–176.

Phinney, J. (1993). A three-stage model of ethnic identity development. In M. E. Bernal & G. P. Knight (Eds.), *Ethnic identity: Formation and transmission among Hispanics and other minorities* (pp. 61–79). Albany: State University of New York Press.

Phinney, J. (2003). Ethnic identity and acculturation. In K. Chun, P. Organista, & G. Marin (Eds.), *Acculturation: Advances in theory, measurement, and applied research* (pp. 63–82). Washington, DC: American Psychological Association.

Phinney, J., & Ong, A. (2007). Conceptualization and measurement of ethnic identity: Current status and future directions. *Journal of Counseling Psychology, 54,* 271–281.

Ponterotto, J. G., Gretchen, D., Utsey, S., Stracuzzi, T., & Saya, R. (2003). The Multigroup Ethnic Identity Measure (MEIM): Psychometric review and further validity testing. *Educational and Psychological Measurement, 63,* 502–515.

Ponterotto, J. G., & Park-Taylor, J. (2007). Racial and ethnic identity theory, measurement, and research in counseling psychology: Present status and future directions. *Journal of Counseling Psychology, 54*, 282–294.

Ponterotto, J. G., & Ruckdeschel, D. (2007). An overview of coefficient alpha and a reliability matrix for estimating adequacy of internal consistency coefficients with psychological research methods. *Perceptual and Motor Skills, 105*, 997–1014.

Ponterotto, J. G., Utsey, S. O., & Pedersen, P. (2006). *Preventing prejudice: A guide for counselors, educators, & parents* (2nd ed.). Thousand Oaks, CA: Sage.

Roberts, R., Phinney, J., Masse, L., & Chenet, R. (1999). The structure of ethnic identity of young adolescents from diverse ethnocultural groups. *Journal of Early Adolescence, 19*, 301–322.

Sellers, R. M., Rowley, S. A., Chavous, T. M., Shelton, J. N., & Smith, M. A. (1997). Multidimensional Inventory of Black Identity: A preliminary investigation of reliability and construct validity. *Journal of Personality & Social Psychology, 73*, 805–815.

Shrake, E., & Rhee, S. (2004). Ethnic identity as a predictor of problem behaviors among Korean American adolescents. *Adolescence, 39*, 601–622.

Spencer, M., & Markstrom-Adams, C. (1990). Identity processes among racial and ethnic minority children in America. *Child Development, 61*, 290–310.

Sue, D. W., & Sue, D. (2008). *Counseling the culturally diverse: Theory and practice* (5th ed.). New York: Wiley.

Suinn, R. M., Richard-Figueroa, K., Lew, S., & Vigil, P. (1987). The Suinn-Lew Asian Self-Identity Acculturation Scale: An initial report. *Educational and Psychological Measurement, 47*, 401–407.

Tabachnick, B. G., & Fidell, L. S. (2007). *Using multivariate statistics* (5th ed.). Boston: Allyn & Bacon.

Trimble, J. E. (2007). Prolegomena for the connotation of construct use in the measurement of ethnic and racial identity. *Journal of Counseling Psychology, 54*, 247–258.

Tsai, G., & Curbow, B. (2001). The development and validation of the Taiwanese Ethnic Identity Scale (TEIS): A "derived etic" approach. *Journal of Immigrant Health, 3*, 199–212.

Waterman, A. S. (1988). Identity status theory and Erikson's theory: Communalities and differences. *Developmental Review, 8*, 185–208.

Worrell, F. (2000). A validity study of scores on the Multigroup Ethnic Identity Measure based on a sample of academically talented adolescents. *Educational and Psychological Measurement, 60*, 439–447.

Yip, T., & Cross, W. (2004). A daily diary study of mental health and community involvement outcomes for three Chinese American social identities. *Cultural Diversity and Ethnic Minority Psychology, 4*, 394–408.

Yoo, H., & Lee, R. M. (2005). Ethnic identity and approach-type coping as moderators of the racial discrimination/well being relation in Asian Americans. *Journal of Counseling Psychology, 52*, 497–506.

24

Native Hawaiian Identity and Measurement

An Ecological Perspective of Indigenous Identity Development

LAURIE D. McCUBBIN AND THU A. DANG

Essentialist notions of race have a long history in society basing physical appearances and phenotypes as indicative of more profound positive and negative characteristics (Stubblefield, 1995), including personality traits, intelligence, cognitive abilities, values, and behaviors. These essentialist notions have influenced the classification and construction of measures in delineating boundaries between racial groups and clarifying membership to one's ethnic or cultural group. In this chapter, we describe the history of colonization; current trends; and social processes facing indigenous groups, specifically Native Hawaiians, in the United States.[1] Essentialist and nonessentialist conceptualizations of race will be presented, with particular attention to decolonization, diaspora, and multiethnicity that challenge essentialist notions of race. Additionally, an alternative ecological paradigm is presented to assist in advancing the efforts in research and measurement in considering different contexts that affect indigenous

identity development. Finally, the relationship between essentialism and measurement will be observed in current measures of Native Hawaiian identity. In conclusion, a discussion of the strengths and limitations of an essentialist perspective will be presented as well as a call for more comprehensive research on indigenous identity development that can help inform legislation and promote self-determination among indigenous communities.

THE HISTORY AND COLONIZATION OF NATIVE HAWAIIANS

According to the current U.S. census (U.S. Census Bureau, 2000), there are 401,162 Native Hawaiians living in the United States, with approximately 60% of Hawaiians living in the state of Hawai'i and 40% on the continental United States. The numbers of people identifying themselves as Native Hawaiians has grown in the past 10 years, with more than 90,000 more Hawaiians identified from 1990 to 2000 (McCubbin, Ishikawa, & McCubbin, 2007). However, despite the increase of people identifying as Native Hawaiian, the actual number of pure Hawaiians has declined to less than 10,000 (Noyes, 1996), representing less than 1% of the total Hawaiian population.

It is argued that the Native Hawaiian (*Kanaka Maoli*—meaning "true" or "real" in Hawaiian) (Blaisdell, 1993) people came to the Hawaiian Islands around 350 A.D. from Polynesia. By the 18th century, the Hawaiian population thrived with a well-established culture. Estimates of the Native Hawaiian population at this time vary from 400,000 (Schmitt, 1968) to 800,000 (Kane, 1997). On January 18, 1778, Captain James Cook arrived in the Hawaiian Islands from Britain, signifying the beginning of the colonization process of the Hawaiian Islands and its indigenous population. After 100 years of Western contact, the indigenous population declined by 90%, with an estimated 53,900 in 1876, because of disease, warfare, and some say despair (Marsella, Oliveira, Plummer, & Crabbe, 1995). With missionaries arriving in the 1920s, Christianity was spread across the islands. While saving the souls of the native peoples, these missionaries also took claim of the land and assumed a great amount of power on the islands (Marsella et al., 1995). Even though the Kingdom of Hawai'i was federally recognized by the U.S. government, a group of American businessmen, with the assistance of the U.S. Navy, invaded the nation and overthrew the last Hawaiian queen, Queen Lili'uokalani. Despite numerous attempts to reinstate the Kingdom of Hawai'i as a sovereign nation, Hawai'i became a territory of the United States in 1898 without a single vote from the Native Hawaiian people, thus establishing the colonization of the indigenous people and the land.

In attempts to make amends for the forced colonization of the Native Hawaiians, in 1921, the U.S. Congress passed the Hawaiian Homes Commission Act, which set aside 200,000 acres of island land to be used to establish homelands for Native Hawaiians with 50% or more Hawaiian blood[2] (Council for Native Hawaiian Advancement, 2005; Hawaii Advisory Committee to the U.S. Commission on Civil Rights, 2001; Spoehr et al., 1998). In 1959, Hawai'i became the 50th state in the United States, culminating in the

federal government returning the ceded lands (i.e., the lands that were once property of the Hawaiian monarchy) to the state. One of the purposes of these ceded lands was for the "betterment of the conditions of Native Hawaiians." The Office of Hawaiian Affairs (OHA) was created in 1978 to manage this share of the ceded land revenues (Bolante, 2003). Its mission includes the preservation of the Native Hawaiian culture, protection of the rights of these indigenous people, and enhancement of the lifestyles of Native Hawaiians (Office of Hawaiian Affairs, 2003). This enhancement and betterment of the conditions for Native Hawaiians have included a variety of activities, such as promoting education and health care for this population. Funding has been provided for early childhood programs, charter schools, creation of indigenous teaching methods and curricula, and scholarships for Hawaiians to pursue higher education (Bernardino, 2008).

The history of oppression and colonization of Native Hawaiians has been recognized by the United States through specific acts and legislation that acknowledges the unique status of Native Hawaiians, which has been viewed as similar to Native Americans and Alaskan Natives—politically, legally, and culturally (Hawaii Advisory Committee, 2001). In 1993, Congress passed a resolution and President Clinton signed Public Law 103–150, which acknowledged the centennial commemoration of the overthrow of the Kingdom of Hawai'i and a formal apology to Native Hawaiians for the improper role of the U.S. military in support of the overthrow (Hawaii Advisory Committee, 2001). Despite this acknowledgment of the colonization of Native Hawaiians and the similarities with other indigenous groups in the United States, as of 2008, Native Hawaiians do not have tribal status, are not recognized as a sovereign entity, and have ambiguous standing in terms of federal recognition. Unfortunately, given the ambiguous legal standing of Native Hawaiians in the United States paired with a lack of awareness and understanding of the cultural genocide and colonization of these indigenous people by most Americans, Native Hawaiians and their respective resources continue to be limited, and those currently available are under threat of elimination.

The agencies and trusts designed to protect and promote Native Hawaiians and their well-being are coming under legal scrutiny, with an increasing number of lawsuits questioning the mission of these organizations. The legal troubles for these institutions, such as the Office of Hawaiian Affairs and Kamehameha Schools, are coming from multiple sources. In the U.S. Supreme Court case of *Rice v. Cayetano* in February 2000, the plaintiff charged that OHA and the voting provisions (e.g., only Native Hawaiians residing in the Hawaiian Islands can vote) were racially discriminatory and violated the Fourteenth and Fifteenth Amendments to the U.S. Constitution (Kauanui, 2005). The U.S. Supreme Court favored the plaintiff, declaring that the OHA voting restrictions violated the Fifteenth Amendment, thus creating the "essential groundwork for further [legal] assaults on Hawaiian lands and people" (Kauanui, 2005, p. 9). Since 2000, several lawsuits have been filed against OHA and private trusts serving Native Hawaiians, charging these institutions with violating the U.S. Constitution by engaging in racial discrimination. For example, Kamehameha Schools has faced some serious legal woes around their admissions preference policy for Native Hawaiian students. Although the school was intended to serve Native Hawaiian children as specified in the will of Princess Bernice Pauahi Bishop (the last descendant of the Hawaiian monarchy), this has been legally challenged in *Doe v. Kamehameha Schools*, declaring that the racial preference policy is unconstitutional. Additionally, although the blood quantum level is enforced for Hawaiian homelands, the Office of Hawaiian Affairs is also being challenged for its deviation from this same practice of providing programs for anyone with any Hawaiian blood quantum. A federal lawsuit was filed by five Native Hawaiians, claiming that OHA was illegally spending dollars by serving Hawaiians with any blood quantum and that programs and funding must adhere to the 50% or more blood quantum regulation.

According to the Statehood Admissions Act, Native Hawaiian refers to "any descendant of the aboriginal peoples inhabiting the Hawaiian Islands in 1778 (prior to Western contact)." Therefore, any person with any blood quantum of Native Hawaiian blood is considered Hawaiian. However, trusts and agencies may be held accountable for requirements of blood quantum when distributing resources for Native Hawaiians (e.g., Hawaiian homelands). With the current legal issues

facing OHA, additional programs funded by this organization may warrant greater due diligence in accounting for blood quantum criteria in programs in education and health care. Additionally, the majority of the programs that OHA funds are accessible only to those Hawaiians who live on the islands, leaving 40% residing in the continental United States without access to these resources.

Given the cultural loss and genocide of Hawaiian people, and the threat to private trusts, institutions, and programs serving Native Hawaiians, the need to have a clear definition of who is Hawaiian is imminent in legal circumstances. Identity development from a psychological perspective is conceptualized as a developmental process (Helms, 2007; Phinney & Ong, 2007), and it can be ambiguous and change over time and in different contexts. Due to the developmental nature of identity and the need to unify around a singular definition of this identity for sociopolitical reasons, one can easily see the conundrum and challenge facing Hawaiians and counseling psychologists in defining and measuring this complex social phenomenon.

DEFINING RACE, ETHNICITY, AND CULTURE AMONG INDIGENOUS PEOPLES

A great amount of energy and concentration has focused on measuring cultural aspects of being Hawaiian and understanding Hawaiian identity. This focus has emerged over the past two decades in relation to public policies, political entities (Government Accountability Office, 2008), and health (McMullin, 2005). Simultaneously, the field of counseling psychology has played a prominent role in the proliferation of measures of identity development with varying definitions of race, ethnicity, and culture (Ponterotto & Mallinckrodt, 2007; Ponterotto & Park-Taylor, 2007). While social scientists debate what constitutes race, ethnicity, or culture, the demand for clarity of Native Hawaiian identification has become critical in order to protect Native Hawaiian rights and funding for education, health care, and land ownership, which are constantly being scrutinized (Government Accountability Office, 2008). As the counseling psychology field conceptualizes the distinctions between race, ethnicity, and culture and the identity measures of identity development (Cokley, 2007; Helms, 2007; Ponterotto & Mallinckrodt, 2007; Trimble, 2007), indigenous peoples' identities persist with permeable boundaries between these terms.

According to Spickard and Burroughs (2000), an ethnic group is a cluster of people who view themselves as connected to one another, have a shared ancestry, and are seen by others as a group entity. Race is based on physical characteristics and associated with having a biological base to establish authenticity. Although recent genetic research has generally refuted this biological notion of race (Graves, 2004; Samuels, 2007), greater consensus has been achieved when race is defined as a socially constructed phenomenon and used as a social and political means to classify people (Cokley, 2007; Helms, 2007; Phinney & Ong, 2007; Spickard & Burroughs, 2000).

Ethnic groups are also viewed as subdivisions of major racial categories such as Asians being a racial group and Japanese, Chinese, Korean, and Vietnamese being ethnic groups subsumed under this racial category. In applying the same line of reasoning, Native Hawaiians may be viewed as an ethnic group under the racial category of Pacific Islanders. Spickard and Burroughs (2000) point out several problems with this line of reasoning, the most prominent of which is the lack of distinction between racial categories and the lack of understanding of the differences between ethnic categories such as Japanese, Korean, and Filipino.

Racialization is another important concept to consider when discussing the differences between race and ethnicity. Race may refer to the physical features of a group of people, and ethnicity may refer to those who share common ancestors and culture. Note, however, that the distinctions between race and ethnicity disappear and the single race category becomes most salient in the presence of acts of racism or discrimination or when "someone does something bad to them on account of their ethnicity" (Spickard & Burroughs, 2000, p. 5). This is the process of racialization, when a dominant group imposes perceived images, stereotypes, or discriminatory actions against a subordinate group on the basis of race. These racialized occurrences (imposing discrimination or stereotypes onto a person based on his or her race or ethnicity) can influence and affect a person's identity development. In order to

examine the measures associated with Hawaiian identity, one needs to look beyond definitions of race and ethnicity found in literature and focus instead on understanding the phenomenon through a racialized lens. Specifically, researchers need to examine the racialized contexts in which indigenous peoples live and the colonial laws under which they live in order to better understand the developmental process toward self-conceptualization as an indigenous person.

ESSENTIALIST AND NONESSENTIALIST PERSPECTIVES OF RACE

Essentialism refers to a philosophical and racialized stance about constructions of race, ethnicity, and culture. Essentialist components of race indicate that certain physical or phenotype characteristics denoted by racial terms are indicative of deeper characteristics that can be either positive or negative (Stubblefield, 1995). The essentialist perspective of Native Hawaiians' physical appearance and racial phenotypes as it relates to negative characteristics has been well-documented in research (Adams, 1934; Hall, 1905; Livesay, 1942; Louttit, 1931a, 1931b; Porteus, 1939; Pratt, 1929). Negative characteristics that have been applied to the Hawaiian race include laziness, low intelligence, mental retardation, and sexual promiscuity. Positive characteristics have also been identified as Hawaiian, including positive personality traits such as being hospitable, easygoing, friendly, generous, and trusting, and having natural talents in music, dance, and the arts.

A nonessential perspective focuses on the issue that the differences in physical appearance do not necessarily mean inherited traits, personality characteristics, or innate talents. Rather, race is a socially constructed category in order to classify people accordingly (Samuels, 2007; Stubblefield, 1995). Measures such as racial identity (Cokley, 2007; Helms, 2007) and ethnic identity (Phinney & Ong, 2007) are based on a nonessentialist perspective focusing instead on the social construction of race and ethnicity and the developmental process of identity.

Measurements of acculturation, dimensions of culture, and enculturation can be viewed as "essentialist" indexes independent of the creators' intentions and thus used by various groups and institutions as a "racial" litmus test (Samuels, 2007) of Hawaiianness. By scoring high on cultural affiliation or Hawaiian acculturation, one can infer the metrics of the essential amount of "Hawaiianness" needed for access to resources such as health care, homelands, and education. The Hawaiian Homelands Act is based on this essentialist notion by using a 50% blood quantum level as a criterion, inferring that those who have 50% or more Hawaiian blood are more "essentially" Hawaiian, score higher on a racial litmus test, and therefore are more deserving or qualified to acquire homesteads.

Where measurement and essentialism intersect is embedded in social justice, affirmative action, and the determination of human rights and access to resources. Specifically, the critical question facing many groups of color is, "What are the criteria for identifying someone as belonging to a group?" (Stubblefield, 1995, pp. 341–342). This is beyond socially determined criteria for belonging to a group of color such as "are you Hawaiian enough?" More specifically, from a social justice perspective, and given the reality of racial oppression in this country and the need to recognize, acknowledge, and rectify past atrocities such as genocide and slavery, how do policymakers decide who is racially essential enough to deserve access to resources such as financial aid and scholarships for education, land rights, and health care? Are psychologists creating measures that were intended to understand and promote positive psychological functioning among indigenous peoples, but now can be used to perpetuate an essentialist paradigm of race and be used by policymakers as a barrier for Native peoples to obtain resources such as land?

THE INTERSECTION OF DECOLONIZATION AND ESSENTIALISM

A new issue is emerging that is unique to indigenous peoples when considering colonization and identity development: What is one's indigenous identity without the context of colonization? How does one become decolonized? One method is to look to the past, to the traditions of the ancestors and practices before the "contamination" by the West began (Smith, 1999). As articulated by Smith (1999), this trend toward decolonization is rooted in the belief that indigenous people

need to remember who they are by looking to the past. Current measures of Native Hawaiian identity may be based on this retrospective examination. This phenomenon of "looking to the past" is part of the decolonizing process that can help move an indigenous group toward the next phase of decolonization—the need to realign together as a unified group toward revolution and/or self-determination (Smith, 1999).

This struggle to decolonize while also maintaining one's indigenous identity can clearly be seen in the Hawaiian language movement and the need to determine what is authentic Hawaiian language. Within the university, present Hawaiian language speakers are really acquiring a second language based on the written word (Wong, 1999). On the other side of the language issue is the past language, spoken by our elders and the need to stay "pure" to the traditions and customs of the past. However, the future is challenging for the Hawaiian language. As with any language, the need to grow and adapt to the changing times can be seen as threatening the authenticity and "purity" of the Hawaiian language spoken by the elders. Essentialism or authenticity is a clear issue in the revitalization of the Hawaiian language (Wong, 1999). The language is also symbolic of the Hawaiian identity as cultural practices, customs, and language are revitalized. How will the Hawaiian identity grow, adapt, and be revitalized in the 21st century? Growth, change, and adaptation can be construed as significant challenges to the essentialist notions of Hawaiianness. Two core social processes that present formidable challenges to the essentialist perspective are diaspora and multiethnicity.

THREATS TO ESSENTIALIST NOTIONS OF RACE: DIASPORA AND MULTIETHNICITY

Variations in the definitions of diaspora can be found in the literature; therefore, the social form of diaspora will be used in this discussion. The social form refers to the dispersion or scattering of a community or group of people with a collective identity from their original homeland, nation, or specified geographical region (Vertovec, 1997). Additionally, Lee and colleagues defined diaspora as an ethnic group that is persecuted, oppressed, and eventually driven from its homeland

and involuntarily relocated to new places or land (Lee, Noh, Yoo, & Doh, 2007). Spickard (2002a) points out that a diasporic model is more appropriate to apply to Pacific Islanders given the history of colonization and the displacement of Hawaiians due to the privatization of land ownership by missionaries and foreign businessmen. Diaspora is also consistent with the continued connectedness between the Native Hawaiians and the land. Diaspora also accounts for the trend of Hawaiians migrating back "home" to the land after leaving for a period of time for education or economic opportunities. This trend has been referred to as return migration (Connell, 2002).

In terms of measuring indigenous identity, does one's identity decrease if one leaves the land? Kauanui (1998) conducted a critical analysis of various statements by Hawaiian leaders, noting that when leaders urge fellow Hawaiians on the continental United States to come home, they are also supporting the argument "that living away from Hawaii means being 'less Hawaiian,' less authentic" (p. 688). Kauanui pointed out that this line of reasoning of the "absentee Hawaiian" who migrates or moves off the islands also can be seen as abandoning the land, the cause, and the Hawaiian people. As most empirical studies focused solely on Hawaiians living on the islands, the impact of diaspora has not been fully addressed in research. This issue of diaspora is critical to understanding the development of identity among indigenous people. Research samples on identity would benefit from inclusiveness of those Hawaiians who live on Native Lands (e.g., homesteads) and those who have migrated to other cities and areas for economic, educational, and personal reasons.

Despite assertions by the Hawaiian community and Hawaiian organizations for indigenous peoples to return home (see Akaka, 1993), how easy is this transition to come "home"? Root (1998) discusses the trauma of "hazing," which is a process that is used to prove one is an insider through a demeaning process of racial and ethnic authenticity testing. Standards to pass these hazing rituals can seem variable and ever changing as they are determined by the one giving the test (Root, 1998). For Hawaiians, especially those coming back to the islands after being away, this authenticity testing can occur on a number of levels, including the family, workplace, community, and social and political organizations. Hazing can have various effects, from being

a stressor for a short period of time; to a repeated chronic abuse pattern traumatizing a person to no longer associate with being a member of a racial or ethnic group, as the "price of acceptance by the ethnic community is too high" (Root, 1998, p. 243).

Osorio (2006) alludes to this authenticity testing of Hawaiian leaders. Hawaiians can assassinate a Hawaiian leader figuratively and literally through spreading rumors, creating suspicion, and getting them out of the islands (Osorio, 2006). Questions emerge regarding the hazing rituals associated with being Native, and more importantly, who decides who passes or fails the litmus test of being "Native." Does internalized oppression manifest itself in the notion of essentialism, and is it acted out using authenticity testing? More research is needed to understand the process of diaspora and authenticity testing/racialized hazing and the respective impacts on indigenous identity development.

Another perspective in understanding the processes of identity development is the Pan-ethnicity movement, which results in lumping together formerly separate ethnic groups into one category (Espiritu, 1992), such as Hawaiians being part of Pacific Islander Americans (Spickard, 2002b). However, this model de-emphasizes the connection to places of origin and focuses more on a collective identity. One example of a new trend of the Pan-ethnic model is multiracial or multiethnic identity that may threaten essentialist notions of race.

Of the Hawaiians living in the United States, 35.1% indicated Hawaiian as their sole racial status (Hart & McCubbin, 2006). However, 39% of Native Hawaiians identified themselves as multiethnic, with 10 different combinations including Japanese Hawaiian, Chinese Hawaiian, Filipino Hawaiian, and Caucasian Japanese Hawaiian. Additionally, 35.2% of the Native Hawaiian population indicated having ancestral Hawaiians; however, this group did not claim Hawaiian ethnicity in the 2000 U.S. census. Also, given the statistics previously mentioned that less than 1% of the Native Hawaiian population is 100% of Hawaiian origin by blood quantum, the estimate of multiethnic Hawaiians could be increased from nearly two thirds (64.9%) to an estimate of 99% of the total population.

What are the effects of being multiethnic on indigenous identity development? Does defining oneself as multiethnic become a threat to one's indigenous identity, or does it strengthen it? The same argument could be made that the Pan-ethnic term "Asian American" makes a Japanese person less Japanese. So, if someone defines himself or herself as a multiethnic individual, does that make him or her less Hawaiian? Osorio (2006) makes a clear distinction about being Hawaiian, stating that "being Hawaiian is ultimately about not wishing to be anything else" (Osorio, 2006, p. 23). This statement can be inferred to mean that to be "essentially Hawaiian," one must see oneself as being solely Hawaiian, nationally, racially, and/or ethnically. By identifying oneself as Hawaiian and other ethnicities, one may be threatening the cause for Hawaiian people (i.e., self-determination). Yet earlier in this same work, he points out that defining one's Hawaiianness by one's knowledge of Hawaiian history, remaining on the islands, and speaking the Hawaiian language does not necessarily mean one is "Hawaiian." Therefore, from a behavioral and geographic perspective, Osorio does not take a pure essentialist stance: A Hawaiian can have a limited knowledge of Hawaiian language or can live in the continental United States. However, politically, as a Hawaiian, one must maintain a sole identity as a Hawaiian and thus remain "pure" to the Hawaiian cause. Therefore, assertions of what is Hawaiian from an essentialist perspective may vacillate depending on the context or the ecological system in which a person is currently functioning, such as one's geographical location or political arena.

To limit this essentialist discussion to individual Hawaiian leaders or Hawaiian scholars would curtail one's understanding of the context and the sociopolitical climate that currently exists around Hawaiians. The soil in which essentialism has grown is embedded, nurtured, and sustained by essentialist policies within the U.S. government and the colonized mind-set that remains prevalent when distributing resources to indigenous peoples. Essentialist notions of race can be interpreted as a product of colonization, slavery, and oppression.

REFRAMING NATIVE IDENTITY: AN ECOLOGICAL PERSPECTIVE FOR INDIGENOUS PEOPLES

A paradigm shift is needed in research to examine indigenous identity development through an ecological framework in order to understand the contextual issues facing Native populations today. This shift is already occurring in counseling psychology (see Coleman, Norton, Miranda, & McCubbin, 2003; Root, 1998, 2000). An ecological model can take into account the aforementioned critical factors affecting indigenous communities: colonization, decolonization, diaspora, and multiethnicity. Additionally, this framework allows for one to expand his or her identity or identities to be more inclusive of multiple dimensions.

Drawing from Bronfenbrenner's (1979) four ecological systems, consisting of the microsystem, mesosystem, exosystem, and macrosystem, each of these systems refers to a nested structure that influences the developing person ranging from proximal relationships (e.g., caregiver and child relationship) to more distal influences, such as government or public policy (Bronfenbrenner, 1979). Additionally, these nested structures have a bidirectional relationship, meaning that one aspect of a system can influence the individual's development as well as the individual can also influence that particular system (i.e., parent to child or child to parent).

The microsystem involves the innermost level of the environment, which consists of the individual and any two-person relationship. The family (also referred to as *'ohana* in Hawaiian) can consist of one's nuclear family (mother, father, and siblings); extended family; informal relationships such as friends and neighbors; and informally adopted relationships, such as relatives connected not by blood but by love (McCubbin et al., 2007). For Hawaiians, the family is the central vehicle through which changing and multiethnic identities are shaped and molded through its schema of values, beliefs, and expectations (McCubbin, 2006). Given the large number of Native Hawaiians who are multiethnic, an individual may be exposed to different cultures or ethnicities growing up, such as Hawaiian, Japanese, and Portuguese, depending on the primary caregiver and other interpersonal relationships in the person's life. How a family expresses its racial heritage can affect an individual's identity development, which may or may not be Native Hawaiian. Also, depending on extended family members' and friends' proximity to an individual, this may affect how salient his or her Hawaiian identity is. For example, living in a house on a Hawaiian homeland may include extended family members, friends, and neighbors all strongly affiliated with being Native Hawaiian, which can affect identity development. However, if one moves to Oregon for college, his or her identity may shift and change as this context changes.

The mesosystem encompasses the interactions and settings that exist in a person's immediate surroundings, such as the family or school. As stated earlier, the family can be a very important socializing influence on an individual's identity development and ethnic schema. The family can provide support and protection for indigenous peoples in times of cultural loss and trauma by colonization. Also, because of the oral tradition, familial stories about colonization can be passed down from generation to generation, which can shape and define one's self-concept as an indigenous person.

The type of school or educational setting in which a child is placed during his or her developmental years also can influence indigenous identity development. In the state of Hawai'i, several educational options may be available, including public schools, private schools, and Native Hawaiian language immersion programs. Children growing up in the continental United States may have fewer options in education for a curriculum designed specifically for Native Hawaiian children. Measures of Hawaiian culture and identity may be influenced by the educational setting each participant attended. Because of diaspora and multiethnicity, children may change school systems. For example, a multiethnic child (Japanese and Hawaiian) may start out in elementary school in a Japanese immersion program, shift to a private school during adolescence focusing on Native Hawaiian cultural immersion, and finish his or her college education at a predominantly white university in another state. These context influences of school systems and their changes in curriculum and foci on different cultures and races (Japanese, Hawaiian, and European American) can affect one's identity development from childhood to early adulthood.

The exosystem refers to the structure of the larger community (Bronfenbrenner, 1979). An example of the exosystem is the neighborhood, which may involve communities on the Hawaiian Islands and/or those in the continental United States. For example, many cultural enclaves exist on the islands and outside of the islands of Hawai'i that focus on a "local" culture, a fusion of Japanese, Chinese, Korean, Portuguese, and Hawaiian cultural practices, languages, and food. Many Native Hawaiians and people from the islands relocate to cities on the West Coast, including Seattle, Las Vegas, Salt Lake City, and Los Angeles. Neighborhoods in these cities may have Hawaiian grocery stores or restaurants that serve Hawaiian foods. These neighborhoods may have hula schools or elders who can teach others the Hawaiian language. However, Hawaiians who move to other states or more rural areas may have less access to these cultural resources, thus affecting their knowledge of Hawaiian culture and the depth of their affiliation with cultural values, beliefs, protocols, and traditions. Also, the timing of diaspora and circular migration in an individual's life (e.g., adolescence or later adulthood during retirement) and the family's developmental stage (e.g., just-married couples or "empty nest" families) can also shape the influence of the exosystem on Hawaiian identity. Institutions and processes in the exosystem need to be taken into consideration when examining identity development and using measures of Hawaiian identity.

The macrosystem includes a core of cultural, political, legal, and economic influences that shape an individual's development (Bronfenbrenner, 1979). At the macro level, indigenous peoples' identity development is affected by legislation and policy decisions such as the use of blood quantum as a criterion for access to land or health and educational programs. It is paradoxical that the responsibility for proving one's indigenous identity is placed on the shoulders of the oppressed group; however, the decision of what is acceptable and used to determine access to resources is in the hands of the colonizer the majority of the time. Indigenous institutions or programs that adhere to the colonial standards and essential definitions of Hawaiianness (e.g., those who live on the islands and identify solely as Hawaiian) are rewarded with funding. The challenge to an indigenous person developing his or her identity is to strive for a balance between cultural heritage, ancestral knowledge, and his or her current adaptation with imperial and colonial laws and practices under the hegemonic doctrine of race. Native institutions must also find their identity and mission within these varying contexts and satisfy various stakeholders and their essentialist criteria of race in order to survive. However, other institutions with predominantly European American leaders do not have this challenge. This delicate balance—trying to balance new experiences and cultures while maintaining an indigenous sense of self—can be challenging and overwhelming at times. Colonial influences on laws and distribution of resources may foreclose one's racial and ethnic identity and result in limiting Native peoples' ability to adapt, grow, and develop.

If a collective definition of Hawaiian identity is not deemed satisfactory and "democratic" in imperial and colonialist terms, the essential rights of Hawaiians (i.e., the right to land, education, health care, and the freedom to define one's self) may be threatened. This conundrum and reality is facing many indigenous groups as they work toward self-determination, sovereignty, and reparations. Therefore, rather than take an essentialist stance of who is indigenous or Native Hawaiian, one is called upon to give weight to the nature of human rights and how this fits the essential definitions of freedom and democracy.

Currently, the essentialist perspective still permeates issues facing Native Hawaiians at the macro level, which in turn affects the microsystem and the individual's development. This influence can be seen clearly upon review of the psychological measures of Hawaiian identity at the individual/microsystem level.

CURRENT MEASURES OF HAWAIIAN IDENTITY

We were purposeful in reviewing measures designed for Native Hawaiians' cultural affiliation and identity (see Table 24.1) and included instruments reported in published articles and dissertations in order to

Table 24.1 Native Hawaiian Measures

Measure	Reference	Item Count	Subscales	Subscales' Reliabilities	Validity
Na Mea Hawai'i: A Hawaiian Acculturation Scale	Rezentes (1993)	34	1. Knowledge of Hawaiian vocabulary 2. Knowledge of Hawaiian customs 3. Knowledge of Hawaiian history 4. Knowledge of Hawaiian culture 5. Participation in Contemporary Hawaiian Culture	n/a	n/a
Da Kine Scale (Hawaii Local Acculturation Scale)	Bautista (2003)	46	1. Pidgin-Island Living 2. Customs-Beliefs 3. Relationships	$\alpha = .92$ $\alpha = .92$ $\alpha = .66$	n/a
Hawaiian Culture Scale—Adolescent Version	Hishinuma et al. (2000)	50	Hawaiian 1. Customs 2. Lifestyles 3. Activities 4. Folklore 5. Causes—Locations 6. Causes—Access 7. Language Proficiency	non-Hawaiian $\alpha = .88$ $\alpha = .87$ $\alpha = .90$ $\alpha = .82$ $\alpha = .96$ $\alpha = .87$ $\alpha = .94$	n/a $\alpha = .88$ $\alpha = .86$ $\alpha = .87$ $\alpha = .76$ $\alpha = .96$ $\alpha = .82$ $\alpha = .94$
He'ana Mana'o O Na Mo'omeheu Hawai'i (Hawaiian Ethnocultural Inventory) (HEI)	Crabbe (2002)	80	1. Beliefs in Hawaiian Cultural Practices 2. Knowledge of Hawaiian Cultural Practices 3. Frequency of Performing Arts 4. Frequency of Ocean Traditions 5. Frequency of Spiritual and Family Customs	$\alpha = .97$ $\alpha = .95$ $\alpha = .96$ $\alpha = .89$ $\alpha = .85$	n/a

identify measures of Native Hawaiians created largely by indigenous scholars/scientists. Three perspectives—acculturation, dimensions of culture, and enculturation—underlie the development of measures for Native Hawaiians. Acculturation refers to the process by which an individual learns to adapt to the majority/host culture after leaving or setting aside his or her home country and culture. This model is commonly used with immigrants coming to the United States. Culture refers to "the unique behavior and lifestyle shared by a group of people, and includes customs, habits, beliefs, and values that shape emotions, behavior, and life pattern" (Tseng, 2003, p. 1). It is learned and passed down through generations and is susceptible to change over time. Enculturation is the process by which an individual learns about her or his native culture.

Two measures were based on acculturation: the Na Mea Hawai'i Scale (Rezentes, 1993) and the Da Kine Scale (Bautista, 2003). Rezentes (1993) believed that a cultural measure of Hawaiianness was needed that also incorporated a biological marker (e.g., the percentage of blood quantum). The Na Mea Hawai'i measures Hawaiian acculturation and consists of five subscales: knowledge of Hawaiian vocabulary, knowledge of Hawaiian customs, knowledge of Hawaiian history, knowledge of Hawaiian culture, and participation in contemporary Hawaiian culture. The 21-item acculturation measure uses responses varying from a "yes," "no," or "don't know" choice to simply filling in a blank, such as percentage of blood quantum. These questions were derived from experts in Hawaiian culture but did not include the expected exploratory factor analysis for confirmation of the subscales.

Rezentes (1993), using a sample consisting of Native Hawaiians, Japanese, and European Americans, reported that Hawaiian participants scored higher than non-Hawaiians in knowledge of Hawaiian history, customs, and culture, and participation in cultural practices including speaking the Hawaiian language, eating Hawaiian foods, attending Hawaiian events, and having Hawaiian spiritual or religious beliefs and customs. Another study (Streltzer, Rezentes, & Arakaki, 1996) did not find a significant relationship between Hawaiian acculturation and depression, anxiety, and the perception of social support among Native Hawaiians. Additionally, when compared to non-Hawaiians, Native Hawaiians did not score significantly higher or lower on measures of psychopathology and psychological well-being. Rezentes (1993) asserts that the Na Mea Hawai'i Scale can be used as a definition of Hawaiian ethnicity, thus using it as a tool to differentiate between Hawaiians and non-Hawaiians. It should be noted, however, that the samples in these studies were only Native Hawaiians living on the Hawaiian Islands.

The second acculturation scale, the 84-item Da Kine Scale (Bautista, 2003), consists of three subscales: Pidgin-island living (Pidgin vocabulary and attitudes toward out-groups); customs-beliefs (attachment toward local culture, preference for things local, and knowledge and practice of local customs); and relationships (collectivism and interpersonal harmony/assertiveness). Bautista's sample also was limited to Hawaiians living in Hawai'i. Native Hawaiians had high scores on Pidgin-island living and customs-beliefs if they were born in, reared in, or attended high school in Hawai'i. Length of residency in the state of Hawai'i was positively correlated with higher Pidgin-island living and customs-beliefs subscale scores but not with the relationships subscale.

Two measures were based on culture and enculturation perspectives. Hishinuma and colleagues (2000) developed the Hawaiian Culture Scale (HCS) specifically for adolescents. In contrast to the previous two measures, the HCS focused on culture and considered developmental processes of cultural affiliation during adolescence. The goals for this measure were to assess the degree to which adolescents affiliated themselves with various dimensions of Hawaiian culture through beliefs, values, customs, and practices. The 50-item instrument has seven Hawaiian cultural subscales with a Likert response format: lifestyles; customs; activities; folklore; causes-locations (land, water, and fishing activism); causes-access (access to the ocean and land activism); and Hawaiian language proficiency. Along with these subscales, the HCS also assesses (a) where they learned about Hawaiian life (family, school, or friends and neighbors); (b) language at home; (c) traditions; (d) blood quantum; and (e) lifestyles. The sociocultural subscales seem to focus on psychology's definition of culture and enculturation (e.g., how one learns about her or his native culture). Similar to Rezentes's measure of Hawaiian acculturation, blood quantum was used to determine the biological measure of being Hawaiian as well as the subscales of socio-cultural aspects associated with being Hawaiian. Hishinuma et al. (2000) found that female Hawaiian participants had higher levels of Hawaiian cultural affiliation than male Hawaiians. Additionally, adolescent Hawaiians with higher levels of education scored significantly higher on the HCS.

Crabbe (2002) also designed a cultural measure, the Hawaiian Ethnocultural Inventory (HEI), which seemed to focus on culture and enculturation. Crabbe (2002) defines "cultural-ethnic identity [as] the degree to which individuals of Native Hawaiian descent culturally identify themselves as Hawaiian" (p. 7). The 80-item measure uses a Likert response and has five subscales: beliefs in Hawaiian cultural practices, knowledge of Hawaiian cultural practices, frequency of performing arts, frequency of ocean traditions, and frequency of spiritual and family customs. Crabbe's sample consisted of both Hawaiians and non-Hawaiians and found that Native Hawaiians scored significantly higher on all five subscales in comparison to non-Hawaiians. Additionally, Native Hawaiians with higher blood quantum level scored higher on knowledge of Hawaiian cultural practices than Native Hawaiians with lower blood quantum levels and non-Hawaiians. Similar to Hishinuma et al.'s (2000) finding, higher levels of education were associated with higher scores on Hawaiian cultural practices.

PSYCHOMETRIC STRENGTHS AND LIMITATIONS OF HAWAIIAN IDENTITY MEASURES

According to Ponterotto and Ruckdeschel (2007), one consistent criterion to determine the strength of measures is reliability, specifically internal consistency as measured by Cronbach's alpha. Many empirical studies fail to take into account the number of items for each subscale and the sample size when looking at internal consistency (Ponterotto & Ruckdeschel, 2007). Using this criterion to evaluate the Hawaiian measures, Na Mea Hawai'i did not report any reliability coefficients for either the entire scale or the subscales. The Da Kine Scale, HCS, and HEI had good to excellent reliabilities for the total scales (see Table 24.1) and the majority of the subscales using Ponterotto and

Ruckdeschel's standards. Only one subscale, relationships in the Da Kine Scale, had a lower score on reliability with an alpha coefficient of .66.

Another psychometric issue when evaluating measures is validity. The Na Mea Hawai'i acculturation measure and the HEI examined face validity by consulting experts in the field of Hawaiian culture to create and evaluate items on the instruments. However, these two scales did not indicate any analyses of convergent or divergent validity. Streltzer et al. (1996) found that higher blood quantum level (greater than or equal to 50%) was positively correlated with Hawaiian acculturation, social desirability, and locus of control. These significant findings may suggest that other variables may be confounding this measure of Hawaiian acculturation, and therefore, further research would be needed to examine this scale with other measures of acculturation in order to establish convergent validity. More research is needed on the other three scales to examine their respective relationships to social desirability, acculturation, cultural affiliation, enculturation, and racial/ethnic identity.

Another major limitation is that three of the measures, the two Hawaiian acculturation measures and the HCS, used only samples from the Hawaiian Islands. The HEI was the only measure that included Hawaiians from the islands and the continental United States. Additionally, these measures were specifically designed for one ethnic group, Native Hawaiians, and cannot be used with other ethnic groups within the racial category of Pacific Islanders. This limits their generalizability and utility with other racial and ethnic groups. The subscales also focus only on Hawaiian cultural aspects rather than on general practices or customs that can be applicable to other indigenous peoples in the United States.

Although all of these measures were designed for Native Hawaiians and their cultural affiliation with being Hawaiian, some researchers used the word "identity" (Crabbe, 2002; Rezentes, 1993) in presenting the measures. However, none of the measures fully takes into account the development processes of identity development as do Phinney (Phinney & Ong, 2007) and Helms (2007). Despite the call to Hawaiians to promote their Native Hawaiian identity for land rights, health care, and education by various political entities, there remains a lack of instruments measuring Hawaiian identity using a nonessentialist paradigm. It is interesting that all the measures used subscales focusing on behaviors, beliefs, values, customs, and language despite using different conceptual frameworks (acculturation, culture, and enculturation). The confusion between race, ethnicity, and culture (Ponterotto & Mallinckrodt, 2007) and identity development also can be seen in these scales.

CONCEPTUAL LIMITATIONS OF HAWAIIAN IDENTITY MEASURES

As indicated earlier in the history of colonization of Native Hawaiians, Hawaiians did not immigrate to the United States but rather were colonized on their own land. Westerners overthrew the Hawaiian government, banned the language, and forced the locals to assimilate to the dominant White culture or leave the islands via migration or death. Therefore, the concept of acculturation with a home and host culture does not fit for Native Hawaiians as their "home" was colonized by the "host" culture. This same argument can be applied to American Indians, Alaskan Natives, and other indigenous groups.

Another issue in these measures is the use of blood quantum level. With less than 1% of Native Hawaiians having "full" Native Hawaiian blood, there is concern of the possible extinction of the Hawaiian race and the loss of elders (kapunas) to pass on Hawaiian culture, traditions, values, and practices. Some interpret this small number of full-blooded Native Hawaiians as an example of assimilation and reinforces a lack of recognition of Native Hawaiians as a separate racial or ethnic group.

CONCLUSION

An ecological model allows researchers to examine the bidirectional relationship at the macrosystem level between sociopolitical influences (such as the Hawaiian Homelands Act and lawsuits against Native Hawaiian institutions) and a person's individual identity development at the microsystem level. The model also can account for influences from the family (mesosystem) and the community (exosystem) that may enhance or restrict one's identity development depending on the context or situation.

An ecological model allows one to consider the multiple issues and contexts that indigenous peoples are facing, including (a) colonial definitions of race in colonial law that determine eligibility of access to resources; and (b) indigenizing identity by self-reflection, adaptation, and adjustment toward self-determination. The ecological model can also help to articulate the decolonization process examining the impact of colonization on multiple levels in family, education, communities, and legislation using both qualitative and quantitative methodologies. Additionally, research can be expanded to understand the relationship between contextual factors and indigenous identity development using both Native Hawaiian indigenous measures and nonessentialist measures such as those based on Phinney's and Helms's models. An ecological perspective can incorporate the critical issues facing many indigenous people today in the 21st century: the influence of colonization, decolonization, diaspora, and multiethnicity on identity development. It is the fundamental premise of this chapter that colonization, decolonization, diaspora, and multiethnicity need to be considered and accounted for in conceptualizing, and consequently factored into, theory development and measurement of Hawaiian identity, and more importantly, lead to greater understanding of indigenous identity development.

NOTES

1. It should be noted that for this chapter, Native Hawaiians and the term *Hawaiian* will refer to "any descendant of the aboriginal peoples inhabiting the Hawaiian Islands in 1778" prior to Western contact in accordance with the 1959 Statehood Admissions Act.

2. Blood quantum is defined by the claimant's report of percent distribution of the individual's ethnic heritage based upon the verifiable birth records or documentation of ancestral histories of the biological parents considered jointly according to the Hawaiian Homes Commission Act.

REFERENCES

Adams, R. (1934). *The unorthodox race doctrine of Hawaii.* New York: McGraw-Hill.

Akaka, M. (1993). Hawaiians come home, your nation needs you. *Ka Wai Ola O OHA/The Living Water of OHA, 10*(11), 14.

Bautista, D. R. (2003). Da Kine Scale: Construction and validation of the Hawaii Local Acculturation Scale. *Dissertation Abstracts International, 64,* 7A.

Bernardino, M. (2008, July). Programs monthly report for July 2008 for the Office of Hawaiian Affairs. Retrieved October 11, 2008, from http://www.oha.org/pdf/OHA_Status_0807.pdf

Blaisdell, K. (1993). The health status of the indigenous Hawaiians. *Asian American and Pacific Islander Journal of Health, 1,* 116–160.

Bolante, R. (2003). What happened to sovereignty? *Honolulu, 116*(3), 94–97.

Bronfenbrenner, U. (1979). *The ecology of human development: Experiments by nature and design.* Cambridge, MA: Harvard University Press.

Cokley, K. (2007). Critical issues in the measurement of ethnic and racial identity: A referendum on the state of the field. *Journal of Counseling Psychology, 54,* 224–234.

Coleman, H. L. K., Norton, R. A., Miranda, G., & McCubbin, L. D. (2003). Ecological perspectives on cultural identity development. In D. Pope-Davis, H. L. K. Coleman, W. M. Lin, & R. L. Toporek (Eds.), *Handbook of multicultural competencies* (pp. 38–58). Thousand Oaks, CA: Sage.

Connell, J. (2002). Paradise left? Pacific Island voyagers in the modern world. In P. Spickard, J. L. Rondilla, & D. H. Wright (Eds.), *Pacific diaspora: Island peoples in the United States and across the Pacific* (pp. 69–86). Honolulu: University of Hawai'i Press.

Council for Native Hawaiian Advancement. (2005). *The Alaka Bill and current lawsuits: National policies for native needs.* Honolulu: Author.

Crabbe, K. M. (2002). Initial psychometric validation of He'ana Mana'o O Na Mo'omeheu: A Hawaiian Ethnocultural Inventory (HEI) of cultural practices. *Dissertation Abstracts International, 63,* 11B.

Espiritu, Y. L. (1992). *Asian American panethnicity: Bridging institutions and identities.* Philadelphia, PA: Temple University Press.

Government Accountability Office. (2008). *Native Hawaiian Education Act: Greater oversight would increase accountability and enable targeting of funds to areas with greatest need* (GAO Publication No. GAO-08–422). Washington, DC: Author.

Graves, J. L., Jr. (2004). *The race myth: Why we pretend race exists in America.* New York: Penguin.

Hall, G. S. (1905). *Adolescence: Its psychology and its relations to physiology, anthropology, sociology, sex, crime, religion, and education* (Vol. 2). New York: D. Appleton.

Hart, H., & McCubbin, H. (2006). *Who are the Hawaiians?* [KeHuli Nei Series, Report 040–01]. Honolulu, HI: Pacific American Foundation.

Hawaii Advisory Committee to the U.S. Commission on Civil Rights. (2001). *Reconciliation at a crossroads: The implications of the Apology Resolution and Rice v. Cayetano for federal and state programs benefiting Native Hawaiians:* Summary report of the August 1998 and September 2000 community forums in Honolulu, HI.

Helms, J. (2007). Some better practices for measuring racial and ethnic identity constructs. *Journal of Counseling Psychology, 54,* 235–246.

Hishinuma, E. S., Andrade, N. N., Johnson, R. C., McArdle, J. J., Miyamoto, R. H., Nahulu, L. B., Makini, G. K., Jr., Yuen, N. Y., Nishimura, S. T., McDermott, J. F., Jr., Waldron, J. A., Luke, K. N., & Yates, A. (2000). Psychometric properties of the Hawaiian Culture Scale—Adolescent Version. *Psychological Assessment, 12,* 140–157.

Kane, H. K. (1997). *Ancient Hawai'i.* Honolulu, HI: Kawainu Press.

Kauanui, J. K. (1998). Off-island Hawaiians "making" ourselves at "home": A [gendered] contradiction in terms? *Women's Studies International Forum, 21,* 681–693.

Kauanui, J. K. (2005). Precarious positions: Native Hawaiians and U.S. federal recognition. *Contemporary Pacific, 17*(1), 1–27.

Lee, R. M., Noh, C. Y., Yoo, Y. C., & Doh, H. S. (2007). The psychology of diaspora experiences: Intergroup contact, perceived discrimination, and the ethnic identity of Koreans in China. *Cultural Diversity and Ethnic Minority Psychology, 13,* 115–124.

Livesay, T. M. (1942). Racial comparisons in test-intelligence. *American Journal of Psychology, 55,* 90–95.

Louttit, C. M. (1931a). Racial comparisons of ability in immediate recall of logical and nonsense material. *Journal of Social Psychology, 2,* 205–215.

Louttit, C. M. (1931b). Test performance of a selected group of part-Hawaiians. *Journal of Applied Psychology, 15,* 43–52.

Marsella, A. J., Oliveira, J. M., Plummer, C. M., & Crabbe, K. M. (1995). Native Hawaiian (Kanaka Maoli) culture, mind, and well-being. In H. I. McCubbin, E. A. Thompson, A. I. Thompson, & J. E. Fromer (Eds.), *Resiliency in ethnic minority families: Native and immigrant American families* (pp. 93–113). Madison: University of Wisconsin Press.

McCubbin, L. D. (2006). The role of indigenous family ethnic schema on well-being among Native Hawaiian families. *Contemporary Nursing Journal: Special Issue: Community & Family Health, 23,* 170–180.

McCubbin, L. D., Ishikawa, M., & McCubbin, H. I. (2007). Kanaka Maoli: Native Hawaiians and their testimony of trauma and resilience. In A. Marsella, J. Johnson, P. Watson, & J. Gryczynski (Eds.), *Ethnocultural perspectives on disaster and trauma: Foundations, issues and applications* (pp. 271–298). New York: Springer.

McMullin, J. (2005). The call to life: Revitalizing a healthy Hawaiian identity. *Social Science & Medicine, 61,* 809–820.

Noyes, M. (1996). Cultural abuse. *Honolulu, 31*(5), 36, 38, 40, 109.

Office of Hawaiian Affairs. (2003). *OHA Mission.* Retrieved April 12, 2005, from http://www.oha.org/cat_content .asp?contentid=20&catid=22

Osorio, J. (2006). On being Hawaiian. *Hulili: Multi-Disciplinary Research on Hawaiian Well-Being, 3*(1), 19–26.

Phinney, J. S., & Ong, A. D. (2007). Conceptualization and measurement of ethnic identity: Current status and future directions. *Journal of Counseling Psychology, 54,* 271–281.

Ponterotto, J. G., & Mallinckrodt, B. (2007). Introduction to the special section on racial and ethnic identity in counseling psychology: Conceptual and methodological challenges and proposed solutions. *Journal of Counseling Psychology, 54,* 219–223.

Ponterotto, J. G., & Park-Taylor, J. (2007). Racial and ethnic identity theory, measurement, and research in counseling psychology: Present status and future directions. *Journal of Counseling Psychology, 54,* 282–294.

Ponterotto, J. G., & Ruckdeschel, D. E. (2007). An overview of coefficient alpha and a reliability matrix for estimating adequacy of internal consistency coefficient with psychological research measures. *Perceptual and Motor Skills, 105,* 997–1014.

Porteus, S. D. (1939). Race and social differences in performance tests. *Genetic Psychology Monographs: Child Behavior, Animal Behavior, and Comparative Psychology, 8*(2), 93–208.

Pratt, H. G. (1929). Some conclusions from a comparison of school achievement of certain racial groups. *Journal of Educational Psychology, 20,* 661–668.

Rezentes, W. C. (1993). Na Mea Hawai'i: A Hawaiian acculturation scale. *Psychological Reports, 73,* 383–393.

Root, M. P. P. (1998). Experiences and processes affecting racial identity development: Preliminary results from the biracial sibling project. *Cultural Diversity and Mental Health, 4*(3), 237–247.

Root, M. P. P. (2000). Rethinking racial identity development. In P. Spickard & W. J. Burroughs (Eds.), *We are a people: Narrative and multiplicity in constructing ethnic identity* (pp. 205–220). Philadelphia: Temple University Press.

Samuels, G. M. (2007). Beyond the rainbow: Multiraciality in the 21st century. In D. Engstrom & L. Piedra (Eds.),

Our diverse society: Race, ethnicity and class: Implications for 21st century America. Washington, DC: NASW Press.

Schmitt, R. C. (1968). *Demographic statistics of Hawai'i: 1778–1965.* Honolulu: University of Hawai'i Press.

Smith, L. T. (1999). *Decolonizing methodologies: Research and indigenous peoples.* New York: St. Martin's.

Spickard, P. (2002a). Introduction: Pacific diaspora. In P. Spickard, J. L. Rondilla, & D. H. Wright (Eds.), *Pacific diaspora: Island peoples in the United States and across the Pacific* (pp. 1–30). Honolulu: University of Hawai'i Press.

Spickard, P. (2002b). Pacific Islander Americans and multiethnicity: A vision of America's future? In P. Spickard, J. L. Rondilla, & D. H. Wright (Eds.), *Pacific diaspora: Island peoples in the United States and across the Pacific* (pp. 40–55). Honolulu: University of Hawai'i Press.

Spickard, P., & Burroughs, W. J. (2000). We are a people. In P. Spickard & W. J. Burroughs (Eds.), *We are a people: Narrative and multiplicity in constructing ethnic identity* (pp. 1–19). Philadelphia: Temple University Press.

Spoehr, H., Akau, M., Akutagawa, W., Birnie, K., Chang, M.-L., Kinney, E. S., Nissanka, S., Peters, D., Sagum, R., & Soares, D. (1998). Ke ala ola pono: The Native Hawaiian community's effort to heal itself. *Pacific Health Dialog, 5*(2), 232–238.

Streltzer, J., Rezentes, W. C., & Arakaki, M. (1996). Does acculturation influence psychosocial adaptation and well-being in Native Hawaiians? *International Journal of Social Psychiatry, 42,* 28–37.

Stubblefield, A. (1995). Racial identity and non-essentialism about race. *Social Theory and Practice, 21*(3), 341–368.

Trimble, J. E. (2007). Prolegomena for the connotation of construct use in the measurement of ethnic and racial identity. *Journal of Counseling Psychology, 54,* 247–258.

Tseng, W. S. (2003). *Clinician's guide to cultural psychiatry.* San Diego, CA: Academic Books.

U.S. Census Bureau. (2000). Racial or ethnic grouping: Native Hawaiian alone or in any combination for data set: Census 2000 Summary File 2 (SF 2) 100-Percent Data. Retrieved on March 8, 2005, at http://factfinder .census.gov/servlet/DTTable?_bm=y&geo_id=01000US &reg=DEC_2000_SF2_U_PCT003:001l062;DEC_2000_ SF2_U_PCT005:001&-ds_name=DEC_2000_SF2_U &-_lang=en&-mt_name=DEC_2000_SF2_U_PCT003& -mt_name=DEC_2000_SF2_U_PCT005&-format=&- CONTEXT=dt

Vertovec, S. (1997). Three meanings of "diaspora" exemplified among South Asian religions. *Diaspora, 6*(3), 277–299.

Wong, L. (1999). Authenticity and the revitalization of Hawaiian. *Anthropology and Education Quarterly, 30,* 94–115.

25

Understanding Whiteness

Previous Approaches and Possible Directions
in the Study of White Racial Attitudes and Identity

LISA B. SPANIERMAN AND JASON R. SOBLE

Understanding whiteness has been a topic of scholarly interest since the work of W. E. B. DuBois (1903, 1935). However, it was not until the post–civil rights era, when scholars of color and their White allies formed a critical mass, that a proliferation of scholarly writings and empirical studies emerged. During this time, scholars initiated specific inquiry into not only how whiteness and White racial attitudes affected other racial groups, but how White individuals were affected by their own racial group membership (e.g., Caditz, 1976; Katz & Ivey, 1977; Terry, 1970). Whereas some scholars have focused on understanding prejudice and discrimination (e.g., Dovidio & Gaertner, 1986) and intergroup relations (see Pettigrew & Tropp, 2006), counseling psychologists have tended to focus more broadly on the feelings, attitudes, and behaviors of White individuals regarding their dominant status in an unjust system. The psychological literature on prejudice is beyond the scope of this chapter, in which our purpose is to explicate and expand theoretical models of White racial identity and attitudes beyond previous reviews of the subject (e.g., Ponterotto, Utsey, & Pedersen, 2006).

In the present chapter, we first review the White racial identity development and White racial consciousness literatures. We describe the central concepts of specific theoretical frameworks and report on existing empirical research on each theory. Next, we revisit the 1990s debate over the utility of White racial identity models versus White racial consciousness types and discuss the current state of the field with regard to this schism. Additionally, we present an emerging theory— psychosocial costs of racism to Whites—as another explanatory framework by which to understand Whites' attitudinal responses to societal racism. We conclude with recommendations for future psychological study of whiteness, emphasizing the need to incorporate the burgeoning interdisciplinary critical whiteness studies literature.

WHITE RACIAL IDENTITY DEVELOPMENT

To describe White racial identity development, scholars have conceptualized a number of different theoretical models or frameworks, each of which offers a slightly different explanation of this process. In general, each model addresses (a) perceptions of one's own racial group membership (i.e., White) and perceptions of people of color, (b) awareness of institutional racism and White privilege, and (c) White supremacist ideology. The various models are multidimensional and dynamic, and each is dependent on dissonance-inducing critical incidents that bring about growth toward more sophisticated statuses or stages. The ultimate goals of healthy White identity development consist of increasing one's critical consciousness of racial issues, exercising greater complexity and flexibility while managing racial material, and abandoning race-based entitlement (Helms, 1995). Below, we review the psychological models of White racial identity development, incorporate empirical research findings, address the strengths and limitations of each model, and provide suggestions for future research.

Rita Hardiman's White Identity Development Process Model

One of the pioneering, yet underutilized, models of White racial identity development was proposed by Rita Hardiman (1982), who qualitatively analyzed the autobiographies of six White antiracist authors who explored racial issues in their lives. She was concerned generally with the psychological effects of racism on dominant group members, and more specifically with the processes by which White individuals develop a healthy (nonracist) White identity. Grounded in the racial identity literature for people of color, as well as the sexual identity development literature, Hardiman's theory focused on racial consciousness (or worldview), dissonance events that triggered change, and the underlying motivation or self-interest for such change. She

based the first three stages of her five-stage developmental model on common themes that she identified in the autobiographies. Drawing on the extant psychological literature (e.g., Cross, 1971; Terry, 1970), she speculated features of the latter two stages. Hardiman referred to Stage 1 as Lack of Social Consciousness, which covers the first few years of life when children initially are unaware of social norms governing appropriate attitudes and behaviors surrounding race and racial interactions. Hardiman explained that White children in this stage become curious about race and, through a number of avenues (e.g., parents, media, and formal education), quickly learn the rules of appropriate racial attitudes and behavior. Subsequently, this socialization process leads to Stage 2, which is classified as Acceptance (of the status quo). It is described as the period in which children are inculcated to the norms of dominant White culture, learning and internalizing beliefs and actions consistent with White supremacist ideology, such as viewing Whites as superior and normal. Whites in this stage generally ignore racial issues and do not realize that "they have been programmed to accept their worldview . . . [which] seems natural" (Hardiman, 1982, p. 171). Whites can (and many do) remain in this stage for their entire lives.

Through a series of contradictions that result in dissonance, some White individuals might progress to Stage 3, Resistance, where they acknowledge the existence of racism in the United States and reject the socialized messages that they once passively accepted. Hardiman (1982) explains that Resistance "represents a dramatic paradigm shift . . . to an ideology that names the dominant group . . . as the source of racial problems" (p. 183). Race becomes increasingly salient during Resistance, and individuals become aware not only that they are racial beings, but also that they have perpetrated racism and benefitted unfairly from White privilege. Consequently, White individuals might experience difficult emotional reactions, such as guilt and anger regarding their participation in a racist system. As Whites abandon their racist beliefs, they might also reject their whiteness, which could results in feelings of grief, loss, and alienation.

The latter two stages, as speculated by Hardiman, are linked to resolution of the aforementioned emotional conflicts. Stage 4, Redefinition, refers to a turning inward—an introspective time when individuals explore what it means to be White. This stage is characterized by an appreciation of differences coupled with a critical consciousness of structural and cultural racism. White individuals might even experience empathy for other Whites who remain in passive acceptance of the status quo, and desire to assist them toward this stage. The aim of Redefinition is to develop a positive sense of White identity without feeling superior to other racial groups. Finally, Stage 5, Internalization, refers to the stage where White individuals integrate their newly established White identity into their overall identity. Whites in this stage will engage spontaneously in social justice behaviors to transform society.

Operationalization. None identified.

Empirical Findings. We find it surprising that a comprehensive theory such as Hardiman's received little to no empirical attention, and we strongly recommend reinvigorating the theory and conducting research to determine whether empirical support exists. Although not intended to test the model explicitly, in her qualitative study of discourses of Whiteness in New Zealand, Gibson (2006) found support for Hardiman's Acceptance stage.

Evaluation and Suggestions for Further Research. Although Hardiman's dissertation was completed in 1982 and analyzed autobiographical texts from the 1940s, 1950s, and 1960s, it seems that many of her assertions are relevant today. For example, passive acceptance of the status quo (i.e., the assumed normativity of Whiteness) continues to be pervasive among White individuals across ethnic and socioeconomic backgrounds. Additionally, qualitative evidence suggests that under certain circumstances, some White individuals experience a paradigm shift, acknowledge the insidiousness of racism, and work toward social justice (e.g., Marx & Pennington, 2003). Alternatively, it would be interesting to examine more contemporary autobiographies of antiracist Whites to determine whether the stages are appropriate today. Because the final two stages of Hardiman's model (i.e., Redefinition and Internalization) were based on speculation, it is particularly important that researchers empirically examine these aspects of the theory. To examine

whether differences exist based on historical periods, we recommend replication of Hardiman's work among contemporary autobiographies. Furthermore, we recommend not only analyzing writings of antiracist Whites, but also those who represent a range of attitudes and beliefs. In Hardiman's theory, there is little mention of more racist White supremacists, and therefore, the theory might need to be augmented. Finally, as Hardiman suggested in 1982, we believe that qualitative research in the form of individual interviews or focus groups could provide important data that could be used to refine the theory.

Janet Helms's Model of White Racial Identity Development

Helms's White racial identity development model is by far the most widely cited and has received the most empirical attention of all White racial identity development models. Developed in 1984, independently from Hardiman, Helms's original conceptualization reflected a linear, developmental process in which Whites increasingly acknowledge institutional racism and White privilege, abandon racism as a feature of one's personality, and enhance their sense of responsibility for dismantling racism. Also similar to Hardiman, the goal is to develop a healthy White identity and to define a sense of self that is not reliant on one's perceived superiority. Helms articulated two general processes of identity development (i.e., abandonment of one's racism and development of a healthy, nonracist White identity), whereas Hardiman focused more specifically on transitions from stage to stage toward internalization of nonracist values and integration of racial identity with other reference group identities.

Helms made several refinements to her original theory to enhance the sophistication, complexity, and conceptual clarity of the model (see Helms, 1990, 1995, 2005). Although initially referred to as stages, Helms (1995) explained that she never intended to profess a linear, developmental sequence, but rather a theory of epigenic statuses, where more primitive statuses are subsumed by more sophisticated statuses. She described statuses as "mutually interactive dynamic processes," such that context is important with regard to the most salient status (Helms, 1995, p. 183). Furthermore,

Helms (1995) elaborated that individuals can exhibit more than one status, although one usually is dominant and most often dictates a person's reactions to racial issues via particular cognitive-emotional information-processing strategies.

The first phase of the model encompasses Contact, Disintegration, and Reintegration, and involves becoming aware of societal racism and abandoning a racist identity. Contact is characterized by adherence to the status quo and denial or lack of awareness of White privilege and racism. The information-processing strategy is avoidance of racial stimuli, characterized by obliviousness of race and racism combined with a pull-yourself-up-by-your-bootstraps mentality (Helms, 1995; Pack-Brown, 1999). Disintegration involves the development of racial awareness, which can cause anxiety and guilt among Whites as they feel forced to choose between loyalty to their own group and the larger moral and humanistic issues that arise in a racist system. Information-processing strategies reflect suppression and ambivalence, in which one is torn between seemingly irreconcilable poles. For example, a White individual may feel conflicted between confronting the racist behavior of a family member while simultaneously fearing rejection or humiliation (Pack-Brown, 1999). Reintegration can emerge as a way to manage the emotions elicited by Disintegration and is characterized by identification and idealization of one's own group as well as anger and intolerance toward racial minorities. Selective perception and negative out-group distortion are the information-processing strategies of this status.

The second, more sophisticated phase (i.e., Pseudoindependence, Immersion/Emersion, and Autonomy) in Helms's model reflects the development of a nonracist, positive White identity. Pseudoindependence is the first stage of redefining a healthy White identity and is characterized by an intellectualized approach to racial issues. In Pseudoindependence, White individuals might look to Black people to explain racism or express a desire to "help" Black people. Helms noted that this status often is associated with liberal guilt and paternalism. Thus, information-processing strategies adhere to principles of reshaping reality and selective perception where White individuals want to prevent themselves from being racist while trying to define their own identity (Helms, 1995; Pack-Brown, 1999). In the updated model, Helms (1990, 1995) added a status (Immersion/Emersion) and thus identified a six-status model. Immersion/Emersion is defined as Whites' search for a deeper understanding of racism and how it has played a role in their lives. Persons in this status often will identify with other White individuals of similar status, and the goal shifts from "helping" Black people to changing Whites. The individual emerges in a type of "rebirth" (Helms, 1990, p. 62) and begins to act in antiracist ways. The information-processing strategies in this status reflect hypervigilance and reshaping. Ultimately, this leads to a strong determination and commitment to antiracism and social advocacy (Helms, 1995; Pack-Brown, 1999). Finally, Autonomy is characterized by an ability to let go of one's racial privilege, as well as a firm commitment to antiracism action. Information-processing strategies reflect flexibility and complexity where White individuals redefine what it means to be White as well as continue to work to avoid actions that reflect racism in their personal lives (Pack-Brown, 1999).

With regard to the counseling process, Helms (1984) argued that racial identity was central to human development, and therefore to the therapy process. Furthermore, she posited an interaction model that consisted of four types of counseling relationships: parallel (counselor and client exhibit same racial identity status), crossed (counselor and client's worldviews are total opposites), progressive (counselor exhibits a higher racial identity status than the client), and regressive (client exhibits a higher racial identity status than the counselor).

Operationalization. The most widely used measure of White racial identity development is the White Racial Identity Attitude Scale (WRIAS) (Helms & Carter, 1990), which is derived from Helms's original five-stage theory. The 50-item inventory consists of five subscales that reflect each of the original five racial identity statuses (10 items each) and measure the salience of each status among White participants. Despite initial psychometric support for the instrument (see Helms, 1990), a number of limitations have been associated with the scale. In particular, researchers have noted consistently low internal consistency estimates for some of the subscales (e.g., $\alpha = .18–.50$ for Contact). Helms (1997) explained that sample homogeneity (i.e., lack of interracial contact) could account for the low reliability estimates, and later, she discussed the limitations of using Cronbach's alpha to assess the utility of a measure (see Helms, 1999, 2005, 2007). And recently, Helms (2007) criticized the use of principal components and factor analysis in response to various researchers' use of these methods to identify different (and psychometrically stronger) factor structures of the WRIAS (e.g., Mercer & Cunningham, 2003). In addition to the independent investigations, two meta-analyses have been conducted on the WRIAS. Across 31 studies, Behrens (1997) found that the structure of the WRIAS is less complex than the theory purports and noted that highly correlated statuses (e.g., Disintegration and Reintegration) might measure the same construct. In an analysis of 38 WRIAS investigations, Helms (1999) argued that systematic measurement errors were at least partly responsible for the poor reliability and validity of the instrument, and she urged researchers to conduct additional psychometric investigation of the WRIAS.

Predating the WRIAS, but receiving far less attention, Claney and Parker (1989) developed the first scale to operationalize Helms's (1984) original theory. The White Racial Consciousness Development Scale (WRCDS) (not to be confused with White racial consciousness theory described later in the chapter) consisted of 15 items, three items for each status. We located only one study that employed the measure, and the researchers expressed serious concerns with its use because of the poor psychometric properties of the scale (Choney & Rowe, 1994). Recently, Lee and colleagues (2007) extended and revitalized the WRCDS, using rigorous procedures such as focus group and individual interviews to generate 85 additional scale items. Exploratory and confirmatory factor analyses resulted in a revised WRCDS scale that consisted of a four-factor, 40-item measure (8 Contact, 14 Reintegration, 9 Pseudoindependence, and 9 Autonomy) that accounted for approximately 52% of the variance. The researchers found adequate internal consistency estimates across two samples.

Lee et al. (2007) highlighted the limitations of their study, such as potential social desirability bias, unequal representation of items in each status, and no items for Immersion/Emersion. Furthermore, they urged researchers to interpret results of their scale cautiously until it is revised further based on additional clarification of Helms's model. Upon reviewing the WRCDS items, we, too, caution the use of this revised measure at this early stage. Because two critical statuses (i.e., Disintegration and Immersion/Emersion) are absent from the inventory, the measure only partially reflects the theory. With regard to the four statuses that are measured in the scale, rather than tapping the complexities and nuances of each status, the WRCDS instead reduces each status to a single (or a few) dimensions, which most often are related to comfort with Black people. The items written to reflect the Contact status, for instance, narrowly pertain to whether participants have had contact with or feel comfortable with Black people and do not capture racial color blindness, which is integral to this status. Even more problematic than the narrow depiction of each status is that many items do not map cleanly onto the theory. For example, the item "In America, people pretty much decide their own fate" is intended to reflect Reintegration, but seems better suited to reflect the color-blind racial perspective found in Contact. Items such as "I do not understand why Blacks are so resentful of White people" and "I have lived in close proximity to Black people" could fit equally well in more than one status. Furthermore, items such as "My family would disown me if I married a Black person" assess perception of one's family racial identity rather than that of the participant. At this stage in instrument development, approximately 20 years after the first measure designed to assess White racial identity and while racial and ethnic minority groups (e.g., Latinos and Asian Americans) quickly are becoming the numerical majority in the United States, we believe that it is essential to move beyond the Black-White binary if researchers are to understand Whites' comprehensive experiences.

Empirical Findings. Despite the methodological limitations of the WRIAS and the WRCDS, Helms's model of White racial identity development has received extensive empirical attention. Generally, findings are consistent with the theory and indicate that some less sophisticated statuses, particularly those reflecting White supremacy, are associated with higher levels of racism (Carter, 1990; Pope-Davis & Ottavi, 1994), color-blind racial attitudes (Gushue & Constantine, 2007), use of primitive ego defense mechanisms (Utsey & Gernat, 2002), and a work ethic that emphasizes getting ahead (Carter, Gushue, & Weitzman, 1994). Contact tends to operate differently from the other, less sophisticated statuses such that higher Contact predicts lower levels of racism (Carter, 1990) and foreclosed and achieved ego identity statuses among women (Miville, Darlington, Whitlock, & Mulligan, 2005). Alternatively, more advanced statuses have been associated with a host of positive outcomes such as lower levels of racial color blindness (Gushue & Constantine, 2007) and higher levels of self-actualization (Tokar & Swanson, 1991), support for particular affirmative action policies (Jacob Arriola & Cole, 2001), positive interracial situations at work (Block, Roberson, & Neuger, 1995), and achieved ego identity statuses among men (Miville et al., 2005).

Gender and age differences also have been identified with regard to White racial identity development. Both Carter (1990) and Pope-Davis and Ottavi (1994), for example, found that college women exhibited significantly higher White racial identity statuses than college men and were thus less likely to hold racist beliefs. Furthermore, participants over the age of 20 were more likely to reflect the more sophisticated racial identity status of Autonomy, whereas younger participants exhibited higher Disintegration and Reintegration (Pope-Davis & Ottavi, 1994).

Counseling psychology researchers have examined how counseling process variables are associated with White racial identity development. For example, findings suggest that White racial identity statuses are associated with perceptions of forming a working alliance with an African American therapist (Burkard, Juarez-Huffaker, & Ajmere, 2003) and preferences for White counselors (Helms & Carter, 1991).

Evaluation and Suggestions for Further Research. In the mid-1990s, as Helms's theory was gaining momentum, a group of scholars (e.g., Rowe & Atkinson, 1995; Rowe, Behrens, & Leach, 1995; Rowe, Bennett, & Atkinson, 1994) criticized the model and its associated instruments. These researchers noted the primary limitations as too similar to (and inconsistent with) racial minority identity models, an emphasis on

Whites' attitudes toward people from other racial groups rather than on White identity and attitudes toward one's own group, the implausible developmental nature of the model, and the limited Black-White binary. Helms and others (e.g., Thompson, 1994) refuted their assertions, claiming that Helms's (1990) theory explicitly focused on Whites' self-awareness, and she noted the extensive differences in racial identity development between Helms's Black and White racial identity models. Thompson (1994) argued that Helms's (1990) theory indeed was developmental, but Rowe and Atkinson (1995) continued to express concern with the nonlinear directionality and cumulative nature of the statuses, which, in their opinion, made empirical testing difficult.

Rigorous intellectual debates ensued between Helms and her critics in the flagship journals of counseling psychology (*The Counseling Psychologist,* 1994; *Journal of Counseling Psychology,* 1997), as well as during the annual convention of the American Psychological Association (1998), and such debate continues today (see Leach, Behrens, & LaFleur, 2002; Rowe, 2006). As noted above, the critics were most concerned that the theoretical framework of White racial identity was not supported empirically (Rowe & Atkinson, 1995; Rowe et al., 1994; Rowe et al., 1995). At the same time, they cautioned against using the WRIAS or WRCDS based on the psychometric limitations (Behrens, 1997; Behrens & Rowe, 1997). Despite Helms's contentions that internal consistency estimates and structural equation modeling are inappropriate with regard to the WRIAS, we, too, caution interpretation of findings. Nevertheless, our initial research program supports aspects of Helms's framework (e.g., empirical support for affective and cognitive attitudes that reflect Contact), and thus we strongly suggest qualitative investigation (e.g., racial life narratives, focus groups, individual interviews, and so forth) to determine whether the statuses are consistent with Whites' experiences. If, in fact, qualitative research supports the theory, then perhaps additional items can be formulated to tap the nuances of each status and create a more precise measure. We believe that the complex nature of each status might make the statuses difficult to assess with brief subscales in a collective measure. Instead, future quantitative research should explore the utility of using established measures in combination to assess individual statuses. For instance, to assess Contact, researchers might combine measures of legitimizing ideologies, avoidance of racial issues, and social distance.

Ponterotto's Model for Counselor Trainees

Derived from the racial identity theories of Cross (1971) and Helms (1984) and based on his personal experience training hundreds of White students in multicultural counseling, Ponterotto (1988) proposed a four-stage developmental model of White racial identity and consciousness among trainees. He was most concerned with White trainees' engagement (or lack thereof) with a multicultural curriculum and how they became aware of their Whiteness and the fact that they have been socialized in a system of subtle racism. Incorporating Cross's Pre-encounter stage enabled Ponterotto to depict an adulthood stage that precedes Helms's Contact status and is similar to Hardiman's childhood lack of social consciousness. Thus, Stage 1, Pre-exposure, is characterized by a lack of awareness of race and racism. White trainees in this stage believe that racism no longer exists in the United States and are oblivious to their own Whiteness. The next stage, Exposure, begins when White counseling trainees are made aware of societal racism as well as racial disparities within the counseling profession. During this stage, trainees typically experience guilt and anger, as well as uncertainty in conveying this newly discovered information to other White individuals for fear of being ostracized and rejected. As students grapple with these emotions, they proceed in one of two directions that represent the third stage, Zealot–Defensive. The zealot represents those trainees who become passionately involved in multicultural issues and social activism, whereas the defensive response reflects anger, skepticism, and withdrawal from multicultural issues. Finally, Stage 4 is labeled Integration and is characterized by critical awareness of racism, along with respect for and appreciation of racial and cultural differences.

Operationalization and Empirical Findings. None identified.

Evaluation and Suggestions for Further Research. Because racial identity development is a crucial element of counselors' multicultural competence in clinical, research, and teaching contexts, one strength of this theory is its specific focus on applied psychology trainees. Thus, we recommend that researchers revive this theory, devise ways to empirically test it, and perhaps reconceptualize and/or refine aspects of the model. For example, we can envision splitting the zealot and defensive responses into two potential stages. Because counseling trainees are a captive audience, this theory can be tested through qualitative methods such as in-class journals, personal narratives and reflection essays, and focus groups of students enrolled in or who have recently completed multicultural classes. Examination of the developmental progression is warranted.

The Key Model: White Male Identity Development

Similar to Hardiman (1982) and Helms's (1984) conceptualization of White racial identity, the ultimate goal in the Key Model is for Whites to acknowledge White privilege; abandon the accompanying sense of entitlement; and develop a healthy, nonracist White identity. In their model, Scott and Robinson (2001) sought to address earlier criticisms of racial identity development frameworks (e.g., the linear nature of stages) and extend Helms's model of White racial identity development. They emphasized that race is one element of a person's identity that interacts with other dimensions, such as gender and sexuality, and thus through a specific focus on the racial identity development of White men, they addressed the intersection between race and gender. Because of the salience of power in men's lives, and taking into account masculine gender role socialization, these scholars surmised that White men's racial identity development might appear different from that of White women. The initial developmental phases entail little self-exploration, whereas higher phases require self-exploration and resolution of some crisis (i.e., dissonance events). The authors described their model as circular in nature, and thus movement can occur in multiple directions. Phases 1 and 2 represent racist types. Phase 1 is called Noncontact and is characterized by ethnocentrism, little knowledge of race, and beliefs in White superiority. Phase 2 is referred to as Claustrophobic and is characterized by beliefs of reverse racism, victim blaming, and an overall feeling of being closed in by other groups who are vying for White male power. Claustrophobics rely on stereotypes for information about racial and ethnic minorities. According to the theory, White men might stay in one of these racist types for their entire lives, either because they were foreclosed or did not engage in critical incidents that created dissonance. The third phase is referred to as Conscious Identity, which develops in response to a dissonance-creating incident or series of events. White men who are Conscious can venture in two possible directions: regress back to being Claustrophobic or emerge into the Empirical Type, in which they begin to acknowledge the existence and effects of racism, as well as recognize their own White privilege. This type is characterized by intellectual understanding, whereby men might engage in reading or discussion on race, reminiscent of Helms's Pseudoindependence. The final phase in the Key Model is referred to as Optimal, which represents a worldview shift and holistic understanding of racial issues. Optimal men value all people, and their struggle for power over people is diminished. These White men use power and privilege in ways that foster equity and redistribution of societal resources.

Operationalization and Empirical Findings. None identified.

Evaluation and Suggestions for Further Research. Although we were unable to identify any empirical research on the Key Model, we find the framework to be promising in that it addresses the intersectionality between gender and race. Sociological researchers have examined White men and women separately with regard to their racial identity and attitudes (see Feagin & O'Brien, 2003; Frankenberg, 1993). This approach makes sense because White privilege is differentially experienced by White individuals depending on their other reference group identities (Neville, Worthington, & Spanierman, 2001). Researchers with an interest in men and masculinity issues could partner with racial identity scholars to develop this intersectionality further to understand more about what it means to be a White man in the United States. Similarly, researchers should explore Whiteness in conjunction with a range of intersecting

identities, such as gay, lesbian, and bisexual men and women. A novel feature of the Key Model is the Claustrophobic type, which seems particularly relevant in a political context of heightened fear of immigrants and terror. With regard to counseling, we hope that additional scholarship on the Key Model will address White male counselors and educators as well as White male clients—who are just as vulnerable and likely to exhibit the racist types. Finally, we recommend that a scale be developed to operationalize this model.

WHITE RACIAL CONSCIOUSNESS

Out of the debates and criticism of White racial identity development theory in the mid-1990s, another model emerged by which to understand Whites' "racial outlook," referred to as *White racial consciousness* (Rowe et al., 1994). Rowe and colleagues (1994) define White racial consciousness as "one's awareness of being White and what that implies in relation to those who do not share White group membership" (pp. 133–134). In contrast to Helms's model, they use types—groupings of attitudes—versus stages or statuses to reflect the nondevelopmental nature of their theory. Movement across types occurs in direct relation to life experiences and observations, and dissonance is the key to change. In the original articulation of the theory (Rowe et al., 1994), White racial consciousness consisted of seven types of racial attitudes that were either *achieved* or *unachieved* (Rowe et al., 1995; Rowe et al., 1994). Similar to Marcia's (1966) ego identity statuses and Phinney's (1989) ethnic identity stages, Rowe and colleagues articulate achievement as dependent on whether one has explored his or her racial attitudes sufficiently and made a commitment to such attitudes. The four achieved types were Dominative, Integrative, Conflictive, and Reactive. Dominative referred to a social dominance perspective that reflects White superiority, whereas Integrative was defined as "a pragmatic view of racial/ethnic minority issues . . . solidly based on moral responsibility" (Rowe et al., 1994, p. 141). Moreover, Integrative attitudes reflect a synthesis of one's sense of Whiteness with sensitivity toward people of color, and persons expressing this type are comfortable interacting with people of color. Conflictive was described as tension between the values of egalitarianism and individualism, where one believes in equality for all, yet does not acknowledge institutional racism and holds individuals personally responsible for any shortcomings. Thus, persons reflecting Conflictive attitudes do not support compensatory policies such as affirmative action, and might even express concerns about perceived reverse racism toward Whites. The Reactive type was depicted as a pro-minority stance in which institutional racism and White privilege are acknowledged. This does not necessarily represent a fully conscious person, however, because Reactive attitudes might reflect only an intellectual understanding of racial issues.

In contrast, the unachieved types lack the necessary combination of exploration and commitment to warrant achievement. Rowe et al. (1994) proposed the unachieved construct to address one of their major critiques of Helms's model, namely, that Whiteness might not be important to some Whites, and therefore, racial identity is not a salient aspect of life experience for all Whites. For example, the Avoidant type reflects an evasion of racial issues altogether. The Dependent type, similar to Marcia's (1966) foreclosure status, reflects one's reliance on others' opinions as the basis for his or her attitudes; and the Dissonant type relates to uncertainty, tentativeness, or confusion about one's racial attitudes. Rowe and colleagues (1994) argued that unachieved types address a potential gap in Helms's theory.

Operationalization. Because development of White racial consciousness theory was tied inextricably to operationalization and initial empirical findings, we continue to discuss theory in this section. Initially, Choney and Behrens (1996) developed the Oklahoma Racial Attitudes Scale-Preliminary (ORAS-P) to measure the seven types described above. They analyzed the psychometric properties of the inventory among six independent samples. Using confirmatory factor analysis, they provided support for the seven distinct types. Later, when independent researchers reduced the multidimensional nature of the theory through factor analysis (e.g., Pope-Davis, Vandiver, & Stone, 1999), the White racial consciousness model was revised and some of the distinct types were collapsed (LaFleur, Rowe, & Leach, 2002). In the revised ORAS manual (LaFleur, Leach, & Rowe, 2003), the researchers

explain that the inventory consists of two separate measures: one dealing with dimensions of racial attitudes and the other with commitments to such attitudes. Specifically, Dominative and Integrative attitudes were combined on a bipolar scale to reflect the dimension of Racial Acceptance. Similarly, the Conflictive and Reactive scales were collapsed to comprise the dimension of Racial Justice. In this revised iteration, the Oklahoma Racial Attitudes Scale, the researchers claimed that the achieved versus unachieved distinction was less important than they originally postulated. Instead, they assessed one's level of commitment to his or her racial attitude type identified in the first measure (i.e., Racial Acceptance and Racial Justice). Although the researchers report adequate internal consistency estimates of the ORAS-P and ORAS, particular subscales have questionable internal consistency estimates in independent research. For example, coefficient alphas for the Dominative and Integrative scales ranged from .50 to .64 (e.g., Castillo et al., 2006; Mueller & Pope, 2003) and for the Avoidant scale ranged from .62 to .65 (e.g., Cumming-McCann & Accordino, 2005; Spanierman & Heppner, 2004).

Empirical Findings. A growing body of research has emerged to examine empirically how White racial consciousness, as measured by the ORAS, relates to various constructs. Data have been obtained from a number of undergraduate and graduate samples. In an unpublished study among 118 White college students, Schmidt and Church (2004) found that the Avoidant White racial consciousness type was associated with lower ego development, whereas the Reactive type was associated with higher ego development. Among psychology graduate students, Castillo et al. (2006) found that Conflictive ($\beta = .63$) and Reactive ($\beta = -.18$) attitudes predicted prejudice, over and above gender, age, and social desirability. Spanierman and Heppner (2004) found that lower scores on Conflictive attitudes were associated with White Empathy, whereas higher scores on this type were associated with higher levels of fear of people of color, as were higher scores on Dominative, Dissonant, and Dependent attitudes. Dissonant and Reactive attitudes also were associated with White Guilt. These moderate associations underscore the links between racial affect and particular White racial consciousness types.

Investigation among various professionals/practitioners also has been conducted. Among student affairs professionals, for example, Mueller and Pope (2003) found that particular demographic characteristics, interest in multicultural issues, and multicultural training experiences were associated with certain racial consciousness types. More specifically, age was negatively associated with unachieved types, suggesting that older participants were less confused about their racial attitudes; identification with a marginalized group was associated with the Reactive (pro-minority) type; multicultural training experiences were positively associated with Reactive attitudes and negatively associated with Avoidant, Dominative, and Conflictive types. Thus, participants who had greater interest in and experience with multicultural issues exhibited more positive attitudes toward people of color. Cumming-McCann and Accordino (2005), among a sample of rehabilitation counselors, noted that lower levels of unachieved attitudes (e.g., Dependent and Dissonant) predicted some forms of multicultural competence, whereas higher scores on Reactive attitudes predicted higher multicultural counseling awareness.

Evaluation and Suggestions for Further Research. A major strength of White racial consciousness theory is its link to rigorous scale development procedures and subsequent empirical research that informed theory modification. Another strength relates to the focus on dissonance as a necessary component for development of achieved attitudes and for change. It seems reasonable, from our experience, that Rowe et al.'s (1994) claim that movement across types, or change in attitudes, is likely not sequential or predictable. Our concerns about White racial consciousness theory relate to perpetuation of the status quo, lack of comprehensiveness of the theory, and inaccuracy that Whiteness is not relevant for some Whites.

Without a social justice focus, which has become increasingly important to counseling psychologists, these scholars (perhaps inadvertently) have perpetuated the status quo. In an effort to remain merely descriptive, they neglected taking an explicit stance on the pervasiveness of institutional and cultural racism in U.S. society, and we were unable to locate any statements in which the researchers affirmed that institutional racism and White privilege actually exist, despite a surge of scholarship in

this area. Therefore, implicitly, the researchers give equal credence to a reality in which the "playing field is tilted" toward Whites or one in which it is tilted toward people of color (LaFleur et al., 2003, p. 5). For example, the Conflictive type, which reflects rugged individualism and a need for fairness and equality, is described as Whites' belief that people of color are unfairly advantaged in U.S. society. The researchers neglect to mention that this perception is a cognitive distortion that reflects color-blind racial ideology and is inconsistent with multicultural psychology's social justice agenda.

Furthermore, the model of White racial consciousness lacks comprehensiveness such that it does not identify a set of attitudes (or type) that represents critical consciousness of racism, empathy for oppressed peoples (without the accompanying paternalism or overidentification), and an antiracism stance. The model never posits a healthy White racial outlook, grounded in an accurate perception of reality. Although one might assume that Integrative or Reactive attitudes reflect positive racial attitudes (or a healthier racial outlook than some of the other types), high scores on the Integrative subscale instead reflect racial color blindness (e.g., "In selecting my friends, race and culture are just not important") or the opposite of Dominative, White supremacist and blatant racist attitudes (e.g., "I believe that minority people are probably not as smart as Whites" [reverse-scored]). Similarly, the Reactive type, which is intended to reflect "strong pro-minority attitudes" (Rowe et al., 1995), instead incorporates paternalistic attitudes (e.g., "Minorities deserve special help in education" and "I believe that it is society's responsibility to help minority people whether they want it or not"). Rowe et al. (1994) perpetuate a pull-yourself-up-by–your-bootstraps mentality among Reactive racial attitudes. They explain that persons with this attitude type

> ignore the implications of individual responsibility and tend to overlook the roles of personal behavior and individual choice as they contribute to the levels of achievement, poverty, and social disorganization experienced by many racial/ethnic minority communities. Instead, such things are seen as the sole result of . . . racism. (p. 140)

Clearly, a tension exists between what the authors believe to be pro-minority and what one would find in the actual scholarship.

Although there is utility in the idea of unachieved types—which represent a lack of exploration and commitment to one's racial outlook—we disagree with the claim that race is not relevant for some Whites, as suggested by Rowe (2006). We believe that the extensive, interdisciplinary critical Whiteness studies literature on the invisibility and normativity of Whiteness speaks to this issue and suggests that a defining feature of White privilege is the ability to ignore it (e.g., Sue, 2004). We believe that race is a defining marker in the United States, and thus is a crucial component in all U.S. Whites' experiences whether they acknowledge it or not. In sum, we recommend further revision of White racial consciousness theory grounded in the extant interdisciplinary literature. If the measure designed to assess the theory lacks comprehensiveness (e.g., no antiracist types), no amount of empirical validation of the measure will extend the theory without broader thinking about the constructs that should be reflected.

PSYCHOSOCIAL COSTS OF RACISM TO WHITES

Adding to the psychological literature on White racial identity development and White racial consciousness, Spanierman and Heppner (2004) theorized an approach to understanding the complexity of White racial attitudes that focused on the costs of racism to White individuals. The term *costs* here refers to the negative cognitive, affective, and behavioral consequences experienced by White individuals as dominant group members in a White supremacist system. Although scholars acknowledge that Whites unfairly benefit from the U.S. system of racial oppression in ways that have been deemed White privilege, it might be less apparent that White individuals also experience negative consequences from living in such a system.

Early conceptual notions of costs outlined the broad ways in which dominant group members are affected by systems of oppression (see Bowser & Hunt, 1981, 1996; Goodman, 2001; Kivel, 2002). Building on this work, Spanierman and Heppner used the conventional psychological tripartite framework (i.e., cognitive, affective, and behavioral) to delineate the psychosocial costs of racism to Whites in a parsimonious, yet comprehensive, manner. Cognitive costs include cognitive

distortions of self (e.g., believing that all achievements are merit based), reality (e.g., denying the existence of racism), or others (e.g., relying on stereotypes). Affective costs refer to emotional consequences of racism, such as sadness or anger about the existence of racism, guilt about one's dominant position in the racial hierarchy, and fear of people of other races. Behavioral costs of racism involve limited or restricted actions, such as living only where other Whites live or censoring oneself in interracial contexts. It is important to note that costs of racism to Whites are conceptualized differently from the ways in which people of color experience consistently detrimental effects of racism. Although the costs to Whites are less egregious, it is crucial that White individuals become engaged in meaningful (and often difficult) discussions about their racial attitudes. Their dominant status allows them to ignore racial issues if they so desire, but also affords them power to use their privilege to create a more equitable society.

Operationalization. To move from the theoretical to the practical, Spanierman and Heppner (2004) developed the Psychosocial Costs of Racism to Whites (PCRW) scale to quantify and measure some of the costs of racism to Whites. This self-report instrument measures the consequences of racism experienced by White individuals and is comprised of three subscales that focus primarily on affective costs of racism: White Empathic Reactions Towards Racism (also known as White Empathy; e.g., anger about the existence of racism), White Guilt, and White Fear of Others (also referred to as White Fear; e.g., limited social relationships outside of one's own racial group). Because emotional responses are particularly salient among Whites with regard to racial issues, researchers examining White racial identity have identified a need for attention to affective states of Whites (e.g., Tokar & Swanson, 1991). Higher PCRW scores are indicative of greater experiences of affective costs of racism. The scale garnered initial psychometric support based on more than 700 observations among a college student sample (Spanierman & Heppner, 2004), and subsequent investigations demonstrated adequate internal consistency estimates for the subscales, ranging from .63 (White Fear) to .85 (White Empathy) among college students (Case, 2007; Spanierman & Heppner, 2004; Spanierman, Poteat, Beer, & Armstrong, 2006), applied psychology graduate students (Spanierman, Poteat, Wang, & Oh, 2008), and a geographically dispersed sample of employed adults (Poteat & Spanierman, 2008).

Empirical Research

Quantitative. In a number of quantitative investigations, researchers found that demographic factors, background characteristics, and race-related constructs have been associated with the PCRW scales. Across samples of undergraduate and graduate students and employed adults, women scored significantly higher than men on White Empathy (Spanierman & Heppner, 2004; Spanierman et al., 2006; Spanierman, Poteat et al., 2008) and White Guilt among graduate psychology students (Spanierman, Poteat et al., 2008). Multicultural education has been positively related to White Empathy and White Guilt, and negatively associated with White Fear (Spanierman & Heppner, 2004; Spanierman, Poteat et al., 2008). White Fear also has been associated with less exposure to and fewer friendships with racial and ethnic minorities among college students (Spanierman & Heppner, 2004). Furthermore, White Empathy has been associated with ethnocultural empathy, and White Empathy and White Guilt have been linked to greater racial awareness, cultural sensitivity (Spanierman & Heppner, 2004), openness to diversity (Poteat & Spanierman, 2008), and various forms of multicultural counseling competence (Spanierman, Poteat et al., 2008). In contrast, White Fear has been related to lower levels of openness to diversity (Poteat & Spanierman, 2008), racial awareness, cultural sensitivity, and ethnocultural empathy (Spanierman & Heppner, 2004).

Identifying Costs of Racism Types. Because the three subscales of the PCRW function in different directions (i.e., White Fear operates differently from White Empathy and White Guilt), a total scale score cannot be calculated (Spanierman & Heppner, 2004). Therefore, to attain a more nuanced and complex portrayal of the costs of racism to Whites by examining the scales in combination, Spanierman et al. (2006) used cluster analysis to identify groups of similar individuals based on their PCRW subscale scores. More specifically, the researchers identified five distinct costs of racism types that represent different constellations of

White Empathy, White Guilt, and White Fear. Among the types, Antiracist reflects the highest levels of White Empathy and White Guilt, coupled with the lowest White Fear. In their investigation, Spanierman et al. (2006) found that this type contained the fewest participants of all the types and consisted of a high proportion of women and self-identified Democrats in the sample. Furthermore, they found that these individuals reported the highest levels of multicultural education, racial diversity among friends, cultural sensitivity, and support for affirmative action among all of the types. Accordingly, individuals in this type exemplified lower levels of color-blind racial attitudes than all other types. The Empathic but Unaccountable type exhibits high White Empathy, without the accompanying White Guilt described above in the Antiracist type. This was most prevalent of the five types among college students. Similar to Antiracist, these individuals reported racial diversity in their friendship group and awareness of blatant racial issues; however, they lacked awareness of racial privilege. Gender representation was balanced, but a high proportion of men in the sample were concentrated in this type. The Fearful Guilt type reflects high levels of White Guilt and White Fear, with low White Empathy. This type is associated with at least some multicultural education and high awareness of racial privilege. The Unempathic and Unaware (Oblivious) type is characterized by low levels of White Empathy and White Guilt, along with moderate White Fear. Similar to Helms's (1990) White racial identity status of Contact, this type displays racial color-blind ideology (see Neville, Lilly, Duran, Lee, & Browne, 2000), in which one is oblivious to issues of race and racism. Spanierman et al. (2006) found that persons in this type were unaware of racial privilege, had little multicultural education, and reported having very few cross-racial friendships. The highest proportion of men was concentrated in this type. Among the five types, the Insensitive and Afraid type exhibited the lowest levels of White Empathy and White Guilt, coupled with the highest scores on White Fear. Moreover, this type reflects the lowest levels of multicultural education, cultural sensitivity, racial awareness, support for affirmative action, and exposure to people of differing racial backgrounds, while also representing the highest proportion of self-identified Republicans (Spanierman et al., 2006).

By and large, experiences of costs of racism are more revealing when examined collectively and improve our understanding of the complex and varied ways in which White individuals respond to societal racism. As we anticipated, subsequent research has found that an individual's costs of racism type is not static. More specifically, Soble (2008) found that students' PCRW types can shift after exposure to a dissonance-inducing stimulus, though it has yet to be determined if any shift is temporary or permanent. In addition, Spanierman, Todd, and Anderson (2009) identified particular patterns with regard to PCRW type change during the course of the first year of college among a sample of White undergraduates.

Qualitative. In a qualitative investigation, Spanierman, Oh et al. (2008) found additional support for the interaction of various costs of racism to Whites. For example, findings suggested that respondents' previous limited experience with people of color influenced their current cognitive and affective responses, such as a lack of critical understanding of White privilege, along with anger toward people of color (i.e., victim blaming). In contrast, participants who had a personal connection with people of color were more likely to express empathy for those oppressed by racism, and sometimes this empathy was connected to a desire to work actively toward dismantling racism. Additionally, respondents who demonstrated high levels of racial sensitivity also experienced a range of emotional responses (e.g., guilt, shame, and empathy), as well as isolation from people of color and other White students on campus.

Evaluation and Suggestions for Further Research. Dating back to earlier work on Whites' self-interest in eradicating racism (e.g., Caditz, 1976; Hardiman, 1982; Terry, 1970), the costs of racism to Whites provide a promising theoretical framework that might make the message more personally relevant for White individuals. Initial empirical findings suggest that the PCRW is an effective tool for measuring particular affective costs of racism as experienced by White individuals. The PCRW types underscore the heterogeneity among Whites with regard to affective responses to racism, and with additional empirical support (e.g., replication) have implications for educational interventions.

At this early stage, further research is needed. For instance, the literature regarding White Guilt is controversial. Although conceptual writings link guilt to barriers to competence or manipulation techniques used by people of color and their White allies to advance their agendas, empirical findings suggest that White Guilt is facilitative of multicultural competence (Spanierman, Poteat et al., 2008). Further research must be conducted to gain a more nuanced understanding of the forms and functions of White Guilt. Additionally, the White Fear subscale of the PCRW is limited, as it focuses only on anxiety and distance from people of color. A more comprehensive articulation of "the fears of White people" (see Jensen, 2005), which includes fear of losing privilege and power, is needed. In some studies, the internal consistency estimates of the White Guilt and White Fear scales have been less than optimal, and therefore additional research must be conducted to enhance those PCRW scales. In general, because the scale measures only affective costs, additional empirical exploration of cognitive and behavioral costs is warranted. We recommend examining the PCRW in conjunction with measures of cognitive complexity and behavioral indexes (e.g., joining an antiracist group). We also suggest additional qualitative research to understand the processes by which Whites develop antiracist dispositions. Researchers could conduct focus groups by PCRW type to detect subtle differences between the types (e.g. Antiracist versus Empathic but Unaccountable).

SUMMARY, IMPLICATIONS, AND FUTURE DIRECTIONS FOR THE PSYCHOLOGICAL STUDY OF WHITENESS

Beginning with Hardiman's (1982) White Identity Development Process Model, a number of scholars (e.g., Helms, 1984; Ponterotto, 1988; Scott & Robinson, 2001) have proposed conceptual models that explain White racial identity in terms of various dynamic stages and statuses through which, the models suggest, White individuals might develop a healthy, nonracist White racial identity. Most early models suggested that White racial identity was developmental and sequential in nature, although Helms complicated this notion in several revisions of her theory. During the mid-1990s, scholars engaged in rigorous intellectual critique and debate of racial identity models, noting, for example, (a) problems inherent in developmental, sequential models; (b) limitations of the Black/White binary; and (c) overemphasis on Whites' attitudes toward Blacks. In response to these debates, White racial identity scholars refined their models to address the criticisms.

Additionally, these debates generated new approaches to the psychological study of Whiteness. A group of scholars, for instance, put forth the White Racial Consciousness model (LaFleur et al., 2002; Rowe et al., 1994), which they described as an alternative to White racial identity. Their approach was grounded in empirical testing of their model and centered on achieved versus unachieved attitude types rather than statuses. Although scholarly debate continued to focus on White racial identity models, which encouraged innovative approaches that were nonsequential and focused on intersecting reference group identities (e.g., Scott & Robinson, 2001), little criticism was directed at the White racial consciousness model. Most recently, a growing body of research has begun to examine the psychosocial costs of racism to Whites in an attempt to explain how living in a racist system, which disproportionately benefits dominant-group members, nonetheless affects them in negative ways. While operationalizing the constructs of White Empathy, White Guilt, and White Fear of people of color, this approach augments prior conceptual work on the topic (e.g., Goodman, 2001; Kivel, 2002) and provides empirical evidence suggesting that racial affect is an important facet of Whiteness.

The present discussion reviews and evaluates the psychological study of Whiteness over the past quarter century, but looking ahead, scholars must continue to refine and develop theoretical models. One useful approach might be to continue synthesizing existing models, thereby integrating key constructs of major theories to capture the most comprehensive frameworks (see, for example, Sabnani, Ponterotto, & Borodovsky, 1991). Another might be to examine the complexities of White privilege attitudes and the various effects of such attitudes on how one feels about his or her racial group membership (see Pinterits, Poteat, & Spanierman, 2009). Scholars must develop innovative theories by which to understand Whiteness that not only encompass prior psychological study, but also include the interdisciplinary field of critical Whiteness studies. The best psychological models will be informed by this rich interdisciplinary literature that includes sociological research, critical race theory, and labor history to gain the most comprehensive understanding.

Because the study of White racial identity and attitudes is complex, operationalization of multifaceted theories has been problematic in a number of ways. It is noteworthy that no psychometrically strong instrument exists to capture the full range of affective, cognitive, and behavioral experiences of White individuals with regard to their racial identity and attitudes. Factor analytic investigations provide inconsistent information and point to alternative constellations of existing WRIAS and ORAS items (e.g., Mercer & Cunningham, 2003; Pope-Davis et al., 1999). Therefore, existing instruments designed to measure White racial identity and White racial consciousness are in need of revision. Lee and colleagues attempted to revise the WRCDS, but the revised measure suffers from some of the same limitations of earlier scales (e.g., focus on Black/White binary). We urge researchers on White racial identity to consult a recent issue of the *Journal of Counseling Psychology* (2007), in which scholars offer strong recommendations regarding assessment of racial and ethnic identity, in general, that could inform future assessment of White racial identity and attitudes. Further investigation also is needed to evaluate and extend the theoretical propositions and related inventories of White racial consciousness and psychosocial costs of racism to Whites, because less empirical research has been conducted in these areas.

Future research also must vary its methodological approaches. In particular, we note that most of the empirical studies to date are correlational in nature (e.g., bivariate correlations, canonical correlations, and multiple regression analyses). As suggested by Ponterotto and Park-Taylor (2007), it is crucial that future research incorporate longitudinal designs to trace Whites' racial identity development. Although some researchers already have begun to do this with regard to change as a result of multicultural training (e.g., Neville et al., 1996) and costs of racism to Whites (Soble, 2008), findings are limited. Some have begun to use innovative approaches, such as profile analyses (e.g., Carter, Helms, & Juby,

2004), to tap into the nuances of White racial identity, and we hope that this work continues. Finally, we believe that rigorous qualitative designs should be employed to inform theory and instrument development. These studies would have the potential to provide thick description (see Ponterotto, 2006) that captures the rich and nuanced nature of the topic.

REFERENCES

Behrens, J. T. (1997). Does the White Racial Identity Attitude Scale measure racial identity? *Journal of Counseling Psychology, 44,* 3–12.

Behrens, J. T., & Rowe, W. (1997). Measuring White racial identity: A reply to Helms (1997). *Journal of Counseling Psychology, 44,* 17–19.

Block, C. J., Roberson, L., & Neuger, D. A. (1995). White racial identity theory: A framework for understanding reactions toward interracial situations in organizations. *Journal of Vocational Behavior, 46,* 71–88.

Bowser, B. P., & Hunt, R. G. (1981). *Impacts of racism on White Americans.* Beverly Hills, CA: Sage.

Bowser, B. P. & Hunt, R. G. (1996). *Impacts of racism on White Americans* (2nd ed.). Thousand Oaks, CA: Sage.

Burkard, A. W., Juarez-Huffaker, M., & Ajmere, K. (2003). White racial identity attitudes as a predictor of client perceptions of cross-cultural working alliances. *Journal of Multicultural Counseling and Development, 31,* 226–244.

Caditz, J. (1976). *White liberals in transition.* New York: Wiley.

Carter, R. T. (1990). The relationship between racism and racial identity among White Americans: An exploratory investigation. *Journal of Counseling & Development, 69,* 46–50.

Carter, R. T., Gushue, G. V., & Weitzman, L. M. (1994). White racial identity development and work values. *Journal of Vocational Behavior, 44,* 185–197.

Carter, R. T., Helms, J. E., & Juby, H. L. (2004).The relationship between racism and racial identity for White Americans: A profile analysis. *Journal of Multicultural Counseling and Development, 32,* 2–17.

Case, K. A. (2007). Raising White privilege awareness and reducing racial prejudice: Assessing diversity course effectiveness. *Teaching of Psychology, 34, 231–235.*

Castillo, L. G., Conoley, C. W., King, J., Rollins, D., Rivera, S., & Veve, M. (2006). Predictors of racial prejudice in White American counseling students. *Journal of Multicultural Counseling and Development, 34,* 15–26.

Choney, S. K., & Behrens, J. T. (1996). Development of the Oklahoma Racial Attitudes Scale-Preliminary Form (ORAS-P). In G. R. Sodowsky & J. Impara (Eds.), *Multicultural assessment in counseling and clinical psychology* (pp. 225–240). Lincoln, NE: Buros Institute of Mental Measurements.

Choney, S. K., & Rowe, W. (1994). Assessing White racial identity: The White Racial Consciousness Development Scale (WRCDS). *Journal of Counseling & Development, 73,* 102–104.

Claney, D., & Parker, W. M. (1989). Assessing White racial consciousness and perceived comfort with Black individuals: A preliminary study. *Journal of Counseling & Development, 67,* 449–451.

Cross, W. E. (1971, July). The Negro-to-Black conversion experience. *Black World,* pp. 13–27.

Cumming-McCann, A., & Accordino, M. P. (2005). An investigation of rehabilitation counselor characteristics, White racial attitudes, and self-reported multicultural counseling competencies. *Rehabilitation Counseling Bulletin, 48,* 167–176.

Dovidio, J. F., & Gaertner, S. L. (Eds.). (1986). *Prejudice, discrimination, and racism.* San Diego, CA: Academic Press.

DuBois, W. E. B. (1903). *Souls of Black folks.* Chicago: A. C. McClurg.

DuBois, W. E. B. (1935). *Black Reconstruction in the United States, 1860–1880.* New York: Free Press.

Feagin, J. R., & O'Brien, E. (2003). *White men on race: Power, privilege, and the shaping of cultural consciousness.* Boston: Beacon Press.

Frankenberg, R. (1993). *White women, race matters: The social construction of Whiteness.* New York: Routledge.

Gibson, H. M. (2006). *The invisible Whiteness of being: The place of Whiteness in women's discourses in Aotearoa/ New Zealand and some implications for antiracist education.* Unpublished doctoral dissertation, University of Canterbury, New Zealand.

Goodman, D. J. (2001). *Promoting diversity and social justice: Educating people from privileged groups.* Thousand Oaks, CA: Sage.

Gushue, G. V., & Constantine, M. G. (2007). Color-blind racial attitudes and white racial identity attitudes in psychology trainees. *Professional Psychology: Research and Practice, 38,* 321–328.

Hardiman, R. (1982). White identity development: A process oriented model for describing the racial consciousness of White Americans. *Dissertation Abstracts International,* DAI-A 43/01.

Helms, J. E. (1984). Toward a theoretical explanation of the effects of race on counseling. *Counseling Psychologist, 17,* 227–252.

Helms, J. E. (Ed.). (1990). *Black and White racial identity development: Theory, research, and practice.* Westport, CT: Greenwood.

Helms, J. E. (1995). An update of Helms's White and people of color racial identity models. In J. G. Ponterotto, J. M. Casas, L. A. Suzuki, & C. M. Alexander (Eds.), *Handbook of multicultural counseling* (pp. 181–198). Thousand Oaks, CA: Sage.

Helms, J. E. (1997). Implication of Behrens (1997) for the validity of the White Racial Identity Attitude Scale. *Journal of Counseling Psychology, 44,* 13–16.

Helms, J. E. (1999). Another meta-analysis of the White Racial Identity Attitude Scale's Cronbach alphas: Implications for validity. *Measurement and Evaluation in Counseling and Development, 32,* 122–137.

Helms, J. E. (2005). Challenging some of the misuses of reliability as reflected in the evaluations of the White Racial Identity Attitudes Scale (WRIAS). In R. T. Carter (Ed.), *Handbook of racial-cultural psychology and counseling: Theory and research* (Vol. 1, pp. 360–390). New York: Wiley.

Helms, J. E. (2007). Some better practices for measuring racial and ethnic identity constructs. *Journal of Counseling Psychology, 54,* 235–246.

Helms, J. E., & Carter, R. T. (1990). Development of the White Racial Identity Inventory. In J. E. Helms (Ed.), *Black and White racial identity development: Theory, research, and practice* (pp. 67–80). Westport, CT: Greenwood.

Helms, J. E., & Carter, R. T. (1991). Relationships of White and Black racial identity attitudes and demographic similarity to counselor preferences. *Journal of Counseling Psychology, 38,* 446–457.

Jacob Arriola, K. R., & Cole, E. R. (2001). Framing the affirmative-action debate: Attitudes toward out-group members and White identity. *Journal of Applied Social Psychology, 31,* 2462–2483.

Jensen, R. (2005). *The heart of Whiteness: Confronting race, racism and White privilege.* San Francisco: City Lights.

Katz, J. H., & Ivey, A. (1977). White awareness: The frontier of racism awareness training. *Personnel and Guidance Journal, 55,* 485–489.

Kivel, P. (2002). *Uprooting racism: How White people can work for racial justice* (Rev. ed.). Philadelphia: New Society Publishers.

LaFleur, N. K., Leach, M. M., & Rowe, W. (2003, June). *Manual: Oklahoma Racial Attitudes Scale.* Unpublished manual.

LaFleur, N. K., Rowe, W., & Leach, M. M. (2002). Reconceptualizing White racial consciousness. *Journal of Multicultural Counseling and Development, 30,* 148–152.

Leach, M. M., Behrens, J. T., & LaFleur, N. K. (2002). White racial identity and White racial consciousness: Similarities, differences, and recommendations. *Journal of Multicultural Counseling and Development, 30,* 66–80.

Lee, S. M., Puig, A., Pasquarella-Daley, L., Denny, G., Rai, A. A., Dallape, A., & Parker, W. M. (2007). Revising the White Racial Consciousness Development Scale. *Measurement and Evaluation in Counseling and Development, 39,* 194–208.

Marcia, J. E. (1966). Development and validation of ego identity status. *Journal of Personality and Social Psychology, 3,* 551–558.

Marx, S., & Pennington, J. (2003). Pedagogies of critical race theory: Experimentations with white preservice teachers. *International Journal of Qualitative Studies in Education, 16,* 91–110.

Mercer, S. H., & Cunningham, M. (2003). Racial identity in White American college students: Issues of conceptualization and measurement. *Journal of College Student Development, 44,* 217–230.

Miville, M. L., Darlington, P., Whitlock, B., & Mulligan, T. (2005). Integrating identities: The relationships of racial, gender, and ego identities among White college students. *Journal of College Student Development, 46,* 157–175.

Mueller, J. A., & Pope, R. L. (2001). The relationship of demographic and experience variables to White racial consciousness among student affairs practitioners. *NASPA Journal, 40,* 149–171.

Neville, H. A., Heppner, M. J., Louie, C. E., Thompson, C. E., Brooks, L., & Baker, C. E. (1996). The impact of multicultural training on White racial identity attitudes and therapy competencies. *Professional Psychology: Research and Practice, 27,* 83–89.

Neville, H. A., Lilly, R. L., Duran, G., Lee, R. M., & Browne, L. (2000). Construction and initial validation of the Color-Blind Racial Attitudes Scale (CoBRAS). *Journal of Counseling Psychology, 47,* 59–70.

Neville, H. A., Worthington, R. L., & Spanierman, L. B. (2001). Race, power, and multicultural counseling psychology: Understanding White privilege and color-blind racial attitudes. In J. G. Ponterotto, J. M. Casas, L. A. Suzuki, & C. M. Alexander (Eds.), *Handbook of multicultural counseling* (2nd ed., pp. 257–288). Thousand Oaks, CA: Sage.

Pack-Brown, S. P. (1999). Racism and White counselor training: Influence of White racial identity theory and research. *Journal of Counseling & Development, 77,* 87–92.

Pettigrew, T. F., & Tropp, L. R. (2006). A meta-analytic test of intergroup contact theory. *Journal of Personality and Social Psychology, 90,* 751–783.

Phinney, J. S. (1989). Stages of ethnic identity development in minority group adolescents. *Journal of Early Adolescence, 9*, 34–49.

Pinterits, E. J., Poteat, V. P., & Spanierman, L. B. (2009). The White Privilege Attitudes Scale: Development and initial validation. *Journal of Counseling Psychology 56*, 417-429.

Ponterotto, J. G. (1988). Racial consciousness development among White counselor trainees: A stage model. *Journal of Multicultural Counseling and Development, 16*, 146–156.

Ponterotto, J. G. (2006). Brief note on the origins, evolution, and meaning of the qualitative research concept "thick description." *Qualitative Report, 11*, 538–549.

Ponterotto, J. G., & Park-Taylor, J. (2007). Racial and ethnic identity theory, measurement, and research in counseling psychology: Present status and future direction. *Journal of Counseling Psychology, 54*, 282–294.

Ponterotto, J. G., Utsey, S. O., & Pedersen, P. B. (2006). *Preventing prejudice: A guide for counselors, educators, and parents* (2nd ed.). Thousand Oaks, CA: Sage.

Pope-Davis, D. B., & Ottavi, T. M. (1994). The relationship between racism and racial identity among White Americans: A replication and extension. *Journal of Counseling & Development, 72*, 293–297.

Pope-Davis, D. B., Vandiver, B. J., & Stone, G. L. (1999). White racial identity attitude development: A psychometric examination of two instruments. *Journal of Counseling Psychology, 46*, 70–79.

Poteat, V. P., & Spanierman, L. B. (2008). Further validation of the Psychosocial Costs of Racism to Whites Scale among a sample of employed adults. *Counseling Psychologist, 36*, 871–894.

Rowe, W. (2006). White racial identity: Science, faith, and pseudoscience. *Journal of Multicultural Counseling and Development, 34*, 235–243.

Rowe, W., & Atkinson, D. R. (1995). Misrepresentation and interpretation: Critical evaluation of White racial identity development models. *Counseling Psychologist, 23*, 364–367.

Rowe, W., Behrens, J. T., & Leach, M. M. (1995). Racial/ethnic identity and racial consciousness: Looking back and looking forward. In J. G. Ponterotto, J. M. Casas, L. A. Suzuki, & C. M. Alexander (Eds.), *Handbook of multicultural counseling* (pp. 218–235). Thousand Oaks, CA: Sage.

Rowe, W., Bennett, S. K., & Atkinson, D. R. (1994). White racial identity models: A critique and alternate proposal. *Counseling Psychologist, 22*, 129–146.

Sabnani, H. B., Ponterotto, J. G., & Borodovsky, L. G. (1991). White racial identity development and cross-cultural counselor training: A stage model. *Counseling Psychologist, 19*, 76–102.

Schmidt, C. A., & Church, A. T. (2004, August). *White racial consciousness formation and ego development.* Poster presented at the annual convention of the American Psychological Association, Honolulu, HI.

Scott, D. A., & Robinson, T. L. (2001). White male identity development: The Key model. *Journal of Counseling & Development, 79*, 415–421.

Soble, J. R. (2008). *The effect of cognitive dissonance induction on racial attitudes and costs of racism types in White individuals.* Unpublished master's thesis, University of Illinois, Urbana-Champaign.

Spanierman, L. B., & Heppner, M. J. (2004). Psychosocial Costs of Racism to Whites scale (PCRW): Construction and initial validation. *Journal of Counseling Psychology, 51*, 249–262.

Spanierman, L. B., Oh, E., Poteat, V. P., Hund, A. R., McClair, V. L., Beer, A. M., & Clarke, A. M. (2008). White university students' responses to societal racism: A qualitative investigation. *Counseling Psychologist, 36*, 839–870.

Spanierman, L. B., Poteat, V. P., Beer, A. M., & Armstrong, P. I. (2006). Psychosocial Costs of Racism to Whites: Exploring patterns through cluster analysis. *Journal of Counseling Psychology, 53*, 434–441.

Spanierman, L. B., Poteat, V. P., Wang, Y-F., & Oh, E. (2008). Psychosocial costs of racism to White counselors: Predicting various dimensions of multicultural counseling competence. *Journal of Counseling Psychology, 55*, 75–88.

Spanierman, L. B., Todd, N. R., & Anderson, C. J. (2009). Psychosocial costs of racism to Whites: Understanding patterns among university students. *Journal of Counseling Psychology, 56*, 239–252.

Sue, D. W. (2004). Whiteness and ethnocentric monoculturalism: Making the "invisible" visible. *American Psychologist, 59*, 761–769.

Terry, R. W. (1970). *For Whites only.* Grand Rapids, MI: William B. Eerdmans.

Thompson, C. E. (1994). Helms's White racial identity development (WRID) theory: Another look. *Counseling Psychologist, 22*, 645–649.

Tokar, D. M., & Swanson, J. L. (1991). An investigation of the validity of Helms's (1984) model of White racial identity development. *Journal of Counseling Psychology, 38*, 296–301.

Utsey, S. O., & Gernat, C. A. (2002). White racial identity attitudes and the ego defense mechanisms used by White counselor trainees in racially provocative counseling situations. *Journal of Counseling & Development, 80*, 475–483.

26

Multiracial-Heritage Awareness and Personal Affiliation (M-HAPA)

Understanding Identity in People of Mixed-Race Descent

SOOJEAN CHOI-MISAILIDIS

People of mixed race descent have had a long history in the United States. However, it was not until 1967, when the U.S. Supreme Court made all antimiscegenation laws illegal in the United States, that the rate of intermarriage increased exponentially (Root, 1996) and the awareness of the growing population of mixed race people in the United States has been heightened. Historically, racial categorization in the United States has been exclusive and absolutist, and therefore, there were no reliable estimates of the number of multiracial people in the United States until the 2000 Census, but there was a general consensus that the number of mixed-race people in the population was growing rapidly (Fernandez, 1996; Johnson et al., 1997; Kerwin & Ponterotto, 1995). Although it is hypothesized that the rate of multiraciality is underreported due to the implications that such endorsements would have in the allocation of resources and in public policy

(Suyemoto, 2004), 6.8 million people, or 2.4% of the U.S. population, were identified as multiracial in the 2000 Census. Demographers estimate that by 2050, approximately 20% of the U.S. population will be multiracial. However, sociopolitical identification of mixed race ancestry, as noted by mechanisms such as the U.S. Census, should be differentiated from the psychological process of forming a multiracial identity.

Although multiracial people have a long history in the United States, it is only within recent years that multiracial people have received significant attention in the research literature. Research prior to this period was largely influenced by the political climate of the times, and subsequently, much of the literature depicted people of mixed-race descent as experiencing pathological levels of maladjustment (Nakashima, 1992; Stonequist, 1937). Much of this early literature was based primarily on clinical samples, and therefore, mixed-race individuals have been depicted as experiencing high levels of psychopathology (Daniel, 1996; Root, 1992). In recent years, as more people of mixed race descent are coming of age in the United States, the view that multiracial people are necessarily maladjusted is being refuted (Shih & Sanchez, 2005). Although theories of racial identity are helpful in informing theories of multiracial identity, the study of multiracial identity merits particular attention because mixed-race people must negotiate their identity within two or more racial contexts. Even when society viewed races as predominantly distinct and discrete (Nakashima, 1992; Thornton, 1996), researchers discovered that some mixed-race individuals were forming identities that successfully integrated all aspects of their racial heritages. The recent literature acknowledges the uniqueness of the multiracial experience and seeks to understand normative and healthy identity among multiracial people.

Many theories of multiracial identity have posited that there is a developmental sequence by which people form a healthy identity (e.g., Kich, 1992; Poston, 1990). In addition, these theories posit that the healthiest and most desirable endpoint of the identity formation process is the attainment of an identity that integrates all aspects of their ancestry. Some researchers have suggested that a multiracial identity reflects the degree of flexibility and fluidity of racial boundaries (Bratter, 2007), but to date, there is no empirical evidence to support the assertion that this is the only healthy outcome of the multiracial identity formation process (Miville, Constantine, Baysden, & So-Lloyd, 2005). This perspective pathologizes those who do not identify as mixed-race individuals and negates other potentially healthy outcomes of the racial identity development process (Anderson, 1993; Nakashima, 1996). Root's (1990) model addresses the limitations of the developmental model by positing that there are four identity resolutions that biracial people may adopt, which allows for more than one possible healthy identity.

There are other notable limitations in the literature. Few empirical studies have been conducted on people of mixed-race descent (Edwards & Pedrotti, 2008), particularly with valid measures (Miville et al., 2005). The shortage of empirical studies can be attributed to an inability to identify multiracial people. Although the data from the 2000 Census estimate the number of mixed-race people

in the United States, researchers have not been able to identify or locate mixed-race people in any systematic way. This difficulty in identifying multiracial individuals has served as a significant barrier to conducting empirical studies of this unique population.

Much of the literature on mixed-race identity consists of qualitative studies focused on specific groups of biracial people, particularly those of mixed African American and European American ancestry (e.g., Gibbs, 1987; Jacobs, 1992; Johnson, 1992; Miller & Miller, 1990; Pedrotti, Edwards, & Lopez, 2008; Wilson, 1984). Because of the small number of participants in these studies, and given the homogeneity of their racial backgrounds, the theories drawn from these studies have limited generalizability to all multiracial people. Qualitative studies have demonstrated that differences between various mixed-race groups exist. The unique sociological, historical, and political experiences of each group are significant in shaping the contexts in which mixed-race individuals form their identity.

Such specified theories fail to account for the shared experiences of all multiracial individuals in the identity formation process (Grove, 1991; Herman, 2004), although it is generally hypothesized that there are commonalities in the experiences of multiracial individuals. The exploration of common issues and processes that all multiracial people encounter in forming an identity is, therefore, warranted (Anderson, 1993; Hall, 1996). Some theorists have attempted to address the limitation in the biracial identity literature by proposing models that are theoretically generalizable to all multiracial populations (e.g., Kich, 1992; Poston, 1990; Root, 1990). However, no published studies have provided research support for these proposed models (Miville et al., 2005; Shih & Sanchez, 2005). Furthermore, some researchers have hypothesized that mixed-race identity is a multidimensional construct (Daniel, 1996) that is fluid and can be influenced by contextual factors (Johnson et al., 1997; Pedrotti et al., 2008). Building upon these tenets, a universal theory of mixed-race identity is offered.

MULTIRACIAL-HERITAGE AWARENESS AND PERSONAL AFFILIATION THEORY

The Multiracial-Heritage Awareness and Personal Affiliation Theory (M-HAPA) (Choi-Misailidis, 2004,

2008a) is an integration of theoretical models proposed by qualitative studies of various biracial groups.

The proposed model of multiracial identity uses a status model for understanding mixed-race identity. As Helms (1994) noted, identity is often more complex than a mere dichotomous commitment to one group over others; for that reason, stage models, which depict the transitions between stages as relatively fixed, neglect the dynamic nature of identity. Identity statuses need not be mutually exclusive. Instead, statuses may be conceptualized as developing in a successive pattern (Helms, 1994) in which statuses that develop later are more cognitively complex and allow the individual to cope with increasingly complex information. However, as Helms (1994) suggested, once an identity status appears, it remains in the individual's personality constellation and is always potentially available to influence the individual's functioning. In the status model, dominant statuses are those that are most frequently reinforced by the environment; in other words, the identity status that an individual adopts most frequently will be the most effective identity the individual can project in his or her interactions with others. Subsequently, dominant statuses have the most influence over an individual's racial identity, but the identity of the individual is hypothesized to be fluid and context specific (e.g., Mass, 1992; Pedrotti et al., 2008; Streeter, 1996; Williams, 1996).

In the M-HAPA model, identity is seen as being fluid and dynamic; as such, individuals are conceptualized as having an identity profile that corresponds to the strength of their agreement with each of the proposed identity statuses. It is hypothesized that multiracial people identify with each of the identity statuses, but the strength of their identification with each status changes across contexts. For some individuals, one identity status may be more dominant than the others across all situations; however, this identification does not preclude the usage of alternate strategies to negotiate their awareness and affiliation as contextual factors change. For other individuals, the predominating identity status will be determined by the context of the given situation. For example, a biracial individual who primarily identifies as a person of mixed-race descent may find that he or she identifies more strongly with neither or one of his or her racial heritages when in different social situations, such as cultural events; in

interactions with various family members; or in neighborhoods with a different racial composition from his or her own.

M-HAPA Theory proposes that identity is composed of two components: an internal mixed-race identity and an external identification with a multiracial heritage. These two facets of identity are distinct, and therefore, it is necessary to differentiate between these two components of multiracial identity. The internal mixed-race identity is conceptualized as a personal, psychological *awareness* of one's ancestry. Evidence of an internal awareness of mixed-race heritage can include an individual's feelings about his or her racial heritages, his or her attitudes and beliefs about multiraciality, his or her sense of belonging with various racial groups, the level of personal appreciation of his or her heritages, and other internal manifestations of his or her racial awareness. In contrast, an external identification, or *personal affiliation* with various racial/ethnic groups, can differ from one's internal awareness and identity. External manifestations of racial identification can include self-identification (such as for the U.S. Census), participation in cultural practices, selection of friends and significant others, relationships with family members, their roles within society, and other external manifestations of an individual's racial affiliations. The external personal affiliation is often influenced more heavily by sociological, historical, and political factors. This concept of an internal identity/external identification should be differentiated from internal and external factors that affect one's mixed-race identity that have been cited extensively in the literature. These factors are discussed later in the chapter.

According to M-HAPA Theory, it is hypothesized that the healthiest outcomes would be anticipated when there is greater congruence between individuals' internal identity and their external racial identification. In cases where there is greater disparity between internal awareness and external personal affiliation, M-HAPA Theory would predict that there would be greater vulnerability to problems with adjustment, mental health concerns, and interpersonal difficulties.

The M-HAPA Theory of mixed-heritage identity consists of three multiracial identity statuses: Marginal Identity Status, Singular Identity Status, and Integrated Identity Status.

Marginal Identity Status. Park (1928) first coined the term *marginal man* to represent a person who lives in two cultural contexts. Some theorists (e.g., Stonequist, 1937) further interpreted marginality as a negative outcome of being a member of two different worlds, yet not completely belonging to either. However, Stonequist's conceptualization of the marginal personality should be differentiated from someone who identifies with Marginal Identity Status. Although there is some contention that Marginal Identity Status exists because it is imposed by societal forces (Anderson, 1993; Kerwin & Ponterotto, 1995; Poston, 1990; Root, 1990), some have argued that Marginal Identity Status constitutes a part of the process of multiracial identity development (Anderson, 1993; Grove, 1991). For mixed-race individuals, the Marginal Identity Status can be described as an awareness of differentness based on race (Kich, 1992; Nakashima, 1988). Marginal Identity Status, in itself, does not necessarily translate into identity problems (Hall, 1992a, 1992b; King & DaCosta, 1996; Root, 1996; Standen, 1996; Weisman, 1996). Some theorists have suggested that Marginal Identity Status may be a viable way of negotiating one's multiraciality in that it allows the mixed-race individual to have a broader perspective because he or she is not limited to or committed to any one racial group (Daniel, 1996).

The Marginal Identity Status is characterized by disconnection from all aspects of one's multiracial heritages. External behaviors associated with the Marginal Identity Status may include a lack of participation in or an avoidance of the cultural practices of one's ethnocultural or racial/ethnic backgrounds. Marginal Identity Status may be characterized by an inability or disinterest in affiliating with one's racial heritages, and also can also be characterized by a lack of affiliation with any racial group. People who subscribe to the attitudes and beliefs associated with Marginal Identity Status may feel disconnected from others because they perceive themselves to be very different from others, especially compared to monoracial individuals. Marginal Identity Status also describes those individuals who may experience feelings of disconnection from friends and peers because of their self-perception of differentness. Individuals who would endorse beliefs and attitudes commonly linked to the Marginal Identity Status

may perceive that their position in society is also marginal because their ambiguous racial heritage does not make them easily classifiable.

The Marginal Identity Status is also associated with internal beliefs and attitudes. For example, individuals who hold attitudes and beliefs associated with the Marginal Identity Status may feel alienated because their mixed-race status precludes them from a sense of membership in society because they are not classified by commonly used racial categories. People who are predominantly of the Marginal Identity Status will lack a sense of belonging with any racial group, and they may neither appreciate nor understand cultural beliefs and practices.

Singular Identity Status. As reviewed in the introduction to this chapter, historically in the United States, people of mixed-race descent have not been allowed to claim multiple racial group memberships because race was viewed as a mutually exclusive classification system (Anderson, 1993; Johnson et al., 1997; Nakashima, 1992; Thornton, 1996). Unofficially, society frequently assigns mixed-race people into particular single racial groups based solely upon physical appearance (Kerwin & Ponterotto, 1995; Nakashima, 1992; Root, 1990). When this affiliation is internalized and the mixed-race individual derives his or her identity from identification and belongingness to one group (Rowe, Behrens, & Leach, 1995), the person has developed a singular identity.

Singular Identity Status is associated with an individual's affiliation with one racial group, to the exclusion of others. An individual who has an identity consistent with Singular Identity Status would be immersed in the cultural practices of only one racial group and to the exclusion of the other racial group or groups in his or her heritage. Singular Identity Status may be manifested in one's selection of friends and dating prospects, as well as through identification with family members who are of the race with which the individual has chosen to identify. The individual whose identity is Singular Identity Status perceives that his or her position in society is equivalent to the status of his or her reference group, regardless of his or her multiraciality. These individuals will feel wholly identified and will feel a sense of belonging to a particular racial reference group. As such, there will be an appreciation of the cultural practices and beliefs of one racial group, but no identification or affiliation with the cultural practices of other racial groups.

Singular Identity Status is also characterized by shifts in identification from one aspect of one's racial heritage to another. In this way, people with Singular Identity Status may explore and experiment with each aspect of their heritage, but in an exclusive fashion, such that they may deny other aspects of their heritage. This fashion of exploring one's identity one group at a time may allow the individual to feel wholly a member of each group, thus providing an essential component in gaining insight into each racial group that comprises one's identity.

Integrated Identity Status. In recent years, consciousness regarding normative multiracial identity has been raised, and subsequently, theorists have acknowledged that mixed-race people can form identities that integrate all aspects of their racial heritage (Kich, 1992; Standen, 1996). Individuals who attain Integrated Identity Status are able to blend all aspects of their racial heritages (Daniel, 1996) and are able to maintain connections with multiple racial groups (Anderson, 1993; Gibbs & Hines, 1992; Hall, 1980; Stephan & Stephan, 1989). Integration of mixed-race identity is an internal manifestation and personal affirmation of one's identification with one's racial groups through the incorporation of multiple groups into one's identity (Brown & Douglass, 1996; Gibbs & Hines, 1992; Hall, 1980; Stephan & Stephan, 1989). Integration of mixed-race identity also has an external component, manifested by the use of multiracial labels claiming simultaneous membership to multiple racial groups, and through participation and affiliation with the racial groups that comprise one's heritage (Daniel, 1996; Hall, 1996; Root, 1992; Thornton, 1996; Williams, 1992). However, an Integrated Identity Status does not necessitate that all racial groups in one's heritage be equally represented or valued within the individual's identity (Kich, 1992). In addition, individuals who achieve Integrated Identity Status are likely to manifest an increased tolerance of differences between racial groups, while appreciating commonalities (Daniel, 1996).

Integrated Identity Status is characterized by an integration of meaningful values and beliefs from each aspect of one's heritage in forming a complete sense of self. There is an appreciation and understanding of all racial groups in one's heritage, participation in the cultural practices and beliefs in each of one's heritages, and the ability to relate to others interpersonally, regardless of racial background. Racial categorization is transcended and an appreciation for diversity is cultivated. Because of their affiliation with all aspects of their racial heritages, individuals with an Integrated Identity Status are able to relate to family members of all racial backgrounds and choose friends and romantic partners from diverse racial groups. There are positive feelings about their racial heritages, appreciation of their multiraciality, and the ability to adapt their identity to situational demands.

M-HAPA Theory presents a comprehensive theoretical framework that is applicable to all people of multiracial descent. Given that there were no valid measures of mixed-race identity in the research literature, the M-HAPA Theory was operationalized into the form of a self-report measure. The scale development and validation research is reviewed in the following section.

MULTIRACIAL-HERITAGE AWARENESS AND PERSONAL AFFILIATION SCALE

Given the difficulty in finding a substantive multiracial population, no measures specifically examining mixed-race identity had been developed and published in the research literature. The Multiracial-Heritage Awareness and Personal Affiliation Scale (M-HAPAs) (Choi-Misailidis, 2004, 2008b) is the first measure of multiracial identity to be developed and empirically tested with a large-scale sample.

The M-HAPAs is a 43-item self-report measure. Each item consists of one sentence devised to assess individuals' awareness of their multiracial heritage, affiliation with their parents' racial groups, beliefs about race, behaviors as a racial being, or relationship to people of various racial groups.

The M-HAPAs was empirically tested on a sample of 364 mixed-race individuals from three universities in Hawai'i. Participants were included in the study if they indicated that they were of mixed racial descent or if they indicated that their parents or grandparents identified with different racial groups. Approximately two thirds of the sample reported that they were biracial;

the remaining one third of respondents reported that their heritage included three or more races. The ages of the participants ranged from 17 to 58.

Exploratory factor analyses revealed that the M-HAPAs is composed of four factors that correspond to the three identity statuses outlined by M-HAPA Theory; however, the analyses revealed that Integrated Identity Status was best conceptualized by two subfactors. These subfactors were Integrated Identity Status—Combinatory Factor and Integrated Identity Status—Universality Factor. Integrated Identity Status—Combinatory Factor represents an identity status in which one has integrated the racial groups comprising one's heritage; individuals who endorse Integrated Identity Status—Universality Factor could be characterized by an appreciation of commonalities among racial groups and a general appreciation for diversity.

The results of the study demonstrated support for the reliability and validity of the M-HAPAs. The Marginal Identity Status subscale was composed of 13 items that described an identity status in which there is no identification with any racial group. Examples of items on the Marginal Identity Status subscale are "I feel disconnected from all racial groups" and "I am not interested in affiliating with any of my parents' racial groups." The Marginal Identity Status subscale demonstrated good internal consistency reliability ($\alpha = .83$); support for construct validity was demonstrated by the negative correlation between the Marginal Identity Status subscale and measures of ethnic identity and attitudes toward other ethnic groups.

The Singular Identity Status subscale represents an identity status in which one identifies solely with one racial group among his or her parents' racial heritages. The Singular Identity Status subscale consists of 13 items, such as "I wish to be identified solely as a member of one of my parents' races" and "I have tried to 'pass' as a member of one of my parents' races." The statistical analyses revealed good internal consistency reliability ($\alpha = .85$) for the Singular Identity Status subscale; support for construct validity was shown by the positive correlation between the Singular Identity Status subscale and a measure of ethnic identity and the negative relationship between the Singular Identity Status subscale with a measure of attitudes toward other ethnic groups.

The Integrated Identity Status—Combinatory Factor subscale was composed of 10 items that described an

identity status characterized by an individual's integration of the racial heritages of both parents. Examples of items on this subscale include "I identify with both my mother's and father's racial heritages" and "I participate in the cultural practices of all groups in my racial heritage." The Integrated Identity Status—Combinatory Factor subscale demonstrated good internal consistency reliability ($\alpha = .83$); support for construct validity was demonstrated by the positive correlation between the Integrated Identity Status—Combinatory Factor subscale and measures of ethnic identity and attitudes toward other ethnic groups.

The Integrated Identity Status—Universality Factor subscale is conceptualized as an identity status in which an individual identifies with people of diverse racial groups and demonstrates an appreciation of commonalities among all people. The Integrated Identity Status—Universality Factor subscale consisted of nine items, such as "I feel connected to many racial groups" and "I have things in common with people of all races." The analyses revealed fair internal consistency reliability ($\alpha = .71$) for the Integrated Identity Status—Universality Factor subscale; support for construct validity was shown by the positive correlation between the Integrated Identity Status—Universality Factor subscale and measures of ethnic identity and attitudes toward other ethnic groups.

Although numerous researchers have shown interest in using the M-HAPAs in other large-scale studies, given the difficulty in conducting research on multiracial people to date, only one other study using the M-HAPAs has been completed. Damann (2008) examined the relationship between multiracial identity status with psychosocial functioning and life satisfaction in a nonclinical sample. In this study, multiracial identity status predicted significant and unique proportions of variance for self-esteem, depression, life satisfaction, and social functioning, as reported by the participants. In addition, multiracial identity status accounted for the greatest variance in social functioning (21%). However, for this sample, confirmatory factor analysis showed a mediocre fit of the data to the model.

The research to date has shown empirical support for the M-HAPA Theory and has demonstrated the utility of the M-HAPAs, but more research is needed to further refine both the theory and the measure.

FACTORS AFFECTING MULTIRACIAL IDENTITY

The research and theoretical literature on people of mixed-race descent have hypothesized that numerous factors affect multiracial identity. Some of these factors are the following:

Phenotype/Appearance. How an individual is perceived and racially categorized can powerfully influence that individual's choice of identity (AhnAllen, Suyemoto, & Carter, 2006; Pedrotti et al., 2008). In some cases, multiracial individuals may identify as one race, but are seen by others as another (Shih & Sanchez, 2005). The effects of this discrepancy have not been systematically studied to date.

Age. Attitudes and beliefs about race are often shaped by early experiences with racial issues (Shih, Bonam, Sanchez, & Peck, 2007). Although it is commonly believed that age and development may influence mixed-race identity (Miville et al., 2005), there have been no longitudinal studies to date that have documented the changes in multiracial identity over the course of the life span.

Name. Although there are no research data to examine its effects, it is hypothesized that one's surname (family name) likely has a significant effect on one's multiracial identity.

Gender. Some qualitative studies have examined gender differences in mixed-race identity (e.g., McClain, 2004; Suyemoto, 2004). However, the results of these studies have been equivocal to date; some have shown that there are no significant differences in multiracial identity between males and females (Suyemoto, 2004), whereas others have shown that men and women do differ, especially with regard to awareness and fluidity of mixed-race identity (McClain, 2004).

Education Level. Studies of the impact of educational level on the expression of a multiracial identity have demonstrated equivocal results. Bratter (2007) found that rejecting racial norms by identifying as multiracial was more commonly found in highly educated families. However, Qian (2004) found that highly educated parents were more likely to identify their children as minority because of their increased awareness of the meaning of being a minority in the United States.

Parents. Again, the literature is equivocal on the effect and role of parents in the expression of a multiracial identity. Connection to racial/ethnic groups is thought to be influenced by parents (Miville et al., 2005; Pedrotti et al., 2008). Some studies have shown that there is less influence on the transmission of identity to the children from the father (Bratter, 2007), whereas other studies have shown that racial identification of children is most likely to reflect the race of the father (Qian, 2004). Yet others have suggested that the disparity in the sociocultural backgrounds of the parents may play a significant role in the racial identification of children (Herring, 1995).

Parents' Marital Status. It is hypothesized that parents' marital status influences the assertion of a multiracial identity because it determines the availability of the parents to facilitate connection of the mixed-race individual with his or her heritages (Miville et al., 2005). In addition, the value and hierarchy of racial groups may be implied in the relationship status of interracial couples. However, the effect of parents' marital status on the identity of mixed-race individuals has not been studied to date.

Extended Family and Other Caregivers. It has been suggested in the literature that extended family and caregivers play a significant role in the identity of multiracial children (Herring, 1995; Miville et al., 2005), but aside from a few studies of parental roles (as discussed above), there is a dearth of research examining the effects of extended family and other caregivers on the identity of mixed-race individuals.

Friends and Significant Others. It is possible that friends and significant others influence an individual's multiracial identity. Conversely, an individual's choice of friends and significant others may be external evidence of the individual's identity and identification. Or, an individual's choice of friends and significant others might have a bidirectional relationship with one's mixed-race identity. No empirical studies have been conducted to test these hypotheses.

Geographical Location. According to the 2000 Census, multiracial individuals are clustered in the western regions of the United States. Therefore, geographical location is another potentially significant variable in determining the heterogeneous experience of mixed-race individuals (Pedrotti et al., 2008). Further studies are needed to determine whether the percentage of mixed-race people is merely greater in these regions, or whether the sociopolitical climate in the western states facilitates multiracial identification.

Community. It is believed that the racial and educational composition of one's neighborhood influences the expression of a multiracial identity (Miville et al., 2005; Qian, 2004), possibly because of the differential treatment that may be given to people of mixed racial descent. The effects of the racial and educational composition of the community on mixed-race identity and identification need to be explored further.

SUMMARY AND RECOMMENDATIONS FOR FUTURE RESEARCH

This chapter has presented a review of the literature on identity among multiracial individuals. The review of the existing research literature revealed numerous theoretical papers and qualitative studies of small homogeneous groups of biracial individuals conducted to find commonalities in the identity development process. Based on these small studies, it is generally assumed that there are commonalities in the identity of all mixed-race people. Despite the fact that large-scale quantitative research is needed to elucidate commonalities in multiracial identity, there is a dearth of empirical research due to difficulties in identifying and locating multiracial individuals, and consequently, there were no valid measures to assess mixed-race identity. The Multiracial-Heritage Awareness and Personal Affiliation (M-HAPA) Theory and Scale are offered to address this limitation in the research literature. Although the research to date has demonstrated empirical support for the M-HAPA Theory and Scale, much more research is needed to refine and strengthen both the theory and the measure.

With regard to multiracial identity, some areas for future research include the following:

Test the M-HAPAs with other samples. In particular, the M-HAPAs should be tested using participants of different age groups and from various geographic regions within the United States and from around the world. Future research should seek to test the measure with other multiracial populations that may not have been represented in previous studies.

Explore the utility of the M-HAPA Theory and Scale for biracial versus multiracial individuals. Studies to date have not differentiated between these groups of mixed-race people; future studies should be mindful of the differences that exist between biracial and multiracial individuals in the development and context of their mixed-race identity.

Evaluate multiracial identity from a life span perspective. No research to date has evaluated multiracial identity longitudinally. Such research may provide insights into the process of mixed-race identity development across the life span.

Determine the relationship between internal awareness and external personal affiliation and their impact on multiracial identity. Internal identity and external affiliations and their roles in determining an individual's mixed-race identity should be examined. M-HAPA Theory posits that internal awareness and external personal affiliation are related, yet independent, facets of multiracial identity. Furthermore, M-HAPA Theory hypothesizes that healthier outcomes would be found when there is greater congruence between a mixed-race person's internal and external identities; conversely, an individual whose internal awareness differs from his or her external affiliations would be more vulnerable to psychosocial difficulties. This complex interplay between internal awareness and external affiliations should be explored further.

Study the effects of contextual factors that determine situational expression or "changes" in multiracial identity. The M-HAPA Theory uses a status model to conceptualize multiracial identity; as such, it posits that even as successively complex identity statuses are formed, other identity statuses remain available to be used as contextual factors change. The role and importance of various contextual factors in determining situational expression, or "changes," in multiracial identity should be explored.

Test the impact of internal and external factors that may influence multiracial identity. Research to date has begun to examine the impact of internal and external factors that may influence mixed-race identity. More investigation is needed to further explicate the effect of internal and external factors.

Explore the outcomes associated with multiracial identity. Research has examined the association between multiracial identity and psychosocial outcomes. Further studies are needed to evaluate the role of mixed-race identity in mental health, psychosocial functioning, self-esteem and self-concept, well-being, resilience, and other psychological outcomes. This area of research would be critical in determining the clinical utility of understanding multiracial identity.

REFERENCES

AhnAllen, J. M., Suyemoto, K. L., & Carter, A. S. (2006). Relationship between physical appearance, sense of belonging and exclusion, and racial/ethnic self-identification among multiracial Japanese European Americans. *Cultural Diversity and Ethnic Minority Psychology, 12,* 673–686.

Anderson, K. S. (1993). *Ethnic identity in biracial Asian Americans.* Unpublished doctoral dissertation, California School of Professional Psychology, Los Angeles.

Bratter, J. (2007). Will "multiracial" survive to the next generation? The racial classification of children of multiracial parents. *Social Forces, 86,* 821–849.

Brown, N. G., & Douglass, R. E. (1996). Making the invisible visible: The growth of community network organizations. In M. P. P. Root (Ed.), *The multiracial experience: Racial borders as the new frontier.* Thousand Oaks, CA: Sage.

Choi-Misailidis, S. (2004). Multiracial-Heritage Awareness and Personal Affiliation: Development and validation of a new measure to assess identity in people of mixed race descent. *Dissertation Abstracts International: Section B. The Physical Sciences and Engineering, 64,* 3556.

Choi-Misailidis, S. (2008a). *Multiracial-Heritage Awareness and Personal Affiliation theory.* Manuscript in preparation.

Choi-Misailidis, S. (2008b). *Multiracial identity: Development and validation of a measure to assess identity in people of mixed racial descent.* Manuscript submitted for publication.

Damann, K. M. (2008). Relation of multiracial identity statuses to psychosocial functioning and life satisfaction. *Dissertation Abstracts International: Section B. The Physical Sciences and Engineering, 68,* 4817.

Daniel, G. R. (1996). Black and White identity in the new millennium: Unsevering the ties that bind. In M. P. P. Root (Ed.), *The multiracial experience: Racial borders as the new frontier.* Thousand Oaks, CA: Sage.

Edwards, L. M., & Pedrotti, J. T. (2008). A content and methodological review of articles concerning multiracial issues in six major counseling journals. *Journal of Counseling Psychology, 55,* 411–418.

Fernandez, C. A. (1996). Government classification of multiracial/multiethnic people. In M. P. P. Root (Ed.), *The multiracial experience: Racial borders as the new frontier.* Thousand Oaks, CA: Sage.

Gibbs, J. T. (1987). Identity and marginality: Issues in the treatment of biracial adolescents. *American Journal of Orthopsychiatry, 57,* 265–278.

Gibbs, J. T., & Hines, A. M. (1992). Negotiating ethnic identity: Issues for Black-White biracial adolescents. In M. P. P. Root (Ed.), *Racially mixed people in America.* Newbury Park, CA: Sage.

Grove, K. J. (1991). Identity development in interracial, Asian/White late adolescents: Must it be so problematic? *Journal of Youth and Adolescence, 20,* 617–628.

Hall, C. C. I. (1980). *The ethnic identity of racially mixed people: A study of Black-Japanese.* Unpublished doctoral dissertation, University of California, Los Angeles.

Hall, C. C. I. (1992a). Coloring outside the lines. In M. P. P. Root (Ed.), *Racially mixed people in America.* Newbury Park, CA: Sage.

Hall, C. C. I. (1992b). Please choose one: Ethnic identity choices for biracial individuals. In M. P. P. Root (Ed.), *Racially mixed people in America.* Newbury Park, CA: Sage.

Hall, C. C. I. (1996). 2001: A race odyssey. In M. P. P. Root (Ed.), *The multiracial experience: Racial borders as the new frontier.* Thousand Oaks, CA: Sage.

Helms, J. E. (1994). The conceptualization of racial identity and other "racial" constructs. In E. J. Trickett & R. J. Watts (Eds.), *Human diversity: Perspectives on people in context.* San Francisco: Jossey-Bass.

Herman, M. (2004). Forced to choose: Some determinants of racial identification in multiracial adolescents. *Child Development, 75,* 730–748.

Herring, R. D. (1995). Developing biracial ethnic identity: A review of the increasing dilemma. *Journal of Multicultural Counseling and Development, 23,* 29–38.

Jacobs, J. H. (1992). Identity development in biracial children. In M. P. P. Root (Ed.), *Racially mixed people in America.* Newbury Park, CA: Sage.

Johnson, D. J. (1992). Developmental pathways: Toward an ecological theoretical formulation of race identity in Black-White biracial children. In M. P. P. Root (Ed.), *Racially mixed people in America.* Newbury Park, CA: Sage.

Johnson, T. P., Jobe, J. B., O'Rourke, D., Sudman, S., Warnecke, R. B., Chavez, N., Chapa-Resendez, G., & Golden, P. (1997). Dimensions of self-identification among multiracial and multiethnic respondents in survey interviews. *Evaluation Review, 21,* 671–687.

Kerwin, C., & Ponterotto, J. G. (1995). Biracial identity development: Theory and research. In J. G. Ponterotto, J. M. Casas, L. A. Suzuki, & C. M. Alexander (Eds.), *Handbook of multicultural counseling.* Thousand Oaks, CA: Sage.

Kich, G. K. (1992). The developmental process of asserting a biracial, bicultural identity. In M. P. P. Root (Ed.), *Racially mixed people in America*. Newbury Park, CA: Sage.

King, R. C., & DaCosta, K. M. (1996). Changing face, changing race: The remaking of race in the Japanese American and African American communities. In M. P. P. Root (Ed.), *The multiracial experience: Racial borders as the new frontier*. Newbury Park, CA: Sage.

Mass, A. I. (1992). Interracial Japanese Americans: The best of both worlds or the end of the Japanese American community? In M. P. P. Root (Ed.), *Racially mixed people in America*. Newbury Park, CA: Sage.

McClain, C. S. (2004). Black by choice: Identity preferences of Americans of Black/White parentage. *Black Scholar, 34*, 43–54.

Miller, R. L., & Miller, B. (1990). Mothering the biracial child: Bridging the gaps between African-American and White parenting styles. *Women and Therapy, 10*, 169–179.

Miville, M. L., Constantine, M. G., Baysden, M. F., & So-Lloyd, G. (2005). Chameleon changes: An exploration of racial identity themes of multiracial people. *Journal of Counseling Psychology, 52*, 507–516.

Nakashima, C. L. (1988). Research notes on Nikkei Hapa identity. In G. Y. Okihiro, S. Hune, A. A. Hansen, & J. M. Liu (Eds.), *Reflections on shattered windows: Promises and prospects for Asian American studies*. Pullman: Washington State University Press.

Nakashima, C. L. (1992). An invisible monster: The creation and denial of mixed-race people in America. In M. P. P. Root (Ed.), *Racially mixed people in America*. Newbury Park, CA: Sage.

Nakashima, C. L. (1996). Voices from the movement: Approaches to multiraciality. In M. P. P. Root (Ed.), *The multiracial experience: Racial borders as the new frontier*. Thousand Oaks, CA: Sage.

Park, R. E. (1928). Human migration and the marginal man. *American Journal of Sociology, 33*, 881–893.

Pedrotti, J. T., Edwards, L. M., & Lopez, S. J. (2008). Working with multiracial clients in therapy: Bridging theory, research and practice. *Professional Psychology: Research and Practice, 39*, 192–201.

Poston, W. S. C. (1990). The biracial identity development model: A needed addition. *Journal of Counseling and Development, 69*, 152–155.

Qian, Z. (2004). Options: Racial/ethnic identification of children of intermarried couples. *Social Science Quarterly, 85*, 746–766.

Root, M. P. P. (1990). Resolving "other" status: Identity development of biracial individuals. In L. Brown & M. P. P. Root (Eds.), *Complexity and diversity in feminist theory and therapy*. New York: Haworth.

Root, M. P. P. (1992). From shortcuts to solutions. In M. P. P. Root (Ed.), *Racially mixed people in America*. Newbury Park, CA: Sage.

Root, M. P. P. (1996). The multiracial experience: Racial borders as a significant frontier in race relations. In M. P. P. Root (Ed.), *The multiracial experience: Racial borders as the new frontier*. Thousand Oaks, CA: Sage.

Rowe, W., Behrens, J. T., & Leach, M. M. (1995). Racial/ethnic identity and racial consciousness: Looking back and looking forward. In J. G. Ponterotto, J. M. Casas, L. A. Suzuki, & C. M. Alexander (Eds.), *Handbook of multicultural counseling*. Thousand Oaks, CA: Sage.

Shih, M., Bonam, C., Sanchez, D., & Peck, C. (2007). The social construction of race: Biracial identity and vulnerability to stereotypes. *Cultural Diversity and Ethnic Minority Psychology, 13*, 125–133.

Shih, M., & Sanchez, D. T. (2005). Perspectives and research on the positive and negative implications of having multiple racial identities. *Psychological Bulletin, 131*, 569–591.

Standen, B. C. S. (1996). Without a template: The biracial Korean/White experience. In M. P. P. Root (Ed.), *The multiracial experience: Racial borders as the new frontier*. Thousand Oaks, CA: Sage.

Stephan, C. W., & Stephan, W. G. (1989). After intermarriage: Ethnic identity among mixed heritage Japanese-Americans and Hispanics. *Journal of Marriage and the Family, 51*, 507–519.

Stonequist, E. V. (1937). *The marginal man: A study in personality and culture conflict*. New York: Russell & Russell.

Streeter, C. A. (1996). Ambiguous bodies: Locating Black/White women in cultural representations. In M. P. P. Root (Ed.), *The multiracial experience: Racial borders as the new frontier*. Thousand Oaks, CA: Sage.

Suyemoto, K. L. (2004). Racial/ethnic identities and related attributed experiences of multiracial Japanese European Americans. *Journal of Multicultural Counseling and Development, 32*, 206–221.

Thornton, M. C. (1996). Hidden agendas, identity theories, and multiracial people. In M. P. P. Root (Ed.), *The multiracial experience: Racial borders as the new frontier*. Thousand Oaks, CA: Sage.

Weisman, J. R. (1996). An "other" way of life. In M. P. P. Root (Ed.), *The multiracial experience: Racial borders as the new frontier*. Thousand Oaks, CA: Sage.

Williams, T. K. (1992). Prism lives: Identity of binational Amerasians. In M. P. P. Root (Ed.), *Racially mixed people in America*. Newbury Park, CA: Sage.

Williams, T. K. (1996). Race as process: Reassessing the "What are you?" encounters of biracial individuals. In M. P. P. Root (Ed.), *The multiracial experience: Racial borders as the new frontier*. Thousand Oaks, CA: Sage.

Wilson, A. (1984). "Mixed race" children in British society: Some theoretical considerations. *British Journal of Sociology, 35*, 42–61.

27

Where Do We Go From Here?

Raising the Bar of What Constitutes
Multicultural Competence in Working With
Lesbian, Gay, Bisexual, and Transgender Communities

LEO WILTON

Today, several people from across the country have experienced a major victory in their lives with the election of Barack Obama—the first Black president of the United States. This election holds special sociohistorical and -political prominence for generations of communities and symbolizes a sense of hope for the future—especially with respect to pursuing a transformative politics that works for the betterment of their communities. Indeed, a multitude of people, including Edna Baldwin, a 102-year-old Black woman from Washington, DC, would not have imagined having the "unthinkable" occur during one's lifetime. On the eve of the election, communities advocating for Barack Obama were represented across boundaries of race/ethnicity, gender, social class, sexuality, and age, thus signifying a sense of hopefulness for the future. Yet at the same time, this historical milestone provides us with an opportunity to reflect on the contradictions that relate to the current realities of the contexts of people's lives and the considerable degree of work that needs to be accomplished during this new era— particularly with respect to challenging hierarchical social structures (e.g., power inequalities) that marginalize and have an impact on the lives of lesbian, gay, bisexual, and transgender (LGBT) communities (e.g., institutionalized forms of homophobia such as discrimination).

In this context, one of the recent major contradictions experienced by LGBT communities relates to the persistent violation of their civil rights. In this respect, the recent passage of Proposition 8 in California modified the state's constitution in two ways: (a) It imposed a legal definition of marriage as between a man and a woman, and (b) it rescinded the right of same-sex couples to marry. The current debate about marriage holds special meaning at this historical moment and needs to be considered within a broader discussion related to the intersection of civil rights struggles. For example, based on the work of Martin (2008), from a historical standpoint, Mildred and Richard Loving as an interracial couple (Mildred Loving was an African American woman and Richard Loving was a White man) experienced institutionalized racism in Virginia when they were both legally exiled from their home by a Virginia court in the late 1950s for obtaining a marriage license in Washington, DC, because segregation laws in the state of Virginia (e.g., Racial Integrity Act) prohibited interracial marriage. At this time, Mildred Loving contacted Robert F. Kennedy, who referred the couple to the American Civil Liberties Union (ACLU). The ACLU brought the case to the U.S. Supreme Court after pursuing the case in court at a variety of levels in Virginia. Consequently, in 1967, the Supreme Court ruled in *Loving v. Virginia* that the miscegenation statute in the state of Virginia was unconstitutional. Following decades of not conducting public interviews regarding the case, Mildred Loving issued a public statement, "Loving for All," on the 40th anniversary of *Loving v. Virginia* on June 12, 2007 (for the full statement, please see Appendix A). In this statement, Mildred Loving articulated a strong position supporting the legal right of same-sex couples to marry:

> Surrounded as I am by wonderful children and grandchildren, not a day goes by that I don't think of Richard and our love, our right to marry, and how much it meant to me to have that freedom to marry the person precious to me, even if others thought he was the "wrong kind of person" for me to marry. I believe that all Americans, no matter their race, no matter their sex, no matter their sexual orientation, should have that same freedom to marry. Government has no business imposing some people's religious beliefs over others. Especially if it denies people's civil rights.

Through this experience, before her death on May 2, 2008, at the age of 68 in Virginia, Mildred Loving provided a powerful testimony regarding the intersectionality of race, gender, social class, and sexuality related to the sociohistorical and -political contexts of civil rights struggles in the United States. This was particularly relevant in connection to the Proposition 8 legislation because Black communities initially were negatively constructed by the news media as having disproportionately voted in favor of this discriminatory legislation when, in fact, this was not the case. A recent report has indicated that a number of factors accounted for the passage of the Proposition 8 legislation that related to age, political party affiliation, political principles, and frequency of attending religious services (Egan & Sherrill, 2009).

Other contemporary issues in LGBT communities involve, but are not limited to, the provision of domestic partnership rights, parental rights, access to quality health care (including mental health such as psychotherapy), work-related discrimination, and the experiences of LGBT-related violence (Cook & Glass, 2008; Pachankis & Goldfried, 2004; Ragins, Singh, & Cornwell, 2007; Ritter & Terndrup, 2002). For example, as there has been an increasing prevalence of LGBT violence over the past few years in the United States, a number of recent cases provide illustrations regarding the impact of the violence: (a) the murder of RaShawn Brazell, a young African American gay man, whose body was found mutilated on a subway platform in Brooklyn, New York; (b) the killing of Sakia Gunn, a young African American lesbian in Newark, New Jersey; and (c) the murder of Jose Sucuzhanay, a young Latino man, whose assailants verbalized anti-immigrant and homophobic comments because they perceived him as being gay for walking arm-in-arm with his brother in Bushwick, an area of Brooklyn, New York. Indeed, there is a critical question that still remains for this new generation at this historical moment: What does civil rights mean for LGBT communities? These contemporary issues relate to the experiences of LGBT communities with respect to the provision of LGBT affirmative counseling. One of the major components of this work relates to incorporating an understanding of the context of the lives of LGBT people and communities (Ritter & Terndrup, 2002), while at the same time serving as an advocate in the work as a scientist-practitioner (Estrada & Rutter, 2008; Fox, 2008). Within this context, the purpose of this chapter is to examine current implications for LGBT affirmative counseling. In this pursuit, the following issues will be examined: the sociohistorical and -political contexts of LGBT affirmative counseling; the role of stigma, marginalization, and mental health in LGBT communities; and implications for the role of practitioners with respect to LGBT affirmative counseling.

SOCIOHISTORICAL AND -POLITICAL CONTEXTS OF LGBT AFFIRMATIVE COUNSELING

It is beyond the scope of this chapter to provide a full account of the historical trajectory of the origins of LGBT affirmative counseling [e.g., the works of Bieschke, Perez, & DeBord (2007), Cabaj & Stein (1996), Greene (1994), Drescher & Merlino (2007), Ritter & Terndrup (2002), and Shidlo, Schroeder, & Drescher (2002) are germane to this area of research]. However, significant milestones have provided the foreground to the emergence of contemporary LGBT affirmative counseling. With the advent of social movements (e.g., civil rights, feminist, LGBT liberation, Vietnam War) and civil rights legislation (e.g., Civil Rights Act of 1964) from the mid-1950s through the early 1970s (Constantine & Wilton, 2004), there has been a growing emphasis on incorporating multicultural constructs (e.g., racial/ethnic/cultural values, identities, and worldviews; gender; social class; sexuality) to the professionalization of psychology (Bernal, Trimble, Burlew, & Leong, 2002; Carter, 2004a, 2004b; Croteau, Bieschke, Fassinger, & Manning, 2008; Fassinger & Arseneau, 2008; Helms & Cook, 1998; Liu & Ali, 2008; Omoto & Kurtzman, 2006; Ponterotto, 2008; Sue & Sue, 2008; Suzuki & Ponterotto, 2008). As will be discussed later in this chapter, much of this work has provided a contemporary focus to the development of multicultural counseling competencies (Worthington, Soth-McNett, & Moreno, 2007) and psychotherapy guidelines in working with lesbian, gay, and bisexual (LGB) clients (Division 44/Committee on Lesbian, Gay, and Bisexual Concerns Joint Task Force on Guidelines for Psychotherapy With Lesbian, Gay, and Bisexual Clients, 2000) (see Appendix B).

Much of the scholarly work on LGBT communities has contributed to the development of a body of literature that has challenged the historical notion of psychopathology associated with LGBT identities (Bayer, 1981; Fox, 2000; Gainor, 2000; Greene, 1994). Based

on the work of Herek, Chopp, and Strohl (2007), one of the earlier scientific studies during the 1950s, funded by the National Institute of Mental Health, on sexuality and psychological health, "The Adjustment of the Male Overt Homosexual," was conducted by Evelyn Hooker, a psychology professor from the University of California at Los Angeles. At a time when conventional wisdom in the mental health professions contended that gay individuals had significant psychological problems in addition to homosexuality, Hooker studied differences in the psychological adjustment that compared gay and heterosexual men based on a series of projective tests (e.g., Thematic Apperception Test, Rorschach Inkblot Test, Make-A-Picture-Story Personality Projective Test). Hooker obtained leading experts to review the findings, without knowledge of the sexual orientation of the participants. The experts could find no evidence of greater psychopathology in either of the two groups, indicating that gay and heterosexual men illustrated similar psychological adjustment. Clearly, Hooker, as a visionary, was at the forefront of conducting scientific studies on sexuality that served as a catalyst to challenge scientific forms of homophobia that were a part of the zeitgeist during this period (Herek et al., 2007).

Significantly, based in part on the pioneering work of studies (like that of Hooker's previously described research) juxtaposed with the sociohistorical and -political contexts of activism of the gay liberation movement (Ritter & Terndrup, 2002), the diagnosis of "homosexuality" as a mental health disorder was reviewed by the American Psychiatric Association and subsequently removed from the second edition of the *Diagnostic and Statistical Manual of Mental Disorders* (*DSM*) in 1973 (Drescher & Merlino, 2007; Shidlo et al., 2002). Moreover, in 1975, the American Psychological Association implemented a resolution supporting the affirmative position regarding homosexuality of the American Psychiatric Association:

> Homosexuality per se implies no impairment in [judgment], stability, reliability, or general social and vocational capabilities; further, the American Psychological Association urges all mental health professionals to take the lead in removing the stigma of mental illness that has long been associated with homosexual orientations. (Conger, 1975, pp. 620–651 as cited by Division 44, 2000)

However, the diagnosis of homosexuality was replaced by sexual orientation disturbance in the *DSM-II*, which was then replaced by ego-dystonic homosexuality in the *DSM-III* (Drescher, Stein, & Byne, 2005). According to Ritter and Terndrup (2002), in 1980, ego-dystonic homosexuality was conceptualized as a "new diagnostic category . . . [that] pathologized psychological distress over same-sex attraction which, in essence, reclassified struggles with homosexuality as a mental disorder" (p. 31) until this diagnostic category was removed from the *DSM-III-R* in 1987.

Nonetheless, the legacy of negatively constructing LGBT identities has persisted as recently illustrated, in part, by the pathology associated with transgender identity (e.g., Male-to-Female [M-T-F] and Female-to-Male [F-T-M]) in the *DSM* (Gainor, 2000; Namaste, 2000; Stryker & Whittle, 2006) and the reemergence of a focus on sexual conversion or reparative therapy (Shidlo et al., 2002). Moreover, a number of scholars have challenged the recent work of Robert Spitzer, who was one of the original influential figures advocating for the depathologizing of homosexuality as a mental health disorder in 1973 (Drescher & Zucker, 2006). In 2001, at the annual meeting of the American Psychological Association, Spitzer presented findings from a study that posited that homosexual individuals could change their sexual orientation to heterosexual (Drescher & Zucker, 2006). However, major professional mental health organizations (e.g., American Psychiatric Association, American Psychological Association, American Counseling Association, and National Association of Social Workers) do not support reparative or conversion therapies. The sociohistorical contexts of negatively constructing LGBT communities and pathologizing LGBT identities have manifested in stigma and have considerable implications for the role of mental health practitioners in the provision of LGBT affirmative counseling.

THE ROLE OF STIGMA, MARGINALIZATION, AND MENTAL HEALTH IN LGBT COMMUNITIES

LGBT communities have experienced stigma and marginalization on a multitude of levels, particularly as related to bias associated with heterosexism and

homophobia (Gibson, Schlosser, & Brock-Murray, 2008; Greene, 1997; Herek, 2007). These sociohistorical and -political realities related to stigma for LGBT communities have been evidenced by recent increases in LGBT-related violence (Gordon & Meyer, 2008; Herek, 2009; National Coalition of Anti-Violence Programs [NCAVP], 2008). For example, in a recent report by the National Coalition of Anti-Violence Programs, there was a 24% increase in LGBT-related violence in the United States in 2007, as compared to 2006, with respect to the total number of victims (NCAVP, 2008). The implications of these findings for mental health practitioners relate to having an understanding of how stigma and marginalization relate to LGBT-related violence. Moreover, these findings provide implications for the development and implementation of strategies to assess violence-related experiences, particularly within the context of how these foci relate to stigma and discrimination.

Furthermore, a growing body of research has demonstrated that experiences with stigma and discrimination have had an impact on the mental health of LGBT individuals (D'Augelli, Grossman, & Starks, 2006; Mays & Cochran, 2001; Meyer, Dietrich, & Schwartz, 2008). Based on a study with a nationally representative sample ($n = 2,917$), Mays and Cochran (2001) found that homosexual and bisexual individuals, as compared to heterosexual individuals, indicated greater lifetime and routine experiences with discrimination. Perceived discrimination was also related to psychological distress and had a deleterious impact on quality of life. Similarly, Meyer et al. (2008) found among 388 LGB individuals in New York City that (a) Blacks indicated a lower prevalence of mental health disorders as compared to Latinos/as and Whites, (b) younger individuals demonstrated fewer mood disorders than older individuals, (c) bisexual individuals demonstrated greater substance use disorders as compared to gay men and lesbians, and (d) Latinos/as had more suicide attempts than Whites. Furthermore, as research has shown that LGBT individuals have reported dissatisfaction with mental health services, in part because of heterosexism and homophobia (Cabaj & Stein, 1996), they indicate a greater likelihood to seek the services of a mental health practitioner (Greene, 2007).

With respect to LGBT people of color, a burgeoning body of research has studied the role that race-, gender-, and sexual orientation-based discrimination has had on greater psychological distress (Arnold & Bailey, in press; Black Gay Men's Research Group, 2007; Diaz, Ayala, Bein, & Henne, 2001; Greene, 1994; Greene, Miville, & Ferguson, 2008; Mays, Cochran, & Rhue, 1993; Ramirez-Valles, 2007; Williams, Wyatt, Resell, Peterson, & Asuan-O'Brien, 2004; Wilson et al., 2009; Wilson & Yoshikawa, 2007). For example, Battle, Cohen, Warren, Fergerson, and Audam (2002), in a large-scale study of Black LGBT communities, indicated that 53% of participants reported racial discrimination, and 42% indicated sexual orientation discrimination. In addition, in this study, 26% of the participants reported sex or gender discrimination (38% for women, 18% for men, and 55% for transgender individuals) and 21% indicated gender appearance (e.g., based on "butch" or "femme" appearance) discrimination. Furthermore, in a large-scale probability sample of 912 Latino gay men from three U.S. cities (Miami, New York, and Los Angeles), Diaz et al. (2001) found that experiences with social oppression (e.g., racism, economic hardship, and homophobia) were predictive of greater psychological distress. Also, in a national report of Latino gay men, Diaz and Ayala (2001) demonstrated that (a) 22% of the men reported being harassed by police because of their ethnicity, (b) 35% of the men reported being treated rudely because of their ethnicity, (c) 64% of the men reported verbal harassment during childhood for being gay/effeminate, and (d) 64% of the men reported having to pretend to be heterosexual in order to be accepted.

Minority Stress Theory (LGBT Communities)

Social stress theory, according to Meyer (2007), posits that social factors, including individual-level experiences, have an impact on the stress of a person, which in turn may have an effect on their quality of mental health. Building on the theoretical premise of social stress theory, Meyer developed a conceptual framework of minority stress that posits that stigma, prejudice, and discrimination experienced by LGBT people serve as specific stressors that have an impact on their psychological distress. He conceptualizes minority stress to refer to the cumulative stressors that individuals from stigmatized groups experience on a routine basis based on their social position in society (e.g., sexual orientation).

Specifically, Meyer (2007) contends that social factors (e.g., homophobia) serve as stressors in the lives of individuals representing stigmatized or marginalized groups (e.g., LGBT persons). Furthermore, three suppositions are indicative of minority stress: (a) Stigmatized groups experience minority stress as a singular stressor beyond general or routine stressors and experience the cumulative effects of both general and minority stress, (b) stigmatized groups experience minority stress on a routine or continuous basis because these stressors are embedded in social structures, and (c) stigmatized groups experience minority stress in connection with social structures that are beyond the influence of the individual.

Based on Minority Stress Theory, as articulated by Meyer (2007), LGBT people as members of stigmatized groups experience greater stress than non-LGBT people (e.g., heterosexuals). Moreover, Meyer (2007) contends that greater levels of stress often result in psychological distress (including mental health disorders). Thus, stress acts as a mediator between social status and the frequency of mental health disorders. According to Meyer (2007), the minority stress model incorporates a distal-proximal component with a focus on the impact of social structures (including social conditions) on the lives of people. The distal dimension refers to the objective events that occur (e.g., individual homophobia), whereas the proximal element relates to the subjective experiences associated with the event (e.g., anticipation of rejection, concealment, internalized homophobia). Empirical evidence has indicated that experiences with stigma and marginalization (e.g., homophobia and heterosexism) relate to greater psychological distress for LGBT people (Mays & Cochran, 2001; Rosario, Schrimshaw, & Hunter, 2008). These theoretical and research findings provide substantial support for the impact of stigma on the mental health of LGBT people.

LGBT AFFIRMATIVE COUNSELING

In 2013, the 40th anniversary since the diagnosis of homosexuality was removed as a mental health disorder from the *DSM* by the American Psychiatric Association will provide the field of mental health with an opportunity to reflect on the progress of the profession with respect to psychotherapeutic practice with LGBT people and communities. Much of the recent work in this area has focused on the development and implementation of guidelines for multiculturally competent practice with LGBT people and communities, particularly within the context of LGBT affirmative counseling (Israel, Gorcheva, Walther, Sulzner, & Cohen, 2008; Pachankis & Goldfried, 2004; Pope, 2006). For example, in 2000, the Committee on Lesbian, Gay, and Bisexual Concerns Joint Task Force on Guidelines for Psychotherapy with Lesbian, Gay, and Bisexual Clients from Division 44 (Society for the Psychological Study of Lesbian, Gay, and Bisexual Issues) of the American Psychological Association established psychotherapeutic guidelines for working with LGB clients (Division 44, 2000). The major objectives of the guidelines for practitioners were to provide (a) a framework for clinical practice with LGB persons; and (b) pertinent guiding principles and strategies with respect to assessment, intervention, LGB identity, couples and relationships, and education and preparation for work as multiculturally competent practitioners.

The psychotherapy guidelines with LGB clients have four areas: attitudes about homosexuality and bisexuality, relationships and families, diversity, and education (Division 44, 2000). This section of the chapter will provide an overview of each of the four areas and then incorporate recommendations for the development of the guidelines, including implications for psychotherapeutic practice with LGBT people and communities.

Attitudes About Homosexuality and Bisexuality

This section provides salient information regarding the sociohistorical and -political context of the diagnostic nomenclature in relation to the pathology of LGB identities (e.g., diagnosis of homosexuality as a mental health disorder). Parallel to this context, the bias and stigma associated with the heritage of the field of mental health in relation to LGBT people poses critical implications for psychotherapeutic practice. This is particularly relevant because research has indicated that LGBT persons experience greater psychological distress compared to heterosexual persons, which often has been connected to experiences of stigma and marginalization (Meyer et al., 2008). A significant component of this work for practitioners relates to self-awareness

regarding their values and beliefs as well as knowledge about pertinent areas of research related to LGB people and communities. Specifically, a consideration of how stigma and marginalization (e.g., heterosexism and homophobia) both on a macro (e.g., large-scale or structural) and micro (e.g., small-scale) level manifest in the lives of LGB people and communities.

With respect to further areas of consideration to the "Attitudes About Homosexuality and Bisexuality" section, an emphasis needs to be placed on the incorporation of the sociohistorical contexts of stigma associated with the (mis)diagnosis of transgender (Male-to-Female and Female-to-Male) people (Gainor, 2000). For example, greater consideration needs to be placed on the historical and current application of the diagnostic categories in the *DSM-IV* in relation to transgender people (e.g., Gender Identity Disorder [GID] in adolescents and adults, GID in children, GID not otherwise specified, and Transvestic Fetishism). Research has shown that transgender people and communities have been neglected and underserved in the areas of research and clinical practice (Burgess, Lee, Tran, & van Ryn, 2007; Grossman & D'Augelli, 2007; Johnson, Mimiaga, & Bradford, 2008). In this respect, current psychotherapeutic guidelines need to address issues of stigma and marginalization for transgender people and communities (Arnold & Bailey, in press). A focus needs to be placed on both intrapersonal (within-group) (e.g., LGBT communities) and interpersonal (outside-of-group) (e.g., non-LGBT communities) experiences with stigma and marginalization for transgender people and communities (e.g., stigma based on genderism [gender expression], gender role socialization, and transphobia) (Arnold & Bailey, in press; Black Gay Men's Research Group, 2007; Hill, 2003).

Relationships and Families

This section focuses on relevant issues related to same-sex couples and families among LGB people and communities. Based on the psychotherapy guidelines with LGB clients (Division 44, 2000), one critical area regarding primary partner relationships among LGB people relates to the development of knowledge of practitioners about same-sex couples; for example, specific factors related to relationship dynamics in same-sex couples (e.g., gender role socialization, developmental phases of same-sex relationships). Furthermore, consideration is provided to issues related to stigma and marginalization for same-sex couples and families (e.g., process of coming out to family members, children, friends, neighbors, coworkers). With respect to institutionalized homophobia (e.g., discrimination on a structural level), legal rights have been significant considerations to same-sex couples and families (e.g., adoption, health care, child custody, parental rights, domestic partnership rights, etc.). Another significant consideration relates to the nonheteronormative structure of families among LGB people (e.g., same-sex parents, inclusion of nonbiological and extended family members [friends] into the family structure). Other relevant issues for same-sex families relate to social support—especially in the midst of experiences of stigma and discrimination. Culture-specific factors in communities of color need to be examined within the context of family-of-origin (e.g., biological family) issues.

In relation to the section on "Relationships and Families" in the psychotherapy guidelines with LGB clients, additional consideration needs to focus on the critical role of racial, ethnic, and cultural norms related to families in LGBT communities of color. For example, the structure and significance of extended family networks within LGBT communities of color call for greater attention to this area (Arnold & Bailey, in press; Black Gay Men's Research Group, 2007; Murill et al., 2008). One current illustration of the role of extended family networks in Black and Latino/a LGBT communities has involved a focus on house ball communities (Arnold & Bailey, in press). House ball communities refer to a community or group of individuals that is connected through houses. These houses serve as fictive kin (e.g., extended family networks) that provide familial, cultural, and supportive social systems for Black and Latino gay and bisexual men as well as transgender women (Murrill et al., 2008). Moreover, according to Arnold & Bailey (in press), house ball communities have served a critical role with respect to the development of home and kinship networks—especially for Black and Latino LGBT youth who may experience disconnection from their biological families (e.g., due to coming out with respect to their gender [transgender] and/or sexuality). Another salient factor for house ball

communities relates to a core value of gender and sexuality expression as an integral part of an individual's racial, gender, and sexual identities. Therefore, consideration to cultural forms of extended family has been relevant for groups that have experienced multiple forms of stigma and marginalization based on their racial, gender, and sexual identities. Equally important, practitioners working with members of house ball communities need to be aware of the resiliency of the communities with respect to providing "intraventions" (e.g., prevention work that occurs organically within the context of house ball communities) (Arnold & Bailey, in press). This illustration of extended family networks (e.g., house ball communities) in LGBT communities of color provides implications for the provision of culturally applicable "intraventions."

Diversity

The section on Diversity in the LGB psychotherapy guidelines (Division 44, 2000) focuses on core issues related to the importance of understanding cultural values and worldviews among LGB people of color. In this regard, the intersection of racial/ethnic, gender, and sexual identities has been relevant to experiences of stigma and marginalization for LGBT people of color. In addition, LGBT people of color develop kinship (e.g., extended family) supportive networks in their communities as a strategy to manage experiences of stigma and marginalization (e.g., racism from White communities [including White LGBT communities] and homophobia from both White communities and communities of color) (Greene, 1997). An emphasis was also placed on developing an understanding of the stressors related to bisexuality (e.g., stigma based on biphobia), LGB youth (e.g., development challenges), generational experiences (e.g., younger and older generations), and LGB people with disabilities.

With respect to generational contexts in LGBT communities, a critical emphasis needs to be placed on HIV-related health disparities. Since the onset of the AIDS epidemic, gay and bisexual men, in particular, have experienced a substantial risk for acquiring the human immunodeficiency virus (HIV) as well as other sexually transmitted infections (STIs) (e.g., chlamydia, gonorrhea, syphilis) (CDC, 2008). Currently, younger generations of gay and bisexual men (especially younger gay and bisexual men of color), as well as women of color, have experienced a considerable increase in the rate of infection of HIV and STIs (CDC, 2008; Greene et al., 2008; Peterson & Jones, 2009). The issue is especially paramount for women of color, including lesbian and bisexual women of color, as research has indicated that sexuality is fluid—placing lesbian and bisexual women at risk for acquiring HIV and other STIs. Similarly, within generational contexts, consideration needs to be provided to health care issues, including human papilloma virus (HPV), among lesbian and bisexual women (Greene et al., 2008). The importance of a focus on health disparities with respect to generational differences in LGBT communities relates to another factor connected with diversity. For example, HIV/STI-related stigma functions differently across generational status in LGBT communities.

Education

Based on the psychotherapy guidelines with LGB clients (Division 44, 2000), the Education section provides an emphasis on the development of knowledge, training, supervision, and consultation for practitioners. For example, research and clinical training need to be incorporated into graduate-level education with a focus on LGB people and communities for practitioners. One of the routine challenges for practitioners has related to the limited focus on LGB issues and clinical training in graduate programs. Moreover, continuing education for practitioners has experienced similar issues with respect to insufficient opportunities for education and clinical training on LGB issues. Another critical element associated with education relates to the practitioner's familiarity with appropriate resources in LGB communities for their clients.

One consideration for providing more focus on the training needs of practitioners involves collaborations with experts who specialize in LGBT issues from community settings. In particular, it would be advantageous for academic training programs to develop partnerships with community-based organizations that specialize in specific LGBT areas or clients (e.g., transgender women, Latina lesbians, Asian gay men). For example, with respect to the current state of prevention interventions,

much of the innovative work focused on LGBT people and issues is being developed and implemented in LGBT communities (Wilton, 2009). It would also be helpful for practitioners to be familiar with Internet-based resources and information that focus on LGBT issues and communities. This is particularly relevant in light of the increasing demand on the Internet as a modality for information and utilization of services. In this pursuit, national surveys of academic training programs and service providers should be developed and implemented (including adequate levels of funding) on a routine basis as a method to assess issues of multicultural competencies (on the macro and micro levels) and mental health needs of LGBT people and communities.

CONCLUSION

The purpose of this chapter was to examine key implications for LGBT affirmative counseling. As such, the objectives were threefold: (a) Provide an account of salient foci that related to the sociohistorical and -political contexts of contemporary LGBT affirmative counseling; (b) examine the role of stigma, marginalization, and mental health in LGBT communities; and (c) explore implications for the role of practitioners in relation to LGBT affirmative counseling. One major element in addressing the mental health needs of LGBT people and communities relates to the development of strategies for LGBT affirmative counseling that focus on stigma and marginalization—especially using conceptual frameworks that are grounded within culturally relevant conceptualizations. Thus, a major part of this work with respect to LGBT people and communities calls for a paradigm shift that places more emphasis on social structures that have an impact on the lives of LGBT people and communities.

REFERENCES

Arnold, E. A., & Bailey, M. M. (in press). Constructing home and family: How the ballroom community supports African American GLBTQ youth in the face of HIV/AIDS. *Journal of Gay and Lesbian Social Services.*

Battle, J., Cohen, C., Warren, D., Fergerson, G., & Audam, S. (2002). *Say it loud, I'm Black and I'm proud: Black Pride Survey 2000.* New York: The Policy Institute of the National Gay and Lesbian Task Force.

Bayer, R. (1981). *Homosexuality and American psychiatry: The politics of diagnosis.* New York: Basic Books.

Bernal, G., Trimble, J. E., Burlew, A. K., & Leong, F. T. L. (Eds.). (2002). *Handbook of racial and ethnic minority populations.* Thousand Oaks, CA: Sage.

Bieschke, K. J., Perez, R. M., & DeBord, K. A. (Eds.). (2007). *Handbook of counseling and psychotherapy with lesbian, gay, bisexual, and transgender clients* (2nd ed.). Washington, DC: American Psychological Association Press.

Black Gay Men's Research Group. (2007). *Black gay research agenda.* New York: Black Gay Men's Research Group and National Black Gay Men's Advocacy Coalition.

Burgess, D., Lee, R., Tran, A., & van Ryn, M. (2007). Effects of perceived discrimination of mental health and mental health services utilization among gay, lesbian, bisexual, and transgender persons. *Journal of LGBT Health Research, 3,* 1–14.

Cabaj, R. P., & Stein, T. S. (Eds.). (1996). *Textbook of homosexuality and mental health.* Washington, DC: American Psychiatric Press.

Carter, R. T. (Ed.). (2004a). *Handbook of racial-cultural psychology and counseling: Theory and research* (Vol. 1). Hoboken, NJ: Wiley.

Carter, R. T. (Ed.). (2004b). *Handbook of racial-cultural psychology and counseling: Theory and research* (Vol. 2). Hoboken, NJ: Wiley.

Centers for Disease Control and Prevention. (2008). HIV prevalence estimates—United States, 2006. *Morbidity and Mortality Weekly Report, 57,* 1073–1076.

Conger, J. J. (1975). Proceedings of the American Psychological Association, Incorporated, for the year 1974: Minutes of the annual meeting of the Council of Representatives. *American Psychologist, 30,* 620–651. Retrieved October 1, 2008, from http://www.apa.org/pi/lgbc/policy/discrimination.html

Constantine, M. G., & Wilton, L. (2004). The role of racial and cultural constructs in the history of the multicultural counseling movement. In R. T. Carter (Ed.), *Handbook of racial-cultural psychology and counseling: Theory and research* (Vol. 1, pp. 64–77). Hoboken, NJ: Wiley.

Cook, A., & Glass, C. (2008). The impact of LGBT policies on ethnic/racial and gender diversity among business school faculty. *Journal of Diversity in Higher Education, 1,* 193–199.

Croteau, J. M., Bieschke, K. J., Fassinger, R. E., & Manning, J. L. (2008). Counseling psychology and sexual orientation: History, selective trends, and future directions. In S. D. Brown & R. W. Lent (Ed.), *Handbook of counseling psychology* (4th ed., pp. 194–211). Hoboken, NJ: Wiley.

D'Augelli, A. R., Grossman, A. H., & Starks, M. T. (2006). Childhood gender atypicality, victimization, and PTSD among lesbian, gay, and bisexual youth. *Journal of Interpersonal Violence, 21,* 1462–1482.

Diaz, R. M., & Ayala, G. (2001). *Social discrimination and health: The case of Latino gay men and HIV risk.* New York: The Policy Institute of the National Gay and Lesbian Task Force.

Diaz, R. M., Ayala, G., Bein, E., & Henne, J. (2001). The impact of homophobia, poverty, and racism on the mental health of gay and bisexual Latino men: Findings from 3 U.S. cities. *American Journal of Public Health, 91,* 927–931.

Division 44/Committee on Lesbian, Gay, and Bisexual Concerns Joint Task Force on Guidelines for Psychotherapy With Lesbian, Gay, and Bisexual Clients. (2000). Guidelines for psychotherapy with lesbian, gay, and bisexual clients. *American Psychologist, 55,* 1440–1451.

Drescher, J., & Merlino, J. P. (Eds.). (2007). *American psychiatry and homosexuality: An oral history.* New York: Routledge.

Drescher, J., Stein, T. S., & Byne, W. (2005). Homosexuality, gay and lesbian identities, and homosexual behavior. In B. J. Sadock & V. A. Sadock (Eds.), *Kaplan and Sadock's comprehensive textbook of psychiatry* (8th ed., pp. 1936–1965). Baltimore, MD: Lippincott, Williams, & Wilkins.

Drescher, J., & Zucker, K. J. (Eds.). (2006). *Ex-gay research: Analyzing the Spitzer study and its relation to science, religion, politics, and culture.* New York: Harrington Park Press.

Egan, P. J., & Sherrill, K. (2009). *California's Proposition 8: What happened, and what does the future hold?* Washington, DC: National Gay and Lesbian Task Force.

Estrada, D., & Rutter, P. A. (2008). Counselors as social advocates: Connecting a lesbian client to social justice. *Journal of LGBT Issues in Counseling, 1,* 121–134.

Fassinger, R. E., & Arseneau, J. R. (2008). Diverse women's sexualities. In F. L. Denmark & M. Paludi (Eds.), *Psychology of women: A handbook of issues and theories* (pp. 484–505). Westport, CT: Praeger.

Fox, R. E. (2000). Bisexuality in perspective: A review of theory and research. In B. Greene & G. L. Croom (Eds.), *Education, research, and practice in lesbian, gay, bisexual, and transgendered psychology: A resource manual* (pp. 161–206). Thousand Oaks, CA: Sage.

Fox, R. E. (2008). Advocacy: The key to survival and growth of professional psychology. *Professional Psychology: Research & Practice, 39,* 633–637.

Gainor, K. A. (2000). Including transgender issues in lesbian, gay, and bisexual psychology: Implications for clinical practice and training. In B. Greene & G. L. Croom (Eds.), *Education, research, and practice in lesbian, gay, bisexual, and transgendered psychology: A resource manual* (pp. 131–160). Thousand Oaks, CA: Sage.

Gibson, D. D., Schlosser, L. Z., & Brock-Murray, R. D. (2008). Identity management strategies among lesbians of African ancestry: A pilot study. *Journal of LGBT Issues in Counseling, 1,* 31–57.

Gordon, A. R., & Meyer, I. H. (2008). Gender nonconformity as a target of prejudice, discrimination, and violence against LGB individuals. *Journal of LGBT Research, 3,* 55–71.

Greene, B. (1994). Lesbian and gay sexual orientations: Implications for clinical training, practice, and research. In B. Greene & G. M. Herek (Eds.), *Lesbian and gay psychology: Theory, research, and clinical applications* (pp. 1–24). Thousand Oaks, CA: Sage.

Greene, B. (1997). Ethnic minority lesbians and gay men: Mental health and treatment issues. In B. Greene (Ed.), *Ethnic and cultural diversity among lesbians and gay men* (pp. 216–239). Thousand Oaks, CA: Sage.

Greene, B. (2007). Delivering ethical psychological services in lesbian, gay, and bisexual clients. In K. J. Bieschke, R. M. Perez, & K. A. DuBord (Eds.), *Handbook of counseling and psychotherapy with lesbian, gay, bisexual, and transgender clients* (2nd ed., pp. 181–189). Washington, DC: American Psychological Association Press.

Greene, B., Miville, M. L., & Ferguson, A. D. (2008). Lesbian and bisexual women of color, racism, heterosexism, homophobia, and health: A recommended intervention and research agenda. In B. C. Wallace (Ed.), *Toward equity in health: A new global approach to health disparities* (pp. 413–426). New York: Springer.

Grossman, A. H., & D'Augelli, R. (2007). Transgender youth and life-threatening behaviors. *Suicide and Life-Threatening Behavior, 37,* 527–537.

Helms, J. E., & Cook, D. A. (1998). *Using race and culture in counseling and psychotherapy: Theory and process.* Upper Saddle River, NJ: Allyn & Bacon.

Herek, G. M. (2007). Confronting sexual stigma and prejudice: Theory and practice. *Journal of Social Issues, 63,* 905–925.

Herek, G. M. (2009). Hate crimes and stigma-related experiences among sexual minority adults in the United States: Prevalence estimates from a national probability sample. *Journal of Interpersonal Violence, 24,* 55–64.

Herek, G. M., Chopp, R., & Strohl, D. (2007). Sexual stigma: Putting sexual minority health issues in context.

In I. H. Meyer & M. E. Northridge (Eds.), *The health of sexual minorities: Public health perspectives on lesbian, gay, bisexual, and transgender populations* (pp. 171–208). New York: Springer.

Hill, D. B. (2003). Genderism, transphobia, and gender-bashing: A framework for interpreting anti-transgender violence. In B. C. Wallace & R. T. Carter (Eds.), *Understanding and dealing with violence: A multicultural approach* (pp. 113–136). Thousand Oaks, CA: Sage.

Israel, T., Gorcheva, R., Walther, W. A., Sulzner, J. M., & Cohen, J. (2008). Therapists' helpful and unhelpful situations with LGBT clients: An exploratory study. *Professional Psychology: Research and Practice, 39,* 361–368.

Johnson, C. V., Mimiaga, M. J., & Bradford, J. (2008). Health care issues among lesbian, gay, bisexual, and transgender and intersex (LGBTI) populations in the United States: Introduction. *Journal of Homosexuality, 54,* 213–224.

Liu, W. M., & Ali, S. R. (2008). Social class and classism: Understanding the psychological impact of poverty and inequality. In S. D. Brown & R. W. Lent (Ed.), *Handbook of counseling psychology* (4th ed., pp. 159–175). Hoboken, NJ: Wiley.

Martin, D. (2008, May 6). Mildred Loving, who battled ban on mixed-race marriage, dies at 68. *The New York Times.* Retrieved May 10, 2008, from http://www.nytimes.com/2008/05/06/us/0610ving.html

Mays, V. M., & Cochran, S. D. (2001). Mental health correlates of perceived discrimination among lesbian, gay, and bisexual adults in the United States. *American Journal of Public Health, 91,* 1869–1876.

Mays, V. M., Cochran, S. D., & Rhue, S. (1993). The impact of perceived discrimination on the intimate relationships of Black lesbians. *Journal of Homosexuality, 25,* 1–14.

Meyer, I. H. (2007). Prejudice and discrimination as social stressors. In I. H. Meyer & M. E. Northridge (Eds.), *The health of sexual minorities: Public health perspectives on lesbian, gay, bisexual, and transgender populations* (pp. 242–267). New York: Springer.

Meyer, I. H., Dietrich, J., & Schwartz, S. (2008). Lifetime prevalence of mental disorders and suicide attempts in diverse, lesbian, gay, and bisexual populations. *American Journal of Public Health, 98,* 1004–1006.

Murrill, C. S., Liu, K. L., Guilin, V., Colón, E. R., Dean, L., Buckley, L. A., Sanchez, T., Finlayson, T. J., & Torian, L. V. (2008). HIV prevalence and associated risk behaviors in New York City's house ball community. *American Journal of Public Health, 98,* 1074–1080.

Namaste, V. K. (2000). *Invisible lives: The erasure of transsexual and transgendered people.* Chicago: University of Chicago Press.

National Coalition of Anti-Violence Programs. (2008). *Anti-lesbian, gay, bisexual, and transgender violence in 2007*. New York: Author.

Omoto, A. M., & Kurtzman, H. S. (Eds.). (2006). *Sexual orientation and mental health: Examining identity and development in lesbian, gay, and bisexual people*. Washington, DC: American Psychological Association Press.

Pachankis, J. E., & Goldfried, M. R. (2004). Clinical issues in working with lesbian, gay, and bisexual clients. *Psychotherapy, 41*, 227–246.

Peterson, J. L., & Jones, K. T. (2009). HIV prevention for Black men who have sex with men in the United States. *American Journal of Public Health, 99*, 1–5.

Ponterotto, J. G. (2008). Theoretical and empirical advances in multicultural counseling and psychology. In S. D. Brown & R. W. Lent (Ed.), *Handbook of counseling psychology* (4th ed., pp. 121–140). Hoboken, NJ: Wiley.

Pope, M. (2006). Culturally appropriate counseling considerations for lesbian and gay clients. In P. B. Pedersen, J. G. Draguns, W. J. Lonner, & J. E. Trimble (Eds.), *Counseling across cultures* (6th ed., pp. 201–222). Thousand Oaks, CA: Sage.

Ragins, B. R., Singh, R., & Cornwell, J. M. (2007). Making the invisible visible: Fear and disclosure of sexual orientation at work. *Journal of Applied Psychology, 92*, 1103–1118.

Ramirez-Valles, J. (2007). "I don't fit anywhere": How race and sexuality shape Latino gay and bisexual men's health. In I. H. Meyer & M. E. Northridge (Eds.), *The health of sexual minorities: Public health perspectives on lesbian, gay, bisexual and transgender populations* (pp. 301–319). New York: Springer.

Ritter, K. Y., & Terndrup, A. I. (Eds.). (2002). *Handbook of affirmative psychotherapy with lesbians and gay men*. New York: Guilford.

Rosario, M., Schrimshaw, E. W., & Hunter, J. (2008). Ethnic/racial disparities in gay-related stress and health among lesbian, gay, and bisexual youths: Examining a prevalent hypothesis. In I. H. Meyer & M. E. Northridge (Eds.), *The health of sexual minorities: Public health perspectives on lesbian, gay, bisexual, and transgender populations* (pp. 427–446). New York: Springer.

Shidlo, A., Schroeder, M., & Drescher, J. (Eds.). (2002). *Sexual conversion therapy: Ethical, clinical, and research perspectives*. New York: Informa Healthcare.

Stryker, S., & Whittle, S. (Eds.). (2006). *The transgender studies reader*. New York: Routledge.

Sue, D. W., & Sue, D. (2008). *Counseling the culturally diverse: Theory and practice* (5th ed.). Hoboken, NJ: Wiley.

Suzuki, L. A., & Ponterotto, J. G. (Eds.). (2008). *Handbook of multicultural assessment: Clinical, psychological, and educational applications* (3rd ed.). Hoboken, NJ: Jossey-Bass.

Williams, J. K., Wyatt, E., Resell, J., Peterson, J., & Asuan-O'Brien, A. (2004). Psychosocial issues among gay- and non-gay-identifying HIV-seropositive African American and Latino MSM. *Cultural Diversity and Ethnic Minority Psychology, 10*, 268–286.

Wilson, P. A., & Yoshikawa, H. (2007). Improving access to quality healthcare among African-American, Asian & Pacific Islander, and Latino lesbian, gay and bisexual populations. In I. H. Meyer & M. E. Northridge (Eds.), *The health of sexual minorities: Public health perspectives on lesbian, gay, bisexual and transgender populations* (pp. 171–208). New York: Springer.

Wilson, P. A., Valera, P., Ventuneac, A., Balan, I., Rowe, M., & Carballo-Diéguez, A. (2009). Race-based sexual stereotyping and sexual partnering among men who use the Internet to identify other men for bareback sex. *Journal of Sex Research, 46*, 1–15.

Wilton, L. (2009). Men who have sex with men of color in the age of AIDS: The sociocultural contexts of stigma, marginalization, and structural inequalities. In V. Stone, B. Ojikutu, K. Rawlings, & K. Smith (Eds.), *HIV/AIDS in communities of color*. New York: Springer.

Worthington, R. L., Soth-McNett, A. M., & Moreno, M. V. (2007). Multicultural counseling competencies research: A 20-year content analysis. *Journal of Counseling Psychology, 54*, 351–361.

Appendix A

Loving for All

BY MILDRED LOVING*

Prepared for delivery on June 12, 2007, the 40th anniversary of the *Loving v. Virginia* announcement When my late husband, Richard, and I got married in Washington, DC in 1958, it wasn't to make a political statement or start a fight. We were in love, and we wanted to be married.

We didn't get married in Washington because we wanted to marry there. We did it there because the government wouldn't allow us to marry back home in Virginia where we grew up, where we met, where we fell in love, and where we wanted to be together and build our family. You see, I am a woman of color and Richard was white, and at that time people believed it was okay to keep us from marrying because of their ideas of who should marry whom.

When Richard and I came back to our home in Virginia, happily married, we had no intention of battling over the law. We made a commitment to each other in our love and lives, and now had the legal commitment, called marriage, to match. Isn't that what marriage is?

Not long after our wedding, we were awakened in the middle of the night in our own bedroom by deputy sheriffs and actually arrested for the "crime" of marrying the wrong kind of person. Our marriage certificate was hanging on the wall above the bed.

The state prosecuted Richard and me, and after we were found guilty, the judge declared: "Almighty God created the races white, black, yellow, malay and red, and he placed them on separate continents. And but for the interference with his arrangement there would be no cause for such marriages. The fact that he separated the races shows that he did not intend for the races to mix." He sentenced us to a year in prison, but offered to suspend the sentence if we left our home in Virginia for 25 years exile.

We left, and got a lawyer. Richard and I had to fight, but still were not fighting for a cause. We were fighting for our love.

Though it turned out we had to fight, happily Richard and I didn't have to fight alone. Thanks to groups like the ACLU and the NAACP Legal Defense & Education Fund, and so many good people around the country willing to speak up, we took our case for the freedom to marry all the way to the U.S. Supreme Court. And on June 12, 1967, the Supreme Court ruled

---

* Together with her husband, Richard Loving, Mildred Loving was a plaintiff in the historic Supreme Court *Loving v. Virginia*, decided 40 years ago June 12, striking down race restrictions on the freedom to marry and advancing racial justice and marriage equality in America.

unanimously that, "The freedom to marry has long been recognized as one of the vital personal rights essential to the orderly pursuit of happiness by free men," a "basic civil right." My generation was bitterly divided over something that should have been so clear and right. The majority believed what the judge said, that it was God's plan to keep people apart, and that government should discriminate against people in love. But I have lived long enough now to see big changes. The older generation's fears and prejudices have given way, and today's young people realize that if someone loves someone they have a right to marry.

Surrounded as I am now by wonderful children and grandchildren, not a day goes by that I don't think of Richard and our love, our right to marry, and how much it meant to me to have that freedom to marry the person precious to me, even if others thought he was the "wrong kind of person" for me to marry. I believe all Americans, no matter their race, no matter their sex, no matter their sexual orientation, should have that same freedom to marry. Government has no business imposing some people's religious beliefs over others. Especially if it denies people's civil rights.

I am still not a political person, but I am proud that Richard's and my name is on a court case that can help reinforce the love, the commitment, the fairness, and the family that so many people, black or white, young or old, gay or straight seek in life. I support the freedom to marry for all. That's what *Loving*, and loving, are all about.

Appendix B

Guidelines for Psychotherapy With Lesbian, Gay, and Bisexual Clients

ATTITUDES TOWARD HOMOSEXUALITY AND BISEXUALITY

Guideline 1: Psychologists understand that homosexuality and bisexuality are not indicative of mental illness.

Guideline 2: Psychologists are encouraged to recognize how their attitudes and knowledge about lesbian, gay, and bisexual issues may be relevant to assessment and treatment and seek consultation or make appropriate referrals when indicated.

Guideline 3: Psychologists strive to understand the ways in which social stigmatization (i.e., prejudice, discrimination, and violence) poses risks to the mental health and well-being of lesbian, gay, and bisexual clients.

Guideline 4: Psychologists strive to understand how inaccurate or prejudicial views of homosexuality or bisexuality may affect the client's presentation in treatment and the therapeutic process.

RELATIONSHIPS AND FAMILIES

Guideline 5: Psychologists strive to be knowledgeable about and respect the importance of lesbian, gay, and bisexual relationships.

Guideline 6: Psychologists strive to understand the particular circumstances and challenges faced by lesbian, gay, and bisexual parents.

Guideline 7: Psychologists recognize that the families of lesbian, gay, and bisexual people may include people who are not legally or biologically related.

Guideline 8: Psychologists strive to understand how a person's homosexual or bisexual orientation may have an impact on his or her family of origin and the relationship to that family of origin.

ISSUES OF DIVERSITY

Guideline 9: Psychologists are encouraged to recognize the particular life issues or challenges that are related to multiple and often conflicting cultural norms, values, and beliefs that lesbian, gay, and bisexual members of racial and ethnic minorities face.

Guideline 10: Psychologists are encouraged to recognize the particular challenges that bisexual individuals experience.

Guideline 11: Psychologists strive to understand the special problems and risks that exist for lesbian, gay, and bisexual youth.

Guideline 12: Psychologists consider generational differences within lesbian, gay, and bisexual populations and the particular challenges that lesbian, gay, and bisexual older adults may experience.

Guideline 13: Psychologists are encouraged to recognize the particular challenges that lesbian, gay, and bisexual individuals experience with physical, sensory, and cognitive-emotional disabilities.

EDUCATION

Guideline 14: Psychologists support the provision of professional education and training on lesbian, gay, and bisexual issues.

Guideline 15: Psychologists are encouraged to increase their knowledge and understanding of homosexuality and bisexuality through continued education, training, supervision, and consultation.

Guideline 16: Psychologists make reasonable efforts to familiarize themselves with relevant mental health, educational, and community resources for lesbian, gay, and bisexual people.

Source: Division 44/Committee on Lesbian, Gay, and Bisexual Concerns Joint Task Force on Guidelines for Psychotherapy With Lesbian, Gay, and Bisexual Clients. (2000). Guidelines for psychotherapy with lesbian, gay, and bisexual clients. *American Psychologist, 55,* 1440–1451.

PART V

Acculturation

Along with the constructs of racial and ethnic identity development covered in Part IV of the *Handbook,* the construct of acculturation has served as a major theoretical anchor for multicultural research and a major clinical anchor for multicultural counseling and assessment. Part V of this *Handbook* consists of two substantive chapters on acculturation research and practice. First, in Chapter 28, Lourdes M. Rivera provides an accessible and thorough review of the role of acculturation in the lives of people adapting to a new cultural environment. Dr. Rivera reviews the history of the acculturation construct in psychology and summarizes leading extant models and conceptualizations of the construct. Next, she reviews measurement and research on acculturation and highlights the challenges in reliably measuring the construct. Dr. Rivera ends her thoughtful chapter with specific directions for needed research on the acculturation construct.

In Chapter 29, prepared by Eric L. Kohatsu, William R. Concepcion, and Patricia Perez, the focus turns to the role of assessing and working with acculturation in the counseling process. The authors highlight five core principles that provide a clear context for the application of acculturation in counseling. Then the authors move to three riveting case studies that demonstrate the application of the core principles in case conceptualization and treatment. The chapter closes with pointed suggestions for mental health professionals working with clients of color. In summary, the two chapters in this section provide a comprehensive overview of theory, research, assessment, and clinical application of acculturation.

28

Acculturation

Theories, Measurement, and Research

LOURDES M. RIVERA

In our increasingly multicultural society, the phenomenon of acculturation has and will continue to play a prominent role in our understanding of and work with ethnic minority populations. Numerous definitions of acculturation have been provided to explain changes that occur at the group (Redfield, Linton, & Herskovits, 1936) and individual (Graves, 1967) level. One of the earliest definitions of acculturation described it as a cultural change process that occurs when individuals from different cultural groups come into continuous contact with one another (Redfield et al., 1936). Contemporary definitions of acculturation have attempted to delineate the multifaceted ways in which this change process manifests itself in various psychosocial (e.g., behaviors, language) (Cuellar, Arnold, & Maldonado, 1995; Marin, 1992) and psychological (e.g., self-esteem, depression) (Balls Organista, Organista, & Kurasaki, 2003) arenas of human functioning. Included in these definitions is the recognition that the environment and individual innate characteristics also influence the acculturation

process (Cuellar et al., 1995, Marin, 1992). Thus, acculturation can be viewed as a dynamic process of change that individuals undergo as they interact with and adapt to a new or different cultural environment; it is an interactive process that occurs along different life domains (e.g., language, values) at different rates of change.

Acculturation has been related to a number of factors in the lives of immigrants and ethnic minorities in the United States, including adherence to cultural values (Marin & Gamba, 2003), issues within family relationships and functioning (Chun & Akutsu, 2003), and physical and mental health issues (Balls Organista et al., 2003; Myers & Rodriguez, 2003; Sam, 2006). Given the relationship between acculturation and overall human functioning, it is one of the most important factors that warrants consideration when working and conducting research with culturally diverse populations (American Psychological Association, 2003; Sam & Berry, 2006).

Although the construct of acculturation continues to receive a great deal of attention in research and practice (Berry, Phinney, Sam, & Vedder, 2006; Chun, Balls Organista, & Marin, 2003; Sam & Berry, 2006), considerable debate continues as to how acculturation should be conceptualized (Cabassa, 2003; Ryder, Alden, & Paulhus, 2000) and measured (Arends-Toth & Van De Vijver, 2007; Kim & Abreu, 2001; Zane & Mak, 2003). Various schools of thought have been proposed regarding how the phenomenon of acculturation should be viewed in order for it to be truly understood. Among these is the strategies approach (Berry, 1997), which focuses on the ways in which individuals engage in the acculturation process; a developmental perspective, which examines acculturation within a developmental framework, particularly when examining acculturation among children of immigrants (Oppedal, 2006); and the perspective of acculturation as culture learning, which emphasizes social skills and social interaction in relation to the acculturation process (Masgoret & Ward, 2006). In short, acculturation is a topic of considerable interest within various psychological and sociological disciplines.

Given the vast amount of research and literature in the area of acculturation, it is not feasible to provide an exhaustive review of acculturation theory, measurement, and research in this chapter. Thus, the goal of this chapter is to provide an overview to assist the reader in beginning to understand and appreciate the complex nature of acculturation and its significance in the lives of culturally diverse populations as they engage in the process of adapting to a different cultural environment (the reader is referred to Chun et al., 2003, and Sam & Berry, 2006, for a more in-depth treatment of the acculturation literature). In this effort, this chapter will focus on how individuals engage in the acculturation process (e.g., strategies) and the factors that may contribute to how individuals negotiate this process.

The first section in this chapter provides an overview of the evolution of the conceptualization of acculturation from a unidimensional to a bidimensional or multifaceted perspective. This overview focuses predominantly on how individuals manage the acculturation process (e.g., strategies) and presents information on the most prominent bidimensional theory in use today (Berry, 1997, 2003). Some examples of recent efforts to expand Berry's theoretical framework in order to encompass a more comprehensive and interactive understanding of the nature of acculturation are also presented. The examples provided here are but a small sampling of the work that is being done in the field; however, they illustrate efforts to build theoretical frameworks that attempt to capture the complexity of this phenomenon and its impact on various areas of human functioning.

The next section focuses on the measurement of acculturation and addresses some of the critical challenges encountered in attempts to accurately measure acculturation given its relation to a number of other variables (e.g., race, ethnicity) and the use of different indicators of acculturation within and across instruments. This is followed by a brief discussion of the literature related to acculturation strategies and some factors that may influence how adolescents engage in the acculturation process. The chapter concludes with a summary and recommendations for the field.

THEORIES

Originally, acculturation was conceptualized as a unidimensional process (Gordon, 1964) within which individuals were seen as giving up or relinquishing aspects of their heritage culture (e.g., beliefs, values, behaviors) as they simultaneously acquired aspects of the new or dominant culture. Within this framework, individuals would eventually assimilate to the new society, thus losing their heritage culture and replacing it with that of the new society. Much criticism has been directed at this conceptualization as it does not allow for alternative methods of acculturating. For example, the unidimensional view of acculturation does not allow for different strategies of negotiating the new culture, such as becoming bicultural (LaFromboise, Coleman, & Gerton, 1993; Ryder et al., 2000). Other criticisms relate to the underlying assumption that exists within this perspective that acculturation occurs only for the new arrivals in a society and that it occurs in isolation of the dominant society's influence (Berry, 1997; Cabassa, 2003; Marin & Gamba, 1996).

Despite these criticisms, there continues to be some support for the unidimensional conceptualization of acculturation. For example, it has been proposed that in situations where a quick assessment of an individual's acculturation status is needed, the unidimensional approach can be beneficial (Flannery, Reise, & Yu, 2001). Thus, given the type of research and level of comprehension being sought, the argument is made that a quick and general assessment of acculturation that is not domain specific may suffice (Flannery et al., 2001). However, for the most part, the unidimensional model of acculturation has given way to more comprehensive and robust bidimensional, multifaceted models of acculturation (Berry, 1997, 2003; Bourhis, Moise, Perreault, & Senecal, 1997; LaFromboise et al., 1993; Navas et al., 2005; Ryder et al., 2000).

BERRY'S ACCULTURATION MODEL

Perhaps the most widely used and researched acculturation framework to date is that proposed by Berry (Berry, 1997). According to Berry's model, as individuals engage in their new environment, they are faced with two issues: the degree to which they wish to hold on to their heritage culture and the degree to which they want to become involved in the new culture or society. Berry proposes that there are four possible acculturation strategies (i.e., assimilation, separation, marginalization, and integration) that represent how individuals go about resolving these two issues.

Individuals who choose the *assimilation* strategy tend to seek to interact with and embrace the new society's culture and adapt the values and behaviors of the new culture while simultaneously rejecting the values and behaviors of the heritage culture. Individuals who use the *separation* strategy wish to maintain their heritage culture and tend to avoid contact with the new society, rejecting the values and behaviors inherent therein. The *marginalization* strategy is used by individuals who have little desire to maintain the heritage culture or to interact with or adopt the values and beliefs of the new society's culture. The fourth strategy is labeled *integration* and denotes the attempt by individuals to simultaneously maintain the heritage culture while interacting with and adapting aspects of the new society's culture (e.g., biculturalism).

The adaptation of these strategies has implications not only for how individuals negotiate the acculturation process, but also for important outcome factors as such as psychosocial and psychological indicators of adjustment. For example, strong empirical support has emerged that indicates that the integration strategy is not only the most favored approach by acculturating individuals (Berry, 1997; Berry et al., 2006), but also the most effective in achieving positive outcomes as relates to higher levels of functioning (Berry, 2003; LaFromboise et al., 1993).

Of particular significance in the bidimensional framework is the evidence that has emerged suggesting not only that acculturation occurs along two dimensions and to varying degrees in different domains, but that a distinction needs to be made between acculturation that takes place in the private (e.g., changes that occur within the family) versus the public (e.g., changes that occur outside of the family) lives of ethnic minorities (Arends-Toth & Van De Vijver, 2007; Navas et al., 2005). Results of a recent study with Turkish immigrants in the Netherlands (Arends-Toth, Van De Vijver, & Poortinga, 2006) indicated that although the Turkish and Dutch cultures were about equally favored in the public domain (suggesting an *integration* attitude), in the private domain, maintenance of the Turkish culture was favored (suggesting a *separation* attitude). Based on these results, the authors propose that a third facet (i.e., domain specificity) be included in assessing the acculturation attitudes of ethnic minorities.

THE INTERACTIVE ACCULTURATION MODEL

Concerns that the four-strategy approach to acculturation may itself be too limiting and that there is a need to examine the acculturation attitudes of members of the receiving society have led to efforts to expand Berry's model (Bourhis et al., 1997; Navas et al., 2005). For example, based on Berry's model of acculturation, Bourhis et al. (1997) proposed the Interactive Acculturation Model (IAM). Within this model, five acculturation strategies are proposed: integration, assimilation, separation, anomie, and individualism. The first three parallel those in Berry's model, and the last two replace *marginalization*. The replacement of *marginalization* with *anomie* and *individualism* attempts to address the difference between individuals who do not identify with either the culture of origin or the new society's culture and may become alienated (resulting in psychosocial or psychological difficulties) and others who may view themselves as individualists and choose not to rely on either cultural perspective to achieve their goals (these individuals may not experience any difficulties related to their individualistic acculturation strategy).

Additionally, taking into consideration that the acculturation process is influenced not only by the attitudes of ethnic minorities but also by the expectations of the receiving society given the dynamic and interactive nature of acculturation, the IAM (Bourhis et al.,1997) incorporates an assessment of the dominant group's acculturation attitudes and expectations of ethnic minorities. By assessing the acculturation attitudes of both ethnic and dominant group members, not only can a more dynamic and comprehensive framework for understanding the acculturation process of different ethnic minority groups be attained, but also a framework for understanding and examining the possible relational outcomes (e.g., conflictual, consensual) between ethnic minority groups and the dominant society is created.

THE RELATIVE ACCULTURATION EXTENDED MODEL

Recently, Navas et al. (2005) proposed the Relative Acculturation Extended Model (RAEM). Taking into consideration that acculturation takes place along various domains, the authors propose that acculturation be assessed along seven domains within the public and private realms (i.e., religious beliefs, principles and values, social relations, family relations, economics, work, and politics and government). In addition, the authors propose that immigrants do not engage in just one acculturation strategy, but that two or more strategies may be used depending on the circumstances and domain being examined. Thus, the authors refer to the minority individual as engaging in a *relative* or *selective* approach to acculturation in which different strategies may be preferred in different domains. Basically, individuals may adapt an integration approach in the public domain (e.g., *politics*) while maintaining a separation approach in the private domain (e.g., *family*). Similar to Bourhis et al. (1997), they propose that the acculturation attitudes or expectations of the dominant society also need to be assessed in order to understand the experiences and strategies used by ethnic minorities within the context of the society in which they reside.

Results of a study conducted with a sample of African immigrants and Spaniards in Spain that used the RAEM (Navas, Rojas, Garcia, & Pumares, 2007) indicated that a complex pattern of acculturation attitudes emerged between the immigrants and the Spaniards within the different domains. The authors report that in the domains of work and economics, both the

African immigrants and the Spaniards preferred the acculturation strategy of *assimilation,* and in the *social* domain, both groups preferred *integration.* However, in the domains of *family, religion,* and *principles and values,* major differences emerged between the groups in that the immigrants preferred the acculturation strategy of *separation,* but the Spaniards preferred that the immigrants engage in *assimilation.* The results of this study highlight the complex nature and process of acculturation for ethnic minority groups and point to issues that may emerge within culturally diverse societies when the dominant society and ethnic minority groups hold opposing acculturation attitudes. Attending to the interaction between the attitudes of the dominant members of a society and those of ethnic minorities allows for a more comprehensive understanding of the acculturation experiences of culturally diverse individuals.

The examples discussed above provide a compelling argument for the need to continue working on the development of comprehensive theoretical models to account for the complex nature of acculturation and the impact of this phenomenon in different areas of human functioning. Recently, Padilla and Perez (2003) argued that the examination of acculturation needs to draw upon social and cognitive psychology as a means of gaining greater insights into the phenomenon of acculturation and the adaptation of ethnic minority groups. The authors stress the need to focus on issues such as social stigma experienced by minority group members in the new society; the influence of the dominant group's attitudes and expectations on the acculturation process of minority group members; an examination of the relative nature of acculturation; and the need to examine the mediating factors (e.g., personal cognitions, characteristics) that contribute to different behaviors on the part of members of minority groups that can be considered to share similar background characteristics (e.g., family structure, socioeconomic status, length of residence in the host society).

As can be discerned from the issues raised above, acculturation is an extremely complex, multifaceted phenomenon that continues to challenge our attempts to easily classify it, measure it, understand it, and incorporate it into research and practice. Much progress is being made as researchers continue to refine and develop theoretical models and methods of measuring acculturation. However, it is a construct that continues to present many challenges in attempts to comprehend its impact on the lives of ethnic minority individuals. It is expected that with continued development of culturally sensitive theory, significant contributions to the understanding of the acculturation phenomenon will be made in the future.

MEASUREMENT

Attempts to understand and explain the phenomenon of acculturation and its impact on various areas of human functioning have resulted in the development of numerous measures of acculturation. Currently, there are measures of acculturation for Asian Americans (e.g., Chung, Kim, & Abreu, 2004), African Americans (e.g., Snowden & Hines, 1999), Hispanic/Latino Americans (e.g., Cuellar et al., 1995; Marin & Gamba, 1996), and Native Americans (e.g., Garrett & Pichette, 2000). Efforts have also been made to develop acculturation measures that could be used with different populations (e.g., Ryder et al., 2000). A recent review of acculturation measures listed 51 such instruments in existence worldwide (Matsudaira, 2006); the overwhelming majority of which were for use with ethnic minority populations residing in the United States.

Despite the abundance of measures of acculturation, much work remains to be done given the great variability that continues to exist in the operationalization and measurement of acculturation (Arends-Toth et al., 2006; Matsudaira, 2006; Zane & Mak, 2003). For example, most measures of acculturation currently use a unidimensional framework for assessing acculturation (Kim & Abreu, 2001; Zane & Mak, 2003). This overreliance on unidimensional measures of acculturation hinders our understanding of this multifaceted and complex phenomenon. Although there have been recent efforts to develop bidimensional, multifaceted measures of acculturation (Chung et al., 2004; Zea, Asner-Self, Birman, & Buki, 2003), additional efforts are needed in this area.

In addition to the limitations on acculturation research related to the use of unidimensional measures, the lack of a consistent method of assessing acculturation also presents a challenge. For example, many measures of acculturation use varied indicators of acculturation within

and between scales (Zane & Mak, 2003), including proxy indicators of acculturation such as language or length of residence in the United States (Cabassa, 2003). This has serious implications for being able to make comparisons across study findings and contributes to the discrepant results often found in acculturation research (Rogler, Cortes, & Malgady, 1991; Unger, Ritt-Olson, Wagner, Soto, & Baezconde-Garbanati, 2007). For example, Unger et al. (2007) recently conducted a study in which they compared three bidimensional measures of acculturation with a sample of Hispanic adolescents. The authors report that across measures, the subscales for U.S./White acculturation were only moderately correlated with each other, as were the subscales for Hispanic/Latino acculturation. These results indicate that these measures are tapping into different acculturation phenomena. Thus, when considering the results of acculturation on different variables of interests, it is important that attention be paid to which indicators of acculturation were used in the study as well as the outcome variables of interest.

Related to the use of multiple indicators of acculturation, the tendency for researchers to collapse scores on measures with multiple indicators (e.g., language, attitudes, values) into a total score of acculturation contributes to a lack of clarity and specificity. Given that it has been established that acculturation occurs at different rates within different life domains (Arends-Toth & Van De Vijver, 2007; Marin & Gamba, 2003), averaging out scores from different domains into a composite acculturation score at best limits our understanding of this complex phenomenon by excluding valuable information from analysis, and at worst can lead to erroneous conclusions about the impact of acculturation on outcome variables of interest.

Another challenge in the measurement of acculturation is the lack of clarity or distinction made between constructs that are often used interchangeably in the literature, such as acculturation and ethnic/racial identity (Helms & Talleyrand, 1997; Phinney, 2003). For example, Phinney (2003; see also Rivera, 2007; Roysircar-Sodowsky & Maestas, 2000) has addressed the relationship that exists between ethnic identity and acculturation and how greater efforts need to be made to separate these constructs. In distinguishing between these two constructs, Phinney (2003) proposed that although ethnic identity is related to acculturation, ethnic identity is more representative of how individuals self-identify with a particular group and how they feel about membership in that group (i.e., identity), whereas acculturation is more representative of the process of adapting to the dominant culture (e.g., language use, skills) in order to function in that new environment and does not necessarily have an impact on one's identity. Thus, although the two constructs may be related, each is tapping into different phenomena.

These multiple and disparate measurement practices contribute to confounding our understanding of acculturation and what factors may be more critical in the understanding of the influence of acculturation (language, behavior, values, etc.) in various areas of human functioning. It has been suggested that in order to advance research on acculturation, more standardized measurement methods need to be established (Arends-Toth & Van De Vijver, 2007), whereas others have suggested that multiple measures of acculturation be used within studies (Unger et al., 2007) in order to tap the different aspects of acculturation. Another strategy that has been proposed in order to obtain a comprehensive understanding of the influence of acculturation on outcome variables of interest, particularly in clinical settings, is that qualitative methods be used in addition to paper-and-pencil instruments (Matsudaira, 2006; Rivera, 2007; Unger et al., 2007). By incorporating a qualitative component into the assessment and measurement of acculturation, it is argued that a broader, more comprehensive and nuanced understanding of the acculturation process in the lives of ethnic minority individuals can be obtained.

ACCULTURATION STRATEGIES

Research on acculturation has increased dramatically in the past few decades, and its influence in virtually every facet of human life and functioning has been recognized (e.g., mental health [Balls Organista et al., 2003]; family functioning [Chun & Akutsu, 2003]). However, what that influence is has not been definitively determined, as the literature on acculturation is replete with apparent contradictory findings (Rogler et al., 1991; Nguyen, Messe, & Stollak, 1999). For example, whereas some studies suggest that acculturating to

the mainstream culture contributes to some positive outcomes (Eyou, Adair, & Dixon, 2000; Nguyen et al., 1999), other studies have reported a negative relationship (Gil, Wagner, & Vega, 2000).

An area of interest that warrants further consideration and that may provide a greater understanding of the complexity of acculturation is the strategies that ethnic minorities and immigrants use in the acculturation process. Although some research has provided support suggesting that the integration strategy may be the most preferred by ethnic minority members and the most conducive to positive adjustment outcomes (Berry et al., 2006; Eyou et al., 2000; LaFromboise et al., 1993), additional research is needed to tease out what integration actually represents to acculturating individuals (Phinney & Devich-Navarro, 1997), in which types of situations and under what circumstances ethnic minority populations are more likely to pursue the integration strategy (Berry et al., 2006; Birman, Trickett, & Buchanan, 2005; Navas et al., 2005), and how this strategy influences different domains of adjustment (Berry et al., 2006; Nguyen et al., 1999). For example, a number of recent studies (Berry et al., 2006; Birman et al., 2005) have indicated that factors such as perceived discrimination and the environment in which acculturation takes place can have an influence on how ethnic minorities engage in the acculturation process. Additionally, studies that examine the relationship between acculturation and adaptation continue to present a complex and intricate picture of the influence of this phenomenon in different life domains (Berry et al., 2006; Nguyen et al., 1999).

In a recent study, Nguyen et al. (1999) examined the relationship between level of involvement in both Vietnamese culture and U.S. culture and various indicators of adjustment for a sample of adolescent Vietnamese living in a predominantly Anglo-American community. Although the authors did not state that they were examining the acculturation strategy of integration, their results do provide some indication of the complex nature of adapting an integration strategy. For example, the authors report that although involvement in the American culture was predictive of positive outcomes on indicators of personal (e.g., self-esteem) and interpersonal (e.g., family relationships) adjustment and school achievement (GPA), involvement in the Vietnamese culture was related to higher levels of psychological distress, while positively predicting family relationships. Thus, from the integration perspective, although involvement in mainstream culture contributed to positive outcomes, involvement in the ethnic culture was more complex, producing both positive and negative outcomes. The authors also report that an interaction effect between adherence to the American and Vietnamese cultures in the prediction of self-esteem emerged in that U.S. cultural involvement positively predicted self-esteem when involvement in the Vietnamese culture was low or moderate, whereas Vietnamese cultural involvement negatively predicted self-esteem when involvement in the U.S. culture was high. These results suggest that a complex relationship exists between various domains of functioning when individuals pursue the integration acculturation strategy.

Another issue that warrants attention as relates to integration is the conceptual definition of this strategy and the different ways in which acculturating individuals may engage in integration. For example, in a study that examined how adolescents viewed themselves in relation to their culture of origin and the mainstream American culture, Phinney and Devich-Navarro (1997) reported that participants in their study could be classified as "blended biculturals," "alternating biculturals," or "separated" adolescents. Those who were classified as "blended" tended to view themselves as both and equally ethnic and American. The "alternating biculturals" indicated that they viewed themselves as more ethnic than American, but also identified situational factors as influencing how they saw themselves at any given point in time. The "separated" adolescents did not view themselves as being bicultural; instead, they identified with the ethnic group and indicated that they did not feel "American." The authors conclude that although most of the adolescents in their study could be classified as bicultural (e.g., integrated), their sense of being bicultural (or integrated) varied based on other factors (e.g., how they perceived the two cultures). These results suggest that even when ethnic minorities engage in what can conceivably be considered the integration strategy of acculturation, it may be occurring in a very idiosyncratic manner.

As relates to preferred acculturation strategies, Berry et al. (2006) conducted a study that included 5,366 ethnically diverse adolescents residing in 13 countries. The authors report that 36.4% of the sample could be classified as having an acculturation profile that indicated that they preferred the integration strategy, 22.5% were classified as having an ethnic profile (i.e., separation), 18.7% as having a national profile (i.e., assimilation), and 22.4% as having a diffuse profile (i.e., marginalization). Thus, although roughly 36% of the sample preferred the integration strategy, 64% were distributed among the other three strategies. An understanding of the circumstances that contribute to ethnic minorities selecting different acculturation strategies is needed.

One possible factor to understanding this pattern of preferred acculturation strategies can be related to the environment in which acculturation takes place. For example, the researchers reported that most of the adolescents classified as having the integration profile resided in ethnically mixed communities within the respective countries, whereas few with this profile fell within the diffuse profile. This finding suggests that the environment in which ethnic minorities reside may have a significant influence on the type of acculturation strategy pursued by ethnic minorities (Berry et al., 2006).

In another recent study, Birman et al. (2005) examined the impact of community context on the acculturation and adaptation process of two groups of adolescents from the former Soviet Union living in the United States for approximately 6 years. The two groups had resettled in two different communities within the same state. One community was described as "concentrated" (consisting of a large percentage of residents with a Russian or Ukranian ancestry) and the other as "dispersed" (indicating more racial/ethnic diversity). The authors report that in the dispersed community, acculturation to American society occurred more quickly compared to the concentrated community. In addition, they report that in the concentrated community, Russian behavioral acculturation was higher, whereas in the dispersed community, American acculturation was higher. These results indicate that the type of community in which adolescents reside may influence how they acculturate to their new environment. The authors suggest that these differences are related to the types of opportunities or "acculturative press" that each of these communities exerts on its members in order to function in that particular environment within the larger society. These findings highlight the need for more research that examines the context in which ethnic minorities acculturate in order to have a better understanding of what factors influence the acculturation process of ethnically diverse populations.

In addition to factors such as the ethnic mix of the environment in which individuals acculturate, studies have indicated that perceived discrimination may also have an impact on how individuals engage in the process of acculturation (Berry et al., 2006; Birman et al., 2005). Birman et al. (2005) reported that perceived discrimination was related to levels of acculturation such that the more discrimination is experienced, the more likely the adolescents in their sample were to reject American identification and hold on to their Russian identity (identity was one of the indicators of acculturation in this study). Berry et al. (2006) also reported that adolescents in the integration profile reported significantly lower levels of perceived discrimination, with the highest level of discrimination being reported by adolescents with the diffuse profile. Thus, it is possible that although an integration approach to acculturation may be more beneficial, the experience of discrimination may deter ethnic minority populations from pursuing this strategy and limit their involvement with the larger society.

Additional research is needed that incorporates factors such as the context in which acculturation takes place, the interactive nature of acculturation within different contexts, factors that affect the process (e.g., perceived discrimination), and the impact that these different variables have on the types of acculturation strategies used by ethnic minority groups. In addition, if integration is the most preferred and adaptive acculturation strategy, more research is needed in order to understand what integration means to individuals engaging in this strategy and to have a better understanding of the varied ways in which individuals integrate the new society while maintaining their culture of origin.

SUMMARY AND CONCLUSIONS

The construct of acculturation continues to garner much attention and research both internationally and in the United States. As the U.S. population continues to grow increasingly more diverse, it is imperative that concerted efforts continue to be made to attain a better

understanding of the process of acculturation and its varied influences in the lives of ethnic minority individuals. Given that 50% of the U.S. population is expected to consist of ethnically and culturally diverse individuals by the year 2050 (U.S. Census Bureau, 2004), this understanding has serious implications in the areas of education, counseling, psychological assessment, and mental health and health care services, as well as the economic well-being of the country. As the prolific literature on acculturation continues to grow, and as scholars continue to work on theory development and measurement strategies, it is expected that a more comprehensive understanding of acculturation will be attained that will contribute to facilitating our continued development as a multicultural society.

However, in order to move forward in our understanding of acculturation and its impact on human functioning, greater efforts need to be directed at incorporating a theoretical framework to the research being conducted and establishing more standardized methods of conceptualizing and measuring acculturation (Arends-Toth & Van De Vijver, 2006, 2007; Cabassa, 2003). Scholars need to pay closer attention to the acculturation models that are being used, the types of measures that are incorporated within research designs, and the underlying factors that influence acculturation that these measures may or may not be tapping into (Kim & Abreu, 2001; Unger et al., 2007; Zane & Mak, 2003).

In order to truly understand the complexity and influence of acculturation in the lives of ethnic minorities, greater attention needs to be paid to the cultural context in which acculturation takes place, and an examination of how the larger society and the dominant culture influence the acculturation process of ethnic minority populations in the United States is also needed (Birman et al., 2005; Bourhis et al., 1997; Navas et al., 2005; Padilla & Perez, 2003). Issues such as discrimination and individual differences within ethnic group members (e.g., personal characteristics, coping) that influence or mediate the process of acculturation also need to be taken into consideration in order to enhance our understanding of this phenomenon (Padilla & Perez, 2003). By incorporating a framework that considers these multiple factors, a more comprehensive understanding of this multifaceted and complex phenomenon can be achieved.

As a society, as researchers, and as practitioners, we also need to pay closer attention to the national and institutional policies and practices within which we operate. As Berry (1997, 2003) has repeatedly discussed, there is a relationship between the policies that pluralistic societies implement and the acculturation process of ethnic minority populations. In order to understand the acculturation process of those we serve and provide the resources and assistance needed to facilitate their ability to function successfully in society and achieve their potential, we must consider these factors as well.

REFERENCES

American Psychological Association. (2003). Guidelines on multicultural education, training, research, practice and organizational change for psychologists. *American Psychologist, 58,* 377–402.

Arends-Toth, J., & Van De Vijver, F. J. R. (2006). Assessment of psychological assessment. In D. L. Sam & J. W. Berry (Eds.), *The Cambridge handbook of acculturation psychology* (pp. 58–77). Cambridge, UK: Cambridge University Press.

Arends-Toth, J., & Van De Vijver, F. J. R. (2007). Acculturation attitudes: A comparison of measurement methods. *Journal of Applied Social Psychology, 37,* 1462–1488.

Arends-Toth, J., Van De Vijver, F. J. R., & Poortinga, Y. H. (2006). The influence of method factors on the relation between attitudes and self-reported behaviors in the assessment of acculturation. *European Journal of Psychological Assessment, 22,* 4–12.

Balls Organista, P., Organista, K. C., & Kurasaki, K. (2003). The relationship between acculturation and ethnic minority mental health. In K. M. Chun, P. Balls Organista, & G. Marin (Eds.), *Acculturation: Advances in theory, measurement, and applied research* (pp. 139–162). Washington, DC: American Psychological Association.

Berry, J. W. (1997). Immigration, acculturation, and adaptation. *Applied Psychology: An International Review, 46,* 5–33.

Berry, J. W. (2003). Conceptual approaches to acculturation. In K. M. Chun, P. Balls Organista, & G. Marin (Eds.), *Acculturation: Advances in theory, measurement, and applied research* (pp. 17–37). Washington, DC: American Psychological Association.

Berry, J. W., Phinney, J. S., Sam, D. L., & Vedder, P. (2006). *Immigrant youth in cultural transition: Acculturation, identity, and adaptation across national contexts.* Mahwah, NJ: Lawrence Erlbaum.

Birman, D., Trickett, E., & Buchanan, R. M. (2005). A tale of two cities: Replication of a study on the acculturation and adaptation of immigrant adolescents from the former Soviet Union in a different community context [Electronic version]. *American Journal of Community Psychology, 35,* 83–101.

Bourhis, R. Y., Moise, L. C., Perreault, S., & Senecal, S. (1997). Towards an interactive acculturation model: A social psychological approach. *International Journal of Psychology, 32,* 369–386.

Cabassa, L. J. (2003). Measuring acculturation: Where we are and where we need to go. *Hispanic Journal of Behavioral Sciences, 25,* 127–146.

Chun, K. M., & Akutsu, P. D. (2003). Acculturation among ethnic minority families. In K. M. Chun, P. Balls Organista, & G. Marin (Eds.), *Acculturation: Advances in theory, measurement, and applied research* (pp. 95–119). Washington, DC: American Psychological Association.

Chun, K. M., Balls Organista, P., & Marin, G. (Eds.). (2003). *Acculturation: Advances in theory, measurement, and applied research.* Washington, DC: American Psychological Association.

Chung, R. H. G., Kim, B. S. K., & Abreu, J. M. (2004). Asian American Multidimensional Acculturation Scale: Development, factor analysis, reliability, and validity. *Cultural Diversity and Ethnic Minority Psychology, 10,* 66–80.

Cuellar, I., Arnold, B., & Maldonado, R. (1995). Acculturation rating scale for Mexican Americans–II: A revision of the original ARSMA scale. *Hispanic Journal of Behavioral Sciences, 17,* 275–304.

Eyou, M. L., Adair, V., & Dixon, R. (2000). Cultural identity and psychological adjustment of adolescent Chinese immigrants in New Zealand. *Journal of Adolescence, 23,* 531–543.

Flannery, W. P., Reise, S. P., & Yu, J. (2001). An empirical comparison of acculturation models. *Personality and Social Psychology Bulletin, 27,* 1035–1045.

Garrett, M. T., & Pichette, E. F. (2000). Red as an apple: Native American acculturation and counseling with or without reservations. *Journal of Counseling and Development, 78,* 3–13.

Gil, A., Wagner, E., & Vega, W. (2000). Acculturation, familism and alcohol use among Latino adolescent males: Longitudinal relations. *Journal of Community Psychology, 28,* 443–458.

Gordon, M. M. (1964). *Assimilation in American life: The role of race, religion, and national origin.* New York: Oxford University Press.

Graves, T. D. (1967). Psychological acculturation in a tri-ethnic community. *Southwestern Journal of Anthropology, 23,* 337–350.

Helms, J. E., & Talleyrand, R. M. (1997). Race is not ethnicity. *American Psychologist, 52,* 1246–1247.

Kim, B. S. K., & Abreu, J. M. (2001). Acculturation measurement: Theory, current instruments, and future directions. In J. G. Ponterotto, J. M. Casas, L. A. Suzuki, & C. M. Alexander (Eds.), *Handbook of multicultural counseling* (2nd ed., pp. 394–424). Thousand Oaks, CA: Sage.

LaFromboise, T., Coleman, H. L. K., & Gerton, J. (1993). Psychological impact of biculturalism: Evidence and theory. *Psychological Bulletin, 114,* 395–412.

Marin, G. (1992). Issues in the measurement of acculturation among Hispanics. In K. F. Geisinger (Ed.), *Psychological testing of Hispanics* (pp. 235–251). Washington, DC: American Psychological Association.

Marin, G., & Gamba, R. J. (1996). A new measurement of acculturation for Hispanics: The Bidimensional Acculturation Scale for Hispanics (BAS). *Hispanic Journal of Behavioral Sciences, 18,* 297–316.

Marin, G., & Gamba, R. J. (2003). Acculturation and changes in cultural values. In K. M. Chun, P. Balls Organista, & G. Marin (Eds.), *Acculturation: Advances in theory, measurement, and applied research* (pp. 83–93). Washington, DC: American Psychological Association.

Masgoret, A., & Ward, C. (2006). Culture learning approach to acculturation. In D. L. Sam & J. W. Berry (Eds.), *The Cambridge handbook of acculturation psychology* (pp. 58–77). Cambridge, UK: Cambridge University Press.

Matsudaira, T. (2006). Measures of psychological acculturation: A review. *Transcultural Psychiatry, 43,* 461–487.

Myers, H. F., & Rodriguez, N. (2003). Acculturation and physical health in racial and ethnic minorities. In K. M. Chun, P. Balls Organista, & G. Marin (Eds.), *Acculturation: Advances in theory, measurement, and applied research* (pp. 17–37). Washington, DC: American Psychological Association.

Navas, M., Garcia, M. C., Sanchez, J., Rojas, A. J., Pumares, P., & Fernandez, J. S. (2005). Relative Acculturation Extended Model: New contributions with regard to the study of acculturation. *International Journal of Intercultural Relations, 29,* 21–37.

Navas, M., Rojas, A. J., Garcia, M., & Pumares, P. (2007). Acculturation strategies and attitudes according to the Relative Acculturation Extended Model (RAEM): The perspectives of natives versus immigrants. *International Journal of Intercultural Relations, 31,* 67–86.

Nguyen, H., Messe, L., & Stollak, G. (1999). Towards a more complex understanding of acculturation and adjustment. *Journal of Cross-Cultural Psychology, 30,* 5–26.

Oppedal, B. (2006). Development and acculturation. In D. L. Sam & J. W. Berry (Eds.), *The Cambridge handbook of acculturation psychology* (pp. 97–112). Cambridge, UK: Cambridge University Press.

Padilla, A. M., & Perez, W. (2003). Acculturation, social identity, and social cognition: A new perspective. *Hispanic Journal of Behavioral Sciences, 25,* 35–55.

Phinney, J. S. (2003). Ethnic identity and acculturation. In K. M. Chun, P. Balls Organista, & G. Marin (Eds.), *Acculturation: Advances in theory, measurement, and applied research* (pp. 63–81). Washington, DC: American Psychological Association.

Phinney, J. S., & Devich-Navarro, M. (1997). Variations in bicultural identification among African American and Mexican American adolescents. *Journal of Research on Adolescents, 7,* 3–32.

Redfield, R., Linton, R., & Herskovits, M. (1936). Memorandum on the study of acculturation. *American Anthropologist, 38,* 149–152.

Rivera, L. M. (2007). Acculturation and multicultural assessment: Issues, trends, and practice. In L. A. Suzuki & J. G. Ponterotto (Eds.), *Handbook of multicultural assessment: Clinical, psychological, and educational applications* (3rd ed., pp. 73–91). San Francisco: Jossey-Bass.

Roysircar-Sodowsky, G., & Maestas, M. V. (2000). Acculturation, ethnic identity, and acculturative stress. In R. H. Dana (Ed.), *Handbook of cross-cultural and multicultural personality assessment* (pp. 131–172). Mahwah, NJ: Lawrence Erlbaum.

Rogler, L. H., Cortes, D. E., & Malgady, R. G. (1991). Acculturation and mental health status among Hispanics. *American Psychologist, 46,* 585–597.

Ryder, A. G., Alden, L. E., & Paulhus, D. L. (2000). Is acculturation unidimensional or bidimensional? A head-to-head comparison in the prediction of personality, self-identity, and adjustment. *Journal of Personality and Social Psychology, 79,* 49–65.

Sam, D. L. (2006). Acculturation and health. In D. L. Sam & J. W. Berry (Eds.), *The Cambridge handbook of acculturation psychology* (pp. 452–468). Cambridge, UK: Cambridge University Press.

Sam, D. L., & Berry, J. W. (Eds.). (2006). *The Cambridge handbook of acculturation psychology.* Cambridge, UK: Cambridge University Press.

Snowden, L. R., & Hines, A. M. (1999). A scale to assess African American acculturation. *Journal of Black Psychology, 25,* 36–47.

Unger, J. B., Ritt-Olson, A., Wagner, K., Soto, D., & Baezconde-Garbanati, L. (2007). A comparison of acculturation measures among Hispanic/Latino adolescents. *Journal of Youth and Adolescence, 36,* 555–565.

U.S. Census Bureau. (2004). *Projected population of the United States, by race and Hispanic origin: 2000 to 2050.* Retrieved May 22, 2008, from http://www.census .gov/ipc/www/usinterimproj/natprojtab01a.pdf

Zane, N., & Mak, W. (2003). Major approaches to the measurement of acculturation among ethnic minority populations: A content analysis and an alternative empirical strategy. In K. M. Chun, P. Balls Organista, & G. Marin (Eds.), *Acculturation: Advances in theory, measurement, and applied research* (pp. 39–60). Washington, DC: American Psychological Association.

Zea, M. C., Asner-Self, K. K., Birman, D., & Buki, L. P. (2003). The Abbreviated Multidimensional Acculturation Scale: Empirical validation with two Latino/Latina samples. *Cultural Diversity and Ethnic Minority Psychology, 9,* 107–126.

29

Incorporating Levels of Acculturation in Counseling Practice

ERIC L. KOHATSU, WILLIAM R. CONCEPCION, AND PATRICIA PEREZ

Acculturation is one of the most widely researched variables in cross-cultural psychology. Since the early 1970s, numerous publications have examined the processes of acculturation, its role in counseling, and its psychological impact on various racial/cultural groups (e.g., Kim, 2006; Kim & Omizo, 2006; Rogler, Cortes, & Malgady, 1991; Roysircar-Sodowsky & Maestas, 2000). The term *racial/cultural groups* is used to emphasize the centrality of race and its impact on one's psychologically identified culture, which is recognized as learned socialization experiences influencing one's behavioral and thought patterns (Carter, 2005a). The term is also used to distinguish it from other popularly used labels such as "multicultural," "ethnic," and "culturally diverse" groups, so as to not dilute or confuse the importance of addressing racial dynamics in counseling practice, training, and research (Carter, 2005a; Helms & Cook, 1999). Recently, several major reviews of the acculturation research have emerged (e.g., Kim & Abreu, 2001; Kohatsu, 2005; Zane & Mak, 2003),

including a chapter in this volume of the *Handbook* (Rivera, Chapter 28), that focused on issues related to its conceptualization, measurement, and relationships to mental health variables.

In spite of this outpouring of book chapters, journal articles, and dissertations on acculturation, surprisingly little information has been published that provides practical suggestions for applying it in counseling, particularly with racial/cultural groups (Leong & Lee, 2006). In addition, researchers have not addressed the procedures to assess acculturation, informally or formally, in counseling. In short, mirroring the historical development of multicultural counseling competencies, the body of work on acculturation appears to lack consistent and meaningful discourse on the applications of acculturation in cross-cultural counseling with different racial/cultural groups. To address these shortcomings, this chapter will present a framework for examining acculturation and illustrate its application through cases based on actual clients.

This chapter will begin by defining acculturation and briefly summarizing some of the persistent problems in the research literature that affect the application of this construct in counseling practice. As a caveat, it is important to note that the focus will be on racial/cultural groups of color in the United States. Second, five core principles that will serve as a framework for understanding and integrating acculturation in counseling will be discussed. Third, an in-depth analysis of three counseling cases using this framework will be offered, including an integrative discussion of issues raised in the cases in light of the five core principles. Fourth, the chapter will conclude with overall recommendations for counselors.

DEFINITIONS OF ACCULTURATION

Lack of precision and consistency in defining acculturation has plagued the field. An integral component of this definitional problem is that researchers have frequently confounded acculturation with other constructs, such as ethnicity, ethnic identity, and assimilation. Similar to other cross-cultural variables, some of the definitions of acculturation have also been influenced by scientific racism in that the dominant White culture was implicitly valued more highly than the incoming, nondominant cultures (e.g., Abe-Kim, Okazaki, & Goto, 2001; Kohatsu, 2005). Finally, how researchers have defined acculturation depended in large part on whether a unidimensional or multidimensional conceptualization was used (e.g., Kohatsu, 2005).

As the most widely used conceptualization, the unidimensional approach defined acculturation on a single continuum, ranging from low to high acculturation to the dominant White culture (Kim & Abreu, 2001; Kohatsu, 2005). As an immigrant/nondominant individual progressed in the acculturation process, it was presumed that a higher degree of White cultural values, beliefs, attitudes, and practices would be incorporated into his or her self-concept. Simultaneously, it also meant that the immigrant/nondominant individual had to discard his or her ethnic cultural values, beliefs, attitudes, and behaviors. The unidimensional approach to acculturation, under much criticism for its inherent racism, has been replaced by multidimensional models.

For this chapter, acculturation, as a multidimensional construct, is defined overall as changes in attitudes, values, practices, and beliefs of both the immigrant/ nondominant group and the host/dominant cultural group. More specifically, acculturation refers to

> the individual's process of learning about and adopting White cultural values, beliefs, attitudes, and behaviors into his or her self-concept . . . [and] the degree to which the person maintains his or her own ethnic culture (or other ethnic cultures) through adherence to cultural values, beliefs, attitudes, and behaviors. (Kohatsu, 2005, p. 209)

Such a definition involves two or more dimensions that are relatively independent from each other. In addition, acculturation, as presented in this chapter, will focus on processes that take place at the individual and/or psychological level.

CORE PRINCIPLES OF ACCULTURATION

Based on a comprehensive review of empirical and theoretical work in acculturation, coupled with our combined counseling experiences, this section of the chapter will highlight five core principles that form the framework for understanding the potential applications of acculturation in counseling.

Core Principle #1: Acculturation Is Complex and Multidimensional

Psychologists continue to struggle with certain aspects of the undeniably complex construct of acculturation (e.g., conceptualization, measurement). Part of this complexity stems from the multiple levels and layers that the processes of acculturation involve. On a macro level, the extent to which one incorporates aspects of the White dominant culture occurs concomitantly with the maintenance or reduction of adherence to one's indigenous culture (e.g., Kim & Abreu, 2001; Kohatsu, 2005; Matsudaira, 2006). On a micro level, the cognitive, affective, and behavioral components of an individual's cultural repertoire interact and, consequently, are constantly being modified during the acculturation process. Furthermore, acculturation is fluid and occurs on multiple levels that intersect simultaneously at any given point in time, over the duration of a client's lifespan and across generations.

Core Principle #2: Acculturation Is Contextually Based

Closely related to the first principle, this one focuses on accounting for the importance of the cultural context in understanding acculturation issues. Acculturation is a phenomenon that is contextually based, in that its meaning shifts from one context to another. Essentially, an ecological approach is adopted in that the multiple social, cultural, and political environments (both macro and micro) in which clients of color function on a daily basis should be accounted for in counseling (e.g., Kohatsu, 2005; Sasao & Sue, 1993). Moreover, these contexts may shift and/or be altered in a short period of time. Therefore, counselors should be wary of adhering to rigid conceptualizations of clients' acculturation status and corresponding experiences. These conceptualizations need to be expanded on and modified to reflect changes taking place in clients.

Core Principle #3: Each Individual Processes Acculturation Issues in Different Ways

In light of the increasing importance given to within-group variables in cross-cultural research, it is also critically important to factor in such distinctions in addressing acculturation issues in counseling. Each person of color processes acculturation in unique ways reflecting his or her particular cultural socialization and interpersonal style. Hence, it behooves counselors to avoid stereotyping clients by overgeneralizing patterns uncovered in research to real clients.

Furthermore, research on acculturation has tended to focus on overt behaviors (e.g., language use, friendship choice, food preference, participation in cultural activities) as a primary means of assessing acculturation (e.g., Kim, 2006; Kim & Abreu, 2001). In counseling, gauging acculturation by using these simple behavioral indicators should not be perceived as synonymous with an overall assessment of acculturation levels in a client. In addition, assessing acculturation is an ongoing process and not a one-shot deal. Counselors should continually monitor and evaluate acculturation throughout the process of counseling. Curiously, current emphasis on using paper-and-pencil acculturation measures in research significantly restricts the assessment of acculturation in counseling.

Core Principle #4: Acculturation Intersects With Racial and Ethnic Identity, as Well as Other Aspects of One's Overall Identity

Although acculturation has generated much research, it is just one of several cross-cultural variables that counselors should factor in when working with clients of color. It is suggested that acculturation intersects with other variables, such as racial and ethnic identity, as well as various components of one's identity (e.g., Kohatsu, 2005). As cultural beings, people do not exist in a vacuum and, likewise, clients should not be conceptualized as devoid of these intersecting factors/variables. Therefore, when addressing acculturation in counseling, it is important to take into account these other mutually influencing variables.

Core Principle #5: Acculturation Processes Should Be Understood From a Race-Based Perspective

As an extension of the ecological approach, the processes of acculturation could be analyzed more fruitfully from a race-based perspective. Carter (2005c) advocated that a race-based approach "assumes that the experience of belonging to a racial group transcends/supercedes all other experiences in the United States" and that "race is the context for understanding culture" (p. xvii). Race exerts a powerful force that affects individuals, including the processes of acculturation, in many ways (Kohatsu, 2005). That is, the sociocultural and racial environments in which people of color find themselves can determine the quality of their acculturation experience. To clarify, the term *sociocultural* refers to societal practices and policies that have an individual's respective culture(s) as a focus (Helms & Cook, 1999). For instance, an African American participating in an all-Black church, compared to a predominantly White church, would have a very different acculturation experience.

In this chapter, the use of Carter's race-based perspective, rather than one focused on ethnicity, reflects more accurately the interpersonal and institutional dynamics in the United States. In contrast, focusing exclusively on ethnicity obscures people's experiences of being treated as perceived members of a particular racial group. According to Helms and Talleyrand (1997), individuals will use ethnicity as a politically correct way of denying or ignoring the importance of sociorace. *Sociorace* refers to race-related processes that occur at the interpersonal or societal level resulting from the imposition of socially defined racial categories (Helms & Cook, 1999; Helms & Talleyrand, 1997).

Both the macro and micro factors of sociorace should be accounted for in unpacking the complexities of acculturation in individuals of color. For instance, counselors must be aware of the importance of adapting skills to navigate the larger system to survive in the United States—a crucial, yet frequently ignored, component of the acculturation process.

These five core principles will be used as the overarching framework to illuminate the use of acculturation in counseling people of color using material from our clients. These cases vary by site/agency, geographical location, duration of counseling, and issues addressed. To maintain the confidentiality of the clients involved, some of the information has been altered. Each client case is, as accurately as possible, a reflection of our clinical experience and not intended to be generalized to other members of the same racial/cultural group.

THE CASE OF JENNY

Jenny is a 28-year-old Southeast Asian American female originally from southern California who has been living in Hawai'i for about 2 years. She is currently in her senior year of college and lives alone off-campus with a pet dog. Jenny's presenting concern was "getting a better perspective in life" and reducing the amount of complaining and pessimism she experiences on a regular basis. She often feels she is a failure and has not accomplished anything significant, which fuels her negativity. Jenny also experiences bouts of anxiety, which make it difficult for her to handle stressful situations and perform well in school (e.g., taking course examinations). Jenny has been taking Paxil and Prozac to help manage anxiety and depression, respectively.

Jenny's concerns also included dealing with interpersonal problems in her family, namely with her 67-year-old mother and, to a lesser extent, her 25-year-old brother. She feels especially frustrated and angry whenever she gets into arguments with her mother.

Jenny believes her internalized anger and impatience with others is a result of their dysfunctional relationship. She is also concerned about her brother, who suffered a severe head injury as a teenager and subsequently experienced cognitive and emotional impairment.

Core Principle #1: Acculturation Is Complex and Multidimensional

Although Jenny's difficulties expressing and managing her emotions (e.g., anger) in adaptive ways was an issue with others in general, it was soon determined that her struggles were rooted in family dynamics. Jenny experienced frustration and anger during verbal conflicts with her mother, but understood that traditional family values she learned while growing up discouraged one from communicating emotions publicly, particularly with older family members. She did not typically express strong emotions with others, which contributed to her struggles of trying to maintain learned traditional cultural practices while adopting the values often espoused by mainstream White American culture (e.g., emotional expressiveness). However, she did not have difficulty expressing disagreement with her mother, with whom she often reported having shouting matches. Jenny's communication style with her mother indicated some level of acculturation to White American culture, in which open expression of opinions contrary to one's elders appeared to occur with comparatively greater frequency. In contrast, Jenny's behaviors may be perceived from an Asian cultural framework as disrespectful to a family member who was senior to her (Chin, Liem, Ham, & Hong, 1993).

Jenny believed her mother wanted to instill in her the value that parents are always to be obeyed, even if it may seem that they are incorrect at times. She further reported that although her mother pursued a college education in the United States, she retained values from her country of origin. Jenny acknowledged, however, that her mother's decision to come to the United States alone could have been a break from the traditional cultural practice of remaining close to family.

Jenny was raised solely by her mother since the age of 12. Even though Jenny's mother had been living in the United States for more than 40 years and received an American college education, she continued to raise her daughter in primarily traditional ways. For example, Jenny often spoke about how her mother was stricter with her than with her brother, who, before his injury, was allowed greater freedoms (e.g., spending time with friends, becoming involved in romantic relationships). Furthermore, Jenny often had sole responsibility of maintaining the house while her mother was busy working. She sometimes envied the freedom that some of her friends appeared to take for granted and felt she needed to lie to her mother just to get a chance to spend time outside of the home.

Jenny's habit of keeping strong emotions (e.g., anger) inside often built up to the point that she verbally exploded onto others, which was often her boyfriend or mother. She also learned not to air family problems, which contributed to her tendencies in keeping emotions bottled up inside. These same tendencies appeared related to the development of physical ailments (e.g., headaches, stomach problems) and an exacerbation of her anxiety. This feeling sometimes overwhelmed her to the point that she removed herself from uncomfortable situations, such as skipping class to avoid anxiety-provoking exams.

Core Principle #2: Acculturation Is Contextually Based

Although Jenny enjoyed her new life in Hawai'i, about one year into her residence she found the pace of life there to be too slow. It may be the case that Asian/Pacific Island values predominate in Hawai'i, which may have made it a different experience from what life was like for her in California. For example, Jenny found it difficult to make friends who were "local" (i.e., born and raised in Hawai'i). However, she was also older than most of her classmates and may have felt they did not share similar life values. Thus, even in this American context, she found it difficult adjusting to local culture. It is perhaps a combination of these experiences that contributed to Jenny's periodic feelings of isolation.

It is also important to be mindful of how Jenny's behaviors may be culturally appropriate in some situations, while recognizing the potential challenges this may present in other contexts. In some cross-racial interactions, for example, it may be more appropriate for her to be expressive and less emotionally private.

Even within her own socioracial group, Jenny may encounter Asian Americans adopting a comparatively more direct, overtly expressive approach.

Core Principle #3: Each Individual Processes Acculturation Issues in Different Ways

Although Jenny's case reflects the common struggles of trying to balance adapting to mainstream White American culture and honoring traditional family cultural values, how she experienced and coped with these issues is unique (Smedley, Myers, & Harrell, 1993). For example, even though Jenny disliked some values upheld in her family (e.g., emphasis on material wealth and accomplishments, unquestioning obedience to elders, and unequal liberties to daughters), she did endorse some of them (e.g., sacrificing individual needs for the family, honoring privacy in family matters).

While, Jenny felt badly about her brother getting injured, she also felt some resentment over having to help raise and take care of him through high school and during her early 20s. Jenny shared that she had to assume a parental role and missed out on various experiences people her age were having because of family responsibilities. Although she now feels happier having moved away from home and living a new life in Hawai'i, she still feels obligated to help her family in whatever way she can.

The concept of getting an education was also highly prized in Jenny's family, and high occupational status was important to her family members. These appear to be values sometimes associated with individuals of Asian background (Sue & Sue, 2008). Jenny, however, felt she did not subscribe to those values and would rather judge and be judged by the quality of one's character.

Core Principle #4: Acculturation Intersects With Racial and Ethnic Identity, as Well as Other Aspects of One's Overall Identity

Jenny felt comfortable discussing her concerns with the psychologist because she perceived he was of similar age and Asian background. She believed individuals of shared racial backgrounds have greater understanding of and sensitivity to one another's experiences. This demonstrates an aspect of racial identity development

(Helms, 1995) in that she perceives that racial similarities can be therapeutically helpful. Jenny may still be trying to balance her cross-cultural experiences living in the United States, but seems to have some level of comfort navigating both her Asian and American identities (Internalization racial identity status).

Jenny may have felt more comfortable opening up in counseling partly because the psychologist self-disclosed about having grown up in the United States. Because length of time spent being exposed to a majority culture has often been a factor associated with influencing acculturation (Sue & Sue, 2008), Jenny's comfort with divulging more of her personal life may have been facilitated by this shared experience. Although not directly spoken, it seemed that Jenny felt the counselor implicitly understood her cultural idiosyncrasies as a result of these perceived racial/cultural similarities. Furthermore, she believed that offering a token gift (e.g., box of cookies) to the psychologist as a sign of appreciation for services rendered was culturally influenced.

Core Principle #5: Acculturation Processes Should Be Understood From a Race-Based Perspective

The culturally sensitive practitioner should be continually mindful that Jenny is living in a society that espouses values different from many of those endorsed in her family. Moreover, the current sociopolitical structures of the United States and its long-standing history with racism do not necessarily make being "different" advantageous in many situations. Residing in Hawai'i or other geographically diverse areas may provide a limited degree of protection from experiences with racial discrimination, but it does not provide complete immunity because of racism's pervasiveness throughout American society. Finally, though Jenny may be able to "talk the talk" and "walk the walk," she still does not represent the generalized notion of how an "American" is envisioned. Despite being American-born and proficient in the English language, White American society will not accept her as a "true" American.

THE CASE OF LUIS AND MONICA

Luis and Monica presented to counseling with significant conflict in their marriage, which they attributed to "communication problems." Luis, a 26-year-old landscape worker from a small town in Mexico, had immigrated illegally to the United States 4 years earlier. Monica was 21 years old and the U.S.-born daughter of Mexican immigrants. They had been married for almost 2 years and had a 1-year-old daughter. Monica had worked full time as a receptionist and attended the local community college part time until she had their baby. Monica valued the time she was spending with her daughter, but was increasingly upset about not being back at work and school, as she had planned prior to the baby's arrival.

One of the major issues this couple faced involved divergent gender role expectations. Monica argued she had the potential to earn a larger salary than Luis, given her bilingual proficiency, higher level of education, and legal status in the United States. Luis asserted he could support the family with his salary and was strongly opposed to her plans of returning to work and school. He managed the couple's finances and indicated he had been saving money so they could soon move out of Monica's parents' home and into their own apartment, possibly in a different city. Monica reported she was very close to her family and did not want to leave.

Luis had recently started attending English classes a few evenings per week and was struggling to pick up the new language, but refused to seek Monica's assistance. During therapy sessions, Monica sometimes used English to insult Luis or to make sarcastic comments, knowing he would be unable to understand. On several occasions, Monica's tone and nonverbal behavior during counseling sessions reflected an expectation that the counselor, who shared some of her cultural characteristics, would agree with her stance. These shared characteristics included being U.S.-born, bilingual, and the daughter of Mexican immigrants.

Core Principle #1: Acculturation Is Complex and Multidimensional

Monica's interest in pursuing academic and professional goals rather than focusing exclusively on the nurturing role of mother indicates a high level of acculturation to the dominant White culture. However, her desire to remain physically and emotionally close to her family of origin reflects a high level of acculturation to her Mexican culture. In fact, this desire reflects a common value among Latinos/as known as *familismo,* which is characterized by cooperation to maintain close ties with family members (Sue & Sue, 2008). Luis's desire to be sole breadwinner of the household reflects strong adherence to traditional cultural values, particularly *machismo.* Despite the negative connotation often attributed to this term, *machismo* actually describes a man's sense of responsibility to provide for his family (Santiago-Rivera, Arredondo, & Gallardo-Cooper, 2002). Luis's recent participation in English classes, however, could indicate a progression toward greater acculturation to the dominant White culture or reflect his increased awareness of how to deal with life in a discriminatory environment.

Core Principle #2:
Acculturation Is Contextually Based

Monica and Luis interact in multiple contexts, which likely exert different amounts of pressure to acculturate to mainstream and/or their ethnic culture. Monica's family of origin, for example, may encourage her to live according to certain gender expectations (e.g., focus on her role as mother) and to keep cultural traditions alive (e.g., celebrate certain holidays, maintain the Spanish language, continue her Roman Catholic upbringing). The school and work settings, on the other hand, may be conducive to greater acculturation to dominant White culture because they increase her exposure to other perspectives and challenge her to take on different roles. For Luis, the family and work environment may underscore the pressure to provide for his family, thereby maintaining a high level of acculturation to his Mexican culture. At school, Luis may be hearing that learning English and adopting U.S. values are required to succeed in this country, ideas that explicitly encourage acculturation to the dominant White culture.

Core Principle #3: Each Individual Processes Acculturation Issues in Different Ways

Monica and Luis are both of Mexican background, but are clearly experiencing distinctly different acculturation processes. One clear behavioral indicator of this is their varying English-language proficiency, which also reflects the difference in their generational status.

However, it is important to keep in mind that a person's language preference may be influenced by factors beyond generational status, including the sociohistorical context in which he or she was raised and the level of comfort in a particular situation (Arredondo & Perez, 2003).

Given this couple's lack of familiarity with mental health services, one important step in the initial sessions involved providing them with information about the counseling process. These clients challenged efforts to develop a collaborative working relationship with each other and with the counselor. Upon further exploration, Luis revealed his expectation of counseling as a directive process, one that involved meeting with a psychologist for no more than a couple of sessions. On several occasions, both expressed their belief that the counselor was the expert and would provide them with advice on how to solve their problems. As Sue and Sue (2008) have noted, the research literature suggests that certain cultural groups, including Latinos and Asian Americans, tend to have a preference for active and more directive forms of therapy.

At the end of one session, Luis inquired about the counselor's marital status and asked if she had children. These questions posed a dilemma, because saying "no" could have reduced her credibility in their eyes, but refusing to respond could have interfered with developing rapport. Avoiding the question was deemed to be detrimental to the developing relationship, and because the counselor was comfortable sharing such information in this situation, she self-disclosed. They responded favorably, honoring her years of education and training, even if she had no firsthand experience related to their situation.

Certain ground rules had to be established to facilitate communication during counseling sessions. The counselor informed Luis and Monica that she would not be taking sides, but instead would work with them as a couple. Even though the similarities in cultural background between the counselor and Monica were most apparent, some similarities with Luis (e.g., familiarity with his home state in Mexico) were also noted as a way of balancing the dynamics. The counselor also discussed Monica's use of English in session, which seemed to be more strategy than genuine language preference, and requested that she make an effort to speak Spanish so that Luis could understand. They agreed that if Monica felt the need to express herself in English, her comments would be translated for Luis.

Monica and Luis self-terminated after the fourth counseling session. This self-termination may have been due to the discrepancy between their expectations of counseling and the services they were receiving. After all, they had already attended four sessions and the counselor had not yet given them advice about how to solve their problem. It is unknown if they attributed this lack of progress to their particular counselor or to the counseling process in general.

This couple's willingness to seek counseling in the first place could be interpreted as demonstrating a high level of acculturation to the dominant White culture, because traditional Mexican cultural values encourage people to resolve problems within the family instead of seeking professional help. However, because two individuals undergoing independent acculturation processes are involved, it would be unwise to conclude that both are at a high level of acculturation to the dominant White culture. In this case, Monica appeared much more comfortable in therapy and less hesitant when disclosing personal information. Luis, on the other hand, tended to be vague in his responses and appeared surprised with some of the details his wife was sharing. Monica and Luis admitted that, because of the stigma that only "crazy people" seek psychological services, they had not told anyone they were in therapy. Interestingly, researchers have found that men who are experiencing high levels of gender role conflict are less willing to seek counseling, and that this relationship is partly influenced by self-stigma associated with seeking therapy (Pederson & Vogel, 2007).

Core Principle #4: Acculturation Intersects With Racial and Ethnic Identity, as Well as Other Aspects of One's Overall Identity

Monica's assertion that she could earn a larger salary than Luis was a blow to his gender identity, even if it was intended as an expression of her own. Luis's views on gender may have interfered in the development of a therapeutic relationship with the counselor and ultimately contributed to termination. Perhaps Luis could not get past the similarities he noticed between the counselor and his wife and doubted that the counselor could be an objective source of assistance.

Luis had faced many recent life changes (e.g., immersion in a new culture, marriage, fatherhood), but lacked the social support network to help him deal with them. Despite Mexico's geographic proximity, Luis had not seen his family since moving to the United States 4 years earlier and spoke with them over the phone only twice a month. As sole breadwinner with a wife and child, the stakes were too high to risk being unable to re-enter the country if he went to Mexico for a visit. Luis reported being discriminated against on a few occasions (e.g., an employer refused to pay him because he knew undocumented Luis would not seek recourse) and added he was likely unaware of additional experiences because of his limited English comprehension.

Core Principle #5: Acculturation Processes Should Be Understood From a Race-Based Perspective

Monica and Luis lived in a community with a large Latino, particularly Mexican, population during a time of increased anti-immigrant and anti-Latino sentiments. To what extent have they, together or independently, internalized some of these negative attitudes? Their distinct educational levels and immigration statuses likely affect how they are treated in society and experience discrimination/prejudice, as well as how they relate to each other. For instance, society may interpret Luis's current inability to speak English as an indication that he lacks motivation. It is possible that the power dynamics in society are reflected in the relationship, with Monica exerting power over Luis because she has legal residence in the United States, has a higher level of education, and is proficient in English. Also, it would be important to explore if Monica endorses certain stereotypes about Mexican immigrants, perhaps behaviors or attitudes she developed growing up in her immigrant household. Finally, given Luis's experiences of discrimination and difficulty adapting to life in the United States, examining his stereotypes about the dominant White culture might shed additional light on their situation.

THE CASE OF TILA

Tila is a 26-year-old Chinese graduate student who was born in China and moved to the United States 4 years ago to pursue graduate studies in international relations.

She came to counseling through a referral from the Women's Center director, who suspected partner abuse. When asked for her thoughts on how she could benefit from counseling services, Tila stated that it was very difficult to speak openly about her specific reason for seeking help because it brought about "strong and uncomfortable" emotions for her.

Tila spent a great deal of time during the first two sessions alluding to a difficulty in her life that caused her stress and sleep loss. She had shared this difficulty only with two close friends and had not discussed it with her family in China because of concern that it would only cause them excessive worry. The counselor tried to normalize the situation for Tila by disclosing that it may sometimes be difficult for some individuals to discuss issues of a personal nature and, by so doing, can bring about feelings of embarrassment and/or shame. The counselor hypothesized that the use of such normalizing statements would help facilitate a safer environment for her (Sue & Sue, 2008). The client nodded in agreement after the disclosure was made.

Once Tila's concerns were openly discussed, she appeared to become more receptive to talking about her personal matters. She eventually spoke of having marital problems with her White American husband and strongly regretted marrying him. It appeared her husband was experiencing deep-seated psychological issues and had trouble regulating his emotions. It was later learned that he also abused substances, was "controlling" of their relationship, and was physically abusive to her. Tila had been trying to learn about the American legal system and how leaving this marriage may jeopardize her eligibility to continue living in the United States.

Core Principle #1: Acculturation Is Complex and Multidimensional

Although Tila has been successful integrating herself into various aspects of mainstream White American culture (e.g., education, independence, cross-cultural friendships, interracial marriage), she continues adhering to many values of her culture of origin (e.g., refraining from discussing personal matters with others, experiencing shame and embarrassment in having difficulty managing personal problems). As counseling continued,

it appeared that a significant proportion of her concerns involved managing cross-cultural differences.

In addition to her husband's mental health concerns, differences in communication patterns may have contributed to presently irreconcilable difficulties in their marriage. More specifically, it seems that Tila's comparatively indirect, high-context communication style conflicted with her husband's direct, emotionally expressive, low-context manner of communicating. Low-context communication styles typically place high value on verbal expression and meaning exactly what one is saying (Hong & Ham, 2001; Stewart & Bennett, 1991). Low-context communication is often to the point, places responsibility on the speaker to understand what is being said, and may be less dependent on the context in which it occurs. High-context communication, in contrast, may place less emphasis on direct verbal expression, incorporates nonverbal and situation-based factors in creating meaning, and places responsibility on the listener to extrapolate value in what is being communicated. There were also times that Tila felt at risk for physical and/or emotional abuse in her marriage, and any discussion around this topic became highly emotionally charged for her.

Core Principle #2: Acculturation Is Contextually Based

At one point during treatment, Tila began a discussion regarding culture's impact on interpersonal relationships. She did not agree with generalized notions of Asians being perceived as more indirect in communication style than White Americans. Tila described an example of how to respond to a party invitation when one is unable to attend. From her experience, Tila reported that Asians would be more likely to "directly," "honestly," and "politely" tell the person inviting that they are unable to attend the party (characteristics that may be more associated with White cultural values). This is different from what she believed someone Asian might be expected to say (i.e., making a noncommittal statement rather than directly saying "no"; saying "yes" but in actuality not meaning to follow through with it).

However, Tila did feel that Whites are comparatively more emotionally expressive and seem less inhibited in showing others their feelings than Asians. Tila shared that she and her husband differed greatly in this respect, which negatively affected their marriage. She also believed that Whites in general might not be as sensitive to or considerate about how their words or deeds can affect others.

Core Principle #3: Each Individual Processes Acculturation Issues in Different Ways

Even though Tila has been living in the United States for more than 4 years, she continues to hold on to many aspects of her family's cultural values. She is uncomfortable sharing personal issues and expressed concern about how her problems can affect family and friends (e.g., she does not want to become a burden to them). This appears to be reflective of traditional Asian values, where thinking of others before one's own needs tends to be more accepted (Sue & Sue, 2008).

At the same time, however, Tila appears to be comfortable enough pursuing both educational and personal aspirations in a country where she originally knew no one. She reported being particularly curious about learning American culture and how it differs from Chinese culture. She appears to have embraced a seemingly individualistic value orientation and has been thriving in her overall experiences in the United States. Furthermore, her openness to new experiences led to an interracial marriage, although it ultimately did not turn out favorably.

Core Principle #4: Acculturation Intersects With Racial and Ethnic Identity, as Well as Other Aspects of One's Overall Identity

Tila's initial and continued reluctance to open up to the psychologist might be based on intersections between acculturation and other identities. For example, it can be hypothesized that the shame and embarrassment she felt about sharing personal matters was heightened with the realization that she was seeing a psychologist of similar racial background. Conversely, this understanding may have also allowed her to feel safer in counseling.

The psychologist's decision to self-disclose was primarily influenced by his training in culturally sensitive counseling approaches. Furthermore, through his own acculturation process, the counselor adopted alternative values regarding self-disclosure that, when used in

situationally appropriate contexts, could be helpful in facilitating the counseling process with some clients. The depth of self-disclosure primarily involved the counselor's sharing of demographic information (e.g., age, being internationally born, immigrant experience), which was mirrored by the client sharing aspects of herself along the same domains.

Tila shared that all of her previous relationships had been with Chinese men, and that her husband was the first White man with whom she had ever had a romantic relationship. Although Tila initially shared that racial and ethnic differences in relationships did not matter to her, she later recognized that a significant portion of her marital conflicts were associated with these factors. When asked about her thoughts on relationships, Tila spoke about how Chinese girls, particularly those from the big cities (e.g., Beijing), "have it made." She expressed her belief that they would often be taken care of and pampered by their partners. Tila's experience living in those areas of China was also that more women could be found in administrative and/or managerial roles, different from her perception of women's place in American society. Tila may have carried some of these expectations regarding "equality with comfort" in her marriage that were somehow not met. Exploring Tila's perception of women's roles in her country of origin became an important part of treatment, as was discussing racial identity dynamics.

Helms (1990) indicated that the racial identity status of both the client and the counselor can influence the therapeutic relationship and process (e.g., racial identity interaction model). More specifically, the counselor's own racial identity status can facilitate or interfere with the counseling process. If, for instance, the psychologist had been operating from the Conformity status (i.e., unaware of race-based dynamics), he may not have been able to sensitively address Tila's struggle to go against traditional cultural values and share her personal experiences with a stranger. Moreover, if the counselor held unresolved issues regarding racial oppression, he may have been unable to address specific cultural behaviors being expressed by his client and be at risk for making erroneous attributions and stereotyping (e.g., that she was being defensive and/or behaving like a "typical" Asian client). Helms and Cook (1999) note the importance of counselors to not only be aware of specific client dynamics in therapy, but also how one's own biases can leak into the therapeutic process.

Continued counseling with Tila could further address various questions that examine the intersections between acculturation and other variables related to identity. For example, how has living in the United States had an impact on Tila's Chinese ethnic identity and evolving Asian racial identity? What stressors has Tila had to navigate due to being a minority in the United States? How has she approached interracial relationships, and how has this affected her life and sense of self?

Core Principle #5: Acculturation Processes Should Be Understood From a Race-Based Perspective

According to Smedley et al. (1993), students of color often have to negotiate the additional stress of being racial/cultural minorities apart from common stressors typically associated with being college students. Living in relatively diverse communities, such as those found in Hawai'i, does not necessarily protect Tila from having race-based experiences.

In conceptualizing Tila's case further, it may be helpful to continue thinking about different intrapersonal and contextual factors she may be experiencing while living in the United States. For example, Tila's behavioral adjustment to American culture (e.g., language) and norms paint only a limited picture of her experience. It may also be important to explore how Tila's self-understanding as someone not just Chinese, but also Asian, has been affected and shaped by living in a society that historically, and currently, evaluates individuals based on racial group membership. Tila's access to specific resources and interpersonal relationships may be influenced by racial dynamics, so it is also helpful to consider how this contributes to her overall concerns and subsequent psychological adjustment. Finally, race-based stressors may also affect Tila's mental health concerns aside from what has been typically associated with acculturative stress (e.g., Carter, Forsyth, Mazzula, & Williams, 2005; Landrine & Klonoff, 1996).

CONCLUSION

The five principles and the corresponding analyses of three cases highlight the critical importance of

acculturation in cross-cultural counseling. As evidenced in this chapter, acculturation is complex and multifaceted, and it manifests in different ways for each client. There are no fixed rules to follow in accounting for acculturation issues in clients, which is also the case with other important cultural factors in counseling. Nor, for that matter, is there a set of specific interventions that works effectively for all clients. Rather than rigidly adhering to a particular model or set of rules, it is suggested that a flexible set of principles that is subject to modification would be the most useful for counselors. This was our intent in proposing the five principles presented in this chapter. In that spirit, then, the following closing thoughts and recommendations are presented as a guide for psychologists to use in dealing more effectively with acculturation issues as they continue their respective paths of providing culturally competent services.

Traditional counseling theories and training models do not comprehensively take into consideration macro-level/ systemic factors that can contribute significantly to clients' presenting concerns (e.g., Sue & Sue, 2008). In order to assist clients more effectively in dealing with acculturation issues, counselors must account for such factors. Consider, for example, clients who tend to keep negative emotions inside. Although understanding that this behavior may serve clients in not offending others, "preserving face," and/or maintaining harmonious relationships, the counselor may also try to assist clients in expanding their repertoire of behaviors, such as being more expressive in certain contexts, to help them navigate the different value systems/environments existing in U.S. society (e.g., Hong & Ham, 2001). Thus, a culturally competent practitioner should acknowledge the role that systemic, contextual factors play in contributing to these individuals' presenting concerns and life situations.

Moreover, these larger systemic forces, including racism, discrimination, political climate, time period, and geographic location, all impinge upon the individual in unique and complex ways (e.g., Sue & Sue, 2008). For instance, specific geographical location (e.g., West Coast vs. East Coast vs. Southwest vs. Pacific Islands) seems to directly affect the ways in which these multiple cultural and environmental variables intersect and affect clients. When addressing acculturation, then, such nuances should always be a part of the counselor's ongoing evaluation and treatment of clients.

As demonstrated in this chapter, counselors should continually evaluate the effects of both macro- and micro-level factors on the acculturation process. Counselors cannot escape from the responsibility of accounting for these systemic factors in consistent ways when working with clients of color. It may also be the counselor's responsibility to be proactive and serve as an advocate for his or her clients (Atkinson, Thompson, & Grant, 1993), as well as assist in some aspects of their acculturation process. It is suggested that mental health professionals

- provide psychoeducational opportunities for both clients and counselors on the multidimensional aspects of acculturation. Counselors who are familiar with acculturation literature (see Rivera, Chapter 28) will be better equipped to explain this important concept in ways that are meaningful to clients.
- facilitate understanding during counseling practice that being different from White mainstream culture does not equate to being deficient. Discussing the existence of multiple realities and promoting self-awareness could be helpful in achieving this task (Arredondo et al., 1996).
- increase awareness that there are often factors in clients' environments (e.g., racial discrimination) that contribute to intrapersonal difficulties (Carter, 2007).
- offer learning experiences (e.g., workshops, presentations) to help participants better understand and work with the various ways individuals interact and communicate with others (and how their own actions affect others). Experiential training modules/activities such as Robert Carter's (2003) racial cultural lab could facilitate this process.
- educate people on the different ways that individuals may experience and handle emotions, as well as their subsequent behavioral expressions.

Incidentally, such psychoeducational interventions focusing on communication skills can occur on an institutional, as well as interpersonal, level in everyday interactions. Such proactive interventions can help individuals develop better awareness of and sensitivity to working with those who experience and express themselves differently from the "normative standards" of White American culture. However, because people

are prone to lapse into stereotyping and overgeneralizing, it is imperative that counselors engage in an ongoing process of evaluating such pitfalls for themselves. Indeed, even with greater awareness of the different communication styles of racial/cultural individuals, there is still the issue of not falling into the trap of using a "cookbook approach" (e.g., stereotyping clients) in counseling.

Acculturation is only one of many variables with which people of color have to contend in the daily struggle to live. By examining acculturation issues in isolation, counselors ignore an incredible matrix of intersecting factors and run the danger of decontexualizing and dehumanizing clients. What is often overlooked in the counseling literature and training is the importance of being open and humble to the incredible cultural richness that each client brings to counseling. That is, counselors should appreciate the complexity, multidimensionality, and dynamic nature of the human condition in its appropriate cultural framework and treat every person uniquely with this perspective in mind. Otherwise, counselors may be setting themselves (as well as the client) up for the perpetuation of stereotyping and prejudicial thinking, which can totally discount the experiences of the human being sitting in the room with them.

Finally, it is critical for mental health professionals to continually self-reflect and be aware of how their personal values, assumptions, and biases can have an impact on the therapeutic process. Such self-appraisal should also include the counselor's own acculturation process and how it may potentially affect clients. Only in being mindful of all these factors can counselors be true facilitators of change and healing.

ACKNOWLEDGMENTS

The first author would like to thank members of his cross-cultural research lab who assisted in the initial stages of preparing this chapter (e.g., collecting articles, preparing summaries of studies)—Michelle Flores, Andrea Salazar, Shannen Vong, and Gloria Wong. In addition, the first author would like to extend his appreciation to his coauthors—both were mentored by him as undergraduates and master's-level graduate students. To complete this project with them as recently graduated professional psychologists has been truly a rewarding and fulfilling experience that cannot be adequately captured in words. The proverbial circle is now complete.

REFERENCES

Abe-Kim, J., Okazaki, S., & Goto, S. G. (2001). Unidimensional versus multidimensional approaches to the asssessment of acculturation for Asian American populations. *Cultural Diversity and Ethnic Minority Psychology, 7*(3), 232–246.

Arredondo, P., & Perez, P. (2003). Counseling paradigms and Latina/o Americans: Contemporary considerations. In F. D. Harper & J. McFadden (Eds.), *Culture and counseling: New approaches* (pp. 115–132). Boston: Allyn & Bacon.

Arredondo, P., Toporek, R., Brown, S. P., Jones, J., Locke, D. C., Sanchez, J., & Stadler, H. (1996). Operationalization of the multicultural counseling competencies. *Journal of Multicultural Counseling and Development, 24,* 42–78.

Atkinson, D. R., Thompson, C. E., & Grant, S. (1993). A three-dimensional model for counseling racial/ethnic minority clients. *Counseling Psychologist, 21,* 257–277.

Carter, R. T. (2003). Becoming racially and culturally competent: The racial-cultural laboratory. *Journal of Multicultural Counseling and Development, 31,* 20–30.

Carter, R. T. (Ed.). (2005a). *Handbook of racial-cultural psychology and counseling: Training and practice* (Vol. 2). Hoboken, NJ: Wiley.

Carter, R. T., Forsyth, J. M., Mazzula, S. L., & Williams, B. (2005b). Racial discrimination and race-based traumatic stress: An exploratory investigation. In R. T. Carter (Ed.), *Handbook of racial-cultural psychology and counseling: Theory and research* (Vol. 2, pp. 447-476). Hoboken, NJ: Wiley.

Carter, R. T. (2005c). Uprooting inequity and disparities in counseling and psychology: An introduction. In R. T. Carter (Ed.), *Handbook of racial-cultural psychology and counseling: Theory and research* (Vol. 1, pp. xv–xxviii). Hoboken, NJ: Wiley.

Carter, R. T. (2007). Racism and psychological and emotional injury: Recognizing and assessing race-based traumatic stress. *Counseling Psychologist, 35,* 13–105.

Chin, J. L., Liem, J. H., Ham, M. A. D. C., & Hong, G. K. (1993). *Transference and empathy in Asian American psychotherapy: Cultural values and treatment needs.* Westport, CT: Praeger.

Helms, J. E. (1990). *Black and White racial identity: Theory, research, and practice.* Westport, CT: Praeger.

Helms, J. E. (1995). An update of Helms's White and People of Color racial identity models. In J. G. Ponterotto, J. M. Casas, L. A. Suzuki, & C. M. Alexander (Eds.), *Handbook of multicultural counseling* (pp. 181–198). Thousand Oaks, CA: Sage.

Helms, J. E., & Cook, D. A. (1999). *Using race and culture in counseling and psychotherapy: Theory and process.* Boston: Allyn & Bacon.

Helms, J. E., & Talleyrand, R. M. (1997). Race is not ethnicity. *American Psychologist, 52,* 1246–1247.

Hong, G. K., & Ham, M. K. (2001). *Psychotherapy and counseling with Asian American clients: A practical guide.* Thousand Oaks, CA: Sage.

Kim, B. S. K. (2006). Acculturation and enculturation. In F. T. Leong, A. G. Inman, A. Ebreo, L. H. Yang, L. M. Kinoshita, & M. Fu (Eds.), *Handbook of Asian American psychology* (2nd ed., pp. 141–158). Thousand Oaks, CA: Sage.

Kim, B. S. K., & Abreu, J. M. (2001). Acculturation measurement: Theory, current instruments, and future directions. In J. G. Ponterotto, J. M. Casas, L. A. Suzuki, & C. M. Alexander (Eds.), *Handbook of multicultural counseling* (2nd ed., pp. 394–424). Thousand Oaks, CA: Sage.

Kim, B., & Omizo, M. (2006). Behavioral acculturation and enculturation and psychological functioning among Asian American college students. *Cultural Diversity and Ethnic Minority Psychology, 12,* 245–258.

Kohatsu, E. L. (2005). Acculturation: Current and future directions. In R. T. Carter (Ed.), *Handbook of racial-cultural psychology and counseling* (pp. 207–231). Hoboken, NJ: Wiley.

Landrine, H., & Klonoff, E. A. (1996). The schedule of racist events: A measure of racial discrimination and a study of its negative physical and mental health consequences. *Journal of Black Psychology, 22,* 144–168.

Leong, F. T. L., & Lee, S. (2006). A cultural accommodation model for cross-cultural psychotherapy: Illustrated with the case of Asian Americans. *Psychotherapy: Theory, Research, Practice, Training, 43,* 410–423.

Matsudaira, T. (2006). Measures of psychological acculturation: A review. *Transcultural Psychiatry, 43,* 462–487.

Pederson, E. L., & Vogel, D. L. (2007). Male gender role conflict and willingness to seek counseling: Testing a mediation model on college-aged men. *Journal of Counseling Psychology, 54,* 373–384.

Rogler, L. H., Cortes, D. E., & Malgady, R. G. (1991). Acculturation and mental health status among Hispanics. *American Psychologist, 46,* 585–597.

Roysircar-Sodowsky, G., & Maestas, M. V. (2000). Acculturation, ethnic identity, and acculturative stress:

Evidence and measurement. In R. H. Dana (Ed.), *Handbook of cross-cultural and multicultural personality assessment* (pp. 131–171). Mahwah, NJ: Lawrence Erlbaum.

Santiago-Rivera, A. L., Arredondo, P., & Gallardo-Cooper, M. (2002). *Counseling Latinos and* la familia: *A practical guide*. Thousand Oaks, CA: Sage.

Sasao, T., & Sue, S. (1993). Toward a culturally anchored ecological framework of research in ethnic-cultural communities [Special issue: Culturally anchored methodology]. *American Journal of Community Psychology, 21,* 705–728.

Smedley, B. D., Myers, H. F., & Harrell, S. P. (1993). Minority-status stresses and the college adjustment of ethnic minority freshmen. *Journal of Higher Education, 64,* 434–452.

Stewart, E. C., & Bennett, M. J. (1991). *American cultural patterns: A cross-cultural perspective* (Rev. ed.). Yarmouth, ME: Intercultural Press.

Sue, D. W., & Sue, D. (2008). *Counseling the culturally diverse: Theory and practice* (5th ed.). New York: Wiley.

Zane, N., & Mak, W. (2003). Major approaches to the measurement of acculturation among ethnic minority populations: A content analysis and alternate empirical strategy. In K. Chun, P. Balls Organista, & G. Marin (Eds.), *Acculturation: Advances in theory, measurement, and applied research* (pp. 39–60). Washington, DC: American Psychological Association.

PART VI

Multicultural Counseling Research

Part VI of the *Handbook* consists of six chapters devoted specifically to conducting multicultural counseling research—a "how-to" of sorts. Chapter 30, written by *Handbook* co-editor Joseph G. Ponterotto, answers the questions: What is it like to be engaged in multicultural research? What are the intrinsic rewards and challenges of a research program in this topical area? Summarizing archival qualitative data on 36 career-long multicultural researchers, Dr. Ponterotto presents a comprehensive snapshot of what it is like to focus one's career on multicultural counseling research.

Quantitative research has long served as a foundation for advancing the knowledge base of multicultural counseling, and in Chapter 31, Germine H. Awad and Kevin O. Cokley provide a concise and accessible guide to conducting quantitative multicultural research. The authors carefully guide the reader through the process of formulating relevant research questions, selecting relevant variables and measures, designing the actual study, interpreting the results accurately, and assessing the validity of the findings.

Extending the quantitative focus in Chapter 31, Kwong-Liem Karl Kwan, Younnjung Gong, and Michael Maestas provide in-depth coverage of issues related to using, adapting, and translating psychological measures and instruments for cross-cultural research and practice. The authors review critical and foundational issues for cross-cultural test usage such as construct equivalence, cultural validity, item desirability, test familiarity, and the impact of testee acculturation

on the testing process. Highlighting the critical constructs addressed in this chapter, the authors report on an original study on the MMPI-2 with a sample of Korean international students. Finally, the authors incorporate an interesting case study to both highlight various testing issues addressed and stimulate further discussion on the topic.

Chapter 33, co-authored by Heather Z. Lyons and Denise H. Bike, guides the reader in understanding, applying, and interpreting qualitative research in multicultural counseling. The authors highlight the particular resonance of qualitative research for multicultural populations who have historically been marginalized, minimized, and silenced. The chapter includes a concise discussion of various research paradigms that are often used to anchor and guide qualitative research. Furthermore, the authors guide readers in the selection of study topics, participants, and research sites; they also review the value and process of gathering a culturally diverse research team, developing the critical research protocol, and carrying out the study. This chapter serves as an exemplar guide to the conduct of culturally competent, ethically vigilant qualitative research.

Clearly, any single paradigm for research is limited. What happens when a researcher joins paradigms in a research study or program of research? In Chapter 34, Vicki L. Plano Clark and Sherry C. Wang effectively guide the reader in applying mixed methods research to multicultural counseling. Mixed methods approaches to counseling research are relatively recent to the counseling literature, and conducting this form of research requires competence in philosophy of science, research paradigms, and specific inquiry approaches and design methods. The authors of this chapter carefully define mixed methods research, outline the variety of mixed methods approaches, review model mixed methods multicultural studies, and guide the reader on the procedures for designing and conducting such studies.

The final chapter in this section (Chapter 35) is written by Timothy B. Smith and addresses a critical question: Is multicultural counseling more effective than regular counseling? That is, are counseling interventions that are culturally contextualized (incorporate culture-specific components) more effective than traditional or general counseling? Dr. Smith reviews the context for this debate and summarizes the results of a groundbreaking meta-analytic study that answers the questions posed above. After reviewing and summarizing the research, the author guides the reader in the implementation of culturally congruent practices supported by the empirical research. Dr. Smith's work over the past decade on evaluating the efficacy of culturally targeted counseling interventions has shed a bright light on the field and has documented the empirical legitimacy of certain culture-specific interventions.

All in all, this section of the *Handbook* provides a comprehensive overview and "how-to" with regard to designing, conducting, and interpreting multicultural research, broadly defined. Collectively, the chapters provide a mini-course on culturally competent and ethically sensitive research in diverse communities.

30

Challenges and Rewards in Conducting Multicultural Counseling Research

A Heuristic, Archival, Phenomenological Study

JOSEPH G. PONTEROTTO

P art VI of this *Handbook* is devoted to research in multicultural counseling. Readers will learn how to critique and conduct quantitative, qualitative, and mixed methods research. They will also read integrative reviews of the multicultural counseling research. However, before getting specifically to the "nuts and bolts" of conducting multicultural counseling research, the *Handbook* editors thought it a good idea to review some of the challenges and rewards of a career in multicultural research. To that end, this chapter presents an archival, heuristic, phenomenological study that summarizes the experiences of 36 established multicultural counseling scholars.

HISTORICAL CONTEXT OF THE STUDY

Recently, Ponterotto (2008) presented a brief review of historical developments in the multicultural counseling field. Borrowing the construct of "moments" (historical periods) from the noted sociologists Denzin and Lincoln (2005), Ponterotto identified five moments in the evolution of the multicultural counseling field. The first moment, "Benign Neglect" (pre-1960s), was characterized by a noticeable absence of multicultural-focused research in counseling journals. Most of the research samples were European Americans, and there appeared to be an underlying assumption that

---

(This chapter is dedicated to the 36 nationally renowned multicultural scholars who, despite their hectic and overextended work schedules, participated in this study. Thank you!)

psychological phenomena were etic (culturally transcendent) in nature. The second moment, "Birth of a Movement" (1960s and 1970s), was facilitated by the civil rights movements of the period and stimulated research into culturally diverse communities, particularly African American communities. An emphasis during this second historical moment was more emic, studying psychological phenomena as they apply to distinct cultural groups. A majority of research designs during this period were between-group designs where select minority groups (particularly African Americans) were compared to White groups; the latter served as the de facto control group, or the group to be emulated.

During the 1980s, a third moment was spawned, "Gaining Momentum and Establishing a Specialty." During this time, exponential growth of empirical research occurred across many diverse racial/ethnic and other minority groups. Also, there was a paradigm shift from the between-cultures focus of the second moment to a focus on within-culture differences. Within-group variables such as racial identity status, level of acculturation, and worldview came into prominence as independent variables in group designs (analyses of variance, multivariate analyses of variance) and as predictor variables in correlational designs (regression, path analysis).

The fourth historical moment was "Maturation and Expansion of a Specialty" (1990s), characterized by a continuing focus on within-group psychological variables and an added focus on evidence-based multicultural practice and counselor competence assessment and accountability. This moment was also characterized by an expanded focus on diverse minority groups, such as biracial and multiracial persons; gay, lesbian, and bisexual groups; the elderly; and so forth. Our current moment is the fifth moment, "Beyond Borders and Disciplines" (2000–present), where there is growing interest in bridging multicultural and international counseling (see Ægisdóttir & Gerstein, this volume, Chapter 17; Casas, Park, & Choe, this volume, Chapter 18), on the intersection of multicultural counseling with other disciplines in psychology such as positive psychology (Pedrotti & Edwards, this volume, Chapter 16), and personnel and personality psychology (Van der Zee & Van Oudenhoven, 2000). There is also a renewed focus on etic psychological constructs that apply across cultural groups, such as the recent work on the multicultural personality (Ponterotto, Utsey, & Pedersen, 2006; Van der

Zee, Zaal, & Piekstra, 2003), and the universal-diverse orientation (Miville et al., 1999).

With a sense of multicultural counseling history in place, let us now locate the context for the study herein described. The sample in the present archival study was primarily engaged in research during the third and fourth moments in the history of multicultural counseling research (1980s and 1990s). Therefore, this study represents a snapshot of the research experiences of a highly select group of scholars during the time when the field of multicultural counseling came into its own as an established specialty within the counseling profession.

Study Rationale

In part, the impetus for this descriptive study stems from my own experiences in multicultural research during the third and fourth historical moments of our field. I had long believed that both the rewards and the challenges in conducting multicultural-focused research were quite unique. And in discussions with colleagues of my generation (those receiving doctoral degrees in the mid-1980s), I began to sense that my experiences were not isolated. A second impetus for this study emanated from the professional literature, particularly that appearing in *The Counseling Psychologist* that focused on the challenges of White and minority scholars in the field (e.g., Fouad & Carter, 1992; Kiselica, 1998; Mio & Iwamasa, 1993). Collectively, these articles support the view that although multicultural counselors and researchers share common struggles and rewards in their work, there are also unique challenges and rewards specific to racial/ethnic minority and majority group (White) scholars and trainees.

The goal of this study was to uncover the particular challenges and rewards of research work in multicultural counseling as perceived by long-standing research experts who have devoted their careers to work in the area. A secondary goal was to examine the stated challenges and rewards across racial/ethnic minority-majority status and gender.

METHOD

Archival Context of Study and Sample

I collected these data throughout 1997, during the latter part of what I labeled the fourth historical moment in the multicultural counseling field (Ponterotto, 2008). The sample consisted of 36 doctoral-level scholars whose research specialty fell in the area of multicultural counseling. Each sample participant was very well published in the area of multicultural counseling, and the majority was affiliated with academic research departments in universities. These researchers came into national prominence particularly during the third and fourth historical moments (1980s and 1990s). The sample was diverse in terms of age, race/ethnicity, gender, and geographic locale. There were 13 females and 23 males in the sample. At the time of the study, 10 participants fell in the 31–40 age range, 15 in the 41–50 age range, 8 in the 51–60 age range, and 3 in the 61–70 age range. Presently, these scholars are in the following age cohorts: Ten participants now fall in the 43–52 age range, 15 in the 53–62 age range, 8 in the 63–72 age range, and 3 in the 73–82 age range. Twelve participants were White (European) Americans (7 males and 5 females), and 24 participants represented racial/ethnic minority groups (8 females and 16 males). More specifically, among the minority females, 2 were Mexican American, 3 were African American, 2 were Asian American, and 1 was biracial. Among the minority males, 4 were Mexican American, 8 were African American, 2 were Asian Indian, 1 was Native American, and 1 was biracial.

PROCEDURE

A target list of multicultural counseling research scholars was developed through a variety of means. Reviews of the literature in counseling over the 1980s and 1990s revealed a number of scholars who were frequent contributors to the multicultural literature. My own networking on multicultural-focused national committees for both the American Psychological Association (Division 17, Counseling Psychology) and the American Counseling Association (particularly the Association for Multicultural Counseling and Development) also yielded names of respected and nationally visible researchers. My goal was to develop a list of 40–50 scholars in the hope that at least 50% would respond to the mail survey. I was careful to include both men and women and scholars representative of diverse racial/ethnic groups and age cohorts.

My final target list consisted of 46 scholars. In mid-October 1997, each scholar was mailed a packet that included the open-ended survey with a self-addressed, pre-stamped return envelope; an invitation cover letter; and a self-addressed, pre-stamped postcard to acknowledge survey completion. Participants who completed the survey and returned the postcard were also entered into a lottery to win a $100 cash prize. The winner of the lottery was a male professor from the southeastern part of the United States. The surveys were to be completed anonymously. After 6 weeks, 30 of 46 participants returned completed surveys for a response rate of 65%. In December 1997, a second mailing was sent to all respondents who had not returned the postcard; an additional six surveys were subsequently received. Therefore, the final sample included 36 of 46 targeted respondents for a response rate of 78%.

SURVEY

The survey consisted of three pages. The first page explained the purpose of the survey and requested basic demographic information: gender, age cohort, and self-defined race and ethnicity. The second and third pages, which were counterbalanced, contained the following two statements: "Challenges I have faced in my multicultural counseling research career include," and "Rewarding aspects of my career in multicultural counseling research have been." Respondents were asked to respond in pen (or typed if preferred) to the statements. A full blank page was included with each statement.

RESEARCH ORIENTATION AND DATA ANALYSIS

My orientation to this archival study was both phenomenological and heuristic in nature. Phenomenology refers to "the study of how people describe things and experience them through their senses" (Patton, 1990, p. 69). The roots of phenomenology as a philosophical tradition in the development of science are often traced back to the German philosopher Edmund H. Husserl (1859–1938) (Moustakas, 1994). According to Patton (1990, p. 69), the guiding phenomenological research query is as follows: "What is the structure and essence of experience of this phenomena [*sic*] for these people?" The goal of the researcher is to capture and describe the basic characteristic or core meaning of this essence.

Heuristics is a form of phenomenology that incorporates the personal experience of the researcher as central to the research process (Moustakas, 1990). Two important points that distinguish heuristic inquiry from the broader phenomenological inquiry are that (a) the researcher has intense interest in and experience with the phenomenon, and (b) the other participants in the study share a similar intensity of experience with the phenomenon. The guiding heuristic probe is "What is my experience of this phenomena [*sic*] and the essential experiences of others who also experience this phenomena [*sic*] intensely?" (Patton, 1990, p. 71).

The phenomenon under consideration in the present study is the experience of being a multicultural counseling researcher as manifested through perceptions of the challenges and rewards of working in the topical area. Given that I have interest in and experience with the phenomenon and was a participant in the study, this phenomenological investigation could be said to include a heuristic component.

Although different phenomenological researchers employ different specific steps to organizing and analyzing their data, some commonality of procedure does exist. Creswell (2007) identified the following steps as common to all psychological phenomenologists: horizonalization, cluster of meanings, textural description, and structural description. *Horizonalization* includes examining research protocols and dividing the essential content into comprehensible statements. For our purposes, we have named these statements "meaning units." These meaning units are then grouped into *clusters of meanings* or major discernible themes. The themes are then tied together to present a general description of the experience. The *textural description* focuses on what was experienced, and the *structural description* focuses on how it was experienced.

These common steps of phenomenological inquiry summarized by Creswell (2007) were used in the present study. More specifically, individual specifications of challenges and rewards were identified and isolated. Each interpretable mention of a reward and challenge was extracted from the data set and classified as a distinct meaning unit. In total, 184 Reward meaning units and 156 Challenge meaning units were specified. Each meaning unit was coded to reflect the gender, race/ethnicity, and age group of the

respondent. Subsequently, each meaning unit was cut out of the survey with a scissor. Initially, meaning units were examined separately for White males, White females, minority males, and minority females. Subsequently, the meaning units were combined across sample cohort groups to identify transcendent challenges and rewards.

To arrive at clusters of meaning or major themes reflected in the meaning units, the cut-out slips of paper were read, re-read, and sorted into common groupings that reflected emergent themes. Tables 30.1 through 30.4 present the major themes and clusters extracted for Challenges and Rewards for the collective sample and for racial/ethnic-specific cohorts.

Consistent with the phenomenological approach that focuses on what people experience and how they interpret their experience, the results that follow rely heavily on direct quotes from the participants. Shorter quotes are worked directly into paragraph text, whereas longer quotes are blocked off for easier reading and comprehension. Following the presentation of results, the discussion section of this chapter attempts to tie the clusters of meaning (themes) together to present a textural and structural description of the phenomenon: challenging and rewarding aspects of a career in multicultural counseling research.

RESULTS

A major goal of this study was to identify professional and/or personal challenges and rewards of a career in multicultural counseling research. A secondary goal, acknowledging a growing body of literature (e.g., Fouad & Carter, 1992; Kiselica, 1998), was to identify challenges and rewards particular to gender and racial/ethnic cohorts. Thus, this results section is organized into sections that reflect both challenges and rewards common to the whole sample, as well as particular challenges and rewards of minority group scholars versus majority group scholars and women versus men.

Challenges

The participants expressed a number of common challenges in pursuing a career in multicultural research. These specific challenges transcended the four within-sample cohorts (minority females, minority males, White females, White males) and fell into four broad categories. The first category focused on attitudes and perceptions of colleagues regarding multicultural scholarship. The second category covered specific challenges in conducting research on the topic of multicultural counseling. The third category addressed personal challenges that the scholars faced in their pursuit of a multicultural research career. Finally, the fourth category focused on challenges in teaching and working with students in multicultural training. In addition to the major categories, clusters (or subcategories) subsumed under the larger categories were identified. Below, I present the major categories and specific clusters along with quotes representative of each cluster. In all cases, the quotes are exact save for some minor editing (spelling, sentence structure, etc.), and the gender and racial/ethnic status of the respondent is specified (see Table 30.1).

Table 30.1   Challenges Faced in a Multicultural Counseling Research Career

Perceptions and Attitudes of Colleagues
Delegitimization of Multicultural Counseling
General Apathy of Majority Culture and Academic Institutions
Colleagues' Inattention or Resistance
Research Challenges
Research Constructs, Design, and Sampling
Journal Editors and Reviewers
Focus and Direction of the Field
Personal Challenges
Staying Abreast of the Field
Self-Doubt and Vulnerability
Unrealistic Expectations
Working With Students and Teaching

Perceptions and Attitudes of Colleagues

By far, the largest grouping of challenges focused on the attitudes and opinions of colleagues regarding multicultural issues generally and the rigor of multicultural research specifically. This category of challenges can be broken down into three related clusters. The first

focused on perceptions of colleagues regarding the legitimacy of multicultural counseling as a distinct topical area along with insulting attitudes regarding the status of research in the field. The second cluster included challenges that deal with the general apathy of the profession regarding multicultural counseling. The final cluster focused on lack of cultural sensitivity in colleagues. We begin with representative quotes from the first cluster.

Delegitimization of Multicultural Counseling. A Mexican American female scholar noted the challenge in "being questioned about the importance, validity, and reason for my research agenda. That is, my research agenda being viewed as a personal and political agenda rather than a research agenda." A White male noted that "one major challenge doing this work at that time [referring to earlier in his career] was with the majority of my colleagues, the counseling and psychology professionals, who did not consider this avenue of work important nor mainstream." A White female noted, "There is some remaining bias of peers that studies on gender or cross-cultural concerns are not very rigorous." A Mexican American male scholar stated, "My colleagues not appreciating the *authenticity* of such research—with this ultimately having an *impact* on my academic career."

The three longer quotes below capture in more detail these related challenges faced by participant scholars. An African American male stated,

> Most of us in the field, I believe, have faced the challenge of academic legitimacy of our work—in one way or another. In the early stages of my work, I had difficulty getting support. Closely related is the fact that I often felt like a Lone Ranger. Nobody in my institutions showed an interest in collaboration. This is an especially difficult challenge for junior faculty attempting to succeed in major research institutions.

An Asian American female presented the following:

> I have had close colleagues indicate to me that multicultural research is a "hot" topic and that anything with this in the title would be published. The subtle message I got was that the research I did was not as scholarly or as rigorous as others. Comments like

this were also made in reference to multicultural presentations at national conferences. I have also heard disparaging remarks made about other, more senior multicultural researchers, which also impacts my feelings of self-efficacy as a multicultural researcher.

Finally, a White male noted,

Though multicultural issues were being embraced by the profession generally at the time I was evolving as an academic, I felt and still feel that there are a couple of unit faculty who do not deem the specialty as rigorous or sophisticated as other subfields in counseling. They do not see multicultural researchers, generally, as strong as they see themselves. They think we are more "political" and "rhetoric oriented." For example, in our students' dissertation proposals, they always want us to link the topic to some other subfield in psychology (e.g., social or cognitive psychology); they do not think the subfield or specialty is really legitimate, that it can stand alone. That is always frustrating to me.

General Apathy of Majority Culture and Academic Institutions. This cluster of noted challenges focused on the perceptions of multicultural scholars that society in general, and academic institutions in particular, are simply disinterested in multicultural issues. A Native American male scholar noted that "the perpetuation of 'lip service' continues to be too common." An Asian Indian male noted that

the major challenges I have faced in multicultural counseling research stem from the personal and professional attitudes of the majority culture. It is quite obvious to me that multiculturalism is downplayed and not sincerely valued by the majority culture. I have witnessed and experienced several situations that support my assertion in many explicit and implicit ways.

Other comments in this cluster focused more directly on institutional apathy. One White male scholar just stated "institutional racism—a hard concept to sell. People just do not get it." A Native American male stated that "the most perplexing challenge continues to be individuals/institutions who are apathetic or uncaring towards dissimilar individuals." Finally, a biracial male scholar noted his experience with

overall discouragement regarding academia's lousy attitude toward multicultural research, issues of diverse curriculum, etc. I never thought it would be this bad when I was a graduate student considering an academic career! It seemed so open and "liberal," and now the "liberals" are some of the worst!

Colleagues' Inattention or Resistance. In this final cluster of this major category, respondents discussed challenges specific to their colleagues and departments. An African American male noted the challenge inherent in "getting colleagues to take seriously the importance of multicultural counseling in the training of students." Another African American male scholar noted "getting senior colleagues with a 'limited' worldview to see the value in or validity of multicultural counseling research." A Mexican American male stated the challenge in "having to continuously educate my colleagues regarding the need to understand and in turn make use of important psycho-social variables that are too frequently ignored (e.g., acculturation, ethnic identity development, etc.)."

A biracial male scholar noted the "lack of acceptance and/or active resistance to multicultural research by other faculty/administrators." Put in a different light, a White female noted "working to avoid defensiveness and adversarial relationships with colleagues and supervisors who do not value diversity." With regard to the multicultural attitudes of colleagues, a few respondents wrote in more detail; two of these longer quotes are presented below. An Asian American female researcher wrote,

I recall going to a social function with 3 White professors. During our dinner conversation, one of them turned to me and asked, "Explain to me this multicultural thing. Tell me what the category 'white' means. I am Italian; this guy's Irish, and she's Jewish. We are not the same so how come we always get lumped together?" I remember this comment so vividly since it was my first year at that institution. I attempted to explain that this was an issue faced by all groups, which they did not seem to understand. There are, I explained, more than 19 different Asian groups, to which they responded with shock. There are also numerous American Indian tribal groups with different languages and histories in the U.S. The same could be said for the Hispanic and African

American groups as well. I do not think that my colleagues got my point (though I felt I was pretty clear). I got so uncomfortable that I ended up changing the subject and then kicking myself because I had not changed their convictions.

An African American female scholar summed up some of her challenges as a more junior professor. She states,

There continues to remain a large number of colleagues claiming that multicultural competency is not important in the context of teaching, research, clinical work, etc. Hence, as an untenured assistant professor in a doctoral program, one of my biggest challenges in my multicultural counseling research career has been to find ways to increase senior faculty members' awareness of the importance of multicultural issues. In particular, because many faculty members in my program do not integrate multicultural issues into their courses or research, some students who enroll in my courses or who conduct research with me are surprised to hear multicultural issues being attended to. Of course, many students express pleasure and relief about my attention to these issues, but other students actively resist this information because they are feeling guilt, fear, discomfort, etc. I believe that if other faculty members in my program actively and consistently attended to multicultural issues in their courses or research, some students would be less resistant to these issues by the time most of them were exposed to me (i.e., their second year of the program). Consequently, I perceive a lack of support regarding my efforts in this area because the faculty and I are "not on the same page" with regard to the importance of these issues.

Research Challenges

Many of the respondents in this study noted challenges in designing and conducting multicultural research. Three related clusters of challenges emerged in this second major category. The first cluster dealt with issues of construct definition, sample access, and instrumentation. The second cluster focused on the challenge of working with journal editors. Finally, the third cluster was more philosophical in nature and addressed challenges in setting a focus or direction for research in the field.

Research Constructs, Design, and Sampling. An African American male noted the challenge in "finding comparable terms for constructs when conducting multicultural counseling research across geopolitical borders." This same scholar talked about the challenge in "defining constructs in multicultural counseling research, for example, racial identity development, African consciousness, and ethnicity/culture/race." In terms of design, a White male scholar noted the need for "challenging mainstream empirical methodologies that insist on the inclusion of control groups as a criterion for viable research."

The difficulty in finding adequate subject pools was also expressed by a number of researchers. An African American male scholar noted the challenge in "getting access to enough Black folks to do my work." An African American female researcher stated, "It is difficult to find enough Visible Racial Ethnic Minority Group members in any single category to satisfy research requirements." A White male researcher was more specific when he noted,

Naturally, I have to work harder to gather quantitative research samples. In my day-to-day work I come more often in contact with Whites than with racial/ethnic minorities. To collect a sample of 300 White university students is rather easy; to collect the same sample size of minority students on many campuses can take five times as long.

Continuing with the challenges of sampling, a White male scholar noted that "conducting research with marginalized populations presents challenges in recruitment of participants, especially in longitudinal or multiple testing methodologies." An African American male noted that

much research in multicultural counseling has been archival or on college populations. It is very difficult to gain access to ethnic minority populations that include children or adults; particularly if you are interested in class-related issues. There is a need for greater collaboration between those who have access and those who have the time to ask questions.

A number of scholars also talked about the challenges in finding adequate psychometric measures for their quantitative-based research. A White female noted "limitations of existing multicultural measures in terms of truly capturing the concepts studied." An African American male researcher noted the challenge in "working to create state-of-the-art psychometric measures that do justice to our theory making."

Journal Editors and Reviewers. There was a clear frustration among the sample in their experiences with journal editors and reviewers. Some representative quotes in this cluster follow. An African American male noted "journal editors who want work that looks like it comes from a well-developed field and do not value the exploratory work that needs to be done." A Mexican American male noted "having journal editors/ reviewers question why I did not use White comparison or control groups in my research." This same scholar noted "having journal reviewers question the validity of such terms as Mexican American and instead insisting on the use of Hispanic."

A White female scholar noted "feeling pressured to describe my qualitative research with a 'quantitative' flavor to satisfy journal editors/reviewers." This same scholar also noted "anxiety related to lack of awareness/ understanding on the part of journal editors and reviewers." Finally, a biracial male scholar noted "submitting articles to mainstream counseling journals which were rejected. Yet it was apparent that the reviewers had no knowledge of multicultural/diversity issues. 'Multicultural' journals then published these articles with no problems."

Focus and Direction of Field. This last cluster under the Research Challenges category focused on general comments on the status of research on the field, and the challenges of focus and direction currently faced by researchers. A Mexican American male noted "dealing with the stereotypes that had basis in previous, poorly developed research on multicultural issues and groups." An Asian American female stated that "multicultural issues are complex, so developing workable approaches to research are challenging." A White male stated that "some variables need to be studied at a very simple level before we can proceed to higher-order inductive concepts (operational definition of racism)." A White female noted the following:

It is extremely difficult to generalize regarding specific ethnic/cultural groups. However, patterns/trends/

tendencies are evident when comparing selected variables between and among various cultural groups. When these patterns are reported, there is always the danger that the researcher will be misunderstood or misquoted.

Regarding the challenges of focus in the field, a Native American male scholar expressed that "too much emphasis remains on putting everything in White/ Black dichotomies. Other minority groups appear to be overlooked, especially in some regions." A White female noted the challenge of "being multifaceted in my approach to cultural diversity when other leaders in the field prefer to see multicultural counseling as 'ethnicity only.'" An Asian Indian male noted the challenge in "the continuing trend to equate multicultural counseling with counseling identifiable groups in society rather than looking at the problems of the society as a whole." Speaking to the general challenges of the field, another Asian Indian researcher stated that

in my judgment, the real challenges of multiculturalism are to fight against the 3 Ps, *poverty, prejudice,* and *persecution.* For almost a century now, psychology has mainly focused on the individual. I think for the 21st century, counselors and psychologists need to become active agents to bring about the social justice to free their clients from the chains and pains of prejudice and poverty.

This same scholar was of the following opinion:

There is now a growing challenge to multiculturalism. There are new designs to dismantle, defocus, and dilute it. The plans are in progress to replace multiculturalism with *diversity*. The well-intentioned agendas to address the issues and concerns of the disabled, gay, and lesbian populations may become injurious to the interests of the ethnic minority groups. In the long term, this might prove as the *erosion of multiculturalism*.

Finally, in this cluster, there were comments regarding the challenges of conducting research that will be of true value to the community itself. A Mexican American male noted his perceived challenge in "conducting research that has pragmatic value—but that is not valued as highly as research that is strongly theory driven." Finally, a Mexican American male noted the challenge in promoting research that has direct pragmatic value—research that can be applied in the counseling dyad. So much research in multicultural counseling, like its counterpart in conventional counseling, is conducted by persons who rarely, if ever, visit a counseling room. Balancing counseling practice with research is difficult.

Personal Challenges

The sample of scholars noted many personal challenges in their research careers. The specific challenges noted appear to fall into three related clusters. The first cluster addressed the challenges of staying current in a rapidly evolving specialty. The second cluster focused on feelings of self-doubt and vulnerability. The final cluster looked at the difficulty in dealing with unrealistic expectations from students, colleagues, and the scholars themselves.

Staying Abreast of the Field. A number of scholars noted the evolving nature of the multicultural specialty. A White male noted that "a fun new challenge is that the literature is bigger than I can master anymore. I recall not so long ago that I felt I knew everything that was going on. No longer true!" An African American male scholar noted the challenge in "feeling that I am staying relevant without losing focus." Finally, an African American female scholar stated the challenge in "maintaining my professional growth and development in an area that continues to develop within the profession, presenting new challenges in training."

Self-Doubt and Vulnerability. A few scholars noted their own self-doubts about their judgment or scholarly contributions. Others discussed feelings of risk in their work. General self-doubt and anxiety about work in the field are reflected in this longer quote by an African American male researcher:

> I was not sure how to get my career started. I knew what my multicultural interests were, but I did not know who could or would be willing to guide me. I had many thoughts about current professionals in this specialty and wanted to ask them questions about how they got started but was too nervous or anxious or thought they would not engage me in dialogue. Writing for publication was a frightening thought. Why? I had never taken a course titled "Writing for

Publication." Another challenge was accepting the thought that I had something significant to write about that would be a contribution to the counseling field.

Self-doubt is also reflected in the following quotes. A White male noted the challenge in "trusting my judgment in how to proceed." A Mexican American female scholar stated,

> I have always believed that multicultural perspectives are essential in research but faced some self-doubts initially because of the lack of literature to support my work. Because of this void, I wondered why others had avoided multicultural perspectives. Yet I persisted.

Speaking to a very personal experience, an African American male scholar stated that

> it took me a long time to get over the charge by a senior scholar that I had ripped off his ideas; it was only when I discovered that he had done this before to other well-known Black scholars that I was finally able to "relax."

Other scholars highlighted the risks they perceived in their research work. An Asian American female researcher stated that

> I have at times worried about how others view my research given that I do not always find what I am hoping to find. Results can be interpreted in racist ways. I feel that I must always have my work reviewed by others to be sure that it cannot be misconstrued by others.

Another Asian American female noted that "because the field is changing, and there is a significant backlash in the popular culture—it can feel a bit risky sometimes to 'put oneself out' in this area."

Unrealistic Expectations. Various scholars talked about the high level of expectation for work and service placed upon them by the campus and local community. An African American male scholar noted unrealistic expectations "from students who want me to be their type of Black and their type of mainstream professor" and "from myself who wants to be the perfect multicultural counseling scholar." A Mexican

American female noted the challenge of "having the time to do the multicultural research as racial/ethnic minority students often gravitate and are directed to my office. I am expected to represent 'diversity' on committees, and manage the requests from the Latino community." An African American female scholar stated the challenge in "being labeled as my program's resident 'expert' in multicultural research without acknowledgment of my competencies in other research areas (i.e., being pigeon-holed)."

A White male scholar noted the challenge in

becoming overextended because of being considered the local expert. Anyone with a cultural question seems to come to me, and I get most students interested in the area. Further, I am on many committees or write the diversity section of national reports for education and psychology.

Finally, an Asian American female scholar noted the following challenge:

What is a multicultural expert? Lately, I have been asking myself this question. I am not an expert on race/ethnicity; in fact, in terms of detail, I know very little about most groups. I know a little about theory, but I am mostly focused on one specific area of multicultural research (intelligence assessment). Students and other faculty, however, have assumed that I am an expert in the entire area and appear shocked when I say that I am not familiar with particular names or topics of research in the area.

Working With Students and Teaching

A good number of respondents noted challenges in working with students and in teaching the multicultural counseling class. A White female scholar noted the challenge in "helping students see themselves as cultural beings when they just feel they are American . . . and helping students deal with their own anger and resentment over being misunderstood and/or maligned while trying to study and communicate across cultures."

A Mexican American male professor noted "resistance among students toward multiculturalism who note that they are tired of hearing about race, class, and gender in their classes." A Native American stated the challenge that "many students still ask, 'Why do I have

to take cross-cultural counseling? My school is one race.' They do not see the true point of multiculturalism." A Mexican American male noted "having nonminority doctoral students appreciate the *importance* and *relevance* of multicultural research—they have been taught quite well (by others) to not view it as *true science!*"

Scholars also noted some of the particular challenges in teaching multicultural counseling. An African American male professor noted the difficulty in "pulling together enough worthwhile research studies for multicultural teaching over the years." A White female scholar noted the challenge in "having the time to cover all the information I feel necessary to include in a multicultural counseling class." This same professor noted the challenge in "trying to convey information about specific cultures and yet not creating other stereotypes in the process."

Challenges Specific to Racial/Ethnic Cohorts

The majority of challenges expressed by the sample were common to the group at large. However, there were some sets of challenges that seemed particular to either racial/ethnic minority or White scholars. In this section, we will first review the challenges unique to minority respondents and then review those unique to White respondents (see Table 30.2).

Table 30.2   Challenges Faced in a Multicultural Counseling Research Career Specific to Racial/Ethnic Status

Racial/Ethnic Minority Researchers
Lack of Role Models and Topic Discouragement
How We Are Silenced
Connecting With Other Multicultural Researchers
White Researchers
Personal Awareness and Bias
Being Accepted as a White Scholar in Multicultural Research

Racial/Ethnic Minority Researcher Challenges

Emerging from the data were three categories of challenges expressed only by racial/ethnic minority scholars. These comments focused on lack of role models and discouragement from pursuing multicultural research, a sense of being silenced, and connecting with other multicultural researchers.

Lack of Role Models and Topic Discouragement. A few minority scholars reported a lack of role models for multicultural research and active discouragement from pursuing the field. An African American female noted, "I had no mentors who could teach me how to do such research." A Mexican American female said that a challenge was "not having any mentors or advisors to help me develop my expertise in multicultural counseling research. Having to do it on my own."

A few scholars talked about being discouraged from pursuing multicultural research. An African American female scholar noted that "I was actively discouraged from doing such research." An African American male noted "being told that if I pursued this area of research, I would not get tenured." Another African American male noted "being told that White students would not want to work with me because they could not relate to the research area."

How We Are Silenced. A small cohort of minority female scholars alluded in their responses to a sense of feeling silenced. An African American female stated, "I have had to deal with issues of censorship, that is, if others do not like what I say or disagree with my perspectives, it (my research) might not get published." A Mexican American female stated

> that the value of "collaborativeness," "group," or "unity" is viewed as being unable to do one's work rather than a value that is reflected by different cultures. Instead, my personal and professional values are viewed as secondary to the academic status quo. I am often left wondering if I am *really* welcome or invited but expected to shut up.

A Mexican American female stated the following:

> As a woman of color, I have also found that different voices are given greater value when it comes to multiculturalism. This lack of inclusivity, regardless of our ethnic and racial backgrounds, is absurd and often divisive. No one owns multicultural counseling research; it is in the public domain. At the same time, as multicultural

researchers and leaders, I believe we need to hold others accountable who proclaim this expertise.

An Asian American female scholar was noting the challenge in being one of only a few people of color in an academic setting; she noted,

> As I have listened to other faculty share their research, I often feel like I am the "race/ethnicity" person. Just the other day, I was sitting in a colloquium and the senior faculty person never described the race/ethnicity breakdown of their sample. I believe that race/ethnicity would be an important variable since the populations they were studying were impoverished and homeless. Actually, I think acknowledging the race/ethnicity of any research sample is important. I sat there with colleagues and fought with myself as to whether I should ask about this. I ended up not mentioning it. I later spoke with a Latino faculty member about this issue since she was also at the colloquium. She shared that she too had noticed that the researcher had not mentioned this information and she felt uncomfortable bringing it up. This could be an example of how we are silenced.

One minority female scholar talked about feeling invisible within the context of a sexist research area. She stated,

> I think that there has been some sexism, too, that I have faced—I often feel invisible as a researcher in the area. I do not enjoy the "pissing contests" (as one researcher put it) when men get together and spend lots of time talking about their latest book or project. It is definitely *not* collaborative.

This same scholar noted as a challenge her experience being sexually harassed. She was the only researcher to relate such an experience, and though not forming a cluster of responses on its own, the harassment experience had such an impact that I include the following quote:

> Being sexually harassed by a prominent White male researcher in the field essentially made me leave what I would call mainstream multicultural counseling research and move into the mainstream of another field, bringing a multicultural focus to that field.

Connecting With Other Multicultural Researchers. Although not a strong cluster in terms of frequency or intensity of mention, there were some revealing comments regarding collegial acceptance. An African American male stated the challenge of "struggling to make a connection to other theorists who do not always seem accessible." Another African American male noted that "a key challenge for me was the willingness to take a position on issues contrary to established multicultural researchers." This same researcher noted that

> finally, a challenge that still haunts me and bothers me today is how closed a society the multicultural researchers are. Some of the established multicultural researchers by their actions and not by their words were not willing and I believe still are not willing to accept or let younger professionals into their "inner circle."

White Researcher Challenges

There appeared to be two clusters of challenge categories that were brought up only by White researchers. The first dealt with the continuing need for self-examination with regard to multicultural awareness and bias. The second cluster focused on the challenges of being a White scholar in the multicultural research area.

Personal Awareness and Bias. A White male noted the following challenge:

> My own history of unconscious racism and ignorance—I feel humbled the more I learn about how little I know. I think I know a lot, but there is constant need to challenge myself. . . . I keep trying and hopefully improving awareness of my White identity.

A White female stated the challenge in "dealing with my own unrecognized cultural bias. I have to always try to be open and learn more about my own worldviews, values, beliefs and prejudices." Finally, a White male researcher summed it up as follows:

> The first challenge was recognizing my own racism and recognizing that my defensiveness about my racism were impediments to my understanding and appreciating the perspectives of some ethnic minority scholars who are leaders in multicultural research. I think I have overcome these obstacles.

Being Accepted as a White Scholar in Multicultural Research. White scholars noted challenges in being accepted by minority colleagues and minority subject pools. There was also a sense of self-questioning regarding the roles one should play in multicultural research. A White female noted simply the challenge of "figuring out how to be a White woman in this field." A White male stated that "there is a sense that I may be limited in the areas of multiculturalism that I can research because I am White. Perhaps these are self-imposed limitations though." A White female noted "being a White person teaching about non-White cultures—there is a question of credibility; also the personal struggle of 'Do I have the right to do this?'"

Some scholars discussed the challenges of conducting research in minority communities. A White female noted the difficulty in "bridging cultural mistrust in respect to obtaining research participants." A White male noted that "I have had 'acceptance challenges' in collecting data in minority communities. At times, understandably, there is suspicion toward me—as a White person and probably as a university academic."

The largest cluster of comments in this category focused on perceived attitudes of minority colleagues. A White male stated, "challenges from non-White friends and colleagues. I feel that I have to prove myself every day and in every way." A White female noted that

> the issue of being a White counseling researcher gets raised more often—it is the only area of research where I have been questioned as to who I am—as opposed to looking at the strengths and weaknesses of my design and conceptualization.

Another White male stated the challenge of "being accepted by ethnic minority colleagues as a credible instructor, researcher, and writer in this area."

Two longer quotes by two male scholars that capture the sentiments of this category are as follows:

> Another challenge has been earning the trust of ethnic-minority researchers, some of whom have judged me to be an unworthy scholar of multiculturalism because I am White. It has been necessary to be genuine (which has always been easy for me), persistent, and non-defensive in response to these judgments about me.

> As a White researcher, there have been times at conferences when I have felt like an outsider, that somehow I

could never understand the nuances of multiculturalism. Further, there have been times when some non-White students see me as lacking credibility until I prove to them that I have something to offer. Interesting, but my sense is that I often experience what many non-Whites have discussed for years regarding credibility.

Rewards

There were a number of expressed rewards that transcended the entire sample regardless of participant race/ethnicity or gender. These rewards could be organized into five categories as follows: the professional and personal meaningfulness of the work, working with students, interacting with and befriending colleagues, the intellectual stimulation and excitement of the field, and the ego-enhancing and material rewards of work in the topical area (see Table 30.3).

Table 30.3   Rewarding Aspects of a Career in Multicultural Counseling Research

---

Professional and Personal Meaningfulness of Work
    Personal Growth, Meaningfulness, and Expression
    Improved Service Delivery to Racial/Ethnic Minority Populations
    Advancing the Profession and Having an Impact on the Field

Working With Students
    Student Mentoring and Role Modeling
    The Multicultural Classroom

Students and Multicultural Research

Interacting With and Befriending Colleagues
    Networking With Colleagues
    Acceptance by and Cohesiveness of Multicultural Professionals

Continuous Learning, Intellectual Stimulation and Challenge, and Excitement
    Continuous Learning and an Expanded Professional Perspective
    Intellectual Challenge and Excitement of Field

Recognition and Material Rewards
    Recognition and Visibility
    Professional Opportunities and Benefits

Professional and Personal Meaningfulness of Work

The largest category of meaning units described the respondents' sense of "meaningfulness and purpose" of their work. Within this broad category, three clusters emerged that focused on personal meaningfulness, the notion of contributing to improved mental health service delivery to racial/ethnic minority populations, and the view of advancing the profession and having an impact on the field.

Personal Growth, Meaningfulness, and Expression. A large cluster of comments addressed participants' personal growth and development as a result of research in the field. For some, it was also a means of self-expression and catharsis. A Mexican American male scholar stated that "first and foremost, it has offered me the opportunity to address a number of my own questions concerning the Mexican American experience—particularly as this pertains to ethnic identity issues I have personally experienced over the years of growing into adulthood." A White female researcher noted that

> my experiences in different cultures and with people of diverse identities (including sexual orientation, ethnicity, disabilities, and age) add to my knowledge base and make me a more interesting person and more able to connect with a variety of people.

Personal awareness and growth are also reflected in the following two quotes. A White male stated, "I have grown a lot personally. Constantly studying multicultural issues led me to examine my own racial identity development and status." Another White male noted that research activity in the field "helped me to grow personally and professionally in a positive way. I am less racist and less ethnocentric and thus am able to appreciate other cultures and . . . peoples in a way I could not before."

Other scholars highlighted the meaningfulness of expression and catharsis in their work, as reflected in this longer quote by an Asian Indian male researcher:

> I derive a great sense of personal satisfaction engaging in multicultural counseling research. In many ways, my research in this area is a reflection of my true-life experiences. For instance, when I write about

prejudice, I can relate to the pains of biases and discrimination afflictions that I had to personally endure. No stories are sweeter than the stories that are born out of our own heart and soul. I find the process of relating and writing about experiences closer to the heart and very *cathartic*. I also perceive myself as an ambassador of the interests of those who are the focus of my multicultural research. It is exciting to fight for those who are downtrodden and hurt. There is a great sense of pride and satisfaction in being the advocate for the oppressed. For me, multiculturalism is a vehicle of voice against past and present injustices.

Improved Service Delivery to Racial/Ethnic Minority Populations. A number of comments focused on the satisfaction inherent in a career that directly benefits racial/ethnic minority clientele. An African American male noted the sense of reward in that "the expertise I develop in multicultural counseling is used in my consultation and clinical work to provide and improve services to ethnic minorities." An African American female noted the reward in "providing training that will develop and enhance professional and personal cultural competencies of students preparing for careers in counseling psychology."

A Native American male scholar talked about the reward in witnessing "the generation of concern for individuals who are genetically mixed. . . . I look forward to the day when these individuals do not have to respond to the question, 'Please choose one.'" This same scholar also noted his sense of reward in observing "how school counselors have improved their delivery of services to student populations. Current school counselors have more content knowledge and process skills to serve diverse students appropriately and sensitively."

Two additional comments in this cluster highlight the reward in conducting research that has pragmatic value to the minority community. A Mexican American male noted a sense of reward in "people of color being very interested in how research findings are converted into real-life solutions." Finally, a Mexican American male experienced a sense of reward in "conducting pragmatic research and working on projects that are of 'real' value to the groups that I research."

Advancing the Profession and Having an Impact on the Field. A significant cluster of reward statements

focused on the meaning inherent in conducting research that advances the field, creates new knowledge, and contributes to a positive social movement. An African American female stated that "the greatest reward of doing multicultural research is feeling like I have contributed to the understanding of diversity in a positive way." A White female scholar stated that conducting research in the area "allowed me to feel as though I am making a much needed contribution to the field of counseling psychology." Another White female scholar noted the meaning in "the chance to help move the field of counseling in the direction of greater sensitivity to individual and group differences." Finally, a biracial female stated that multicultural research "is incredibly important work to me—intrinsically rewarding. I feel as if I have had an impact on bringing a multicultural perspective to vocational psychology. Not the only voice, but one of a few."

Some of the comments in this cluster focused on the concept of creating or contributing to new knowledge. An African American male expressed reward in "creating new knowledge and information to advance the field." A Native American male scholar expressed reward in "having some part in the expansion of the research literature in multicultural counseling." An African American male scholar expressed reward in "developing and sharing a theory of multicultural counseling: Transcendent Counseling."

A few comments in this cluster focused specifically on work with journals, committees, and professional organizations as reflected in the following three quotes. An African American male felt reward in heading "the *Journal of Multicultural Counseling and Development*, having a positive impact on the multicultural literature, helping worthy authors to get published, and improving the quality and the size of the journal." A Mexican American male noted reward in "my current involvement on APA's Committee on Ethnic Minority Affairs." Finally, a Native American male noted that "another reward is evidenced in the addressing of multicultural issues and concerns by the professional organizations. Even though lip service continues to exist, the opposite is rapidly expanding."

A final subgroup of reward statements in this cluster focused on being part of something new and different— a social movement of sorts. An African American male talked of "charting new territory." A Mexican

American male noted a sense of reward in "helping to develop a new field." An African American male stated, "I feel I am part of a history-making process. My work has made a difference, and from what I can tell, it continues to add value to the discourse on Black identity dynamics." Another African American male noted a reward in "being involved in the multicultural movement since its origin in concept and terminology, and being involved in the 'racial/ethnic movement in counseling' since a doctoral student in 1969."

Focusing more on the social impact nature of research careers were the following statements. A White male noted "being able to see social change as a result of my research." A White female stated, "I feel like I am part of a social movement that gives my life meaning. I am committed to social justice for diverse people." Finally, another White female stated that "I have a strong commitment to fairness and social justice—work on multicultural counseling can contribute to a more 'just' mental health delivery system."

Working With Students

A second major category of rewards that transcended all cohorts within the sample was working with students. The expressed rewards fell into three related clusters. First were the rewards of mentoring and role modeling for students. The second cluster focused on the rewards of the multicultural counseling class. The final cluster in this category dealt with the joy of working with students specifically on multicultural research.

Student Mentoring and Role Modeling. Many respondents talked generally of the joy and pleasure of mentoring students and serving as role models for them. For example, a Mexican American male scholar talked simply of the pleasure of "mentoring students toward careers in multicultural research." An African American male scholar stated that "I can model and mentor multicultural counseling competence for ethnic minority and nonminority students to increase access to the field for culturally sensitive professionals."

At times, the comments grouped in this cluster were race-specific. A number of scholars talked about the specific reward of training racial/ethnic minority students. One White male scholar noted the reward in "the chance to train underrepresented students and help them obtain positions in which they can influence the field through their research and by serving as models for others." A biracial scholar noted the reward in "mentoring racial/ethnic minority students; recruiting them to our program; making this [training] a good experience for them." A White male scholar noted the rewards in modeling for White trainees, through transmitting the message that "you can be of White, heterosexual, male, European background and do work in this area."

The Multicultural Classroom. A second cluster of stated rewards in working with students focused on the classroom experience, challenging the students, and witnessing their personal and professional growth. A White female scholar specified the following rewards: "hearing students view the world and events within it in a culturally sensitive manner" and "having students discover their cultural origins and be interested to know more about their backgrounds." A Mexican American male respondent stated clearly that "one of my greatest joys is bringing an ethnic minority professional voice into the classroom and being able to challenge students to develop an awareness of their own ethnic identity—particularly White students who often report not having one."

Related to the rewards in teaching students multicultural counseling are the expressed rewards of feedback from current and former students. A Mexican American female scholar noted the sense of personal reward in "having students directly and indirectly tell me that the work I am doing and how I approach classes lets them know that their realities are acknowledged and integral to learning and to the field of counseling psychology." A White female professor noted the reward in "having former students say how valuable my course was to them and how they are using information and materials from the course at their work sites."

Students and Multicultural Research. The third cluster of expressed rewards in the student category focused on working with students specifically in multicultural research. An Asian American female scholar stated that "it is rewarding to work with graduate students and to see their growth and development as researchers." A

White female scholar noted the reward in "witnessing students' increasing interest in participating in multicultural research."

Other comments in this cluster focused on the rewards of working with doctoral students as research collaborators. For example, an African American male specified the sense of reward in "working with doctoral dissertations on the topic and co-authoring with doctoral students and graduates." Another African American male scholar commented that "over the past 7 years, I have been able to attract outstanding doctoral students who want to work on my research teams. These students have become my most valuable collaborators."

Interacting With and Befriending Colleagues (A Wonderful Network of Colleagues)

Virtually all of the respondents talked about the great rewards of meeting colleagues in the multicultural field. The comments in this category could be organized into two major clusters. The first cluster encompassed the personal and professional rewards of establishing networks of colleagues across the country (and internationally) in the multicultural field. It was apparent that collegial relationships turned to important friendships for many respondents. The second cluster of comments focused specifically on feelings of being accepted by the multicultural professional community. Also falling within this cluster were comments regarding the rewards of mentoring and being mentored by colleagues in the area. Finally, there was a sense in this cluster that the multicultural network was perhaps more cohesive and close than networks in other specialty areas of the counseling profession.

Networking With Colleagues. A number of comments just described the rewards in finding a network of colleagues with similar interests. A Mexican American male scholar specified the reward in "developing collaborative relationships with colleagues who share research interests." A White male researcher noted the value in "learning from and with my colleagues who share my values and interests." Another White male specified the reward in "collaboration with international colleagues and U.S.-based colleagues on multicultural research issues." A Mexican American male

noted his joy in "working with racial/ethnic minority colleagues who have helped to pioneer the field." Finally, a White female scholar noted the reward in "being associated with and learning from and with other individuals who are seriously committed to issues of cultural diversity."

There was a sense among some respondents that their national network of multicultural specialists helped fill a void left by individual academic departments. As one African American female academic noted,

> I work in an academic program that does much lip-service to the "idea" of multiculturalism, but that does little to advance or promote multicultural competency in our students. However, when I am feeling discouraged about their inaction related to multicultural issues, I can call on a host of individuals across the nation who will infuse energy and motivation in me about our mutual interest, and I begin to feel recharged.

Working with colleagues nationwide in the multicultural area provided extensive professional development and support. This reward is exemplified in the well-organized comment of an African American female scholar who notes,

> The fellowship and support of other colleagues involved in multicultural counseling research have been critical to my professional and personal life. Colleagues have (a) stimulated my thinking in this area, (b) provided research ideas, (c) served as my primary professional support system, and (d) been generous in allowing me to use their work (e.g., instruments they developed, existing data sets, etc.) to further the profession's knowledge about multicultural issues in counseling.

Within this first cluster of rewards, there was a subset that noted specifically the development of friendships through initially collegial relationships. A White male noted the pleasure of "meeting and befriending numerous people from other cultures." A White female noted that "I meet most of my friends through work, and because I am interested in the multicultural field, my friends are quite diverse." An Asian American female noted, "I have begun to establish a long-distance network of peers interested in the same general areas. We talk and do projects collaboratively, which is a great experience. I enjoy working on research teams and making new friends related to my areas of interest." A White male stated, "I have developed wonderful friendships with other scholars of multiculturalism through my research interests."

Acceptance by and Cohesiveness of Multicultural Professionals. The second cluster of comments in the Colleague category focused on feelings of acceptance and belonging, on the rewards of mentoring or being mentored by colleagues, and on the sense that the multicultural network was extremely close and supportive. An Asian American female noted, "Recently, I have met people who I believe to be 'star researchers,' and they have been so welcoming. I think about how great it is to be in a profession with these kinds of people. What a thrill!" A White male stated, "Importantly, as a White man, I felt very welcomed by my minority mentors/colleagues. That was a powerful experience for me, and it motivated me to do more and better work in the area. I also felt very supported by senior White scholars in the area."

Other comments falling into this cluster focused on the construct of mentoring. An Asian American female stated that "there have been mentors and professors who have supported me for so long." Others talked about the rewards of serving as mentor. A biracial male noted satisfaction in "mentoring other racial/ethnic minority faculty." A Mexican American female specified the reward of "the mentoring of new professionals."

Finally, two longer quotes highlight the sense among some respondents that the multicultural scholars' network is particularly close and cohesive. One White male stated the sense of reward in

> the wonderful network of colleagues, mentors, mentees, and friends I have established through the multicultural specialty network. I have felt embraced, welcomed, cared-for, looked-out for and so on by my colleagues. I don't know if colleagues in other counseling specialties build the same depth of support that we seem to have in the multicultural community.

Another White male presented a more academic reward description of the same notion:

> According to anthropological, sociological, and psychological research, often the possibility exists that

minority groups tend to become cohesive in order to secure a common voice. Because of the small number of multicultural counseling researchers, I believe that this has occurred in the field. It is nice to have great colleagues who are "fighting for the cause."

Continuous Learning, Intellectual Stimulation and Challenge, and Excitement

Virtually all of the respondents talked in some way about how their work in the field has helped them to expand their intellectual perspective and challenge their creativity and flexibility. They also talked about the fun and excitement of being involved in multicultural research. Under this category are two related clusters of rewards. The first deals with the continuous learning highlighted by researchers, and the second deals with the creativity, challenge, and excitement of being part of the multicultural field.

Continuous Learning and an Expanded Professional Perspective. A White male scholar stated the following reward: "extending my knowledge and awareness of healing far beyond Western mental health practices to embrace other disciplines such as history, anthropology, sociology, public health, education, economics, social work, and political science." A White female respondent specified that work in the field "provided me with a greater appreciation of the value-laden nature of all theoretical and research approaches." Along the same lines, a White male noted, "learning to retain multiple, often opposing, 'truths' or perspectives that are all valid." Finally, an Asian Indian male talks of his professional growth in the following way:

> [The] most rewarding aspect of my involvement in multicultural counseling research has been a deeper understanding of how cultural norms and values influence the behavior of individuals, groups, and intergroup relations. Almost everything that human beings do, either as individuals or as members of particular groups that they identify with, is influenced directly or indirectly by cultural norms and values.

Intellectual Challenge and Excitement of Field. The second cluster of rewards in this category addressed the flexibility, complexity, excitement, and joy of working in the field. An Asian American female noted that "it is gratifying to be creative with qualitative and innovative methods." A White male scholar expressed one reward as "being able to be interdisciplinary and borrow and transform ideas from other fields such as geography and physics." A White female expressed the following:

> Engaging in multicultural counseling research has allowed me to combine my personal and professional interests in the area of diversity, including racial and ethnic attitudes, gender attitudes, and power dynamics. This has been both intellectually and emotionally stimulating and exciting.

Speaking to the complexity and challenge of a research career in the field, a White male simply listed the "intellectual challenge" as a reward. Another White male noted "struggling with and overcoming methodological challenges and problems." Finally, a White female noted, "I like the complexity of the problems in trying to do multicultural research—issues of design, selection of variables, managing majority culture bias— all make for complex and challenging thinking."

A number of scholars highlighted the sheer excitement and joy they experienced in their multicultural research work. An African American female noted that "it is exciting to identify future research possibilities in this domain, and find ways to investigate them." An African American male noted that "it is exciting to work with new ideas, to integrate what has gone before into new perspectives." A White male said, "Being excited by an idea or conclusion, for example, not being able to sleep because of the stimulation, or seeing a student come up with something I had not seen before."

A few of the reward statements focused more on the joy of working in the field. A White male remarked, "It is a lot of fun—I would do it even if I did not get paid." Finally, an African American male put it this way:

> Although I work very hard, and the stress level can at times get out of hand, the fact of the matter is I am extremely fortunate that my "job" is fun and constantly full of joy. Whether it is seeing a young student come into intellectual bloom, find results that confirm a hypothesis, or write a new chapter that truly captures the heart of a topic and instantly engages the reader, each of these "rewards" make my work highly fulfilling.

Recognition and Material Rewards

A good number of respondents across race and gender noted the recognition and material rewards of their research careers in multicultural counseling. This category of rewards can be grouped into two clusters. The first deals with esteem-related rewards of recognition and respect arising out of visible publication records in the field. The second cluster deals with more materialistic rewards such as professional opportunity and advancement, income, and travel.

Recognition and Visibility. Speaking of the recognition that came from specializing in multicultural counseling, one Mexican American male scholar noted that "it is rewarding to be recognized in the community, the campus, and the professional arena as a contributor to the field." An African American male noted the reward in "becoming recognized as an expert in the field." An African American female commented that "I have met lots of people from all over the world who use my work." An Asian American female states, "I must admit that it is quite a thrill to see my name in print and to be recognized by others as someone who has something to offer our profession." Finally, an African American male noted a more lengthy reward:

> Although I never thought it would be an issue for me, my self-confidence in my overall ability improved as a result of my pursuit of this career. My knowledge of the counseling field expanded and other professionals in the multicultural field began to respect my views. As a teacher, students and fellow teachers would seek me out more often for my views on a range of topics even if the subject had nothing to do with multicultural issues. At the university, the central administration began to appoint me to significant university committees.

Professional Opportunities and Benefits. This second cluster of comments focused on material rewards accruing from research visibility in the field. These comments can be organized along travel benefits, financial opportunities, and general professional development rewards. An African American female stated, "I have had the opportunity to travel to places I never thought I would see." A White male noted the "opportunity to travel and work in over 20 countries and the opportunity to work with numerous cultures within the United States."

Referring to financial benefits, a White male stated that "having published in the area, I had some visibility and it led the way to speaking engagements that helped support my low teaching income." An African American female said, "I get paid to ask questions about race and culture."

With regard to general career opportunities an Asian Indian male noted that

> my knowledge, skills, and research interests in multiculturalism have provided many professional opportunities that may otherwise might never have been possible. As a matter of fact, my first faculty position at the university level became a possibility only because of my multicultural counseling research background. . . . In addition to my research interests in multiculturalism, my skin color also became an *insignia* of expertness in this area. Because of this "perceived expertness," more and more consulting and professional opportunities became available.

An African American male stated directly that a reward of his work was "getting tenured because of my multicultural counseling research." Finally, a White male noted the following:

> Multicultural specialization (along with publishing on the topic) helped my career. I dove into multicultural issues in the mid-1980s, and the profession was at the time embracing the subfield. It made me more marketable as training programs were looking to build their multicultural strength by hiring first minority, and second, majority scholars specializing in the area.

Rewards Specific to Racial/Ethnic and Gender Cohorts

Careful scrutiny of the rewards across groupings yielded no dominant reward differences across groups. There were a few mini-clusters of rewards that seemed to be connected to a particular group, but the meaning units identified in such cases were generally few in number. Nonetheless, we found the statements of reward interesting, revealing, and worth quoting (see Table 30.4).

Table 30.4 Rewarding Aspects of a Career in Multicultural Counseling Research Specific to Racial/Ethnic Status

Racial/Ethnic Minority Researchers
    Colleagues' Increasing Interest in Multicultural Counseling
    Acknowledgment of Family

White Researchers
    Affirmation by Minority Colleagues and Influencing Other White Scholars

Racial/Ethnic Minority Researcher Expressed Rewards

Two mini-clusters of rewards specified by racial/ethnic minority scholars in the sample reflected satisfaction in witnessing colleagues' growing acceptance and interest in multicultural issues, and the notion of family acknowledgment.

Colleagues' Increasing Interest in Multicultural Issues. Three of the eight minority women in the sample all noted a sense of reward in witnessing increasing multicultural interests among colleagues. Although one might imagine this to be a reward that transcended the groups, these comments were found only among the minority women. An African American female stated, "I have been able to influence colleagues who thought they were not interested in multicultural counseling research." Another African American female noted that "of primary importance to me is the fact that there are increasing numbers of our colleagues who believe in the importance of such issues." Finally, a Mexican American female noted a sense of reward in "the response of colleagues who have found a new interest in multicultural counseling."

Acknowledgment of Family. A second mini-cluster in the minority grouping focused on remarks regarding family. Although not noted by many scholars, the family comments are revealing and we include them here. A Mexican American female listed the following as a reward of her research career: "Feeling like I am honoring the past efforts of my family—my father worked three jobs—who helped finance my education. That is, the work I am doing in multicultural counseling research reflects who I am and acknowledges my family." An African American male, in speaking of his increasing recognition as a research scholar, stated, "Family members and relatives began to state they had a scholar in the family even though I did not feel like I was a scholar."

White Researcher Expressed Rewards

Two unique responses were found among the White sample cohort. Although not forming actual clusters of responses, the quotes are revealing and worth presenting. The reward statements focus on affirmation by minority colleagues and effectiveness in influencing other White scholars.

Affirmation by Minority Colleagues and Influencing Other White Scholars. A White female noted the sense of reward in "having persons of color and other cultural identities affirm my work and presentations." A White male stated that

> since Whites make up the majority of researchers, instructors, and administrators, I believe that Whites need to become more focused on multiculturalism. Being White, I can discuss multiculturalism with other Whites as "one of them." Multicultural research then becomes something other than what "minorities" do.

DISCUSSION

You have just read a very lengthy Results section that included numerous themes, clusters, and individual quotes. Perhaps reading all of the distinct quotes was a little overwhelming. In this Discussion section, I attempt to tie things together in narrative form by summarizing the major challenges and rewards noted by our sample.

It is important to remember that the 36 participants in this study represented a select sample. All of the research scholars were specialists in multicultural counseling and had been working in the area for a number of years. Each participant was well published in the field, had conducted numerous empirical studies, had mentored students in multicultural research, and was active nationally in multicultural issues. The sample was diverse in terms of age, race, ethnicity, gender, and geographic locale. Let us now turn to a review of the

major challenges and rewards of a career in multicultural counseling research.

Major Challenges

Perhaps the major challenge expressed by our collective sample was dealing with the negative, disparaging attitudes of colleagues and the larger profession toward multicultural issues generally and the status of multicultural research specifically. Many in the sample felt that some of their colleagues both inside and outside their institutions regarded multicultural counseling as a "fringe" discipline, and as a political orientation more than a scientific discipline. Multicultural scholars felt that some colleagues (including journal editors and reviewers) deemed multicultural research as less valid, scientific, and rigorous than research in other specialties within counseling psychology. There was an impression that some in the profession gave "lip service" to the importance of multicultural issues, but in reality thought little of the topic and expended little effort embracing cultural perspectives in their own lives and work. Overall, dealing with colleagues regarding the legitimacy and importance of multicultural issues in counseling research and practice was a source of great stress and emotional drain for many in the sample.

A second group of challenges expressed by the sample was the general difficulty in designing and conducting multicultural counseling research. There was a perception that the multicultural counseling field is relatively new, and that well-defined constructs and theories are lacking. Consequently, designing research studies and posing research questions is a challenge. Furthermore, a number of participants expressed challenge in recruiting participants for their research. First, for quantitative research, there is difficulty in finding large sample sizes in some areas for particular racial/ethnic group cohorts. Second, given the mistrust of academic researchers by some in the minority communities, there may be resistance to psychological research. Members of the sample also expressed a challenge in finding well-validated, culturally appropriate instrumentation for quantitative research.

Within the research challenge grouping, a number of scholars expressed frustration over dealing with journal editors and manuscript reviewers. There was a sense that some reviewers and editors of mainstream counseling journals lacked sensitivity to and expertise in multicultural research. Dealing with editors and responding to reviewers' criticisms seemed to be a source of significant frustration for a number of researchers in our sample.

The final category of challenges expressed in this grouping was the perception that multicultural counseling was a complex field and that clear direction for research in the field was not available. There was a sense among some participants that the field is still in its early stages and that it was a challenge to decide the proper direction for research in the area. There seemed to be confusion over what constructs were most important to study and how to study them. There was also a sense of challenge in conducting research that benefited the minority communities directly.

A third major category of challenges was more personal in nature. Personal challenges included coping and managing with the perception of unrealistic expectations placed upon participants by students, colleagues, and even themselves. Scholars had at times faced issues of self-doubt about their work and contributions, and they also felt at risk and vulnerable during their research pursuits and presentations. Another challenge in this area was staying abreast of and personally managing the outpouring of material and literature related to such a rapidly evolving and growing field.

The final category of challenges focused on working with students on multicultural issues and teaching the multicultural counseling class. Some members of the sample reported feelings of frustration in working with students who were very unaware culturally and who were resistant to multicultural training. It was clear among the sample that teaching a multicultural counseling course was particularly challenging with respect to designing the class and managing student affective reactions to the material presented and topics discussed.

In addition to the above challenges that transcended the sample as a whole, there were also groups of challenges specific to majority and minority respondents. Racial/ethnic minority scholars noted the challenges in their professional development due to lack of role models in multicultural research. In fact, some minority scholars in our sample were actively discouraged from pursuing multicultural research. A number of minority women talked about feeling silenced by the profession. Although there was a façade of invited participation, these women felt their voices were not really heard or valued. One female scholar talked about male dominance in the field. Finally, a few minority scholars noted that it was tough breaking into the inner circle of multicultural scholars, and that there was little tolerance for dissenting philosophical positions within the network.

White scholars also expressed some unique challenges. A number of these researchers talked about the challenge in initially and periodically confronting their own socialization bias, ethnocentrism, and racism. Taking a close, honest look at oneself is often a difficult and emotionally draining process. Finally, White scholars also expressed challenges in being accepted by the minority community—both minority research colleagues and minority subject pools.

Major Rewards

The 36 research scholars who participated in this study found their work very rewarding. Multicultural research, practice, and training were very meaningful to participants in terms of personal growth, awareness, and expression. There was a strong sense of reward and satisfaction expressed in working toward the improvement of mental health service delivery to racial/ethnic minority populations. There was also pride and reward in contributing to defining a specialty and advancing the field through original research inquiry.

Another category of rewards expressed by virtually all respondents was the pleasure in working with students in research mentoring and teaching. Many students are very enthusiastic about multicultural research and practice, and respondents were stimulated intellectually in their collaborative work with students. The specialty of multicultural counseling attracts students of varying racial/ethnic backgrounds and lifestyles, and the researchers perceived their interactions with culturally diverse students as very rewarding. The scholars' relationship with students specializing in multicultural research was clearly perceived as very special.

A major reward category for our sample was the collegial and friendship networks established with other multicultural scholars across the country. These relationships were empowering, exciting, and intellectually stimulating. The scholars felt that their networks were particularly close and supportive. Interestingly, some scholars who perceived their own academic departments and/or institutions as lacking in cultural pluralism were bolstered and energized by contact with culturally focused colleagues from other institutions. Finally, a majority of respondents felt warmly embraced and welcomed into the multicultural counseling specialty.

A fourth major reward category revolved around the intellectual stimulation and challenge associated with multicultural research. The respondents were clearly excited and enthused by their work; they loved their research activities and did not consider them "work." Respondents sensed that they were always learning something new in this evolving and growing specialty of multicultural counseling.

The fifth and final reward category expressed by the sample concerned the esteem and material rewards associated with national recognition for their work. The sample participants are well known in the field, their work is often referenced, their books are often read, and their phone numbers are often called by students and scholars around the world. There was a sense of pride and joy expressed in others' acknowledgment of their work and contributions. This national visibility also brought about more material rewards, such as travel and financial opportunities.

Unlike the Challenge category presented earlier, no strong clusters of rewards emerged that were unique to racial/ethnic cohorts. There were what I called mini-clusters identified that revolved around acknowledgment of family, colleagues' increasing attention to multicultural issues for the minority respondents, and affirmation by minority colleagues and the sense of being able to reach other Whites on multicultural matters for the White respondents.

FINAL COMMENTS ON CHALLENGES AND REWARDS

Interestingly, many sources of reward for the participants were at times also sources of challenge,

and vice versa. For example, although working with and interacting with students constituted a major reward category, students at times also were perceived as a challenge in the scholars' work. Whereas interacting and working with colleagues was a great satisfaction to the subject pool, colleagues also constituted the greatest challenge category as well. The sample considered the research process intellectually stimulating and rewarding, but the complexity of the research area also was a source of challenge and frustration for some in the sample. The personal growth and expression common to work in the area that were seen as rewards were also seen as challenges in that "growth" multiculturally involves challenging your pre-existing worldview and confronting your own ethnocentrism. The reward cluster that focused on helping to improve service delivery to minority communities also had a companion challenge cluster that focused on attempts to conduct research that had ultimate pragmatic value for the community. Finally, the rewards of national visibility and recognition also carry with them the challenges of high service expectations from different constituencies inside and outside the university.

My hope is that the reader has some understanding of the challenges and rewards of a career in multicultural counseling research as heard through the voices of one group of multicultural scholars that was actively publishing multicultural research during the third and fourth historical moments (1980s and 1990s) of the multicultural counseling field. Whether you have or will experience the same rewards and challenges as the 36 scholars in this study is, of course, a question. Although there is no guarantee that you will reap the same rewards or endure the same challenges as our sample of researchers, it is likely that you have experienced or will experience some of the rewards and challenges highlighted throughout this chapter. Like all studies, the present one is replete with limitations and interpretive cautions. It is now important to turn our attention to a discussion of these limitations.

LIMITATIONS AND RESEARCH DIRECTIONS

There are a number of limitations to the present study. First, as an archival study, the present study presents a glimpse of, or snapshot into, a historical period in the development of a counseling specialty. It is highly likely that newer generations of scholars (those receiving their doctorates during the latter part of the fourth historical moment and during the fifth and present historical moment (1995–present) have had quite different experiences as they shape their careers as multicultural counseling researchers. For example, the counseling profession by and large now sees multiculturalism as a core of the profession rather than as an addendum or appendix to the counseling profession. Some of the challenges (e.g., scholarly legitimization) faced by many in the present sample as well as nationally identified "pioneers" in the field (see Chapters 1–12 of this and the previous edition of this *Handbook*) may not exist today. Then again, some challenges may continue to exist, and that is one area for future research in this topical area. What are the challenges and rewards of a career in multicultural counseling research faced by scholars who came into their own during the present fifth historical moment in the development of multicultural counseling?

A second limitation is the exploratory and shallow nature of the methodology I employed in this study. The use of one-time, open-ended written responses is perhaps the least penetrating way to probe the experiences and views of a group of research participants. Polkinghorne (1994) notes that "the use of subjects' written productions for the data set has typically resulted in restrained and scant descriptions" (p. 510). I found this to be the case in the present study, save for a number of responses that were more detailed and revealing in nature. Furthermore, collecting all of my data at one specific point in time precluded the use of "theoretical sampling," where data collection and analysis alternate, and where the researcher can therefore fill in gaps of information with follow-up or modified questions (see Polkinghorne, 1994; Ponterotto, 2005). I would like to see extended and follow-up research on this topic using established qualitative methods of grounded theory (Charmaz & Henwood, 2008; Fassinger, 2005), phenomenological inquiry (Eatough & Smith, 2008; Giorgi & Giorgi, 2008; Wertz, 2005), and consensual qualitative research (Hill et al., 2005). The results of such small-sample qualitative studies could lead to the development of a quantitative instrument that could be used

for large-sample representative national sampling to study this topic.

Naturally, my sample was not random and was not intended to be. Generalizing the major themes and clusters to other multicultural counseling scholars must be done with great caution. We must remember that males outnumbered females almost two to one, and there was a marked underrepresentation of Native American Indian scholars. One wonders if more females had been sampled whether the themes of "feeling silenced" and "invisible" would have been strengthened, and whether issues of sexual harassment may have come to the fore. It is likely that although the survey was intended to be anonymous, female researchers may have been hesitant to discuss harassment issues in such an aloof response format. Here, skillful, confidential, in-depth, face-to-face, long interviews (see McCracken, 1988; Polkinghorne, 2005) may have been more revealing. Having a female co-researcher would also seem to be a very important consideration in this context.

Furthermore, there were aspects of the extant data set that were not examined. For example, we did not consider sample cohort differences based on geographic locale. Do multicultural scholars working in the Midwest (a predominantly Anglo populace) experience similar challenges and rewards as scholars working in the Northeast or Southwest (with a larger population of non-Anglos)? Also, we did not consider age or generational differences in multicultural research experiences. Although there were only three scholars in the 61–70 age range at the time of the study, I did note some comments regarding how the field has evolved and changed over time. It might have been revealing to compare the responses of the 31- to 40-year-old and 41- to 50-year-old sample cohorts with the 51- to 60-year-old and 61- to 70-year-old cohorts. Furthermore, an interesting question would be to study the experience of our present emerging multicultural counseling scholars, such as those receiving their doctorates in this fifth historical moment (year 2000 to present).

It is likely that some of the experiences of reward and challenge identified by our multicultural specialists would be found among research scholars in other areas. I cannot claim that all of the themes and clusters identified are unique to multicultural scholars. For example, it is likely that nationally visible scholars in career counseling or marriage and family counseling also struggle with research challenges and unrealistic expectations. These scholars also have very rewarding experiences with students and colleagues, and they, too, reap esteem and material rewards from their publishing and resultant national visibility. Clearly, some of the themes identified are common to the general academic research experience. Further research may examine similarities and differences of research experiences among scholars in different specialties within counseling psychology.

Finally, the fact that I, the chapter author, was a participant in the study may be interpreted as both a strength and a limitation. Within the heuristic mode of qualitative inquiry, my own interest in and experience with the issues is central to the study. My voice helped to make sense of and interpret the comments of the other 35 research participants. On the other hand, despite my own self-monitoring, there is the chance of selecting representative quotes that affirm my own experiences as a multicultural researcher and as a White researcher. Naturally, all of the limitations noted here can serve as directions for further research on the topic. It is my hope that this exploratory study has both stimulated the readers' interest in multicultural research and provided ideas for further inquiry.

REFERENCES

Charmaz, K., & Henwood, K. (2008). Grounded theory. In C. Willig & W. Stainton-Rogers (Eds.), *The Sage handbook of qualitative research in psychology* (pp. 240–259). London: Sage.

Creswell, J. W. (2007). *Qualitative inquiry & research design: Choosing among five approaches* (2nd ed.). Thousand Oaks, CA: Sage.

Denzin, N. K., & Lincoln, Y. S. (2005). Introduction: The discipline and practice of qualitative research. In N. K. Denzin & Y. S. Lincoln (Eds.), *The Sage handbook of qualitative research* (3rd ed., pp. 1–32). Thousand Oaks, CA: Sage.

Eatough, V., & Smith, J. A. (2008). Interpretive phenomenological analysis. In C. Willig & W. Stainton-Rogers (Eds.), *The Sage handbook of qualitative research in psychology* (pp. 179–194). London: Sage.

Fassinger, R. E. (2005). Paradigms, praxis, problems, and promise: Grounded theory in counseling psychology research. *Journal of Counseling Psychology, 52,* 156–166.

Fouad, N. A., & Carter, R. T. (1992). Gender and racial issues for new counseling psychologists in academia. *Counseling Psychologist, 20,* 123–140.

Giorgi, A. P., & Giorgi, B. (2008). Phenomenological psychology. In C. Willig & W. Stainton-Rogers (Eds.), *The Sage handbook of qualitative research in psychology* (pp. 165–178). London: Sage.

Hill, C. E., Knox, S., Thompson, B. J., Williams, E. N., Hess, S., & Ladany, N. (2005). Consensual qualitative research: An update. *Journal of Counseling Psychology, 52,* 196–205.

Kiselica, M. S. (1998). Preparing Anglos for the challenges and joys of multiculturalism. *Counseling Psychologist, 26,* 5–21.

McCracken, G. (1988). *The long interview.* Newbury Park, CA: Sage.

Mio, J. S., & Iwamasa, G. (1993). To do or not to do: That is the question for White cross-cultural researchers. *Counseling Psychologist, 21,* 197–212.

Miville, M. L., Gelso, C. J., Pannu, R., Liu, W., Touradji, P., Holloway, P., & Fuertes, J. N. (1999). Appreciating similarities and valuing differences: The Miville-Guzman Universality-Diversity Scale. *Journal of Counseling Psychology, 46,* 291–307.

Moustakas, C. (1990). *Heuristic research: Design, methodology, and applications.* Newbury Park, CA: Sage.

Moustakas, C. (1994). *Phenomenological research methods.* Thousand Oaks, CA: Sage.

Patton, M. Q. (1990). *Qualitative evaluation and research methods* (2nd ed.). Newbury Park, CA: Sage.

Polkinghorne, D. E. (1994). Reaction to special section on qualitative research in counseling process and outcome. *Journal of Counseling Psychology, 41,* 510–512.

Polkinghorne, D. E. (2005). Language and meaning: Data collection in qualitative research. *Journal of Counseling Psychology, 52,* 137–145.

Ponterotto, J. G. (2005). Qualitative research in counseling psychology: A primer on research paradigms and philosophy of science. *Journal of Counseling Psychology, 52,* 126–136.

Ponterotto, J. G. (2008). Theoretical and empirical advances in multicultural counseling and psychology. In S. D. Brown & R. W. Lent (Eds.), *Handbook of counseling psychology* (4th ed., pp. 121–140). New York: Wiley.

Ponterotto, J. G., Utsey, S. O., & Pedersen, P. B. (2006). *Preventing prejudice: A guide for counselors, educators, and parents* (2nd ed.). Thousand Oaks, CA: Sage.

Van der Zee, K., & Van Oudenhoven, J. P. (2000). The Multicultural Personality Questionnaire: A multidimensional instrument of multicultural effectiveness. *European Journal of Personality, 14,* 291–309.

Van der Zee, K., Zaal, J. N., & Piekstra, J. (2003). Validation of the Multicultural Personality Questionnaire in the context of personnel selection. *European Journal of Psychology, 17,* 77–100.

Wertz, F. J. (2005). Phenomenological research methods for counseling psychology. *Journal of Counseling Psychology, 52,* 167–177.

31

Designing and Interpreting Quantitative Research in Multicultural Counseling

GERMINE H. AWAD AND KEVIN O. COKLEY

Historically, counseling psychology has emerged as one of the subdisciplines in psychology that has acknowledged and addressed the central role of culture in human behavior (Ivey, 1977; Locke, 1990). However, although the importance of culture in clinical or therapeutic settings has been recognized by counseling psychologists for some time, the importance and centrality of culture in research endeavors has not been as widely recognized. Traditionally, Western psychology has focused primarily on individual-level explanations independent of contextual issues. The research implications for strict individual-level explanations include relegating the role of cultural variables to the status of nuisance variables or error variance that has to be controlled for. It would be misleading, however, to say that the recognition of the importance of culture has characterized the approach of all psychologists. Long before the current interest in what is now called multicultural research, ethnic minority psychologists were interested in the impact of culture in research endeavors.

For example, early on, some African American psychologists challenged the appropriateness of using traditional quantitative research methods and traditional psychological constructs for research on Black people, and instead advocated using more culturally relevant research methods that integrated culturally relevant constructs (Dixon, 1976). Other African American psychologists believed that traditional quantitative research methods could be used to explore more culturally relevant issues in research for Black people (Boykin, Franklin, & Yates, 1979). Although the philosophical debate about the use of traditional quantitative research methods on ethnic minority populations is not going to be resolved any time soon, we believe it is nevertheless important to have a basic understanding of research methods in order to competently design and interpret quantitative research in multicultural counseling.

This chapter presents issues in designing and interpreting quantitative multicultural research. The first section addresses the formulation of research questions pertinent to multicultural research with an emphasis on the comparative research framework. The second section discusses design choice and study set-up with a focus on choosing appropriate variables and measures. The final section presents issues related to validity and interpretation of study findings.

FORMULATING THE RESEARCH QUESTION

The first step of a study is the formulation of the research question. After an extensive literature review, research questions often arise after noting gaps in the literature. For multicultural research, questions concerning applicability and generalizability to diverse populations are common. Many early psychological theories did not account for the experiences of people of color, and the impact of culture was largely ignored. Therefore, many studies in the multicultural psychology literature included testing the applicability of mainstream psychological theories on communities of color.

Heppner, Wampold, and Kivlighan (2008) suggest several techniques to help new researchers identify a research topic and formulate a question that are applicable to multicultural research. First and foremost, they suggest reading as much as possible in the topic area of interest. In addition to reading journal articles and books, individuals should also read compilations such as psychological encyclopedia sets and handbooks (such as this one). Because multicultural research is multidisciplinary by nature, it is also suggested that individuals look beyond the field of psychology to related disciplines (e.g., anthropology, sociology, gender studies, ethnic studies, economics, journalism) to inform their cultural work (Quintana, Troyano, & Taylor, 2001).

According to Drew (1980), three types of research questions may be developed for a study. The first, the descriptive question, essentially describes certain phenomena, events, or behaviors. Descriptive questions are designed to ask "What is happening?" and may be assessed using surveys, interviews, focus groups, and observation. The second category of research questions is the relationship question, which assesses the degree to which two or more variables are related to one another. Relationship questions tend to use correlational statistical methods ranging from bivariate correlations

to more complex procedures, such as structural equation modeling or hierarchical linear modeling. The third type of question or hypothesis is the difference question. Difference questions assess differences between individuals in one or more categories. Individuals can be compared to one another based on treatment received, region of country, or social category membership, to name a few. These types of questions are especially pertinent to multicultural research. In many multicultural studies, minority group members are often compared to majority group members or other minority or cultural groups. These types of questions can be analyzed using correlational methods such as regression as well as experimental or quasi-experimental methods such as factorial analysis of variance. In many ways, these types of studies helped elucidate some of the shortcomings of psychological theories in terms of applicability to certain cultural groups. Although these studies have been helpful in identifying some of the generalizability issues of psychological theories, they have also produced some undesirable consequences.

Hegemony or Good Science? Reflections on the Comparative Research Framework

A noted issue about conducting multicultural research with racial and ethnic minority populations has involved an epistemological concern regarding what has been called the comparative research framework. This concern was brought to light most provocatively in an article written by Daudi Azibo (1988) in which he recounts presenting a colloquium while applying for a faculty position. During his colloquium, he presented empirical research involving two instruments, Robert Williams's Black Personality Questionnaire (Wright & Isenstein, 1978) and Joseph Baldwin's African Self-Consciousness Scale (Baldwin & Bell, 1985). Upon conclusion of his presentation, a European American professor asked why he didn't include a White control group, to which Azibo asked what he would be controlling for. After indicating that the constructs would be meaningless to European Americans, Azibo characterized the European American professor's response as "red-faced, mouth-open stare, and marked discomfort" (p. 19). Azibo reported that he made the statement "Whites or Europeans are no longer the standard by which the psychology of people is judged," which he attributes to Khatib and Nobles (1977, pp. 97–98). Azibo concluded this introduction by indicating that this episode represented a problem of hegemony.

More recently, the second author (Kevin Cokley) was making a presentation to the American Psychological Association Minority Fellowship Program (MFP) Fellows when one of the Fellows asked a question regarding an experience she had submitting a grant. Similar to the Azibo account, part of the feedback she received was a request to include a White control group. The MFP Fellow was frustrated because intuitively, she did not feel that a White control group was necessary, but pragmatically, she was also feeling the pressure to secure a grant. So, her question was whether there was a reference that she could cite that would defend her decision to not use a White control group. Another MFP Fellow also shared a similar concern. The presenter immediately gave them the Azibo citation and briefly explained to them the core elements of his argument. In light of these incidents, and undoubtedly other untold examples, a more thorough discussion of the comparative research framework is warranted.

Comparative research in psychology has a long history and typically involves comparing two or more samples in order to discover commonalities and differences. The objective of comparative research is to establish general scientific principles about human behavior using the scientific method. A central element of the scientific method involves conducting experimental research versus other methods such as correlational research. For the purposes of this discussion, only two guiding principles of experimental research are emphasized: causality and control. Causality involves several assumptions: (a) The cause and the effect are contiguous, or closely related in space; (b) the cause must precede the effect in time; and (c) there is a necessary connection between the cause and the effect (Plutchik, 1968). The primary purpose of experimental research is to establish the causes of events or phenomena. The principle of control is central to experimental research. The only way that meaningful conclusions can be drawn from research is to effectively deal with the source of bias in some way (Plutchik, 1968). In experimental research, the problem of bias is dealt with in one of three ways: (a) avoiding the sources of bias, (b) evenly distributing

the effects of bias across various conditions, and (c) measuring the bias and determining its relative contribution (Plutchik, 1968). Both concepts—causality and control—have direct bearing on the comparative research framework.

The epistemological foundation of the comparative research framework rests on John Stuart Mill's method of difference canon. Mill was a British philosopher who, like physical and social scientists, was interested in trying to determine the causes of things (Plutchik, 1968). He identified several rules, or canons, for establishing cause and effect relationships. The canon most relevant to the comparative research framework is the method of difference. Azibo (1988) was the first scholar of color to link the method of difference canon with the comparative research framework, but in doing so, he failed to provide an explicit definition of method of difference. Instead, he focused on the methodological requirement of the method of difference canon. The method of difference canon, as articulated by Mill (1872), states the following:

> If an instance in which the phenomenon under investigation occurs, and an instance in which it does not occur, have every circumstance in common save one, that one occurring only in the former, the circumstance in which alone the two instances differ, is the effect, or the cause, or an indispensable part of the cause, of the phenomenon. (p. 256)

Stated another way, let's say that there are two essentially equal conditions that differ in only one meaningful way. These conditions are referred to as the experimental group and the control group. The difference is that one condition, the experimental group, is exposed to an intervention, treatment, or manipulation, whereas the other condition, the control group, is not. If a change is observed in the experimental group and not the control group, the effect can be attributed to the impact of the intervention, treatment, or manipulation. This method forms the basis of experimental research and is considered to be the exemplar of rigorous scientific research. With a more thorough understanding of Mill's method of difference, let's re-examine the scenario provided by Azibo.

One perspective is that the question "Why didn't you use a White control group?" did not come from a hegemonic worldview. Instead, it may be argued that the question was simply coming from a value of the scientific method in experimental research that, as previously identified, requires that all sources of bias are controlled for in order to draw meaningful conclusions about the results. In this case, the European American faculty member appeared to be operating under the assumption that the relatively new and unknown construct (at least unknown to European American faculty) of African self-consciousness could be considered a legitimate, and thus valid, construct for African Americans only if it could be shown that African Americans differed from European Americans.

However, another perspective is that the question did indeed come from a hegemonic worldview. This perspective is supported by the fact that the European American faculty member thought it was necessary to use a *White* control group. If he had been operating from a truly nonhegemonic perspective, he could have asked why a non-White (e.g., Hispanic/Latino, Asian American, Native American) control group wasn't used. This would have provided evidence that he wasn't operating from a Eurocentric hegemonic perspective and was truly interested only in demonstrating that African self-consciousness was a more valid and relevant construct for African Americans than other ethnic groups. Instead, he automatically assumed that a White control group was necessary, and therein lays the hegemonic problem. Azibo's (1988) recommendations for when comparative research is appropriate include the following: (a) when the nature of the research question compels comparisons across racial or ethnic groups, such as when one is interested in reporting on the differences in demographic and societal indexes such as income, health status, and unemployment rates; and (b) when the nature of the construct compels comparisons because ethnic or racial differences are an inherent part of the construct, such as the previous example involving African self-consciousness. According to Azibo, comparative research is inappropriate when the racial or ethnic groups are not equated on any relevant variables involving culture. Azibo goes on to state that whenever constructs are involved, culture is relevant. Taken to an extreme, some may dismiss Azibo's position as being rigid and impractical; however, Phinney (1996) later echoed his sentiments by stating that when

doing group comparisons, ethnic groups should be matched on all relevant variables. Interestingly, she then states that groups can never be matched on all relevant demographic variables. The implications for research are, among other things, that ethnic groups that are comparison groups should not be used as control groups.

CHOOSING THE DESIGN AND SETTING UP THE STUDY

Ideally, the research question should drive the type of design chosen for a particular study. Often, other factors such as statistical and methodological strengths of the researcher and feasibility of implementation drive design decisions. As a result, some may formulate their research question based on the statistical and methodological procedures with which they are most comfortable. Engaging in such a practice is akin to using the same power tool regardless of appropriateness for every household maintenance job. The goal of any research design is to answer the research question or test hypotheses while limiting extraneous variables and plausible rival hypotheses.

Kazdin (1980) identified three general research design typologies: experimental, quasi-experimental, and correlational designs. Each design comes with its own set of strengths and weaknesses, and the researcher must take these into consideration when attempting to answer the research question. One must weigh the issues of experimental control (internal validity) and generalizability (external validity) before the study is carried out. The tensions between external and internal validity have been widely documented in the literature (e.g., Cook & Campbell, 1979; Heppner et al., 2008; Sue, 1999). Multicultural research has especially suffered from the undue weight placed on internal validity (Sue, 1999). Sue argued that selective enforcement of validity rules has yielded a disproportionate emphasis on internal validity, and issues of external validity in psychology have been largely ignored. Studies that are concerned with questions of causation tend to emphasize internal validity over external validity because a great deal of experimental control is needed to demonstrate a causal link between variables. The more experimental controls a researcher employs to rule out plausible rival hypotheses, the less generalizable the study becomes.

Historically, psychology has been less concerned with issues of external validity, as evidenced by the wide use of convenience samples largely composed of introductory psychology students. One rationale given for the underemphasis of generalizability (external validity) is the idea that psychology is mostly concerned with relationships among variables instead of population representativeness (Aron, Aron, & Coups, 2006). Inherent in this line of thinking is the assumption that psychological theories are objective and universal for all people, and therefore, generalizability is not as important. Clearly, this view neglects the fact that culture is crucial to all human behavior, and to ignore it is to practice bad science. Furthermore, the bias in favor of experimental designs in psychology allows for only one type of question to be answered: causal.

The goals of science include description, prediction, determination of causes of behavior, and explanation of behavior (Cozby, 1997). The overemphasis on experimental design and internal validity neglects the other goals of science that do not involve the determination of causal links. Because certain areas within multicultural research are less developed, it is necessary to engage in the descriptive aspects of science. If one does not know very much about an area of research for an ethnic group, one must gather as much information as possible, and most of the time, these initial data-gathering steps involve descriptive data. One mainstream cultural example is the current wave of research on brain mapping and psychological traits. Many of these studies are in the early stages where researchers are simply documenting what areas of the brain are activated when exposed to certain stimuli. Because this area of research is in its infancy, researchers must gather as much information as possible before they move on to more causal or complex relationship questions. When any research area is in its infancy, initial research questions tend to be more descriptive, and questions assessing deep-level explanations and causal relationships develop after more basic descriptive questions are answered.

One relatively easy way to increase the generalizability of studies is to include diverse group members in study samples. Although the mere presence of minorities in a study sample is not sufficient, the representation of ethnic populations in early psychological research

studies was abysmal. Minority groups were usually included only in research studies where the superiority of Caucasian groups was being tested in some way (e.g., intelligence) and the inferiority of minority groups was assumed (Gould, 1996). When there was not a deliberate inclusion of minorities, they were largely ignored in psychological research. Within the past 30 years, the number of journals dedicated to minority populations has grown (e.g., *Hispanic Journal of Behavioral Sciences, Cultural Diversity and Ethnic Minority Psychology, Journal of Black Psychology, American Indian and Alaska Native Mental Health Research*). Nevertheless, ethnic minorities are still underrepresented in mainstream psychological journals. Imada and Schiavo (2005) conducted a content analysis of 16 psychology journals to assess the number of empirical articles on Latino, African American, Native American, and Asian minority groups. Furthermore, they included the same journals used in Graham's (1992) content analysis, which focused on the presence of African American participants in studies published from 1970 to 1989. Results of Imada and Schiavo's study indicated that of all the articles published in six APA journals (*Developmental Psychology, Journal of Educational Psychology, Journal of Clinical and Consulting Psychology, Journal of Personality and Social Psychology, Journal of Counseling Psychology, Journal of Applied Psychology*) from 1990 to 1999, only 4.7% studied ethnic minority populations where minorities were the focus of the study, or analyses were conducted by race in multiethnic samples that included Whites. Results also indicated that non-APA journals published a higher percentage of articles (8.7%) than did APA journals during the same time period. African Americans remain the most examined group in the psychological literature, followed by Hispanics, Asians, and Native Americans. Of all the APA journal articles that examined ethnic minority populations, the *Journal of Counseling Psychology* contributed the largest percentage of articles at 12.9%, followed by the *Journal of Consulting and Clinical Psychology* at 6.8%. The *Journal of Personality and Social Psychology* provided the lowest percentage of studies at 2.5%.

As Imada and Schiavo's (2005) results indicate, counseling psychology has made the greatest strides in increasing the representation of ethnic minorities in mainstream psychology research. Because the American Psychological Association is the largest professional psychological organization responsible for regulating accreditation for professional psychological programs, it is imperative that a greater number of empirical articles appear in its journals. The inclusion and acknowledgment of culture in psychology will become mainstream only when studies about ethnic minorities are published in mainstream psychological journals. Increasing diverse populations in psychological studies is a necessary first step in increasing the level of external validity of all psychological research.

Choosing Study Variables: Proximal Versus Distal Variables

One of the challenges in conducting multicultural research involves how individuals approach conducting research with diverse populations. In other words, do individuals thoughtfully conceptualize and plan research with specific ethnic, cultural, or racial variables in mind, or do they simply collect data with the hope of finding something interesting because they have a sample that includes ethnic minorities? This is a fundamental question of what constitutes multicultural research. The perspective taken in this chapter is that research should be considered multicultural only when it involves intentionality; that is, the researcher(s) approaches the research project with a specific population(s) in mind, with specific ethnic, racial, or cultural constructs in mind, and with specific types of research questions. Appropriate multicultural research questions include, but are not limited to, research questions that (a) address deficits in, or build upon, knowledge about a cultural group, or (b) challenge the relevance or appropriateness of existing psychological theories for a particular cultural group.

Multicultural research sometimes focuses on providing explanations for observed differences between ethnic groups, or on providing explanations for what is believed to be a cultural phenomenon. However, intentionality is often lacking from this research focus, making it questionable as being multicultural research. Nowhere is the importance of intentionality more obvious than in the concepts of distal and proximal variables. Literally defined, *distal* is away or farthest from

the point of origin, whereas *proximal* is defined as toward or closest to the point of origin. Distal variables include variables that are often referred to as demographic variables, such as race, ethnicity, sex, socioeconomic status, generation status, language, and age (see Table 31.1). When analyzing data sets, researchers usually run descriptive statistics on the demographic variables, and they often compare the scores of the variables of interest along demographic lines (e.g., Are there differences in variable X along race, sex, socioeconomic status, etc.?). Upon finding differences, researchers often attribute the differences to the demographic variables themselves. Here, the demographic variables are distal variables because they do not directly explain why the differences exist in the first place. For example, if Chinese Americans score higher on an anxiety scale than Mexican Americans, the researcher would attribute the difference to some vague notion of cultural differences simply because the ethnic groups involved are different. However, we are reminded by Phinney (1996) that ethnicity alone is insufficient to explain psychological phenomena. Simply put, Chinese Americans are not higher on anxiety simply because they identify themselves as Chinese Americans. A better question would seek to identify the specific cultural variables that might explain the difference in scores.

One sign that multicultural research has started to mature occurs when researchers begin to identify more proximal variables. Proximal variables are more psychological in nature and include variables such as

Table 31.1   Examples of Distal and Proximal Variables to Explain Group Differences

Distal Variables	Proximal Variables
Race	Racial Identity
Sex	Ethnic Identity
Ethnicity	Gender Identity
Gender	Acculturation
Income	Familial Roles
Education	Individualism/Collectivism
Occupation	Spirituality/Religiosity
Generational Status	Communication Styles
Major	Worldview
Religion	Power Distance

acculturation, ethnic or racial identity, spirituality, values, individualism, and collectivism (see Table 31.1). Proximal variables are closer to the phenomenon of interest than distal variables, and they explain the observed phenomenon more directly and parsimoniously. In the previous example, let's say that we included the variable loss of face. We may discover that Chinese American students disproportionately feel pressure to excel in school, and the concern of shaming their family is contributing to their depression. Therefore, it becomes obvious that the distal variable of ethnicity is inadequate to explain the higher anxiety, whereas the proximal variable of loss of face provides a more direct explanation for the difference. Checking the box Chinese American on the demographic form does not explain why they are higher in anxiety than Mexican Americans!

In addition to including proximal variables in research, multicultural researchers must properly operationally define the constructs used in their study. Operational definitions make it possible for research questions to be tested empirically. These definitions allow for researchers to specify how variables are to be measured during the course of the study (Kerlinger, 1973). Many cultural studies refer to variables such as race, ethnicity, and culture. Cokley and Awad (2008) review the many different conceptualizations of these terms offered in the literature, and clearly, there is little consensus in how these terms are defined in multicultural research. Therefore, it is especially important to operationally define terms in every study. Clear operationalization of variables is a criterion for all research studies and not an issue exclusive to multicultural research.

Choosing Study Measures

Once the variables and research design have been chosen for a study and operational definitions have been decided upon, the next step involves choosing instruments to effectively measure your study variables. Arguably, the most important qualities of an instrument are reliability and validity. According to classical test theory, there are three types of reliability: interjudge, retest, and internal consistency (Charter, 2003). The type of reliability discussed and used most commonly in psychological research is internal consistency reliability

(Charter, 2003; Cokley, 2007; Hogan, Benjamin, & Brezinksi, 2000; Thompson, 2003). Scores from psychological instruments must be considered minimally reliable before any conclusions can be made about study findings. Therefore, reliability is the first condition that must be met before one can assess the validity of a study.

Several scholars have recommended guidelines for minimally acceptable levels of internal consistency for psychological measures in psychology (Ponterotto & Ruckdeschel, 2007). Internal consistency reliability refers to intercorrelations among scale items where items with high intercorrelations are assumed to be measuring the same construct (DeVellis, 1991). Therefore, according to classical test theory, items should be highly correlated with one another. Cronbach's coefficient alpha is the most widely used measure of internal consistency. Typically, internal consistency estimates in psychological research studies range from .70, which is considered minimally acceptable, to .95, which is considered excellent or desirable (Charter & Feldt, 2000; Nunnally & Bernstein, 1994). Ponterotto and Ruckdeschel (2007) offered a more sophisticated matrix for estimating acceptable coefficient alpha levels that takes into consideration number of items on a scale and sample size. Generally, the matrix suggests that scales with fewer items given in studies with lower sample sizes may yield lower Cronbach's alpha levels that still may be considered acceptable, whereas scales with a greater number of items given to a large sample of participants should have more stringent standards given that reliability estimates tend to be inflated for scales with many items and those given to large samples.

Low internal consistency estimates are usually one of the first signs that a measure is not functioning properly with a particular sample. Low reliability estimates may arise for several reasons. In multicultural research, the most common reason for low levels of reliability is that a scale may be used on a cultural population for which it was not originally created and validated. Less than stellar reliability estimates in this case may be a reflection of a deeper validity issue where the construct under investigation may have a different meaning for the sample under consideration. Other reasons include not following adequate scale construction protocol, which includes an iterative item generation process, pilot testing, and rigorous sampling and validation procedures. Kerlinger (1973) presented his MAXMINCON principle for test development, which posits that variance of individuals should be *max*imized, error variance should be *min*imized, and extraneous variables should be *con*trolled. Not following adequate procedures can lead to the creation of scales with double-barreled, leading, and loaded questions (Nardi, 2003). According to DeVellis (1991), there are eight primary steps to scale development: (a) determine what you want to measure, (b) generate an item pool, (c) determine measurement format, (d) request review of the initial item pool by subject matter experts, (e) include validation items, (f) administer items to a development sample, (g) evaluate items, and (h) optimize scale length. Scale validation is also an additional, necessary step, especially for ethnic groups for which scales were not initially created (see DeVellis, 1991, or Lee & Lim, 2008, for a more in-depth discussion of scale construction).

Internal consistency is only one type of reliability that is assessed in psychological research. Other types of reliability, such as test-retest reliability, should also be evaluated. Furthermore, the presence of adequate reliability in a study does not mean that the measure is valid. Reliability is therefore a necessary but insufficient condition for validity. If a study includes measures that are not reliable, one cannot begin to assess validity because of the inconsistency and error involved in the measurement of the construct.

INTERPRETATION, CULTURE, AND VALIDITY

Validity in research typically refers to "truth." According to Cook and Campbell (1979), one can never know the truth in research but can only approximate it. Typically, when issues of validity are discussed in psychological research, internal and external validity are highlighted. In addition to external and internal validity, Cook and Campbell discuss two additional types of validity, statistical conclusion and construct validity. In this section, we will define each type of validity and the threats pertaining to each one. We will focus on the threats that are most pertinent to multicultural research (for an in-depth review of validity types and threats, see Cook & Campbell, 1979, or Heppner et al., 2008).

Statistical Conclusion Validity

Statistical conclusion validity refers to questions relating to covariation among variables. Therefore, this type of validity assesses whether or not the correct conclusion has been made regarding variable relationships. A researcher may ask, "Did I make the right decision with regard to whether or not the variables in my study are related to one another?" Multicultural research, for the most part, is not any more susceptible to statistical conclusion validity threats than other types of studies except for issues relating to sample size and power. In many studies, low statistical power may lead a researcher to commit a Type II error and incorrectly accept the null hypothesis (i.e., conclude that a relationship does not exist). This issue is exacerbated in multicultural research, where recruitment of certain ethnic minority populations is more difficult. Statistical power is partly dependent on sample size, and if an adequate number of ethnic minority participants is not achieved, then it is quite likely that a researcher will conclude incorrectly that a relationship among study variables does not exist.

In addition to issues of low power, unreliability of measures is also a possible threat to statistical conclusion validity. As discussed earlier, adequate reliability of measures is imperative in all research, but the use of measures that have been previously normed and constructed for middle-class White participants on ethnic minority communities presents additional issues in multicultural research. The use of such measures increases error variance and may mask significant relationships among variables in multicultural research. Therefore, one should try to use measures that have been created, validated, or adjusted for the population of interest. Another, related threat to statistical conclusion validity is the unreliability of treatment implementation. This issue may be salient in studies where treatment implementation is given in more than one language. Because direct translation of treatment protocol is not always possible, there may be slight differences in treatment execution that may lead to lack of standardization and result in increased error variability.

Internal Validity

As discussed earlier, internal validity has been the most emphasized validity in psychological research

(Sue, 1999). Internal validity refers to the extent that a researcher can conclude a causal relationship among variables. The most common way to increase internal validity in a study is to rule out plausible rival hypotheses. Informed by Campbell's (1968, 1969) discussion of threats to internal validity, Brislin, Lonner, and Thorndike (1973) suggest the plausible rival hypothesis approach to cross-cultural methodology, which refers to the idea that a researcher should always list all of the potential explanations for study results that may go beyond initial study hypotheses posited. Several threats to internal validity may be more salient for those conducting multicultural research. One threat that may be more likely to arise while carrying out multicultural research is local history. A history threat is characterized by an event that occurs between a pretest and a posttest in a study that is not part of the intervention. For example, suppose someone is conducting an intervention to increase health and mental health utilization among African Americans and European Americans. The intervention may include activities designed to increase trust in institutions as well as educational information pertaining to the benefits of seeking health treatment. As this study is well under way, Hurricane Katrina hits the Gulf Coast and participants of the study witness the slow response of the U.S. government to those in the affected regions. At the end of the 6-week intervention, researchers administer posttest questionnaires assessing future intentions to use health services and trust in institutions and find that both trust and intentions to use services decreased from the pretest for the African American group but not for the European American group. If the researchers infer that the intervention was not successful for African Americans and caused trust and health utilization intentions to decrease, then they would be overlooking the plausible rival hypothesis that the hurricane introduced a history threat. African Americans who were part of the intervention may have lost faith in U.S. institutional systems and also increased their level of suspicions about whether or not the U.S. government really cares about the welfare of African Americans. This example demonstrates a Selection × History effect where one group was disproportionately affected by the history effect.

Another possible threat that may occur in the previous example is attrition. Suppose that after witnessing the events of Hurricane Katrina, participants enrolled in the intervention designed to increase health utilization drop out because they perceive the researchers to be part of the system that caused the delayed response to Hurricane Katrina victims. As a result, posttest scores would not reflect the effects of the intervention because the original composition of participants was altered. Attrition may result in a more serious threat if the dropout is differential.

Individuals working with immigrant populations may have to be cognizant of maturation threats to internal validity that may be due to participants' level of acculturation. For example, suppose that there was a year-long intervention designed to increase reporting of sexual abuse among immigrant women. The intervention consisted of assertiveness training among other activities. At the beginning of the intervention, participants are given a pretest to assess the likelihood that they would report abuse in addition to other measures. Posttests given at the end of the intervention indicated an increase in the likelihood of the women in the intervention to report sexual abuse. The researchers concluded that the intervention was successful in building assertiveness for the group of immigrant women. An explanation that the researchers failed to acknowledge was the role that acculturation played in increasing the likelihood that the women would report abuse. Many immigrants are not aware of all of the laws or norms of the United States until they spend time in the country. The more exposure they have to social norms and societal laws in general, the more likely they will be aware of sexual abuse laws. Some immigrant women come from countries that may not offer the level of protection that is available in the United States, and therefore, they may not be aware that they have legal rights when it comes to sexual abuse. As length of residence in the United States increases, the level of acculturation increases. Another threat related to acculturation is testing. As immigrants whose first language is not English acculturate to the dominant culture, they increase their level of language proficiency. This issue may lead to gains from pretest to posttest in an intervention solely because of the acquisition of language skills over the course of time. With every administration of follow-up or posttest measures, their language skills increase and understanding of wording on intervention measures increases.

Arguably, one of the most common and harmful threats to internal validity is selection. This threat arises when random assignment of participants fails to occur. In field research studies, many times it is very difficult to randomly assign participants to a treatment or comparison group. Researchers often depend on self-selection as a recruitment strategy. Selection is a particularly problematic issue in multicultural research because researchers tend to compare groups based on ethnic or racial group membership. Obviously, ethnic or racial group membership cannot be assigned randomly. Furthermore, the use of the distal variables of race and ethnicity may mask more pertinent variables related to the outcome of interest. At times, researchers may make erroneous causal conclusions based solely on a participant's membership in a group.

External Validity

External validity refers to generalizability of a study across people, settings, and times (Cook & Campbell, 1979). Multicultural researchers have significantly contributed to the understanding and acknowledgment of the importance of external validity in psychological studies (Quintana et al., 2001; Sue, 1999). In psychological studies, external validity most often refers to generalization *across* populations as opposed to generalization *to* populations. It is rare to find that psychologists obtain a random sample of participants to generalize to a population of interest. In psychological studies, it is important that the population of interest is clearly identified. Researchers must specify the population to which they wish to generalize before the study is executed. Although some scholars contend that one must have a representative sample to make general conclusions about psychological phenomena, it may be inappropriate to combine individuals from ethnic groups if the constructs are culturally laden. To do so may obscure important cultural differences between groups.

Construct Validity

Construct validity refers to the extent to which study variables (i.e., independent and dependent variables) accurately represent the constructs that they claim to measure (Cokley & Awad, 2008; Heppner

et al., 2008). Related to external validity in multicultural research, construct validity assesses whether or not psychological constructs are generalizable across cultural groups. Because most instruments in psychology have been developed and normed on White middle-class participants, issues of construct validity are especially crucial to multicultural research. Issues of construct equivalence are prevalent in work that involves ethnic minority populations. For example, the concept of self-esteem is foreign to certain collectivist cultures, where the idea of the self extends beyond the individual. Defining a construct in one way that neglects other possible definitions is an example of a mono-operation threat and inadequate preoperational explication of study constructs (Cook & Campbell, 1979).

An instrument is considered biased if accuracy levels differ for minority and majority groups or if they measure different traits for each group (Reynolds, 1982). One tool that can be used to determine if the underlying factor structure of an instrument is similar for majority and minority groups is factor analysis (Reynolds, 1982; Tabachnick & Fidell, 2001). If the factor structure differs between the groups, then one can conclude that there may be an issue with construct validity. Other methods in addition to factor analysis should be used to determine construct validity. Furthermore, measurement invariance across groups is not sufficient evidence of construct equivalence (Byrne & Watkins, 2003). Because of construct underrepresentativeness (Shadish, Cook, & Campbell, 2002), a measure may not address all of the pertinent aspects of a construct across different cultural groups. Therefore, it is imperative that researchers examine measures carefully before disseminating them to ethnic groups.

As Cokley and Awad (2008) point out, there are some strategies that researchers can use to conduct more culturally competent studies. The first strategy reviewed is the use of mixed methodology. The cardinal rule of research studies is that a method should be informed first and foremost by the research question. If researchers abided by this rule, there might be less of a debate between quantitative and qualitative researchers. Mixed methods employ both quantitative and qualitative approaches in the same study with the intent of adequately answering the research question (Plano Clark & Wang, this volume). Qualitative approaches are especially appropriate for exploring new areas in psychology where very little information is available, whereas quantitative approaches allow for greater generalizability. Mixed methods also allow researchers to clarify findings that may be perplexing. For example, if an instrument was originally normed and validated on a White middle-class sample and used with an ethnic minority group, including qualitative questions pertaining to the meaning of the questionnaire may help elucidate how the measure differs for both groups.

Another strategy outlined is the use of pilot testing. A thorough pilot test will help circumvent some of the issues that may arise during the main study implementation. This is especially important for research with cultural groups that are understudied. In addition, pilot testing may allow researchers to understand how constructs may differ between groups by examining participants' understanding of instruments used in research. In addition to pilot testing, researchers should involve members of the ethnic group that they are examining in the conceptualization, implementation, and interpretation of a study.

As multicultural research becomes more integrated into mainstream psychological research, there will not be a need for chapters such as these. A paradigm shift needs to occur in psychology where culture is acknowledged as an integral element in everyday human interactions. If the role of culture was recognized as an important determinant of human behavior, then excluding issues related to culture would be considered bad science. All psychological research should adhere to validity standards to ensure that valid conclusions are achieved. Neglecting the role of culture in psychology not only ignores issues pertinent to ethnic minority groups but also contributes to the myopic view that all psychological theories are universal. The infusion of culture in mainstream psychology will only continue to strengthen the discipline as a whole and increase overall understanding of human behavior.

REFERENCES

Aron, A., Aron, E., & Coups, E. (2006). *Statistics for psychology* (4th ed.). Upper Saddle River, NJ: Prentice Hall.

Azibo, D. A. (1988). Understanding the proper and improper usage of the comparative research framework. *Journal of Black Psychology, 15,* 81–91.

Baldwin, J. A., & Bell, Y. R. (1985). The African Self-Consciousness Scale: An Africentric personality questionnaire. *Western Journal of Black Studies, 9,* 61–68.

Boykin, A. W., Franklin, A. J., & Yates, J. F. (Eds.). (1979). *Research directions in Black psychology.* New York: Russell Sage Foundation.

Brislin, R. W., Lonner, W. J., & Thorndike, R. M. (1973). *Cross-cultural research methods.* New York: Wiley.

Byrne, B. M., & Watkins, D. (2003). The issue of measurement invariance revisited. *Journal of Cross Cultural Psychology, 34,* 155–175.

Campbell, D. T. (1968). A cooperative multinational opinion sample exchange. *Journal of Social Issues, 24,* 245–258.

Campbell, D. T. (1969). Perspective artifact and control. In R. Rosenthal and R. Rosnow (Eds.) *Artifact in behavioral research* (pp.351–382). New York: Academic Press.

Charter, R. A. (2003). A breakdown of reliability coefficients by test type and reliability method, and the clinical implications of low reliability. *Journal of General Psychology, 130,* 290–304.

Charter, R. A., & Feldt, L. S. (2000). The relationship between two methods of evaluating an examinee's difference scores. *Journal of Psychoeducational Assessment, 18,* 125–142.

Cokley, K. O. (2007). Critical issues in the measurement of ethnic and racial identity: A referendum on the state of the field. *Journal of Counseling Psychology, 54*(3), 224–234.

Cokley, K. O., & Awad, G. H. (2008). Conceptual and methodological issues in multicultural research. In P. P. Heppner, D. M. Kivlighan, & B. E. Wampold, (Eds.), *Research design in counseling* (3rd ed., pp. 365–384). Belmont, CA: Wadsworth.

Cook, T. D., & Campbell, D. T. (1979). *Quasi-experimentation: Design and analysis issues for field settings.* Boston: Houghton Mifflin.

Cozby, P. C. (1997). *Methods in behavioral research* (6th ed.). Mountain View, CA: Mayfield.

DeVellis, R. F. (1991). *Scale development: Theory and applications.* Newbury Park, CA: Sage.

Dixon, V. (1976). Worldview and research methodology. In L. King, V. Dixon, & W. Nobles (Eds.), *African philosophy: Assumptions and paradigms for research on Black persons* (pp. 51–93). Los Angeles: Fanon Center.

Drew, C. F. (1980). *Introduction to designing and conducting research* (2nd ed.). St. Louis, MO: C. V. Mosby.

Gould, S. J. (1996). *The mismeasure of man* (2nd ed.) New York: Norton.

Graham, S. (1992). Most of the subjects were White and middle class: Trends in published research on African Americans in selected APA journals, 1970–1989. *American Psychologist, 47,* 629–639.

Heppner, P. P., Wampold, B. E., & Kivlighan, D. M. (2008). *Research design in counseling* (3rd ed.). Belmont, CA: Wadsworth.

Hogan, T. P., Benjamin, A., & Brezinski, K. L. (2000). Reliability methods: A note on the frequency and use of various types. *Educational and Psychological Measurement, 60,* 523–531.

Imada, T., & Schiavo, R. S. (2005). The use of ethnic minority populations in published psychological research, 1990–1999. *Journal of Psychology, 139,* 389–400.

Ivey, A. E. (1977). Cultural expertise: Toward systematic outcome criteria in counseling and psychological education. *Personnel and Guidance Journal, 55,* 296–302.

Kazdin, A. E. (1980). *Research design in clinical psychology.* New York: Harper & Row.

Kerlinger, F. N. (1973). *Foundations of behavioral research* (2nd ed.). New York: Holt, Rinehart & Winston.

Khatib, S., & Nobles, W. (1977). Historical foundation of African psychology and their philosophical consequences. *Journal of Black Psychology, 4,* 91–101.

Lee, D., & Lim, H. (2008). Scale construction. In P. P. Heppner, D. M. Kivlighan, & B. E. Wampold (Eds.), *Research design in counseling* (3rd ed., pp. 494–510). Belmont, CA: Wadsworth.

Locke, D. (1990). A not so provincial view of multicultural counseling. *Counselor Education and Supervision, 30,* 18–25.

Mill, J. S. (1872). A *system of logic, ratiocinative and inductive: Being a connected view of the principles of evidence, and the methods of scientific investigation* (8th ed.). London: Longmans, Green.

Nardi, P. M. (2003). *Doing survey research: A guide to quantitative methods.* Boston: Allyn & Bacon.

Nunnally, J. C., & Bernstein, I. H. (1994). *Psychometric theory* (3rd ed.). New York: McGraw-Hill.

Phinney, J. (1996). When we talk about American ethnic groups, what do we mean? *American Psychologist, 51,* 918–927.

Plutchik, R. (1968). *Foundations of experimental research.* New York: Harper & Row.

Ponterotto, J. G., & Ruckdeschel, D. E. (2007). An overview of coefficient alpha and a reliability matrix for estimating adequacy of internal consistency coefficients with psychological research measures. *Perceptual and Motor Skills, 105,* 997–1014.

Quintana, S. M., Troyano, N., & Taylor, G. (2001). Cultural validity and inherent challenges in quantitative methods for multicultural research. In J. G. Ponterotto, J. M. Casas, L. A. Suzuki, & C. A. Alexander (Eds.), *Handbook of multicultural counseling* (pp. 604–630). Thousand Oaks, CA: Sage.

Reynolds, C. R. (1982). The problem of bias in psychological assessment. In C. R. Reynolds & T. B. Gutkin (Eds.), *The handbook of school psychology* (pp. 178–208). New York: Wiley.

Shadish, W. R., Cook, T. D., & Campbell, D. T. (2002). *Experimental and quasi-experimental designs for generalized causal inference.* Boston: Houghton Mifflin.

Sue, S. (1999). Science, ethnicity, and bias: Where have we gone wrong? *American Psychologist, 54,* 1070–1077.

Tabachnick, B. G., & Fidell, L. S. (2001). *Using multivariate statistics* (4th ed.). Boston: Allyn & Bacon.

Thompson, B. (2003). *Score reliability: Contemporary thinking on reliability issues.* Thousand Oaks, CA: Sage.

Wright, B. J., & Isenstein, V. (1978). *Psychological tests and minorities* (DHEW Publication No. ADM. 78–482). Washington, DC: Government Printing Office.

32

Language, Translation, and Validity in the Adaptation of Psychological Tests for Multicultural Counseling

KWONG-LIEM KARL KWAN, YOUNNJUNG GONG, AND MICHAEL MAESTAS

Cross-cultural application of psychological tests has been of research interest to psychologists working with populations in other countries as well as cultural groups different from the normative sample within the same country where the tests were developed. Most studies in the counseling and psychology literature involved the translation (i.e., items were literally translated into a different language version) or adaptation (i.e., some item wording or content of the original version was modified) (van de Vijver & Leung, 1997) of psychological tests developed in the United States for populations outside the United States (e.g., John Holland's Self-Directed Search) (Reardon & Lenz, 1998). For example, between 2000 and 2005, among the 15 studies published in major journals related to counseling psychology that involved translation of instruments, Ægisdóttir, Gerstein, and Çinarbas (2008)

found that all the instruments were translated from English-language measures based in the United States. Many studies also examined the validity of a translated version of the original instrument for populations that are different from the normative sample within the same country (e.g., the Spanish version of the Beck Depression Inventory-II for Mexican American medical patients) (Beck, Steer, & Brown, 1996; Penley, Wiebe, & Nwosu, 2003). Some translated tests have been adapted for clinical application using norms established with samples in various countries (e.g., international adaptation of the Minnesota Multiphasic Personality Inventory [MMPI]-2) (Butcher, 1996), whereas other translated tests derived specific norms from various racial and ethnic samples in the country where the test was developed (e.g., adaptation of the Cultural Adjustment Difficulties Checklist for Central and South American immigrants in the United States) (Sodowsky & Lai, 1997; Torres & Rollock, 2004).

Translation accuracy and precision of both the language and concepts of the original instruments are the most critical and fundamental building blocks when adapting an assessment instrument for cross-cultural use. The ultimate goal of translation, however, is to establish cross-cultural validity, which refers to an evaluation of whether inferences drawn from test scores for the test's normative sample carry the same meaning or serve the same function for a culturally different sample (Kwan & Maestas, 2008; Messick, 1989). In addition to language issues, the cross-cultural validity of a psychological test can be affected by systematic differences in item endorsement by people from different countries or cultures. In other words, even though the language of the translated items best captures items in the original version, item content may elicit reactions or perceptions that result in differential responses by people from different cultures. Item desirability, item familiarity, and perceived shamefulness of certain responses on the MMPI-2, for example, have been discussed as some of the cultural factors that account for differences in score distributions by national and ethnic groups (Butcher, 1996; Cheung, 1985; Cheung, Song, & Zhang, 1996; Gong & Kwan, 2001; Sue, Keefe, Enomoto, Durvasula, & Chao, 1996).

Establishing cross-cultural validity of an adapted test is more than an issue of language and translation. To minimize threats to cultural validity, it also entails a critical evaluation of the cultural relevance of item content and concepts, as well as an "insider's" astuteness to discern and identify cultural nuances that may affect item endorsement and score patterns of the linguistically different group. Competence in cross-cultural application of psychological tests is an ethical mandate (American Psychological Association, 2002). The ethical concern is particularly salient when test scores form the basis of diagnosis (e.g., personality disorder), classification (e.g., intelligence level), placement (e.g., gifted or remedial classes), or other clinical and evaluative decisions. At the group level, failure to establish cross-cultural validity may result in incorrectly labeling and stereotyping an entire national or cultural group, which is a form of cultural discrimination (APA Ethical Standards, 3.01). For bilingual people within a country, such as the many immigrants in the United States, whether the original English version or the translated version should be used in clinical settings remains an empirical question.

In this chapter, we seek to address cross-cultural application of psychological tests from both a scientist and a practitioner perspective. In the first section, we review the test property issue of equivalence. In the second section, we focus on the test taker characteristics of item desirability, acculturation, and test familiarity. Throughout the chapter, we emphasize the thesis that cultural adaptation of psychological tests is more than a language translation issue. For cultural validity to be established, it is critical to understand the culture of the people and identify cultural orientations (e.g., response style) that influence item endorsement and contribute to test scores, especially scores that deviate significantly from the norms derived from the source sample. Few empirical studies on the evaluation of cross-cultural applicability of clinical tests, however, have been reported in the counseling literature. In this chapter, we report an empirical study that explored the relationships among cultural orientations (response frequency, perceived desirability, and perceived shamefulness of item endorsement); defensiveness; and endorsement of MMPI-2 items with a sample of Korean international students in the United States. We conclude by applying knowledge in the conceptual and empirical literature reviewed in this chapter to approach a clinical scenario.

TEST CHARACTERISTICS: CULTURAL VALIDITY, EQUIVALENCE, AND TEST BIAS

Scholars in cross-cultural, social, and personality psychology have written extensively on the concept of test equivalence (Brislin, 1986; van de Vijver, 2001; van de Vijver & Leung, 1997) that has significant implications for research and practice in multicultural counseling and assessment (Ægisdóttir et al., 2008; Butcher, 1996). Equivalence refers to the reliability of scores between the original and translated versions of an assessment instrument. Four types of equivalence have been postulated to guide and evaluate cultural adaptation of psychological tests: linguistic equivalence, conceptual equivalence, functional equivalence, and metric equivalence. Messick

(1989) has contended that validity—an overall evaluative judgment of the degree to which empirical evidence and theoretical rationales support the adequacy and appropriateness of interpretations and actions on the basis of test scores—subsumes all test properties (e.g., reliability, stability). Messick (1995) has reiterated that validity is not a property of the test or assessment instrument, but the meaning of the test scores, which is a function not only of the test items, but also of the *people responding and the contexts of assessment* (italics added; p. 741). What needs to be valid is not the test score, but the meaning or interpretation of the score, and any action consequences that the meaning entails (Messick, 1995).

Equivalence, in essence, is an issue of cultural validity, and an empirical question of "the extent to which score meaning and action implications hold across persons or population groups and across settings or contexts" (Messick, 1995, p. 741). If a score (range) indicates a certain diagnosis (e.g., mild retardation), equivalence or cultural validity assesses whether the same inference or interpretation can be derived from the same score (range) when a test is translated or adapted and administered to a culturally different sample. Equivalence and validity are often discussed in terms of test scores and test properties. Yet Messick (1989, 1995) has stressed the importance of reorienting the focus from sheer psychometric issues (e.g., reliability coefficient, replication of factor structure) to consequences on people (e.g., labeling, diagnosis) when considering the issue of validity. Equivalence and cultural validity are people characteristics as described or interpreted by the test score—validity describes the people a test purports to assess, and equivalence further delineates the cultures of the people a test seeks to compare. Test validity is subjected to threats when a construct is inadequately operationalized, when test items are inadequately developed, and when respondents are inadequately sampled. Similarly, test equivalence can be hampered by biases when a construct is inaccurately assumed to be cross-culturally relevant, when items are poorly translated or adapted, and when systematic cultural factors that moderate item responses remain unidentified. Test biases are nuisance factors that reduce the function of a translated or adapted psychological test to validly compare cultural groups (van de Vijver & Leung, 1997). The four types of equivalence and the respective biases will be discussed in the following sections.

Linguistic Equivalence. Linguistic equivalence assesses whether the wording of the translated or adapted test accurately captures the item content of the original version and in a language that the target group understands. Establishing linguistic equivalence entails close agreement between the language versions of a given test, which is a function of the integrity of the translation methodology. The translation-and-back-translation strategy has often been used to establish linguistic equivalence (Brislin, Lonner, & Thorndike, 1973). In brief, the original-language version of a test is first translated by one or a committee of bilingual people into the target-language version, which is then translated back to the original-language version by another independent team of bilingual people. The two versions (i.e., original-language version and translated version in the original version's language) are then compared toward further refinement to enhance and establish equivalence. Beyond language and translation, it is also necessary to determine if item content of the original version needs to be modified or changed (i.e., test adaptation). Item unfamiliarity is one of the factors for test bias. If respondents in the target cultural group are not familiar with the item content in the original version, the best translation cannot reduce the test bias caused by the lack of understanding. For example, when the MMPI was adapted in Chinese societies, the test item "I like 'Alice in Wonderland' by Lewis Carroll" was replaced by the item "I like to read 'Journey to the West, a Story of the Adventures of the Monkey King,'" which is a popular folk story in Chinese societies that presumably served the same function as the item in the English MMPI. Although both items were eventually eliminated in the (Chinese) MMPI-2, the adaptation was necessary to control for random responding due to unfamiliarity with item content. Best practices in establishing linguistic equivalence, therefore, necessitate the formation of a bilingual team instead of relying on a single person, and identification of translators who are knowledgeable in languages, the target culture, and assessment in psychology (Hambleton & de Jong, 2003; van de Vijver & Hambleton, 1996).

Conceptual Equivalence. Conceptual equivalence assesses whether psychological concepts have similar meanings; definitions; and (behavioral, attitudinal, and emotional) manifestations across cultures. A fundamental issue addressed by conceptual equivalence is whether a psychological concept or construct even exists in different cultures, and it tries to determine how etic or emic the constructs are across cultures. Etic assumes universality of a construct (i.e., a construct exists across cultures), whereas emic refers to locality of a construct (i.e., a construct is indigenous to a given culture). Determining the conceptual equivalence of a psychological test cannot be separated from examining the etic/emic nature of the construct it purports to assess. Emic constructs are conceptually nonequivalent across cultures. The fourth edition, text revision of the *Diagnostic and Statistical Manual of Mental Disorders* (*DSM-IV-TR*) (American Psychiatric Association, 2000), for example, identified a number of culture-bound syndromes, which connotes mental illnesses purported to be indigenous and specific to particular cultures. A construct becomes an imposed etic or pseudo-etic when it is erroneously assumed to be culturally equivalent (Dana, 1993); that is, a construct as assessed through items on a test is treated as universally applicable and cross-culturally relevant when it is not.

Even when a construct exists in a different culture, researchers also need to determine if there are common and culturally specific ways in which an etic construct is understood, operationalized, and manifested. For example, the etic construct of eating connotes different behavioral and experiential meanings for people who eat through oral feeding (e.g., a healthy group) and people who can eat only through intravenous feeding (e.g., a patient group). If a test of eating pleasure developed in the healthy group's practice language (e.g., food texture, taste) is administered to the patient group, the construct of eating pleasure is not conceptually equivalent and the items cannot be applied to the patient group. Despite the best of translation and subsequent statistical manipulation, we echo Ægisdóttir et al.'s (2008) comment that "it is not until the equivalence of the concepts under study have been determined that a meaningful cross-cultural comparison can be made" (p. 194).

Given its critical role in reducing test bias, the issue of conceptual equivalence will be elaborated further by *taijin kyofusho,* a psychological disorder in Japan characterized by persistent social avoidance due to an intense fear that the appearance, movements, or functions of one's body would be offensive to other people. The fear and avoidance is accompanied by subjective distress and physiological symptoms such as blushing, copious sweating, and rigid facial expression. Several subtypes of *taijin kyofusho* have also been delineated: *sekimen-kyofu,* the phobia of blushing; *shubo-kyofu,* the phobia of a deformed body; *jikoshisen-kyofu,* the phobia of eye-to-eye contact; and *jikoshu-kyofu,* the phobia of having foul body odor. As a formal diagnosis in the Japanese diagnostic system, *taijin kyofusho* spells out the emotional, behavioral, and physiological symptoms of a psychological disorder that are similar to the social phobia diagnosis in the U.S.-based *DSM-IV.* *Taijin kyofusho,* or social phobia, regardless of the language label, has some degree of conceptual equivalence as the construct (regardless of the language label) conveys similar conceptual meaning and diagnostic function in Japan and the United States. At the same time, there are also variations in how the construct is operationalized and symptoms are manifested. The key differentiating feature between the Japanese and *DSM-IV*'s conceptualization of social phobia is the attribution for social avoidance—Japanese patients attribute their fear and social avoidance to the perceived negative impact of their presence and their body parts, whereas American patients attribute their fear and social avoidance to the perceived threat of the environment or situation.

Although it is recognized as a formal diagnosis in Japan, *taijin kyofusho* is relegated as a culture-bound syndrome by the *DSM-IV.* Suzuki, Takei, Kawai, Minabe, and Mori (2003), however, have questioned the locality or folk status of *taijin kyofusho* as designated by the *DSM-IV.* Suzuki et al. argued that with the exception of a subtype of *taijin kyofusho* (*jikoshisen-kyofu,* or phobia of eye-to-eye contact), the majority of diagnostic criteria are congruent with symptoms of social phobia as commonly conceived. In the context of maintaining harmony with the social collective, attributing one's social anxiety to one's inadequacy instead of projecting perceived or actual threat to other people is a socially apt mechanism of symptom expression. In addition, channeling psychological distress through physical symptoms is not unique to the Japanese culture. In fact, the *DSM-IV* acknowledged the dualistic (i.e., mental and physical) sources of psychological disorders—there is much "physical" in "mental" disorders and much "mental" in "physical" disorders, and the term *mental* persists in the title of *DSM-IV-TR* because an appropriate substitute has not been found (American Psychiatric Association, 2000, p. xxx). In the case of *taijin kyofusho,* the collectivistic-individualistic basis of attribution and the mental-physical basis of symptom expression are implicit cultural orientations that designate the same construct as a formal diagnosis in one culture and emic or indigenous in another. When determining conceptual equivalence, it is important to discern that the criteria used to determine the emic-etic distinction are configured within the cultural orientations of cross-cultural scholars.

Functional Equivalence. Whereas conceptual equivalence evaluates whether there are cultural variations in the behaviors or attitudes that define a given construct, functional equivalence assesses if behaviors serve similar functions in different cultures. In other words, if a psychological test includes certain behavioral, attitudinal, or affective items to define and assess a given construct in one culture (e.g., maintaining eye contact indicates assertiveness), functional equivalence questions whether the same behavior, attitude, or affect has alternative meanings in another culture (e.g., maintaining eye contact indicates disrespect). Despite the best translation, test bias occurs if construct variations as reflected in the test items are not identified in the cross-cultural adaptation of psychological tests. In the case of *taijin kyofusho,* items about the attribution of social avoidance to body parts or body odor that are perceived to be offensive are probably not as appropriate and culturally relevant to assess social phobia in the United States. On the other hand, when a U.S.-based social phobia measure is adapted in Japan, these somatic and self-attribution items will need to be added to enhance its diagnostic function. Consider the Liebowitz Social Anxiety Scale (LSAS; http://www.socialanxiety support.com/disorder/liebowitz) which assesses respondents' level of fear and avoidance associated with a range of social interaction (e.g., "Resisting a high pressure sales person," "Eating in public") and performance (e.g., "Acting, performing, or speaking in front of an audience," "Working while being observed") situations in the United States. Whereas the items "Expressing disagreement or disapproval to someone you don't know

very well," "Looking someone who you don't know very well straight in the eyes," and "Being the center of attention" are appropriate behavioral indicators of social phobia in the United States, endorsement of these items in the pathology (i.e., fear and avoidance) direction may indicate deference, respect, and modesty as expected in Japan and other collectivistic societies. We emphasize that evaluation of functional equivalence *at the item level,* therefore, is important to reduce test bias in the cross-cultural adaptation of psychological tests.

Metric Equivalence. Metric equivalence compares and examines the psychometric and statistical properties (e.g., factor structure, scales and subscales, score distributions) of a psychological test administered to various cultural groups in the same language (e.g., comparing different racial groups in a society, such as the English MMPI-2 between Asian American and White American college students) (Sue et al., 1996) or in multiple language versions (e.g., comparing different national groups, such as examining Chinese MMPI-2 performance using the Chinese version of MMPI-2) (Cheung et al., 1996). In particular, metric equivalence determines whether the same score within the same scales or subscales could connote different meanings or indicate different levels of the construct as assessed by the measure. When establishing metric equivalence, it is assumed that similarities in or replications of measurement characteristics indicate that the understanding of test items and the meaning associated with the same response (e.g., a rating of 2 or 5 on a continuous five-point Likert scale) is consistent across culturally different respondents. In the most ideal case, congruence in full score comparability (i.e., scores yield the same distributions and connote the same meaning between the cultural groups) provides the strongest evidence of equivalence between two versions of a translated or adapted test (van de Vijver, 2001; van de Vijver & Leung, 1987). In reality, cultural groups often yield different normative metrics on the same scale; consequently, different criteria (e.g., cutoff score for diagnostic decision) need to be determined to enhance descriptive or diagnostic precision of scale scores. For example, despite establishing translation equivalence of the original and Chinese versions of MMPI/MMPI-2, Cheung et al. (1996) noted that significant elevations were found among Chinese normal subjects and psychiatric patients in mainland China, particularly on F Scale (Infrequency), Scale 2 (Depression), and Scale 8 (Schizophrenia). Although elevations on these scales indicate similar diagnosis between Chinese and U.S. psychiatric patients, normal Chinese also produced significantly higher scores on these scales that would be considered pathological if the U.S. norms were applied. To control for potential overpathologizing bias, the Chinese Infrequency Scale was empirically derived and a different set of cutoff scores was recommended for clinical use (Cheung, Song, & Butcher, 1991).

In sum, when applying a psychological test to a different cultural or national group, researchers need to evaluate test equivalence at multiple levels: Is the translation accurate? Does the construct assessed by the original test exist in the target culture? Are there cultural variations in how a construct (as assessed by test items) is defined or manifested? Is there item content that needs to be modified? Are there items that need to be deleted or added? Do scale scores on different versions of a test serve uniform functions or connote similar meanings?

TEST TAKER CHARACTERISTICS: ITEM DESIRABILITY, ACCULTURATION, AND PERCEIVED SHAMEFULNESS

Test adaptation serves the ultimate goal to determine if and to what extent different language versions of a psychological test can be applied to people in a different culture. Along with test properties, it is perhaps more important to examine the influence of the culture of the target population on test performance. Specifically, it is necessary to discern subtle mental set and cultural orientation that people apply when responding to test items that may account for scale score differences between cultural groups. As previously reviewed, even when linguistic equivalence was sufficiently established and when similar factor or scale structures were extracted for translated or adapted measures, scale score differences are still often observed between cultural groups on many psychological tests (e.g., MMPI-2). A number of moderators have been conceptually postulated and empirically shown to account for score differences among cultural groups: item desirability, item familiarity, and level of acculturation. In the following section, the role these moderators play in the cultural application of

psychological tests will be reviewed using research in MMPI-2 as an illustration. We will report an empirical study (Gong & Kwan, 2001) (first presented at APA, but published in this chapter for the first time) examining the relationship between defensiveness and scoring of items in the pathological directions by Koreans in the United States who were administered the English MMPI-2.

Item Desirability. The perceived desirability of item content as well as certain responses to item content have been found to moderate item endorsement that accounted for differential response patterns among cultural groups. In particular, items with psychopathology and related content may be perceived as less desirable, which may inhibit people from endorsing the item in the scored direction. In an earlier cross-cultural study, Cheung (1985) found differences in the perceived desirability of endorsing "True" responses to MMPI items between college students in Hong Kong and the United States. Using a 9-point Likert scale (1 = *very undesirable* and 9 = *very desirable*), at least a one-point difference was found between the two samples. Eight items showed at least a 50% endorsement difference between the two samples, and the perceived desirability of 24 (40%) items on the Depression (D) scale and 26 (33%) items on the Schizophrenia (Sc) scale were found to be discrepant. Cheung delineated several categories according to the item content of scales D and Sc: social behavioral and interpersonal relationship, attitude of nonchalance, acceptance of low arousal and low activity level, modesty as a virtue, and admitting of their problems. Eight items showed at least a 50% endorsement difference between the Chinese and U.S. samples; it was also found that the mean desirability ratings between the two samples were significantly different by more than one rating point on the 9-point Likert scale. These results indicate that the meaning of the same response (i.e., True or False) to items may reflect respondents' perception of the item's desirability instead of their true response to item content. As such, item desirability constitutes a subtle source of measurement error.

Level of Acculturation. Level of acculturation has been found empirically (Sue et al., 1996) to moderate Asian Americans' MMPI-2 responses. Using Asian American and White American college samples, Sue et al.

reported that low-acculturated Asian American students produced the most elevated scores on most MMPI-2 scales, followed by that of high-acculturated Asian American students, whose scale scores were significantly higher than those of White American students. Group differences of scale scores were found to be statistically significant for the Infrequency (F), Hypochondriasis (Hs), Depression (D), Psychopathic Deviate (Pd), Paranoia (Pa), Psychasthenia (Pt), Schizophrenia (Sc), and Social Introversion (Si) scales. Results indicated the moderating effect of acculturation on MMPI-2 scale elevations. Although the elevated scores produced by Asian Americans with lower levels of acculturation may suggest stress associated with cultural adjustment, it is more difficult to interpret the elevated scores produced by the high-acculturated Asian American group. The stress correlates of low-acculturated Asian Americans' elevated MMPI-2 profiles, however, remain an empirical question.

Item Familiarity, Shamefulness, and Symptom Tolerance. Item familiarity assessed to what extent the characteristic assessed by test items was perceived to be familiar to the participant's cultural group. Shamefulness assessed how shameful it would be for a person from his or her cultural group to endorse items in the pathology direction. Symptom tolerance assessed how upsetting it would be for a person from his or her cultural group to endorse each item. Okazaki (1995) investigated the moderating effects of item familiarity, perceived shamefulness of item content, and symptom tolerance on Asian Americans' MMPI-2 item endorsement patterns. Okazaki hypothesized that cultural differences between Asian and Caucasian Americans exist to the extent to which people perceive item content to be familiar, shameful, and upsetting, and that such differences contribute to response discrepancy. Results showed that Asian Americans perceived the item content of MMPI-2 to be less familiar, more shameful, and more upsetting than did their White American counterparts. The relationships of perceived familiarity, shamefulness, and item tolerance with MMPI-2 item endorsement were different across the three cultural dimensions. Compared to those of White Americans, Asian Americans produced weaker associations of MMPI-2 item endorsement both with shamefulness

and item tolerance. The correlations of item familiarity and MMPI-2 item endorsement were not significantly different between Asian and White Americans. Okazaki (1995) suggested that the relationship between the perceived cultural dimensions of items and the actual endorsement might not be as direct.

To further explore and illustrate the role of cultural orientations in the cross-cultural application of the MMPI-2, Gong and Kwan (2001) examined defensiveness, item desirability, and perceived shamefulness associated with responses to MMPI-2 items that were previously found to have significant endorsement discrepancy between Korean and U.S. samples.

EFFECTS OF CULTURAL ORIENTATIONS ON MMPI-2 ITEM ENDORSEMENT OF KOREANS IN THE UNITED STATES

Using a translated version of the MMPI-2 in Korea, Han (1996) found significantly different scale score distributions between the Korean and U.S. normative samples. Similar to other Asian MMPI studies (Butcher, 1996; Butcher & Pancheri, 1976), Koreans produced significantly elevated mean scale scores on all MMPI-2 basic scales when compared with those of U.S. normative samples, with the exception of the Lie (L) and Defensiveness (K) scales. In subsequent item analyses, 98 "extreme items" that showed a 25% or more endorsement difference between the Korean and U.S. normative samples were identified. Extreme items were distributed across all basic scales with a range from 7% (scales L and F) to 30% (scale D) of the total number of items in the respective scales. Several categories were derived upon examination of these items' content: (a) interpersonal and social attitudes, (b) depressive affect, (c) obsessiveness-compulsiveness, (d) rare sensory experience, and (e) health concern-somatization. Han suggested that unique cultural aspects in Korean society were related to such response discrepancies.

To investigate whether cultural orientations and defensiveness affect item perception and endorsement, Gong and Kwan (2001) asked Korean international students in the United States to rate the response frequency, desirability, and perceived shamefulness of these MMPI-2 "extreme items" (Han, 1996). Specifically, each extreme item was presented with a response (i.e., either True or False) in the scored direction (i.e., the response was indicative of symptoms and contributed to scale elevation). Three identical sets of extreme items were presented to assess participants' perceptions of response frequency, item desirability, and perceived shamefulness associated with endorsing items in the scored direction. The questions used to assess response frequency, item desirability, and perceived shamefulness were as follows: "How frequently would Koreans give this response?" "How desirable would it be for Koreans to give this response?" and "How shameful would it be for Koreans to give this response?" To control for random responding due to lack of language proficiency, participants were allowed to use an English-Korean dictionary and were encouraged to ask the researcher (Gong) for item explanations. In addition, to standardize clarifications of MMPI-2 items that Korean students might not understand, Korean translations of 32 words that Gong considered difficult were provided on a separate sheet. Fifty-seven Korean international students rated extreme items using a 9-point Likert scale (1 = *very infrequent/very undesirable/not shameful at all* and 9 = *very frequent/very desirable/very shameful*). The standardized reliability coefficients (α) of measures of response frequency, item desirability, and perceived shamefulness for the sample were .86, .90, and .95, respectively. Given the amount of time and the potential fatigue associated with responding to a large number of MMPI-2 items and rating the same set of extreme items three times, only extreme items that constituted the basic scales (i.e., 67 out of 98 extreme items) were used.

Participants' defensiveness was assessed using the Superlative Scale (scale S, Butcher & Han, 1995), which is selected from among a number of defensiveness measures for both conceptual and empirical reasons. Conceptually, S scale was developed to assess attempts to proclaim overly positive self-presentation that would not be detected by conscious distortion as measured by the L (i.e., Lie) scale. Unlike other defensiveness measures (e.g., the K, or Correction, scale) that were derived from clinical samples, the S scale was developed with normal samples (i.e., pilot applicants or those being screened in personnel settings), which is more appropriate for the nonclinical sample in this study. Empirically, the S scale has been found to be more sensitive than other scales to detect dissimulation (Nichols & Greene, 1997;

Nicholson et al., 1997). In cross-cultural assessment, Sue et al. (1996, p. 209) also recommended that the S scale be used because the K scale may not be as effective for controlling defensiveness. The S scale consists of 50 items derived empirically from MMPI-2 to measure attitude to present oneself in a positive light. Twenty-nine of these items were found in the basic scales; the remaining 21 items were also included in the present study to assess participants' defensiveness. Butcher and Han (1995) reported internal consistencies of .86 for men and .85 for women in the normative sample. Five factors were identified through a component analysis: Beliefs in Human Goodness, Serenity, Contentment with Life, Patience and Denial of Irritability and Anger, and Denial of Moral Flaws (Butcher & Han, 1995).

Table 32.1 reported the Korean sample's T-scores on clinical scales by gender. Tables 32.2 through 32.5 compared Korean T-scores to those of Chinese international students (Stevens, Kwan, & Graybill, 1993) and college students in the MMPI-2 normative sample (Butcher et al., 1989). Consistent with previous studies, Korean students scored significantly higher than White American students on most clinical scales. To examine whether cultural orientations influence item endorsement, the direct effects of the response frequency,

Table 32.1 T-Scores of Female and Male Korean International Students

Scale	Male (n = 30)		Female (n = 26)	
	M	SD	M	SD
L	62.3	12.4	56.5	11.2
F	60.6	15.1	70.9	17.7
K	53.7	11.9	50.1	10.9
Hs	57.7	9.4	63.2	10.6
D	62.6	12.4	67.7	11.8
Hy	54.8	10.7	58.9	10.9
Pd	58.9	7.6	59.5	11.1
Mf	48.7	8.6	61.1	11.5
Pa	59.4	11.8	64.4	13.3
Pt	61.9	11.3	65.9	11.1
Sc	63.9	12.1	68.9	9.3
Ma	58.1	10.7	57.0	14.1
Si	57.8	8.7	61.2	9.3

Table 32.2 Comparisons of Mean T-Scores for Korean International Students, U.S. College Students, and Chinese International Students

	Male			Female		
Scale	Koreans (n = 30)	U.S.[a] (K-U)[b] (n = 515)	Chinese[c] (K-C)[d] (n = 10)	Koreans (n = 26)	U.S.[a] (K-U)[b] (n = 797)	Chinese[c] (K-C)[d] (n = 15)
L	62.3	49 (13.3)	54.6 (7.7)	56.7	46 (10.7)	63.0 (−6.3)
F	60.6	52 (8.6)	60.7 (−0.1)	71.2	54 (17.2)	59.0 (12.2)
K	53.7	48 (5.7)	48.2 (5.5)	49.9	47 (2.9)	55.3 (−5.4)
Hs	57.7	49 (8.7)	54.6 (3.1)	62.7	51 (11.7)	60.7 (2.0)
D	62.6	47 (15.6)	52.5 (10.1)	67.3	48 (19.3)	61.7 (5.6)
Hy	54.8	48 (6.8)	50.1 (4.7)	57.2	50 (7.2)	59.7 (−2.5)
Pd	58.9	51 (7.9)	51.0 (7.9)	58.1	52 (6.1)	55.9 (2.2)
Mf	48.7	49 (−0.3)	46.9 (1.8)	61.8	51 (10.8)	59.9 (1.9)
Pa	59.4	52 (7.4)	59.3 (0.1)	63.6	53 (10.6)	56.5 (7.1)
Pt	61.9	54 (7.9)	57.6 (4.3)	66.0	56 (10.0)	57.7 (8.3)
Sc	63.9	56 (7.9)	62.1 (1.8)	69.4	56 (13.4)	61.6 (7.8)
Ma	58.1	57 (1.1)	55.4 (2.7)	57.4	55 (2.4)	56.3 (1.1)
Si	57.8	48 (9.8)	57.5 (0.3)	61.7	49 (12.7)	51.9 (9.8)

a. From Butcher et al. (1990).

b. T-score difference between Korean and U.S. samples.

c. From Stevens et al. (1993).

d. T-score difference between Korean and Chinese samples.

Table 32.3 Comparisons of Non-K-Corrected Raw Scores for Korean International Students and U.S. College Students

	Male					Female				
	Koreans (n = 30)		U.S.[a] (n = 515)			Koreans (n = 26)		U.S.[a] (n = 797)		
Scale	M	SD	M	SD	t	M	SD	M	SD	t
L	6.3	2.8	3.3	2.2	5.78*	4.9	2.3	2.8	1.9	4.63*
F	7.9	4.8	5.3	3.9	2.91*	9.8	5.2	4.9	3.6	4.74*
K	16.9	5.6	14.4	4.7	2.44	15.1	5.1	13.8	4.6	1.31
Hs	6.9	6.9	5.1	4.0	1.41	11.5	5.7	6.9	4.5	4.07*
D	24.3	6.2	17.0	4.7	6.34*	28.7	5.5	19.6	5.0	8.39*
Hy	23.0	5.0	20.4	4.6	2.78*	25.8	4.2	22.2	4.8	4.31*
Pd	20.0	3.7	17.8	4.8	3.09*	20.4	4.8	17.8	5.0	2.72
Mf	25.3	4.3	25.2	5.0	−.12	31.4	4.7	34.9	4.2	−3.76*
Pa	12.7	3.2	10.9	3.3	3.02*	14.3	3.7	11.1	3.3	4.45*
Pt	15.2	8.4	14.1	7.7	.70	20.8	8.9	16.5	7.7	2.47
Sc	17.5	10.2	15.0	9.1	1.31	22.9	9.5	15.5	8.7	3.93*
Ma	19.7	5.3	20.4	4.5	−.74	18.9	5.6	18.8	4.5	.14
Si	31.6	7.8	23.7	8.6	5.34*	37.4	8.8	26.7	8.7	6.10*

a. From Butcher et al. (1990).

*p < .01.

Table 32.4　Comparisons of Non-K-Corrected Raw Scores for Korean and Chinese International Students

	Male					Female				
	Koreans (n = 30)		Chinese[a] (n = 10)			Koreans (n = 26)		Chinese[a] (n = 15)		
Scale	M	SD	M	SD	t	M	SD	M	SD	t
L	6.3	2.8	4.6	2.4	1.89	4.9	2.3	6.3	2.6	−1.69
F	7.9	4.8	8.0	5.4	−.03	9.8	5.2	6.3	4.7	2.21
K	16.9	5.6	14.5	2.6	1.86	15.1	5.1	17.4	14.1	−.60
Hs	6.9	6.9	7.0	5.3	−.04	11.5	5.7	9.1	5.0	1.40
D	24.3	6.2	19.4	5.2	2.45	28.7	5.5	26.0	5.8	1.49
Hy	23.0	5.0	20.8	5.6	1.10	25.8	4.2	26.6	5.4	−.46
Pd	20.0	3.7	17.6	3.4	1.89	20.4	4.8	17.9	4.5	1.71
Mf	25.3	4.3	24.1	4.7	0.71	31.4	4.7	32.0	3.5	−.48
Pa	12.7	3.2	12.7	2.9	0.0	14.3	3.7	12.1	10.6	.78
Pt	15.2	8.4	15.3	8.8	−.03	20.8	8.9	14.2	8.2	2.42
Sc	17.5	10.2	19.0	11.8	−.35	22.9	9.5	15.8	7.8	2.60
Ma	19.7	5.3	19.5	4.1	.11	18.9	5.6	18.3	4.7	.42
Si	31.6	7.8	32.3	6.7	−.27	37.4	8.8	29.7	4.9	3.59*

a. From Stevens et al. (1993).

*p < .01.

Table 32.5　Gender Difference on Defensiveness and Three Cultural Orientations

	Male (n = 30)		Female (n = 26)			
Scales	M	SD	M	SD	t	Sig.
Scale S	53.23	10.72	48.96	10.88	1.48	.15
Frequency	5.54	.60	5.3	.46	.06	.95
Desirability	4.78	.63	4.6	.70	.82	.42
Shamefulness	4.32	.91	4.6	.84	−1.21	.29

perceived desirability, and shamefulness and their respective indirect effects via defensiveness on MMPI-2 scores are explored. Three specific hypotheses were tested. First, the more item endorsement in the scored direction is perceived as frequent, the lower defensiveness and less suppressed MMPI-2 scale scores will be. Second, the more item endorsement in the scored direction is perceived as desirable, the lower defensiveness and less suppressed MMPI-2 scale scores will be. Third, the more item endorsement in the scored direction is perceived as shameful, the more defensiveness and more suppressed MMPI-2 scale scores will be (see Figure 32.1). Three separate hierarchical regression analyses were conducted for each MMPI-2 clinical scale, with response frequency, item desirability, and

perceived shamefulness being the respective predictor variable (PV1), defensiveness being the PV2, and T-score of the respective MMPI-2 clinical scale being the criterion variable. The PV1 value was computed based on the mean ratings of extreme items that fell under the respective clinical scales. For example, 17 extreme items were found in scale Sc; thus, mean ratings of the respective cultural dimensions of the 17 items were calculated and used as the predictor for the regression analysis of scale Sc. T-scores were used for clinical scales and the defensiveness scale. Comparisons of male and female students' scores on defensiveness and the three cultural orientations are provided in Table 32.5. Results of the hierarchical regression analyses are summarized in Table 32.6.

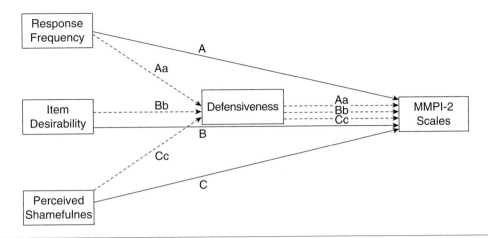

Figure 32.1   Relationships of Response Frequency, Item Desirability, and Perceived Shamefulness With MMPI-2 Scale Scores Moderated by Defensiveness

Note: A/B/C indicates direct effect of response frequency/item desirability/perceived shamefulness on MMPI-2 scales. Aa/Bb/Cc indicates indirect effect of response frequency/item desirability/perceived shamefulness on MMPI-2 scales via defensiveness.

Table 32.6   Result of Hierarchical Regression Analyses for Response Frequency, Item Desirability, Perceived Shamefulness, and Defensiveness Explaining Scale Scores

Scale	Variable	B	SE B	β	R^2	ΔR^2
Hs	Step1					
	Frequency	1.54	1.24	.17	.03	
	Desirability	.75	.99	.10	.01	
	Shamefulness	−.07	.94	−.01	.00	
D	Step1					
	Frequency	4.87	2.24	.28*	.08*	
	Desirability	2.89	2.18	.18	.03	
	Shamefulness	−1.21	1.70	−.09	.01	
	Step2					
	Frequency	4.45	2.15	.26*	.18*	.10*
	Defensiveness	−.35	.14	−.31*		
Hy	Step1					
	Frequency	3.12	2.03	.20	.04	
	Desirability	1.62	1.92	.11	.01	
	Shamefulness	.36	1.40	.04	.00	
Pd	Step1					
	Frequency	2.55	1.79	.19	.04	
	Desirability	−.43	1.26	−.05	.00	
	Shamefulness	−1.05	1.32	−.11	.01	

(Continued)

Table 32.6 (Continued)

Scale	Variable	B	SE B	β	R²	ΔR²
Mf	Step 1					
	Frequency	−2.68	2.04	−.18	.03	
	Desirability	−2.69	1.92	−.19	.04	
	Shamefulness	−1.59	1.47	−.15	.02	
Pa	Step1					
	Frequency	−3.24	1.93	−.22	.05	
	Desirability	−2.30	1.41	−.22	.05	
	Shamefulness	2.46	1.66	.19	.04	
Pt	Step1					
	Frequency	2.65	1.74	.20	.04	
	Desirability	1.58	1.54	.14	.02	
	Shamefulness	1.25	1.37	.12	.02	
Sc	Step1					
	Frequency	3.44	1.68	.27*	.08*	
	Desirability	2.74	1.36	.27*	.07*	
	Shamefulness	.82	1.42	.08	.01	
	Step2 (w/ Frequency)					
	Frequency	1.24	1.51	.09	.34**	.27**
	Defensiveness	−.51	.11	−.55**		
	Step2 (w/ Desirability)					
	Desirability	.77	1.24	.08	.34**	.27**
	Defensiveness	−.51	.11	−.55**		
Ma	Step1					
	Frequency	2.01	1.92	.14	.02	
	Desirability	3.79	1.56	.32*	.10*	
	Shamefulness	−2.63	1.47	−.24	.06	
	Step2					
	Desirability	3.56	1.61	.30*	.11	.01
	Defensiveness	−.08	.13	−.09		
Si	Step1					
	Frequency	−.02	1.92	−.00	.00	
	Desirability	−.47	1.97	−.03	.00	
	Shamefulness	−.61	1.26	−.07	.00	

*p < .05; **p < .01.

Relationships Among Response Frequency, Defensiveness, and Clinical Scales. Response frequency was positively correlated with scales Hs, D, Hy, Pd, Pt, Sc, and Ma and was found to be a significant predictor of the D (β = .28, R² = .08) and Sc (β = .27, R² = .08) scales. Given the significant relationship with the criterion variables, two separate regression analyses were conducted subsequently to test whether response frequency has an indirect effect on scales D and Sc via defensiveness. For scale D, both response frequency ($\beta = .26$) and defensiveness ($\beta = -.31$) were significant predictors when they were entered together in the subsequent regression equation. The increased explained variance by defensiveness was significant ($\Delta R^2 = .10$), and the decreased β value (.02) of familiarity (i.e., indirect effect of response frequency on scale D via defensiveness) was minimal. Therefore, results suggest that the direct effect of response frequency, as indicated by the regression coefficient in a second regression analysis, was stronger than the indirect effect through defensiveness on scale D. For scale Sc, defensiveness was found to be the only variable that contributed significantly to the explained variance ($\beta = -.55$, $\Delta R^2 = .27$) when response frequency and defensiveness were both entered in the subsequent regression equation ($R^2 = .34$). Given that the direct effect of response frequency on scale Sc was not significant in the subsequent regression analysis ($\beta = .09$), results suggest that the indirect effect of response frequency on scale Sc via defensiveness is stronger than its direct effect.

Relationships Among Item Desirability, Defensiveness, and Clinical Scales. Item desirability was positively associated with scores on the Hs, D, Hy, Pt, Sc, and Ma scales. Item desirability significantly explained scales Sc ($\beta = .27$, $R^2 = .07$) and Ma ($\beta = .32$, $R^2 = .10$). In other words, the total effect of item desirability on scales Sc and Ma was significant. Two separate regression analyses were conducted subsequently to test whether item desirability has an indirect effect on scales Sc and Ma via defensiveness. For scale Sc, defensiveness was found to be the single variable that contributed significantly to the explained variance ($\beta = -.55$, $\Delta R^2 = .27$) when item desirability and defensiveness were entered together in the subsequent regression equation ($R^2 = .34$). Direct effect of item desirability on scale Sc was not significant ($\beta = .08$). Given the significant total effect and the insignificant direct effect of item desirability on scale Sc, the results suggest that item desirability has a stronger indirect effect via defensiveness than direct effect on scale Sc. For scale Ma, defensiveness did not increase the explained variance significantly ($\beta = -.09$,

$\Delta R^2 = .01$) when item desirability and defensiveness were entered together in the subsequent regression equation. Direct effect of item desirability, as indicated by regression coefficient, on scale Ma was significant ($\beta = .30$). Results suggest that the direct effect of item desirability is stronger than its indirect effect via defensiveness on scale Ma.

Relationships Among Perceived Shamefulness, Defensiveness, and Clinical Scales. Results of regression analyses showed inconsistent relationships of perceived shamefulness with MMPI-2 scale scores. Perceived shamefulness was negatively correlated with scales Hs, D, Pd, Mf, Ma, and Si, and positively correlated with scales Hy, Pa, Pt, and Sc. None of these relationships was statistically significant. Thus, subsequent regression analysis with defensiveness as a second predictor was not conducted.

Response frequency was found to have a significant total effect (i.e., combined effect including direct and indirect effect via defensiveness) on scales D and Sc. Subsequent regression analyses adding defensiveness as a second predictor variable showed that the direct effect of response frequency is stronger than its indirect effect via defensiveness on scale D. Response frequency, however, has a stronger indirect effect via defensiveness than a direct effect on scale Sc, which is consistent with the hypothesis. As participants perceive extreme item content to be frequently endorsed, their defensiveness associated with endorsing item in the scoring direction may decrease, resulting in an elevated scale Sc. Total effects of item desirability on scales Sc and Ma were found to be significant. The effect of item desirability on scale Sc was more indirect via defensiveness, which is consistent with the hypothesis. When item content is perceived to be desirable in Korean society, participants may be less defensive when admitting certain items or symptoms, resulting in an elevated scale. Item desirability showed a stronger direct effect than an indirect effect via defensiveness on scale Ma. Thus, Korean students are likely to endorse items in scale Ma when items are perceived to be desirable, and the impact of item desirability on endorsing items in scale Ma may be relatively independent of level of defensiveness. In summary, response frequency and/or item desirability significantly explained scores of scales D, Sc, and Ma either directly or indirectly via defensiveness. Given that scales D and Sc have been found consistently to be elevated among Asian Americans (see Kwan, 1999), results of the current study suggest that the elevated scores of scales D and Sc may be related to the perceived response frequency and item desirability of item content of those scales.

Overall, results of this study suggest that perceived response frequency and item desirability influence Korean international students' MMPI-2 scale scores. Korean international students endorsed more items in the scored direction on scales D, Sc, and Ma when items were perceived to be frequent and/or desirable. Each of the culture-related variables explained between 7% and 10% of the variances of scales D, Sc, and Ma. Therefore, counselors need to consider the potential contributions of response frequency and item desirability when interpreting Korean MMPI-2 profiles. The moderating effect of defensiveness on response MMPI-2 scale scores, however, was not consistent across the cultural orientations. The validity of the relationships is also limited by the small sample size ($N = 57$).

CULTURAL APPLICATION OF PSYCHOLOGICAL TESTS: CLINICAL IMPLICATIONS AND RESEARCH DIRECTIONS

We introduce the following case study as a stimulus for discussion:

> During the course of psychotherapy, it was decided that psychological testing would help a Chinese immigrant client better articulate emotions and the White American therapist gain more insights into the client's coping styles. The client left China during his late teenage years and had lived in the United States for 7 years. The therapist found the client somewhat fluent in English with occasional grammatical errors amidst a strong accent. While preparing for testing, the therapist realized that a translated Chinese version of the selected psychological test is available with extensive normative data collected from the client's country of origin. Concerned that language proficiency might bias test results and interpretation, the therapist discussed with the client whether the English version or the Chinese version would be preferred.

TEST LANGUAGE CONSIDERATIONS AND SUMMARY

Based on the review of the conceptual and empirical literature, it is apparent that language proficiency is a critical factor that contributes to measurement and diagnostic errors if test takers do not (fully) understand test items. Although many psychological tests have been translated into other language versions with norms derived from samples in the respective countries, it is unlikely that translated versions of these instruments are available and used in clinical settings in the United States. If the test is administered in its original language different from the client's (e.g., immigrants and international students), it is important to ask if vocabulary, idiomatic expressions, and item content require knowledge of the source culture that the culturally different test taker has difficulty understanding. Even when a translated version is available, culture-based items that are not modified or adapted can still contribute to test bias in that unfamiliarity with item content could lead to random responding that masks the true meaning of item response. In the process of establishing linguistic equivalence, therefore, it is necessary to conduct research studies that identify these culture-based items and explore their effects on test scores.

When interpreting test scores, it is necessary to evaluate whether, and the extent to which, the inference or meaning derived from the original cultural group can be applied to the culturally different test taker. Evaluating conceptual equivalence and metric equivalence is important because culturally different samples (within and outside the United States) have often produced test scores that are significantly different from the normative samples of the original version of psychological tests. Before attributing meaning to test scores that deviate from the norm in the abnormality, deficiency, or psychopathology direction, researchers and clinicians should also consider a number of issues: whether the construct as measured by the test items exists in the test taker's culture, whether endorsing behavioral/attitudinal/affective items in the scored direction connote meanings different from the items' intended purpose, and whether there are subtle factors that influence test response systematically. When adapting a test to measure a psychological phenomenon with an etic label (e.g., social phobia), researchers and clinicians also need to observe and discern if there are other cognitive, emotional, and physiological manifestations common to people in the target culture that need to be included. Maintaining an emic approach to inquiry facilitates exploration of variations and refinement of etic constructs.

It is imperative for clinicians to know the test norms of culturally different groups, as well as research that examined factors that contribute to significant differences between cultural groups. Metric equivalence studies have indicated that various subtle culture-related factors, including acculturation and item desirability, moderate test responses. These moderating factors, which have a significant effect on test scores, are often not explicit to researchers and clinicians. In clinical assessment, it is good practice to gauge the client's experience of testing and explore whether his or her perception and reactions provoked by test items may have an impact on test response. Bilingual researchers who possess language skills *and* knowledge of culture and measurement need to be recruited when conducting test equivalence research. Beyond language translation, research on test equivalence should further focus on the issue of cultural validity and on controlling test bias that may lead to mislabeling or misdiagnosing people from another culture by an imported test.

REFERENCES

American Psychiatric Association. (2000). *Diagnostic and statistical manual of mental disorders* (4th ed., text rev.). Washington, DC: Author.

American Psychological Association. (2002). Ethical principles of psychologists and code of conduct. *American Psychologist, 57*, 1060–1073.

Beck, A. T., Steer, R. A., & Brown, G. K. (1996). *Manual for the Beck Depression Inventory-II*. San Antonio, TX: Psychological Corporation.

Brislin, R. W. (1986). The wording and translation of research instruments. In W. J. Lonner & J. W. Berry (Eds.), *Field methods in cross-cultural research* (pp. 137–164). Beverly Hills, CA: Sage.

Brislin, R. W., Lonner, W. J., & Thorndike, R. M. (1973). *Cross-cultural research methods*. New York: Wiley.

Butcher, J. N. (Ed.). (1996). *International adaptations of the MMPI-2*. Minneapolis: University of Minnesota Press.

Butcher, J. N., Dahlstrom, W., Graham, J. R., Tellegen, A., & Kaemmer, B. (1989). *MMPI-2: Manual for administration and scoring*. Minneapolis: University of Minnesota Press.

Butcher, J. N., Graham, J. R., Dahlstrom, W. G., & Bowman, E. (1990). The MMPI-2 with college students. *Journal of Personality Assessment, 54*, 1–15.

Butcher, J. N., & Han, K. (1995). Development of a MMPI-2 scale to assess the presentation of self in a superlative manner: The S scale. In J. N. Butcher & E. D. Spielberger (Eds.), *Advances in personality assessment* (pp. 35–50). Hillsdale, NJ: Lawrence Erlbaum.

Butcher, J. N., & Pancheri, P. (1976). *A handbook of cross-cultural MMPI research*. Minneapolis: University of Minnesota Press.

Cheung, F. M. (1985). Cross-cultural considerations for the translation and adaptation of the Chinese MMPI in Hong Kong. In J. N. Butcher & C. D. Spielberger (Eds.), *Advances in personality assessment* (Vol. 4, pp. 131–158). Hillsdale, NJ: Lawrence Erlbaum.

Cheung, F. M. (1995). *The Chinese Minnesota Multiphasic Personality Inventory manual*. Shatin, Hong Kong: Chinese University Press.

Cheung, F. M., Song, W-Z., & Butcher, J. N. (1991). An infrequency scale for the Chinese MMPI. *Psychological Assessment, 4*, 648–653.

Cheung, F. M., Song, W., & Zhang, J. (1996). The Chinese MMPI-2: Research and applications in Hong Kong and the People's Republic of China. In J. B. Butcher (Ed.), *International adaptations of the MMPI-2* (pp. 137–161). Minneapolis: University of Minnesota Press.

Dana, R. H. (1993). *Multicultural assessment perspectives for professional psychology*. Boston: Allyn & Bacon.

Gong, Y., & Kwan, K.-L. K. (2001, August). *Effects of perceived item desirability, familiarity, and shamefulness on the MMPI-2 patterns of Korean students in the U.S.* Paper presented at the annual meeting of the American Psychological Association, San Francisco.

Hambleton, R. K., & de Jong, J. H. A. L. (2003). Advances in translating and adapting educational and psychological tests. *Language Testing, 20*, 127–134.

Han, K. (1996). The Korean MMPI-2. In J. N. Butcher (Ed.), *International adaptations of the MMPI-2: Research and clinical applications* (pp. 88–136). Minneapolis: University of Minnesota Press.

Kwan, K.-L. K. (1999). MMPI and MMPI-2 performance of the Chinese: Cross-cultural applicability. *Professional Psychology: Research and Practice, 30*, 260–268.

Kwan, K.-L. K., & Maestas, M. (2008). MMPI-2 and MCMI-III performances of non-White populations in the United States: What we (don't) know and where we go from here. In L. A. Suzuki & J. G. Ponterotto (Eds.), *Handbook of multicultural assessment* (3rd ed., pp. 425–446). San Francisco: Jossey-Bass.

Lonner, W. J. (1985). Issues in testing and assessment in cross-cultural counseling. *Counseling Psychologist, 13,* 599–614.

Lonner, W. J., & Berry, J. W. (Eds.). (1986). *Field methods in cross-cultural research.* Beverly Hills, CA: Sage.

Messick, S. (1989). Validity. In R. L. Linn (Ed.), *Educational measurement* (3rd ed., pp. 13–103). New York: Macmillan.

Messick, S. (1995). Validity of psychological assessment: Validation of inferences from persons' responses and performance to scientific inquiry into score meaning. *American Psychologist, 50,* 741–749.

Nichols, D. S., & Greene, R. L. (1997). Dimensions of deception in personality assessment. *Journal of Personality Assessment, 68,* 251–266.

Nicholson, R. A., Mouton, G. J., Bagby, R. M., Buis, T., Peterson, S. A., & Buigas, R. A. (1997). Utility of MMPI-2 indicators of response distortion: Receiver operating characteristic analysis. *Psychological Assessment, 9,* 471–479.

Okazaki, S. (1995, August). *Cultural dimensions underlying Asian-White differences on the MMPI-2.* Paper presented at the annual meeting of the American Psychological Association, New York.

Penley, J. A., Wiebe, J. S., & Nwosu, A. (2003). Psychometric properties of the Spanish Beck Depression Inventory-II in a medical sample. *Psychological Assessment, 15,* 569–577.

Reardon, R. C., & Lenz, J. G. (1998). *The self-directed search and related Holland career materials: A practitioner's guide.* Lutz, FL: Psychological Assessment Resources.

Sodowsky, G. R., & Lai, E. W. M. (1997). Asian immigrant variables and structural models of cross cultural distress. In A. Booth, A. C. Crouter, & N. Landale (Eds.), *Immigration and the family: Research and policy on U.S. immigrants* (pp. 211–237). Mahwah, NJ: Lawrence Erlbaum.

Stevens, M. J., Kwan, K.-L. K., & Graybill, D. (1993). Comparison of MMPI-2 scores of foreign Chinese and Caucasian-American students. *Journal of Clinical Psychology, 49,* 23–27.

Sue, S., Keefe, K., Enomoto, K., Durvasula, R. S., & Chao, R. (1996). Asian American and White college students' performance on the MMPI-2. In J. B. Butcher (Ed.), *International adaptations of the MMPI-2* (pp. 206–218). Minneapolis: University of Minnesota Press.

Suzuki, K., Takei, N., Kawai, M., Minabe, Y., & Mori, N. (2003). Is *taijin kyofusho* a culture-bound syndrome? *American Journal of Psychiatry, 160,* 1358.

Torres, L., & Rollock, D. (2004). Acculturative distress among Hispanics: The role of acculturation, coping, and intercultural competence. *Multicultural Counseling and Development, 32,* 155–167.

van de Vijver, F. J. R. (2001). The evolution of cross-cultural research methods. In D. Matsumoto (Ed.), *Handbook of culture and psychology* (pp. 77–97). New York: Oxford University Press.

van de Vijver, F. J. R., & Hambleton, R. K. (1996). Translating tests: Some practical guidelines. *European Psychologist, 1,* 89–99.

van de Vijver, F. J. R., & Leung, K. (1997). *Methods and data analysis for cross-cultural research.* Thousand Oaks, CA: Sage.

Ægisdóttir, S., Gerstein, L., & Çinarbas, D. C. (2008). Methodological issues in cross-cultural counseling research: Test equivalence, bias, and translations. *Counseling Psychologist, 36,* 188–219.

33

Designing and Interpreting Qualitative Research in Multicultural Counseling

HEATHER Z. LYONS AND DENISE H. BIKE

Despite the well-documented need in the counseling literature to integrate the voices of the understudied, Fine (1994), among others (e.g., Denzin, 2005), warned qualitative researchers against the "colonizing discourse of the 'Other'" (p. 70). In doing so, she invoked the following passage from bell hooks:

> No need to hear your voice when I can talk about you better than you speak about yourself. . . . I want to know your story. And then I will tell it back to you in a new way. Tell it back to you in such a way that it has become mine, my own. . . . I am still author, authority. I am still the colonizer. (hooks as cited in Fine, 1994, p. 70)

In other words, research that distances, objectifies, or pathologizes the understudied can cause more harm than good. However, when conducted competently, qualitative research holds the potential to empathically represent, involve, and benefit understudied populations in the counseling literature (Guba & Lincoln, 2005; Pedersen, 1991; Polkinghorne, 2005). Indeed, the use of qualitative research has gained credibility as a means of evaluating the effectiveness of psychotherapy (Stiles et al., 2006). Furthermore, qualitative research has been thought to be particularly appropriate for the study of multicultural counseling because it allows (a) researchers to consider the multifaceted nature of identity and the sociocultural contexts of those at the center of research; (b) researchers to better understand understudied phenomena or populations; (c) participants to feel comfortable with data collection methods (e.g., interviews); and (d) communities to have easier access to the results, which are derived from and reported in a familiar voice (Choudhuri, 2005; Morrow, Rakhsha, & Castaneda, 2001).

Despite the confluence between what understudied populations need and what qualitative research offers, qualitative studies continue to represent few of the published studies in psychology and counseling journals (Hoyt & Bhati, 2007). This may be in part because few researchers learned qualitative methods in their graduate programs (Ponterotto, 2005b; Walsh-Bowers, 2002). Thus, they are unfamiliar with qualitative methods, which are derived from anthropology and sociology, as opposed to the more familiar, quantitative methods, which are derived from the natural sciences (Hoshmand, 1999).

Reflecting this crossroads, our own entry into qualitative research was marked by both excitement (at the possibilities for our research) and befuddlement (over how to conduct multicultural qualitative research competently). Thankfully, we were able to rely on experts in a variety of paradigms and methods, some available guides (e.g., Hill, Thompson, & Williams, 1997; Miles & Huberman, 1994), trial, and lots of error. Given that multiculturally competent qualitative research that benefits understudied populations is needed and that researchers and practitioners need direction in order to conduct and consume it, in this chapter, we will reflect on the process of qualitative research. That notwithstanding, this chapter is not meant to be an instructional manual but rather a deliberation on exemplar and best practices. We cover topic, sample, and site selection; research team and instrument development; and data collection, analysis, and interpretation.

DISCLAIMERS

When writing this chapter, we attempted to strike a balance between organizing the chapter in a way accessible to those more accustomed to quantitative positivistic or postpositivistic paradigms while realizing that this organization (or any organization, for that matter) might deceptively lead readers to assume that qualitative approaches can be thoroughly and accurately understood in a neat and orderly manner. (See Heppner, Kivlighan & Wampold, 1999, for an extended discussion on the differences between qualitative and quantitative research.) First, although we present the qualitative research process in stages, this linear progression is somewhat artificial and used only for heuristic purposes. Most qualitative methods are iterative in nature, as the vertical double-sided arrow

on Table 33.1 indicates. It is the exception when qualitative research occurs as a series of discrete stages.

Second, we present examples of qualitative methods (e.g., phenomenology, feminist theory) along with common research strategies employed when using those methods. This, too, is a somewhat artificial association. In reality, there is much more flexibility in strategies used in qualitative research. Strategies that we defined as belonging to one paradigm may be borrowed by another (see Fassinger, 2005; Patton, 2002).

Third, we present examples of qualitative methods and the paradigms with which they are typically associated. The flexibility of these associations is indicated by the double-sided horizontal arrow running along the top of Table 33.1, indicating a continuum. Researchers using the same method may differ in terms of ontology (i.e., definitions of truth and reality), epistemology (i.e., relationship between researcher and participant), and axiology (i.e., conceptualization of researcher values). In summary, this means that the paradigm classifying the same method may vary. For example, even though grounded theory has been classified under the constructivist paradigm (Fassinger, 2005; Ponterotto, 2002), ask any random grounded theorist about his or her paradigmatic loyalties and the answer might range from postpositivist to critical (Fassinger, 2005; Highlen & Finley, 1996). Similarly, consensual qualitative research (CQR) (Hill et al., 2005; Hill et al., 1997) has been defined as constructivist, postpositivistic, or a combination of the two (see Hill et al., 2005; Ponterotto, 2005a; Yeh & Inman, 2007).

A final disclaimer of sorts typical of qualitative research is called *bracketing*. In constructivist approaches, it is common for researchers to identify their own biases (i.e., relevant life experiences and identities) and expectations (i.e., previous exposure to relevant academic literatures) for readers (Hill et al., 1997). Bracketing not only acts as documentation of the reflexivity that should occur throughout the research process, but also allows readers to better understand the lens through which data were interpreted (Morrow, 2005). To that end, let us introduce ourselves. We are researchers who, despite over a decade each of involvement in qualitative methods, continue to consider ourselves novices as we realize the great time investment necessary to become proficient in

Table 33.1   Notable Features of Qualitative Research "Stages" in Postpositivistic, Constructivistic-Interpretive, and Critical-Ideological Paradigms

Stages	Postpositivistic	Constructivism-Interpretivism	Critical-Ideological
Sample Methods	Content analysis, CQR	Grounded theory, phenomenology	Participatory action research, feminist theory, queer theory, critical race theory
Identifying a Topic	Culling literature to develop research questions that will advance the field or fill in existing gaps by attempting to challenge existing theory	Selecting a topic that will help delineate the meaning of constructs (e.g., working alliance, ethnic identity) and/or result in model or theory generation	Identifying a topic of practical relevance to participants that will result in collaborative strategies for participant and community improvement, empowerment, and emancipation
Sample and Site Selection	Homogeneous sample selected prior to data collection	Theoretical sampling, purposeful sampling	Sample would represent various aspects of relevant community with participants possessing complementary knowledge and experiences
Research Team Construction	Emphasis is placed on selecting research team members who are knowledgeable of relevant literatures	Team members are selected who are able to engage in self-reflection and identification of biases	Research team necessarily involves equitable participation by community members ("co-investigators") with complementary skill sets and knowledge
Data Collection	Use of structured or semi-structured interview or observation protocols in an attempt to standardize data collection across participants	Interviews, naturalistic observation, focus groups, and other methods that allow researchers to fully immerse themselves in the participants' lives or phenomenon under investigation	Use of data collection methods that involve all segments of relevant community with an emphasis on collecting data that will flesh out community needs and the nature of helpful collaboration
Analysis	Assessing rater agreement or consensus on data categorization	Iterative process that cycles and recycles through data collection, interpretation, and hypothesis generation	As in other steps, community members are involved in analysis, documented critical/ideological studies have used a variety of analysis methods
Interpretation	Researchers attempt to make objective interpretations that offer possible theory falsification	Researchers' biases and other relevant experiences are recognized in interpretations that may result in model or theory generation	Interpretations highlight study's practical utility and challenge societal power differentials and existing social structure

any qualitative method. This is particularly true for us, as it is for any researcher beginning from a quantitative positivistic or postpositivistic stance. The development of our qualitative research identity was sparked by our recognition of the limitations of using strictly quantitative methods to study our largely multicultural topics of interest, which include the work experiences of African Americans of a range of social classes and gay men and lesbians (Heather Z. Lyons) and social class (Denise H. Bike). These tend to be multifaceted topics benefitting from an understanding of context: topics ripe for qualitative inquiry. At this point, we would identify with the constructivist paradigm. However, we have experience with postpositivistic qualitative (Lyons, 1997) and mixed methods (Lyons & O'Brien, 2006) research, and we have aspirations to conduct research from a critical-ideological paradigm, particularly participatory action research.

SELECTING A TOPIC, SAMPLE, AND SITE

Topic Selection

When designing a qualitative research study, specificity of topic may depend on the researchers' paradigm (Guba & Lincoln, 2005; Miles & Huberman, 1994; Polkinghorne, 2005). Postpositivists (those closest to quantitative researchers on a continuum of structure and a priori assumptions) are more likely to comb the literature for what is missing or misrepresented and fine-tune their topic based on formal research questions. Topic selection for postpositivists is tied closely to their goal of theory verification and hypothesis testing. Lyons and O'Brien (2006), for example, used their qualitative study of the work experiences of middle- and upper-middle-class African Americans to confirm the validity of the Theory of Work Adjustment with this population. At the other end of the spectrum, constructivist-interpretive and critical-ideological researchers allow the specific details of their topic to emerge because of the emphasis on discovery. (See Guba & Lincoln, 2005, and Ponterotto, 2005a, for a complete review of the differences between paradigms.) Constructivists, specifically, will select topics that allow for the generation of theories, hypotheses, and research questions. As an example, Beckstead and Morrow (2004)

sought to understand the unique experiences of Mormons seeking conversion therapy. From this exploration emerged a new model of the motivations for seeking conversion therapy that challenged earlier ideas and suggested new treatment strategies. Fundamentally, and regardless of paradigm, in order to select a topic that is meaningful to the field and to participants, multiculturally competent qualitative researchers must know the population intimately (Merchant & Dupuy, 1996), whether that is accomplished through immersion in the extant literature or through close involvement with participants' communities.

Sample Selection

When selecting a sample, qualitative researchers consider size and variety. Sample size is small in qualitative research in order to manage time and enable in-depth exploration (Miles & Huberman, 1994). From the participants' perspective, smaller size provides more time for interviews, leaving participants and researchers feeling less rushed and put-upon by the process. As Flores et al. (2007) observed in their work with a small sample of Latino/a immigrants to the United States, having time to interact informally before interviews aligned with their participants' cultural expectations. From the researchers' perspective, problems can arise from having too small or too large a sample. Data collected from too few participants lack stability across cases and risk "thin" data (Miles & Huberman, 1994). Data from too many may mean that researchers pass the point of saturation (i.e., the data become repetitive and major themes recur). Furthermore, more participants increase the demand on researchers' time and ability to engage deeply with participants (Fassinger, 2005). For instance, in a study of Filipinos living in poverty (Tuason, 2008), keeping the sample size small allowed team members to spend the day with participants as they worked, an arrangement that would have been prohibitive with a large sample size.

When deciding how much variety to seek in a sample, opinions vary with paradigms. Constructivists prefer slightly larger samples because they lead to greater heterogeneity (e.g., Fassinger, 2005). Casting a wider net can be valuable to researchers who depend on the sample as the source of emergent theory, as in Remafedi and

Carol's (2005) exploration of tobacco use prevention strategies preferred by lesbian, gay, bisexual, and transgender (LGBT) youth. Their sample was large (30 people) and varied (it included current and former smokers; urban and suburban youth; and "a mix of persons of different gender identities, ages, and races/ethnicities" [p. 250]). Postpositivists, on the other hand, recommend a homogeneous sample for stability across experiences (Hill et al., 2005; Miles & Huberman, 1994). As with other design considerations, when it comes to sample selection, multiculturally competent qualitative researchers seek to balance their needs with their topic's and their participants' needs.

Finally, and perhaps most importantly, participants should be selected who will not be harmed by and may benefit from the qualitative research process. Haverkamp's (2005) seminal discussion of qualitative research ethics described the unique and asymmetrical nature of relationships in qualitative research. For this reason, the ethical guidelines that dictate positivistic and postpositivistic research may fail to consider what may be ethical and beneficial for those participating in qualitative research. This consideration may be of particular importance when considering the needs of understudied populations.

Site Selection

Most qualitative research takes place in the field to provide the researchers with "a sense of the lived world of research participants . . . in which the behaviors of interest might normally be expected to occur" (Hoyt & Bhati, 2007, p. 204). Equally important is the researchers' consideration of the impact of site selection on their participants as well as participants' welfare (Haverkamp, 2005). As such, site selection considerations are a commingling of methodology, logistics, and participants' needs. For example, in a study of cross-cultural supervision issues, Burkard et al. (2006) used phone interviews to provide for participants' comfort, privacy, and confidentiality. Arranged at the supervisees' convenience and in a location of their choice, this method met participants' and researchers' needs. On the other hand, Lyons et al. (2009) chose a church outreach center in which to conduct interviews with materially poor African Americans. This reduced demands on

participants—they were interviewed while waiting for services—and provided them with the comfort of "home turf." However, noise occasionally interfered with the sound quality, and interviewers sometimes struggled to secure privacy. Such examples demonstrate the trade-offs inherent in balancing qualitative researchers' needs with their participants' needs when selecting a site.

PUTTING TOGETHER A RESEARCH TEAM

Because of the up-close and personal nature of qualitative research, team members' cultural characteristics and competencies will play a role throughout the process (Choudhuri, 2003; Guba & Lincoln, 2005). Unlike in quantitative research, where researcher variables are ostensibly controlled for to reduce confounding, in qualitative research, these factors are excavated and acknowledged as part of the interactive process of knowledge building that takes place during the research process. This occurs by different methods, for different purposes, and to varying degrees, depending on the researchers' paradigm (see Table 33.1). Because people possess different cultural characteristics, skills, and traits desired in a qualitative researcher, diversity in each of these areas has its merits. Thus, team members' experiences and abilities complement each other as they contribute to the process.

Cultural Characteristics

The diversity of a qualitative research team in terms of race, ability status, gender, social class, sexual orientation, nationality, and language can prove to be a strength. Dissimilarities force team members to explain (and thereby to examine) how their experiences shape their understanding of participants' experiences. Language dissimilarity can be particularly helpful because team members must consider the assumptions underlying their use of language. Furthermore, diversity can affect the salience value a team has in the field. The points of similarity that researchers share with informants can provide intimate access to participants and can help researchers anticipate and respond nondefensively to challenges from participants about the purpose of their research. Language, racial/ethnic, and experiential similarities between researchers and participants can also improve communication throughout the process. For example, in a study of the resettlement experiences of people with mobility disabilities in post-conflict Sierra Leone, one of the researchers (who had lived and worked among the population) spoke both Krio and English, which helped while translating and conducting the interviews (dos Santos-Zingale & McColl, 2006).

Skills and Characteristics

Certain intra- and interpersonal skills add value to a multiculturally competent qualitative research team. *Creativity*—the ability to generate original insights and unconventional ideas, view material naively, and identify novel constructs—is a key skill for a multiculturally competent qualitative team member. As more exposure to and greater depth of experience with other cultures are predictive of this skill (Leung, Maddux, Galinsky, & Chiu, 2008), it can be argued that team members from any cultural minority (ethnographic, demographic, status-related, or attributional) have developed this ability because of their immersion in both the dominant culture and their own. Naturally, team members should also demonstrate *multicultural competence*, including the possession of a sophisticated racial identity status, the ability to self-reflect on culture, and prior experience with the population. *Counseling skills* are valuable as well. They provide team members with the ability to self-reflect, conduct interviews dialogically, and engage respectfully and compassionately with participants and each other.

Because of the time- and labor-intensive nature of qualitative research, team members should also be *responsible* and *committed*. Qualitative research has a significant data management component that often can be broken into parts and delegated to team members, fostering agency and commitment to the project over the long term. Hill et al. (1997) also recommend choosing team members who are *outspoken* and *diplomatic*. Such qualities lend themselves to positive and productive interactions in the field as well as with each other.

DEVELOPING A RESEARCH INSTRUMENT

Although recognizing that other methods of qualitative data collection exist (e.g., e-mail—Kim, Brenner, & Liang, 2003; document analysis—Hughes & Heycox, 2008; observation—Breen, 2008), this discussion is focused on in-person interviews, the most widely used method in qualitative research (Hoyt & Bhati, 2007; Krahn & Putnam, 2003; Polkinghorne, 2005). Interviews are particularly useful when working with understudied populations because they can allay barriers related to native language, reading level, and unfamiliarity or distrust of traditional questionnaire formats (Lyons & Bike, 2007). Conducting interviews in participants' native languages and revising the reading level to meet the "zero-order level of communications" (Berg, 2001, p. 77) demonstrates respect for participants' cultural needs and preferences. It also reduces the likelihood of misinterpretations or multiple interpretations of the questions. For example, in a study of undocumented Latino/a workers in the Midwest—whose spare time is precious and whose cultural mistrust (or "healthy paranoia") may be understandably high—the researchers conducted interviews in participants' homes and in their native language (Flores et al., 2007). As another example, Tuason's (2008) team interviewed affluent Filipinos living in the United States in English but employed a translated protocol when interviewing Filipinos living in poverty in their native land. The researchers recognized that, although most of these participants were bilingual, they were more comfortable speaking in their native language.

When designing the interview protocol, decisions must also be made about structure, purpose, and transparency about the purpose of the interview (Kvale, 1996; Suzuki, Ahluwalia, Arora, & Mattis, 2007). An *unstructured interview*, where questions and follow-ups are generated during the interview (Berg, 2001), is more often used by constructivist-interpretive researchers because of the emphasis these researchers place on discovery. Furthermore, constructivist-interpretive researchers generally use methods that help them either prevent or recognize the influence of their own biases and expectations, which might be more probable with an unstructured interview. In a *structured interview*, the questions and the order in which they are asked are standardized (favoring a postpositivist perspective). *Semi-structured interviews* strike a balance between these extremes. The researchers prepare questions and thematically relevant probes in advance of the interview.

However, interviewers may adjust the questions and their order during the interview to capitalize on each participant's contributions.

When designing the interview, multiculturally competent qualitative researchers should adapt "methods of inquiry and data collection to the systematic inequality inherent in the relationship between the researcher and the researched" (Blauner & Wellman, 1982, p. 103). Interviewers control the topic, length, and direction of the interview—albeit to different extents depending on the level of structure (Kvale, 1996). The asymmetry of power between researcher and informant can be compounded when researchers are from a powerful population relative to the participants' (Choudhuri, 2003; Guba & Lincoln, 2005). Thus, researchers should be mindful of the potential of this power differential to interfere with participant agency and interview responses by attending to the order, type, and wording of the questions.

Berg (2001) suggested starting an interview with neutral demographic questions to establish rapport. However, one may question the neutrality of demographic questions. Several other researchers have suggested beginning the interview with a "grand-tour question," which frees the participant to take the discussion where he or she is interested in going rather than being led by the researcher (Hill et al., 1997; Spradley, 1979). This may also allow participants to experience self-efficacy. After breaking the ice and opening with a broad question, Suzuki et al. (2007) proposed moving on to topic-specific questions. Finally, to acknowledge that participating in an interview has an effect on the participant and the resultant data, qualitative researchers may ask about the participants' interview experience (Kvale, 1996; Suzuki et al., 2007). Such experience-of-interview questions also serve as a debriefing, offering a valuable opportunity for participants to gain closure by reflecting upon their experience (Kvale, 1996).

Piloting

Throughout the literature, qualitative researchers emphasize the importance of piloting interview questions with a representative sample (e.g., Berg, 2001; Hill et al., 2005; Hill et al., 1997). From a postpositivistic standpoint, making arrangements to pilot protocols

(i.e., interviewing a small number of participants from the target population using a draft of the interview protocol) will reduce the need for revisions after the interviews have begun (Hill et al., 2005). From a constructivist-interpretive perspective, piloting can be a time for initial emergence of the topic's underlying structure in relation to the people sampled (Guba & Lincoln, 2005). From the critical-ideological paradigm, the benefit of piloting may be that it begins to sensitize researchers to the power differential and helps foster rapport.

Bracketing

After piloting and revising the protocol, each team member can be interviewed using the protocol, which may assist with bracketing (Hill et al., 1997). As mentioned at the beginning of this chapter, *bracketing* is the process by which researchers' biases and expectations are identified and presented. Using this means of bracketing provides additional practice conducting interviews. More importantly, it allows team members to gain a deeper understanding of their relationship to the experiences under investigation. While post-positivists are more likely to employ bracketing to lessen or control for the effect of researchers' biases and expectations on the study (Hill et al., 1997), constructivist-interpretive and critical-ideological researchers may use bracketing to foster awareness of the co-construction of knowledge (Guba & Lincoln, 2005).

Subjectivity and Reflexivity

Because qualitative researchers are their own instrument, additional self-examination is highly valuable and can be accomplished through subjectivity and reflexivity (Morrow, 2005). In the context of cultural competency, *subjectivity* is the recognition that researchers' worldviews influence the questions they ask as well as how data are collected, analyzed, and interpreted. *Reflexivity* refers to investigators' ability to articulate their cultural worldview, understand their salience to participants, and consider their impact during each stage of the research process and, ultimately, its outcomes. For example, dos Santos-Zingale and McColl (2006) reflexively recognized that independence, which is subjectively valued in their Western culture, can raise problems when people with disabilities need additional support—an observation implanted within Western-based literature. However, in their sample of resettled Sierra Leone occupants, interdependency was the norm in the community-oriented society. The researchers' self-reflection enabled them to understand that the need for assistance was not perceived as distressing in itself; the lack of available assistance was.

Team members' prior assumptions of and attitudes toward the participants and the topic under investigation can arise from both personal and professional exposure to a culture, or lack thereof. Whether researchers share group identifications with participants or not, these locations create assumptions that can affect the research process. With regard to professional biases and assumptions, these may arise from familiarity with the extant literature and from team members' prior knowledge of topic- or population-related theory. Whether personal or professional, previously held views and ideas must be discussed to further elucidate them and how they may come into play during the research process (Hill et al., 1997; Hill et al., 2005; Morrow, 2005). Such an examination should include cultural similarities and differences, over- or under-identification, and sympathetic postures. Positive biases can play as big a role as negative biases.

DATA COLLECTION

Maintaining Flexibility and Focus

Flexibility is built into the semi-structured and unstructured interview formats, and interviewers should make use of it while monitoring its use mindfully. Participants can take open-ended questions in unanticipated directions—a desired outcome in multicultural research, but one that must be skillfully guided for best results (Hill et al., 1997; Rubin & Rubin, 1995). Qualitative researchers can exercise the freedom to follow topic- and theme-relevant tangents but should stay mindful of the need to guide participants who get significantly off track back to the prepared questions or to theme-relevant probes (Kvale, 1996; Rubin & Rubin, 1995). At the same time, interviewers should remain aware that, because of the asymmetry of power and our skills as therapists, participants may find themselves sharing

more than they wish to (Fassinger, 2005; Haverkamp, 2005; Morrow, 2007).

Therefore, multiculturally competent qualitative researchers provide for participants before, during, and after the interview. For instance, they can precede the interview with an explanation of its general purpose and the process. During the interview, a similar respect for the participants' self-efficacy and boundaries should be demonstrated. Rubin and Rubin (1995) remind qualitative researchers to remain open to redesigning a question if the need becomes apparent. Hill et al. (2005) noted that revising questions is common—and acceptable when kept track of for the write-up. For example, Suzuki, Prendes-Lintel, Wertlieb, and Stallings (1999) realized the need to reword one of the questions posed to adults who had been unaccompanied child refugees from Cuba (known as Pedro Pans). The question—How did the refugee experience affect your "current sense of stability?" (p. 125)—contained negative connotations reflecting the researchers' worldview. They changed it to "How does the refugee experience affect you now?" (p. 126), a neutral probe that transferred the agency to the participants.

Debriefing the Interviewers

Qualitative interviewers often debrief by making notes about interviews soon after completion, while the experience is still fresh (Kvale, 1996). Particularly with under-studied populations, the *concrete principle* of recording thoughts from a descriptive rather than an interpretive perspective is recommended (Spradley, 1979), as this allows for greater communication of participants' voices. These field notes can describe interpersonal impressions as well as observations about the participants' behavior, the environment, and "observer effects" (Arnold, 1982, p. 58). Such information can provide a valuable context that may be missing from the transcript, even if it was present during the interview.

In qualitative research, another key source of data is what may be termed the *participant effect*—the changes that researchers undergo as a function of experiencing life on the participants' terms. Thus, through group debriefing, interviewers may find that some expectations and biases were confirmed and others contradicted. Because subjectivity plays a role in the qualitative research process by design (Kvale, 1996; Morrow, 2007), such shifting perceptions should be noted for the write-up. In addition to perceptual shifts, group debriefing can also uncover a broadening of the researchers' knowledge about participants and their topic prior to data analysis. Beginning to gain insight from the data during the debriefing stage can be encouraging and exciting. The qualitative research process is so inherently time- and labor-intensive (Miles & Huberman, 1994) that small payoffs in the form of perceptual shifts and new insights can engender some much-needed stamina for the remaining stages of the process.

DATA ANALYSIS

Although data analysis has been variously defined, we use this term to mean the process of organizing and classifying data, leading to pattern and relationship recognition that prepares researchers for interpretation or meaning generation. Similarly, Patton (2002) suggested that *data analysis* is the process by which you "recognize patterns in qualitative data and turn those patterns into meaningful categories and themes" (p. 463). A cursory search of data analysis strategies used in the multicultural counseling literature reveals a robust showing by the constant comparative method (Strauss & Corbin, 1990), usually as part of grounded theory, and more recently, CQR strategies (i.e., creating domains, core ideas, and cross analysis) (Hill et al., 2005; Hill et al., 1997). The popularity of these methods has been attributed to their accessibility given their similarity to strategies employed by postpositivistic researchers (Fassinger, 2005; Hill et al., 1997; Krahn & Putnam, 2003) and accompanying manuals (e.g., Hill et al., 1997) that instruct researchers in language accessible to those previously unaccustomed to qualitative research.

In light of the popularity of data analysis strategies informed by grounded theory and CQR, novice researchers and consumers may be surprised to learn that more than 20 qualitative data analysis strategies have been identified (see Leech & Onwuegbuzie, 2007). Each of these methods prescribes a variety of strategies and processes used to analyze data. Multicultural counseling researchers should select a method with cognizance of the following factors, to name a few: the extent to which the method reflects the paradigmatic allegiance of the researchers, the consistency of the method with the paradigm used to frame the research questions, the type of data collected, and researcher competence. Arguably, the most important consideration is for the method that will convey respect for participants, whether through permission of consent and comfort during data collection or through methods that communicate their "voice" and culture.

Among such diversity of methods, there are similarities (Marshall & Rossman, 1995; Patton, 2002). Elements common to the most popular data analysis strategies include (a) developing a category system, (b) coding the data, (c) recognizing meaningful or related patterns, and (d) considering alternative explanations for the data. First, category systems are developed to reflect a structure inherent in the "raw field notes and verbatim transcripts [that] constitute the undigested complexity of reality" (Patton, 2002, p. 463). Patton likened this step to creating an index for the data during which researchers decide what topics are relevant for inclusion in this index. Depending on the paradigm employed, this category system will be inductively (postpositivist) or deductively (constructivist-interpretive and critical-ideological) developed. For example, dos Santos-Zingale and McColl (2006) determined their coding domains prior to developing the interview protocol in their Sierra Leone study (an approach that they identified as positivist in their Method section). At the other end of the qualitative spectrum, Suzuki et al. (1999) identified themes while reading the transcribed interviews from the Pedro Pan population they studied, as did Remafedi and Carol (2004) in their study of LGBT youth smokers (exemplifying a more constructivist approach).

Next, the researchers code the data by placing them into the categories created, which may take several passes. It is during this process that the quality of the codes can be judged. Specifically, the codes are considered useful when they display *internal homogeneity* (similarity in the data within a category), and *external heterogeneity* (differences between categories) (Guba, 1978). Next, researchers attempt to identify meaningful or related patterns in the data, considering the ways in which relationships between categories might suggest an emerging model or theory (Highlen & Finley, 1996). Finally, the researchers consider alternative explanations for the data using *triangulation*. That is, alternative accounts might be sought by employing multiple data coders representing a variety of cultural backgrounds similar and dissimilar to the study participants, gaining member checks (i.e., what do the participants think of categories, models, and conclusions drawn up to this point?), and using mixed methods (Highlen & Finley, 1996; Ponterotto, 2005a). Naturally, these identified elements of data analysis will not meet with complete agreement with all methods or paradigms. Multiculturally competent qualitative researchers thoroughly review potential data analysis methods from the source as well as exemplar studies in detail before engaging in analysis.

INTERPRETATION

As has been stated previously, the iterative nature of the qualitative research process makes it ineffectual to separate interpretation from other aspects of the research process. This is particularly true of the relationship between interpretation and analysis. We acknowledge this relationship between analysis and interpretation and caution researchers to preserve it. For the purposes of this discussion, however, we define *interpretation* as the aspect of the qualitative research process during which meaning is constructed and communicated for the purposes of describing, explaining, or disputing phenomena, or generating models and theories (Guba & Lincoln, 2005; Miles & Huberman, 1994). In other words, analysis, in the qualitative view, entails organizing data; interpretation entails finding the meanings that lie within them.

Data interpretation in qualitative multicultural counseling research carries with it a particular responsibility: respect for and duty to the community of investigation. Researchers must include those represented in interpretation in meaningful ways that benefit those represented, ideally beginning at the start of research (e.g., meaningful involvement in and by the community of investigation). However, as Haverkamp (2005) identified, what benefits a community will vary based on participants' cultural backgrounds. Depending on the researchers' paradigm, community involvement in the form of "member checks" will consist of asking participants to vet transcripts and tentative interpretations (postpositivist researchers); having participants offer

their own interpretations, which may compete with researchers' interpretations; serving to highlight researcher bias (constructivist-interpretivist researchers); or engaging participants as co-creators in the interpretation process (critical-ideological researchers). Use of such member checks helps fulfill moral responsibility to participants and improves the quality of the interpretations. This may be true whether quality is judged by the research's trustworthiness, the reflection of participants' historical experiences, the encouragement that readers act on behalf of participants, or the ability to challenge naïveté (see Guba & Lincoln, 2005). Tuason (2008), who took a grounded theory approach, employed several of these methods when interpreting data collected from materially impoverished Filipinos, including member checks and focus groups. Lyons et al. (2009), using the postpositivist CQR approach, employed both member checks and an external auditor who specialized in vocational issues with multicultural populations, the topic of the study.

When writing up interpretations, respect for participants can be accomplished, in part, by remaining close to the data. This occurs, in part, through the generous use of informant quotes as is allowed by the chosen paradigm and corresponding method. Liberal use of quotes not only speaks to the quality of the research (Fassinger, 2005; Hoyt & Bhati, 2007) but also is appreciated by informants, who are empowered by, find more accessible and fair, and prefer research interpretations that use direct but confidential quotes over interpretations without quotes (Corden & Sainsbury, 2006).

CONCLUSION

I ascribe a basic importance to the phenomenon of language. . . . To speak means to be in a position to use a certain syntax, to grasp the morphology of this or that language, but it means above all to assume a culture, to support the weight of a civilization. (Fanon, 1967, pp. 17–18)

Multicultural populations are under- and misrepresented in the counseling literature. Qualitative research is well suited to correct this situation when conducted competently because of the close relationships that can be formed between researchers, participants, and communities; the creation of multifaceted depictions of community needs and assets; and the potential for communities to access and benefit from results generated by qualitative research. To help the counseling community increase its comfort and familiarity with this genre, we presented a reflection on how culturally competent qualitative research is conducted beginning with topic, sample, and site selection; moving to research team and instrument development; and then, finally, data collection, analysis, and interpretation. Culturally competent qualitative research can be a powerful tool when it reflects the daily lives of participants in their words, in their settings, and on their terms.

REFERENCES

Arnold, D. O. (1982). Qualitative field methods. In R. B. Smith & P. K. Manning (Eds.), *Qualitative methods: Volume II of handbook of social science methods* (pp. 49–78). Cambridge, MA: Ballinger.

Beckstead, A. L., & Morrow, S. L. (2004). Mormon clients' experiences of conversion therapy: The need for a new treatment approach. *Counseling Psychologist, 32,* 651–690.

Berg, B. L. (2001). *Qualitative research methods for the social sciences* (4th ed.). Needham Heights, MA: Allyn & Bacon.

Blauner, B., & Wellman, D. (1982). The researcher and the researched. In R. B. Smith & P. K. Manning (Eds.) *Qualitative methods: Volume II of handbook of social science methods* (pp. 101–113). Cambridge, MA: Ballinger.

Breen, G. (2008). Interpersonal, intragroup conflict between Southern Baptist pastors: A qualitative inquiry examining contributing factors. *Pastoral Psychology, 56,* 249–268.

Burkard, A. W., Johnson, A. J., Madson, M. B., Pruitt, N. T., Contreras-Tadych, D. A., Kozlowski, J. M., Hess, S. A., & Knox, S. (2006). Supervisor cultural responsiveness and unresponsiveness in cross-cultural supervision. *Journal of Counseling Psychology, 53,* 288–301.

Choudhuri, D. D. (2003). Qualitative research and multicultural counseling competency. In D. B. Pope-Davis, H. L. K. Coleman, W. M. Liu, & R. L. Toporek (Eds.), *Handbook of multicultural competencies in counseling and psychology* (pp. 267–282). Thousand Oaks, CA: Sage.

Choudhuri, D. D. (2005). Conducting culturally sensitive qualitative research. In M. Constantine & D. W. Sue (Eds.), *Strategies for building multicultural competence in mental health and educational settings* (pp. 269–282). Hoboken, NJ: Wiley.

Corden, A., & Sainsbury, R. (2006). Exploring "quality": Research participants' perspectives on verbatim quotations. *International Journal of Social Research Methodology: Theory & Practice, 9,* 97–110.

Denzin, N. K. (2005). Emancipatory discourses and the ethics and politics of interpretation. In N. K. Denzin & Y. S. Lincoln (Eds.), *The Sage handbook of qualitative research* (pp. 933–958). Thousand Oaks, CA: Sage.

dos Santos-Zingale, M., & McColl, M. A. (2006). Disability and participation in post-conflict situations: The case of Sierra Leone. *Disability & Society, 21,* 243–257.

Fanon, F. (1967). *Black skins, white masks.* New York: Grove.

Fassinger, R. E. (2005). Paradigms, praxis, problems, and promise: Grounded theory in counseling psychology research. *Journal of Counseling Psychology, 52,* 156–166.

Fine, M. (1994). Working the hyphens: Reinventing self and other in qualitative research. In N. K. Denzin & Y. S. Lincoln (Eds.), *Handbook of qualitative research* (pp. 70–82). Thousand Oaks, CA: Sage.

Flores, L. Y., He, Y., Jordan, S. E., Medina, V., Mendoza, M. M., Ojeda, L., et al. (2007, August). *Culturally competent qualitative research with Latino immigrants.* Paper presented at the 115th annual meeting of the American Psychological Association, San Francisco.

Guba, E. G. (1978). *Toward a methodology of naturalistic inquiry in educational evaluation* [Monograph 8]. Los Angeles: UCLA Center for the Study of Evaluation.

Guba, E. G., & Lincoln, Y. S. (2005). Paradigmatic controversies, contradictions, and emerging confluences. In N. K. Denzin & Y. S. Lincoln (Eds.), *The Sage handbook of qualitative research* (3rd ed., pp. 191–216). Thousand Oaks, CA: Sage.

Haverkamp, B. E. (2005). Ethical perspectives on qualitative research in applied psychology. *Journal of Counseling Psychology, 52,* 146–155.

Heppner, P. P., Kivlighan, D. M., & Wampold, B. E. (1999). *Research design in counseling.* Belmont, CA: Wadsworth.

Highlen, P. S., & Finley, H. C. (1996). Doing qualitative analysis. In F. T. L. Leong & J. T. Austin (Eds.), *The psychology research handbook: A guide for graduate students and research assistants* (pp. 177–192). Thousand Oaks, CA: Sage.

Hill, C. E., Knox, S., Thompson, B. J., Williams, E. N., Hess, S. A., & Ladany, N. (2005). Consensual qualitative research: An update. *Journal of Counseling Psychology, 52,* 196–205.

Hill, C. E., Thompson, B. J., & Williams, E. N. (1997). A guide to conducting consensual qualitative research. *Counseling Psychologist, 25,* 516–572.

Hoshmand, L. T. (1999). Locating the qualitative research genre. In M. Kopala & L. A. Suzuki (Eds.), *Using qualitative methods in psychology* (pp. 15–24). Thousand Oaks, CA: Sage.

Hoyt, W. T., & Bhati, K. S. (2007). Principles and practices: An empirical examination of qualitative research in the *Journal of Counseling Psychology*. *Journal of Counseling Psychology, 54,* 201–210.

Hughes, M., & Heycox, K. (2008). Using observation for reflective practice with older people. *Educational Gerontology, 34,* 185–205.

Kim, B. S. K., Brenner, B. R., Liang, C. T., & Asay, P. A. (2003). A qualitative study of adaptation experiences of 1.5-generation Asian Americans. *Cultural Diversity and Ethnic Minority Psychology, 9,* 156–170.

Krahn, G. L., & Putnam, M. (2003). Qualitative methods in psychological research. In M. C. Roberts & S. S. Ilardi (Eds.), *Handbook of research methods in clinical psychology* (pp. 176–195). Malden, MA: Blackwell.

Kvale, S. (1996). *Interviews: An introduction to qualitative research interviewing.* Thousand Oaks, CA: Sage.

Leech, N. L., & Onwuegbuzie, A. J. (2007). An array of qualitative data analysis tools: A call for data analysis triangulation. *School Psychology Quarterly, 22,* 557–584.

Leung, A. K., Maddux, W. W., Galinsky, A. D., & Chiu, C. (2008). Multicultural experience enhances creativity. *American Psychologist, 63,* 169–181.

Lyons, H. Z. (1997). *Ethnic identity choices for Black-White biracial individuals: Social influences and consequences.* Unpublished senior honors thesis, Northeastern University.

Lyons, H. Z., & Bike, D. H. (2007, August). *Culturally competent data collection in qualitative research: Sharing strategies and lessons learned.* Paper presented at the 115th annual meeting of the American Psychological Association, San Francisco.

Lyons, H. Z., & O'Brien, K. M. (2006). The role of person-environment fit in the job satisfaction and tenure intentions of African American employees. *Journal of Counseling Psychology, 53,* 387–396.

Lyons, H. Z., O'Brien, K. M., Bike, D. H., Raughley, B., Im, J. G., Smith, H. L., et al. (2009). *Meanings ascribed to work by African American men experiencing chronic unemployment.* Manuscript in preparation.

Marshall, C., & Rossman, G. B. (1995). *Designing qualitative research* (2nd ed.). Thousand Oaks, CA: Sage.

Merchant, N., & Dupuy, P. (1996). Multicultural counseling and qualitative research: Shared worldview and skills. *Journal of Counseling & Development, 74,* 537–541.

Miles, M. B., & Huberman, A. M. (1994). *Qualitative data analysis: An expanded sourcebook* (2nd ed.). Thousand Oaks, CA: Sage.

Morrow, S. L. (2005). Quality and trustworthiness in qualitative research in counseling psychology. *Journal of Counseling Psychology, 52,* 250–260.

Morrow, S. L. (2007). Qualitative research in counseling psychology: Conceptual foundations. *Counseling Psychologist, 35,* 209–235.

Morrow, S. L., Rakhsha, G., & Castaneda, C. L. (2001). Qualitative research methods for multicultural counseling. In J. G. Ponterotto, J. M. Casas, L. A. Suzuki, & C. M. Alexander (Eds.), *Handbook of multicultural counseling* (2nd ed., pp. 575–603). Thousand Oaks, CA: Sage.

Patton, M. Q. (2002). *Qualitative research & evaluation methods* (3rd ed.). Thousand Oaks, CA: Sage.

Pedersen, P. B. (1991). Multiculturalism as a generic approach to counseling. *Journal of Counseling & Development, 70,* 6–12.

Polkinghorne, D. E. (2005). Language and meaning: Data collection in qualitative research. *Journal of Counseling Psychology, 52,* 137–145.

Ponterotto, J. G. (2002). Qualitative research methods: The fifth force in psychology. *Counseling Psychologist, 30,* 394–406.

Ponterotto, J. G. (2005a). Qualitative research in counseling psychology: A primer on research paradigms and philosophy of science. *Journal of Counseling Psychology, 52,* 126–136.

Ponterotto, J. G. (2005b). Qualitative research training in counseling psychology: A survey of directors of training. *Teaching of Psychology, 32,* 60–62.

Remafedi, G., & Carol, H. (2005). Preventing tobacco use among lesbian, gay, bisexual, and transgender youths. *Nicotine & Tobacco Research, 7,* 249–256.

Rubin, H. J., & Rubin, I. S. (1995). *Qualitative interviewing: The art of hearing data.* Thousand Oaks, CA: Sage.

Spradley, J. P. (1979). *The ethnographic interview.* New York: Holt, Rinehart and Winston.

Stiles, W. B., Hurst, R. M., Nelson-Gray, R., Hill, C. E., Greenberg, L. S., Watson, J. C., Borkovek, T. D., Castonguay, L. G., & Hollon, S. D. (2006). What qualifies as research on which to judge effective practice? In J. C. Norcross, L. E. Beutler, & R. F. Levant (Eds.), *Evidence-based practices in mental health: Debate and dialogue on the fundamental questions* (pp. 56–130). Washington, DC: American Psychological Association.

Strauss, A., & Corbin, J. M. (1990). *Basics of qualitative research: Grounded theory procedures and techniques.* Thousand Oaks, CA: Sage.

Suzuki, L. A., Ahluwalia, M. K., Arora, A. K., & Mattis, J. S. (2007). The pond you fish in determines the fish you catch: Exploring strategies for qualitative data collection. *Counseling Psychologist, 35,* 295–327.

Suzuki, L. A., Prendes-Lintel, M., Wertlieb, L., & Stallings, A. (1999). Exploring multicultural issues using qualitative methods. In M. Kopala & L. A. Suzuki (Eds.), *Using qualitative methods in psychology* (pp. 123–133). Thousand Oaks, CA: Sage.

Tuason, T. G. (2008). Those who were born poor: A qualitative study of Philippine poverty. *Journal of Counseling Psychology, 55,* 158–171.

Walsh-Bowers, R. (2002). Constructing qualitative knowledge in psychology. *Canadian Psychology, 43,* 163–179.

Yeh, C. J., & Inman, A. G. (2007). Qualitative data analysis and interpretation in counseling psychology: Strategies for best practices. *Counseling Psychologist, 35,* 369–403.

34

Adapting Mixed Methods Research to Multicultural Counseling

VICKI L. PLANO CLARK AND SHERRY C. WANG

Researchers in the discipline of counseling psychology are encouraged to develop an ever-widening assortment of research methodologies for addressing their research questions (e.g., Gergen, 2001; Polkinghorne, 1991). Traditionally, researchers in the field have turned to quantitative research and focused on measuring trends and testing hypotheses. In recent years, a growing number of researchers have embraced qualitative research and are applying it to understand individuals' perspectives and experiences, generate theories, and give voice to marginalized groups (Ponterotto, 2002). With an increasing awareness and acceptance of qualitative research, some counseling psychology researchers are combining these two approaches within mixed methods research studies (Hanson, Creswell, Plano Clark, Petska, & Creswell, 2005; Hoyt & Bhati, 2007; Plano Clark, 2005). Such combinations can be advantageous when either method alone is insufficient for addressing the problem of interest (Johnson & Onwuegbuzie, 2004; Tashakkori & Creswell, 2007; Tashakkori & Teddlie, 2003). While offering much potential, combining quantitative and qualitative methods can also be challenging, requiring counseling psychologists to demonstrate expertise in two approaches, negotiate the complexity of combining approaches to study a topic, and publish the combined results successfully (Hanson et al., 2005; Plano Clark, 2005; Ponterotto & Grieger, 2007).

One way that researchers learn about the use of a new research approach like mixed methods is by examining published examples within a discipline. Such reviews document the successful use of the method in the discipline, provide researchers with disciplinary exemplars, and uncover nuances that develop as a method

Authors' Note: The authors thank their colleagues in the Office of Qualitative and Mixed Methods Research at the University of Nebraska–Lincoln for their valuable feedback on previous drafts of this manuscript.

is applied within a discipline's context. To date, scholars have studied the use of mixed methods research across a wide array of broad disciplines (Creswell & Plano Clark, 2007), including counseling psychology (Hanson et al., 2005; Plano Clark, 2005; Worthington, Soth-McNett, & Moreno, 2007). Little work, however, has focused on the use of mixed methods within a specific subfield such as multicultural counseling. Therefore, multicultural counseling researchers lack information about how mixed methods research is being applied to study multicultural counseling topics.

There are many reasons why multicultural counseling researchers may want to consider mixed methods research. Mixed methods approaches allow researchers to include the strengths of qualitative research for understanding the perspectives of diverse individuals and developing culturally sensitive relationships (Ponterotto, 2002; Sanchez-Hucles & Jones, 2005). A combination of quantitative and qualitative approaches helps researchers to fully benefit from the different advantages of these diverse methods (Hoyt & Bhati, 2007) and potentially reduce the gap between theory and research (Worthington et al., 2007). Mixed methods is also well suited for research conducted with diverse populations and by researchers who have a social justice perspective, allowing research to be designed that is collaborative, meets the needs of diverse participants, and produces results useful for promoting change (Mertens, 2003). Combining quantitative and qualitative information also mirrors the process that counselors use in practice when they merge quantitative assessments with qualitative information about a client's experiences and the meaning of those experiences (Plano Clark, 2005).

Multicultural counseling researchers need to learn about mixed methods research to adequately interpret published studies, determine its appropriateness for their own research situations, and design studies using this approach that are rigorous and culturally sensitive. This understanding can be advanced through an examination of mixed methods studies from the multicultural counseling literature to learn how researchers are adapting mixed methods to study multicultural counseling issues. Such an examination will provide multicultural counseling researchers with an introduction to mixing methods and exemplars of this approach. It will also provide researchers from any discipline with a discussion of the nuances that emerge when mixed methods approaches are applied to address multicultural topics and participants.

The purpose of this chapter, therefore, is to examine how mixed methods research is being adapted to study multicultural counseling issues. We begin by first providing a definition of mixed methods research from the larger mixed methods literature. Next, we describe our strategies for locating published studies that applied mixed methods to study topics of interest to multicultural counseling. We then discuss key features of the selected studies as examples of both mixed methods research and multicultural research. Finally, we conclude by offering recommendations for multicultural counseling researchers interested in conducting mixed methods research with multicultural sensitivity.

DEFINING MIXED METHODS RESEARCH

Mixed methods research is an approach to research in which a researcher collects, analyzes, and integrates quantitative and qualitative research in a single study or a program of inquiry to best understand a problem (Tashakkori & Creswell, 2007). Fundamental to this definition is that a researcher is combining quantitative and qualitative research. Creswell and Plano Clark (2007) note that this combination can be thought of as both a method and a methodology. As a method, mixed methods research emphasizes the collection and analysis of quantitative data (e.g., the use of numeric scores and statistical analyses) and qualitative data (e.g., the use of text and image data and thematic analyses) and how the two sets of results are combined, or integrated, into a larger interpretation.

Considered as a methodology, mixed methods research includes discussions that attend to the philosophical foundations of this research approach and the implications of underlying assumptions about reality, how knowledge is gained, and the role of values for conducting mixed methods studies (Tashakkori & Teddlie, 1998). Historically, these discussions have focused on the differences between two prominent worldviews for conducting research: postpositivism (e.g., belief in a singular reality, objectivity, deductive logic) and constructivism (e.g., belief in multiple constructed realities, subjectivity, inductive logic). A dialectical stance for mixed methods is that researchers explicitly use both worldviews such that an improved understanding emerges from the resulting tensions and contradictions (Greene & Caracelli, 2003). Other scholars argue that worldviews such as pragmatism (Tashakkori & Teddlie, 2003) or transformative-emancipatory perspectives (Mertens, 2003) provide a foundation for conducting mixed methods research. Based on these differing perspectives of mixed methods research, our examination of the use of mixed methods within multicultural counseling research focused on issues related to both method and methodology within published research articles.

IDENTIFYING MULTICULTURAL COUNSELING EXEMPLARS OF MIXED METHODS RESEARCH

Building on our collective background knowledge about mixed methods research and multicultural counseling, we examined the literature to identify recent examples of mixed methods used to study multicultural counseling topics. We followed search procedures used and refined across numerous disciplines, including counseling psychology (Hanson et al., 2005; Plano Clark, 2005), primary care medicine (Plano Clark, 2005), and family science (Plano Clark, Huddleston-Casas, Churchill, Green, & Garrett, 2008), to locate sample studies. We delimited the current literature search to research studies published within the past 10 years to focus on recent examples. Articles were identified using combinations of the following search terms in the electronic databases of PsycINFO and Web of Science: mixed methods, multimethod*, quantitative AND qualitative, multicultural, cultural*, diversity, and counsel* (where * indicates a wildcard character). We included articles for analysis if they were empirical studies published in peer-reviewed journals. Dissertations, book chapters, nonempirical commentaries, and literature reviews were not included. We identified 12 articles representing 11 mixed methods studies that met the definition of mixed methods research (i.e., collected, analyzed, and combined quantitative and qualitative research). Some articles were published in mainstream counseling psychology journals, but others appeared in journals that were not specific to counseling. We chose to include all that focused on topics relevant to multicultural

counseling, such as multicultural competencies, cultural adaptation, and programs for challenging oppression.

Recent writings in mixed methods (e.g., Creswell & Plano Clark, 2007; Hanson et al., 2005) framed our thinking about the use of mixed methods, but we also remained open to identifying issues and approaches that best described how mixed methods research is actually being used in practice. As we read each study, we analyzed how the authors implemented their mixed methods approach (the methods) and any indications of the worldview(s) that informed the approach (the methodology). In addition, we noted the elements that demonstrated the researchers' applications of this approach within a multicultural context. The following section presents the findings that emerged across the collection of studies.

MIXED METHODS EXEMPLARS FROM MULTICULTURAL COUNSELING RESEARCH

We examined the collection of studies in two different ways. We first considered them as applications of mixed methods research and considered how the authors implemented this approach. We present an overview of the different approaches used and their key mixed methods features. In addition, we considered them as examples of conducting mixed methods research with multicultural topics and diverse populations. We present a separate discussion that describes the researchers' strategies for implementing mixed methods with cultural sensitivity.

The Studies as Examples of Mixed Methods Research

Our examination of the 11 selected studies identified three approaches for applying mixed methods research in multicultural counseling research: one-phase, multiphase, and embedded. These approaches are summarized in Table 34.1, including citations to the corresponding articles. We provide an overview of each approach with specific examples drawn from the identified studies. After describing the major approaches, we also examine three key mixed methods features that differentiated the studies by and/or within approach.

Table 34.1　Mixed Methods Approaches as Applied Within Multicultural Counseling Research

	One-Phase Approach	*Multiphase Approach*	*Embedded Approach*
Exemplars	• Bikos et al. (2007a, 2007b) • Butler-Byrd, Nieto, and Senour (2006) • Diemer, Kauffman, Koenig, Trahan, and Hsieh (2006) • Edwards and Lopez (2006) • Whaley and McQueen (2004)	• Morelli and Spencer (2000) • Poasa, Mallinckrodt, and Suzuki (2000) • Swagler and Ellis (2003) • Tuckwell (2001)	• Varjas et al. (2006) • Williams (2005)
Timing[a]	Concurrent: • Quantitative + Qualitative	Sequential: • Qualitative → Quantitative • Quantitative → Qualitative • Qualitative → Quantitative → Qualitative • Quantitative → Qualitative → Quantitative	Concurrent and sequential
Priority[b]	Equal priority Quantitative priority	Equal priority Quantitative priority Qualitative priority	Quantitative priority
Integration[c]	Merge Results: • Compare and contrast two sets of results in discussion • Transform qualitative results into a numerical score and analyze statistically with quantitative data	Connect Phases: • Design quantitative phase to test hypotheses from qualitative phase • Develop questionnaire items based on qualitative results • Design qualitative interview questions to follow up on quantitative results • Use qualitative focus groups to explain the nature of the relationships among variables	Embed Within a Design: • Collect qualitative data during an experimental intervention to study the process • Collect qualitative data from experimental group after an intervention to study the process • Use qualitative data to understand cultural contexts before designing an intervention

a. Timing is the chronological relationship describing when the quantitative and qualitative methods are used in the study.

b. Priority is the relative emphasis of the use of quantitative and qualitative research to address the study's purpose.

c. Integration is how the quantitative and qualitative results are related to each other within the study.

One-Phase Mixed Methods Studies. We classified five of the studies as using a one-phase approach because the authors reported conducting their quantitative and qualitative research during the same phase of the study. In these studies, the authors chose to combine quantitative and qualitative research in order to develop a more complete picture of a complex phenomenon (Bikos et al., 2007a, 2007b; Edwards & Lopez, 2006), reach more valid conclusions based on consistencies across multiple types of evidence (Butler-Byrd, Nieto, & Senour, 2006; Whaley & McQueen, 2004), or assess relationships between qualitative and quantitative information (Diemer, Kauffman, Koenig, Trahan, & Hsieh, 2006).

To accomplish these goals, the authors of these studies collected and analyzed their quantitative and qualitative data during the same time frame of the research process. The two data sets were first analyzed separately and then the separate results were combined. Four of the studies combined the results by comparing and contrasting the two sets of findings during the discussion and interpretation, even in one case where the two sets of results were reported in a pair of companion articles published in one journal issue (Bikos et al., 2007a, 2007b). Diemer et al. (2006) combined their data sets in a different way. They analyzed their qualitative responses, used a framework to quantitize the responses, and used these "quantitized" data in subsequent statistical analyses. This quantification of qualitative information indicated an overall quantitative priority to this study, whereas in some of the other studies, the two methods appeared to be equally important for addressing the overall purpose of the study.

This set of one-phase studies represents a common approach for conducting mixed methods research. In the literature, these one-phase designs have been referred to as parallel/simultaneous (Tashakkori & Teddlie, 1998), concurrent triangulation (Creswell, Plano Clark, Gutmann, & Hanson, 2003), and convergence (Creswell, 1999). Although the studies' authors did not use these names for their approaches, some provided clear indications as to their one-phase approach. Example statements included the following: "Our longitudinal data were collected concurrently throughout the project; equal weight was given to the quantitative and qualitative data; and data were analyzed separately, compared, and contrasted" (Bikos et al., 2007a, p. 30) and "both quantitative and qualitative data were collected at the same time, and the primary methodology was quantitative" (Edwards & Lopez, 2006, p. 281).

Multiphase Mixed Methods Studies. The second type of mixed methods approach we found consisted of studies that employed the quantitative and qualitative methods in distinct phases, one after the other. For studies using a multiphase mixed methods approach, one method alone proved to be inadequate to address the multicultural topic of interest. For example, Poasa, Mallinckrodt, and Suzuki (2000) described the need to collect qualitative data that "allowed explorations of indigenous notions" (p. 37) to follow up and help explain cultural differences measured quantitatively.

Morelli and Spencer (2000) needed to use a mixed methods approach to first explore and then measure trends about the use of multicultural and antiracist education practices. The other two examples represented programs of inquiry that used different methods in multiple phases to build on emergent findings (Swagler & Ellis, 2003; Tuckwell, 2001).

The multiphase studies were straightforward to classify because the authors collected and analyzed their quantitative and qualitative data at different times and in two or three distinct phases. For each phase, the authors collected and analyzed one type of data (qualitative or quantitative) and based on those results, planned and implemented a subsequent phase (quantitative or qualitative). Two of the studies began with a quantitative phase (Poasa et al., 2000; Tuckwell, 2001), and the other two began qualitatively (Morelli & Spencer, 2000; Swagler & Ellis, 2003). The authors made connections between the phases in different ways, including designing a quantitative phase to test hypotheses generated from a qualitative phase, developing questionnaire items based on qualitative results, posing qualitative interview questions to follow up on quantitative results, and using qualitative focus groups to explain the nature of the relationships among variables. Some studies appeared to place heavier emphasis on the initial quantitative or qualitative phase, whereas others treated each phase equally as its own study.

These multiphase studies encompass a range of sequential mixed methods designs discussed in the literature. Although most mixed methods design typologies include sequential designs (e.g., Creswell & Plano Clark, 2007), the discussion is often limited to two-phase studies differentiated by the method used in the initial phase. Three-phase "sandwich" approaches, however, have been mentioned in the mixed methods literature (e.g., Miles & Huberman, 1994; Sandelowski, 2003). In multicultural counseling research, we found as many examples of three-phase approaches as two-phase approaches. Therefore, iterating between methods in a deliberate sequence appears to be a viable approach. As with the one-phase designs, the authors used specific language to signal their use of multiple phases, such as "a two-phase multimethod field design" (Morelli & Spencer, 2000, p. 169) and "a series of studies" (Swagler & Ellis, 2003, p. 421).

Embedded Mixed Methods Studies. The third mixed methods approach that we identified represented studies where authors embedded qualitative methods within a larger quantitative experimental and evaluative design (Varjas et al., 2006; Williams, 2005). These studies differed from the others because the authors framed their studies with a design traditionally associated with quantitative methods, but also incorporated qualitative methods to enhance the implementation and interpretation of the larger quantitative study. For example, Williams (2005) conducted a pretest-posttest nonequivalent comparison group design to test the effectiveness of a cultural competence training intervention. She also had questions about the process by which cultural competence develops and therefore included sources of qualitative data within her experimental study. Varjas et al. (2006) used qualitative information to "learn the culture" (p. 40) of a school before designing an intervention aimed at improving the environment for gay, lesbian, bisexual, transgender, questioning, and intersex youth.

Although the embedded studies were guided by quantitative methodology, the researchers collected and analyzed qualitative data at various points of time during the study, including before, during, and after the intervention. The timing of the qualitative methods depended on its purpose for enhancing the overall study's goals. Williams (2005) organized her findings by individual and group and reported both the quantitative outcome results and the qualitative process results for each category. In this way, the qualitative findings "supplemented" (p. 123) the quantitative experimental results. Varjas et al. (2006) described using qualitative information at numerous points in time and in numerous ways throughout their overall evaluation and experimental process to design and assess the effectiveness of the intervention.

These two studies are examples of an embedded mixed methods approach (Creswell & Plano Clark, 2007; Greene & Caracelli, 1997). The name of this design indicates that one type of method (in this case, qualitative) is embedded within a design traditionally associated with the other method (in this case, a quantitative experimental design). In embedded designs, the two methods are often used to address different questions (such as about process and outcomes) and one method plays a supporting role to enhance or augment the other method. For example, Williams (2005) described her overall study in the following way: "The study used a pretest-posttest nonequivalent comparison group design, and evaluation was based on both quantitative and qualitative data collections" (p. 111).

Looking across these different approaches to conducting mixed methods research, we see that the researchers made several decisions while designing their studies. These decisions relate to the timing of the quantitative and qualitative methods, how they are mixed or integrated, and their relative priority. Different options for these decisions as illustrated in the example studies are summarized in Table 34.1 and discussed in more detail in the following sections.

Timing Within the Mixed Methods Studies. The chronological timing for implementing the quantitative and qualitative methods is a defining characteristic of any mixed methods approach (Teddlie, Tashakkori, & Johnson, 2008). In general, researchers have two options for the timing of their mixed methods studies: concurrent or sequential (Morse, 1991). In studies with concurrent timing, researchers collect, analyze, and interpret the two types of data during one phase (i.e., during the same time frame), such as in the Bikos et al. (2007a, 2007b) study. Researchers conducting sequential studies collect, analyze, and interpret the methods in two (or more) phases, using the results from one method to inform the subsequent method. The quantitative or the qualitative methods may be implemented first in sequential studies, as illustrated by the multiphase studies listed in Table 34.1.

Although many mixed methods discussions describe timing as an either-or choice, this was not always the case in the multicultural counseling studies. For example, Williams's (2005) study included both a concurrent (i.e., collecting qualitative information at the same time as the quantitative measures) and a sequential (i.e., follow-up interviews) aspect to her qualitative data collection. In addition, Tuckwell (2001) used a three-phase sequential timing (quantitative → qualitative → quantitative) to study racial and cultural dynamics in the counseling process.

Integration Within the Mixed Methods Studies. In addition to timing, the concept of integration has become central to thinking about mixed methods research (Teddlie & Tashakkori, 2006) and represents another key methodological decision. Integration, also known as mixing, refers to the way or ways by which a researcher explicitly relates the quantitative and qualitative aspects of a mixed methods study. It is not enough for both methods to be present; researchers should combine them so that they learn more from the combination than just the separate sets of results. The examined studies illustrate three major ways that authors integrate in a mixed methods study: merging results, connecting between phases, and embedding to enhance a design (Creswell & Plano Clark, 2007).

The studies using a one-phase approach all demonstrated mixing by merging results. For example, Edwards and Lopez (2006) merged the results of their two data sets and noted that the findings were "integrated to reveal areas of convergence as well as areas in which the data suggested discrepant findings or helped to provide a context for the data" (p. 281). Diemer et al. (2006) demonstrated an approach to merging that occurs during data analysis by describing their integration process as follows: "The obtained qualitative data were coded by the research team and 'quantitized' . . . for subsequent quantitative analyses" (p. 449). In contrast to merging, the multiphase studies mixed by making connections between phases. Poasa et al. (2000) noted that they collected qualitative data in a second phase "to expand and . . . elaborate on" (p. 42) the quantitative results. Swagler and Ellis (2003) connected in several ways, such as posing hypotheses and conducting a quantitative phase "to build on and test further the findings from Study 1 [qualitative]" (p. 426). Williams (2005) provides an example of integrating by embedding when she embedded supplemental qualitative data to "contribute additional information" (p. 123) and enrich the quantitative outcome results.

Priority Within the Mixed Methods Studies. In addition to timing and integration, scholars often consider the relative priority given to the quantitative and qualitative methods for addressing a mixed methods study's purpose (Morgan, 1998; Morse, 1991). The two methods may be equally important, or one method may be prioritized more than the other (e.g., see the different classifications across the 11 studies found in Table 34.1).

Ideally, researchers explicitly indicate the priority with a statement such as "equal weight was given to the quantitative and qualitative data" (Bikos et al., 2007a, p. 30). This information conveys an important aspect of the relationship between the methods within a mixed methods study. If the priority is not explicitly stated by the authors, then judgments may be based on characteristics such as the overall study purpose (explanation and/or exploration), the relative extent and sophistication of the quantitative and qualitative components, sampling procedures (random and/or purposeful), and criteria used to judge the study's quality (generalizability and/or rich description).

The priority of mixed methods studies is an important consideration for many because it ties to the worldviews and assumptions that researchers bring to their studies (Greene, Caracelli, & Graham, 1989; Morse, 1991). Quantitative and qualitative research represent important paradigmatic differences, including different cultures and assumptions for conducting multicultural counseling research (Hoyt & Bhati, 2007; Ponterotto, 2002). Over the years, many writers have problematized paradigmatic issues such as ontology (the nature of reality), epistemology (how we gain knowledge), and axiology (the role of values) for those considering mixed methods research (see the historical review in Tashakkori & Teddlie, 1998). The central premise of these debates was that quantitative and qualitative research cannot be "mixed" because of their paradigmatic differences. Today, these debates have largely quieted, but researchers still need to carefully reflect on the role of paradigms and assumptions within their mixed methods studies.

Creswell and Plano Clark (2007) summarized three stances on paradigms in mixed methods research, and we found examples of each in the identified multicultural counseling studies. One stance is that there is a "best" paradigm for mixed methods research, such as pragmatism or a transformative-emancipatory perspective (Tashakkori & Teddlie, 2003). For example, Edwards and Lopez (2006) noted that their study of the development of a critical consciousness "was conceptualized from a pragmatic theoretical paradigm" (p. 281). A second stance is for researchers to use both the post-positivist and constructivist paradigms in a dialectic (Greene & Caracelli, 2003). Bikos et al. (2007a, 2007b) provide an example of this approach as they published the two components of their study in separate manuscripts due to "the distinctiveness of the scientific paradigm and philosophies of science" (p. 6) behind the quantitative and qualitative research. Swagler and Ellis (2003) emphasized that they followed a "paradigm for qualitative research" (p. 421) for their qualitative phase, highlighting the different assumptions from the quantitative phase of their study. Finally, researchers might use different paradigms based on the nature of their purpose and study design (Creswell & Plano Clark, 2007), such as Williams (2005), who embedded qualitative data within a traditional postpositivist experimental design.

The Studies as Examples of Multicultural Research

In addition to examining the methodology of the studies as examples of mixed methods research, we also considered them as exemplars for conducting multicultural research using a mixed methods approach. In conducting mixed methods research, researchers are faced with a variety of opportunities as well as challenges to integrate cultural sensitivity into the methodological process. All of the studies considered topics of interest to multicultural counseling, and most included participants that represented diverse and/or marginalized groups, including African Americans; Native Americans; Mexican Americans; Taiwanese students with sojourner status in the United States; and gay, lesbian, bisexual, transgender, questioning, and intersex youth. We noted decisions reported in the studies that reflected the authors' strategies for conducting research with multicultural participants. We conducted a thematic analysis of our notes, and seven categories emerged to describe the multicultural elements of the studies' methods. The following themes provide examples as to how the authors of the identified studies conducted culturally sensitive mixed methods research.

Defining the Problem Based on Experiences and Need for Social Change. Researchers indicated a multicultural perspective as they conceptualized the research problem. For example, Swagler was motivated to start her line of research based on her awareness of difficulties experienced by Taiwanese friends and students, as

well as the underrepresentation of this group within the counseling literature (Swagler & Ellis, 2003). Other scholars conveyed that they selected their research topic and theoretical framework as a means to bring about social change (Diemer et al., 2006; Morelli & Spencer, 2000). One group waited to define the problem until after having first developed a partnership with the community of interest and then selecting a problem based on its needs (Varjas et al., 2006).

Selecting Methods That Best Fit With the Study Topic and Participants. Researchers selected their research design by taking into consideration the cultural context of their study as well as participants' experiences. For example, scholars incorporated qualitative methods into their research so as to not impose the researchers' worldviews onto participants' experiences and perspectives (Poasa et al., 2000; Swagler & Ellis, 2003). Qualitative methods were also used to understand the cultural context of the participants to best design an intervention that meets their unique cultural needs (Varjas et al., 2006). In addition, the use of pluralistic methodologies were highlighted as being the best approach to use in order to examine complex phenomena related to racial and cultural research (Tuckwell, 2001).

Using Multicultural Research Teams. Research teams play an important role in conducting culturally sensitive research. Researchers highlighted the relevance of selecting members based on their familiarity with the study topic and their prior experiences with the study population. For example, in Bikos and colleagues' (2007a, 2007b) study with female expatriate spouses in Turkey, the authors purposefully selected a research team composed of four Turkish and four American members. Edwards and Lopez (2006) also assembled a multiethnic team that included members who identified themselves as Latina/White, Mexican American, and European American in a study examining the experiences and attitudes of Mexican American youth. The importance of multicultural teams was emphasized with regard to the collection and analysis of data. Swagler and Ellis (2003) selected interviewers and coders who were both familiar and unfamiliar with Taiwanese culture and the purpose of the research study in order to be sensitive and to attend to potential bias.

Collaborating With Gatekeepers. Gaining entry into a community is an integral component to conducting culturally sensitive multicultural mixed methods research. This process included soliciting help from various administrators (Edwards & Lopez, 2006) and from presidents of cultural organizations (Swagler & Ellis, 2003), and even providing a separate section in a report about the process of "gaining entry" with the help of community leaders to recruit participants in Western Samoa (Poasa et al., 2000). Community collaboration also includes having stakeholders in the project, and researchers emphasized the importance of bridging research with the community and community-based agencies (e.g., Varjas et al., 2006; Whaley & McQueen, 2004).

Acknowledging Researcher Subjectivity. The primary researchers' knowledge of the study content and their own level of awareness of the cultural groups participating in the study are important assets to a multicultural research study. In some studies, researchers included separate sections to detail the "subjectivity" of the researcher and specific background experiences relevant to the study content (e.g., Swagler & Ellis, 2003). Other researchers also explicitly acknowledged their familiarity with the research participants and used this knowledge to guide methods decisions and interpretations (e.g., Diemer et al., 2006; Tuckwell, 2001).

Considering Linguistic Differences. With regard to conducting studies with participants who are not native English speakers, researchers used strategies for linguistic sensitivity. Poasa and colleagues (2000) conducted translation and back-translation for their study materials with Samoan study participants, whereas Edwards and Lopez (2006) translated consent materials from English into Spanish for the parents of Mexican adolescent participants. Even when researchers were not fluent in the language of participants, one noted that speaking at least a little of their language can help to establish rapport with participants (Swagler & Ellis, 2003).

Being Sensitive to Within-Group Cultural Contexts. Researchers demonstrated cultural sensitivity by acknowledging differences within groups and not treating all ethnic or minority groups as homogeneous. For example, Swagler and Ellis (2003) described the unique cultural contexts of Taiwanese as compared with other Chinese groups, Edwards and Lopez (2006) focused on Mexican Americans as having their own culture within the general Hispanic culture, and Poasa et al. (2000) indicated the importance of considering two Samoan cultures for their study. Although not focused on groups defined by diversity, Williams (2005) also argued for the importance of considering individual processes in addition to group processes.

CONCLUDING COMMENTS

This chapter has provided a definition of mixed methods research and demonstrated that studies that combine quantitative and qualitative research are being conducted and published successfully in the area of multicultural counseling research. Among the studies examined, there are currently at least three approaches for mixing quantitative and qualitative methods in the field: one-phase, multiphase, and embedded. These approaches differ in terms of researchers' reasons for mixing methods, the chronological timing of the methods, and how the results of the two methods are mixed. In addition, researchers used different priorities and worldviews for designing their research studies across the approaches.

This collection of studies presents an interesting picture of how mixed methods research is currently being adapted by multicultural counseling researchers. Compared to other disciplinary reviews conducted by Plano Clark (Hanson et al., 2005; Plano Clark, 2005; Plano Clark et al., 2008), the authors of this group of studies made noticeably more use of mixed methods terminology, and they provided more sophisticated discussions of their use of mixed methods, including issues such as timing, priority, and mixing. Perhaps this is indicative of researchers gaining increased awareness of this approach. Also, although Ponterotto (2002) cautioned multicultural counseling researchers against using both methods concurrently, we found similar numbers of studies using concurrent approaches as using approaches across two or more phases. This prevalence of concurrent mixed methods designs in the literature has been found previously in other disciplines such as counseling psychology (Hanson et al., 2005) and family science (Plano Clark et al., 2008). Finally, researchers' reports of multiphase designs that included more than two distinct sequential phases provide interesting models for reporting mixed methods programs of inquiry.

Along with providing models of innovative mixed methods designs, this group of studies also suggested a rich collection of strategies for conducting mixed methods research that is culturally sensitive. Some of these strategies could apply to quantitative, qualitative, or mixed methods research (such as the use of multicultural teams). Others, however, spoke to the specific advantages that can occur when researchers are open to using diverse and pluralistic methods. These strategies add to other methodological discussions that seriously consider the role of the researcher when studying diverse populations and how research design can reflect multicultural concerns. The works by Mertens (2003) and Green, Creswell, Shope, and Plano Clark (2007) both emphasized how to incorporate diversity and cultural issues within each step of the research process, from defining the problem to reporting the results. As such, the themes reported in this chapter correspond to many of the same issues raised by these authors. We found, however, that some of our emergent categories, such as research teams, have implications across multiple steps. All of the studies we examined suggested valuable insights for using mixed methods research and conducting multicultural research. We noted a general trend, however, that studies strongest in methodology were not always strongest in multicultural competency, and vice versa. Therefore, it appears that researchers could benefit from increased discussion about and awareness of issues related to combining methodological and multicultural emphases. We encourage all multicultural counseling researchers to seriously reflect on both their methods and their multicultural strategies, and to share the lessons learned with the community in their research reports.

Although mixed methods studies may not be prevalent, we have found that the field of multicultural counseling is open to diverse methodologies, including mixed methods, and researchers need to be aware of major features associated with quantitative, qualitative, and mixed methods research approaches. This awareness helps researchers to critically interpret research studies in the field. In addition, knowing about different research approaches helps researchers choose the approach that best fits their purpose for conducting

research. If a quantitative or qualitative approach alone is inadequate, then researchers should consider whether their research questions might be best served by a mixed methods approach.

Mixed methods research is an appealing option for many researchers; it simply makes sense to combine the strengths of quantitative and qualitative approaches. These strengths, however, can be realized in multicultural counseling only if researchers apply mixed methods approaches in a thoughtful and informed way that is methodologically *and* culturally competent. Perhaps learning to work with these two worldviews and approaches within one study can be considered analogous to learning to take multiple viewpoints in counseling diverse populations. That is, mixed methods research may present numerous challenges, but it also offers the potential for meaningful insights and improved understandings when done well.

Drawing on the framework of multicultural counseling competencies (Sue, Arredondo, & McDavis, 1992), researchers need to develop beliefs and attitudes, knowledge, and skills for conducting and interpreting mixed methods research that is culturally sensitive. To help with the design and interpretation of multicultural mixed methods studies, we conclude by suggesting six multimethological and multicultural competencies useful for conducting and interpreting multicultural counseling mixed methods research:

1. Before mixing methods, first develop an understanding about what it means to conduct rigorous qualitative research in addition to rigorous quantitative research. Recognize that these approaches represent different assumptions, cultures, and methods of research (Neuman, 2006). Having expertise in both separately will enhance your ability to combine them in effective ways.

2. Develop an understanding of the assumptions and worldviews that you bring to conducting research, and articulate these assumptions for your mixed methods study. Consider whether a pragmatic (Tashakkori & Teddlie, 2003), transformative-emancipatory (Mertens, 2003), or dialectical (Greene & Caracelli, 2003) stance provides the best foundation for your research.

3. Examine the assumptions and worldviews that you bring to your topic, and use strategies and methods

to ensure that you are open to learning how they may differ from your participants' assumptions and world-views about the topic.

4. Offer an explicit rationale describing why your study's purpose requires you to use mixed methods research and how the approach fits the multicultural contexts of the study.

5. Become familiar with the mixed methods literature, and use mixed methods terminology, concepts, and citations in your published report. Examine recent mixed methods books for more formal discussions of these issues (e.g., Bergman, 2008; Creswell & Plano Clark, 2007; Greene, 2007; Plano Clark & Creswell, 2008; Ridenour & Newman, 2008; Teddlie & Tashakkori, 2009).

6. Consider mixed methods decisions (such as timing, priority, and integration) and multicultural decisions (such as team membership and use of researcher experiences), and discuss these decisions as important aspects within the design of your study.

REFERENCES

Bergman, M. (Ed.). (2008). *Advances in mixed methods research: Theories and applications.* London: Sage.

Bikos, L. H., Çiftçi, A., Güneri, O. Y., Demir, C. E., Sümer, Z. H., Danielson, S., DeVries, S., & Bilgen, W. A. (2007a). A longitudinal, naturalistic inquiry of the adaptation experiences of the female expatriate spouse living in Turkey. *Journal of Career Development, 34,* 28–58.

Bikos, L. H., Çiftçi, A., Güneri, O. Y., Demir, C. E., Sümer, Z. H., Danielson, S., DeVries, S., & Bilgen, W. A. (2007b). A repeated measures investigation of the first-year adaptation experiences of the female expatriate spouse living in Turkey. *Journal of Career Development, 34,* 5–27.

Butler-Byrd, N., Nieto, J., & Senour, M. N. (2006). Working successfully with diverse students and communities: The community-based block counselor preparation program. *Urban Education, 41,* 376–401.

Creswell, J. W. (1999). Mixed-method research: Introduction and application. In G. J. Cizek (Ed.), *Handbook of educational policy* (pp. 455–472). San Diego, CA: Academic Press.

Creswell, J. W., & Plano Clark, V. L. (2007). *Designing and conducting mixed methods research.* Thousand Oaks, CA: Sage.

Creswell, J. W., Plano Clark, V. L., Gutmann, M., & Hanson, W. (2003). Advanced mixed methods research designs. In A. Tashakkori & C. Teddlie (Eds.), *Handbook of mixed methods in social and behavioral research* (pp. 209–240). Thousand Oaks, CA: Sage.

Diemer, M. A., Kauffman, A., Koenig, N., Trahan, E., & Hsieh, C. (2006). Challenging racism, sexism, and social injustice: Support for urban adolescents' critical consciousness development. *Cultural Diversity and Ethnic Minority Psychology, 12,* 444–460.

Edwards, L. M., & Lopez, S. J. (2006). Perceived family support, acculturation, and life satisfaction in Mexican American youth: A mixed-methods exploration. *Journal of Counseling Psychology, 53,* 279–287.

Gergen, K. J. (2001). Psychological science in a postmodern context. *American Psychologist, 56,* 803–813.

Green, D. O., Creswell, J. W., Shope, R. J., & Plano Clark, V. L. (2007). Grounded theory and diversity. In A. Bryant & K. Charmaz (Eds.), *The handbook of grounded theory* (pp. 444–464). London: Sage.

Greene, J. C. (2007). *Mixed methods in social inquiry.* San Francisco: Jossey-Bass.

Greene, J. C., & Caracelli, V. J. (Eds.). (1997). *Advances in mixed-method evaluation: The challenges and benefits of integrating diverse paradigms* [New Directions for Evaluation, No. 74]. San Francisco: Jossey-Bass.

Greene, J. C., & Caracelli, V. J. (2003). Making paradigmatic sense of mixed methods practice. In A. Tashakkori & C. Teddlie (Eds.), *Handbook of mixed methods in social and behavioral research* (pp. 91–110). Thousand Oaks, CA: Sage.

Greene, J. C., Caracelli, V. J., & Graham, W. F. (1989). Toward a conceptual framework for mixed-method evaluation designs. *Educational Evaluation and Policy Analysis, 11,* 255–274.

Hanson, W. E., Creswell, J. W., Plano Clark, V. L., Petska, K. S., & Creswell, J. D. (2005). Mixed methods research designs in counseling psychology. *Journal of Counseling Psychology, 52,* 224–235.

Hoyt, W. T., & Bhati, K. S. (2007). Principles and practices: An empirical examination of qualitative research in the *Journal of Counseling Psychology. Journal of Counseling Psychology, 54,* 201–210.

Johnson, R. B., & Onwuegbuzie, A. J. (2004). Mixed methods research: A research paradigm whose time has come. *Educational Researcher, 33,* 14–26.

Mertens, D. M. (2003). Mixed methods and the politics of human research: The transformative-emancipatory perspective. In A. Tashakkori & C. Teddlie (Eds.), *Handbook of mixed methods in social and behavioral research* (pp. 135–164). Thousand Oaks, CA: Sage.

Miles, M. B., & Huberman, A. M. (1994). *Qualitative data analysis: An expanded sourcebook* (2nd ed.). Thousand Oaks, CA: Sage.

Morelli, P. T. T., & Spencer, M. S. (2000). Use and support of multicultural and antiracist education: Research-informed interdisciplinary social work practice. *Social Work, 45,* 166–175.

Morgan, D. L. (1998). Practical strategies for combining qualitative and quantitative methods: Applications to health research. *Qualitative Health Research, 8,* 362–376.

Morse, J. M. (1991). Approaches to qualitative-quantitative methodological triangulation. *Nursing Research, 40,* 120–123.

Neuman, W. L. (2006). *Social research methods: Qualitative and quantitative approaches* (6th ed.). Boston: Pearson Education.

Plano Clark, V. L. (2005). Cross-disciplinary analysis of the use of mixed methods in physics education research, counseling psychology, and primary care. *Dissertation Abstracts International, 66,* 02A.

Plano Clark, V. L., & Creswell, J. W. (2008). *The mixed methods reader.* Thousand Oaks, CA: Sage.

Plano Clark, V. L., Huddleston-Casas, C. A., Churchill, S. L., Green, D. O., & Garrett, A. L. (2008). Mixed methods approaches in family science research. *Journal of Family Issues, 29,* 1543–1566.

Poasa, K. H., Mallinckrodt, B., & Suzuki, L. A. (2000). Causal attributions for problematic family interactions: A qualitative, cultural comparison of Western Samoa, American Samoa, and the United States. *Counseling Psychologist, 28,* 32–60.

Polkinghorne, D. E. (1991). Two conflicting calls for methodological reform. *Counseling Psychologist, 19,* 103–114.

Ponterotto, J. G. (2002). Qualitative research methods: The fifth force in psychology. *Counseling Psychologist, 30,* 394–406.

Ponterotto, J. G., & Grieger, I. (2007). Effectively communicating qualitative research. *Counseling Psychologist, 35,* 404–430.

Ridenour, C. S., & Newman, I. (2008). *Mixed methods research: Exploring the interactive continuum* (2nd ed.). Carbondale: Southern Illinois University Press.

Sanchez-Hucles, J., & Jones, N. (2005). Breaking the silence around race in training, practice, and research. *Counseling Psychologist, 33,* 547–558.

Sandelowski, M. (2003). Tables or tableaux? The challenges of writing and reading mixed methods studies. In A. Tashakkori & C. Teddlie (Eds.), *Handbook of mixed*

methods in social and behavioral research (pp. 321–350). Thousand Oaks, CA: Sage.

Sue, D. W., Arredondo, P., & McDavis, R. J. (1992). Multicultural counseling competencies and standards: A call to the profession. *Journal of Counseling and Development, 70,* 477–486.

Swagler, M. A., & Ellis, M. V. (2003). Crossing the distance: Adjustment of Taiwanese graduate students in the United States. *Journal of Counseling Psychology, 50,* 420–437.

Tashakkori, A., & Creswell, J. W. (2007). The new era of mixed methods. *Journal of Mixed Methods Research, 1,* 3–7.

Tashakkori, A., & Teddlie, C. (1998). *Mixed methodology: Combining qualitative and quantitative approaches.* Thousand Oaks, CA: Sage.

Tashakkori, A., & Teddlie, C. (Eds.). (2003). *Handbook of mixed methods in social and behavioral research.* Thousand Oaks, CA: Sage.

Teddlie, C., & Tashakkori, A. (2006). A general typology of research designs featuring mixed methods. *Research in the Schools, 13,* 12–28.

Teddlie, C., & Tashakkori, A. (2009). *Foundations of mixed methods research.* Thousand Oaks, CA: Sage.

Teddlie, C., Tashakkori, A., & Johnson, B. (2008). Emergent techniques in the gathering and analysis of mixed methods data. In S. Hesse-Biber & P. Leavy (Eds.), *Handbook of emergent methods* (pp. 389–413). New York: Guilford.

Tuckwell, G. (2001). "The threat of the other": Using mixed quantitative and qualitative methods to elucidate racial and cultural dynamics in the counselling process. *Counselling and Psychotherapy Research, 1,* 154–162.

Varjas, K., Meyers, J., Henrich, C. C., Graybill, E. C., Dew, B. J., Marshall, M. L., Williamson, Z., Skoczylas, R. B., & Avant, M. (2006). Using a participatory culture-specific intervention model to develop a peer victimization intervention. *Journal of Applied School Psychology, 22,* 35–57.

Whaley, A. L., & McQueen, J. P. (2004). An Afrocentric program as primary prevention for African American youth: Qualitative and quantitative exploratory data. *Journal of Primary Prevention, 25,* 253–269.

Williams, C. C. (2005). Training for cultural competence: Individual and group processes. *Journal of Ethnic & Cultural Diversity in Social Work, 14,* 111–143.

Worthington, R. L., Soth-McNett, A. M., & Moreno, M. V. (2007). Multicultural counseling competencies research: A 20-year content analysis. *Journal of Counseling Psychology, 54,* 351–361.

35

Culturally Congruent Practices in Counseling and Psychotherapy

A Review of Research

TIMOTHY B. SMITH

As demonstrated across the chapters of this *Handbook*, the field of multicultural counseling and psychology is varied and complex. However, to simplify and generalize, one of its foundational assumptions is that cultural contexts exert profound influence on individuals and their mental health. More concisely, culture counts (U.S. Department of Health & Human Services, 2001).

Even skeptics of multicultural psychology acknowledge the influence of culture. However, they do question its salience with respect to mental health practices (e.g., Patterson, 2004). If psychotherapy can be effective without attending to cultural contexts, why bother with multiculturalism? Can we avoid stereotyping/mistreating individuals when we emphasize cultural collectives? Are not many intrapsychic factors (childhood experiences, family dynamics, reinforcement history, irrational cognitions, etc.) more relevant to

mental health than macro-level cultural contexts? From such a perspective, culture counts, but not as much as individual-level factors.

Tension in the broader profession results from these divergent perspectives regarding the salience of multiculturalism. Should cultural considerations be primary (equivalent to other components of mental health interventions, including individual-level factors) or secondary (nonequivalent to individual-level factors, which are the focus of traditional mental health interventions)? This distinction is neither subtle nor trivial. It concerns the very foundation upon which mental health interventions are designed and implemented. If cultural considerations are primary, then contemporary mental health interventions require revision to better meet the needs and experiences of clients not aligned with Western worldviews, and new interventions specific to diverse cultural groups are needed. Thus the debate often centers on how to best serve ethnic minority clients not acculturated to European American society. For such populations, what constitutes an effective mental health intervention?

Much of the confusion about and polarization between multicultural and traditional approaches may be attributable to the historically sparse research literature specific to ethnic minority groups (Sue, 1999; Sue et al., 2006). However, during the past decade, adequate research evidence has accumulated to the point that substantive questions may be posed of the literature. Empirical research, although not unflawed, is seen as the arbiter of professional debates, such as the efficacy of psychotherapy and the role of cultural variables in psychotherapy (primary or secondary). Given this state of affairs, one of the most decisive research questions that could be posed is, *Are mental health interventions that are intentionally made congruent with clients' cultural contexts more effective than traditional practices?* If a large body of empirical data supports an affirmative response to this question, then multiculturalism may be deemed not only legitimate within but integral (primary) to mental health interventions. However, if the data are inconclusive or deemed inadequate, then multiculturalism will remain marginalized (secondary) as an egalitarian ideal, possibly worthy of public praise but privately labeled as "impractical" or worse. All other things being equal, empirical evidence should determine which path will be taken; this chapter will attempt to provide direction.

The chapter begins with a general description of culturally congruent practices within mental health therapy. A list of rationale for how such practices could improve existing mental health interventions is provided. Subsequently, the chapter focuses attention on empirical data from studies of such practices. The chapter concludes with a discussion of why such practices might be effective and presents a hypothesis that could become the focus of future inquiry.

MENTAL HEALTH INTERVENTIONS: THE NEED FOR CULTURALLY CONGRUENT PRACTICES

At a basic level, counseling and psychotherapy include three components: the therapist, the client, and the intervention enacted in the context of the client-therapist relationship. Traditionally, the focus of counseling and psychotherapy research has been on the efficacy and effectiveness of the intervention itself (e.g., competing theoretical paradigms, managed care), with relatively less attention given to characteristics/abilities of the therapist or to expectations/resources of the client (Atkinson, Bui, & Mori, 2001). Current emphasis on empirically supported treatments reflects the larger trend: Thousands of research studies investigate nuances of treatment, whereas studies of therapist competence or client resource networks receive less attention.

An opposite trend characterizes the multicultural literature, which has attempted to fill the gaps in the traditional literature by explicitly emphasizing therapist factors (i.e., multicultural awareness, knowledge, and skills) and client factors (i.e., acculturation, ethnic/racial identity, experiences with discrimination). The contributions of the multicultural literature in raising awareness of those areas are groundbreaking, but the impact upon counseling and psychotherapy interventions in practice settings has been less prominent. This chapter asserts that applying the principles of multicultural psychology can lead to improved mental health interventions. Although in any approach, the components of client, therapist, and intervention necessarily overlap, this chapter focuses discussion on intervention factors that are less emphasized in multicultural literature.

What Constitutes Culturally Congruent Practice? Culturally congruent practices in mental health interventions are consistent with clients' conceptualization of the problems, means for solving problems, and goals regarding outcomes (Sue, 1988). Such practices include providing services in clients' preferred language, modifying the length/frequency of sessions, using culturally congruent terminology and concepts, involving family members or friends, consulting with persons familiar with a client's culture to facilitate accurate understanding, and so on. A specific example would be a treatment program for Native Alaskans based on that population's cultural concepts, integrating traditional healing practices (Fisher, 1996).

Because such practices go beyond what is typically provided in traditional counseling and psychotherapy, they are commonly referred to as "cultural adaptations" to treatment. Nevertheless, scholars promoting multicultural competency contend that therapy should involve such practices as a matter of course (Arredondo & Toporek, 2004; Pedersen, 1990). Hence, rather than referring to *adaptations*, a term that may imply exceptions or unusual effort, this chapter uses the term *culturally congruent practices* (see also the related term *ethnocultural psychotherapy* in Sue, 2000).

Why Address Macro-Level Cultural Variables in Mental Health Interventions for Individuals? Provision of culturally congruent practices is based on an assumption that clients will experience greatest improvement when they understand and value the interventions provided in therapy. For example, in most cases, clients may value a humanistic, conversational approach to therapy, but in some cases, the normative expectations regarding "professional help" involve receiving prescriptive advice to resolve dilemmas (e.g., Zane, Morton, Chu, & Lin, 2004). The effectiveness of therapy thus depends on the utilization of existing client worldviews and on client readiness to engage in change through certain ways over others.

To put this concept into perspective, it may be useful to put ourselves in the place of the client. On experiencing distress and seeking assistance from a mental health provider, which would we find most helpful: treatment that required us to adapt to the worldview of the professional or therapy in which the professional worked within our own worldview? Although the optimal solution might actually be found in a blend of these two extremes, a client might tend to favor a balance decidedly tipped toward having his or her own worldview valued and understood. Seen from a client's perspective, then, there is little question about whether psychotherapy should be made congruent with cultural contexts. By incorporating macro-level cultural worldviews, therapists match the perspective of individuals who share that worldview.

Nevertheless, because researchers and therapists tend to make decisions based on reasons other than client preferences, some additional rationale for changes in mental health interventions may warrant consideration. As a fiscal consideration, culturally congruent mental health practices affect client utilization and retention. The number of mental health providers across the world

has increased markedly over the past four decades, growth that is directly proportional to the willingness of the population to pay for psychotherapy (either directly or indirectly through insurance premiums or public funding). Yet people of color tend to underutilize mental health services compared to people of European origin (U.S. Department of Health & Human Services, 2001). Research has demonstrated that clients of color are more likely to seek out and remain in therapy when interventions are congruent with their personal values and beliefs (Coleman, Wampold, & Casali, 1995; Flaskerud & Nyamathi, 2000). If therapists would integrate clients' cultural perspectives into treatment, then utilization and retention rates for people of non-European origin would likely increase over time (Hall, 2001), further enhancing growth of mental health services worldwide.

Culturally congruent practices have also been shown to enhance client outcomes in psychotherapy. Race and culture moderate how mental health symptoms are interpreted and expressed (e.g., Atkinson et al., 2001; Varela et al., 2004). Racial and cultural groups have similar yet distinct perspectives about well-being. People of color often fear that their particular beliefs/ worldviews will be misunderstood by mental health professionals (e.g., Cinnirella & Loewenthal, 1999; Whaley, 2001). Multicultural competency in treatment has the potential to augment the effectiveness of that treatment by such factors as strengthening the therapeutic alliance and drawing upon existing client resources (e.g., Vasquez, 2007).

Considering concepts and ideas across cultures can benefit therapists' own conceptualization of well-being and treatment. Practices and traditions of cultures across the world have effectively enhanced coping, resilience, and healing (e.g., Garrett, 1999). Such traditions and insights can make valuable contributions to contemporary therapeutic practices, which historically have been based exclusively on European and North American healing traditions (e.g., Katz, 1985; Sue & Sue, 2008). For example, the recently popular "mindfulness-based cognitive therapy" and "acceptance and commitment therapy" are based on Buddhist teachings (e.g., Hayes, Follette, & Linehan, 2004). Researchers are increasingly recognizing the wisdom in traditional cultural and religious practices and values that have enhanced mental health and prevented mental illness for generations in other areas of the world (Koenig, McCullough, & Larson, 2001; Richards & Bergin, 2000).

Pragmatic observation also supports multiculturalism as essential to effective practice. Because each human is in many ways unique, no single approach or technique will work with every person or group (Smith, 2004). This problem of generalizability has yet to be addressed adequately in mental health research (Sue, 1999). In our theories and training, we attempt to generalize from one client to the next, but in the real world, treating all clients alike ensures incompetence. If differentiation across clients is essential, it makes sense to understand and apply factors that account for client differences (i.e., age, abilities, ethnicity, family composition and history, gender, race, socioeconomic background, etc.).

Finally, ethically and even morally, the best practice is to incorporate cultural values and symbols when working with people for whom those values have meaning (Arredondo & Toporek, 2004; James & Foster, 2006; Smith, Richards, Granley, & Obiakor, 2004). Making practices congruent with the characteristics and needs of those who seek mental health assessment or treatment is a professional responsibility. Ethical standards of the American Psychological Association (APA, 2002) and American Counseling Association (ACA, 2005) include cultural considerations, and these organizations have provided specific guidelines relevant to multicultural considerations (APA, 2003).

Given the several benefits covered above, culturally congruent practices seem not only viable but integral to effective mental health services. Nevertheless, such arguments have been made for decades (i.e., Sue & Zane, 1987). Despite the continuous publication of logical arguments like these and the continuous publication of hundreds of observations regarding the benefits of culturally congruent practices by clinicians working with clients of color, contemporary mental health practices differ little from those of 30 years ago, well prior to the recent "multicultural revolution" (Sue, Bingham, Porché-Burke, & Vasquez, 1999). Although practitioners have increasingly become aware of the need for multicultural competence through repeated calls in the literature (e.g., Hall, 1997), the implementation of culturally congruent practices lags well behind this general awareness (Constantine & Sue, 2005, 2006; Sue & Sue, 2008).

Given this discrepancy, it may be useful to consider a historical parallel to the contemporary acceptance/ application of multicultural counseling and psychotherapy. Although now largely forgotten, for many decades doubts were expressed about the efficacy of psychotherapy itself (i.e., Eysenck, 1952, 1993). Under scrutiny, psychotherapists were sometimes defensive, citing logical arguments and generating hundreds of case studies to prove their position. Psychotherapists believed in their own work, but they generally lacked respect within the larger community. It was not until the first major synthesis of empirical data (Smith & Glass, 1977) conclusively demonstrated the efficacy of psychotherapy that the whole terms of the debate changed. The question of efficacy had been answered conclusively: Psychotherapy works. The focus of scholarship turned to nuances of effectiveness (e.g., psychotherapy with specific conditions, with specific components, with specific intensity/duration, etc.). Meta-analytic data had provided the field with legitimacy and with the associated confidence to promote mental health services among insurance providers, federal and state legislators, and the general public.

Perceptions of counseling and psychotherapy 40 years ago parallel some views of culturally congruent practices within the mental health professions today. The idea receives general support, but limited implementation in practice. Claims by advocates of culturally congruent practices are politely acknowledged but not always applied within the larger profession, let alone local clinics. Given the historical precedent for empirical data to provide confidence sufficient to radically change perceptions and practices, this chapter will shift focus from logical rationale to empirical evidence.

Empirical Evaluations of Culturally Congruent Mental Health Practices

Systematic methods for reviewing empirical research, called meta-analyses, have greatly improved the confidence of the mental health field in identifying overall trends across numerous research studies (Cooper, 1998; Labin, 2008). Because they are systematic, comprehensive, and replicable, meta-analyses have replaced the need for conducting narrative literature reviews; the results of a meta-analysis provide the most reliable summary of the literature.

A Meta-Analysis of Culturally Congruent Mental Health Interventions. In 2006, a meta-analysis of 76 studies demonstrated the effectiveness of culturally congruent mental health interventions (Griner & Smith, 2006). Across a wide variety of studies, interventions that intentionally included cultural considerations (e.g., Africentric interventions for African Americans, *Cuento* therapy for Latino youth, traditional healing practices integrated with therapy for native Hawaiians) were more beneficial to clients than those that did not (Cohen's $d = .45$, or a difference of about one half of a standard deviation). This finding maintained across a variety of settings and participant characteristics: For example, studies with participants of different gender, race/ethnicity, and level of distress all yielded equivalent average effect sizes. Thus, the benefits of culturally congruent interventions appeared to generalize across many circumstances.

Additional findings of the meta-analysis included several factors that likely moderated the effectiveness of culturally congruent interventions. Key among these were three variables related to the salience of culture from the perspective of the client. First, a statistically significant correlation ($r = .29$) between the average age of participants and the effect size from each study indicated that adults tended to benefit more from culturally congruent interventions than did children and adolescents. This finding is presumably due to differences in the salience of culture (enculturation) across age groups, with adults typically identifying with cultural values more than children or adolescents (e.g., Kwak, 2003). Second, interventions in which clients had access to services delivered in their preferred language (i.e., bilingual therapists) were much more helpful for clients ($d = .49$) than services apparently conducted exclusively in English with clients who were apparently not native English speakers ($d = .21$). Third, interventions that were specific to a particular racial/ethnic group were more effective ($d = .49$) than interventions delivered to a mixed group of participants from different races/ethnicities ($d = .12$). Thus, interventions apparently tailored to meet the needs of a specific group (e.g., a "life enhancement" treatment designed for elderly Cuban Americans) (Szapocznik, Santisbetan, Hervis, & Spencer, 1981) were more effective than those in which interventions included general multicultural considerations (e.g., clinics generically oriented to cultural

groups) (Mathews, Glidden, Murray, Forster, & Hargreaves, 2002). The common theme across these three findings is that the more congruent an intervention was with clients' cultural worldviews, the more effective it was in helping them.

Although enhanced client satisfaction with services was the outcome variable most affected by culturally congruent interventions ($d = .93$), client retention also improved to some degree ($d = .30$). Across studies that evaluated reductions in client mental health symptoms, the average improvement relative to control groups was $d = .39$ (a little more than one third of a standard deviation of difference). Taken as a whole, the results of the meta-analysis provided a wake-up call to the profession. Data now support what scholars investigating culturally congruent interventions had been emphasizing for decades (e.g., Sue & Zane, 1987).

Additional Considerations About the Meta-Analytic Data. Meta-analyses have multiple advantages over traditional literature reviews (Cooper, 1998; Labin, 2008). However, meta-analyses are also subject to several criticisms, including mixing articles with similar yet distinct research methodologies, outcome variables, and so on (e.g., Eysenck, 1993). Although these concerns apply generally to all meta-analyses, these specific concerns could also be leveled at the meta-analysis just described (Griner & Smith, 2006). One might ask whether the results of that meta-analysis would have been different if (a) studies including any European American participants had been excluded, (b) studies using only experimental designs had been examined, and (c) studies investigating only mental health interventions with clinical populations had been included. These and related questions will be addressed through analyses conducted with the data collected by Griner and Smith that were not reported in the original publication.

Of the studies reviewed in the meta-analysis, 10 included European Americans as part of the sample (either as a comparison group or as a small percentage of those receiving the intervention). Excluding those 10 studies resulted in an overall effect size of $d = .48$ (95% CI $= .39$ to $.57$), virtually the same as the originally reported value of $d = .45$ (95% CI $= .36$ to $.53$). Moreover, after subsequent analyses of the variables found to moderate the results of the overall study (i.e., age, language of services, culture-specific services), the results remained unchanged. Thus, the original findings of the meta-analysis could not be attributed merely to the presence of some European American participants in studies with participants from a variety of racial backgrounds.

Many of the studies reviewed in the meta-analysis involved comparison groups without an equivalent control group (i.e., untreated persons on a waiting list), and some of them involved pre- to posttest changes with a single group. Given the multiple limitations associated with those research designs, a subsequent analysis with the data from only the 48 studies using experimental designs yielded an overall effect size of only slightly lower magnitude ($d = .39$, 95% CI = .29 to .48) than findings across all 76 studies. Additional analyses of the moderating variables also replicated the results obtained with the full 76 studies. Thus these analyses confirm the overall findings of the meta-analysis as published.

Finally, because the meta-analysis reviewed a wide variety of intervention studies that considered (a) preventative mental health (i.e., social skills training for at-risk youth) and (b) substance abuse treatment/ prevention, as well as (c) psychotherapy and related mental health interventions (i.e., family therapy), it would be important to distinguish the findings accordingly. Nevertheless, the average effect sizes were equivalent across these three different types of services ($d = .36$, .45, and .46, respectively, $p > .10$), with psychotherapy-type interventions being more effective than the other two types of interventions. These findings again confirmed the original published results: Mental health interventions that are culturally congruent with clients of color are much more effective than services provided without such considerations.

Data Interpretation. The data of the meta-analysis by Griner and Smith (2006) are open for interpretation. These analyses are based on relatively few research reports—76 studies, in contrast to the 375 studies involved in the original meta-analysis of psychotherapy effectiveness conducted by Smith and Glass in 1977. Moreover, dozens of meta-analyses involving hundreds of additional efficacy studies on traditional psychotherapy

have been conducted since 1977. Thus, even with the substantive findings of the single meta-analysis of culturally congruent practices (Griner & Smith, 2006), additional evidence (possibly dozens of efficacy studies using rigorous designs and controls) may be required before the entire profession becomes completely convinced of the need to completely infuse cultural considerations into traditional practices.

Similarly, a skeptic of multiculturalism might consider the differences observed between practices that are and are not culturally congruent to be only moderate in magnitude (as per guidelines provided by Cohen, 1987). However, the differences observed in the data (Griner & Smith, 2006) are of the same magnitude observed when comparing psychotherapy with a licensed psychologist to a placebo treatment, such as a social support group run by a trained undergraduate (Lambert, 2005). To put this comparison into perspective, if an effect of this magnitude ($d = .45$) were consistently found between one type of mental health treatment and another (e.g., humanistic vs. cognitive-behavioral therapy or one psychopharmacological agent vs. another), the less effective treatment would no longer be considered empirically justified. Therefore, so long as the meta-analytic data prove replicable, every mental health intervention should be made culturally congruent.

Implementation of Culturally Congruent Practices

All other things being equal, empirical evidence should guide the infusion of culturally congruent practices throughout counseling and psychology. If so, then direction is clear: Culture is of primary, not secondary, import.

Given the demonstrated relevance of cultural issues, traditional mental health interventions or those designed without explicit cultural congruence for people not already aligned with European/European American worldviews will benefit from revision. Even when traditional interventions appear to be effective with clients of color (Miranda et al., 2005), deliberate inclusion of cultural considerations will likely enhance their effectiveness. Moreover, nontraditional interventions designed to meet the needs of specific populations are now accepted. In any case, these two approaches, refinement of traditional interventions and promulgation of new interventions grounded in clients' cultures, will both benefit from using conceptual frameworks for culturally congruent practice (Castro, Barrera, & Martinez, 2004).

Conceptual Guidelines. How should culturally congruent practices be designed and implemented? At the most fundamental level, such practices should be congruent with the client's cultural values, conceptualization of change, and expectations regarding normative behavior (Sue, 1988). When mental health interventions include multicultural considerations yet fail to account for these foundational principles, the role of culture remains superficial, distanced from client experience (see related concepts of ecological and social validity) (Bernal, Bonilla, & Bellido, 1995). Although traditional therapy can be improved by adding culturally relevant components, such as using the *Kaffa* ceremony with Ethiopian refugees (Loewy, Williams, & Keleta, 2002), optimally such integration of cultural variables occurs across the entire treatment. Thus, *the optimal focus of culturally congruent practice is alignment with client experiences* rather than the specific cultural components used to facilitate that alignment.

Recognizing the risks of nominal or unsystematic inclusion of cultural considerations in therapy, several authors have provided conceptual frameworks to aid therapists in implementing practices that are truly culturally congruent. For example, Castro et al. (2004) indicate that culturally congruent practices should not only involve patently compatible cultural concepts but also attend to cognitive, affective-motivational, and environmental factors. Moreover, such practices should go beyond content to include form: channel of delivery (e.g., group/family rather than individual), location of delivery (e.g., community center/church rather than clinic), and qualities of the therapist (Castro et al., 2004). In short, there are a variety of ways in which cultural mismatches can continue despite nominal attention to clients' cultural backgrounds.

Guillermo Bernal and colleagues (Bernal & Saez-Santiago, 2006; Bernal et al., 1995) have generated useful guidelines for professionals attempting to provide culturally congruent practices. Their framework contains eight dimensions:

1. *Language*—Conduct therapy in the preferred language of the client.
2. *Persons*—Match client-therapist on salient variables to enhance the therapeutic alliance and client expectations.
3. *Metaphors*—Use expressions, objects, and concepts already embedded within the client's culture.
4. *Content*—Apply cultural knowledge about values, customs, and traditions.
5. *Concepts*—Conceptualize the presenting problem consistent with clients' cultural worldviews.
6. *Goals*—Identify and facilitate clients' desired outcomes.
7. *Methods*—Use procedures in treatment that align with clients' cultural worldview and goals.
8. *Context*—Consider the social, economic, and political realities that affect the client.

These eight elements should inform the development of culturally congruent practices and can be used in the future to evaluate the quality (i.e., ecological and social validity) of interventions described in the literature. For example, Domenech-Rodríguez and Wieling (2005) have demonstrated a useful application of these eight elements when developing a systematic procedure for working with Latino/a parents and their children. Systematic demonstrations such as these will go a long way toward improving the quality of culturally congruent practices.

At present, the field could benefit from increased systematization in implementing these guidelines (Bernal & Saez-Santiago, 2006; Bernal et al., 1995). A review of the literature demonstrates that adherence to these guidelines is highly variable: About one half of the elements (an average of 3.8 out of 8) characterize studies that attempt to promote culturally congruent practice (as identified through post hoc analyses of studies identified by Griner & Smith, 2006). The practices described within studies typically include some but not all of the eight elements: Eighty-four percent provided therapy in the clients' preferred language, 61% matched clients with therapists of similar ethnic/racial backgrounds, 29% used metaphors/objects from client cultures, 84% included explicit mention of cultural content/values, 21% adhered to the client's conceptualization of the presenting problem, 11%

solicited outcome goals from the client, 44% modified the methods of delivering therapy based on cultural considerations, and 49% addressed clients' contexts by either providing external services (24%) or discussing contextual issues (33%). These findings prompt greater attention to the elements that are relatively deficient in current efforts to implement culturally congruent practices (i.e., metaphors, concepts, goals, and methods). Given the inconsistent adherence to best practices in studies presently available in the literature, it is likely that future multifaceted practices following all eight guidelines may result in greater therapeutic benefits than those observed in the meta-analysis of prior research findings (Griner & Smith, 2006).

Why Are Culturally Congruent Interventions More Effective Than Traditional Interventions? The conceptual guidelines suggested by Bernal and colleagues (1995) are based on sound reasoning, years of clinical practice, and research findings from related fields of inquiry. However, the conceptual models are broad, accounting for a multiplicity of salient factors. They articulate key considerations but do not specify underlying causal mechanisms. Until causal mechanisms are specified, conceptual guidelines will necessarily remain comprehensive—broad enough to capture the associated complexity.

Therefore, it may prove useful to consider possible reasons *why* culturally congruent practices might improve client outcomes. Identifying such factors may help focus future research efforts and could result in refined conceptual models that lead to more widespread implementation of culturally congruent practices.

One hypothesis worth testing is that several underlying (indirect) factors may better account for the efficacy of culturally congruent mental health practices than the (direct) practices themselves. The inclusion of cultural components in therapy (e.g., sharing folk stories or cultural maxims) is likely not the sole reason why clients improve. Improvements observed in clients may be due primarily to more general factors. Atkinson et al. (2001) articulated three generic reasons relevant to client/therapy matching: compatibility of racial/ethnic identity, beliefs about the causes of problems, and beliefs

about which treatments are effective for those problems. The logic is that if client and therapist complement one another on these factors, the therapy provided will be more efficacious than otherwise.

The fact that the data from the meta-analysis (Griner & Smith, 2006) failed to ascertain differences across several intervention components (e.g., content, method, modality, duration) supports the hypothesis that general factors, rather than treatment-specific factors, explain the enhanced effectiveness of culturally congruent practices compared to traditional practices. The specific type of intervention provided may matter much less than the fact that the intervention remains congruent with clients' experiences and worldviews.

The parallel concept advocated in the psychotherapy literature has been termed the *common factors* approach (see Frank, 1982; Rosenzweig, 1936). From this perspective, no single approach or theoretical orientation works better than any other; rather, the efficacy of any treatment depends on how it well it promotes the client-therapist relationship, client expectations for improvement, and so on (e.g., Wampold, 2000, 2001). Any form of psychotherapy works, to the extent that it provides these common factors.

By this logic, culturally congruent practices align well with common factors (Atkinson et al., 2001). It is not the act of allowing a client to recite cultural maxims in session or pour libations in honor of deceased ancestors that reduces the client's symptoms; rather, it is the fact that such acts have multiple indirect effects, which include implicitly honoring the client by honoring his or her family members, referring to external resources and role models, drawing upon spiritual resources, and enhancing the level of intimacy in the client-therapist relationship. Examples of indirect effects broken down by three common factors are provided in Table 35.1. Multiple indirect effects, such as those listed in the table, have great power collectively. Therefore, a hypothesis worth evaluating in future research concerns the summative effects of culturally congruent practices: Even one culturally congruent component in treatment should be better than omission of cultural considerations, but the most efficacious interventions should be those that result in multiple indirect effects.

Table 35.1 Common Factors and Associated Indirect Effects That May Account for the Effectiveness of Culturally Congruent Mental Health Practices

Client/Therapist Mutual Understanding

    Implicit interpersonal valuing (affirmation)

    Implicit structure/frame for the encounter (familiarization)

    Attention to interpersonal similarities (cohesion)

    Validation (normalization)

    Enhanced communication fluidity and accuracy

Client/Therapist Mutual Responsiveness

    Reduced interpersonal anxiety (enhanced trust)

    Improved expectations for outcome (hopefulness)

    Willingness to engage (personal investment)

    Pledges/commitments with one another (co-created bonds)

    Acknowledged interdependence (equality)

    Demonstration of appropriate social skills (in vivo modeling)

Mutually Satisfactory Therapeutic Actions

    Recognition and reinforcement of client strengths and coping methods

    Rehearsal of realistic alternatives for coping

    Involvement of client support networks (connectivity and accountability)

    Communal reintegration (forgiveness/reconciliation)

    Symbolic healing (ritual/ceremony/imagery)

    Spiritual perspectives; invitations for intervention from spiritual sources

    Plans for/acceptance of an unknown future

    Description of compatible examples to emulate

    Acknowledgment of cultural values/principles that may guide decisions/actions

Note: The three categories above generally correspond with the common notions of therapeutic alliance (broken down into understanding/responsiveness) and therapeutic interventions. The terms are purposefully altered to denote the reciprocal influence of client and therapist.

Informed Interventions Versus Misuse. If culturally congruent practices are to become the norm in the profession, then a danger posed by this proliferation concerns the possible misuse of those practices, such as by misapplication (e.g., improper timing or mismatch with client expectations) or by misappropriation (i.e., cultural thievery, which is using precepts from indigenous cultures for personal gain or without consent of or collaboration with acknowledged representatives of the host culture). Competence in traditional schools of psychotherapy (e.g., Adlerian, interpersonal, reality therapy, etc.) requires extensive supervision and practice. How could a therapist possibly become competent in culturally congruent practices without similar supervision and skill refinement (Ladany, Friedlander, & Nelson, 2005)? Well-intentioned therapists may integrate relevant cultural concepts (e.g., acceptance of fate as a way to enhance inner peace and thus decrease symptoms of depression) that may actually harm clients under some circumstances (i.e., fatalism without the larger cultural concept of unity/oneness could prompt thoughts of suicide). Similarly, therapists must attend to within-group heterogeneity (Zane, Hall, Sue, Young, & Nunez, 2004), such that the inclusion of a cultural practice does not perpetuate a different set of assumptions/stereotypes when working with individuals who may differ widely from cultural norms. In short, interventions are merely tools that can be used to promote or detract from well-being. The focus of therapy should remain on the client and his or her context, with interventions matching accordingly. Hence, the emphasis that this chapter has placed on culturally congruent practices must be matched by a larger professional emphasis upon ethics, training, and ongoing professional development.

CONCLUSION

For many years, scholars have affirmed that culturally congruent practices are more effective than traditional practices with ethnic minority clients (e.g., Hall, 1997; Sue, 2003; Zane, Hall et al., 2004). They were right. Culturally congruent practices are more effective than practices that do not account for clients' cultural contexts.

Therefore, culture should be a primary, not secondary, consideration in the development and implementation of mental health interventions with clients who do not align with European American worldviews. However, it must be emphasized that this perspective, merging individual-level and macro-level conceptualizations, does not denote contradiction. It is not an either/or scenario. Individual-level factors will always be a focus of psychotherapy, and those individual factors are better understood when simultaneously accounting for larger contexts. Thus, multiculturalism is not merely a macro-level abstraction but a necessary overlay to understand each individual client.

Historically, counseling and psychotherapy practices have undergone constant revision. To wit, we rarely see clients five times per week, and we use methods not wholly dependent upon Freud, Skinner, or Rogers. Change is constant in the profession, and the need to develop, evaluate, and maintain culturally congruent mental health practices should impel improvement. Based on the principles of multicultural competence (e.g., Arredondo & Toporek, 2004; Constantine & Sue, 2005, 2006), psychotherapy can better meet the needs of clients whose worldviews are not presently represented by traditional paradigms. Irrespective of differences that may emerge across the content and method of culturally congruent practices, the essential features will be accessibility, interpersonal connectivity, worldview congruity, and utility (usefulness). How we have been trained as counselors and psychotherapists may

not be what our clients may need. What do they need? How can we respond?

REFERENCES

American Counseling Association. (2005). *Code of ethics.* Alexandria, VA: Author.

American Psychological Association. (2002). Ethical principles of psychologists and code of conduct. *American Psychologist, 57,* 1060–1073.

American Psychological Association. (2003). Guidelines on multicultural education, training, research, practice, and organizational change for psychologists. *American Psychologist, 58,* 377–402.

Arredondo, P., & Toporek, R. (2004). Multicultural counseling competencies = ethical practice. *Journal of Mental Health Counseling, 26,* 44–55.

Atkinson, D. R., Bui, U., & Mori, S. (2001). Multiculturally sensitive empirically supported treatments: An oxymoron? In J. G. Ponterotto, J. M. Casas, L. A. Suzuki, & C. M. Alexander (Eds.), *Handbook of multicultural counseling* (2nd ed., pp. 542–574). Thousand Oaks, CA: Sage.

Bernal, G., Bonilla, J., & Bellido, C. (1995). Ecological validity and cultural sensitivity for outcome research: Issues for the cultural adaptation and development of psychosocial treatments with Hispanics. *Journal of Abnormal Child Psychology, 23,* 67–82.

Bernal, G., & Saez-Santiago, E. (2006). Culturally centered psychosocial interventions. *Journal of Community Psychology, 34,* 121–132.

Castro, F. G., Barrera, M., & Martinez, C. R. (2004). The cultural adaptation of prevention interventions: Resolving tensions between fidelity and fit. *Prevention Science, 5*(1), 41–45.

Cinnirella, M., & Loewenthal, K. M. (1999). Religious and ethnic group influences on beliefs about mental illness: A qualitative interview study. *British Journal of Medical Psychology, 72,* 505–524.

Cohen, J. (1987). *Statistical power analysis for the behavioral sciences.* Hillsdale, NJ: Lawrence Erlbaum.

Coleman, H. L. K., Wampold, B. E., & Casali, S. L. (1995). Ethnic minorities' rating of ethnically similar and European American counselors: A meta-analysis. *Journal of Counseling Psychology, 42,* 55–64.

Constantine, M. G., & Sue, D. W. (2005). *Strategies for building multicultural competence in mental health and educational settings.* Hoboken, NJ: Wiley.

Constantine, M. G., & Sue, D. W. (2006). *Addressing racism: Facilitating cultural competence in mental health and educational settings.* Hoboken, NJ: Wiley.

Cooper, H. (1998). *Synthesizing research: A guide for literature reviews* (3rd ed.). Thousand Oaks, CA: Sage.

Domenech-Rodríguez, M., & Wieling, E. (2004). Developing culturally appropriate, evidence-based treatments for interventions with ethnic minority populations. In M. Rastogin & E. Wieling (Eds.), *Voices of color: First person accounts of ethnic minority therapists* (pp. 313–333). Thousand Oaks, CA: Sage.

Eysenck, H. J. (1952). The effects of psychotherapy: An evaluation. *Journal of Consulting Psychology, 16,* 319–324.

Eysenck, H. J. (1993). Forty years on: The outcome problem in psychotherapy revisited. In T. R. Giles (Ed.), *Handbook of effective psychotherapy* (pp. 3–20). New York: Plenum.

Fisher, D. G. (1996). Therapeutic community retention among Alaska Natives: Akeela House. *Journal of Substance Abuse Treatment, 13,* 265–271.

Flaskerud, J. H., & Nyamathi, A. M. (2000). Attaining gender and ethnic diversity in health intervention research: Cultural responsiveness versus resource provision. *Advances in Nursing Science, 22*(4), 1–15.

Frank, J. D. (1982). Therapeutic components shared by all psychotherapies. In J. Harvey & M. Parks (Eds.), *Psychotherapy research and behavior change* (pp. 5–38). Washington, DC: American Psychological Association.

Garrett, M. T. (1999). Understanding the "medicine" of Native American traditional values: An integrative review. *Counseling & Values, 43,* 84–98.

Griner, D., & Smith, T. B. (2006). Culturally adapted mental health interventions: A meta-analytic review. *Psychotherapy: Theory, Research, Practice & Training, 43,* 531–548.

Hall, C. C. I. (1997). Cultural malpractice: The growing obsolescence of psychology with the changing U.S. population. *American Psychologist, 52,* 642–651.

Hall, G. C. N. (2001). Psychotherapy research with ethnic minorities: Empirical, ethical, and conceptual issues. *Journal of Consulting and Clinical Psychology, 69,* 502–510.

Hayes, S. C., Follette, V. M., & Linehan, M. M. (2004). *Mindfulness and acceptance: Expanding the cognitive-behavioral tradition.* New York: Guilford.

James, S., & Foster, G. (2006). Reconciling rules with context: An ethical framework for cultural psychotherapy. *Theory & Psychology, 16,* 803–823.

Katz, J. H. (1985). The sociopolitical nature of counseling. *Counseling Psychologist, 13,* 613–624.

Koenig, H. G., McCullough, M. E., & Larson, D. (2001). *Handbook of religion and health.* New York: Oxford University Press.

Kwak, K. (2003). Adolescents and their parents: A review of intergenerational family relations for immigrant and non-immigrant families. *Human Development, 46*(2–3), 115–136.

Labin, S. N. (2008). Research synthesis: Toward broad-based evidence. In N. Smith & P. Brandon (Eds.), *Fundamental issues in evaluation* (pp. 89–110). New York: Guilford.

Ladany, N., Friedlander, M. L., & Nelson, M. (2005). Heightening multicultural awareness: It's never been about political correctness. In N. Ladany, M. Friedlander, & M. Nelson (Eds.), *Critical events in psychotherapy supervision: An interpersonal approach* (pp. 53–57). Washington, DC: American Psychological Association.

Lambert, M. J. (2005). Early response in psychotherapy: Further evidence for the importance of common factors rather than "placebo effects." *Journal of Clinical Psychology, 61,* 855–869.

Loewy, M. I., Williams, D. T., & Keleta, A. (2002). Group counseling with traumatized East African refugee women in the United States: Using the Kaffa ceremony intervention. *Journal for Specialists in Group Work, 27,* 173–191.

Mathews, C. A., Glidden, D., Murray, S., Forster, P., & Hargreaves, W. A. (2002). The effect of treatment outcomes of assigning patients to ethnically focused inpatient psychiatric units. *Psychiatric Services, 53,* 830–835.

Miranda, J., Bernal, G., Lau, A., Kohn, L., Hwang, W., & LaFromboise, T. (2005). State of the science on psychosocial interventions for ethnic minorities. *Annual Review of Clinical Psychology, 1,* 113–142.

Patterson, C. H. (2004). Do we need multicultural counseling competencies? *Journal of Mental Health Counseling, 26,* 67–73.

Pedersen, P. (1990). The multicultural perspective as a fourth force in counseling. *Journal of Mental Health Counseling, 12,* 93–95.

Richards, P. S., & Bergin, A. E. (Eds.). (2000). *Handbook of psychotherapy and religious diversity.* Washington, DC: American Psychological Association.

Rosenzweig, S. (1936). Some implicit common factors in diverse methods of psychotherapy. *American Journal of Orthopsychiatry, 6,* 412–415.

Smith, M. L., & Glass, G. V (1977). Meta-analysis of psychotherapy outcome studies. *American Psychologist, 32,* 752–760.

Smith, T. B. (Ed.). (2004). *Practicing multiculturalism: Affirming diversity in counseling and psychology.* Boston: Allyn & Bacon.

Smith, T. B., Richards, P. S., Granley, M., & Obiakor, F. (2004). Practicing multiculturalism: An introduction. In

T. B. Smith (Ed.), *Practicing multiculturalism: Affirming diversity in counseling and psychology* (pp. 3–16). Boston: Allyn & Bacon.

Sue, D. W., Bingham, R., Porché-Burke, L., & Vasquez, M. (1999). The diversification of psychology: A multicultural revolution. *American Psychologist, 54,* 1061–1069.

Sue, D. W., & Sue, D. (2008). *Counseling the culturally diverse: Theory and practice* (5th ed.). Hoboken, NJ: Wiley.

Sue, S. (1988). Psychotherapeutic services for ethnic minorities: Two decades of research findings. *American Psychologist, 43,* 301–308.

Sue, S. (1998). In search of cultural competence in psychotherapy and counseling. *American Psychologist, 53,* 440–448.

Sue, S. (1999). Science, ethnicity, and bias: Where have we gone wrong? *American Psychologist, 54,* 1070–1077.

Sue, S. (2000). Ethnocultural psychotherapy. In A. E. Kazdin (Ed.), *Encyclopedia of psychology* (Vol. 3, pp. 265–267). Washington, DC: American Psychological Association.

Sue, S. (2003). In defense of cultural competency in psychotherapy and treatment. *American Psychologist, 58*(11), 964–970.

Sue, S., & Zane, N. (1987). The role of culture and cultural techniques in psychotherapy: A critique and reformulation. *American Psychologist, 42,* 37–45.

Sue, S., Zane, N., Levant, R. F., Silverstein, L. B., Brown, L. S., Olkin, R., & Taliaferro, G. (2006). How well do both evidence-based practices and treatment as usual satisfactorily address the various dimensions of diversity? In J. C. Norcross, L. E. Beutler, & R. F. Levant (Eds.), *Evidence-based practices in mental health: Debate and dialogue on the fundamental questions* (pp. 329–337). Washington, DC: American Psychological Association.

Szapocznik, J., Santisbetan, D., Hervis, O., & Spencer, F. (1981). Treatment of depression among Cuban American elders: Some validational evidence for a life enhancement counseling approach. *Journal of Consulting and Clinical Psychology, 49,* 752–754.

U.S. Department of Health & Human Services. (2001). *Mental health: Culture, race, and ethnicity—A supplement to mental health: A report of the Surgeon General.* Rockville, MD: Author.

Varela, R. E., Vernberg, E. M., Sanchez-Sosa, J. J., Riveros, A., Mitchell, M., & Mashunkashey, J. (2004). Anxiety reporting and culturally associated interpretation biases and cognitive schemas: A comparison of Mexican, Mexican American, and European American families. *Journal of Clinical Child and Adolescent Psychology, 33,* 237–247.

Vasquez, M. J. (2007). Cultural difference and the therapeutic alliance: An evidence-based analysis. *American Psychologist, 62,* 878–885.

Wampold, B. E. (2000). Outcomes of individual counseling and psychotherapy: Empirical evidence addressing two fundamental questions. In S. D. Brown & R. W. Lent (Eds.), *Handbook of counseling psychology* (pp. 711–739). New York: Wiley.

Wampold, B. E. (2001). *The great psychotherapy debate: Models, methods and findings.* Hillsdale, NJ: Lawrence Erlbaum.

Whaley, A. L. (2001). Cultural mistrust: An important psychological construct for diagnosis and treatment of African Americans. *Professional Psychology: Research and Practice, 32,* 555–562.

Zane, N., Hall, G. C. N., Sue, S., Young, K., & Nunez, J. (2004). Research on psychotherapy with culturally diverse populations. In M. J. Lambert (Ed.), *Handbook of psychotherapy and behavior change* (5th ed., pp. 767–804). New York: Wiley.

Zane, N., Morton, T., Chu, J., & Lin, N. (2004). Counseling and psychotherapy with Asian American clients. In T. B. Smith (Ed.), *Practicing multiculturalism: Affirming diversity in counseling and psychology* (pp. 190–214). Boston: Allyn & Bacon.

PART VII

Spiritual and Religious Issues in Counseling

Part VII of the *Handbook* contains four chapters on spiritual and religious issues in counseling. Although early in the multicultural counseling movement spiritual issues in counseling were seldom addressed, in the past decade, the constructs of spirituality and religiosity have received increased attention among multicultural counselors and researchers. In Chapter 36, Lewis Z. Schlosser, Pamela F. Foley, Ellyn Poltrock Stein, and Jason R. Holmwood open this section by reporting on an original content analysis of the place of religious issues in counseling psychology research. The authors document that over a recent 13-year period, there was a serious lack of attention to spiritual and religious issues in counseling research. Dr. Schlosser and his colleagues then offer well-reasoned interpretations for the field's neglect of religious issues in counseling, explain why counselors should attend to religious issues in their practices, and offer helpful and specific suggestions for needed research on the topic.

Muninder K. Ahluwalia and Noreen K. Zaman examine issues relevant to counseling Muslims and Sikhs within the context of a post-9/11 U.S. society (Chapter 37). After the attacks on the United States on 9/11, there was and continues to be a backlash of hate and violence directed toward Muslims and Sikhs. U.S. society, including its counseling profession, knows relatively little about the spiritual beliefs and practices of Muslims and Sikhs relative to other religious/spiritual groups. The authors of this chapter provide an excellent primer that educates counseling professionals on

the experiences, beliefs, and practices of Muslims and Sikhs. Furthermore, helpful and specific implications for culturally responsive counseling interventions with U.S. Muslim and Sikh clients are outlined.

In Chapter 38, John J. Cecero introduces a series of spiritual exercises as a component of integrative, spiritually oriented counseling and psychotherapy. The author convincingly highlights the general importance of integrating spirituality into the counseling process. Next, Dr. Cecero presents a series of spiritual exercises rooted in the work of St. Ignatius Loyola. The exercises are compatible with a broad range of counseling interventions and models, and although they are targeted primarily to Christian clients, existential goals of the exercises transcend many religions (e.g., meaning of suffering, gratitude, love).

The final chapter in Part VII of this *Handbook*, authored by John Huang (Chapter 39), addresses counseling clients from Eastern religions and spiritualities. Dr. Huang provides a clear and helpful review of the background of major Eastern religions, reviews the assessment of religiosity during the counseling process, summarizes Eastern-specific counseling interventions, and concisely reviews select Western therapeutic interventions that may be more consonant with Eastern spiritualities (e.g., Acceptance and Commitment Therapy, Dialectical Behavior Therapy). Finally, Dr. Huang presents an interesting case study of a Southeast Asian refugee that demonstrates important assessment and intervention points highlighted throughout the chapter.

36

Why Does Counseling Psychology Exclude Religion?

A Content Analysis and Methodological Critique

LEWIS Z. SCHLOSSER, PAMELA F. FOLEY,
ELLYN POLTROCK STEIN, AND JASON R. HOLMWOOD

In this chapter, we summarize the results of a content analysis of research on religious issues in three major counseling psychology journals over the 13-year period from 1994 to 2006. Of the 1,914 studies reviewed from the *Journal of Counseling Psychology*, *The Counseling Psychologist*, and the *Journal of Counseling & Development*, only 51 (.027%) were focused on religion. The chapters' content demonstrates a lack of a clear definition of and distinction between religion and spirituality, and an even split between conceptual and empirical approaches. Beyond the results of the content analysis, some reasons are offered for counseling psychology's lack of attention to religion and why counseling psychologists should attend to religion in their research and clinical practice.

INTRODUCTION

The importance of culture as a critical consideration in research and practice is widely recognized within the American Psychological Association (APA) and the specialty of counseling psychology. Since Pedersen's (1991) seminal article on multiculturalism as the "fourth force" in psychology, there has been a virtual explosion of research on cultural diversity. The quantity and quality of the scholarly work that has focused specifically on multicultural topics speaks to the importance of these issues. In addition, several chapters in the most recent edition of the *Handbook of Counseling Psychology* (Brown & Lent, 2008) are specifically focused on cultural issues. Furthermore, the approval into policy of the Guidelines on Multicultural Education, Training, Research, Practice, and Organizational Change for Psychologists (American Psychological Association, 2002) by the APA highlights the importance of providing culturally responsive treatment to an ever-diversifying client population. In sum, multiculturalism has firmly established itself as the fourth force in psychology, and it continues to grow.

Although the multicultural movement has gained prominence and recognition, not all aspects of cultural diversity have enjoyed the same amount of attention. Specifically, issues of race and ethnicity have dominated the extant multicultural literature. And, as noted by Sue (2003), it is necessary and critical to focus on race because of the perpetuation of racism in the United States and its detrimental effects on people of color. We agree that race is a critical factor, but we also contend that other dimensions of culture, which are briefly acknowledged in the Multicultural Guidelines (American Psychological Association, 2002), must not be overlooked. In particular, we believe that religion is an important yet understudied aspect of diversity; other scholars agree with our stance (e.g., Pope-Davis, Ligiero, Liang, & Codrington, 2001; Schlosser, 2003). Failure to consistently consider religious issues as part of multicultural psychology has contributed to the lack of attention to religious issues in counseling psychology graduate training; this, in turn, limits the cultural competence of professionals treating clients of diverse religious backgrounds and the number of researchers who consider religion as an important construct.

Specialty journals now exist (e.g., *Counseling and Values, Journal for the Scientific Study of Religion*) whose mission is focused on issues of religion and spirituality. Although the existence of these journals is important for the field, the majority of counseling psychologists are not likely to read *Counseling and Values* or other similar publications. In fact, this type of specialty journal is likely to be read only by people with specific relevant interests. To gain consistent attention in the professional literature, a topic needs to be published in journals with a wide readership. In the case of counseling psychology, three such journals are the *Journal of Counseling Psychology, The Counseling Psychologist,* and the *Journal of Counseling and Development*. Counseling psychologists are in a unique position to consider religion in the therapeutic setting and to conduct research on religion. This is because two core unifying themes of counseling psychology are (a) an emphasis on person-environment interactions, and (b) a focus on human strengths (Gelso & Fretz, 2001). As such, counseling psychologists are concerned with identity development and the interaction between an individual and her or his social surroundings. Because religion is part of the social environment, it follows that religion is likely to have played a role in shaping people's development, and thus, it is crucial that counseling psychologists be trained to attend to these issues. Furthermore, survey data indicate that a large number of individuals in the United States believe in G-d and/or practice religion (Kosmin, Mayer, & Keysar, 2001). Hence, counseling psychologists could attend to religion as both a positive contributor to identity and an adaptive coping mechanism.

One of the issues we faced in constructing this study is the frequency with which religion and spirituality are equated in the existing literature. Religion and spirituality are separate yet related constructs that appear to be erroneously viewed as interchangeable because of a perceived commonality (Knox, Catlin, Casper, & Schlosser, 2005). Before proceeding, it is important to define religion and spirituality and delineate their similarities and differences. *Religion* is often defined as a system of ritual behaviors, worship, faith, and tradition that organizes and binds people together (Fukuyama & Sevig, 1999). In this way, religion is seen as being associated with structure and community. In contrast, spirituality is defined as "the 'breath' that animates life; or a sense of connection to oneself, others, and to that which is beyond self and others (e.g., G-d, love, the transcendent, universal energy)" (Knox et al., 2005, p. 287). Dyson, Cobb, and Forman (1997) differentiate these constructs by noting that whereas spirituality typically refers to a personal or individual relationship with a higher power, religion is often viewed as a socially constructed organization with rules and structures. Burkhardt (1989) observed that people may express their spirituality through their religion, yet at the same time, religion may also prescribe rules and procedures that can inhibit the expression of one's individual spirituality. Despite various definitions in the existing literature, as noted by Pargament (1999), there is no consensus in the field regarding definitions of religion and spirituality. Therefore, although we sought to focus on religion's place in or absence from counseling psychology research, we decided to include spirituality in this review because of the perceived interrelatedness of the two constructs, as well as the likelihood of their intersection in the extant research (Knox et al., 2005).

In the field of counseling psychology, previous content analyses have focused on research in the *Journal of Counseling Psychology* (Buboltz, Miller, & Williams, 1999), research on racial/ethnic minority issues (Ponterotto, 1988), and research on lesbian and gay male issues (Buhrke, Ben-Ezra, Hurley, & Ruprecht, 1992); however, there has not yet been a systematic examination of religion in counseling psychology research. Hence, the purpose of the study was to explore the quantity and quality of research on religion and spirituality in three of the major journals associated with counseling psychology. We sought to (a) see what kind of research on religion, if any, was being published in these journals, and (b) assess the quality and methodological rigor of the extant research.

METHOD

Judges

Five counseling psychology doctoral students served as judges in this study. In addition, two assistant professors administered the project and helped define and clarify the methodology.

Procedure

The *Journal of Counseling Psychology* (JCP), *The Counseling Psychologist* (TCP), and the *Journal of Counseling and Development* (JCD) are three of the journals that are most closely associated with counseling psychology (Buhrke et al., 1992; Ponterotto, 1988). As such, these were the target journals for our content

analysis. We decided to include full-length articles and brief reports in our review, but to exclude test reviews, book reviews, letters to the editor, introductions to special sections/issues, and reactions to research; this is consistent with previously conducted content analyses (e.g., Buhrke et al., 1992; Ponterotto, 1988).

We developed an initial coding form by brainstorming with a team of two assistant professors and six doctoral students in counseling psychology; we also sought consultation with a respected researcher with experience conducting content analyses. We decided to target the years 1994 to 2006 because of the temporal proximity to Pedersen's (1991) seminal article on multicultural counseling. Given the time delay from manuscript submission to article publication, we reasoned that it would take time for authors to begin publishing with greater frequency on multicultural issues; thus, we allowed 3 years following the publication of Pedersen's article.

We first attempted to pilot our coding scheme on the issues of JCP, TCP, and JCD that were published between 1990 and 1992, but we failed to find any articles related to religion and/or spirituality. So, we opted to review recent issues of *Counseling and Values* in succession to refine our coding system. As a result of our first review (Volume 46, Issue 3), we made minor changes to the coding system specifically for cases in which the term *religion* or *spirituality* is inferred rather than stated (e.g., when "G-d" is mentioned, it is coded as religion, but when "higher power" is mentioned, it is coded as spirituality). We also added several questions to our coding system (e.g., Is religion mentioned in the title?). At this point, the estimate of our interrater reliability was 97%. Our next review (Volume 46, Issue 2) prompted us to define what we meant by multicultural research (i.e., research is considered multicultural when it is focused on group comparisons based on some aspect of cultural identity or when examining aspects of a specific cultural group). It also helped shape some exclusionary criteria regarding religion and spirituality (e.g., if religion or spirituality is mentioned, but is not the intent of the article [e.g., if G-d is mentioned in a case study of therapy, but the article is not focused on religion or spirituality], then it is not coded as mentioning religion or spirituality). At this point, the estimate of our interrater reliability was 99%. We conducted a third and final pilot review (Volume 47, Issue 1), and obtained an interrater reliability estimate of 97%. Over these three pilots, we were able to establish very good interrater reliability estimates (i.e., 98%).

In the formal content analysis, then, we reviewed each article in its entirety to determine whether it focused on religion, spirituality, or both. We also searched to see if religion, spirituality, or both were mentioned (a) anywhere in an article, (b) in the title of an article, or (c) in the discussion section of an article (i.e., as an implication or suggestion for future research). In addition, because researchers—particularly in qualitative studies—often provide demographic self-descriptions, we looked to see if the religious identity of the participants or the authors was provided in any of the articles. If a particular article was determined to have a multicultural focus, then we looked to see if religion or spirituality was included as a multicultural variable. Next, each article was then reviewed and classified as either theoretical/conceptual or empirical; within the empirical studies, we examined each sample population described.

Finally, we reviewed the extant research to provide a methodological critique.

RESULTS

During the 13 years from 1994 to 2006, there were 1,914 articles and brief reports published in the three surveyed journals. Of those, only 51 (0.027%) were focused on religion, spirituality, or both. Table 36.1 displays a breakdown of the number of articles by journal and by year. The JCD published the most articles of this type, 24 of 748 (.032%), whereas JCP published the fewest such articles, 13 of 659 articles (.019%). The 51 articles were examined for focus and content as described above. Of those 51 articles, 20 focused solely on religion-related issues, 15 focused solely on spirituality-related issues, and 16 either focused on both religion and spirituality or failed to distinguish between the two constructs.

Looking specifically at religion, 10 of the 20 identified articles (50%) were empirical and 10 (50%) were

Table 36.1   Number of Articles Concerning Religion and Spirituality and Number of Total Articles for the Three Major Counseling Psychology Journals

Year	Number of Religious- and Spiritual-Related Articles			Number of Total Articles	
	JCP	TCP	JCD	Total	Percentage[a]
1994	0/60	0/40	1/99	1/199	0.005
1995	0/62	0/44	0/98	0/204	0.000
1996	0/54	0/33	0/51	0/138	0.000
1997	0/45	0/31	0/43	0/119	0.000
1998	0/48	0/28	1/40	1/116	0.009
1999	2/47	0/34	4/65	6/146	0.041
2000	0/45	1/35	2/52	3/132	0.023
2001	2/54	2/35	0/51	4/140	0.028
2002	0/46	1/48	2/52	3/146	0.021
2003	3/43	0/49	3/51	6/143	0.042
2004	0/41	8/45	3/40	11/126	0.087
2005	6/64	0/49	3/55	9/168	0.054
2006	0/50	2/36	5/51	7/137	0.051
Total	13/659	14/507	24/748	51/1914	0.027
Percentage[a]	0.019	0.028	0.032	0.027	—

Note: JCP = Journal of Counseling Psychology, TCP = The Counseling Psychologist, JCD = Journal of Counseling & Development.
a. Percentage of total articles that concern religious or spiritual issues.

theoretical or conceptual pieces. Of the conceptual pieces, topics included conversion therapy, Jewish issues, the impact of September 11th, recommendations for counseling practice, international issues, and indigenous healing. The 10 empirical articles focused on several topics, including religious commitment/orientation, the use of self-help books by religious practitioners, group therapy behavior, Jewish identity, and religious involvement and psychological well-being; there was also a meta-analysis on religion-accommodative counseling.

The 10 articles reporting empirical research described a total of 14 studies. One of the articles described an instrument development project and used five different data collections, whereas another article used two data collections to examine the constructs of interest. Another of the articles was a meta-analysis of five studies. Each of the other articles described singular studies; the methods used include survey/correlational analogues, qualitative methods, and quasi-experimental designs. Across the empirical studies identified (excluding the meta-analysis), sample sizes ranged from 10 to 5,472, and the religious identity of the participants was consistently identified. Christians were the overwhelming majority of the participants in most of the studies; in fact, two of the studies included only Christians in their sample. In comparison, only two studies did not include any Christian participants; one study compared Muslim, Jewish, and Druze teens, and another investigated the identity of adult American Jews.

In Table 36.2, the instances of religion and spirituality being present in the target journals are displayed, including (a) being mentioned anywhere in the article, (b) being in the title of the article, and (c) being an implication (e.g., suggestion for future research). We also include the number of articles in which the religious identity of the participants or the authors was provided.

Finally, we investigated the degree to which religion was included within or omitted from articles specifically addressing multicultural (MC) issues. If an article was coded as MC, we then searched the text to determine whether religion and/or spirituality were included along with other MC variables (e.g., race, gender). Overall, there were 804 articles we identified as MC articles, with 318 (40%) such articles in *JCP*, 293 (36%) in *JCD*, and 193 (24%) in *TCP*. Of those 804, 235 (29%) included religion and/or spirituality as a MC variable. The breakdown by journal is as follows: fifty out of 318 articles (16%) in *JCP*; 128 out of 293 articles (44%) in *JCD*, and 57 out of 193 articles (30%) in *TCP*.

DISCUSSION

First, we discuss our findings from the content analysis and highlight the salient aspects of the analysis. Then, we turn our attention to nine propositions regarding why religion has been largely ignored in counseling psychology. We also highlight three reasons why

Table 36.2   Instances of Religion and Spirituality Being Present in the Three Major Counseling Psychology Journals

Content	JCP	TCP	JCD	Total
Religion mentioned anywhere	61	80	128	269
Religion in title of article	11	14	14	39
Religion of sample provided	36	8	11	55
Religion of authors provided	1	2	4	7
Religion as implication	29	20	65	114
Spirituality mentioned anywhere	29	43	102	174
Spirituality in title of article	3	0	10	13
Spirituality as implication	15	8	57	80
Total number of articles	659	507	748	1,914

Note: JCP = Journal of Counseling Psychology, TCP = The Counseling Psychologist, JCD = Journal of Counseling & Development.

counseling psychologists should attend to religion, and close with some recommendations for the future.

Content Analysis

The purpose of this study was to examine and describe the literature on religion appearing in three main counseling psychology journals. The results of our review reveal that religion or religious issues rarely appear in these journals. Hence, research concerning religion is underrepresented in the counseling psychology literature. This certainly appears to be the case when comparing the representation of religion with other MC variables. For example, Buhrke et al. (1992) found 0.65% (43 of 6,661) of articles focused on LGBT issues over a 12-year period, and Ponterotto (1988) found 5.7% (53 of 934) of articles had a racial/ethnic minority focus over an 11-year period. Considering that the vast majority (i.e., 81%) of Americans affiliate with an organized religion (Kosmin et al., 2001), it seems that religion's absence from the counseling psychology literature is a serious shortcoming for the profession.

Of course, it is quite possible that a fair amount of empirical research is being conducted on the topic of religion. However, if this is so, it is either being published in specialty journals or is not being published at all. This raises the possibility that this kind of research is not being accepted by journal editors of mainstream counseling psychology journals. The problem here, which has been previously noted and discussed as it pertains to research on lesbian and gay male issues (Buhrke et al., 1992), is that articles must appear in the mainstream journals for a topic to be seen as important, and articles such as these should not be limited to specialty journals. In addition, roughly half of the articles in this review were empirical in nature. This appears consistent with the findings from Buhrke et al.'s (1992) content analysis of research on lesbian women and gay men (i.e., 40% of articles were empirical). This suggests that research on religion is at a very beginning stage, perhaps in a similar place to where research on lesbian women and gay men was at the beginning of the 1990s.

The results also speak to the role of religion in multicultural psychology. The frequency with which religion is mentioned at all suggests that religion and spirituality are being considered somewhat by scholars engaging in multicultural research. We believe, however, that our findings are likely an overestimate of what is actually present in the literature, for two reasons. First, religion and spirituality were typically used interchangeably in the extant literature; this led to an overestimation in our findings because many studies were counted for both terms. Second, our inclusion criteria were minimal. When religion or spirituality was included as a multicultural factor, it was often limited to one sentence (e.g., being included in a definition of multiculturalism). However, the articles rarely focused on religion as a multicultural factor; this is why we believe counseling and multicultural psychology has largely excluded religion.

Why Does Counseling Psychology Exclude Religion?

It is our proposition that several factors have contributed to the subtle, yet consistent message that religion is not an important factor in the theory, research, and practice of counseling psychology. Certainly, religion has been relegated to a status beneath race, gender, and sexual orientation as an important cultural variable (Schlosser, 2003). We believe that nine factors have contributed to this problem: (a) Christian privilege, (b) the historical evolution of psychology's multicultural movement, (c) problems with the definitions of multicultural terms, (d) psychology's relationship with religion, (e) the "Oppression Olympics," (f) the invisibility of religious identity, (g) problems with religious identity development models, (h) the complexity of religious issues, and (i) antisemitism. Each of these will be amplified below.

Christian Privilege. Christian privilege is an invisible, unacknowledged power, and in a fashion not unlike White, male (McIntosh, 1998), and heterosexual (Simoni & Walters, 2001) privilege, it is largely an unconscious process (Schlosser, 2003). Privilege, in all its forms, is a pervasive, ingrained part of the status quo, and homeostasis operates to ensure that privilege does not change hands (i.e., from Whites, men, heterosexuals, and Christians). In the current U.S. society, if one doesn't identify with a religious group, it is likely that Christianity will be assumed. To that end, in 1999, the United States was 83% Christian, and for sake of comparison,

82% White (U.S. Census Bureau, 2000). Christians might perceive that Christianity does not provide a unifying identity because of the heterogeneity within the group known as Christian (e.g., Protestant, Catholic, Latter-Day Saints). This perception is partly based on historically strong animosities between some Christian denominations, who do not believe that they have much in common with each other. However, this statement serves to mask important aspects of similarity, which maintains Christian privilege. In a discussion of religious privilege, Christians might identify with another aspect of their cultural identity (e.g., race, gender); however, the invoking of other aspects of identity is a common defense against acknowledging one's privileged status. For example, in a discussion of race, a White person may try to focus on some other aspect of identity as a means of escaping the difficult discussion regarding his or her own racial privilege. In sum, assumptions of the universality of Christianity are likely to have contributed to the invisibility of religion in counseling psychology.

Historical Evolution of Psychology's Multicultural Movement. Another possibility for why religion has not been examined grows from the origin of psychology's multicultural movement. The civil rights movement, led mostly by women and people of color, was focused on obtaining equal rights for oppressed people. This naturally led into the shift in psychology to pay attention to cross-cultural issues. Eventually, this developed into a more inclusive definition of diversity to include other salient aspects of identity beyond race (e.g., gender, sexual orientation, age, ability status, religion). Despite being a part of the more inclusive definition, religion has received far less scholarly attention in counseling psychology. We would like to be explicit here in that we do not want to criticize the MC movement. In fact, it is because of the hard work and dedication of people committed to civil rights that we can even begin discussing the importance of religion in the context of cultural diversity. Our goal is to increase the inclusion of important variables such as religion, not to be divisive and critical of the multicultural movement. We agree with Sue (2003), who states that it is necessary to focus on race because of its salience, and we also agree with Sue's assertion that racism is an unavoidable

consequence of being raised in the United States. However, we believe that to exclude the importance of other issues such as religion inherently neglects other important aspects of people's identities.

Problems With Definitions of Multicultural Terms. One of the more controversial topics that may have contributed to the neglect of religion is the confusion over terms commonly used in multicultural psychology. Specifically, we are referring to the terms *race* and *ethnicity*. It is our contention, and we are not alone in our thinking, that religion can be an ethnic identity (Ali, Liu, & Humedian, 2004; Moradi & Neimeyer, 2005; Schlosser, 2006). Biologically, race has been defined as "an inbreeding, geographically isolated population that differs in distinguishable physical traits from other members of the species" (Zuckerman, 1990, p. 1297, as cited in Atkinson, 2004). As noted by several authors (e.g., Atkinson, 2004; Helms & Cook, 1999), however, there is no consensus on a biological definition of race, and the biological definitions of race have been widely criticized. To many, race is seen as a socially constructed term (Helms & Cook, 1999). The first definition put forth from a social perspective was Cox (1948): "any people who are distinguished or consider themselves distinguished, in social relations with other peoples, by their physical characteristics" (p. 402, as cited in Atkinson, 2004). An ethnic group has been defined as "a group of people who live, or once lived, in close proximity to one another and, as a consequence, share ways of thinking, feeling, and behaving, learning from similar life circumstances shared over generations" (Fouad & Brown, 2000, p. 381). It should be readily apparent that these definitions are quite different; in fact, scholars have argued that race and ethnicity are not the same (Helms & Cook, 1999). That being said, it is our contention that race and ethnicity have become confounded over the years. For example, in most survey research, participants are instructed to indicate their "race/ethnicity." This approach acknowledges the frequent confounding of the Latino or Hispanic ethnicity with race, but it also introduces a new problem. Membership in a religious group fits within Fouad and Brown's conception of ethnic group; however, these groups (e.g., Jews, Muslims) are not provided as choices under "race/ethnicity" because they are ethnic groups that are not specifically recognized in the current sociopolitical structure (Ali et al., 2004; Moradi & Neimeyer, 2005; Schlosser, 2006). The overall result is that religion is omitted from consideration as ethnicity and race are commingled.

Psychology's Relationship With Religion. As a profession, psychology has strived to be seen as more scientific, and thus to be on equal footing with the "hard" sciences (e.g., biology). The divide between science and religion goes back far into history; for example, the Catholic Church was known to persecute scientists (e.g., Galileo) who put forth research that countered the Vatican's edicts. In modern times, religion and faith are often seen as antithetical to science (as they are concepts that cannot be quantified or measured with any reliability or validity), and the social sciences have been separated from the physical or "real" sciences based on a similar premise. Psychology, however, has long sought to be viewed as a valid science. To that end, divorcing ourselves as psychologists from religion would help other scientists come to view psychology as having equal stature. The development of the logical positivist tradition in psychology is likely related to this desire to be accepted as a legitimate science. As suggested by Sue, Bingham, Porché-Burke, and Vasquez (1999), the logical positivist tradition in psychology may bias many against religion and spirituality. In addition to this bias toward quantitative research methods, observable data, and the search for objective reality, psychologists are trained in graduate school to avoid dichotomies like right and wrong. For example, dichotomous thinking is a diagnostic criterion for borderline personality disorder. The major Western religions, on the other hand, often espouse "right" or "wrong" behaviors. Because psychologists see concepts like dichotomous thinking and external locus of control as evidence of psychopathology, it is no surprise that psychology and religion have been at odds for some time. It should come as no surprise that psychologists as a whole are less religious than the general population, and that therapy clients are much more likely to be religious and/or spiritual than their therapists (Bergin & Jensen, 1990). Because of this disparity, Bergin and Jensen suggested that psychologists may have a "blind spot" in regard to the importance of such issues.

The Oppression Olympics. The Oppression Olympics (Martinez, 1994) refers to the game we play when discussing histories of persecution: namely, who is the most oppressed, and whose pain is the worst? Unfortunately, when we play this game, nobody wins. What was the worst human suffering? The genocide of Native Americans by European settlers? Six million Jews killed in the Holocaust? More than 200 years of African slavery, including millions who lost their lives in the Maafa or postslavery racism? The Japanese internment during World War II and the eventual use of weapons of mass destruction at Hiroshima and Nagasaki? The answer is that they (and other atrocities committed against various cultural groups) were all horrific. The problem with the Oppression Olympics is that people and groups who could be natural allies end up fighting with one another for limited resources. Because of finite resources, people must advocate for their own group to be seen as having the most important needs. Of course, in order to be the "most oppressed," you are also saying that other groups have suffered less than your group. This leads to schisms between the groups (Schlosser, Talleyrand, Lyons, & Baker, 2007) that, when combined with the small numbers of religious minorities in the United States (i.e., non-Christians), have contributed to religion being relegated as less important in the hierarchy of the oppressed. In sum, once you start to play in the Oppression Olympics, it is very hard to stop.

The Invisibility of Religious Identity. Another reason for the neglect of religion is that, like sexual orientation and some ability statuses, religious identity is invisible. Despite the persistent stereotypes, unless a person wears a visibly identifiable marker (e.g., yarmulke for Jews, hijab for Muslims), she or he can "pass" and not be identified as belonging to a specific religious group. Of course, passing has inherent advantages and disadvantages. Being able to pass often, but not always, ensures safety. However, it also ensures that one has to neglect or deny an important or perhaps most central aspect of identity. Finally, the invisibility of religious identity contributes to the assumption of Christian universality in the United States (Schlosser, 2003).

Problems With Religious Identity Development Models. The limited number of extant models of religious identity development provides another reason why there is limited research on religion in counseling psychology. Given the profession's focus on developmental issues, it is surprising that there are no published religious identity models. In addition, past definitions of religious identity have been focused solely on the religious aspects of group membership and have neglected the important secular (i.e., cultural) component of many religions, especially groups that are religious minorities in the United States.

The Complexity of Religious Issues. Religious issues are complex, difficult to define, and difficulty to study for a variety of reasons. One factor is the tremendous within-group variability that exists among the various religious groups. Within each religion, there are often various denominations or subgroups, as well as degrees of observance. This increases the complexity and may cause people to avoid these issues altogether. Another complicating factor is that religion has been labeled by many as a taboo topic in social settings. As a result, people are often uncomfortable talking about religion; this silence only serves to maintain Christian privilege (Schlosser, 2003). In addition, some people don't talk about their own religion for fear of being seen as a zealot. Another complicating factor is that people have the ability to choose to leave their religion of origin. For example, individuals could decide to convert to another religion or declare themselves atheists or agnostics. In addition, the frequent confounding of religion and spirituality has certainly complicated matters. Religion and spirituality are different constructs, but as mentioned previously, they are often linked together. The world has also witnessed acts of murder and genocide committed in the name of religion both historically (e.g., the Crusades) and more recently (e.g., terrorism), and this has also likely contributed to the discomfort regarding religion. Finally, there is a concern that expressing religion may contribute to the perpetuation of oppression against LGBT individuals. That is, to believe in some religious traditions (e.g., conservative Christianity) is to affirm a worldview that justifies negative attitudes against LGBT individuals; some might avoid religion completely to avoid this possibility.

Antisemitism. Finally, antisemitism (Schlosser & MacDonald-Dennis, 2006) is also partly responsible for the exclusion of religion from counseling psychology research. As noted by other scholars (e.g., Langman, 1999; Schlosser, 2006; Weinrach, 2002), Jewish issues have, at times, been excluded from discussions of diversity. In fact, Weinrach found that only 16 (37.2%) of 43 textbooks published in the United States on multicultural issues between 1995 and 2000 included any listing for antisemitism, Jew, Jews, Jewish, and/or Judaism in the table of contents or index. If counseling psychologists attend to religion, then they will have to attend to Jewish issues consistently in the multicultural discourse, as well as appropriately describe and include Jews. This would be a major undertaking, as there is confusion as to whether Jews constitute a religion, an ethnic group, or a sociopolitical racial group. Any fully inclusive model of assessing demographic characteristics would have to appropriately attend to Jewish issues, and the current taxonomies are just not equipped to do so (Schlosser, 2006).

Why Should Counseling Psychologists Attend to Religion?

We next discuss three reasons why we should embrace religion as a critical component of cultural competence in counseling psychology research and practice: (a) the importance of religion in the lives of our clients, (b) the psychological impact of religious minority status, and (c) the role of religion in our work as psychologists and our own personal lives.

Religion in the Lives of Our Clients. Research indicates that most of our clients view their lives as grounded in faith (Hoge, 1996), and this is especially true for people of color (Sue & Sue, 2003) and people with disabilities (Vash, 1994). As a result, many potential clients are likely to believe that religion would be important to address in therapy. However, potential clients often seek religious guidance rather than professional help, in part because of a perception that mental health professionals will not understand their concerns or may pathologize their religious beliefs (Richards & Bergin, 2000). Asking a client about her or his religious beliefs may provide an opportunity to demonstrate a respect for these beliefs, and it may even strengthen the therapeutic alliance. This idea, however, remains a question for future empirical attention.

As noted previously, religion may be a source of strength and guidance for our clients, and as counseling psychologists, we are uniquely trained for attending to these factors. However, it is equally important to recognize possible religious factors in psychological disorders. In some cases, suffering may be conceptualized as a result of religious offenses that the individual has committed. Suicide and same-gender sexual attraction have particular religious implications within a wide range of religious traditions, such that a highly religious client may be ashamed of even having these thoughts. However, Richards and Bergin (2000) note that clients may not discuss suicidal feelings, for example, because of a fear that clinicians would minimize or misunderstand their distress. By extension, psychotherapy researchers will be missing important components related to distress and healing unless religion is included as a variable in studies.

Religion as a Minority Status. As noted by Schlosser (2003), it is important to consider the importance of religious minority status within a Christian country, which is a generally neglected cultural variable. Being in any minority status can be a significant source of stress, and this may be overlooked if religion is not considered as an important variable in both research and practice. Furthermore, a religious minority status may be in addition to another (or several) minority statuses. For example, Muslims, Sikhs, Jains, Hindus, Buddhists, and members of other minority religious groups are typically also people of color. It is essential, however, not to infer a client's religion based solely on racial or ethnic identity. Culturally competent psychologists should consider religion as an important component of a client's cultural identity and worldview and as an important variable in psychological research.

Religion in the Lives of Psychologists. Research has previously documented that psychologists tend to be less religious than the clients who seek treatment from them (Bergin & Jensen, 1990). However, Shafranske (1996) suggested that findings of some earlier studies may have presented an oversimplified view of this, which is supported by a recent study of therapists (Smith & Orlinsky, 2004). This study found that 94% of the participants reported having been raised in a religious

tradition. Despite this, only 65% of the U.S. sample reported having a current religious affiliation. Although this fits the image of the nonreligious psychologist, Smith and Orlinsky also reported that the majority (51%) of the sample was described as outwardly secular but holding religious values, and 27% of the sample reported both traditional communal religiosity and high personal spirituality. This suggests that the drift away from organized religion does not necessarily coincide with a loss of internal religiosity.

To the extent that religion forms a dimension of culture, these findings are not surprising. Children raised in religious environments do absorb those values. Lifelong values, in turn, shape the career choices and ethical systems of adults, who may be unaware of the religious roots of what they may view as a personal value system. As a helping profession, psychology shares important values with several of the world's major religions. Counseling psychology, in particular, has embraced a strong commitment to social justice, which is represented in the Hebrew principle of *Tikkun Olam*. This commandment, to "heal" or "repair" the world, is embedded in Jewish culture and is surely a factor in the high proportion of Jews who choose careers in the helping or healing professions (Foley, 2005; Langman, 1999; Schlosser, 2006). These ideas, particularly in terms of charity and care for others, are also reflected in the social values of the other two Abrahamic religions, Christianity and Islam. It would be naïve to assume that those who shaped the field of psychology, who had predominantly Jewish and Christian roots, developed a system of psychological ethics independent of their own value systems.

However, these religious roots are obscured by an effort to remain "value neutral" in research and practice. One of the ways in which this appears is in the growing trend toward a focus on spirituality rather than religion, which allows an individual to draw from some aspects of religion while minimizing the perceived focus on restrictive sets of rules. Ironically, it is less possible to be value neutral without recognizing and acknowledging that psychological principles, theories, and ethics are as much a value system as any system of religious values. Shafranske and Malony (1996) emphasized that value neutrality in psychotherapy is an illusion; rather, the values of the client and therapist both inevitably influence the process. Because psychological ethics are rooted in a predominantly Western system of religious values, it is also important to understand areas in which these ethics may conflict with those of other religious groups.

Finally, we encourage counseling psychologists to embrace and seek to understand their own religion and religiosity, which may provide a source of strength in the tasks we face as helping professionals—tasks that are often associated with burnout. Although we do face challenges in reconciling some religious doctrine with a culturally sensitive approach to research and practice, our own religions offer considerable resources and sources of meaning in our lives. If we are truly comfortable with our own religious roots, we will be better prepared to provide culturally competent care. Cultural competence, then, requires an ability to join with our clients' religious strengths to facilitate their growth and healing, and to attend to religion as a critical component of a client's cultural identity.

Suggestions for Future Research

Whereas multicultural literature has typically mentioned religion as an important topic, multicultural theory and research have largely ignored religion and focused on race and gender, with sexual orientation garnering increased attention recently. Although race and other cultural variables are of critical importance, so, too, is religion. However, the extant meta-message is that religion is an important part of the multicultural movement in principle, but not in practice. The lack of attention to religious issues or the cursory mentioning of its importance downplays the interrelationships that exist between cultural variables and identities. Further work needs to be done to address the exclusion of religion from multicultural theory, research, and training. In addition, our results led us to make some specific recommendations regarding the role of religion in counseling psychology research.

Religion, Not Spirituality. Based on our results, it appears that researchers often view religion and spirituality as interrelated constructs. To understand the role of religion in counseling psychology theory, research, and practice, it must be separated from spirituality in research and

practice. One idea for encouraging research on religion would be to have a special issue of a mainstream journal focused specifically on religion. It is important to note that spirituality is certainly important, and should be studied on its own as well—it just should not be inextricably and erroneously linked to religion.

Reporting Religion in Research Studies. One of our findings is that religious identity was rarely reported for the participants of the research, and even less so for the authors of research. Hence, we believe that researchers need to attend to religion more by inquiring about the religious identity of their study participants. In doing so, we will become better aware of whom we are studying and if there are differences between and within religious groups.

Religion of Origin as a Developmental Variable. As psychologists, we have begun to recognize the importance of attending to racial and cultural socialization experiences (Helms & Cook, 1999). With that in mind, it follows that we should attend to one's religion of origin (i.e., the religious tradition in which one was raised). This is because the religion of origin is highly likely to affect aspects of development, especially where values are concerned. Even if one has chosen not to practice this same or any religion as an adult, the effects of being raised with or without a religious tradition do not go away. One's religion of origin is likely to have shaped, at least in part, one's cultural socialization experiences. Hence, it is important to begin attending to religion of origin in the theory, research, and practice of counseling psychology.

Religious Identity Models. Religious identity models, which are currently few, need to attend to both the specific issues about each of the major religious groups (e.g., Christian, Jewish, Muslim, Hindu) *and* to the minority/majority experience (as in Helms's White and people of color models) (Helms & Cook, 1999). Furthermore, these models must consider both the religious and secular/cultural aspects of religion.

CONCLUSION

In closing, this study has increased our awareness about the neglect of religion by counseling psychologists. In keeping with the tenets of our profession, counseling psychologists have a responsibility to be aware of, knowledgeable about, and skilled in the treatment of and research concerning issues for culturally diverse people; cultural diversity must include religious diversity. In order for this to happen, more research needs to reach counseling psychologists through the mainstream journals. Hopefully, this article will serve as a call to scientists and practitioners alike regarding the importance of religion in our work as counseling psychologists.

REFERENCES

Ali, S. R., Liu, W. M., & Humedian, M. (2004). Islam 101: Understanding the religion and therapy implications. *Professional Psychology: Research and Practice, 35,* 635–642.

American Psychological Association. (2002). *Guidelines on multicultural education, training, research, practice, and organizational change for psychologists.* Washington, DC: Author.

Atkinson, D. R. (2004). Defining populations and terms. In D. R. Atkinson (Ed.), *Counseling American minorities* (6th ed., pp. 3–26). New York: McGraw-Hill.

Bergin, A. E., & Jensen, J. P. (1990). Religiosity of psychotherapists: A national survey. *Psychotherapy: Theory, Research, Practice, Training, 27,* 3–7.

Brown, S. D., & Lent, R. W. (Eds.). (2008). *Handbook of counseling psychology* (4th ed.). New York: Wiley.

Buboltz, W. C., Miller, M., & Williams, D. J. (1999). Content analysis of research in the *Journal of Counseling Psychology* (1973–1998). *Journal of Counseling Psychology, 46,* 496–503.

Buhrke, R. A., Ben-Ezra, L. A., Hurley, M. E., & Ruprecht, L. J. (1992). Content analysis and methodological critique of articles concerning lesbian and gay male issues in counseling journals. *Journal of Counseling Psychology, 39,* 91–99.

Burkhardt, M. (1989). Spirituality: An analysis of the concept. *Holistic Nursing Practice, 3,* 69–77.

Dyson, J., Cobb, M., & Forman, D. (1997). The meaning of spirituality: A literature review. *Journal of Advanced Nursing, 26,* 1183–1188.

Foley, P. F. (2005, August). Why counseling psychologists should get religion. In L. Z. Schlosser (Chair), *Tikkun Olam: Bringing and keeping religion in the multicultural family.* Symposium conducted at the 113th annual meeting of the American Psychological Association, Washington, DC.

Fouad, N. A., & Brown, M. T. (2000). Role of race and social class in development: Implications for counseling psychology. In S. W. Brown & R. W. Lent (Eds.), *Handbook of counseling psychology* (3rd ed., pp. 379–408). New York: Wiley.

Fukuyama, M. A., & Sevig, T. D. (1999). *Integrating spirituality into multicultural counseling.* Thousand Oaks, CA: Sage.

Gelso, C. J., & Fretz, B. R. (2001). *Counseling psychology* (2nd ed.). Pacific Grove, CA: Brooks/Cole.

Helms, J. E., & Cook, D. A. (1999). *Using race and culture in counseling and psychotherapy: Theory and process.* Boston: Allyn & Bacon.

Hoge, D. R. (1996). Religion in America: The demographics of belief and affiliation. In E. P. Shafranske (Ed.), *Religion and the clinical practice of psychology* (pp. 21–41). Washington, DC: American Psychological Association.

Knox, S., Catlin, L., Casper, M., & Schlosser, L. Z. (2005). Addressing religion and spirituality in psychotherapy: Clients' perspectives. *Psychotherapy Research, 15,* 287–303.

Kosmin, B. A., Mayer, E., & Keysar, A. (2001). *American Religious Identification Survey.* Retrieved on August 1, 2005, from http://www.gc.cuny.edu/faculty/research_studies/aris.pdf

Langman, P. F. (1999). *Jewish issues in multiculturalism: A handbook for educators and clinicians.* Northvale, NJ: Aronson.

Martinez, E. (1994). *Seeing more than Black and White.* Retrieved on October 28, 2005, from http://www.zmag.org/zmag/articles/mrtinez2.htm

McIntosh, P. (1998). White privilege: Unpacking the invisible knapsack. In M. McGoldrick (Ed.). *Re-visioning family therapy: Race, culture, and gender in clinical practice.* (pp. 147–152). New York: Guilford.

Moradi, B., & Neimeyer, G. J. (2005). Diversity in the ivory white tower: A longitudinal look at faculty race/ethnicity in counseling psychology academic training programs. *Counseling Psychologist, 33,* 655–675.

Pargament, K. I. (1999). The psychology of religion *and* spirituality? Response to Stifoss-Hanssen, Emmons, and Crumpler. *International Journal for the Psychology of Religion, 9,* 35–43.

Pedersen, P. B. (1991). Multiculturalism as a generic approach to counseling. *Journal of Counseling and Development, 70,* 6–12.

Ponterotto, J. G. (1988). Racial/ethnic minority research in the *Journal of Counseling Psychology*: A content analysis and methodological critique. *Journal of Counseling Psychology, 35,* 410–418.

Pope-Davis, D. B., Ligiero, D. P., Liang, C., & Codrington, J. (2001). Fifteen years of the *Journal of Multicultural Counseling and Development*: A content analysis. *Journal of Multicultural Counseling and Development, 29,* 226–238.

Richards, P. S., & Bergin, A. E. (2000). Toward religious and spiritual competency for mental health professionals. In P. S. Richards & A. E. Bergin (Eds.), *Handbook of psychotherapy and religious diversity* (pp. 3–26). Washington, DC: American Psychological Association.

Schlosser, L. Z. (2003). Christian privilege: Breaking a sacred taboo. *Journal of Multicultural Counseling and Development, 31,* 44–51.

Schlosser, L. Z. (2006). Affirmative psychotherapy for American Jews. *Psychotherapy: Theory, Research, Practice, Training, 43,* 424–435.

Schlosser, L. Z., & MacDonald-Dennis, C. (2006). Anti-Semitism. In Y. Jackson (Ed.), *Encyclopedia of multicultural psychology* (pp. 44–45). Thousand Oaks, CA: Sage.

Schlosser, L. Z., Talleyrand, R. M., Lyons, H. Z., & Baker, L. M. (2007). Racism, antisemitism, and the schism between Blacks and Jews in the United States: A pilot intergroup encounter program. *Journal of Multicultural Counseling and Development, 35,* 116–128.

Shafranske, E. P. (Ed.). (1996). *Religion and the clinical practice of psychology.* Washington, DC: American Psychological Association.

Shafranske, E. P., & Malony, H. N. (1996). Religion and the clinical practice of psychology: A case for inclusion. In E. P. Shafranske (Ed.), *Religion and the clinical practice of psychology* (pp. 561–586). Washington, DC: American Psychological Association.

Simoni, J. M., & Walters, K. L. (2001). Heterosexual identity and heterosexism: Recognizing privilege to reduce prejudice. *Journal of Homosexuality, 41,* 157–172.

Smith, D. P., & Orlinsky, D. E. (2004). Religious and spiritual experience among psychotherapists. *Psychotherapy: Theory, Research, Practice, Training, 41,* 144–151.

Sue, D. W. (2003). *Overcoming our racism: The journey to liberation.* San Francisco: Jossey-Bass.

Sue, D. W., Bingham, R. P., Porché-Burke, L., & Vasquez, M. (1999). The diversification of psychology: A multicultural revolution. *American Psychologist, 54,* 1061–1069.

Sue, D. W., & Sue, D. (2003). Counseling the culturally diverse: Theory and practice (4th ed.). New York: Wiley.

U.S. Census Bureau. (2000). *2000 statistical abstract of the United States.* Retrieved August 11, 2004, from http://www.census.gov/prod/2001pubs/statab/sec01.pdf

Vash, C. L. (1994). *Personality and adversity: Psychospiritual aspects of rehabilitation.* New York: Springer.

Weinrach, S. G. (2002). The counseling profession's relationship to Jews and the issues that concern them: More than a case of selective awareness. *Journal of Counseling & Development, 80,* 300–314.

37

Counseling Muslims
and Sikhs in a Post-9/11 World

MUNINDER K. AHLUWALIA AND NOREEN K. ZAMAN

In the years since September 11, 2001 (hereafter 9/11), there has been an increase in attention to and awareness of the experiences of Muslims and Sikhs in America. Less favorable public opinion (Nisbet & Shanahan, 2004; Pew Research Center, 2003, 2005) and media portrayal (Brookshire, 2004; Ibrahim, 2003) of Muslims in America have contributed to an increasingly hostile sociopolitical climate. The media have consistently and repeatedly displayed images of suspected terrorists—people with "Islamic-sounding" names, those who "appear" Muslim, and men who wear turbans. Because of these images in the United States, Sikhs are misidentified as Muslim and *therefore* terrorists. Alongside this growing interest, the post-9/11 era has witnessed a dramatic backlash against U.S. Muslims and Sikhs with a sharp increase in and record high rates of discrimination, hate crimes, and religious profiling (Council on American-Islamic Relations, 2007; United Sikhs, n.d.). Although these two communities practice two distinct religions, they have been affected similarly by the current climate in the United

States and, in particular, the backlash since 9/11. Among South Asians, Sikhs and Muslims in the United States were most affected by hate crimes and discrimination after 9/11, with 64% of Sikhs and 41% of Pakistani Muslims feeling afraid for their physical safety (Rajghatta, 2006). As a result, Muslim and Sikh Americans are currently in a precarious situation, left vulnerable to poor physical and psychological outcomes resulting from increased stress and challenges.

Unfortunately, the scientific community has been slow to respond to this urgent problem. Emerging empirical evidence has demonstrated the deleterious effects of post-9/11 discrimination on psychological distress in Muslims (e.g., Hallak & Quina, 2004; Moradi & Hasan, 2004; Sheridan, 2006). Little has been written on the experiences of Sikhs. Nonetheless, the experiences of U.S. Muslims and Sikhs continue to be underrepresented in the social sciences literature. The purposes of this chapter are to broaden the psychological understandings of the experiences, perspectives, beliefs, and practices of Muslims and Sikhs, and to provide mental health clinicians with specific implications and suggestions for culturally responsive therapeutic interventions when working with U.S. Muslims and Sikhs.

COUNSELING MUSLIMS

In order to effectively provide services in the Muslim community, it is critical to understand the cultural and historical background of the group. This section addresses the religious tenets of Islam and their relationship to mental health treatment. In addition, sociopolitical issues currently affecting the Muslim community will be discussed, along with attention to mental health values.

Who Are Muslim Americans?

With an estimated 1.3 billion Muslims worldwide, Islam is the second largest religion in the world after Christianity (Esposito & Mogahed, 2008). In the U.S. Census, official statistics of Muslims are difficult to obtain as religious data are not collected. However, commonly accepted estimates indicate that the Muslim population in America constitutes approximately 7 million individuals (Haniff, 2003). After Judaism, Islam is the second largest religious minority in America (Kelly, Aridi, & Bakhtiar, 1996). Furthermore, Islam is one of the fastest growing religious groups in the country and is projected to be the second largest religion in the United States by the year 2010 (Bagby, 1994). Muslims are a compound of diverse racial and ethnic groups of individuals in the United States. In addition, American Muslims vary in their religiosity, values, cultural traditions, adherence to schools of Islam, socioeconomic status, immigration history, level of acculturation, and integration into American society.

According to the Pew Research Center for the People & the Press and The Pew Forum on Religion & Public Life (2007), among U.S. Muslims, approximately two thirds (65%) are first-generation immigrants and one third (35%) are born in the United States. Of the foreign-born immigrants, roughly one third are from the Arab region (37%) and one quarter are from South Asia (27%). Of the U.S.-born group, 20% are African American. In addition to these three large ethnic groups, American Muslims include a range of other races and ethnicities. Despite the preponderance of immigrants, 77% of U.S. Muslims are citizens (Pew Research Center, 2007), and 82% are registered voters (Zogby International, 2004). As of 1998—the latest date for which statistics are available—more than 9,000 Muslims were on active duty in the U.S. Armed Forces (U.S. Department of Defense, 1998, as cited in the Institute for Social Policy & Understanding, 2004). With the burgeoning number of Muslims integrating themselves into the political and social framework of American society (Kelly et al., 1996), it is imperative that mental health providers demonstrate knowledge of how religion, cultural heritage, historical background, and life experiences inform the Muslim American understanding of the world (Sue, Arredondo, & McDavis, 1992).

What Do Muslim Americans Believe?

Islam, alongside Judaism and Christianity, is considered an Abrahamic faith tradition in that it traces its origins to the patriarch Abraham. As the founder of a sustained monotheistic society anchored in free will and human equality, Abraham is revered as an important prophet in Islam (Abdul Rauf, 2004). Muslims also believe in other prophets prior to Muhammad (e.g., Adam, Moses, Noah, Jesus), in scriptures revealed to these prophets (e.g., Old and New Testament), in the existence of angels (e.g., Gabriel), and in a day of judgment in which individuals will be held accountable for their actions.

The mosaic of Muslim Americans is woven together by the common thread of Islam. Shaping the lives of all Muslims is the belief in the five fundamental pillars of Islam:

1. Shahadah (Declaration of Faith): "There is no deity, but God, and Muhammad is his messenger"

2. Salat: the performance of prayer five times daily

3. Zakat: the annual distributing of 2.5% of one's accumulated wealth to the poor

4. Sawm: fasting from sunrise to sunset during the holy month of Ramadan

5. Hajj: the pilgrimage to the holy city Mecca at least once in a lifetime, if physically and financially capable (Abdul Rauf, 2004).

Embedded in practice of the five pillars is the concept of group orientation. This value of collectivism emphasizes the awareness of, and responsibility to, one's community (Banawi & Stockton, 1993). Furthermore, Muslims throughout the world consider themselves citizens of the *ummah*, the Islamic concept of community.

Muslims believe that Islam is more than a set of beliefs, but an entire way of life with prescribed guidelines and principles encompassing all aspects of daily living. The Qur'an and other scriptures provide Muslims with answers to questions about life, death, relationships, divorce, family, depression, suicide, politics and government, marriage, sex, education, rituals, and practice (Abudabbeh & Aseel, 1999; Banawi & Stockton, 1993; Carolan, Bagherinia, Juhari, Himelright, & Mouton-Sanders, 2000; Daneshpour, 1998; Mahmoud, 1996). These guidelines are to be practiced with moderation and flexibility (Banawi & Stockton, 1993). Examples of specific behaviors that are forbidden to both sexes include the consumption of pork, alcohol, and drugs; unchaperoned interactions between men and women; premarital sex; homosexuality; and death by suicide. Examples of specific practices that are encouraged include modest dress for men and women (which, for women, may encompass varying levels of covering); heterosexual marriage for the purposes of procreation and enjoyment; and respect, honor, and duty toward one's parents, extended family, and community over oneself (e.g., Carolan et al., 2000).

As Islam spread across the globe, it was integrated into the cultural and ethnic value systems of disparate nations. As a result, religious practice and cultural practice may be so highly intertwined as to appear inextricable from the perspective of Muslims and non-Muslims alike. One such example is the role of women. Although gender equity is highly prized in Islam, the practice and implementation of it has been significantly affected by patriarchal values of the host cultures. Furthermore, many Muslim women may view men and women's roles as complementary to each other, rather than comparable. This reconceptualization of traditionally Western notions of feminism holds both chosen professional roles and chosen family roles in high esteem (e.g., Ali, Mahmood, Moel, Hudson, & Leathers, 2008; Podikunju-Hussain, 2006).

With What Recent Challenges Have Muslim Americans Been Confronted?

Since 9/11, the United States has witnessed a dramatic backlash against Islam and Muslims alike. In 2001

alone, reported hate crimes against Muslims and people of Middle Eastern descent increased by 1,600% from the previous year (Federal Bureau of Investigation: Uniform Crime Reporting Program [FBI], 2002). In November 2002, the U.S. Federal Bureau of Investigation documented 481 hate crimes against Arabs and Muslims in the United States during 2001, a massive increase from the 28 cases reported in 2000 (Anderson, 2002). With every passing year since the 9/11 attacks, reported discriminatory acts against Muslims have continued to escalate. In 2004, the Council on American-Islamic Relations (CAIR) processed a total of 1,522 incident reports of civil rights cases, constituting a 49% increase from the 1,019 incidents in 2003 (Council on American-Islamic Relations, 2005). In 2005 and 2006, the number of civil rights complaints continued to rise by 30% and 25%, respectively (Council on American Islamic Relations, 2005, 2006). The 2006 data mark the highest number of Muslim civil rights complaints ever reported in CAIR's 12-year history (Council on American-Islamic Relations, 2007). The various incidents reported include, but are not limited to, "due process" arrests, employment discrimination, airport profiling, verbal harassment, intimidation, vandalism, physical assault, and murder (Council on American-Islamic Relations, 2005, 2006, 2007; FBI, 2002).

This increase in discrimination, in tandem with the general lack of knowledge about Islam (Nisbet & Shanahan, 2004; Pew Research Center, 2003, 2005), unfavorable media portrayal (Brookshire, 2004; Ibrahim, 2003), and the charge of defending basic religious freedom (Podikunju-Hussain, 2006) creates a perilous situation for Muslim Americans.

In response to the unique challenges currently facing Muslim Americans, varying coping strategies have emerged in the literature. On one hand, Muslim Americans may counter sociopolitical realities with a protective stance. For example, they may keep a low profile, turn to inner circles of support, and find comfort in sharing with each other (Hallak & Quina, 2004; Livengood & Stodolska, 2004). On the other hand, Muslim Americans may embrace a proactive stance. They may become more politically active, see themselves as "Ambassadors of Islam," take pride in their religion and religious identity, and participate in interfaith communication and outreach activities (Livengood & Stodolska, 2004; Peek, 2005). Awareness of the larger sociopolitical system within which Muslim Americans live, and its impact on the individual, is an important aspect of multicultural competence (Sue et al., 1992) in counseling.

What About Muslims and Mental Health Values?

Despite the fact that general concepts of human psychology were discussed in the Qur'an well before its birth as a formal science in the Western world, psychotherapy is neither a religiously nor a culturally accepted channel of support for Muslims (Banawi & Stockton, 1993). In general, Muslims tend to find comfort and healing in their faith, and rely primarily on their mosque (Abudabbeh & Aseel, 1999; Ali, Milstein, & Marzuk, 2005; Hallak & Quina, 2004) and family (Abudabbeh & Aseel, 1999; Carolan et al., 2000) as sources of social support. Indeed, 74% of U.S. mosques provide marital and family counseling services directly to their congregants (Bagby, Perl, & Froehl, 2001) and approximately half of U.S. *imams*—Muslim religious leaders—provide up to 5 hours of counseling per week to their communities (Ali et al., 2005).

When religious leaders, family, and trusted friends are unsuccessful, Muslims may turn to mental health professionals for support. The decision to seek out a Muslim or non-Muslim counselor is likely to be a function of the individual's religious identity (Kelly et al., 1996; Shafi, 1998) and may be shaped by the centrality of religion to the presenting problem (Shafi, 1998). Additionally, the cultural value of saving face may manifest itself in Muslim Americans purposely seeking mental health services from providers outside of their community (Abudabbeh & Aseel, 1999). This may be particular true when the individuals' experiences are counter to religious expectations and cultural values, and accompany a sense of shame or fear of judgment (Shafi, 1998).

Research has suggested that although religious similarity may not be an integral factor of counseling (e.g. Atkinson, Wampold, Lowe, Matthews, & Ahn, 1998; Helms & Carter, 1991), cultural awareness is (Shafi, 1998). Kelly and colleagues (1996) found that approximately half of the Muslims in their study would be open to working with a non-Muslim counselor. However, more than 85% would want their counselor to have an understanding of Islamic values (Kelly et al., 1996). Among highly religious Muslims, Islamic values

have been found to be more conservative and conventional than traditional counselor values (Kelly, 1995).

COUNSELING SIKHS

In this section, a brief overview of Sikhs in America, the religious tenets of Sikhism (including religious and cultural values), and sociopolitical issues currently affecting the community will be discussed. A focus will be on challenges that Sikh Americans are experiencing, and then mental health values and coping will be discussed.

Who Are Sikh Americans?

Sikhism is the fifth largest organized religion in the world (Leifker, 2006), and estimates suggest that there are between 23 million (United Sikhs, n.d.) and 25 million Sikhs worldwide (Singh, 2003). Despite this group's presence, psychologists understand very little about Sikhs' experiences and their worldview.

Sikhs are a religious minority in India and comprise approximately 2% of the population. Although Punjab is considered home to the majority of Sikhs, there is a significant Sikh diaspora. Sikhs live in states throughout India as well as many other countries. Sikh migration to other countries began more than 100 years ago, primarily with the goal of economic gain (Chilana, 2005). There are approximately 500,000 Sikhs in the United States (*Resolution on Hate Crimes Against Sikh-Americans*, n.d.). Sikhs have settled throughout the United States but are largely in cities such as New York, Los Angeles, Chicago, and San Francisco. As stated before, because the U.S. Census does not collect statistics on religious adherence, there is a paucity of information in this area. Although most Sikhs are Indian in origin, some Sikhs have converted from other religions and racially are not Asian American, such as the White American Sikhs in New Mexico. As with Muslims, Sikhs, even with their small number, are integrated into American society. Although most Americans associate Sikhs with doctors, engineers, computer-related professions, and taxi drivers, there are Sikhs in all areas of employment.

What Do Sikh Americans Believe?

Although there are millions of Sikhs worldwide and Sikhism has been around for many centuries, the majority of the U.S. population knows very little about Sikhs. Followers of the Sikh religion are called Sikhs, a term meaning "disciples," "learners" (Chilana, 2005, p. 108), or seekers of truth. As Singh (1998) explains, the religion emerged in the 15th century in the state of Punjab in northern India. The founder of the religion, Guru Nanak, was born in 1469 A.D. into a Hindu family during a time of Mughal rule, which was a time of perilous conflict between the Muslims and Hindus. In addition, within the Hindu community, there was a strong division between the upper- and lower-caste Hindus. Guru Nanak preached the unity of humankind and fought against oppression (i.e., of Hindus under Mughal rule, of lower-caste Hindus by upper-caste Hindus, and of women by men). "Nanak rejected rituals, asceticism, monasticism and formalism in favor of egalitarianism (including complete equality of the sexes), social order, communal harmony and charity" (Singh, 2004, p. 94).

The 10th guru, Guru Gobind Singh, pronounced the holy book and named his successor, Guru Granth Sahib or Adi Granth. The Sikh holy book includes scriptures thought to encompass the living spirits of the Gurus (Singh, 2004). In fact, Sikhs give it the same respect and authority as they would a human Guru (Gatrad, Jhutti-Johal, Gill, & Sheikh, 2005).

Simran (meditation on God's name) is one technique to bring one closer to the spiritual self. "A Sikh receives guidance from the Guru scripture by performing a prayer (*ardas*) in front of the scripture, and then randomly opening the scripture to read a sacred passage (*vaak*)" (Sandhu, 2004, p. 36). Sandhu describes a Sikh model for suffering and healing based in large part on the scriptures. Everything evolves from and revolves around *Ek Onkar*, the essence that unifies all diversity. The individual is multilayered, with *atma* (the spiritual core), *surti* (consciousness), *chitr gupt* (the hidden record or the unconscious), *antahkaran* (the mind), and *sareer* (the physical body). *Dukh*, or suffering, is related to the cycle of transmigration. In fact, many Sikhs believe that the suffering they experience in the current life is a consequence of actions they performed in previous lives (e.g., the Guru Granth Sahib states, "As you sow, so shall you reap" [Sandhu, 2004, p. 39]). Internal sources of suffering also include passions or vices, such as anger or greed, as the causes of distress. Sandhu explains that according to the Guru Granth Sahib, when experiencing

external sources of suffering, such as inequality, oppression, and discrimination, Sikhs must overcome the feeling of being a victim, take personal responsibility, and transform his or her own circumstances. The process of healing involves a realization of the spiritual self and consciousness spiraling through *panj khand* (five spheres): *dharma* (righteousness), *guian* (knowledge), *saram* (effort), *karam* (grace), and *sach* (truth).

Chilana (2005) states, "The teachings in the Guru Granth Sahib direct Sikhs to believe in universal brotherhood and the oneness of humanity, and to work for the welfare of everyone regardless of race, religion, nationality, or social position" (p. 109). In fact, social justice and fighting against oppression of any kind against anyone is the foundation of the religion. *Seva*, community service, is a key concept in Sikhism and is considered another way to become closer to one's spiritual self.

As Singh (2004) explains, Sikhism is monotheistic and believes that there is only one God, who is timeless and formless, and whose existence is power and love. Although Sikhs believe in *hukam*, or the will of God, they also believe people have been given free will. The five vices or passions—lust, anger, undue attachment to possessions or people, greed, and false pride—should be resisted. The ability to truly resist these vices, however, is seen as something aspirational, rather than something that can be accomplished easily. Alcohol use is prohibited in Guru Granth Sahib because "Drink makes one forget god" (Ahuja, Orford, & Copello, 2003, p. 840), impairs one's judgment, and makes one irrational. Alcohol consumption, however, does take place among Sikhs, and when individuals drink to excess, it can lead to alcohol-related disorders (Cochrane & Bal, 1990) and negatively affect the family (Ahuja et al., 2003).

Sikh men and women are required to wear the "five Ks" (symbols), which are as follows: *kes* (uncut hair, which is considered a gift of God); *kanga* (a small comb to keep the hair tidy); *kachhehara* (underwear or riding breeches, a symbol of commitment to purity); *kara* (a steel band worn on the right wrist, as a reminder of the bond between a Sikh and the Guru, and for the need for restraint); and the *kirpan* (a small sword that is a reminder to fight for freedom and justice) (Singh, 2004, p. 93). Men cover their head with turbans, and although some women wear turbans, most either do not cover their head or use a *chuni* (headscarf). Throughout

Indian history, turbans were worn by princes and kings. Indeed, among Sikhs, turbans are a matter of pride, and they are seen as the "crown of spirituality" (Chilana, 2005, p. 109). The turban is also seen as something very private and is not to be removed by anyone other than the wearer.

With What Recent Challenges Have Sikh Americans Been Confronted?

Ghuman (1997) found that Sikh adolescents opposed assimilation and separation and believed in integration.

> Overall, the Sikh boys and girls support gender equality, want to retain their language, would like freedom to meet young people in youth clubs, want to visit their English friends' homes, want to attend their places of worship, and want to fulfill their parents' wishes. (Ghuman, 1997, p. 31)

Although Ghuman studied Sikhs in England, much of the same attitude toward integration into mainstream society is also reflected in Sikhs in the United States. Inherent in their desire to integrate within the dominant culture and retain their own, Sikhs experience conflict that arises from belonging to two different cultures and being a minority religious group in a predominantly Christian country.

In the United States, Sikhs are both a racial minority and a religious minority. By having several identities that diverge from the dominant, mainstream group in the United States, Indian Americans are seen as multiply different (Yoshi, 2006). When those Indian Americans are also immigrants, additional factors (e.g., cultural and linguistic differences such as ethnic dress and accented speech) magnify the effects of being different. It should be noted that each religious group within the racial category of Indian Americans is placed in a different position: Muslims are considered "dangerous," Sikhs "strange," and Hindus "exotic yet safe" (Yoshi, 2006). In the United States, particularly after 9/11, Sikhs are often misidentified as being Muslim and are thus seen as strange (at best) and dangerous (most often).

Hate Crimes, Profiling, and Discrimination. The most appalling consequences of the misidentification of Sikhs have come in the form of hate crimes, racial and religious profiling, and discrimination. In a report on South Asian American Communities, 83% of Sikhs said that they or someone they knew personally had experienced a hate crime or incident (Rajghatta, 2006). Shortly after the attacks on 9/11, Americans were inundated with images of a particular manifestation of Islam; media portrayal of Afghani Muslims showed men wearing turbans and long beards. Specifically, the images of Osama bin Laden, an Arab, and Mohammed Omar, an Afghani, became associated in the American mainstream mind with Sikh men because of the visual image of the turban and beard. Americans (including not only White but also Black and East Asian Americans) incorrectly perceived Sikh Americans as Muslims because of their false understanding of Muslims' appearance as including a turban and beard (Goodstein & Lewin, 2001). Although Sikhs have experienced discrimination because of their names; skin color; style of dress; and for immigrants, speech, two of the five Ks, long *kes* covered with a turban and the *kirpan,* are the most often-cited reasons for hate crimes and discrimination.

The mistaken association of Sikh cultural implements with terrorism has led to a large number of verbal and physical attacks as Sikhs go about their everyday lives. The first post-9/11 death was the murder of Balbir Singh Sodhi in Arizona. Sodhi, a 51-year-old Sikh gas station attendant in Mesa, Arizona, was killed on September 15, 2001, by a man police described as angry about the 9/11 attacks in New York City and Washington, DC. He associated the turban, a Sikh article of faith, with terrorism. As of 2006, 800 hate crimes against Sikhs in the United States were reported after 9/11 (Leifker, 2006).

The discrimination that Sikhs face, however, is because of not only individual acts of racism but also institutionalized racism and oppression, including the following: government, criminal justice systems, legal systems, educational systems, sports associations, media, airports, and the workplace. On September 17, 2001, U.S. Representative John Cooksey explained to a network on a Louisiana radio station that anyone "wearing a diaper on his head should expect to be interrogated as a possible suspect in the investigations of the terrorist attacks" (Puar & Rai, 2002, p. 137). This incident illustrates how Sikhs were targeted and encountered severe repercussions both from the backlash after the 9/11 terror attacks but also from subsequent laws and policies (Puar & Rai, 2002), such as the PATRIOT Act and airport racial profiling. Sikhs have been routinely and repeatedly mistaken for "terrorists" and unjustly stopped at airport security. Within the community, it is clear what is meant when someone says, "Flying while Sikh." In a violation of their civil rights, Sikhs have been forced to take off their turbans so they can be checked for weapons. Because of its religious meaning, however, the turban cannot be simply removed in public, like a hat.

One in 10 Sikhs report that they have been refused employment because of their religious identity (Indeck, 2008). Following 9/11, reactionary "no turban" policies were instituted at workplaces, with discriminatory effects on the Sikh community (The Wing Luke Asian Museum, n.d.). Two high-profile cases of individuals who worked with Sikh community organizations were those of Amric Singh and Sat Hari Singh Khalsa (The Wing Luke Asian Museum, n.d.). In 2001, Amric Singh was fired from the New York Police Department (NYPD) because he refused to remove his turban. He filed suit against the NYPD in 2002, and more than 2 years later, the case was resolved in favor of Singh and the Sikh community. In 2004, subway train operator Kevin Harrington (Sat Hari Singh Khalsa) filed suit against the New York City Transit, which had ordered him to stop wearing his turban, put a Metropolitan Transportation Authority logo on his turban, or be demoted in his job, despite a 23-year career as a train operator wearing a turban. Harrington refused and was demoted to a yard job, where he would have no customer interaction (Sikh Coalition, n.d.). Sikh children were also subjected to bullying and harassment. Indeck (2008) reports that half of the Sikh students in New York have been harassed at school because of their religion or national origin.

Sikhs are required to wear a *kirpan,* and the public commonly mistakes the *kirpan* for a dangerous weapon or an instrument used for violence. Therefore, in the United States, Sikhs wearing the *kirpan* in public venues, such as schools, workplaces, and in air travel, has become controversial. The *kirpan* is symbolic rather than functional and can range from less than an inch (placed on a *kanga* or as a locket around the neck) to a 3-foot ceremonial sword (Singh, 2004). The typical 8-inch *kirpan* is less dangerous than a blunt dinner knife. In schools and workplaces, however, there have been cases where *kirpans* have been banned. Sikhs carrying *kirpans* were threatened with probation, losing their jobs, and even criminal charges (Sikh Coalition, n.d.). In addition, "No tolerance weapons policies on school grounds have included the kirpan . . . forcing Sikhs to deny their religion and identity at the earliest of ages" (The Wing Luke Asian Museum, n.d.).

In addition to the 9/11 attacks in the United States, there are other events in recent history in which Sikhs have experienced discrimination and oppression. In June 1984, the Indian army, under the direction of the Prime Minister Indira Gandhi, attacked the Golden Temple, the most sacred site for Sikhs. In this attack, innocent Sikhs were killed and historical documents and buildings were destroyed. In retaliation, her two Sikh bodyguards killed her. "This horrendous event, and the Delhi riots that followed the assassination of Prime Minister Indira Gandhi, during which Sikhs were massacred, remain the most critical forces in the generation of a universal Sikh identity" (Banchu, 1991, p. 5). Three days and nights of unchecked violence resulted in the death of approximately 4,000 Sikhs. Again, this was a trauma that has stayed with Sikhs—both those who had firsthand experience and those who bore witness—and contributes to many Sikhs' feelings that India is no longer their homeland. Similar to the 9/11 attacks, the July 7, 2005, bombings in London, England, resulted in a backlash against Sikhs (The Pluralism Project, n.d.). With the backlash in the United States and England, some Sikhs questioned the welcome of their adopted countries.

What About Sikhism, Mental Health, and Coping?

Sikhs experience mental health issues just as any community does; however, psychotherapy is not often seen as a culturally viable option. Sikhs will often turn to their family, community, and faith prior to seeking out mental health services. Scriptures, in particular, are considered a traditional healing source (Sandhu, 2004). Depending on the presenting problem and factors such as generational status, level of acculturation, religiosity, and so on, Sikhs may or may not seek out the assistance of an Indian mental health practitioner for any number of reasons (e.g., because finding a Sikh clinician is improbable, because of shame around mental health issues).

In a post-9/11 world, misidentification and discrimination of Sikhs has continued with tragic consequences, including increases in mental health disorders such as depression, anxiety, and posttraumatic stress disorder (PTSD). Sikhs have responded through various coping mechanisms. Many Sikhs felt the need to show their solidarity with the United States and their patriotism. They held vigils and covered their gurdwaras with American flags. Some Sikhs went as far as wearing red, white, and blue turbans to show the public that they were not terrorists and were, in fact, patriots of the country (Puar & Rai, 2002). Although some Sikhs turned away from their religion, others turned toward it for strength and support.

Many Sikhs coped with the attacks of 9/11 by responding to those in need through *seva* to the larger community around them. For example, an immediate response to 9/11 by Sikh taxi drivers in New York City was to provide free taxi service to those who were volunteering in the rescue efforts and for individuals searching for family members (Murphy, 2008). Others donated blood to the Red Cross (Puar & Rai, 2002) and became involved in interfaith activities. Some Sikhs focused their energies on educating the American public about their religion after 9/11. In fact, many Sikh organizations, such as Sikh Coalition and United Sikhs, were engaged in defending the rights of those who were victims of hate crimes and discrimination. In addition, individuals and organizations alike have been instrumental in providing education and training about Sikhs. One example of an individual's effort is Jasbir Singh (2006), who developed the multimedia curriculum program *The Sikh Next Door*, which aims to teach tolerance through educating U.S. students and communities about Sikhs and Sikhism. Created in response to the bullying and harassment that Sikh students experienced, this program is the first Sikh curriculum program designed specifically for American schools.

For some Sikhs, *simran* and *seva* have not been enough to combat the effects of discrimination and to heal themselves. They feel disconnected from their spiritual self and have a "crisis of faith." These Sikh men, in particular, cut their hair, shaved their beard, and abandoned their turban when they (or someone they know) encountered hate crimes and discrimination. Although some may have felt relief at this action, it also often caused a great amount of grief and feelings of loss for individuals, their families, and the community.

HOW CAN CLINICIANS BEST HELP MUSLIM AND SIKH AMERICANS?

There has been an increase in mental health-related problems and difficulties among Muslims and Sikhs as a result of hate crimes and discrimination after 9/11. They have experienced physical and verbal attacks, as well as nonverbal gestures, resulting in significant emotional consequences. Given that clinicians historically receive training that is primarily developed from a Eurocentric model for White, middle-class Americans (Davis-Russell, 2003; Wyatt & Parham, 1985), it is important that clinicians become aware of culturally sensitive approaches to working with Muslim and Sikh Americans.

In addition, it is important not to view religious beliefs and Western psychology as divergent and contradictory. In the Sikh religion, for example, there are several observable parallels between Western psychology and Sikh religious beliefs. The Sikh worldview, along with its model of the person, suffering, and healing, has parallels in psychological concepts in psychoanalytic, cognitive, behavioral, family systems, feminist, reality, humanistic, and gestalt therapies (Sandhu, 2004). Sandhu outlines how the Sikh worldview is similar to Western existentialism:

> (1) The anxiety of suffering arising from a person's struggle for permanence is a condition of life; (2) the sense of separation from others leads to feelings of isolation and instills an underlying fear of non-being; (3) the awareness of the inevitability of death can cultivate thoughts and actions in order to make life more meaningful; and (4) persons are responsible for their own lives, their actions, their failures, and to constructively change their lives. (p. 43)

An essential component of cultural competence in working with Muslim and Sikh Americans is an awareness of the religions and the typical value orientations associated with them. Through this appreciation for the religions, clinicians may be better equipped to respond empathically, respectfully, and in therapeutically beneficial ways (Kelly et al., 1996; Podikunju-Hussain, 2006). However, despite potentially shared values within the

Islamic worldview, there continues to be much diversity, and sometimes conflict, in the interpretation and practice of Islam within an American context (Hodge, 2005). In addition to the intermingling of cultural and religious values, historical, social, political, economic, and familial factors may contribute to individuality among American Muslims (Altareb, 1996; Carolan et al., 2000; Podikunju-Hussain, 2006). When considering Sikhs, it is also important to understand them as individuals with unique beliefs and histories embedded within the contexts of family, community, and the larger society. As a result, clinicians working with Muslims and Sikh Americans are encouraged to explore the cultural values that accompany the client into the therapeutic encounter.

As with all cross-cultural counseling interactions, rapport and alliance building are critical to effective treatment when counseling Muslims and Sikhs. This is particularly true with Muslim clients given the stigma regarding mental health treatment (Abudabbeh & Aseel, 1999; Hodge, 2005), issues of mistrust (Ali, Liu, & Humedian, 2004), and a hesitancy to disclose personal information (Carolan et al., 2000). Mahmoud (1996) discusses the importance of exploring the individual's spiritual belief system in an effort to establish rapport; it may serve to communicate recognition, respect, and appreciation for their religious and spiritual values. It may also allow for opportunities to discuss potential reluctance to seeking mental health services (Abudabbeh & Aseel, 1999; Ali et al., 2004). At the same time, however, the post-9/11 era has resulted in Muslims experiencing greater hypervigilance regarding how they are perceived by others (Podikunju-Hussain, 2006). Sikhs are also alert to how others respond to them—both verbally and nonverbally. Thus, clinicians must be careful not to assess religious values prematurely, so as to seem suspicious of religious activity. It is important that clinicians understand and believe the reality of intolerance, hate, and discrimination that Muslims and Sikhs encounter on a regular basis.

The initial phase of clinical work may include exploration of whether or not the presenting concern is connected to a religious expectation and/or a cultural expectation. For some clients, this may be a unique opportunity to assess the ways in which their cultural reference groups have influenced their worldview (Altareb, 1996). With highly religious individuals, it

may be important for them to feel as though their spiritual and religious values are an accepted part of the therapeutic process and an integral part of the solution (Podikunju-Hussain, 2006). Mental health clinicians may consider learning about the client's presenting concern from an Islamic perspective, either in discussion with the client or in consultation with Muslim colleagues, religious leaders, and Islamic organizations (Altareb, 1996). Books (e.g., history books and scriptures) and films (e.g., *Mistaken Identity: Sikhs in America*) may help them understand the cultural and sociopolitical context. In addition, consultation with Sikh colleagues, community leaders, and organizations may also be beneficial.

Muslim and Sikh clients may experience greater levels of discomfort with self-disclosure and seeking mental health services when the presenting concern relates to behavior that is prohibited by the religion or culturally taboo. For example, the candid discussion of alcohol, drugs, dating, sex, rape, sexual abuse, homosexuality, and discontent with family or community may be not only shameful for the client, but also contribute to fears of negative judgments (Shafi, 1998). As explicated earlier in this chapter, there is considerable variability regarding religious and cultural value systems held by Muslim and Sikh Americans; moreover, there are meaningful intergroup differences among U.S. Muslims and Sikhs (e.g., Latino Muslim converts vs. Afghani Muslim refugees; Indian American Sikhs vs. White American Sikhs). Clinicians are encouraged to be aware of religious and cultural values without overlooking intergroup and individual differences. It is also important that mental health clinicians not confuse cultural practices with religious practices (e.g., female genital mutilation) (Abu-Sahlieh, 1994; Joseph, 1996).

Clinicians working with Muslim and Sikh American clients are encouraged to be aware of their own perceptions, stereotypes, and beliefs about Islam and the Sikh religion. As such, they have a duty to identify and avoid making false assumptions about their clients. For example, public opinion of *hijab* (i.e., headscarf) indicates that it is understood to be oppressive of women. However, in a study of African American Muslim women, Byng (1998) explains the ways in which the Muslim experience of *hijab* is one that is liberating from physical and sexual objectification. Similarly, some may see the turban as outdated and "traditional," whereas for many Sikhs, the turban is a symbol of pride in their faith. Although not all Sikhs wear a *kirpan,* there are clients who do. It is important for mental health practitioners working with Sikhs to respect the religious traditions of their clients, while also ensuring the safety of the client and others (Singh, 2004). For example, Singh (2004) emphasizes the importance of discussing any concerns openly but sensitively with clients in an in-patient psychiatric center, explaining the concerns about safety while not challenging or judging Sikh religious traditions.

Sue and colleagues (1992) indicate that mental health clinicians have a responsibility to consider the greater sociopolitical context within which both they and their clients participate. As such, clinicians are cautioned not to invalidate the experiences of their Muslim and Sikh American clients. In a study by Sheridan (2006), it was found that despite 55% of Muslims reporting increased tension and conflict within their communities, 25% stated that others inferred them to be paranoid about racism and religious discrimination. Discriminatory experiences in public realms of life may be difficult to broach with a religiously and culturally different clinician (Podikunju-Hussain, 2006). Thus, when Muslim and Sikh clients take risks to introduce real or perceived discrimination, it is vital that the clinician exercise sensitivity in validating and honoring the client's experience.

Sikhs who experience discrimination have gained assistance from community organizations such as United Sikhs, Sikh Coalition, and the Sikh American Legal Defense and Education Fund (SALDEF). Muslim organizations, such as the Council on American-Islamic Relations, provide similar services to the Muslim community. These organizations have played an important role in that they understand the religious and cultural implications. They have also broadened their scope by providing assistance and relief efforts for not only their own communities, but other communities as well. In addition, these organizations have served to provide referrals in instances when mental health issues arise. It is also important for clinicians to engage in dialogue with these organizations to provide culturally appropriate services.

CONCLUSION

It is hoped that the information provided in this chapter will promote understanding among mental health professionals of the ways in which Muslims' and Sikhs' cultural heritage, historical background, and life experiences shape their understanding of the world (Sue et al., 1992) and approach to mental health treatment. As Singh (2004) states, it is important to allow ethnic and religious minority clients to feel that their value and belief systems are not only understood, but also respected.

REFERENCES

Abdul Rauf, F. (2004). *What's right with Islam: A new vision for Muslims and the West.* New York: Harper.

Abudabbeh, N., & Aseel, H. A. (1999). Transcultural counseling and Arab Americans. In J. McFadden (Ed.), *Transcultural counseling* (2nd ed., pp. 283–296). Alexandria, VA: American Counseling Association.

Abu-Sahlieh, S. A. (1994). To mutilate in the name of Jehovah or Allah: Legitimization of male and female circumcision. *Medicine & Law, 13,* 575–622.

Ahuja, A, Orford, J., & Copello, A. (2003). Understanding how families cope with alcohol problems in the UK West Midlands Sikh community. *Contemporary Drug Problems, 30,* 839–873.

Ali, O. M., Milstein, G., & Marzuk, P. M. (2005). The imam's role in meeting the counseling needs of Muslim communities in the United States. *Psychiatric Services, 56,* 202–205.

Ali, S. R., Liu, W. M., & Humedian, M. (2004). Islam 101: Understanding the religion and therapy implications. *Professional Psychology: Research and Practice, 35,* 635–642.

Ali, S. R., Mahmood, A., Moel, J., Hudson, C., & Leathers, L. (2008). A qualitative investigation of Muslim and Christian women's views of religion and feminism in their lives. *Cultural Diversity and Ethnic Minority Psychology, 14,* 38–46.

Altareb, B. Y. (1996). Islamic spirituality in America: A middle path to unity. *Counseling and Values, 41,* 29–38.

Anderson, C. (2002, November 25). FBI reports jump in violence against Muslims. *Associated Press.*

Atkinson, D. R., Wampold, B. E., Lowe, S. M., Matthews, L., & Ahn, H. (1998). Asian American preferences for counselor characteristics: Application of the Bradley-Terry Luce model to paired comparison data. *The Counseling Psychologist, 26,* 101–123.

Bagby, I. (1994). *Muslim resource guide.* Fountain Valley, CA: Islamic Resource Institute.

Bagby, I., Perl, P. M., & Froehl, B. T. (2001). *The mosque in America: A national portrait.* Washington, DC: Council on American-Islamic Relations.

Banawi, R., & Stockton, R. (1993). Islamic values relevant to group work, with practical applications for the group leader. *Journal for Specialists in Group Work, 18,* 151–160.

Banchu, P. (1991). Ethnicity constructed and reconstructed: The role of Sikh women in cultural elaboration and educational decision-making in Britain. *Gender & Education, 3*(1), 45–61.

Brookshire, M. D. (2004). Press coverage of Muslims and Islam after September 11, 2001. *Masters Abstracts International, 43*(04).

Byng, M. D. (1998). Mediating discrimination: Resisting oppression among African-American Muslim women. *Social Problems, 45,* 473–487.

Carolan, M. T., Bagherinia, G., Juhari, R., Himelright, J., & Mouton-Sanders, M. (2000). Contemporary Muslim families: Research and practice. *Contemporary Family Therapy: An International Journal, 22,* 67–79.

Chilana, R. S. (2005). Sikhism: Building a basic collection on Sikh religion and culture. *Reference & User Services Quarterly, 45,* 108–116.

Cochrane, R., & Bal, S. (1990). The drinking habits of Sikh, Hindu, Muslim and white men in the West Midlands: A community survey. *British Journal of Addiction, 85,* 759–769.

Council on American-Islamic Relations. (2005). *The status of Muslim civil rights in the United States: Unequal protection.* Washington, DC: Author.

Council on American-Islamic Relations. (2006). *The status of Muslim civil rights in the United States: The struggle for equality.* Washington, DC: Author.

Council on American-Islamic Relations. (2007). *The status of Muslim civil rights in the United States: Presumption of guilt.* Washington, DC: Author.

Daneshpour, M. (1998). Muslim families and family therapy. *Journal of Marital and Family Therapy, 24,* 355–368.

Davis-Russell, E. (2003). Integrating multicultural issues into graduate clinical psychology training. In P. Bronstein & K. Quina (Eds.), *Teaching gender and multicultural awareness: Resources for the psychology classroom* (pp. 399–346). Washington, DC: American Psychological Association.

Esposito, J. L., & Mogahed, D. (2008). *Who speaks for Islam? What a billion Muslims really think.* New York: Gallup Press.

Federal Bureau of Investigation: Uniform Crime Reporting Program. (2002). *Hate crime statistics: 2001.* Retrieved February 12, 2007, from http://www.fbi.gov/ucr/01hate.pdf

Gatrad, R., Jhutti-Johal, J., Gill, P. S., & Sheikh, A. (2005). Sikh birth customs. *Archives of Disease in Childhood, 90,* 560–563.

Ghuman, P. A. S. (1997). Assimilation or integration? A study of Asian adolescents. *Educational Research, 39,* 23–35.

Goodstein, L., & Lewin, T. (2001, September 19). Victims of mistaken identity, Sikhs pay a price for turbans. *New York Times.* Retrieved on December 18, 2008, from http://query.nytimes.com/gst/fullpage.html?res=9C06EE D9123BF93AA2575AC0A9679C8B63

Hallak, M., & Quina, K. (2004). In the shadows of the Twin Towers: Muslim immigrant women's voices emerge. *Sex Roles, 51,* 329–338.

Haniff, G. M. (2003). The Muslim community in America: A brief profile. *Journal of Muslim Minority Affairs, 23,* 303–311.

Helms, J. E., & Carter, R. T. (1991). Relationships of White and Black racial identity attitudes and demographic similarity to counselor preferences. *Journal of Counseling Psychology, 38,* 446–457.

Hodge, D. R. (2005). Social work and the house of Islam: Orienting practitioners to the beliefs and values of Muslims in the United States. *Social Work, 50,* 162–173.

Ibrahim, D. A. (2003). Framing of Arabs and Muslims after September 11th: A close reading of network news. *Dissertation Abstracts International: Section A: Humanities and Social Sciences, 64*(12).

Indeck, S. H. (2008, April 15). Prejudice with the Sikh religion people in the United States. *Ground Report.* Retrieved on May 28, 2008, from http://www.ground report.com/Lifestyle

Institute for Social Policy and Understanding. (2004). *The USA Patriot Act: Impact on the Arab and Muslim American community.* Retrieved May 31, 2007, from http://www.ispu.us/files/PDFs/patriot%20act%20_2–04 %20-%20with%20cover_.pdf

Joseph, C. (1996). Compassionate accountability: An embodied consideration of female genital mutilation. *Journal of Psychohistory, 24,* 2–17.

Kelly, E. W. J. (1995). *Spirituality and religion in counseling and psychotherapy: Diversity in theory and practice.* Alexandria, VA: American Counseling Association.

Kelly, E. W. J., Aridi, A., & Bakhtiar, L. (1996). Muslims in the United States: An exploratory study of universal and mental health values. *Counseling and Values, 40,* 206–218.

Leifker, D. (2006). Investigating anti-Sikh discrimination in a post 9/11 world. *Sikh Spectrum.* Retrieved on May 28, 2008, from http://www.sikhspectrum.com/112006/ denise.htm

Livengood, J. S., & Stodolska, M. (2004). The effects of discrimination and constraints negotiation on leisure behavior of American Muslims in the post-September 11 America. *Journal of Leisure Research, 36,* 183–208.

Mahmoud, V. (1996). African American Muslim families. In M. McGoldrick, J. Giordano, & J. K. Pearce (Eds.), *Ethnicity and family therapy* (2nd ed., pp. 112–128). New York: Guilford.

Moradi, B., & Hasan, N. T. (2004). Arab American persons' reported experiences of discrimination and mental health: The mediating role of personal control. *Journal of Counseling Psychology, 51,* 418–428.

Murphy, A. (2008). Sikhs respond to September 11. *Asia Source.* Retrieved December 18, 2008, from http://query.nytimes.com/gst/fullpage.html?res=9C06EED9123BF93AA2575AC0A9679C8B63

Nisbet, E. C., & Shanahan, J. (2004). *Restrictions on civil liberties, views of Islam, and Muslim Americans.* Ithaca, NY: Cornell University, Media and Society Research Group.

The Pluralism Project. (n.d.). *Discrimination & national security initiative: Project description.* Retrieved May 28, 2008, from http://www.pluralism.org/affiliates/kaur_sidhu/index.php

Peek, L. (2005). Becoming Muslim: The development of a religious identity. *Sociology of Religion, 66,* 215–242.

Pew Research Center for the People & the Press and the Pew Forum on Religion & Public Life. (2003, July 24). *Religion and politics: Contention and consensus.* Retrieved February 12, 2007, from http://people-press.org/reports/pdf/189.pdf

Pew Research Center for the People & the Press and the Pew Forum on Religion & Public Life. (2005, July 26). *Fewer say Islam encourages violence: Views of Muslim-Americans hold steady after London bombings.* Retrieved February 12, 2007, from http://people-press.org/reports/pdf/252.pdf

Pew Research Center for the People & the Press and the Pew Forum on Religion & Public Life. (2007, May 22). *Muslim Americans: Middle class and mostly mainstream.* Retrieved May 31, 2007, from http://pewresearch.org/assets/pdf/muslim-americans.pdf

Podikunju-Hussain, S. (2006). Working with Muslims: Perspectives and suggestions for counseling. In G. R. Walz, J. C. Bleuer, & R. K. Yep (Eds.), *Vistas: Compelling perspectives on counseling* (pp. 103–106). Alexandria, VA: American Counseling Association.

Puar, J. K., & Rai, A. S. (2002). Monster, terrorist, fag: The war on terrorism and the production of docile patriots. *Social Text, 20,* 117–148.

Rajghatta, C. (2006, September 11). Sikhs, Muslims bore the brunt of 9/11 backlash. *Times of India.* Retrieved May 25, 2008, from http://timesofindia.indiatimes.com/World/US/Sikhs-Muslims-bore-the-brunt-of-911-backlash/articleshow/1980135.cms

Resolution on Hate Crimes Against Sikh-Americans: Congressional Briefing Package. (n.d.). Retrieved May 15, 2008, from http://www.sikhcoalition.org/CongressBriefingPacket.pdf

Sandhu, J. S. (2004). Sikh model of the person, suffering, and healing: Implications for counselors. *International Journal for the Advancement of Counselling, 26,* 33–46.

Shafi, S. (1998). A study of Muslim Asian women's experiences of counselling and the necessity for a racially similar counsellor. *Counselling Psychology Quarterly, 11,* 301–314.

Sheridan, L. P. (2006). Islamophobia pre- and post-September 11th, 2001. *Journal of Interpersonal Violence, 21,* 317–336.

Sikh Coalition. (n.d.). *2004 legal protection—Highlights.* Retrieved May 20, 2008, from http://www.sikhcoalition.org/ar2004_legal.asp

Singh, G. (1998). *A history of the Sikh people (1469–1988).* New Delhi: Allied Publishers Limited.

Singh, J. (2006). Who is the Sikh next door? *Independent School, 65,* 9.

Singh, M. (2003). Power in Punjab. *Christianity Today, 47,* 24–25.

Singh, S. P. (2004). Caring for Sikh patients wearing a kirpan (traditional small sword): Cultural sensitivity and safety issues. *Psychiatric Bulletin, 28,* 93–95.

Sue, D. W., Arredondo, P., & McDavis, R. J. (1992). Multicultural counseling competencies and standards: A call to the profession. *Journal of Multicultural Counseling and Development, 20,* 64–88.

United Sikhs. (n.d.). *About Sikhs.* Retrieved May 27, 2008, from http://www.unitedsikhs.org/aboutsikhs.php?PHPSESSID=6c1a24f48f84700d1a28c5bc9f5d4e48

The Wing Luke Asian Museum. (n.d.). *Being a Sikh in a Western world.* Retrieved October 2, 2007, from http://www.wingluke.org/pages/sikhcommunitywebsite/beingasikhinawesternworld.html

Wyatt, G. E., & Parham, W. D. (1985). The inclusion of culturally sensitive course materials in graduate school and training programs. *Psychotherapy: Theory, Research, Practice, Training, 22,* 461–468.

Yoshi, K. Y. (2006). The racialization of Hinduism, Islam, and Sikhism in the United States. *Equity & Excellence in Education, 39,* 211–226.

Zogby International. (2004, October 19). *Muslims in the American public square: Shifting political winds and fallout from 9/11, Afghanistan, and Iraq.* Retrieved May 31, 2007, from www.zogby.com/AmericanMuslims2004.pdf

38

The *Spiritual Exercises* in Counseling and Therapy

JOHN J. CECERO, S. J.

"I'm feeling okay, but I'm still not living the life I should be living." This is a comment of a client who has been in psychotherapy with me for more than a year of weekly sessions. A middle-aged married professional, he was referred to me to treat chronic depression and anxiety symptoms related to an unrelenting perfectionism, an inability to feel good enough about his work and to relax. He had been evaluated extensively in the year preceding our work and was prescribed an antidepressant that he continues to take, believing that it has certainly helped him to recover from the depths of depression and to sustain an adequate level of functioning at work and at home. In the therapy, we have been challenging his perfectionism through cognitive and behavioral interventions. The client has learned that he doesn't have to meet everyone's expectations perfectly and that he can ask for help when he is unsure about how to respond in any given situation. He has also been challenged to balance work and play time, and to include some spontaneity in his ordinary week. He reports that he is feeling better since implementing these strategies over time, yet still

he believes that he is fundamentally living the wrong life. When queried about the origin of this existential concern, the client pointed out that in college, he believed strongly that God was directing him both to his current profession and marriage, but that it has turned out that God misdirected him. Although he was a very spiritual young person, he harbors such strong feelings of resentment and disappointment in God that he can no longer turn to his faith as a source of support and guidance in life.

In the context of psychotherapy, this case presents some challenging questions. It appears that the client clearly connects his lack of enthusiasm for life with a spiritual conflict, and although the traditional cognitive and behavioral interventions are helpful, they are not in themselves targeting this ultimate concern. Should the therapist ignore this concern, because its content is outside the professional parameters of psychotherapy? Or should the counselor refer the client to a religious professional for pastoral counseling or spiritual direction? Or should the therapist attempt to address these concerns within psychotherapy?

Even if the counselor were inclined to address issues of anger and disappointment with God, so as to include a spiritual focus in the client's quest for purpose in life, there are few, if any, psychotherapy manuals to inform or direct the interventions. At the same time, there are models of spiritual healing, growth, and transformation that might greatly assist a practitioner in addressing these concerns. One such model is the *Spiritual Exercises* of St. Ignatius Loyola, written between March 1522 and February 1523 by the saint as he was undergoing and recording a series of personal spiritual experiences. The original Spanish text of the *Exercises* was translated into two Latin versions (the *Versio Prima* and the Vulgate) and approved by Pope Paul III in 1548. This 16th-century manual of spiritual strategies, practices, and techniques has been employed with great success for more than 500 years by spiritual guides aiming to accompany individuals who are searching for a more secure attachment to God, the development of a clear sense of purpose in life, the discovery of meaning in suffering, and a profound sense of gratitude and love in life. It is a flexible manual that can be tailored to the specific spiritual needs of a client, with clear goals and assessment strategies to guide the application of these exercises and progress toward healing and transformation.

The principal aim of this chapter is to introduce these spiritual exercises as a component of an "integrative spiritually oriented psychotherapy" (Sperry, 2005) by describing how their use may permit a counselor to expand the treatment focus to include spiritual issues, conflicts, and concerns in the promotion of adjustment and transformation.

RATIONALE FOR A SPIRITUALLY ORIENTED PSYCHOTHERAPY

Despite a burgeoning research literature that supports a positive relationship between spirituality and physical and mental health (Paloutzian & Park, 2005), there are very few psychotherapy models to guide therapists in addressing the pressing spiritual questions and concerns that are brought to treatment sessions (Richards & Bergin, 2002; Sperry & Shafranske, 2005). Although cognitive, behavioral, interpersonal, and psychodynamic therapeutic theories and techniques have been successfully employed to facilitate healing from symptoms that

are associated with a range of disorders, including depression, anxiety, trauma exposure, substance abuse, and personality disorders, there are few existing therapeutic models to address some of the core spiritual needs and issues that clients bring to therapy. These spiritual concerns include the search for eternal identity and connection with the divine, a sense of transcendent purpose and meaning in life, a spiritual understanding of suffering and death (Richards & Bergin, 2002, pp. 101–110), and a deeper sense of gratitude and love of God and others.

Now, one might argue that such concerns are the proper domain of religion and pastoral practice rather than psychotherapy. However, there are practical and clinical reasons for addressing these concerns in psychotherapy. In the first place, despite the apparent prevalence of spirituality in this country, relatively few Americans are turning to traditional religious venues with their spiritual concerns. For example, although 85% of respondents to a 2002 Gallup poll reported that faith gives meaning and purpose to their lives (Sperry & Shafranske, 2005, pp. 16–17), a full 54% of Americans also reported that "churches and synagogues have lost the real spiritual part of religion" (Roof, 1999, p. 89). As a consequence of this widespread perception, people are, in fact, bringing their spiritual concerns to psychotherapy. In addition, there are solid clinical reasons for addressing these concerns. In the first place, religious and spiritual beliefs are essential components of an individual's coping repertoire (Pargament, 2002), so that in the face of trial or distress, attention to these beliefs may assist the clinician's efforts at facilitating adjustment. Second, spiritual beliefs are often disrupted in the wake of trauma, and this disturbance may be a cause of considerable anxiety, anger, and even despair. According to Park (2005), the amount of discrepancy between global or spiritual beliefs and particular attributions may account for stress in the wake of traumatic situations like the death of a loved one, an accident, or some other significant assault on physical or emotional integrity. As a result, in using or adjusting spiritual beliefs to make sense of particular events, the clinician is likely reducing stress and promoting emotional well-being. Third, Sperry and Shafranske (2005, pp. 21–23) point out that the search for significance or meaning is a spiritual quest that prompts some people to seek psychotherapy, even in the absence of urgent stressors or traumatic crises, and that this quest is in itself a legitimate psychotherapeutic objective.

An important decision facing the counselor who is open to addressing the spiritual issues and concerns of the client is timing; that is, when should one begin to address these concerns in the course of psychotherapy? The answer to this question depends on one's assumptions about the relationship of the psychological and spiritual dimensions of human experience. If one assumes that the psychological dimension is primary, then standard psychotherapeutic models and techniques will be employed first. Then, once a measure of therapeutic gain has been achieved, the spiritual issues will be addressed in the work. Alternatively, if the assumption is that the spiritual dimension is primary, then these issues will be the focus of the work from the very beginning of psychotherapy.

Each of the relatively few existing models of spiritually oriented psychotherapy bears certain assumptions about the relationship between the spiritual and psychological dimensions of human experience (Sperry & Shafranske, 2005, pp. 23–24). Some claim that they are fundamentally different, others that they are the same, and each model assigns primacy to one or the other. The model that is most consistent with the one proposed in this chapter is the one advanced by Sperry (2005), which he calls "integrative spiritually oriented psychotherapy." According to this model, "The psychological and spiritual dimensions of human experience are considered to be related, with the spiritual having primacy because spirituality is understood to be our response to our most basic longing and desire" (p. 307). According to Sperry's model, the goal of psychotherapy is both to cure and to heal. Sperry defines cure in terms of traditional psychotherapy goals, namely, symptom relief and more adaptive functioning. Healing, on the other hand, is associated with self and social transformation, and this goal necessarily involves the spiritual and moral dimensions of human experience. For example, in order to assist someone to live a purposeful life, and not just one that is relatively free from neurotic suffering, the counselor needs to pay attention to spiritual concerns about one's relationship to the global and transcendent values that are often related to one's relationship to God. From this perspective, especially toxic impediments to healing include those "lifetraps" (Cecero, 2002), or fear themes,

that undermine one's relationship to God and significant others, and in so doing get in the way of a purposeful life. As I point out in my book *Praying Through Lifetraps: A Psychospiritual Path to Freedom* (Cecero, 2002), the assessment and treatment of these lifetraps through Schema Therapy (Young, Klosko, & Weishaar, 2003) may be profitably complemented by attention to spiritual wisdom, prayer methods, and techniques to confront each of the lifetraps.

THE SPIRITUAL EXERCISES WITHIN PSYCHOTHERAPY

Among the various spiritual strategies to integrate in psychotherapy, the spiritual exercises of St. Ignatius Loyola stand out as uniquely useful tools to employ within psychotherapy because of their thematic organization and its implications for assessment and intervention.

As a collection of spiritual practices and techniques, the spiritual exercises are to be conducted in the context of solitude and prayer, and they have served as a powerful guide for spiritual renewal over the past five centuries. These exercises originated with Ignatius and reflect the rich mystical experiences of a personal conversion that led him from a life of self-interest to one of true freedom, manifested in a more complete experience of gratitude and love for the Creator and all humanity. Ignatius proposed a twofold goal of these exercises for those who would practice them: "the overcoming of self and the ordering of one's life on the basis of a decision made in freedom from any disordered attachment" (Holgate, 2003, p. 10). In other words, the aim of the exercises is to radically confront oneself and one's inordinate attachments so as to live a more balanced and ultimately more productive and fulfilling life. The fundamental spiritual assumption of the exercises is that such balance relies on a secure attachment to God, who is the source of unconditional love.

The exercises are organized into four "weeks," or thematically related practices and techniques that challenge the exercitant with a decision point. Meissner (1999) suggests that

at each stage of spiritual growth, the self is confronted with a decisive crisis.... Each crisis must be faced and worked through, and only insofar as each is successfully resolved, can the self move on to the next crisis. At each step, there is required a decisive commitment, an acceptance of the values inherent in that level of development, and the consequent reconstruction within the self. (p.74)

The spiritual exercises are compatible with a broad range of psychotherapeutic interventions and as such are ideal candidates in the composition and operationalization of an "integrative spiritually oriented psychotherapy," with the dual goals of symptom relief and transformation (Sperry, 2005). The orientation, developmental perspective, goals, and flexibility of the exercises are entirely consistent with all four of the theoretical assumptions proper to integrative spiritually oriented psychotherapy, as outlined by Sperry (2005, pp. 311–314). First of all, the fundamental assumption of the exercises is that a proper orientation to God serves as the primary source of well-being, gives meaning and purpose to life, enables adaptive suffering, and motivates gratitude and love for the world. This spiritual orientation certainly does not exclude the importance of attention to other dimensions of human experience in psychotherapy—the biological, psychological, and social—but it clearly asserts its primacy over them. Second, as described above, the exercises are organized thematically in two parts. The first week focuses primarily on healing, or moving from a state of disordered affections and attachments to one of healthy attachment to God. This week is consistent with the "pathology model," as described by Sperry (p. 312), where psychotherapy aims to relieve symptoms and promote more adaptive functioning. However, the aim of the exercises extends beyond this model in its subsequent weeks, focusing instead on the development of optimal functioning, where the individual is challenged to grow beyond adequate adjustment to living a purposeful and virtuous life. This "developmental focus," according to Sperry, is a hallmark of integrative spiritually oriented psychotherapy. Third, the goal of the exercises is conversion or transformation, primarily from fear to freedom, and specific exercises that are intended to foster this conversion, as well as strategies to evaluate the extent of conversion, are provided in Weeks 2, 3, and 4. Finally, and perhaps most importantly, the exercises are intended for adaptation to the specific assets and needs of the individual, and Annotations are provided to guide their use for healing and/or transformation purposes. The Annotations provide guidance on when to lead a person only through the first week, where the goal is healing, and when to proceed to subsequent weeks toward the goal of transformation. This flexibility is entirely consistent with integrative spiritually oriented psychotherapy, where treatment is tailored to healing, as in using the exercises to foster lifetrap recovery, or toward transformation, where the exercises are used to foster freedom, gratitude, and love.

First Week

Key Spiritual Concerns:
Who Is God? Who Am I Before God?

During each week of the spiritual exercises, the exercitant is confronted with a particular life decision, often in the context of an existential crisis about issues of self-worth, freedom, and purposeful living. Exercises and techniques are also provided to assist with achieving some resolution to these crises. In addition, there are also assessment tools within each week to measure the extent to which one has achieved spiritual progress toward those goals.

In the First Week of the exercises, there are two existential questions presented to the exercitant for at least partial resolution: Who is God? Who am I before God? From a spiritual perspective, the images of God and of self are dynamic and interrelated. Ignatius begins the exercises by having the exercitant meditate on the many expressions of the love of God and his or her own inherent self-worth because of this freely offered divine love. Callaghan (2003) writes, "What Ignatius does in the *Exercises,* it seems to me, is to enable me to recognize and to tell myself ever-new stories of the ways in which my life is caught up in God's love" (p. 31). May (1977) contends that the search for this God experience responds to a basic human drive—along with sex, food, shelter, and community—and that its content is the need to belong to the ultimate source of reality, or God. Holgate (2003) points out that the positive ego-ideal of the exercitant as one who belongs to God is the context for all future considerations and exercises in this week. More specifically, it forms the background for a reflection on the First Principle and Foundation, which reads as follows:

> God freely created us so that we might know, love, and serve him in this life and be happy with him forever. God's purpose in creating us is to draw forth from us a response of love and service here on earth, so that we may attain our goal of everlasting happiness with him in heaven.
>
> All things in this world are gifts of God, created for us, to be the means by which we can come to know him better, love him more surely, and serve him more faithfully.
>
> As a result, we ought to appreciate and use these gifts of God insofar as they help us toward our goal of loving service and union with God. But insofar as any created things hinder our progress toward our goal, we ought to let them go.
>
> In everyday life, then, we should keep ourselves indifferent or undecided in the face of all created gifts when we have an option and we do not have the clarity of what would be a better choice. We ought not to be led on by our natural likes and dislikes even in matters such as health or sickness, wealth or poverty, between living in the east or in the west, becoming an accountant or a lawyer.
>
> Rather, our only desire and our one choice should be that option which better leads us to the goal for which God created us. (Fleming, 1978, p. 23)

This Principle and Foundation is intended as a challenging and provocative consideration at the beginning of the exercises, one that confronts the exercitant with a radical choice about how to respond to God's love. The ideal response is presented in this consideration, namely, a life that is free from all attachments, lived in radical surrender to the will of God. Holgate (2003) continues, "With the consideration of the Principle and Foundation, it is possible that some doubts about their (exercitants') self-image may creep in" (p. 12). Fears and doubts about letting go of perceived needs (e.g., reputation, health, security) in order to realize this level of surrender and freedom are a common experience in the face of this consideration. It nudges the exercitant beyond the comfort of basking in the love of God, and toward a kind of restlessness before this radical exigency. In his description of the experience of the First Week, Barry (1973) observes that after several days of praying in thanksgiving and praise, "the retreatant begins to experience a sense of alienation, of impotence, and of desolation" (p. 104). Holgate (2003) contends that these doubts and insecurities are increased by exercises on sinfulness that immediately follow this Principle and Foundation. Meissner (1999) explains in psychoanalytic terms that "the guilt and shame connected with a deep recognition of one's sinfulness puts the exercitant's ego-ideal under pressure and begins the process of transformation of the sinful self" (p. 120).

How can I, who is selfish, or limited, or guilty, be at the same time so loved by God? This is the fundamental question with which the exercitant is invited to wrestle at this point in the exercises. In her comparison of the methodology of the spiritual exercises to Jungian psychotherapy, Meadow (1989) contends that this first stage of the exercises corresponds to the confession stage of therapy, wherein the individual is challenged to face secrets and confront one's own fallibility on the road to self-acceptance. Meadow cites Jung:

> The first beginnings of all treatment are to be found in its prototype, the confessional. . . . As soon as people were capable of conceiving the idea of sin, they had recourse to psychic concealment. . . . The maintenance of secrets acts as a psychic poison which alienates the possessor from community . . . has a destructive effect . . . [and] cuts off the unfortunate possessor from communion with . . . fellow-beings. (Jung, 1933, p. 31)

As stated above, the major goal of the First Week, with its exercises on God's love, the Principle and Foundation, and on sinfulness, is to transform one's image of God and self. Holgate (2003) observes that "In the First Week, an exercitant can deepen [his or her] sense of God's love by discovering how it remains untouched despite [his or her] fallibility and sinfulness" (p. 12). The aim of this First Week is to strengthen the exercitant's confidence in unconditional divine love, so as to promote self-acceptance. In other words, despite limitations and shortcomings, God chooses to love the person, and so people are invited to love themselves. Moreover, this portrayal of God's love and the self-love that it engenders will foster the freedom from attachments and false securities that will be the foundation for a life directed more by purpose than by fear.

As signposts and assessment tools for measuring the extent to which one's images of God and self have been revised are the experiences of consolation and desolation. Ignatius describes these experiences in the Rules for the Discernment of Spirits that he appends to the *Exercises,* and he provides one set of rules for the First Week and another set for the Second Week. In the First Week, consolation is described as

> when we find our life of faith, hope, and love so strengthened and emboldened that the joy of serving God is foremost in our life. More simply stated, consolation can be found in any increase of our faith, our hope, and our love. (Fleming, 1978, p. 207)

By contrast, desolation is described as "when we find ourselves enmeshed in a certain turmoil of spirit or weighed down by a heavy darkness; when we experience . . . a certain restlessness and . . . thoughts of rebelliousness, despair, or selfishness" (Fleming, 1978, p. 207). Aufauvre (2003) distinguishes between depression and desolation, noting that whereas the focus of the problem for the depressed person revolves around images of self and others, in the case of desolation, the focus is on one's image of God and primarily around how the effects of consolation have disappeared. In the context of the First Week, then, the hallmark of spiritual progress toward a more secure relationship with God, confidence in God's love and in one's own inherent self-worth, is the predominance of the experience of consolation, and specifically of gratitude. Fleming (1983) writes,

> The sense of "finishing" the Week would come from the God-given peace (i.e., consolation) of at once experiencing oneself as a sinner and being loved and saved as such by God. God's abiding mercy is a real experience, deeper down but just as factual as our own sinfulness. The stress which Ignatius puts on gratitude in the First Week is significant in making a judgment about a retreatant's readiness to move on to the Second Week. (p. 9)

Second Week

Key Spiritual Concern: *What Is My Purpose in Life, According to God's Plan?*

In a recent article, "Spiritual Assessment in Clinical Practice," Puchalski (2006) writes, "Meaning and purpose are things that all people seek; the inability to find that meaning and purpose can lead to depression and anxiety" (p.152). For people with a spiritual orientation who are searching for meaning and purpose in their lives, it may be especially profitable for the counselor to employ some of the strategies and techniques of the Second Week of the spiritual exercises. The goals of this Week are twofold: (a) Fashion a purposeful and generous response to God's love, and (b) motivate this generous response through a deepening identification with the person and mission of Jesus Christ. Accordingly, the plan of the Week follows three phases: first, a series of meditations designed to clarify the values that are necessary to respond to God's love and to lead a purposeful life; second, a series of contemplations designed to deepen a mature relationship with Christ as the prime motivation for living according to these values; and finally, an exercise of Election, what Meissner (1999) calls "the central dynamic point of the *Exercises*" (p. 189), whereby the exercitant is invited to make some specific choices in the way he or she incarnates these values in choosing a particular state of life.

As a bridge to link the First and Second Weeks, Ignatius proposes the meditation on The Kingdom of Christ (91–99). In this meditation, he first describes the call of a noble king to all who would follow, and then parallels that description with the call of Christ to all humanity (95):

> It is my will to win over the whole world, to conquer sin, hatred, and death—all the enemies between humanity and God. Whoever wishes to join me in this mission must be willing to labor with me, so that by following me in suffering, he may follow me in glory.

For a person who may have achieved some sense of God's enduring love yet still lacks a clear sense of vocation or purpose in life, this meditation begins the shift of focus in the Second Week away from the reorganization and reconstruction of the self and toward positive growth (Meissner, 1999, p. 175). To use an Eriksonian paradigm, there is a call to generativity and service here that follows the identity consolidation of the First Week. This call involves a great deal of imagination, as the individual is challenged to consider his or her own mission in life as a participation in and contribution to the grand design of reshaping the world according to the plan outlined by Christ.

The Second Week goes on to present two key exercises that are designed to elaborate upon that plan and clarify the essential values necessary to carry it out: the meditation on the Two Standards and the meditation on Three Types of Persons. These exercises are intended to assist the exercitant with the internalization of core values.

The Two Standards meditation directs the exercitant's imagination to recreate in great detail the battlefields on which Satan and Christ make very different appeals to discipleship. The plan of evil and good is elaborated upon by each figure, and the individual stands before each one to consider his respective values, objectives, and strategies. First, in looking at Satan, the exercitant is directed as follows:

> I try to grasp the strategy of Satan as he attempts ever to enslave men and women and the world according to his design. People find themselves tempted to covet riches, and then because they possess some thing or things they find themselves seeking and accepting the honor and esteem of this world. From such honor arises the false sense of identity and value in which false pride has its roots.
>
> So, the strategy is simple: riches (or "this is mine") to honor (or "look at me") to pride (or "I AM . . ."). By these three steps, the evil one leads to all other vices. (137–142)

Then, the exercitant is invited to consider the strategy of Jesus:

> I notice how gently, but insistently, Jesus continues to call followers of all kinds and sends them forth to spread his good news to all people, no matter what their state or condition. Jesus adopts a strategy which is just the opposite of Satan: Try to help people, not enslave or oppress them. His method: Attract men and women to the highest spiritual poverty, and should it please God, and should he draw them to want to choose it, even to a life of actual poverty. Being poor, they will be led to accept and even to desire the insults and contempt of the world. The result will be a life of true humility.
>
> Jesus' strategy is simple: If I have been graced with the gift of poverty, then I am rich; if I have nothing, I

have no power and I am despised and receive the contempt of the world; if I have nothing, my only possession is Christ and this is to be really true to myself—the humility of a person whose reality lies in being created and redeemed in Christ. (143–146)

The two key values that are embodied in the strategy of Christ are indifference and service. Reminiscent of the First Week meditation on the First Principle and Foundation, this exercise on the Two Standards reiterates the goal of living a life that is free from all attachments, lived in radical surrender to the will of God, for the sake of service to others. This detachment is so central to the goal of the exercises that it is taken up again and elaborated upon in the exercise immediately following the Two Standards, namely, the meditation on the Three Types of Persons.

Depicting three ways of responding to the challenge of living a life that is relatively free from inordinate attachments to riches, honor, and pride, the meditation on Three Types of Persons invites the exercitant to consider these types or responses:

The First Type—"a lot of talk, but no action"

> This person keeps saying that he would like to stop being so dependent on all the things which he possesses and which seem to get in the way of his giving his life unreservedly to God . . . but when death comes, he is too busy about his possessions to have taken any step toward serving God. (153)

The Second Type—"to do everything but the one thing necessary"

> This person would like to be free of all attachments that get in the way of his relationship with God. But he would rather work harder or fast or pray more—really just do anything but face the problem which he feels holds him back in his relationship with God. (154)

The Third Type—"to do Your will is my desire"

> This person's whole effort is to be in balance. Whatever seems better for the service and praise of God is his whole desire and choice. Meanwhile, he strives to act in such a way that he seemingly is free of any attachments. (155)

All of the considerations and meditations presented thus far in the *Exercises* aim to clarify the necessary values of detachment and service to God and others. However, the internalization of these values relies on a personalization of them. As Meissner (1999) explains,

> To internalize such standards and norms means to personalize them, to make them a functioning part of one's own inner psychic reality. In the process of inter-nalization, therefore, such values are modified, changed, given a uniqueness and specificity within the personal-ity of which they are a part. They must become an inte-gral and functioning part of the person. (p. 78)

Moreover, this personalization is achieved in the context of a relationship with Jesus. In other words, the motivation for detachment and service is not the intrin-sic attractiveness of such a lifestyle to be adopted as one's own, but rather the invitation of a personal Jesus to imitate his pattern of living. For this reason, Ignatius turns the attention of the exercitant from these medita-tions to a series of contemplations on the person and life of Jesus, so that they can grow in knowledge and love of him. Barry (1978) notes, "The experience of many retreatants in this week . . . is that they are developing an adult relationship to the living Lord Jesus" (p. 174).

Unlike the meditations and considerations that have been presented up to this point, which rely on the fac-ulty of reason for pensive reflection, contemplation is an imaginative and sensual approach to the living per-son of Jesus. It is the medium for achieving an intimate knowledge of Jesus that is the foundation and model of detachment and service. Au (2001) claims that the basic thrust of Ignatian contemplation is to dispose us to meet the risen Jesus at the deepest level of our beings and to actualize this experience by living more fully a committed Christian life. Pointing out the similarities between the spiritual exercises and Gestalt therapy, Au further notes that the method of contemplation relies on the senses and imagination, where the exercitants are invited to immerse themselves in a Gospel scene and to use all of their senses to recreate it with them-selves in it and taking an active part in the dialogue and action. Au compares this Ignatian contemplation to the three-step approach of Gestalt dream work, whereby the therapist first invites the client to recount the dream as it happened, then to describe how he or she would

like to reenact it with him- or herself and the other characters, and finally to take the part of the different characters or aspects of the dream. The aim of this method is to emphasize the importance of self-awareness, especially in developing a relationship to Jesus. Au elaborates on the contemplative or Gestalt procedure with Scripture:

> First, read the account of an event or mystery in Scripture, like the cure of the blind beggar Bartimaeus at the end of the Way section in Mark's Gospel (10:46–52). Second, identify with one of the onlookers and describe the action from his or her point of view. Do this as if the event were actually unfolding right now in front of your eyes. Third, insert yourself into the event by identifying with one of the active participants in the scene. As you experience what is happening in the Gospel scene, be aware of what you are thinking, sens-ing, and feeling, your entire subjective response. (p. 20)

Au (2001) concludes that by allowing the parts of oneself, identified with one or another character in the Gospel scene, to interact with Jesus, an intimacy with him ensues, and the exercitant is transformed. Au cites the theologian Spohn (1985), who underscores the effects of Ignatian contemplation along these lines:

> As we tangibly and visually move into their narrated encounter with the Lord, we find in ourselves some echo of their response. If Peter could be forgiven, so can I. If the father could welcome home the prodigal son, then my fears of God's anger are without foun-dation. We learn to "ask for what we want" in these contemplations by the example of these characters in the story. They raise our expectations and open us to hear the Lord's word to us today. (p. 8)

From a Jungian perspective, Callaghan (2003) observes that because the symbols of Christianity take up all the key themes in human living, an engagement of these symbols through Ignatian contemplation is transfor-mative. He asserts,

> Encountering the central symbols around which I order my life changes me: it cannot do otherwise. In the *Exercises*, Ignatius puts me regularly in contact with the key symbols of my living: should we be surprised if I am transformed by this repeated experience? (p. 29)

In the temporal sequence of the *Spiritual Exercises,* the last segments of the Second Week, and arguably the "centerpiece of the *Exercises*" (Meissner, 1999, p. 205) are the Election and its prelude, the Three Degrees of Humility. Having fostered a repeated exposure to the person of Jesus and to the varied and often fragmented aspects of oneself in relationship to this person through the contemplations on his life, Ignatius returns to the central goals of the Week, namely, to fashion a purposeful and generous response to God's love through specific decisions about how to live one's life.

The internalization of spiritual values, namely, detachment and service, and identification with Christ are once again the themes of the Three Degrees of Humility, with each degree representing a more complete realization of these values. According to the First Degree of Humility, "I would want to do nothing that would cut me off from God—not even were I made head of all creation or even just to save my own life here on earth" (165). The Second Degree exemplifies the detachment that has been advocated at the start in the First Principle and Foundation:

> The only principle of choice in my life is to seek out and do the will of my Father. With this habitual attitude, I find that I can maintain a certain balance in my inclinations to have riches rather than poverty, honor rather than dishonor, or to desire a long life rather than a short one. (166)

With the Third Degree of Humility, however, Ignatius introduces "a whole range of higher spiritual values which have no limit, no higher cut-off point, and in which the self advances to higher and higher levels of realization and synthesis" (Meissner, 1999, p. 202). In the Third Degree,

> I so much want the truth of Christ's life to be fully the truth of my own that I find myself, moved by grace, with a love and a desire for poverty in order to be with the poor Christ; a love and a desire for insults in order to be closer to Christ in his own rejection by people; a love and a desire to be considered worthless and a fool for Christ, rather than to be esteemed as wise and prudent according to the standards of the world. (167)

The Election in the *Spiritual Exercises* refers to the process of making important life choices that are rooted in the spiritual values of detachment and service and motivated by a deep and lasting identification with the person of Jesus. Ignatius proposes three times for making the Election. The first time occurs when "God our Lord so moves and attracts the will that a devout soul, without hesitation, or the possibility of hesitation, follows what has been manifested to it" (175). Clearly, this is a relatively peaceful time for making a life choice, without many doubts or fears to encumber the process. The foundation for this choice is a profoundly clear spiritual experience.

The second and third times for making the Election, however, are more complex and also more frequently the experience of people seeking the right path in life. In the second time, there is more affective fluctuation in response to considerations of choices: "Quite frequently we experience a time of alternating certainties and doubts, of exhilarating strength and debilitating weakness, of consolation and desolation" (176). As described above, the emotional experiences of consolation and desolation are the tools for determining whether a particular choice is in synchrony with one's life purpose. In this Second Week, however, the experience of consolation and desolation is more nuanced than in the First Week, and Ignatius provides a separate set of Rules for the Discernment of Spirits for the Second Week. For people who are already advanced in their pursuit of a spiritual path, where the decision is not between obvious good and bad choices but more likely between two good choices, the affective experience of consolation (i.e., peace, joy, enthusiasm, and so on) may not automatically confirm the rightness of the decision. Ignatius introduces the notion that an "angel of darkness" may be disguised as an "angel of light" (333); in other words, that affective consolation may lead one to believe erroneously that his or her decision is the right one, whereas the "thought and action may be more self-focused, turning us away from God" (333). In this case, the exercitant is encouraged to trace backward the course of thoughts to the very beginning, so as to catch the influence of more selfish thinking.

Au (2001, p. 21) points out that Ignatian decision making relies on a complementary dynamic of thoughts and feelings. Whereas the confirmation of a right decision in the second time of Election prioritizes affective experience, in the form of consolation and desolation, it also requires the application of reasoning to confirm that experience.

In the third time of Election, for the exercitant who is not experiencing any affective movements when considering a particular course of action, where "nothing seems to be going on . . . we are placid, having neither consolation or desolation" (177), Ignatius proposes three rational techniques for arriving at a correct choice in life. First, he suggests that the exercitant list and weigh the advantages and disadvantages of a particular decision (181), and to weight them according to their motives, such that those that are less selfish and more directed to the fulfillment of one's overall purpose in life, as described in the First Principle and Foundation, will receive more weight. Consistent with the observation of Au (2001) on the complementary dynamic of thoughts and feelings in this mode of decision making, the exercitant is then instructed to confirm the decision "by bringing it into the ambit of the Second or First Time" (183). In other words, this rational process must be integrated with affective and religious experience in order to complete the discernment. In a similar way, alternate rational techniques include giving advice to someone else who may be faced with a similar decision (185) or considering the alternatives from the perspective of one's deathbed, where one would ask, "What would be the decision that I would want to have made now?" (186). Once again, the exercitant is instructed to consider the answers to these questions in the light of his or her emotional and religious experience: "After a period of testing, if positive feelings (peace, joy, hope, confidence) dominate, it is clear then that affectivity has joined with intelligence to produce an harmonious effect" (Au, 2001, p. 21).

Third Week

Key Spiritual Concern:
How Can I Find Meaning in Suffering?

Just as the Second Week aims at a clarification and concrete realization of the spiritual values of detachment and service in the context of an ever-deepening identification with the person and life of Jesus, the Third Week is designed to strengthen those values through a more complete identification with his suffering and death. In this Third Week, the exercitant is confronted with the harsh realities of the Passion, including the human experiences of limitation, betrayal, abandonment, physical pain, and ultimately death. Ignatius invites the exercitant to feel these experiences with Jesus in order to find meaning in them. Meissner (1999) writes,

> The pain and sorrow of the exercitant likewise have meaning to the extent that they join the sufferings of Christ. That pain can only become redemptive to the extent that it chooses and wills what God wills, joins its suffering with the intentionality of Christ suffering. (p. 229)

Within the context of psychotherapy, the person who is struggling to cope with suffering in life may greatly benefit from the exercises of this Third Week, as a medium of meaning and hope through the pain.

Meadow (1989) articulates the goal of the Third Week as the development of "compassionate intimacy" that entails a willingness to suffer with Christ (p. 185). She compares this Third Week to the third stage of psychotherapy, in a Jungian framework, which is that of education. She cites Jung, "The patient must be, as it were, prodded into other paths and this always requires an educating will" (p. 185). This education in psychotherapy is not primarily a matter of imparting information or clarifying values, as might be more characteristic of the Second Week, but instead provokes a confrontation with resistances to living according to those values, especially in the face of suffering and death. Fears, doubts, and insecurities often surface in the context of Third Week exercises, and this is exactly what Ignatius encourages the exercitant to ask for in prayer: "It belongs to the Passion to ask for grief with Christ in grief, anguish with Christ in anguish, tears and interior pain at such great pain which Christ suffered for me" (203). The purpose of these prayers is to suffer with Christ, not to seek ready solutions to the problem of evil, but to join him in these dark moments of human existence.

Throughout the contemplations on the Passion of Christ, the exercitant is encouraged to engage the "application of senses" (206), that is, to use all five senses to enter into each of these scenes with as much affective presence as possible. Citing the noted theologian Karl Rahner (1967), Meissner (1999) writes,

Ignatius again calls for the "application of senses" to help the exercitant not only consider, but experience, with Christ the sense of lonesomeness and forsakenness that go with his separation from the Father who has abandoned him to suffer this agony that is part and parcel of his humanity as it is ours. (p. 230)

This complete surrender of self to the will of God, with Jesus, is the spiritual foundation for meaning making through human suffering. As Meadow (1989) points out, it finds its parallel in Jungian psychotherapy, in the education phase, where

> the opening up of the unconscious always means the outbreak of intense spiritual suffering. . . . One is never helped in . . . suffering by what one thinks for oneself, but only by revelations of a wisdom greater than one's own. It is this which lifts one out of . . . distress. (Jung, 1933, pp. 240–241)

Ignatian spirituality, as evidenced perhaps most explicitly in this Third Week of exercises, is not an anodyne to spiritual and existential anguish. Instead, it is a venue for finding meaning in human suffering. By freely choosing to join one's own pain and suffering to the Passion of Christ, the exercitant is more deeply immersed in human suffering, but with a different perspective and motivation. The realities of pain and death are inevitable, and yet the attitude with which one approaches them, or in this case chooses them, can make all the difference.

The success of this Week is gauged by the extent of freedom and peace with which the person approaches human suffering. Citing the reflections of a seasoned director of the spiritual exercises, Fr. Dom Maruca, on the signposts of progress in this Third Week and readiness to move on to the Fourth and final Week, Meadow (1989) records the following:

> Some experienced simply a quieting down with deep peace even in the midst of distress; this made it possible for them to surrender to the mysteries beyond their comprehension along with willingness to continue suffering with Christ. Others experienced a great growth in faith, and some felt empowered with new courage. Others found their rage against unjust systems moderated, and they knew they would be able to persevere. Still others felt compelled to follow

God's mandate and protest to the limit against the particular types of injustice and oppression in which they and their people were entangled. All seemed to experience a peaceful tension that combined pain and hope. (p. 187)

Fourth Week

Key Spiritual Concern:
How Do I Lead a Virtuous Life?

In the Fourth Week of the exercises, the exercitant is invited to contemplate and rejoice in the glory of the Risen Christ, as a prelude to the final exercise, the Contemplation on the Love of God (230–237). The joy of this Week is the ultimate outcome of the anguish and pain of the Third Week, and the goal of this Week is to turn the exercitant's attention away from the self-consciousness of the previous Weeks and toward the consolidation of a life plan rooted in love and service. Meadow (1989, pp. 188–189) compares this Week to the fourth stage of Jungian psychotherapy, which is transformation, where the patient and therapist are focused on implementing the insights and conversion experiences of the therapeutic encounter into daily living. This Week may be especially useful to the person in psychotherapy who desires to live a more virtuous life but is uncertain about how to connect his or her spirituality to the practical demands of love and service. Unlike many psychotherapies that tend to foster individual self-fulfillment over community well-being (Sperry, Carlson, & Kjos, 2002), the Fourth Week's focus on transformation is not entirely for personal benefit; it has communal dimensions.

In the Contemplation on the Love of God, what Meissner (1999) calls "the culmination and pinnacle of the spirituality of the *Exercises*" (p. 237), the process for ongoing transformation is described, proceeding from gratitude to love and finally self-donation through a life of service. For Ignatius, the motivation and grounding for a virtuous life is rooted in a deep and abiding awareness of one's giftedness at the hand of a loving God.

CONCLUSION

Although the application of these spiritual exercises in psychotherapy is especially suited for Christian clients, their overarching existential themes of life purpose; the meaning of suffering; and the values of freedom, gratitude, and love render them useful for a broader application. For example, other spiritual and religious traditions might employ their structure and thematic organization to grapple with the same existential concerns within the context of their own identifications of the transcendent. In any case, these spiritual exercises are a promising tool for counselors to use to address the ageless spiritual questions and concerns that explicitly or implicitly underlie the presenting issues in psychotherapy.

REFERENCES

Au, W. (2001). Gestalt therapy and the spiritual exercises of St. Ignatius. *Presence: An International Journal of Spiritual Direction, 7*(3), 17–29.

Aufauvre, B. V. (2003). Depression and spiritual desolation. *The Way, 42*(3), 47–56.

Barry, W. J. (1973). The experience of the First and Second Weeks of the spiritual exercises. *Review for Religious, 32*, 102–109.

Barry, W. J. (1978). On asking God to reveal Himself in retreat. *Review for Religious, 37*, 171–176.

Cecero, J. (2002). *Praying through lifetraps: A psychospiritual path to freedom*. Totowa, NJ: Resurrection Press.

Callaghan, B. (2003). Do teddy bears make good spiritual directors? Ignatius Loyola meets Donald Winnicott. *The Way, 42*(3), 19–32.

Fleming, D. (1978). *The spiritual exercises of St. Ignatius Loyola: A literal translation and contemporary reading*. St. Louis, MO: The Institute of Jesuit Sources.

Fleming, D. (1983). The Ignatian spiritual exercises: Understanding a dynamic. In D. L. Fleming (Ed.), *Notes on the spiritual exercises of St. Ignatius Loyola: The best of the review*. St. Louis, MO: Review for Religious.

Holgate, R. (2003). Growing into God. *The Way, 42*(3), 7–18.

Jung, C. G. (1933). *Modern man in search of a soul*. New York: Harcourt, Brace, and World Harvest Book.

May, G. (1977). The psychodynamics of spirituality: A follow-up. *Journal of Pastoral Care, 3* (2), 84–90.

Meadow, M. J. (1989). Four stages of spiritual experience: A comparison of the Ignatian exercises and Jungian psychotherapy. *Pastoral Psychology, 37*(3), 172–191.

Meissner, W. (1999). *To the greater glory: A psychological study of Ignatian spirituality*. Milwaukee, WI: Marquette University Press.

Paloutzian, R., & Park, C. (Eds.). (2005). *Handbook of the psychology of religion and spirituality*. New York: Guilford.

Pargament, K. (2002). The bitter and the sweet: An evaluation of the costs and benefits of religiousness. *Psychological Inquiry, 13*(3), 168–181.

Park, C. (2005). Religion and meaning. In R. Paloutzian & C. Park (Eds.), *Handbook of the psychology of religion and spirituality* (pp. 295–314). New York: Guilford.

Puchalski, C. (2006). Spiritual assessment in clinical practice. *Psychiatric Annals, 36*(3), 150–156.

Richards, P., & Bergin, A. (2002). *A spiritual strategy for counseling and psychotherapy*. Washington, DC: American Psychological Association.

Roof, W. C. (1999). *Spiritual marketplace: Baby boomers and the remaking of American religion*. Princeton, NJ: Princeton University Press.

Sperry, L. (2005). Integrative spiritually oriented psychotherapy. In L. Sperry & E. Schafranske (Eds.), *Spiritually oriented psychotherapy* (pp. 307–329). Washington, DC: American Psychological Association.

Sperry, L., Carlson, J., & Kjos, D. (2002). *Becoming an effective therapist*. Englewood Cliffs, NJ: Prentice-Hall.

Sperry, L., & Schafranske, E. (Eds.). (2005). *Spiritually oriented psychotherapy*. Washington, DC: American Psychological Association.

Spohn, W. C. (1985). The biblical theology of the pastoral letter and Ignatian contemplation. *Studies in the Spirituality of American Jesuits, 17*(4), 8–9.

Young, J., Klosko, J., & Weishaar, M. (2003). *Schema therapy: A practitioner's guide*. New York: Guilford.

39

Counseling Persons From Eastern Religions and Spiritualities

JOHN HUANG

This chapter integrates some of the literature on counseling people from Eastern religions and spiritualities. The term *spirituality* is used because it is more inclusive, meaning "relating to spirit and inspiration," not necessarily involving organized religion. The chapter will provide a brief background on Eastern religions, discuss assessment of religiosity, describe interventions that stem directly from Eastern traditions, discuss culturally congruent Western treatments, and illustrate clinical applications with a case study. Needless to say, the information provided will be brief due to necessity. A whole book could be written on these issues!

The topic of counseling people from Eastern spiritualities is important because of the need to respect the spiritual diversity represented by this growing population. According to Richards and Bergin (2005), about 1.3% of the U.S. population, or 3.6 million people, hail from Eastern religions. However, it is not clear if these statistics reflect the large number of people who are starting to practice Eastern spiritualities. For instance,

Finn and Rubin (2000) discuss how there has been an extremely large increase in the number of Buddhist meditation centers in the United States since the 1940s. Furthermore, there has been an increase of regular practitioners of yoga and meditation in the past few decades, but some of them do not consider themselves Hindus or Buddhists. Coleman (2001, as cited in Miklaus, 2007) estimates that Buddhists alone could constitute as much as 1.3% of the U.S. population. Hence, knowledge and skills in working with these growing populations will be in more demand during one's psychological career.

BACKGROUND

There are many religions that can be considered "Eastern." However, for the sake of brevity, this chapter focuses on Buddhism, Confucianism, Hinduism, and Taoism. For a more comprehensive review of these religions, see Richards and Bergin (2000, 2005), Miklaus (2007), Ho (1995), Sharma (2000), and Wong (1997).

Buddhism. Buddhism originated in India 2,500 years ago, founded by Gautama Buddha, and then later spread throughout all of Asia (Bowman & Baylen, 1994). It is described as a philosophy (i.e., wisdom and an analysis of beliefs), a religion (i.e., devotion to an ultimate reality), and a psychology (Miklaus, 2007). Different branches of Buddhism have different practices and beliefs. In general, most Buddhists do not believe in a God or Gods, although some sects may do so. Some common beliefs include reincarnation and karma. The principle of karma states that good, charitable deeds are rewarded (by divine or the "universe"), and unethical deeds result in retribution (Wong, 1997). Many believe that karma from a past life can affect the current life. The cycle of karma can also occur during one's current lifetime.

Another major principle of Buddhism is that in order to transcend and be free from suffering (which is the main goal of Buddhism), one must let go of one's "self." The reason that people suffer is because they see their "selves" as independent and stable. For instance, throughout peoples' lives, they strive to acquire possessions and status, and compare their acquisitions to what others have. They see themselves as separate from others and compete with them. People identify with their material things as well as with their histories, status, and personalities. According to Buddhism, the belief in the illusion that the self is separate and stable is "born of primal ignorance" (Ho, 1995, p. 121). Who we really are is not those things but an eternal, interconnected One. Perhaps the words *awareness* or *soul* may be used to describe who we really are. An analogy that has been used to describe this concept is that we are all actors in a play, with this physical world as a stage. For example, I am currently playing a psychologist named "John" who is writing a book chapter, but this is not the ultimate reality. The ultimate reality is one interconnected consciousness, and our identities can be shed like the labels that they are. The Oneness reflects how everything around us is Divine and we are all part of Divine. A somewhat imperfect example of interconnectedness in Western thinking occurs in family systems theory, where a single family member is an interactive element of a whole unit. The person cannot be fully understood out of the context of the family. Buddhists believe that the person cannot be taken out of the context of everyone and everything else.

According to Buddhism, there is also no such thing as a stable "self" because it (and everything else in the world) is always changing. Thoughts and desires are highly unstable, always arising and passing. Thus, impermanence is another important Buddhist principle (Bowman & Baylen, 1994). Working for personal goals such as wealth or power goes against the true nature of the self, because everyone is interrelated and material gains do not last anyway. Nothing lasts forever.

According to Buddhism, to truly understand the interconnected and impermanent nature of the self, one must meditate (Bowman & Baylen, 1994). By meditating, one personally experiences the temporary and ephemeral quality of thoughts and desires. They arise and pass in one's mind. One learns to be equanimous to sensations, not craving one sensation over the other, because attachment to feeling reinforces the separateness and stability of the self (Reynolds, 1976) and leads to suffering.

There are many forms of meditation as well, and one common process involves sitting with legs crossed and back straight, and focusing on one's breath. Shapiro and Zifferblatt (1976) have described how this is done in Zen meditation where one focuses on the breath to sharpen one's awareness. As one sits, focusing on the breath, thoughts and images will arise. Then one practices remaining equanimous with whatever thoughts or sensations arise by being aware of them, but not reacting to them. After that, one goes back to concentrating on the breath. Eventually, the thoughts will become less and less frequent, resulting in a peaceful awareness of other external and internal stimuli (Shapiro & Zifferblatt, 1976).

Confucianism. Like Buddhism, Confucianism emphasizes that people are relational beings (Wong & Ujimoto, 1998). Confucius's teachings have been integrated into Chinese society since the 5th century B.C. Ho (1995) described the teachings as "an ethic governing human relationships" (p. 116). These teachings have spread to many countries in Asia, including Japan, Korea, and Vietnam. According to Confucianism, one's individualistic and personal goals do not define one's behaviors, but one's relationships do. Wong and Ujimoto (1998) write that specific behaviors for specific roles are delineated. For instance, they describe the Five Cardinal Relationships according to Confucianism (the relations between ruler and subject, father and son, husband and wife, older brother and younger brother, and friend and friend). The person who is higher in the hierarchy is the authority and has power over the lower members in the hierarchy. There is also an emphasis on reciprocity, interdependence, and interconnectedness among people (Ho, 1995; Wong & Ujimoto, 1998). The person's identity is a relational and collective one, not an individual one.

Ho also writes that self-realization is the ultimate purpose of life, which involves self-cultivation, personal growth, virtue, and sincerity. He describes that in order to achieve self-realization, one must control one's impulses such as love, hate, joy, and anger. One keeps them in their proper place to maintain the hierarchies. Thus, interpersonal harmony is important for self-realization, and the needs of the group take precedence over the needs of the individual.

Confucianism is mainly a description of how society, government, and family relationships should ideally work, and it is not a main form of religion or spirituality in that it does not typically talk about deities or a higher power. However, it does have some religious elements in that it describes living with virtue and proper conduct (Richards & Bergin, 2005) as well as self-realization.

Hinduism. Hinduism predates Buddhism by more than a thousand years (Richard & Bergin, 2005), but they have many similarities because much of Buddhism arose out of Hinduism. For instance, belief in reincarnation, karma, impermanence, interconnectedness, and meditation practice are common throughout Hinduism as well. The discussion on these topics in the section on Buddhism also applies to Hindus and will not be repeated because of the need for brevity.

However, one important difference is the emphasis and belief in a God or Gods. Some who practice Hinduism are polytheistic, whereas others are monotheistic (Richards & Bergin, 2005). However, most of them believe in an ultimate reality, similar to the Buddhist principle of interconnectedness and oneness. Richards and Bergin describe this as pantheism, where "all is God, and God is all" (Percesepe, 1991, p. 469, as cited in Richards & Bergin, 2005).

Sharma (2000) provides a good overview of Hinduism and describes how the religion recognizes that people are diverse and that there are many paths to God. This is also reflected in the number of different deities in the religion, which can be said to represent the different aspects of God. For instance, the God Brahma reflects the creator aspect of God, and the Goddess Lakshmi brings prosperity. There are also different rituals that are done in Hindu practice for different purposes. For example, Sharma (2000) reports that common rituals involve fire and making offerings (such as food or flowers) to the Gods. Finally, in Hinduism, there is a belief that time is cyclical and not linear. Hindu texts describe that the universe goes through a cycle of creation and then destruction, spanning roughly 4 million years (Sharma, 2000).

Taoism. The foundations of Taoism have origins from several thousand years ago in the shamanic traditions of ancient China (Wong, 1997). For instance, the magical practices of Taoism, which involve making talismans and invoking the powers of deities and spirits, were practiced by the shamans. The philosopher Lao-tzu, who was born during the 1st century B.C., is credited with writing the Tao-te ching, which describes Taoism's principles. "Tao" is translated in many ways, including Way, Path, Nature, Mind, Reason, Law, and even God (Liu, 1979). Taoism and Taoist concepts, such as the "Tao," are also very similar to Vedic/Indian spiritual traditions (Bhopal, 1986).

Taoism is also both a religion and a philosophy, and it principally focuses on doing charitable work; living in harmony with nature and with change; living spontaneously; and connecting with the divine, or "sacred powers" (Wong, 1997). The focus on doing charitable work is due to the belief in karma.

Taoists advocate living in harmony with nature and change because resisting the natural order of how things work creates suffering (Ehrlich, 1986). A common analogy is to be like water, which flows naturally with its environment. This is related to how the self is seen as an extension of the cosmos, an ecological extension of a system or the environment. Thus, there is not a hierarchical view of the self or society because all things are equal: Nature treats everyone and everything without discrimination, and so should we (Ehrlich, 1986). For instance, when it rains, everyone gets wet, no matter his or her social status. Similar to the other

Eastern spiritualities, there is a de-emphasis on the self, and selflessness is a goal. By not focusing on the self, one can act spontaneously and in harmony with society and nature (Ho, 1995). Finally, connecting with the divine is the focus of Ceremonial Taoism (Wong, 1997). By performing certain rituals, Ceremonial Taoists believe that people create a bond with the sacred powers and are bestowed protection and blessings.

Ho (1995) describes that the Tao also entails many contradictions and polarities. For instance, the Tao is all encompassing, yet indescribable, and according to the tradition, a sage is also like a little child. This is because nature consists of the interaction and unity of opposites (Ehrlich, 1986). For example, a sage is like a child because he or she can see beauty and magic in simple activities, like children often do. Similarly, in nature, the male and female must always be in balance, and they are intimately related.

Common Themes: There are some commonalities between the Eastern spiritualities, including acceptance; nondualism (not being separate from divine); belief in reincarnation; interconnectedness; experiential focus; present focus; use of meditation; and holism (that the mind, body, and spirit are connected). These commonalities should be emphasized when appropriate, as discussed in the following sections on interventions.

ASSESSMENT

My approach to assessment is probably not as technical as others would like. In clinical, nonresearch practices, very few counselors (none known to me) give clients spirituality questionnaires, even though quite a few are available. Nevertheless, Richards and Bergin (2005) provide a detailed overview of assessment issues, questions, and questionnaires. For instance, they discuss the 10-item Religious Commitment Inventory, which measures adherence to religious worldviews and behaviors, and the 24-item Spiritual Transcendence Scale, which assesses the degree to which one experiences a connection with nature that is beyond (transcending) death. Richards and Bergin also describe how Hill and Hood (1999) have a handbook titled *Measures of Religiosity,* which reviews more than 120 measures related to religion.

My preference is to have a dialogue with the client about his or her spiritual beliefs, and the spirituality assessment literature does inform how it is conducted. Helpful questions include "What are your spiritual beliefs?" "What do you believe happens when you die?" "How do you think the universe works (e.g., is there a divine plan, or is it random)?" I also discuss how the clients' spiritual beliefs help them make meaning in their lives, especially of difficulties, and if they believe that a benevolent higher power helps them or watches over them. Similarly, it is important to assess if there are spiritual practices such as prayer or meditation that help them cope. These are some of the dimensions Richards and Bergin (2005) mention. They also discuss how rapport and understanding can be enhanced by the counselor talking openly and genuinely about these issues.

In addition, it is important to assess how connected a person is with his or her spiritual path because some people from Eastern spiritualities may adhere to only some of the practices and beliefs. For instance, many Westerners meditate and are interested in Eastern religions, but do not worship any of the Gods or do not call themselves "Hindu." On the other hand, some Asians from Eastern religions may pray to the Gods but do not meditate. Furthermore, not everyone from Eastern spiritualities adheres to the teaching of oneness such that the self is de-emphasized. Some may accept the idea, but many may not fully understand or experience it. It is perhaps one of the most difficult teachings to internalize, where one is truly experiencing the interconnectedness and oneness of all beings. However, with practice (e.g., meditation), glimpses of this reality are more common.

EASTERN THERAPEUTIC INTERVENTIONS

Some treatment interventions stem directly from Eastern spiritual traditions. This chapter will discuss three of them: meditation, mantra repetition, and alternative medicine. Some comments on implementing these interventions are also included.

Meditation. First of all, meditation was already discussed in the previous section on Buddhism, which provided an example of a Zen technique. Walsh (1995) expressed that meditation itself is a form of therapy, which has physiological as well as psychological benefits for clients. For instance, meditation has been found to effectively reduce anxiety (Kabat-Zinn, Massion, Kristeller, & Peterson, 1992), and, combined with cognitive therapy, it prevents depression relapse (Segal, Williams, & Teasdale, 2002). Brown and Ryan (2003) also found that mindfulness meditation was associated with decreased anger and higher positive affect and self-esteem.

Mindfulness has been gaining popularity, and it basically consists of three components: Being in the present moment, with full awareness, with an accepting and nonjudgmental attitude. A common form of mindfulness meditation, similar to the Zen exercise described earlier, involves focusing full awareness on the sensation of breathing, which anchors one in the present moment. When distractions occur, such as thoughts, feelings, or sounds, the acceptance and nonjudgmental attitude is practiced as one redirects the attention back to the breath without resisting the distractions.

Counselors have many opportunities to get training in mindfulness. Psychology continuing education workshops are available that focus on mindfulness, and training is important if one wishes to incorporate it into treatment. In addition to being better able to help clients, therapists gain many other benefits. Meditation can be used to help the counselor increase self-care. Also, Shapiro, Schwartz, and Bonner (1998) found that teaching mindfulness to medical students increased their empathy. Grepmair, Mitterlehner, and Nickel (2008) conducted a study where a Zen master taught meditation to therapists-in-training. Compared to a control group of therapists, the meditating therapists had better treatment outcomes with their inpatients (e.g., on the Symptom Checklist-90). Some resources to obtain training include http://www.meditationandpsychotherapy.org/ and http://health.ucsd.edu/specialties/psych/mindfulness/

Mantra Repetition. Mantra repetition is practiced by many Hindus as well as some Buddhists. It consists of repeating a word or words that have a spiritual meaning. In a randomized control design, Bormann, Gifford, et al. (2006) found that mantra repetition in an HIV population reduced anger and intrusive thoughts while increasing spiritual faith and connectedness. Bormann,

Oman, et al. (2006) also found that the practice helped to reduce stress in a veteran and hospital employee population, using a pre-post design without a control group.

Mantra repetition can also be taught to a client, but trainings are not as ubiquitous as they are for mindfulness. Jill Bormann, PhD, does trainings in the southern California area. I recommend that therapists first practice meditation and mantra repetition if they want to teach it to clients. This way, they can speak about the techniques with more experience and confidence. They are also excellent ways of enhancing self-care.

Alternative Medicine. The other type of intervention that is related to Eastern spiritualities is complementary and alternative medicine. There are indigenous approaches to healing that conceptualize the mind, body, and spirit as connected and whole. Gogtay, Bhatt, Dalvi, and Kshirsagar (2002) cite that 65%–80% of the world's population uses these traditional, non-Western systems of health care. Some more popular approaches include Ayurvedic medicine (originating from India) and acupuncture (originating in China). These healing modalities are not always considered traditional practices of Eastern spirituality per se, but many consumers of alternative medicine also practice Eastern spirituality. In addition, there is much overlap in terms of the principles behind them.

Kaptchuk (2002) provides a good overview of acupuncture and describes that the system of healing is based on Taoist principles of yin and yang. The purpose of the healing approach is to bring balance back to the body's "qi," or life energy, by using needles to stimulate different energy points in the body. Kaptchuk (2002) reports that research supports the efficacy of acupuncture in treating nausea from surgery and chemotherapy, as well as certain pain conditions, especially dental pain. The study describes that much research has been done in treatment of other conditions (e.g., pulmonary disease, addiction, stroke) with equivocal results.

There has also been some research on mental disorders and acupuncture. Hollifield, Sinclair-Lian, Warner, and Hammerschlag (2007) conducted a randomized controlled pilot study with PTSD. They found that acupuncture as well as cognitive-behavioral therapy had large treatment effects when compared to a waitlist control. In addition, many studies have examined depression.

Leo and Ligot (2007) reviewed randomized controlled studies and concluded that even though there may be a general trend that acupuncture may be as effective as antidepressants, they still feel that the evidence is inconclusive due to the limitations of the studies (e.g., small sample sizes, lack of longitudinal data). They say further research is needed.

In terms of Ayurvedic medicine, Gogtay et al. (2002) write that the term comes from the Sanskrit words *ayuh*, meaning "life," and *veda*, meaning "knowledge." They report that it is the oldest system of medicine in the world and the most commonly practiced alternative medicine in India. It is similar to acupuncture in that it is based on conceptualizing the mind, body, and spirit as connected as well as maintaining a balance of the five basic natural elements (air, water, fire, earth, and space). Some of the modalities that they use include herbs (also used in acupuncture), diet, exercise, and sometimes meditation.

Some studies show that Ayurveda may be effective for treating diabetes (Shekelle et al., 2005); high cholesterol (Singh, Vinjamury, et al., 2007); asthma (Singh, Khorsan, et al., 2007); osteoarthritis (Singh et al., 2003); and sleep-onset insomnia (Farag & Mills, 2003). This makes sense because many pharmaceuticals are also based on herbal compounds. Winters (2006) also states that an herb commonly used in Ayurveda, *withania somnifera*, has antioxidant, anti-inflammatory, and antistress attributes and slows down cancer growth in animal and human cell studies.

Alternative medicine is probably more effective as an adjunct to treatment for persons from Eastern spiritualities. It takes more training for a therapist to be able to use these modalities, and referring to a qualified expert is usually more practical. However, it can be difficult to ascertain if the acupuncturist or Ayurvedic doctor is competent. Currently in the United States, acupuncturists require licensure in order to practice, but Ayurvedic doctors do not. The research on acupuncture shows that detrimental effects are extremely uncommon with trained professionals (Kaptchuk, 2002). It is also important to note that any licensed or unlicensed professional can vary in his or her expertise. Furthermore, Gogtay et al. (2002) talk about some safety issues to be aware of when receiving Ayurveda, which include the fact that some of the mineral supplements they use may contain heavy metals such as lead. Therefore, it is important for a psychologist to find out more information about alternative medicine practitioners and talk to members of the community about them. There is potential benefit in these treatments, and one must exercise caution.

WESTERN THERAPEUTIC INTERVENTIONS

Some Western therapies are more congruent with the common themes and values of Eastern spiritualities. Some of the treatments have direct connections, such as incorporating principles of mindfulness. Others have philosophical and theoretical similarities to Eastern religions in other ways that will be described.

The Western therapies are touched upon briefly in the following sections. The sections also discuss the way in which many of the Western treatments were directly or indirectly influenced by Eastern values or spiritualities. Then, a few comments about implementing each therapy are included. The use of these treatments should be considered when counseling someone from an Eastern religion because the underlying theory or interventions may be more congruent with his or her worldview. This is also especially true for incorporating (if possible) the Eastern interventions mentioned above. It is important to note that the Western treatments are also effective with clients from non-Eastern cultural and spiritual backgrounds. However, very little research has been done on the effectiveness of these treatments with Asian Americans or people from Eastern spiritualities. This is especially true with some of the newer treatments, such as acceptance and commitment therapy. A few of the areas where there is some research on this issue are discussed briefly in the respective sections.

Acceptance and Commitment Therapy (ACT). Steve Hayes developed ACT, which incorporates principles of mindfulness and focusing on behavior that is in accordance with one's values and purpose (Hayes, Masuda, Bissett, Luoma, & Guerrero, 2004). Hayes et al. describe that psychopathology can be caused by unbalanced attempts to control feelings, thoughts, and memories; not letting oneself directly experience what is occurring in the present moment; and lack of clarity about what one's life values are and not acting in congruence with them. They reviewed the preliminary research on ACT's effectiveness, which demonstrates that it is helpful in reducing anxiety, depressive symptoms, opiate abuse, and the rehospitalization rate of patients with psychosis.

ACT is a manualized treatment that may be useful for treating clients from Eastern religions. Embedded within this treatment are some of the principles, such as acceptance and mindfulness, that are probably congruent with this population's worldview. Therefore, using this modality in whole or in part is recommended. Training in ACT is readily available; see www.contextual psychology.org for more information.

Dialectical and Behavior Therapy (DBT). Marsha Linenhan (1993) developed DBT in order to treat borderline personality disorder and its parasuicidal symptoms. It incorporates cognitive-behavioral therapy; skills training (e.g., emotion regulation, interpersonal skills); and mindfulness. The treatment focuses on validating the client's experience and synthesizing paradoxical or opposing feelings and perspectives. It conceptualizes that borderline personality is caused by biological precursors and an invalidating environment. Hayes et al. (2004) report that DBT has also been found effective in reducing opiate abuse, suicidal behaviors in clients with borderline personality, and binging/purging behavior in clients with bulimia.

Similar to the rationale for using ACT, DBT is manualized and is probably useful for treating clients from Eastern religions, especially for the diagnoses and problems just mentioned. Its focus on synthesis is similar to Taoism's emphasis on the unity of opposites, and the emphasis on mindfulness also fits with Eastern religious practices. Training in DBT is also available, and more information is provided at www .behavioraltech.org.

Behavior Therapy. De Silva (1984) writes that there are similarities between traditional behavior therapy and Buddhism. He notes that behaviorist principles are demonstrated in Buddhist writing and stories. For example, de Silva relates a story about a monk who had difficulty staying with the monastic life because he was attached to his worldly possessions—a pot of seed beans and a spade. He left the monastic life seven times to live a layperson's life because he enjoyed planting the seeds, growing them, eating them, and saving some seeds in his pot to plant in the next season. However, in order to fully commit to monkhood, he threw away his pot of seeds and spade because they were his main attachment to his other life. De Silva talks about how this story illustrates the principle of stimulus control, where an unwanted behavior is regulated by eliminating a stimulus or trigger that elicits it. He also writes about other behavior principles such as modeling, reciprocal inhibition, aversion therapy, use of rewards, and social skills training, which are illustrated by Buddhist writings and stories.

Implementing behavior therapy and teaching principles of behavior to clients from Eastern spiritualities therefore may be congruent with their background. Similar principles already exist between behaviorism and certain Eastern spiritualities, especially Buddhism. Furthermore, the use of parables and stories can be used as an intervention. They can be used to illustrate and teach certain principles and are common in many Eastern spiritual practices. If the counselor is familiar with Eastern writings and stories, sometimes they can be discussed with patients to help them think about their problems in a different way. Similarly, Costantino, Malgady, and Rogler (1986) developed cuento therapy, using Puerto Rican folktales as a way of helping at-risk Puerto Rican children learn adaptive behaviors and bridge bicultural conflict. They found that the intervention was more effective at reducing anxiety and aggression compared to an art/play therapy control group. Thus, making counseling more culturally and religiously sensitive can involve such creative techniques.

There has not been much research on the cultural sensitivity of behavior therapy with people from Eastern religions, or with Asian Americans. However, some studies have applied this treatment with some benefit. For example, Huey and Pan (2006) found that behavior therapy, compared to a control group, was more effective for Asian Americans with phobias. Another study examined behavior therapy in the context of parent training, with some beneficial results in reducing ADHD symptoms in Japanese American children (Iwasaka et al., 2002).

Cognitive-Behavioral Therapy (CBT). CBT also seems a good fit for people from Eastern religions because of some overlapping principles. For example, the way in which CBT theory states that negative thoughts can lead to negative affect is related to the emphasis in Buddhism—and to a degree in Hinduism and Taoism—on how thoughts affect our experience of the world, many times creating suffering and making our experience inaccurate. In a sense, cognitive restructuring occurs with mindfulness because the person learns to relate to his or her environment in a different way, with an emphasis on acceptance. Similarly, Ellis's rational-emotive behavioral therapy emphasizes a form of acceptance that he describes as frustration tolerance. Ellis wrote that he borrowed from Eastern philosophies and names Buddha as one of his influences (Ellis & MacLaren, 1998).

Therefore, including CBT in treatment with this population can be beneficial and potentially effective. Studies have shown that Asian Americans (Huang, 2004) and Asian Indians (Gupta, 2000) may benefit from this type of treatment. Integrating certain CBT interventions into counseling may be helpful, especially teaching clients how thoughts affect our emotions, how we distort our thinking, and how to look at our situations in alternative ways. These interventions are similar to how Eastern spiritualities encourage people to distance themselves from their thoughts so that they are not as attached to them. A complete, comprehensive CBT protocol may also be useful as well as the specific interventions.

Systems Theory. Goldenberg and Goldenberg (1995) describe how systems theory takes into account the many contexts and social roles in which a client operates, both within and outside the family. The people and institutions with which a client comes into contact interact so that they can affect the client and vice versa. It is also important to remember that an individual who practices an Eastern religion usually does so within a context. Many times, there is a community that supports and teaches the practices and beliefs. It can be informal, such as a meditation group or yoga class, or more institutionalized, such as a Hindu temple. Helping a client access social support from the community can be a crucial intervention. As a counselor, getting more

in touch with the community and visiting some of these places may be very helpful. Encouraging clients to attend temple events or services can help them better cope with their issues and enhance their support system.

Canda and Phaobtong (1992) studied the benefits of Buddhist temples for Southeast Asian refugees. They noted that the temples provided food, clothing, and shelter, as well as psychological, social, and spiritual support. The monks sometimes counseled the refugees or performed healing rituals for their physical or mental illnesses. Supporting indigenous methods of healing and folk beliefs can also help build rapport with the client.

Psychodynamic Therapy. Many psychodynamic therapists have compared their approach with principles of Buddhism. Miklaus (2007) describes how psychoanalysis is similar to Buddhism in that both involve cultivation of insight for transformation of suffering, and both emphasize experiential methods to investigate the dynamics of one's personal reality. This is also true for Taoism and Hinduism. Miklaus also describes that, in terms of the therapist being mindful, many have compared a meditative state to how Freud recommends an "evenly hovering attention" while working with a client.

Many of the psychodynamic therapists who practice meditation seem to work with clients from Eastern religions who are more acculturated to the United States (e.g., Finn & Rubin, 2000). Some authors have indicated that a more directive form of treatment for more traditional Asian Americans may be more culturally appropriate (Chin, 1998; Park, 1999). Thus, psychodynamic theories may not be the best fit with all clients from Eastern religions, especially those who are less acculturated and may prefer an emphasis on directiveness and hierarchy. However, more detailed education on how psychodynamic treatments are beneficial may help the client better understand them and increase his or her willingness to engage in them. Also, more acculturated Eastern clients may have a better fit with psychodynamic treatment.

CASE STUDY

The case study presented is an amalgam of clients that I have treated when working with Southeast Asian refugees at a community mental health center. A case study can be helpful in illustrating how to incorporate some of the recommendations mentioned earlier.

"Seyla" (not the client's real name) is a divorced, mono-lingual Cambodian woman in her late forties. She has two boys, ages 8 and 13, and is a welfare recipient. As a teenager, she witnessed the deaths of some of her family members by the bloody Khmer Rouge regime. She was forced to do hard manual labor and faced starvation. After a few months she escaped, spending 2 years in a Thai refugee camp. She eventually immigrated to the United States. She presents with some depressive symptoms as well as PTSD symptoms, especially nightmares, insomnia, hypervigilance, irritability, and avoidance of memories and situations that remind her about her trauma.

Counseling was done with the help of a translator/case manager. During the intake, the purpose was to build rapport with the patient while getting a background. With PTSD and refugee populations, I do not go into a detailed trauma account early in treatment because of the risk of retraumatization and early dropout. Instead, the session focused on assessing and developing the client's coping skills. In the first session, I taught a deep-breathing technique so the client could see a concrete benefit from treatment. It was also a segue into teaching her mindfulness, because deep breathing can help clients associate the breath with relaxation. We also discussed her spiritual beliefs, and she identified herself as Buddhist. She said that she believed in karma and probably believed in reincarnation, but was not sure about how it worked. She described that she occasionally went to the temple for services. She also identified some concrete goals, including decreasing her insomnia and depressive symptoms.

In the second session, I provided psychoeducation on sleep hygiene. For example, I discussed things to avoid before bed such as caffeine, nicotine (also a stimulant), sugar, TV, or too much exercise. We also practiced a mindfulness technique that fits well with CBT principles. I first gave the client some background on CBT. I taught her how our thoughts affect our feelings and how the mind often tends to focus on past, current, or future negative situations. I emphasized focusing on the present moment, sometimes taking constructive action and other times resting if we have done everything in our power to deal with our situation. The mindfulness technique, based on Thich Nhat Hanh's (1992) work, involved repeating relaxing thoughts to facilitate rest and relaxation. The repetition of relaxing thoughts was used to replace negative thoughts. I instructed the client that for this meditation, every time she inhaled, to silently say to herself, "breathing in I calm my body," relaxing her body a little more each time. As she continued to do that, I then told her that every time she exhaled, to silently say to herself, "breathing out I calm my mind." We practiced silently and mindfully for about 5 minutes, repeating these statements over and over. A discussion followed, and she reported that she felt more relaxed. I praised her and encouraged her to practice at home, telling her that the more she practices, the stronger the intervention.

In later sessions, we did a basic mindfulness breathing exercise, described earlier in the chapter. I also taught her relaxation imagery exercises. I audiotaped the meditation and relaxation sessions so that she could listen and practice at home. In terms of addressing her depressive symptoms, I encouraged her to use her temple as social support. We talked about how isolating and staying at home gave her more time to focus on her negative thoughts about her financial situation and her symptoms. She was also invited to the regular outings that the mental health center sponsored in order to decrease isolation. The client followed through quite often, reporting that she enjoyed the social activities at her temple and at the center.

I also used storytelling as a way of teaching certain principles. De Silva describes a story about a woman whose baby dies, and, grief stricken, she turns to Buddha for help in bringing her baby back. He tells her that he can help her, but first she needs to bring a pinch of mustard seeds from a house that has never experienced death. She starts wandering from village to village and over time finds that every home she comes across has had death and that she is not the only one who has lost a baby. Eventually, she returns to Buddha, saying that she understood his teaching, and he expands on the principle of impermanence.

I told the story to the client, illustrating the teaching of acceptance. The discussion in session focused on the importance of accepting some of her current symptoms and then taking action to deal with them. However, I pointed out how she tends to mentally resist and try to push away symptoms, such as her intrusive thoughts about her trauma. Instead, she was told to imagine the symptoms and intrusive thoughts as a 2-year-old having a tantrum. Instead of yelling at the toddler trying to get it to stop, I encouraged her to refocus her attention onto the most constructive behavior at that moment. With real toddlers throwing tantrums, ignoring them is often an appropriate intervention, and eventually, they stop. Similarly, I educated her how the intrusive thoughts eventually pass, and sometimes, trying to make them go away makes things more difficult. This focus on acceptance with constructive action is emphasized in ACT.

During the next few sessions, we reviewed coping skills such as exercising, staying busy, and connecting socially. The client eventually reported that meditation and relaxation helped her manage her insomnia, even though she still woke up in the middle of the night. She also stated that her social support was improving, having some benefit in decreasing her depressive symptoms. However, I left the agency to go to another job and had to transfer her care. Nevertheless, she acknowledged some gains made in treatment because of the interventions discussed.

CONCLUSION

In summary, a number of treatments and recommendations can be helpful in working with clients from Eastern spiritualities and religions. A very brief overview was discussed, and I encourage those interested in more information to read the recommended readings. There is a growing interest in the topic of spirituality and counseling. In addition, the number of people interested in Eastern religions is growing, and it is also influencing the way that we do treatment. Learning and integrating these approaches can benefit not only clients from Eastern spiritualities, but the general population as well.

REFERENCES

Bhopal, R. S. (1986). The inter-relationship of folk, traditional and Western medicine within an Asian community in Britain. *Social Science & Medicine, 22,* 99–105.

Bormann, J. E., Gifford, A. L., Shively, M., Smith, T. L., Redwine, L., Kelly, A., Becker, S., Gershwin, M., Bone, P., & Belding, W. (2006). Effects of spiritual mantram repetition on HIV outcomes: A randomized controlled trial. *Journal of Behavioral Medicine, 29,* 359–376.

Bormann, J. E., Oman, D., Kemppainen, J. K., Becker, S., Gershwin, M., & Kelly, A. (2006). Mantram repetition for stress management in veterans and employees: A critical incident study. *Journal of Advanced Nursing, 53,* 502–512.

Bowman, R. L., & Baylen, D. (1994). Buddhism as a second-order change psychotherapy. *International Journal for the Advancement of Counseling, 17,* 101–108.

Brown, K., & Ryan, R. (2003). The benefits of being present: Mindfulness and its role in psychological well-being. *Journal of Personality and Social Psychology, 84,* 822–848.

Canda, E. R., & Phaobtong, T. (1992). Buddhism as a support system for Southeast Asian refugees. *Social Work, 37,* 61–67.

Chin, J. L. (1998). Mental health services and treatment. In L. C. Lee & N. W. S. Zane (Eds.), *Handbook of Asian American psychology* (pp. 485–504). Thousand Oaks, CA: Sage.

Costantino, G., Malgady, R. G., & Rogler, L. H. (1986). Cuento therapy: A culturally sensitive modality for Puerto Rican children. *Journal of Consulting & Clinical Psychology, 54,* 639–645.

De Silva, P. (1984). Buddhism and behaviour modification. *Behaviour Research and Therapy, 22,* 661–678.

Ehrlich, M. P. (1986). Taoism and psychotherapy. *Journal of Contemporary Psychotherapy, 16,* 23–38.

Ellis, A., & MacLaren, C. (Eds.). (1998). *Rational emotive behavior therapy: A therapist's guide.* San Luis Obispo, CA: Impact Publishers.

Farag, N. H., & Mills, P. J. (2003). A randomised-controlled trial of the effects of a traditional herbal supplement on sleep onset insomnia. *Complementary Therapies in Medicine, 11,* 223–225.

Finn, M., & Rubin, J. B. (2000). Psychotherapy with Buddhists. In P. S. Richards & A. E. Bergin (Eds.), *Handbook of psychotherapy and religious diversity* (pp. 317–340). Washington, DC: American Psychological Association.

Gogtay, N. J., Bhatt, H. A., Dalvi, S. S., & Kshirsagar, N. A. (2002). The use and safety of non-allopathic Indian medicines. *Drug Safety, 25,* 1005–1119.

Goldenberg, I., & Goldenberg, H. (1995). Family therapy. In R. J. Corsini & D. Wedding (Eds.), *Current psychotherapies* (5th ed., pp. 356–385). Itasca, IL: Peacock.

Grepmair, L., Mitterlehner, F., & Nickel, M. (2008). Promotion of mindfulness in psychotherapists in training. *Psychiatry Research, 158,* 265.

Gupta, R. (2000). Treatment of depression in an elderly Asian Indian male: A cognitive behavioral approach. *Clinical Gerontologist, 22,* 87–90.

Hanh, T. N. (1992). *Peace is every step: The path of mindfulness in everyday life.* New York: Bantam.

Hayes, S. C., Masuda, A., Bissett, R., Luoma, J., & Guerrero, L. F. (2004). DBT, FAP and ACT: How empirically oriented are the new behavior therapy technologies? *Behavior Therapy, 35,* 35–54.

Hill, C. H., & Hood, R. W. (1999). *Measures of religiosity.* Birmingham, AL: Religious Education Press.

Ho, D. Y. F. (1995). Selfhood and identity in Confucianism, Taoism, Buddhism, and Hinduism: Contrasts with the West. *Journal for the Theory of Social Behaviour, 25,* 115–134.

Hollifield, M., Sinclair-Lian, N., Warner, T. D., & Hammerschlag, R. (2007). Acupuncture for posttraumatic stress disorder: A randomized controlled pilot trial. *Journal of Nervous and Mental Disease, 195,* 504–513.

Huang, J. S. (2004). Enhancing cultural responsiveness to Asian culture and practices during the initial session of therapy (Doctoral dissertation, University of California, Santa Barbara). *Dissertation Abstracts International: Section B: The Sciences & Engineering, 64,* 4040.

Huey, S. J., & Pan, D. (2006). Culture-responsive one-session treatment for phobic Asian Americans: A pilot study. *Psychotherapy: Theory, Research, Practice, Training, 43,* 549–554.

Iwasaka, H., Iida, J., Kawabata, Y., Chikaike, M., Onishi, T., & Kishimoto, T. (2002). Efficacy of a parent training program as attention deficit/hyperactivity disorder (AD/HD) therapy. *Japanese Journal of Child and Adolescent Psychiatry, 43,* 483–497.

Kabat-Zinn, J., Massion, A. O., Kristeller, J., & Peterson, L. G. (1992). Effectiveness of a meditation-based stress reduction program in the treatment of anxiety disorders. *American Journal of Psychiatry, 149,* 936–943.

Kaptchuk, T. J. (2002). Acupuncture: Theory, efficacy, and practice. *Annals of Internal Medicine, 136,* 374–383.

Leo, R. J., & Ligot, J. S. (2007). A systematic review of randomized controlled trials of acupuncture in the treatment of depression. *Journal of Affective Disorders, 97,* 13–22.

Linenhan, M. (1993). *Cognitive-behavioral treatment of borderline personality disorder.* New York: Guilford.

Liu, D. (Ed.). (1979). *The Tao and Chinese culture.* New York: Schocken.

Miklaus, W. L. (2007). Buddhism and Western psychology: Fundamentals of integration. *Journal of Consciousness Studies, 14,* 4–49.

Park, S. S. (1999). A test of two explanatory models of Asian-American and White students' preferences for a directive counseling style. *Dissertation Abstracts International: Section A: Humanities & Social Sciences, 59,* 3746.

Reynolds, D. K. (1976). *Morita psychotherapy.* Berkeley: University of California Press.

Richards, P. S., & Bergin, A. E. (Eds.). (2000). *Handbook of psychotherapy and religious diversity.* Washington, DC: American Psychological Association.

Richards, P. S., & Bergin, A. E. (Eds.). (2005). *A spiritual strategy for counseling and psychotherapy* (2nd ed.). Washington, DC: American Psychological Association.

Segal, Z. V., Williams, J. M. G., & Teasdale, J. D. (2002). *Mindfulness-based cognitive therapy for depression: A new approach to preventing relapse.* New York: Guilford.

Shapiro, D. H., & Zifferblatt, S. M. (1976). Zen meditation and behavior self-control: Similarities, differences, and clinical applications. *American Psychologist, 31,* 519–532.

Shapiro, S. L., Schwartz, G. E., & Bonner, G. (1998). Effects of mindfulness-based stress reduction on medical and premedical students. *Journal of Behavioral Medicine, 21,* 581–599.

Sharma, A. R. (2000). Psychotherapy with Hindus. In P. S. Richards & A. E. Bergin (Eds.), *Handbook of psychotherapy and religious diversity* (pp. 317–340). Washington, DC: American Psychological Association.

Shekelle, P. G., Hardy, M., Morton, S. C., Coulter, I., Venuturupalli, S., Favreau, J., & Hilton, L. K. (2005). Are Ayurvedic herbs for diabetes effective? *Journal of Family Practice, 54,* 876–886.

Singh, B. B., Khorsan, R., Vinjamury, S. P., Der-Martirosian, C., Kizhakkeveettil, A., & Anderson, T. M. (2007). Herbal treatments of asthma: A systematic review. *Journal of Asthma, 44,* 685–698.

Singh, B. B., Mishra, L. C., Vinjamury, S. P., Aquilina, N., Singh, V. J., & Shepard, N. (2003). The effectiveness of Commiphora mukul for osteoarthritis of the knee: An outcomes study. *Alternative Therapies in Health & Medicine, 9,* 74–79.

Singh, B. B., Vinjamury, S. P., Der-Martirosian, C., Kubik, E., Mishra, L. C., Shepard, N. P., et al. (2007). Ayurvedic and collateral herbal treatments for hyperlipidemia: A systematic review of randomized controlled trials and quasi-experimental designs. *Alternative Therapies in Health & Medicine, 13,* 22–28.

Walsh, R. (1995). Asian psychotherapies. In R. J. Corsini & D. Wedding (Eds.), *Current psychotherapies* (5th ed., pp. 547–559). Itasca, IL: Peacock.

Winters, M. (2006). Ancient medicine, modern use: Withania somnifera and its potential role in integrative oncology. *Alternative Medicine Review, 11,* 269–277.

Wong, E. (Ed.). (1997). *The Shambhala guide to Taoism.* Boston: Shambhala.

Wong, P. T. P., & Ujimoto, K. V. (1998). The elderly: Their stress, coping, and mental health. In L. C. Lee & N. W. S. Zane (Eds.), *Handbook of Asian American psychology* (pp. 165–209). Thousand Oaks, CA: Sage.

Multicultural Health Counseling: The Intersection of Physical and Mental Health

In Part VIII of the *Handbook,* teams of authors address health-related counseling issues relevant to racial and ethnic minorities; women; and lesbian, gay, and bisexual individuals. The section opens in Chapter 40 with co-authors Carolyn M. Tucker, Katherine D. Daly, and Keith C. Herman addressing the intersection of mental and physical health for racial and ethnic minorities. The authors address race- and ethnic-based disparities in health and health care, and they introduce their customized multicultural health counseling model. The important role of mental health professionals in promoting the health of the nation is highlighted, and specific strategies for applying customized multicultural health counseling are presented.

Chapter 41, by Merle A. Keitel, Erica Tennenbaum, and Heather Cunha Amato, focuses on a lifespan perspective of women's physical health. The authors attend particularly to puberty, pregnancy and childbirth, and menopause. Challenging the medical profession's tendency to "medicalize" these normative developmental transitions, the authors call for a broader understanding of women's health within the context of biological, psychological, and sociocultural factors. To illustrate their points and demonstrate treatment issues, Drs. Keitel, Tennenbaum, and Cunha Amato present a detailed, life-span case study that is both riveting and highly informative.

The final chapter in Part VIII is written by Eric C. Chen, Ryan Androsiglio, and Vicky Ng and focuses on stress and health risks in lesbian, gay, and bisexual individuals. Anchoring their conceptualization in minority stress theory, the authors review the stressors faced by this diverse population in adolescence, adulthood, and late adulthood. Major health risks such as depression, suicide, and substance abuse are discussed within minority stress theory and developmental contexts. Counseling implications informed by developmental contextualism and social justice are discussed. Finally, Drs. Chen, Androsiglio, and Ng present two vivid and detailed case studies highlighting key points made throughout the chapter.

40

Customized Multicultural Health Counseling

Bridging the Gap Between Mental and Physical Health for Racial and Ethnic Minorities

CAROLYN M. TUCKER, KATHERINE D. DALY, AND
KEITH C. HERMAN

Promotion of health is one of the highest priorities within the United States. The impetus for making this nation's health a priority is the growing prevalence and costs associated with burdensome health problems such as obesity, diabetes, and hypertension that will likely bankrupt our nation in the near future if left unaddressed. A national-level response to this reality was "Healthy People 2010," an initiative launched in 1979 based on the Surgeon General's report titled *Healthy People* (U.S. Department of Health and Human Services, 2008) with the goal of improving the health of the nation by 2010 through federally funded and grassroots programs designed to increase health-promoting behaviors among children, adults, and families. Many programs that were part of "Healthy People 2010" were aimed at improving the health statuses and reducing health disparities of racial/ethnic minority groups and groups with low socioeconomic status.

However, health disparities continue to plague our nation and have emerged in recent years as a problem of national concern. Health disparities are defined as differences in health statuses and outcomes and in health care quality between non-Hispanic Whites and some racial/ethnic minority groups, among racial/ethnic minority groups, and between lower socioeconomic status (SES) groups and higher SES groups. It is particularly noteworthy that health disparities have had a disproportionately negative impact on racial/ethnic minorities, particularly African Americans and Hispanics (Agency for Healthcare Research and Quality [AHRQ], 2004).

There is growing recognition in the United States that culturally sensitive health care and health promotion are critical to reducing health disparities among the multicultural population that constitutes the United States. Given that cultural factors intersect with various internal and external factors (e.g., biological, psychological, social/environmental, and economic factors) to influence health status, health care quality, and health outcomes, culturally sensitive biopsychosocial approaches have much potential for guiding intervention efforts to promote health and improve health care quality (Betancourt, Green, Carrillo, & Ananeh-Firempong, 2003). Yet the vast number of cultures and subcultures in the United States and the individual differences within even the smallest of these subcultural groups creates enormous challenges for providers aspiring to deliver culturally sensitive care. Ongoing efforts to train physicians and other health care providers to become more culturally competent and/or culturally sensitive are inadequate and have been criticized for fostering stereotyping of patients. Such stereotyping can be avoided and health disparities can be reduced through health care that is patient-centered and culturally sensitive/competent (Tucker et al., 2008).

Lipkin and colleagues (Lipkin, Putnam, & Lazare, 1995) asserted that patient-centeredness is conveyed by practitioners through (a) having the knowledge, attitudes, and skills to elicit the patient's unique health-related story; (b) promoting trust in the patient-provider relationship; (c) clarifying and understanding the patient's symptoms; (d) conceptualizing the patient's illness from a biopsychosocial model; and (e) fostering an ongoing relationship with the patient (e.g., by expressing unconditional positive regard, respecting patient autonomy, expressing commitment, and finding ways to overcome barriers to patient-provider communication). Beach, Saha, and Cooper (2006) asserted that patient-centered care interacts with culturally competent care:

> To the extent that patient-centered care is delivered universally, care should become more equitable. Conversely, to the extent that cultural competence enhances the ability of health care systems and providers to address individual patients' preferences and goals, care should become more patient-centered. (p. 9)

Many counseling psychologists, clinical psychologists, and counselors are uniquely prepared to facilitate patient-centered, culturally sensitive health promotion and health care that will help reduce health disparities. This is the case because these professionals are typically trained to provide client-centered counseling as part of their basic core counseling training, regardless of the theory of counseling they embrace, and they are typically

trained to have expertise in the areas of multicultural counseling theory, research, and practice. Indeed, multicultural counseling competencies have been defined and advocated by the Society of Counseling Psychology of the American Psychological Association (APA) (Sue et al., 1998), the American Counseling Association (Roysircar, Arredondo, Fuertes, Ponterotto, & Toporek, 2003), and the APA (2003). Given the well-established interactive relationship between physical health and mental health (Satcher & Pamies, 2006), it is not surprising that increasing numbers of psychologists and counselors with multicultural competence and client-centeredness training are engaged in physical health promotion as well as mental health promotion, especially in physical health care settings.

The purpose of this chapter is to highlight the roles of counseling psychologists, clinical psychologists, and counselors in helping to promote the health of the nation and in helping to reduce health disparities. First, we briefly discuss the existence of health disparities and the multilevel factors that influence these disparities. Next, we define customized multicultural health counseling and highlight its implications for effective health promotion, and ultimately for reducing health disparities. Finally, we present specific examples and recommendations for engaging in customized multicultural health counseling.

RACE/ETHNICITY AND DISPARITIES IN HEALTH AND HEALTH CARE QUALITY AND ACCESS

Racial/ethnic minorities as compared to non-Hispanic Whites are more likely to have serious health problems that threaten the quality and length of their lives. For example, in 2005, the Centers for Disease Control and Prevention's National Center for Chronic Disease Prevention and Health Promotion (NCCDPHP) reported that compared to non-Hispanic Whites, (a) African American, Asian American, and Puerto Rican infants experience higher mortality rates; (b) Hispanics and Asian Americans experience higher rates of stomach cancers; (c) African Americans experience a higher incidence of heart disease deaths; (d) African Americans are more affected by hypertension (40% greater prevalence); and (e) African Americans, Hispanics, American

Indians, and Alaska Natives are two to three times more likely to have diagnosed diabetes (http://www.cdc.gov/nccdphp/).

Because racial/ethnic minorities are overrepresented in the lower SES groups, they are more likely to experience health problems that are associated with low SES. Compared to higher SES groups, persons from lower SES groups are more likely to experience obesity, diabetes, heart disease, low birth weight, and illness-related death (AHRQ, 2004). Additionally, compared to higher SES groups, lower SES groups are more likely to experience the following health care access-related disparities: (a) less entry into the health care system, (b) structural barriers within the system, (c) poorer patient-provider communication, and (d) lower levels of provider cultural competency and/or cultural sensitivity (AHRQ, 2004).

Regarding entry into the health care system, many studies suggest that racial/ethnic minorities and individuals from low SES backgrounds are more likely to be either uninsured or underinsured, even when they have stable jobs (Doty & Holmgren, 2004; Hoffman, Schoen, Rowland, & Davis, 2001), and consequently, they are less likely to receive preventive health care and needed treatment for health problems (Klein, Glied, & Ferry, 2005). Examples of evidence of structural barriers within the health care system include the findings that (a) African Americans and the uninsured are more likely to report waiting more than 1 hour at the emergency room for semi-urgent or non-urgent care, and to report leaving the emergency room without ever being seen (AHRQ, 2003); and (b) 25% of pharmacies in predominantly non-White neighborhoods carried opioid analgesic supplies compared to 72% of pharmacies in predominantly White neighborhoods (Morrison, Wallenstein, Natale, Senzel, & Huang, 2000).

Examples of research findings suggesting that patient-provider communication contributes to race/ethnicity-related health disparities include findings that American Indians and Alaska Natives, Asian Americans, African Americans, Hispanics, low-income populations, and individuals without a high school diploma are more likely than non-Hispanic Whites, individuals with middle and high income levels, and individuals who attended college, respectively, to report poor communication with their physicians (AHRQ, 2003). Additionally,

research indicates that doctors are less likely to engage African American patients in conversation compared to non-Hispanic White patients, and the tone of visits with African American patients was generally less friendly than with non-Hispanic White patients (Johnson, Roter, Powe, & Cooper, 2004). Finally, many health experts have asserted that race/ethnicity-related health disparities are negatively associated with provider cultural competence and cultural sensitivity and have called for research to support these assertions (Betancourt, Green, Carrillo, & Park, 2005; Tucker et al., 2008).

Compared to non-Hispanic Whites, some racial/ethnic minorities experience a lower quality of health care even given similar health problems and health insurance status (Institute of Medicine, 2002). For instance, African Americans and Hispanics are less likely than non-Hispanic Whites to receive analgesics at emergency care facilities (Todd, Deaton, D'Adamo, & Goe, 2000). African Americans, Asian Americans, Pacific Islanders, American Indians, and Alaska Natives are all less likely to receive a kidney transplant within 3 years of renal failure compared to non-Hispanic Whites (AHRQ, 2003). Differences in health care quality associated with race/ethnicity may also interact with income and gender. For example, African Americans enrolled in Medicare experience higher rates of amputations than non-Hispanic Whites (Gornick et al., 1996), and African Americans and women are less likely than non-Hispanic Whites and men to be referred for cardiac catheterization (Shulman, Berlin, & Escarce, 1999).

It has also been well documented that being a racial/ethnic minority, female, and/or from a low SES group places one at risk for discrimination and prejudice, which in turn have been linked to stress, racism-related stress, and other psychological problems. Such psychological problems are associated with common physical health problems such as obesity and hypertension. These physical health problems often contribute to psychological symptoms such as depression, low self-esteem, and anxiety (Clark, Anderson, Clark, & Williams, 1999).

Particularly noteworthy is that the nature of the associations between physical health problems and psychological symptoms often differs by race/ethnicity and/or culture. For example, Molloy and Herzberger (2004) found that obesity is associated with low self-esteem among non-Hispanic White adolescents and

Hispanic adolescents but is associated with high self-esteem among African American adolescents. These authors attributed their findings to cultural differences in the conceptualization of obesity. Such documented associations between physical and psychological health together highlight the complexity of the health of racial/ethnic minorities and of the disparities that negatively affect these individuals.

RACE/ETHNICITY AND HEALTH WITHIN A REAL-WORLD CONTEXT

Having knowledge of the multiple factors that affect the physical health of racial/ethnic minorities as well as acknowledging the complexity of the relationship between race/ethnicity and health are important for identifying counseling strategies to promote the physical and psychological health of multicultural groups and individuals. Anderson (1998) suggested a multilevel analysis system for understanding the factors that contribute to health status/outcomes. The specific factors of focus in this multilevel analysis system are the following: biological factors (i.e., organ systems, cellular, and molecular); social/environmental factors (e.g., sociocultural groupings and economic resources); and behavioral/psychological factors (e.g., diet, exercise, stress appraisal, and coping).

Biological Factors. Examples of findings that support the view that biological factors influence health are the following: (a) certain health conditions tend to cluster in specific populations (e.g., Collins et al., 2003) and (b) the effectiveness of pharmaceutical treatment regimens has been linked to differences in drug receptors and drug enzymes among racial/ethnic groups (e.g., Lin, 2001). Such findings have prompted the recent development of controversial race-specific medications (Bloche, 2004) and promoted a campaign of genetic research geared toward reducing and/or eliminating health disparities (Collins et al., 2003). However, a number of criticisms and cautions have been raised to deter this genetic research campaign, and other criticisms and cautions have emerged in response to the occurrence of this campaign. For example, Johnson et al. (1995) identified flawed assumptions that underlie the genetic model of racial differences in health. More

recently, in a comprehensive overview of the issues surrounding genetic research and health disparities, Sankar et al. (2004) outlined several problematic issues, such as how overemphasizing genetics could divert attention from the primary factors in the occurrence of health disparities.

Social/Environmental Factors. There is growing consensus that the most prominent factors that influence the health of racial/ethnic minorities and individuals from lower socioeconomic backgrounds are social and environmental factors such as economics, culture, and sociopolitical power (e.g., Johnson et al., 1995). Specific examples of economic factors include not being able to purchase healthier foods such as fresh vegetables versus canned vegetables that are typically higher in sodium, and not being able to live in safer neighborhoods where there are bike paths and recreation centers that are conducive to maintaining daily recommended physical activity. Some examples of cultural factors in health status include having culture-related beliefs about health and illness that preclude taking medicines prescribed by physicians, and eating culture-specific foods that are often high in fat and sodium. Examples of social and political factors that affect the health of racial/ethnic minorities include placing polluting factories near the neighborhoods of racial/ethnic minorities and low-income families, and placing health-promoting facilities in locations that are not easily accessible to most members of racial/ethnic minority communities.

Behavioral/Psychological Factors. The positive influence that health-promoting behaviors (e.g., exercising, eating less sodium, drinking water rather than sweetened beverages) has on the health of all individuals has been well documented by the NCCD-PHP. Stress management has also been identified as an important aspect of a health-promoting lifestyle. Lower levels of skills for managing stress have been linked to depression, anxiety, and other psychological problems that negatively affect health (Ng & Jeffery, 2003). Given that stress often accompanies racial/ethnic minority status, including racism-related stress (Clark et al., 1999), it is particularly important to consider coping skills as a factor in the health of racial/ethnic minorities.

IMPLICATIONS OF THE MULTIPLE HEALTH INFLUENCE FACTORS FOR CUSTOMIZED MULTICULTURAL HEALTH COUNSELING

Many of the factors that affect the health of racial/ethnic minorities are to a large degree beyond the control of those with low family incomes. Indeed, these individuals often do not have the economic resources or the social political power to leverage health care access and health care quality that facilitate health promotion and illness prevention and promote positive health outcomes. Moreover, many of the factors influencing the health of racial/ethnic minorities, such as racism and discrimination, are intractable and thus will require long-term systemic solutions. While we await such systemic solutions, it is imperative that we address more easily modifiable aspects of health promotion, such as changing health-related behaviors.

It is important that interventions designed to increase health-promoting behaviors among racial/ethnic minorities, particularly those who have low family incomes, include a focus on empowering these individuals to engage in their own health promotion and to elicit health care quality and access under whatever conditions that exist in their lives. Psychologists and counselors with training in multicultural counseling are particularly prepared to facilitate this health self-empowerment. Specifically, these professionals can (a) provide customized multicultural health counseling, which includes a focus on health self-empowerment, and (b) train physical health care providers for engaging in this counseling as part of their health care delivery to the multicultural populations they serve.

CUSTOMIZED MULTICULTURAL HEALTH COUNSELING

Traditional Versus Customized Multicultural Health Counseling. The traditional conceptualization of multicultural counseling is that it involves using acquired knowledge, skills, awareness, and experiences for effectively providing counseling to culturally diverse clients (Sue et al., 1998). Based on this traditional definition of multicultural counseling, it is reasonable to extrapolate that the term *multicultural health counseling* involves using multicultural counseling principles to address the physical health problems of clients/patients with the recognition that physical health problems often have psychological causes and consequences that need to be assessed and addressed as well. However, it is our contention that multicultural counseling as traditionally defined and practiced is based on the knowledge, skills, awareness, and experiences that "expert" professionals (e.g., psychologists and counselors) deem important for effectively counseling culturally diverse clients/patients. Using this traditional definition may unintentionally undermine the empowerment of clients/patients and may not sufficiently include counseling behaviors and attitudes that clients/patients view as important.

The first author, Carolyn M. Tucker, has coined the term *customized multicultural health counseling* as an alternative to traditional multicultural counseling models. Customized multicultural health (CMH) counseling is defined by culturally diverse clients/patients—the "true experts" for determining the health counseling that they need. CMH counseling is guided by the views of culturally diverse clients/patients regarding the specific knowledge, skills, awareness, and experiences that (a) enable them to feel comfortable, trusting, and respected in the counseling process and environment; and (b) empower them to address their physical and mental health needs or elicit the help required to address these needs.

CMH counseling involves (a) empowering clients/patients to identify behaviors, skills, and attitudes of their own and of others (e.g., family and friends), including the psychologist/counselor present, that enable these clients/patients to engage in health-promoting behaviors and to elicit/obtain desired health care quality from their health care providers, administrators, and others; and (b) teaching clients/patients how to use these behaviors, skills, and attitudes to obtain desired health care access and quality. Health-promoting behaviors include eating a healthy breakfast daily; eating fruits and vegetables two to three times a day; eating whole-grain foods; eating foods/snacks low in calories, fat, and sodium; drinking water and low-sugar and low-sodium beverages; engaging in medium- to high-intensity physical activity for at least 30 minutes to 1 hour daily; and limiting television and video screen time (common sedentary activities) to 2 hours or less per day. These health-promoting behaviors are consistent with those advocated in "Healthy People 2010."

CMH Counseling With Racial/Ethnic Minorities for Health Promotion. In addition to being aware of the multiple factors that affect the physical and mental health of racial/ethnic minorities and the interaction of physical and mental health, CMH providers/counselors use a model for guiding their assessment and intervention activities. Health Self-Empowerment (HSE) Theory (Tucker, Butler, Loyuk, Desmond, & Surrency, in press) offers a framework/model for implementing counseling strategies and interventions and associated assessments so as to achieve the aims of increasing health-promoting behaviors and sustaining them over time. HSE Theory is a culturally sensitive theory that acknowledges the influence of social/environmental variables (e.g., poverty, limited health promotion and health care access) and other variables on health behaviors and health status, but asserts that given the intractable nature of these variables in ethnic minority and low-income communities, self-empowerment-oriented self-variables are key target variables for understanding and modifying the health behaviors of individuals who live in these communities. Specifically, HSE Theory asserts that engagement in health-promoting behaviors and avoidance of health risk behaviors are influenced by the following four literature-based, modifiable, self-empowerment-oriented, cognitive-behavioral self-variables: (a) health motivation, (b) health self-efficacy, (c) self-praise of health-promoting behaviors, and (d) active coping strategies/skills for managing stress so as to avoid its potentially negative impact on health status (e.g., blood pressure).

In a direct examination of the HSE Theory variables as predictors of engagement in both a health-promoting lifestyle (HPL) and individual health-promoting behaviors among low-income African American mothers and non-Hispanic White mothers ($N = 96$), it was found that these predictor variables together accounted for significant variance in level of engagement in an HPL (Tucker et al., in press). Additionally, health motivation, health self-efficacy, health self-praise, and active coping skills/strategies were significant individual predictors of one or more individual health-promoting behaviors.

CMH Counseling to Promote Patient Engagement in Health-Promoting Behaviors Through Use of HSE Theory. In CMH counseling, psychologists and counselors specifically target HSE Theory variables (health motivation, health self-efficacy, health self-praise, and active coping) to achieve the goal of increasing health promoting behaviors among their clients/patients. These professionals can promote health motivation in their clients/patients in many ways, including by encouraging their clients/patients to do the following: (a) Consider health-promoting behaviors as ways of expressing love for themselves and for their children and significant others; (b) think of the fact that through engaging in health-promoting behaviors, they can, to a large degree, control the quality of their lives and avoid dying early and leaving behind all that they worked hard to obtain (e.g., their home, money, and partner/spouse); (c) set small-step health promotion goals that they can achieve (e.g., walking 10 steps more each day toward the nationally recommended goal of 10,000 steps daily); and (d) identify ways to express love for their family members that increases family engagement in health-promoting behaviors.

Health self-efficacy can be facilitated among clients/patients by inviting them to identify low-cost or no-cost behaviors in which they can engage to control their weight, blood pressure, and cholesterol, such as the following: (a) choosing not to add salt to one's food; (b) reading the nutrition label on all foods before buying/eating them; (c) choosing products with the lowest sodium, fat, and cholesterol; (d) finding a physical activity/walking partner such as a co-worker, family member, or friend; (e) choosing not to buy/eat junk foods; (f) talking to a friend or someone else when stressed rather than eating; (g) cooking with olive oil rather than oils high in saturated or trans fats; and (h) using recipes for cooking healthy versions of favorite foods.

Self-praise can be taught to clients/patients by giving them some examples of this type of praise, such as saying, "I am so proud of myself for choosing an apple for dessert rather than a slice of cheesecake," and "I am worthy of giving my health priority, and I am proud of myself for doing so." It can be explained that, for various reasons (e.g., jealousy, cultural norms), family members often do not provide desired supportive praise of one's health-promoting behaviors, and thus, it is important to praise one's own self for health promotion efforts, behaviors, and outcomes.

Finally, active coping can be promoted in CMH counseling by teaching clients/patients stress management, anxiety management, anger management, and depression management skills and strategies with an emphasis on encouraging these clients/patients to choose those skills and strategies or identify other such skills and strategies for self-managing their emotions rather than allowing others to control their emotions and thus control their health. Use of these skills and strategies by clients/patients can be facilitated by informing them of research involving individuals like themselves that evidence the linkages between emotions (e.g., stress) and health status/outcomes (e.g., blood pressure).

The customizing (individualizing) aspect of CMH counseling can be facilitated by challenging clients/patients to identify the motivators of and barriers to health-promoting behaviors (which the first author also calls health-smart behaviors) that they personally experience. Once this information is obtained, the identified personal motivators can be encouraged and verbally reinforced, and the identified personal barriers can be discussed for the purpose of assisting clients/patients in identifying ways of overcoming these barriers under the conditions that exist in their lives. The first author is in the process of developing a Motivators of and Barriers to Health-Smart Behaviors Inventory (MB-HSBI)–Adult and Youth Versions on which clients/patients can rate the degree to which each item on the age-appropriate version is a motivator of or barrier to health-promoting behaviors. The items on the MB-HSBI–Adult Version and the items on the MB-HSBI–Youth Version were generated by culturally diverse adult focus groups and youth focus groups, respectively. Currently, the psychometric properties of both the MB-HSBI–Adult Version and the MB-HSBI–Youth Version are being evaluated using culturally diverse national samples of adults and youth, respectively. Use of both versions of the MB-HSBI or similar types of inventories is a time-efficient way of engaging in CMH counseling.

CMH Counseling With Racial/Ethnic Minorities for Fostering Satisfactory Health Care Access and Quality. CMH counseling can be an important vehicle for empowering patients/clients to obtain satisfactory health care access and health care quality, both of which lower the likelihood of costly serious health problems. Much of this empowerment involves providing patients/clients with needed information and skills for obtaining desired health care.

CMH counseling to foster health care access, particularly among racial/ethnic minorities, involves (a) providing patients/clients with health literacy facilitating information (e.g., information regarding available health care services and patients'/clients' health care rights and responsibilities), and doing so in a language and format that are easily understood by culturally diverse patients/clients; and (b) teaching patients/clients skills (e.g., assertiveness and advocacy skills) for obtaining desired health care access. Although such health information provision and teaching are often particularly needed by patients/clients with low education levels and/or patients/clients for whom English is a second language, these counseling interventions should be respectfully offered to these and other patients/clients and should occur only with their expressed desire for these interventions. It is also the case that counseling psychologists, counselors, and other health promotion professionals ideally should join with community leaders and health policy experts in racial/ethnic minority and low-income communities to advocate for needed health care access when such access does not exist.

CMH counseling to foster health care quality, particularly among racial/ethnic minorities, involves teaching patients/clients behaviors, skills, and attitudes for obtaining/inspiring patient-centered, culturally sensitive health care (Tucker et al., 2008). This type of health care has the following specific characteristics: (a) it emphasizes displaying patient/client-desired, modifiable provider and staff behaviors and attitudes; implementing health care site policies; and displaying physical health care center environment characteristics and policies that culturally diverse patients/clients identify as indicators of respect for their culture and that enable these patients/clients to feel comfortable with, trusting of, and respected by their health care providers and office staff; (b) it conceptualizes the patient-provider relationship as a partnership that emerges from patient centeredness; and (c) it is patient empowerment oriented (Tucker et al., 2008).

Use of Culturally Sensitive Assessments in CMH Counseling With Racial/Ethnic Minorities. It is important that CMH counseling to improve health care quality begins with assessing the specific provider behaviors and attitudes and health care site characteristics and policies that patients/clients involved in such counseling view as contributing to them feeling comfortable/uncomfortable, trusting/untrusting, and respected/disrespected, and that contribute to them feeling that their culture is respected. This type of assessment is especially important in CMH counseling with racial/ethnic minorities given that trust of one's provider, feeling respected by one's provider, and feeling respected in the health care delivery process have been linked to health care satisfaction and treatment adherence of racial/ethnic minority patients (Tucker et al., 2008).

Health care quality-related assessment in CMH counseling can be facilitated through the use of the Tucker-Culturally Sensitive Health Care Inventory (T-CSHCI)–Patient Form. This is an inventory on which patients rate the degree to which they experience provider behaviors and attitudes, staff behaviors and attitudes, and health care site physical characteristics and policies that racially and culturally diverse patients view as indicators of culturally sensitive health care (i.e., that enable them to feel comfortable, trusting, respected, etc.). Patients/clients who complete the T-CSHCI–Patient Form can also add desired provider/staff behaviors and attitudes and health care site characteristics and policies that are not already on it, and rate the degree to which they experience these added behaviors, attitudes, policies, and site characteristics. On a clinical tool version of the T-CSHCI–Patient Form, patients/clients can also identify the behaviors, attitudes, policies, and site characteristics that are most important to them. Patient data obtained from the T-CSHCI–Patient Form and from the clinical tool version of this inventory can help enable CMH counseling.

In CMH counseling to foster racial/ethnic minority clients'/patients' satisfaction with their health care access and/or health care quality, it is also important to assess these patients'/clients' health beliefs and conceptualizations of health and illness. The fact that racial/ethnic minorities often hold health beliefs and conceptualizations that are different from those of their typically middle- to upper-class, non-Hispanic White providers (Huff, 1999), and that these differences may interfere with various aspects of health care, make it especially important for psychologists/counselors and health care providers to assess and discuss these health beliefs.

It is also important that psychologists/counselors determine whether the client/patient in CMH counseling has family/friends that will support her/his efforts to inspire patient-centered culturally sensitive health care and to obtain and use health literacy-facilitating information. However, the decision to involve family members in providing such support should remain with the patient/client and should not be an alternative to a lack of culturally sensitive health care services, such as provision of a certified interpreter.

Perhaps most importantly, the assessment aspect of CMH counseling to foster racial/ethnic minority patients' satisfaction with their health care access and/or health care quality should focus on identifying the client's/patient's health care access and quality goals. Clarity regarding these goals is often facilitated through use of the earlier mentioned health literacy-facilitating information. Additionally, it is important to assess the client's/patient's skills and behavioral repertoire for obtaining desired health care access and quality.

The skills that enable clients/patients in general and racial/ethnic minority clients/patients in particular to obtain desired health care access and/or health care quality include the following: (a) assertiveness skills (e.g., skills for making requests and for giving positive and negative feedback to health care providers/counselors in constructive and respectful ways); (b) anxiety and stress management skills (e.g., skills for overcoming anxiety and stress, respectively, that occur at and outside of the counseling or health care setting); (c) behavior management skills (e.g., use of praise of specific provider and clinic office support staff behaviors for which an increase is desired by the patient); and (d) cognitive-behavioral anger management skills (e.g., skills for constructively managing anger prompted by disrespectful and racist health care provision behaviors). These skills can be taught using Meichenbaum's (1977) self-empowerment-oriented cognitive modeling and self-instruction training approach. This approach empowers the learner (i.e., each patient) by using a step-by-step teaching and learning method that makes learning simple and easy. This approach also uses demonstration modeling and role-plays as well as learning theory-based strategies. These strategies include (a) using praise and encouragement in response to efforts to learn and actual learning of new behaviors, attitudes, and skills; and (b) encouraging the learners to praise themselves for their efforts to use and actual use of target behaviors, attitudes, and skills.

It is particularly important that racial/ethnic minority clients/patients be asked their opinion and preferences regarding behaviors, skills, and strategies discussed with them in CMH counseling, as only these patients know whether what is discussed in counseling is applicable in their everyday lives and environments, both of which are typically very different from those of psychologists/ counselors and health care providers. These clients/ patients should also be asked to consider how the behaviors, skills, and strategies discussed with them in CMH counseling fit with their health beliefs. For example, the client/patient who believes that God controls his or her health and that the body is a holy temple can be asked to consider how God might work through providers to bless him or her with health and how eating healthy might fit with his or her belief that the body is a holy temple.

General Counseling Strategies Important in CMH Counseling

A number of general counseling strategies are important in providing CMH counseling to any client/patient. These general strategies include (a) assessing the client's/ patient's health goals/desires; (b) assessing the psychosocial factors (e.g., health status of parents, health beliefs/conceptualizations, health behaviors of family and friends, and socioeconomic factors) that influence the client's/patient's health behaviors and attitudes; and (c) using counseling interventions to facilitate the client's/patient's knowledge and skills for obtaining satisfactory health care.

It is also important that CMH counseling of any client be patient-centered and culturally sensitive, and thus reflective of the fact that all individuals, including non-Hispanic White clients/patients, have cultures that need to be considered in the health counseling process. Additionally, it is important to conceptualize health counseling as a partnership in which the psychologist or counselor and the client work together to improve the health of the client/patient in ways that facilitate mutual respect. Central to these partnerships are providers who demonstrate empathy, compassion, and responsiveness in relation to the assessed needs, values, and preferences of their patients, and patients who are actively involved in identifying these needs, values, and preferences (Paterson, 2001). These partnerships have been associated with increased treatment adherence by patients (Beck, Daughtridge, & Sloane, 2002), improvements in the health statuses of patients, and reductions in misdiagnoses of patients' health problems due to poor patient-provider communication (Michie, Miles, & Weinman, 2003). Furthermore, research suggests that patients typically want to be active partners in their health care (Michie et al., 2003).

General Counseling Strategies Particularly Important in CMH Counseling With Racial/Ethnic Minorities

Some strategies are particularly important in CMH counseling with racial/ethnic minority clients/patients. One of these strategies is promoting client/patient empowerment. There is agreement among researchers who have studied empowerment of Blacks (Solomon, 1976) and Hispanics (Paterson, 2001) that empowerment of minorities must include enabling them to experience a psychological sense of personal and interpersonal control, and attending to social, political, and legal factors that influence this perceived control.

It is also important that in CMH counseling, psychologists and counselors show their respect for racial/ ethnic and cultural differences by overtly communicating their commitment to being nonjudgmental about health beliefs and practices that are not generally accepted by health care providers. In addition to verbally communicating their openness to nontraditional, culturally relevant health practices, CMH psychologists and counselors ideally can demonstrate their commitment to cultural sensitivity by displaying culturally diverse artwork, having health literature and brochures in various languages available to clients/patients, and including an expressed commitment to culturally sensitive health promotion and health care in a mission statement listed directly on the health care intake form. This strategy is responsive to research findings indicating that individuals of different cultural backgrounds from their health care providers (a) may construct their own meanings and explanations for illness, and these constructions may conflict with the traditional Western biomedical model of medicine (Borrayo & Jenkins, 2003; Kundhal & Kundhal, 2003); (b) may misrepresent symptoms to their health care providers, as certain illnesses and symptoms (e.g., symptoms of depression in many Asian cultures) are stigmatized in different cultures (Kundhal & Kundhal, 2003); and (c) may not inform their health care providers of their use of complementary and alternative medicines such as herbal remedies (Robinson & McGrail, 2004), even though nondisclosure of the use of these medicines can interfere with traditional medicines and thus negatively affect patients' well-being and chances of survival (Tasaki, Maskarinec, Shumay, Tatsumura, & Kakai, 2002).

Another important strategy that should be used by psychologists/counselors in CMH counseling with racial/ethnic minority clients/patients is use of clear, simple language as well as use of a professional interpreter if doing so is desired by a particular client/patient. These actions are important given the finding that American Indians and Alaska Natives, Asian Americans, African Americans, Hispanics, low-income populations, and individuals without a high school diploma are more likely than non-Hispanic Whites, individuals with middle and high income levels, and individuals who attended college, respectively, to report poor communication with their physicians (AHRQ, 2003).

Given research findings suggesting that African American clients/patients may come to counseling with a history of having received less engaged/supportive health care treatment than non-Hispanic White clients/patients, it is also particularly important that psychologists and counselors actively engage African American clients/patients in the discussion of their health, and show sensitivity, reassurance, and support in their interactions with their clients/patients. The need for additional efforts to engage minority clients/patients is also supported through research findings that doctors were found to be less likely to engage African American patients in conversation compared to non-Hispanic White patients, and that the tone of visits with African American patients was generally less friendly than with non-Hispanic White patients (Johnson et al., 2004).

Strategies for Becoming an Effective CMH Psychologist or Counselor for Racial/Ethnic Minorities

Some important strategies for becoming an effective CMH psychologist or counselor for racial/ethnic minorities include doing the following:

1. Spending time shadowing health care providers in health care settings, and spending time with tribal medicine providers, healers, and pastoral counselors who engage in health counseling toward the goal of learning firsthand the health care and health promotion challenges experienced by racial/ethnic minorities similar to those served in one's CMH counseling practice

2. Participating in health fairs and other health promotion events in communities where one's clients/patients live

3. Learning about the biological, physiological, psychological, and cultural aspects of and treatment regimens for health problems (e.g., hypertension, diabetes, and obesity) that are common among racial/ethnic minorities

4. Inviting clients/patients to involve their family members in the health counseling process, as changing to a healthy lifestyle (e.g., buying and eating more vegetables) typically involves/affects all family members

5. Learning to speak the language of the clients/patients served, and/or advocating for increased training as well as certification of professional interpreters who can assist with the CMH counseling process (Youdelman & Perkins, 2005)

6. Pursuing CMH counseling positions in health care and/or health promotion settings by educating providers and administrators in these settings on the interaction of physical and mental health problems and culture, and on how CMH counseling can likely improve the health outcomes of their patients.

Future Directions for Promoting CMH Counseling

Psychologists and counselors trained in CMH counseling can assume leadership in training physical health care providers in the provision of this counseling as these providers often serve the masses of racial/ethnic minorities. Furthermore, lay and professional physical health care providers typically have long-term relationships with their patients/clients and thus are well positioned to provide health counseling that can occur over time, even if opportunities for this counseling do not occur consistently. Once becoming informed about CMH counseling, physical health care providers as well as psychologists and counselors will likely serve as advocates for involvement of racial/ethnic minorities in such counseling.

To a large degree, the future of CMH counseling rests with demonstrating its effectiveness through outcome research that targets culturally diverse clients/patients. It is important that this research is itself culturally sensitive in that it involves (a) the inclusion of qualitative research aspects; (b) participation of some racial/ethnic minority psychologists and counselors; (c) use of language, education, and culturally appropriate assessments; and (d) inclusion of former racial/ethnic minority clients/patients as well as community members as research planning and implementation partners. It is only through demonstrating the impact of CMH counseling on health status and outcomes that the needed training resources to advance this counseling will become available.

The potential benefits of CMH counseling include a reduction in health and health care disparities, most of which have a disproportionately negative impact on racial/ethnic minorities. These potential benefits, in turn, have great potential for improving the health status of all Americans, and thereby help reduce the escalating costs of health care that plague our nation.

REFERENCES

Agency for Healthcare Research and Quality. (2003). *National healthcare disparities report* (HHS Publication). Rockville, MD: Government Printing Office.

Agency for Healthcare Research and Quality. (2004). *National healthcare disparities report* (HHS Publication). Rockville, MD: Government Printing Office.

American Psychological Association. (2003). Guidelines on multicultural education, training, research, practice, and organizational change for psychologists. *American Psychologist, 58,* 377–402.

Anderson, G. F. (1998). *Multinational comparisons of health care: Expenditures, coverage, and outcomes* [Report]. New York: Commonwealth Fund.

Beach, M. C., Saha, S., & Cooper, L. A. (2006). *Patient centeredness and cultural competence: Their relationship and role in healthcare quality* [Report]. New York: Commonwealth Fund.

Beck, R., Daughtridge, R., & Sloane, P. (2002). Physician-patient communication and outcomes: A systematic review. *Journal of the American Board of Family Practice, 15,* 25–38.

Betancourt, J. R., Green, A. R., Carrillo, J. E., & Ananeh-Firempong, O. (2003). Defining cultural competence: A practical framework for addressing racial/ethnic disparities in health and health care. *Public Health Reports, 118,* 293–303.

Betancourt, J. R., Green, A. R., Carrillo, J. E., & Park, E. R. (2005). Cultural competence and health care disparities: Key perspectives and trends. *Health Affairs, 24*(2), 499–505.

Bloche, M. G. (2004). Race-based therapeutics. *New England Journal of Medicine, 351,* 2035–2037.

Borrayo, E. A., & Jenkins, S. R. (2003). Feeling frugal: Socioeconomic status, acculturation, and cultural health beliefs among women of Mexican descent. *Cultural Diversity and Ethnic Minority Psychology, 9*(2), 197–206.

Clark, R., Anderson, N. B., Clark, V. R., & Williams, D. R. (1999). Racism as a stressor for African Americans: A biopsychosocial model. *American Psychologist, 54,* 805–816.

Collins, F. S., Patrinos, A., Jordan, E., Chakravarti, A., Gesteland, R., & Walters, L. (2003). New goals for the U.S. Human Genome Project: 1998–2003. *Science, 282*(5389), 682–689.

Doty, M. M., & Holmgren, A. L. (2004). *Unequal access: Insurance instability among low-income workers and minorities* [Report]. New York: Commonwealth Fund.

Gornick, M. E., Eggers, P. W., Reilly, T. W., Mentnech, R. M., Fitterman, L. K., Kucken, L. E., & Vladeck, B. C. (1996). Effects of race and income on mortality and use of services among Medicare beneficiaries. *New England Journal of Medicine, 335,* 791–799.

Hoffman, C., Schoen, C., Rowland, D., & Davis, K. (2001). Gaps in health coverage among working-age Americans and the consequences. *Journal of Health Care for the Poor and Underserved, 12*(3), 272–289.

Huff, R. M. (1999). Cross cultural concepts of health and disease. In R. M. Huff & M. V. Kline (Eds.), *Promoting health in multicultural populations* (pp. 23–40). Thousand Oaks, CA: Sage.

Institute of Medicine, Board of Health Sciences Policy, Committee on Understanding and Eliminating Racial and Ethnic Disparities in Health Care. (2002). *Unequal treatment: Confronting racial and ethnic disparities in health care.* Washington, DC: National Academy of Science.

Johnson, K. W., Anderson, N. B., Bastida, B., Kramer, B. J., Williams, D., & Wong, M. (1995). Panel II: Macrosocial and environmental influences on minority health. *Health Psychology, 14,* 601–612.

Johnson, R. L., Roter, D., Powe, N. R., & Cooper, L. A. (2004). Patient race/ethnicity and quality of patient-physician communication during medical visits. *American Journal of Public Health, 94,* 2084–2090.

Klein, K., Glied, S., & Ferry, D. (2005, September). *Entrances and exits: Health insurance churning, 1998–2000* (Issue Brief No. 855). New York: Commonwealth Fund.

Kundhal, K. K., & Kundhal, P. S. (2003). Cultural diversity: An evolving challenge to physician-patient communication. *Medical Student Journal of the American Medical Assocation, 289,* 94.

Lin, K. (2001). Biological differences in depression and anxiety across races and ethnic groups. *Journal of Clinical Psychiatry, 62*(13), 13–19.

Lipkin, M., Putnam, S. M., & Lazare, A. (Eds.). (1995). *The medical interview: Clinical care, education, and research.* New York: Springer.

Meichenbaum, D. H. (1977). *Cognitive-behavior modification: An integrative approach.* New York: Plenum.

Michie, S., Miles, J., & Weinman, J. (2003). Patient-centeredness in chronic illness: What is it and does it matter? *Patient Education and Counseling, 51,* 197–206.

Molloy, B. L., & Herzberger, S. D. (2004). Body image and self-esteem: A comparison of African American and Caucasian women. *Sex Roles, 38*(7), 631–643.

Morrison, R. S., Wallenstein, S., Natale, D. K., Senzel, R. S., & Huang, L. L. (2000). We don't carry that: Failure of pharmacies in predominantly non-white neighborhoods to stock opioid analgesics. *New England Journal of Medicine, 342,* 1023–1026.

Ng, D. M., & Jeffery, R. W. (2003). Relationships between perceived stress and health behaviors in a sample of working adults. *Health Psychology, 22,* 638–642.

Paterson, B. (2001). Myth of empowerment in chronic illness. *Journal of Advanced Nursing, 34,* 574–581.

Robinson, A., & McGrail, M. R. (2004). Disclosure of CAM use to medical practitioners: A review of qualitative and quantitative studies. *Complementary Therapies in Medicine, 12,* 90–98.

Roysircar, G., Arredondo, P., Fuertes, J. N., Ponterotto, J. G., & Toporek, R. L. (2003). *Multicultural counseling competencies, 2003: Association for Multicultural Counseling and Development.* Alexandria, VA: American Counseling Association.

Sankar, P., Cho, M. K., Condit, C. M., Hunt, L. M., Koenig, B., Marshall, P., Lee, S. S., & Spicer, P. (2004). Genetic research and health disparities. *Journal of the American Medical Assocation, 291,* 2985–2989.

Satcher, D., & Pamies, R. J. (Eds.). (2006). *Multicultural medicine and health disparities.* New York: McGraw-Hill.

Shulman, K. A., Berlin, J. A., & Escarce, J. J. (1999). Race, sex, and physicians' referrals for cardiac catheterization. *New England Journal of Medicine, 341,* 286.

Solomon, B. B. (1976). *Black empowerment: Social work in oppressed communities.* New York: Community University Press.

Sue, D. W., Carter, R. T., Casas, J. M., Fouad, N. A., Ivey, A. E., Jensen, M., LaFromboise, T., Manese, J. E., Ponterotto, J. G., & Vazquez–Nutall, E. (1998). *Multicultural counseling competencies: Individual and organizational development.* Thousand Oaks, CA: Sage.

Tasaki, K., Maskarinec, G., Shumay, D. M., Tatsumura, Y., & Kakai, H. (2002). Communication between physicians and cancer patients about complementary and alternative medicine: Exploring patient perspectives. *Psycho-Oncology, 11,* 212–220.

Todd, K. H., Deaton, C., D'Adamo, A. P., & Goe, L. (2000). Ethnicity and analgesic practice. *Annals of Emergency Medicine, 35,* 11–16.

Tucker, C. M., Butler, A. M., Loyuk, I. S., Desmond, F. F., & Surrency, S. (in press). Predictors of a health promoting lifestyle and behaviors among low-income African American mothers and White mothers of chronically ill children. *Journal of the National Medical Association.*

Tucker, C. M., Herman, K. C., Ferdinand, L. A., Bailey, T. R., Lopez, T. M., & Beato, C. (2008). Providing patient-centered culturally sensitive health care: A formative model. *Counseling Psychologist, 35,* 679–705.

U.S. Department of Health and Human Services. (2008). *Healthy people 2010.* Retrieved June 1, 2008, from http://www.healthypeople.gov/

Youdelman, J. D., & Perkins, J. (2005). *Providing language services in small health care provider settings: Examples from the field.* Retrieved November 1, 2005, from http://www.cmwf.org/publications/publications_show .htm?doc_id=270667

41

Gender and Physical Health

A Lifespan Perspective on Women's Fertility

MERLE A. KEITEL, ERICA TENNENBAUM,
AND HEATHER CUNHA AMATO

Gender roles in the United States have shifted and blended over the past several decades, becoming less stringent and narrowly defined, yet gender stereotypes and expectations persist. Feminists encourage girls and women to be assertive, yet women who behave assertively are frequently mislabeled as aggressive.

> The cultural conception of womanhood is fraught with contradictions and impossibilities. The most obvious is the issue of body image, wherein the cultural ideal is unattainable for most women and is defined as directly contradictory to the bodily changes of female development from child to adult. (Compitello, 2003, p. 243)

The theme of physical transformation pervades the mythology and literature of virtually every human society. The physical alterations undergone by women during the life cycle provide especially compelling imagery—growth of breasts and widening of the hips at puberty, swelling of the breasts and abdomen during pregnancy, the act of giving birth, and the cessation of the menses during menopause. These "are highly visceral and often visible events that announce themselves to . . . the external world in general" (Trad, 1990, pp. 341–342). As noted by the Boston Women's Health Collective (2005),

> For women, life can often seem like a beauty pageant. Throughout every phase of our lives, from childhood to maturity, our appearance is judged, critiqued, [and] compared to those of our peers, sisters, women in the media, or imaginary ideals. (p. 3)

Women's bodies fluctuate considerably through the lifespan, yet the media perpetuate a link between physical attractiveness and thinness. Not surprisingly, higher body mass index (BMI) has been associated with lower well-being in women but not in men in a large national nonclinical sample (Bookwala & Boyar, 2008). In comparison to men, women also have more anxiety about becoming overweight (Muth & Cash, 1997) and

517

may experience greater social stigma for being overweight (e.g., Chen & Brown, 2005). Yet the "thin ideal" is unrealistic for women, in general, and particularly for women during puberty, pregnancy, and menopause.

Gender expectations that encourage women to sacrifice their own self-care practices (e.g., exercise, relaxation, and good nutrition) to take care of others infringes upon time to maintain their own health. Women also face numerous barriers to accessing medical care, such as insufficient funds to pay for transportation to treatment facilities, being unable to take days off from work to attend medical appointments, and difficulties arranging child care coverage (Altmaier et al., 2003). Because women are overrepresented in lower socioeconomic status (SES) groups, they also face more exposure to health risks such as obesity, smoking, and alcohol consumption (Wise, Carmichael, Belar, Jordan, & Berlant, 2001) that affect their general and reproductive health. Another barrier to women's health is that, traditionally, health care providers have been men and clinical trials were almost exclusively conducted on men.

This chapter examines the interface of gender and health by focusing on puberty, pregnancy and childbirth, and menopause. Physicians tend to medicalize these normative transitions, and a broader conceptualization is clearly needed that incorporates not only biological factors but also psychological and sociocultural factors. Health issues are always embedded within the context of women's lives and roles. When health professionals ignore social and cultural contexts, and when they do not listen to their patients or take the time to answer their questions, treatment adherence suffers (e.g., Shearer & Evans, 2001). Thus, open communication between patients and doctors is critical not only for all women experiencing normative physical transitions, but especially for adolescents, who may feel embarrassed to share details about their pubertal experience.

PUBERTY, MENSTRUATION, AND SEXUALITY

Puberty

Puberty is often considered to mark the beginning of adolescence (e.g., Biro & Dorn, 2005; Diorio & Munro, 2003). However, it is a complex process that actually begins prenatally (Boxer, Tobin-Richards, &

Petersen, 2001). The pubertal process lasts about 4 years and begins and ends about 2 years earlier for girls than for boys. Although the visible physical changes are most evident during adolescence, the underlying hormonal process that sets puberty into motion starts much earlier, at approximately age 7 (Boxer et al., 2001). The rate of bodily change that occurs during puberty is second only to the rate of growth during infancy. However, unlike an infant, an adolescent has developed a consciousness through which the striking changes of puberty are experienced (Boxer et al., 2001). There is a complex interplay among the biological, social, and psychological domains of development during puberty.

Puberty is marked by the development of secondary sex characteristics, such as body hair and breasts (Biro & Dorn, 2005), increases in total body fat, and height. The reaching of the essential "metabolic level," or fat/lean ratio, heralds the start of puberty in boys and girls (Boxer et al., 2001). Relatively late in puberty, adolescent girls experience menarche, or the onset of menstruation. This event has long been used as a marker of puberty onset because it occurs suddenly; is easy to measure by self-report (Blumstein Posner, 2006); and is a biologically, culturally, and psychologically significant event in a young woman's life. In many cultures, menarche signifies the transition from childhood to womanhood (Rembeck, Moller, & Gunnarsson, 2006). In the majority of non-Western cultures, it is often recognized with special rituals (Rembeck et al., 2006); in most Western societies, however, menarche is treated with "hygienic silence," which contributes to shame and stigma (e.g., Rembeck et al., 2006).

This hygienic silence seems to have religious roots. The Old Testament, Leviticus 15:19–33, emphasizes a woman's uncleanliness and the negative consequences of touching anything "soiled" by a menstruating woman (Petro Harper, 2004).

> Anything that she lies on during her impurity shall be unclean; and anything that she sits on shall be unclean. . . . And if a man lies with her, her impurity is communicated to him; he shall be unclean seven days; and any bedding on which he lies shall become unclean. (Plaut, Bamberger, & Hallo, 1981, p. 853)

Thus, in Judaism, Orthodox Jews follow niddah, a ritual exclusion for 7 days following the end of menstruation where a woman remains separate from her husband and checks for traces of blood daily (Petro Harper, 2004). When bleeding ceases, she prepares to immerse herself in the mikvah, a ritual bath with a natural water source, to symbolically cleanse her body. Other religious traditions, such as Islam and Hinduism, also place restrictions on menstruating women (i.e., refraining from intercourse or participation in religious ceremonies).

Across numerous cultures, menstruation has negative connotations. A custom in modern American Jewish families, for example, is slapping a girl across the face when she has her first period. For many mothers and daughters today, this is a light tap on the cheek, and the origins of the tradition tend not to be questioned. However, the implications are negative, either indicating "slapping some sense" into a newly fertile girl or "awakening" a child into her role as a Jewish woman (Appel-Slingbaum, 2000).

In other societies, menarche is celebrated as a rite of passage. For instance, a Nayar girl of India is secluded and then visited by neighboring women, who dress her in new clothes, followed by a ceremonial bath with friends and a large feast (Petro Harper, 2004). In the Navajo Kinaalda 4-day ceremony for girls, menarche is a time of happiness and rejoicing. The Kinaalda is regarded as the most important "personality shaping" in a young girl's life and is believed to set her life on course (Markstrom & Iborra, 2003).

Pubertal timing, particularly timing of menarche, has received considerable focus over the past two decades (e.g., Blumstein Posner, 2006). Researchers have investigated whether girls are entering puberty at an earlier rate, and if so, why. Blumstein Posner found little support that menarche is occurring earlier for adolescent girls in industrialized countries. In fact, she reported that menarcheal age has remained constant over the past 50 years. Yet several other studies found that girls are experiencing menarche sooner and have implicated environmental stressors such as divorce, absence of a father, and interpersonal conflict (e.g., Hoier, 2003). Recent studies also have provided inconsistent results on racial and ethnic differences in the timing of menstruation. Some studies found that African American girls had an earlier onset of puberty than White girls (Obeidallah, Brennan, Brooks-Gunn, Kindlon, & Earls, 2000). However, other studies reported that Latinas reached menarche earlier than their White and African American peers (Chumlea et al., 2003). Numerous studies have connected low SES to early menarche (Blumstein Posner, 2006). One explanation is that lower SES individuals tend to have higher rates of obesity. Adolescents with a higher percentage of body fat are more likely to exhibit earlier maturation (e.g., Blumstein Posner, 2006). Further research is needed to determine the role that race, ethnicity, and SES play in potential timing differences.

Traditionally, early onset of puberty has been associated with negative consequences for girls, including difficulties relating socially, behavior problems, negative body image, disordered eating, substance abuse, earlier first sexual experiences, and sexual promiscuity (e.g., Blumstein Posner, 2006). Lanza and Collins (2002) found that girls who mature earlier were more likely than their peers to use alcohol, cigarettes, and marijuana in seventh and eighth grades. Although startling, these negative psychosocial effects do not necessarily last into later adulthood (Blumstein Posner, 2006).

Physical pubertal changes force a young woman to reassess her conception of her body and how this fits into her existing conception of herself (Graber & Sontag, 2006). Due to these dramatic transformations, and the fact that peer acceptance is often based on appearance, adolescent girls commonly experience a sense of dissatisfaction with their bodies (e.g., Rembeck et al., 2006). Appearance then not only becomes a marker of group identification and social status (Graber & Sontag, 2006), but affects potential romantic relationships and feelings of physical attractiveness, which directly relate to a girl's sense of her own sexuality.

Sexuality

Puberty and sexual development are, by definition, intertwined. However, sexuality is more than simply intercourse or sexual "risks"; rather, "it encompasses feelings about oneself, reappraisals of the self, attitudes, and behaviors" (Graber & Sontag, 2006, p. 24). In the Western world, societal anxiety about adolescent female sexuality has inhibited young women's abilities to positively consolidate their sexuality into their identities (Blumstein Posner, 2006).

Young women are receiving mixed cultural messages concerning their sexuality. In most Western cultures, the media bombard girls with images of sex. On the other hand, sex education classes have socialized children to view sex as a dangerous game (Blumstein Posner, 2006). Fear is provoked by discussion of sexually transmitted diseases, loss of educational opportunities, and the negative consequences of teenage pregnancy. Cultural norms have made it more difficult for young women, particularly minorities, to speak openly and seek advice about their sexuality. For instance, Latinas were found to be less likely to discuss sexual topics with their mothers because of fears of punishment and false judgments (Guilamo-Ramos et al., 2006).

Fine and McClelland (2007) argued that contemporary public policies considerably limit young women's access to information and health care regarding sexual behavior and sexual desire, reduce supports available to young women, and limit the professional license of educators and health workers. Although intended to "protect our youth," these policies negatively affect girls' sexual and reproductive lives. For example, in 12 states, sex under the age of 16, 17, or 18 is presumed illegal, regardless of consent or the age difference between the partners.

Implications for Counseling

Mental health professionals can help adolescent females discuss touchy topics such as gender identity, self-esteem, body image, pregnancy, and birth control. Puberty is a crucial time, and girls may experience excitement, confusion, and anxiety. Therapists who are aware of and sensitive to diverse cultural and/or religious beliefs can help girls understand the significant psychological and physical changes that occur in order to successfully integrate these changes into their identity. Individual and group counseling can help to validate girls' experiences of puberty and may expand their capacity to cope with changing bodies and roles.

PREGNANCY AND CHILDBIRTH

Pregnancy and childbirth are life-altering endeavors. Across races and religions, women who become pregnant get to witness their bodies' extraordinary ability to create, sustain, and ultimately birth another human being. Notwithstanding the wonder and joy, pregnancy also typically introduces stressors for a mother-to-be. More specifically, challenging issues regarding body image, sexuality, and identity often arise. Of course, timing and expectations contribute significantly to one's emotional and psychological outlook on pregnancy. Given the limited scope of this chapter, our focus is on planned and anticipated pregnancies.

Physical Changes and Body Image

Early in a woman's first trimester, her sense of herself as a mother is often strengthened by physical signs and symptoms (Cunha Amato, 2007). According to Eisenberg, Murkoff, and Hathaway (2002), the most typical visible signs of pregnancy are (a) amenorrhea (absence of menstruation), (b) morning sickness, (c) frequent urination/incontinence, (d) tender/swollen breasts, (e) darkening of areola (area around nipple) and elevation of tiny glands around nipple, (f) food cravings, and (g) fatigue/sleepiness. These bodily changes are perceived by some as exciting. Others experience them as a loss of control over their bodies and become anxious. In response to this anxiety, some women develop obsessive or compulsive behaviors in an attempt to have power over their external world because their internal world is, in a sense, on autopilot and out of their control. Similarly, visible evidence (i.e., sonogram) of a growing being within one's body can produce a range of emotions from elation to intrusion and even fear. Trad (1990) noted that among the psychological changes expectant women experience is the "initial relationship to the fetus as a foreign and threatening growth, and the eventual recognition that the fetus is evolving into an emergent and separate object" (p. 342).

Perhaps the most notable and inevitable change that an expectant mother faces is an enlarging uterus/abdomen. Research findings reveal relationships among greater weight, lower self-esteem, and depressive symptomatology (Cameron et al., 1996). As noted by the Boston Women's Health Collective (2005), "One could sadly joke that there are two kinds of women in the United States: those who are fat, and those who are afraid of becoming fat. Our self-worth is often tied to the numbers on the bathroom scale" (p. 13). Societal pressures to be thin contradict the weight gain that is essential to healthy fetal development. Indeed, pregnant women may experience their bulging bellies and expanding hips and breasts as simply getting fat. This perception may create emotional strain (Fairburn & Welch, 1990) and instigate prepartum dysphoria. Cultural differences exist, however, in how weight affects women's self-esteem. Specifically, African Americans are less vulnerable to the negative emotional effects of weight because of differing cultural expectations that affect self-judgments about weight status (Thompson, Altabe, Johnson, & Stormer, 1994). Certainly, such findings have implications for women's health care as concerns about weight gain may negatively affect prepartum health behavior, such as dieting or overexercising while pregnant. Moreover, the risk for developing prepartum dysphoria is clinically relevant as it may affect attitudes toward childbearing, and it has been moderately linked to postpartum depression (Nicolson, 1999).

During the last trimester, the emergence of varicose veins; hemorrhoids; indigestion/acid reflux/heartburn; leg cramps; lower back pain/sciatica; swelling of extremities (i.e., hands/fingers, ankles/feet); ligament stretching (e.g., symphysis pubis dysfunction); and Braxton Hicks contractions (Lees & McCartan, 2007) may compromise psychological well-being. The latter four symptoms can make regular daily activities such as walking and sitting difficult, and even painful. Although they may be suffering, some women minimize their physical discomfort or feel silenced by the cultural myth of the self-sacrificing pregnant woman.

Hormonal Changes and Sexuality

According to Lees and McCartan (2007), another significant, though not visible, change for pregnant women is increased production of progesterone and estrogen and the introduction of two new hormones: (a) human chorionic gonadotrophin and (b) human placental lactogen. Increased progesterone maintains one's pregnancy by relaxing certain muscles to prevent preterm labor, dilating blood vessels to lower blood pressure, slowing down the digestive system, and contributing to the preparation of the breasts for breast-feeding. Progesterone also alters mood, heightens body temperature, accelerates breathing rate (which may make it difficult to breathe), and triggers nausea. Estrogen also helps prepare a woman's body for pregnancy, childbirth, and postpartum nurturance by strengthening the womb wall to cope with powerful

contractions of labor, softening body tissues to allow the ligaments and joints to stretch, and stimulating a pregnant woman's nipples to facilitate the development of milk glands (Lees & McCartan, 2007). Elevated estrogen levels also are associated with irritability, mood swings, irrationality, weepiness, and other emotions ranging from fear and misgivings to joy and elation (Eisenberg et al., 2002).

Heightened hormonal activity increases blood flow to the genitals, which, for some women, increases sexual desire (Boston Women's Health Collective, 2005). However, increased desire may be tempered by fatigue, nausea, pain, fear, or discomfort with changing body size and self-image. The latter two factors may be exacerbated by a husband's/partner's rejecting reaction to engaging in sexual intimacies and/or intercourse. In accordance with Freud's "Madonna-Whore complex," the husband/partner of an expectant woman may begin to see his wife/partner as a mother figure—a Madonna figure—and thus no longer considers her a possible object of sexual attraction. As one might imagine, this perspective may instigate confusion and concern for women.

Sense of Identity/Self-Efficacy as a Mother

Women must find ways to redefine themselves, first as pregnant women, then as new mothers (Smith, 2004). This period of coming to view oneself as a mother-to-be and then a mother is a complicated process of personal reflection and integration, which entails far more than one's changing physical appearance. Typically, across cultures and races, girls are expected to nurture others, and, from early on, they imitate their mothers and grandmothers by playing house and baby-sitting. "These acts of nurturing and the identity of motherhood become part of the pictures women paint of themselves as they grow from childhood into adulthood" (Cunha Amato, 2007, p. 49). Although research has demonstrated that both socialization (Smith, 2004) and biological drives (Lerner, 2003) may contribute to the development of maternal identity, several studies suggest that sense of self as a mother is established during pregnancy (Leifer, 1980). Thus, it can be argued that during the transitional phase of pregnancy, a woman's identity forever changes from being an individual to being a prospective mother.

Supports—Prenatal Care and Childbirth Preparation

Monthly prenatal visits with a midwife or obstetrician can help to normalize experiences, concerns, and fears. Unfortunately, access to prenatal care is less available to lower SES women, who, given high correlations with poor nutrition, lack of support, and inadequate education about childbearing and childbirth (Goodman & Emory, 1992), are particularly in need of this care. Women, especially those in their first pregnancy, commonly fear pain and/or potential complications with either a vaginal birth or cesarean section. In addition to speaking candidly with a physician or midwife, a childbirth education class, which teaches women and their partners about the process of labor and delivery, can be very helpful. Furthermore, at the 4- to 6-week postpartum follow-up visit, it is important for the OB-GYN or midwife to discuss issues of diet, nutrition, exercise, sexuality, and contraception; assess postpartum depression symptoms; and refer to a mental health professional if indicated.

Baby Blues/Postpartum Depression and Counseling

Although becoming a mother is routinely expected to be a "happy event" (Nicolson, 1999, p. 162), numerous women become depressed in the first months following childbirth (Lee, 1997). Ultimately, Nicolson identified, from his qualitative study on 24 women, an important paradox. Women are happy to be mothers to their children, but unhappy at the losses that early motherhood inflicts upon their lives, including loss of or declines in autonomy and time, appearance, femininity, sexuality, and occupational identity. A recent qualitative study by Ruzza, Keitel, Balzano, and Forte (2008) suggested that first-time mothers after age 40 do not experience loss of autonomy or sadness regarding changes in appearance, femininity, or sexuality, but they did report other losses, such as the loss of the opportunity for their child to have a sibling and losses related to their aging parents. Most women experience some mood lability within the first few weeks of giving birth, commonly called "baby blues" (Boston Women's Health Collective, 2005). However, about 10%–15%

of women will suffer more severe and persistent depressive symptoms (i.e., postpartum depression). "The difference between postpartum depression and the baby blues is that postpartum depression often affects a woman's well-being and keeps her from functioning well for a longer period of time" (National Women's Health Information Center, 2005, p. 3). The most severe form of postpartum depression is postpartum psychosis, which occurs in only 1 or 2 out of every 1,000 births and typically appears in the first 6 weeks postpartum. According to the Office on Women's Health, symptoms may include delusions, hallucinations, sleep disturbances, and obsessive thoughts about the baby (National Women's Health Information Center, 2005).

Notwithstanding biological evidence that changing hormone levels can cause chemical changes in the brain that lead to depression, as well as the fact that depression is a hereditary illness that runs in some families (National Women's Health Information Center, 2005), social and relational elements may certainly elicit and/or contribute to a woman's postpartum depression. Such factors might include fatigue, increased demands (i.e., child care duties with no increase in support), and changes in relationship with partner/spouse as new parents face many lifestyle changes such as sleep deprivation and mastering infant caregiving tasks (Feeney, Hohaus, Noller, & Alexander, 2001). Finally, women's expectations of being a new mother commonly differ from the reality. Studies have found that when experiences of being a new mother were not as positive as expected, then marital satisfaction declined (Harwood, McLean, & Durkin, 2007).

Whether women are suffering from postpartum depression or simply struggling with the transition to motherhood, counseling may provide a safe space to process and cope with complicated and confusing emotions such as frustration, elation, pride, guilt, and despair. Because speaking negatively about the experience of being a new mother is taboo, talking to an objective and nonjudgmental mental health professional might provide a sense of security.

THE MENOPAUSAL TRANSITION

Menopause, the permanent cessation of menstrual periods, marks the end of a woman's reproductive years. Natural menopause occurs gradually over a 5- to 10-year period, usually between ages 45 and 55, but it can be triggered by surgery (e.g., hysterectomy), radiation, and/or chemotherapy (Northrup, 2001). Symptoms are typically more debilitating for women undergoing induced menopause. In the United States, the median age of menopause is 51 years (North American Menopause Society, 2007). The age at which a woman's mother had her last period is probably the best predictor of the age at which a woman reaches menopause; however, the nature of one's mother's experience of the menopausal transition is not predictive of her daughter's experience. According to the North American Menopause Society (2007), about 6,000 U.S. women reach menopause every day (almost 2 million per year).

As menopause approaches, menstrual periods typically become less regular. By the age of 40, a number of hormonal changes associated with perimenopause have already commenced. By age 44, many women have begun to experience periods that either increase or decrease in duration, intensity, and flow, and about 80% of women begin skipping periods altogether (Northrup, 2001). Hormonal changes include a decrease in progesterone and estrogen, and higher blood levels of androgens relative to estrogen (Robinson Kurpius & Foley Nicpon, 2003). Many women are confused about whether or not they are in the menopausal transition. Menopausal symptoms, a thorough physical examination, medical history, and blood tests to monitor hormone levels may help to clarify this, but hormone levels normally fluctuate, so blood tests alone cannot reliably confirm menopause.

It is important to note that findings across many nations indicate that the majority of women pass through the menopausal transition with relatively little or no discomfort (Lock, 1993). Obermeyer (2000) noted that despite this, menopausal women do report uncomfortable symptoms in nearly all societies that have investigated it. In the United States, between 80% and 85% of American menopausal women complain of unpleasant symptoms that in more than 50% of cases compromise women's quality of life (North American Menopause Society, 2000). Robinson Kurpius and Foley Nicpon (2003) report research that indicates that anxiety, depression, and low marital quality predict the report of menopausal symptoms. Menopause most

dramatically affects quality of life during the peri- and early postmenopausal stages (Dennerstein, 1996).

Women in perimenopause tend to report the following symptoms: decreased sex drive; irregular or otherwise abnormal periods (most often excessive vaginal bleeding); bloating; breast swelling and tenderness; mood swings; weight gain (particularly around the abdomen and hips); cold hands and feet; and headaches, especially premenstrually. Hot flashes may begin during perimenopause and continue after the last menstrual period. Reported symptoms for postmenopausal women include night sweats, heart palpitations, migraine headaches, vaginal dryness and/or painful intercourse, recurrent urinary tract infections, urinary stress incontinence, dry skin (particularly around the eyes), bone loss, insomnia, and fuzzy thinking. However, because menopause occurs at about the same time as other significant life events such as children leaving home, the birth of grandchildren, marital tensions, and the declining health or death of parents, it is difficult to determine whether these reported symptoms are biologically/hormonally based or a function of life stage. Generally, psychological health has been more associated with lifestyle variables and physical health status than the fluctuating hormone levels associated with menopause (Dennerstein, 1996). Menopause has been conceptualized as a medical issue, rather than a normative life transition that is a cause for celebration (e.g., no more bothersome menstrual cramps, bloating, premenstrual symptoms, need to purchase tampons or sanitary napkins, no need for birth control), and thus the adverse effects have been emphasized. It has been suggested by Matthews (1992) that the expectation that menopause is a negative experience has resulted in a self-fulfilling prophecy. Irritability, mood swings, and memory problems have been attributed to menopause, yet women at midlife have other stressors that are likely to result in these symptoms. It is possible that hot flashes (flushes) and night sweats might interfere with sleeping and that lack of sleep may cause irritability. One study by Thurston, Blumenthal, Babyak, and Sherwood (2006) showed, however, that self-reports of hot flashes did not correspond to objectively measured hot flashes, and it was the self-reports of hot flashes rather than actual hot flashes that were related to sleep problems. Insomnia in midlife may also be caused by anxiety and depression resulting not necessarily from the biological changes associated with menopause but by overload of demands, caring for children and elderly parents while working full-time, having the lion's share of responsibility for domestic tasks, and declining marital satisfaction.

Stress can also add to memory problems that midlife individuals experience but that women often attribute to perimenopause. It is estimated that 60% of women who experience the menopausal transition perceive themselves to have memory problems; however, a recent cross-sectional analysis of data from a study by Luetters et al. (2007) indicated that cognitive functioning was not related to menstrually defined menopause status or hormone levels. Women in midlife have so many commitments that it may be more difficult for them to remember things as well as they once did. To complicate matters further, we live in a youth-oriented culture in the United States, and midlife tends to bring weight gain and other signs of aging. Interest in sex is another area of contradictory findings. Whereas some women report an increase in libido related to freedom from concerns about pregnancy, others report losing interest in sex. This can be related to hormonal fluctuations, but may also be related to stress, fatigue, and relationship problems. Research is only beginning to tease out the biological, social, and psychological contributors to symptoms attributed to menopause.

Menopause Is Not a Universal Experience

Culture clearly influences how women respond to the menopausal transition. Hall, Callister, Berry, and Matsumura (2007) described differences among what they label traditional, immigrant, and modern cultures across many countries. Women in traditional cultures tend to raise large families and focus on child-rearing and domestic responsibilities. Hall et al. (2007) integrated the results of numerous qualitative studies and concluded that although many women had positive experiences as they progressed through menopause, ambivalent feelings were common. For example, menopausal women in Thailand speak of midlife as being both "natural and miserable." In Arabic, the term for menopause, *sinn al ya,* connotes a period of misery (Obermeyer, 2000). In countries where fertility and having large families are highly valued, rural women report that going through menopause instigates anxiety that their husbands might replace

them with younger women. The fear is magnified when women are dependent on their husbands for physical, financial, and social reasons (e.g., Aaron, Muliyil, & Abraham, 2002). In traditional societies that are male-dominated, few, if any, privileges are associated with menopause (Aaron et al., 2002). Women feel depressed about children leaving home because they no longer feel needed (Elliot, Berman, & Kim, 2002).

There is considerable variability in how modern women perceive menopause, from completely insignificant, to a nuisance, to a debilitating medical condition. Menopause and its attendant physical changes, as markers of women's aging, may be associated with low self-esteem and diminished self-worth, particularly for women for whom a youthful appearance was central to identity (Davis, 1997). On the other hand, some women embrace menopause as a time of freedom and the opportunity to embrace a new life where they can pursue their personal interests rather than sacrificing their own needs for the benefit of their families, and a time when they feel more comfortable in their own skin.

The SWAN study (Luetters et al., 2007) followed a multiethnic (non-Hispanic Caucasian, African American, Hispanic, Japanese American, and Chinese American) community sample of 16,000 American adult women ranging in age from 40–55 at the time of screening. After controlling for age, education, financial status, and health, Caucasian women were found to report more symptoms, particularly psychological symptoms (tension, depression, irritability, forgetfulness, and headaches). African American women reported more vasomotor symptoms and vaginal dryness but had more positive attitudes toward menopause than White women. Chinese American and Japanese American women reported the fewest symptoms overall. Interestingly, Japanese women living in Japan had fewer vasomotor symptoms than third-generation Japanese American women, suggesting that diet may be related to vasomotor symptoms. Clearly, cultural differences exist even within a country.

TREATMENTS

Menopausal Hormone Therapy

Menopausal hormone therapy (MHT) was formerly known as hormone replacement therapy until scientists noted that hormones, rather than being replaced, were balanced to create a particular hormonal climate. According to the National Institutes of Health (NIH, 2007), results from the Women's Health Initiative indicated that MHT does provide relief for women suffering from moderate to severe hot flashes, or vulvar and vaginal dryness or atrophy. It was also found that women on hormone therapy (HT) had fewer fractures. Unfortunately, treatment with estrogen plus progestin increased the risk of heart attack, stroke, blood clots, and breast cancer; offered no protection against mild cognitive impairment; and increased the risk of dementia (study included only women 65 and older). Taking estrogen alone led to increased risk of stroke and blood clots, uncertain effect for breast cancer, and no difference in risk for colorectal cancer or heart attack. Therefore, the NIH (2007) recommends that women follow the Food and Drug Administration's (FDA's) advice on hormone (estrogen alone or estrogen plus progestin) therapy. Although HT can prevent postmenopausal osteoporosis, it should be considered only for women at significant risk of osteoporosis who cannot take nonestrogen medications. If a woman decides to do HT, the FDA recommends that it be at the lowest doses for the shortest duration needed to achieve goals. Postmenopausal women who use or are considering HT should do a risk-benefit analysis and talk with their physicians.

Complementary Treatments

Many women are concerned about the potentially harmful effects of MHT, so more research needs to be conducted on nonpharmacological treatment of menopausal symptoms. Preliminary research has been conducted on exercise, yoga, meditation, cognitive- behavioral therapy, and dietary supplements.

Physical activity may reduce perceived severity of menopausal symptoms and increase feelings of well-being (Elavsky & McAuley, 2005). Women at all stages of menopause, particularly those who are sedentary, should be encouraged to exercise to prevent adverse symptoms of menopause, including vasomotor symptoms. Regular physical activity is associated with higher self-esteem and fewer menopausal complaints.

Yoga and walking programs (Elavsky & McAuley, 2005) and a mental silence form of meditation (Manocha, Semmar, & Black, 2007) have been found to modestly reduce vasomotor symptoms in menopausal women. According to the NIH, botanicals that contain or act like estrogens (e.g., soy and herbs, such as black cohosh) may effectively treat hot flashes. However, limited research has yielded conflicting results on the safety and effectiveness of these products. Some antidepressants, although not yet approved for the treatment of hot flashes, have been shown in clinical trials to be a moderately effective treatment. Lifestyle changes can offer some relief from hot flashes and other menopausal symptoms, especially those that are mild to moderate (e.g., dressing to avoid being too warm; reducing stress; avoiding spicy foods, alcohol, and caffeine; getting enough sleep; and being physically active).

CONCLUSION

Mental health professionals in training should be educated on the interface between physiological, sociocultural, and psychological issues across the lifespan so that they may more easily recognize and competently help female clients manage these normative transitions. Such training would promote greater empathy and thus allow for more open therapeutic relationships where girls and women would feel comfortable to introduce material they have perceived as taboo. It seems critical for mental health professionals to acknowledge and validate to clients the connection between psychological and biological issues and to translate intimidating medical terms into more understandable language. Additionally, by encouraging clients to discuss these topics in individual and group treatment, they may begin to feel more at ease talking to other women about their experiences.

Other ways to help reduce the sense of isolation and shame many girls and women feel during these transitions is to enhance public awareness. Through research and practice, mental health professionals can influence the media by encouraging the dissemination of more appropriate and realistic images and expectations of women. Furthermore, professional organizations such as the American Psychological Association, the American Psychiatric Association, and the American Counseling Association should create task forces to inform policy statements and encourage the conduct and presentation of research on women's health. Finally, because education related to psychological and physical development is imperative during adolescence, school counselors and psychologists can be instrumental in designing curricula and creating programs that promote insight and positive acceptance through open small group discussion rather than strictly through the provision of information.

In the United States, the overemphasis on youth, beauty, and thinness along with the medicalization of these transitions complicates and potentially harms women as they journey through puberty, pregnancy, and menopause. Unlike many non-Western cultures, American society fails to celebrate these beautiful milestones throughout a female's life. We hope that continued psychological research and education in areas of women's health will enable women to not only accept these changes, but also value and embrace these natural transitions.

A CASE STUDY

To help illustrate the physical and psychosocial issues attendant to puberty, pregnancy, and menopause, we created a fictional case that depicts primarily normative issues. Although all of the difficulties presented in the case may not occur for every woman, we hope that reading about one woman's experience of these life transitions will highlight and humanize the issues that typically emerge, and promote empathy for current and future clients.

Marissa's mother slapped her face and wished her "Mazel Tov" (congratulations/good luck), yet Marissa was in no mood to celebrate getting her period. She felt confused and overwhelmed by all the changes she was experiencing. Marissa, an 11-year-old Caucasian American Conservative Jewish adolescent, lives in an affluent suburban New York community with her parents and 15-year-old sister. She is the first of her friends to have visible signs of puberty, which has left her feeling bigger and less pretty, and thus insecure. In an attempt to keep her growing breasts from appearing so prominent, she has started to round her shoulders and to avoid boys, who try to snap her bra and tease her at school. This attention from boys was exciting, but also embarrassing, leaving her unsure of how to respond. Marissa wishes she could talk to her older sister about her feelings but does not think she would understand as

her sister is thin and popular, and has a boyfriend. She is hesitant to talk with friends because they do not seem to be experiencing the same changes. Consequently, she feels very alone.

After several weeks of missing gym, her teacher sent her to the school counselor, Ms. Devino. Marissa became tearful when the counselor asked why she was avoiding gym. She explained that she had had menstrual cramps, and felt very self-conscious undressing in front of her peers. Ms. Devino was empathic and reassured Marissa that even if she couldn't see the changes her friends were undergoing, they would soon be visible. She also let her know that the weight she had gained was an expected and healthy change for this stage of development. Marissa was relieved to have someone to talk to and felt less alone. Together, Marissa and Ms. Devino brainstormed strategies for increasing her comfort about participating in gym (e.g., using the bathroom stall to change) and decided to continue meeting weekly. Eventually, Marissa spoke to her friends and was surprised to learn they were jealous of her because they couldn't wait to get their periods and wear a bra.

Marissa graduated 15 years later with a master's degree in nutrition and started her career as a nutritionist and personal trainer. After working several years, she became pregnant and was delighted at the prospect of becoming a mother. However, as the enormity of the situation began to sink in, she became terrified. For the first time in her life, she felt the responsibility of another human being whose physical and mental development was totally and utterly dependent on her. Marissa was also overwhelmed by the rapid and uncontrollable physical and emotional changes she was experiencing. These changes reminded her of the insecure feelings she had as an adolescent. In an effort to maintain a sense of control, Marissa became regimented about what she would eat and drink. As the weeks passed, Marissa's husband worried about her increasingly obsessive behaviors and, although she always spoke about them as nutritional choices for the baby, he felt she was also being weight conscious. Truthfully, after years of discipline, Marissa was proud of her body and was scared that the pregnancy would make her unattractive. Additional concerns about weight gain came from her work. As a nutritionist and personal trainer, her appearance was important.

Although rationally she knew she was pregnant and not just fat, she felt self-conscious about clients' first impressions of her. Moreover, as her pregnancy progressed, she could no longer demonstrate certain exercises because of their position or intensity. Finally, Marissa worried about her job security at the gym because the paid maternity leave was only 8 weeks. Would she be physically ready to return to work after only 8 weeks? These worries about work contributed to some depressive symptoms that persisted through her pregnancy. Finally, as scheduled, Marissa delivered a healthy baby girl, Rachel.

Three years later, she gave birth to a son, Adam. Adam was colicky as a baby, and Marissa experienced him as far more challenging than Rachel, so her mother came for a week to help. The day before her mother left, she was carrying her baby past the top of the stairs when she had an incredible urge to throw him down. She carried Adam to his room and sat on the bed, shaken and crying. She was appalled that she could have such an awful thought. It occurred to her to ask her mother to stay, but simply could not bring herself to disclose her awful thought or the fear it had instilled in her. To others, it appeared as though she was beginning to manage and her physical recovery was seemingly complete, yet she felt totally incompetent and ill-prepared.

As Adam's crying persisted, so did thoughts of harming him. After several weeks, perhaps due to the sleep deprivation, Marissa began having what seemed to be auditory hallucinations. She would hear babies crying all the time. Thinking Adam was again wailing, she would run upstairs to check on him, only to find him sleeping soundly. After this occurred repeatedly, Marissa finally confided in her husband. He minimized her experience and suggested she try to nap more, which was impossible given her daily routine of cooing at Adam, playing with Rachel, changing diapers, and doing laundry. Although she kept up appearances, Marissa felt increasingly surprised that no one noticed that she was quietly disappearing.

Marissa's breaking point came 10 weeks after Adam was born when she placed a screaming Adam in his crib, Rachel in front of a video, went out to her garage, and started her car. Sobbing, Marissa called her husband at work and announced that she was leaving. Hearing her desperation, her husband immediately

returned home. Marissa shared with him the full extent of her depression, and together, they determined that Marissa needed help with child care and treatment by a psychologist specializing in postpartum depression.

After 6 weeks of individual weekly treatment, Marissa was referred to a postpartum counseling group. Here she experienced the kind of healing that comes from knowing "you are not alone." In fact, when she first heard the universal message of Postpartum Support International—"You are not alone. You are not to blame. You will be well. Your experience is real."—she cried tears of relief.

Fast forward, many years later, Marissa is 48, her 19-year-old daughter Rachel is living away at college, and her son Adam, a junior in high school, is 16. Although employed as a nutritionist, she was also responsible for the great majority of housework and child care responsibilities. It was difficult to balance work and family, and Marissa often felt guilty that she wasn't doing either well. Personal time, such as exercise and relaxation, was not prioritized. To be the ideal mother, wife, and employee, Marissa thought she had to put everyone's needs ahead of hers. Rather than asserting herself with her boss to reduce her hours or to obtain more help with domestic responsibilities, Marissa pushed herself to meet her own unrealistic expectations. Now that her children were grown, Marissa had time to reflect on her life. She and her husband had grown distant over the years as Marissa buried her resentments regarding her husband's lack of participation in family life. He frequently traveled for business, and even when he was home, he was immersed in his work. She felt taken advantage of and unappreciated. She had virtually no interest in sex and was self-conscious about the weight she had gained around her middle. She sought counseling for this resurgence of depressive symptoms.

Fortunately, the counselor who saw Marissa did a thorough biopsychosocial assessment. Was she still menstruating? If so, were her periods regular? How was she eating, sleeping? What medications, if any, was she taking? When was her last annual physical or visit to a gynecologist? It turns out that Marissa was in perimenopause. She reported waking up from hot flashes and mild night sweats and then found it difficult to resume sleep. As a consequence, she was tired and irritable, which also negatively affected her relationships with her husband and son. On top of everything,

Marissa was shuttling her mother back and forth to the doctor. Marissa reported that yesterday she had spent a half hour looking for her glasses, and they were on top of her head. She feels like she needs to write everything down because she is so forgetful.

It is clear that many issues needed to be untangled to understand how much of her distress was biologically versus psychologically based. Was Marissa's lack of sexual desire related to her long-standing resentment of her husband? Were hormonal factors contributing to her decreased desire for sex? Were anxiety and depression solely contributing to the sleeping difficulties, or were her vasomotor symptoms significant to the problem? Were her reports of menopausal symptoms related to her anxiety, depression, and marital dissatisfaction? The counselor was able to normalize Marissa's concerns in terms of what was normative biologically, socially, and culturally. She encouraged Marissa to get back to a regular exercise routine and helped her realize that exercising with friends would give her some social time as well as the benefits of stress reduction and weight loss. With an exercise program in place, Marissa was given some strategies to help with the insomnia, such as using relaxation procedures when she awakened during the night to help her get back to sleep. Once Marissa felt more rested, they shifted attention to the marital relationship. Marissa confronted the difficulties in her relationship with her husband, and they began marriage counseling. The counselor explained that Marissa's forgetfulness was likely due to stress and anxiety rather than hormones. Cognitive therapy helped to decrease Marissa's quest for perfection, and through discussions with the counselor, she felt less compelled to please everyone in her life. This allowed her to say no to requests for her time. As she started "supporting her own magnificence," her husband began to appreciate her more and made concerted efforts to reduce his own workload and spend more time with her.

REFERENCES

Aaron, R., Muliyil, J., & Abraham, S. (2002). Medico-social dimensions of menopause: A cross sectional study from rural India. *National Medical Journal of India, 15,* 14–17.

Altmaier, E. M., Fraley, S. S., Homaifer, B. Y., Maloney, R., Rasheed, S., & Rippentrop, A. E. (2003). Health counseling: Assessment and intervention. In M. Kopala & M. Keitel (Eds.), *Handbook of counseling women* (pp. 323–344). Thousand Oaks, CA: Sage.

Appel-Slingbaum, C. (2000). The tradition of slapping our daughters. Retrieved February 18, 2008, from http://www.mum.org/slap.htm

Biro, F. M., & Dorn, L. D. (2005). Puberty and adolescent sexuality. *Pediatric Annals, 34,* 777–784.

Blumstein Posner, R. (2006). Early menarche: A review of research on trends in timing, racial differences, etiology and psychological consequences. *Sex Roles, 54,* 315–322.

Bookwala, J., & Boyar, J. (2008). Gender, excessive body weight, and psychological well-being in adulthood. *Psychology of Women Quarterly, 32,* 188–195.

Boston Women's Health Collective. (2005). *Our bodies, ourselves: A new edition for a new era.* New York: Simon & Schuster.

Boxer, A. M., Tobin-Richards, M., & Petersen, A. C. (2001). Puberty: Physical change and its significance in early adolescence. *Theory into Practice, 22,* 85–90.

Cameron, R., Grabill, C., Hobfoll, S., Crowther, J., Ritter, C., & Lavin, J. (1996). Weight, self-esteem, ethnicity, and depressive symptomatology during pregnancy among inner-city women. *Health Psychology, 15,* 293–297.

Chen, E. Y., & Brown, M. (2005). Obesity stigma in sexual relationships. *Obesity Research, 13,* 1393–1397.

Chumlea, W. C., Schubert, C. M., Roche, A. F., Kulin, H. E., Lee, P. A., Himes, J. H., & Sun, S. S. (2003). Age at menarche and racial comparisons in US girls. *Pediatrics, 111,* 110–113.

Compitello, V. (2003). Through the eye of the needle. In M. Kopala & M. Keitel (Eds.), *Handbook of counseling women* (pp. 243–255). Thousand Oaks, CA: Sage.

Cunha Amato, H. (2007). *A qualitative investigation of the psychological and emotional experiences of recurrent miscarriage.* Unpublished doctoral dissertation, Fordham University.

Davis, C. (1997). Body image, exercise, and eating behaviors. In K. R. Fox (Ed.), *The physical self: From motivation to well-being* (pp. 143–175). Champaign, IL: Human Kinetics.

Dennerstein, L. (1996). Well-being, symptoms, and the menopausal transition. *Maturitas, 23*(2), 147–157.

Diorio, J. A., & Munro, J. (2003). What does puberty mean to adolescents? Teaching and learning about bodily development. *Sex Education, 3,* 119–131.

Eisenberg, A., Murkoff, H. E., & Hathaway, S. E. (2002). *What to expect when you're expecting.* New York: Workman.

Elavsky, S., & McAuley, E. (2005). Physical activity, symptoms, esteem, and life satisfaction during menopause. *Maturitas, 52,* 374–385.

Elliot, J., Berman, H., & Kim, S. (2002). A critical ethnography of Korean Canadian women's menopause experience. *Health Care for Women International, 23,* 377–388.

Fairburn, C., & Welch, S. (1990). The impact of pregnancy on eating habits and attitudes to shape and weight. *International Journal of Eating Disorders, 9,* 153–160.

Feeney, J., Hohaus, R., Noller, P., & Alexander, L. (2001). Attachment, insecurity, depression, and the transition to parenthood. *Personal Relationships, 10,* 475–493.

Fine, M., & McClelland, S. (2007). The politics of teen women's sexuality: Public policy and the adolescent female body. *Emory Law Journal, 56,* 993–1038.

Goodman, S., & Emory, E. (1992). Perinatal complications in births to low socioecomomic status schizophrenic and depressed women. *Journal of Abnormal Psychology, 101,* 225–229.

Graber, J. A., & Sontag, L. M. (2006). Puberty and girls' sexuality: Why hormones are not the complete answers. *New Directions for Child and Adolescent Development, 112,* 23–38.

Guilamo-Ramos, V., Dittus, P., Jaccard, J., Goldberg, V., Casillas, E., & Bouris, A. (2006). The content and process of mother-adolescent communication about sex in Latino families. *Social Work Research, 30,* 169–181.

Hall, L., Callister, L. C., Berry, J. A., & Matsumura, G. (2007). Meanings of menopause: Cultural influences on perception and management of menopause. *Journal of Holistic Nursing, 25,* 106–118.

Harwood, K., McLean, N., & Durkin, K. (2007). First-time mothers' expectations of parenthood: What happens when optimistic expectations are not matched by later experiences. *Developmental Psychology, 43,* 1–12.

Hoier, S. (2003). Father absence and age at menarche: A test of evolutionary models. *Human Nature, 14,* 209–233.

Lanza, S. T., & Collins, L. M. (2002). Pubertal timing and the onset of substance use in females during early adolescence. *Prevention Science, 3,* 69–82.

Lee, C. (1997). Social context, depression and the transition to motherhood. *British Journal of Health Psychology, 2,* 93–108.

Lees, C., & McCartan, G. (2007). *Pregnancy & birth: Your questions answered.* New York: Dorling Kindersley.

Leifer, M. (1980). *Psychological effects of motherhood: A study of first pregnancy.* New York: Praeger.

Lerner, H. (2003). *Miscarriage: Why it happens and how best to reduce your risks—A doctor's guide to the facts.* Cambridge, MA: Perseus.

Lock, M. (1993). *Encounters with aging: Mythologies of menopause in Japan and North America.* Berkeley: University of California Press.

Luetters, C., Huang, M. H., Seeman, T., Buckwalter, G., Meyer, P. M., Avis, N. E., Sternfeld, B., Johnston, J. M., & Greendale, G. A. (2007). Menopause transition stage and endogenous estradiol and follicle-stimulating hormone levels are not related to cognitive performance: Cross-sectional results from the Study of Women's Health Across the Nation (SWAN). *Journal of Women's Health, 16,* 331–344.

Manocha, R., Semmar, B., & Black, D. (2007). A pilot study of a mental silence form of meditation for women in perimenopause. *Journal of Clinical Psychology in Medical Settings, 14,* 266–273.

Markstrom, C., & Iborra, A. (2003). Adolescent identity formation and rites of passage: The Navajo Kinaalda ceremony for girls. *Journal of Research on Adolescence, 13,* 399–425.

Matthews, K. A. (1992). Myths and realities of menopause. *Maturitas, 54,* 1–9.

Muth, J. L., & Cash, T. F. (1997). Body image attitudes: What difference does gender make? *Journal of Applied Social Psychology, 27,* 1438–1452.

National Institutes of Health. (2007). Menopausal hormone therapy information. Retrieved from http://www.nih.gov/PHTindex.htm

National Women's Health Information Center. (2005). *Depression during and after pregnancy.* Retrieved August 1, 2008, from http://www.womenshealth.gov/faq/depression-pregnancy.pdf

Nicolson, P. (1999). Loss, happiness, and postpartum depression: The ultimate paradox. *Canadian Psychology, 40,* 162–178.

North American Menopause Society. (2007). Terms and statistics. Retrieved from http://www.menopause.org/aboutmeno/overview.aspx

Northrup, C. (2001). *The wisdom of menopause.* New York: Bantam.

Obeidallah, D., Brennan, R., Brooks-Gunn, J., Kindlon, D., & Earls, F. (2000). Socioeconomic status, race, and girls' puberty maturation: Results from a project on human development in Chicago neighborhoods. *Journal of Research on Adolescence, 10,* 443–464.

Obermeyer, C. M. (2000). Menopause across cultures: A review of the evidence. *Menopause, 7,* 184–192.

Petro Harper, K. (2004, May 3). Menstruation, rites of passage, and culture. Retrieved February 18, 2008, from http://www.kathrynpetroharper.com/mindful/2004/05/03menstruation-rites-of-passage-and culture/

Plaut, W. G., Bamberger, B. J., & Hallo, W. W. (1981). *The Torah: A modern commentary.* New York: Union of American Hebrew Congregations.

Rembeck, G. I., Moller, M., & Gunnarsson, R. K. (2006). Attitudes and feelings towards menstruation and womanhood in girls at menarche. *Acta Pediatrica, 95,* 707–714.

Robinson Kurpius, S. E., & Foley Nicpon, M. (2003). Menopause and the lives of midlife women. In M. Kopala & M. Keitel (Eds.), *Handbook of counseling women* (pp. 269–276). Thousand Oaks, CA: Sage.

Ruzza, C., Keitel, M., Balzano, J., & Forte, G. (2008, August). *First-time motherhood after age forty: A phenomenological inquiry.* Poster presentation at the annual meeting of the American Psychological Association, Boston.

Shearer, H. M., & Evans, D. R. (2001). Adherence to health care. In S. S. Kazarian & D. R. Evans (Eds.), *Handbook of cultural health psychology* (pp. 115–138). New York: Academic Press.

Smith, M. (2004). Figures of speech: The rhetorical construction of pregnancy identification. *Dissertation Abstracts International Section A: Humanities & Social Sciences, 64*(10-A), 3538.

Thompson, J., Altabe, M., Johnson, S., & Stormer, S. (1994). Factor analysis of multiple measures of body image disturbance: Are we all measuring the same construct? *International Journal of Eating Disorders, 16,* 311–315.

Thurston, R. C., Blumenthal, J. A., Babyak, M. A., & Sherwood, A. (2006). Association between hot flashes, sleep complaints, and psychological functioning among healthy menopausal women. *International Journal of Behavioral Medicine, 13,* 163–172.

Trad, P. (1990). On becoming a mother: In the throes of developmental transformation. *Psychoanalytic Psychology, 7,* 341–361.

Wise, E. A., Carmichael, S. K., Belar, C. D., Jordan, C. B., & Berlant, N. E. (2001). Women's health: A cultural perspective. In S. S. Kazarian & D. R. Evans (Eds.), *Handbook of cultural health psychology* (pp. 445–473). New York: Academic Press.

42

Minority Stress and Health of Lesbian, Gay, and Bisexual Individuals

A Developmental-Contextual Perspective

ERIC C. CHEN, RYAN ANDROSIGLIO, AND VICKY NG

Despite significant progress in our understanding and support of lesbian, gay, and bisexual (LGB) individuals over the past several decades, the formation and integration of an LGB identity is a complex and often stressful process (DiPlacido, 1998; Maguen, Floyd, Bakeman, & Armistead, 2002). Unlike racial minority individuals who are raised in families and communities that are supportive of their minority identity, LGB individuals often struggle, silently and alone, to develop and integrate their gay identity. In the context of their sexual minority status, LGB individuals experience stigma, prejudice, and discrimination, which create a hostile and stressful social environment. The incongruence between their needs and the societal structures and environment results in minority stress, ranging from experiencing negative gay-relevant life events (e.g., loss of employment, home, custody of children) to more chronic daily hassles (e.g., hearing antigay jokes). Few

LGB persons are able to avoid the stress associated with their minority status; when they experience difficulties coping with greater psychological distress, a wide range of health problems may result (D'Augelli, 2002). Research has supported links between minority stress and mental health problems, depression, high-risk sexual behaviors among gay and bisexual men, excessive cigarette smoking, and heavy alcohol consumption among lesbian and bisexual women (cf. Grossman, 2006). There is also evidence, however, that LGB individuals demonstrate resilience to negative health outcomes despite—or because of—minority stress. Thus, it is important to examine the complex dynamics of the linkage between minority stress and health outcomes as well as the factors that affect these relations.

Despite the high rates of depression, anxiety, suicidality, and other behavioral problems documented among LGB individuals in general, and among LGB youth in particular (cf. D'Augelli, 2002; Luhtanen, 2003), many LGB individuals do not differ from heterosexuals in psychological adjustment (Gonsiorek, 1991). Evidently, resourceful LGB individuals learn to cope with high levels of minority stress remarkably well, whereas LGB individuals who have nonsupportive relationships *and* ingrained internalized homophobia perhaps are more likely to experience increases in psychosomatic problems. Counseling professionals working with LGB clients will benefit from a close examination of the linkage between stress and health problems across the lifespan that need to be considered in the design and delivery of prevention and intervention strategies.

In accordance with the purpose of the other chapters in this section, this chapter examines stress and coping among LGB individuals, mainly through the lens of a minority stress framework (cf. Meyer, 2003). Because of space constraints, we focus our discussion in this chapter mainly on LGB individuals as a group, over-looking within-group differences among them. Lesbians, bisexual persons, and gay men, for example, all have different abilities to pass as heterosexual, not to mention other dynamics, such as gender role expectation and differing social attitudes, which may influence their LGB identity development and coming-out process differently (Fassinger, 1995). Furthermore, to reduce overlap with a growing body of literature on counseling LGB individuals, particularly affirmative counseling approaches (cf. Chen, Stracuzzi, & Ruckdeschel, 2004; Crisp & McCave, 2007), we highlight the complex relationship between minority stress and health risks, offering broad counseling implications—rather than specific counseling intervention strategies—that are developmentally appropriate and relevant to the contextual circumstances.

The remainder of this chapter is comprised of three main sections. In the first section, we summarize the model of minority stress and coping as a framework for understanding the health risks of LGB individuals. The model describes stress processes, including the experience of prejudice events, expectations of rejection, hiding and concealing, internalized homophobia, and ameliorative coping processes. Next, specific impacts of minority stress on LGB individuals' health are highlighted in relation to three different life stages: adolescence, adulthood, and late adulthood. Presented in the final section are counseling

practice implications, accompanied by case illustrations. The chapter concludes with some closing comments.

MINORITY STRESS AND COPING

Minority Stress Model

Linking social identity theory, research on the mental health of LGB individuals, and the literature on stress and coping (cf. Lazarus & Folkman, 1984), Meyer's (2003) minority stress framework is useful for understanding the LGB experience and effects of minority stress within the context of strengths and vulnerabilities in the larger environment and in the individual.

The concept of minority stress should be distinguished from general stressors, which are commonly experienced by all individuals, such as job loss or death of a parent. LGB individuals experience additional and unique stressors because of their status as a social minority group, and as such, their minority stress tends to be chronic and socially based. In this view, minority stress results from stable, underlying social and cultural structures rather than specific individual events or conditions that characterize general stressors. According to Meyer (2003), LGB individuals' health problems are a function of an excess of social stressors related to stigma and prejudice. LGB individuals' minority status is inextricably linked to their sexual identity, which can be a source of stress related to their perception of themselves as a stigmatized and devalued social minority.

In Meyer's (2003) view, minority stressors can be described along the continuum from the distal, objective, or direct end to the proximal, subjective, or indirect end. Distal stressors tend to be less dependent on one's perception because individuals under similar circumstances will likely encounter similar adaptational demands. By contrast, stressors that are more proximal tend to be more closely linked to one's identity as lesbian, gay, or bisexual. A heterosexual teenager who is perceived by his peers as gay, for instance, will be as likely as a gay teenager to experience distal—but not proximal—minority stress as targets of their peers' prejudice toward LGB individuals.

As illustrated in Figure 42.1, the four main minority stressors relevant to LGB individuals, from the distal to the proximal, are (a) external, objective, antigay

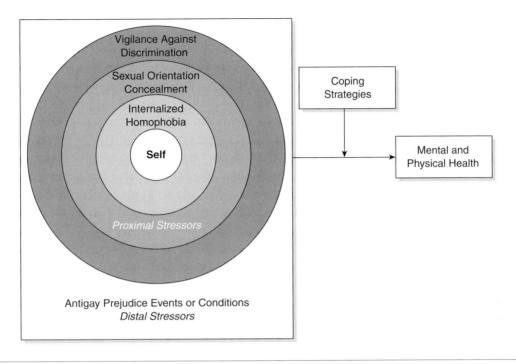

Figure 42.1 Minority Stressors, Coping Strategies, and Health

prejudice events or conditions; (b) vigilance as a defense against potential rejection and discrimination; (c) concealment of one's sexual orientation; and (d) internalized homophobia.

External, Objective, Antigay Prejudice Events or Conditions. It has been well documented that LGB individuals observe or encounter various forms of antigay violence and discrimination on the basis of their sexual orientation. In addition to acute prejudice events, such as harassment, loss of employment, or custody of children, LGB individuals may experience stress more commonly in relation to chronic daily hassles such as hearing antigay jokes. The powerful cumulative impact of such external social conditions and structures on LGB individuals is evidenced in that LGB youths are even more likely than adults to be victimized by antigay prejudice events, thus increasing their health problems. Few LGB individuals are able to fully avoid the stress resulting from antigay prejudice events and conditions, but they make decisions to minimize their stress, such as changing jobs, or keeping an LGB sexual orientation a secret, for example.

Vigilance as a Defense Against Potential Rejection and Discrimination. In response to antigay prejudice events, observed or experienced, LGB individuals perceive themselves as a stigmatized and unvalued social minority group. They maintain vigilance as a self-protective strategy in their interactions with others to anticipate, avoid, and reduce the likelihood of violence or rejection. The necessary degree of vigilance and, by extension, the stress level vary depending on the context (e.g., work, family, school) and the likelihood of negative rejection. For LGB youths, for instance, such experiences of rejection and victimization may occur from the friends and family to whom they turn for support and acceptance. Not only do they learn from these experiences of rejection to have to constantly monitor the degree of potential rejection from others in future social situations, they also need to prepare their own emotional responses and cope with the consequences accordingly.

Concealment of One's Sexual Orientation. For LGB individuals, it is stressful to constantly evaluate the implications of hiding a concealable social stigma attached to their sexual orientation. The issue of concealment of sexual orientation is linked to the aforementioned stressors and involves a continuous decision-making process of whether, who, when, and how to disclose in each social situation. When LGB individuals conceal their sexual orientation, their social stigma is more invisible. As such, the external stressor of negative life events or chronic hassles may be less relevant because others do not know their sexual orientation. On the other hand, they may experience additional stress of increasing their vigilance to keep their sexual orientation a secret. In their constant effort to conceal from others their own sexual orientation, they also perpetuate antigay attitudes in themselves and further deepen their internalized homophobia. A positive LGB identity will become increasingly difficult to form.

By contrast, when LGB individuals are open about their sexual orientation, their minority status is more visible to others, thus increasing their risk of experiencing a greater number of antigay life events and hassles. They may also experience the additional stress of vigilance as a defense against potential rejection and discrimination. In being open to others about their sexual orientation, however, they assert themselves as equal members of society, shifting from the role of victims to the role of resilient actors. Their gay-affirmative stance also facilitates development of a positive LGB identity, gradually reducing the stress of internalized homophobia.

Internalized Homophobia. Internalized homophobia is a proximal stressor for LGB persons that manifests as a result of internalization of negative feelings and attitudes toward homosexuality. These antigay societal attitudes are incorporated in childhood into LGB individuals' self-concept, representing chronic strains that contribute to self-doubt or, worse, self-hatred. Increased levels of internalized homophobia make it difficult to form a positive LGB identity, and as such, some LGB individuals may engage in self-destructive behaviors that threaten their well-being.

Minority Stress and Coping Strategies

Although Meyer (2003) suggests a distal-proximal distinction among the minority stressors, he notes that the distinction between subjective and objective conceptualization of stress is often blurred because of the important role of cognitive appraisal in the stress and coping linkage (Lazarus & Folkman, 1984). In response to a stressful event or situation, individuals' coping strategies will vary depending on their appraisal of the nature of the stressor (chronic or situational) as well as the extent to which the stressor is believed to surpass their personal capabilities. When the stressor is perceived as chronic or as surpassing personal capabilities, *problem-focused coping* efforts are used to directly address the problem by eliminating the stressor. By contrast, when faced with stressful events perceived as situational, individuals may resort to *emotion-focused coping* (e.g., social support, blaming others) to lessen emotional distress or to *avoidance coping* strategies (e.g., delayed confrontation, withdrawal) to evade the stressor.

Although minority stress could potentially lead to negative health outcomes among members of sexual minorities, resourceful LGB individuals learn to use effective coping strategies in response to high levels of minority stress. For LGB youths in a school environment where they experience daily hassles of antigay attitudes, their use of avoidance coping (e.g., concealing their sexual orientation) or emotion-focused coping (e.g., participating in a support group for LGB students) or both depends, to a large extent, on their perceived level of support from teachers and parents. In response to the stressor of an antigay work environment, LGB adults may decide to employ problem-focused coping, such as lodging a complaint with the management. Alternatively, they may decide to minimize their stress through avoidance coping, such as changing workplaces, or keeping their sexual orientation a secret through the use of various sexual identity management strategies. LGB teachers, for example, may engage in any of the four different types of strategies to manage their sexual identity in the work environment: *passing* (i.e., fabricating information so that they can be perceived as heterosexual), *covering* (i.e., censoring information or avoiding topics and situations that may result in being perceived as LGB individuals), *implicitly out* (i.e., being open about themselves but not explicitly labeling themselves as LGB), and *explicitly out* (i.e., being open about themselves and explicitly identifying to others as being LGB individuals) (Griffin, 1992).

In conclusion, the range and use of coping strategies will hinge upon the specific situational context, the meaning given to the event, as well as the LGB individual's assessment of his or her coping capacity. Because coping strategies are not mutually exclusive, problem-focused, emotion-focused, and avoidance coping strategies may be used simultaneously.

IMPACT OF MINORITY STRESS ON LGB INDIVIDUALS' HEALTH ACROSS THE LIFESPAN

LGB individuals, because of their sexual minority status, experience discrimination that is often accompanied by psychological distress. The combined effects of chronic stressful events, daily hassles, constant vigilance, and internalized homophobia may create intense mental and health risks for LGB individuals. LGB individuals who have difficulties dealing with their minority status are at even greater risk for developing health problems. In the spirit of facilitating an articulation of this risk, we focus now on the impact of minority stress on the health of those LGB individuals with nonsupportive relationships *and* ingrained internalized homophobia at three different life stages, with specific attention to factors that ameliorate stress and contribute to their health.

Adolescence

Adolescence and early adulthood are times of exploration, experimentation, instability, self-focus, discovery, and identity formation (Arnett, 2007). Many normative developmental challenges at this stage include, among others, maintaining a healthy social network, experiencing intimacy through personal relationships, managing school and work, negotiating autonomy within the family, and exploring ideas and feelings about sexuality. In addition to these challenges, many LGB youths first experience questions about their sexual orientation during their identity struggles in adolescence, which are often compounded by social isolation, such that they may be at greater risk for gay-related stressors than their older counterparts.

Depression. LGB youths are at an increased risk of being victims of harassment, abuse, and violence, because disclosure of their sexual orientation is often met with aggression, demoralization, and prejudice. To reduce the risk of harassment and violence at school, some LGB youths cope by trying to pass as heterosexual, cover aspects of their sexual identity, or "compartmentalize" their LGB identity separately from their heterosexual identity (Bohan, 1996). They also become increasingly vigilant to avoid becoming targets of antigay violence. For LGB youths experiencing victimization, symptoms of depression may emerge from a sense of helplessness coupled with anger toward the perpetrators as well as themselves (Williams, Connolly, Pepler, & Craig, 2005). Depression generally includes feelings such as hopelessness, irritability, loneliness, sluggishness, and sleep disturbances. Depression among adolescents in particular may also be characterized by aggression, antisocial behavior, school failure, anxiety, and poor peer relations (Yaylayan, Viesselman, Weller, & Weller, 1992). Environmental stressors that are uniquely present for LGB youths (e.g., loss of friendships, peer victimization, abuse at home or at school) increase the possibility of experiencing depressive symptoms (Martin & D'Augelli, 2003). LGB youths who have internalized homophobic attitudes and beliefs, for instance, may struggle with the development of a positive sense of LGB identity. These negative views about their sexual identity may turn inward toward their general sense of self and thus contribute to depressive symptoms, increasing their risk of suicide. Parents can play an important role in providing a supportive environment for their LGB children and help prevent negative outcomes. Parental support, acceptance, and protection have been demonstrated to be significant protective factors among LGB victims of abuse and harassment (D'Augelli, 2002).

From a minority stress perspective, concealing sexual orientation from friends and family members is one example of a proximal stressor. Depressive symptoms have been found to be more pronounced among LGB youths who report being less open about their sexual orientation, whereas those who are able to disclose their sexual orientation to others report fewer symptoms of depression (D'Augelli, 2002). The stress of negotiating dual identities as LGB and as heterosexual and the struggle to keep one identity hidden takes a toll on LGB youths' physical and mental health. Having to hide or split away from an undesirable aspect of one-self may lead to a more generalized negative view of the self and result in low self-esteem and depression.

Suicide. There is convincing evidence that LGB youths' risk for suicide is more than two times greater than their heterosexual counterparts (D'Augelli, Hershberger, & Pilkington, 2001; Kitts, 2005). The increased prevalence of suicidality among LGB youth is linked to the absence of coping skills and supportive relationships and to the presence of minority stress. In a meta-analysis of six studies examining precipitating factors among LGB youth who attempted suicide, Remafedi (1999) found that suicide attempts were associated with stressors spanning the range of distal (objective) to proximal (subjective) sources of minority stress. These stressors include school dropout, acquaintances' suicide attempts, homelessness, substance abuse, psychiatric disorders such as depression (objective events or conditions), victimization by peers, family problems (increasing vigilance for negative events), lack of social supports, early awareness of being gay (contributing to the internalization of negative societal attitudes), and gender nonconformity (impeding the concealment of sexual orientation). These findings highlight the importance of supportive relationships in helping LGB youths cope with stressors such as abuse and victimization, which increase the risk of suicide (Saewyc et al., 2006).

In a study on suicidality patterns and sexual orientation (D'Augelli et al., 2001) among 116 LGB youth who attempted suicide, 54% made their first attempt before coming out to others, 27% made the attempt during the same year they came out, and 19% made the attempt after coming out. Although LGB youths who conceal their sexual orientation attempt suicide more often, those who come out are not immune from suicide risk. It seems that stress from concealing one's sexual orientation and the fear of incurring the social consequence of coming out are significant precipitating factors. Many made suicide attempts during the year that they came out, perhaps because of acute repercussions from family, friends, and community members. For LGB youths who attempt suicide after being out for more than a year, perhaps distal and proximal stressors lead to feelings of hopelessness and resignation.

Whether or not a suicide attempt is made, coming out is a turbulent and potentially distressing transition for all LGB youths. During this developmental milestone, important sources of social support for the well-being and identity development of LGB youths include positive relationships with peers and adults (D'Augelli, 2002; Russell, Seif, & Truong, 2001).

Adulthood

Workplace Stress and Burnout. One particularly salient area of minority stress for LGB adults involves their vocational activities and work environment. Constant encounters of heterosexism or antigay attitudes and the pressure to conceal one's sexual orientation have been found to contribute to adverse physiological consequences for LGB workers, including headaches, ulcers, and feelings of chronic exhaustion (Waldo, 1999). For LGB workers, direct and indirect workplace discrimination is also a common experience. Direct discrimination in the workplace could include verbal and physical harassment, bullying, and unsafe or hostile work environments. Indirect discrimination is often more difficult to distinguish and could include being overlooked for career promotions, social exclusion by coworkers, and not being able to receive the same health benefits as heterosexual couples. Prolonged exposure to these kinds of working conditions, regardless of the type of occupation, can cause psychological distress, possible physical harm, and somatic symptoms such as fatigue and headaches.

Working in a heterosexist environment can also be a socially and relationally isolating experience for LGB workers, and can be considered a risk factor for minority stress. LGB individuals who experience internalized homophobia may not readily share their sexual orientation with others out of fear of discrimination or feelings of shame. Those who are constantly subjected to stigmatization because of their minority status may also be at increased risk for symptoms of physical distress, such as high blood pressure (Cochran & Mays, 2007; Waldo, 1999). For LGB workers, such stigmatization may impair their ability to form close relationships in the workplace, which can result in feelings of isolation, manifestation of depressive symptoms, and development of other negative physical symptoms.

Substance Abuse. Researchers have found that LGB individuals engage in recreational drug use, including drugs such as ecstasy and methamphetamine, at a higher rate than the general population (Green & Galatowitsch, 2006). One explanation for the higher rate of substance abuse in the LGB population is their experiences of minority stress, including rejection, low social support, stress related to leading a double life, and fear of HIV/AIDS (Ratner, 1993). LGB individuals experiencing pervasive feelings of shame and the difficulties of contending with discrimination and heterosexism may resort to drugs and alcohol as a maladaptive coping mechanism (Weber, 2008). Indeed, there is evidence that heavy drinking is associated with experience of antigay discrimination and harassment (Satre, 2006). LGB individuals with a negative LGB identity may also consume alcohol or drugs, legal or illegal, as a way to reduce their discomfort and inhibitions about sex or their fear about HIV/AIDS, which may inadvertently compromise their judgment about safe sex practices.

Another contributing factor is the availability of gay culture and LGB-friendly environments. In small towns, gay bars may be the only established meeting place for LGB individuals to socialize (Chernin & Johnson, 2003). When drinking, smoking, and other drug use are encouraged in the gay bars, LGB individuals may use substances as a result of experiences of peer pressure and as a way to conform to norms concerning drug use. Abstaining from the use of alcohol and drugs may then result in ostracism. Excessive dependence on bars as a social setting may contribute to the onset and maintenance of drug use. These drugs are not just limited to recreational drugs or "club drugs" such as ecstasy and crystal meth, which are increasingly popular in urban gay cultures, but can also include prescription drug abuse and steroid abuse in gay men. Given that physical attractiveness and appearance are highly valued among gay men, those who are concerned about or unsatisfied with their body image may use steroids to develop a more masculine physique. Such societal and peer group pressures and the experience of minority stressors can result in substance abuse among LGB individuals and should be recognized and explored as negative coping behaviors that adversely affect the health of LGB adults (Green & Galatowitsch, 2006; Weber, 2008).

HIV/AIDS. Another pressing concern of LGB adults is related to the effects of the HIV and AIDS epidemic. Following the AIDS crisis in the late 20th century, safe sex education in schools often implicitly links homosexuality with HIV and AIDS, further increasing stigma and stress among LGB individuals. HIV-positive LGB individuals, in addition to having to contend with their unique medical needs, must also deal with the stresses of their minority status even within the LGB community. HIV-positive gay men, for example, may be reluctant to disclose their HIV status to their sexual partner because of fear of rejection, thus perpetuating the HIV epidemic. Perceived instances of minority stress as a result of HIV status may lead to a decrease in quality of life and poorer physical health outcomes in LGB adults (Cochran & Mays, 2007).

Research suggests that positive attitudes toward homosexuality are related to more positive mental health for HIV-positive individuals, whereas having a negative outlook or hiding sexual orientation can result in higher levels of depression and hopelessness, and lower self esteem (Ironson et al., 2005). Gay and bisexual men with low self-esteem or who experience social isolation may not feel comfortable requesting that their sexual partners practice safe sex because of fear of rejection. HIV/AIDS continues to be a concern among LGB individuals and contributes to their experiences of minority stress. This stigma and stress can lead to negative health behaviors such as not engaging in safe sexual practice. Another potentially negative reaction to minority stress is the refusal to seek health care services until their illness has progressed to a severe or fatal stage, which can then lead to more severe health complications.

Late Adulthood

The effects of minority stress on health are often magnified among LGB adults as they age. The demands on LGB elders to cope with stress in relation to their sexual orientation continue as they enter late adulthood, and they face challenges and stigma attached to their double minority status because of heterosexism and ageism. Like other heterosexual elders, they also encounter ageism, and similar to their younger LGB cohorts, they also experience heterosexism. Differences between ageism and heterosexism need to be noted, however. No one attributes aging to individual choice, for example. The general public does not urge older adults to avoid acting old, whereas LGB individuals are likely to experience negative reactions when they express their romantic attractions in public. Equally important, evidence suggests that ageism in the LGB community may be more prevalent than in the general public (Kimmel, Rose, Orel, & Greene, 2006). As they experience physical changes of aging, older LGB adults, and gay men in particular, may have to confront prejudice and discrimination on both fronts: heterosexism and ageism in society at large as well as ageism in the LGB culture that values youth and physical attractiveness. Not surprisingly, they may find their needs unaddressed within the youth-oriented LGB community, further increasing their sense of marginalization and isolation.

For the current generation of LGB elders, the experience and impact of living with, surviving, and losing friends and partners to the AIDS crisis at its peak in the late 20th century cannot be underestimated. Many LGB adults were challenged to cope with repeated loss of individuals in their support network. Distressing as they may be, these experiences also provided opportunities to confront and prepare for death and dying—issues that often accompany the normal process of aging. They may thus develop a stronger support network and greater coping skills than heterosexuals as they grow older.

For other LGB elders, however, the experience of discrimination and stigma following the AIDS crisis may be more intensified, particularly when they continue to struggle with feelings such as survivor's guilt and negative attitudes toward themselves and other LGB individuals. With these feelings and internalized homophobia, LGB elders may be unwilling to engage in the larger LGB community, leading to an increasing sense of social isolation as they tackle the challenges associated with growing older.

In a survey of older LGB adults (Grossman, D'Augelli, & O'Connell, 2001), most participants reported excellent or good mental health, particularly among those who lived with a partner, had higher-than-average incomes, experienced limited lifetime victimization, and had social support networks. Furthermore, four out of five participants were found to have lower levels of internalized homophobia and a more positive LGB identity. Consistent with findings in other studies, Grossman et al. concluded that results suggest an overall mastery among LGB elders of the minority stress associated with their developmental years.

Given the diversity among LGB individuals, however, the stress and struggles of LGB elders with limited coping resources should not be minimized. In fact, the normal process of aging may leave some LGB elders increasingly vulnerable to the stressors of internalized homophobia and concealment of one's sexual orientation, leading to feelings of depression, suicidality, and maladaptive responses such as alcohol consumption. In contrast to contemporary cohorts, for instance, LGB individuals of prior generations historically had little or no support services in their struggles with stress and marginalization as a social minority. They also came of age at a time in society when heterosexism and homophobia were more overt and powerful than they are today. Partly due to experiences or expectations of antigay attitudes and discrimination, LGB elders, particularly when HIV-positive, may view health service providers with caution. Out of fear that they may receive poor quality care or treatment, they may cope with the stress of stigma by maintaining vigilance, concealing their sexual orientation to health professionals, or, worse, postponing their routine medical care visits. Each of these coping strategies may potentially compromise their health needs.

As LGB adults age, social support plays an increasingly vital role in mitigating the effects of minority stress on health, because they are more likely than their heterosexual counterparts to live alone (Grossman, 2006). Some LGB adults may experience alienation from their family of origin and, in response, build networks of close friends that act as substitutes for biological family relationships. Without active involvement and integration with the LGB community, LGB elders may experience an increasing sense of social isolation, particularly when they reside in geographically remote areas or are homebound because of their health.

Even when LGB individuals live with partners, they are not immune from minority stress. Retirement facilities and nursing homes may have institutional policies that are discriminatory and create additional minority stress. Romantic intimacy for same-sex couples, for example, becomes a source of stress for them not experienced by heterosexuals in society at large. Similarly, hospitals may have policies that limit visitation to blood relatives and exclude same-sex partners. When their partners die, LGB elders may experience "disenfranchised grief" (Blevins & Werth, 2006) as a result of societal denial of the right to mourn a same-sex relationship unrecognized by law. In addition to the lack of emotional recognition and validation of their loss, they face additional stress when they are denied insurance benefits and homestead survivorship rights as surviving same-sex partners. Evidently, addressing concerns and barriers, perceived or real, at the individual and structural levels for LGB elders in the use of health services remains an important priority for health professionals.

COUNSELING IMPLICATIONS

Counseling Practice Informed by Developmental Contextualism

Because minority stress and coping are highly individualized, mental health professionals need to attend to the developmental and contextual factors that affect the health of LGB clients. *Developmental contextualism* (Ford & Lerner, 1992) provides a useful framework for counselors in understanding the LGB individual through a lifespan conceptualization of human development, attention to relational and contextual factors, and a balanced view of strengths and risks. In this view, the individual's development is conceived as influenced on multiple levels by various systems and subsystems within one's environment, or context. Furthermore, the individual is viewed as an active agent of change who endeavors to influence the surrounding environment across time.

Developmental contextualism is consistent with Lazarus and Folkman's (1984) view of stress in relation to surrounding contexts where the effects of social structures on the individual depend largely on how they are experienced proximally, within the personal contexts of thought, feeling, and action. It is important for the counselor to understand the differences in developmental experiences among LGB individuals of different generations. A careful examination of their stressors and the complicated dynamics involved in managing their LGB identity within their environment is essential.

Contemporary LGB youths are aware of their same-sex attraction at earlier ages, have language to explore and affirm their identities, disclose their sexual orientation to others earlier, and find greater support from their families and from other LGB individuals of all ages in physical and digital environments. In contrast to LGB individuals of the current generations, LGB elders with internalized homophobia experience difficulties with their gay identity integration in a different and more complex manner than their younger counterparts. Having come of age against the backdrop of a powerfully heterosexist and homophobic social environment, older LGB adults' experience of stigma may be more intensified than that of their younger counterparts. In a similar vein, the intersection of social change and historical cohort suggests that future generations of LGB elders will have markedly different experiences of aging from those in the baby-boomer generation in the United States.

Within the counseling context, if LGB youths present stress related to the early stage of the coming-out process, for example, attention needs to be paid to whether they have the coping skills and resources necessary to negotiate the stresses in that process. A cost-benefit analysis of antecedents and consequents of self-disclosure of sexual orientation in their environment (e.g., schools, workplace) should be explored further.

Regardless of the developmental stage of LGB clients, counselors need to raise questions about their clients' level of internalized homophobia. Addressing barriers to identity integration, such as unrealistic fears regarding disclosure and negative perceptions of LGB individuals, may facilitate LGB identity integration and contribute to greater mental and physical health. Although supportive social interactions and involvement in the LGB community can reduce distress, prevention and interventions that focus exclusively on providing a supportive network may not be maximally beneficial for improving their well-being. Counselors can also work with clients in individual or group therapy to address issues of shame and internalized homophobia, on one hand, and facilitate their LGB identity development, on the other.

Counseling Practice Incorporating Social Justice

Because LGB individuals' minority stress is related to social mores and norms, helping the LGB client cope with external stressors is of limited value. Counselors have the responsibility to serve as agents of change by incorporating social justice-based perspectives in their work (e.g., Bell, 1997; Chen, in press; Vera & Speight, 2003), underscoring issues of equity and social responsibility. Because equity is often impeded by current social, systemic, and institutional practices, social justice perspectives seek to achieve structural transformation at a systemic level rather than limiting psychological interventions to the individual. In fact, when LGB clients' elevated level of distress and psychological maladjustment are in response to the larger context of social inequalities, prejudice, and discrimination, interventions at the individual level could unintentionally disempower LGB clients by locating and treating "pathology" within them and by excluding alternative treatments that address larger sociocultural realities.

Reflecting on their social justice work in counseling psychology, Goodman et al. (2004) offer recommendations that may offer implications for counseling practice incorporating social justice: ongoing self-examination, sharing power with underprivileged groups, giving voice to those who feel silenced, raising consciousness among clients and professionals, focusing on strengths instead of weaknesses, and leaving marginalized clients with tools. Giving voice to an invisible and devalued segment of our society is integral to achieving social justice, as it affirms their perspectives and sensitizes the general public to the needs of LGB individuals and the communities to which they belong. In a counseling group, for instance, the counselor's active attempts to elicit and validate LGB members' experiences are critical in helping them redefine themselves as individuals whose presence and participation in society is valued and respected.

A related component of social justice work is to build on individual strengths and develop coping strategies that promote self-determination and self-fulfillment, consistent with the hallmark of developmental contextualism. Specifically, counselors can help LGB clients identify themselves as resilient individuals with unique perspectives that can help them use their support systems to overcome individual difficulties and contribute to societal transformation.

A social justice perspective also challenges counselors to embrace the advocate role in their practice

(Atkinson, Thompson, & Grant, 1993). Specifically, efforts need to be directed at decreasing organizational tolerance of heterosexism and all forms of discrimination, subtle or direct, based on sexual orientation. When counselors serve as consultants to organizations regarding issues of workplace climate and policy issues for LGB workers, for instance, it is important to explore issues of organizational tolerance of heterosexism, experiences of heterosexism, and internalized homophobia. They may call attention to the following questions: Are there policies that prohibit discrimination based on sexual orientation, and, equally important, are there policies to address it when it occurs? Do workplaces support LGB employees in addressing health concerns through employee assistance programs, health insurance benefits, or support groups? Are policies in place to provide same-sex partner benefits? Counselors may also underscore the importance of increasing acceptance of LGB employees through organizational practices such as diversity training and welcoming same-sex partners at work-social functions. Because external variables can facilitate or inhibit LGB individuals' disclosure of their sexual orientation, counselors have the responsibility to effect change at schools, workplaces, and organizations to ensure that they are supporting LGB clients and, in turn, reducing health risks and enhancing their educational attainment or job satisfaction and organizational commitment.

CASE ILLUSTRATION

Case 1

Michael, white, aged 15, lives in a conservative, rural neighborhood in the Midwest with his family. Michael's parents are active members of their church. An only child, he is often alone and has trouble fitting in with his peers, especially other boys. He has witnessed other boys in school being bullied and called names like "faggot," and he is nervous around other students who he has heard use these words before.

Michael keeps his same-sex attractions a secret, except when he uses the family computer late at night to chat with other gay men. Recently, Michael has come to trust Jake, a man in his 30s with whom he has been chatting for a few weeks. Jake sent Michael an e-mail message inviting him to see his apartment. Michael went to Jake's apartment and, after drinking some beer, found himself being coerced to have unprotected sex with Jake. Confused yet curious, and wanting Jake to like him, Michael did not object. On his way home, Michael struggles with strong emotions of shame, guilt, hurt, and anger. Later that night, he takes a whole bottle of Vicodin, prescribed for his mother's back pain.

Discussion. Michael is faced with a number of interconnected psychosocial stressors from both his home and school environments. An assessment from a minority stress perspective further describes these stressors as ranging from distal to proximal. Some of Michael's distal stressors include homophobic teasing at school and perhaps a moral standard held by his religious community about LGB individuals. A natural reaction to being the target of or witnessing verbal or physical abuse is to become more vigilant in anticipating future abuse. Michael, aware of which classmates are most likely to ridicule him, either avoids contact with these students or carefully negotiates interactions with them to avoid incurring their contempt. Given his religious upbringing, Michael may also struggle with how he would be received by his church community if he discloses his sexual orientation. Internalizing the view that being LGB is inherently immoral or abnormal contributes to Michael's negative self-concept. Without an accepting community or sense of belonging, Michael turns to the Internet to learn more about himself and about other individuals like him. The betrayal Michael experiences when he was abused by Jake would likely deepen his negative view of self. These psychosocial stressors, coupled with Michael's own internal struggle of reconciling negative messages about being LGB from his church, school, or family lead to waves of strong emotions, particularly anger, desperation, and hopelessness, and ultimately, his suicide attempt.

In light of his minority stress, Michael has thus far employed emotion-focused and avoidance coping strategies. By concealing his sexual orientation, seeking support from other LGB individuals on the Internet, and avoiding conflicts at school, Michael has adapted to these stressors as well as could be expected, given his age and lack of support in his environment.

In working with Michael, the counselor needs to examine his stressors and also how Michael managed to negotiate the distal and proximal stressors in various contexts. His experimentation with various emotion-focused and avoidance coping strategies could be reframed as a sign of his strength and resiliency. Given the negative messages and attitudes from his environment that Michael may have internalized, helping Michael move toward an integrated identity that incorporates his religious beliefs and sexual orientation would include exploring and confronting negative perceptions that Michael has about LGB individuals.

A focus on the perceived contextual supports, or lack thereof, needs to balance individual differences and needs with the effects of environmental influences. Following Michael's suicide attempt, his parents are aware of his struggles with his sexual orientation. Assuming that family counseling is an option, the counselor needs to assist Michael's parents in extending and communicating their support to him. Equally important, in response to antigay messages and attitudes from others, his parents also need emotional support as they explore, experience, and cope with minority stress because of their status as parents of LGB individuals. His parents may struggle with conflicting, if not ambivalent, needs: to support Michael, on one hand, and to affirm their religious beliefs, on the other. As such, it may be more adaptive that the whole family does not disclose Michael's sexual orientation to others while they, individually and together, develop the necessary coping skills and emotional resources during the counseling process. In addition to personal counseling, an LGB support group would be beneficial for Michael because of the therapeutic value of universality and connection with others who share his struggles (Chen, Thombs, & Costa, 2003).

From a social justice perspective, the counselor can take initiative in educating Michael's parents and, further, advocating for LGB student issues to move the school community toward systemic change. In so doing, these efforts will likely reduce future suicide attempts by LGB students like Michael. As a school counselor, specific endeavors include providing sensitivity training workshops for school personnel to learn how to identify and intervene with antigay incidents, or facilitating gay-straight student groups to decrease homophobia at school.

Case 2

Tasha is a single, 30-year-old, black lesbian woman. She is an accomplished county prosecutor. Despite her impressive track record of success, however, she is increasingly frustrated that she has been passed over repeatedly for nomination to the position of Assistant District Attorney. She strongly believes in the importance of separating her personal life from her work, and few of her colleagues are aware of her sexual orientation. Tasha has recently entered into counseling following a referral by her primary care physician. She initially stated to her doctor that she was feeling generally fatigued and that she was having problems with insomnia, which she attributed to her current workplace situation. After completion of a thorough physical exam that did not yield any health concerns, her doctor suggested that she seek a counselor to discuss her workplace concerns.

In her initial counseling sessions, Tasha states that her career is her top priority, and she envisions herself being promoted to district attorney in a few years. In addition, she states that she is experiencing a great deal of stress at work lately after being assigned a new case in which the defendant, a 39-year-old man, Jake, was convicted in the statutory rape of a 15-year-old boy, who was hospitalized following a suicide attempt. As a lesbian woman herself—which she disclosed to the counselor with trepidation near the end of the second session—she has spent an enormous amount of time on this case and feels that it highlights the disparity in the types of social support networks available for LGB individuals of all ages. Her most recent romantic relationship ended 3 years ago when she was appointed county prosecutor, and she has dated only infrequently since that time. Tasha has been afraid to initiate any romantic relationships in recent years as she fears criticism from those in the LGB community for not being open about her sexual orientation. Recently, she has found herself consuming alcohol more heavily and more often than before. Although she has been able to recover from her binge drinking episodes with only small side effects, she is increasingly concerned about her drinking.

Discussion. Tasha seems to experience many of the health-related consequences of minority stress among LGB adults. These health concerns have a reciprocal effect on her psychological well-being in that she continues to feel fatigued. The stress she is experiencing in her workplace as a result of hiding her sexual orientation may be the precursor to her increased alcohol consumption, an indicator of a negative coping strategy. Additionally, her unsuccessful attempts to be promoted to Assistant District Attorney may cause her to further question her triple minority status as a woman, a lesbian, and a person of color.

In order to ameliorate the negative health symptoms Tasha has reported, it would be helpful for her to engage in counseling to express her feelings openly and to learn new coping strategies in response to her stress and workplace burnout. In working with Tasha, the counselor must explore the possibility that her negative physical symptoms may be outward manifestations of her inner turmoil. By making the important connection between her mental health and her physical health, Tasha would likely feel some relief from her physical symptoms and continue to explore other factors that contributed to her minority stress. In addressing Tasha's concerns of possible workplace discrimination, the counselor can role-play with her varying scenarios of approaching her supervisor to discuss her concerns. In so doing, she would be empowered to become her own advocate and to confront some of her fears of discrimination.

In accordance with the social justice perspective, the counselor could assist Tasha in identifying her personal strengths as a way to enhance the therapeutic process and moderate her responses to her environmental stressors. In addition, she needs to be encouraged to act as an advocate for the LGB community in order to feel more connected to the LGB population. In so doing, she also uses her strengths to assist others who may be experiencing similar instances of minority stress.

CONCLUDING REMARKS

Since the beginning of the millennium, there has been growing recognition and legalization of same-sex partnerships both in the United States and abroad. Although the issue of same-sex partnerships has often generated intense debates, it also calls public attention to the needs and experiences of LGB couples by giving voice to an otherwise silent, invisible social minority group. If the broadening legal scope of marriage serves as a window into the future health of LGB individuals as a whole—as the American Psychiatric Association's (1973) depathologizing of homosexuality did several decades earlier in our society when homosexuality was perceived as abnormal by the general public—we as counseling professionals are uniformly optimistic about a future in which LGB clients' experience of minority stress will be greatly reduced and their health enhanced in response to the increasing acceptance of homosexuality as a normal sexual orientation, changing laws and social mores in the digital age.

REFERENCES

American Psychiatric Association. (1973). *Diagnostic and statistical manual of mental disorders* (2nd ed.). Washington, DC: Author.

Arnett, J. J. (2007). Suffering, selfish, slackers? Myths and reality about emerging adults. *Journal of Youth and Adolescence, 36,* 23–29.

Atkinson, D. R., Thompson, C. E., & Grant, S. K. (1993). A three-dimensional model for counseling racial/ethnic minorities. *Counseling Psychologist, 21,* 257–277.

Bell, L. A. (1997). Theoretical foundations for social justice education. In M. Adams, L. A. Bell, & P. Griffin (Eds.), *Teaching for diversity and social justice: A source book* (pp. 3–15). New York: Routledge.

Blevins, D., & Werth, J. L., Jr. (2006). End-of-life issues for LGBT older adults. In D. Kimmel, T. Rose, & S. David (Eds.), *Lesbian, gay, bisexual, and transgender aging: Research and clinical perspectives* (pp. 206–226). New York: Columbia University Press.

Bohan, J. S. (1996). *Psychology and sexual orientation: Coming to terms.* New York: Routledge.

Chen, E. C. (in press). Cultivating organizational culture and climate for social justice and empowerment. In M. G. Constantine (Ed.), *Social justice and empowerment initiatives in psychology and education.* New York: Wiley.

Chen, E. C., Stracuzzi, T. I., & Ruckdeschel, D. E. (2004). Affirmative counseling with gay men. In D. Atkinson & G. Hackett (Eds.), *Counseling diverse populations* (3rd ed., pp. 388–411). New York: McGraw-Hill.

Chen, E. C., Thombs, B., & Costa, C. (2003). Building connection through diversity in group counseling: A dialogical perspective. In D. B. Pope-Davis, H. L. K. Coleman, W. M. Liu, & R. L. Toporek (Eds.), *Handbook of multicultural competencies in counseling & psychology* (2nd ed., pp. 456–477). Thousand Oaks, CA: Sage.

Chernin, J. N., & Johnson, M. R. (2003). *Affirmative psychotherapy and counseling for lesbians and gay men.* Thousand Oaks, CA: Sage.

Cochran, S. D., & Mays, V. M. (2007). Physical health complaints among lesbians, gay men, and bisexual and homosexually experienced heterosexual individuals: Results from the California quality of life survey. *American Journal of Public Health, 97,* 2048–2055.

Crisp, C., & McCave, E. (2007). Gay affirmative practice: A model for social work practice with gay, lesbian, and bisexual youth. *Child & Adolescent Social Work Journal, 24,* 403–421.

D'Augelli, A. R. (2002). Mental health problems among lesbian, gay, and bisexual youths ages 14 to 21. *Clinical Child Psychology and Psychiatry, 7,* 433–456.

D'Augelli, A., Hershberger, S., & Pilkington, N. (2001). Suicidality patterns and sexual orientation-related factors among lesbian, gay, and bisexual youths. *Suicide and Life-Threatening Behavior, 31,* 250–264.

DiPlacido, J. (1998). Minority stress among lesbians, gay men, and bisexuals: A consequence of heterosexism, homophobia, and stigmatization. In G. M. Herek (Ed.), *Stigma and sexual orientation: Vol. 4. Understanding prejudice against lesbians, gay men, and bisexuals* (pp. 138–159). Thousand Oaks, CA: Sage.

Fassinger, R. E. (1995). From invisibility to integration: Lesbian identity in the workplace. *Career Development Quarterly, 44,* 148–167.

Ford, D. L., & Lerner, R. M. (1992). *Developmental contextual theory: An integrative approach.* Newbury Park, CA: Sage.

Gonsiorek, J. C. (1991). The empirical basis for the demise of the illness model of homosexuality. In J. C. Gonsiorek & J. D. Weinrich (Eds.), *Homosexuality: Research implications for public policy* (pp. 115–136). Newbury Park, CA: Sage.

Goodman, L. A., Liang, B., Helms, J. E., Latta, R. E., Sparks, E., & Weintraub, S. R. (2004). Training counseling psychologists as social justice agents: Feminist and multicultural principles in action. *Counseling Psychologist, 32,* 793–837.

Green, A. I., & Galatowitsch, P. (2006, August). *Crystal methamphetamine and sexual sociality in an urban gay subculture: An elective affinity.* Paper presented at the annual meeting of the American Sociological Association, Philadelphia.

Griffin, P. (1992). From hiding out to coming out: Empowering lesbian and gay educators. In K. M. Harbeck (Ed.), *Coming out of the classroom closet* (pp. 167–196). Binghamton, NY: Harrington Park Press.

Grossman, A. H. (2006). Physical and mental health of older lesbian, gay, and bisexual adults. In D. Kimmel, T. Rose, & S. David (Eds.), *Lesbian, gay, bisexual, and transgender aging: Research and clinical perspectives* (pp. 53–69). New York: Columbia University Press.

Grossman, A. H., D'Augelli, A. R., & O'Connell, T. S. (2001). Being lesbian, gay, bisexual, and 60 or older in North America. *Journal of Gay and Lesbian Social Services, 13,* 23–40.

Ironson, G., O'Cleirigh, C., Fletcher, M. A., Laurenceau, J. P., Balbin, E., Klimas, N., Schneiderman, N., & Solomon, G. (2005). Psychosocial factors predict CD4 and viral load change in men and women with human immunodeficiency virus in the era of highly active antiretroviral treatment. *Psychosomatic Medicine, 67,* 1013–1021.

Kimmel, D., Rose, T., Orel, N., & Greene, B. (2006). Historical context for research on lesbian, gay, bisexual, and transgender aging. In D. Kimmel, T. Rose, & S. David (Eds.), *Lesbian, gay, bisexual, and transgender aging: Research and clinical perspectives* (pp. 1–19). New York: Columbia University Press.

Kitts, R. L. (2005). Gay adolescents and suicide: Understanding the association. *Adolescence, 40,* 621–628.

Lazarus, R. S., & Folkman, S. (1984). *Stress, appraisal, and coping.* New York: Springer.

Luhtanen, R. K. (2003). Identity, stigma management, and well-being: A comparison of lesbians/bisexual women and gay/bisexual men. *Journal of Lesbian Studies, 7,* 85–100.

Maguen, S., Floyd, F. J., Bakeman, R., & Armistead, L. (2002). Developmental milestones and disclosure of sexual orientation among gay, lesbian, and bisexual youths. *Journal of Applied Developmental Psychology, 23,* 219–233.

Martin, J. I., & D'Augelli, A. (2003). How lonely are gay and lesbian youth? *Psychological Reports, 93,* 486.

Meyer, I. H. (2003). Prejudice, social stress, and mental health in lesbian, gay, and bisexual populations: Conceptual issues and research evidence. *Psychological Bulletin, 129,* 674–697.

Ratner, E. (1993). Treatment issues for chemically dependent lesbians and gay men. In L. Garnets & D. Kimmel (Eds.), *Psychological perspectives on lesbian and gay male experiences* (pp. 567–578). New York: Columbia University Press.

Remafedi, G. (1999). Sexual orientation and youth suicide. *Journal of the American Medical Association, 282,* 1291–1292.

Russell, S. T., Seif, H., & Truong, N. L. (2001). School outcomes of sexual minority youth in the United States: Evidence from a national study. *Journal of Adolescence, 24,* 11–27.

Saewyc, E. M., Skay, C. L., Pettingell, S. L., Reis, E. A., Bearinger, L., & Resnick, M. (2006). Hazards of stigma: The sexual and physical abuse of gay, lesbian, and bisexual adolescents in the United States and Canada. *Child Welfare, 85,* 195–213.

Satre, D. D. (2006). Use and misuse of alcohol and drugs. In D. Kimmel, T. Rose, & S. David (Eds.), *Lesbian, gay, bisexual, and transgender aging: Research and clinical perspectives* (pp. 131–151). New York: Columbia University Press.

Vera, E. M., & Speight, S. L. (2003). Multicultural competence, social justice, and counseling psychology: Expanding our roles. *Counseling Psychologist, 31,* 253–272.

Waldo, C. R. (1999). Working in a majority context: A structural model of heterosexism as a minority stress in the workplace. *Journal of Counseling Psychology, 46,* 218–232.

Weber, G. N. (2008). Using to numb the pain: Substance use and abuse among lesbian, gay and bisexual individuals. *Journal of Mental Health Counseling, 30,* 31–48.

Williams, T., Connolly, J., Pepler, D., & Craig, W. (2005). Peer victimization, social support, and psychosocial adjustment of sexual minority adolescents. *Journal of Youth and Adolescence, 34,* 471–482.

Yaylayan, S., Viesselman, J. O., Weller, E. B., & Weller, R. A. (1992). Depressive mood disorders in adolescents. *Adolescent Medicine, 3,* 41–50.

PART IX

Counselor Social Justice in Action: Lessons From the Field

The topic of social justice has risen to prominence in the counseling field, such that it now represents one of our defining identities distinguishing us from other mental health and psychology specialties. Thus, defining characteristics of the counseling profession could be said to include a normative, life-span developmental perspective; a psychoeducation and prevention focus; an integrated multicultural emphasis; a positive, strengths-based perspective; a focus on career and work as it relates to quality of life; and a commitment to social justice and advocacy. The ascendance of social justice to a primary position in our field is reflected in a major new handbook for social justice in counseling (Toporek, Gerstein, Fouad, Roysircar, & Israel, 2006).

This section includes five chapters on social justice that focus on K–12 schools, colleges and universities, and the larger community. In Chapter 43, Alan W. Burkard, Michael J. Martinez, and Casey A. Holtz highlight the relevance of the "academic achievement gap" in the larger discussion of social inequality. Social justice and equality throughout life begin with our children and our schools, and the role of school counselors is critical in closing the current achievement gap based on race, ethnicity, and socioeconomic status. The authors review the philosophical foundation of school counseling reform, and they outline specific and emerging issues for school counseling practice, including service

to all students, education and career planning, college readiness, English-language learners, school climate and safety, and multidisciplinary collaboration.

Chapter 44, co-authored by Roger L. Worthington, Jeni Hart, and Taleb S. Khairallah, focuses on the critical role that counselors can and should play as diversity change agents in higher education. The authors review numerous change agent roles that counselors can play in this regard: research, curriculum reform and teaching, and advocacy. Dr. Worthington and colleagues also review the impact of emerging national trends regarding efforts to diversify the campus, including the Chief Diversity Officer model, campus climate assessments, depolarizing the diversity discourse and the use of "difficult dialogue" paradigms, the impact of recent anti-affirmative action efforts and Supreme Court cases, and the impact of war and serving returning veterans on campus.

In Chapter 45, a faculty and student collaborative team of authors address responding to hate on a college campus. The author team was Charlene Alexander, a co-editor of this *Handbook,* Stefania Ægisdóttir, Lawrence H. Gerstein, Erin Snyder, Doris Kirkpatrick, Michael O'Heron, Elizabeth Sellers, Rebecca Hansen, Marlon Rollins, and Timothy Gordon. The chapter focuses on innovative multicultural interventions implemented at the authors' home institution, Ball State University. The authors review their "Stop Hate

Campaign," a rapid response to a hate incident on campus. Anchored in an established ecological model, the authors vividly describe the program and its impact. A second intervention described by the authors focused on responding to a request by the university president to examine bias issues occurring in the athletic department. This program involved a comprehensive and multifaceted climate assessment of the athletics department. Both programs/interventions described in this chapter can serve as exemplar models for other campuses.

Chapter 46 is co-authored by Michael D'Andrea and Judy Daniels, two visionary and career-long contributors to, and advocates for, social justice. Drs. D'Andrea and Daniels were among the first counselors to direct in-depth attention to issues of social justice, equity, racism, and unearned privilege. In this chapter, the authors highlight the link between psychosocial health and social justice, review and critique existing multicultural organizational development theories, and propose and demonstrate the application of their own thoughtfully integrated theory on social justice organizational development (SJOD). The chapter includes a comprehensive campus-based case study of the SJOD model.

Chapter 47, by Rebecca L. Toporek, Diane Dodge, Felicia Tripp, and Laura Alarcón, closes out this section of the *Handbook*. The authors focus on collaborative, community engagement social justice work. They highlight important roles for social justice-oriented counselors, namely those of clinician, consultant, advocate, and researcher. A major emphasis of the chapter is on describing a highly successful relationship between Seven Tepees, a youth program addressing social change, and San Francisco State University's Department of Counseling. As a result of their collaborative work, the authors review realizations and recommendations that emerged from their efforts. The chapter closes with critical implications for training counselors for social justice community engagement.

REFERENCE

Toporek, R. L., Gerstein, L. H., Fouad, N. A., Roysircar, G., & Israel, T. (Eds.). (2006). *Handbook of social justice in counseling psychology: Leadership, vision, and action.* Thousand Oaks, CA: Sage.

43

Closing the Achievement Gap

A Social Justice Imperative for School Counseling

ALAN W. BURKARD, MICHAEL J. MARTINEZ, AND CASEY A. HOLTZ

The current public scrutiny of our school systems is unprecedented. The educational reform movement, legislation action through the No Child Left Behind Act of 2001, educational research (Noguera, 2003; Portes, 2005), and commissioned reports (Kuh, Kinzie, Buckley, Bridges, & Hayek, 2006; National Commission on Excellence in Education, 1983) have made us abundantly aware that at least some of our children are unsuccessful in schools and that schools are failing many children. Perhaps a natural consequence of such attention is to look for which group or groups are to blame for academically unsuccessful students or the inadequacies of our schools, particularly our public schools. Interestingly, many would contend that we know how to teach children and to help them learn effectively (Darling-Hammond, 2000). So, why do we continue to have problems helping children achieve academically in school? Many believe that the current problems in education are due to social inequality (Noguera, 2003), which manifests as an *academic*

achievement gap. This gap in achievement is based on the unequal performance on academic achievement measures that occurs between students from various ethnic/racial and socioeconomic groups.

There is considerable evidence supporting the existence of social inequality in education and an achievement gap. Academic gaps between ethnic/racial and socioeconomic groups begin to emerge in elementary school, particularly in reading and math, and persist into middle and high school (Portes, 2005). Although African American, Hispanic, and Native American students have made significant gains in math and reading scores in recent years, these scores continue to lag significantly behind Asian American and White students (National Assessment of Educational Progress [NAEP], 2007). Furthermore, over the 16-year period from 1990 to 2005, grade point averages (GPAs) were significantly higher for Asian American and White students in comparison to African American and Hispanic students. Additionally, high school/GED completion rates are 94% and 90% for Asian Americans and Whites, respectively, but the rates drop to 81% for African Americans and 63% for Hispanics (NAEP, 2004). As a final example, drop-out rates for Hispanic students were 22.4% in 2005, whereas Whites were at 6% and African Americans were at 10.4% (NAEP, 2005). The evidence supporting the social inequalities among these aforementioned groups in our schools is compelling, and suggests that students of color and students from lower economic groups are not provided with adequate educational opportunities (Kuh et al., 2006; Lee, 2005), which may cause one to wonder how to intervene. The solution to closing the achievement gap will necessitate a systemic and collaborative effort by all educational professionals and stakeholders.

Many believe that school counselors are essential professionals in furthering efforts to close the achievement gap (Education Trust, 1997; Hart & Jacobi, 1992; House & Sears, 2002; Martin, 2002). School counselors have a systemic perspective of students and the school, and are the educational professionals best positioned to intervene on behalf of students when barriers to equity and access are present (Martin, 2002). Interestingly, critical reviews of school counseling practice (Education Trust, 1997; Hart & Jacobi, 1992; Rosenbaum, 1976) found that school counselors often were not using their training effectively to advocate for students, were unprepared to provide leadership related to closing the achievement gap, and often served as barriers to student access to relevant and rigorous coursework. Consequently, school counselors essentially helped to maintain the social inequities that were problematic in schools.

A few organizations have emerged to address these concerns and lead reform efforts of school counseling practice. Starting in 1996, the Education Trust embarked on the Transforming School Counseling Initiative to change school counselor preparation (Martin, 2002). The goal of this initiative was to position school counselors as integral educational leaders in school reform, with the long-term intention of closing the achievement gap, particularly for poor and ethnic minority students. In addition to the Education Trust initiatives, the American School Counselor Association (ASCA) published the *National Standards for School Counseling Programs* (Campbell & Dahir, 1997) and later the *ASCA National School Counseling Model* (ASCA, 2005). The

National Standards consist of content standards for students in the academic, career, and personal/social domains, and offer guidelines for the knowledge, skills, and attitudes that all students should acquire through participation in a school counseling program. To support school counselors in the implementation of these standards, the ASCA National School Counseling Model was published. This model provided a comprehensive framework that addressed the philosophical foundation of, delivery of school counseling services to, management of, and accountability-evaluation components of a school counseling program (Bowers, Hatch, & Schwallie-Giddis, 2001). This model was founded on the work of Gysbers and others (e.g., Gysbers & Henderson, 2000; Gysbers & Moore, 1981; Myrick, 1997) and philosophically aligns with the themes of social justice, leadership, collaboration, systemic change, data-driven practice, and advocacy for all students. Finally, the College Board recently formed the National Office of School Counselor Advocacy (NOSCA) to influence school counselor preparation regarding college readiness counseling. NOSCA focuses its efforts on preservice training of school counselors, research on college readiness, and legislative lobby efforts (Martin & Lee, 2007). Although each of the preceding organizations addresses different aspects of school counselor preparation and practice, they all share a common focus on encouraging leadership among school counselors with the intent of creating equal access to opportunities for all students. Closing the achievement gap, then, becomes a social justice imperative for all school counselors.

In this chapter, we are specifically concerned with the role of school counselors in addressing the achievement gap. As context, we focus first on the philosophical beliefs that serve as a foundation for school counselor training and practice. Next, we will concern ourselves with emerging issues affecting school counseling practice as well as training of school counselors. Finally, we will draw some conclusions about important future directions and points of collaboration.

PHILOSOPHICAL FOUNDATION OF SCHOOL COUNSELING REFORM

At the heart of school counseling reform that is focused on closing the achievement gap is a philosophical paradigm shift in school counseling practice. Although reform has resulted in several philosophical changes for school counselors, the following three beliefs are specifically important to addressing the achievement gap.

Equity and Access

If school counselors are to address student achievement gaps successfully, equity and access must become the goal of all school counseling programs (House & Martin, 1998). Perhaps at the foundation of this belief is the notion that all students can achieve at high levels and that the role of the school counselor is to ensure that all students have access to educational opportunities to support their potential (Hart & Jacobi, 1992). This social justice perspective suggests that school counselors must correct injustices in our schools by challenging biased school practices such as restricting access to advanced placement courses, placing the lowest performing students with the least skilled teachers, or offering little assistance to students and their parents regarding postsecondary planning. In addition to challenging biased and restrictive practices, school counselors can also increase equity and access by developing guidance curricula that empower students in the classroom (e.g., organizational skills, study skills, test-taking strategies, time management); educate students and their families about academic coursework that ensures that students are college ready (i.e., college awareness, college preparedness); and provide resources to students and their families that would support academic success at elementary, secondary, and postsecondary levels (House & Hayes, 2002; Lee, 2005). Thus, social advocacy becomes the cornerstone skill in ensuring that equity and access have been addressed adequately in our schools (Bailey, Getch, & Chen-Hayes, 2007).

Multicultural Competence

If school counselors are to address student concerns regarding equity and access, they must be culturally competent and provide culturally responsive school counseling services (Lee, 2001). In fact, ASCA (2004) adopted the following position statement on cultural diversity: "Professional school counselors have the skills necessary to collaborate with students, parents and school personnel to identify attitudes and policies that impede the learning process of culturally diverse students" (p. 1). Such a position illustrates the importance of cultural competence to school counseling. The first conceptualization of cultural competence was based on Sue et al.'s (1982) model of awareness, knowledge, and skills. Awareness refers to counselors' understanding of their worldview and the effect that their own cultural conditioning has on their attitudes, behaviors, and interactions with others. School counselors are also expected to be knowledgeable of their students' cultural worldviews and to develop skills that are appropriate for working with culturally diverse students. This original conceptualization of cultural competence served as the foundation for what later became the multicultural counseling competencies adopted by the Association of Multicultural Counseling and Development (Sue, Arredondo, & McDavis, 1992). School counselors use their cultural competencies to lead efforts in educating others on how social, cultural, and systemic barriers impede academic achievement, development, and advancement of marginalized groups (e.g., racial/ethnic minorities; low socioeconomic status students; lesbian/gay/bisexual/transgender students; students with disabilities) and use their skills to intervene on students' behalf (Hipilito-Delgado & Lee, 2007).

Systemic Perspective

Finally, a systemic approach to school counseling is important to attain long-term academic and personal success for all students (Behring, 2002). School counselors have to be mindful of the various interconnected systems (e.g., family, school, community) that influence all children's lives (Sink & Stroh, 2003). This perspective is especially important to many schools' mission of academic achievement and represents a commitment to ensuring that all children, regardless of socioeconomic status or race/ethnicity, have the opportunity to achieve (Lee, 2005). School counselors can align themselves with the newly transformed role of school counseling by becoming advocates and leaders for all students and their families (Bemak & Chung, 2005). For example, in addition to partnering with students, school counselors should align with parents to provide them with skills and knowledge on how to gain access to important resources (Bemak, 2000). School counselors are also in a position to build relationships with teachers (Amatea, Daniels, Bringman, & Vandiver, 2004), principals, and administrators who can assist in working toward social change and decreasing the achievement gap (Bemak, 2000; Lee, 2005), and also collaborate with community agencies that provide important services for children and families (Cox & Lee, 2007). By shifting to a more systemic approach, school counselors are able to be proactive and visible leaders in educational reform (e.g., decreasing the achievement gap) and thereby contribute to the central mission of schools (House & Hayes, 2002).

EMERGING ISSUES FOR SCHOOL COUNSELING PRACTICE

Based on the philosophical changes in school counseling, a new vision of school counseling practice is rapidly emerging in this country. This new perspective encourages school counselors to relinquish their roles as substitute teachers, schedule coordinators, record keepers, and psychotherapists within schools, and to develop roles as educational leaders, social advocates, prevention experts, counselors, collaborators, consultants, and evidence-based practitioners (ASCA, 2005). School counselors use these roles to develop a comprehensive program designed to provide services to *all students* (ASCA, 2005; Gysbers, 1997; Gysbers & Henderson, 2000). Furthermore, the comprehensive school counseling program is based on standards that address students' academic, career, and personal/socio-emotional needs (Campbell & Dahir, 1997), but fundamentally support academic success and student achievement. The attention to supporting student achievement brings into focus the achievement gap that exists for students of color and economically disadvantaged groups. The following discussion describes programmatic changes important to practicing school counselors and closing achievement gaps.

Service to All Students

Traditional models of school counseling have often emphasized duties, processes, or services—paradigms that Gysbers (1997) believes lead to poorly organized and ineffective services for students and their families. With these traditional models, school counselors often had little rationale or focus for their responsibilities, and consequently, it was exceedingly unclear if school counselors had any effect on student outcomes, particularly in academic achievement. Because of the lack of role clarity, school counselors were vulnerable to being assigned administrative duties that often had little or nothing in common with supporting student growth and development (ASCA, 2005; Burnham & Jackson, 2000; Scarborough, 2005). Under these traditional models, school counselors worked with relatively few students in the school. To address these concerns, theorists (Gysbers & Henderson, 2000; Myrick, 1997) encouraged school counselors to develop comprehensive school counseling programs (CSCPs) that are based upon prevention and standards (i.e., academic, career, personal/social-emotional) (Campbell & Dahir, 1997). CSCPs are designed to reach all students and increase accountability for student achievement outcomes. CSCPs are composed of four components: philosophical foundation, delivery system, management, and accountability (see ASCA, 2005, for a detailed description of each component). Contemporary school counselors, then, stand in sharp contrast to those school counselors who continue to operate as therapists in schools and often reach a minimal number of students. ASCA's (2005) National Model for School Counseling Programs stands as one prominent example of a CSCP, and an increasing number of state departments of education are endorsing comprehensive models for the school counselors in their state.

Emerging research on CSCPs is promising and provides some support for the claim that these programs do indeed increase student academic achievement (Lapan, Gysbers, & Petroski, 2003; Lapan, Gysbers, & Sun, 1997; Sink & Stroh, 2003). Operating on the premise and research that CSCPs support student academic achievement, these programs would appear to be an important social justice initiative that could hold promise for closing the achievement gap. Alarmingly, Lapan, Gysbers, Cook, Bragg, and Robbins (2006) found that schools with high percentages of students of color and economically disadvantaged students had fewer school counselors and had higher school counselor-to-student ratios than did schools with lower percentages of students of color and economically disadvantaged students. Additionally, in comparison to schools with lower percentages of students of color and economically disadvantaged students, schools with higher percentages of these student groups were less likely to have fully enacted CSCPs. The implications of this research are disturbing and suggest that students who are most in need of service are the least likely to have access to a school counselor or receive assistance through a fully developed school counseling program. These findings are not unlike prior research that indicated that students of color and economically disadvantaged students have difficulty accessing school counselors for assistance (Lee & Ekstrom, 1987). Given the positive outcomes for academic achievement when students experienced a CSCP, it is important that school counselors educate themselves about and seek to implement CSCPs in their schools.

Educational and Career Planning

An important component of the delivery system in a CSCP is educational and career planning. School counselors are positioned to significantly influence students' selection of academically rigorous programs that promote academic achievement, thus addressing the achievement gap. However, school counselors historically have acquired the administrative duty of scheduling student classes, a responsibility that many still have today (Perusse, Goodnough, Donegan, & Jones, 2004). This duty has little to do with academic and career planning, and has placed school counselors in the position of administrative gatekeepers for rigorous academic classes (Hart & Jacobi, 1992). As gatekeepers, school counselors became responsible for assisting students in the selection of their academic track. These decisions were often based on performance in classes and on standardized tests, and test performance determined whether students were encouraged to enroll in either a vocational/noncollege or a precollege track. Research on educational choice suggests that students and their families often made choices about academic tracks with little to no information about the potential implications of such a decision, and that a disproportionately large number of students of color and economically disadvantaged students were placed into noncollege tracks (Oakes & Lipton, 1990; Rosenbaum, 1976).

Consequently, students of color or economically disadvantaged students were not afforded the opportunity nor encouraged to take more rigorous classes. Interestingly, research indicates that rigorous academic course plans, particularly math classes, were better predictors of student success in college than high school rank, GPA, or background variables such as economic status or ethnicity/race (Adelman, 1999). Additionally, completion of math courses was found to be particularly important to postsecondary success for African American and Latina/o students along with those from lower socioeconomic groups. Trusty (2004) and Trusty and Niles (2003) also found a strong connection between students who took extensive math and science classes and postsecondary success. Furthermore, their research revealed the importance of school attendance, extracurricular involvement, and parent involvement. Unfortunately, the disproportionate placement of students of color and economically disadvantaged students into less rigorous academic coursework appears to continue to be present in high schools today (U.S. Department of Education, 2001a), perhaps a reason that students from these groups continue to struggle at the postsecondary level. The evidence appears compelling, then, that assisting students of color and of lower economic groups in selecting more challenging academic programs is one important method school counselors can use to close the achievement gap.

To encourage selection of more rigorous academic programs, school counseling programs should develop a plan to systematically offer educational and career planning to all students as early as middle school, and readiness for educational and career planning should begin in elementary school through developmental guidance activities (Herr & Cramer, 1996). Many states now require that high school students have developed educational plans in ninth grade and that these plans be reviewed periodically with school counselors and parents. For example, schools in Wisconsin that seek federal money through Carl Perkins are required to have educational plans in place for all students. Educational and career planning services for students should include student appraisal, educational advising and counseling, and transition planning (ASCA, 2005). Additionally, workshops should be offered to parents to provide them with knowledge regarding postsecondary educational and career options to support their child's decision making. In sum, school counselors should have organized services for educational and career planning that help students and their families make informed decisions about their coursework in both middle and high school.

College Readiness

To be work ready today, it is believed that students need, at a minimum, 2 years of postsecondary education (Carnevale & Desrochers, 2003; Hecker, 2001). Furthermore, growth in careers that require postsecondary education degrees, particularly college and advanced degrees, is expected to rise in the foreseeable future (U.S. Bureau of Labor Statistics, 2007). Relatedly, research on students' interest in attending college indicates that roughly 90% of students plan to go to college, but less than 40% actually meet the college eligibility requirements upon graduation from high school (Kirst & Bracco, 2004) and only 23% go on to receive a degree (American Council on Education, 2002). Additionally, research also suggests that fewer than 12% of students who intend to apply to college are actually familiar with college admission requirements (Venezia, Kirst, & Antonio, 2004). So, teachers often become a primary source of college information, but unfortunately, few teachers know accurate information on college admission requirements (Venezia et al., 2004). Further confounding the problems at the postsecondary level, national data indicate that large percentages of students seek remedial education at 2-year (63%) and 4-year (40%) institutions, but only 34% of these students who seek help go on to complete their 2- or 4-year degrees (U.S. Department of Education, 2001a). Degree persistence is also a concern, as only 50% of 2-year degree students and about 25% of 4-year degree students persist beyond the first year of their programs. Such findings indicate that students are often not ready to attend college, and seek information from educational professionals who may not be well informed about important college readiness criteria. Furthermore, the statistics regarding college completion rates are startling and highlight an important achievement gap between racial/ethnic groups that may be partially indicative of college readiness. For instance, college entrance rates for African American,

Latina/o, and White students have increased dramatically since 1971; however, as of 2006, White students were 88% more likely to complete a college education than African American students and 95% more likely than Latina/o students (Baum & Ma, 2007). The achievement gap in college persistence and completion rates suggests that students and families from ethnic/racial and economically disadvantaged groups need college readiness preparation.

As a goal related to closing the achievement gap, college readiness preparation begins with educational and career planning processes; should address educational goal setting, career exploration, and selection of appropriate middle and high school courses; and provide information regarding college admissions requirements, financial aid, and campus life (Tierney, Corwin, & Colyar, 2005). This information should be repeated at several points through students' progression through middle and high school. Families should also be provided with such information, because parents and guardians are particularly influential in students' postsecondary and career decision making (Merchant, 2004). As suggested earlier, the educational and career planning process should specifically address the importance of taking rigorous academic coursework to prepare for college. For additional ideas regarding college readiness preparation, readers are directed to the *College Counseling Sourcebook: Advice and Strategies From Experienced School Counselors* (College Board, 2007).

One group of students that may find college readiness preparation particularly challenging is first-generation college students, and recent figures from the College Board (2007) suggest that 37% of the 2005 Scholastic Aptitude Test (SAT) cohort were first-generation college students. Many different types of students can be identified as first generation, but the 2005 figures indicated that 46% of the first-generation SAT cohort were ethnic/racial minority students and that a large majority of this SAT cohort were also from economically disadvantaged families. These first-generation students are likely to have multiple needs with regard to college readiness. Similar to all students, first-generation students need assistance with educational planning for college and ensuring that their academic programs completed during high school meet college eligibility requirements. Their families should also be provided such information through educational planning confer-ences and workshops designed to provide information and advice about college. First-generation students also may need additional academic assistance with regard to college readiness, for these students indicated inten-tions of seeking such assistance on college campuses. More specifically, 65% indicated the intention to seek academic assistance, 46% wanted study skills assis-tance, 41% intended to seek assistance with math, and 33% wanted help with writing skills. These figures regarding intentions for help seeking on campus high-light important areas of intervention for school coun-selors, particularly with regard to time management, organizational skills, and study skills. School coun-selors could also support the educational concerns (i.e., math, writing) by encouraging selection of rigorous coursework in high school and by collaborating with teachers to offer tutoring to support skill development and an increased sense of self-efficacy regarding acade-mic abilities. These kinds of services will be essential to college readiness and persistence for first-generation students and their families.

English Language Learners

The current transformation of the professional school counselor's role must also include attention to the sig-nificant number of immigrants in U.S. schools and the many challenges they face (Bemak & Chung, 2003), for these students are particularly at risk of being aca-demically unsuccessful in school (Park-Taylor, Walsh, & Ventura, 2007). For example, English Language Learner (ELL) students must contend with English lan-guage acquisition; lack of social support networks; racial labeling; and, in some cases, posttraumatic stress disorder (Williams & Butler, 2003). Research also indi-cates that learning a new language can predispose an ELL student to anxiety and social isolation (Spomer & Cowen, 2001), which may be exacerbated by teachers who have little, if any, formalized training in addressing ELL students' needs (Bemak & Chung, 2003). School counselors potentially could be an important support for ELL students, but research suggests that ELL stu-dents had little contact with school counselors, were unable to communicate with counselors in their native language, and generally felt isolated and disconnected

from the rest of the school (Clemente & Collison, 2000). In addition to challenges at school, ELL stu-dents often face challenges at home. These students often acculturate more rapidly than their parents, which lead to conflicts as family roles change. Additionally, these students acquire English more rapidly than their parents, a position that leaves these students with little support and feeling further isolated as they seek to navi-gate the educational system (Bemak & Chung, 2003).

Many states require ELL teachers to achieve and demonstrate cross-cultural competencies in education, but no such requirements exist for school counselors (McCall-Perez, 2000; Schwallie-Giddis, Anstrom, Sanchez, Sardi, & Granato, 2004). Furthermore, school counselors indicated feeling uncomfortable working with cultu-rally and linguistically diverse families and learning to navigate the cultural differences of ELL students (Schwallie-Giddis et al., 2004). Additionally, translators often are not available to assist, further compounding school counselors' frustration in communicating with ELL students and their families (Schwallie-Giddis et al., 2004). Unfortunately, ELL students are less likely to seek out assistance from counselors than English-speaking students (Montgomery, Roberts, & Growe, 2003), even though ELL students have higher needs for school counselor support and services (McCall-Perez, 2000). If school counselors are to be effective in reaching ELL students, they should promote cooperative small group learning, coordinate study skills training, build a climate of respect for cultural diversity, and focus on student strengths rather than lack of English proficiency (Bemak & Chung, 2003). School counselors should seek profes-sional development opportunities related to working with ELL students (Williams & Butler, 2003). Interestingly, when school counselors are prepared to work with ELL students, the students show an increase in English literacy, improvement in mastery of academic content, and better transitions in schools, particularly postsecondary transitions (McCall-Perez, 2000).

School Climate and Safety

In the wake of several school shootings and other violence, there has been an increased emphasis placed on school safety and school climate (Crepeau-Hobson, Filaccio, & Gottfried, 2005). This concern is valid according to a recent survey of more than 80,000 schools that found that 96% of high schools reported violent crimes (i.e., rape, sexual battery, physical attack with or without a weapon) from 2003 to 2004 (Guerino, Hurwitz, Noonan, & Kaffenberger, 2006); 94% of middle schools and 74% of elementary schools also reported violent crimes. In addition to criminal violence, bullying is one of the most common forms of student aggression in schools (Oliver, Hoover, & Hazler, 1994; Whitted & Dupper, 2005). Bullying includes verbal and physical harassment, isolationism, and cyberbullying (Strom & Strom, 2005). Alarmingly, 42% of middle school students reported being a victim of weekly bullying (Guerino et al., 2006), and to a lesser degree, high school students (21%) and elementary school students (24%) also reported weekly bullying. Furthermore, two thirds of the students surveyed nationally reported they were verbally or physically harassed or assaulted during the past year because of their perceived or actual appearance, gender, sexual orientation, gender expression, socioeconomic status, race/ethnicity, disability, or religion (Gay, Lesbian, and Straight Education Network, 2005).

Such violence in schools can negatively affect normal development in students (Becker & Luthar, 2002), and students who do not feel safe in school are more likely to experience depression (Loukas & Robinson, 2004) and decreased self-esteem and self-efficacy (Kuperminc, Leadbeater, & Blatt, 2001). In addition to the psychological and social implications of school climate and school safety, school environment (e.g., perceived cohesion) and perceived safety are directly related to student academic achievement (Kosciw, 2004; McEvoy & Welker, 2000). Bullying and harassment threaten student perceptions of school as a safe place, which creates an aversive environment and disrupts learning in all areas (Newman-Carlson & Horne, 2004). Conversely, students who have a sense of community and belonging to school experience showed increased levels of engagement and academic performance (Loukas & Robinson, 2004). Clearly, addressing student safety is important to academic achievement and quite possibly closing the achievement gap.

School counselors are in a unique position to improve students' feelings of safety at school (Fontes, 2003). For example, school counselors use developmental guidance and small group activities that address conflict resolution strategies (Flannery et al., 2003), and social skills training (Moote, Smythe, & Woodarski, 1999). Many bullying and violence prevention programs (e.g., Frey et al., 2005; Grossman et al., 1997; Hirschstein, Edstrom, Frey, Snell, & MacKenzie, 2007; Olweus, 2001) were found to be effective in reducing the impact of school violence and decreasing the number of disciplinary problems (see Nation, 2007, for an overview of these programs). Other researchers debate the impact that these programs have on actual bullying behaviors but have discovered that these programs enhance teachers' knowledge and efficacy regarding intervention and enhance student social competence, self-esteem, and peer acceptance (Merrell, Gueldner, Ross, & Isava, 2008). Additionally, school counselors can serve as trainers and consultants for teachers, parents, and staff (Lickona, Schaps, & Lewis, 2003; U.S. Department of Education, 2007), which may include diversity education, social justice education, and problem solving. Finally, school counselors should contribute to the development of school policies and procedures that can improve the safety of the entire school (Fontes, 2003).

Multidisciplinary Collaboration

To address all of the concerns above that are important to closing the achievement gap, school counselors must think of themselves as a part of a multidisciplinary collaboration team within the school. For instance, career exploration and development can and should be a coordinated school effort. To illustrate, one high school in the Milwaukee, Wisconsin, area requires students to write an extensive English paper on a job-shadowing experience that examines roles and responsibilities regarding a career area, likes and dislikes about the job, necessary academic and professional preparation, and labor market projections for future employment. These papers are then used in collaboration with junior and senior year educational planning during sophomore conferences. This example illustrates how an academic assignment can address an important area of career development and represents collaboration between the English department and the school counseling program to achieve this goal. Although there are many areas of potential collaboration, one important area to consider may be the students who come to school struggling with mental health concerns.

For example, it is estimated that 20% of children and adolescents experience a mild to moderate mental health concern, and serious mental health concerns hover around 5% (U.S. Department of Health and Human Services, 2000). Theorists have suggested that student service professionals (e.g., school counselors, social workers, psychologists, nurses) should collaborate to address the mental health concerns in schools (Adelman & Taylor, 2000). Identifying areas for collaboration between these professional groups could improve services where needed. One mechanism for encouraging collaboration would be through the development of an advisory council (ASCA, 2005). The advisory council reviews CSCP goals, interventions, and program outcomes, and ideally would provide assistance in program development and offer recommendations for program improvement. Closing the achievement gap would be enhanced through these types of collaborative efforts.

EMERGING ISSUES FOR SCHOOL COUNSELOR TRAINING

If school counselors are to contribute effectively to closing the achievement gap, graduate programs must change the training of future professionals. At the foundation of this change is the importance of multicultural competency, and many concur that school counselors must be capable of providing services that are sensitive to and appropriate for students from diverse cultural backgrounds (Holcomb-McCoy, 2007; Lee, 2001; Pedersen & Carey, 2003). However, graduate programs must address more than cultural sensitivity training and help school counseling graduates develop specific skills to intervene. As addressed earlier, this approach requires that graduate training programs teach student advocacy, systemic change, prevention, and data-driven and accountability practices, with social justice as the philosophical heart and soul of the program. The next section provides a synthesis of important concerns or trends in the training of future school counselors and offers potential resources for making such changes.

School Counseling for All Students

Future school counselors should be prepared to develop programs that focus on the whole school and provide services to all students (Gysbers & Henderson, 2000; Hart & Jacobi, 1992; House & Sears, 2002; Martin, 2002). Furthermore, closing the achievement gap will require that graduates be trained to provide comprehensive and prevention-based services that are developed and informed by data specific to schools. CSCP models (e.g., ASCA, 2005; Gysbers & Henderson, 2000) offer the most promising approach to achieving these goals, and school counseling training should prepare students with the attitudes, knowledge, and skills to implement programs that meet the needs of individual students while also addressing important school climate concerns (Burkard, Holtz, Martinez, Alexander, & Hyatt, 2008; Holcomb-McCoy, 2007; Lee, 2001). Graduate programs seeking to align their training with this approach should review Education Trust program guidelines (see www2.edtrust.org/EdTrust/Transforming+School+Counseling/current.htm). Additionally, ASCA (2008) recently published the *School Counselor Competencies*, which are an important resource to graduate programs in developing program curricula and refining school counselor training. These competencies align with the Council for Accreditation of Counseling and Related Educational Programs (CACREP) standards for school counseling programs, and will be an important asset in advancing training for school counseling students. Finally, to implement CSCPs, school counselors will need strong leadership skills. As such, graduate programs will need to provide leadership training, particularly focusing on the politics of education, curriculum development, and school management and finance concerns.

Postsecondary Counseling

There is a great deal of consensus among educational leaders that graduate programs in school counseling must teach postsecondary counseling skills if they are to assist in closing the achievement gap (Kirst & Venezia, 2004; Martin & Lee, 2007; Portes, 2005; Tierney et al., 2005). A recent report by the Joyce Ivey Foundation (2008), however, identified few graduate programs in school counseling that offered such preparation. At this time, few resources are available to assist in preparing school counseling graduate students for postsecondary counseling (Martin & Lee, 2007). Graduate programs will want to familiarize themselves with College Board (2007) resources and the college counseling competencies developed by the National Association of College Admission Counselors (NACAC, 2000). Additionally, NOSCA (Martin & Lee, 2007) is currently planning to develop a graduate curriculum for postsecondary counseling and eventually hopes to publish a text in this important area. For the foreseeable future, training programs should expect postsecondary decision making, and postsecondary transitions will be important to school counseling program planning and to the development of school improvement goals related to closing the achievement gap. Given this emerging emphasis on PK–16 education, graduate programs in school counseling should develop curricula that support skill development in this important area.

School Safety and Climate

Students, parents, and our communities are demanding that our schools be safe, and school counseling graduates need to be prepared to address school climate and safety concerns. Safe schools that have positive learning environments would seem to be essential to addressing any existing achievement gaps. Important school climate and safety concerns include violence, discrimination, bullying and harassment, and gang activity (Fontes, 2003). Little research is available on graduates' preparedness to address such concerns in schools, although one recent investigation of racial conflicts and harassment suggests that school counselors feel ill prepared to address such concerns (Burkard et al., 2008). It is recommended that graduate programs address assessment, intervention, and prevention of violence in schools. For example, graduate programs should familiarize trainees with early warning signs of violence, prevention and intervention strategies, and crisis response. Trainees should also be taught to integrate prevention strategies into their CSCP through the guidance curriculum, and these programs need to address topics such as communication and decision-making skills, acceptance and appreciation of differences, and conflict resolution skills. Finally, trainees need to develop leadership skills with regard to school safety and climate, specifically learning how to contribute to the development of school and district policies that promote positive learning environments for all students.

Evidence-Based Practice

Although we have focused on the necessity of closing the achievement gap as a social justice concern for school counselors, it should also be stated that this focus is a federal mandate. In January 2002, the No Child Left Behind Act (U.S. Department of Education, 2001b) was signed into federal law. NCLB mandates regular testing, provides sanctions for schools that do not provide evidence that students are learning, and requires schools to demonstrate that they are making progress toward closing the achievement gap between academically high- and low-performing students. Additionally, educational practices and interventions in schools need to be validated empirically. These criteria require that school counselors develop strong skills in program evaluation and school accountability practices. Graduate programs typically require research and/or statistics classes as core requirements, and CACREP, the primary accrediting body for school counseling programs, has also established clear standards regarding research training for school counselors (www.cacrep .org/2001Standards.html). Despite these requirements, many school counselors have low self-efficacy beliefs regarding their research skills (Astramovich, Coker, & Hoskins, 2005), and accountability components are usually the least developed aspects of a CSCP (Burkard, Gillen, & Martinez, 2008). Furthermore, 75% of school counseling graduates recently indicated that they needed more training in evaluation and accountability practice (Astramovich et al., 2005). Graduate training programs, then, need to provide training regarding empirically based school counseling practices (Dimmitt, Carey, & Hatch, 2007). Several models currently exist that offer guidelines for integrating data-based decision making in school counseling programs (see Dimmitt et al., 2007; Isaacs, 2003; Kaffenberger & Young, 2007; Poynton & Carey, 2006; Reynolds & Hines, 2001; Stone & Dahir, 2007). These models could easily be integrated into research courses. Additionally, it is generally recognized that such training should address needs assessment, evaluation of outcome research, intervention evaluation, and overall program evaluation.

Finally, training programs should introduce students to the National Center for School Counseling Outcome Research as an important resource in promoting accountability practice in school counseling programs.

CONCLUSIONS

In reflecting on this chapter and its content, one may wonder if much has changed in school counseling since Sciarra's (2001) chapter in the second edition of the *Handbook of Multicultural Counseling*. For instance, the role of school counselors remains a concern, the Education Trust continues to address the transforming school counseling initiative, the achievement gap remains a focus, and postsecondary success and preparation are also of concern to the field. We would argue that much has changed. Social justice and closing the achievement gap have moved from being a marginal focus for school counselors to the primary focus. Although some may continue to argue that school counselors should be the mental health experts in schools, ASCA and Education Trust continue to work toward redefining school counselor roles and encouraging their development as educational leaders in the development of a comprehensive school counseling program that is integral to addressing student achievement. This perspective does not abandon the mental health concerns of students; rather, it sharpens the focus of school counseling by encouraging a true prevention-based model of practice with the intent of influencing all students' academic achievement. Similarly, college readiness and preparation counseling are also coming into focus, particularly as the field moves from a PK–12 view toward a PK–16 perspective. Consequently, school counselors are making progress in redefining their professional roles as student advocates and leaders who promote and develop opportunities for all students to attain high academic achievement.

REFERENCES

Adelman, C. (1999). *Answers in the toolbox: Academic intensity, attendance patterns, and bachelor's degree attainment.* Washington, DC: U.S. Department of Education.

Adelman, C., & Taylor, L. (2000). Shaping the future of mental health in schools. *Psychology in the Schools, 37,* 49–60.

Amatea, E. S., Daniels, H., Bringman, N., & Vandiver, F. M. (2004). Strengthening counselor-teacher-family connections: The family-school collaborative consultation project. *Professional School Counseling, 8,* 47–55.

American Council on Education. (2002). *Minorities in higher education 2001–2002: 19th annual status report.* Washington, DC: Author.

American School Counselor Association. (2004). *Position statement: Cultural diversity.* Retrieved from http://www.schoolcounselor.org/content.asp?contentid=249

American School Counselor Association. (2005). *The ASCA national model: A framework for school counseling programs* (2nd ed.). Alexandria, VA: Author.

American School Counselor Association. (2008). *School counselor competencies* [Brochure]. Washington, DC: Author.

Astramovich, R. L., Coker, J. K., & Hoskins, W. J. (2005). Training school counselors in program evaluation. *Professional School Counseling, 9,* 49–59.

Bailey, D. F., Getch, Y. Q., & Chen-Hayes, S. F. (2007). Achievement advocacy for all students through transformative school counseling programs. In B. T. Erford (Ed.), *Transforming the school counseling profession* (2nd ed., pp. 98–120). Upper Saddle River, NJ: Pearson.

Baum, S., & Ma, J. (2007). *Education pays: The benefits of higher education for individuals and society.* Washington, DC: College Board.

Becker, B. E., & Luthar, S. S. (2002). Social-emotional factors affecting achievement outcomes among disadvantaged students: Closing the achievement gap. *Educational Psychologist, 37,* 197–214.

Behring, S. T. (2002). School counseling in the twenty-first century: A systemic multicultural approach. In C. D. Johnson & S. K. Johnson (Eds.), *Building stronger school counseling programs: Bringing futuristic approaches into the present* (pp. 131–141). Greensboro, NC: ERIC.

Bemak, F., & Chung, R. C. (2003). Multicultural counseling with immigrant students in schools. In P. B. Pedersen & J. C. Carey (Eds.), *Multicultural counseling in schools: A practical handbook* (2nd ed., pp. 84–104). Boston: Pearson.

Bemak, F., & Chung, R. C. (2005). Advocacy as a critical role for urban school counselors: Working toward equity and social justice. *Professional School Counseling, 8,* 196–202.

Bemak, K. (2000). Transforming the role of the counselor to provide leadership in education reform through collaboration. *Professional School Counseling, 3,* 323–331.

Bowers, J., Hatch, T., & Schwallie-Giddis, R. (2001). The brainstorm. *School Counselor, 39,* 16–19.

Burkard, A. W., Gillen, M., & Martinez, M. J. (2008). *The effect of comprehensive school counseling programs on student academic and behavioral outcomes.* Manuscript in preparation.

Burkard, A. W., Holtz, C., Martinez, M. J., Alexander, C. M., & Hyatt, C. (2008, July). *Racial conflict in middle and high schools.* Symposium conducted at the annual meeting of the American School Counselor Association, Atlanta, GA.

Burnham, J. J., & Jackson, C. M. (2000). School counselor roles: Discrepancies between actual practice and existing models. *Professional School Counseling, 4,* 41–49.

Campbell, C. A., & Dahir, C. A. (1997). *The national standards for school counseling programs.* Alexandria, VA: American School Counseling Association.

Carnevale, A. P., & Desrochers, D. M. (2003). Preparing students for the knowledge economy: What school counselors need to know. *Professional School Counseling, 6,* 228–236.

Clemente, R., & Collison, B. (2000). The relationships among counselors, ESL teachers, and students. *Professional School Counseling, 3,* 339–348.

College Board. (2007). *College counseling sourcebook: Advice and strategies from experienced school counselors* (4th ed.). New York: Author.

Cox, A. A., & Lee, C. C. (2007). Challenging educational inequities: School counselors as agents of social justice. In C. C. Lee (Ed.), *Counseling for social justice* (2nd ed., pp. 3–14). Alexandria, VA: American Counseling Association.

Crepeau-Hobson, M. F., Filaccio, M. L., & Gottfried, L. (2005). Violence prevention after Columbine: A survey of high school mental health professionals. *Children & Schools, 27,* 157–165.

Darling-Hammond, L. (2000). How teacher education matters. *Journal of Teacher Education, 52,* 166–173.

Dimmitt, C., Carey, J. C., & Hatch, T. (2007). *Evidence-based school counseling: Making a difference with data-driven practices.* Thousand Oaks, CA: Corwin.

Education Trust. (1997). *Education watch: The 1997 Education Trust State and National data book.* Washington, DC: Author.

Flannery, D. J., Vazsony, A. T., Liau, A. K., Guo, S., Powell, K. E., Atha, H., Vesterdal, W., & Embry, D. (2003). Initial behavior outcomes for the PeaceBuilders Universal School-Based Violence Prevention Program. *Developmental Psychology, 39,* 292–308.

Fontes, L. A. (2003). Reducing violence in multicultural schools. In P. B. Pedersen & J. C. Carey (Eds.), *Multicultural counseling in schools: A practical handbook* (2nd ed., pp. 211–233). Boston: Pearson.

Frey, K. S., Hirschstein, M. K., Snell, J. L., Edstrom, L. V., MacKenzie, E. P., & Broderick, C. J. (2005). Reducing playground bullying and supporting beliefs: An experimental trial of the STEPS TO RESPECT program. *Developmental Psychology, 41,* 479–491.

Gay, Lesbian, and Straight Education Network. (2005). *From teasing to torment: School climate in America: A survey of students and teachers.* New York: Author.

Grossman, D. C., Neckerman, H. J., Koepsell, T. D., Liu, P., Asher, K. N., Beland, K., Frey, K., & Rivara, F. P. (1997). Effectiveness of a violence prevention curriculum among children in elementary school: A randomized controlled trial. *Journal of the American Medical Association, 277,* 1605–1611.

Guerino, P., Hurwitz, M. D., Noonan, M. E., & Kaffenberger, S. M. (2006). *Crime, violence, discipline, and safety in U.S. public schools: Findings from the School Survey on Crime and Safety: 2003–04* (NCES 2007–302). Washington, DC: U.S. Government Printing Office.

Gysbers, N. C. (1997). A model comprehensive guidance program. In N. C. Gysbers & P. Henderson (Eds.), *Comprehensive guidance programs that work II* (pp. 1–24). Greensboro, NC: ERIC/CASS.

Gysbers, N. C., & Henderson, P. (2000). *Developing and managing your school guidance program* (3rd ed.). Alexandria, VA: American School Counseling Association.

Gysbers, N. C., & Moore, E. J. (1981). *Improving guidance programs.* Englewood Cliffs, NJ: Prentice-Hall.

Hart, P. J., & Jacobi, M. (1992). *From gatekeeper to advocate: Transforming the role of the school counselor.* New York: College Board.

Hecker, D. E. (2001). Occupational employment projections to 2010. *Monthly Labor Review, 124,* 57–84.

Herr, E. L., & Cramer, S. H. (1996). *Career guidance and counseling through the life span: Systemic approaches* (5th ed.). New York: HarperCollins.

Hipilito-Delgado, C., & Lee, C. (2007). Empowerment theory for the professional school counselor: A manifesto for what really matters. *Professional School Counseling, 10,* 327–332.

Hirschstein, M. K., Edstrom, L. V. S., Frey, K. S., Snell, J. L., & MacKenzie, E. P. (2007). Walking the talk in bullying prevention: Teacher implementation variables related to initial impact of the STEPS TO RESPECT program. *School Psychology Review, 36*(1), 3–21.

Holcomb-McCoy, C. (2007). *School counseling to close the achievement gap: A social justice framework for success.* Thousand Oaks, CA: Corwin.

House, R. M., & Hayes, R. L. (2002). School counselors: Becoming key players in school reform. *Professional School Counseling, 5*, 249–256.

House, R. M., & Martin, P. J. (1998). Advocating for better futures for all students: A new vision for school counselors. *Education, 119*, 284–291.

House, R. M., & Sears, S. J. (2002). Preparing school counselors to be leaders and advocates: A critical need in the new millennium. *Theory into Practice, 41*, 155–162.

Isaacs, M. L. (2003). Data-driven decision making: The engine of accountability. *Professional School Counseling, 6*, 288–295.

Joyce Ivey Foundation. (2008). *The eleven-month challenge: 22 recommendations for improving the transition from high school to college.* Ann Arbor, MI: Author.

Kaffenberger, C., & Young, A. (2007). *Making data work.* Washington, DC: American School Counselor Association.

Kirst, M. W., & Bracco, K. R. (2004). Bridging the great divide: How the K–12 and postsecondary split hurts students, and what can be done about it. In M. W. Kirst & A. Venezia (Eds.), *From high school to college: Improving opportunities for success in postsecondary education* (pp. 1–30). San Francisco: Jossey-Bass.

Kirst, M. W., & Venezia, A. (2004). *From high school to college: Improving opportunities for success in postsecondary education.* San Francisco: Jossey-Bass.

Kosciw, J. G. (2004). *The 2003 National School Climate Survey: The school-related experiences of our nation's lesbian, gay, bisexual and transgender youth.* New York: Gay, Lesbian, and Straight Education Network.

Kuh, G. D., Kinzie, J., Buckley, J. A., Bridges, B. K., & Hayek, J. C. (2006). *What matters to student success: A review of the literature.* Retrieved May 19, 2008, from http://nces.ed.gov/npec/pdf/kuh_team_report.pdf

Kuperminc, G. P., Leadbeater, B. J., & Blatt, S. J. (2001). School social climate and individual differences in vulnerability to psychopathology among middle school students. *Journal of School Psychology, 39*, 141–159.

Lapan, R. T., Gysbers, N. C., Cook, A., Bragg, S., & Robbins, J. (2006, June). *Improving school counseling programs and school counselor training.* Symposium conducted at the annual meeting of the American School Counselor Association, Chicago.

Lapan, R. T., Gysbers, N. C., & Petroski, G. F. (2003). Helping seventh graders be safe and successful: A statewide study of the impact of comprehensive guidance and counseling programs. *Professional School Counseling, 6*, 186–197.

Lapan, R. T., Gysbers, N. C., & Sun, Y. (1997). The impact of more fully implemented guidance programs on the school experiences of high school students: A statewide evaluation study. *Journal of Counseling and Development, 75*, 292–302.

Lee, C. C. (2001). Culturally responsive school counselors and programs: Addressing the needs of all students. *Professional School Counseling, 4*, 257–261.

Lee, C. C. (2005). *Multicultural issues in counseling.* Alexandria, VA: American Counseling Association.

Lee, V. E., & Ekstrom, R. B. (1987). Student access to guidance counseling in high school. *American Educational Research Journal, 24*, 287–310.

Lickona, T., Schaps, E., & Lewis, C. (2003). *Eleven principles of effective character education.* Washington, DC: Character Education Partnership.

Loukas, A., & Robinson, S. (2004). Examining the moderating role of perceived school climate in early adolescent adjustment. *Journal of Research on Adolescence, 14*, 209–233.

Martin, P. J. (2002). Transforming school counseling: A national perspective. *Theory into Practice, 41*, 148–153.

Martin, P. J., & Lee, V. E. (2007, November). *Research, training, and legislation for school counseling.* Symposium conducted at the College Board Counselor Education Summit, Washington, DC.

McCall-Perez, Z. (2000). The counselor as advocate for English language learners: An action research approach. *Professional School Counseling, 4*, 13–22.

McEvoy, A., & Welker, R. (2000). Antisocial behavior, academic failure, and school climate: A critical review. *Journal of Emotional and Behavioral Disorders, 8*, 130–140.

Merchant, B. (2004). Roadblocks to effective K–16 reform in Illinois. In M. W. Kirst & A. Venezia (Eds.), *From high school to college: Improving opportunities for success in postsecondary education* (pp. 115–150). San Francisco: Jossey-Bass.

Merrell, K. W., Gueldner, B. A., Ross, S. W., & Isava, D. M. (2008). How effective are school bullying intervention programs? A meta-analysis of intervention research. *School Psychology Quarterly, 23*(1), 26–42.

Montgomery, P. S., Roberts, M., & Growe, R. (2003). *English language learners: An issue of educational equity.* Lafayette: University of Louisiana Press. (ERIC Document Reproduction Service No. ED 027915)

Moote, G. T., Smythe, N. J., & Woodarski, J. S. (1999). Social skills training with youth in school settings: A review. *Research on Social Work Practice, 9*, 427–465.

Myrick, R. D. (1997). *Developmental guidance and counseling: A practical approach* (3rd ed.). Minneapolis, MN: Educational Media Corporation.

Nation, M. (2007). Empowering the victim: Interventions for children victimized by bullies. In J. E. Zins, M. J. Elias, & C. A. Maher (Eds.), *Bullying, victimization, and peer harassment: A handbook of prevention and intervention* (pp. 239–255). New York: Haworth.

National Assessment of Educational Progress. (2004). *NAEP 2004 trends in academic progress.* Washington, DC: U.S. Department of Education, National Center for Education Statistics.

National Assessment of Educational Progress. (2005). *NAEP 2005 trends in academic progress.* Washington, DC: U.S. Department of Education, National Center for Education Statistics.

National Assessment of Educational Progress. (2007). *NAEP 2007 trends in academic progress.* Washington, DC: U.S. Department of Education, National Center for Education Statistics.

National Association for College Admission Counseling. (2000). *Statement on counselor competencies.* Alexandria, VA: Author.

National Commission on Excellence in Education. (1983). *A nation at risk: The imperative for educational reform.* Washington, DC: Government Printing Office.

Newman-Carlson, D., & Horne, A. M. (2004). Bully busters: A psycho-educational intervention for reducing bullying behavior in middle school students. *Journal of Counseling and Development, 82,* 259–268.

Noguera, P. A. (2003). *City schools and the American dream.* New York: Teachers College Press.

Oakes, J., & Lipton, M. (1990). Tracking and ability grouping: A structural barrier to access and achievement. In J. I. Goodlad & P. Keating (Eds.), *Access to knowledge: An agenda for our nation's schools* (pp. 187–204). New York: College Entrance Examination Board.

Oliver, R., Hoover, J. H., & Hazler, R. (1994). The perceived roles of bullying in small-town Midwestern schools. *Journal of Counseling & Development, 72,* 416–421.

Olweus, D. (2001). *Olweus' core program against bullying and antisocial behavior: A teacher handbook.* Bergen, Norway: Research Center for Health Promotion (The HEMIL Center).

Park-Taylor, J., Walsh, M. E., & Ventura, A. B. (2007). Creating healthy acculturation pathways: Integrating theory and research to inform counselors' work with immigrant children. *Professional School Counseling, 11,* 25–35.

Pedersen, P. B., & Carey, J. C. (2003). *Multicultural counseling in schools: A practical handbook* (2nd ed.). Boston: Pearson.

Perusse, R., Goodnough, G. E., Donegan, J., & Jones, C. (2004). Perceptions of school counselors and school

principals about the national standards for school counseling programs and the transforming school counseling initiative. *Professional School Counseling, 7,* 152–159.

Portes, P. R. (2005). *Dismantling educational inequality: A cultural-historical approach to closing the achievement gap.* New York: Peter Lang.

Poynton, T. A., & Carey, J. C. (2006). An integrative model of data-based decision making for school counseling. *Professional School Counseling, 10,* 121–130.

Reynolds, S. E., & Hines, P. L. (2001). *Vision-to-action: A step-by-step activity guide for systemic educational reform* (6th ed.). Bloomington, IN: American Student Achievement Institute.

Rosenbaum, J. E. (1976). *Making inequality: The hidden current of high school tracking.* New York: Wiley.

Scarborough, J. L. (2005). The School Counselor Activity Rating Scale: An instrument for gathering process data. *Professional School Counseling, 8,* 274–284.

Schwallie-Giddis, P., Anstrom, K., Sanchez, P., Sardi, V. A., & Granato, L. (2004). Counseling the linguistically and culturally diverse student: Meeting school counselors' professional development needs. *Professional School Counseling, 8,* 15–23.

Sciarra, D. T. (2001). School counseling in a multicultural society. In J. G. Ponterotto, J. M. Casas, L. A. Suzuki, & C. M. Alexander (Eds.), *Handbook of multicultural counseling* (pp. 701–728). Thousand Oaks, CA: Sage.

Sink, C. A., & Stroh, H. R. (2003). Raising achievement test scores of early elementary school students through comprehensive school counseling programs. *Professional School Counseling, 6,* 352–364.

Spomer, M. L., & Cowen, E. L. (2001). A comparison of the school mental health referral profiles of young ESL and English-speaking children. *Journal of Community Psychology, 29,* 69–82.

Stone, C. B., & Dahir, C. A. (2007). *School counselor accountability: A measure of student success* (2nd ed.). New York: Prentice-Hall.

Strom, P. S., & Strom, R. D. (2005). Cyberbullying by adolescents: A preliminary assessment. *Educational Forum, 70,* 21–35.

Sue, D. W., Arredondo, P., & McDavis, R. (1992). Multicultural counseling competencies and standards: A call to the profession. *Journal of Counseling and Development, 70,* 477–486.

Sue, D. W., Bernier, J. B., Durran, M., Feinberg, L., Pedersen, P., Smith, E., & Vasquez-Nuttall, E. (1982). Position paper: Cross-cultural counseling competencies. *Counseling Psychologist, 10,* 42–52.

Tierney, W. G., Corwin, Z. B., & Colyar, J. E. (2005). *Preparing for college: Nine elements of effective outreach.* Albany: State University of New York Press.

Trusty, J. (2004). *Effects of students' middle-school and high-school experiences on completion of the bachelor's degree* (Research Monograph no. 1). Amherst: University of Massachusetts, Center for School Counseling Outcome Research.

Trusty, J., & Niles, S. G. (2003). High-school math courses and completion of the bachelor's degree. *Professional School Counseling, 7,* 99–107.

U.S. Bureau of Labor Statistics. (2007). *Employment outlook: 2006–16.* Retrieved April 12, 2008, from http://www.bls.gov/opub/mir/2007/11/content.htm

U.S. Department of Education. (2001a). *The condition of education.* Washington, DC: National Center for Education Statistics.

U.S. Department of Education. (2001b). *PL 107–100, The No Child Left Behind Act of 2001.* Retrieved May 14, 2008, at www.ed.gov/policy/elsec/leg/esea02/index.html

U.S. Department of Education. (2007). *Mobilizing for evidence-based character education.* Jessup, MD: Author.

U.S. Department of Health and Human Services. (2000). *Report of the Surgeon General's Conference on Children's Mental Health: A national action agenda.* Rockville, MD: Author.

Venezia, A., Kirst, M. W., & Antonio, A. L. (2004). *Betraying the college dream: How disconnected K–12 and postsecondary education systems undermine study aspirations.* Retrieved May 19, 2008, from http://www.stanford.edu/group/bridgeproject/betrayingthecollegedream.pdf

Whitted, K. S., & Dupper, D. R. (2005). Best practices for preventing or reducing bullying in schools. *Children and Schools, 27,* 167–175.

Williams, F. C., & Butler, S. K. (2003). Concerns of newly arrived immigrant students: Implications for school counselors. *Professional School Counseling, 7,* 9–14.

44

Counselors as Diversity Change Agents in Higher Education

ROGER L. WORTHINGTON, JENI HART, AND TALEB S. KHAIRALLAH

A wealth of scholarship has demonstrated that the historical context of higher education has been characterized by a substantial degree of exclusion—meaning that women, racial-ethnic minorities, people with disabilities, sexual minorities, individuals from low socioeconomic status backgrounds, and particular religious groups were often intentionally or unintentionally barred from admission (Chesler, Lewis, & Crowfoot, 2005; Smith & Associates, 1997; Sue, 1995). As a result, the American Association of Colleges and Universities (AACU, 1995) challenged higher education institutions to create and articulate a commitment to inclusion, fairness, and equality by developing inclusive environments that cultivate diversity and celebrate differences in which all people are welcomed, heard, and valued equally. Across the past 20 years, research suggests that diversity on college campuses is associated with (a) increased learning, (b) greater interpersonal competencies, (c) increased self-confidence among students, (d) fewer irrational prejudices, (e) substantive gains in critical thinking, (f) more involvement in civic and community service, and (g) higher earning potential after graduation (Antonio, 2001; Blimling, 2001; Chang, 1996; Gurin, 1999; Hurtado, 2001; Jayakumar, 2007; Smith & Associates, 1997). Within that context, colleges and universities are engaged in systematic efforts to become more proficient, knowledgeable, and responsive with respect to diversity issues (American Psychological Association [APA], 2003).

At present, diversity efforts in higher education can be viewed as both burgeoning and under threat. Even as national statistics increasingly show positive growth in the numbers of students from underrepresented group members achieving their higher education goals (U.S. Census Bureau, 2008a), it is readily apparent that women, people of color, and other traditionally underrepresented groups continue to be unequally or disproportionally represented throughout higher education in faculty, administrative, and other academic leadership roles (Garcia, 2007; Glazer-Raymo, 1999, 2008). There are emerging national trends among major institutions to increase spending on diversity recruitment of students and faculty (Clayton-Pedersen, Parker, Smith, Moreno, & Teraguchi, 2007), devote more resources to promote a positive campus climate for diversity (Gose, 2006), and elevate chief diversity officers (CDOs) to cabinet-level administrative positions (Williams & Wade-Golden, 2008). At the same time, significant resistance to the goals and values of diversity continues to surface, including, but not limited to, challenges to affirmative action in hiring, admissions, and scholarships from executive, legislative, and judicial branches of government and well-funded political groups (D'Souza, 1998; Horowitz, 2007; Moses, Marin, & Yun, 2008). These conflicting themes of growth and deficit, and promise and challenge produce contradictions in which societal demands require greater diversity and competencies to function effectively in the global multicultural marketplace at the same time that political, economic, and legal constraints continue to hinder efforts to be responsive.

With a long-standing tradition of training for diversity competencies, the counseling profession has the potential to play a significant role in how higher education institutions respond to the dynamics of economic, political, and institutional forces that both hinder and support the quest for faculties and student bodies who reflect the diversity of the broader population and enhance educational outcomes. This chapter focuses on the numerous change agent roles that counselors can play in higher education in the service of pursuing and achieving broad-based diversity goals.

DEEPENING SOCIAL, CULTURAL, AND POLITICAL DIVIDES IN HIGHER EDUCATION

According to the U.S. Census Bureau (2009), as of July 1, 2008 (the most current data available), non-Hispanic Whites constituted only 66% of the total population (199.5 million) and grew at a rate of only 0.3% during the 1-year period between July 1, 2007 to July 1, 2008. Hispanics constituted 15% of the total population (exceeding 46.9 million) with a growth rate of 3.3% for the same 1-year period. African Americans/Blacks accounted for 13.5% of the U.S. population (41.1 million), followed by Asians (5%), American Indian/Alaska

Natives (1.6%), and Native Hawaiians and other Pacific Islanders (0.4%). Overall, the nation's minority population reached 34% of the total in 2008 (104.6 million). However, the Current Population Survey (CPS) (U.S. Census Bureau, 2008a) identified ongoing disparities in higher education attainment between racial-ethnic groups. Specifically, the CPS estimated that 28.7% of the total population aged 25 and older held a bachelor's degree or higher, with Asians achieving the highest proportion (52.1%), followed by non-Hispanic Whites (31.8%), Blacks (18.5%), and Hispanics (12.7%). (Note that the CPS does not report information for American Indian/Alaska Natives, or separately for Native Hawaiians and other Pacific Islanders.) Many assume that a higher education degree is important. Moreover, the 2005 Annual Social and Economic Supplement data reinforce the economic value of a college education (U.S. Census Bureau, 2006). Among workers 18 and over with a bachelor's degree, average earnings were $51,600 a year, whereas those with a high school diploma earned $28,600, and those without a high school diploma averaged $19,200. Furthermore, workers with an advanced degree made an average of $78,100.

Although people of color have begun to make inroads and advances with respect to educational attainment and income over the past 30 years (U.S. Census Bureau, 2004), the long-standing history of inequities provides advantages to Whites in these areas that tend to be cyclical (Council of Economic Advisors for the President's Initiative on Race, 1998). That is, Whites are more likely than people of color to attend schools with smaller class sizes and to have access to computers in public schools and at home during their education. This provides the foundation on which Whites are more likely to both attend and graduate from a college or university; earn higher incomes; retain employment during a recession; have health insurance and gain access to health care; and survive some life-threatening illnesses (e.g., cancer, heart disease, diabetes). In addition, the resulting economic advantages also translate into having greater access to low-risk home mortgage loans and home ownership, spending a smaller proportion of income on housing, and experiencing better housing conditions. Ultimately, Whites are more likely than people of color to invest in the stock market, have retirement accounts, and gain a substantial net worth, which provides opportunities for their children to attend schools with smaller class sizes, have access to computers, and so on, in a cycle that perpetuates the educational and economic inequities that existed in previous generations (Neville, Worthington, & Spanierman, 2001).

When considering gender, women have earned 57% of bachelor's degrees since 1982 (Corbett, Hill, & St. Rose, 2008). Despite the higher percentages of women graduating from postsecondary education, men are earning college degrees at their highest historical rate. Although women's earnings have improved compared to men, 2005 data show that women's median earnings were 77% of men's for those who work full-time, no matter what education level they attained (Corbett et al., 2008). Through their analysis, Corbett et al. dispelled the myth that there is a "boy crisis" in higher education (i.e., fewer men are going to college and earning degrees); however, they do report that when enrollment, achievement, and salaries are disaggregated by race/ethnicity, serious concerns continue to exist for low-income students, Hispanic students, and African American students of all genders.

As religious pluralism becomes an increasingly important focus within counseling and higher education, important new data have emerged in recent years about religious diversity in higher education. For example, the UCLA Higher Education Research Institute (HERI, 2005) has reported that about 80% of college students attended religious services in the past year and that they discussed religion/spirituality with friends and family. Furthermore, about 40% also considered it "essential" or "very important" to "follow religious teachings" in their everyday lives, and nearly half (48%) said that it is "essential" or "very important" that college encourage their personal expression of spirituality. This is in contrast to findings that 31.2% of the professors surveyed gave no religious preference, and about 23.4% of respondents reported being either atheists or agnostics, a figure that is much higher than the 6.9% of the U.S. population as a whole who said they did not believe in God or did not know if God existed and believed there was no way to find out (HERI, 2006). When asked whether "colleges should be concerned with facilitating students' spiritual development," only a minority of faculty (30%) agreed; however, in a national survey of college juniors, most reported that their professors have never encouraged discussion of spiritual or religious matters and never provide opportunities for discussing the meaning or purpose of life (HERI, 2006).

In addition to greater attention to religious diversity, there has also been a parallel trend regarding political diversity (a hot-button topic we will return to later). The *American Freshman National Norms for Fall 2006* (Pryor et al., 2007) indicated that there is a deepening political divide among entering first-year students in higher education. "Liberal" was at the highest level since 1975 (30.7%). "Conservative" was at the highest point in the history of the Freshman Survey. Only 43.3% of college freshmen identified as "middle-of-the-road." Both "liberal" (28.4%) and "conservative" (23.9%) each increased by 1.3 percentage points from 2005. In contrast, there has been extensive debate about the extent to which academic faculties contain and reflect an inherent liberal bias (e.g., Bauerlein, 2006; Gravois, 2007; Will, 2007) with political think tanks promoting research data that would indicate a professoriate overloaded with liberals at astronomical numbers as objectionable as 30 to 1 in the field of anthropology (Klein & Stern, in press), 10 to 1 among major universities (Horowitz & Lehrer, 2003), and a shift from 39% to 72% between 1984 to 1999 (Rothman, Lichter, & Nevitte, 2005). In more methodologically sound research, however, the dominance of liberal professors does not appear to be quite so lopsided (Zipp & Fenwick, 2006) and may be explained more effectively by the personal values and career goals of self-identified liberals versus conservatives than by systemic biases against conservative thought or thinkers (Woessner & Kelly-Woessner, 2008).

The deepening social, religious, cultural, and political divisions within the broader society are being played out in dynamic and often controversial ways within higher education and among those who have vested interests in the missions, goals, and products of the academy. These changes call for all those involved in higher education to take notice and to consider the extent to which these critical issues should be addressed. Specifically, counselors, among others in higher education, must consider whether they have a responsibility to address diversity and multiculturalism in their roles as diversity change agents.

WHAT IS A CHANGE AGENT IN HIGHER EDUCATION?

Transformation in higher education is a difficult and slow process (Eckel & Kezar, 2003). Furthermore, when thinking about those who are in positions to transform higher education, more often than not, academic leaders who are part of the traditional organizational structure of the university or college are assumed to be those responsible for change (Hart, 2009). According to Egan (1985), a *change agent* refers to any person playing a role in creating, redesigning, operating, reconfiguring, or transforming an institution, organization, or system. Within the context of our topic, the focus is on changing oppressive social environments in higher education and helping identify the systemic or contextual sources of problems and methods of resolving them (Atkinson, Morten, & Sue, 1998). Thus, change agents in higher education can have influence at different levels (from micro to macro) of the social context.

Certainly, the traditional institutional leadership is in a position to act as change agents for diversity issues; however, change agents also include less traditionally considered leaders throughout the academy. Hart (2005, 2007, 2008) and other scholars (Brown-Glaude, 2008) have shown how faculty have been change agents around issues of diversity. Their empirical work on faculty as change agents suggests that anyone who is committed to social justice and works to improve the climate for all is truly a change agent. This means that many scholars and practitioners within higher education can be and often are change agents, including the following:

- Faculty
- Career center staff
- Counseling center staff
- Student health staff
- Wellness center staff
- Academic advisors
- Academic retention service staff
- Diversity offices staff (e.g., women's center, multicultural center, LGBT center, disability services)
- Student affairs staff (e.g., residential life, student activities, recreation, judicial, programming)

The work of these change agents is evidenced in many ways and can produce effects at the highest levels of the organizational structure as well as on more interpersonal and individual levels. Generally speaking, the broadest level of systemic change often takes place only after achieving support from faculty governance and key top administrators, but there are many ways that faculty, students, and staff can be key figures in organizing and facilitating grassroots change efforts that build momentum from the bottom up. The next section provides examples of how research, curricular transformation and teaching, and advocacy can be levers for institutional transformation, guided by change agents. In addition, Grieger and Toliver's (2001) chapter in an earlier edition of this book provides specific suggestions for enhancing multiculturalism in higher education.

Research

As part of faculty work, research plays a significant role. For certain faculty, conducting scholarly inquiry and sharing their findings is part of their responsibility as change agents. In fact, faculty who identify as feminist scholars, multicultural scholars, and queer and critical theorists consider activism fundamental to the work that they do. Said differently, these scholars conduct research about issues of diversity and multiculturalism in order to critique the status quo and to influence change for those who are marginalized; this is an aspect of what it means to be a change agent in higher education. Many of these same scholars also participate in research about and for their own colleges and universities. Sometimes, this work is not done in order to publish a book chapter or journal article, but rather to empirically and critically study multicultural issues that can influence policymakers on campus, very much like the campus climate work described later. Hart, Grogan, Litt, and Worthington (2008) identify this type of research as *scholarly service* and advocate that it be recognized and rewarded by institutional leaders as scholarship.

Research, however, is not only a role that faculty play. More and more, we see practitioners conducting rigorous research (Rhoades, 2006), not only for publication and presentation externally, but in order to make data-driven decisions for their units and campuses. Evidence of this sort of inquiry is through the development and execution of campus climate studies

(Harper & Hurtado, 2007). Those conducting such work are likely change agents themselves, but they certainly set the stage for other change agents to use the findings and recommendations to transform a campus climate to one that is more multicultural (e.g., Worthington, Navarro, Loewy, & Hart, 2008). A more detailed discussion about the nature of campus climate research appears below.

Curricular Transformation and Teaching

Much like the research function of a college or university, the teaching function now is shared by many constituents of an institution. Faculty have a central role in teaching and curricular decisions, but more and more, professional staff, including counselors and administrators, are part of the formal curriculum. Historically, these individuals have been crucial to the education that happens outside the classroom and supports learning that occurs inside the classroom (i.e., the co-curriculum). As a result, any of these educators can serve as change agents in their work related to teaching and the development of the curriculum and co-curriculum.

In the late 1970s and early 1980s, many colleges and universities were involved in curricular transformation efforts. The National Endowment for the Humanities funded projects to integrate women's studies into the larger institutional curriculum on many campuses (Aiken, Anderson, Dinnerstein, Lensink, & MacCorquodale, 1988), and similar, but often unfunded projects continue today to create departments and programs with a emphasis on multicultural issues (e.g., Black studies, Chicano/Hispanic/Latino studies, women's and gender studies, Native American studies, and queer studies). In addition to discrete departments and programs that focus on diversity, individual faculty and groups of faculty have intentionally designed courses that integrate diversity throughout the course content. Adams, Bell, and Griffin (1997) offer four approaches to integrate multiculturalism into the curriculum, whether in an individual course or more widely constructed: contribution approach, additive approach, transformation approach, and social justice approach. As teachers move from one approach to another, the commitment to multiculturalism and activism increases, as does the likelihood that these educators are change agents for diversity.

Transforming the curriculum so that it is multicultural is one aspect of the teaching endeavor. Another component, and one that is more day-to-day, is the pedagogical approaches that educators take as they interact with students. Teachers who are change agents are conscious of and intentionally address issues in their classes that exclude others. For instance, teachers confront myths and stereotypes like "non-native English speakers are less intelligent," "women are less capable in math and science," and "all Asians are inherently good students." They also confront discriminatory and harassing remarks; do not expect individual students to speak for their entire race, religion, sex, gender, sexual orientation, and/or other identity characteristics; and prepare activities and assignments that are accessible to all students in the class. In addition, they facilitate difficult dialogues in respectful and thoughtful ways so that all points of view can be considered (Landis, 2008; Nash, Bradley, & Chickering, 2008). To be change agents as educators, skill is necessary. And skillful educators are aware of how students experience their own learning and perceive teachers' actions, are critically reflective about their teaching, and do whatever it takes to help students learn (Brookfield, 2006).

Advocacy

Thanks in large part to influences from multicultural and feminist psychology, advocacy has emerged as an important professional activity for counselors and counseling psychologists. Advocacy is commonly referred to as the third leg of the three-legged stool of professional activities, which include practice and research activities (Fouad, 2002). Advocacy can occur across many domains, and counselors are especially well positioned to contribute to each because of their unique skill set. These domains include public policy/legislative agendas, campus advocacy, and student organization advocacy.

The ascension of the role of advocacy has brought attention from national organizations representing counselors and psychologists. The American Mental Health Counselors Association and the American Counseling Association (ACA) have both organized public policy offices. However, the most visible effort arguably has been put forth by the American Psychological

Association (APA). APA has organized multiple advocacy efforts that are coordinated by each of its directorates, which include practice, education, public interest, and science. APA has also extended its approach beyond the other organizations by recruiting state-level federal advocacy coordinators (FACs) as well as reaching out to members who may not belong to state associations by organizing divisional FACs as well as its graduate student organization APAGS advocacy coordination teams. These various organizations are active in recruiting members to lobby legislators and advising them about the impact of pending legislation. This is a critical outlet for counselors who are invested in social justice and understand the widespread impact of federal and state legislation.

In addition to policy advocacy at the federal and state levels, counselors are able to provide advocacy on a local level. Many psychologists and counselors write letters to the editors in local newspapers in order to bring awareness to neglected issues or redress misrepresentations in media. Counselors are further involved in campus advocacy in whatever role they work. This is evident in supporting efforts to make services more accessible to various underrepresented segments of the campus community in the most appropriate fashion. This may include assisting students in forming campus organizations that address their needs or providing a voice to a group that had been lacking one thus far.

EMERGING NATIONAL TRENDS: POTENTIAL ISSUES ON A CHANGE AGENT'S AGENDA

Myriad hot-button issues are salient for today's change agents. Some of the issues described below present challenges to multicultural work on campus, whereas others provide opportunities to advance diversity and multicultural agendas on campus and throughout higher education.

Emergence of the Chief Diversity Officer Model

In their landmark study, Williams and Wade-Golden (2008) have identified the chief diversity officer (CDO) as one of the fastest growing administrative positions in higher education. According to their research,

responsibilities of CDOs include efforts to (a) improve access and equity for underrepresented groups of students, faculty, staff, and administrators; (b) assess and improve the campus climate for diversity; (c) use research and scholarship to provide insight into the experiences of marginalized and underrepresented groups on campus; and (d) infuse diversity into the curriculum in multiple ways that ensure the educational benefits of diversity. As Gose (2006) points out, a host of highly regarded institutions across the country have created and expanded the scope of the CDO over the past 5 years, including Harvard; the University of California, Berkeley; the University of Texas at Austin; the University of Virginia; the University of Missouri; and Washington State University, to name only a few. Nevertheless, institutions differ widely in terms of (a) the level and scope of administrative authority given to the CDO (from "director" to "assistant/associate vice provost," to "vice president"); (b) the organizational structure of the division headed by the CDO (from single-person offices to unit-based operations to broad-based, multifaceted divisional structures); (c) the level of fiscal resources dedicated to the unit (e.g., operating budgets in the tens of thousands through the tens of millions of dollars); and finally (d) the level and types of qualifications required to perform the duties of the CDO (e.g., with degrees ranging from the bachelor's to the PhD or JD, and career tracks arising out of tenured academic faculty positions through nonacademic staff positions in student affairs or human resources or coming from the business sector outside the university) (see Williams & Wade-Golden, 2008, for an analysis of these wide variations across institutions).

Thus, the CDO must have the vision, interpersonal style, and communication skills to work collaboratively with people from the broadest spectrum of backgrounds and perspectives at all levels of the university system and community. The CDO must pursue positive change in organizational culture and climate through efforts to assess, analyze, implement, monitor, and modify policies and procedures that will increase diversity and inclusiveness. Within that context, the CDO must engage a broad base of stakeholders and constituents in the diversity strategic planning process and identify key strategic advantages that will facilitate progress toward goals and objectives. There is enormous complexity in managing the sometimes rival demands of different groups of students, faculty, staff, alumni, community members, donors, legislators, and political groups. The CDO must have the capacity to engage these "difficult dialogues" with balance, realism, integrity, perseverance, patience, and humility. Counselors and psychologists working in higher education contexts have unique training and skills to place them on a career track that might result in appointment to a CDO position (usually after many years of demonstrated research, service, and/or teaching diversity issues in a higher education context).

In 2007, the National Association of Diversity Officers in Higher Education (NADOHE) was established in response to the growing need for higher education to leverage and maximize investments in diversity initiatives, provide opportunities for cross-institutional exchange and fertilization of ideas, and enhance professional standards among diversity workers. It has become the principal organization of the chief and senior diversity officers in higher education. In its first year of existence, NADOHE had 109 charter institution members. The first national conference of NADOHE was held in conjunction with the national meeting of the American Council on Education in Washington, DC, in February 2007, and the second conference was in San Diego in February 2008. In addition, NADOHE established the *Journal of Diversity in Higher Education* (*JDHE*) in cooperation with the APA journals, and the first two issues of *JDHE* appeared in print in March and June 2008, featuring the scholarship of several counseling psychologists (Garriott, Love, & Tyler, 2008; Kivlighan, 2008; Spanierman, Neville, Liao, Hammer, & Wang, 2008; Worthington et al., 2008).

Campus Climate Research

The campus climate for diversity and inclusion has become a central focus of efforts to enhance diversity processes and outcomes in 21st-century higher education, especially for the purposes of informing diversity strategic planning (Hurtado, Milem, Clayton-Pedersen, & Allen, 1998). Given the intricacy of the concept of diversity, as well as the complexity of institutions of higher education, the study of campus climate can seem overwhelming and fraught with potential challenges. According to Hurtado et al. (1998), there are four climate-related factors internal to and within the control of individual colleges and universities: (a) compositional

or structural diversity, (b) the psychological dimension of the climate, (c) the behavioral dimension of the climate, and (d) an institution's history and legacy of inclusion or exclusion. Assessment of compositional or structural diversity refers to identifying the presence of members of previously underrepresented groups and evaluating the quality or comprehensiveness of efforts to increase the numerical or proportional diversity of students, staff, and faculty. Assessment of the psychological dimension of diversity refers to examination of perceived racial conflict and discrimination, the extent to which particular groups feel singled out because of their background, and perceptions of institutional support/commitment related to diversity. The behavioral dimension of campus climate is generally assessed using reports of enrollment in diversity courses, interactions or contact experiences between and among different groups, and participation (or lack thereof) in campus programs and diversity activities (and may at times include evaluations of the quality of those interactions). Assessments of an institution's history and legacy of inclusion or exclusion should include both recent and distant history with respect to exclusion and discriminatory practices, as well as successes and failures of past efforts to enhance diversity and inclusion.

Effective researchers must be aware of the potential trade-offs between scientific validity, practical implementation issues, resources/costs, and the applied utility of different approaches to campus climate research. They must also understand how the institutional contexts of fiscal, political, organizational, historical, human, and local diversity issues will influence their approach to conducting campus climate research. Counselors and psychologists are often equipped to assist campus administrators in developing appropriate strategies for the design, implementation, and diffusion of successful campus climate research and findings (e.g., Ancis, Sedlacek, & Mohr, 2000; Gloria, Castellanos, Lopez, & Rosales, 2005; Gloria, Hird, & Navarro, 2001; Gloria & Ho, 2003; Gloria & Robinson Kurpius; 2001; Gloria, Robinson Kurpius, Hamilton, & Willson, 1999; Spanierman et al., 2008; Worthington et al., 2008).

Depolarizing the Discourse

For many higher education faculty and administrators, the need for addressing controversial topics from a *difficult dialogues* paradigm has reached a critical point, as a number of political groups begin to launch attacks that are perceived to threaten academic freedom and politicize the university in ways that will be destructive to fundamental missions of the academy. The Ford Foundation Difficult Dialogues Initiative was launched in 2006 on 43 institutions across the country "to promote academic freedom and religious, cultural, and political pluralism on college and university campuses" (Thomas Jefferson Center for the Protection of Freedom of Expression, 2008). Although the funded programs varied widely in scope and content, a variety of themes were apparent, including (a) differentiating dialogue from debate; (b) focusing on the development of critical thinking skills for students in the classroom through deliberation and dialogue; (c) promoting a climate of respect, safety, and inquiry where cultural, religious, and political differences may produce a divisive atmosphere in the classroom; (d) addressing the roles of academic freedom, freedoms of speech and expression, academic responsibility, and intellectual pluralism in managing difficult dialogues; and (e) negotiating inherent tensions between social justice advocacy and inclusion efforts, on one hand, and constitutional freedoms on the other (Boggs, Worthington, Khairallah, & Wagner, 2008; Landis, 2008; Nash et al., 2008; O'Neill, 2008; Worthington, Hodge, & Ladehoff, 2008). Thus, whether a particular classroom discussion centers on the Iraq war; the theology of Islam or the politics of Islamic countries; Israeli-Palestinian relations; the teaching of intelligent design in secondary education; the use of stem cells in medical, biological, and life sciences; the nature of sexual orientation and sexual identity politics; debates over immigration in the United States; the impact of racial identity in political discourse; or any number of other hot-button issues, the focus of the Difficult Dialogues Initiative is to prepare students (and faculty) to engage constructively in dialogues that deepen and enhance understanding across cultural, political, and religious divides.

The discovery of new knowledge and the resolution of social problems vitally depend on critical thinking, effective communication, collaboration, and truth-telling among those with differing cultural, religious, and ideological perspectives; yet sophisticated new political groups have begun to attack these fundamental ideals of higher education. In 2007, David Horowitz, president of the David Horowitz Freedom Center, unveiled a new campaign aimed at college campuses designed to encourage college students to reject "anti-American teachings" and recognize the threat of radical Islam, which he described as "terrorism awareness" (Chronicle of Higher Education, 2007). Since establishing the Center for the Study of Popular Culture in 1989, now the David Horowitz Freedom Center, Horowitz has become a national figure in attacks against what he calls the "leftist" academy, claiming that radical liberals have overtaken higher education and indoctrinated students to feminism, multiculturalism, and anti-Americanism. The Southern Poverty Law Center identified Horowitz and his organization as one of an array of foundations and think tanks that have entered the mainstream "to support efforts to make bigoted and discredited ideas respectable" (Berlet, 2003)—with Horowitz focusing his efforts primarily on higher education. To be clear, according to FBI statistics, the most common forms of hate crimes involve racial, ethnic, religious, or sexual orientation bias, and campuses are among the top locations for such acts. Anti-Semitism is the leading form of religious hate crime, followed by anti-Islamic bias. Anti-Islamic incidents have become more prevalent since the first Gulf War, in the aftermath of 9/11, and with the war in Iraq. According to the Southern Poverty Law Center (2008a, 2008b), hate groups in the United States have grown by 48% between 2000 to 2007, from 602 to 888 respectively, stating that "The growth of these groups is being helped by conspiracy theories and other racist propaganda about immigrants that is being spread by mainstream politicians and pundits" (2008b, para. 7). As in the cases of other topics covered in this chapter, counselors working as change agents have the potential to play significant roles in the processes and outcomes of campus dialogues, difficult dialogues, on sensitive subjects that cross-cut cultural, political, and religious divides that have been described as "culture wars" in the United States.

Anti-Affirmative Action Efforts and Supreme Court Cases

Affirmative action has been a critical issue in higher education for decades, and there have been renewed efforts to dismantle it in the courts and in state referenda. The initial intent of affirmative action policies was to correct decades of racial discrimination in employment, education, and housing. The first two major cases against it were presented to the U.S. Supreme Court within 10 years after affirmative action was first implemented (i.e., *DeFunis v. Odegaard,* 1974; *University of California Regents v. Bakke,* 1978). The *Bakke* case against the University of California became a landmark decision governing affirmative action in higher education in which Justice Lewis Powell authored the majority opinion, stating that race could be one of numerous factors used in college admissions, but that it may not be the sole factor in making admissions decisions. However, because the nine justices ruling in the case were in concurrence on only parts of the majority opinion and there were five separate dissenting opinions written against portions of the Powell opinion, *Bakke* has widely been interpreted as an unsettling split decision that produced rulings both supporting and limiting affirmative action in educational admissions. More recently, in two cases against the University of Michigan (*Grutter v. Bollinger,* 2003; *Gratz v. Bollinger,* 2003), the U.S. Supreme Court rendered yet another split decision. In the first decision, the court ruled that the University of Michigan admissions policy that awarded points to people of color on the basis of race/ethnicity (along with points awarded for such things as children of alumni, athletes, and men enrolling in nursing programs) was unconstitutional. In the second decision, the Court upheld the policy of the University of Michigan Law School that gave consideration to increasing diversity within the law school and among those in the legal professions by using race as one factor in determining admissions.

A critical aspect of these major Supreme Court rulings is that they have established the standard of *strict scrutiny,* the most rigorous standard of judicial review, in the consideration of race and ethnicity in decisions that confer opportunities or benefits. Under the standard of strict scrutiny, institutions must demonstrate that their "race-conscious" policies are "narrowly tailored" to serve a "compelling interest" in promoting the educational benefits of a diverse student body (Coleman & Palmer, 2006). Justice Sandra Day O'Connor wrote the majority decision for *Grutter v. Bollinger,* which stated that the Constitution

does not prohibit the . . . narrowly tailored use of race in admissions decisions to further a compelling interest in obtaining the educational benefits that flow from a diverse student body. . . . In order to cultivate a set of leaders with legitimacy in the eyes of the citizenry, it is necessary that the path to leadership be visibly open to talented and qualified individuals of every race and ethnicity.

Nevertheless, after successfully using state referenda in California, Washington, and Michigan with devastating effects on admissions for African Americans and Latino/a students (e.g., Chapa, 2005; Grodsky & Kurlaender, 2006; Moses et al., 2007; Rendón, Novack, & Dowell, 2005), Ward Connerly and others have continued to challenge race-conscious affirmative action through referenda designed to make it unconstitutional in several more states, initially focusing on Arizona, Colorado, Missouri, Nebraska, Nevada, Oregon, South Dakota, Wyoming, and Utah, but ultimately narrowing his 2008 efforts to only five states (Arizona, Colorado, Missouri, Nebraska, and Oklahoma). Connerly failed to obtain enough signatures to put his referenda on the ballots in Oklahoma, Arizona, and Missouri (the first losses encountered by Connerly using "civil rights" terminology as a tactic in attacking a central strategy of the civil rights movement), but petition drives in Colorado and Nebraska were ultimately successful in placing the anti-affirmative action referenda on the ballots in those states for the November 2008 election. Although the ballot initiative passed in Nebraska by a similar margin as in Washington and California (58% voting in favor of the ban), the measure in Colorado was narrowly defeated (51%–49%). In addition, Connerly has vowed to return to states where court battles helped to defeat his efforts, possibly in 2010.

Impact of War

The current armed conflicts in Afghanistan and Iraq differ significantly from previous wars such as Vietnam, Korea, and World Wars I and II because of various factors. The current conflicts resemble the Vietnam war in the questioning of the necessity of the conflict from its outset because many individuals saw it as a war of choice rather than necessity. However, significant differences exist, as seen in the absence of organized and sustained protests such as those seen in the 1960s. The context of the war appears to draw less tension because of the perceived threat of terrorism and the absence of a formal draft. However, some have referred to these wars as being fueled by an economic draft that operates to recruit individuals who seek "to gain job skills, experience and educational opportunities absent from their civilian lives" (Zweig, 2008, para. 1). This creates a special concern for counselors who are concerned with social justice and the differential impact of financial incentives on the poor. Although to date, fewer people are affected overall than in the Vietnam war, there is a significant difference in the aftermath of war because of the higher survival rates for veterans as a result of improvements in body armor and advances in health care. This increased survival rate has led to a significant increase in the demand for career and rehabilitation services as veterans with significant functional losses return home.

Since the inception of the counseling field, counselors have been invested in the welfare of returning soldiers and have designed services to assist in their successful reintegration into society and academic settings. The influence of this investment is seen in the efforts by various institutions to provide a "veteran-friendly" campus. This issue continues to receive significant focus, as noted by the American Council on Education's 2008 summit titled "Serving Those Who Serve: Higher Education and America's Veterans." This event allowed higher education leaders to engage in candid conversation about issues faced by America's veterans as they resume their education after wartime service. As with the other salient issues described above, counselors and psychologists are well poised to bring attention to the special needs of returning soldiers and to provide services that address their needs in higher education.

Progress in Guidelines

The growth in the multicultural field has led to the adoption and revision of guidelines across national organizations. Such guidelines can be seen in the early work of counselors and counseling psychologists. APA's early efforts in developing guidelines resulted in the "Guidelines for Providers of Psychological Services to Ethnic, Linguistic, and Culturally Diverse Populations"

(American Psychological Association, 1993). This document served as a template for other organizations that were looking to establish practice guidelines for their members, including ACA, the National Board for Certified Counselors, the Association for Specialists in Group Work, and even noncounseling organizations such as the National Association of Social Workers.

This document was exemplary in its coverage of the necessary skills for providing culturally appropriate services. It also set the stage for the next step in guideline development as multicultural scholars found this document lacking in several areas. As a result, efforts to develop a more comprehensive statement led to the "Guidelines on Multicultural Education, Training, Research, Practice, and Organizational Change for Psychologists." This document was endorsed by the APA's governing body in 2002 and is considered policy until 2009. The APA council of representatives will have the option to continue or revise this policy at that time. The implications of this document are widespread as articulated in Guideline 3: "As educators, psychologists are encouraged to employ the constructs of multiculturalism and diversity in psychological education" and Guideline 6: "Psychologists are encouraged to use organizational change processes to support culturally informed organizational (policy) development and practices."

Additional competencies continue to be identified and endorsed by counselor organizations. In 2003, the ACA Governing Council endorsed a set of advocacy competencies that were drafted by Lewis, Arnold, House, and Toporek (American Counseling Association, 2003). The document provides a comprehensive framework for organizing advocacy activities across domains of activity and interventions, which allows training programs to conduct assessments about training effectiveness and the counselor's readiness to adopt the role of change agent.

CONCLUSIONS

Threats and opportunities to create and sustain a diverse multicultural community in higher education continue to confront those who are committed to social justice. Counselors are among the scholars, practitioners, and scholar-practitioners who are in a position to act as change agents and contribute to multicultural transformation. Discrete and continuing efforts through research, curriculum and teaching, the co-curriculum, direct services, administration, and advocacy are among myriad ways that counselors can realize their work for change. Furthermore, given the larger societal, cultural, and political context in which higher education exists, diversity change agents must be attuned to the complexities that continue to influence the higher education landscape. As emerging issues unfold, counselors must remain vigilant in monitoring national and local trends and situating them within a diverse contextual framework that is broadening beyond race/ethnicity and gender. As a result of their unique set of skills, counselors espouse broadly defined roles and seek opportunities that allow them to intervene across widespread campus initiatives. Counselors must remain flexible in their approaches to address societal demands because of the potential to make significant contributions toward improving social justice in higher education.

REFERENCES

Adams, M., Bell, L. A., & Griffin, P. (Eds.). (1997). *Teaching for diversity and social justice: A sourcebook*. New York: Routledge.

Aiken, S. H., Anderson, K., Dinnerstein, M., Lensink, J. N., & MacCorquodale, P. (Eds.). (1988). *Changing our minds: Feminist transformations of knowledge*. Albany: State University of New York Press.

American Association of Colleges and Universities. (1995). *The drama of diversity and democracy: Higher education and American commitments*. Washington, DC: Author.

American Counseling Association. (2003). Advocacy competencies. Retrieved June 30, 2008, from http://www .counseling.org/Files/FD.ashx?guid=680f251e-b3d0–4f77–8aa3–4e360f32f05e

American Psychological Association. (1993). Guidelines for providers of psychological services to ethnic, linguistic, and culturally diverse populations. *American Psychologist, 48*(1), 45–48.

American Psychological Association. (2003). Guidelines on multicultural education, training, research, practice, and organizational change for psychologists. *American Psychologist, 58*(5), 377–402.

Ancis, J. R., Sedlacek, W. E., & Mohr, J. J. (2000). Student perceptions of campus cultural climate by race. *Journal of Counseling & Development, 78*(2), 180–185.

Antonio, A. L. (2001). Diversity and the influence of friendship groups in college. *Review of Higher Education, 25*(1), 63–89.

Atkinson, D. R., Morten, G., & Sue, D. W. (1998). *Counseling American minorities* (5th ed.). Boston: McGraw-Hill.

Bauerlein, M. (2006). How academe shortchanges conservative thinking. *Chronicle of Higher Education, 53*(17), B6.

Berlet, C. (2003, Summer). Into the mainstream: An array of right-wing foundations and think tanks support efforts to make bigoted and discredited ideas respectable. *Intelligence Report*. Retrieved on October 1, 2008, from http://www.splcenter.org/intel/intelreport/article.jsp?aid=50

Blimling, G. S. (2001). Editorial: Diversity makes you smarter. *Journal of College Student Development, 42*(6), 517–519.

Boggs, K. A., Worthington, R. L., Khairallah, T., & Wagner, J. (2008, March). *When religious freedom intersects with social justice advocacy*. Workshop presented at the International Counseling Psychology Conference: Creating the Future: Counseling Psychologists in a Changing World, Chicago, IL.

Brookfield, S. D. (2006). *The skillful teacher*. San Francisco: Jossey-Bass.

Brown-Glaude, W. (Ed.). (2008). *Backbone and nerves of steel: Faculty leadership for diversity in higher education*. New Brunswick, NJ: Rutgers University Press.

Chang, M. J. (1996). *Racial diversity in higher education: Does a racially mixed student population affect educational outcomes?* Unpublished doctoral dissertation, University of California, Los Angeles.

Chapa, J. (2005). Affirmative action and percent plans as alternatives for increasing successful participation of minorities in higher education. *Journal of Hispanic Higher Education, 49*(3), 181–196.

Chesler, M. A., Lewis, A. E., & Crowfoot, J. E. (2005). *Challenging racism in higher education: Promoting justice*. Lanham, MD: Rowman & Littlefield.

Chronicle of Higher Education. (2007, February 1). David Horowitz's latest venture aims to awaken students to Islamic peril. Retrieved October 30, 2008, from http://chronicle.com/news/article/1599/david-horowitzs-latest-venture-aims-to-awaken-students-to-islamic-peril

Clayton-Pedersen, A. R., Parker, S., Smith, D. G., Moreno, J. F., & Teraguchi, D. H. (2007). *Making a real difference with diversity: A guide to institutional change*. Washington, DC: Association of American Colleges and Universities.

Coleman, A. L., & Palmer, S. R. (2006). *Admissions and diversity after Michigan: The next generation of legal and policy issues*. New York: College Board.

Corbett, C., Hill, C., & St. Rose, A. (2008). *Where the girls are: The facts about gender equity in education.* Washington, DC: American Association of University Women Educational Foundation.

Council of Economic Advisors for the President's Initiative on Race. (1998). *Changing America: Indicators of social and economic well-being by race and Hispanic origin.* Washington, DC: U.S. Government Printing Office.

DeFunis v. Odegaard, 416 U.S. 312, 350 (1974).

D'Souza, D. (1998). *Illiberal education: The politics of race and sex on campus.* New York: Free Press.

Eckel, P. D., & Kezar, A. J. (2003). *Taking the reins: Institutional transformation in higher education.* Westport, CT: Greenwood.

Egan, G. (1985). *Change agent skills in helping and human services settings.* Monterey, CA: Brooks/Cole.

Fouad, N. A. (2002). 2001 presidential address. Dreams for 2010: Making a difference. *Counseling Psychologist, 30*(1), 158–166.

Garcia, M. (2007). Democracy, diversity, and presidential leadership. *Liberal Education, 93*(3), 22–27.

Garriott, P. O., Love, K. M., & Tyler, K. M. (2008). Anti-Black racism, self-esteem, and the adjustment of White students in higher education. *Journal of Diversity in Higher Education, 1*(1), 45–58.

Glazer-Raymo, J. (1999). *Shattering the myths: Women in academe.* Baltimore: Johns Hopkins University Press.

Glazer-Raymo, J. (2008). The feminist agenda: A work in progress. In J. Glazer-Raymo (Ed.), *Unfinished agendas: New and continuing gender challenges in higher education.* Baltimore: Johns Hopkins University Press.

Gloria, A. M., Castellanos, J., Lopez, A. G., & Rosales, R. (2005). An examination of academic nonpersistence decisions of Latino undergraduates. *Hispanic Journal of Behavioral Sciences, 27*(2), 202–223.

Gloria, A. M., Hird, J. S., & Navarro, R. L. (2001). Relationships of cultural congruity and perceptions of the university environment to help-seeking attitudes by socio-race and gender. *Journal of College Student Development, 42*(6), 545–562.

Gloria, A. M., & Ho, T. A. (2003). Environmental, social, and psychological experiences of Asian American undergraduates: Examining issues of academic persistence. *Journal of Counseling & Development, 81*(1), 93–105.

Gloria, A. M., & Robinson Kurpius, S. E. (2001). Influences of self-beliefs, social support, and comfort in the university environment on the academic nonpersistence decisions of American Indian undergraduates. *Cultural Diversity & Ethnic Minority Psychology, 7*(1), 88–102.

Gloria, A. M., Robinson Kurpius, S. E., Hamilton, K. D., & Willson, M. S. (1999). African American students' persistence at a predominantly white university: Influence of social support, university comfort, and self-beliefs. *Journal of College Student Development, 40*(3), 257–268.

Gose, B. (2006, September 29). The rise of the chief diversity officer. *Chronicle of Higher Education, 53*(6), B1.

Gratz v. Bollinger et al., 539 U.S. 241 (2003).

Gravois, J. (2007, January 26). The battle over studies of faculty bias. *Chronicle of Higher Education, 53*(21), A8.

Grieger, I., & Toliver, S. (2001). Multiculturalism on predominantly white campuses: Multiple roles and functions for the counselor. In J. Ponterotto, J. M. Casas, L. Suzuki, & C. Alexander (Eds.), *Handbook of multicultural counseling* (2nd ed., pp. 825–848). Thousand Oaks, CA: Sage.

Grodsky, E., & Kurlaender, M. (2006, October 27). *The demography of higher education in the wake of affirmative action.* Paper presented at the Equal Opportunity in Higher Education: The Past and Future of Proposition 209 meeting, Berkeley, CA.

Grutter v. Bollinger et al., 539 U.S. 241 (2003).

Gurin, P. (1999). *The compelling need for diversity in education.* Expert report prepared for the lawsuits *Gratz and Hamacher v. Bollinger, Duderstadt, the University of Michigan, and the University of Michigan College of LS&A,* U.S. District Court, Eastern District of Michigan, Civil Action No. 97–75231; and *Grutter v. Bollinger, Lehman, Shields, the University of Michigan, and the University of Michigan Law School,* U.S. District Court, Eastern District of Michigan, Civil Action No. 97–75928 [Online]. Retrieved May 24, 2007, from http://www.umich.edu/~urel/admissions/legal/expert/gurintoc.html

Harper, S. R., & Hurtado, S. (2007). Nine themes in campus racial climates and implications for institutional transformation. In S. R. Harper & L. D. Patton (Eds.), *Responding to the realities of race on campus* (pp. 7–24). San Francisco: Jossey-Bass.

Hart, J. (2005, Summer). Activism among feminist academics: Professionalized activism and activist professionals. *Advancing Women in Leadership, 18.* Retrieved June 7, 2005, from http://www.advancingwomen.com/awl/social_justice1/Hart.html

Hart, J. (2007). Creating networks as an activist strategy: Differing approaches among academic feminist organizations. *Journal of the Professoriate, 2*(1), 33–52.

Hart, J. (2008). Mobilization among women academics: The interplay between feminism and professionalization. *National Women's Studies Association Journal, 20*(1), 184–208.

Hart, J. (2009). Creating faculty activism and grassroots leadership: An open letter to aspiring activists. In A. Kezar (Ed.), *New horizons for leadership development of faculty and administrators in higher education* (pp. 169–184). Sterling, VA: Stylus.

Hart, J., Grogan, M., Litt, J., & Worthington, R. (2008). Institutional diversity work as intellectual work. In W. Brown-Glaude (Ed.), *Doing diversity in higher education: Faculty leaders share challenges and strategies* (pp. 61–80). New Brunswick, NJ: Rutgers University Press.

Higher Education Research Institute. (2005). The spiritual life of college students: A national study of college students' search for meaning and purpose. Retrieved June 20, 2008, from http://spirituality.ucla.edu/spirituality/reports/FINAL_REPORT.pdf

Higher Education Research Institute. (2006). Spirituality and the professoriate: A national study of faculty beliefs, attitudes and behaviors. Retrieved June 30, 2008, from http://spirituality.ucla.edu/results/spirit_professoriate.pdf

Horowitz, D. (2007). *Indoctrination U: The left's war against academic freedom.* New York: Encounter Books.

Horowitz, D., & Lehrer, E. (2003). Political bias in the administrations and faculties of 32 elite colleges and universities. Retrieved June 30, 2008, from http://www.studentsforacademicfreedom.org/news/1898/lackdiversity.html

Hurtado, S. (2001). Linking diversity and educational purpose: How diversity affects the classroom environment and student development. In G. Orfield & M. Kurlaender (Eds.), *Diversity challenged: Evidence on the impact of affirmative action* (pp. 187–203). Cambridge, MA: Harvard Civil Rights Project.

Hurtado, S., Milem, J. F., Clayton-Pedersen, A. R., & Allen, W. R. (1998). Enhancing campus climates for racial/ethnic diversity: Educational policy and practice. *Review of Higher Education, 21*(3), 279–302.

Jayakumar, U. M. (2007). *Can higher education meet the needs of an increasingly diverse society and global marketplace? Campus diversity and cross-cultural workforce competencies.* Unpublished doctoral dissertation, University of California, Los Angeles.

Kivlighan, D. M. (2008). Compositional diversity and the research productivity of PhD graduates. *Journal of Diversity in Higher Education, 1*(1), 59–66.

Klein, D. B., & Stern, C. (in press). How politically diverse are the social sciences and humanities? Survey evidence from six fields. *Academic Questions.*

Landis, K. (2008). *Start talking: A handbook for engaging difficult dialogues in higher education.* Anchorage: University of Alaska Press.

Moses, M., Marin, P., & Yun, J. (2008, April). *Affirmative action's fate: Are 20 more years enough?* Paper presented at the American Educational Researcher's Association annual meeting, New York.

Nash, R. J., Bradley, D. L., & Chickering, A. W. (2008). *How to talk about hot topics on campus: From polarization to moral conversation.* San Francisco: Jossey-Bass.

Neville, H. A., Worthington, R. L., & Spanierman, L. B. (2001). Race, power, and multicultural counseling psychology: Understanding white privilege and color-blind racial attitudes. In J. G. Ponterotto, J. M. Casas, L. A. Suzuki, & C. M. Alexander (Eds.), *Handbook of multicultural counseling* (2nd ed., pp. 257–288). Thousand Oaks, CA: Sage.

O'Neill, R. (2008). *Academic freedom in the wired world: Political extremism, corporate power, and the university.* Cambridge, MA: Harvard University Press.

Pryor, J. H., Hurtado, S., Saenz, V. B., Korn, J. S., Santos, J. L., & Korn, W. S. (2007). *The American freshman: National norms for fall 2006.* Los Angeles: Higher Education Research Institute.

Rendón, L., Novack, V., & Dowell, D. (2005). Testing race-neutral admissions models: Lessons from California State University–Long Beach. *Review of Higher Education, 28*(2), 221–243.

Rhoades, G. (2006). The higher education we choose: A question of balance. *Review of Higher Education, 29*(3), 381–404.

Rothman, S., Lichter, S. R., & Nevitte, N. (2005). Politics and professional advancement among college faculty. *Forum, 3*(1). Retrieved October 1, 2008, from http://www.bepress.com/cgi/viewcontent.cgi?article=1067&context=forum

Smith, D. G., & Associates. (1997). *Diversity works: The emerging picture of how students benefit.* Washington, DC: Association of American Colleges and Universities.

Southern Poverty Law Center. (2008a, Spring). Extremist propaganda: Fake "hate" crimes embarrass far right. *Intelligence Report.* Retrieved October 1, 2008, from http://www.splcenter.org/intel/intelreport/article.jsp?aid=889

Southern Poverty Law Center. (2008b, Spring). The year in hate: Active U.S. hate groups rise to 888 in 2007. *Intelligence Report.* Retrieved October 1, 2008, from http://www.splcenter.org/intel/intelreport/article.jsp?aid=886

Spanierman, L. B., Neville, H. A., Liao, H. Y., Hammer, J. H., & Wang, Y. F. (2008). Participation in formal and informal campus diversity experiences: Effects on students' racial democratic beliefs. *Journal of Diversity in Higher Education, 1,* 108–125.

Sue, D. W. (1995). Multicultural organizational development: Implications for the counseling profession. In J. G. Ponterotto, J. M. Casas, L. A. Suzuki, & C. M. Alexander (Eds.), *Handbook of multicultural counseling* (pp. 474–492). Thousand Oaks, CA: Sage.

Thomas Jefferson Center for the Protection of Freedom of Expression. (2008). Difficult dialogues initiative: Promoting pluralism and academic freedom on campus. Retrieved October 1, 2008, from http://www.difficult dialogues.org/

University of California Regents v. Bakke, 438 U.S. 265 (1978).

U.S. Census Bureau. (2004). Educational attainment in the United States: 2003. Retrieved October 1, 2008, from http://www.census.gov/prod/2004pubs/p20-550.pdf

U.S. Census Bureau. (2006). 2006 Annual Social and Economic Supplement (ASEC) of the Current Population Survey (CPS). Retrieved October 1, 2008, from http://pubdb3.census.gov/macro/032006/perinc/new02_001.htm

U.S. Census Bureau. (2008a). Educational attainment in the United States: 2007. Retrieved June 30, 2008, from http://www.census.gov/population/www/socdemo/education/cps2007.html

U.S. Census Bureau. (2008b). U.S. Hispanic population surpasses 45 million: Now 15 percent of total. Retrieved October 30, 2008, from http://www.census.gov/Press-Release/www/releases/archives/population/011910.html

Will, G. F. (2007, October 14). Code of coercion. *Washington Post.* Retrieved June 30, 2008, from http://www.washingtonpost.com/wp-dyn/content/article/2007/10/12/AR2007101202151.html

Williams, D. A., & Wade-Golden, K. C. (2008). *The chief diversity officer: A primer for college and university presidents.* Washington, DC: American Council on Education.

Woessner, M., & Kelly-Woessner, A. (2008). Why conservatives don't get doctorates. In R. Maranto, R. Redding, & F. Hess (Eds.), *Reforming the politically correct university.* Washington, DC: American Enterprise Institute Press.

Worthington, R. L., Hodge, S., & Ladehoff, P. (2008, April). *Principles in facilitating difficult dialogues on immigration policy.* Paper presented at Cambio de Colores-Change of Colors conference: Latinos in Missouri: Uniting Cultures-Uniendo Culturas, Columbia, MO.

Worthington, R. L., Navarro, R. L., Loewy, M., & Hart, J. (2008). Color-blind racial attitudes, social dominance orientation, racial-ethnic group membership and college students' perceptions of campus climate. *Journal of Diversity in Higher Education, 1,* 8–19.

Zipp, J. F., & Fenwick, R. (2006). Is the academy a liberal hegemony? *Public Opinion Quarterly, 70*(3), 304–326.

Zweig, M. (2008, March 31). The war and the working class. Retrieved October 1, 2008, from http://www.thenation.com/doc/20080331/zweig

45

Responding to Hate on a College Campus

The Stop Hate Campaign and a Multicultural Climate Assessment

CHARLENE ALEXANDER, STEFANÍA ÆGISDÓTTIR,
LAWRENCE H. GERSTEIN, ERIN SNYDER,
DORIS KIRKPATRICK, MICHAEL O'HERON, ELIZABETH SELLERS,
REBECCA HANSEN, MARLON ROLLINS, AND TIMOTHY GORDON

"Change will not come if we wait for some other person or some other time. We are the ones we've been waiting for."

Barack Obama

Reflecting on the election of Barack Obama, it is quite clear that for institutions to change, change requires bold vision and action. President Obama's victory started as a grassroots movement with ordinary citizens banding together to enact change in our political system. Similarly, counseling psychology has its roots in social justice, and as the profession continues to grow and mature, the social context in which we live will continue to shape our work (Vera & Speight, 2003; Watson, 1983). The interest in social justice seems to be gaining more attention in the counseling

psychology literature (Toporek, Gerstein, Fouad, Roysircar, & Israel, 2006; Vera & Speight, 2003) as well as becoming an increasingly emphasized curriculum component at several counseling psychology graduate training programs across the United States and abroad, including ours at Ball State University (BSU).

The following sections of this chapter detail the response of counseling psychology faculty and students to specific incidents on the BSU campus. The first response occurred in 2005 and involved students, faculty, administrators, and the community. This response focused on a model of collaboration, pulling from feminist, multicultural, and ecological models of change. The second response occurred between 2007 and 2008 and involved two faculty members and students in the Department of Counseling Psychology and staff and students within the athletic department. This response reflects the social justice organizational development (SJOD) theory outlined by D'Andrea and Daniels in Chapter 46 of this *Handbook*. Each response is described in detail here to provide the reader with specific examples of how counseling psychologists can respond and be advocates for change when confronted with racially motivated incidents on a college campus.

THE STOP HATE CAMPAIGN

(ERIN SNYDER,
DORIS KIRKPATRICK,
MICHAEL O'HERON,
ELIZABETH SELLERS,
REBECCA HANSEN, MARLON
ROLLINS, TIMOTHY GORDON,
AND LAWRENCE H. GERSTEIN)

During the fall semester of 2005, several BSU students of color, international students, and students with minority religious backgrounds experienced racially motivated harassment while walking across campus. The incidents were public and prolific enough to bring wider public attention to such discriminatory and reprehensible behavior. Abusers in vehicles traveling on the two main campus thoroughfares shouted racial epithets, threw eggs, and in one case fired a water gun at a female student (Moody, 2005). Frustrated students filed complaints with campus authorities, and some felt that the university was not doing enough to address the situation. As members of the BSU community, we (students and faculty of counseling psychology) were also frustrated by what had happened. We were outraged that the harassment had occurred and concerned about what steps the university would take to combat this violence. We were outraged not only as human beings but also as members of the counseling psychology community, a community that had recently begun talking more in depth about our roles as advocates for

change not only with individual clients but also on a larger societal level.

In this section of the chapter, we will discuss our acquaintance with "immersive learning" as we worked for social justice goals as part of our training experience in the Department of Counseling Psychology and Guidance Services (CPSY) at BSU. To accomplish this, we embraced Bronfenbrenner's (1977, 1979) ecological model, which defines how the individual interacts with, influences, and is affected by her or his environment. We also incorporated Neville and Mobley's (2001) adaptation of this model for social justice work. This ecological model of multicultural counseling psychology processes (EMMCPP) was developed to help practitioners understand that multicultural counseling competencies exist on a broader scale than what exists in a one-to-one counseling relationship, and that therapeutic change must go beyond the individual.

As a part of our graduate training, 10 counseling psychology students enrolled in a special issues class focused on social justice and its relation to counseling psychology were required to develop a project addressing social justice issues. The students proposed that all members of the class work together as a group with their professor to accomplish some task with a potentially bigger impact than could be achieved individually. As advocates for change ourselves, we wanted to make the largest difference we could on campus. We believed that addressing the racial incidents at BSU was important, but we also wanted our message to be one of hope and one that would acknowledge the voices of hope and equality.

In our social justice class, discussion of this project, the Stop Hate campaign, became focused around creating a banner to be displayed on campus that would bring attention to the problem of discrimination on campus and encourage appreciation of differences. We wanted to get individuals from the campus and surrounding community to sign the banner, demonstrating the overall awareness of discrimination and the community's desire to be tolerant and accepting of others. We had a steep learning curve for doing social justice work in the community—from the rather innocuous idea of putting up a sign against hate on campus to the culmination of unfurling a banner five stories high and three stories wide with more than 3,500 signatures on it (see Photo 45.1a and Photo 45.1b). In truth to feminist and

Photo 45.1a   Stop Hate Banner on Building

Stop Hate Banner on Bracken Library at Ball State University, April 2006.

Photo 45.1b   Graduate-Level Social Justice Class and Stop Hate Banner

Members of the Counseling Psychology Social Justice Class at Ball State University, April 2006. 1st Row (L to R): Casey Martin, Erin Snyder, Rebecca Hansen, Doris Kirkpatrick, and Elizabeth Sellers. Back Row (L to R): Tim Gordon, Michael O'Heron, Lawrence Gerstein, Marlon Rollins, and Scott Olenick.

multicultural models of change (Goodman et al., 2004), though, the outcome of our project had as much to do with the support of the community and the collaboration of several community and campus organizations and departments, including staff from the Physical Plant, as it did with our own efforts to get our message out.

A COLLABORATIVE MODEL OF SOCIAL JUSTICE IN ACTION

In order to share power within our class and in the larger community, we focused on a collaborative model of change. As we began this project, our professor, Dr. Lawrence Gerstein, encouraged us to be mindful and intentional in our work. We were expected to use what we knew about ourselves, our community, and counseling psychology to maximize the effect of our intervention, and we were, of course, encouraged to "look to the literature" to guide our process. From our training, we knew that who we were as people should match who we were as counselors (Edwards & Bess, 1998), or in this case, advocates. As multicultural counselors, we looked to ecological, feminist, social justice, and multicultural models to guide our work.

Although the desire to promote positive social change is ignited by affective, intellectual, and pragmatic dimensions (Vera & Speight, 2003), counselors cannot rely solely on intrapersonal resources to engage in social change. In order to more fully understand how social justice movements develop and how mobilization ensues on a broader scale, a contextual understanding that illustrates the role of environmental dimensions is necessary.

Neville and Mobley's (2001) adapted model is composed of five subsystems: (a) *the individual/person system,* which includes general factors such as personality style, self-esteem, and self-efficacy, and sociocultural factors such as race, ethnicity, sexual orientation, acculturation, and multicultural competencies; (b) the *microsystem,* which includes general factors such as the family, neighborhood, and training environment, and sociocultural factors such as cultural competence of mental health centers and multicultural organizations; (c) the *mesosystem,* which includes the interaction of the family and mental health professionals and the

interaction of these professionals with teachers; (d) the *exosystem,* which includes general factors such as the health care system, managed care, and the legal system, and sociocultural factors such as social policies or laws (e.g., affirmative action) and civil rights movements; and (e) the *macrosystem,* which includes general factors such as the political and economic structure, and sociocultural factors such as social identity structures and hierarchies, and dominant stereotypes about sociocultural groups.

Santiago-Rivera, Talka, and Tully (2006) recommended that social justice-informed counseling interventions should overlap all five of Neville and Mobley's (2001) subsystems as a means to facilitate positive social change. Similarly, we believed that our efforts to mobilize and foster support in a quick and efficient manner needed to happen across all the subsystems and was necessary for the success of our Stop Hate campaign.

Goodman et al. (2004) proposed another social justice model. Their model outlined six principles from feminist and multicultural perspectives of counseling that might be helpful in performing and teaching social justice work: (a) ongoing self-examination, (b) sharing power, (c) giving voice, (d) facilitating consciousness raising, (e) building on strengths, and (f) leaving clients with the tools for social change. A brief description of each of these principles follows.

Ongoing Self-Examination. Goodman et al. (2004) argued that ongoing self-examination is essential to performing social justice work. Counseling psychologists must be aware of their assumptions, biases, and values that contribute to their understanding of the communities they support, their own goals, and their commitment that impels their work. Additionally, counseling psychologists should be aware of the power dynamics that exist between themselves and the communities they serve.

Sharing Power. Inherent in multicultural and feminist perspectives is also the importance of sharing power between the practitioner and the client. This is also extremely important in social justice work. Sharing power can be achieved when counseling psychologists view their role as co-learners with the community and establish themselves as resources rather than experts. This role facilitates the community's sense of ownership and self-efficacy and helps members see themselves as effective agents for change. This can also help to empower groups as a whole over the individual (Goodman et al., 2004).

Giving Voice. Both feminist and multicultural perspectives propose that oppressed groups have "lost their voice," or their ability to be heard in the dominant culture. An essential role of the counselor, therefore, is to help reamplify their voices by advocating for oppressed groups in counseling and in the larger social context (Goodman et al., 2004). Again, Goodman et al. argued that this principle of giving voice to oppressed groups should be employed in social justice work. They proposed two ways of accomplishing this: approaching communities with the belief that they know what help they need, and finding ways to bolster the voices of community members so that they can express what they need and want, act on their strengths, and fulfill their vision.

Facilitating Consciousness Raising. Both feminist and multicultural perspectives advocate the idea of raising awareness about the role that social, political, and historical forces play in individual difficulties. Both perspectives emphasize the importance of helping individuals understand how sexism, racism, and discrimination of all sorts contribute to their difficulties. Counseling psychologists performing social justice work can broaden this principle by raising consciousness with community groups rather than with individual clients (Goodman et al., 2004). In essence, by raising awareness of the socio-economic and cultural factors that contribute to oppression, counseling psychologists can empower both individuals and larger communities to make positive, constructive social change.

Building on Strengths. Counseling psychologists, in general, emphasize the importance of helping persons recognize their own strengths and their ability to make positive change. In the social justice context, counseling psychologists can help communities see the strengths inherent in their systems. They can then help community members develop ways to build on these strengths (Goodman et al., 2004).

Leaving Clients With the Tools for Social Change. Just as in individual counseling, one goal of social justice work is to help the community thrive after an intervention. Counseling psychologists serving as social justice advocates should talk with community members about what tools will be necessary to help maintain the changes that were made. This discussion should include plans for continuing change after collaboration with the psychologist ends and ways of expanding community resources (Goodman et al., 2004). Simply stated, counseling psychologists should engage community members in a way that their own presence becomes unnecessary and the community ultimately can maintain change and thrive on its own. In essence, the counseling psychologist's role is to teach community members how to be their own change agents.

Goodman et al. (2004) suggested that the principles just discussed might be applied across a broad range of social justice practices, such as policy development, program design, community intervention, and research. Because we were, as a class, both doing and learning how to engage in social justice work, relying on these principles seemed useful. In addition, feminist and multicultural perspectives fit well with our individual and collective theoretical orientations and belief systems.

OUR EXPERIENCE WITH STOP HATE

Based on the collaborative model of social justice work outlined above, our goals for the Stop Hate campaign were threefold: Send a message to the campus that BSU appreciates diversity and will not tolerate discrimination; bring together students, university administrators, and campus organizations and departments for this common goal; and induce campus discussion about the racial incidents and our message of tolerance and acceptance. What started out as a class discussion exploded into a campus-wide reaction against racism, hate, and oppression.

Creating the Stop Hate! Banner

Our main strategy to accomplish our goals involved the creation of a banner. As stated earlier, we believed that by displaying a banner on campus, it would bring attention to the problem of discrimination and potentially encourage the appreciation of differences. As a class, we decided we could create our own banner if everyone contributed a little money for materials and his or her time and effort. One strategy that had a positive impact on our effort at the beginning of this project was the establishment of an online class message board. This device helped to facilitate our capacity to exchange ideas about the banner project. In the realm of project organization, this message board was an essential tool in helping the banner project move forward as quickly as it did.

Through our various communications, we decided to put a design on the banner. This design was to include the word "hate" surrounded by a circle with a line through it. We obtained approval from the president of the university to drape the banner on the main library. This location ensured maximum exposure to our message through pedestrian and motorist traffic.

After finalizing the exact design of the project using our message board to exchange ideas, it seemed more sensible to paint the design on a tarp. We purchased a giant tarp (50' × 30') of the sturdiest grade we could find. We also purchased latex semi-gloss indoor/outdoor paint and paintbrushes at Lowes. These initial materials cost around $100, and the class members were delighted that the banner might be created so inexpensively.

After completing the painting of the banner, we started collecting signatures on it. The next 2 weeks were a blur because we were actively engaged in the signature collection process and continuing to meet all of our other academic responsibilities. These 2 weeks, however, were very encouraging because we had excellent help at the banner-signing table from various members of our department and even students from other programs. Even so, it was exhausting work.

Getting the Message to the Community

The next step was getting the message out. Recruiting volunteers and collaborators was essential to help spread the word and to staff the table to collect signatures prior to having the banner displayed. At different times, we collected signatures in the lobby and outside of Teachers College, and in one of the main eating locations on campus.

Having multiple collaborators on the entire project was important to demonstrate that the community as a whole would not tolerate discrimination and that it agreed with the message of "Stop Hate!" as one that needed to be communicated strongly (Ellis, 2002). This was also important in order to share power, give a voice, and facilitate raising consciousness in the community (Goodman et al., 2004). What started as a simple plan on campus to recruit volunteers to help staff the table grew to a much larger outreach to the BSU community, as well as the surrounding Muncie, Indiana, community. The outreach and the securing of collaborators and sponsors became a symbol of solidarity against discrimination and hate.

Our department chairperson, Dr. Sharon Bowman, agreed to contact the department chairs at Teachers College in which CPSY is housed. Dr. Bowman asked the chairs if they would support the Stop Hate campaign by spreading the word and encouraging people to be involved. Posters were printed and displayed throughout the department and college announcing the dates to sign the banner, requesting volunteers to help with gathering signatures, and explaining the purpose of the banner. In addition, the CPSY department Web site advertised the campaign and displayed information and pictures of the campaign's progress. E-mails were sent to all the students, staff, and faculty members on campus explaining the purpose of the Stop Hate campaign and soliciting volunteers to help with the project.

The response that we received from the BSU community and Muncie amazed us all. We received many offers to help volunteer and gather signatures prior to unfurling the banner from undergraduate students, graduate students, faculty, and staff. Volunteers from the School of Social Work, the CPSY department, and the counseling center staffed the signature table. Through 2 weeks of gathering signatures, we were able to reach out to the BSU community to raise awareness and provide information about how to combat discrimination. The Muncie community also responded by demonstrating their support as cosponsors, and by signing the banner.

At the end of 2 weeks, we had 48 volunteers who helped gather signatures; 67 cosponsors (e.g., African Connection, Center for Peace and Conflict Studies, Muncie Chapter of the National Organization for Women, Office of the President of Ball State University); 3,552 signatures, and countless other people who participated in spreading the word and working toward ending discrimination. This process of collaboration helped teach the students about social justice, but also helped teach the community how to make changes in the atmosphere of the campus and in people's lives, in essence fulfilling Goodman et al's principle of leaving clients with the tools to continue the process.

In order to further our cause, we also took advice from Palmer (2004) and advocated a multidisciplinary approach to social justice. For the Stop Hate campaign, we attempted to model this approach by collaborating with a multicultural education class in the Department of Educational Studies. The instructor of the course, Dr. Jayne Beilke, allowed the students to join the Stop Hate campaign as part of another class project. The premise of the class was based on bell hooks's "oppositional gaze" (hooks, 1992). According to hooks, the oppositional gaze stares in the face of domination. By setting one's eyes on oppression, s/he transforms the oppression, giving power to those who are oppressed. hooks (1992) believed that by acknowledging and asserting control over oppressive images and structures that attempt to marginalize, dominate, and exclude, these images and structures can be transformed. By developing a distinctive Web site, Dr. Beilke's students used their knowledge and technological skills to represent hooks's philosophy of challenging structures of domination (see http://jbeilke.iweb.bsu.edu/politicsofhate/index.htm). This collaboration gave a universal and continuous platform to showcase the Stop Hate campaign and demonstrated the necessity for social action across disciplines. To view pictures of the entire campaign, visit www.bsu.edu/counselingpsychology/phdcounpsych.

The local, regional, and university print, radio, and television media were also contacted to promote the Stop Hate campaign and our message to combat discrimination at BSU. Media representatives from the class managed all press releases, media inquiries, and requests for interviews.

The most media exposure the Stop Hate campaign received was on the editorial page of the campus newspaper. Over the course of the campaign, numerous editorials and letters to the editor were published in the campus newspaper. Reactions expressed in these editorials ranged from strong support to highly critical and negative. The reactions expressed in the more critical editorials tended to fall into two categories. First,

several people spoke to the belief that displaying a banner against hate cannot simply combat racism and prejudice. And second, some individuals shared the belief that hate was a basic human emotion, and that by trying to eliminate hate, the campaign was attempting to limit human experiences.

This dialogue on the editorial page proved to be one of the most challenging moments for the Stop Hate campaign organizers. Each member of the campaign possessed a deep sense of social justice and the inherent equality of all people. Hearing such critical responses to our deeply held beliefs and our personal investment in the campaign created at times strong feelings of irritation, aggravation, and anger for everyone involved. Learning to cope with these feelings in light of the mission of the campaign was one of our most powerful and poignant learning experiences.

Frustrating as it was, in the end, this dialogue was what the members of the Stop Hate campaign had desired from the campaign. At the conclusion of the campaign, in an open letter to the campus community published in the university newspaper, as organizers we congratulated all of the individuals who made the campaign what it was. Sentiments of gratitude were shared with everyone who had experienced discrimination on campus and who had shared their stories, giving all the organizers the strength and resolve to move forward with the challenging campaign. Finally, our open letter thanked those individuals who wrote critical editorials against the campaign for lending their voices and keeping the dialogue going.

CLIMATE ASSESSMENT OF THE ATHLETICS DEPARTMENT

(CHARLENE ALEXANDER AND STEFANÍA ÆGISDÓTTIR)

When intervening at the organizational level, existing theories of multicultural organizational development such as the ones presented by Adler (1986) and Cross, Bazron, Dennis, and Isaacs (1989), which are helpful in describing organizational development from a multicultural perspective, are limited in that they do not provide the needed direction for counseling psychologists engaging in organizational advocacy efforts. Therefore, a theoretical framework provided by D'Andrea and Daniels in Chapter 46 of this *Handbook* is used to guide the following discussion of a climate assessment of the BSU athletics department directed and performed by two faculty members in the counseling psychology department at BSU.

D'Andrea and Daniels articulated a social justice organizational development (SJOD) theory that includes the following assumptions: (a) Organizations operating from a multicultural framework promote a greater level of social justice; (b) the manifestation of organizational oppression is perpetuated by oppressive policies and practices that maintain the status quo within the organization, and therefore, it is the responsibility of counselors to confront these prejudices when they are made aware of them; (c) organizations can change and develop into compassionate entities; (d) individuals within organizations are each unique and have varied states of consciousness that are evidenced in the ways organizations respond or fail to respond to multicultural crises; and (e) counselors have a significant role in modeling practices that are multiculturally affirming and that resist oppression and social injustice. D'Andrea and Daniels also insisted it is imperative for counselors to be advocates for change in the varied contexts within which they work and live. With D'Andrea and Daniels's framework in mind, we now present the process of our assessment of the climate at the BSU athletics department.

Organizations Operating From a Multicultural Framework Promote a Greater Level of Social Justice

On June 26, 2007, Dr. Charlene Alexander (a CPSY faculty) received a phone call from Ball State University's president, Dr. Jo Ann Gora, requesting a meeting to discuss a recent incident at BSU. At this meeting, Dr. Gora debriefed Dr. Alexander about events occurring the previous weekend during which the BSU basketball coach found racially charged notes in several locations within the athletics department. Dr. Gora also requested that, in light of these events, a climate assessment of the athletic department should be conducted to determine the size of this problem within the entire athletic department and whether the climate in this particular department was supportive to persons of color. Dr. Alexander was also instructed to make recommendations to President Gora based on the assessment's findings.

Dr. Alexander was given a few hours to reflect on this assignment, and after consultation with her chair and the college dean, she immediately asked Dr. Stefanía Ægisdóttir (a CPSY faculty) who was leaving the country the following day to join her in conducting this climate assessment. Once a decision was made to undertake this task, Dr. Alexander met with university staff and helped prepare the press release that was issued the following day. The incident was described in Ball State University's student newspaper as follows:

> Members of the Ball State University men's basketball coaching staff found notes that included racial slurs in the basketball office over the weekend. . . . A total of seven notes with the words "nigger," "liar" and "cheater" written on them were found at about 8 a.m. Sunday. (Jones & Wood, 2007)

Dr. Gora was adamant that the university would not tolerate these incidents and that all resources would be used to identify the perpetrator(s) and they would be punished to the fullest extent. Following are excerpts from the text of the president's announcement:

> Harassment will not be tolerated!
> I have some unsettling news, and I wanted you to hear it directly from me rather than in the media. Over the weekend, harassing materials of a racial nature targeted toward members of the men's basketball coaching staff were found in their office area. Our campus police launched an immediate investigation into the matter and will continue working the case until some concrete answers are revealed. . . . No one should ever have to endure an attack such as this. Let me be clear, the acts that were committed were repugnant, and they certainly do not reflect the values of this campus. I pledge to the coaching staff and to the team that their safety is of our utmost concern, and we will take every action to find the people who perpetrated this intolerable act. These actions will never shake our commitment of promoting diversity at Ball State and of standing up for everyone in our campus community. Along with conducting a full police investigation, we are also going to conduct a

complete assessment of the work environment within the athletics department—beginning immediately. To that end, . . . I have asked Charlene Alexander and Stephania Aegisdottir—both from the counseling psychology department and experts on the topic of multiculturalism in the workplace—to lead the inquiry. Their goal will be to gauge the climate within athletics to determine whether it is supportive to all people. We need to assess whether this weekend's incident is an isolated one or indicative of broader problems that need to be corrected.

A hostile work environment will not be tolerated. Should the report reveal any inconsistencies with our commitment to a supportive work environment and diversity, action to remedy those discrepancies will be swift.

It should be clear to the reader at this time that support for addressing issues of organizational oppression were supported by the university's administration at the highest level. Twenty-seven news outlets across the country picked up this story, and there were several requests for interviews. The climate assessment conducted by the faculty in the counseling psychology department was distinct from the legal investigation of the incidents involving the basketball coach. The legal investigation included several attorneys and the university police, and its results are not presented in this chapter. What follows, then, is a description of the different phases of this climate assessment and the lessons taken from performing a climate assessment of this scope and magnitude. Additionally, to ensure the confidentiality guaranteed to participants in this assessment, no specifics of the report submitted to the president are included. We will, however, briefly describe some of the organizational changes made within the university's athletics department as a result of the assessment.

The climate assessment included four phases. In Phase 1, we met with staff and students in each athletics area to inform them about the assessment process and to solicit their input. Phase 2 involved developing and administering a survey regarding the department's climate. Phase 3 consisted of a series of 1-hour in-depth, follow-up interviews with a small number of survey respondents. And, finally, in Phase 4, we analyzed the survey and interview data, summarized the results, and presented our recommendations to the president.

The Manifestation of Organizational Oppression Is Perpetuated by Oppressive Policies and Practices. It is the Responsibility of Counselors to Confront Prejudices When Made Aware of Them

Phase 1: Meetings With Stakeholders

Meetings With Athletics Staff. This stage of the assessment entailed meetings with athletic department staff that began shortly after the press release. The assistance of two doctoral students in counseling psychology was solicited to help conduct these meetings and take notes about issues and concerns raised by the staff. These meetings were all held outside the athletic department and lasted approximately 30 minutes to 1 hour. This phase of the assessment was important for several reasons. First, it was considered imperative to explain each phase of the climate assessment to the staff, ensure their participation, answer any questions they might have about the process, and minimize any misperceptions of how information obtained from the assessment might be used. During these meetings, we also explained the anticipated time line for completing the climate assessment.

Second, also during these meetings, those involved were given an opportunity to collaborate in the climate assessment process by identifying any additional areas of concern they thought should be included in the climate assessment. Thus, any concerns in addition to race and ethnicity were noted. Finally, because of the media attention of this incident on campus, it was important to alleviate any fears and insecurities the staff felt related to the incident and the assessment. For instance, Dr. Alexander discussed issues of confidentiality, the potential benefits of a climate assessment, and the importance of their cooperation with the process. As expected, during this phase, on several occasions, we encountered a tremendous amount of resistance. Some participants did not trust that any tangible results would come out of this assessment, whereas others believed that the university would act swiftly to address any areas needed for improvement. Furthermore, during the ensuing weeks of meeting with the athletic staff and hearing their concerns, it was decided to delay the start of the formal climate assessment until the legal investigation was concluded. This decision was considered extremely important in ensuring that those involved in the assessment would recognize a clear distinction between the legal investigation and the climate assessment.

Following these meetings with staff, it also became clear that the climate survey would have to expand beyond issues of race and ethnicity as several other areas of concerns were identified by the staff. Thus, at this point, it was communicated to the president that the scope of our assessment would need to be extended beyond the original parameters identified. Our request was granted, and we received permission from the BSU president to amend the assessment to address a wider range of topics and areas of concern within the athletics department.

Meetings With Student Athletes. Several meetings were also conducted with student athletes. These included men's baseball, basketball, football, golf, tennis, men's volleyball, women's basketball, cross-country track, field hockey, golf, gymnastics, soccer, softball, swimming and diving, tennis, and women's volleyball teams. As with the athletics staff, student athletes were informed about the process and anticipated time line for the climate assessment. During these meetings, student athletes also had an opportunity to ask questions about the climate assessment, were informed about confidentiality of responses, and were encouraged to participate in the process. They were also asked to identify areas of concern that they believed would be important to include in a survey developed for student athletes.

It became apparent following the meetings with the student athletes that they reported similar concerns regarding the athletics department as the staff did. In addition, the students raised unique concerns about their roles as students at BSU and members of the Muncie community.

Observations at the End of Phase 1

Once the press release from BSU was issued, we were struck by how the university community responded. For instance, university staff were eager to provide assistance with room reservations, materials, and resources for the initial meetings. Others volunteered to assist in any way possible. There was a general sense of ownership in the entire process by the university community. At the same time, we received unsolicited input from a number of sources, and the team had to reflect on the emotional impact of the assessment at several stages.

In some instances, we heard painful testimonies of individuals who recounted their experiences of discrimination on campus and in the Muncie community. Others were concerned with the public perception and negative attention these events were shedding on the university. We were also impressed by how open our student athletes were. On several occasions, the coaching staff had predicted that students would be resistant, whereas our experience was quite the opposite. On several occasions, the meetings went over the time allotted to address their concerns about the assessment process and to hear their stories. We also experienced that many students wanted guarantees that specific changes would occur within the athletics department—changes that we could not guarantee. Many times, we found ourselves reassuring the students that our report and recommendations would reflect the data and input gathered from the participating stakeholders.

President Gora is a zealous advocate and believes in taking swift action. Her concern for all students and staff was quite evident at several times throughout this phase of the assessment. However, in order to protect the integrity of the climate assessment process, we decided not to discuss this with the president until the climate assessment was complete.

Phase 2: Development and Administration of Measures

Surveys. Shortly after the public announcement that a climate assessment of the BSU athletics department would be conducted, we received invitations to review existing climate assessment surveys that were designed specifically for athletic departments at other institutions throughout the United States. The survey we adapted to assess participants' perception of the climate in the BSU athletics department was derived from the Athletic Climate Assessment Form (student and staff versions) developed by Dr. Peggy Stockdale, Professor of Psychology at Southern Illinois University, Carbondale

(SIU-C). After reviewing the questions on the SIU-C measure, it was determined that numerous items had to be changed and adapted to fit the BSU context. We also developed new items reflecting the concerns identified in our meetings with students and staff as well as items that we considered important additions based on our knowledge of the multicultural literature. In order to do this, we reviewed notes taken during the meetings with students and staff and identified the themes that emerged. We compared these themes with the themes we identified in the SIU-C survey and expanded its coverage to better fit the BSU context. We also decided at this time to develop three sets of surveys, one for each group targeted (student athletes, staff, and former staff). Next, the team engaged in several rounds of item development and reviews to ensure that all themes that were identified were included in each version of the survey and that each theme contained numerous items. We also decided on a rating scale for the items. Furthermore, we included several open-ended questions to ensure that stakeholders' voices were heard. Next, the final versions of the surveys were reviewed by each member of the team for clarity. It is worth noting that we opted to also survey former staff members of the athletics department to determine if their departure from the university had anything to do with the climate within the department. Online and paper versions of the survey were constructed in response to requests from students and staff. The surveys were pilot tested to establish the amount of time required to complete each version of the survey and for feedback about its clarity.

Time Line. As stated earlier, the administration of the climate survey was put on hold until the conclusion of the legal investigation of the incidents prompting the climate assessment. The climate survey was not distributed until after October 24, 2007, which was the date that the university attorneys and police completed their legal investigation. The decision to separate these two processes ensured that these two assessment procedures would not interfere with one another, and it increased the likelihood for relevant stakeholders' participation in the survey. Thus, on October 26, 2007, all athletics department staff and student athletes who had requested an online version of the survey were e-mailed a link to the survey. Subsequently, those who had requested a

paper version of the survey were contacted to complete the survey at scheduled group meetings. All participants were assured about the confidentiality of their responses, but were invited to participate in a follow-up interview during which they could address any additional concerns and issues not tapped in the survey items. They were provided with contact information (e-mail address and phone numbers) of the two faculty members in charge of the assessment to schedule interviews.

Observations Following Phase 2 of the Assessment

Although we had to wait for the legal investigation to conclude before administering the climate survey, this additional time provided the assessment team an opportunity to develop surveys geared specifically to the unique issues relevant to the BSU athletics department. Additionally, during this time, one of the directors of the assessment received phone calls from attorneys not associated with this case and other interested parties requesting the results of the assessment. Thus, it became more apparent that these two types of investigations needed to be separated.

Phase 3: Postsurvey Interviews

Phase 3 of the assessment entailed the final data collection and was performed after all survey data had been collected. As stated previously, students and staff were offered the opportunity to participate in an individual interview if they had any additional information or concerns to share. All participants who indicated such an interest were contacted to schedule an interview time. These interviews lasted for about 1 hour and were conducted in a conference room in the Department of Counseling Psychology and Guidance Services. The interviews were all completed within a 2-day period. Both Drs. Alexander and Ægisdóttir were present during the interviews, and each one kept separate notes on the information shared by the volunteers. The interviews began with a standard open-ended question. The responses were then followed-up with questions to add to the depth of the information that was shared. All persons who were interviewed were informed about the confidentiality of the information that they shared.

Observations of Phase 3

It became clear to us during this phase how important it was for both staff and students to share with us their concerns about the climate within the athletic department. By soliciting information from stakeholders about what they perceived as the problem, describing to them the purpose of this assessment, and getting their input about how to best reach them with our survey, their interest and investment in the process was maximized. Also, by employing a mixed methodology using closed- and open-ended response options on the survey and by gathering additional information through individual interviews with interested stakeholders, we were able to get an in-depth view of the participating stakeholders' concerns, hopes, and insights about the climate in the athletics department.

Counselors Have a Significant Role to Play in Modeling Practices That Are Multiculturally Affirming and Resist Oppression and Social Injustice

Data Analyses and Dissemination. Phase 4 of the climate assessment involved data analysis and dissemination of results. The three versions of the survey were analyzed separately. Furthermore, both quantitative and qualitative methods were used to analyze the responses from the three targeted groups. The closed-ended questions on the surveys, which included a rating scale, were factor analyzed separately for each set of data to identify underlying dimensions or themes. Then, within each dimension, responses to each question were reported in terms of frequencies in addition to providing an overall summative score for each dimension. It was noteworthy that the dimensions emerging from the factor analyses were somewhat in line with the themes we had identified earlier in the item development process. However, because of different experiences of each one of the targeted groups (students, staff, former staff) and not completely identical items, the meaning or content of each dimension varied somewhat between groups. Factor analyzing the responses thus helped us organize our findings and better identify the unique concerns that were raised by each of the groups.

The open-ended questions and the interview responses were analyzed using qualitative methods. That is, they

were categorized based on general themes that were then categorized into subthemes. Number of responses emerging within each theme were tallied and reported. Additionally, representative examples from each one of the themes and categories were presented.

At the conclusion of our climate assessment, and after finishing the report, which included the methodology used, results, and detailed recommendations organized by the themes that emerged in the data, Drs. Alexander and Ægisdóttir submitted the report to President Gora on January 14, 2008. About a week later, Drs. Alexander and Ægisdóttir met with President Gora to go over the findings and recommendations.

Organizations Can Change and Develop Into Compassionate Entities

On January 30, 2008, the president and the director of the athletic department held a news conference to announce the reorganization and change in leadership of the athletic department. The headline of the student newspaper read:

> Athletics department is reorganized; new leadership committee is formed.
>
> After a year of multiple NCAA rule violations, being placed on a two-year's probation by the NCAA and a former coach's initial claims of a racially hostile work environment, the university announced the athletics department will undergo significant changes.

The university's athletic director pledged to increase communication within the department and to create a safe environment where both staff and student-athletes could be safe and successful. An African American associate director was given increasing responsibility within the department.

Individuals Within Organizations Are Each Unique and Have Varied States of Consciousness. These States of Consciousness Can Be Seen in the Ways Organizations Respond or Fail to Respond to Multicultural Crises

It is apparent that the administration of BSU responded promptly to the racial incidents on campus and contacted relevant personnel to assess the situation—the CPSY faculty to perform a multicultural climate assessment and relevant legal entities to conduct an investigation of the criminal aspects of the incident. It is also became apparent to those of us who performed the climate assessment that the various stakeholders perceived the racial incidents in diverse ways, and that additional concerns were raised that we considered important to address in our climate assessment to help restore the morale and tension that had developed in the department prior to and after the incident. Furthermore, as the directors of the assessment, we found ourselves to be mediators between the administration of BSU, the administration of the athletics department, and the staff and students within the department. It became extremely important for us to make sure that the voices of the staff and students were heard and that we develop concrete recommendations that we believed could be realized within the organization. Furthermore, in addition to meeting with the president to discuss the results and our recommendations, we met with the athletics director to make sure he understood clearly the recommendations that we made. This also provided him with an opportunity to ask specific questions about the assessment process and details of the report.

EVALUATION OF STRENGTHS AND LIMITATIONS

Overall, those of us involved in these social justice initiatives at BSU—the Stop Hate campaign and the climate assessment of the athletics department—believe we had a positive impact on the BSU campus. The Stop Hate campaign involved developing a 50- × 30-foot banner that was prominently displayed on one side of the main library building, which is a centralized location on campus. More than 3,500 people signed the banner, 15 newspaper articles were written in response to the campaign, and a number of interviews were conducted on Fox News and Indiana Public Radio. The climate assessment and the legal investigation conducted at BSU resulted in a different level of awareness of the impact of hate speech within the athletic department; they also resulted in the departure of key personnel and a reorganization of the governance of the athletics department. All of these accomplishments

brought into the spotlight not only the racial incidents that had occurred on campus, but also the grassroots responses of the BSU community to these indefensible attacks against persons of color.

Just as important were the lessons we all learned from planning and implementing these campaigns—that is, the personal *is* political. The Stop Hate campaign was an immersive experience in social justice work that shaped how one can expand one's role from being a counselor to a social justice advocate. The climate assessment charged counseling psychologists with expertise in multicultural counseling to intervene in a way that was multiculturally affirming. The role of the counselor becomes that of a public (or sometimes private) servant. Our client becomes the community and our community the client. The most effective methods of building alliances and trust remain the same and are necessary for transformation in both arenas. In this process, the counselor must "lay down the mantle of special recognition" and engage in effective collaboration with other stakeholders. These projects challenged our ability to think and work systemically and realistically, and to work collaboratively not only with each other, but with people and groups possessing both significantly more and less power than us.

In the Stop Hate campaign, we also learned about our limitations. The significance of social justice work is larger than class projects. We could not do everything we wanted to do. After the project ended, maintaining the longevity of the goals and a presence in the university community was a primary challenge. We discussed continuing the campaign after the banner had been taken down, but diffusion of responsibility set in and our motivation seemed to subside. We *were* able to join with the Multicultural Task Force on campus, which established a number of discussion forums related to combating discrimination on campus. Our hope by joining forces was that we could give a continued voice to students affected by discrimination. Although the Stop Hate campaign has been less active since May 2005, remnants of the campaign can still be seen around campus—students wearing T-shirts created by the Office of Student Affairs with our logo and Stop Hate stickers plastered on bulletin boards and flyer kiosks across campus. New students may not know the history of these images, but the images themselves still convey our message.

We also discussed the idea of forming a social justice student group within the CPSY department that would serve to inform students of social justice activities occurring on campus as well as provide chances to take part in these activities. This group was formed by incoming students (not involved in the campaign) at the CPSY department in the Fall of 2008. In addition, students and faculty involved in the campaign proposed a doctoral cognate in social justice in the CPSY department that was recently adopted by our university. We plan to continue to draw from the Goodman et al. (2004) theoretical model, and our hope is that the Stop Hate campaign will thrive even more within our department and throughout campus.

The Stop Hate campaign taught us a great deal about social activism. We grew as a class as well as individually. The experience of organizing and implementing a campaign sparked an interest to continue social justice work for many of us. It helped us realize that we are capable of raising awareness and effecting change, as well as reassured us that we have the support of our faculty and campus.

Those of us involved in the athletics department climate assessment saw and experienced significant positive changes following the assessment, however we were not able to share our findings with all stakeholders. The results and recommendations are the property of the president. Although we are confident that the president's response to the climate assessment reflects most of our recommendations, we, the directors, are not in a position to share the results and discuss our recommendations. Initially, we encountered resistance by some stakeholders who were concerned that our findings would not be made public. At the discretion of the BSU president, some results and recommendations were made public and some were not, in an effort to safeguard the identity of key personnel and students. Although this was not a desired outcome, it was a necessary outcome.

REFERENCES

Adler, N. J. (1986). *Cultural synergy: Managing the impact of cultural diversity. The 1986 annual: Developing human resources.* San Diego, CA: University Associates.

Bronfenbrenner, U. (1977). Toward an experimental ecology of human development. *American Psychologist, 32,* 513–531.

Bronfenbrenner, U. (1979). *The ecology of human development: Experiments by nature and design.* Cambridge, MA: Harvard University Press.

Cross, T. L., Bazron, B. J., Dennis, K. W., & Isaacs, M. R. (1989). *Towards a culturally competent system of care.* Washington, DC: Georgetown University Child Development Center.

Edwards, J. K., & Bess, J. M. (1998). Developing effectiveness in the therapeutic use of self. *Clinical Social Work Journal, 26*(1), 89–105.

Ellis, S. J. (2002). *The volunteer recruitment book (and membership development).* Philadelphia: Energize.

Goodman, L. A., Liang, B., Helms, J. E., Latta, R. E., Sparks, E., & Weintraub, S. R. (2004). Training counseling psychologists as social justice agents: Feminist and multicultural principles in action. *Counseling Psychologist, 32,* 793–837.

hooks, b. (1992). *Black looks: Race and representation.* Boston: South End Press.

Jones, L., & Wood, R. (2007). University responds to racism: Thompson's staff finds harassing notes in men's basketball office. *Ball State Daily News.*

Moody, E. (2005, November 17). Students encounter racism. *Ball State Daily News.*

Neville, H. A., & Mobley, M. (2001). Social identities in contexts: An ecological model of multicultural counseling psychology processes. *Counseling Psychologist, 29,* 471–486.

Palmer, L. K. (2004). The call to social justice: A multidiscipline agenda. *Counseling Psychologist, 32,* 879–885.

Santiago-Rivera, A. L., Talka, K., & Tully, A. W. (2006). Environmental racism: A call to the profession for community intervention and social action. In R. L. Toporek, L. H. Gerstein, N. A. Fouad, G. Roysircar, & T. Israel (Eds.), *Handbook for social justice in counseling psychology* (pp. 185–199). Thousand Oaks, CA: Sage.

Toporek, R. L., Gerstein, L. H., Fouad, N. A., Roysircar, G., & Israel, T. (2006). Future directions for counseling psychology: Enhancing leadership, vision, and action in social justice. In R. L. Toporek, L. H. Gerstein, N. A. Fouad, G. Roysircar, & T. Israel (Eds.), *Handbook for social justice in counseling psychology: Leadership, vision, and action* (pp. 533–552). Thousand Oaks, CA: Sage.

Vera, E. M., & Speight, S. L. (2003). Multicultural competencies, social justice, and counseling psychology: Expanding our roles. *Counseling Psychology, 31,* 253–272.

Watson, E. C., Jr. (1983). Counseling psychology vs. clinical psychology: Further explorations on a theme or once more around the "identity" maypole with gusto. *Counseling Psychologist, 11*(4), 76–92.

46

Promoting Multiculturalism, Democracy, and Social Justice in Organizational Settings

A Case Study

MICHAEL D'ANDREA AND JUDY DANIELS

The multicultural movement represents a powerful force that is forging transformational changes in the counseling profession (D'Andrea & Daniels, 2008). The genesis of this transformational force can be traced to the late 1960s and early 1970s, when the United States was in the midst of a social revolution. This was an era when many civil rights advocates, Black revolutionaries, and allies of the feminist movement worked to tear down the walls of oppression and injustice that characterized our society at that time. In addressing such issues, these persons sought to more fully realize the promise of justice and democracy by striving to dismantle an unjust power hierarchy that privileges members of the dominant cultural-racial group in the United States at the expense of individuals in other devalued groups (Rothenberg, 2008).

Initially led by a relatively small number of Black counselors and psychologists, the birth of the multicultural counseling movement focused on the ineffective and harmful psychological outcomes that ensue from using culturally biased helping theories and practices among clients in diverse client populations. These calls for more culturally and racially responsive mental health care were followed by similarly articulated demands for other corrective actions by a growing number of Asian American, Latino/a, and Native American counselors as well as feminist and gay/lesbian/bisexual/transgender advocates. One of the central similarities that bonded these different multicultural-social justice advocates was their interest in forging transformative changes in the mental health professions that would result in the delivery of more effective and respectful services in an increasingly diversified society (Sue & Sue, 2003).

Pragmatically speaking, these advocacy efforts resulted in numerous changes that stimulated a greater level of cultural competence in the profession. Among the changes that occurred in this regard included the

591

development and implementation of new training practices (Grieger & Toliver, 2001), research methods, and counseling services (Sue & Sue, 2003), all of which reflect a greater cultural awareness, knowledge, and skill set (Daniels & D'Andrea, 2003).

From a more idealistic perspective, such changes were catalyzed by a drive to promote more inclusionary decision-making practices and cultural competence in our society in general and the mental health professions in particular (D'Andrea & Daniels, 2008). The motivation that guided these broader ideals was fueled in part by an increasing understanding of the intimate links that exist between psychosocial health and social justice. To address this linkage, multicultural-social justice counseling advocates emphasize the need for mental health practitioners to implement new roles and services when working to stimulate the well-being of larger numbers of persons from diverse groups and backgrounds than has been done in the past.

Acknowledging the Intimate Links Between Psychosocial Health and Social Justice

There are a couple of fundamental reasons why multicultural-social justice counseling advocates encourage counselors to embrace new professional roles that enable them to more effectively stimulate environmental-organizational changes that promote a greater level of democracy and justice in our society. First, these persons are knowledgeable of the research findings that describe the negative psychosocial impact that millions of persons in devalued and oppressed cultural-racial groups experience as a result of being routinely subjected to various forms of racism, sexism, classism, heterosexism, ageism, ableism, and other injustices. This includes overt and intentional forms of the above-stated "isms" as well as the perpetuation of covert injustices that are embedded in the policies and practices of the organizations and institutions that comprise the infrastructure of our contemporary society (Jones, 1997).

Many culturally biased and covert discriminatory practices continue to be perpetuated in our nation's justice, health care, economic, and educational systems. Some of the specific negative outcomes that result from such unjust and discriminatory practices in these organizational-institutional systems include

the disproportionate number of Black and Latino/a persons who are incarcerated in our prison systems; lower quality and differential medical treatment provided to persons of color compared to their White counterparts; lower family incomes and higher unemployment rates among Black, Latino/a, and Native American persons; and higher high school drop-out and lower college graduation rates among students of color in contrast to White students (Miller & Garran, 2008).

Given the adverse psychosocial effects that the above-mentioned injustices have on the well-being of millions of persons in our society, it is important for counselors to expand their professional roles to address these structural problems. In doing so, counselors are encouraged to extend the work they do in primarily offering direct client services (i.e., individual counseling) to include multicultural-social justice advocacy interventions. These latter interventions are intentionally designed to alleviate the adverse psychosocial impact that millions of persons experience as a result of being routinely subjected to various forms of structural oppression and injustice by ameliorating the discriminatory and unjust practices that continue to be perpetuated in organizational, institutional, and community settings.

We have attempted to contribute to such advocacy efforts by developing and implementing a new organizational development theory that addresses some of the above-mentioned injustices. The following sections of this chapter describe this new model and other multicultural organizational development frameworks that preceded it. We also describe a case study that outlines specific intervention strategies that were implemented to ameliorate various forms of organizational injustice at a university in the western region of the United States. When presenting this case study, we list some of the positive and negative outcomes that ensued from implementing these interventions in a large organizational setting as well as acknowledge the promise and pitfalls of using such interventions in other organizational settings in the future.

MULTICULTURAL ORGANIZATIONAL DEVELOPMENT THEORIES

Early theoretical publications related to multicultural organizational development are based on the work of Adler (1986), Barr and Strong (1987), Foster, Jackson,

Cross, and Hardiman (1988), and Cross, Bazron, Dennis, and Isaacs (1989). Although these theoretical models provide helpful descriptions of the stages of multicultural organizational development, they fail to detail the types of intervention strategies that counselors can use to foster a greater level of cultural diversity, social justice, and democratic decision making in organizational settings. Most also fail to provide research findings that validate their theoretical premises.

D'Andrea, Daniels, and their colleagues (D'Andrea & Daniels, 1995; D'Andrea et al., 2001) were among the first to publish research findings related to the effectiveness of using organizational development strategies to promote multiculturalism, social justice, and democratic principles (e.g., inclusionary decision-making policies and practices) within professional counseling and psychology organizations. The successes and limitations of their work as multicultural organizational development change agents were detailed in their 1995 publication and updated in a second article published in 2001.

Sue and Sue (2003) helped to further expand the knowledge base in multicultural organizational development by publishing additional theoretical works in this area. Their efforts resulted in a new model that extends the efforts of the above-mentioned theorists and researchers.

Zalaquett, Foley, Tillotson, Dinsmore, and Hof (2008) recently published research findings that verified the short- and long-term efficacy of using specific interventions to stimulate a greater level of acceptance of multiculturalism and social justice in organizational settings. These organizational interventions are based on the recommendations made by D'Andrea and Daniels (1995), D'Andrea et al. (2001), and Sue and Sue (2003). The research published by Zalaquett and his colleagues represents an important contribution in this area because it is one of the few investigative reports that describes counselors' effectiveness in using organizational development interventions to foster a greater level of institutional support for multicultural-social justice issues in university settings over time.

Limitations of the Existing Multicultural Organizational Development Knowledge-Base

One of the major limitations associated with the existing multicultural organizational development (MOD)

knowledge base involves the *softening down* of the goals, purposes, and interventions used in doing such work. This softening down is manifested in a number of ways:

1. A reluctance of MOD advocates to explicitly name the various injustices and forms of institutional oppression that continue to be perpetuated in organizational settings (i.e., organizational racism, institutional classism, epistemological racism, etc.)

2. An overemphasis on the goal of promoting diversity initiatives in organizations (which enables many organizational leaders to sidestep the perpetuation of more controversial forms of injustice and oppression in such settings)

3. The failure of MOD theorists to discuss the sort of professional and personal courage that is necessary to exercise when confronting the negative impact that various forms of organizational injustice and institutional oppression have on millions of people in the United States.

After critically analyzing the existing MOD knowledge base and evaluating the strengths and limitations of our earlier work in this area, we decided to make a number of changes as multicultural-social justice organizational development theorists and researchers. These efforts resulted in the development of a new organizational theory that shares a number of similarities and differences with the other multicultural organizational development theories mentioned earlier. Later in this chapter, a case study is presented that describes the implementation of this new theoretical model. Before doing so, the following section discusses the basic assumptions that underlie what we refer to as the social justice organizational development (SJOD) theory.

THEORETICAL ASSUMPTIONS UNDERLYING THE SJOD FRAMEWORK

Assumption #1: The first assumption that guides the SJOD theory is based on a strong belief in the "revolutionary potential of multiculturalism to promote a greater level of justice and democracy in our nation" (D'Andrea et al., 2001, p. 225). Far from operating from romantic notions about the transformational potential of the multicultural movement, the SJOD model is based on our own knowledge about the ways that other social justice advocates have operated from a similar principle as they successfully worked against the odds to foster significant organizational, institutional, and societal changes in the United States. Much of this knowledge comes from a critical assessment of the successes of various organizational-institutional development interventions that were implemented by individuals in the civil rights, women's, poor people's, disability, and peace movements in the past.

Assumption #2: The second assumption relates to our recognition that most of the forms of injustice and oppression that continue to exist in our contemporary society are perpetuated by culturally biased, undemocratic, and oppressive organizational and institutional policies and practices. These unjust, undemocratic, and oppressive practices are designed to maintain particular hierarchies of power that privilege individuals in the dominant cultural-racial group while negatively affecting many people in other devalued and marginalized groups (Rothenberg, 2008).

Culturally competent counselors are knowledgeable of the adverse psychological impact that such power and privilege have on millions of persons in devalued groups as well as among members of the dominant group (Bowser & Hunt, 1996). They also are committed to using their knowledge and skills as multicultural advocates to ameliorate unjust, undemocratic, and oppressive policies and practices that continue to be operative in organizational settings (Sue, Arredondo, & McDavis, 1992).

Assumption #3: The third assumption that underlies the SJOD theory is grounded in a particular perspective of human development. This perspective embraces the notion that individuals and human systems (e.g., organizations, institutions, and communities) are characterized by an innate evolutionary propensity to develop into more complex, compassionate, and justice-oriented persons and entities (Gilligan, 1982; Kohlberg, 1984). Although the SJOD theory is based on the work of numerous human development experts, including Carol Gilligan (female development), Lawrence Kohlberg (moral development), Janet Helms (racial identity development), Jane Loevinger (ego development), and Joseph Ponterotto (White racial identity development), it also

draws from Donald Beck and Christopher Cowan's (2006) theory of organizational development.

One of the major contributions of Beck and Cowan's theory relates to its description of five developmental phases of organizational change. This includes what Beck and Cowan refer to as the *Alpha Fit* (a time of relative stability within organizations); the *Beta Condition* (a time of uncertainty, questioning, and frustration); the *Gamma Trap* (a state of anger manifested by various individuals who are distressed with controversial questions that are raised by other people during the Beta Condition); the *Delta Surge* (a time of excitement and rapid change that includes the integration of new ideas expressed during the Beta Condition and Gamma Trap); and the building of a *New Alpha* (a time of consolidating and institutionalizing ideas generated during the Beta Condition, Gamma Trap, and Delta Surge phases).

Assumption #4: The fourth assumption acknowledges that individuals in organizations operate from different states of consciousness. These diverse states of consciousness relate to different developmental capacities that people have realized during their lives. They include, but are not limited to, the diverse cognitive (problem solving), social (interpersonal styles and skills), and moral (ethical reasoning) capacities that people realize in their lives. These identifiable developmental capacities account for the different ways people respond to various organizational issues and legitimize and maintain specific kinds of institutional practices in school, university, employment, military, religious, social, and community settings. The continued legitimization and maintenance of these organizational practices directly and indirectly affect all of our lives.

Beck and Cowan (2006) refer to these different developmental capacities and states of consciousness as *memes*. The unique and identifiable memes that are reflected in the thinking and behavior of persons operating from different developmental capacities result in distinct levels of understanding and different degrees of commitment to promote multiculturalism, social justice, and democratic decision making in organizational settings.

Assumption #5: The fifth assumption that underlies the SJOD theory relates to the important role that counselors can play in modeling the courage that is necessary to resist pressure to conform to organizational policies and practices that perpetuate various forms of cultural oppression and social injustice. This assumption is consistent with Dr. Martin Luther King, Jr.'s teachings about the moral responsibility people have to address social injustice wherever it exists. This includes working to eradicate injustices that are overtly or covertly perpetuated in organizational settings where counselors are employed (King, 1987; Washington, 1986).

Dr. King (1987) acknowledged that it requires a certain state of consciousness and courage to resist conforming to social-organizational conditions that perpetuate injustice and undemocratic practices. Because the fifth theoretical assumption of the SJOD theory is directly derived from Dr. King's philosophy of social and organizational change, it is useful to emphasize the difficult moral challenges counselors face in dealing with organizational leaders and workers who willingly foster and conform to unjust organizational policies and practices even after being made aware of the ways that the organization perpetuates various forms of social injustice, cultural-racial oppression, and undemocratic decision making in our society (Giroux, 2006).

This assumption emphasizes the importance of seeking out and working with other social justice allies in the organization whose consciousness, developmental capacity/meme, and personal courage do not make them as vulnerable to conforming to social pressures. However, as Dr. King explained, it is equally important for individuals to implement actions on their own when they are aware of the negative impact that unjust and oppressive organizational, institutional, and community policies and practices have on other people's health and well-being. He stressed this point further by noting that individuals have the moral responsibility to act on injustices despite the threats and controversy that accompany such individual action, even when other persons around them are hesitant to do so.

With this in mind, the SJOD theory asserts that it is particularly important for counselors to assert the courage of their convictions by implementing interventions that are intentionally designed to address various forms of injustice and cultural oppression that continue to be perpetuated in the organizational practices where they work. Although difficult, it is particularly important to do so when the majority of persons in the organization where one is employed are operating from a state of consciousness that inhibits them from doing so themselves.

IMPLEMENTING NEW ROLES AND INTERVENTIONS TO PROMOTE SOCIAL JUSTICE ORGANIZATION DEVELOPMENT: A CASE STUDY

Space restrictions limit our ability to discuss all of the roles, interventions, and projects implemented in this case study. However, the following section summarizes some of the roles and strategies that were used to promote organizational changes at a university in the western region of the United States. These strategies were grounded in the SJOD theory. After briefly describing these aspects of the case study, we summarize an evaluation of these efforts by discussing the positive and negative outcomes that ensued from each intervention strategy.

Implementing the SJOD Theory at the Departmental Level

From 1999 to 2003, a small number of social justice advocates in a counselor education department directed time and energy mobilizing other faculty members and students in discussions about the ways that their own department unintentionally perpetuates institutional racism by continuing to use a culturally biased epistemology and instructional strategies in its graduate programs. These mobilization efforts resulted in a series of educational and consultation meetings where faculty members were afforded opportunities to discuss some of the specific ways that institutional racism is unintentionally perpetuated in counseling programs by many good-hearted, well-meaning faculty members.

The counselor educators who led this initiative understood that the effective implementation of this aspect of the SJOD project necessitated the use of a set of roles and services that is different from what many counselors are trained to use in their work. In this regard, the counselor educators involved in this intervention operated as community organizers by mobilizing faculty members and students into discussion groups where individuals in the department could learn about and raise questions regarding the ways that institutional racism was alleged to be perpetuated in counselor education programs in general and their own department in particular. The counselor educators leading this effort also accepted the role of "educator" by providing reading materials that describe how this complex problem is manifested in their profession and department. They also took on the "consultant role" by meeting with interested faculty members and students in individual consultation meetings to discuss these issues in greater detail upon request.

Positive outcomes: Several positive outcomes ensued from this intervention, as follows:

a. A changed discourse at faculty meetings that focused on the injustices and oppression that were unintentionally perpetuated in their counseling department by using culturally biased epistemologies with graduate students as well as the department's history of disproportionately hiring White male faculty members to tenure-track faculty positions;

b. Acknowledgment by some faculty members that one practical way to ameliorate such injustice was to have course instructors agree to address various multicultural counseling competencies in explicit and deliberate ways in all of their courses; and

c. Agreement among some of the faculty members to implement instructional changes in the department that address some of the social injustices and cultural oppression that are perpetuated by using culturally biased counseling theories and practices in their graduate courses. This agreement was institutionalized in the department when three of the six faculty members agreed to formally endorse the multicultural counseling competencies (Sue et al., 1992) by committing themselves to explicitly stating which competencies would be addressed in their courses as outlined in their course syllabi.

In organizational development terms, these positive outcomes reflected some of the ways that the implementation of the SJOD model at the departmental level fostered changes that encouraged movement from

a. the Alpha fit phase (a time of relative stability) to

b. the Beta Condition (a period in which faculty members were challenged to consider some of the ways that institutional racism was unintentionally perpetuated in their department) to

c. the Gamma Trap (a phase characterized by frustration and anger as some faculty members became increasingly frustrated by the allegations that the department helped to perpetuate various forms of institutional racism and cultural oppression) and finally to

d. the Delta Surge phase (where some of the faculty members integrated new ideas that were discussed within the meetings in their courses).

Negative outcomes: In addition to the positive outcomes mentioned above, this SJOD intervention resulted in a number of negative outcomes in this counselor education department:

a. Increased divisions among faculty members who supported the endorsement of the multicultural counseling competencies versus those faculty members who expressed resentment about the ways that this action violated their "academic freedom"

b. Negative gossiping about what was perceived as "pushy" and "intimidating" attempts to lobby support for this initiative by some faculty members who were antagonistic and displeased with such social justice organizational development advocacy efforts

c. Negative comments that were made by some faculty members among persons outside of the department as well as with administrators in the College of Education where the department was situated. As a result of such negative gossiping, the counselor educators who led this initiative became increasingly viewed as individuals who used "bullying" and "intimidating" tactics to promote "their cause."

Implementing the SJOD Theory at the College Level

In addition to addressing the complex problem of institutional racism in their department, the counselor educators mentioned above expanded their efforts to effect changes in the College of Education (COE) where their department was situated. These efforts were implemented from 2000 to 2007.

This component of the intervention began in the summer of 2000 by taking on the roles of "consultant," "educator," and "social justice advocate" in meetings that one of the counselor educators set up with a senior administrator in the college. The consultation, educational, and advocacy services used at this time were designed to address the covert ways that institutional racism and sexism were perpetuated in the COE.

The above-mentioned social justice advocacy efforts included providing the senior administrator with research and theoretical publications that describe how the complex problems of institutional racism and sexism are commonly manifested in institutions of higher education. These articles also described the direct and indirect impact of these injustices on millions of persons in marginalized groups in the United States (including many persons in marginalized and devalued groups in the city where their university was located).

The consultation-education-advocacy meetings continued through the fall of 2000 and spring of 2001. During that time, it became increasingly clear that the senior administrator was not genuinely interested in or supportive of addressing the complex problems of institutional racism and sexism as they were allegedly being perpetuated in the COE. The senior administrator's lack of interest and support in helping to eradicate such systemic problems represented a serious barrier to implementing other organizational changes that would effectively address these complex problems beyond the advocates' own department.

Like their efforts to gain support from their departmental colleagues, the counselor educators involved in implementing the SJOD theory at the college level recognized that they had overestimated the developmental readiness and personal courage of the senior administrator and other persons in the college to address these controversial organizational problems. Recognizing the importance of more accurately assessing the developmental meme and state of consciousness of those individuals who would be key in helping to address such complex organizational problems, the counselor educators leading this effort decided that it was necessary to take time to reassess the potential for change in the college by more carefully reevaluating the senior administrator and other persons' developmental readiness to deal with such problems. Consequently, they became more systematic and intentional in their assessment of these individuals than they had been in the past. By modifying the developmental assessment strategies developed by Hy and Loevinger (1996), the counselor educators using the SJOD in their work setting gained what they believed were more accurate assessments of the senior administrator's and other persons' developmental readiness in dealing with the complex problems of institutional racism and sexism in the COE.

Using the modified assessment strategy mentioned above, the counselor educators discussed the reactions that the senior administrator and other persons in the COE had with them when discussing the complex ways that institutional racism and sexism continued to be perpetuated in society at large and within the college in particular. The reactions of these persons provided the counselor educators with a rich source of qualitative data that helped them assess more accurately the developmental readiness of the senior administrator and other persons in the COE to deal with the social justice issues.

The assessment process that the counselor educators used led them to conclude that the senior administrator appeared to be operating from Loevinger's (1986) Self-Protective/Conformist Stages of ego development and the "Red Meme" of Beck and Cowan's organizational development theory when called upon to deal with the complex problems of institutional racism and sexism in the college. Interestingly, the counselor educators also found that many other faculty members, students, and staff persons in the COE exhibited a similar developmental readiness to deal with these issues as well.

Persons operating from these developmental memes or states of consciousness predictably exhibit self-protective tendencies when called upon to help change organizational policies and practices that allegedly perpetuate institutional racism and sexism in their work settings. These self-protective tendencies are typically reflected in a general unwillingness to discuss, investigate, or otherwise address the complex problems of institutional racism and sexism in organizational settings reportedly largely out of fear of the negative reactions other people might have to their addressing such controversial issues in the workplace. Furthermore, the developmental characteristics associated with Loevinger's self-protective/conformist stages and Beck and Cowan's Red meme commonly lead persons operating from such dispositions to respond in negative and hostile ways to individuals who advocate for changes in the status quo that include eradicating covert forms of institutional racism and sexism that are perpetuated in organizational settings (D'Andrea & Daniels, 2008).

It is also important to point out that persons operating from the Red meme and self-protective/conformist stages do not like to have their authority questioned in organizational settings. When these persons feel that their authority is being questioned, they are likely to use whatever formal and informal organizational policies, practices, and power they can to maintain their own power and privileged position within the organization (Beck & Cowan, 2006).

After much consideration of the developmental barriers and increasing resistance and hostility that were encountered from the senior administrator and other faculty members, staff persons, and students in the college as a result of their efforts to implement the SJOD initiative, the counselor educators felt morally compelled to file a formal complaint. This complaint included

a. a detailed description of the various ways that institutional racism and sexism were allegedly manifested in the college;

b. a formal request for corrective action; and

c. an organizational assessment tool that one of the counselor educators developed and provided to the senior administrator to measure the degree to which these alleged problems might be perpetuated in the college. This assessment tool provided guidelines that administrators could use to assess the racial-ethnic disparities that exist in the composition of administrators, faculty members, staff persons, and even janitorial workers employed in the organization as well as the ways that epistemological racism was perpetuated in the courses offered by faculty members in the college.

By following established organizational policies in filing this complaint, it was hoped that the senior administrator would conduct an investigation of the alleged problems, report the findings, and make recommendations for corrective action as outlined by the University Board of Regents' policies. Although the senior administrator is responsible for investigating any formal complaint that is filed with his office, this individual failed to conduct a formal investigation of the initial 2000 complaint regarding the ways that institutional racism and sexism are allegedly perpetuated in the COE. The senior administrator also failed to investigate two additional complaints alleging the same concerns that one of the counselor educators again filed between February and June 2006. Not only did the senior administrator refuse to investigate and report the findings of such an investigation, but this individual began to increasingly initiate what were perceived to be retaliatory actions against the counselor educators who implemented the SJOD theory in the college.

The growing pressure that resulted from these perceived forms of retaliation suggested that it was important for the counselor educators to gain support from resources outside the university system. This support was found in state and national human rights agencies as well as in securing legal assistance from a private attorney. One of the counselor educators involved in this project was particularly fortunate to find an attorney who had a reputation for tackling difficult cases that were similar to the situation he was experiencing at the university.

By taking the time to accept the role as purveyors of these agencies and resources, the counselor educators became more knowledgeable of their legal rights when promoting SJOD strategies in their workplace. They also learned a great deal about the legal protections one is afforded when individuals are subjected to what they believe to be retaliation at the workplace. As a result of securing support from these resources, the counselor educators learned the importance of becoming knowledgeable about local, state, and national human rights agencies (e.g., the Federal Equal Employment Office, the State Commission of Civil Rights, the American Civil Liberties Union, etc.) when implementing SJOD initiatives in their workplace.

The increasing hostility, discrimination, and retaliation to which the counselor educators involved in the present study perceived themselves being subjected by senior administrators and their associates at the university led to the filing of numerous formal complaints with legal and quasi-legal offices that were both internal and external to the university. As a result of filing formal complaints with agencies that were external to the university, the counselor educators found themselves acquiring the defensive power that is necessary to assert when experiencing what they perceived to be retaliatory and harassing actions by various persons in their work setting as a result of implementing the SJOD theory. This included using faculty union grievance procedures and arbitration hearings in attempting to seek fair redress regarding what they perceived to be false and unsubstantiated accusations made against themselves while implementing the SJOD theory at their university. These defensive actions also included filing lawsuits and other legal complaints related to various forms of retaliation and harassment that the counselor educators perceived themselves to be subjected as a result of their continuing work in this area.

Positive outcomes: A number of positive outcomes followed from what became an increasingly contentious situation. Among the positive changes were an increased level of discourse among administrators, faculty members, and students in the college regarding the complex problems of institutional racism and sexism. The importance of promoting a greater level of discourse related to these complex problems is particularly important given the unique role and function that institutions of higher education play in promoting democracy in our society (Giroux, 2006).

Another positive organizational change that was stimulated by the increasing discourse on issues related to racism and sexism in the college involved a noticeable shift within the organizational culture of the college. This shift was manifested in the sort of dynamic changes that Beck and Cowan (2006) insist are necessary for organizational development to occur. Such changes are manifested when organizations move beyond the Alpha Fit (a time of relative stability and unquestioned acceptance of the status quo) to the Beta Condition (a period of increased questioning and critical analysis of the organization) that may foster movement to the Gamma Trap (a phase marked by heightened frustration and anger by persons supportive of the status quo and dissatisfied with those individuals who raise criticisms about the organization).

It is important to note that the controversy that was stimulated by the counselor educators' continued efforts to address the ways that institutional racism and sexism were allegedly perpetuated in the COE represent some of the ways that other social justice advocates can stimulate these developmental dynamics in organizational settings. In doing so, the counselor educators involved in this intervention hoped that the college would experience a Delta Surge (a time in which the organization would begin to integrate the new ideas generated by an increased organizational discourse regarding social justice) and finally move to a New Alpha phase (where the organization would begin to incorporate new ways of thinking and behaving).

A third positive outcome that resulted from their efforts to implement the SJOD theory in the college related to actions taken by the COE's Faculty Senate in the 2006–2007 academic year. During the Spring 2006 semester, one of the counselor educators involved in implementing the SJOD theory initiated formal discussions with this organizational body regarding the need for faculty members to investigate and address allegations about the ways that institutional racism continued to be perpetuated in their organization. As a result of these discussions, the Faculty Senate unanimously agreed to conduct a "discovery" of these allegations.

This discovery process involved having the members of the Faculty Senate's Diversity Committee gather relevant data regarding the demographic composition of the student body, administration, and faculty in the college. It also involved identifying and interviewing persons in the COE and university at large who could provide additional information related to the allegations of institutional racism in the college.

As a result of these efforts, the Diversity Committee drafted a detailed report of its findings along with recommendations for corrective action. The report was submitted to the full Faculty Senate for approval. The full Faculty Senate formally approved the report and recommendations for corrective actions in May 2007. This report was presented to the dean of the college at that time.

It is important to point out that the formal action taken by the Faculty Senate represented the possibility of stimulating new policies and practices that could help address the problem of institutional racism in the college. By implementing these recommendations, the college could potentially move from the Beta Condition (that was manifested in the increasing discourse and questions about institutional racism in the college) to the Delta Surge phase (where a greater commitment to deal more effectively with the complex problem of institutional racism could be reflected in new organizational action plans).

A fourth positive outcome that emerged from implementing the SJOD model in the college involves the galvanizing of both local and national support for these social justice advocacy efforts. Not only was this support helpful when the counselor educators leading this initiative increasingly came under attack by persons who viewed their efforts in antagonistic and oppositional ways, but it also led to building new connections with other social justice advocates at the university and in the greater community where the university is located.

A fifth positive outcome relates to the important strategy of using legal assistance when implementing the SJOD theory at one's workplace. In this regard, one of the counselor educators involved in this case study filed two lawsuits against the university for violating his 1st (free speech) and 14th (due process) Amendment rights. This individual secured positive settlements in both of these lawsuits. In 2006, the second counselor educator was able to reach a separate legal and monetary settlement related to complaints she had also filed, some of which related to false allegations that had been made about her.

Negative outcomes: One of the negative outcomes that resulted from their efforts to expand the SJOD initiative in the COE was reflected in the increasing negative reactions these counselor educators experienced from other administrators, faculty members, students, and staff persons who were antagonistic to such efforts. These antagonisms were concretely manifested when three faculty members and one administrator filed what were perceived as being false allegations against one of the counselor educators for what was termed his "threatening, bullying, and harassing behavior." Two of these complaints have undergone review by the university president's office and found to be "without cause." The remaining complaints are currently under review in arbitration processes that are supported by the faculty union.

A third negative outcome that resulted from their work in this area relates to the personal toll that the hostility these counselor educators experienced had on their personal lives. Although expressing much gratefulness for the support that was provided by the Faculty Senate in approving the Diversity Committee's report and recommendations as well as the support offered by the faculty union, other legal experts in the community, and many students and colleagues in the field, it is important to state the obvious. That is, the ongoing stressors they experienced from the various antagonisms they encountered when implementing the SJOD theory in their work had an adverse impact on different aspects of their overall health and well-being. Without elaborating further on the health hazards that are associated with doing this sort of work, the counselor educators involved in this social justice advocacy simply pointed out that the predictable negative personal and organizational reactions that are likely to occur as a result of implementing SJOD interventions in one's work setting can adversely affect

an individual's health and career in different ways. These hazards need to be taken into consideration when counselors think about exercising the professional roles and services that are described in this chapter.

SUMMARY AND CONCLUSIONS

In summary, it is suggested that the SJOD offers much promise in helping to foster the realization of a greater level of justice and democratic decision making in large organizations in general and particularly in large public universities. When reporting on the specific positive outcomes that ensued from their efforts to implement the SJOD theory at a university in the western region of the United States, the persons involved in this initiative suggested that all of the outcomes discussed in this chapter directly and indirectly helped to foster a greater level of active and participatory democracy in the organization as a result of openly and consistently confronting different injustices at their workplace.

It is equally important to discourage the reader from concluding that the efforts and outcomes described in this case study were solely the responsibility of the counselor educators involved in this case study. Rather, it is vital to note that the progress that was made in stimulating new ways of thinking about and implementing social justice and democratic principles in this organizational setting is also due to the collective work of other faculty members, students, and community members who are committed to promoting similar outcomes at the university where this intervention was implemented.

The following list of achievements summarizes some of the positive outcomes that ensued from the work of the two counselor educators discussed in this case study as well as the ongoing efforts of other persons who are committed to promoting social justice and democracy at this university. This list includes a summary of the positive outcomes reported in this chapter as well as other accomplishments that were not mentioned in the preceding discussion. These accomplishments include the following:

a. The endorsement of the multicultural counseling competencies at the department level in an effort to promote more just, respectful, and culturally responsive training opportunities for graduate students;

b. The hiring of the first African American female faculty member for a tenure-track position in the department where the SJOD project was first initiated;

c. The establishment of an independent student empowerment and advocacy organization in the same department in 2004;

d. The development of a detailed report by the Faculty Senate's Diversity Committee that substantiated how institutional racism is perpetuated in the college and outlined recommendations to ameliorate this complex problem in the future;

e. Successful efforts to remediate some of the ways that administrators allegedly misused their organizational power when the social justice advocates involved in the case study implemented the SJOD theory at their workplace;

f. The recent hiring of two women in high administrative positions at the university;

g. The remodeling of a number of restrooms and the reconstruction of doorways and completion of curb-cutting projects to increase accessibility of the College among persons with disabilities;

h. The implementation of new sensitivity training workshops for coaches and student-athletes in an effort to address the forms of hostility that were reportedly directed to women and gay/lesbian/bisexual persons in the university's athletic department.

This list of accomplishments illuminates how the implementation of the SJOD theory helped to partially realize the unfulfilled promise for social justice and democracy at one large university in the western part of the United States, but it is important to also summarize some of the pitfalls associated with implementing this theoretical model in this particular organizational setting. The first pitfall relates to the time and energy that is necessary to effectively realize the kinds of positive outcomes reported in this chapter. With this in mind, it is readily recognized that it is difficult for many counselors and counselor educators to direct the time and energy that is necessary to effectively implement this theoretical model given their demanding schedules and professional responsibilities.

A second major pitfall involves the negative impact that counselors may experience from persons who are antagonistic to having social justice initiatives implemented in their organizations and the types of hostility one is likely to encounter as a result of engaging in this kind of work. This hazard is linked to the potential negative outcomes that can occur in one's overall health as a result of engaging in this important work.

Recognizing the insidious implications of this factor, it is important that counselors engaged in this sort of social justice advocacy make a personal commitment to live a lifestyle that is based on wellness principles. Such a commitment necessitates individuals to strive to consciously maintain a healthy diet as well as make time for physical exercise, family fun, and other social-recreational-cultural activities. These activities are particularly important in rejuvenating one's energy reserves and drive to continue the vital work that needs to be done in this area. It is also important to establish support networks both locally and nationally that can offer personal as well as professional support when stressors begin to overtax one's coping abilities.

Despite the very real, dangerous, and stressful pitfalls associated with implementing the SJOD model in organizational settings, the potential benefits to promote justice, peace, and democracy in society outweigh many of the negative outcomes that may ensue in doing so. Hopefully, this case study will stimulate new thinking about the roles counselors can play in helping to build a more democratic, peaceful, just, and saner society by addressing various injustices that are perpetuated in one's work setting.

REFERENCES

Adler, N. J. (1986). *Cultural synergy: Managing the impact of cultural diversity. The 1986 annual: Developing human resources.* San Diego, CA: University Associates.

Barr, D. J., & Strong, L. J. (1987, May). Embracing multiculturalism: The existing contradictions. *ACU-I Bulletin,* pp. 20–23.

Beck, D. E., & Cowan, C. C. (2006). *Spiral dynamics: Mastering values, leadership, and change.* Malden, MA: Blackwell.

Bowser, B. P., & Hunt, R. G. (Eds.). (1996). *Impacts of racism on White Americans* (2nd ed.). Thousand Oaks, CA: Sage.

Cross, T. L., Bazron, B. J., Dennis, K. W., & Isaacs, M. R. (1989). *Towards a culturally competent system of care.* Washington, DC: Georgetown University Child Development Center.

D'Andrea, M., & Daniels, J. (1995). Promoting multiculturalism and organizational change in the counseling profession: A case study. In J. G. Ponterotto, J. M. Casas, L. A. Suzuki, & C. M. Alexander (Eds.), *Handbook of multicultural counseling* (pp. 17–33). Thousand Oaks, CA: Sage.

D'Andrea, M., & Daniels, J. (2008, April). *Promoting social justice in organizational settings: Extending the struggle for psychological liberation.* Paper presented at the Fourth Interamerican Congress on Counseling Culture, Community and Counseling: Connections for a Flourishing Life. Managua, Nicaragua.

D'Andrea, M., Daniels, J., Arredondo, P., Ivey, A., Ivey, M. B., Locke, D. C., O'Bryant, B., Parham, T. A., & Sue, D. W. (2001). Fostering organizational changes to realize the revolutionary potential of the multicultural movement: An updated case study. In J. G. Ponterotto, J. M. Casas, L. A. Suzuki, & C. M. Alexander (Eds.), *Handbook of multicultural counseling* (2nd ed., pp. 222–253). Thousand Oaks, CA: Sage.

Daniels, J., & D'Andrea, M. (2003, November). Promoting multicultural and social justice counseling. *Counseling Today, 46,* 36–38.

Foster, B. G., Jackson, G., Cross, W. E., & Hardiman, R. (1988). *Workforce diversity and business.* Alexandria, VA: American Society for Training and Development.

Gilligan, C. (1982). *In a different voice.* Cambridge, MA: Harvard University Press.

Giroux, H. (2006). Higher education under siege: Implications for public intellectuals. *Thought and Action, 22,* 63–78.

Grieger, I., & Toliver, S. (2001). Multiculturalism on predominately White campuses: Multiple roles and functions. In J. G. Ponterotto, J. M. Casas, L. A. Suzuki, &

C. M. Alexander (Eds.), *Handbook of multicultural counseling* (2nd ed., pp. 825–848). Thousand Oaks, CA: Sage.

Hy, L. X., & Loevinger, J. (1996). *Measuring ego development.* Mahwah, NJ: Lawrence Erlbaum.

Jones, J. M. (1997). *Prejudice and racism* (2nd ed.). New York: McGraw-Hill.

King, C. S. (1987). *The words of Martin Luther King, Jr.* New York: Newmarket.

Kohlberg, L. (1984). *Essays on moral development: Vol. 2. The psychology of moral development.* New York: Harper & Row.

Loevinger, J. (1986). *Paradigms of personality.* New York: Freeman.

Miller, J., & Garran, A. M. (2008). *Racism in the United States: Implications for the helping professions.* Belmont, CA: Thomson Higher Education.

Rothenberg, P. S. (Ed.). (2008). *White privilege: Essential readings on the other side of racism* (3rd ed.). New York: Worth.

Sue, D. W., Arredondo, P., & McDavis, R. (1992). Multicultural counseling competencies and standards: A call to the profession. *Journal of Counseling & Development, 70,* 477–486.

Sue, D. W., & Sue, D. (2003). *Counseling the culturally diverse: Theory and practice* (4th ed.). New York: Wiley.

Washington, J. M. (Ed.). (1986). *A testament of hope: The essential writings of Martin Luther King, Jr.* San Francisco: Harper & Row.

Zalaquett, C. P., Foley, P. F., Tillotson, K., Dinsmore, J., & Hof, D. (2008). Multicultural and social justice training for counselor education programs and colleges of education: Rewards and challenges. *Journal of Counseling & Development, 86,* 323–329.

47

Social Justice and Community Engagement

Developing Relationships Beyond the University

REBECCA L. TOPOREK, DIANE DODGE,
FELICIA TRIPP, AND LAURA ALARCÓN

Contributing to social justice in the community provides opportunities for making counseling and psychology relevant in addressing significant problems faced by individuals and communities. Many clients face daily challenges, not always created by intrapsychic conflict but by issues that arise out of external systems and barriers. Psychologists and counselors can engage and partner with communities facing the greatest disparities to address these issues at multiple levels and through a range of constructive roles. By forming these alliances, professionals and communities become a stronger force toward social justice and greater well-being.

The intent of this chapter is to encourage professionals, students, and educators to enhance relationships across settings and create alliances and partnerships

that work toward social justice. We assert that community engagement presents a vital opportunity to enact social change in a way that is more informed and more relevant to the needs of those who might have less power and are affected most greatly by inequity and injustice. First, a general discussion of social justice and community engagement will provide a brief foundation for multilevel involvement in communities. Second, we will present a case study of a partnership between a nonprofit agency (Seven Tepees Youth Program) and a higher education institution (the career counseling graduate program at San Francisco State University) to illustrate, in an intimate way, the growth of a relationship across two entities that have different structures, cultures, and languages, but a shared commitment to

Authors' Note: Additional thanks to Kym Glanville and Gabriel Martinez for their contributions to this partnership.

social justice. Third, we will present recommendations for future directions for training and collaboration across organizations.

In writing this chapter as partners, we disclosed to each other many of our unspoken assumptions and experiences and were surprised to find that the process of developing a working partnership was a bit like the development of an intimate relationship. Although literature exists regarding collaborative work between universities and community agencies, there is a paucity of literature describing the process by which the collaborations develop. In deconstructing our process, we hope to expose some of the perceived obstacles that both parties encountered that could have potentially hindered the collaboration process to help others embarking on such a venture. We will also share recommendations for developing partnerships between organizations that reflect principles of social justice, social change, multicultural competence, and community engagement.

SOCIAL JUSTICE: MULTIPLE LEVELS OF INTERVENTION AND RELEVANT ROLES

Counselors and psychologists have worked in the interest of social justice through empowerment efforts with clients (e.g., Holcomb-McCoy & Mitchell, 2007; McWhirter, 1994), influencing public policy (e.g., Buki, 2007; Herr, 2003), advocacy (e.g., Kiselica & Robinson, 2001; Toporek, Lewis, & Crethar, 2009), implementation of multicultural competence and guidelines (American Psychological Association, 2003; Sue, Arredondo, & McDavis, 1992), and numerous other examples. A significant recognition in the social justice literature is the need to address oppression at all levels reflecting the influence of context and environment on well-being and development (Bronfenbrenner, 1977). For example, in the development of the American Counseling Association (ACA) Advocacy Competencies (Lewis, Arnold, House, & Toporek, 2002), domains of competence include individual, school or community, and societal levels. The model also acknowledges that, at times, advocacy is done in partnership with the client or community, and at other times, it is done on behalf of the client or community.

Similarly, the recent *Handbook for Social Justice in Counseling and Psychology* provided numerous examples of social justice work at multiple levels, such as individual, community, and policy or legislative (Toporek, Gerstein, Fouad, Roysircar, & Israel, 2006). Across these levels, overarching themes embedded in the social justice interventions included community involvement, interdisciplinary collaboration, multilevel or systemic approaches, patience with the pace of change, commitment, fidelity, and veracity. At each of these levels of intervention, a broader range of roles allows the counseling and psychology professional to address social justice issues. We will now focus specifically on relevant professional roles within the context of community engagement and counseling and psychology.

Social Justice, the Community, and Constructive Roles

Although the commitment to social justice in counseling and psychology has fluctuated over time, individual and collective actions have helped shape current perspectives. In particular, feminist, multicultural, prevention, and community counseling and psychology have presented philosophies and practices that support the evolution of social justice encompassing a wider range of practitioner roles. These roles reflect the multilevel influences on clients' well-being and suggest that broader conceptualization of professionals' roles is both ethical and appropriate, particularly in the face of oppression and marginalization (Atkinson, Thompson, & Grant, 1993; Lewis, Lewis, Daniels, & D'Andrea, 1998; Sue et al., 1998; Vera & Speight, 2003). For example, Reese and Vera (2007) called for counseling psychologists to move beyond individual counseling and psychotherapy to engage in culturally relevant advocacy, prevention, and outreach. Atkinson and his colleagues identified eight roles that may be appropriate given the client's acculturation, locus of problem etiology, and focus of intervention. Some of these included advocate, consultant, counselor, psychotherapist, and change agent. Recognizing the breadth of expertise that counselors and psychologists can bring to the context of community engagement toward greater social justice, we have chosen to frame our discussion around four roles: counselor, advocate, consultant, and researcher. It is important to note that although these roles may vary, multicultural competence at all levels (e.g., Sue et al., 1998) is a critical foundation.

Counselor and Clinician. There is a paucity of literature regarding the social justice potential of the counselor and clinician roles. Morrow, Hawxhurst, Montes de Vegas, Abousleman, and Castaneda (2006) noted that feminist and multicultural perspectives identify sociopolitical aspects of clients' experiences and recognize the ways in which individual clinical work can address larger political realities. For example, Ponterotto, Utsey, and Pedersen (2006) addressed the ways in which counselors and psychologists can work toward preventing prejudice by facilitating awareness and skills among children, adults, and colleagues. Community counseling has also identified roles for counselors acting against oppression as critical components of practice (Lewis et al., 1998). Counseling for empowerment (McWhirter, 1994) integrates the clinician's understanding of the sociopolitical context within counseling and facilitates clients becoming change agents in their own lives and as members of their communities. In addition, multicultural counseling emphasizes the role of cultural context and sociopolitical histories in working with clients (Sue et al., 1992). Providing services as a community-engaged professional increases the likelihood that the cultural context of the community and the forces that influence the wellness of clients will be integrated more appropriately into clinical work.

Consultant. The role of consultant brings the expertise of the professional to address community needs. The tools of a consultant include, among others, assessment, program design, evaluation, public information, and facilitator of group process. We wish to expand the conceptualization of this role with the frame of an emancipatory communitarian approach. This approach brings depth to the consultant role as we think of the contributions of counselors and psychologists through a social justice lens.

> The overarching goal of this orientation is to increase the personal and collective power of people who are powerless and, in so doing, to reduce domination. Perhaps more than other approaches, communitarian practice would emphasize collaboration and power sharing. Groups who are served would be enabled to negotiate the contents, procedures, processes, and ethical parameters of psychological interventions. (Prilleltensky, 1997, p. 528)

Advocate. On a broad scale, multicultural and feminist counseling and psychology have noted the need for human service professionals to advocate for clients either through empowerment or in addressing the external barriers faced by clients (e.g., Lewis et al., 1998; Toporek & Liu, 2001). The ACA Advocacy Competencies Model was designed to assist counselors in serving ethically and effectively in the advocate role (Lewis et al., 2002). Although each of the advocacy competency domains necessarily integrates context and community, two of the six domains of advocacy competence specifically focus on the counselor's role of advocacy within the community. As counselors and psychologists recognize the impact of larger social issues on clients' well-being, they can work with their clients on addressing those issues through collective, organized, or social action.

Researcher. The role of researcher provides the opportunity to assist communities in projecting their voice and potential solutions to a broader audience. It is important to note that communities may perceive researchers with some wariness given that there is a history within psychology of conducting research without clear and immediate benefit to the community (Marker, 2003). There is a growing movement to connect more clearly the needs of the community with the research process. One of the most often-cited research approaches in relation to social justice is community-based participatory action research. This approach facilitates collaboration between the investigator and participants to identify issues and assess them in a manner that promotes greater sociopolitical awareness and change in the community itself (Fetterman, 2000; Taylor, Braveman, & Hammel, 2004). Engaging participants in an integral way in the investigation ensures that the needs of the community drive the process and that their questions are being researched, and it dictates how the data are analyzed and collected. Although participants take a lead in this process, investigators may serve as consultants or play multiple roles, including community organizer, meeting facilitator, activist, and resource person (Taylor et al., 2004), that support the participants' goals and activities.

Morsillo and Prilleltensky (2007) described action research as a collaborative process in which the participants and researchers jointly design the research based on the community members' concerns and needs. They state that "the very process of identifying issues and devising actions empowers participants" (p. 728). Morsillo and Prilleltensky assert that this process in itself creates social change.

Each of the roles described here may be enacted through an individual level, a community level, and a societal level. In this chapter, we endeavor to illustrate how these roles may be relevant by presenting a case of collaboration between a university entity and a community entity. In the writing process, we discovered that the richness of our developmental process was as important as the identification of the roles we had set out to illustrate.

CASE STUDY OF A BUDDING RELATIONSHIP

Building alliances across settings allows for greater breadth of expertise and resources and ultimately can help to increase the visibility and awareness of the issues faced by a community. Additionally, these partnerships provide opportunities for a cross cultural dialogue and experience whereby the culture of the different parties may differ in terms of definitions of success, the way time is used, how accountability is measured, and language and communication patterns. Sometimes, the social justice intentions of all parties may not be enough to assume the automatic development of a smooth partnership. Negotiating those differences and creating a positive and productive partnership can be complex.

In their seminal work, Goodman and her colleagues (2004) emphasized that to implement social justice, more work needed to be done to connect with communities and address systemic issues. They outlined principles for social justice in counseling that are relevant across levels of intervention, including "a) ongoing self-examination; b) sharing power; c) giving voice; d) facilitating consciousness raising; e) building on strengths; and f) leaving clients with the tools for social change" (p. 798). Goodman and her colleagues suggested that these principles, grounded in feminist and multicultural counseling, could help guide the work with and for

communities to address the oppression and marginalization. Literature on community engagement also serves as a framework (e.g., Commission on Community-Engaged Scholarship in the Health Professions, 2007; Fawcett et al., 1995) and emphasizes the benefit of bringing the resources of the academic environment to the strengths and knowledge of the community regarding critical problems.

The case example of the community partnership with Seven Tepees illustrates a number of the principles outlined by Goodman et al. (2004) as well as the roles mentioned above, including those of consultant and researcher. We will begin by briefly describing Seven Tepees and the career counseling specialization at San Francisco State University. We will devote significant space to the agency as an entity because of the social change impact that this agency has in working with urban youth of color. We will then deconstruct the evolution of our relationship and discuss reflections and recommendations.

SEVEN TEPEES: A YOUTH PROGRAM ADDRESSING SOCIAL CHANGE THROUGH YOUTH EMPOWERMENT AND ENGAGEMENT

Seven Tepees was founded to counter systemic issues of social injustice by working directly with the youth most affected by racism, poverty, violence, and academic failure. The program is located in the Mission District of San Francisco and serves predominantly Latino and African American youth. The mission of Seven Tepees is to teach youth the skills they need to make positive life choices and create their own success. The program is designed with the hope that the positive effects of youths' growth and success will ripple out to their families, communities, and future generations.

In 1995, Daniel Weinstein, a retired San Francisco Juvenile Courts Supervising Judge, cofounded Seven Tepees with the aim of helping youth avoid the juvenile justice system. The unique program design is both long term and comprehensive in scope. Seven Tepees seeks to develop youth over a period of 7 years, from 6th to 12th grade, bridging the transitions between school levels, during a time when many marginalized students drop out of school. Each youth in the program is provided with comprehensive services in tutoring, academic and social case management, enrichment, mentoring, job training, parent training, environmental overnight trips, small group art and health education sessions, and counseling and individual therapy. In addition, increasing numbers of youth and families attend small group sessions aimed at overcoming culturally embedded feelings of stigmatism surrounding mental health issues. In all of these counseling modalities as well as in the program milieu, Seven Tepees engages an eclectic and culturally sensitive approach, with a focus on individual strengths and reinforcing positive family and community systems. The philosophy is based on the belief that all individuals have unique promise and purpose. Youth do not need to be rescued, but need to be provided positive experiences and opportunities, support, and guidance for their natural resiliency and gifts to evolve.

The name Seven Tepees Youth Program was given by cofounder Hully Fetiçó, a Native American Song Dancer. "Seven" represents the 7 years that youth are with the organization, as well as seven directions: North (Earth), South (Fire), West (Water), East (Wind), Above (the ancestors), Beneath (world), and You (fire or spark inside you) (H. Fetiçó, personal communication, November 13, 2008). The organization began as a summer camp where youth lived in seven tepees, each representing a different continent. As the program grew in complexity, the name remains as a reminder of the core values of native traditions: community building and respect for nature. A core belief is that connecting with nature has a healing quality for people who have experienced violence (more than 70% of the youth involved in Seven Tepees have experienced a death from violence in their immediate circle).

Seven Tepees values a systems perspective in its efforts to empower youth. Youth learn about their own history and cultural identity, and they explore their own personal goals and dreams for their community and society at large. Youth leaders design programs and activities during the academic year, and a personal growth retreat is held annually where youth explore identity, as well as personal and communal challenges. The youth-designed projects are often oriented toward social change. In one project in the San Francisco Mission District, a group of high school students designed a photography class centered on the concept of gentrification. Through it, they researched and photographed their neighborhoods, culminating in a gallery show. Based on this experience, the youth designed and facilitated a workshop on gentrification at a citywide youth conference. In another youth project, a group working with an expressive arts counselor explored the impact of violence in their lives and wrote the lyrics and beat to a hip-hop song called "Hella Ways to Get Up in This World," which described positive and negative ways to "make it" in the teen world in which they live. The youth recorded the song and performed it at a local theater, generating a sense of community and self-esteem, as none was a professional musician. In other projects, youth have served as delegates to city agencies, presented on youth violence to the mayor's office, and served on planning committees for the program.

Currently, Seven Tepees has embarked on an extension of college and career transition programming to neighborhood public schools. Seven Tepees has developed initial partnerships with middle and high schools with low records of retention, graduation, and college placement. This is where the partnership between Seven Tepees and the San Francisco State University Career Counseling Specialization Community Engagement Team began.

The Career Counseling Specialization at San Francisco State University

The career counseling specialization is one of six accredited master's-level counseling training programs in the Department of Counseling at San Francisco State University, a large urban university. Core values of the program, and of the university, include social justice, multicultural competence, and community engagement. The program attracts an ethnically and economically diverse pool of candidates, many of whom have had experience working in nonprofit organizations, community-based organizations, and educational institutions. In the career counseling specialization classes, students prepare workshops and presentations as well as culminating papers that reflect the complexities and realities of the surrounding communities, such as career counseling with undocumented students and immigrants, acculturation, oppression, and issues for clients with limited English skills.

San Francisco State University's counseling program maintains extensive contacts with college and university career and counseling centers as well as nonprofit and governmental organizations. All graduate students in the department are required to complete 2 years of field placement in the community, most of which serve low-income and ethnically diverse communities. Consequently, there is constant effort to develop and maintain a level of relationship with community organizations to ensure healthy field placement experiences for students. In addition, the coordinator of the career counseling specialization has written extensively on multicultural counseling competence, social justice, and advocacy (e.g., Arredondo et al., 1996; Pope-Davis et al., 2002; Toporek, 2006, 2009; Toporek et al., 2006; Toporek & Pope-Davis, 2005; Toporek & Reza, 2001).

Creating a Career and College Transition Program for Youth

The career and college transition program envisioned by Seven Tepees aims to increase the rates of students who graduate from high school and move on to college, and subsequently careers, increasing the overall power of individuals and families in a low-income and mostly immigrant community. By increasing the college and earning potential of students from communities with low academic success, immigrant families, and low financial resources, the imbalance of power is gradually shifted. In addition, this type of program can increase the potential of youth to contribute to their community in a broader range of ways while developing their ethnic, vocational, and community identity. By emphasizing social change, contributions to family and community, and self-growth, the program strives to facilitate youth in the development of a positive adult identity. These goals reflect the core values of Seven Tepees and San Francisco State University.

The initiation and implementation of this collaborative project centered on the ideals of community engagement and social justice and consequently invited the complexities inherent in such an approach.

The Evolution of a Relationship

There are excellent resources on community engagement and collaborative work between university entities and community agencies, the components necessary to establish a collaborative partnership, and the tools that can be useful in such an endeavor (e.g., Solberg, Howard, & Blustein, 2002; Toporek et al., 2006). Yet one of the aspects not often described in the literature is the process through which a relationship and community partnership develops. The human element of developing a trusting relationship within a working relationship is worth attention given the different cultures of the two types of organizations. On one hand, there may be a shared commitment to core values such as social justice, service to the community, and the importance of increasing access to opportunities, but there also exist different languages, worldviews, organization cultures, and resources, among other things.

As noted above, in the writing of this chapter, we reflected on the development of our partnership and found humor in the similarities between dating and the evolution of the partnership between our two organizations. We will describe the process of building the relationship highlighting some of the key issues, challenges, and successes. The analogy of dating may help to communicate some of the emotional components and behaviors that lay behind the professional behavior. To be clear, this was a professional partnership, yet some of the hesitations, misunderstandings, and communication patterns are not completely dissimilar to two individuals striving to build a healthy, intimate relationship. Table 47.1 frames the process in terms of this intimacy, complementing the description below chronicling the development of the professional partnership. Although the entire project also requires the involvement of schools and parents, this chapter focuses on the relationship between Seven Tepees and the university because it serves as the foundation for other collaborations.

Table 47.1 The Evolution of a Relationship

Agency "Inside Voice"	Stages of Relationship Building	University "Inside Voice"
See the need and have the vision	Seeking a compatible partner	Want more community engagement but so many other projects going; no time to seek new relationships
Who can fulfill this need? This program seems to fit the criteria: proximity, expertise, mission	Curiosity	Could be a good opportunity, need to see what the commitment would be. What does the name say?
They seem interested and like they might bring a lot to the relationship	Attraction	Seems like a great agency, congruent values, genuine
This could be great!	Excitement and admiration	This could be great!
Do they use the same language?	Look to see if it's a match	Are they able to work within our constraints?
I don't want to scare them away; don't want to seem too needy	Testing the waters	Let's see if we can do something within our means
Do they really understand our kids? Not ready to feel safe but we want them involved, maybe we can work with it	Building trust	Do they really want our involvement?
We'd love to have them work with us, but we can do most of it ourselves if needed	Do we have what it will take for a successful relationship?	Time? Is our expertise relevant to them?
What do they think of us?	What are they really thinking?	What do they think of us?
I think *this* could work	Initial commitment What does the commitment look like? How is it demonstrated?	I think *this* could work
Do they really want to work with us long term? We need to show that we can do it on our own	Trouble in paradise Disillusionment or confusion Mixed messages Approach-avoidance	Do they really want us? What is it they want from us?
Ok, they seem committed. They have demonstrated some understanding of our kids. It feels safer	Calibration and recommitment	We finally understand what this is about, but this needs a much bigger commitment if it is going to work
We are committed and will welcome them into our house, to recognize them as partners to our youth and staff	Meeting the family	We are committed and will assert our presence respectfully into the life of the agency, take the time to become a known entity to the youth

Precontact: Seeking a Compatible Partner. In reflecting on our developmental process, a model emerged that seemed to summarize how our two entities came together, what we brought to the process, and the core values we shared that helped the developmental process to progress even during times of uncertainty (see Figure 47.1).

Each partner involved had specific goals, expectations, visions, and ideas that formed a foundation for our work together. Some of these included the core values noted in the center circle in Figure 47.1. The director of Seven Tepees had identified the need to develop a career and college transition program for their youth

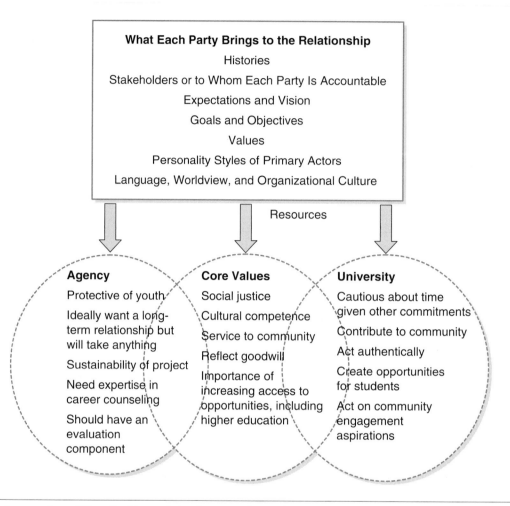

Figure 47.1   Intersection of Two Entities and the Common Ground

and had acquired a grant to fund it. Knowing that the program needed interns, and that outside expertise may be a benefit, she began to look for programs that might fit the need. The coordinator of the career counseling specialization was committed to the ideals of community engagement, multiculturalism, and social justice. However, given other writing projects, teaching responsibilities, current field placement relationships, and national community engagement efforts, she was not actively seeking an extensive committed partnership. Still, she was passively seeking to expand social justice internship opportunities for trainees.

It is important to understand this backdrop to contextualize the starting point of the relationship. It is on this foundation that the two entities enter the relationship and through which motivations, reactions, and later responses appear.

Initial Contact: Curiosity, Attraction, Excitement, and Admiration. After surveying local programs, the director of Seven Tepees contacted the career counseling specialization coordinator, sharing that they had received a grant and that they would be building a new program component. They were interested in discussing their plans as well as the possibility of developing internship positions. From the perspective of the career counseling coordinator, developing additional field placement sites for students was desirable, and the prospect of offering program development opportunities for students was intriguing. Yet she felt wary of the level of commitment needed. They made a plan to meet and talk further about the ideas that Seven Tepees had and the career counseling program requirements for field sites. At this stage of the process, the community agency was certain that it wanted assistance and knew the types of assistance it needed. However, the director was tentative in proposing that, indicating only the minimum desire (interns) in order to not "scare away" a potential partner. The career coordinator was cautious to not promise too much given other obligations and the enormity of the potential program development task. Her unspoken assumptions were that, beyond providing interns, any involvement should be true to the principles set forth by Goodman and her colleagues (2004)—specifically, the principles of sharing power, leaving the client with the tools, and building on strengths; as well as the aspects of social justice work presented by Toporek et al. (2006) that the pace would be slow; the need for commitment, veracity, and fidelity would need to be respected; the process may require multilevel approaches; the relationship should maintain equitable power; and the actions should primarily benefit the community, leave the partner with tools, and build on existing strengths.

At this point, each entity independently assessed the other party as well as the congruity of goals and objectives. Reflecting on assumptions and biases we might bring as well as the mutual benefits was an important yet unspoken part of this process. In uncovering common values and the promise of fulfilling social justice opportunities, we chose to pursue the next step of the relationship.

The Next Step: Testing the Waters and Building Trust. We met and further developed our understanding of each other, trying to assess the compatibility of our respective expectations, requirements, and organizational culture, and the extent to which the other party could adhere to our needs. Although some of this was made explicit, shared understanding was somewhat surface level.

In this meeting, questions of trust, safety, and viability arose. Specifically, the university's requirement of audiotaping all client sessions raised concern on the part of Seven Tepees given the vulnerability of the youth and their previous protocol. The initial excitement of the potential partnership and attraction was tempered by the perceived threat and concern. However, the agency

chose to pursue the internship and continue discussion in the hope that these concerns could be allayed. There was clearly a power differential that was insurmountable in that the taping requirement was a "nonnegotiable" issue. Yet, in an effort to try to reestablish the power balance, the coordinator wanted to communicate their relevance and the desirability of their interns as well as offer reassurance regarding the safety of taping. Another development that deepened the potential of the partnership was the addition of a graduate student who expressed an interest in working with the coordinator on a research project. Consequently, a small research and community engagement team (hereafter referred to as the Career Counseling Specialization Community Engagement Team, or CCET) was created to potentially work on the project. This created more motivation to follow through and, at the very least, try to help Seven Tepees begin developing its program.

In the next meeting between Seven Tepees and the CCET, questions about commitment, direction, and the roles and expectations continued. Although both parties engaged independently in self-reflection, these experiences were not explicitly shared. Seven Tepees had hired a coordinator of the budding program, and from their perspective, this communicated that they were serious and committed to this program. At the same time, Seven Tepees shared some ideas based on a previous university partnership. Knowing that a similar program would be logistically unlikely, CCET became concerned that they may not be able to fulfill the expectations of Seven Tepees. There was also uncertainty regarding the power dynamics at the agency, given the new hire, and where CCET might fit. CCET offered, as a start, to advocate for an internship as well as provide consultation regarding best practices in school-to-work transition and a reference list of similar programs in area schools as a means of offering some tools that Seven Tepees would be able to use, regardless of whether CCET was able to remain involved. Essentially, we both offered continued connection even in the face of uncertainty regarding the future of the relationship.

Building the Relationship: What Do They Really Want? This phase of the relationship was marked by divided attention, difficulty maintaining communication, and assumptions on both sides regarding uncertainty about the desire and commitment of the other party. With infrequent communication, lack of clarity, and uncertainty, each party worked to define its goals independently. The agency maintained its goal of developing an internship and leaving the door open for further involvement; however, there were lags in communication due to personnel issues. From the CCET's perspective, an internship was possible if the agency could adhere to the requirements and provide the necessary information. Although CCET still felt some uncertainty about whether Seven Tepees actually wanted the documents previously proposed, they continued working on them in an effort to follow through and stay connected.

Recalibration and Recommitment: Should We Stay Together? There were several pivotal events that prompted a recalibration accompanied by a deepening of commitment to the partnership. In addition to a shifting of agency personnel, an additional graduate student with expertise in school-to-work programs joined the CCET, and the best practices and survey of existing programs documents were provided to the agency. Yet the event with an unanticipated positive effect was a meeting held in the CCET office. Up to this point, the meetings had been held at the agency, in part for logistical reasons but also because the career coordinator believed that for community engagement and sharing power, it was important to meet in the community. However, the meeting at the office allowed the community member to see where the university partner "lived." The décor of the office reflected the multicultural commitment of the career program, and resources regarding social justice and advocacy were visible. In discussing some of the best practices in the career development curriculum, an incidental discussion ensued regarding the subtle discrimination behaviors faced by people of color of which the youth in the program might be peripherally aware. This prompted the CCET to share the framework of "microaggressions" and provide a relevant article by Sue, Capodilupo, and Torino (2007) that was coincidentally lying on the desk. In writing this chapter, Seven Tepees later indicated that that experience was pivotal because it signaled a genuine commitment to multiculturalism as well as an understanding of what their youth faced. A deepened understanding of shared values and philosophies was revealed as well as a commitment for

continued work together. Although this commitment was genuine, there was still ambiguity concerning the extent of the commitment and involvement each partner had to the other; however, the bond was significantly strengthened making the relationship more resilient. Following the meeting, the CCET met and discussed uncertainty about the extent to which the agency was willing to involve them with the youth and staff. Being cognizant of the different roles that counselors using a social justice framework need to assume to be effective, the career coordinator expressed that if this partnership was going to work, it was going to involve respectfully asserting and inserting themselves into the agency on a regular basis and becoming a known entity to all involved, thus highlighting the need for participatory research and advocacy.

Making a Commitment: Meeting the Family. As noted earlier, in the process of writing the chapter collaboratively, we chose to bring all of our assumptions, misunderstandings, and hopes to the surface. Consequently, we both agreed that this was a good match and that we would like to work together with the understanding that there would need to be time invested together, getting to know each other better, the CCET getting to know the youth, and the agency actively involving the CCET on a deeper and longer term basis. Although there were still uncertainties at this phase, becoming involved in each other's "lives" signaled that the relationship was worth the work and that the potential partnership was promising. The phases of development solidified mutual trust and understanding of the core values and commitment to the youth, multiculturalism, and social justice.

The Status of the Relationship

Seven Tepees and the CCET are immersed in developing a comprehensive transition program that consists of a 12-week career curriculum, a 3-year curriculum, structure for a youth portfolio, and an intern training program and manual, as well as participatory action research and program evaluation.

The transition program is grounded in Seven Tepees' experiences with their youth, the community, and the schools, as well as CCET's consultation and knowledge of relevant literature (e.g., Blustein et al., 2002; Solberg et al., 2002; Vera, Daly, Gonzales, Morgan, & Thakral, 2006) and curriculum design, counseling training, and program evaluation expertise. The program development process will also integrate involvement by school personnel, as well as youth and their parents. The curriculum focuses on teaching important "soft skills" for academic success, such as (a) personal and organizational skills needed to attend classes, focus attention, and organize projects; (b) setting of familial and social expectations for college graduation; (c) greater self-understanding, including identity and role within their community as well as the potential impact they can have on positive change; and (d) empowered responses to overt racism and micro-aggressions, including exploration of adopting a more empowered identity within the youths' own communities. The curriculum is grounded in school-to-work-to-life, career development, youth empowerment, multicultural, social justice, community development, and sociopolitical identity development literature.

Seven Tepees has successfully developed relationships with two inner-city high schools that are excited about having the program offered through their school. In the 2008–2009 academic year, two college and career counseling interns served youth in these high schools along with 2 Seven Tepees staff members, implementing the career curriculum and working individually with youth to identify and overcome blocks to achieving their career goals. An additional aspect of the program is in development within Seven Tepees' comprehensive program facilitating youths' development through the more intensive 3-year curriculum and portfolio development process. CCET is working to structure an intern training process to facilitate interns in understanding the social justice roles of counseling, advocacy, consulting, and research in this environment. The preliminary evaluation of the first year is taking place using basic data regarding numbers of students served, activities and events provided, college and financial aid applications completed, and other indicators. A more complex program evaluation component is being developed to integrate qualitative assessment and involves the students, school staff, Seven Tepees, staff, CCET, and the above consultants. Eventually, it is hoped that the program will involve parents more directly in the program and evaluation process.

The collaboration between Seven Tepees and San Francisco State University creates a training ground for developing culturally competent professionals to serve school sites under the guidance of a nonprofit, and it provides a model for ongoing evaluation, improvement, and sustainability. In addition, it provides opportunities for advocacy training and social justice as well as program development and evaluation experience. With attention to maintaining an effective collaboration, this program may serve as a model for university and nonprofits to work together to promote positive social change.

Realizations and Recommendations

A number of recommendations arose in the process of reflecting on our relationship development. First, a candid discussion of values and philosophies is useful at the outset. Yet the trust and "proof" of these values requires time and demonstration. Second, sharing material that helps the other understand "what you are about" can be useful. For example, any work that the academic has done that communicates commitment and knowledge that is relevant to the concerns at hand may be offered in partnership. It is important that this is shared in collaboration of resources as opposed to communicating superior expertise. Third, sharing resources as well as meeting spaces can help each party understand more about where the other "lives" and who their "family" is. Fourth, establishing clear expectations and roles is critical. This can be in the form of a memorandum of understanding, yet it needs to be regularly revisited and revised. This is particularly true when parties involved come from different organizational cultures, use different languages, and are expected to produce different types of outcomes. Fifth, each party should be clear about what it wants or needs to get out of the partnership. Although service to community is a worthwhile goal, there may be other benefits that would be helpful to communicate. For example, collaboration on publication, expanding students' opportunities, and other outcomes may be useful to communicate such that there is greater transparency of how this would be a "win-win" relationship. It is important that each party is clear with itself and others regarding what benefit it expects to receive in forming this relationship.

The lessons learned in developing community-university partnerships can be time intensive and require a range of skills beyond psychotherapeutic theory and approaches. The process of training counselors and psychologists to engage ethically and effectively with community entities is important to address.

IMPLICATIONS FOR SOCIAL JUSTICE COMMUNITY ENGAGEMENT TRAINING

Although the resurgence of social justice in counseling psychology is relatively new, there have been some notable works providing recommendations for training to address social justice (e.g., Ali, Liu, Mahmood, & Arguello, 2008; Goodman et al., 2004; Green, McCollum, & Hays, 2008). Still, an investigation of issues and concerns of counselor educators would be beneficial in assessing the ways in which they feel prepared and committed to integrating social justice advocacy training into counselor education. In addition, it is important to note that many practicing counselors and psychologists have not been exposed to training in social justice advocacy. There is a critical need for continuing education resources that can help to fill this gap. Moreover, there is variation in the degree of commitment and belief in the extent to which social justice and advocacy are relevant to counseling and psychology. Consequently, the field may benefit from continued discourse regarding the need and appropriateness of counselors and psychologists to be involved in addressing societal problems that influence the well-being of the families and individuals.

As illustrated by the case study, it is important for counseling trainees to have an understanding of the various roles that a counselor must employ to facilitate collaboration across organizations. The case study demonstrates that such collaborations present opportunities as well as challenges for training.

Counselor: Empowerment and the Role of the Counselor Within the Community

In the counselor role, trainees often want to make a difference in their individual clients' lives. However, when these clients face large social issues, such as community violence and poverty, the size and nature of these issues can leave trainees feeling powerless and anxious yet may also stir a new sociopolitical awareness. Training programs can help counter the feelings of helplessness by including social issues into training, encouraging trainees to take action on these issues and develop alliances within the community. Providing an understanding of the role of empowerment in counseling and the specific skills regarding individual and systemic levels of practice allows trainees to try on this role with guidance of the community leaders.

Advocate: Learning How to Promote Change Within Systems

In order to prepare trainees to be counselor advocates, there is a need to integrate advocacy theory, research, and practice into the curriculum, as well as integrate knowledge and experience from social justice work in other disciplines. A curriculum that emphasizes systems theories, community building, and multicultural and social justice competencies can help trainees to understand how systems are structured and improve their community awareness. Similarly, addressing the skills necessary to develop community partnerships in a way that honors the complexities of the community is challenging yet vitally important. Advocacy competencies (Lewis et al., 2002) provide a useful structure for considering different levels of intervention as well as skills and knowledge needed for advocacy implementation.

Similar to concerns expressed by practitioners, trainees may also question the feasibility of advocacy and outreach into the community (Helms, 2003). Establishing strong community partnerships that integrate advocacy roles into the clinical experience can help acknowledge a broader definition of direct client hours.

Consultant: Training for Community Collaboration in Program Design and Evaluation

Enhancing social justice in the community through consultation training can include examples such as incorporating community-based social justice projects into clinical experiences as well as integrating relevant systemic discussions in assessment, theory, and research courses. In this way, students have a foundation from which to draw when they begin the practical tasks of consultation in their practicum or internship. Emphasis on developing skills in public speaking, networking, and team building can establish the capability to build relationships, develop a collective movement, and inspire action while working in community-based social justice projects. Two examples of programs that have integrated these components effectively into counselor training are the Community-Based Block Counselor Education Program at San Diego State University (Butler-Byrd, Nieto, & Senour, 2006) and the Counselor Education Program at George Mason University (Talleyrand, Chung, & Bemak, 2006).

Researcher: Training Students to Investigate Community Needs and Effective Social Justice

In the role of researcher, trainees have the option to acquire investigative skills that may complement their work as consultants, change agents, and advocates for communities and organizations. Applied and collaborative research approaches such as community-based participatory action research (e.g., Fawcett et al., 1995) can be taught through community-based research projects, similar to the field experience requirement connected with the consultant role. Providing students with a framework and skills for developing effective community relationships, informed by multicultural competence, helps to build the foundation needed to engage in appropriate and meaningful social justice research.

COMMUNITY ENGAGEMENT: AN AVENUE FOR SOCIAL JUSTICE SERVICE AND TRAINING

The current emphasis on social justice recognizes the breadth of forces that impinge on the well-being of clients and their communities and the role that counselors and psychologists play in contributing to greater equity across populations. It is important that this movement is not simply academic, philosophical, or enacted from a place of cultural encapsulation. Engaging with communities and stakeholders in culturally informed ways demands greater complexity of process and provides the opportunity to build stronger and more relevant alliances. To do this effectively and ethically while

reflecting cultural competence requires conscious inclusion within training and practice. Thoughtful community engagement along with purposeful curriculum can provide students with opportunities to become counselors, advocates, researchers, and consultants and increase the likelihood that psychological interventions will reflect the realities of their clients' lives.

REFERENCES

Ali, S. R., Liu, W. M., Mahmood, A., & Arguello, J. (2008). Social justice and applied psychology: Practical ideas for training the next generation. *Journal for Social Action in Counseling and Psychology, 1*(2). Retrieved from http://www.psysr.org/jsacp/Ali-V1N2-08.pdf

American Psychological Association. (2003). Guidelines on multicultural education, training, research, practice, and organizational change for psychologists. *American Psychologist, 58,* 377–402.

Arredondo, P., Toporek, R., Brown, S., Jones, J., Locke, D., Sanchez, J., & Stadler, H. (1996). Operationalization of multicultural counseling competencies. *Journal of Multicultural Counseling and Development, 24*(1), 42–78.

Atkinson, D. R., Thompson, C. E., & Grant, S. K. (1993). A three-dimensional model for counseling racial/ethnic minorities. *Counseling Psychologist, 21*(2), 257–277.

Blustein, D. L., Chaves, A. P., Diemer, M. A., Gallagher, L. A., Marshall, K. G., Sirin, S., & Bhati, K. S. (2002). Voices of the "forgotten half": The role of social class in the school-to-work transition. *Journal of Counseling Psychology, 49,* 311–323.

Bronfenbrenner, U. (1977). Lewinian space and ecological substance. *Journal of Social Issues, 33*(4), 199–212.

Buki, L. P. (2007). Reducing health disparities: The perfect fit for counseling psychology. *Counseling Psychologist, 35*(5), 706–715.

Butler-Byrd, N., Nieto, J., & Senour, M. N. (2006). Working successfully with diverse students and communities. *Urban Education, 41*(4), 376–401.

Commission on Community-Engaged Scholarship in the Health Professions. (2007). Linking scholarship and communities: The Commission on Community-Engaged Scholarship in the Health Professions. Retrieved on November 14, 2007, from http://depts.washington.edu/ccph/pdf_files/commissionpresentation2.pdf

Fawcett, S. B., Paine-Andrews, A., Francisco, V. T., Schultz, J. A., Richter, K. P., Lewis, R. K., Williams, E. L., Harris, K. J., Berkley, J. Y., Fisher, J. L., & Lopez, C. M. (1995). Using empowerment theory in collaborative partnership for community health and development. *American Journal of Community Psychology, 23*(5), 677–697.

Fetterman, D. (2000). *Foundations of empowerment evaluation.* Thousand Oaks, CA: Sage.

Goodman, L. A., Liang, B., Helms, J. E., Latta, R. E., Sparks, E., & Weintraub, S. R. (2004). Training counseling psychologists as social justice agents: Feminist and multicultural principles in action. *Counseling Psychologist, 32*(6), 793–837.

Green, E. J., McCollum, V. C., & Hays, D. G. (2008). Teaching advocacy counseling: A social justice paradigm of awareness, knowledge, and skills. *Journal for Social Action in Counseling and Psychology, 1*(2). Retrieved from http://www.psysr.org/jsacp/Green-V1N2-08.pdf

Helms, J. E. (2003). A pragmatic view of social justice. *Counseling Psychologist, 31*(3), 305–313.

Herr, E. L. (2003). The future of career counseling as an instrument of public policy—Career counseling in the next decade. *Career Development Quarterly, 52*(1), 8–17.

Holcomb-McCoy, C., & Mitchell, N. A. (2007). Promoting ethnic/racial equality through empowerment-based counseling. In C. Lee (Ed.), *Counseling for social justice* (2nd ed., pp. 137–157). Alexandria, VA: American Counseling Association.

Kiselica, M. S., & Robinson, M. (2001). Bringing advocacy counseling to life: The history, issues, and human dramas of social justice work in counseling. *Journal of Counseling and Development, 70*, 387–397.

Lewis, J., Arnold, M. S., House, R., & Toporek, R. L. (2002). *ACA advocacy competencies.* Retrieved September 13, 2008, from http://www.counseling.org/Publications/

Lewis, J. A., Lewis, M. D., Daniels, J. A., & D'Andrea, M. J. (1998). *Community counseling: Empowerment strategies for a diverse society* (2nd ed.). Pacific Grove, CA: Brooks/Cole.

Marker, M. (2003). Indigenous voice, community, and epistemic violence: The ethnographer's "interests" and what "interests" the ethnographer. *International Journal of Qualitative Studies in Education, 16*(3), 361–375.

McWhirter, E. H. (1994). *Counseling for empowerment.* Alexandria, VA: American Counseling Association.

Morrow, S. L., Hawxhurst, D. M., Montes de Vegas, A. Y., Abousleman, T. M., & Castaneda, C. L. (2006). Toward a radical feminist multicultural therapy: Renewing a commitment to activism. In R. L. Toporek, L. H. Gerstein, N. A. Fouad, G. Roysircar, & T. Israel (Eds.), *Handbook for social justice in counseling psychology: Leadership, vision, and action* (pp. 231–247). Thousand Oaks, CA: Sage.

Morsillo, J., & Prilleltensky, I. (2007). Social action with youth: Interventions, evaluation, and psychopolitical validity. *Journal of Community Psychology, 35*(6), 725–740.

Ponterotto, J. G., Utsey, S. O., & Pedersen, P. B. (2006). *Preventing prejudice: A guide for counselors, educators and parents* (2nd ed.). Thousand Oaks: CA: Sage.

Pope-Davis, D. B., Toporek, R. L., Ligiero, D., Ortega, L., Bashshur, M. L., Brittan-Powell, C. S., Liu, W. M., Codrington, J., & Liang, C. (2002). A qualitative study of clients' perspectives of multicultural counseling competence. *Counseling Psychologist, 30*(3), 355–393.

Prilleltensky, I. (1997). Values, assumptions, and practices: Assessing the moral implications of psychological discourse and action. *American Psychologist, 52*(5), 517–535.

Reese, L. E., & Vera, E. M. (2007). Culturally relevant prevention: The scientific and practical considerations of community-based programs. *Counseling Psychologist, 35*(6), 763–778.

Solberg, V. S., Howard, K. A., & Blustein, D. L. (2002). Career development in the schools: Connecting school-to-work-to-life. *Counseling Psychologist, 30*(5), 705–725.

Sue, D. W., Arredondo, P., & McDavis, R. J. (1992). Multicultural counseling competencies and standards: A call to the profession. *Journal of Counseling & Development, 70*(4), 477–486.

Sue, D. W., Capodilupo, C. M., & Torino, G. C. (2007). Racial microaggressions in everyday life: Implications for clinical practice. *American Psychologist, 62*(4), 271–286.

Sue, D. W., Carter, R. T., Casas, J. M., Fouad, N. A., Ivey, A., Jensen, M., LaFromboise, T., Manese, J. E., Ponterotto, J. G., & Vazquez-Nutall, E. (1998). *Multicultural counseling competencies: Individual and organizational development.* Thousand Oaks, CA: Sage.

Talleyrand, R. M., Chung, R. C. Y., & Bemak, F. (2006). Incorporating social justice in counselor training programs: A case study example. In R. L. Toporek, L. H. Gerstein, N. A. Fouad, G. Roysircar, & T. Israel (Eds.), *Handbook for social justice in counseling psychology: Leadership, vision, and action* (pp. 44–54). Thousand Oaks, CA: Sage.

Taylor, R. R., Braveman, B., & Hammel, J. (2004). Developing and evaluating community-based services through participatory action research: Two case examples. *American Journal of Occupational Therapy, 58*(1), 73–82.

Toporek, R. L. (2006). An integrative approach for competencies: Career counseling, social justice advocacy and the multicultural counseling competencies. *Career Planning and Adult Development Journal, 21*(40), 34–50.

Toporek, R. L. (2009). Counseling from a cross-cultural and social justice posture. In C. M. Ellis & J. Carlson (Ed.), *Cross cultural awareness and social justice in counseling* (pp. 1–22). New York: Routledge.

Toporek, R. L., Gerstein, L. H., Fouad, N. A., Roysircar, G., & Israel, T. (Eds.). (2006). *Handbook for social justice in counseling psychology: Leadership, vision, and action.* Thousand Oaks, CA: Sage.

Toporek, R. L., Lewis, J. & Crethar, H. C. (2009). Promoting systemic change through the Advocacy Competencies. Special Section on ACA Advocacy Competencies. *Journal of Counseling and Development, 87,* 260–268.

Toporek, R. L., & Liu, W. M. (2001). Advocacy in counseling psychology: Critical issues of race, class, and gender. In D. B. Pope-Davis & H. L. K. Coleman (Eds.), *The intersection of race, class and gender in counseling psychology* (pp. 385–413). Thousand Oaks, CA: Sage.

Toporek, R. L., & Pope-Davis, D. B. (2005). Exploring the relationships between multicultural training, racial attitudes, and attributions of poverty among graduate counseling trainees. *Cultural Diversity and Ethnic Minority Psychology, 11*(3), 259–271.

Toporek, R. L., & Reza, J. V. (2001). Context as a critical dimension of multicultural counseling: Articulating personal, professional, and institutional competence. *Journal of Multicultural Counseling and Development, 29*(1), 13–30.

Vera, E. M., Daly, B., Gonzales, R., Morgan, M., & Thakral, C. (2006). Prevention, advocacy, outreach: Social justice work with Latino youth. In R. L. Toporek, L. H. Gerstein, N. A. Fouad, G. Roysircar, & T. Israel (Eds.), *Handbook for social justice in counseling psychology: Leadership, vision, and action* (pp. 86–99). Thousand Oaks, CA: Sage.

Vera, E. M., & Speight, S. L. (2003). Multicultural competence, social justice and counseling psychology: Expanding our roles. *Counseling Psychologist, 31,* 253–272.

PART X

Advances in Multicultural Assessment and Counseling

Part X of this *Handbook* consists of five developmentally sequenced chapters addressing the latest development in multicultural counseling and assessment for children, adolescents, adults, later-life adults, and families. The section opens with Chapter 48, co-authored by Jennie Park-Taylor, Allison B. Ventura, and Vicky Ng, and focuses on multicultural assessment with children. This team of authors covers important intake, diagnostic, and psychological assessment issues when working with culturally diverse youth. They review procedures for culturally centered counseling and therapy with racial and ethnic minority youth, with a special focus on immigrant children. The authors highlight the value of cuento therapy in working with minority youth, and they introduce the Children's Acculturation Story Pictogram (CASP) as an acculturation assessment tool for immigrant children.

Chapter 49 focuses on advances in multicultural assessment and counseling with adolescents, and is prepared by Christine J. Yeh and Kwong-Liem Karl Kwan. These authors anchor their practical suggestions in an ecological and social justice model, and they convincingly highlight the centrality of social relationships and connectedness when working with culturally diverse adolescents. Thus, the authors advocate counselors working from more systemic and relational models rather than the traditional individually based counseling models. In working from an ecological model, counselors must

consider and work within the context of peer relationships, family environment, school and academic situation, and the community and cultural influences. The authors nicely bring their thorough discussion together with a vivid and in-depth case study of a second-generation Chinese American adolescent female.

Co-authors Alex L. Pieterse and Matthew J. Miller move to a focus on adult multicultural assessment in Chapter 50. These authors provide a state-of-the-art review of major advances in multicultural assessment occurring during the past decade. The chapter opens with realistic scenarios highlighting the challenges of assessment across cultures. The authors then summarize recent models, frameworks, and tools for multicultural assessment. Included in the chapter are reviews of assessments for acculturation, racial-cultural stressors, and the multicultural personality. The chapter closes with concise and helpful discussion of the clinical interview, clinician bias, and the relevance of a social justice perspective to multicultural assessment. Included in the chapter is a very helpful clinician checklist that can guide counselors in their multicultural assessment work.

Chapter 51, written by Luis A. Vázquez, Merranda Marín, and Enedina García-Vázquez, focuses on an often neglected group: culturally diverse, later-life adults. The chapter opens with a poignant and riveting real-life case study involving the mother of the chapter's senior author. The chapter provides an up-to-date

demographic profile of the growing population of culturally diverse, later-life individuals. Culturally competent assessment of culturally diverse later-life adults is
covered in depth, and a number of invaluable resources
for counselors are noted throughout the chapter. This
chapter serves as a foundational resource for counselors working with culturally diverse, later-life adults
and their extended families.

George V. Gushue, Daniel T. Sciarra, and Brenda X.
Mejía close out Part X with Chapter 52, focusing on multicultural family assessment and counseling. The authors
anchor their discussion in postmodern approaches to
treatment and review collaborative language systems
therapy, solution-focused therapy, and narrative therapy.
The authors highlight both between-group and within-
group perspectives (e.g., differences due to acculturation
or cultural identity) that should be considered in understanding culturally diverse families. Major issues discussed in the chapter are integrated into two rich and
vivid case studies that highlight the complexity and layers
of family counseling within cultural contexts, and also
offer the clinician specific models for intervention.

48

Multicultural Counseling and Assessment With Children

JENNIE PARK-TAYLOR, ALLISON B. VENTURA, AND VICKY NG

Major demographic shifts in the U.S. youth population have been associated with changes in the way in which pediatric-focused health and mental health professionals have approached their work with their patients/clients. Professional changes in practice are particularly visible in the implementation of multicultural standards and guidelines. For instance, the recent publications of the Declaration of Professional Responsibility: Medicine's Social Contract With Humanity (American Medical Association [AMA], 2002); the National Association of Social Workers (NASW) Standards for Cultural Competence in Social Work Practice (NASW, 2001); the Guidelines on Multicultural Education, Training, Research, Practice and Organizational Change for Psychologists (American Psychological Association [APA], 2003); and the American School Counselor Association's position statement (ASCA, 2004) are some examples of professional-wide changes that demonstrate a professional movement toward cultural competence in child-focused clinical practice.

Taking race, ethnicity, and culture into consideration when working with youth is also a clear priority of governmental bodies that are focused on health. For example, in 1999, the Surgeon General's office published its first report specifically on mental health with a supplement that focused on culture, race, and ethnicity. The office also conducted a conference on children's mental health in an effort to work collectively to eliminate cultural and socioeconomic disparities in children's mental health (U.S. Public Health Service, 2000). The conference report pointed to concerns for ethnic and racial minority youth, two of which included the increasing incidences of mental health misdiagnosis among minority youth and the disproportionate use of government systems such as welfare or juvenile justice rather than schools or other proactive settings for mental health treatment (U.S. Public Health Service, 2000).

In the present chapter, we first discuss intake, diagnostic, and psychological assessment considerations when working with ethnic/racial minority children. We then discuss multicultural counseling and culture-centered therapy with ethnic/racial minority youth. Although our chapter highlights practical considerations when working with all ethnic/racial minority children, given contemporary immigration rates (Portes & Rumbaut, 2001), there is a focus on clinical work with immigrant youth. Finally, we end the chapter highlighting an innovative, culture-centered form of therapy called cuento therapy and a qualitative acculturation tool designed specifically for young immigrant children called the Children's Acculturation Story Pictogram (CASP).

INTAKE AND DIAGNOSIS WITH ETHNIC/RACIAL MINORITY CHILDREN

There are a number of barriers to providing culturally competent care, but perhaps one of the greatest hurdles during the initial intake assessment is the lack of diagnostic tools that are sensitive and comprehensive enough to capture cultural variability in the symptomatic expression and experience of and coping with psychological disorders. Although the *Diagnostic and Statistical Manual of Mental Disorders, Fourth Edition, Text Revision (DSM–IV–TR)* (APA, 2000) includes a culture-specific section in the text, an appendix of culture-bound syndromes, and an outline for cultural formulation to enhance the cross-cultural applicability of the manual, scholars argue that it continues to be insufficient in addressing cultural variability (Roysircar, 2005).

Beyond the lack of culturally sensitive diagnostic instruments, another major barrier to culturally competent care in intake assessment is related to variations in levels of cultural competence among clinicians (Acevedo-Polakovich et al., 2007; Ecklund & Johnson, 2007). The significance of this barrier cannot be overstated, because although culturally sensitive psychological tools and instruments are clearly essential, if a clinician lacks cultural competence, the presence or absence of culturally sensitive psychological tools almost becomes irrelevant. The lack of culturally sensitive diagnostic tools, limitations in cultural competence among clinicians and other barriers (e.g., institutional and systemic barriers) may contribute to clinicians making type I (overpathologizing) and type II (underdiagnosing) errors with ethnically/racially diverse clients (Roysircar, 2005). Although clinicians make both types of errors, evidence suggests that

they are more likely to overpathologize versus underdiagnose their ethnic/racial minority clients (Roysircar, 2005; U.S. Department of Health and Human Services, 2001; Whaley, 1997).

Although clinicians are responsible for continuously developing their cultural competence (APA, 2003), recently published guidelines may help increase the cultural sensitivity of intake procedures (e.g., Aklin & Turner, 2006; Ecklund & Johnson, 2007; Hays, 1996). In considering a client's identity, Hays's (1996) development of the A-D-D-R-E-S-S-I-N-G strategy reminds clinicians to examine multiple areas of influence (age, developmental issues, disabilities, religion/spirituality, ethnicity, socioeconomic status, sexual orientation, indigenous origins, national origins, and gender). Similarly, going beyond individual factors and examining the significance of an individual's sociocultural context, Natasi and associates (2004) have developed a participatory culture-specific model for school psychology practice that integrates ecological-developmental theory, ethnographic and participatory action research, and participatory consultation.

Culture in Intake

Beyond the exploration and assessment of an individual client's reference groups that Hays (1996) suggests, culturally competent clinicians also respect and understand the role of culture as one that is significant pre-, during, and post-treatment. Culture affects whether or not ethnic/racial minority individuals will seek treatment and how they might respond to outreach. Ethnic/racial minority children and their families may perceive a mental health facility as foreign and even hostile or frightening, and such perceptions can affect the way a child or parent responds to the mental health diagnostic examination (Gibbs & Huang, 2003). Thus, at first contact, clinicians should explain the process and work from a psychoeducational framework that integrates cultural factors and communicates an affirmation of culture (Ecklund & Johnson, 2007).

Culture must be taken into account if accurate diagnosis and effective treatment plans are to be made for ethnic/racial minority child clients, because culture not only affects normative behaviors, it also influences the ways individuals express psychiatric symptoms (Canino

& Spurlock, 2000). For instance, in some cultures, it is not unusual to view a child's disturbed behavior as related to a physical or spiritual disorder, and consequently, talking about the behavior is not expected to cure it. Furthermore, cultural expectations of child development and behavior vary across cultures in such a way that crucial traits such as cooperativeness and dependence, and the acquisition of language and motor skills, acquire different meanings in different cultures (Canino & Spurlock, 2000). Although clinicians clearly should have a foundation in human development—as this literature provides a guide for the expected milestones and associated behaviors during childhood—caution should be used as these behaviors conform to Western nosological considerations and may not apply to less acculturated children (Johnson-Powell, 1997).

Collecting Comprehensive Information

The major goal of intake is to collect as much data as is necessary to make an accurate diagnosis or recommendation. However, given the potential salience of cultural variables for ethnic/racial minority clients, when conducting intake assessments with these individuals, clinicians are faced with the additional task of collecting comprehensive culture-specific data. For example, Pynoos and associates (2001) recommended that the following areas are necessary in a comprehensive assessment of an immigrant/refugee child client: frequency and nature of traumatic reminders; level of physiological and psychological reactivity; other traumas and losses; medical conditions and treatment; secondary adversities and stressors; and any developmental consequences, including those that affect peer, academic, and family functioning. In order to collect all of the information that these authors recommend, a clinician would need to collect information from a variety of sources.

When assessing ethnic/racial minority child clients, it is important to collect collateral information from other sources, such as parents, additional caretakers, and teachers (Berthold, 2007). Starting with a comprehensive family history that includes data from multiple sources provides a contextual basis pertinent to the diagnostic process. Family data are particularly important because families transmit cultural values and beliefs, spirituality, assignment of roles, problem-solving

strategies, communication patterns, and biases to their children. Given the significance of this information, clinicians perform better when they assume a learning position and acknowledge their need to know more about the family's history and culture (Canino & Spurlock, 2000).

A complete school history of the child should also be gathered before a diagnosis is determined. This is particularly important for new immigrant youth because schools often represent the gateway for learning the norms of the new culture. Permission to talk to teachers and school counselors should be obtained to address academic performance, cognitive skills, language development, social behaviors and interactions, and temperament.

Once intake assessments are completed, recommendations for treatment and/or further testing are usually provided to parents/caretakers and sometimes to education and mental health professionals. In the following section, we first outline some considerations when conducting psychological tests with ethnic/racial/linguistic minority youth, and then we discuss multicultural counseling with ethnic/racial minority youth.

PSYCHOLOGICAL TESTS WITH ETHNIC/RACIAL/LINGUISTIC MINORITY YOUTH

Standardized psychological instruments (e.g., cognitive, behavioral, personality) are used for a variety of purposes. For instance, psychological assessments are used to facilitate intake and determine appropriate treatment modality, determine accurate diagnosis, and/or address specific concerns (e.g., questions about learning disabilities). Although the use of psychological tests with youth has a long history, the growing diversity among the nation's population has spurred an increased interest in considering the ways in which these tests are used with, and the implications of, tests for ethnic/racial/linguistic minority youth (Rhodes, Ochoa, & Ortiz, 2005). The next section provides some preassessment, assessment, and postassessment considerations in testing with ethnic/racial minority children.

Preassessment and Assessment Considerations

Once a referral is made for psychological testing with an ethnic/racial/linguistic minority child, one of the first steps a clinician needs to take is to determine the appropriate tests to be included in the assessment battery. Conducting psychological assessments with ethnic/racial/linguistic minority youth is challenging and complex in large part because standardized psychological instruments are conceived and developed from a particular culture and language, and thus are fundamentally culturally bound and driven (Vazquez-Nuttall et al., 2007). For instance, DiCerbo and Barona's (2000) review of the literature suggests that controversy continues regarding the adequacy of current IQ tests to measure the cognitive ability level of ethnic/racial/linguistic minority youth. Because the culture of many ethnic/racial minority youth may be very different from the cultural foundation of psychological instruments, there may be a need to use varied assessment methods such as qualitative and dynamic testing in order to accurately assess the minority child (Vazquez-Nuttall et al., 2007).

Questions about the validity of standardized tests come to the forefront when one is considering using tests that were originally developed and standardized for one group (e.g., U.S.-born, monolingual, English-speaking, European American youth) with ethnic/racial/linguistic minority youth (Vazquez-Nuttall et al., 2007). For instance, the two specific facets of diversity that Vazquez-Nuttall and associates posit strongly affect the evaluation process are English-language ability and acculturation. Although different types of validity (e.g., construct, content, predictive) need to be examined in determining whether or not a standardized test is appropriate to use with a specific target population, validity is generally understood as the extent to which theory and evidence support interpretations of test scores garnered by proposed uses of a particular test (AERA, APA, & NCME, 1999).

When there are questions regarding the construct and predictive validity of test scores based on group membership, issues of test bias emerge (Helms, 2006). Although an examination of the validity, reliability, and cultural bias of standardized instruments is certainly essential, Helms (2006) argues that an investigation of test fairness also needs to be addressed. Test fairness is differentiated from test validity in that the former is related to individual attributes (e.g., meaning of racial group membership to individuals) that may result in systematic mean group differences, and the latter is related to whether test scores are related to the

criteria similarly across groups (Helms, 2006). The scope of this chapter does not allow for a more in-depth discussion of test validity, reliability, bias, and fairness, but the reader may go to the following sources for further information: Aiken & Yen (2003), AERA et al. (1999), Helms (2006), and Wall and Walz (2004).

In deliberating which standardized instruments should be included in an assessment battery for an ethnic/racial/linguistic minority child, Dana (2000) suggests that the clinician examine the extent of cultural/linguistic differences between the child and the dominant culture to determine whether the instruments can be used as they are or whether modifications of available measures and/or culture-/language-specific instruments need to be integrated. Although there are a variety of possible accommodations to standardized tests and testing conditions, they are all accompanied by their own challenges. For instance, because literal translations of tests can be detrimental to the assessment's validity (Greenfield, 1997), translated instruments need to be tested for reliability and validity within the targeted cultural group (Dimmit, 1995) before they are used. The use of interpreters is also problematic because of the lack of training and expertise of many interpreters, the absence of standards for the use of interpreters in testing, and the diversity in dialects and accents within any given language (Vazquez-Nuttall et al., 2007).

Despite challenges in developing new and adapted tests for specific minority groups, some authors have assumed the challenges. For instance, acculturation instruments are currently available for various racial and ethnic groups. Readers are referred to the following measures: Acculturation Rating Scale for Mexican Americans-II (Cuéllar, Arnold, & Maldonado, 1995), Acculturation Scale for Southeast Asians (Anderson et al., 1993), Latino/Latina Adolescent Acculturation Scale (Felíx-Ortiz, Newcomb, & Myers, 1994), and the African American Acculturation Scale (Landrine & Klonoff, 1994). It should be noted that most acculturation assessments, including the ones listed above, were developed and normed for either adolescent or adult populations and may be neither applicable to nor appropriate for children.

In the area of projective personality assessment, Tell Me a Story (TEMAS) (Constantino, Malgady, & Rogler, 1988) was created as a culturally sensitive revision of the Thematic Apperception Test. The 23 TEMAS stimulus cards are designed to be culturally relevant and gender sensitive. The minority cards show predominantly Hispanic and Black individuals, whereas the nonminority cards depict mostly nonminority characters. TEMAS has promising construct-related validity, but has yet to establish criterion-related validity and to demonstrate that it is better than the TAT in assessing the personality characteristics of minority children (Center for Psychological Studies, 2008).

In the area of cognitive assessment, the WISC-III Spanish and the WISC-IV Spanish (Wechsler, 2005) have been developed for youth (ages 6 to 16 years) who are English-language learners and relatively new to American culture. Norms for the WISC-IV Spanish were carefully calibrated to the WISC-IV English (Wechsler, 2003) with a sample of children whose parents originated from several countries of origin—Mexico, Cuba, Dominican Republic, Puerto Rico, and Central and South America— with test items modified to minimize cultural bias across multiple regions of origin. However, the vast majority of actual items on the WISC-IV Spanish are direct translations of those included on its English counterpart, with a few replacements and adjustments broadly defined as "adaptations" by test developers (Clinton, 2007, p. 8). Because of the abundance of direct translations and limited adaptations to culturally specific aspects of testing, learning, and problem solving, the ability to measure the same constructs and processes in the WISC-IV Spanish compared with the WISC-IV remains uncertain (Clinton, 2007). Despite these limitations, the WISC-IV Spanish provides a generally reliable and valid measure of overall intelligence and more specific cognitive processes for children who report greater linguistic proficiency in Spanish than English and are relatively new to the United States. For a unique cross-cultural perspective of the WISC-III, the reader is referred to *Culture and Children's Intelligence: Cross-Cultural Analysis of the WISC-III* (Georgas, Weiss, van de Vijver, & Saklofske, 2003), which provides an overview of the WISC-III construction, translation, and adaptation in 16 different cultures, as well as its clinical use with different ethnic groups.

Finally, after research, supervision, and deliberation regarding which tests would be valid, culturally appropriate, and necessary to answer the referral question(s), the clinician also needs to be mindful of the client's level of comfort with the assessment procedure (Brems,

1998). Test-taking behavior and comfort level with the testing environment may vary across cultures and need to be considered when determining whether a particular type of assessment is appropriate for a particular client (Cofresí & Gorman, 2004).

Postassessment Considerations

Culturally competent assessment does not end once the battery of standardized tests has been administered. In addition to test administration, there are two major components of the culturally competent assessment: culturally competent report writing and feedback procedures (Allen, 2007; Dana, 2005). Conducting psychological assessments with ethnic/racial/linguistic minority youth is clearly a complex endeavor in that all of the components of the assessment procedure require an integration of cultural factors, and in the final stage of assessment, an accurate reporting of these steps along with an integration of cultural information collected during earlier stages must be included (Allen, 2007).

According to Dana (2005), all multicultural assessment reports should include the following elements: (a) a description of the quality of the relationship between the client and clinician; (b) a description of cultural information and its use in interpretations; (c) any potential confounds that may contribute to bias; and (d) summarization of findings, recommendations, and limitations. In the written communication of assessment results, the language should be clear and, as much as possible, jargon free. This is not only beneficial to the child client's families, but also important for third parties, who often request the testing but are not psychologists. If possible, it may also be important to write a brief summary of the report in the primary language of the client's parent.

The face-to-face feedback session is a critical component of multicultural assessment because it represents another important opportunity for a collaboration to take place between the client/client's family and the clinician. For instance, the client/client's family's interpretation and reflections of the results may lead to further elaboration and the emergence of important cultural data that would ultimately strengthen the validity of the test (Dana, 2005). Many times, the assessment report includes a recommendation for counseling, in which case the clinician may want to research mental health facilities that offer culturally competent care. In the following section, we discuss multicultural counseling.

Multicultural Counseling With Ethnic/Racial Minority Youth

Clinicians who provide counseling for children from racially, ethnically, and culturally diverse backgrounds must provide comprehensive and culturally sensitive care (Canino & Spurlock, 2000). But how does a clinician know if he or she is culturally sensitive and competent enough to treat an ethnic/racial minority child? Several key documents, such as the multicultural competencies by Sue, Arredondo, and McDavis (1992) and the Guidelines on Multicultural Education, Training, Research, Practice, and Organizational Changes for Psychologists (APA, 2003), can aid mental health providers in understanding themselves as racial or cultural beings in clinical settings (Constantine & Sue, 2005).

Beyond professional guidelines, scholar-practitioners have developed models of multicultural counseling. For instance, Liu and Clay (2002) proposed a five-step model to inform case conceptualization and treatment planning with racially/ethnically diverse child clients, as follows: (a) evaluating which cultural aspects are relevant; (b) determining the level of skills and information necessary for competent treatment and possible referral; (c) determining how much, when, and how to incorporate cultural issues; (d) examining the potential list of treatments and understanding the cultural assumptions of each; and (e) implementing the treatment using the cultural strengths. Liu and Clay's model is general and can be applied when working from a variety of modalities (e.g., individual or group). Although decisions related to treatment modality are often determined by intake clinicians or intake teams, there may be some benefits associated with modalities other than traditional individual psychotherapy.

La Familia y el Grupo: Going Beyond Individual Counseling

Treatment of ethnic/racial minority youth may be most effective when it is not solely focused on individual therapy, but expanded to include family, group, and community approaches, and school involvement.

Treatment that involves family and kinship networks is culturally appropriate given the connectedness among children and their families and the respect for the hierarchical structure and roles of the family members that family-integrated treatment demonstrates (Canino & Spurlock, 2000). Many minority families believe the behavior of one member is a reflection of the whole family unit and may often feel shame and guilt, which may lead to resistance to seeking outside help. In such cases, it is important to provide the family with psychoeducation about the process of therapy, the child's diagnosis, and specific ways that therapy can help the child.

Just as children benefit from the support of their families, they also can benefit from peer support and therapeutic community involvement. Group approaches are especially successful with children from cultures that value cooperation and the group above the individual. More specifically, conducting group counseling sessions with a social skills and discussion component can respond to the myriad of feelings that children experience (Thomas, Solorzano, & Cobb, 2007). Beyond family and peer involvement, engaging the school and the community in interventions with ethnic/racial minority youth is also recommended (Thomas et al., 2007).

La Escuela y La Communidad: Going Beyond Outreach

Given that children spend the majority of their time in schools, mental health providers have a clear role in consulting with schools when issues arise (Thomas et al., 2007). School consultation is a way of providing indirect services to the minority child by problem solving with important individuals who have a stake in the child's education. Clinicians can enhance the school's cultural sensitivity by (a) increasing the awareness of minority identity development and its effects on interpersonal behavior and achievement, (b) increasing the awareness of sociocultural differences in learning styles and behavior, (c) increasing the awareness of systemic factors that impede progress for minority students, and (d) facilitating professional development in the area of multicultural education and curriculum (Duncan, 1994). By acting as a liaison, clinicians can also help coordinate services/resources in the school and the community to maximize child development.

The culturally responsive clinician must also be "willing to engage in outreach and facilitate the mobilization of other resources for any positive, meaningful change to occur in the child's life" (Thomas et al., 2007, p. 73). Accordingly, the clinician may need to seek support from indigenous support systems in the community (e.g., the church, indigenous healers, and respected community leaders) to aid the comprehensive approach to treatment.

General guidelines and recommendations are certainly helpful in providing a framework for clinicians, but specific treatment approaches provide insight into the practical applications of these recommendations. The following sections provide an overview of a specific culture-centered form of therapy called cuento therapy and an introduction to an acculturation instrument for immigrant youth called the Children's Acculturation Story Pictogram (CASP).

Los Cuentos: A Culture-Centered Model of Multicultural Counseling

Folktale or cuento therapy (Constantino, Malgady, & Rogler, 1986), which was developed for Puerto Rican children, represents an innovative and effective approach to multicultural counseling with Hispanic youth (Altarriba & Santiago-Rivera, 1994; Tharp, 1991). Cuentos, or folktales, involve characters that portray beliefs, customs, and values of the Puerto Rican culture. In developing cuento therapy, Constantino and associates conducted a study to examine the effectiveness of their intervention. In their study, a series of cuentos were read to 210 high-risk kindergarten through third-grade children by their bilingual/bicultural therapists and their mothers, with a follow-up discussion fostering the exploration of the meaning of the tales. The folktales were either traditional in nature or adapted to incorporate issues related to the process of acculturation and life in the United States. Results indicated that cuento therapy significantly reduced trait anxiety over a 1-year period in comparison with control groups, who received traditional therapy or no intervention at all. Cuento therapy also resulted in higher Wechsler Intelligence Tests for Children-Revised (WISC-R) Comprehension subtest scores, and lowered levels of observed aggression.

Although cuento therapy may represent an innovative, culturally relevant form of psychological treatment for a specific population, results from efficacy studies that use standardized cognitive ability tests (CATs) (e.g., WISC-R) should be interpreted with caution given some of the limitations of CATs with minority individuals. Furthermore, although best practice in clinical work demands that clinicians use interventions that are efficacious with the population with which they are working, nontraditional forms of treatment, such as cuento therapy, may have benefits that are difficult to measure with traditional assessment tools. Thus, the recent recommendation that future studies on ethnic and racial identity incorporate constructivist qualitative research (Ponterotto & Park-Taylor, 2007) can also be applied to further investigations of the effectiveness of culture-centered interventions like cuento therapy. Next, we describe a qualitative acculturation instrument that attempts to gather important cultural adjustment information from immigrant youth.

The Children's Acculturation Story Pictogram

The CASP is a projective drawing and story-telling instrument that aims to gather information from immigrant children about their subjective acculturation experiences. The CASP includes a drawing exercise followed by a narrative interview, which is individually administered by the researcher. The CASP drawing exercise is composed of a 6-page paper booklet, which appears physically similar to a blank children's storybook (please see Appendix A). The participant is asked to complete the instrument by drawing as many pictures as necessary to depict what he or she went through to become adjusted to living in the United States. Once the participant completes the drawing task to his or her satisfaction, he or she is asked to share the story of the drawings with the researcher orally. By allowing the child an opportunity to explain his or her drawings in his or her own words, the instrument allows for further clarification of possibly unclear elements of the drawings and a richer explanation of the acculturation process from the participant's perspective. The interview is audiotaped and transcribed for coding and analysis purposes. The total time for administration of the drawing exercise and the interview is approximately 30 minutes.

Although many, if not most, acculturation instruments make use of paper and pencil or verbal data, these may be neither the only nor the most effective ways to collect information from immigrant and first-generation youth about their acculturation. If one considers developmental and linguistic factors specific to immigrant youth, collecting nontraditional forms of data (i.e., drawings and stories) may indeed represent a more effective way to collect information about their experiences. Considering developmental stage, school-age youth may be less comfortable answering interview questions about their experience and more comfortable talking about their experiences indirectly (i.e., pictorially or through stories).

The development of the CASP represents the second iteration of a previously developed qualitative instrument (Children's Acculturation Report-Drawings, or CAR-D) that focused on immigrant children's pictograms of the process an immigrant might go through to become American (Park-Taylor, 2004). As part of a larger previous study, 199 immigrant and nonimmigrant elementary students completed the CAR-D. The principal investigator coded and analyzed the content of the entire set of participants' pictograms. Based on an initial review of the drawings from both immigrant and nonimmigrant participants, there were a number of emergent acculturation themes: (a) English-language acquisition; (b) becoming accepted or rejected by others; (c) completing the requirements for citizenship; (d) becoming successful in school and in life; (e) adjusting to a new culture, which included adopting various American customs and coping with unmet expectations; and (f) a multidimensional understanding of cultural adjustment that incorporated more than one of the above themes (Park-Taylor, 2004).

The CAR-D instrument provided rich pictorial data regarding children's perceptions of "what an immigrant might go through to become American," but coding and analysis of drawings were challenging and limited because of ambiguity in interpreting the drawings in isolation (please see Appendix B). Given the significance of triangulation (Patton, 2002) in qualitative research, the CASP was developed so that both pictorial and narrative data could be retrieved from one instrument.

The CASP was administered to nine immigrant children living in the metropolitan Northeast. Participants' ages ranged from 9 to 14 (mean = 10.6), and the majority immigrated to the United States before the age of 6. Participants identified various countries of origin, and most identified that English was not their first language. The consensual qualitative research (CQR) approach developed by Hill, Thompson, and Williams (1997), and a coding system specifically designed to analyze drawings, which was developed by Haney, Russell, and Bebell (2004), were used for data-coding/analysis purposes. Results revealed the following domains: migration experiences, school experiences, family experiences, language, and contrast between country of origin and the United States (please see Appendix C for results table) (Park-Taylor, Ventura, Ng, Budianto, & Sinha, 2008).

In the future, the CASP should be administered to a larger sample. The CASP is intended to have multiple functions. First, it may be useful in clinical and educational interventions with immigrant youth. For example, school counselors may use the CASP either as a means for collecting information about their students' cultural adjustment concerns or as a way to connect with immigrant youth and promote a healthy integrative style of adjustment. The CASP can also be used in educational and psychological research with immigrant youth either in conjunction with traditional self-report instruments as part of a mixed method study design or on its own for qualitative explorations. Although the CASP was developed for immigrant youth, for nonimmigrant ethnic and racial minority youth, future iterations of the CASP may use different prompts that would elicit distinct cultural adjustment data. For instance, an African American child who is new to a predominantly Caucasian American school might be asked, "Think back from the time you first came to this school until now. Please draw pictures that tell the story of your experience as a new student."

CONCLUSION

As our nation becomes increasingly diverse, multicultural counseling and assessment with ethnic/racial minority youth are areas within applied psychology that clearly warrant further attention. Previous multicultural scholars and practitioners have laid a substantial foundation through the development of multicultural guidelines, competencies, and models, and the creation and examination of various standardized and culture-specific psychological instruments, but current and future psychologists will need to extend and expand upon this healthy platform. The multicultural counseling and assessment literature suggests that future work should focus on developing and enhancing the multicultural competence of clinicians as well as the cultural appropriateness/validity of both treatment approaches and assessment instruments. Furthermore, as is highlighted by cuento therapy and the CASP instrument, future practice and assessment may benefit from nontraditional approaches to reaching out to, communicating with, and gathering data from ethnic/racial minority youth. Finally, although culturally competent clinicians and culture-centered and valid assessment instruments are clearly necessary components of multicultural counseling and assessment with ethnic/racial minority youth, psychologists are also well positioned to and responsible for making changes at institutional and policy levels that may positively affect the health and well-being of ethnic/racial minority child clients (APA, 2003).

REFERENCES

Acevedo-Polakovich, I. D., Reynaga-Abiko, G., Garriott, P. O., Derefinko, K. J., Wimsatt, M. K., Gudonis, L. C., & Brown, T. L. (2007). Beyond instrument selection: Cultural considerations in the psychological assessment of U.S. Latinas/os. *Professional Psychology: Research and Practice, 38,* 375–384.

Aiken, M., & Yen, W. M. (2003). *Psychological testing and assessment* (11th ed.). Boston: Allyn & Bacon.

Aklin, W. M., & Turner, S. M. (2006). Toward understanding ethnic and cultural factors in the interviewing process. *Psychotherapy: Theory, Research, Practice, Training, 43,* 50–64.

Allen, J. (2007). A multicultural assessment supervision model to guide research and practice. *Professional Psychology: Research and Practice, 38,* 248–258.

Altarriba, J., & Santiago-Rivera, A. L. (1994). Current perspectives on using linguistic and cultural factors in counseling the Hispanic client. *Professional Psychology: Research and Practice, 25,* 388–397.

American Educational Research Association, American Psychological Association, & National Council on Measurement in Education. (1999). *Standards for educational and psychological testing.* Washington, DC: American Educational Research Association.

American Medical Association. (2002). *Declaration of professional responsibility: Medicine's social contract with humanity.* Available: http://www.ama-assn.org/ama/upload/mm/369/decofprofessional.pdf

American Psychiatric Association. (2000). *Diagnostic and statistical manual of mental disorders* (4th ed., text rev.). Washington, DC: Author.

American Psychological Association. (2003). Guidelines on multicultural education, training, research, practice, and organizational changes for psychologists. *American Psychologist, 58,* 377–402.

American School Counselor Association. (2004). Ethical standards for school counselors. Retrieved from http://www.schoolcounselor.org/content.asp?contentid=173

Anderson, J., Moeschberger, M., Chen, M. S., Jr., Kunn, P., Wewers, M. E., & Guthrie, R. (1993). An acculturation scale for Southeast Asians. *Social Psychiatry and Psychiatric Epidemiology, 28,* 134–141.

Berthold, S. M. (2007). Transcultural approaches in working with traumatized refugee and asylum-seeking children, youth, and their families. In N. E. Cohen, T. V. Tran, & S. Y. Rhee (Eds.), *Multicultural approaches in caring for children, youth, and their families* (pp. 269–311). Boston: Pearson.

Brems, C. (1998). Cultural issues in psychological assessment: Problems and possible solutions. *Journal of Psychological Practice, 4,* 88–117.

Canino, I. A., & Spurlock, J. (2000). *Culturally diverse children and adolescents: Assessment, diagnosis, and treatment* (2nd ed.). New York: Guilford.

Center for Psychological Studies. (2008). *Nova Southeastern University: Tell Me a Story.* Retrieved May 11, 2008, from http://www.cps.nova.edu/~cpphelp/TEMAS.html

Clinton, A. (2007). Test review: Wechsler, D. (2005). Wechsler Intelligence Scale for Children Fourth Edition Spanish. San Antonio, TX: Psychological Corporation. *Journal of Psychoeducational Assessment, 25,* 285–314.

Cofresí, N. I., & Gorman, A. A. (2004). Testing and assessment issues with Spanish-English bilingual Latinos. *Journal of Counseling & Development, 82,* 99–106.

Constantine, M. G., & Sue, D. W. (2005). The American Psychological Association's guidelines on multicultural education, training, research, practice, and organizational psychology: Initial development and summary. In M. G. Constantine & D. W. Sue (Eds.), *Strategies for building multicultural competence in mental health and educational settings* (pp. 3–15). Hoboken, NJ: Wiley.

Constantino, G., Malgady, R. G., & Rogler, L. H. (1986). Cuento therapy: A culturally sensitive modality for

Puerto Rican children. *Journal of Consulting and Clinical Psychology, 54*, 639–645.

Constantino, G., Malgady, R., & Rogler, L. (1988). *TEMAS (Tell-Me-A-Story) manual*. Los Angeles: Western Psychological Services.

Cuéllar, I., Arnold, B., & Maldonado, R. (1995). Acculturation Rating Scale for Mexican Americans-II: A revision of the original ARSMA scale. *Hispanic Journal of Behavioral Sciences, 17*, 275–304.

Dana, R. H. (2000). An assessment-intervention model for research and practice with multicultural populations. In R. H. Dana (Ed.), *Handbook of cross-cultural and multicultural personality assessment* (pp. 5–16). Mahwah, NJ: Lawrence Erlbaum.

Dana, R. H. (2005). *Multicultural assessment: Principles, applications, and examples*. Mahwah, NJ: Lawrence Erlbaum.

DiCerbo, K. E., & Barona, A. (2000). A convergent validity study of the differential ability scales and the Weschler Intelligence Scale for Children-Third Edition with Hispanic children. *Journal of Psychoeducational Assessment, 18*, 344–352.

Dimmit, J. (1995). Adult Self-Perception Profile (ASPP) Spanish translation and reassessment for a rural, minority population. *Western Journal of Nursing Research, 17*, 203–217.

Duncan, C. F. (1994). Cross-cultural school consultation. In C. C. Lee (Ed.), *Counseling for diversity: A guide for school counselors and related professionals* (pp. 129–141). Boston: Allyn & Bacon.

Ecklund, K., & Johnson, W. B. (2007). Toward cultural competence in child intake assessments. *Professional Psychology: Research and Practice, 38*, 356–362.

Félix-Ortiz, M., Newcomb, M. D., & Myers, H. (1994). A multidimensional measure of cultural identity for Latino and Latina adolescents. *Hispanic Journal of Behavioral Sciences, 16*, 99–115.

Georgas, J., Weiss, L. G., van de Vijver, F. J. R., & Saklofske, D. H. (Eds.). (2003). *Culture and children's intelligence: Cross-cultural analysis of the WISC-III*. San Diego, CA: Academic Press.

Gibbs, J. T., & Huang, L. N. (2003). *Children of color: Psychological interventions with culturally diverse youth* (2nd rev. ed.). San Francisco: Jossey-Bass.

Greenfield, P. (1997). You can't take it with you: Why ability assessments don't cross cultures [Special issue: Intelligence & Lifelong Learning]. *American Psychologist, 52*, 1115–1124.

Haney, W., Russell, M., & Bebell, D. (2004). Drawing on education: Using drawings to document schooling and support change. *Harvard Educational Review, 74*, 241–272.

Hays, P. A. (1996). Culturally responsive assessment with diverse older clients. *Professional Psychology: Research and Practice, 27*, 188–193.

Helms, J. E. (2006). Fairness is not validity or cultural bias in racial-group assessment: A quantitative perspective. *American Psychologist, 61*, 845–859.

Hill, C., Thompson, B., & Williams, E. (1997, October). A guide to conducting consensual qualitative research. *Counseling Psychologist, 25*, 517–572.

Johnson-Powell, G. (1997). The culturologic interview. In G. Johnson-Powell & J. Yamamoto (Eds.), *Transcultural child development* (pp. 349–364). New York: Wiley.

Landrine, H., & Klonoff, E. A. (1994). The African American Acculturation Scale: Development, reliability, and validity. *Journal of Black Psychology, 20*, 104–127.

Liu, W. M., & Clay, D. L. (2002). Multicultural counseling competencies: Guidelines in working with children and adolescents. *Journal of Mental Health Counseling, 24*, 177–187.

Natasi, B. K., Moore, R. B., & Varjas, K. M. (2004). *School-based mental health services: Creating comprehensive and culturally specific programs*. Washington, DC: American Psychological Association.

National Association of Social Workers. (2001). *NASW standards for cultural competence in social work practice*. Washington, DC: Author.

Park-Taylor, J. (2004). Towards the development of the Children's Acculturation Report. *Dissertation Abstracts International: Section B: The Sciences and Engineering, 65*(12-B), 6690.

Park-Taylor, J., Ventura, A. B., Ng, V., Budianto, L., & Sinha, J. (2008, April). *The Children's Acculturation Story-Pictogram (CASP): Development and initial findings*. Poster presented at the annual meeting of the American Educational Research Association, New York.

Patton, M. Q. (2002). *Qualitative evaluation and research methods* (3rd ed.). Thousand Oaks, CA: Sage.

Ponterotto, J., & Park-Taylor, J. (2007, July). Racial and ethnic identity theory, measurement, and research in counseling psychology: Present status and future directions. *Journal of Counseling Psychology, 54*, 282–294.

Portes, A., & Rumbaut, R. G. (2001). *The story of the immigrant second generation: Legacies*. Los Angeles: University of California Press.

Pynoos, R. S., Kinzie, J. D., & Gordon, M. (2001). Children, adolescents, and families exposed to torture and related trauma. In E. Gerrity, T. M. Keane, & F. Tuma (Eds.), *The mental health consequences of torture* (pp. 211–225). New York: Kluwer Academic/Plenum.

Rhodes, R. L., Ochoa, S. H., & Ortiz, S. O. (2005). *Assessing culturally and linguistically diverse students: A practical guide.* New York: Guilford.

Roysircar, G. (2005). Culturally sensitive assessment, diagnosis, and guidelines. In M. G. Constantine & D. W. Sue (Eds.), *Strategies for building multicultural competence in mental health and educational settings* (pp. 19–38). Hoboken, NJ: Wiley.

Sue, D. W., Arredondo, P., & McDavis, R. J. (1992). Multicultural counseling competencies and standards: A call to the profession. *Journal of Multicultural Counseling and Development, 20,* 64–88.

Tharp, R. G. (1991). Cultural diversity and treatment of children. *Journal of Consulting and Clinical Psychology, 59,* 799–812.

Thomas, A. R., Solorzano, L., & Cobb, H. C. (2007). Culturally responsive counseling and psychotherapy with children and adolescents. In H. T. Prout & D. T. Brown (Eds.), *Counseling and psychotherapy with children and adolescents: Theory and practice for school and clinical settings* (pp. 64–93). Hoboken, NJ: Wiley.

U.S. Department of Health and Human Services. (2001). *Mental health: Culture, race, and ethnicity: A supplement to Mental health: A report of the Surgeon General.* Rockville, MD: Author.

U.S. Public Health Service. (2000). *Report of the Surgeon General's Conference on Children's Mental Health: A national action agenda.* Washington, DC: U.S. Department of Health and Human Services.

Vazquez-Nuttall, E., Li, C., Dynda, A. M., Ortiz, S. O., Armengol, C. G., Walton, J. W., & Phoenix, K. (2007). Cognitive assessment of culturally and linguistically diverse students. In G. B. Esquivel, E. C. Lopez, & S. Nahari (Eds.), *Handbook of multicultural school psychology* (pp. 265–288). Mahwah, NJ: Lawrence Erlbaum.

Wall, J. E., & Walz, G. R. (Eds.). (2004). *Measuring up: Assessment issues for teachers, counselors, and administrators.* Greensboro, NC: CAPS Press.

Wechsler, D. (2003). *Wechsler Intelligence Scale for Children–Fourth edition.* San Antonio, TX: Psychological Corporation.

Wechsler, D. (2005). *Wechsler Intelligence Scale for Children–Fourth Edition Spanish.* San Antonio, TX: Psychological Corporation.

Whaley, A. L. (1997). Ethnicity/race, paranoia, and psychiatric diagnoses: Clinician bias versus sociocultural differences. *Journal of Psychopathology & Behavioral Assessment, 19,* 1–20.

Appendix A

The Children's Acculturation Story Pictogram (CASP)

Directions:

Think back from the time you moved to America until now. Please draw pictures that tell the story about your experience in America as a new immigrant.
Use as many pages as you need to complete your story.

Appendix B

The Children's Acculturation Report-Drawings (CAR-D)

Directions: Please draw pictures that tell the story of what an immigrant might go through to become American. Please use as many boxes as you need to complete your story.

Appendix C

Initial CASP Domains

Domain	Categories	Frequency
Migration Experiences	Mode of Transportation	Typical
	Feelings	Typical
School Experiences	Target of Bullying	Variant
	Friendship Development	General
	School Characteristics	Typical
Family Experiences	Family Separations & Step-Migration	Typical
	Parental Acculturation	Typical
	Extended Family Support	Typical
	Living Arrangements	Typical
Language	Friendships	Typical
	Bilingual vs. Monolingual Classes	Typical
	Barrier to Acculturation	Typical
	Academic	Typical
	English Acquisition	Typical
Contrast Between Country of Origin (COO) & USA	Feelings About COO (pos or neg or mixed)	Typical
	Environmental Differences (building structures, level of congestion, clean, city characteristics)	Typical
	Lifestyle Differences (SES, living arrangements, cousins live nearby)	Typical

49

Advances in Multicultural Assessment and Counseling With Adolescents

An Ecological Perspective

CHRISTINE J. YEH AND KWONG-LIEM KARL KWAN

According to the 2008 U.S. Census Bureau (U.S. Census Bureau, 2008a), there are more than 79 million racial and ethnic minorities, which make up approximately 26% of the total population. Less than 25 years from now, racial and ethnic minority groups are projected to account for almost 40% of adults and 48% of children in the United States (U.S. Census Bureau, 2008b). Children and youth under the age of 18 years comprise 25% of the total United States population: Of these youth, 48% are racial and ethnic minorities; 20% are Latino/a, 15% are Black/African American, 4% are Asian, 2% are multiracial, 1% are American Indian/Alaskan Native, and 1% are Native Hawaiian/Pacific Islander (Anne E. Casey Foundation, 2008). Twenty-two percent of youth in the United States are from immigrant families.

More than 17% of children and adolescents are living below the poverty level. Thirty-five percent of

Black/African American, 35% of American Indian, 28% of Latino/a, and 12% of Asian and Pacific Islander children and youth are living in poverty (Fass & Cauthen, 2007). These demographic statistics not only highlight the vast racial and cultural diversity of adolescents in the United States, but also underscore a need for reconceptualizing mental health counseling services for this growing group.

This chapter provides a critical look at advances in multicultural counseling and assessment practices with racially and culturally diverse adolescents. We present these approaches from ecological (see Bronfenbrenner, 1994) perspectives with a strong emphasis on the role of counselors as social justice change agents (Goodman et al., 2004). We also discuss the reciprocal relationships between youth and their relevant social contexts (Trickett & Formoso, 2008). Specifically, because research has demonstrated that racial and ethnic minorities often use social support networks when coping with social and academic problems (Colbert & Magouirk Colbert, 2003; Yeh & Wang, 2000), connections with family, peers, school personnel, and community members are essential when developing appropriate counseling interventions for culturally diverse adolescents. Because of these collectivistic cultural values, multicultural counseling practices must shift from primarily individually based models to more systemic and relational approaches.

Cultural Values and Coping

Traditional counseling models focus on individual, verbally oriented, insight-focused direct communication and do not incorporate the interdependent nature of many cultural groups' values and beliefs (Sue & Sue, 2003). Individual therapy is the dominant paradigm for counseling psychologists and other mental health professionals, but this form of intervention may be culturally inappropriate for cultural groups that emphasize forebearance, universality, belonging, social networks, and family relationships (Yeh, Arora, & Wu, 2006).

Culturally diverse adolescents may find humanistic, psychodynamic, existential, and other theoretical orientations confusing because they may not be familiar with the role of the counselor and what to expect from one-on-one therapy. They may also feel uncomfortable with emotional expression or sharing their family problems with a stranger. The mismatch between traditional therapy models and culturally diverse worldviews further contributes to the well-documented research on ethnic minority underuse of counseling and mental health services (Sue & Sue, 2003). The lack of bilingual counselors and school-, community-, and culturally based services may also contribute to high rates of underuse among diverse adolescents.

The link between cultural values, identity, and coping strategies has been explored in various ways (see Ponterotto, Anderson, & Grieger, 1986). Collectivistic coping refers to strategies for dealing with a stressful situation that involve social support networks, such as relatives, authority figures, community members, and friends (Cook & Wiley, 2000; Yeh, Arora, & Wu, 2006). Many cultural groups perceive mental health and coping in different ways (Lopez & Guarnaccia, 2000). For example, for African Americans, coping

strategies incorporate harmony with nature, spirituality, and collective consciousness (Chiang, Hunter, & Yeh, 2004; Utsey, Adams, & Bolden, 2000). Latino/a communities have coping strategies that incorporate church, home care, folk healers and medicines, and indigenous healers, as well as connection to ancestors and supernatural forces (Zea & Garcia, 1996).

In order to be successful with diverse youth, conceptualizations of mental health services must include indigenous patterns of coping (Yeh, Hunter, Madan-Bahel, Chiang, & Kwong, 2004). For example, researchers have demonstrated that Asian immigrants deal with mental health problems by seeking help from parents and older relatives, friends (Atkinson, Whiteley, & Gim, 1990), community members such as religious leaders and colleagues from social organizations (Yeh, Inman, Kim, & Okubo, 2006), and authority figures such as teachers and school staff (Yeh, Chang, Arora, Kim, & Xin, 2003).

Ecological Approaches to Counseling and Assessment

Bronfenbrenner (1994) has proposed a development-in-context theory that counselors can adapt to construct ecological counseling and assessment schemas. According to Bronfenbrenner, human development is nested within five environmental systems that exert bidirectional influences within and between the systems. The *microsystem* consists of an individual's biology and immediate settings (e.g., family, neighborhood, school, peers). The *mesosystem* comprises links and connections between multiple immediate environments (e.g., child and school, family and neighborhood). The *exosystem* involves developmental influence from a setting in which the individual does not have an active role (e.g., availability of school choices based on distance from home). The *macrosystem* encompasses the cultural context (e.g., political system, racial/racist climate), including the values and customs of the society. The *chronosystem* refers to the sociohistorical circumstances and conditions that accompany or transition throughout the individual's course of life (i.e., zeitgeist such as liberation from slavery, legalization of gay marriage).

Because culturally diverse adolescents tend to adapt their coping strategies depending on the situation, environment, and social system (Coleman, Casali, & Wampold, 2001), an ecological approach to counseling must incorporate the flexible, reciprocal, and dynamic nature of youths' relationships and identities (Trickett & Formoso, 2008). To best provide counseling to culturally diverse youths, it is imperative to understand their peer, family, school, and community contexts. Moreover, counselors must find ways to collaborate with these various systems to validate and empower youth effectively.

Peer Context

It is well documented that peer relationships affect adolescents' behavior and social experiences in profound ways (e.g., Allen, Porter, McFarland, Marsh, & McElhaney, 2005), and positive peer attachment is associated with lower levels of depression and stress (Licitra-Kleckler & Waas, 1993). Group work, in particular, can be effective for culturally diverse youth who value social relationships and cooperation (Bemak & Chung, 2003). Counselors may foster healthy relationships by promoting cross-cultural sharing, creating peer mentoring groups, and developing programs for peer conflicts and peer pressure (Lee & Cort, 2008).

In research on collectivistic practices in coping, Yeh et al. (2003) found that culturally diverse youth tended to rely on racially and culturally similar peers for social support when coping with a stressful event, such as discrimination or alienation. Conceptual writings specific to culturally diverse immigrant youth (Espiritu & Wolf, 2001) have also noted the importance of peer connections in buffering the impact of culture shock, family conflict, immigrant status, and discrimination.

Family Context

Counselors must also seek to understand the family environment and setting when working with culturally diverse adolescents. Families provide entrée into the role dynamics, cultural values and beliefs, gender expectations, lifestyle preferences, communication patterns, immigration histories, and socialization practices (Jones Thomas, 2005). Counselors must consider how youth define "family" in terms of membership (nuclear, immediate, extended, etc.) and associated roles (see McGoldrick, Giordano, & Pearce, 1996).

Racial-cultural factors that affect diverse youth are underscored through family interactions with counselors. For example, Latina/o and Asian American families have great respect for elders, strict gender roles, and an emphasis on extended family relationships. Similarly, African American families highly value extended family and have flexible roles in the family system (Jones Thomas, 2005). Various theorists have expressed the importance of involving family members in counseling practices (see Patterson, 2008). To best serve culturally diverse adolescents, counselors should assess family members' immigration history, socioeconomic status, occupational history, language use, role expectations, parenting styles, and acculturation level, among other things (Jones Thomas, 2005). Specific, culturally based questions (Paniagua, 2005) and cultural genograms (Adachi Sueyoshi, Rivera, & Ponterotto, 2001) have been suggested as useful methods to examine family cultural beliefs and practices.

The parent-child relationship is critical for culturally diverse youth who migrated to the United States with at least one parent (Fuligni, 1997). For immigrant families, being able to adapt effectively to environmental change can help in the process of adjustment to a new culture. For example, a cultural priority on family cohesion may help families remain intact, thereby providing a more stable and secure environment for children. However, research studies have shown that adapting to a new set of cultural norms is difficult and may contribute to family conflict, especially among Asian immigrants (Bemak & Chung, 2003; Yeh et al., 2005). As children mature, cultural gaps between parents and children become more pronounced, in part because children of immigrant families tend to adopt individualistic values that contradict with their more traditional parents (Buki, Ma, Strom, & Storm, 2003). Intergenerational family conflict may, in turn, have negative consequences on youths' psychological functioning (Lee & Liu, 2001). In addition, many culturally diverse youth have numerous familial obligations that they must learn to balance and maintain (Fuligni, Yip, & Tseng, 2002).

Schools Context

To date, culturally diverse youth living in urban poverty rarely receive mental health services because of lack of insurance and few monetary resources (Atkins et al., 1998). A few decades ago, schools began offering counseling and mental health services, and recent research indicates that schools are the ideal environment to promote social and emotional development (Roeser, Eccles, & Freedman-Doan, 1999), cultural adjustment, academic achievement (Borrero, 2006), empowerment (Borrero, 2007; Caldwell, Oldfield, Beech, & Price, 2008), and career development (Shea, Ma, & Yeh, 2007).

Presently, schools are increasingly offering counseling services and interventions, providing 70%-80% of psychological services received by youth (Rones & Hoagwood, 2000). In recent years, several studies have investigated the efficacy of using school-based mental health services for children living in low-income, urban communities (Atkins et al., 2006). Atkins et al. developed a school-based mental health services program for low-income African American youth in Chicago public schools and found that services were correlated with improved academic performance and classroom and home behavior (Atkins et al., 2006).

Schools serve as an organized forum where students can seek help. Schools are often the only counseling option due to economic, social, and cultural factors. Because students and parents are unlikely to be informed about outside resources for counseling services, on-site school counselors can provide interventions that are integrated into the daily schedule of youths' lives. In fact, ethnic minority youth in general, and immigrant adolescents in particular, often lack knowledge of how to seek help when they experience mental health problems (Bemak & Chung, 2003). Increased accessibility to mental health services for immigrant adolescents is critical due to the high costs of individual counseling and other linguistic and cultural barriers to mental health services. School-based interventions may effectively address mental health concerns and foster positive student development. Schools offer a unique avenue to help adolescents become educated about help-seeking strategies and resources (Yeh & Pituc, 2008).

Trickett and Formoso (2008) refer to "schools as agents of socialization as well as education: that is, they provide a context for socializing students as well as serving an explicitly educational function through the formal curriculum" (p. 80). To best serve culturally diverse adolescents, it is important to integrate social and emotional learning in the academic curriculum in order to further use schools to foster positive mental health among students. School settings not only serve culturally diverse youth and their peers, but they may also help parents navigate a new cultural setting through various activities that provide information and resources about their children's development (Trickett & Formoso, 2008).

Community and Cultural Context

The role of the community context is also important to understand when counseling culturally diverse adolescents. Communities provide resources that include specific support systems (e.g., churches, synagogues, cultural centers, etc.) (Yeh, Inman et al., 2006). For example, among many immigrant communities, families tend to settle in ethnic enclaves because of factors such as language barriers and racism experienced in mainstream settings (Loo, 1998). These community settings have the potential to offer a set of indigenous resources that addresses the unique needs of this population. This ranges from instrumental support to meet everyday needs (e.g., housing, employment, immigration services) to accommodating psychological and spiritual needs (e.g., indigenous healers, elders, etc.) (Yeh et al., 2004). The community context may serve to validate immigrant identities and experiences while decreasing the likelihood of encountering discrimination on the job or in everyday life (Louie, 2001). However, the current literature on integrating community support into youth counseling services is lacking.

One method for improving community and counselor relationships is through the use of a community board (McKay & Paikoff, 2007). Community boards are composed of a group of collaborative individuals such as counselors, parents, teachers, and community members who work together to develop innovative interventions. Such collaboration provides voice and power to specific members in the community, including religious leaders, businesses, elders, family members, indigenous healers, youth activists, and youth counselors, to name a few. A community board with stakeholders is essential when using an ecological perspective because it can create a space for interventions to emerge from the worldviews and values of community members. Community members may be excellent liaisons for counselors of diverse youth because they may have firsthand cultural and linguistic knowledge of the clients' backgrounds. Community collaborators may also have perceived cultural credibility because they reside in the same neighborhood and socioeconomic setting as the adolescent.

Social Justice Perspectives in Counseling Adolescents

According to Goodman et al. (2004), an ecological and systems perspective (Bronfenbrenner, 1979) is consistent with a social justice goal because such work may occur on three different levels: the *microsystem* (e.g., families), the *mesosystem* (e.g., communities), and the *macrosystem* (e.g., policies and structures). Change must occur not only within the adolescents, but also across the systems, structures, organizations, and policies affecting youths' experiences. These changes are intended to improve access and equitable conditions for oppressed and marginalized groups (Goodman et al., 2004).

When working with culturally diverse adolescents, counselors should think of themselves as potential agents of social change because they are in a position to advocate for equitable conditions and policies. With this goal in mind, Goodman et al. (2004) articulate several main principles for social justice counseling approaches, programs, interventions, and policy development: (a) ongoing self-examination, (b) sharing power, (c) giving voice, (d) facilitating consciousness raising, (e) building on strengths, and (f) leaving clients with the tools to work toward social change.

Through community and family collaboration, counselors can provide opportunities for culturally diverse adolescents' voices to be heard. This approach allows clients to share their story and history and incorporates important aspects of the clients' social, familial, and cultural world. Trust and credibility between counselors and clients is better established when there is less theorizing and more active listening (Sue & Zane, 1987). With ongoing and shared partnerships with youth, counselors may foster positive cultural identity, empower communities, and facilitate systemic change from meaningful exchanges from key stakeholders (Goodman et al., 2004). Counselors must learn to effectively assess clients' identities as embedded in a larger social and cultural context; examine the influence of political history, acculturation, and immigration; explore the role of community and family; examine language and translation issues; and investigate preferred indigenous coping strategies.

Counseling practices are inextricably linked to the multicultural assessment of culturally diverse adolescents. In the following section, we describe critical issues in multicultural assessment from an ecological perspective. Assessment is discussed in terms of multicultural competencies, the development of ecological schemas, client assessment, and counselor assessment. A case study is also presented to demonstrate the application of an ecological schema model.

Multicultural Assessment From an Ecological Perspective

Assessment provides a significant foundation for conceptualization, diagnosis, and intervention. Psychological assessment reflects the interaction between the means by which data are gathered and the meanings ascribed to data by counselors. How counselors gather, process, interpret, and integrate client data has direct and ethical implications on therapeutic process and outcome. Similar to objective or projective psychological tests, counselors are instruments in the assessment and diagnostic process, and are subjected to threats of reliability and validity. Counselors can be unreliable and invalid tools when assessment questions do not correspond to the presenting concerns (i.e., errors in symptom perception), when client data are understood or interpreted out of context (i.e., errors in normative reference), and when an inappropriate approach or construct is used to conceptualize clinical data (i.e., errors in diagnosis). These assessment errors are related to counselor training orientation and value orientation (or worldview), which are shaped by academic and cultural socialization environments.

When working with racially and culturally diverse adolescents, counselors' racial biases, lack of cultural knowledge, and deficit in skills to form cross-cultural relationships all introduce sources of errors in the assessment process. Models of multicultural counseling competencies have provided guidelines to enhance the cultural validity of counselors as an assessment instrument. In general, these guidelines delineated counselor awareness (i.e., self-knowledge); knowledge of racially and culturally diverse people; and skills (e.g., in clinical, consulting, and supervising settings) as core components of multicultural counseling competencies (Arredondo et al., 1996; Sue, Arredondo, & McDavis, 1992). Although knowledge of the characteristics of racial and ethnic groups provides normative information, the characteristics may be a source of bias if counselors fail to consider within-group variations in psychological assessment. What is more critical is counselor knowledge of the socialization experiences associated with individuals' racial and ethnic heritage, and the contextual forces (e.g., White privilege, racism) within which socialization experiences take place and from which identity configures. In fact, the *Guidelines on Multicultural Education, Training, Research, Practice, and Organizational Change* (APA, 2002) is guided by the principles that

> ethical conduct of psychologists is enhanced by knowledge of differences in beliefs and practices that emerge from socialization through racial and ethnic group affiliation and membership; . . . understanding and [recognition of] the interface between individuals' socialization experiences based on ethnic and racial heritage; . . . [and] recognition of the ways in which the intersection of racial and ethnic group membership with other dimensions of identity (e.g., gender, age, sexual orientation, disability, religion/spiritual orientation, educational attainment/experiences, and socioeconomic status) enhances the understanding and treatment of all people. (p. 20)

Developing an Ecological Assessment Schema

It is necessary to adopt an ecological approach when conducting assessment with culturally diverse adolescents. Rather than focusing solely on the individual, it is critical for counselors to also identify and assess the contributions of systemic forces that trigger and sustain clients' presenting concerns and symptoms. Without an ecological assessment schema, counselors will miss out on significant contextual information when conducting clinical interviews, resulting in misattributing clients' psychological problems to deficits or pathology within the individuals. When assessing adolescents in racially oppressive and hostile environments, the ability to

place their psychological and behavioral problems in the proper racial and sociopolitical context is an issue of professional competence and ethical practice.

CASE STUDY

The application of the ecological assessment schema can be illustrated by a second-generation Chinese American adolescent girl who was referred by her teacher and parents for assessment for underachieving in school. According to her parents, the client was a "perfect child" who was performing well academically until her middle school years. Her teachers and parents observed that she applied herself only minimally in classes and to homework while investing her time and energy in pursuing social relationships primarily with her White peers. Her parents were particularly upset as they wanted her to be placed in a gifted curriculum to pave her way to enter a prestigious university. Both the teachers and parents wanted the therapist to conduct intelligence testing to determine the client's potential to be a gifted student.

Client Assessment

Along with cognitive and intellectual testing (i.e., concerns, deficits, or pathology within the individual), an assessment of the *microsystem* (i.e., interactions with parents, peers, teachers) revealed that the adolescent girl detested teachers' and parents' expectations to achieve "like my older brother and Asians do." In addition, she always downplayed her "Asianness" so she could be accepted by her peers in the predominantly White school and neighborhood. In her mesosystem (i.e., connections between microsystems), her battle with the academic expectations of her parents and teachers made it difficult for her to trust authority figures, such as her guidance counselor, Sunday school teacher at church, and the counselor as she believed "you guys are only trying to make me study more." Her popularity among her White classmates reinforced her preference for White peers. At the same time, she alienated herself from other Asian peers as they reminded her of "those brainy cousins mom and dad always told me about." In her *exosystem* (i.e., a setting in which the individual does not play an active role but exerts influence on development), a group of Chinese immigrant residents in the community decided to open a weekend Chinese-language school. Her parents forced all their children to attend, which further fueled her rebelliousness against her Chinese American identity. In her *macrosystem* (i.e., society and its cultural values), she became increasingly aware of how her family values (e.g., subordination to parents) differed from the individual autonomy that the larger culture and her schoolmates embraced. Although she grew up in a *chronosystem* (i.e., sociocultural circumstance and conditions) where multiculturalism and diversity are encouraged in national and local politics, she felt angry and conflicted when teachers singled her out as the "expert" or as "representative" of Asian culture in school.

Although intellectual assessment did not indicate any cognitive deficits, assessment of the ecological systems found that the client's underachievement was a deliberate attempt to seek social acceptance and to not fit into the Asian American model minority stereotype. In other words, the underachievement concern was driven by acculturation conflicts within the family and racial identity conflict within herself. Based on the assessment data, the focus of intervention shifted from the client's academic ability (i.e., internal attributes) to contextual factors that triggered the client's (mal)adaptive strategies (of underachievement), and therapy/consultation was extended to significant people in the client's family (i.e., parents) and school (i.e., teacher, guidance counselor) systems. Counselor competence to identify and explore the contributions of factors in the ecological system thus enhances conceptual and diagnostic precision and reduces overpathologization of adolescent clients whose racial and ethnic background predisposes them to identify conflict and stress.

The ecological model provides clear directions for where counselors need to gather information in the clinical interview and assessment process. For adolescents whose race is perceived or self-perceived as different from their immediate environment (e.g., an African American student/family in a predominantly White school/neighborhood), how racial salience configures in the respective ecological system has direct and indirect effects on identity development and the youths' psychosocial experience. How race and ethnicity are

rejected or integrated into one's identity can lead to intrapersonal, interpersonal, and intergenerational conflict and stress that, in turn, can be manifested in various forms of (mal)adjustment and counseling concerns.

Acculturation and racial identity development are critical cultural variables that moderate the identity and stress experience and expression among racially diverse clients (Paniagua, 2005). Psychological assessment needs to incorporate sociocultural (e.g., immigrant/U.S.-born status, racial composition in immediate environment) and psychocultural (e.g., differential acculturation within the family; experience with racism; see Kwan, 1999; Ponterotto, Gretchen, & Chauhan, 2003) information that is embedded in the respective ecological systems.

For example, in the microsystem, counselors need to gather information of birthplace of origins (immigrant or U.S.-born), age of immigration, and length of stay in the United States of the adolescent and family members as generation level has implications for an individual's ethnic group identification and family acculturation conflicts. In the mesosystem, counselors can assess the adolescents' contact opportunities with various racial and ethnic groups, and their (positive or negative) experiences in these interactions. Racial exposure and interaction opportunities, including immersion in their own ethnic culture (e.g., language school, ethnic grocery store) also configures within the exosystem, such as the economy (e.g., employment opportunities), population characteristics (e.g., influx or attrition of people from same ethnic group), and education policies (e.g., bilingual curriculum adopted by school board) in the community. Knowledge and assessment of the exosystem is especially important because it exerts indirect developmental influences beyond the adolescent's control. In the macrosystem, the counselor needs to discern the racial climate (e.g., attitude toward racial diversity, overseas establishment) of the community, and how the adolescent client copes with experience of racial salience—a heightened awareness that one is different due to racial visibility leads to certain feelings and coping behaviors that would be different had race not been perceived (by self and/or by others) as visible in the immediate environment (Kwan, 2005)—within the community.

The sociocultural data gathered across ecological systems are instrumental for counselors in assessing how adolescents' concerns (e.g., depression, rebelliousness, underachievement) are moderated by the following: (a) acculturative stress when members from different generations within the family espouse different modes of acculturation (e.g., assimilation to vs. rejection of U.S. cultural values), (b) cultural identity conflict triggered by experience of racism while attempting to reject their own ethnic identity, and (c) social alienation when peers and community afford differential treatment based on the adolescents' racial salience.

Counselor Assessment

In addition to knowledge of culturally diverse clients, counselor awareness/self-knowledge is an important dimension of multicultural counseling competence. Similar to clients, counselor racial attitude and identity development also takes place within an ecological system. As such, counselors need to examine how their own racial socialization history affects their relationships with people who are racially and culturally different. Just as clients may distrust a counselor because of adverse experiences with the racial group the counselor represents, counselors' unexamined racial assumptions and unintentional racism can bias the interview and assessment process.

Along with examination of racial assumptions and biases, counselors need to consider a number of equivalence issues when psychological assessment is guided or supplemented by a diagnostic system and testing developed for and normed with samples different from culturally diverse adolescents. Conceptual equivalence evaluates the extent to which psychological constructs developed in a particular culture or for a particular population can be considered universal. Linguistic equivalence determines the extent to which translated versions of assessment instruments can be adapted as valid measures. Metric equivalence concerns the representativeness of a normative sample to culturally different groups. The three equivalence issues caution counselors lest one cultural perspective is applied as the standard against which all other cultures are compared. The *Diagnostic and Statistical Manual of Mental Disorders, Fourth*

Edition, Text Revision (American Psychiatric Association, 2000) states that

> A clinician who is unfamiliar with the nuances of an individual's cultural frame of reference may incorrectly judge as psychopathology those normal variations in behavior, belief, or experience that are particular to the individual's culture. . . . Varied cultural backgrounds affect the content and form of the symptom presentation (e.g., depressive disorders characterized by a preponderance of somatic symptoms rather than sadness in certain cultures), preferred idioms for describing distress, and information on prevalence when it is available. . . . Culture-bound syndromes and the provision of an outline for cultural formulation are designed to . . . increase sensitivity to variations in how mental disorders may be expressed in different cultures and will reduce the possible effect of unintended bias stemming from the *clinician's own cultural background* [italics added]. (p. 687)

To clarify what it means to use a cultural and multicultural ecological perspective in counseling and assessing culturally diverse youth, we provide some sociocultural and psychocultural data in the respective ecological systems (see Table 49.1). We hope that counselors will explore (with clients and within themselves) the various systems in which youth interact in order to provide a proper context for a racial interview, assessment, and counseling intervention. In addition, Table 49.1 provides ideas for counselors to engage in social justice and ecological approaches to counseling that seek to empower and give voice to culturally diverse youth (Goodman et al., 2004).

It is a challenging task to document best practices for working with culturally diverse youth when the context is ever changing. From an ecological perspective (see Trickett & Formoso, 2008), counselors must adopt a "learning how to learn" perspective that adjusts to the fluid and dynamic nature of adolescents' lives (Trickett & Formoso, 2008). Counselors must be open to a diverse range of cultural experiences, values, structures, and behaviors and must learn to consider microsystem, macrosystem, mesosystem, and chronosystem levels of intervention and assessment. The nature of future demographic shifts underscores the need to work effectively with and empower marginalized communities while

Table 49.1   Ecological Approach to Counseling Diverse Adolescents

Bronfenbrenner's Ecological Systems	*Sociocultural Data*	*Psychocultural Data*	*Counselor Practices and Approaches (Goodman et al. 2004)*
Chronosystem: Socio-historical conditions & circumstances of the time (i.e., zeitgeist)	Immigration policy Affirmative action Racial characteristics/of political leaders	Reactions to discrimination policies Coping with awareness of White privilege	Advocate to change racist policies Raise consciousness about structures that limit fair access
Macrosystem: Cultural context & societal values	Racial composition in community Dominant cultural values & practice	Experience of racial salience & effects on racial identity development	Work with communities to give voice
Exosystem: System that exerts indirect influence on adolescent	Exposure to/involvement in organized racial & ethnic communities Cultural orientation of curriculum	Effects of (in)voluntary contact/involvement on ethnic identity development	Help provide youth with tools for change Raise awareness of important systems
Mesosystem: Connections between microsystems	Opportunity/frequency of racial interactions	Nature of/experience from racial group interaction	Validate racialized experience Find ways for youth to share power in racial interactions
Microsystem: Psychological understanding of self through interactions in family, school, neighborhood	Birth place of origin Age of immigration Length of stay in the United States	Stress/Conflicts due to generation difference in modes of acculturation and ethnic group identification	Promote voice and sharing across generations Build on strengths in family systems In corporate counselor and client self-examination

simultaneously exploring one's own worldviews, values, biases, and racial and ethnic identities.

REFERENCES

Adachi Sueyoshi, L., Rivera, L., & Ponterotto, J. G. (2001). The family genogram as a tool in multicultural career counseling. In J. G. Ponterotto, J. M. Casas, L. A. Suzuki, & C. M. Alexander (Eds.), *Handbook of multicultural counseling* (2nd ed., pp. 655–671). Thousand Oaks, CA: Sage.

Allen, J. P., Porter, M. R., McFarland, F. C., Marsh, P., & McElhaney, K. B. (2005). The two faces of adolescents' success with peers: Adolescents' popularity, social adaptation, and deviant behavior. *Child Development, 76,* 747–760.

American Psychiatric Association. (2000). *Diagnostic and statistical manual of mental disorders* (4th ed., text rev.). Washington, DC: Author.

American Psychological Association. (2002). *Guidelines on multicultural education, training, research, practice, and organizational change for psychologists.* Washington, DC: Author.

Anne E. Casey Foundation. (2008). *Kids Count data center.* Retrieved July 16, 2008, from http://www.aecf.org/Major Initiatives/KIDSCOUNT.aspx

Arredondo, P., Toporek, R., Brown, S. P., Jones, J., Locke, D. C., Sanchez, J., & Stadler, H. (1996). Operationalization of the multicultural counseling competencies. *Journal of Multicultural Counseling and Development, 24,* 42–78.

Atkins, M. S., Frazier, S. L., Birman, D., Adil, J. A., Jackson, M., Graczyk, P. A., Talbott, E., Farmer, A. D., Bell, C. C., & McKay, M. M. (2006). School-based mental health services for children living in high poverty urban communities. *Administration and Policy in Mental Health, 33*, 146–159.

Atkins, M. S., McKay, M. M., Arvanitis, P., London, L., Madison, S., Costigan, C., Haney, P., Zevenbergen, A., Hess, L., Bennett, D., & Webster, D. (1998). An ecological model for school-based mental health services for urban low-income aggressive children. *Journal of Behavioral Health Services & Research, 25*, 64–75.

Atkinson, D. R., Whiteley, S., & Gim, R. H. (1990). Asian-American acculturation and preferences for help providers. *Journal of College Student Development, 31*, 155–161.

Bemak, F., & Chung, R. C. Y. (2003). Multicultural counseling with immigrant students in schools. In P. B. Pedersen & J. C. Carey (Eds.), *Multicultural counseling in schools: A practical handbook* (2nd ed., pp. 84–104). Boston: Pearson Education.

Borrero, N. (2006). *Promoting academic achievement for bilingual middle school students: Learning strategies for young interpreters.* Unpublished doctoral dissertation, Stanford University, Stanford, CA.

Borrero, N. (2007). Promoting cultural and linguistic diversity in American public schools: Fostering the assets of bilingual adolescents. *International Journal of Diversity in Organizations, Communities, and Nations, 7*(1), 195–203.

Bronfenbrenner, U. (1979). *The ecology of human development: Experiments by nature and design.* Cambridge, MA: Harvard University Press.

Bronfenbrenner, U. (1994). Ecological models of human development. In T. Husen & T. N. Postlethwaite (Ed.), *The international encyclopedia of education* (2nd ed., pp. 1643–1647). New York: Elsevier Science.

Buki, L. P., Ma, T.-C., Strom, R. D., & Storm, S. K. (2003). Chinese immigrant mothers of adolescents: Self-perceptions of acculturation effects on parenting. *Cultural Diversity & Ethnic Minority Psychology, 9*, 127–140.

Caldwell, L. D., Oldfield, R., Beech, B. M., & Price, V. (2008). African American empowerment in secondary school counseling. In H. L. K. Coleman & C. J. Yeh (Eds.), *Handbook of school counseling* (pp. 195–208). New York: Taylor & Francis.

Chiang, L., Hunter, C. D., & Yeh, C. J. (2004). Coping attitudes, sources, and practices among Black and Latino college students. *Adolescence, 39*, 793–815.

Colbert, R. D., & Magouirk Colbert, M. (2003). School counselor involvement in culture-centered education reform. In P. B. Pedersen & J. C. Carey (Eds.), *Multicultural counseling schools: A practical handbook* (2nd ed., pp. 3–20). Boston: Allyn & Bacon.

Coleman, H. L. K., Casali, S. B., & Wampold, B. E. (2001). Adolescent strategies for coping with cultural diversity. *Journal of Counseling & Development, 79*, 356–364.

Cook, D. A., & Wiley, C. J. (2000). Psychotherapy with members of African American churches and spiritual traditions. In P. S. Richards & A. E. Bergin (Eds.), *Handbook of psychotherapy and religious diversity* (pp. 369–396). Washington, DC: American Psychological Association.

Espiritu, Y.-L., & Wolf, D. (2001). The paradox of assimilation: Children of Filipino immigrants in San Diego. In R. G. Rumbaut & A. Portes (Eds.), *Ethnicities: Children of immigrants in America* (pp. 157–186). Berkeley: University of California Press.

Fass, S., & Cauthen, N. (2007, November). *Who are America's poor children? The official story.* National Center for Children in Poverty. Retrieved July 16, 2008 from http://www.nccp.org/publications/pub_787.html

Fuligni, A. J. (1997). The academic achievement of adolescents from immigrant families: The roles of family background, attitudes, and behavior. *Child Development, 68*, 351–363.

Fuligni, A. J., Yip, T., & Tseng, V. (2002). The impact of family obligation on the daily activities and psychological well-being of Chinese American adolescents. *Child Development, 73*, 302–314.

Goodman, L. A., Liang, B., Helms, J. E., Latta, R. E., Sparks, E., & Weintraub, S. R. (2004). Training counseling psychologists as social justice agents: Feminist and multicultural principles in action. *Counseling Psychologist, 32*, 793–837.

Jones Thomas, A. (2005). Family counseling and psychotherapy in racial-cultural psychology: Case applications. In R. T. Carter (Ed.), *Handbook of racial-cultural counseling: Training and practice* (Vol. 2, pp. 364–378). Hoboken, NJ: Wiley.

Kwan, K.-L. K. (1999). Assessment of Asian Americans in counseling: Evolving issues and concerns. In D. S. Sandhu (Ed.), *Asian and Pacific-Islander Americans: Issues and concerns for counseling and psychotherapy* (pp. 229–249). Comack, NY: Nova Science.

Kwan, K.-L. K. (2005). Racial salience: Conceptual dimensions and implications for racial and ethnic identity development. In R. Carter (Ed.), *Handbook of racial-cultural psychology and counseling: Theory and research* (Vol. 1, pp. 115–131). New York: Wiley.

Lee, R. M., & Liu, H. T. (2001). Coping with intergenerational family conflict: Comparison of Asian American, Hispanic, and European American college students. *Journal of Counseling Psychology, 48,* 410–419.

Lee, S., & Cort, K. (2008). Immigrant children and youth in schools. In H. L. K. Coleman & C. J. Yeh (Eds.), *Handbook of school counseling* (pp. 95–110). New York: Taylor & Francis.

Licitra-Kleckler, D. M., & Wass, D. A. (1993). Perceived social support among high-stress adolescents: The role of peer and family. *Journal of Adolescents Research, 8,* 381–402.

Loo, C. M. (1998). *Chinese America: Mental health and quality of life in the inner city.* Thousand Oaks, CA: Sage.

Lopez, S. R., & Guarnaccia, P. J. (2000). Cultural psychopathology: Uncovering the social world of mental illness. *Annual Review of Psychology, 51,* 571–598.

Louie, V. (2001). Parents' aspirations and investments: The role of social class in the educational experience of 1.5- and second-generation Chinese Americans. *Harvard Educational Review, 71,* 438–474.

McGoldrick, M., Giordano, J., & Pearce, J. K. (Eds.). (1996). *Ethnicity and family therapy* (2nd ed.). New York: Guilford.

McKay, M. M., & Paikoff, R. L. (2007). *Community collaborative partnerships: The foundation for HIV prevention research efforts.* New York: Taylor & Francis.

Paniagua, F. A. (2005). *Assessing and treating culturally diverse clients: A practical guide* (3rd ed.). Thousand Oaks, CA: Sage.

Patterson, T. (2008). Families in context: An essential component of school counseling. In H. L. K. Coleman & C. J. Yeh (Eds.), *Handbook of school counseling* (pp. 449–458). New York: Taylor & Francis.

Ponterotto, J. G., Anderson, W. H., & Grieger, I. Z. (1986). Black students' attitudes towards counseling as a function of racial identity. *Journal of Multicultural Counseling and Development, 11,* 11–26.

Ponterotto, J. G., Gretchen, D., & Chauhan, R. V. (2003). Cultural identity and multicultural assessment: Quantitative and qualitative tools for the clinician. In L. A. Suzuki, J. G. Ponterotto, & P. J. Meller (Eds.), *Handbook of multicultural assessment: Clinical, psychological, and educational applications* (2nd ed.). New York: Wiley.

Roeser, R., Eccles, J., & Freedman-Doan, C. (1999). Academic functioning and mental health in adolescents. *Journal of Adolescent Research, 14,* 135–174.

Rones, M., & Hoagwood, K. (2000). School-based mental health services: A research review. *Clinical Child and Family Psychology Review, 3,* 223–241.

Shea, M., Ma, P.-W., & Yeh, C. J. (2007). Development of a culturally specific career exploration group for urban Chinese immigrant youth. *Career Development Quarterly, 56,* 62–73.

Sue, D. W., Arredondo, P., & McDavis, R. J. (1992). Multicultural competencies and standards: A call to the profession. *Journal of Multicultural Counseling and Development, 20,* 64–88.

Sue, D. W., & Sue, D. (2003). *Counseling the culturally diverse: Theory and practice* (4th ed.). Hoboken, NJ: Wiley.

Sue, S., & Zane, N. (1987). The role of culture and cultural techniques in psychotherapy: A critique and reformulation. *American Psychologist, 42,* 37–45.

Trickett, E. J., & Formoso, D. (2008). The acculturative environment of schools and the school counselor: Goals and roles that create a supportive context for immigrant adolescents. In H. L. K. Coleman & C. J. Yeh (Eds.), *Handbook of school counseling* (pp. 79–94). New York: Taylor & Francis.

U.S. Census Bureau. (2008a). *2006 American Community Survey.* Retrieved on December 28, 2008, from http://factfinder.census.gov/servlet/table

U.S. Census Bureau. (2008b). *U.S. Population Projections.* Retrieved on January 4, 2009, from http://www.census.gov/population/www/projections/summarytables.html

Utsey, S. O., Adams, E. P., & Bolden, M. (2000). Development and initial validation of the Africultural Coping Systems Inventory. *Journal of Black Psychology, 26,* 194–215.

Yeh, C. J., Arora, A. K., & Wu, K. (2006). A new theoretical model of collectivistic coping. In P. T. P. Wong & C. J. Wong (Eds.), *Handbook of multicultural perspectives on stress and coping* (pp. 55–72). New York: Springer.

Yeh, C. J., Chang, T., Arora, A., Kim, A. B., & Xin, T. (2003, August). *Reliability, validity and factor analysis of the Collectivistic Coping Scale.* Poster presented at the annual meeting of the American Psychological Association, Toronto, Canada.

Yeh, C. J., Hunter, C. D., Madan-Bahel, A., Chiang, L., & Kwong, A. (2004). Indigenous and interdependent perspectives of healing: Implications for counseling and research. *Journal of Counseling and Development, 82,* 410–419.

Yeh, C. J., Inman, A., Kim, A. B., & Okubo, Y. (2006). Asian American collectivistic coping in response to 9/11. *Cultural Diversity and Ethnic Minority Psychology, 12,* 134–148.

Yeh, C. J., Ma, P.-W., Madan, A., Hunter, C. D., Jung, S., Kim, A., Akitaya, K., & Sasaki, K. (2005). The cultural negotiations of Korean immigrant youth. *Journal of Counseling & Development, 83,* 172–181.

Yeh, C. J., & Pituc, S. T. (2008). Understanding yourself as a school counselor. In H. L. K. Coleman & C. J. Yeh (Eds.), *Handbook of school counseling* (pp. 63–78). New York: Taylor & Francis.

Yeh, C. J., & Wang, Y. W. (2000). Asian American coping attitudes, sources, and practices: Implications for indigenous counseling strategies. *Journal of College Student Development, 41,* 94–103.

Zea, M. C., & Garcia, J. (1996). *Psychological interventions and research with Latino populations.* Upper Saddle River, NJ: Prentice Hall.

50

Current Considerations in the Assessment of Adults

A Review and Extension of Culturally Inclusive Models

ALEX L. PIETERSE AND MATTHEW J. MILLER

"Never look for a psychological explanation unless every effort to find a cultural one has been exhausted."

Margaret Mead quoting William Fielding Ogburn,
one of her mentors at Columbia University

Assessment has been described as "a process of evaluation that includes both qualitative (e.g., background information, observation) and quantitative (e.g., standardized test scores) data as part of the evaluation process" (Suzuki, Kugler, & Aguiar, 2005, p. 300). The purpose of assessment within counseling can be viewed as gaining an "in-depth understanding of the factors that influence the client's experience, perception, and presentation of her or his problems" (Grieger & Ponterotto, 1995, p. 357). Given the well-documented emphasis on incorporating racial and cultural variables within the counseling process (American Psychological Association, 2003; Moodley & Palmer, 2006), the inclusion of a cultural perspective in the assessment process has come to be viewed as a clinical, ethical, and social justice imperative (Dana, 2005; Mattaini, 2005). Over the past two decades, scholars have sought to provide a rationale and outline for the inclusion of cultural variables within the assessment process (Dana, 2005; Grieger, 2008; Grieger &

Ponterotto, 1995; Malgady, Rogler, & Constantino, 1987; Ridley, Hill, & Li, 1998). Collectively, these authors argue that cultural insensitivity is associated with a number of detrimental outcomes in the counseling process. These outcomes include a lower utilization of counseling services by persons of color, the mischaracterization of psychological distress for these individuals, a failure to consider important cultural elements associated with client support and sources of well-being, and the application of ineffective therapeutic interventions. Moreover, with the utility of culturally sensitive psychotherapeutic interventions now well established (Griner & Smith, 2006), some have argued that a lack of cultural inclusion in the assessment process is consistent with a breach of ethical standards (Dana, 2005; Ridley, Tracey, Pruitt-Stephens, Wimsatt, & Beard, 2008). The current chapter therefore will provide an overview and update of major developments in multicultural assessment over the past decade. We will discuss the clinical utility of measures assessing acculturation, racial/cultural stressors, and multicultural personality, and will explore the role of clinician bias as a significant source of error in the assessment process. Finally, we outline a counselor checklist as a template for the effective assessment of adults within counseling and psychology and equate the failure to employ cultural assessment with a form of ethical malpractice.

MULTICULTURAL ASSESSMENT— RHETORIC VERSUS REALITY

The past decade has witnessed the publication of a number of important frameworks and models for undertaking culturally inclusive assessment procedures (Dana, 2005; Grieger, 2008; Ridley et al., 1998). Yet the following two real-life scenarios highlight the tension that exists between the conceptual considerations of multicultural assessment and actual day-to-day practices.

Scenario #1: A psychological assessment was undertaken on a Chinese female immigrant who had been admitted for evaluation of depression and posttraumatic stress disorder following an apparent suicide threat. The psychological battery prescribed by the consulting psychologist included the Thematic Apperception Test— a projective technique in which individuals are asked to respond to neutral visual stimuli set in an American

context. In view of a language barrier between the client and clinician, an interpreter was employed. The assessment proceeded with the client responding to the cues, the clinician responding to the interpreter, the interpreter requesting clarification of the cues, and so on, without any sense of the reliability of the translation or the validity of the stimuli in relation to the client's racial and cultural background. Furthermore, a clinical interview was undertaken that focused primarily on the duration and severity of the client's symptoms.

Scenario #2: The client, a 28-year-old Latino, was undergoing cognitive and personality assessment in order to establish competency for trial. The psychological battery included standard assessments such as the Minnesota Multiphasic Personality Inventory (MMPI) and the Wechsler Adult Intelligence Scales (WAIS), as well as an extensive clinical interview. The clients' case was discussed at a weekly case conference, and reference was made to specific cultural and historical variables that the clinician felt had affected the client's development and current behavioral pattern. After conveying appreciation for the thoughtful overview of the client's case, the lead psychologist proceeded to emphasize the need to get to the "bottom line," namely, the client's MMPI profile and scores on the WAIS.

These two scenarios are not uncommon and illustrate the challenges associated with the implementation of a culturally inclusive approach to effective assessment within the counseling and psychotherapeutic process. The specific challenges highlighted in these cases include the overreliance and inflated value placed on quantitative data, the primary role of the assessment procedure being diagnostic, the application of a universal perspective to the understanding of psychological distress/mental illness, and the failure to recognize the manner in which cultural and racial experiences inform performance and profiles on various normative tests (Dana, 2005; Malgady & Colon-Malgady, 2008). Perhaps most troubling is the ongoing need to legitimize the nature of cultural and racial constructs as critical psychological processes and not peripheral information that most probably has little to do with the "bottom line." Assuming for a moment the adoption of a culturally inclusive critique to the assessment process outlined in the two previous scenarios, what we might learn is that the undertaking of a culturally inclusive assessment is often a function of the clinician's cultural awareness, requires a thoughtful and informed choice of psychological instrumentation, includes a negotiation of the economic and political aspects of mental health treatment, and represents a consistent challenging of Eurocentric notions of psychological health and psychological distress (Dana, 2005). As the function of this chapter is to explicate some of the processes and choices involved in multicultural assessment, our first order of business will be to provide a brief context in which to understand the term *multicultural*.

Multiculturalism

Carter and Qureshi (1995) provided a useful typology of the manner in which cultural differences in counseling are conceptualized. Specifically, they offered four typologies: universal, ubiquitous, race-based, and pannationalist. A review of the current understanding of multiculturalism in the counseling literature will reveal that the ubiquitous approach, an approach that views culture as representative of any group-related identity (gender, ability, sexual orientation, ethnicity, race, social class, etc.), is the most frequently employed understanding of multiculturalism (see Arredondo et al., 1996; D'Andrea & Heckman, 2008; Sue & Sue, 2003). The following approaches to multicultural assessment therefore are reflective of models that adopt the ubiquitous understanding of cultural differences and thus provide important frameworks in which to perform a culturally inclusive assessment procedure.

CULTURALLY INCLUSIVE ASSESSMENT PROCEDURES

Multicultural Assessment Procedure

The multicultural assessment procedure (MAP) formulated by Ridley et al. (1998) is designed to offer an assessment protocol that is practical, is driven by theory, and can be scientifically validated. To this end, the MAP comprises four phases: collecting culturally salient data via multiple methodologies; formulating a working hypothesis through accurate interpretation of the data; testing the hypothesis via cultural and clinical data and refining the hypothesis as necessary; and

providing an assessment report that is accurate and complete, and that reflects a process of hypothesis testing (see McKitrick, Edwards, & Sola, 2007). The central assessment device of the MAP is the clinical interview. The clinical interview, unlike standard assessment interviews, explicitly includes references to such variables as acculturation, language, religious practices, racism and prejudice, and cultural values affecting communication. Furthermore, a hallmark of the MAP is the emphasis that Ridley et al. place on the need to recycle through the assessment process. Thus, the assessment process as outlined by the MAP is dynamic, not static; is cyclical, not linear; and seeks to incorporate cultural variables as central to all phases of the assessment process.

Cultural Assessment Framework and Interview Protocol

The Cultural Assessment Framework and Interview Protocol (CAIP) (Grieger, 2008) is the most recent comprehensive approach to culturally inclusive assessment and also highlights the clinical interview as the most critical tool in accurate assessment. As outlined by Grieger, the CAIP contains 11 categories required for a culturally inclusive assessment and application. These 11 categories are problem conceptualization and attitudes toward helping; cultural identity; level of acculturation; family structure and expectations; level of racial and cultural identity development; experience with bias; immigration issues; existential/spiritual issues; counselor characteristics and behaviors; implications of cultural factors between the counselor and client; and summary of cultural factors and implications for diagnosis, case conceptualization, and treatment (see p. 140). Although adopting an inclusive approach to assessment, Grieger acknowledges that not all difference is equivalent and highlights the role of bias, discrimination, racism, and white privilege as variables with potentially toxic ramifications for clients of color. The CAIP provides a consistent and explicit focus on cultural variables that might inform the clients' experience of distress or pathology. Additionally, the CAIP attends to the dynamics of difference that may occur between the client and counselor and incorporates this process variable as an important part of the assessment procedure.

Multicultural Assessment Intervention Process Model

The Multicultural Assessment Intervention Process (MAIP) model formulated by Dana (1998, 2005) is designed to incorporate universal and culture-specific variables within the assessment process. Presented as a flow chart not unlike the diagnostic tree of the *DSM-IV-TR*, the clinician is guided through a series of steps based on seven questions. Question 1 begins with a consideration of universal (etic) or cultural (emic) orientation specificity. Question 2 reminds the clinician to assess cultural orientation with choices that include Anglo, Assimilated, Bicultural, Marginal, and Traditional. Question 3 draws attention to the need for a diagnosis. If a diagnosis is deemed necessary, Questions 4 and 5 highlight a consideration of instrumentation. Here, the clinician has an opportunity to assess the extent to which measures have been standardized on the population of interest and to choose between culture-specific, universal standard, or modified instruments. Question 6 requests an assessment of cultural stress, which becomes a part of the consideration for Question 7, the establishment of a diagnosis and the mode of intervention, again with the choice referencing either culture-specific intervention or a combined universal and culture-specific intervention. It is important to note that the premise of the MAIP is that of a cross-cultural pairing between client and counselor, that is, where differences exist between the client and counselor based on racial, ethnic, or cultural background.

Culturally Valid Assessment Procedures

A final approach is offered by Roysircar-Sodowsky and Kuo (2001), who have provided the following set of procedural guidelines for culturally valid assessment: (a) the use of language that clients understand and the building of rapport, (b) assessment of acculturation, (c) the selection of appropriate measures of assessment, (d) the use of translated measures with linguistic and construct equivalence, (e) information gained from observational assessment, (f) the use of multiple methods of assessment, (g) a cautious approach to using computerized reports because of the omission of cultural and social-racial effects and the emphasis on pathology, and (h) the employment of racial and ethnic consultants.

It is clear that there is much consistency in these models of multicultural assessment, and, if implemented, they should provide the foundation for a culturally inclusive mode of psychological assessment. As Dana (1996) has argued, the primary rationale for an assessment procedure that incorporates culture as a central construct for diverse racial and ethnic groups is that competent assessment can also "determine the quality of ensuing interventions and the extent to which these interventions are utilized by multicultural groups" (p. 482). Validation of this claim can be seen in the recent meta-analysis undertaken by Griner and Smith (2006), in which the utility of culture-sensitive interventions produced effect sizes that exceeded those associated with traditional modes of counseling and psychotherapy. Furthermore, due to the growing acknowledgment of the intersecting nature of identities associated with race, gender, ethnicity, and social class (see Pope-Davis & Coleman, 2003), the guiding principles associated with the above models could be considered the foundation of competent practice irrespective of the cultural background or orientation of the client. In other words, the incorporation of culture within the counseling process should be viewed as an element of general competence and not only considered within the rubric of multicultural competence. The principles of multicultural competence as applied to psychological assessment need to be viewed as critical elements associated with general competence and ethical practice (Ridley et al., 2008).

ACCULTURATION, RACIAL-CULTURAL STRESSORS, AND MULTICULTURAL PERSONALITY

Given the continued racial and ethnic hierarchy within the United States (Marger, 2008) and the fact that gender, ability, and related identities are experienced within the context of racial and ethnic hierarchies, we now turn our attention to variables that are located more directly within race and cultural socialization (see Helms & Richardson, 1997). Here we will provide a brief review of acculturation, racial-cultural stressors, and multicultural personality and will provide recommendations for the accurate assessment of these important constructs. Additionally, we refer the reader to Table 50.1, which lists a range of potential instruments that could be adapted for use within the clinical setting.

Table 50.1 Instruments for the Assessment of Acculturation, Racial-Cultural Stressors, and Multicultural Personality

Scale	Domains of Assessment	Subscales	Number of Items	Reliability[a]	Validity Evidence	Utility
Acculturation						
Native American Acculturation Scale (Garrett & Pichette, 2000)	Language, identity, friendships, behaviors, generational/geographic background, attitudes	N/A	20	Total: .91	N/A	Ninth-grade reading level, includes an assessment interview
Stephenson Multigroup Acculturation Scale (Stephenson, 2000)	Language, cultural knowledge, social interactions, media and food preferences	Ethnic Society Immersion, Dominant Society Immersion	32	Total: .86 Subscales: .90 to .97	Criterion-related, convergent	Developed for use across ethnic groups
Asian American Multidimensional Acculturation Scale (Gim Chung, Kim, & Abreu, 2004)	Cultural identity, language, cultural knowledge, food consumption	AAMAS-Culture of Origin, AAMAS-Asian American, AAMAS-European American	45	Subscales: .78 to .89 Test-Retest: .75 to .89	Criterion-related, convergent, discriminant, factorial	Bilinear measure Assesses pan-ethnic orientation Appropriate across Asian ethnic groups
Asian American Values Scale–Multidimensional (Kim, Li, & Ng, 2005)	Asian American cultural value dimensions	Collectivism, Conformity to Norms, Emotional Self-Control, Family Recognition Through Achievement, Humility	42	Total: .89 Subscales: .78 to .90 Test-Retest: .73 to .92	Convergent, criterion-related, discriminant, factorial	Assesses nonbehavioral aspects of acculturation
Abbreviated Multidimensional Acculturation Scale (Zea, Asner-Self, Birman, & Buki, 2003)	Language competence, cultural competence and knowledge, cultural identity	AMAS-ZABB U.S. American, AMAS-ZABB Culture of Origin	42	Subscales: .83 to .97	Criterion-related, convergent, discriminant, factorial	Assesses cultural competence Adaptable for use with different groups
Racial/Cultural Attitudes						
Color-Blind Racial Attitudes Scale (Neville, Lilly, Duran, Lee, & Browne, 2000)	Cognitive dimensions of color-blind racial attitudes	Unawareness of Racial Privilege, Institutional Discrimination, Blatant Racial Issues	20	Total: .91 Subscales: .70 to .83 Test-Retest: .34 to .80	Criterion-related, discriminant, factorial	Self-assessment in counselor training Provides an index of unawareness of racism

(Continued)

Table 50.1 (Continued)

Scale	Domains of Assessment	Subscales	Number of Items	Reliability[a]	Validity Evidence	Utility
Psychosocial Costs of Racism to Whites Scale (Spanierman & Heppner, 2004)	Affective, cognitive, and behavioral dimensions of psychological costs of racism	White Empathic Reactions Toward Racism, White Guilt, White Fear of Others	16	Subscale: .63 to .85 Test-Retest: .69 to .95	Criterion-related, convergent, discriminant, factorial	Self-assessment in counselor training
Scale of Ethnocultural Empathy (Wang et al., 2003)	Intellectual empathy, empathic emotions, communicative empathy	Empathic Feeling and Expression, Empathic Perspective Taking, Acceptance of Cultural Differences, Empathic Awareness	31	Total: .91 Subscales: .71 to .90 Test-Retest: .64 to .86	Convergent, discriminant, criterion-related, factorial	Assesses empathy in multicultural settings
Africultural Coping Systems Inventory (Utsey, Adams, & Bolden, 2000)	Coping attitudes and behaviors that reflect an African-centered worldview	Collective Coping, Ritual-Centered Coping, Spiritual-Centered Coping, Cognitive/Emotional Debriefing	30	Subscales: .76 to .82	Factorial	Assesses coping strategies and sources of internal strengths
Multicultural Personality						
Miville-Guzman Universality-Diversity Scale (Miville et al., 1999)	Cognitive, behavioral, and affective components of social attitudes toward diversity	N/A	45	Total: .89 to .94 Test-Retest: .94	Criterion-related, discriminant	Assesses degree of acceptance of differences and similarities among people
Multicultural Personality Questionnaire (Van der Zee & Van Oudenhoven, 2000, 2001)	Personality dimensions associated with multicultural effectiveness	Cultural Empathy, Openmindedness, Emotional Stability, Social Initiatives, Flexibility	78	Subscales: .81 to .91 Test-Retest: .64 to .79	Criterion-related, convergent, factorial	Assesses training needs for employees with international experience
Racial-Cultural Stressors						
Index of Race-Related Stress–Brief Version (Utsey, 1999)	Psychological and emotional stress related to experiences of racism	Cultural Racism, Institutional Racism, Individual Racism	22	Subscales: .69 to .78	Convergent, criterion-related, factorial	Ninth-grade reading level

Scale	Domains of Assessment	Subscales	Number of Items	Reliability[a]	Validity Evidence	Utility
Asian American Racism Related Stress Inventory (Liang, Li, & Kim, 2004)	Psychological stress associated with experiences of racism	Socio-Historical Racism, General Racism, Perpetual Foreigner Racism	29	Total: .90 to .95 Subscales: .75 to .93 Test-Retest: .73 to .87	Convergent, discriminant, factorial	Specific to the sociopolitical experiences of Asian Americans
Asian American Family Conflicts Scale (Lee, Choe, Kim, & Ngo, 2000)	Parent and child relationship and interaction	FCS–Likelihood, FCS–Seriousness	20	Subscale: .89 to .91 Test-Retest: .80 to .85	Convergent, criterion-related, factorial	Brief measure of conflict due to cultural differences
Acculturative Stress Inventory for Children (Suarez-Morales, Dillon, & Szapocznik, 2007)	Stress due to acculturation across language, culture, and environment	Perceived Discrimination, Immigrant-Related Stress	20	Total: .82 Subscales: .72 to .79 Test-Retest: .77 to .93	Convergent, discriminant, criterion-related, factorial	Developed specifically for children
Perceived Ethnic Discrimination Questionnaire (Brondolo et al., 2005)	Frequency, types, and sources of discrimination	Lifetime Discrimination, Exclusion/Rejection, Stigmatization, Threat/Aggression, Work/School Discrimination, Media Discrimination, Discrimination Against Family, Discrimination in Various Settings, Past-Week Discrimination	70	Subscales: .75 to .99	Convergent, concurrent, discriminant	Primarily research on fifth-grade reading level
General Ethnic Discrimination Scale (Landrine, Klonoff, Corral, Fernandez, & Roesch, 2006)	Perceived ethnic discrimination for all populations	Lifetime Discrimination, Recent Discrimination, Appraised Discrimination	18	Subscales: .93 to .94	Factorial	Primarily research oriented

a. Reliability coefficient unless otherwise stated.

In this table, we have provided information regarding structure and psychometric properties, specific domains of assessment, and potential utility of a number of the selected instruments that we believe have applicability to both assessment and training (see Table 50.1).

Acculturation has been broadly defined as "those phenomena which result when groups of individuals having different cultures come into continuous first-hand contact, with subsequent changes in the original cultural patterns of either or both groups" (Redfield, Linton, & Herskovits, 1937, p. 149). Acculturation is an important variable for racial and ethnic minorities (Ponterotto, Baluch, & Carielli, 1998) and has been referred to as one of the more dominant forces in research focusing on the experiences of racially and ethnically diverse populations (Kohatsu, 2005). Although the acculturation process occurs on both a societal and an individual level (Berry, 2003), individual acculturation (sometimes referred to as *psychological acculturation*) is typically the focus of most counseling assessments and refers to the cultural change of the individual as a result of continuous exposure to a second culture (Graves, 1967). Over the past decade, the study of the acculturation process of diverse populations has seen a number of advances (cf. Chun, Balls Organista, & Marín, 2003; Kohatsu, 2005; Sam & Berry, 2006). Although a review of this expansive body of literature is beyond the scope of this chapter, we wish to highlight two major advances: the linear and domain-specific nature of acculturation.

Linear Nature. Historically, there have been two common ways of conceptualizing how individuals experience the acculturation process: the unilinear and bilinear conceptual models. The unilinear model of acculturation was the first to appear in the literature and suggests that acculturation occurs along a single continuum with one's culture of origin on one end and the second culture at the other. According to the unilinear model, over time, an individual internalizes and adapts to a second culture (often referred to as the dominant or majority culture and usually referring specifically to European American culture) while necessarily and simultaneously losing ties with her or his culture of origin (Gordon, 1978). More recently, the bilinear model of acculturation, which asserts that an individual can

develop and maintain competence in a new culture while still retaining ties and competence in his or her culture of origin, has come into favor because it provides a more nuanced framework for understanding the way in which an individual orients him- or herself to multiple cultural contexts (cf. Chun et al., 2003; Kim & Abreu, 2001; Miller, 2007; Ryder, Alden, & Paulhus, 2000). Bilinear acculturation literature often includes the term *enculturation* to describe an individual's adherence and orientation to his or her culture of origin (Kim & Abreu, 2001). Thus, according to the bilinear model of acculturation, competence in the new culture (acculturation) can be conceptualized along one continuum and competence in the culture of origin (enculturation) can be conceptualized along another, distinct continuum (Cuellar, Arnold, & Maldonado, 1995). For example, a Hmong female might demonstrate a high level of engagement in European American culture (e.g., English-language proficiency, espousal of European American values, interacting with European Americans) while at the same time maintaining a high level of engagement in her culture of origin (e.g., fluency in language associated with culture of origin, participation in cultural traditions, espousal of values from culture of origin, interacting with other Hmong individuals).

Domain-Specific Nature. In addition to describing acculturation in terms of linearity, it is also possible to conceptualize the process as occurring across different dimensions or life domains (Szapocznik, Scopetta, Kurtines, & Aranalde, 1978). For example, acculturation can occur across such domains as (a) language ability, use, and preference; (b) social interactions and norms; (c) communication style; (d) family life, childrearing; (e) daily living habits; (f) culture-specific activities, practices, and traditions; (g) education, work, and school; (h) cultural identity; (i) worldview, belief systems, and values; and (j) cognitive processes (Arends-Tóth & van de Vijver, 2006). Furthermore, an individual may vary in levels of acculturation across these different dimensions or life domains (Tsai, Ying, & Lee, 2000). In other words, just because an individual demonstrates a high level of competence in a second culture language (e.g., English) does not mean that the individual also engages in other second culture domains with the same frequency and/or degree.

Recommendations for Assessing Acculturation. First, given the numerous acculturation measures available, we encourage counselors to be strategic in the measures they select and attend to the consistency between the acculturation domains of interest and the assessment protocol selected to operationalize acculturation. Second, we encourage researchers to use domain-specific bilinear measures (e.g., ARSMA-II) (Cuellar et al., 1995) or assessment protocols when interested in assessing acculturation. As previously noted, relying on unilinear measures will likely provide an incomplete understanding of the acculturation process. Third, given the complexity of the acculturation process, we encourage researchers to avoid relying on demographic or categorical variables (e.g., language spoken or number of years in the United States) as the sole indicators of acculturation. Such indicators fail to capture the numerous life domains that are involved in the acculturation process and therefore are not well suited to advance our understanding in this area (cf. Quintana, Troyano, & Taylor, 2001). In fact, in order to assess acculturation, it is likely that counselors will need to employ multiple acculturation protocols on more than one occasion. Fourth, we would suggest that counselors continue to incorporate acculturation/enculturation (cf. Kim, Atkinson, & Yang, 1999) in the practice of assessment. Accounting for the way in which individuals maintain and develop cultural values might further elucidate the experiences of culturally diverse populations.

Racial-Cultural Stressors

Client stress associated with race and culture can be thought of as occurring along two dimensions: stress associated with bias, discrimination, and prejudice, and stress associated with the acculturation process.

Racism-related stress refers to the "race-related transactions between individuals or groups and their environment that emerge from the dynamics of racism, and that are perceived to tax or exceed existing individual and collective resources or threaten well-being" (Harrell, 2000, p. 44). Racism-related stress has been linked to decreased psychological well-being (Pak, Dion, & Dion, 1991; Yoo & Lee, 2005), decreased physical health (Harrell, Marcellus, & Kalu, 1998), and cognitive impairment (Salvatore & Shelton, 2007) in racially

and ethnically diverse populations. In the following paragraphs, we highlight three important issues: the multifaceted nature, pervasive nature, and subjective nature of racism-related stress.

Multifaceted Nature. Experiences of racism can occur from interactions across individual, institutional, and cultural life domains, and racism-related stress can be experienced through racism-related life events, vicarious life experiences, daily racism microstressors, chronic contextual stressors, collective experiences, and transgenerational transmission (cf. Harrell, 2000). Recently, daily racism microstressors and/or microaggressions have been purported to be important components in understanding modern racism (Harrell, 2000). Pierce (1995) described microaggressions as "subtle, innocuous, preconscious, or unconscious degradations and putdowns" (p. 281). Furthermore, Pierce noted, "microaggressions may seem harmless, but the cumulative burden of a lifetime of microaggressions can theoretically contribute to diminished mortality, augmented morbidity, and flattened confidence" (p. 281). More recently, Sue et al. (2007) have built on this description and applied it more broadly by stating that microaggressions can be viewed as "brief and commonplace daily verbal, behavioral, or environmental indignities, whether intentional or unintentional, that communicate hostile, derogatory, or negative racial slights and insults toward people of color" (Sue et al., 2007, p. 273).

Pervasive Nature. The possibility of experiencing racism-related stress is an unfortunate daily reality for people of color (Utsey, 1999). "To live with the threat of racism means planning, almost every day of one's life, how to avoid or defend oneself against discrimination" (Essed, 1990, p. 260). Not surprisingly, people of color are likely to expend a considerable amount of psychological, emotional, and physical energy dealing with racism-related stress (Harrell, 2000; Utsey, Bolden, & Brown, 2001)—energy that could be used in other pursuits (e.g., workplace advancement, personal development, social justice advocacy). Utsey et al. have described six categories associated with reactions to racism, which could provide a useful framework for the assessment of racial stressors. The six categories are race-related trauma, racism-related fatigue, anticipatory racism reaction, race-related distress, racism-related confusion, and racism-related frustration. These categories represent a fairly comprehensive description of the types of psychological and emotional sequelae associated with experiencing and responding to racist events (Carter, 2007).

Subjective Nature. Although acts of racism are at times subtle and ambiguous, the psychological, emotional, and physical effects are insidious (Carter, 2007; Dovidio & Gaertner, 1986; Harrell, 2000). The individual's perception of the race-related event is of central importance to understanding the impact of racism-related stress (Harrell, 2000). In addition, the severity of the racism-related stress is more a function of the individual's perception and reaction rather than the specific racist act (Carter, 2007). An individual's perception of racism is likely affected by some combination of such factors as racial identity, stress reactivity, and personality (cf. Bolger & Zuckerman, 1995; Sellers & Shelton, 2003). Note that within a society that is built on the foundation of racial categorization and accompanying racism, individuals of color can also experience an internalization of racist beliefs and attitudes, also referred to as a false consciousness (Fanon, 1967). The manner in which beliefs of inferiority have been internalized is also an important consideration when thinking of the pervasive nature of racism (Speight, 2007).

Recommendations for Assessing Racism-Related Stress

First, when assessing racism-related stress, it is important to consider both the level of exposure and the level of reactivity to racism-related stressors (cf. Bolger & Zuckerman, 1995). In other words, it is important to consider *how much* and *how stressful* when assessing racism-related stress in people of color. Furthermore, Carter (2007) suggests giving more attention to the meaning and salience of clients' self-reports of racism-related stress and less attention to one-size-fits-all paradigms of assessment (e.g., *DSM-IV-TR*). Second, when determining the magnitude of racism-related stress, it is most effective to allow the client to set the parameters for what is and is not stressful (cf. Carter, 2007). In other words, certain events may or may not be perceived as

racist and/or stressful depending on the client, context, and so on. Third, regardless of using formal or informal assessment protocol, it is essential to evaluate multiple racism-related stressors across individual, institutional, and cultural domains. Similar to the domain-specific assessment of acculturation, when assessing racism-related stress, context is paramount. Fourth, because racism can be subtle (cf. Dovidio & Gaertner, 1986), it is important to consider the degree to which the selected assessment protocol taps into racism-related stressors in terms of nuance. For example, does the protocol assess only overt, concrete acts of racism (e.g., being called a derogatory racial slur), or does it also tap into subtler daily microaggressions? Finally, it is likely that most people of color experience stress related to experiences of racism, and we do not suggest that the perception and stress experience is the same for all people of color (Alvarez, Juang, & Liang, 2006). We encourage counselors to also consider how the sociopolitical context specific to clients' racial group membership affects the appropriateness of assessing racism-related stress.

Acculturative Stress

The acculturation process can result in physical, biological, relational, and psychological change (Berry & Kim, 1988) and therefore, can be stressful. *Acculturative stress* has been defined as "a reduction in the health status of individuals, and may include physical, psychological, and social aspects" (Berry et al., 1987, p. 492) that result in a reduction in that can lead to anxiety, depression, and psychosomatic symptoms (Oh, Koeske, & Sales, 2002; Williams & Berry, 1991). Acculturative stress includes perceived and/or actual difficulties across a number of life domains including language, education, work, intercultural interactions, values, and worldviews (Oh et al., 2002; Roysircar-Sodowsky & Maestas, 2000). In addition, the perceived incompatibility between one's culture of origin and the second culture can also be a point of stress (Benet-Martinez, 2003). Factors associated with acculturative stress include level of education, level of acculturation, and contact with other culture (Berry et al., 1987).

Probabilistic Nature. Acculturation does not necessarily lead to a stress reaction (Williams & Berry, 1991).

Instead, a number of factors moderate (buffer or exacerbate) the level of stress associated with the acculturation process, including the nature (i.e., level of acceptance of diversity) of the "host" society; the nature (e.g., voluntary, involuntary, refugee) of the acculturating group; pre-immigration history; social class; acculturation status (integration, assimilation, separation, marginalization); social and family support; and one's perceived ability to deal with the culture-specific stress (Berry et al., 1987; Rodriguez, Myers, Bingham Mira, Flores, & Garcia-Hernandez, 2002; Williams & Berry, 1991).

Recommendations for Assessing Acculturative Stress. First, when assessing acculturative stress, it is important to differentiate between acculturation-specific stress and other (e.g., racism related) stressors (cf. Rodriguez et al., 2002). It is therefore essential to select a measure of acculturative stress that taps life domains specific to the acculturation process. Second, depending on clients' generational status, years in the United States, and exposure to a second culture, different aspects of acculturative stress might be most salient. For example, for recent immigrants, assessing difficulties associated with the culture might be most relevant, whereas stress related to culture-of-origin difficulties might be more appropriate for later-generation individuals or those who have lived in the United States for their entire lives (Roysircar-Sodowsky & Maestas, 2000). Finally, because higher levels of perceived efficacy in dealing with acculturative stress are likely to reduce the negative impact of the stress experience, it might be important to (formally or informally) assess the client's perceived ability to deal with acculturative stress across a number of life domains (e.g., language, family environment, social interactions, perceived cultural incompatibilities, etc.).

Multicultural Personality

Recently, scholars have begun to investigate what has been described as the multicultural personality (cf. Ponterotto, Costa, & Werner-Lin, 2002; Ramirez, 1999; Van Der Zee & Van Oudenhoven, 2000, 2001). The *multicultural personality* consists of a number of traits and skill sets, including the following: emotional stability; a developed and secure sense of racial/ethnic identity; openness and commitment to cultural diversity; a sense of spirituality and connectedness with others; empathy, cognitive flexibility, and cultural curiosity; self-reflection and awareness of worldview, beliefs, biases regarding race, sexual orientation, and privilege; sense of humor; and multiple role competence (Ponterotto, Utsey, & Pedersen, 2006). In addition, individuals with a multicultural personality are likely to be engaged in social justice advocacy (Burkard & Ponterotto, 2008). At the conceptual level, the multicultural personality is compelling in that scholars suggest it might affect one's ability to thrive (vocationally, relationally, etc.) in an increasingly diverse society. It is also thought to have a positive impact on one's psychological and overall well-being (Burkard & Ponterotto, 2008). Recent empirical evidence has indicated a positive association between the multicultural personality and self-esteem, interpersonal functioning, and psychological adjustment and well-being (cf. Brummett, Wade, Ponterotto, Thombs, & Lewis, 2007; Burkard, Ponterotto, Johnson, & Costa, 2007; Ponterotto et al., 2007).

Recommendations for Assessing Multicultural Personality

First, it might be important to consider whether the trait or skill (or both) components of multicultural personality are most relevant for one's assessment needs (cf. Burkard & Ponterotto, 2008). Traits are stable aspects of personality, whereas skill level is dynamic (i.e., can change). Therefore, multicultural personality skills (e.g., ability to understand culturally diverse perspectives) might be an especially relevant target of assessment because both strengths and areas for improvement could be identified. In addition, skills assessment could be used to aid in planning counseling interventions. Second, to date, no measure encapsulates all aspects of multicultural personality articulated in the literature (Burkard & Ponterotto, 2008; Ponterotto et al., 2006). Therefore, if appropriate, one might use multiple pre-existing measures to capture the breadth of the multicultural personality. Finally, assessing multicultural personality might be especially salient for individuals traveling internationally and/or those working in culturally diverse environments. Assessment results could highlight individual strengths and also identify areas for improvement.

Utility of Quantitative Methods in Assessing Specific Racial-Cultural Factors

At present, there are a growing number of measures designed to assess psychological processes associated with acculturation, racial-cultural stressors, and multicultural personality (see Table 50.1). Although most of the measures have been used within the context of research, we suggest that these measures could be adapted for use within the assessment process. The use of measures designed primarily for research need to be adapted with caution to the clinical domain, but most measures contain sufficient information to give the clinician a sense of the meaning associated with a score. For example, the General Ethnic Discrimination Scale (GEDS) (Landrine et al., 2006) allows for the assessment of both the frequency and the appraised stressfulness of discrimination-related experiences. The scoring protocol simply involves adding the numeric value of the responses for each subscale. If the score is high, it reflects greater levels of the construct being assessed. As opposed to clinical scales that might include cut-off scores whereby a clinician can decide the extent of distress or pathology, the measures outlined in Table 50.1 provide the clinician with additional methods of obtaining important cultural information that represents critical data toward establishing a diagnosis or challenging a presumptive hypothesis (Ridley et al., 1998). As such, the use of such instruments fits well with the assessment procedures described in the earlier sections of this chapter.

CLINICIAN BIAS AND THE CLINICAL INTERVIEW

The Clinical Interview

The clinical interview has been described as the primary vehicle for gathering accurate information and as such is viewed as the "cornerstone of obtaining an accurate diagnosis and providing a target treatment" (Wiger & Huntley, 2002, p. 1). Some authors maintain what we view as a false dichotomy between the clinical interview as part of standard assessment procedures and the multicultural clinical interview as presenting an addition to the standard assessment (see McKitrick et al., 2007). Although the institutionalization of a Eurocentric worldview within counseling and psychology has necessitated a need to emphasize racial and cultural variables, we argue

that the culturally inclusive assessment should be viewed as *standard* assessment procedure. Indeed, the interview protocol outlined by Grieger (2008) is one that would enhance the quality of information gathered during the assessment process irrespective of the racial or cultural composition of the counseling or clinical dyad. It has been noted that people of color are projected to become a collective majority in the next few decades (Sue & Sue, 2003). Although this statistic does provide a sense of urgency to the call for culturally inclusive assessment, we cannot overlook the fact that all psychological assessment and intervention is inherently cultural in nature. As such, clinicians are as much a product of their cultural socialization as are their clients, irrespective of the specific cultural, racial, or ethnic group to which they belong. From this perspective, the most critical variable associated with a culturally inclusive assessment is the clinician, the instrument through which the assessment is undertaken. Kaufman (1994) has stated that the clinician has to be better than the instruments he or she employs, a statement that has particular relevance to the area of cultural inclusivity in the assessment process.

Clinician Bias as a Source of Error

The notion of error is generally associated with instrumentation, psychometric validity, and behavioral observation (Hartmann, Barrios, & Wood, 2004; Messick, 2005). However, if an accurate assessment is predicated on the reduction of error, then an ongoing self-assessment of "clinician error" (i.e., bias and ethnocentricity) becomes a central aspect of the assessment procedure (see Suzuki et al., 2005). Clinician error can be understood from the perspective of cultural orientation. Castillo (1997) provides a helpful framework within which to appreciate the role of culture within the assessment process. Specifically, Castillo argues that culture serves four fundamental functions. It provides a symbolic representation of the world; it allows for the construction and communication of realities; it directs individuals in relation to their interaction with the environment; and finally, it evokes affective processes that stem directly from the representational, constructive, and directive function of culture as a system of meaning. In relation to clinician bias, error can occur when clinicians fail to see their cultural worldview as *a* worldview and not *the* worldview. What becomes challenging for clinicians within the United States is the manner in which Eurocentric models of illness have been applied universally (Dana, 1998). Note that the system of diagnosis as outlined in the *DSM-IV-TR* is thought to have universal applicability, thereby underscoring the notion that Western or Eurocentric notions of mental illness have universal applicability. While the most recent edition of the *DSM* does offer guidelines for culture-specific diagnosis, it fails to acknowledge that the diagnostic system in the *DSM-IV-TR* itself is a cultural representation of reality. Thus, perhaps the most effective antidote to clinician bias is a recognition by the clinician of the manner in which his or her cultural socialization informs his or her evaluation of racial and cultural data. If the clinician is willing to view a client's racial and cultural experience as a legitimate, valid, and core aspect of the client's psychological functioning, the potential for bias is significantly reduced. If, however, the clinician holds a view that cultural and racial phenomena are secondary to what he or she views as universal processes of psychological distress, then the potential for error is significantly enhanced.

The final area of bias is associated with the interaction that is generated between the client and clinician, and the quality of the therapeutic relationship that ensues. Constructs such as cultural mistrust (Whaley, 2001), racial identity (Helms, 1995), and cultural worldview (Ibrahim, 1991) are variables that directly affect the qualitative nature of the counseling interaction and as such have a direct bearing on the type of information solicited during an assessment procedure, as well as the manner in which the clinician interprets the information. According to Hays (2008),

> At first, recognizing the complexity of cultural influences is more difficult than either ignoring these influences or simplifying them into a singular dimension. But in the long run, recognizing this complexity can lead therapists to a much deeper understanding of our clients and ourselves (p. 18)

Given the complexity associated with cultural influences and the tendency, particularly for novice clinicians, to feel overwhelmed in the process of incorporating culture within the assessment process, we have outlined a clinician checklist (see Table 50.2) as an attempt to provide a concrete self-assessment that clinicians can use to ensure accountability when undertaking assessment that, by definition, is culturally inclusive. Note that the checklist in essence summarizes some of the central points offered in this review and emphasizes the points we have offered on the utility of quantitative assessment and the potential for clinician error in the clinical interview.

Table 50.2 Clinician Checklist

Self-Awareness

- ☐ I have undertaken an inventory of my biases and socialization processes that might hinder my ability to undertake an effective assessment.
- ☐ I have reviewed the manner in which differences and similarities between the client and myself will affect our interaction.
- ☐ I have explored the manner in which my worldview might inform my interpretation of the client's experience.
- ☐ I have given thought to how my racial group membership might impede or enhance my relationship with the client.

Qualitative Assessment

- ☐ I have implemented a culturally inclusive assessment protocol that includes a focus on family, community, racial/cultural stressors, cultural identity, and client worldview.
- ☐ I have obtained observational data from additional sources such as family network and community networks.
- ☐ I have included a focus on the client's internal and external sources of strength.
- ☐ I have clearly outlined to my client the purpose of the interview and invited my client to collaborate or partner with me in the assessment process.
- ☐ I have incorporated within my assessment observational behavior that addresses cultural aspects of communication between the client and myself.
- ☐ I have included observations of the manner in which the client responded to, and interacted with, the quantitative assessments.

(Continued)

Table 50.2 (Continued)

Quantitative Assessment

☐ I have used only diagnostic instruments that have been validated on the racial-ethnic group of my client.
☐ I have included a quantitative assessment of identity, multicultural personality, worldview, acculturation, and racial/cultural stressors.
☐ I have included normative scores from the client's racial-cultural group when using standardized measures.
☐ I have clearly outlined the limitations of standardized measures as they apply to my client and where they are appropriate.
☐ I have used culture-specific instruments as needed.

CULTURAL ASSESSMENT AS A SOCIAL JUSTICE IMPERATIVE

The lack of consideration of cultural variables within counseling and psychology has been discussed from the perspective of ethics and malpractice (Fouad & Arredondo, 2006; Hall, 1997). Specifically, psychological interventions that fail to address the cultural component of a client's experience can be considered to be practice that is inconsistent with the ethical standards articulated by professional associations such as the American Psychological Association (2002) and the American Counseling Association (2006). As Ridley et al. (2008) argue, "No other ethical issue compares in importance to making an accurate, sound, and comprehensive assessment of clients" (p. 22). Given the plethora of information available with regard to culturally inclusive assessment (Dana, 2005), as well as the emerging evidence supporting the utility of culturally adapted interventions (Griner & Smith, 2006), assessment procedures that do not incorporate culture could now be viewed from the perspective of clinical malpractice.

Additionally, the social justice movement within counseling and psychology stresses the need for psychologists to be cognizant of the manner in which psychological and counseling interventions such as inappropriate testing procedures might further discriminate and oppress individuals from nondominant groups within the United States (e.g., people of color; gay, lesbian, bisexual, and transgendered individuals; individuals living in poverty; and First Nations or indigenous individuals and groups) (Crethar, Torres-Rivera, & Nash, 2008; Duran, Firehammer, & Gonzalez, 2008; Toporek, Gerstein, Fouad, Roysircar, & Israel, 2006). From a social justice perspective, assessment procedures that incorporate racial and cultural variables when relevant are seen as a fundamental human right.

SUMMARY AND CONCLUSION

The need to attend to cultural variables within assessment is now considered to be standard practice, yet the extent to which counselors and psychologists implement culturally inclusive assessment on a day-to-day basis remains unclear. As highlighted in this chapter, a number of assessment protocols centralize multicultural variables and as such provide excellent guides toward a culturally inclusive assessment protocol. This chapter has also emphasized the process of acculturation, the presence of racial-cultural stressors, and those attributes of personality considered to be multicultural as important variables to include in the assessment process. Finally, the role of the clinician cannot be overemphasized, as the clinician is the instrument through which a culturally inclusive assessment is undertaken. Although multicultural assessment is now more widely accepted, there remains a need to further highlight the ethical nature of multicultural assessment and to require that all clinicians display a minimal level of competence in their ability to assess clients of all cultural backgrounds. Until those requirements can be fully met, there remains the potential for ethical malpractice and the provision of ineffective services to people of color and other nondominant cultural groups within the United States and abroad.

REFERENCES

Alvarez, A. N., Juang, L., & Liang, C. T. H. (2006). Asian Americans and racism: When bad things happen to "model minorities." *Cultural Diversity and Ethnic Minority Psychology, 12,* 477–492.

American Counseling Association. (2006). ACA code of ethics. *Journal of Counseling & Development, 84,* 235–254.

American Psychological Association. (2002). Ethical principles of psychologists and code of conduct. *American Psychologist, 57,* 1060–1073.

American Psychological Association. (2003). Guidelines on multicultural education, training, research, practice, and organizational change for psychologists. *American Psychologist, 58,* 377–402.

Arredondo, P., Toporek, R., Pack Brown, S., Jones, J., Locke, D., Sanchez, K., & Stadler, H. (1996). Operationalization of the multicultural counseling competencies. *Journal of Multicultural Counseling and Development, 24,* 42–78.

Arends-Tóth, J., & van de Vijver, F. J. R. (2006). *Assessment of psychological acculturation.* New York: Cambridge University Press.

Benet-Martinez, V. (2003). *The Riverside Acculturation Stress Inventory (RASI): Development and psychometric properties.* Technical Report, Department of Psychology, University of California at Riverside.

Berry, J. W. (2003). Conceptual approaches to acculturation. In K. M. Chun, P. Balls Organista, & G. Marín (Eds.), *Acculturation: Advances in theory, measurement, and applied research* (pp. 17–37). Washington, DC: American Psychological Association.

Berry, J. W., & Kim, U. (1988). Accultural and mental health. In P. R. Dasen, J. W. Berry, & N. Sartorius (Eds.), *Health and cross-cultural psychology: Toward applications* (pp. 207–236). Newbury Park, CA: Sage.

Bolger, N., & Zuckerman, A. (1995). A framework for studying personality in the stress process. *Journal of Personality and Social Psychology, 69,* 890–902.

Brondolo, E., Kelly, K. P., Coakley, V., Gordon, T., Thompson, S., Levy, E., Cassells, A., Tobin, J. N., Sweeney, M., & Contrada, R. J. (2005). The Perceived Ethnic Discrimination Questionnaire: Development and preliminary validation of a community version. *Journal of Applied Social Psychology, 35,* 335–365.

Brummett, B. R., Wade, J. C., Ponterotto, J. G., Thombs, B., & Lewis, C. (2007). Psychological well-being and a multicultural personality disposition. *Journal of Counseling and Development, 85,* 73–81.

Burkard, A. W., & Ponterotto, J. G. (2008). Cultural identity, racial identity, and the multicultural personality. In L. A. Suzuki & J. G. Ponterotto (Eds.), *Handbook of multicultural assessment: Clinical, psychological, and educational applications* (3rd ed., pp. 52–72). San Francisco: Jossey-Bass.

Burkard, A. W., Ponterotto, J. G., Johnson, A., & Costa, C. I. (2007). *The multicultural personality: A preliminary investigation.* Manuscript under review.

Carter, R. T. (2007). Racism and psychological and emotional injury: Recognizing and assessing race-based traumatic stress. *Counseling Psychologist, 35,* 13–105.

Carter, R. T., & Qureshi, A. (1995). A typology of philosophical assumptions in multicultural counseling and training. In J. G. Ponterotto, J. M. Casas, L. A. Suzuki, & C. M. Alexander (Eds.), *Handbook of multicultural counseling* (pp. 239–262). Thousand Oaks, CA: Sage.

Castillo, R. J. (1997). *Culture and mental illness: A client-centered approach.* Boston: Brooks/Cole.

Chun, K. M., Balls Organista, P., & Marín, G. (Eds.). (2003). *Acculturation: Advances in theory, measurement, and applied research.* Washington, DC: American Psychological Association.

Crethar, H. C., Torres-Rivera, E., & Nash, S. (2008). In search of common threads: Linking multicultural, feminist, and social justice counseling paradigms. *Journal of Counseling & Development, 86,* 269–278.

Cuellar, I., Arnold, B., & Maldonado, R. (1995). Acculturation Rating Scale for Mexican Americans-II: A revision of the original ARSMA scale. *Hispanic Journal of Behavioral Sciences, 17,* 245–304.

Dana, R. H. (1996). Culturally competent assessment practice in the United States. *Journal of Personality Assessment, 66,* 472–487.

Dana, R. H. (1998). Multicultural assessment of personality and psychopathology in the United States: Still art, not yet science, and controversial. *European Journal of Psychological Assessment, 14,* 62–70.

Dana, R. H. (2005). *Multicultural assessment: Principles, applications and examples.* Mahwah, NJ: Lawrence Erlbaum.

D'Andrea, M., & Heckman, E. F. (2008). A 40-year review of multicultural counseling outcome research: Outlining a future research agenda for the multicultural counseling movement. *Journal of Counseling and Development, 86,* 356–363.

Dovidio, J. F., & Gaertner, S. L. (Eds.). (1986). *Prejudice, discrimination, and racism.* San Diego, CA: Academic Press.

Duran, E., Firehammer, J., & Gonzalez, J. (2008). Liberation psychology as the path toward healing cultural wounds. *Journal of Counseling & Development, 86,* 288–295.

Essed, P. (1990). *Everyday racism: Reports from women of two cultures.* Claremont, CA: Hunter House.

Fanon, F. (1967). *Black skin White masks* (C. L. Markmann, Trans.). New York: Grove Press.

Fouad, N. A., & Arredondo, P. (2006). Evaluating cultural identity and biases. In N. A. Fouad & P. Arredondo (Eds.), *Becoming culturally oriented: Practical advice for psychologists and educators* (pp. 15–34). Washington, DC: American Psychological Association.

Garrett, M. T., & Pichette, E. G. (2000). Red as an apple: Native American acculturation and counseling with or without reservation. *Journal of Counseling and Development, 78,* 3–13.

Gordon, M. M. (1978). *Human nature, class and ethnicity.* New York: Oxford University Press.

Gim Chung, R. H., Kim, B. S. K., & Abreu, J. M. (2004). Asian American Multidimensional Acculturation Scale: Development, factor analysis, reliability, and validity. *Cultural Diversity and Ethnic Minority Psychology, 10,* 66–80.

Graves, T. D. (1967). Acculturation, access, and alcohol in a tri-ethnic community. *American Anthropologist, 69,* 306–321.

Grieger, I. (2008). A cultural assessment framework and interview protocol. In L. A. Suzuki & J. G. Ponterotto (Eds.), *Handbook of multicultural assessment: Clinical, psychological, and educational applications* (pp. 132–161). San Francisco: Jossey-Bass.

Grieger, I., & Ponterotto, J. G. (1995). A framework for assessment in multicultural counseling. In J. G. Ponterotto, J. M. Casas, L. A. Suzuki, & C. M. Alexander (Eds.), *Handbook of multicultural counseling* (pp. 357–374). Thousand Oaks, CA: Sage.

Griner, D., & Smith, T. (2006). Culturally adapted mental health interventions: A meta-analytic review. *Psychotherapy: Theory, Research, Practice, and Training, 43,* 531–548.

Hall, C. C. (1997). Cultural malpractice: The growing obsolescence of psychology with the changing U.S. population. *American Psychologist, 52,* 642–651.

Harrell, S. P. (2000). A multidimensional conceptualization of racism-related stress: Implications for the well-being of people of color. *American Journal of Orthopsychiatry, 70,* 42–57.

Harrell, S. P., Marcellus, M. M., & Kalu, J. (1998). Racism, stress and disease. In R. L. Jones (Ed.), *African American mental health.* Hampton, VA: Cobb & Henry.

Hartmann, D. P., Barrios, B. A., & Wood, D. D. (2004). Principles of behavioral observation. In S. N. Haynes & E. M. Heiby (Eds.), *Comprehensive handbook of psychological assessment* (Vol. 3, pp. 108–127). Hoboken, NJ: Wiley.

Hays, P. A. (2008). *Addressing cultural complexities in practice* (2nd ed.). Washington DC: American Psychological Association.

Helms, J. E. (1995). Update of Helm's White and People of Color racial identity models. In J. G. Ponterotto, J. M. Casas, L. A. Suzuki, & C. M. Alexander (Eds.), *Handbook of multicultural counseling* (pp. 181–198). Thousand Oaks, CA: Sage.

Helms, J. E., & Richardson, T. Q. (1997). How "multiculturalism" obscures race and culture as differential aspects of counseling competency. In D. B. Pope-Davis & H. L. K. Coleman (Eds.), *Multicultural counseling competencies: Assessment, education, training, and supervision.* Thousand Oaks, CA: Sage.

Ibrahim, F. A. (1991). Contribution of cultural worldview to generic counseling and development. *Journal of Counseling & Development, 70,* 13–19.

Kaufman, A. S. (1994). *Intelligence testing with the WISC-III.* New York: Wiley.

Kim, B. S. K., & Abreu, J. M. (2001). Acculturation measurement: Theory, current instruments, and future directions. In J. G. Ponterotto, J. M. Casas, L. A. Suzuki, & C. M. Alexander (Eds.), *Handbook of multicultural counseling* (2nd ed., pp. 394–424). Thousand Oaks, CA: Sage.

Kim, B. S. K., Atkinson, D. R., & Yang, P. H. (1999). The Asian values scale: Development, factor analysis, validation, and reliability. *Journal of Counseling Psychology, 46,* 342–352.

Kim, B. S. K., Li, L. C., & Ng, G. (2005). The Asian American Values Scale–Multidimensional: Development, reliability, and validity. *Cultural Diversity and Ethnic Minority Psychology, 11,* 187–201.

Kohatsu, E. L. (2005). Acculturation: Current and future directions. In R. T. Carter (Ed.), *Handbook of racial-cultural psychology and counseling* (pp. 207–231). Hoboken, NJ: Wiley.

Landrine, H., Klonoff, E. A., Corral, I., Fernandez, S., & Roesch, S. (2006). Conceptualizing and measuring ethnic discrimination in health research. *Journal of Behavioral Medicine, 29,* 79–93.

Lee, R. M., Choe, J., Kim, G., & Ngo, V. (2000). Construction of the Asian American Family Conflicts Scale. *Journal of Counseling Psychology, 47,* 211–222.

Liang, C. T. H., Li, L. C., & Kim, B. S. K. (2004). The Asian American Racism-Related Stress Inventory: Development, factor analysis, reliability, and validity. *Journal of Counseling Psychology, 51,* 103–114.

Malgady, R. G., & Colon-Malgady, G. (2008). Building community test norms: Considerations for ethnic minority populations. In L. A. Suzuki & J. G. Ponterotto (Eds.), *Handbook of multicultural assessment: Clinical, psychological, and educational applications* (pp. 34–51). San Francisco: Jossey-Bass.

Malgady, R. G., Rogler, L. H., & Constantino, G. (1987). Ethnocultural and linguistic bias in mental health evaluation of Hispanics. *American Psychologist, 42,* 228–234.

Marger, M. (2008). *Race and ethnic relations: American and global perspectives* (8th ed.). Belmont, CA: Wadsworth.

Mattaini, M. A. (2005). Mapping practice: Assessment, context, and social justice. In A. K. Stuart (Ed.), *Mental disorders in the social environment* (pp. 62–82). New York: Columbia University Press.

McKitrick, D. S., Edwards, T. A., & Sola, A. B. (2007). Multicultural issues. In M. Hersen & J. C. Thomas (Eds.), *Handbook of clinical interviewing with adults* (pp. 64–78). Thousand Oaks, CA: Sage.

Messick, S. (1995). Validity of psychological assessment: Validation of inferences from persons' responses and performances as scientific inquiry into score meaning. *American Psychologist, 50,* 741–749.

Miller, M. J. (2007). A bilinear multidimensional measurement model of Asian American acculturation and enculturation: Implications for counseling interventions. *Journal of Counseling Psychology, 54,* 118–131.

Miville, M. L., Gelso, C. J., Pannu, R., Liu, W., Touradji, P., Holloway, P., & Fuertes, J. (1999). Appreciating similarities and valuing differences: The Miville-Guzman Universality-Diversity Scale. *Journal of Counseling Psychology, 46,* 291–307.

Moodley, R., & Palmer, S. (2006). *Race, culture and psychotherapy: Critical perspectives in multicultural practice.* London: Routledge.

Neville, H. A., Lilly, R. L., Duran, G., Lee, R. M., & Browne, L. (2000). Construction and initial validation of the Color-Blind Racial Attitudes Scale (CoBRAS). *Journal of Counseling Psychology, 47,* 59–70.

Oh, U., Koeske, G. F., & Sales, E. (2002). Acculturation, stress, and depressive symptoms among Korean immigrants in the United States. *Journal of Social Psychology, 142,* 511–526.

Pak, A., Dion, K. L., & Dion, K. K. (1991). Social-psychological correlates of experienced discrimination: Test of the double jeopardy hypothesis. *International Journal of Intercultural Relations, 15,* 243–253.

Pierce, C. M. (1995). Stress analogs of racism and sexism: Terrorism, torture, and disaster. In C. V. Willie, P. P. Rieker, B. M. Kramer, & B. S. Brown (Eds.), *Mental health, racism, and sexism* (pp. 277–298). Pittsburgh, PA: University of Pittsburgh Press.

Ponterotto, J. G., Baluch, S., & Carielli, D. (1998). The Suinn-Lew Asian self-identity acculturation scale (SL-ASIA): Critique and research recommendations. *Measurement & Evaluation in Counseling & Development, 31,* 109–124.

Ponterotto, J. G., Costa, C. I., Brobst, K., Spelliscy, D., Mendelsohn-Kacanski, J., Scheinholtz, J., & Martines, D. (2007). Multicultural personality dispositions and psychological well-being. *Journal of Social Psychology, 147,* 119–136.

Ponterotto, J. G., Costa, C. I., & Werner-Lin, A. (2002). Research perspectives in cross-cultural counseling. In P. B. Pedersen, J. G. Draguns, W. J. Lonner, & J. E. Trimble (Eds.), *Counseling across cultures* (5th ed., pp. 395–420). Thousand Oaks, CA: Sage.

Ponterotto, J. G., Utsey, S. O., & Pedersen, P. B. (2006). *Preventing prejudice: A guide for counselors, educators, and parents* (2nd ed.). Thousand Oaks, CA: Sage.

Pope-Davis, D. B., & Coleman, H. L. K. (Eds.). (2003). *The intersection of race, class, and gender in multicultural counseling.* Thousand Oaks, CA: Sage.

Quintana, S. M., Troyano, N., & Taylor, G. (2001). Cultural validity and inherent challenges in quantitative methods for multicultural research. In J. G. Ponterotto, J. M. Casas, L. A. Suzuki, & C. M. Alexander (Eds.), *Handbook of multicultural counseling* (2nd ed., pp. 604–630). Thousand Oaks, CA: Sage.

Ramirez, M. (1999). *Multicultural psychotherapy: An approach to individual and cultural differences* (2nd ed.). New York: Pergamon.

Redfield, R., Linton, R., & Herskovits, M. J. (1937). Memorandum for the study of acculturation. *American Anthropologist, 38,* 149–152.

Ridley, C., Hill, C., & Li, L. (1998). Multicultural assessment: Reexamination, reconceptualization, and practical application. *Counseling Psychologist, 26,* 827–910.

Ridley, C. R., Tracey, M. L., Pruitt-Stephens, L., Wimsatt, M. K., & Beard, J. (2008). Multicultural assessment validity: The preeminent ethics issues in psychological assessment. In L. A. Suzuki & J. G. Ponterotto (Eds.), *Handbook of multicultural assessment: Clinical, psychological, and educational applications* (pp. 22–33). San Francisco: Jossey-Bass.

Rodriguez, N., Myers, H. F., Bingham Mira, C., Flores, T., & Garcia-Hernandez, L. (2002). Development of the Multidimensional Acculturative Stress Inventory for adults of Mexican origin. *Psychological Assessment, 14,* 451–461.

Roysircar-Sodowsky, G., & Kuo, P. Y. (2001). Determining cultural validity of personality assessment: Some guidelines. In D. Pope-Davis & H. L. K. Coleman (Eds.), *The intersection of race, class, & gender: Implications for multicultural counseling* (pp. 213–239). Thousand Oaks, CA: Sage.

Roysircar-Sodowsky, G., & Maestas, M. V. (2000). Acculturation, ethnic identity, and acculturative stress: Evidence and measurement. In R. H. Dana (Ed.), *Handbook of cross-cultural and multicultural personality assessment* (pp. 131–172). Mahwah, NJ: Lawrence Erlbaum.

Ryder, A. G., Alden, L. E., & Paulhus, D. L. (2000). Is acculturation unidimensional or bidimensional? A head-to-head comparison in the prediction of personality, self-identity, and adjustment. *Journal of Personality and Social Psychology, 79,* 49–65.

Salvatore, J., & Shelton, J. N. (2007). Cognitive costs of exposure to racial prejudice. *Psychological Science, 18,* 810–815.

Sam, D. L., & Berry, J. W. (Eds.). (2006). *The Cambridge handbook of acculturation psychology.* New York: Cambridge University Press.

Sellers, R. M., & Shelton, J. N. (2003). The role of racial identity in perceived racial discrimination. *Journal of Personality and Social Psychology, 84,* 1079–1092.

Spanierman, L. B., & Heppner, M. J. (2004). Psychosocial Costs of Racism to Whites scale (PCRW): Construction and initial validation. *Journal of Counseling Psychology, 51,* 249–262.

Speight, S. L. (2007). Internalized racism: One more piece of the puzzle. *Counseling Psychologist, 35,* 126–134.

Stephenson, M. (2000). Development and validation of the Stephenson Multigroup Acculturation Scale (SMAS). *Psychological Assessment, 12,* 77–88.

Suarez-Morales, L., Dillon, F. R., & Szapocznik, J. (2007). Validation of the Acculturative Stress Inventory for Children. *Cultural Diversity and Ethnic Minority Psychology, 13,* 216–224.

Sue, D. W., Capodilupo, C. M., Torino, G. C., Bucceri, J. M., Holder, A. M. B., Nadal, K. L., & Esquilin, M. (2007). Racial microaggressions in everyday life: Implications for clinical practice. *American Psychologist, 62,* 271–286.

Sue, D. W., & Sue, D. (2003). *Counseling the culturally diverse: Theory and practice* (4th ed.). Hoboken, NJ: Wiley.

Suzuki, L. A., Kugler, J. F., & Aguiar, L. J. (2005). Assessment practices in racial-cultural psychology. In R. T. Carter (Ed.), *Handbook of racial-cultural psychology and counseling* (Vol. 2, pp. 297–315). Hoboken, NJ: Wiley.

Szapocznik, J., Scopetta, M. A., Kurtines, W., & Aranalde, M. D. (1978). Theory and measurement of acculturation. *Revista Interamericana de Psicología, 12,* 113–130.

Toporek, R. L., Gerstein, L. H., Fouad, N. A., Roysircar, G., & Israel, T. (Eds.). (2006). *Handbook of social justice in counseling psychology: Leadership, vision, and action.* Thousand Oaks, CA: Sage.

Tsai, J. L., Ying, Y., & Lee, P. A. (2000). The meaning of "being Chinese" and "being American": Variation among Chinese American young adults. *Journal of Cross-Cultural Psychology, 31,* 302–332.

Utsey, S. O. (1999). Development and validation of a short form of the Index of Race-Related Stress (IRRS)—Brief Version. *Measurement and Evaluation in Counseling and Development, 32,* 149–167.

Utsey, S. O., Bolden, M. A., & Brown, A. L. (2001). Visions of revolution from the spirit of Frantz Fanon: A psychology of liberation for counseling African Americans confronting societal racism and oppression. In J. G. Ponterotto, J. M. Casas, L. A. Suzuki, & C. M. Alexander (Eds.), *Handbook of multicultural counseling* (2nd ed., pp. 290–310). Thousand Oaks, CA: Sage.

Utsey, S. O., Adams, E. P., & Bolden, M. (2000). Development and initial validation of the Africultural Coping Systems Inventory. *Journal of Black Psychology, 26,* 194–215.

Van Der Zee, K. I., & Van Oudenhoven, J. P. (2000). The Multicultural Personality Questionnaire: A multidimensional instrument of multicultural effectiveness. *European Journal of Personality, 14,* 291–309.

Van Der Zee, K. I., & Van Oudenhoven, J. P. (2001). The Multicultural Personality Questionnaire: Reliability and validity of self and other ratings of multicultural effectiveness. *Journal of Research in Personality, 35,* 278–288.

Wang, Y., Davidson, M. M., Yakushko, O. F., Savoy, H. B., Tan, J. A., & Bleier, J. K. (2003). The Scale of Ethnocultural Empathy: Development, validation, and reliability. *Journal of Counseling Psychology, 50,* 221–234.

Whaley, A. L. (2001). Cultural mistrust: An important psychological construct for diagnosis and treatment of African Americans. *Professional Psychology: Research and Practice, 32,* 555–562.

Wiger, D., & Huntley, D. (2002). *Essentials of interviewing.* New York: Wiley.

Williams, C. L., & Berry, J. W. (1991). Primary prevention of acculturative stress among refugees: Application of psychological theory and practice. *American Psychologist, 46,* 632–641.

Yoo, H. C., & Lee, R. M. (2005). Ethnic identity and approach-type coping as moderators of the racial discrimination/well-being relation in Asian Americans. *Journal of Counseling Psychology, 52,* 497–506.

Zea, M. C., Asner-Self, K. K. Birman, D., & Buki, L. P. (2003). The Abbreviated Multidimensional Acculturation Scale: Empirical validation with two Latino/Latina samples. *Cultural Diversity and Ethnic Minority Psychology, 9,* 107–126.

51

Advances in Multicultural Assessment and Counseling With Culturally Diverse Older Adults

LUIS A. VÁZQUEZ, MERRANDA MARÍN,
AND ENEDINA GARCÍA-VÁZQUEZ

A Shared Experience

An elder named Juanita reaches for my hand while sitting in her wheelchair as we roll through an adult senior care facility. Juanita doesn't know who I am, but holds my hand with great trust as we share our time together. We roll through the corridors, we wave at other elder adults or stop to say hello, and at other times stay and chat for a while. She speaks only Spanish, smiling often because those around her speak only English. She looks up at me to translate, because I have become her ambassador to the other elder adults in the facility. It is time for lunch. Our journey in the wheelchair comes to a slow stop at a table with a plate of food that Juanita stares at in a strange way. I explain in Spanish what's on her plate and how good it is for her. I, too, have decided to eat the same things. Juanita stares at me and begins to laugh as I fasten a large napkin to cover her blouse in case of spills. I carefully help feed Juanita and chat about little things that she likes to talk

about, such as the weather, other people, gossip, and *las novelas* (Spanish soap operas). When lunchtime ends, I carefully clean Juanita, then we roll back to her room.

There, she loves to watch Spanish *novelas*. We sit together and she repeats everything she sees on the television, and it sounds like what happened in the *novela* happened in real life just yesterday. Juanita shares these incidents with great enthusiasm and worry as to what will happen next to everyone in the *novela*. As time passes throughout the day, it is time for Juanita to rest. She often looks at me and asks, "Quien eres?" Who are you? "Vienes mañana?" Will you come tomorrow? I gently hold her hand and kiss her on the forehead and say, "Si, vengo mañana." Yes, I will be here tomorrow. I cover her with a warm blanket and walk down the hallway with tears in my eyes. I have come to accept that Juanita's time is near and she will soon cross over to the spirit world.

During the visits to the senior facility, I became very acquainted with the staff. I began to explore the possibility

667

of having bilingual staff and ways for the staff to communicate with Juanita, because her doctors also spoke only English. The staff director shared her difficulties in finding bilingual staff in a small Midwestern town. I decided to explore options that might help Juanita and elders like herself. I developed cards that showed actions that the staff wanted Juanita to do with them and trained the staff to ask Juanita to teach them the Spanish words for those actions. Soon, the staff began to use short Spanish phrases with Juanita. Through a collaborative approach and challenging conversations with the director, we were able to identify two bilingual workers for the facility and found out that one worker in the facility knew how to speak Spanish, but was shy to use her language skills. I worked closely with this staff member. Her confidence increased, and the director realized what a valuable skill this worker could share with the patients. The director and I talked about incentives for the worker for using her language skills. A strong, positive relationship began to develop with the worker and her director. During this same time, another elder adult was admitted to the facility that spoke only Spanish. She had become Juanita's roommate.

The days passed, and I became very familiar with the staff. They had no idea how much they helped Juanita, who had become much more comfortable with them, and how much they helped me. The staff often shared Spanish phrases with me, and I strongly encouraged them and praised them for their work. I visited the senior citizen facility for 12 consecutive days from 7:30 am to 8:00 pm every day. I made friends with many residents and spent a great amount of time with Juanita. At times, I listened to other sons and daughters who had their elders in the facility and helped them form a support group. Some even began to have lunch together. At the end of the 12 days, it was time to return home to my own family across the country. The last day visiting the facility was one of the hardest days of my life.

A few weeks later, Juanita had crossed over to the spirit world. Juanita spent the last month before she crossed over in the senior citizen facility with daily visits from three of my siblings and me. All of us spent many nights after our visits reflecting on our early years with Juanita. At times we laughed, and at other times we cried.

Juanita was in the last stages of Alzheimer's. The days I spent with her were very precious and, at the same time, some of the emotionally hardest days I had lived through with my mother, Juanita. She needed a level of care that none of us could provide—24 hours a day in the last weeks of her life. We needed help. This was the hardest decision we had to face, because it went against every cultural value with which we grew up in our family. There were many difficult discussions with a great deal of emotion expressed until we reached our decision. It was so hard that I spent many nights crying in my sleep dealing with this decision.

It's been more than a year since I was rolling down the hallway at the senior citizen facility. I can still feel her hand in mine as she would look up at me and ask, "Quien eres?" Who are you? And where are we going? I came to realize that I, Luis A. Vázquez, had become a familiar stranger.

Who Are the Culturally Diverse Older Adults, and Why Are They Important?

Careful examination of the culturally diverse older adult is essential in the promotion of quality care. One cannot provide quality of care if we are not aware of demographic and cultural issues that could affect such care. Overall life expectancy rates in the United States suggest that people are living longer and healthier lives. In 2000, average life expectancy at birth rose to 76.9 from 47.3 in 1900 (U.S. Census Bureau, 2005). Moreover, increases in immigration and high birth rates have contributed to a diversification among the older adult. In fact, such noted changes in demographics have led to a trend now referred to as "the browning of America" in lieu of the noted "graying of America" (Hayes-Bautista, Hsu, Perez, & Gamboa, 2002, p. 15). In 2003, nearly 83% of the older adult population, defined as those 65 years and older, was made up of non-Hispanic Whites, whereas Blacks, Hispanics, and Asians accounted for 8%, 6%, and 3%, respectively (U.S. Census Bureau, 2005). Projections indicate that by 2030, the composition of the elderly population will be more diverse, thereby calling attention to health-related issues unique to this segment of the population (U.S. Census Bureau, 2005).

Factors such as cultural and language differences as well as physical isolation and lower income typically make U.S. health care services difficult for persons of color (AARP, 2008). Furthermore, caring for culturally diverse older adults also has an impact on the family system. In 2003, older adult Black, Asian, and Hispanic women were more likely to live with relatives as compared to older adult non-Hispanic White women (U.S. Census Bureau, 2005). Overall, people of color receive a lower quality of health and medical care than the non-Hispanic White population (Institute of Medicine, 2002).

The health care preferences among people of color can be attributed to issues related to trust, cultural values, traditional healing practices, and language communication. A history related to the Tuskegee experiments with syphilis and sterilization in African American men is simply one example of racially motivated disparities in health care (Shavers, Lynch, & Burmeister, 2000). These disparities are also related to a history of separate hospitals for people of color, creating high levels of distrust. The idea among minority groups of often self-sacrificing, minimizing mental and physical illness, with an external view of illness, greatly affects participation in quality health care. Among several of the ethnic minority groups, some of the traditional practices have been passed down from the elders through herbal remedies, spiritual healing practices for illnesses, healing ceremonies, and sweat lodges. The strong adherence to these beliefs and the lack of acknowledgment of these beliefs among mainstream health care givers creates many misunderstandings. Finally, the lack of health care givers and the system's inability to communicate with its patients in their native language has also created many disparities in quality of care, misdiagnosis, and a strong lack of trust. The issues discussed have led to the exacerbation of the illnesses that affect each of the ethnic groups.

Across African Americans, Latino/a Americans, Native Americans, and Asian Americans, the prevalence of diabetes is 2.2 to 3 times higher than that of their White counterparts (Johnson & Smith, 2002). Hypertension and high blood pressure develop earlier and at a much higher rate for African Americans and Native Americans than for their White counterparts. African American men have higher rates of cancer, followed by African American women, who are more likely to die from breast cancer. The irony is that White women are more often diagnosed with breast cancer. Cancer death rates are also increasing in Latino/a

Americans and Native Americans. Access to and quality of mental health services has been dismal for minority populations due to limited bilingual counselors and lack of preventive services, along with a lack of understanding of cultural issues for minority group members. It is evident that understanding health disparities is a complex process among the various ethnic/racial older adults.

There is considerable research that shows that health-related issues correlate at various levels with socioeconomic status (Yen & Syme, 1999). Health care providers and health systems often attribute the lack of people of color participating in health care as an economic issue and not a racial/ethnic issue. However, even when using a multivariate analysis that includes socioeconomic status, cultural context, family structure, residential stability, race/ethnicity, and language differences, disparities in health care usage by people of color does not disappear (Johnson & Smith, 2002). This implies that we need to educate ourselves on understanding the processes and preferences that continually result in different outcomes for minority populations in their use of health care.

The heterogeneity of within-group differences directly affects how culturally diverse older adults use health care services to meet their needs. There are three cultures that must merge: the culture of the health profession and how it acculturates its students; the culture of the health care professional and how it affects how he or she serves others; and the culture of the patient and how it affects the process. The combination of each of these cultures has an impact on the success of the outcome, which affects the quality of life for culturally diverse older adults (Johnson & Smith, 2002). A discussion of these three cultures would necessitate a chapter for each; however, a brief explanation of how they affect each other is noteworthy at this point.

The culture of the health profession trains and teaches students the definition of wellness, appropriate behaviors for their patients, and appropriate values for health care. For example, very few training programs have a course on poverty, culture, and gerontology to help trainees understand how these factors have a direct impact on the decision-making process in accessing quality care. Many programs also lack a rural health course to help students understand the decisions that many patients have to make when living in rural areas, great distances from any health care facility. There is also a lack of understanding and training in programs about how to work with interpreters/translators when the professional is not able to speak the native language of the patient (Vázquez, 2004). Finally, very few programs do an adequate job of teaching students the meaning and processes of traditional healing practices across cultures. Of course, it would be impossible to learn about every culture. On the other hand, it behooves every program to educate and train students on how to research, explore, interpret, and understand how cultural information can affect the decision-making process of patients in health care. A revamping of curriculum and a re-education of faculty in relation to the understanding of the impact of culture is necessary in order to reverse the health disparities that are currently present in the health care profession (Vázquez & García-Vázquez, 2003).

The culture of the health care professional is of utmost importance in helping trainees understand how they affect their patients. As trainees, professionals are taught to acculturate to the program's values and view of health care. In translation, this means to adopt the worldview and identity set forth by the program for health care. However, it is very important for the health care professional to understand how his or her worldview and identity affect his or her view of health care. The professional needs to understand how his or her values are similar to and different from the program of training—in what areas he or she has compromised or adopted the values of the program in place of his or her values. Self-awareness of the professional's biases, prejudices, and views of health care and openness in helping the patient understand his or her own values about health care will help lead to a quality and successful outcome for the patient. The ability of the professional to explore and understand the patient's values requires cultural competence in working with the diversity of the patient. Above all, understanding the culture of the patient is the most important variable in understanding the process and outcome of success for the quality of care for the patient. The patient's worldview of wellness, history with health care, family structure, environmental issues, and understanding of quality of care will enhance the success in any type of treatment that is agreed upon with the patient. The

following paragraphs open the discussion to what has developed in the advancement of multicultural assessment and counseling with culturally diverse older adults.

Multicultural assessment is based on the foundations of awareness, knowledge, and skills of the patient's culture, the professional, and the knowledge provided through training from health care programs. Included in these foundations is the development of cultural competence. Cultural competence cannot be achieved without cultural wisdom. First and foremost, competence cannot be achieved without first understanding and exploring the patient's culture. But how do you operationalize each of these terms to create the understanding necessary to work with the advances in multicultural assessment and counseling with culturally diverse older adults?

Cultural competence can be defined as

> the integration and transformation of knowledge, information, and data about individuals and groups of people into specific clinical standards, skills, service approaches, techniques, and marketing programs that match the individual's culture and increase the quality and appropriateness of health care and outcomes. (Davis, 1997, p. 3)

Cultural wisdom refers to the accumulated learning through life that has been gained through experience by the professional in understanding the culturally diverse older adult. This accumulated learning includes levels of sensitivity and processing, while at the same time integrating the information and data in relation to the culture of the health care system, the patient, and the professional. The process of understanding and exploring cultures has been best defined through the methodology of ethnography within the discipline of anthropology (Kleinman & Benson, 2006). Ethnography places at the highest level the thorough understanding of a person's native culture. Ethnography is the study of observing a person's life through the world in which he or she lives at a certain time/context of society, including learning the person's language, social patterns, and cultural beliefs of being. The ability for a health care provider to conduct a mini-ethnographic assessment with his or her patient will set the stage for appropriate treatment followed by a high-quality outcome. For the professional working with the population of culturally diverse older adults, engaging in this process sets the foundation in formulating the cultural wisdom necessary to engage at the highest level of cultural competence when meeting the needs of the patient. For the culturally diverse older adult, several important issues must be explored given the impact an assessment may have on his or her quality of life.

Assessment for the Culturally Diverse Older Adult

Great care must be taken in the assessment of culturally diverse older adults. The results of an assessment are used to determine eligibility for services, diagnose and treat, and generate information for policy changes and health care. They are also used as tools for training health care providers. Overall, problems with current care for older adults are fragmented, with a lack of availability of health care for many older adults, care that is insensitive to culturally diverse older adults, and a lack of sharing among professionals affecting the quality of life for older adults. "Effective treatment for older adults in general is predicated on health care that is coordinated among various professionals that form an integrated health care team to serve the needs of an older adult" (American Psychological Association [APA] Presidential Task Force, 2008, p. 37). Issues that may especially affect culturally diverse older adults have been mentioned earlier in this chapter—poverty, language barriers, and lack of access to health care. Other issues include fraud perpetrated on older adults, severe isolation in their own ethnic/racial group, grandparents raising grandchildren, and the abuse of elders.

According to the *Blueprint for Change: Achieving Integrated Health Care for an Aging Population* (2008), a report from the APA Presidential Task Force, integrated, diverse, interdisciplinary health care is the optimal approach for advancement of assessment and coordinated health care. This would be the optimal approach for culturally diverse older adults. There are six basic skill areas that a health care professional, such as a psychologist or counselor, needs to enhance his or her ability to provide optimal integrated health care for culturally diverse older adults. These areas consist of having knowledge of aging and adult development; knowledge related to clinical issues; assessment knowledge and skills; intervention knowledge and skills; consultation, program development, and research skills; and knowledge that results in cultural competency.

Knowledge in aging and adult development begins with a mini-ethnographic study of one's own culture, beliefs and attitudes about aging, stereotypes that a professional may hold about elder adults, and how these attitudes may affect his or her ability to serve culturally diverse older adults. Knowledge of the natural aging process includes such common issues as diminishing physiological symptoms, community support issues, and diminished capacity, to name a few. Awareness of the importance of relationships for older adults, dealing with losses, along with being able to have the capacity to integrate cultural information for treatment is of utmost importance in providing optimal care in an integrated health care team. In addition, the counselor/psychologist must be able to differentiate between what effects medication may have on older adults versus what are causes of the natural aging process. Finally, the counselor/psychologist must also be aware of the capacity of healthy older adults and their abilities to perform in intimate relationships and independent living.

Knowledge related to clinical issues is directly related to the ability to recognize and assess symptoms of normal aging for cognitive functioning and sensory deficits. The competence to differentiate these symptoms from mental and physical pathologies that are not directly related to the side effects of medication is very important in understanding any underlying mental conditions that are being presented by the older adult. Another area of concern is assessing the ability of older adults to make autonomous decisions and how family issues affect these decisions, especially in families that are ill-equipped to deal with such issues. Finally, there is a responsibility to be aware of any psychological, emotional, or physical abuse by those who are responsible for caring for the older adult.

Assessment knowledge and skills are a shared responsibility of the integrative health care team. The integrative team may include a social worker, medical doctor, nurse, counselor/psychologist, pastor, cultural healer, senior citizen home director, and a family member. The integrative team can be established based on, for example, the needs presented by the older adult, the various support systems available to the older adult, the family structure and impact on care, financial resources, language needs, and cultural healing practices. All of these issues can affect who would best serve on the integrative team, including their skills in assessing the older adult's needs from various contexts. The integration of the various knowledge points of view in a comprehensive assessment by each team member will serve to increase the quality of the services received by the older adult.

Intervention knowledge and skills are directly related to the use and implementation of the knowledge gathered from the assessment of the integrative team in creating appropriate interventions at all levels of the older adult's needs. Overall, this is probably the most challenging phase of providing the most advanced creative interventions for culturally diverse older adults by the counselor/psychologist. "He or she should be familiar with modifications of interventions for persons with sensory and communication difficulties, physical disabilities, low education and literacy, and poor or not existent English speaking skills" (APA Presidential Task Force, 2008, p. 34). Other areas of importance to be included are cultural healing practices, community support, and the structure of the family. Implied with culturally sensitive interventions is awareness of the skills related to the understanding of how the various factors manifest themselves as challenges, as well as acceptance by the culturally diverse older adult of the prescribed interventions by the integrative team.

Skills in consultation, program development, and research are areas in need of serious consideration in working with older adults. With the change in demographics, significant increases have been noted in the number of older adults in this country, especially among culturally diverse older adults. Therefore, it is critical that knowledge in managing consultations and creating successful programs with older adults, families, and communities needs further development. Consultation skills across the various integrative team members, whether they are traditional cultural healers or other health care professionals, are essential in helping the various integrative team members to understand the diversity of belief systems related to the development of interventions for the culturally diverse older adult. The skills to develop programs from the information gathered through the integrative team can be a template for other integrative teams working with culturally diverse

older adults in the delivery of services. Data-driven research, both qualitative and quantitative, is necessary to validate the process and outcome resulting from the question as to why disparities still occur even after controlling for socioeconomic status, for example, among culturally diverse older adults. The training in developing the skills discussed in this section is necessary for ongoing development of appropriate services, knowledge, and accessibility to quality health care for older adults.

Knowledge that results in cultural competency is a lifelong pursuit, and exposure to a variety of cultures and an accumulation of knowledge over time leads to the development of cultural wisdom. Working with issues of diversity can be very challenging because it requires making a major commitment to a deep awareness of how we contribute to the success or failure of creating a diverse multicultural environment that is nonthreatening, supportive, and safe for all. The development of cultural competence through the process of experiencing cultural wisdom is the skill that enhances our understanding of the within- and between-group experiences of culturally diverse patients. We believe that as professionals, we learn by this process, which results in the ongoing development of diverse relationships, engaging in collaborations and interactions with diverse cultures, while learning and discovering how ideas affect diversity initiatives. Committing to becoming culturally competent is a lifestyle commitment to diversity. Strong interpersonal skills and an open mind, combined with a delayed judgment of one's cultural experiences and compassion to truly understand another's cultural experiences, has a direct impact on the quality of service toward culturally diverse older adults. Throughout the various knowledge areas, the counselor/psychologist may have to serve several roles at different times, such as leader, collaborator, facilitator, and integrator, across issues of diversity in relation to fellow health care workers, family, community, and programs of diversity, and also contribute to the development of strategic plans for intervention through a team approach.

It is imperative to understand that all of the areas of information regarding special populations and expertise described throughout this chapter are necessary requirements in providing advanced multicultural assessments and counseling with culturally diverse older adults. With this in mind, multiculturalism can be defined for the culturally diverse older adult as a collaborative process that recognizes, appreciates, and respects the multiple dimensions of diversity and emphasizes how participants, practices, and institutions have an impact on a person's location in a social structure of health care delivery (Yee, 2002). Multicultural assessment for the culturally diverse older adult includes areas such as social characteristics, socioeconomic status, cultural context, family structure, residential stability, language, community-based support, civil capacity, physiological capacity, psychiatric and emotional factors, psychological cognitive factors, and side effects of medication versus true diminished capacities. The variety of areas presented in the multicultural assessment requires the cooperation and collaboration of several professional disciplines in the health care field. The importance of the latest advancements in assessment for each discipline is what provides the highest potential for success for the culturally diverse older adult's capacity and ability to be successful in meeting his or her quality-of-life needs. Space does not permit an explanation of the latest multicultural advancements in assessment for each discipline. However, there have been some reconceptualizations of assessment for counselors and psychologists regarding older adults.

Advancements in Assessments

An excellent resource for understanding assessment issues is *Assessment of Older Adults With Diminished Capacity: A Handbook for Psychologists* (American Bar Association, 2008). Diminished capacity depends on the type of transaction or decision under consideration and the particular legal standard of capacity used in the state (p. 15). This handbook was developed to give psychologists a framework to assess six civil capacities with which older adults often have to contend in making quality-of-life decisions. The six areas of assessment for capacities are medical consent, sexual consent, financial matters, testamentary matters, ability to drive, and independent living. Embedded in each assessment is the area of values and preferences. In this area, culturally relevant information that may affect the assessment of the area of capacity is considered in the development of an informed decision for the older adult. Such variables include a person's race, ethnicity,

culture, gender, sexual orientation, and religion (p. 26). According to the American Bar Association (2002), if the person's values are long-standing throughout his or her life and have been consistent for that person, it may be an indicator of capacity. It must also be noted that in the field of multicultural psychology, a person's values can change through critical incidents, creating significant changes in his or her values of life. In addition, other factors such as religion, cultural beliefs, social networks, and family can heavily influence changes in a person's values. It is imperative that a thorough assessment of any life-altering changes be done for older adults in order to attend to the important issue of assessing for capacity in the areas listed in this section.

The *Blueprint for Change* publication (APA Presidential Task Force, 2008) validates the need for coordinated health care for the older adult. A basic integrated health care model is presented that involves team support. This includes individual assessments, shared information, team goals, an intervention plan, and strategies leading to the individual delivery of care. Earlier in this chapter, the knowledge and skills necessary to participate in this model are presented for the counselor/psychologist. However, of utmost importance are the eight principles of integrated health care: (a) integrated teams are sensitive to ageism and its influence on treatment decisions; (b) psychologists become familiar with core roles of other health care team members; (c) models of health care processes and beliefs may differ among team members; (d) conflict among team members is natural and can lead to strengthening or weakening of the team; (e) psychologists benefit from applying conflict resolution skills to team conflicts; (f) health care teams communicate in increasingly diverse ways; (g) health care teams are sensitive to issues of multicultural diversity and marginalization; and (h) assessment of treatment and treatment outcomes should be ongoing (pp. 38–46).

Even though all the principles are very important in providing aspirations for integrative health care, Principles 1 and 7 are directly related to the aspirations for advancement in assessment for older adults. Principle 1 describes issues related to discriminatory practices toward older adults and awareness about ageism among the integrative care team (p. 38). This principle demands that all team members be aware of their biases and prejudices toward older adults and how it may affect their views toward a strength-based perspective on treatment. Principle 7 explains the aspiration of team members to be sensitive to multicultural issues and the marginalization of older adults. In this principle, multiculturalism is described as "referring to the interactions between individuals from minority ethnic and racial groups in the United States and the dominant European American culture" (p. 45). Implied in this principle is that the health care giver has an understanding of the sociopolitical-economic-educational history of the ethnic/racial minority and the impact of this history on the quality of health care for this population. This history is useful in understanding the interpersonal dynamics between ethnic/racial populations and European Americans as presented across the health care systems. Dismantling the interpersonal dynamics that create barriers to cultural issues leads to appropriate interventions and treatment in delivering quality care for culturally diverse older adults. It is evident that these two principles serve as the foundation for modifying the mainstream training of counselors and psychologists in the area of health care. Ongoing development of knowledge and training is essential in becoming multiculturally competent with culturally diverse older adults.

ADDITIONAL RESOURCES FOR COUNSELORS

The American Society on Aging (ASA) is an organization that was developed in 1954 that may be helpful in developing a practitioner's multicultural competence. The organization is committed to improving the quality of life for older adults and their families. It is dedicated to the training needs among its membership in order to increase knowledge and skills related to the quality of care for older adults. The organization has a diversity of members that include practitioners, counselors, educators, policymakers, and researchers, to name a few. The diversity of membership emulates the multidisciplinary perspectives taken among integrative health care teams in their sharing of knowledge and support for older adults. Within ASA, a Minority Concerns Committee (MCC) was established in 1983 to serve as a monitoring and consulting committee to the ASA in keeping its commitment to quality care for older adults, especially culturally diverse older adults.

The organization also publishes a Diversity Impact Report that evaluates diversity in ASA in the areas of membership, training, education, research, and publications. Joining such an organization serves as a strong support for professionals interested in the quality of care of culturally diverse older adults.

There are committees and divisions in the American Psychological Association that may be beneficial for psychologists with interests in the quality of life for older adults to join (APA, 2008a, 2008b). The committee on aging is very active in researching issues related to older adults and diversity. The Society of Clinical Geropsychology (Division 12, Section II) emphasizes the development of quality of care in areas of mental health and delivery of services to older adults. Adult Development and Aging (Division 20) is another division dedicated to adult development, research, and service of older adults. Psychologists in the private sector who work with older adults or do research in adult development are encouraged to join in order to share their knowledge and information with others with the same interests. The American Counseling Association has the Division for the Association for Adult Development and Aging that is dedicated to adult development and aging issues, sharing information and enhancing professional development for counselors (ACA, 2008). There are several other organizations across the country that can meet the diversity of needs among counselors/psychologists who are dedicated to working with culturally diverse older adults. It is important that knowledge, training, education, and research be shared about culturally diverse older adults in order to continually develop best practices that increase the quality of health care and decrease health disparities.

SUMMARY

The demographic changes of culturally diverse older adults in the United States dictate the need for culturally sensitive, quality health care. The health care provider's ability to explore and evaluate data that lead to multicultural wisdom will result in multicultural competence in health care for the older adult. The six basic areas of knowledge and civil capacities mentioned in this chapter are beneficial in helping the practitioner understand the role of assessment for the culturally diverse older adult. Competence in these combined areas by counselors/psychologists and being an integrative health care team member provide the foundation for best practices when working with the culturally diverse older adult. Membership in organizations dedicated to issues of aging that provide continuing education and research, along with much needed support, is necessary for counselors/psychologists working with the challenges faced by culturally diverse older adults. Aging is part of the cycle of life, caring for others is a commitment to humanity, and sharing knowledge to eliminate barriers to improving quality of life is an aspiration to reach for counselors/psychologists.

The process of saying goodbye as you watch a person's mind diminish over time is a painful experience. Working through those emotional issues with my own mother was a devastating process as I moved from being a son to becoming a familiar stranger. There were so many challenges to face, such as the quality of care, capacity to make decisions in several areas, language issues, consulting with numerous professionals, being involved in the training of staff at the senior citizen center, senior daycare, and finances. It was an overwhelming experience for me—one that will be with me for the rest of my life. Through the love from my immediate family, support from many friends, and unbelievable professionals dedicated to older adults, I learned more from my mother than I ever imagined. I am sure that my experience is one of many that happen across the country.

REFERENCES

AARP. (2008). *A portrait of older minorities.* Retrieved October 10, 2008, from http://www.aarp.org/research/reference/minorities/aresearch-import-509.html

American Bar Association. (2002). *Model rules of professional conduct.* Washington, DC: Author.

American Bar Association Commission on Law and Aging and the American Psychological Association. (2008). *Assessment of older adults with diminished capacity: A handbook for psychologists.* Washington, DC: American Bar Association and American Psychological Association.

American Counseling Association. (2008). Divisions of American Counseling Association. Retrieved December 15, 2008, from http://www.counseling.org/AboutUs/Divisions BranchesAndRegions/

American Psychological Association. (2008a). Committees of the American Psychological Association. Retrieved

December 15, 2008, from http://www.alaapa.org/about/governancetfcommitteesupdate.html

American Psychological Association. (2008b). Divisions of the American Psychological Association. Retrieved December 15, 2008, from http://www.apa.org/about/division.html

American Psychological Association Presidential Task Force on Integrated Health Care for an Aging Population. (2008). *Blueprint for change: Achieving integrated health care for an aging population.* Washington, DC: American Psychological Association.

Davis, K. (1997). Race, health status, and managed care. In L. Epstein & F. Brisbane (Eds.), *Cultural competence series.* Rockville, MD: Center for Substance Abuse Prevention.

Hayes-Bautista, D. E., Hsu, P., Perez, A., & Gamboa, C. (2002). The "browning" of the graying of America: Diversity in the elderly population and policy implications. *Generations: Journal of the American Society on Aging, 26*(3), 15–24.

Institute of Medicine. (2002). *Unequal treatment: Confronting racial and ethnic disparities in health care.* Washington, DC: National Academy Press.

Johnson, J. C., & Smith, N. (2002). Health and social issues associated with racial, ethnic and cultural disparities. *Generations: Journal of the American Society on Aging, 26*(3), 25–32.

Kleinman, A., & Benson, P. (2006). Anthropology in the clinic: The problem of cultural competence and how to fix it. Retrieved from http://www.plosmedicine.org/article/info:doi/10.1371/journal.pmed.0030294

Shavers, V. L., Lynch, C. F., & Burmeister, L. F. (2000). Knowledge of the Tuskegee study and its impact on willingness to participate in medical research studies. *Journal of the National Medical Association, 92,* 563–572.

U.S. Census Bureau. (2005). *65+ in the United States: 2005* (CPO Publication No. P23–209). Washington, DC: U.S. Government Printing Office.

Vázquez, L. A. (2004). Lost in translation. *California Psychologist, 37*(6), 13–15.

Vázquez, L. A., & García-Vázquez, E. (2003). Teaching multicultural competence in the counseling curriculum. In D. B. Pope-Davis, H. L. K. Coleman, W. M. Liu, & R. L. Toporek (Eds.), *Handbook of multicultural competencies* (pp. 546–561). Thousand Oaks, CA: Sage.

Yee, D. (2002) Recognizing diversity, moving toward cultural competence. *Generations: Journal of the American Society of Aging, 26*(3), 5–7.

Yen, I. H., & Syme, S. L. (1999). The social environment and health: A discussion of the epidemiologic literature. *Annual Review of Public Health, 20,* 287–308.

52

Family Counseling

Systems, Postmodern, and Multicultural Perspectives

GEORGE V. GUSHUE, DANIEL T. SCIARRA, AND BRENDA X. MEJÍA

The multicultural sensitivity of family therapy has been a debated topic for quite some time. Classic models such as structural family therapy (SFT) (Minuchin, 1974; Minuchin & Fishman, 1981), strategic family therapy (Haley, 1987), and Bowen family systems therapy (Bowen, 1966; Kerr & Bowen, 1988) have all been criticized from a multicultural perspective. These models presume to possess universally valid concepts to judge the health of a family's functioning without regard to cultural differences that might relativize the definition of "health." In contrast, more recent models (sometimes referred to as postmodern therapies) reject universal concepts applied to family functioning and view each family as an entity unto itself. These models include collaborative language systems therapy (Anderson 1997, 2001; Anderson & Goolishian, 1988), solution-focused therapy (Berg & de Shazer 1993; Miller & de Shazer, 1998, 2000), and narrative therapy (White, 1991; White & Epston,

1990). The first part of this chapter will give a brief overview of these different therapeutic approaches.

SYSTEMS MODELS OF FAMILY THERAPY

Therapist driven, these models have in common the belief and use of pre-existing conceptual schemes to understand family processes that transcend cultural differences. They view the family as a system in which members are interconnected to create a single organism (Minuchin & Fishman, 1981). As a result, behaviors are co-created and maintained over time. However, a change in one member's behavior will inevitably cause a compensatory change in another part of the family system. In order to understand this system, a structural frame is imposed upon the observable data to understand the often complex world of family interactions. The major elements of this framework are subsystems, boundaries, circular causality, and triangles.

677

Subsystems

In families, some members unite with others to perform a common function or shared activity. These functionally united segments are called *subsystems* that develop and change over time and exercise more or less influence in the history of family's development. Common subsystems in a family are the *spousal subsystem* (a term long used by family therapists to refer to either gay or straight couples), the *parental or executive subsystem,* and the *sibling subsystem.* The spousal subsystem develops patterns for dealing with conflict. For example, conflict may be dealt with through direct exchange, and so remain contained within the subsystem. On the other hand, one or both members of the spousal subsystem may seek allies outside of the subsystem or detour away from conflict by turning toward other things and/or people as a distraction. Children, if present in the family, are often the focus of detoured spousal conflict. Family therapists pay careful attention to the parental or executive subsystem, being alert to such problems as parents not working together, invalidating each other, and/or ceding too much authority to their children. A potential bias in this model is that many behavioral problems in children are traced to a dysfunctional parental subsystem (Minuchin & Fishman, 1981; Minuchin, Montalvo, Guerney, Rosman, & Schumer, 1967). A source of displaced authority often lies in the parents' inability to work together in dealing with their children. Children quickly learn to play one parent against the other, a tactic that gives the children too much control in the system.

The third major subsystem in the family is the *sibling subsystem.* Although children in a family (optimally) live most of their lives under the umbrella of care and management provided by the parental subsystem, they do—or should—have significant interactions among themselves that do not directly involve the adult caregivers. One reason that intergenerational coalitions, detouring of spousal conflict toward children, and the parentification of young children are deemed dysfunctional by therapists is the violation of the integrity of the sibling subsystem.

Boundaries

Family subsystems are differentiated by boundaries— invisible barriers that demarcate and define the relationship among the different subsystems (Nichols & Schwartz, 2006). Moreover, the family system as a whole is differentiated by a boundary that creates both psychological and physical distance between the family and the extrafamilial world.

Boundaries are assessed along a continuum from *rigid* to *diffuse.* A rigid boundary between subsystems produces a *disengaged* relationship between the members of the respective subsystems, whereas a diffuse boundary produces *enmeshed* relationships. For example, the SFT therapist would see the overinvolvement of a parent in the lives of his or her children as the result of a diffuse boundary between the parental and sibling subsystems. Signs of a rigid boundary between the parental and sibling subsystems can include a disregard for a child's difficulty, unreturned phone calls to school personnel, repeated inability to make meetings concerning the child, and a general inability to foster support when needed.

SFT assumes that problematic families have subsystem boundaries that are too diffuse and/or too rigid. Children who are enmeshed with one or both parents may receive wonderful care and support, but at the expense of independence and autonomy (Nichols & Schwartz, 2006). Parent-child enmeshment also entails a negative impact on the spousal subsystem, allowing little time and opportunity for the partners to be alone with each other. The likely result is a nonfulfilling spousal relationship.

In contrast, families with rigid boundaries have members who are independent of, yet isolated from, one another. On the positive side, children from disengaged families learn to be resourceful and to not shy away from tasks that require perseverance and mastery. On the negative side, such children will not have experienced the warmth, nurturance, and affection so prevalent in families with more permeable boundaries.

Circular Causality

The concept of circular causality is central to systems thinking. In opposition to a linear understanding of behavior (A causes B, which causes C), which searches for explanations in the past, circular causality views behavior within a system as being maintained in the present by repetitive, circular interactive loops. The linear understanding of A causing B causing C is thus replaced by the understanding of A causing B, which, in turn, causes A.

When applied to families, the concept of circular causality produces the view that a family member's behavior is both caused by and causes the other members' behavior. It is never a question of "who started it" or "who is to blame," because all family members are assumed to be co-responsible for maintaining any and all patterned behaviors enacted within the family. An example might be a punitive father and his acting-out son. The son's acting out causes the father to be punitive, which in turn elicits further acting out on the son's part. Mother intervenes by coddling her son, because she cannot stand seeing him cry. Father feels undermined and punishes the son even more.

Triangulation

Bowen (1966) believed that a family's problems often stemmed from an individual's lack of differentiation from and among family members. He introduced the concept of *triangles* into family counseling in order to explain this lack of differentiation. When two undifferentiated people in a relationship face anxiety, there is a tendency to draw in a third party as a way of reducing the couple's anxiety. In families, this usually takes the form of children being triangulated into conflicts between their parents. A triangulated person is not allowed to differentiate, which in turn can lead to symptomatic behavior. For example, family counselors recognize that a daughter's behavior depends on her relationship with her mother, which depends on the mother's relationship with her husband or partner. Bowen believed all behavior to be basically triadic rather than dyadic.

POSTMODERN MODELS OF FAMILY THERAPY

These models, also referred to as *idiographic* models, tend to understand each family not as a system, but as a culture unto itself, and that therapy is the meeting of two cultures: that of the family and that of the therapist (Paré, 1995, 1996). To impose upon a family an external conceptual scheme (i.e., something from a foreign culture) is a form of colonialism (Sciarra & Simon, 2008). We briefly summarize three of these postmodern therapies: collaborative language systems therapy (Anderson, 1997, 2001; Anderson & Goolishian,

1988), solution-focused therapy (Berg & de Shazer, 1993; Miller & de Shazer, 1998, 2000), and narrative therapy (White, 1991; White & Epston, 1990).

Collaborative Language Systems Therapy

A language systems therapist pays careful attention to key language that a family uses in order to make sense of their own situation. The therapist's task is to ask questions to elicit meanings from the family to explain the presenting problem. Such questioning is necessary to evoke the idiosyncratic meanings that heretofore have not been spoken in order to solve the problem. The language systems approach is based on the vaporous nature of meaning so that once sufficient and adequate meaning of the problems is elicited, the problem will be dissolved (Sciarra & Simon, 2008; Simon, 2003).

Solution-Focused Therapy

Similar to the language systems approach, the solution-focused therapist approaches the therapeutic encounter with no pre-existing conceptual scheme to understand the family. However, rather than paying attention to the unique meanings a family has attached to the presenting problem, the therapist focuses on the family's idiosyncratic solutions to the problem. The therapist is more interested in what the family is already doing, albeit in a very small way, to deal with the problem and alleviate its impact upon the family. The family is doing something, and the therapist's task is to make the family aware of that something and then amplify it. The therapist does not impose solutions upon the family. Rather, the therapist discovers what the family is already doing to solve the problem and helps them to apply such solution(s) more generally and consistently.

Narrative Therapy

Similar to language systems therapy and solution-focused therapy, *narrative therapy* believes in each family's unique capacity to create meaning from its presenting problem. The narrative model differs, however, in viewing a family's local conversation as derivative of broader sociocultural discourses that diminish a family's unique wisdom (Sciarra & Simon, 2008).

Dominant and nondominant cultural practices are seen as inherently dehumanizing and limit a family's authentic expression (Griffith & Griffith, 1994). The goal of therapy is similar to the other postmodern therapies: the liberation of a family's knowledge, wisdom, and meaning-making capacity. To achieve this goal, narrative therapy effectuates a conversation that focuses on the destructive effects of cultural discourse at the societal level. Narrative therapy would see any conceptual scheme imposed upon the family by the classic models as yet another corrosive effect of dominant cultural discourse.

MULTICULTURAL PERSPECTIVES ON FAMILY THERAPY

For the past quarter century, an increasing amount of clinical and scholarly attention has been paid to the role of culture in family functioning and interactions. Cultural systems of worldviews, meanings, beliefs, and behaviors are thought to form a larger system in which particular family systems are embedded (Sue & Sue, 2003). Various models have been employed to understand how culture influences family functioning. Some have focused primarily on differences between cultural groups (emic), whereas others have examined within-group cultural (idioemic) differences (Johnson, 1990). The following paragraphs will briefly outline one between-group and two within-group approaches to understanding the role of culture in families. The implications of the postmodern (idiographic) critique for these models of cultural difference between and among families will also be considered.

A Between-Group Perspective

The emic approach examines broad cultural patterns that inform family life and highlight important between-culture differences. How are Irish families different from Italian families? How are both of these different from Salvadoran or Arab families? Is the meaning assigned to "family" primarily nuclear or extended? How does a particular culture define differences in gender roles, and how do these apply to expectations of the roles of father and mother? What constitutes culturally sanctioned expressions of emotion? Is the

individual or the family given primacy in decision making? Factors such as these affect differences in what is considered optimal family functioning from one culture to the next. Whether a given action is judged to be healthy or pathological is determined by reference to culturally specific norms for that behavior. For instance, a grown man who speaks to his mother on the telephone every day might be considered enmeshed from one cultural perspective but normal from another, depending on the culture-specific criteria for determining rigidity or diffuseness in subsystem boundaries. A young adult who defers to her family's educational or career plans for her future might be considered submissive from a perspective that places primacy on individual choice, but appropriate from a cultural perspective that favors a collectivistic decision-making process. The between-group approach highlights cultural differences in the meanings assigned to particular behaviors in family systems. Depending on the cultural context, the same interaction might be interpreted as adaptive or pathological. Emic models call for an appreciation of cultural differences in normative family behavior and functioning.

Within-Group Perspective 1: Acculturation

Idioemic perspectives focus on within-group cultural differences. Such models endeavor to account for cultural differences between families or individuals of the same cultural or ethnic group. The primacy of family (familismo) may be an important feature of a Mexican culture in general, but to what extent is that true for this particular family presenting for treatment? A collectivistic family outlook is often described as a central aspect of Chinese culture, but how true is it for each of the members of the second-generation Chinese family sitting in the consulting room? A number of researchers and clinicians have used the model of acculturation to understand cultural differences observed within families. This model envisions the interaction between two cultures, usually in the context of immigration, as the traditional cultural worldview, beliefs, and behaviors of the immigrating family adapt to the expectations of the dominant culture of the host country.

Numerous models of acculturation have been proposed, with some highlighting different domains of acculturation. Thus, one may function in a more acculturated way at work and a more traditional way at home. Other models stress that in addition to being more highly attuned to the dominant culture or one's traditional culture, other possibilities exist (e.g., Berry, 1990). Thus, one may function equally well in both cultures (bicultural) or may feel alienated from both cultures (marginalized). Other authors have noted that children of immigrants adapt to the dominant culture more rapidly than their parents. Thus, from this perspective, differing cultural perspectives and worldviews may be represented in a given family. One example of using acculturation in family treatment is offered by what Szapocznik and his colleagues (Szapocznik & Kurtines, 1993; Szapocznik, Kurtines, Santisteban, & Pantin, 1997) have called bi-cultural effectiveness treatment (BET). In this approach, clinicians make the differences in worldviews between subsystems explicit and use these differences to help the family to understand the issues that lead them to present for treatment. One aspect of BET is helping individuals and subsystems within the family acknowledge and accept the cultural differences that exist among them.

Within-Group Perspective 2: Cultural Identity

A second idiographic perspective is that of cultural identity. Helms's (1995) models of racial and cultural identity highlight individual differences in orientation to both one's own racial or cultural group and others with which one is in contact. Like models of acculturation, these models suggest that what is important is not one's cultural designation per se, but rather how deeply one embraces or distances oneself from the values and worldviews typical of one's own cultural group and to what extent one embraces the values of other cultures. Helms (1995) outlined different ego identity statuses to describe differing configurations of orientation. Unlike acculturation, which describes the experience of nondominant cultural groups (adaptation to the dominant culture), Helms proposed models for both dominant and nondominant groups. Her model can be applied to a wider range of families and family therapists. Gushue (1993; Gushue & Sciarra, 1995) proposed an extension of Helms's model to family therapy and suggested that therapists needed to account for potential differences in values, beliefs, and

behaviors both between members or subsystems of the same family and between members of the family and the therapist based on differences in cultural identity. Based on Helms's (1984) interaction model, Gushue suggested potential family and therapeutic dynamics resulting from differences in cultural orientation.

Implications of the Postmodern Critique for Family Cultural Models

The problems with the nomothetic position (all families are alike) have been noted above. The universal dynamics that are privileged as "normal" in such an approach reflect the patterns of functioning of the dominant culture. Similarly, to suggest that all families of a particular culture are alike runs the risk of stereotyping and, understood from the postmodern perspective, yet another form of colonialism. However, to suggest that each family is utterly unique discounts the influence of the cultural systems in which the family is embedded. The mirror image of universalism, the postmodern (idiographic) perspective arrives at a similar conclusion: an abrogation of the importance of culture in understanding family functioning. Recently, Sciarra and Simon (2008) explored some of the implications of the postmodern approaches of family treatment for traditional paradigms of family therapy. They proposed a "nomothetic/ideographic blend" of postmodern and traditional models as a way of balancing both the universal and the unique aspects of a given family's functioning and illustrate this by presenting a hybrid of the structural family therapy and collaborative language system models. Perhaps a similar approach may be taken on the emic and idioemic dimensions just described, as clinicians seek to understand cultural differences within and between families.

The postmodern approaches highlight the importance of listening to families' narratives and allowing them to define their own experience. Sciarra and Simon (2008) suggested that universal models of family functioning might guide therapists' assessment by indicating critical areas to explore, whereas idiographic (postmodern) models might assist in determining if problems exist and how they should be construed. In a similar way, between-group and within-group models of family cultural patterns might suggest areas for inquiry regarding potential cultural dimensions in the family's presentation. However, the clinician will have to listen for the family's own definition (or lack thereof) of important between-group cultural areas such as *familismo*, collective decision making, gender roles, and respect for elders, among others. In the same way, the clinician will need to attend to idiographic differences in worldview or cultural values in the linguistic formulations of individuals and subsystems within the family. Should the therapist feel that the family is describing a dynamic that it experiences as problematic and that cultural differences within the family in some way influence that dynamic, then he or she will need to describe these in the family's own terms—the unique intersection of this family's own culture and dynamics and those of the larger systems in which the family is embedded. Similarly, the therapist can try to help identify the idiosyncratic solutions the family is proposing to address these idioemic cultural conflicts.

The preceding discussion suggests three domains for consideration in understanding family dynamics. First, traditional universal models of family therapy point to general areas that may be examined and that may or may not warrant clinical attention in a family presenting for treatment, such as the quality of the boundaries between the parental and child subsystems. Second, the multicultural models suggest that these traditional areas for inquiry can be understood only within a culturally specific context. For example, norms for the optimal boundaries between subsystems vary from culture to culture, and certain areas of family functioning may be more salient for one culture than another. Moreover, the within-group cultural difference models call attention to the fact that different families and different members of the same family may endorse these cultural norms to a greater or lesser extent. Third, the postmodern perspectives highlight the importance of attending to a family's own idiosyncratic integration of cultural norms and of listening to their own definitions of problems in their functioning, as well as solutions they may be enacting.

CASE 1: LISA AND KAREN

Karen and Lisa have come to the first session of family therapy because they are concerned about their son's behavioral changes in the past 3 months. Lisa, a 31-year-old Caucasian lawyer who specializes in immigration law, and Karen, a 33-year-old African American associate professor of special education, are an interracial couple from an upper-middle-class background who were married 5 years ago. Lisa and Karen are fluent in Spanish, a commonality that attracted them to one another. After exclusively dating for 1 year, the couple married in Massachusetts and subsequently had a small ceremony among family and friends to celebrate their union.

Lisa and Karen always had dreams of having children. A year ago, they began to consider adopting a child. Both women grew up with brothers and decided that it would be best to adopt a boy given their positive personal experiences growing up with their brothers. They began the adoption process but were rejected several times by various agencies because of discriminatory policies against same-sex couples. After facing many obstacles in the domestic adoption process, the couple decided to pursue an international adoption, which they thought was "more promising" than the domestic adoption. Once again, they found that most international adoption agencies had discriminatory restrictions and practices against same-sex parents, with some even requiring affidavits of heterosexuality. Frustrated with the laws, Lisa and Karen decided to conceal their relationship, and Lisa pursued the adoption as the official adoptive parent. Both Lisa and Karen report feeling "sad and frustrated" at having to keep Karen "invisible" in the adoption process, but "we didn't have another option." Although this was a difficult decision for them, they concluded, "It was the only way we would become parents." Ultimately, they decided to adopt a child from a Spanish-speaking country given their bilingual skills.

Seven months ago, Lisa and Karen traveled to Guatemala and fell in love with Carlos, an 8-year-old boy who had been living in a foster home for 2 years. Carlos seemed to immediately connect with Lisa and was excited to learn that he would be living in the United States. Lisa promised him, "You will have all of the toys you want and your own room." At first, the couple reports that the adoption was "completely joyful." Lisa was thrilled to have a son whom she could name after her father, Jonathan. After discussing it, Karen went along with Lisa's wish, and they decided to change Carlos's name to "Jonathan," whom seemed indifferent to his new name.

Jonathan began attending a private school that had an English program for second-language learners. According to the couple, Jonathan's transition into his new family was "seamless." He liked school and the attention and love of two parents. He enjoyed playing board games and talking to Lisa and Karen. In the past month, however, Lisa and Karen noticed that Jonathan began to withdraw. He preferred to stay in his room, where he mostly watched television in Spanish and played video games. When he was asked to turn off the television, he became angry and insisted, "Please, just 15 more minutes." Lisa, who is permissive and affectionate, gave in to him to avoid seeing him get angry at her, whereas Karen, who is authoritarian and stern, turned the television off and walked away. Karen says that Jonathan "needs to learn how to follow rules," and Lisa states that "he is just being a kid." Karen has noticed that when she is disciplining Jonathan, he begins to weep and says, "me quiero ir a mi casa" (I want to go home). Subsequently, Lisa often undermines her instructions to Jonathan.

They also found a picture of Jonathan's foster mother under his pillow. Jonathan speaks with her once a month, an agreement that was made during the adoption process. Lisa and Karen, however, wonder if this was a good idea. They thought that the "distress of uprooting" would be lessened if Jonathan remained in contact with his foster mother. Jonathan also dislikes sleeping in his room by himself because he says he feels "scared"; consequently, Lisa has begun to lie in bed with him to help him fall asleep. Karen disapproves because she thinks Lisa is "spoiling him too much." Jonathan has begun to ask Lisa, "Why do I have two moms? The kids at school don't have two moms." Recently, he has come home saying, "The kids at school say I'm lying. They don't believe me that I have two moms."

Balancing the demands of work and parenting has been a challenging adjustment for the couple. They report "we have less time for each other," as Lisa is usually attending to Jonathan. Karen feels "distant" and is beginning to question "whether adopting was a good idea after all," but is afraid to share her feelings with Lisa for fear that it may drive them further apart. Karen says that she was raised with an "orientation to family" and assumed that having a son would bring her and Lisa closer together. Although she loves Jonathan, she states that she is harboring "resentment" about the adoption experience. She feels "angry at the discrimination we faced and about having to remain invisible and for not being recognized as his mother under the law."

Discussion: Case 1

A number of the perspectives described earlier can be used to understand different aspects of this case. For instance, the systems models draw attention to the unraveling of boundaries between subsystems in this family. Seen from this perspective, Jonathan (a.k.a. Carlos) has been triangulated into the relationship between Lisa and Karen. The diffuse boundary around the executive subsystem has become compromised: Lisa and Jonathan are enmeshed and Karen is on the outside. Karen and Lisa disagree on parenting decisions, and each acts in her own way. Karen accuses Lisa of "spoiling" Jonathan, and Lisa undermines Karen's attempts at setting limits. Seen from a systems perspective, Jonathan's recent behavior may be calling attention to dysfunction in the executive subsystem. One of the first tasks for the therapist working from a systems framework would be to help Lisa and Karen rediscover one another, bond as parents, and reestablish the boundary between the executive and child subsystems. In addition, it seems that the role of Jonathan's "third mom" (his foster mother) must be explicitly acknowledged and clarified.

Both between-culture and within-culture perspectives suggest additional dimensions to consider in this case. A number of cultural fault lines run through this family system. Lisa and Karen have formed their identities within the overarching Anglo American culture of the United States, whereas at age 8, Jonathan has been raised within the values and beliefs of Latin America. Moreover, although they are both from the United States, Karen and Lisa may or may not have differing worldviews and views about family, given their differing racial/cultural group memberships. Potentially, a therapist working with this family may be addressing three differing sets of cultural assumptions about intimacy, emotion, expression of affection, boundaries, and roles for parents and children. A therapist would need to explore the cultural context of statements like "he needs to learn how to follow rules" and "he's just being a kid." What culturally based standards might inform these differing judgments about Jonathan's behavior? What are some of the cultural assumptions underlying Karen's statement about "orientation to family" and her belief that having a child would bring Lisa and her closer together? Does the prevailing racial ideology of the United States have anything to do with the unequal alliances that Jonathan has forged with his parents? Although Jonathan's retreat to his room with Spanish-language television and a picture of his foster mother may be understood on many levels, one reading would be to see it as an attempt to reclaim a world of meaning, values, interpersonal dynamics, and affection that was taken from him in his transformation from Carlos to Jonathan. Jonathan and his adoptive mothers may not share a set of assumptions about what a family should look like—part of family counseling will be to create a space for them to engage in that task.

Although between-culture differences may appear salient when considering the members of the family in this case, within-group cultural differences may also play an important role in understanding this family. For instance, the constructs of cultural identity (Helms, 1995) and racial color-blind ideologies (Neville, Lilly, Duran, Lee, & Browne, 2000) have been employed to understand how people differ in their orientations to race and culture. From these perspectives, Lisa may be seen as expressing a color-blind orientation to race and culture (i.e., highlighting universal aspects of human experience while minimizing or denying cultural differences). For instance, she appears to have few misgivings about changing Carlos's name to Jonathan, in memory of a member of her own family. From the account presented, Lisa prefers not to see (or at least to minimize) Carlos's culture and family history. She may have underestimated the difficulties that this transition would pose for Carlos, the fact of which he is reminding her with his current behavior. Seen from this perspective, Lisa may need help in broadening her cultural identity—forging one that allows her to better see and value difference (versus emphasizing universality).

The family that Lisa, Karen, and Jonathan have formed has also been profoundly affected by the larger cultural systems of which it is a part. As a lesbian couple,

buffeted by discrimination, Lisa and Karen made the decision to have Karen "disappear." How was this decision made, and how do both partners feel about it now? From the account above, Lisa clearly seems to have forged a different relationship with Jonathan, promising him toys before the adoption, naming him after her father, indulging his behavior, lying with him as he falls asleep. To what extent are some of these dynamics a reflection of the unequal terms of adoption that the couple found themselves forced to accept? The couple decided to adopt a Latin American child only because their initial efforts were thwarted by discriminatory adoption policies within the United States. Did they fully anticipate the added cross-cultural issues that would arise because of this change in strategy? The influence of larger cultural systems may also be noted in Jonathan's report about the reaction of the kids in school to the fact that he has two moms. Is there an available community of other same-sex parent families that might provide both Jonathan and his parents with a counterbalance to societal homophobia?

The postmodern models were the final set of theories discussed above. Traditional family theories stress what are thought to be universal dynamics; between-culture models highlight norms for particular cultural groups. Postmodern models emphasize the unique ways in which each family incorporates (or does not incorporate) universal and culture-specific norms. For instance, a narrative approach would encourage Karen and Lisa to examine the ways in which systems of cultural oppression (e.g., heterosexism and White privilege) have contributed to prevent them from re-storying their lives to live in greater harmony with each other and reach their own (not someone else's) prescriptions for relationships and child rearing.

A collaborative language systems approach would urge therapists to listen to the family's own discourse to elicit their understanding of the problem for which they seek treatment. From this perspective, the family presents a number of metaphors that offer a key to how it experiences its dilemma. For instance, Lisa and Karen report their frustration at having to make Karen invisible for the purposes of adoption. Issues of visibility and invisibility permeate this case. The larger cultural system could not tolerate seeing both partners at once. What dynamics in the executive subsystem led to

Karen's being chosen to be the invisible one? It seems that a large part of the current problem is that she has remained invisible even within the family since the adoption. Lisa has named their child and appears to take the lead in setting the parenting standards. Karen's decisions/recommendations are overruled. Perhaps Karen's continued invisibility has contributed to Jonathan's enmeshment with his other mother. On the other hand, a number of aspects of Jonathan's culture and family history have also been rendered invisible—he now withdraws to his room to visit his hidden culture and family. From the case, it is clear that the invisibility of these two members is very painful for the family as a whole. To adopt the family's language, what can be done to make Karen and Jonathan/Carlos more visible? Invisibility provides only one possible point of entry into this family's description of what it is experiencing. Similar explorations of the unique meanings that the family attaches to words such as "distance" and "uprooting" could also prove helpful in assisting a therapist and the family construct an idiosyncratic cultural narrative of the events that led them to seek treatment.

CASE 2: ROCÍO AND ANTONIO

Rocío, a 36-year-old woman born in El Salvador, came to therapy with her sister, Adriana, 27, and her 7-year-old daughter, Jasmin. Fourteen years prior, Rocío left El Salvador seeking better educational and occupational opportunities. As the oldest of three children, Rocío was expected to help care for her younger siblings. After completing night school and learning to speak English, she found a job as a sales clerk in a department store where she works 40 hours a week. Six years ago, Rocío and Adriana reunited after Rocío helped her sister immigrate. Adriana is Jasmin's *madrina* (godmother).

Eight years ago, Rocío married Antonio, a 37-year-old Peruvian man who immigrated to the United States 12 years ago and has been working steadily as a cab driver for the past 5 years. Antonio usually works more than 65 hours a week to provide financial support to his family. A year ago, Antonio was involved in a car accident that left him with a herniated disk and back pain. After a month of recuperating, he returned to working long hours to pay for his medical expenses.

When Jasmin was born, Rocío assumed the responsibility of homemaker and caretaker while her husband "works long hours to support us." Rocío reports that Antonio "tells Jasmin to obey me, but he does not discipline her. He likes to play with her since he never sees her." Rocío worries that Jasmin will not have "respeto" (respect) for Antonio when she gets older. The couple is expecting their second child, a son, whom they plan to name "Christian." They decided to give their children "American names" because "they are American citizens."

Although Rocío is "happy" to be expecting a son, she reports feeling "stressed" at having to care for Jasmin and a newborn. Antonio tells her that "she should be happy that we are having a son and stop worrying about it." Rocío notes that she "loves" her husband, and he is "responsible," but "sometimes he doesn't understand that we can't follow the gender traditions." For example, she would like him to help more with the housework, like "sweeping the floor." Antonio supports Rocío by taking his daughter to school, but due to his limited English fluency, Rocío is the one who communicates with the school staff.

The couple lives in New York and has few family members and friends in the area. Adriana, Rocío's sister, works part-time and helps her care for Jasmin. Antonio also has an aunt and two cousins who live nearby, but sees them only on special occasions because of his long working hours. One of his male cousins is Jasmin's *padrino* (godfather), who sends her birthday presents every year. Rocío hopes that as soon as Antonio obtains his citizenship, he will bring his mother from El Salvador to help care for their son. Both Antonio and Rocío are green card holders and have submitted applications for U.S. citizenship.

According to Rocío, a month ago, her husband happily reported to a U.S. citizenship interview at the U.S. Citizen and Immigration Services office. He was aware that a background check was required as part of the naturalization process to assess for criminal law violations. Although he knew that he had outstanding unpaid parking fines, Antonio was prepared to explain his financial situation due to medical expenses and his plans for resolving the outstanding fees. Unfortunately, under current deportation policies, undocumented immigrants, as well as legal permanent residents, can be deported for minor and nonviolent crimes. Six hours after his U.S. citizenship interview, Antonio was deported to El Salvador for unpaid traffic fines. In despair, Rocío describes, "He was torn from us. He couldn't even call to say goodbye." Rocío was not informed that he would be removed and heard from Antonio 3 days after his deportation. Neither Rocío nor her daughter are likely to be deported because Rocío is a green card holder and her daughter Jasmin is an American citizen.

Since the deportation, Rocío has been feeling "sad and depressed." She has lost her appetite, has difficulty sleeping and concentrating, and feels agitated. She has noticed that Jasmin has become "clingy," is wetting her bed, and cries easily. For instance, she has noticed that she now cries every time she leaves her with her sister Adriana. At school, the teacher has noticed that Jasmin has difficulty paying attention and seems to be "daydreaming." Prior to losing her father, Jasmin, who turns 8 years old next month, was "as happy as she could be" and academically gifted. When she talks to her father on the phone, she cries and asks him, "Why did you leave us?" Antonio has told Rocío that he "does not sleep or eat." Rocío has contacted her church pastor, who is helping her find a lawyer who can help bring her husband back. Her pastor is also trying to help her to accept "this horrible situation" and believes that "si Dios quiere" (if God wills), Antonio will be able to return.

Rocío has come to family therapy with Jasmin and Adriana, after being referred by her physician who is concerned about her symptoms of depression and the consequences of Antonio's forced separation from both Rocío and her daughter.

Discussion: Case 2

Prior to deportation, Rocío and Antonio, admittedly happily married, differed with regard to disciplining their daughter, Jasmin. A structural family therapist would investigate the couple's capacity to parent together and effectively. An initial hypothesis would be that father, in his desire to have a close relationship with his daughter, undermines mother by undoing certain rules and expectations imposed by Rocío. A plausible question might be, Does a coalition exist between father and daughter against mother? In terms of boundaries, one might ask, Is there an overly diffuse boundary between

father and daughter, making for a less clear separation between the executive subsystem and the sibling subsystem? The culturally sensitive structuralist, however, would consider seriously the long hours worked by an immigrant father who wants to maximize his time with his daughter without being a disciplinarian. In addition, the therapist would consider differing forms of second-culture acquisition that have fathers rooted in traditional Latino culture, where mothers are expected to do the caretaking and fathers are responsible for protecting and providing for the family. For Rocío, gender roles appear more blurred as she expects her husband to participate in the household chores, which suggests a move toward the dominant culture's erosion of gender stereotypes. Adopting a strategy from the collaborative language approach, the therapist might have them talk about Rocío's use of the word "discipline" and what this means. It is possible that their respective cultural and family backgrounds have allowed them to understand "discipline" in different ways. The narrative therapist would listen to their respective stories for oppressive cultural determinants around Antonio's needing to be a "good father" to his daughter.

This pre-deportation family frame can contribute to helping the family after Antonio's separation. Cognizant that the family has suffered a terrible loss and that both mother and daughter are suffering symptoms of depression, the structuralist's goal remains to empower Rocío as a capable executor of her children. Currently functioning as a single mother and also sharing the grief of her daughter can result in a diffuse boundary, reduce Rocío's executive role, and thus contribute even more to Jasmine's feelings of vulnerability. The culturally sensitive therapist would consider Rocío's reliance on others outside the family (e.g., her sister, the pastor) not as weakness but as culturally appropriate ways of strengthening her executorship. In addition, the culturally aware therapist would consider the difficulties Rocío might have in developing trust in light of the deportation, and the therapist being seen as a handmaiden of the dominant culture responsible for separating her husband from his family. Through the lens of acculturation, Rocío's history indicates her capacity to transcend culturally inherited gender stereotypes by going to school and learning English, getting a job, contributing financially to her family, and understanding that her husband should help out with the housework, traditionally regarded as "women's" work. The therapist can build on Rocío's acculturation to strengthen her role of executor, relying on the mainstream/dominant culture that provides numerous models of survival for female-headed households. The counselor will take into account Rocío's cultural identity status to determine her ability to access healthy mechanisms that reside in both her native culture and the dominant Eurocentric culture of the United States.

None of this is meant to minimize the grief that Rocío and her daughter are experiencing, but the multicultural sensitive family therapist takes into consideration the positives of the cultural system(s) in which the family is embedded. In this case, the therapist can effectuate a biculturalism within the family by integrating the role of women in U.S. society along with Rocío's own cultural tradition of reliance upon extended family members to sustain her executorship in the family. A traditionalist might look with suspicion on the fact that Rocío comes to a family therapy session with her sister; the multiculturalist might consider it an asset. The structuralist would want to make sure that the sister is supporting and not undermining Rocío's executive role in the family, as this is a key element in reducing Jasmin's symptoms, which are clearly related to an increased sense of vulnerability.

Consideration can also be given to the use of some of the postmodern approaches to help with the family's grief over the loss of father. Although the grief process may have a universal quality to it, the multicultural family counselor recognizes that different cultures grieve differently and that the grief process can be unique to a particular family. Careful attention should be paid to the use of the words "sad" and "depressed" and the meanings attached to these words by both Rocío and her daughter. What is unspoken in this family? Up until now, they seemingly have done everything right to pursue a better life in this country and the American dream. Rocío and Antonio wanted their children to have "American" names because they are "American citizens." Pursuing this use of language, the family therapist might uncover newfound meaning attached to "American," especially in light of Antonio's abrupt and unexpected deportation. What meaning does Rocío give to such an action by government authorities? The narrative therapist would listen carefully to how the internalization of the cultural prescription of the "American dream" has become an oppressive one for the family from which they need to be freed in order to move on with their lives. Finally, the solutions-focused approach would isolate what the family is already doing to help the situation (e.g., relying on extended family, the church) and try to amplify these "solutions." An all-important question is: What makes the situation better or worse, because no problem exists to the same degree 24 hours a day, 7 days a week? Using a solutions approach, the multicultural family counselor would emphasize drawing upon the various cultural systems (e.g., church, the Latino importance of the *padrino*, the use of the dominant culture's legal system) in order to promote the family's effectiveness in not only dealing with their grief but also working toward reconciling the father with his family.

In this chapter, we have compared various therapeutic models of family therapy. We discuss both emic and idioemic perspectives as well as the inevitable tensions that exist between nomoethic and idiographic approaches. We also presented relevant vignettes and described salient dynamics and suggestions that a therapist working with the families may want to consider. By applying the different perspectives presented to the cases, we hope to advance a more flexible approach to working with families: extended, same-sex, single-parent, and nuclear. Because all families share both universal and unique dynamics, family therapists are called to integrate a multicultural perspective from which the family may be understood. When working with a family, therapists can highlight the families' strengths and uniqueness while also specifying their universal aspects. Through an integrative approach, a therapeutic space that facilitates psychological well-being for all families can be created.

REFERENCES

Anderson, H. (1997). *Conversation, language, and possibilities: A postmodern approach to therapy.* New York: Basic Books.

Anderson, H. (2001). Postmodern collaborative and person-centered therapies: What would Carl Rogers say? *Journal of Family Therapy, 23,* 339–360.

Anderson, H., & Goolishian, H. A. (1988). Human systems as linguistic systems: Preliminary and evolving ideas about the implications for clinical theory. *Family Process, 27,* 371–394.

Berg, I. K., & de Shazer, S. (1993). Making numbers talk: Language in therapy. In S. Friedman (Ed.), *The new language of change: Constructive collaboration in psychotherapy* (pp. 5–24). New York: Guilford.

Berry, J. W. (1990). Psychology of acculturation: Understanding individuals moving between cultures. In R. W. Brislin (Ed.), *Applied cross-cultural psychology* (pp. 232–253). Newbury Park, CA: Sage.

Bowen, M. (1966). The use of family theory in clinical practice. *Comprehensive Psychiatry, 7,* 345–374.

Griffith, J. L., & Griffith, M. E. (1994). *The body speaks: Therapeutic dialogues for mind-body problems.* New York: Basic Books.

Gushue, G. V. (1993). Cultural-identity development and family assessment: An interaction model. *Counseling Psychologist, 21,* 487–513.

Gushue, G. V., & Sciarra, D. T. (1995). Culture and families: A multidimensional approach. In J. G. Ponterotto, J. M. Casas, L. A. Suzuki, & C. M. Alexander (Eds.), *Handbook of multicultural counseling* (pp. 586–606). Thousand Oaks, CA: Sage.

Haley, J. (1987). *Problem-solving therapy: New strategies for effective family therapy* (2nd ed.). San Francisco: Jossey-Bass.

Helms, J. E. (1984). Toward a theoretical explanation of the effects of race on counseling: A black and white model. *Counseling Psychologist, 13,* 695–710.

Helms, J. E. (1995). An update of Helms's White and People of Color racial identity models. In J. G. Ponterotto, J. M. Casas, L. A. Suzuki, & C. M. Alexander (Eds.), *Handbook of multicultural counseling* (pp. 181–198). Thousand Oaks, CA: Sage.

Johnson, S. D., Jr. (1990). Toward clarifying culture, race, and ethnicity in the context of multicultural counseling. *Journal of Multicultural Counseling and Development, 18,* 41–50.

Kerr, M. E., & Bowen, M. (1988). *Family evaluation: An approach based on Bowen theory.* New York: Norton.

Miller, G., & de Shazer, S. (1998). Have you heard the latest rumor about . . . ? Solution-focused therapy as a rumor. *Family Process, 37,* 363–377.

Miller, G., & de Shazer, S. (2000). Emotions in solution-focused therapy: A re-examination. *Family Process, 39,* 5–23.

Minuchin, S. (1974). *Families and family therapy.* Cambridge, MA: Harvard University Press.

Minuchin, S., & Fishman, H. C. (1981). *Family therapy techniques.* Cambridge, MA: Harvard University Press.

Minuchin, S., Montalvo, B., Guerney, B., Rosman, B., & Schumer, F. (1967). *Families of the slums.* New York: Basic Books.

Neville, H. A., Lilly, R. L., Duran, G., Lee, R. M., & Browne, L. (2000). Construction and initial validation of the Color-Blind Racial Attitudes Scale (CoBRAS). *Journal of Counseling Psychology, 47,* 59–70.

Nichols, M. P., & Schwartz, R. C. (2006). *Family therapy: Concepts and methods* (7th ed.). Boston: Allyn & Bacon.

Paré, D. A. (1995). Of families and other cultures: The shifting paradigm of family therapy. *Family Process, 34,* 1–19.

Paré, D. A. (1996). Culture and meaning: Expanding the metaphorical repertoire of family therapy. *Family Process, 35,* 21–42.

Sciarra, D. T., & Simon, G. M. (2008). Assessment of diverse family systems. In L. A. Suzuki & J. G. Ponterotto (Eds.), *Handbook of multicultural assessment: Clinical, psychological, and educational applications* (3rd ed., pp. 247–272). San Francisco: Jossey-Bass.

Simon, G. M. (2003). *Beyond technique in family therapy: Finding your therapeutic voice.* Boston: Allyn & Bacon.

Sue, D. W., & Sue, D. (2003). *Counseling the culturally diverse: Theory and practice* (4th ed.). Hoboken, NJ: Wiley.

Szapocznik, J., & Kurtines, W. (1993). Family psychology and cultural diversity: Opportunities for theory, research and application. *American Psychologist, 48,* 400–407.

Szapocznik, J., Kurtines, W., Santisteban, D. A., & Pantin, H. (1997). The evolution of structural ecosystemic theory for working with Latino families. In J. G. Garcia & M. C. Zea (Eds.), *Psychological interventions and research with Latino populations* (pp. 166–190). Boston: Allyn & Bacon.

White, M. (1991). Deconstruction and therapy. *Dulwich Centre Newsletter, 3,* 21–40.

White, M., & Epston, D. (1990). *Narrative means to therapeutic ends.* New York: Norton.

PART XI

Multicultural Career Counseling and Development: Updates on Theory and Practice

The final section of this third edition of the *Handbook of Multicultural Counseling* focuses on career theory, research, and practice from multicultural perspectives. Career issues have always been a defining focus of the counseling and counseling psychology professions. The section opens with two state-of-the-art chapters reviewing the relevance and validity of two major career theories across cultures. Following this theoretical overview, three chapters present practical, research-supported career counseling models and interventions for culturally diverse individuals across the life span. Collectively, the five chapters comprising this section provide a concise mini-course on culturally relevant career theory and culturally informed career counseling practice.

The section opens in Chapter 53 with co-authors Robert W. Lent and Hung-Bin Sheu addressing the cross-cultural applicability of social cognitive career theory (SCCT). SCCT is a comprehensive, vibrant, and research-directing theory that is considered landmark for the counseling profession. Is this theory valid across cultures? Drs. Lent and Sheu open the chapter by reviewing SCCT's basic elements and predictive models. They then move to a careful and integrative review of select illustrative individual studies as well as to meta-analytic findings testing SCCT constructs within and across diverse cultures. Importantly, the authors direct readers to promising and important areas for needed research, including culture-specific model testing, modifying or expanding the SCCT model by adding culture-specific mechanisms or factors, emphasizing construct-relevant and valid research measures, and expanding methodologies to develop and test the model, including cross-sectional and longitudinal studies as well as qualitative research.

Chapter 54, written by multicultural pioneer Nadya A. Fouad (see Fouad, 2001) and co-author Neeta Kantamneni, focuses on the longstanding and popular Holland theory of career development. The authors first summarize the main tenets of John Holland's theory and then review empirical research testing various aspects of the theory. A major emphasis in the chapter is on assessing the validity of Holland's theory across diverse cultural groups within and outside the United States. Within this topical area, the authors integrate the research on measure equivalence across cultures, racial and ethnic group differences, structural differences in makeup of the model, and the congruence hypothesis. The chapter closes by detailing seven specific suggestions for needed research. Each of these research suggestions is prime material for doctoral dissertations and ongoing multicultural career research.

In Chapter 55, Margo A. Jackson, Cesar A. Leon, and Mira Zaharopoulos address culturally competent career interventions with adolescents who are vulnerable to discrimination. Thus this chapter moves the discussion from theoretical validity (Chapters 53 and 54) to practical application that is theoretically and empirically informed. The chapter opens with a clear discussion of the relevance of career interventions in facilitating positive identity and educational achievement with adolescents of color. The reality and detrimental impact of discrimination for diverse adolescents is highlighted, and the importance of career interventions that deal with bias preparation and resilience enhancement is emphasized. Importantly, the chapter addresses counselors' own resistance in working with culturally diverse adolescents and outlines resources for counselor training around these issues. Dr. Jackson and colleagues also critique relevant research on the topic, outline key developmental tasks for adolescents transitioning from school to work, and highlight implications for designing culturally relevant career interventions for diverse adolescents.

Mark Pope is the author of Chapter 56, and he provides a comprehensive discussion on career counseling with culturally diverse adults. Dr. Pope opens the chapter with a concise review of the history and context for multicultural career counseling with adults. He then moves to the importance of counselor self-assessment of their own biases relevant to counseling others. His discussion builds nicely off of the discussion of counselor resistance in the previous chapter. Dr. Pope reviews a number of client-focused interventions and issues that

counselors will want to consider, including discrimination, group career counseling, role of the family, dual-career couples, career testing, the role of internalized oppression, and "coming out" or disclosing cultural membership. The chapter closes with a discussion of program-focused interventions and social justice/advocacy interventions. Dr. Pope has provided comprehensive and applied coverage of career counseling for culturally diverse adults.

This third edition of the *Handbook* closes with Chapter 57, with V. Scott Solberg and Judith M. Ettinger writing on career development in older culturally diverse adults. The chapter focuses on designing career development strategies for older adults from diverse backgrounds who do not have the option of retiring. The authors anchor their discussion around three points: a social justice perspective, the integration of developmental and person-environment fit theories, and the counselor's own cultural awareness levels. The authors effectively contextualize their intervention suggestions around case studies of three culturally diverse older adults. The chapter provides a comprehensive understanding of career challenges of culturally diverse older adults as well as provides concrete, tested strategies for career development and counseling interventions with this diverse and rapidly growing segment of our population.

REFERENCE

Fouad, N. A. (2001). Reflections of a nonvisible racial/ethnic minority. In J. G. Ponterotto, J. M. Casas, L. A. Suzuki, & C. M. Alexander (Eds.), *Handbook of multicultural counseling* (2nd ed., pp. 55–63). Thousand Oaks, CA: Sage.

53

Applying Social Cognitive Career Theory Across Cultures: Empirical Status

ROBERT W. LENT AND HUNG-BIN SHEU

Social cognitive career theory (SCCT) was developed to help explain the career development of a broad range of persons (Lent, Brown, & Hackett, 1994, 2000). It brings together variables (e.g., interests, values, abilities) from a number of prior career theories, using Bandura's (1986, 1997) general social cognitive theory as a unifying framework. Most significantly for the present purposes, it is also intended to incorporate cultural and other contextual factors that pervade the career development process but that have not always been the explicit focus of earlier career theories. To create a more comprehensive picture of career development—and to respond to criticisms that career theorists had too often ignored the environment and the ways in which it can limit individuals' work options and progress (e.g., Fitzgerald & Betz, 1994)—SCCT focuses on factors that enable people to assert agency (i.e., personal control, volition) in their own career development as well as factors that can promote, impede, or even override agency.

Career and choice are two terms that have been the subject of controversy in vocational psychology. One may question whether the concept of career and the assumptions of traditional career theories are relevant for many workers (Smith, 1983; Warnath, 1975), particularly those whose occupational options are circumscribed by such sociostructural barriers as discrimination, poverty, or substandard education (Fitzgerald & Betz, 1994). From this perspective, the notion of career implies a certain economic strata and freedom from various contextual constraints, conferring the unfettered ability to steer one's own occupational ship. Some writers prefer the term *work* or working as being more inclusive (Blustein, 2006), recognizing that most people work but not everyone is sufficiently privileged to enjoy a career. The notion of *choice* has also long been critiqued in the vocational literature (Fitzgerald & Betz, 1994). It is clear that most people are simply not free to do whatever they wish to do in the world of work. Rather, *career choice* is at least a two-way street.

691

People select occupations, but they are also selected for them (Vroom, 1964). That is, the environment plays an undeniable, potent role in helping to determine who gets to do what and where, for how long, and with what sorts of rewards.

SCCT uses the term *career* in a generic and inclusive sense to encompass the sequence of work positions that persons occupy throughout their occupational lives (Super, 1980). It can also refer to the type (e.g., house-painter, piano teacher) and continuity of work that people perform. Such a definition does not imply that careers will necessarily be linear, stable, or free of constraints. In addition to work selection and adjustment, SCCT focuses on the periods of work preparation and entry; on transitions from school to work, between work options, and from work to retirement; and, more recently, on the interface between work and nonwork life roles. Although they may mean somewhat different things to different writers, in SCCT, *career* is synonymous with the terms *occupation, vocation,* and *work*. Moreover, in SCCT, *choice* refers to the process through which people select and pursue a particular occupational option or options—with full appreciation for the fact that choice is seldom if ever "free," that it typically entails compromise, and that the choice process takes place within a social, economic, historic, and cultural context.

It is difficult, if not impossible, to envision a career trajectory that is devoid of environmental influence. Indeed, the *social* in social cognitive career theory is intended to capture the essential roles that other people play throughout an individual's work life. We all encounter others who convey messages about our capabilities, who teach us, who provide models of different career options, who transmit values about what is important in life, who encourage or discourage our dreams, who open or close myriad doors. And, of course, individuals' social worlds are embedded in a cultural context. Among other things, cultures offer general templates regarding how, when, and by whom career choices should be made and what values they should be designed to fulfill (e.g., helping others, seeking personal satisfaction)—though the influence of a particular culture is open to wide within-group variations, and in multicultural environments, individuals absorb multiple and sometimes conflicting messages about what career paths, work conditions, and reinforcers are more or less

acceptable. Other contextual factors, such as the quality of education one has received, discrimination, and the financial resources of one's family, also enable or deter particular career options for particular persons.

Needless to say, the process of career choice and development is complex and multifaceted, and an adequate explanatory scheme will need to deal with factors that are both internal and external to the person. Contemporary career choice and development theories deal with person and contextual factors to varying degrees and in different ways, and all are intended to apply to a fairly wide range of persons. Although their range of cultural applicability may be subjected to expert critical analysis, we believe that cross-cultural validity is, ultimately, an empirical question (e.g., Lent & Worthington, 2000).

Our goal in this chapter is not to discuss the hypothetical merits of etic versus emic career theories. Instead, it is, more modestly, to consider the cross-cultural applicability of SCCT, a general theory of career development designed to lend itself to culture-specific tests and modifications (Lent et al., 1994). We first provide a brief overview of SCCT's basic elements and predictive models. We then offer a review of research that has applied the theory to diverse populations. Given space limitations and the number of culture-relevant applications of SCCT that have been generated in recent years, we can only provide a selective review here. We will, therefore, focus on tests of SCCT with racial-ethnic groups in the United States, relying mainly on a recent meta-analysis (Sheu et al., 2008). We will also note, albeit briefly, examples of theory extensions in other cultural contexts outside of the United States. More detailed presentations of SCCT and its research base, applications to particular groups (e.g., persons of color; women; persons with disabilities; lesbian, gay, bisexual, and transgender [LGBT] workers; persons outside of the United States), and practical implications can be found elsewhere (e.g., Betz, 2008; Brown & Lent, 1996; de Bruin, 1999; Fabian, 2000; Hackett & Byars, 1996; Lent, 2005; Morrow, Gore, & Campbell, 1996).

SCCT's INTEREST AND CHOICE MODELS

The original exposition of SCCT presented three interlocking models of academic and vocational (a) interest formation, (b) choice, and (c) performance and persistence (Lent et al., 1994). A fourth model, focusing on educational and work satisfaction, was recently added (Lent & Brown, 2006a). These models encompass an overlapping set of person, environmental, behavioral, and experiential variables that, together, are assumed to guide the process of career development throughout the life span. Given space limitations, our coverage will focus on the interest and choice models. These models have thus far attracted the majority of studies of SCCT, many of which have included consideration of diversity (especially gender, race, ethnicity, culture) and contextual factors. The interest and choice models are both embedded in Figure 53.1.

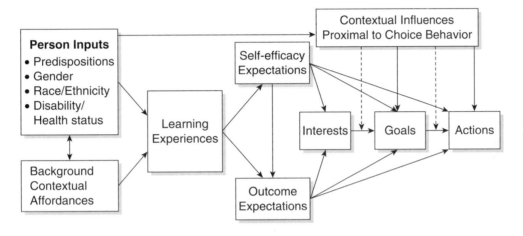

Figure 53.1 Model of Person, Contextual, and Experiential Factors That Help Shape Career-Related Interest and Choice

Note: Direct relations between variables are indicated with solid lines; moderator effects (where a given variable strengthens or weakens the relations between two other variables) are shown with dashed lines. Adapted, with permission, from Lent, Brown, and Hackett (1994).

SCCT's Cognitive Person Variables

SCCT highlights three key "person variables" that develop through repeated interaction with the environment and that also offer some measure of agency in career development: *self-efficacy beliefs, outcome expectations,* and *personal goals.* Self-efficacy beliefs refer to "people's judgments of their capabilities to organize and execute courses of action required to attain designated types of performances" (Bandura, 1986, p. 391). Social cognitive theory views self-efficacy as a dynamic set of self-beliefs that are specific to particular performance domains and contexts. It has been studied within a wide array of Holland themes, academic subjects, and work contexts, but the greatest concentration of research has examined self-efficacy in relation to science, technology, engineering, and mathematics (STEM) domains.

Self-efficacy beliefs develop via four primary types of learning experience: (a) personal performance accomplishments, (b) vicarious learning, (c) social persuasion, and (d) physiological and affective states (Bandura, 1997). Personal success and failure experiences are generally assumed to exert the greatest influence on self-efficacy, although observations of others' performance experiences, social support or discouragement, and one's affective state while engaged in particular activities can also have important effects on self-efficacy.

Outcome expectations are beliefs about the consequences of performing particular behaviors. Whereas self-efficacy beliefs are concerned with the central question, "Can I do this?" outcome expectations are directed at the complementary question, "If I try doing this, what will happen?" People are assumed to consider both self-efficacy and outcome expectations in choosing which school and work-related activities to pursue and which ones to avoid. Self-efficacy may be an especially influential determinant relative to choice options that involve complex skills or potentially costly or difficult courses of action. However, there can also be situations in which self-efficacy is high but outcome expectations are low. For example, women or students of color may be confident in their math and science capabilities but still refrain from elective courses or advanced study in these topics if they anticipate encountering such negative consequences as a chilly interpersonal environment, discrimination, or an absence of socially relevant role models.

Personal goals may be defined as one's intention to engage in a particular activity or to produce a particular outcome (Bandura, 1986). Through goal setting, people envision a possible career option (or options) and the steps necessary to attain it. Goal setting allows people an important route for organizing and guiding their own career behavior, although, of course, goal progress ultimately depends as well on a variety of factors over which the individual may have limited, if any, control. SCCT maintains that the relationship of goals to self-efficacy and outcome expectations is a reciprocal one: People ordinarily set goals that are consistent with their self-efficacy and outcome expectations, and the outcomes of goal pursuit also have an impact on subsequent self-efficacy and outcome expectations. For example, success at goal pursuit may strengthen beliefs about personal efficacy and the anticipation of future positive outcomes.

Other Person, Contextual, and Experiential Variables

Self-efficacy, outcome expectations, and goals do not develop in a void. Rather, they are intimately linked to a number of other key aspects of persons and their contexts, such as gender, race, ethnicity, culture, and socioeconomic status. SCCT is concerned with the psychological and social—rather than mere physical—aspects of demographic factors such as race or sex. These factors are viewed within SCCT as statuses that are socially conferred and constructed, and thus their primary relevance to career choice and development stems not from their biological properties but rather from the sort of learning experiences, supports, and barriers that people who look a certain way or who come from a particular background are afforded within a particular cultural context.

It is particularly useful to consider how variables such as gender and ethnicity affect the context in which self-efficacy and outcome expectations develop. Hackett and Betz (1981), who initiated the study of career self-efficacy, were concerned with uncovering the reasons why women often underuse their abilities in selecting among career options. In their theoretical analysis, they noted that gender role socialization biases the access that boys and girls have to the learning experiences necessary for developing a strong sense of efficacy at traditionally male- versus female-typed activities. For instance, boys are more likely to receive encouragement for pursuing science-related activities and thus are at an advantage for developing the skills and self-efficacy that help nurture STEM career paths. Moreover, there is a progressive narrowing of options with respect to STEM (and other) options because failure to gain elective coursework and experiences and to do well at earlier levels restricts access to later courses and academic majors. Likewise, Hackett and Byars (1996) pointed out how gender, culture, and opportunity affect the acquisition of self-efficacy beliefs in persons of color, particularly African American women.

Interest and Choice Hypotheses

SCCT's formal hypotheses about interest development and career choice are concerned with how the above variables operate together to either foster or deter educational and occupational paths. Briefly, the basic predictions of the interest model posit that "interest in an activity is likely to blossom and endure when people (1) view themselves as competent (self-efficacious) at the activity and (2) anticipate that performing it will produce valued outcomes (positive outcome expectations)" (Lent, 2005, p. 106). Conversely, people may become disinterested in or even averse to activities at which they possess low self-efficacy and pessimistic outcome expectations.

SCCT's choice model assumes that people are most likely to set and pursue career choice goals that are consistent with their vocational interests as well as with their self-efficacy beliefs and outcome expectations. Choices are also co-forged by environmental and cultural factors. In particular, SCCT highlights the role of environmental supports and barriers that accompany particular choice goals, predicting that people are more likely to select and pursue a particular career path when they experience strong environmental supports and weak environmental barriers in relation to this path.

Moreover, the theory maintains that people do not always have the luxury to pursue their preferred career paths or ones that are consistent with their interests. For instance, personal interests may need to be compromised in the choice process due to family dictates or economic realities. Under such conditions, people are likely to select among available options based less on their interest than on their self-efficacy, outcome expectations, and environmental supports and barriers in relation to these options. In collectivist cultures, for instance, choice may be more of a family decision than an individual one, with key family members being likely to provide differential support and resources for the pursuit of family-approved options.

In sum, gender, ethnicity, and other "social address" variables may partly affect career interest and choice through the differential learning experiences that give rise to self-efficacy and outcome expectations. For example, by virtue of how environmental resources are allocated with respect to race and SES, certain students may receive poorer quality educational experiences and access to a truncated range of vocational role models, thereby dampening their self-efficacy and outcome expectations regarding career options that require higher education. Environmental (e.g., social, cultural, material) factors are also linked to the structure of opportunity within which people set and implement their educational and career goals. Thus, SCCT focuses on the several routes by which person, contextual, and experiential factors interact to shape the course of career choice and development.

CROSS-CULTURAL RESEARCH STATUS

There has been a good deal of research testing the basic hypotheses of SCCT's interest and choice models with persons of color in the United States as well as a smaller but growing body of research studying SCCT's models in other countries and cultural contexts. Some of the research has examined bivariate relations among particular sets of SCCT variables, such as the relation of self-efficacy to choice goals. We will first cite illustrative studies that have tested fuller (i.e., multivariate) versions of the interest and choice models with U.S.

minority as well as cross-national samples. We will then present meta-analytic findings that have tested these models with both racial-ethnic minority and majority samples. The latter findings are particularly important because they involve the synthesis of data over multiple studies and allow an empirical basis for assessing the cross-cultural validity of SCCT. We will confine our review to interest in and choice of STEM-related courses and majors because this domain has been the focal point for much of the research on SCCT, most U.S. racial-ethnic minority groups are underrepresented in STEM fields, and space limitations preclude a more extensive literature review.

Illustrative Studies

The earliest multivariate tests of SCCT's interest and choice hypotheses tended to focus on the core cognitive person variables of self-efficacy, outcome expectations, interests, and choice goals, without including contextual variables (e.g., social supports and barriers). Fouad and Smith (1996) examined SCCT in a sample of 380 inner-city middle school students, most of whom were either Hispanic or African American. Consistent with hypotheses, they found that self-efficacy and outcome expectations jointly predicted interests in math and science activities and, together with interests, helped explain students' goals to pursue math- and science-related courses and career paths in the future. Studying a sample of 164 Black college students, Gainor and Lent (1998) examined the core cognitive person variables, along with measures of racial identity attitudes, as predictors of interest and choice in math and science pursuits. The social cognitive predictions of interests and choice were found to hold across levels of racial identity attitudes, and the latter were largely unrelated either to the interest or choice criteria.

Recognizing the important role of the environment in the choice process, tests of SCCT's choice model have gradually begun to examine the ways in which social-contextual variables, such as supports, barriers, and family influences, operate along with the cognitive person variables to help shape students' choice goals. For example, Tang, Fouad, and Smith (1999) added measures of acculturation, socioeconomic status, and family involvement to self-efficacy and interests as predictors of career choice in a sample of 187 Asian American students. They found that interests, which typically serve as good predictors of choice across a variety of cultural contexts (Hansen, 2005), did not predict the traditionality of Asian American students' career choices once the effects of self-efficacy, acculturation, and family involvement were taken into account. These findings suggest that, under certain conditions (e.g., a collectivist cultural context), personal interests may give way to other variables, such as perceptions of personal capabilities and familial input, in the setting of career goals.

Another important development in the testing of SCCT has been the comparison of model fit within racial-ethnic minority and majority samples. In one such study, Lent et al. (2005) examined the predictive validity of the choice model in two samples, one composed of 221 (mostly African American) students from historically Black universities and the other containing 266 (mostly European American) students from a predominantly White university. Students in both samples were mostly in their first or second years as engineering majors. A multiple-group structural equation analysis indicated that the model accounted well for academic interests and choices across both groups of students. Support was also found for the model in subsamples of men and women. These findings were replicated and extended in a recent, larger scale study of students in the computing disciplines (Lent, Lopez, Lopez, & Sheu, 2008). These types of studies are useful because, by directly testing the invariance of model fit across different groups, one can examine empirically the degree to which SCCT's predictions are applicable across culture, race, gender, and other dimensions of diversity.

Finally, research has also begun to test SCCT's tenability in different cultural groups outside of the United States. For instance, Lent, Brown, Nota, and Soresi (2003) studied 796 high school students in northern Italy. The students completed measures of self-efficacy, outcome expectations, interests, social supports and barriers, and occupational aspirations across all six Holland themes. The results indicated that the model generally fit the data well for all themes. However, as has been found in U.S. tests of the choice model (e.g., Lent et al., 2005), supports and barriers tended to relate to the choice criteria indirectly through self-efficacy, rather than directly. Paixão, da Silva, and Leitão (2007) obtained similar findings in a replication of this study with Portuguese high school students.

Meta-Analytic Findings

Several meta-analyses have been conducted to integrate the findings of this rapidly growing literature. Most of these analyses have calculated traditional bivariate effect sizes (e.g., weighted mean correlations) over groupings of individual studies. For example, in a meta-analysis of 53 samples containing, collectively, nearly 38,000 participants, Rottinghaus, Larson, and Borgen (2003) found that self-efficacy correlated strongly with interests ($r = .59$). In an earlier meta-analysis, Lent et al. (1994) found moderate to strong (.40–.60) theory-consistent correlations among self-efficacy, outcome expectations, interests, and choice goals over smaller subsets of studies.

Such meta-analyses are helpful in testing SCCT's bivariate hypotheses (e.g., that self-efficacy should relate to interests). However, they cannot adequately test the network of relations among sets of variables that are specified by the theory (e.g., self-efficacy is hypothesized to relate to interests both directly and indirectly through outcome expectations). Because they focus on relations among pairs of variables, without taking into account the presence of other predictors, bivariate meta-analyses are likely to overestimate the relation of a particular predictor to a criterion variable. Moreover, such meta-analyses do not examine indirect, or mediator, pathways; neither do they assess the overall fit of a multivariate model to the data. While bivariate meta-analyses can examine race or other diversity dimensions as moderators of particular predictor-criterion relations (e.g., is self-efficacy a better predictor of interests in group A or B?), existing meta-analyses have not yet delved much into this issue.

A new class of methods, which may be termed *meta-analytic path analysis,* has been developed that allows investigators to surmount some of the limitations of bivariate meta-analysis. Sheu et al. (2008) recently conducted a meta-analytic path analysis of studies testing SCCT's choice model (which subsumes the basic predictions about interest development). They used a two-stage structural equation modeling procedure (TSSEM;

Cheung & Chen, 2005) that enables the synthesis of entire correlation matrices (rather than just a single correlation) over studies. The first step of the analysis involves identifying subsets of studies that yield homogeneous correlation matrices. In the second step, the pooled correlation matrices from these studies are subjected to path analysis.

Sheu et al. (2008) identified studies that had examined either of two versions of SCCT's choice model in the context of STEM-related choices: (a) a four-variable version, including self-efficacy, outcome expectations, interests, and choice goals, or (b) a six-variable model, consisting of the same four variables plus environmental supports and barriers. The four-variable model tests emerged earlier and are more numerous than the six-variable tests. For the purpose of examining race as a moderator of variable relations, Sheu et al. also categorized the samples into (a) racial minority, (b) racial majority, and (c) combined race groups, based on whether they were primarily composed of one racial group or were relatively heterogeneous with respect to race.

The four-variable model accounted for around one third to one half of the variation in interests and choice for all three groups (racial minority, three samples, $n = 540$; combined race, five samples, $n = 5,835$; and racial majority, three samples, $n = 295$). In addition, except for one path in the combined race group, each of the paths among self-efficacy, outcome expectations, interests, and choice goals yielded significant coefficients for each group. These path coefficients (ranging between .10 and .49) reflected mostly small to medium effect sizes. On balance, the findings suggest that (a) self-efficacy and outcome expectations together explain substantial variation in interests; (b) self-efficacy, outcome expectations, and interests each explain unique variation in choice; and (c) the relations of self-efficacy and outcome expectations to choice are generally both indirect (mediated by interests) and direct.

Although the meta-analytic findings for the four-variable model version were largely consistent with SCCT for each of the three groups, there was some variability among the three groups in terms of the magnitude of specific path coefficients. For instance, the direct path from self-efficacy to choice goals was larger for the racial minority group than for the other two groups, and the path from outcome expectations to choice goals was larger in the combined race and racial majority groups than for the racial minority group. The paths from interest to choice, meanwhile, were roughly equivalent across all three groups.

Sufficient data were available to test the six-variable model in only two of the groups (racial minority, two samples, $n = 376$; combined race, three samples, $n = 700$). The basic SCCT model fit the data well in the racial minority group and less optimally in the combined race group. Once again, the model explained large amounts of variation in both interests and choice goals, and the paths linking self-efficacy, outcome expectations, interests, and choice goals were mostly significant and of small to moderate size for both groups. Environmental supports were linked to choices mostly indirectly (through self-efficacy and outcome expectations) rather than directly for both groups. Barriers generally offered limited unique predictive value.

As in the case of the four-variable model variation, there were some differences in path coefficients as a function of racial group. Specifically, self-efficacy appeared to be a better predictor of both interest and choice in the racial minority than in the combined race group, whereas outcome expectations constituted a stronger predictor of choice in the combined race group than in the racial minority group. The two groups did not differ, however, in terms of the path coefficients from interests, supports, or barriers to choice.

The differential predictive utility of self-efficacy over outcome expectations for the racial minority group is intriguing, particularly since it is contrary to what some authors had posited. For example, Leong and Brown (1995) argued that, because of discrimination and other forms of bias, outcome expectations may constitute a more salient explanatory mechanism than self-efficacy for ethnic minorities. It is challenging to interpret the opposite pattern revealed by the Sheu et al. (2008) meta-analysis for a few reasons. For instance, the meta-analysis did not include variables (like differential access to sources of self-efficacy and outcome expectations, such as career role models or occupational information) that could help explain how these percepts develop and function in different racial-ethnic groups. Also, the findings are based on relatively small sets of studies that used a limited number of measures.

Our caveats suggest the need for more research on the basis for and stability of racial-cultural differences among the predictors of interest and choice in SCCT. On the other hand, while their basis may not be entirely clear, the overall pattern of findings—both from individual studies and meta-analyses—suggests that the basic choice model offers explanatory utility across minority and majority racial-ethnic groups in the United States. Moreover, at a clinical level, the findings suggest the value of assessing self-efficacy beliefs within the context of academic and major choice interventions with racial minority clients— and, potentially, of efforts to strengthen self-efficacy in instances where unrealistically low self-efficacy may be constraining choice goals or actions (Brown & Lent, 1996; Hackett & Byars, 1996).

SUMMARY AND FUTURE DIRECTIONS

Culture-focused research on SCCT might take a number of fruitful directions. We will highlight several specific directions in this section.

Model Testing Within Particular Racial-Ethnic Groups and Across Cultural Contexts

Given the nature of the studies that have been conducted to this point, the Sheu et al. (2008) meta-analysis involved aggregation of data over different racial-ethnic minority samples (and African Americans were the largest group in most of the minority samples). Thus, there is a continuing need to study SCCT predictions in Hispanic, Asian, and Native American samples. Such studies will allow future meta-analyses to examine the issue of model invariance across particular racial-ethnic groups (rather than only across racial majority and combined racial-ethnic minority samples).

It would also be valuable to study further the degree to which SCCT's basic models fit the data across culture, gender, and other forms of diversity. To this point, most of the cross-cultural tests of SCCT have applied the interest and choice models to groups of U.S. minority and majority student samples. Additional research is needed on how well these models fare in other cultural contexts outside of the United States. Cross-national research on SCCT has begun but has mostly involved Western European samples to this

point (e.g., Lent et al., 2003; Paixão et al., 2007). Extension to other countries representing more diverse cultural orientations (e.g., Asia, Africa, the Middle East, South America, Eastern Europe) would be valuable. It would also be useful to subject the SCCT models of performance and satisfaction to cross-cultural research (e.g., Lent, Taveira, Sheu, & Singley, 2009). Such research could help to establish the range of applicability of SCCT's various career development models.

Inclusion of Diverse Cultural Mechanisms

Lent et al. (1994) described SCCT as a "broad framework [that] could be elaborated further to better capture the issues, challenges, and obstacles that especially characterize the career development of particular groups" (p. 117). Their view was that, while SCCT may serve as a useful general perspective on career development, it could also be fine-tuned in an emic sense by incorporating contextual and experiential factors that may be relatively unique to particular groups. Thus far, several studies have included culture-specific factors, such as acculturation (Tang et al., 1999) and racial identity attitudes (Gainor & Lent, 1998), into tests of SCCT's choice model with particular racial-ethnic groups.

In adding culture-specific variables to SCCT studies, the key challenge lies in articulating *how*, conceptually, they should operate in relation to SCCT's core person variables (e.g., self-efficacy). Should they be expected, for instance, to be part of the distal contextual affordances that help to shape children's learning experiences and, ultimately, self-efficacy and outcome expectations? Might they inform the proximal contextual factors that, in turn, affect the framing or pursuit of choice goals during active phases of choice making? Might they themselves be recast in social cognitive terms (e.g., collectivist values could be incorporated into outcome expectation measures)? Or might they function as moderators of particular variable relationships in SCCT (e.g., do interest-choice relations diminish or strengthen under different cultural conditions)? Building a clear conceptual bridge between SCCT and cultural variables that emanate from other theories is necessary to avoid the pitfalls of "cafeteria-style theorizing in which constructs are plucked from divergent theories and strung together" (Bandura, 1995, p. 354) without much forethought about how, why, or even if they should fit together.

Measurement Considerations

Proper tests of SCCT require adequate measures. Lent and Brown (2006b) offered a measurement guide for conceptualizing and assessing SCCT's core constructs. Among their recommendations, Lent and Brown suggested that outcome variables be properly linked to SCCT (i.e., that they reflect criteria that SCCT is designed to explain) and that predictors and outcome variables align appropriately with one another in terms of behavioral domain, level of specificity, and temporal frame (e.g., if choice of STEM fields is the outcome criterion, each of the SCCT predictors should be specific to this domain). While these measurement prescriptions are of general relevance to tests of SCCT, they are particularly relevant to cross-cultural tests. Deficient measures cannot provide an adequate basis for testing hypotheses within a particular culture, much less across cultures.

Many culture-specific factors (e.g., racial identity, acculturation, worldview, collectivism) are measured in relatively global fashion. For instance, racial identity attitudes are presumed to remain constant across behavioral domains. This poses both a measurement and, as suggested above, a conceptual challenge to studying them in conjunction with SCCT's domain-specific variables. Part of the solution may lie in articulating and then testing plausible pathways through which the two sets of variables may interrelate. For instance, broader cultural factors may be conceptualized as affecting the nature of domain-specific self-efficacy building experiences or the contextual supports and barriers to which particular students are exposed. Or certain cultural factors, such as collectivistic cultural values, may be posited to moderate particular variable relations within SCCT.

Toward Diversity of Methodological Tools

SCCT's cross-cultural validity can be assessed in two general ways. First, studies can test the theory's predictions within a particular cultural context. A second strategy is to directly compare model fit across two or more distinct groups. The first strategy is useful in exploring the cultural scenarios in which SCCT is more or less tenable, but the second strategy allows for more precise assessment of whether model fit (or particular path coefficients) is stronger in one group or another. Ultimately, of course, findings need to be aggregated across individual studies to strengthen inferences about cross-cultural validity. However, multiple-group structural equation modeling (SEM) offers a flexible statistical tool for implementing the second strategy, allowing direct comparison of multivariate model fit across two or more cultural groups, within individual studies (e.g., Lent et al., 2005; Lent et al., 2008).

To properly interpret the results of cross-cultural comparison studies, one must ascertain the conceptual and measurement equivalence of the variables of interest across cultural groups. Conceptual equivalence means that a psychological construct has the same meaning across cultures (van de Vijver, 2001). Measurement equivalence involves the extent to which an instrument is operationalizing a construct in an equivalent manner across groups (Byrne, Shavelson, & Muthén, 1989). For instance, does social support mean the same thing in two samples, one representing a collectivist and the other an individualist culture? Does a particular measure of social support bear the same psychometric properties in these two samples? An affirmative answer to both questions is necessary to increase confidence that a test of cross-cultural validity is itself valid. See Miller and Sheu (2008) and Sheu and Sedlacek (2009) for detailed discussion of these two forms of equivalence.

Finally, future cross-cultural research on SCCT will, ideally, employ diverse research methods and designs, tailored to the specific research questions of interest. For instance, a comprehensive understanding of the role of culture in career development may require a methodologically diverse research program that includes cross-sectional studies (e.g., do particular cultural factors relate to choice goals either directly or indirectly through self-efficacy or the learning experiences that shape it?), longitudinal studies (e.g., do cultural socialization experiences predict subsequent self-efficacy beliefs?), qualitative methods (e.g., how do different groups perceive the impact of particular person or social variables on their career choice goals?), and experimental designs (e.g., what generic or group-specific intervention elements can be used to foster the career development of persons from particular cultures?).

CONCLUSIONS

We offered an overview of SCCT, particularly its interest and choice models, and reviewed research applying these models to racial-ethnic majority and minority samples in the United States as well as to international samples. Our review suggests the continuing need to explore the role that cultural factors play relative to SCCT and, by extension, other theories of career development. Several conceptual and methodological issues related to the inclusion of cultural factors within studies of SCCT were also discussed. Additional research will allow a better appreciation of the parts of the SCCT models that are broadly applicable across cultures and those that are culture specific. This type of knowledge may, in turn, assist practitioners in designing and delivering better, more culturally appropriate career counseling services.

REFERENCES

Bandura, A. (1986). *Social foundations of thought and action: A social cognitive theory*. Englewood Cliffs, NJ: Prentice Hall.

Bandura, A. (1995). On rectifying conceptual ecumenism. In J. E. Maddux (Ed.), *Self-efficacy, adaptation, and adjustment: Theory, research, and application* (pp. 347–375). New York: Plenum.

Bandura, A. (1997). *Self-efficacy: The exercise of control*. New York: Freeman.

Betz, N. E. (2008). Advances in vocational theories. In S. D. Brown & R. W. Lent (Eds.), *Handbook of counseling psychology* (4th ed., pp. 357–374). New York: John Wiley.

Blustein, D. L. (2006). *The psychology of working: A new perspective for career development, counseling, and public policy*. Mahwah, NJ: Lawrence Erlbaum.

Brown, S. D., & Lent, R. W. (1996). A social cognitive framework for career choice counseling. *Career Development Quarterly, 44*, 354–366.

Byrne, B. M., Shavelson, R. J., & Muthén, B. (1989). Testing for the equivalence of factor covariance and mean structures: The issue of partial measurement invariance. *Psychological Bulletin, 105*, 456–466.

Cheung, M. W. L., & Chen, W. (2005). Meta-analytic structural equation modeling: A two-stage approach. *Psychological Methods, 10*, 40–64.

de Bruin, G. P. (1999). Social cognitive career theory as an explanatory model for career counselling in South Africa.

In G. B. Stead & M. B. Watson (Eds.), *Career psychology in the South African context* (pp. 91–102). Pretoria, South Africa: J. L. van Schaik.

Fabian, E. S. (2000). Social cognitive theory of careers and individuals with serious mental health disorders: Implications for psychiatric rehabilitation programs. *Psychiatric Rehabilitation Journal, 23*, 262–269.

Fitzgerald, L. F., & Betz, N. E. (1994). Career development in cultural context: The role of gender, race, class, and sexual orientation. In M. L. Savickas & R. W. Lent (Eds.), *Convergence in theories of career choice and development* (pp. 103–117). Palo Alto, CA: Consulting Psychologists Press.

Fouad, N. A., & Smith, P. L. (1996). A test of a social cognitive model for middle school students: Math and science. *Journal of Counseling Psychology, 43*, 338–346.

Gainor, K. A., & Lent, R. W. (1998). Social cognitive expectations and racial identity attitudes in predicting the math choice intentions of Black college students. *Journal of Counseling Psychology, 45*, 403–413.

Hackett, G., & Betz, N. E. (1981). A self-efficacy approach to the career development of women. *Journal of Vocational Behavior, 18*, 326–336.

Hackett, G., & Byars, A. M. (1996). Social cognitive theory and the career development of African American women. *The Career Development Quarterly, 44*, 322–340.

Hansen, J. C. (2005). Assessment of interests. In S. D. Brown & R. W. Lent (Eds.), *Career development and counseling: Putting theory and research to work* (pp. 281–304). New York: John Wiley.

Lent, R. W. (2005). A social cognitive view of career development and counseling. In S. D. Brown & R. W. Lent (Eds.), *Career development and counseling: Putting theory and research to work* (pp. 101–127). New York: John Wiley.

Lent, R. W., & Brown, S. D. (2006a). Integrating person and situation perspectives on work satisfaction: A social-cognitive view. *Journal of Vocational Behavior, 69*, 236–247.

Lent, R. W., & Brown, S.D. (2006b). On conceptualizing and assessing social cognitive constructs in career research: A measurement guide. *Journal of Career Assessment, 14*, 12–35.

Lent, R. W., Brown, S. D., & Hackett, G. (1994). Toward a unifying social cognitive theory of career and academic interest, choice, and performance [Monograph]. *Journal of Vocational Behavior, 45*, 79–122.

Lent, R. W., Brown, S. D., & Hackett, G. (2000). Contextual supports and barriers to career choice: A social cognitive analysis. *Journal of Counseling Psychology, 47*, 36–49.

Lent, R. W., Brown, S. D., Nota, L., & Soresi, S. (2003). Testing social cognitive interest and choice hypotheses across Holland types in Italian high school students. *Journal of Vocational Behavior, 62,* 101–118.

Lent, R. W., Brown, S. D., Sheu, H., Schmidt, J., Brenner, B. R., Gloster, C. S., et al. (2005). Social cognitive predictors of academic interests and goals in engineering: Utility for women and students at historically Black universities. *Journal of Counseling Psychology, 52,* 84–92.

Lent, R. W., Lopez, A. M., Lopez, F. G., & Sheu, H. (2008). Social cognitive career theory and the prediction of interests and choice goals in the computing disciplines. *Journal of Vocational Behavior, 73,* 52–62.

Lent, R. W., Taveira, M., Sheu, H., & Singley, D. (2009). Social cognitive predictors of academic adjustment and life satisfaction in Portuguese college students: A longitudinal analysis. *Journal of Vocational Behavior, 74,* 190–198.

Lent, R. W., & Worthington, R. L. (2000). On school-to-work transition, career development theories, and cultural validity. *Career Development Quarterly, 48,* 376–384.

Leong, F. T. L., & Brown, M. T. (1995). Theoretical issues in cross-cultural career development: Cultural validity and cultural specificity. In W. B. Walsh & S. H. Osipow (Eds.), *Handbook of vocational psychology: Theory, research, and practice* (2nd ed., pp. 143–180). Mahwah, NJ: Lawrence Erlbaum.

Miller, M. J., & Sheu, H. (2008). Conceptual and measurement issues in multicultural psychology research. In S. D. Brown & R. W. Lent (Eds.), *Handbook of counseling psychology* (4th ed., pp. 103–120). New York: John Wiley.

Morrow, S. L., Gore, P. A., & Campbell, B. W. (1996). The application of a sociocognitive framework to the career development of lesbian women and gay men. *Journal of Vocational Behavior, 48,* 136–148.

Paixão, M. P., da Silva, J. T., & Leitão, L. M. (2007, September). *Occupational considerations in a sample of Portuguese adolescents: Replicating Lent et al. (2003) study.* Paper presented at the meeting of the International Association for Educational and Vocational Guidance, University of Padova, Padova, Italy.

Rottinghaus, P. J., Larson, L. M., & Borgen, F. H. (2003). The relation of self-efficacy and interests: A meta-analysis of 60 samples. *Journal of Vocational Behavior, 62,* 221–236.

Sheu, H., Lent, R. W., Miller, M. J., Hennessy, K. D., Duffy, R. D., & Brown, S. D. (2008). *Testing the interest and choice hypotheses of social cognitive career theory in relation to science, technology, engineering, and mathematics domains: A meta-analytic path analysis.* Unpublished manuscript.

Sheu, H., & Sedlacek, W. E. (2009). Cross-cultural issues in counseling research. In C. C. Lee, D. A. Burnhill, A. L. Butler, C. P. Hipolito-Delgado, M. Humphrey, O. Muñoz, et al. (Eds.), *Elements of culture in counseling* (pp. 226–241). Boston: Allyn & Bacon.

Smith, E. J. (1983). Issues in racial minorities' career behavior. In W. B. Walsh & S. H. Osipow (Eds.), *Handbook of vocational psychology: Vol. 1. Foundations* (pp. 161–222). Hillsdale, NJ: Lawrence Erlbaum.

Super, D. E. (1980). A life-span, life-space approach to career development. *Journal of Vocational Behavior, 13,* 282–298.

Tang, M., Fouad, N. A., & Smith, P. L. (1999). Asian Americans' career choices: A path model to examine factors influencing their career choices. *Journal of Vocational Behavior, 54,* 142–157.

van de Vijver, F. J. R. (2001). The evolution of cross-cultural research methods. In D. Matsumoto (Ed.), *The handbook of culture and psychology* (pp. 77–97). New York: Oxford University Press.

Vroom, V. H. (1964). *Work and motivation.* New York: John Wiley.

Warnath, C. (1975). Vocational theories: Direction to nowhere. *Personnel & Guidance Journal, 53,* 422–428.

54

Cultural Validity of Holland's Theory

NADYA A. FOUAD AND NEETA KANTAMNENI

Person-environment fit models have played an important role in vocational psychology over the past century. Since Frank Parsons's (1909) tripartite model, career development researchers and practitioners alike have focused on helping individuals gain a better understanding of themselves, the world of work, and the relationship between themselves and work. Stemming from Parsons's model, theories of person-environment fit have focused on analyzing the self in relation to the world of work, with an emphasis on matching people to work environments that best fit their personality and interests. The most widely researched and employed framework of person-environment fit is Holland's theory of vocational personalities and work environments (Betz, 2008; Spokane & Cruza-Guet, 2005; Swanson & Gore, 2000).

This chapter reviews the central tenets of Holland's theory, reviews U.S. research related to the theory, and discusses the ways that the theory has been operationalized through interest inventories. We then discuss evidence of the cultural validity of the theory (Leong & Brown, 1995; Quintana, Troyano, & Taylor, 2001).

As Leong and Brown (1995) and Quintana et al. (2001) suggested, cultural validity is a form of construct validity: How well does the theory and its related constructs function in different cultures? Holland's theory is culturally valid if the measures are equivalent across cultures, if the constructs are related in similar ways across cultures, and if the usefulness of the theory is similar across cultural groups. This is critical to know because Holland's model is used as a basis for interest inventories and career assessment programs all over the world (Betz, 2008).

HOLLAND'S THEORY

Holland's theory was initially proposed in 1959 (Holland, 1959). Holland (1997) noted that the initial development of the theory was influenced by both his experiences as a practitioner and as a developer of the Vocational Preference Inventory (Holland, 1958). The applicability and operationalization of the theory have continued to be strong influences in the popularity and usefulness of the theory 50 years later. Holland's

(1997) theory is based on the premise that career choice is an expression of an individual's personality and that a reciprocal relationship exists between people and their environments. Both people and environments can be characterized as one or a combination of six different personality and environment types (Realistic, Investigative, Artistic, Social, Enterprising, and Conventional; RIASEC). Briefly stated, Realistic interest types are interested in mechanics, construction, and repair activities as well as working with nature and outdoors; Investigative interest types enjoy obtaining scientific knowledge, uncovering and gathering new facts, and analyzing and interpreting data; Artistic types tend to have aesthetic qualities and value self-expression through artistic work; Social types enjoy working with others collaboratively and nurturing/caring for others; Enterprising types enjoy leading others and obtaining economic success; and Conventional types prefer strong attention to detail, accuracy, and organization.

The structure of interest types is assumed to be hexagonal, with the six interest types arranged in an invariant order (Holland, 1997). The order is Realistic, Investigative, Artistic, Social, Enterprising, and Conventional (RIASEC). Adjacent types are predicted to be more similar, and types directly opposite each other (e.g., Investigative-Enterprising) on the hexagon are most dissimilar. Labeled the calculus hypothesis, the structure of RIASEC interest types is an essential component of Holland's theory. The distances between the types or environments are assumed to be inversely proportional to one another, and the types are presumed to be equidistant around the hexagon.

Holland (1997) proposes that cultural and personal factors interact with one another to create a characteristic set of attitudes and skills for each of these personality types. Similarly, environments can be characterized by a combination of personality types. People are presumed to search for environments that enable them to express their attitudes and use their skills. Individuals are also hypothesized to avoid environments that require undesirable responsibilities (e.g., an individual with Artistic interests is likely to avoid a Conventional work environment because of the attention to detail and organization skills required of that environment). Holland's model is based on the fundamental premise that a match between an individual's interests and

work environment leads to optimal career choices. Theoretically, Holland's theory asserts that if individuals' personality types are assessed, individuals' vocational outcomes may be predicted, such as job satisfaction and tenure, and counselors can help individuals make satisfying occupational choices.

Holland (1997) has four constructs associated with the six personality types: consistency, differentiation, identity, and congruence. The consistency hypothesis proposes that the shorter the distance between interest types in the hexagonal pattern, the more similar the interests are, and thus the stronger and more consistent the rewards of the environment. For example, Realistic and Investigative interests are close in proximity to one another; therefore, these two interest themes more closely resemble one another when compared to other interest categories. Investigative and Enterprising interests are far from one another in proximity, and thus these interest categories are dissimilar to one another. Theoretically, consistency is hypothesized to be related to vocational preference; individuals who possess consistent interests (e.g., Realistic and Investigative) are expected to have more predictable vocational choices than those who have inconsistent interests (e.g., Realistic and Social).

The second construct, differentiation, is the difference between an individual's highest and lowest themes. Some individuals and environments are more clearly defined than others (Holland, 1997), and the more clearly defined, the narrower the interests. An individual may closely resemble only a single interest type and show very little resemblance to other types; another individual may resemble several interest types. The same is true for environments; some environments closely resemble one interest type, and others resemble several interest types. A differentiated individual or environment is characterized by resembling only a single type, whereas an undifferentiated individual or environment is characterized by an equal number of the six interest types and will not indicate preference for any one of the RIASEC types (Holland, 1997). Differentiation is hypothesized to predict career choice; differentiated individuals are expected to have more predictable career choices than undifferentiated individuals.

The third construct, identity, is the clarity, consistency, and stability of an individual's vocational goals and interests (Holland, 1997). A highly identified individual has consistent and stable career interests, whereas as a low identified individual has inconsistent interests that change often. Holland's theory also assumes that environments have an identity. Environments that are highly defined are related to clear, stable, and consistent environmental goals, whereas environments that are poorly identified possess unclear and inconsistent environmental goals. High levels of vocational identity are predicted to be related to job tenure, level of performance, and job satisfaction.

The fourth and perhaps most central construct is congruence (Holland, 1997). Different types of people create different environments; career choices are "congruent" when there is a match between personality type and work environment. Congruent work environments provide the opportunities and rewards needed for job satisfaction and fulfillment. For example, individuals who possess Investigative interests prosper in Investigative work environments. Conversely, incongruence occurs when there is not a match between an individual's personality type and the work environment. This would occur, for example, if a Realistic individual chooses to work in a Social work environment. A Social work environment would not provide the same rewards and fulfillment for a Realistic individual as it would for a Social individual. Congruence is expected to predict vocational outcomes; a higher degree of congruence between personality and work environment is hypothesized to be positively related to increased job satisfaction, tenure, stability, and success.

In conclusion, Holland's theory is based on the premise that gaining an understanding of a person's personality and work environment can provide knowledge about his or her vocational choices and can help predict vocational outcomes, such as job satisfaction and tenure. Career counseling from this perspective would focus on helping clients identify their first, second, and third personality type; help them identify the typology of potential environments; and help clients identify the steps needed to enter congruent occupations.

Research on Holland's Theory

Holland's (1997) theory is the most researched and used theory in vocational psychology (Fouad, 2007; Swanson & Gore, 2000), but researchers have not equally examined all parts of the theory. In support of Holland's theory and the importance of interests in vocational choice within the United States, Betz, Borgen, and Harmon (2006) and Rottinghaus, Betz, and Borgen (2003) found that interests accounted for a significant amount of variance in occupational choices. Most of the research on Holland's theory has been conducted with U.S. populations, primarily in two main areas of examination: the congruence hypothesis and the dimensionality and structure of interests in various samples. Researchers have largely overlooked the investigation of Holland's differentiation and consistency hypotheses (Betz, 2008).

A plethora of studies have investigated Holland's congruence hypothesis (Assouline & Meir, 1987; Tsabari, Tziner, & Meir, 2005), examining whether people make career choices that are congruent with their interests. As a whole, these studies have found that people tend to choose congruent environments (Betz, 2008). For example, Tracey and Robbins (2005) examined whether a fairly diverse group of middle and high school U.S. students (71% Caucasian, 18% racial-ethnic minority, and 11% other) made congruent career choices (e.g., their intended college majors were congruent with their measured interests) and found support for the congruence hypothesis for middle school and high school students. Specifically, they found that congruence increased between 8th and 10th grades, yet decreased by 12th grade. The authors suggest that this may be attributable to the other influences for seniors in high school, rather than a reflection of the development of congruence.

A separate body of literature has examined the relationship between congruence and various job outcomes mostly for employed adults, focusing on the role of congruence in job tenure and retention. Theoretically, congruence is hypothesized to predict job satisfaction. Several meta-analyses have examined the relationship between congruence and job satisfaction (e.g., Assouline & Meir, 1987; Spokane, Meir, & Catalano, 2000; Tranberg, Slane, & Ekeberg, 1993; Tsabari et al., 2005), finding a small relationship ($r = 0.17–0.22$) between them. For example, Spokane et al. (2000) found that congruence explained only 5% of the variance in job satisfaction. Furthermore, many of these meta-analyses did not report the sample characteristics of the studies included in their analyses, with the exception of Spokane et al. (2000; 4 of the 66 studies reported samples from diverse backgrounds) and Tsabari et al. (2005; 9 of the 38 studies examined samples in Israel), making it difficult to assess the role of culture on congruence. As a whole, these studies provided little support for Holland's hypothesis that congruence in career choice is related to positive job outcomes, demonstrating only a small relationship between congruent career choices and job satisfaction; they also did not incorporate an analysis of cultural influences on congruence (with the exception of Tsabari et al., 2005, which will be discussed more fully below).

Considerable research has also examined the structure of interests hypothesized by Holland (1997). Research on the structure of interests has examined whether interests fall in the circular RIASEC order Holland postulated as well as the more stringent circulant model that emphasizes the equidistant nature of the hexagonal structure. Findings have supported the circular RIASEC pattern of interests across gender and ethnicity (Armstrong, Hubert, & Rounds, 2003; Rounds & Tracey, 1996), although mixed results were found for the equidistant, hexagonal pattern (Armstrong et al., 2003; Fouad, 2002). Research also indicated the presence of gender differences, with findings indicating differential preferences for specific types of interests; men scored higher in Realistic interests and women scored higher in Social interests (Fouad, 2002; Tracey & Robbins, 2005). These studies will be discussed more fully below.

EVIDENCE OF CULTURAL VALIDITY

Cultural validity of a theory is an indication of how well the constructs of the theory function across cultures, whether the hypothesized relationships among constructs are similar across cultures, and whether the hypothesized relationships to external criteria are similar across cultures. Thus, evidence of the cultural validity of Holland's theory would focus on whether the six vocational personality types are found in various cultural groups, if the relationship among those types are in the same RIASEC order, and if the constructs are associated in similar ways to vocational outcomes such as satisfaction and stability in a job. It is also critical to know if the tools used to operationalize the theory are linguistically and functionally equivalent across cultures.

We will focus in this section first on the operationalization of Holland's (1997) theory through interest inventories, discuss evidence of differences in interests across racial-ethnic groups, examine differences or similarities in the structure of interests across groups, and discuss research related to Holland's central constructs (e.g., congruence) across diverse samples.

Equivalence of Measures Across Cultures

Holland's (1997) theory has been operationalized by the creation of interest inventories that assess the six types proposed by the theory. The intuitive appeal of the hexagonal framework, as well as the large amount of research on the theory, has led to the integration of Holland's framework into interpretive materials even for instruments not originally developed to measure Holland's theory. For example, although the Strong Vocational Interest Blank was originally developed as an atheoretical, empirically keyed instrument, Holland's theory was integrated into the Strong in 1974 with the General Occupational Themes and continues today as an overarching framework for all parts of the Strong. These instruments are intended to help individuals select potential careers and occupations for future exploration. Some of the instruments help identify interest areas (e.g., Career Decision-Making System, Self-Directed Search, Unisex Edition of the ACT Interest Inventory [UNIACT]), others identify interest areas and similarity to professionals in various occupational fields (e.g., Strong Interest Inventory [SII], Kuder Career Planning System). The latter scales are intended to predict occupational satisfaction as an aid to occupational decision making.

Although each of these assessments operationalizes Holland's theory and, as such, possesses Holland's central themes at their core, each instrument was created to measure interests in a different manner. Differences in measurement type, philosophy, and scale construction have generated some of the greatest controversies in vocational psychology. These have been most evident in how test developers have handled the differences in vocational interests between men and women.

The first instruments (e.g., Strong Vocational Interest Blank, Kuder Occupational Interest Survey) acknowledged those differences in the creation of separate interest inventories for men and women. The rationale for this was stated by E. K. Strong in 1943: "It was felt that women might not possess interests which would pertain to any large degree to occupations" (p. 568). Strong was an empirical scientist; he was noting the fact that most women at that time did not choose to have a career but instead chose to work until marriage. In some occupations, men and women were similar, but enough occupations were different that he recommended two separate interest inventories. The inventories were different in items, and although several of the scales were the same, the women's scales included less professional occupations (e.g., model, secretary).

The consciousness raising of the women's movement of the 1960s and 1970s led to greater awareness that interest inventories can "unintentionally emphasize socialized sex differences and . . . have limited the options of individual men and women" (Walsh & Betz, 2001, p. 425). The Strong Vocational Interest Blank was explicitly accused of creating and reinforcing sex-restricted options for women. In 1974, the men's and women's forms were merged. However, men and women in the same occupation often had different interests; therefore, they were kept in separate occupational criterion groups (or comparison groups). This practice continues even in the most recent revision. Indeed, Fouad (2002) found that gender differences on the Strong Interest Inventory had a large effect size ($\eta^2 = .19$) in measured interests, whereas racial-ethnic differences in measured interests were small ($\eta^2 = .02$).

Other interest inventories, developed during the controversies in the 1970s, explicitly considered gender differences in either the item development or in the interpretation of the results. Developers of the ACT Program created the UNIACT with the express purpose of minimizing gender differences (Swaney, 1995). Thus, the 90 items on the UNIACT were chosen to provide career options that would be similar for both high school boys and girls. Items that displayed large gender differences were eliminated from the instrument. However, Holland argued that sex differences are a realistic representation of the world of work, and eliminating sex differences in a scale trivialized those differences. Holland (Holland, Fritzsche, & Powell, 1994) used raw scores in the Self-Directed Search, with

the result that there are large differences between men's and women's scores on the Realistic and Social scales. The literature in the late 1970s and 1980s contained several heated debates between Prediger and Holland over the implications of these decisions (e.g., Holland, 1976; Holland, Gottfredson, & Gottfredson, 1975; Prediger, 1976; Prediger & Hanson, 1976). The Self-Directed Search and the UNIACT continue to approach the issue of gender differences in different ways.

It is important to understand the influence of the concern about gender differences in the operationalization of Holland's constructs when evaluating the research in the rest of this chapter. All of the major interest inventories were substantially redesigned or revised to address gender differences in the 1970s and 1980s. There is convergent and discriminant validity that they operationalize Holland's theory in similar ways but not identically. For example, Savickas, Taber, and Spokane (2002) found that similarly named scales on five interest inventories correlated only moderately well. All were designed to assess interests, but each was developed with different underlying philosophical assumptions and scaling methods that influence the results. Inventories that minimize gender differences, for example, assess a range of activities common to both boys and girls. The resulting scales tap the areas of interests that are common between boys and girls, and use of the inventory helps to suggest career options that are similar for both genders. But the resulting inventories may not wholly sample the domain of interests for either gender.

Instruments have not been developed in the same way to tap the interests across all racial-ethnic groups; rather, they have been developed to assess preference for activities for individuals from the U.S. majority culture. Most test developers of the revisions of interest inventories have made every attempt to find racially-ethnically diverse samples for validation studies. However, since inventories were not developed from within the cultural perspective of each racial-ethnic group, the domain of activities created for majority culture populations may not adequately represent the range of activities preferred by racial-ethnic minority populations. For example, a review of the items on the SII indicates that most of the items are individualistically oriented, which may not represent the domains of interests for collectivistically oriented cultural groups. As we note later, much more research is needed on this.

Racial-Ethnic Group Differences

Psychologists began to be interested in examining the validity of Holland's theory for ethnic minority populations in the United States in the 1970s and 1980s (Fouad, 2002). The early research investigated mean differences between racial-ethnic groups, and later research focused on structural differences among racial-ethnic groups. This research was intended to provide evidence for the applicability of Holland's theory to diverse groups, and, indeed, Holland's theory has been examined extensively in U.S. Asian (e.g., Goh, Lee, & Yu, 2004; Haverkamp, Collins, & Hansen, 1994; Tak, 2004; Tang, 2002), Latino(a) (e.g., Flores, Spanierman, Armstrong, & Velez, 2006; Fouad & Dancer, 1992; Hansen, Sarma, & Collins, 1999), and African American populations (Swanson, 1992).

Researchers initially investigated the applicability of Holland's theory by examining mean differences among Holland themes for individuals from minority populations. These studies examined whether the interests of racial-ethnic groups differed from one another and found significant mean differences between Chinese Americans and European Americans (Sue & Kirk, 1972), African Americans and European Americans (Carter & Swanson, 1990), and Saudi men and American men (Dagenais, 1987). For example, Carter and Swanson examined eight studies that investigated the psychometric validity of Holland's theory with African Americans. With the exception of one sample of professionals, the rest of the samples examined in Carter and Swanson's (1990) review were college students. They found that African Americans and European Americans differed in their pattern of interests; African Americans scored higher on Social, Enterprising, and Conventional themes but scored lower on Realistic and Investigative themes when compared with European Americans.

Fouad (2002) argued that these initial studies focusing on between-group mean differences documented the presence of "stereotypic" interests for specific minority populations. Her critique included several concerns: that previous research had focused too much on between-group comparisons, relied heavily on small samples,

and used inappropriate analyses. Fouad (2002) addressed these concerns by examining both differences within and between racial-ethnic groups in a large sample of both professionals and students, focusing on the effect sizes related to the differences in racial-ethnic groups. Similar to previous studies, racial-ethnic differences were found in interest themes, although the effect size of these differences was small ($\eta^2 = .02$). The only significant difference between the ethnic groups was found in the Investigative General Occupational Themes; Asian Americans scored higher than Caucasians, African Americans, Latinos, and Native Americans.

Fouad (2002) concluded that racial-ethnic groups do not practically differ on interests as measured by the SII. However, as discussed earlier, it is important to note that the items on the SII were initially developed to provide responses on a broad range of activities common across occupational groups in the United States. In addition, although these studies investigating mean differences among racial-ethnic groups are useful in examining the applicability of Holland's theory to diverse groups, they may lead to inappropriately highlighting stereotypic interests. Researchers have called for more sophisticated investigations that examine the structural differences between and within groups as well as item analyses.

Structural Differences

Research investigating the cultural validity of Holland's theory has focused most intensively on the structural differences in interests among racial-ethnic groups, partly in response to criticisms that Holland's theory has been investigated primarily in Caucasian samples (Subich, 2005). This research has focused on whether the structure of interests for minority populations falls in the hexagonal pattern hypothesized by Holland (1997) with equidistances between Holland themes as well as a simpler circular model without an assumption of equidistance. This line of research is particularly important because it assesses whether the structural assumption underlying Holland's theory is found within diverse racial-ethnic groups, indicating that perceptions of the world of work are similar across groups. Previous investigations have used several different analytical techniques to analyze the structure of interests, including randomization tests of hypothesized order, confirmatory factor analysis, multidimensional scaling, and, most currently, circular unidimensional scaling. Frequently, correspondence indices are used to test whether the structure of interests falls in Holland's hypothesized order (RIASEC), yet these analyses do not test whether Holland types are equidistant apart from one another. Both confirmatory factor analyses and multidimensional scaling have been used to examine the more stringent, equidistant model. Recently, circular unidimensional scaling has also been used to investigate the hexagonal nature of interests.

Between-Group Investigations of Structural Differences. Several studies have investigated the structural differences among racial-ethnic groups. For example, a meta-analysis by Rounds and Tracey (1996) examined the fit of the RIASEC structure of interests for African Americans, Native Americans, Latino(a)s, and Asian Americans. With a few exceptions, samples included mostly high school and college students. Using 20 correlation matrices from studies using a variety of instruments, they found that Holland's circular model was not a good fit for U.S. ethnic samples. They also examined 76 international matrices representing 18 countries, including Australia, Brazil, Canada, Colombia, France, Guyana, Iceland, Indonesia, Israel, Japan, Malaysia, Mexico, New Zealand, Pakistan, Papua New Guinea, Paraguay, Portugal, and Taiwan, and found that Holland's circular order fit better with U.S. benchmark samples than for international samples. Overall, this meta-analysis found general support for Holland's model, although their findings questioned the fit of Holland's model with minority and international student samples.

Fouad, Harmon, and Borgen (1997) explored the structure of interests across large samples of African American, Latino(a), Asian American, and Caucasian American employed adults. Using a randomization test and multidimensional scaling, the authors tested the fit of the participants' scores with Holland's (1997) model. They found the predicted circular order of the six occupational types for all racial-ethnic groups, yet their findings did not support Holland's equidistant hypothesis when measured using the SII. Specifically, Asian American men did not fit the hexagonal equidistant structure hypothesized by Holland. Fouad et al.'s

findings suggest that Holland's model may be applied to individuals from diverse minority backgrounds. Day, Rounds, and Swaney (1998) found similar results in their investigation of structural differences in African American, Mexican American, Native American, Asian American, and Caucasian American college-bound high school students who completed the UNIACT interest assessment. They found that both Holland's circular order and the more stringent hexagonal order fit well with all groups in their sample with this instrument; specifically, they found that all racial-ethnic groups fit Holland's equidistant hexagonal hypothesis. As we discussed, however, the items on the UNIACT represent a relatively narrow range of activities, and thus the items on which racial-ethnic groups differ may not be included on the inventory.

More recently, Armstrong et al. (2003) examined the structure of interests using circular unidimensional scaling, an analytical technique that is more advanced than previously used analytical techniques because it simultaneously assesses for both order and distance between RIASEC categories. The results from this study provided support for the circular nature of interests across racial-ethnic samples of employed adults and college-bound high school students, although only limited support was found for the equidistant, hexagonal model of interests. The equidistant model fit better for Asian American females and Caucasian American males and females than for other minority groups, such as Latino men or African American women. Armstrong et al. argue that their inability to find support for the hexagonal model suggests that the distinctions hypothesized by Holland between interest types are culturally bound; equidistant distinctions between interest types may not be equally meaningful to all racial-ethnic groups in this study. This finding calls into question the applicability of Holland's structural hypothesis to racial-ethnic minorities within the United States, thus also questioning the cultural validity of Holland's theory to U.S. racial-ethnic minority populations.

Investigations of Structural Differences in Specific Cultural Groups. Whereas the previous studies examined structural differences among racial-ethnic groups, several studies have investigated the structure of interests within specific cultural groups. Hansen et al. (1999)

investigated the applicability of Holland's (1997) hexagonal model to a sample of 127 Chicana(o)/Latina(o) university students in the upper Midwest. Multidimensional scaling analyses found that data from both males and females deviated from Holland's hypothesized hexagonal pattern. Although male participants demonstrated the RIASEC circular pattern, female participants demonstrated the RIAESC pattern instead, suggesting that Holland's proposed circular order does not fit with this Latina college student sample. Flores et al. (2006) also investigated the validity of the Holland's structural hypothesis with a sample of 487 Mexican American high school students and found similar results. Using circular unidimensional scaling, Flores et al. found that Holland's structural hypothesis did not fit their Mexican American sample as well as it fit the normative samples of the SII; the circular order for Latinos was RAISEC rather than the RIASEC. In addition, interest types were not found to be equidistant from one another. An earlier study by Fouad and Dancer (1992) also found deviation from the RIASEC ordering in a sample of Mexican student engineers who possessed a RIASCE order of interests. Fouad and Dancer also did not find support for the equidistant hexagonal pattern of interests in either their professional or student Mexican samples. As a whole, these studies shed light on the applicability of Holland's structural hypothesis with Latino(a) population; very limited research has supported the hexagonal nature of interests for Latino(a) samples, and research has evidenced deviation in Latino(a) samples from Holland's RIASEC circular order of interests.

Swanson (1992) examined the structure of interests for 357 African American college students. Multidimensional scaling analyses found that data from both males and females fell in a circular RIASEC order. Partial support was found for the hexagonal pattern of interests; E and C were closer than hypothesized by Holland (1997) for females, and the hexagonal shape was not found for males. This suggests that Holland's calculus hypothesis may fit better for the African American females in this sample than for the African American males. Similar to previous studies, findings from this study supported the circular RIASEC order for African American students but did not support the equidistant hypothesis.

Several studies have examined the structure underlying the vocational interests of Asian and Asian American populations. Haverkamp et al. (1994) used multidimensional scaling to compare the structure of interests from a sample of 168 Asian American university students to a sample of 285 Caucasian college students and found a strong fit of the circular nature of interests for the Asian American participants. Mixed results were found for the hexagonal pattern of interests. The equidistant hypothesis was somewhat supported for Asian American females but not for Asian American males; a closer relationship was found between E–C and R–I interest categories than predicted. Tak (2004) examined the structure of interests in a sample of 829 Korean college students and found a good fit with Holland's circular order of interests; however, again, only partial support was found for the hexagonal structure of interests. Investigating the structure of interests in two samples of 166 and 247 Chinese students, Tang (2002) and Goh et al. (2004) found that neither the circular nor the hexagonal RIASEC order fit.

Two studies have examined the applicability of Holland's theory with Native American and Native Hawaiian populations. Hansen, Scullard, and Haviland (2000) investigated the use of the SII with a sample of 176 Native American students. Using a randomization test and multidimensional scaling, they found a good fit with Holland's circular order for both males and females; results also indicated that the hexagonal structure of interests fit better with female participants than with male participants. A more dichotomous arrangement of interest categories was found for males, with R–I–A clustering together and C–E–S clustering together. Oliver and Waehler (2005) investigated the structure of interests in a sample of 156 Native Hawaiian college students and community members and found support both for the structure of interests, supporting the validity of Holland's RIASEC order.

In conclusion, the applicability of Holland's theory with U.S. racial-ethnic minority populations has been studied extensively for decades, with much of the research focusing on the structure of interests for racial-ethnic minority populations (many of whom were college students), demonstrating some structural differences. As stated earlier, to assess for cultural validity, we need to examine whether Holland's (1997) constructs are relevant and function in the same manner across cultures. The studies described above indicate that, for the most part, Holland's circular order hypothesis appears to be found in most samples studied. However, most of the samples were college students, and many racial-ethnic differences were found in the hexagonal pattern of interests, suggesting that minority groups may perceive the world of work in a similar manner (e.g., support for the circular order of interests), yet not in an identical manner (e.g., lack of support for the equidistant order of interests). More research is needed to investigate the applicability of Holland's theory with minority populations, particularly in investigating specific cultural groups (Tracey, Watanabe, & Schneider, 1997).

Item Analysis. Although researchers have argued that analyses need to be conducted to examine differences at an item level, very little research has explored item differences, with only one study to date examining racial-ethnic group differences at the item level. Fouad and Walker (2005) used differential bundle functioning (DBF) to examine item responses on the General Occupational Themes for participants from five different racial-ethnic groups: African American, Asian or Pacific Islander, Latino(a), Native American, and Caucasian. Item bundles were created by identifying groups of items related to activities in each of the General Occupational Themes; previous literature was used to group items that may be differentially endorsed by members of specific groups. Fouad and Walker found high levels of DBF, indicating that racial-ethnic groups differentially endorse particular sets of items due to the items measuring a secondary trait in addition to the trait the scale intended to measure. Fouad and Walker conclude that the items on the SII may not reflect true racial-ethnic group differences in interests but instead may have additional meanings across racial-ethnic groups due to role modeling and cultural expectations.

Congruence Hypothesis

Although a considerable amount of research has examined Holland's congruence hypothesis (e.g., Assouline & Meir, 1987; Spokane et al., 2000; Tranberg et al., 1993; Tsabari et al., 2005), as noted above, only a few studies have examined the validity of the congruence hypothesis in diverse samples. A few researchers have investigated the role of cultural and contextual factors in the expression of interests and have found, overall, that contextual factors appear to play a role in the expression of interests and the congruence between measured and expressed interests. This is of particular importance because a central assumption in Holland's theory is that interests are directly related to choice.

Tang, Fouad, and Smith (1999) examined the influence of cultural factors, such as acculturation, on the relationship between measured interests and career choices for Asian American college students. Tang et al. found that acculturation influenced the relationship between interests and career choices; individuals who were less acculturated were more influenced by family expectations in expressing career choices rather than by their interests. Gupta and Tracey (2005) also investigated the influence of familial duty on congruence and found that Asian Indian college students expressed higher adherence to the value of dharma and were less congruent in their expressed and measured interests when compared to Caucasians. Yet, Gupta and Tracey did not find that dharma significantly predicted congruence. Together, these studies indicate that contextual influences such as cultural values and acculturation may influence congruence, yet more research is needed to gain a further understanding.

Limited research has also examined the predictive value of the congruence hypothesis in job outcomes. Leong, Austin, Sekaran, and Komarraju (1998) examined the relationship between Holland's (1997) constructs of differentiation, consistency, and congruence with job and occupational satisfaction in a sample of 172 employed workers in India. They found no relationship between congruence, differentiation, or consistency and job satisfaction; furthermore, they did not find that congruence predicted job or occupational satisfaction, suggesting that Holland's predictive value of congruence on positive job outcomes may be not be applicable in Indian society.

A recent meta-analysis by Tsabari et al. (2005) investigated the moderating influence of two contextual variables, culture and age, on interest congruence and job satisfaction for predominately employed adults. Tsabri et al. found support for the moderating relationship of both age and culture on the strength of the congruence–job satisfaction relationship; individuals who were younger in age are better predictors of the congruence hypothesis than individual in older groups (over 30 years). Culture (Israel vs. United States) was also found to have a moderating influence in interest congruence and job satisfaction; a stronger relationship between congruence and job satisfaction was found in individualistic societies (Israel vs. United States). Leong et al.'s (1998) study and Tsabari et al.'s meta-analysis are among the first to examine the role of cultural factors in interest congruence. Their studies provide a preliminary indication that cultural differences do indeed play a role in Holland's congruence hypothesis, suggesting that the construct of congruence may not have the same relevance or may function differently for individuals from different cultural backgrounds. Yet, more research is needed to gain a further understanding of the influence contextual factors have on Holland's congruence hypothesis (e.g., examining how various cultural factors such as acculturation, cultural values, and family influence congruence between interests).

FUTURE DIRECTIONS

We have reviewed the evidence of the cultural validity of Holland's theory, and some of the evidence indicates that Holland's theory may be applied across cultural groups in the United States. However, we also argue that much more research is needed to fully examine the cultural validity of Holland's theory with U.S. minority populations as well as international populations. We recommend several areas for future research to examine the cultural validity of Holland's theory; many of these are interrelated.

1. Much of the cultural research reviewed in this chapter has examined the cultural validity of Holland's theory from an etic perspective rather than an emic perspective. More research needs to examine the cultural validity of Holland's theory from an emic perspective that emphasizes the investigation of vocational interests and the role of interests in career decisions from a culture-specific perspective.

2. Related to Recommendation 1, more research needs to develop interest inventories that are rooted within a cultural context for racial-ethnic minority individuals. Most of the research has been conducted on racial-ethnic minority college students, and more research is needed on the applicability of Holland's theory to other non-college-bound racial-ethnic minority adolescents.

3. More research is needed to examine whether items on current interest inventories using Holland's theory capture the domains of interests for collectivistically oriented cultural groups. Then, the structure of interests should be examined with new or expanded interest inventories.

4. We need to examine whether the domain of vocational personality types may be captured with six personality types across cultural groups and if the structure of those types is the same. In other words, a fundamental question is whether Realistic, Investigative, Artistic, Social, Enterprising, and Conventional themes exist across culture and if they exist in the same order.

5. We need to know whether the theory may be applied in the same way across cultures. The theory presumes, for example, that interests are a central, motivating factor in occupational choice. However, in some cultures, interests are a minor factor in vocational choices, and family expectations are a much greater predictor of career choice. Thus, the usefulness of the constructs of the theory needs to be examined across cultural groups.

6. More research also needs to examine whether Holland's central constructs are related in a similar manner across cultures (e.g., is congruence related to job satisfaction and tenure for all cultures, or do other factors moderate this relationship?).

7. More research is needed to examine the influence that contextual factors (e.g., acculturation, cultural values, family expectations) have on all of Holland's central constructs.

REFERENCES

Armstrong, P. I., Hubert, L., & Rounds, J. (2003). Circular unidimensional scaling: A new look at group differences in interest structure. *Journal of Counseling Psychology, 50,* 297–308.

Assouline, M., & Meir, E. I. (1987). Meta-analysis of the relationship between congruence and well-being measures. *Journal of Vocational Behavior, 31,* 319–332.

Betz, N. E. (2008). Advances in vocational theories. In S. D. Brown & R. W. Lent's (Eds.), *Handbook of counseling psychology* (4th ed., pp. 357–374). New York: John Wiley.

Betz, N. E., Borgen, F. A., & Harmon L. (2006). Vocational confidence and personality in the prediction of occupational group membership. *Journal of Career Assessment, 14,* 36–55.

Carter, R. T., & Swanson, J. L. (1990). The validity of the Strong Interest Inventory with Black Americans: A review of the literature. *Journal of Vocational Behavior, 36,* 195–209.

Dagenais, F. (1987). Vocational Preference Inventory (Holland): Mean scores for samples of Saudi and American men. *Psychological Reports, 60,* 630.

Day, S. X., Rounds, J., & Swaney, K. (1998). The structure of vocational interests for diverse racial-ethnic groups. *Psychological Science, 9,* 40–44.

Flores, L. Y., Spanierman, L. B., Armstrong, P. I., & Velez, A. D. (2006). Validity of the Strong Interest Inventory and Skills Confidence Inventory with Mexican American high school students. *Journal of Career Assessment, 14,* 183–202.

Fouad, N. A. (2002). Cross-cultural differences in vocational interests: Between-group differences on the Strong Interest Inventory. *Journal of Counseling Psychology, 49,* 283–289.

Fouad, N. A. (2007). Work and vocational psychology: Theory, research and applications. *Annual Review of Psychology, 58,* 543–564.

Fouad, N. A., & Dancer, L. S. (1992). Cross-cultural structure of interests: Mexico and the United States. *Journal of Vocational Behavior, 40,* 129–143.

Fouad, N. A., Harmon, L. W., & Borgen, F. H. (1997). Structure of interests in employed male and female members of U.S. racial-ethnic minority and nonminority groups. *Journal of Counseling Psychology, 44,* 339–345.

Fouad, N. A., & Walker, C. M. (2005). Cultural influences on responses to items on the Strong Interest Inventory. *Journal of Vocational Behavior, 66,* 104–123.

Goh, D. S., Lee, J. A., & Yu, J. (2004). Factor structure of the Strong Interest Inventory with a Chinese high school sample. *Journal of Psychology: Interdisciplinary and Applied, 138,* 171–183.

Gupta, S., & Tracey, T. J. G. (2005). Dharma and interest-occupation congruence in Asian Indian college students. *Journal of Career Assessment, 13,* 320–336.

Hansen, J. I. C., Sarma, Z. M., & Collins, R. C. (1999). An evaluation of Holland's model of vocational interests for Chicana(o) and Latina(o) college students. *Measurement and Evaluation in Counseling and Development, 32,* 2–13.

Hansen, J. I. C., Scullard, M. G., & Haviland, M. G. (2000). The interest structures of Native American college students. *Journal of Career Assessment, 8,* 159–172.

Haverkamp, B. E., Collins, R. C., & Hansen, J. C. (1994). Structure of interests and Asian-American college students. *Journal of Counseling Psychology, 41,* 256–264.

Holland, J. L. (1958). A personality inventory employing occupational titles. *Journal of Applied Psychology, 42,* 336–342.

Holland, J. L. (1959). A theory of vocational choice. *Journal of Counseling Psychology, 6,* 35–45.

Holland, J. L. (1976). The virtues of the SDS and its associated typology: A second response to Prediger and Hanson. *Journal of Vocational Behavior, 8,* 349–358.

Holland, J. L. (1997). *Making vocational choices: A theory of vocational personalities and work environments* (3rd ed.). Odessa, FL: Psychological Assessment Resources.

Holland, J. L., Fritzsche, B. A., & Powell, A. B. (1994). *The self-directed search (SDS): Technical manual.* Odessa, FL: Psychological Assessment Resources, Inc.

Holland, J. L., Gottfredson, G. D., & Gottfredson, L. S. (1975). Read our reports and examine the data: A response to Prediger and Cole. *Journal of Vocational Behavior, 7,* 253–259.

Leong, F. T. L., Austin, J. T., Sekaran, U., & Komarraju, M. (1998). An evaluation of the cross-cultural validity of Holland's theory: Career choices by workers in India. *Journal of Vocational Behavior, 52,* 441–455.

Leong, F. T. L., & Brown, M. T. (1995). Theoretical issues in cross-cultural career development: Cultural validity and cultural specificity. In W. B. Walsh & S. H. Osipow (Eds.), *Handbook of vocational psychology: Theory, research, and practice* (2nd ed., pp. 143–180). Hillsdale, NJ: Lawrence Erlbaum.

Oliver, K. E., & Waehler, C. A. (2005). Investigating the validity of Holland's RIASEC typology among Native Hawaiians. *Journal of Counseling Psychology, 52,* 448–452.

Parsons, F. (1909). *Choosing a vocation.* Boston: Houghton.

Prediger, D. J. (1976). Do raw scores deserve a D minus? A reply to Holland. *Measurement & Evaluation in Guidance, 9,* 136–138.

Prediger, D. J., & Hanson, G. R. (1976). Holland's theory of careers applied to women and men: Analysis of implicit assumptions. *Journal of Vocational Behavior, 8,* 167–184.

Quintana, S. M., Troyano, N., & Taylor, G. (2001). Cultural validity and inherent challenges in quantitative methods for multicultural research. In J. G. Ponterotto, J. M. Casas,

L. A. Suzuki, & C. M. Alexander (Eds.), *Handbook of multicultural counseling* (2nd ed., pp. 604–630). Thousand Oaks, CA: Sage.

Rottinghaus, P. J., Betz, N. E., & Borgen, F. H. (2003). Validity of parallel measures of vocational interests and confidence. *Journal of Career Assessment, 11*, 355–378.

Rounds, J., & Tracey, T. J. (1996). Cross-cultural structural equivalence of RIASEC models and measures. *Journal of Counseling Psychology, 43*, 310–329.

Savickas, M. L., Taber, B. J., & Spokane, A. R. (2002). Convergent and discriminant validity of five interest inventories. *Journal of Vocational Behavior, 61*, 139–184.

Spokane, A. R., & Cruza-Guet, M. C. (2005). Holland's theory of vocational personalities in work environments. In S. D. Brown & R. W. Lent (Eds.), *Career development and counseling: Putting theory and research to work* (pp. 24–41). Hoboken, NJ: John Wiley.

Spokane, A. R., Meir, E. I., & Catalano, M. (2000). Person-environment congruence and Holland's theory: A review and reconsideration. *Journal of Vocational Behavior, 57*, 137–187.

Strong, E. K., Jr. (1943). *Vocational interests of men and women.* Stanford, CA: Stanford University Press.

Subich, L. M. (2005). Career assessment with culturally diverse individuals. In B. W. Walsh & M. L. Savickas (Eds.), *Handbook of vocational psychology: Theory, research, and practice* (3rd ed., pp. 397–422). Mahwah, NJ: Lawrence Erlbaum.

Sue, D. W., & Kirk, B. A. (1972). Differential characteristics of Chinese American students. *Journal of Counseling Psychology, 20*, 142–148.

Swaney, K. (1995). *Technical manual: Revised unisex edition of the ACT Interest Inventory.* Iowa City, IA: American College Testing.

Swanson, J. L. (1992). The structure of vocational interests for African-American college students. *Journal of Vocational Behavior, 40*, 144–157.

Swanson, J. L., & Gore, P. A. (2000). Advances in vocational psychology theory and research. In S. D. Brown & R. W. Lent (Eds.), *Handbook of counseling psychology* (3rd ed., pp. 233–269). New York: John Wiley.

Tak, J. (2004). Structure of vocational interests for Korean college students. *Journal of Career Assessment, 12*, 298–311.

Tang, M. (2002). A comparison of Asian American, Caucasian American, and Chinese college students: An initial report. *Journal of Multicultural Counseling & Development, 30*, 124–134.

Tang, M., Fouad, N. A., & Smith, P. L. (1999). Asian Americans' career choices: A path model to examine factors influencing their career choices. *Journal of Vocational Behavior, 54*, 142–157.

Tracey, T. J. G., & Robbins, S. B. (2005). Stability of interests across ethnicity and gender: A longitudinal examination of grades 8 through 12. *Journal of Vocational Behavior, 67*, 335–364.

Tracey, T. J. G., Watanabe, N., & Schneider, P. L. (1997). Structural invariance of vocational interests across Japanese and American cultures. *Journal of Counseling Psychology, 44*, 346–354.

Tranberg, M. S., Slane, S., & Ekeberg, S. E. (1993). The relation between interest congruence and satisfaction: A meta-analysis. *Journal of Vocational Behavior, 42*, 253–264.

Tsabari, O., Tziner, A., & Meir, E. I. (2005). Updated meta-analysis on the relationship between congruence and satisfaction. *Journal of Career Assessment, 13*, 216–232.

Walsh, W. B., & Betz, N. E. (2001). *Tests and assessment* (4th ed.). Upper Saddle River, NJ: Prentice Hall.

55

Multiculturally Competent Career Counseling Interventions With Adolescents Vulnerable to Discrimination

MARGO A. JACKSON, CESAR A. LEON, AND MIRA ZAHAROPOULOS

As access to the means for long-term financial security and life-affirming growth, work can provide the means for self sufficiency, sustenance and care for loved ones, and prosocial contributions to our communities and larger society (Blustein, 2006; Peterson & Gonzalez, 2005; Richardson, 1993). Individuals' work roles are not only vital aspects of their identities but also can enable or impede fulfillment of human potential. Yet from an ethical perspective, access to educational and occupational options and achievement remain severely limited for members of groups vulnerable to discrimination and merit multiculturally competent interventions (American Psychological Association [APA], 2003). Adolescence is not only a critical period for career development generally but also might present unique developmental opportunities to intervene constructively with members of groups vulnerable to discrimination.

Similar to Jackson, Holder, and Ramage (2008), we interpret the term *culturally diverse* to mean that individuals belong to or identify with various cultural groups (e.g., by race, ethnicity, gender, age, socioeconomic status, health/disability status, sexual orientation, and religious affiliation). Thus, individuals may vary not only in their worldviews but also in their access to power and privilege or vulnerability to discrimination. Competent psychological assessment and intervention requires attention to the cultural contexts of and meanings attributed by both clients and counselors (Byars-Winston & Fouad, 2006; Krishnamurthy et al., 2004). In particular, counselors have an ethical responsibility to attend to the specific cultural factors of vulnerability to discrimination relevant to individuals of racial-ethnic minority groups (Ridley, 2005). In this chapter, we focus more narrowly on members of racial-ethnic minority groups in the United States (similar to the focus of the multicultural guidelines for psychologists; APA, 2003), and we use the terms *culturally diverse, multicultural,* and *of color* in reference to these group memberships.

In the first section of this chapter, we summarize how career development interventions facilitate positive identity development and educational and occupational achievement with adolescents of color. Then, we discuss how discrimination vulnerability is a barrier to optimal vocational identity development for these youth. Next, we advocate for incorporating into career development interventions helpful approaches to bias preparation and resilient strategies for coping with discrimination. We review explanations for counselor resistance to acknowledging discrimination influences as well as resources for constructively challenging biases toward providing more multiculturally competent career interventions with adolescents vulnerable to discrimination.

In the second section of this chapter, we describe our definitions of the terms *career development interventions* and *career counseling,* and we note the viewpoints that ground our discussion. We highlight contributions and limitations of research findings on the effectiveness of career development interventions with relevance for adolescents of color. We summarize key career development tasks for adolescents in school-to-work transitions (Lent, Hackett, & Brown, 1999), a theoretically grounded and potentially useful framework from which to develop multiculturally competent career interventions with adolescents vulnerable to discrimination. Finally, we review selected studies of career development interventions that incorporate and evaluate the impact of the four types of learning experience sources of self-efficacy postulated by Bandura (1977), and we discuss implications for designing effective career development interventions with culturally diverse adolescents.

CAREER DEVELOPMENT INTERVENTIONS FACILITATE POSITIVE IDENTITY DEVELOPMENT AND EDUCATIONAL/OCCUPATIONAL ACHIEVEMENT

The key psychosocial developmental challenge to resolve during adolescence according to Erikson (1963) is to negotiate role conflicts and build a coherent sense of identity from understanding one's abilities, values, relationships, life history, and cultural expectations (Douvan, 1997). Career counseling and psychoeducational interventions designed to facilitate career development (i.e., for planning and making decisions about occupations and education) can promote positive identity development. Furthermore, research evidence has demonstrated career interventions that help students learn to effectively negotiate vocational development processes (such as identifying, exploring, and gaining knowledge about their occupational and educational interests, abilities, values, beliefs, options, and goals) also help students develop more positive academic motivation and educational achievement (Baker & Taylor, 1998; Evans & Burck, 1992; Lapan, Gysbers, & Sun, 1997). Adolescents' future career options depend on achieving educational success, and students who understand the connections between school and their career paths are better prepared to succeed in school (Kenny, Blustein, Haase, Jackson, & Perry, 2006). Thus, one approach to promoting optimal development with all students—and in particular, to reducing the educational and occupational achievement gaps for culturally diverse adolescents vulnerable to discrimination—may be to facilitate effective career interventions in schools and communities.

Barrier to Optimal Vocational Identity Development: Vulnerability to Discrimination

Adolescents of color—beyond their disproportionate representation associated with systemic barrier risk factors such as low income, urban environments, and restricted educational achievement that limit their future career development and well-being (Arbona, 2000; Constantine, Erickson, Banks, & Timberlake, 1998)—face an additional developmental challenge to their building a positive identity in their vulnerability to discrimination. Adolescents of color experience a range of negative messages, both overt and covert, from racial and ethnic discrimination that can have harmful psychological effects (Gibbons et al., 2007; Greene, Way, & Pahl, 2006). In addition to witnessing overt racist events, adolescents of color have reported experiencing covert racial-ethnic microaggressions on a common and frequent basis (Alvarez, Juang, & Liang, 2006; Rosenbloom & Way, 2004). Racial microaggressions—defined as "brief and commonplace daily verbal, behavioral, and environmental indignities, whether intentional or unintentional, that communicate hostile, derogatory, or negative racial slights and insults toward people of color" (Sue et al., 2007, p. 271)—are forms of discrimination that strike at the core of the group identities of people of color. "Adolescents are acutely attuned to external messages that provide guidelines for how they see themselves and their futures (Phinney, 2001), raising their vulnerability to negative social experiences, such as discrimination" (Grossman & Liang, 2008, p. 3).

INCLUDING FOCUS ON BIAS PREPARATION

Although not yet well integrated in career development interventions, potentially relevant research has begun to investigate protective factors that might buffer against the negative effects of vulnerability to discrimination for adolescents of color. Protective factors include positive racial-ethnic identity (Rivas-Drake, Hughes, & Way, 2008), peer support (Grossman & Liang, 2008), collectivistic and interdependent cultural value orientations, and religion and spirituality coping and social support mechanisms (Constantine & Sue, 2006). In addition to building on protective factors buffering discrimination vulnerability toward positive vocational identity development, career interventions with adolescents of color might include helping them learn constructive coping strategies. Jackson and Nutini (2002) identified themes of contextual and psychological barriers and resources for career-related learning through interviews with adolescents vulnerable to discrimination (low-income, urban middle school students, predominantly African Americans and Latinos/as). The authors discussed how one theme that emerged as a possible psychological resource *and* barrier to career development was the belief by many participants that equal opportunity and no barriers exist for all people to attend college or pursue the career of their choice regardless of race, ethnicity, gender, or biracial/bicultural characteristics. This attitude might reflect an early status of racial identity development (e.g., conformity;

Helms & Cook, 1999) and could serve as a resource to motivate adolescents of color to expand their learning opportunities, aspirations, and achievement in academic and career development. Alternatively, this belief could serve as a barrier when confronted with inevitable discrimination if adolescents of color have not developed resilient strategies for coping, persisting, and constructively negotiating the potentially negative effects on their evolving identity and career development.

Efforts to design helpful career interventions for adolescents of color that include building effective resources for coping with discrimination might beneficially draw on research that examines the strategies that families and communities of color use to promote their children's positive racial-ethnic identity and prepare them to succeed in the face of racial bias or *racial socialization* practices (e.g., Hughes, 2003). One recent study found that racial socialization messages that African American parents transmitted to their adolescent children at a moderate (optimal) level of preparation for bias (vs. low or high levels) served as a buffer to perceived discrimination with these youth (Harris-Britt, Valrie, Kurtz-Costes, & Rowley, 2007). Interpreted from the perspective of racial identity theories (e.g., Cross & Vandiver, 2001; Helms & Cook, 1999), we suggest these findings imply that low levels of preparation for bias are reflected in earlier statuses of racial identity development that may focus on the ideals of equal opportunity but leave adolescents of color unprepared to cope effectively with discrimination. An additional implication of Harris-Britt et al.'s (2007) findings is that high-level approaches to preparation for bias that focus more exclusively on discrimination awareness (e.g., reflected in the immersion-emersion stages or statuses of racial identity development; Cross & Vandiver; Helms & Cook) may not serve as effective buffers to the negative psychosocial effects of discrimination. More optimal moderate-level approaches to preparation for bias that include teaching both awareness of discrimination and constructive coping strategies (reflected in the racial identity stages or statuses of internalization or integrated awareness), however, may be more effective. Because most current approaches to career development intervention with adolescents of color do not include preparation for bias, we argue this is a missing key element for facilitating their vocational identity development and achievement in education and career domains. Further research is needed to develop culturally relevant approaches to constructively addressing discrimination and integrating these approaches into effective career development interventions.

We submit that interventions designed to facilitate optimal vocational identity development with adolescents vulnerable to discrimination should include specific objectives and effective methods for constructively dealing with discrimination. Multiculturally competent career development interventions with these youth should include a focus on bias preparation by increasing recognition of protective resources, improving access to sources of support, and learning resilient coping strategies. Furthermore, the evolving research literature on perceptions of not only *barriers* but also sources of *support* for career development (e.g., Kenny et al., 2007; Lent, Brown, & Hackett, 2000) may helpfully inform efforts to design intervention components on bias preparation for constructively negotiating the influences of discrimination with diverse adolescents.

RESISTANCE TO ACKNOWLEDGING DISCRIMINATION AND INTEGRATING BIAS PREPARATION IN CAREER INTERVENTIONS

It follows, then, that counselors (of color and Caucasians) who design and implement career development interventions with adolescents vulnerable to discrimination must themselves have well-developed multicultural competences (APA, 2003; Arredondo et al., 1996; National Career Development Association, 1997), as reflected in the highest levels of racial identity development (e.g., internalization or integrated awareness; Cross & Vandiver, 2001; Helms & Cook, 1999; Sue et al., 1998). On one hand, sound evidence has shown that racial discrimination continues to exist, on both overt and covert levels, and it adversely affects the physical and psychological well-being of people of color, including adolescents (Alvarez et al., 2006; Sue et al., 2007; Thompson & Neville, 1999; U.S. Department of Health and Human Services, 2001). Yet on the other hand, we submit that most counselors themselves (those of color as well as Caucasians) experience strong resistance to acknowledging these painful realities and

thus are impeded in constructively addressing potential discrimination influences in their counseling practice, in general, and career counseling interventions, in particular.

At least in part, most people, including counselors, have blind spots or biases relevant to racial discrimination issues that tend to be ingrained and unexplored (Abreu, 2001; Sue, 2003). Several authors have offered explanations for why it may be difficult for counselors to recognize, acknowledge, and deal constructively with identifying their own biases and role in discrimination that may affect their clients of color. For example, on some level, most counselors are unlikely to accept responsibility for continued and pervasive racial discrimination in their local and broader communities because they take for granted the myth of meritocracy and deny personal prejudice and privilege. Counselors—regardless of their membership in dominant or marginalized groups in U.S. society—are acculturated to some extent to the beliefs, values, and behaviors of Caucasian Americans by virtue of their extended academic experience and their professional training in psychology (Ridley, 2005). Therefore, counselors are likely to believe in the *myth of meritocracy,* that democratic choice and opportunity are equally available to all, and thus be surprised at or discount evidence to the contrary (McIntosh, 1998; Sue, 2003). Many counselors believe their own educational and professional success can be attributed solely to their own efforts and ability while failing to recognize the uneven playing field of advantages that only some may take for granted—for example, embedded systemic privileges afforded by gender, race, ethnicity, socioeconomic class, sexual orientation, or health status. One implication for career counseling interventions with adolescents vulnerable to discrimination is that counselors may fail to recognize this vulnerability and not incorporate helpful approaches to bias preparation and resilient strategies for coping with discrimination.

Potentially more harmful are the negative stereotypes and prejudiced attitudes and beliefs that counselors (and others) may subtly and unconsciously harbor toward adolescents of color, such as attributing their academic and behavioral difficulties to their own (or their parents') laziness, apathy, or lack of intellect. In contrast to overt hate crime events that people generally associate with prejudice and discrimination, it is counselors' own personal lack of awareness of how social biases affect their own judgments and behavior toward marginalized group members that is most insidious and harmful (Sue, 2003). Social scientists have established that even though most people (including counselors) embrace egalitarian values toward racial diversity, they harbor toward people of color negative perceptual biases that are automatic, unconscious, and normative (Fiske, 1998). Counselors in the multicultural training process of confronting such socially and ethically undesirable biases may understandably become defensive about exploring, acknowledging, and ameliorating their personal attitudes and beliefs toward clients of color (Abreu, 2001). As valuable resources to facilitate counselors' progress through this challenging yet vital process of exploring their biases and developing more multiculturally competent counseling approaches, Abreu (2001) recommended that counselors learn about theory and research on stereotypes and perceptual bias.

In their incorporation of multicultural metacognition strategies to an expanded model of culturally appropriate career counseling (CACCM), Byars-Winston and Fouad (2006) have provided another potentially valuable resource for helping counselors uncover and reflect on their personal biases and constructively adjust their assessments and interventions throughout the career counseling process. As one method to challenge racial and other unhelpful biases to clinical judgment, Byars-Winston and Fouad advocated "for counselors' development of metacognitive awareness of their [own] cultural context and how their thinking and perceptions may influence the way they view clients' cultural contexts throughout the course of intervention" (p. 191). One implication for career counseling interventions with adolescents vulnerable to discrimination is that counselors who are consciously engaged throughout the process in self-monitoring and challenging their racial biases (e.g., by attending to the reflective questions posed in Byars-Winston and Fouad's model) may be more likely to recognize current and potential discrimination influences in their work with these youth and be more able to incorporate helpful approaches to bias preparation and coping with discrimination.

In the next section of this chapter, we highlight empirical contributions and limitations relevant to multiculturally competent career interventions with adolescents of color. We summarize career developmental tasks salient in adolescence for school-to-work transitions (Lent et al., 1999), and we suggest how this theoretically grounded framework may be useful for developing multiculturally competent career interventions with adolescents vulnerable to discrimination. First, we describe definitions of the terms *career development interventions* and *career counseling,* and we note the viewpoints that ground our discussion.

DEFINITION OF TERMS AND VIEWPOINTS

We ascribe to Spokane's (1991) broad definition of career development interventions as any activity designed to empower individuals to cope effectively with career development tasks. With particular relevance for adolescents of color, we focus on career development interventions that facilitate positive identity development, educational achievement, and healthy transitions during middle and high school and from school to college and work. We submit that career development interventions designed and implemented by professional counselors provide the value added of the context and process of counseling relationships in which to establish rapport, define goals, evaluate progress, and negotiate transitions. Career counseling interventions (a) can be administered to individuals or groups, (b) typically include psychoeducational goals, and (c) are likely most effective when attentive to and integrated with the contexts of individuals' other personal life issues, including mental health issues (Blustein, 2008; Fouad & Bynner, 2008; Hinkelman & Luzzo, 2007; Krumboltz, 1993).

While career development interventions with adolescents can be implemented through various settings (e.g., through community-based and family service organizations or school-university-community partnerships), recent literature in counseling psychology is grounded in applications to school-linked interventions (Kenny, Waldo, Warter, & Barton, 2002; Walsh, Galassi, Murphy, & Park-Taylor, 2002). As noted earlier, adolescents' access to future career options depends on their achieving educational success, and career development interventions have been shown to affect academic achievement. In light of the significant educational achievement disparities for adolescents of color compared to Caucasians (Education Trust, 2006; National Center for Education Statistics, n.d.), school-based interventions may provide particularly useful venues for promoting the career development of adolescents vulnerable to discrimination (Howard & Solberg, 2006; Solberg, Howard, Blustein, & Close, 2002).

Theory serves as a vital bridge between science and practice (Murdock, 2006). Career development interventions need to be grounded in theory so that counselors have a basis to evaluate and explain what aspects are effective, under what conditions, and with whom through empirical research that, in turn, informs and improves evolving knowledge about effective practices. Furthermore, by using theory to ground interventions, counselors make their assumptions explicit and their biases more accessible to constructively challenging evaluation and revision (e.g., through metacognitive strategies in the expanded model of culturally appropriate career counseling recommended by Byars-Winston & Fouad, 2006).

EFFECTIVENESS OF CAREER DEVELOPMENT INTERVENTIONS

Research evidence from meta-analyses synthesizing the results of numerous studies has found support for the effectiveness of career counseling interventions in helping clients make vocational decisions and career choices (Oliver & Spokane, 1988; Ryan, 1999; Whiston, Sexton, & Lasoff, 1998). This research is grounded in a history of useful career development theories (Lent & Worthington, 2000; Savickas & Lent, 1994) and is based on the development of psychometrically sound vocational assessment instruments and methods applied in the context of (a) professional ethics codes (e.g., American Counseling Association, 2005; APA, 2002), (b) testing standards (American Educational Research Association, American Psychological Association, & National Council on Measurement in Education, 1999), and (c) guidelines for competencies in career counseling (National Career Development Association, 1997).

By further examining the results of Ryan's (1999) meta-analytic research, Brown and Ryan Krane (2000) and Brown et al. (2003) identified five strategies or

critical components that incrementally contributed to the effectiveness of career counseling intervention outcomes: (1) written exercises (committing their career goals and plans to writing), (2) individualized interpretation and feedback (e.g., regarding career self-assessment), (3) in-session occupational information exploration, (4) modeling opportunities, and (5) social support building.

Whiston, Brecheisen, and Stephens (2003) conducted a meta-analysis to compare the effectiveness of different formats for delivery of career counseling interventions. Their results suggested that counselor assistance (e.g., with self-directed computer-guided interventions) and structured group formats were more effective than totally self-directed interventions or less structured group formats. Too few studies had been conducted with an individual career counseling format to compare the relative effectiveness to other career intervention formats.

Thus, evidence to date from meta-analytic research supports the general effectiveness of career development interventions at a moderate magnitude (i.e., effect size; Cohen, 1988). In addition, this literature suggests testable hypotheses about which career intervention characteristics and components might be investigated to improve effectiveness (Brown et al., 2003; Miller & Brown, 2005).

Relevant to school-based career development interventions for adolescents of color, several resources review relevant multicultural issues and recommend strategies (e.g., American School Counselor Association, 2002; Fusick & Charkow Bordeau, 2004). Nevertheless, the "lack of specificity about interventions in the career development and academic achievement literature . . . is a problem for school counselors and policymakers in an era of limited resources. The nation's school counselors need concrete guidance on what career development activities can give them the most leverage in promoting student success" (Dykeman et al., 2003, p. 276).

Moreover, empirical knowledge is relatively scant regarding the influence of the multicultural contexts and issues of both clients and counselors on the effectiveness of career counseling intervention outcomes (Heppner & Heppner, 2003; Miller & Brown, 2005). Relevant to our discussion in the first part of this chapter, Byars-Winston and Fouad (2006) have provided a model (including multiculturally competent metacognitive strategies throughout the process of career counseling) that may be useful for examining the influence of *counselors'* multicultural issues on the effectiveness of career interventions, particularly with adolescents vulnerable to discrimination. However, this remains an area for needed empirical investigation. In addition, far too little is known to date on the role that the multicultural contexts and issues of *clients* may have on the effectiveness of career counseling intervention outcomes, in general, and how counselors might effectively tailor career development interventions to the needs and goals of adolescents of color, in particular. Further empirical research is needed to investigate these questions with qualitative and mixed methods, as well as quantitative research methodological approaches, to give voice to the experiences of adolescents of color relevant to their career development (e.g., through interviews and narrative; Chaves et al., 2004; Kenny et al., 2007; Pizzolato, 2007).

The outcome research on career development interventions "seems to treat all clients, regardless of presenting concerns and goals, not only as if they are alike but also as if clients' gender, race/ethnicity, and sexual orientation have inconsequential influences on their responsiveness to counseling or the outcomes they might attain" (Miller & Brown, 2005, p. 451). For example, many studies included in meta-analyses failed to provide data on demographic characteristics of their samples beyond gender. Furthermore, although the conceptual literature is evolving on the career development experiences of members of culturally diverse and marginalized groups, the effectiveness of career counseling models designed for these groups has not yet been systematically evaluated or empirically tested. For example, the Culturally Appropriate Career Counseling Model proposed by Fouad and Bingham (1995) and expanded by Byars-Winston and Fouad (2006) merits empirical investigation of its strengths and limitations for informing and evaluating interventions with adolescents of color.

CAREER DEVELOPMENT TASKS FOR ADOLESCENTS

Lent et al. (1999) proposed career development tasks salient in adolescence for school-to-work transitions that offer one theoretically grounded framework with potential for developing multiculturally competent career interventions with adolescents vulnerable to discrimination. Developmental tasks for adolescents include negotiating transitions between middle school, high school, and college or work (Eccles et al., 1993; Lent et al., 1999; Turner & Lapan, 2005b). Both universal and culture-specific theoretical perspectives can be usefully applied in studying and promoting the school-to-work transitions of racial-ethnic minority students (Lent & Worthington, 2000). The integrative social cognitive career theory (SCCT; Lent, Brown, & Hackett, 1994, 2000) has grounded many such efforts over the recent past decades (Gainor, 2006). As Lent et al. (1999) noted,

> Anchored in Bandura's (1986) general social cognitive theory, SCCT focuses on several "agentic" variables (self-efficacy, outcome expectations, goals)—and on how they interact with other person and environmental variables (e.g., gender, race/ethnicity, social supports and barriers)—in the context of people's career development. (p. 297)

From the perspective of SCCT, Lent et al. (1999) proposed six developmental tasks to promote the process of school-to-work transitions with youth, beginning in the elementary and middle school years and then proceeding through the high school years and beyond. The first three career development tasks, which are prominent for students during the elementary and middle school years and then are repeatedly revisited and refined throughout high school and thereafter, include (1) acquiring constructive (vs. maladaptive) self-efficacy beliefs and outcome expectations, (2) forming interests relevant to careers (as well as abilities, values, and other attributes), and (3) developing linkages to define provisional career goals or aspirations (e.g., interest-goal connections). The additional three of six career development tasks salient for adolescents, which facilitate successful transitions from high school to work or college and beyond, are (4) translating goals into actions, (5) developing school or work-related performance skills, and (6) negotiating transition supports and barriers that individuals envision and encounter in pursuing their goals. The sixth career development task discussed by Lent et al.—negotiating transition barriers and supports—is particularly relevant to our discussion in the first part of this chapter on integrating bias preparation in career development interventions with adolescents vulnerable to discrimination.

Lent et al.'s (1999) six career development tasks for school-to-work transitions provide a useful framework from which to develop career interventions with adolescents vulnerable to discrimination. In addition to its theoretical grounding in SCCT (a theory that has generated a surge of research on the career development of culturally diverse group members; Subich, 2005; Tien, 2007), this framework has been used to critique the strengths and limitations of recent research on culturally appropriate assessment tools to promote career development with students in middle and high school (Jackson et al., 2008). Culturally appropriate assessment tools, methods, and practices are required to inform and implement effective interventions (APA, 2003; Garfield & Krieshok, 2002; Krishnamurthy et al., 2004). Furthermore, assessment as a collaborative process in counseling can serve as a helpful intervention in itself (Krishnamurthy et al., 2004).

CAREER DEVELOPMENT INTERVENTIONS BASED ON FOUR TYPES OF LEARNING EXPERIENCES OR SOURCES OF SELF-EFFICACY

Acquiring constructive self-efficacy beliefs is not only a key variable in SCCT (Lent et al., 1994) but also a foundational career development task for adolescence and beyond (Lent et al., 1999). Understanding self-efficacy beliefs is particularly important in career assessment and counseling with individuals from groups prone to unrealistically underestimate their capabilities or be constrained in the range of career options they perceive as accessible (Betz, 2004). Defined as one's confidence in one's ability to perform a given behavior or task, self-efficacy beliefs have been shown to influence whether individuals will initiate a behavior and the degree of effort they will expend to sustain the behavior in the face of obstacles (Bandura, 1997). Relevant to academic and occupational achievement, self-efficacy beliefs have been hypothesized to relate to the initiation of career-related activities, persistence despite

obstacles, and eventual success (Lent et al., 1994). In light of the disparities in academic and occupational achievement for people of color, attention is merited to include acquiring constructive self-efficacy beliefs as components in career development interventions with adolescents vulnerable to discrimination.

Four types of learning experiences that lead to the development of self-efficacy expectations were postulated by Bandura (1977)—performance accomplishments, vicarious learning, social/verbal persuasion, and physiological/emotional arousal. These four types of learning experiences offer a basis for understanding career-related self-efficacy expectations, as well as for designing career development interventions that facilitate acquiring constructive self-efficacy beliefs.

Yet, in her review of career self-efficacy research, Betz (2007) noted that despite the postulated importance of these four learning experience sources of self-efficacy, surprisingly little attention has been paid to operationalizing them for empirical investigations or using them as a guide for developing career counseling interventions. Notable exceptions discussed by Betz were three exemplary quasi-experimental studies that demonstrated evidence of effectiveness of structured group interventions targeting career-related self-efficacy in a specific domain using and assessing the impact of all four types of learning experiences. Although all three studies were conducted with predominantly Caucasian college students, their interventions target members of groups who face barriers to career development and illustrate examples of well-designed and effective career interventions that strategically incorporate and assess the impact of the four learning experience sources of self-efficacy proposed by Bandura (1977).

Exemplary Studies of Career Efficacy-Enhancing Interventions

Sullivan and Mahalik (2000) investigated the effectiveness of a group career counseling intervention designed to increase the career-related self-efficacy of college women ($n = 61$, ages 18–43, median age 21). Participants in the intervention condition ($n = 31$) were divided among five treatment groups at three universities in New England. The intervention was conducted over 6 weeks in 90-minute sessions, and the content incorporated the four types of learning experience sources of self-efficacy. For example, participants in the intervention condition (a) focused on successful performance accomplishments in constructing a vocational history, (b) participated in vicarious learning by interviewing a successful female role model about her career decision-making process, (c) experienced verbal persuasion and encouragement through facilitators' positive affirmations, and (d) constructively attended to physiological anxiety arousal through relaxation exercises and adaptive self-talk. Results indicated that, compared with the control group, women who completed the intervention significantly improved in career decision-making self-efficacy and vocational exploration and commitment, and they maintained those gains at a 6-week follow-up.

Foltz and Luzzo (1998), in a study with non-traditional-aged college students (ages 26–54, mean age 33), evaluated the effectiveness of a career counseling workshop intervention to increase career decision-making self-efficacy that incorporated the four sources of self-efficacy beliefs. Participants (29 women and 37 men at a large public university in the Southeast) were randomly assigned to either an experimental treatment group or a delayed-treatment control group of 6 to 8 students per group. The content of the two-session workshop (2 hours per session) incorporated discussion of personal career accomplishments, positive verbal persuasion, exposure to role models, and strategies for anxiety reduction. The study found that participation in the workshop had a significant, positive effect on the career decision-making self-efficacy of these nontraditional college students.

Women continue to be significantly underrepresented in traditionally male-dominated careers, such as in sciences and engineering, which led Betz and Schifano (2000) to investigate the effects of an intervention designed to increase the self-efficacy expectations of college women in Realistic Holland (1997) vocational theme activities (e.g., assembling, building, repairing, operating machinery, and using tools). Participants ($n = 54$, ages 18–25, mean age 19, from an introductory psychology course) were selected for the study who scored low in Realistic confidence but at least moderately high in Realistic interests. Betz (2007) further described this study's 7-hour, three-session experimental group intervention,

which "included all four of Bandura's sources of efficacy information and included the following content areas: hand tool identification and usage; building and repairing useful objects such as bookcases, lamps, and sink drain pipes; and architectural design and engineering" (p. 416). The course of instruction included periodic breaks to facilitate structured relaxation exercises, positive self-talk, and group support. The modeling component was addressed by an instructional group tour of campus construction sites conducted by a woman who was the chief university architect. The component of performance accomplishment was addressed at the end of the intervention when each young woman was given the task of repairing a broken lamp and a light bulb to test her success, which occurred in every case. At posttreatment, compared to the control group, women who participated in the intervention showed a statistically significant increase in their Realistic vocational self-efficacy expectations.

These three studies (Betz & Schifano, 2000; Foltz & Luzzo, 1998; Sullivan & Mahalik, 2000) provide empirical evidence supporting the effectiveness of career development interventions for enhancing career-related self-efficacy in targeted domains by incorporating the four types of learning experiences postulated by Bandura (1977). In addition, the studies' authors provide useful examples of the content of the efficacy-enhancing learning experiences they used in these career development interventions. Adaptations of the intervention effectiveness study by Betz and Schifano (2000) to increase efficacy in math- and science-related disciplines may be particularly relevant for culturally diverse adolescents whose academic achievement in math and science courses can facilitate (or impede) their access into higher education and career options in these disciplines. As women and people of color continue to be significantly underrepresented in higher paying careers in science, technology, engineering, and math (or STEM) disciplines, efforts to effectively intervene with youth have been supported, for example, by the National Science Foundation (Ferreira, 2007; Kerr & Kurpius, 2004).

We suggest that another implication for designing career interventions with adolescents of color concerns the potential for using efficacy-enhancing learning experiences to facilitate STEM career choices and persistence with youth who have interest but not confidence in STEM disciplines. As Betz and her colleagues have noted, the optimal conditions for facilitating choice are when *both* interests and confidence are at moderate to high levels (Betz & Rottinghaus, 2006; Betz & Schifano, 2000). Research has found that racial-ethnic minority individuals, including high school students, have endorsed high interests in math and engineering activities (Fouad & Walker, 2005). For those adolescents with moderate interest but low self-efficacy in STEM-related activities—that is, "in cases in which there is interest without high levels of confidence, Bandura's (1977) sources of efficacy information can be used to increase self-efficacy and thus possibly expand career options" (Betz, 2007, p. 415).

Studies of Career Efficacy-Enhancing Interventions With Culturally Diverse Adolescents

Recent reviews of research on the role of self-efficacy in career development—although predominated by college student samples—have included some studies with samples of culturally diverse adolescents (Betz, 2007; Gainor, 2006; Lindley, 2006). In the following section, we focus our discussion of these studies on those that assessed the impact of self-efficacy-based interventions (i.e., program evaluation and quasi-experimental designs). We highlight four studies with middle school students and three studies with high school students examining the effectiveness of self-efficacy-based interventions designed to facilitate career decision-making skills or expand exploration of occupational or educational options deemed nontraditional (or disproportionately represented) by their gender or race/ethnicity.

Career Intervention Studies With Diverse Middle School Students. Dawes, Horan, and Hackett (2000) conducted a study to examine the effectiveness of a technology education program for promoting interest and self-efficacy in technical and scientific careers with seventh- and eighth-grade students in an urban Southwest community (approximately 62% Caucasian, 20% Mexican American, and 7% African American students). Participants (*n* = 169) were stratified by grade level and randomly assigned to either a technology

education or control curriculum (in art). Over a 7-week period, the technology education program aimed to foster exploration in the students' choice of 3 (of 21 possible) technical and scientific career module options, and it incorporated three of the four theory-based types of efficacy-enhancing learning experiences (performance accomplishments, social encouragement, and vicarious learning). Pre- and posttest measures assessed technical/scientific self-efficacy and career interest, but no treatment effects were found.

As one plausible explanation for these nonsignificant results, Dawes et al. (2000) suggested that participants in the technology program may have selected activities in which they already had high interest and confidence, and thus they would not show much higher posttreatment levels. If so, this supports Betz and Schifano's (2000) rationale for targeting theoretically based efficacy-enhancing career interventions with individuals who have moderate to high levels of interest but low confidence in a STEM domain to promote self-efficacy and potentially expand career options. We wonder if another possible explanation for no treatment effects found by Dawes et al. may be that the intervention did not explicitly incorporate addressing cultural influences such as bias awareness and constructive strategies for negotiating barriers for women and people of color in STEM education and careers.

In contrast, evidence was found supporting the effectiveness of an intervention that did attend to the importance of sociocultural influences on participants' career development (O'Brien, Dukstein, Jackson, Tomlinson, & Kamatuka, 1999). The Career Horizons Program for youth at risk for educational or vocational underachievement was described and evaluated by Karen O'Brien and colleagues (1999). Middle school students (*n* = 57, mean age 12) from low-income, culturally diverse backgrounds (including 62% who identified as people of color) participated in a 1-week summer program on a college campus (a result of a university-community-parent collaboration). The program set goals consistent with the middle school competencies recommended by the National Occupational Information Coordinating Committee. In addition to facilitating specific discussions and infusing activities that explored with participants cultural and societal influences on their career decision-making and vocational success, the program incorporated the four hypothesized facilitators of self-efficacy. The authors noted that the program provided student participants with opportunities for (a) multiple success experiences (performance accomplishments), (b) observing scientists and staff (carefully chosen to reflect the diverse racial-ethnic backgrounds of the participants) to demonstrate competence in performing academic and career-related tasks (vicarious learning), (c) developing confidence in their abilities and receiving positive feedback about their efforts from staff members specifically trained to use such facilitative verbal persuasion, and (d) learning how to constructively express anxiety and concerns, as well as build on positive emotional experiences, to regulate emotional arousal to adaptive levels. Following the Career Horizons Program, data from measures assessing career interests and self-efficacy suggested that participants considered a greater number of careers, selected careers congruent with their interests, and demonstrated enhanced confidence in performing tasks related to investigating, selecting, and implementing career choices. As noted by Gainor (2006), one limitation of this study, as with other program evaluation versus quasi-experimental designs, was the lack of a control group as a means to determine whether improvements in career-related self-efficacy could more likely be attributed directly to the intervention or other factors.

Another program evaluation study found preliminary support for the effectiveness of a career development intervention to increase medical career self-efficacy with diverse adolescents (Speight, Rosenthal, Jones, & Gastenveld, 1995). Students in the ninth grade (10 boys, 35 girls, mostly Caucasians and African Americans) participated in Medcamp, a 3-day problem-based career intervention that incorporated all four theoretical antecedents for developing self-efficacy. Findings from a measure completed at the beginning and end of the program showed significant increases on all three self-efficacy subscales and the greatest effect on participants' self-efficacy specific to medical-related skills, similar to those demonstrated in the case history used in the program.

Turner and Lapan (2005a) used a quasi-experimental design (with treatment and delayed-treatment control groups) to evaluate the effectiveness of a career intervention designed to increase adolescents' interests and self-efficacy in occupations deemed nontraditional for their gender. Participants were middle school students (*n* = 160, mean age 13) from two culturally diverse public middle schools in a lower- to middle-class mid-sized community in the Midwest. The authors (professors and vocational psychologists) designed and implemented a three-module computer-assisted career intervention (the Mapping Vocational Challenges Career Development Program) to facilitate exploration activities and processing discussions with groups of 10 to 15 students. Compared to the control group, intervention participants demonstrated significant increases in self-efficacy for career planning and exploration as well as educational and vocational development. Furthermore, the intervention was successful in demonstrating significant increases in girls' interests in the Holland (1997) vocational themes of Realistic, Enterprising, and Investigative careers as well as boys' interests in Artistic, Social, and Conventional careers (i.e., in occupations considered nontraditional for their gender). While the intervention did not intentionally incorporate Bandura's (1977) four sources of self-efficacy, it did explicitly help participants to explore and challenge the relationship between their individual career interests and their perceptions of gender-typing and gender appropriateness of various careers. The latter approach, we submit, is of potential value as preparation for bias with adolescents exploring career options in which their gender is underrepresented.

Career Intervention Studies With Diverse High School Students. Kraus and Hughey (1999) investigated the effectiveness of a 4-week psychoeducational career intervention program with 11th-grade students who were culturally diverse (mostly Caucasians and African Americans) and attended an urban high school in the Midwest. The intervention was administered by a counselor and designed to help participants learn skills in career self-assessment, obtain occupational information, and apply these skills and information to career decision-making and choice. The intervention also incorporated elements of performance accomplishments and verbal persuasion. Participants (*n* = 60) were randomly assigned to a treatment or control group, with an equal number by gender in each. No significant differences were found between the treatment and control groups in career decision-making self-efficacy or career indecision. However, the intervention appeared effective in raising the career decision-making self-efficacy of the female participants. The authors noted the limitation of no pretest data collection to determine the possible confound of preexisting differences in participants' levels of career indecision and self-efficacy for decision making.

In a nonrandomized quasi-experimental design, O'Brien et al. (2000) examined the effectiveness of a career exploration program for high school students at risk for academic and vocational underachievement. Participants (n = 65; mean age 16) were low-income, predominantly African American students, who attended an Upward Bound Summer Institute. The treatment group (n = 26) attended five 50-minute sessions throughout the 5-week summer program. The intervention incorporated the four sources of self-efficacy (Bandura, 1977) and used interactive activities to help students learn more about themselves and the world of work to develop their self-efficacy for career decision making and broaden their career opportunities. Another component of the intervention included discussions about and practice with strategies for career decision making and overcoming obstacles to career development. The findings suggested that this intervention was effective in increasing participants' confidence in performing tasks in the process of career decision making.

Kerr and Kurpius (2004) evaluated the effectiveness of TARGETS—an intervention designed to enhance career identity and exploration, build science self-efficacy and self-esteem, and reduce risky behaviors—with low-income, culturally diverse adolescent girls who earned high grades in math and science but were at risk for not achieving high math/science potential (e.g., due to poverty, low self-esteem, unsafe behaviors, or low support by family for goals). Participants (n = 502, mean age 15) ranged from 6th- to 12th-graders (the majority in 10th grade) from high schools throughout Arizona (rural, urban, suburban, and reservation). Those who identified their ethnicity included 33% Caucasian, 27% Hispanic, 22% Native American, 11% African American, and 4% Asian American. A full-day intervention, the TARGETS program components included assisting participants assess their values, exploring their beliefs related to self-esteem and

educational self-efficacy, experiencing a guided imagery exercise focusing on a perfect workday 10 years in the future, completing career interest and personality inventories and receiving individual interpretations, and taking part in a group discussion of barriers (including risky behaviors) to self-understanding, goal setting, and career attainment. At the end of the intervention, participants reported increased career search behaviors that would expand their knowledge about careers in math and science. In addition, these math/science-gifted yet at-risk girls showed increases from pretest to follow-up at 3 to 4 months in their self-esteem, school self-efficacy, and future self-efficacy. Their risk for suicidality decreased over this period.

One implication of this study's findings for designing effective career counseling interventions with adolescents vulnerable to discrimination is the importance of integrating salient personal or mental health issues (Krumboltz, 1993; Skorikov & Vondracek, 2007). We also noted that a strength of the TARGETS intervention (Kerr & Kurpius, 2004)—as well as the interventions described by O'Brien and colleagues (1999, 2000)—was the component addressing participants' barriers to career development. Including this component is consistent with Lent et al.'s (1999) sixth career development task (negotiating barriers and supports) for adolescents in school-to-work transitions. A growing body of research suggests that addressing perceptions of barriers as well as supports to career development is of particular importance with adolescents of color and youth in low-income educational contexts (Jackson, Kacanski, Rust, & Beck, 2006; Kenny et al., 2007; McWhirter, Hackett, & Bandalos, 1998).

CONCLUSION

The scant research evidence to date suggests preliminary support for the effectiveness of career counseling interventions with adolescents of color that strategically incorporate the four learning experience sources of self-efficacy proposed by Bandura (1977). In addition, there is preliminary research support for interventions with culturally diverse adolescents that include opportunities to constructively address barriers and supports for career development, particularly for building career decision-making self-efficacy and expanding consideration of occupational/educational options deemed nontraditional (or disproportionately represented) for their gender or race/ethnicity. These interventions are consistent with the career development tasks for adolescents in school-to-work transitions of (a) building constructive self-efficacy and outcome expectations for their education/career interests, goals, and achievement and (b) adaptively negotiating barriers and supports (Lent et al., 1999).

There is a dearth of empirical knowledge to date on the influence of the multicultural contexts and issues of both clients and counselors on the effectiveness of career counseling intervention outcomes. Therefore, future research that links theoretical contributions relevant to multicultural counseling issues with the broader literature evaluating the effectiveness of career development interventions may offer potentially useful hypotheses and questions to investigate toward improving practical applications. We submit that one challenging area that merits increased attention in career counseling theory, research, and practice is in addressing the influences of discrimination. With adolescents vulnerable to discrimination (a relatively unexamined barrier to optimal vocational identity development and educational/career achievement), we advocate for incorporating into career development interventions helpful approaches to bias preparation and resilient strategies for coping with discrimination.

REFERENCES

Abreu, J. M. (2001). Theory and research on stereotypes and perceptual bias: A didactic resource for multicultural counseling trainers. *The Counseling Psychologist, 29,* 487–512.

Alvarez, A. N., Juang, L., & Liang, C. T. (2006). Asian Americans and racism: When bad things happen to "model minorities." *Cultural Diversity and Ethnic Minority Psychology, 12,* 477–492.

American Counseling Association. (2005). *ACA code of ethics.* Retrieved July 15, 2008, from http://www.counseling.org/Resources/CodeofEthics/TP/Home/CT2.aspy

American Educational Research Association, American Psychological Association, & National Council on Measurement in Education. (1999). *Standards for educational and psychological testing.* Washington, DC: American Educational Research Association.

American Psychological Association. (2002). Ethical principles of psychologists and code of conduct. *American Psychologist, 57,* 1060–1073.

American Psychological Association. (2003). Guidelines on multicultural education, training, research, practice, and organizational change for psychologists. *American Psychologist, 58,* 377–402.

American School Counselor Association. (2002). *The ASCA national model: A framework for school counseling programs.* Herndon, VA: Author.

Arbona, C. (2000). The development of academic achievement in school aged children: Precursors to career development. In S. D. Brown & R. W. Lent (Eds.), *Handbook of counseling psychology* (pp. 270–309). New York: John Wiley.

Arredondo, P., Toporek, R., Brown, S., Jones, J., Locke, D. C., Sanchez, J., et al. (1996). *Operationalization of the multicultural counseling competencies.* Alexandria, VA: Association for Multicultural Counseling and Development.

Baker, S. B., & Taylor, J. G. (1998). Effects of career education interventions: A meta-analysis. *Career Development Quarterly, 46,* 376–385.

Bandura, A. (1977). Self-efficacy: Toward a unifying theory of behavioral change. *Psychological Review, 84,* 191–215.

Bandura, A. (1997). *Self-efficacy: The exercise of control.* New York: Freeman.

Betz, N. E. (2004). Contributions of self-efficacy theory to career counseling: A personal perspective. *Career Development Quarterly, 52,* 340–353.

Betz, N. E. (2007). Career self-efficacy: Exemplary recent research and emerging directions. *Journal of Career Assessment, 15,* 403–422.

Betz, N. E., & Rottinghaus, P. (2006). Current research on parallel measures of interests and confidence for basic dimensions of vocational activity. *Journal of Career Assessment, 14,* 56–76.

Betz, N. E., & Schifano, R. S. (2000). Evaluation of an intervention to increase realistic self-efficacy and interests in college women. *Journal of Vocational Behavior, 56,* 35–52.

Blustein, D. L. (2006). *The psychology of working.* Mahwah, NJ: Lawrence Erlbaum.

Blustein, D. L. (2008). The role of work in psychological health and well-being: A conceptual, historical, and public policy perspective. *American Psychologist, 63,* 228–240.

Brown, S. D., & Ryan Krane, N. E. (2000). Four (or five) sessions and a cloud of dust: Old assumptions and new observations about career counseling. In S. D. Brown & R. W. Lent (Eds.), *Handbook of counseling psychology* (3rd ed., pp. 740–766). New York: John Wiley.

Brown, S. D., Ryan Krane, N. E., Brecheisen, J., Castelino, P., Budisin, I., Miller, M., et al. (2003). Critical ingredients of career choice interventions: More analyses and new hypotheses. *Journal of Vocational Behavior, 62,* 411–428.

Byars-Winston, A. M., & Fouad, N. A. (2006). Metacognition and multicultural competence: Expanding the culturally appropriate career counseling model. *Career Development Quarterly, 54,* 187–201.

Chaves, A. P., Diemer, M. A., Blustein, D. L., Gallagher, L. A., DeVoy, J. E., Casares, M. T., et al. (2004). Conceptions of work: The view from urban youth. *Journal of Counseling Psychology, 51,* 275–286.

Cohen, J. (1988). *Statistical power analysis for the behavioral sciences* (2nd ed.). Hillsdale, NJ: Lawrence Erlbaum.

Constantine, M. G., Erickson, C. D., Banks, R. W., & Timberlake, T. L. (1998). Challenges to the career development of urban racial and ethnic minority youth: Implications for vocational intervention. *Journal of Multicultural Counseling and Development, 26,* 83–95.

Constantine, M. G., & Sue, D. W. (2006). Factors contributing to optimal human functioning in people of color in the United States. *The Counseling Psychologist, 34,* 228–244.

Cross, W. E., Jr., & Vandiver, B. J. (2001). Nigrescence theory and measurement: Introducing the Cross Racial Identity Scale (CRIS). In J. G. Ponterotto, J. M. Casas, L. A. Suzuki, & C. M. Alexander (Eds.), *Handbook of multicultural counseling* (2nd ed., pp. 371–393). Thousand Oaks, CA: Sage.

Dawes, M. E., Horan, J. J., & Hackett, G. (2000). Experimental evaluation of self-efficacy treatment on technical/scientific career outcomes. *British Journal of Guidance and Counselling, 28,* 87–99.

Douvan, E. (1997). Erik Erikson: Critical times, critical theory. *Child Psychiatry & Human Development, 28,* 15–21.

Dykeman, C., Wood, C., Ingram, M., Pehrsson, D., Mandsager, N., & Herr, E. (2003). The structure of school career development interventions: Implications for school counselors. *Professional School Counseling, 6,* 272–278.

Eccles, J. S., Midgley, C., Wigfield, A., Buchanan, C., Reuman, D., Flanagan, C., et al. (1993). Development during adolescence: The impact of stage/environment fit on young adolescents' experiences in schools and families. *American Psychologist, 48,* 90–101.

Education Trust. (2006). *Education watch: The nation. Key education facts and figures: Achievement, attainment and opportunity from elementary school through college.* Retrieved July 31, 2008, from http://www2.edtrust.org/edtrust/summaries2006/USA.pdf

Erikson, E. H. (1963). *Childhood and society.* New York: Norton.

Evans, J. H., & Burck, H. D. (1992). The effects of career education interventions on academic achievement: A meta-analysis. *Journal of Counseling & Development, 71,* 63–68.

Ferreira, M. M. (2007). The development of a learning community through a university-school district partnership. *School Community Journal, 17,* 95–111.

Fiske, S. T. (1998). Stereotyping, prejudice, and discrimination. In D. T. Gilbert, S. T. Fiske, & G. Lindzey (Eds.), *The handbook of social psychology* (4th ed., Vol. 2, pp. 357–411). Boston: McGraw-Hill.

Foltz, B. M., & Luzzo, D. A. (1998). Increasing the career decision-making self-efficacy of nontraditional college students. *Journal of College Counseling, 1,* 35–44.

Fouad, N. A., & Bingham, R. P. (1995). Career counseling with racial and ethnic minorities. In W. B. Walsh & S. H. Osipow (Eds.), *Handbook of vocational psychology* (2nd ed., pp. 331–366). Hillsdale, NJ: Lawrence Erlbaum.

Fouad, N. A., & Bynner, J. (2008). Work transitions. *American Psychologist, 63,* 241–251.

Fouad, N. A., & Walker, C. M. (2005). Cultural influences on responses to items on the Strong Interest Inventory. *Journal of Vocational Behavior, 66,* 104–123.

Fusick, L., & Charkow Bordeau, W. (2004). Counseling at-risk Afro-American youth: An examination of contemporary issues and effective school-based strategies. *Professional School Counseling, 8,* 102–115.

Gainor, K. A. (2006). Twenty-five years of self-efficacy in career assessment practice. *Journal of Career Assessment, 14,* 161–178.

Garfield, N. J., & Krieshok, T. S. (2002). Assessment and counseling competencies and responsibilities: A checklist for counselors. In J. T. Kapes & E. A. Whitfield (Eds.), *A counselor's guide to career assessment instruments* (4th ed., pp. 65–72). Tulsa, OK: National Career Development Association.

Gibbons, F. X., Hsiu-Chen, Y., Gerrard, M., Cleveland, M. J., Cutrona, C., Simons, R. L., et al. (2007). Early experience with racial discrimination and conduct disorder as predictors of subsequent drug use: A critical period hypothesis. *Drug and Alcohol Dependence, 88,* S27–S37.

Greene, M., Way, N., & Pahl, K. (2006). Trajectories of perceived adult and peer discrimination among Black, Latino, and Asian American adolescents: Patterns and psychological correlates. *Developmental Psychology, 42,* 218–238.

Grossman, J. M., & Liang, B. (2008). Discrimination distress among Chinese American adolescents. *Journal of Youth and Adolescence, 37,* 1–11.

Harris-Britt, A., Valrie, C. R., Kurtz-Costes, B., & Rowley, S. J. (2007). Perceived racial discrimination and self-esteem in African American youth: Racial socialization as a protective factor. *Journal of Research on Adolescence, 17,* 669–682.

Helms, J. E., & Cook, D. A. (1999). *Using race and culture in counseling and psychotherapy.* Boston: Allyn & Bacon.

Heppner, M. J., & Heppner, P. P. (2003). Identifying process variables in career counseling: A research agenda. *Journal of Vocational Behavior, 62,* 429–452.

Hinkelman, J. M., & Luzzo, D. A. (2007). Mental health and career development of college students. *Journal of Counseling and Development, 85,* 143–147.

Holland, J. L. (1997). *Making vocational choices* (3rd ed.). Odessa, FL: Psychological Assessment Resources.

Howard, K. A. S., & Solberg, V. S. H. (2006). School-based social justice: The Achieving Success Identity Pathways Program. *Professional School Counseling, 9,* 278–287.

Hughes, D. (2003). Correlates of African American and Latino parents' messages to children about ethnicity and race: A comparative study of racial socialization. *American Journal of Community Psychology, 31,* 15–33.

Jackson, M. A., Holder, A. M. B., & Ramage, M. T. (2008). Culturally competent vocational assessment with at-risk adolescents in middle-high school. In L. A. Suzuki & J. G. Ponterotto (Eds.), *Handbook of multicultural assessment: Clinical, psychological, and educational applications* (3rd ed., pp. 273–298). San Francisco: Jossey-Bass.

Jackson, M. A., Kacanski, J. M., Rust, J. P., & Beck, S. E. (2006). Constructively challenging diverse inner-city youth's beliefs about educational/career barriers and supports. *Journal of Career Development, 32,* 203–218.

Jackson, M. A., & Nutini, C. D. (2002). Hidden resources and barriers in career learning assessment with adolescents vulnerable to discrimination. *Career Development Quarterly, 51,* 56–77.

Kenny, M. E., Blustein, D. L., Haase, R. F., Jackson, J., & Perry, J. C. (2006). Setting the stage: Career development and the student engagement process. *Journal of Counseling Psychology, 53,* 272–279.

Kenny, M. E., Gualdron, L., Scanlon, D., Sparks, E., Blustein, D. L., & Jernigan, M. (2007). Urban adolescents' constructions of supports and barriers to educational and career attainment. *Journal of Counseling Psychology, 54,* 336–343.

Kenny, M. E., Waldo, M., Warter, E. H., & Barton, C. (2002). School-linked prevention: Theory, science, and practice for enhancing lives of children and youth. *The Counseling Psychologist, 30,* 726–749.

Kerr, B., & Kurpius, S. E. R. (2004). Encouraging talented girls in math and science: Effects of a guidance intervention. *High Ability Studies, 15,* 85–102.

Kraus, L. J., & Hughey, K. F. (1999). The impact of an intervention on career decision-making self-efficacy and career indecision. *Professional School Counseling, 2,* 384–390.

Krishnamurthy, R., VandeCreek, L., Kaslow, N. J., Tazeau, Y. N., Miville, M. L., Kerns, R., et al. (2004). Achieving competency in psychological assessment: Directions for education and training. *Journal of Clinical Psychology, 60,* 725–739.

Krumboltz, J. D. (1993). Integrating career and personal counseling. *Career Development Quarterly, 42,* 143–148.

Lapan, R. T., Gysbers, N. C., & Sun, Y. (1997). The impact of more fully implemented guidance programs on the school experiences of high school students: A statewide evaluation study. *Journal of Counseling and Development, 75,* 292–302.

Lent, R. W., Brown, S. D., & Hackett, G. (1994). Toward a unifying social cognitive theory of career and academic interest, choice, and performance [Monograph]. *Journal of Vocational Behavior, 45,* 79–122.

Lent, R. W., Brown, S. D., & Hackett, G. (2000). Contextual supports and barriers to career choice: A social cognitive analysis. *Journal of Counseling Psychology, 47,* 36–49.

Lent, R. W., Hackett, G., & Brown, S. D. (1999). A social cognitive view of school-to-work transition. *Career Development Quarterly, 47,* 297–311.

Lent, R. W., & Worthington, R. L. (2000). On school-to-work transition, career development theories, and cultural validity. *Career Development Quarterly, 48,* 376–384.

Lindley, L. D. (2006). The paradox of self-efficacy: Research with diverse populations. *Journal of Career Assessment, 14,* 143–160.

McIntosh, P. (1998). Unpacking the invisible knapsack. In M. McGoldrick (Ed.), *Revisioning family therapy: Race, culture, and gender in clinical practice* (pp. 147–152). New York: Guildford.

McWhirter, E. H., Hackett, G., & Bandalos, D. L. (1998). A causal model of the educational plans and career expectations of Mexican American high school girls. *Journal of Counseling Psychology, 45,* 166–181.

Miller, M. J., & Brown, S. D. (2005). Counseling for career choice: Implications for improving interventions and working with diverse populations. In S. D. Brown & R. W. Lent (Eds.), *Career development and counseling: Putting theory and research to work* (pp. 441–465). Hoboken, NJ: John Wiley.

Murdock, N. L. (2006). On science-practice integration in everyday life: A plea for theory. *The Counseling Psychologist, 34,* 548–569.

National Career Development Association. (1997). *Career counseling competencies.* Retrieved July 31, 2008, from http://www.ncda.org/pdf/counselingcompetencies.pdf

National Center for Education Statistics. (n.d.). *America's children in brief: Key national indicators of well-being, 2008: Education.* Retrieved July 31, 2008, from http://www.childstats.gov/americaschildren/edu.asp

O'Brien, K. M., Bikos, L. H., Epstein, K. L., Flores, L. Y., Dukstein, R. D., & Kamatuka, N. A. (2000). Enhancing the career decision-making self-efficacy of Upward Bound students. *Journal of Career Development, 26,* 277–293.

O'Brien, K. M., Dukstein, R. D., Jackson, S. L., Tomlinson, M. J., & Kamatuka, N. A. (1999). Broadening career horizons for students in at-risk environments. *Career Development Quarterly, 47,* 215–229.

Oliver, L. W., & Spokane, A. R. (1988). Career intervention outcome: What contributes to client gain? *Journal of Counseling Psychology, 35,* 447–462.

Peterson, N., & Gonzalez, R. C. (2005). *The role of work in people's lives: Applied career counseling and vocational psychology* (2nd ed.). Belmont, CA: Wadsworth.

Pizzolato, J. E. (2007). Impossible selves: Investigating students' persistence decisions when their career-possible selves border on impossible. *Journal of Career Development, 33,* 201–223.

Richardson, M. S. (1993). Work in people's lives: A location for counseling psychologists. *Journal of Counseling Psychology, 40,* 425–433.

Ridley, C. R. (2005). *Overcoming unintentional racism in counseling and therapy* (2nd ed.). Thousand Oaks, CA: Sage.

Rivas-Drake, D., Hughes, D. D., & Way, N. (2008). A closer look at peer discrimination, ethnic identity, and psychological well-being among urban Chinese American sixth graders. *Journal of Youth and Adolescence, 37,* 12–21.

Rosenbloom, S. R., & Way, N. (2004). Experiences of discrimination among African American, Asian American, and Latino adolescents in an urban high school. *Youth & Society, 35,* 420–451.

Ryan, N. E. (1999). *Career counseling and career choice goal attainment: A meta-analytically derived model for career counseling practice.* Unpublished doctoral dissertation, Loyola University, Chicago.

Savickas, M., & Lent, R. W. (Eds.). (1994). *Convergence in career development theories: Implications for science and practice.* Palo Alto, CA: CPP Books.

Skorikov, V. B., & Vondracek, F. W. (2007). Positive career orientation as an inhibitor of adolescent problem behaviour. *Journal of Adolescence, 30,* 131–146.

Solberg, V. S., Howard, K., Blustein, D. L., & Close, W. (2002). Career development in the schools: Connecting school-to-work-to-life. *Counseling Psychologist, 30,* 705–725.

Speight, J. D., Rosenthal, K. S., Jones, B. J., & Gastenveld, P. M. (1995). Medcamp's effect on junior high school students'

medical career self-efficacy. *Career Development Quarterly, 43,* 285–295.

Spokane, A. R. (1991). *Career interventions.* Englewood Cliffs, NJ: Prentice Hall.

Subich, L. M. (2005). Career assessment with culturally diverse individuals. In W. B. Walsh (Ed.), *Handbook of vocational psychology: Theory, research, and practice* (pp. 397–421). Mahwah, NJ: Lawrence Erlbaum.

Sue, D. W. (2003). *Overcoming our racism: The journey to liberation.* San Francisco: Jossey-Bass.

Sue, D. W., Capodilupo, C. M., Torino, G. C., Bucceri, J. M., Holder, A. M. B., Nadal, K. L., et al. (2007). Racial microaggressions in everyday life: Implications for clinical practice. *American Psychologist, 62,* 271–286.

Sue, D. W., Carter, R. T., Casas, J. M., Fouad, N. A., Ivey, A. E., Jensen, M., et al. (1998). *Multicultural counseling competencies: Individual and organizational development.* Thousand Oaks, CA: Sage.

Sullivan, K. R., & Mahalik, J. R. (2000). Increasing career self-efficacy for women: Evaluating a group intervention. *Journal of Counseling and Development, 78,* 54–62.

Thompson, C. E., & Neville, H. A. (1999). Racism, mental health, and mental health practice. *The Counseling Psychologist, 27,* 155–223.

Tien, H. S. (2007). Annual review: Practice and research in career counseling and development—2006. *Career Development Quarterly, 56,* 98–140.

Turner, S. L., & Lapan, R. T. (2005a). Evaluation of an intervention to increase non-traditional career interest and career-related self-efficacy among middle-school adolescents. *Journal of Vocational Behavior, 66,* 516–531.

Turner, S. L., & Lapan, R. T. (2005b). Promoting career development and aspirations in school-age youth. In S. D. Brown & R. W. Lent (Eds.), *Career development and counseling: Putting theory and research to work* (pp. 417–440). Hoboken, NJ: John Wiley.

U.S. Department of Health and Human Services. (2001). *Mental health: Culture, race, and ethnicity* (Supplement to Mental Health: Report of Surgeon General [Inventory No. SMA01–3613]). Washington, DC: Author.

Walsh, M. E., Galassi, J. P., Murphy, J. A., & Park-Taylor, J. (2002). A conceptual framework for counseling psychologists in schools. *The Counseling Psychologist, 30,* 682–704.

Whiston, S. C., Brecheisen, B. K., & Stephens, J. (2003). Does treatment modality affect career counseling effectiveness? *Journal of Vocational Behavior, 62,* 390–410.

Whiston, S. C., Sexton, T. L., & Lasoff, D. L. (1998). Career-intervention outcome: A replication and extension of Oliver and Spokane (1988). *Journal of Counseling Psychology, 45,* 150–165.

56

Career Counseling With Diverse Adults

MARK POPE

Some may think that providing effective career counseling to culturally diverse adults may be the same as helping individuals from majority cultures identify and pursue their career goals. Following the historical axiom of Frank Parsons (1909), the founder of the career counseling movement, it was very simple—"in the choice of a vocation there are three broad factors: (1) a clear understanding of yourself; . . . (2) a knowledge of the requirements and conditions for success . . . in different lines of work; (3) true reasoning on the relation of these two groups of facts" (p. 5). If you have been paying attention in your multicultural counseling classes, you already have an idea that this might not be exactly accurate for every person.

Although the foundation of providing career counseling to culturally diverse adults is similar, the nuances that lead to assisting these adults in mastering their career issues are quite important and can be determinant in achieving successful outcomes. Bowman (1995) stated that "the structure (of career counseling) can make the career counselor's job easier, because there is less variability to contend with, but can also cause

complacency and lull the career counselor into believing that a pat or uniform approach will work with all clients, regardless of race, gender, age, and so on" (p. 152). In this chapter, I hope to help you develop a framework to approach these career counseling issues that you will certainly encounter in your practice.

Historically, the literature on career counseling with adults is only about 100 years old (Parsons, 1909), and as with any body of research in the social sciences that deals with such a general phenomenon, it begins with studies and observations of the dominant cultures (in the United States, such groups were White, male, able bodied, heterosexually oriented, college educated, etc.). It is only in the past 30 years that we have seen an extension of that research emerge, beginning to focus on the career development and career behavior of individuals from nondominant cultures in the United States. The focus of much of this new research has been on description rather than explanation. This chapter focuses on that new research along with the special interventions that have been identified in that emerging literature.

It is not within the scope of this chapter to detail each of the issues that are different from the dominant culture or different from each other culture. There are already many excellent writings on such issues—some in this book along with others in our literature. I will, however, use examples to highlight some of these issues in the context of the provision of career counseling services to adults from diverse backgrounds.

Furthermore, in this chapter, I use the term *culturally diverse adults* as an identifier for individuals who are from nondominant or nonmajority cultures within the United States (Pope, 1995c). In this chapter, both *dominant* and *majority* imply numeric quantity and/or power. I also want to acknowledge that I understand that culture is complex. A person is composed of many cultures: Witness the African American, lesbian, disabled veteran who is in her 70s, is a vegan, and lives on a farm. In this example, each of these is a culture, but they get refracted through one person, a person who may walk into our office seeking help with a career decision. This is a person not of one but of many cultures, each having prominence or salience at one time or even sometimes at the same time, depending on the situation at hand. It can all be overwhelming in its complexity. It is my role to help you be successful in these situations.

This chapter is divided into five parts: history and context, counselor self-preparation for working with culturally diverse adults, individual counseling interventions useful for counseling with culturally diverse adults, workplace programs useful to address the special issues that such individuals present, and appropriate advocacy or social action interventions. Issues of multiple cultural identities are also addressed throughout this chapter.

HISTORY AND CONTEXT

Less than 30 years ago, there was little research addressing career counseling with culturally diverse adults (Bowman, 1993; Croteau & Thiel, 1993; Phillips, Strohner, Berthaume, & O'Leary, 1983; Pope, 1995a; Young, Marshall, & Valach, 2007). In the past three decades in particular, there has been a steady increase in such research (Flores, Berkel, et al. 2006; Koegel, Donin, Ponterotto, & Spitz, 1995; Loveland, Buboltz, Schwartz, & Gibson, 2006). Important publications in

the career counseling field regarding culturally diverse adults have included books (Betz & Fitzgerald, 1987; Diamant, 1993; Gelberg & Chojnacki, 1996; Leong, 1995) and special issues of journals (Croteau & Bieschke, 1996; Leong & Pope, 2002; Pope, 1995b), as well as special chapters in several multicultural counseling and career counseling texts (Flores, Navarro, & Ojeda, 2006; Leong & Brown, 1995; Orzek, 1992), along with the many individual articles in the refereed journals of our profession (e.g., Arbona, 1990; Bowman, 1993; Gainor & Forrest, 1991; Hoyt, 1989; Leong, 1985; Fouad, 1993; Juntunen et al., 2001; Martin, 1991; Pope, 1995a; Pope et al., 2004; Rivera, Chen, Flores, Blumberg, & Ponterotto, 2007).

The good news is that, for the career counselor or vocational psychologist who is seeking practical advice on how to provide such career counseling services, there is now a growing body of literature to plumb for knowledge of how to intervene appropriately in the lives of culturally diverse adults. The literature, however, on the intersection of these cultural variables—for example, gay and lesbian culture—with ethnicity and race has not expanded at that same pace.

The context in which many culturally diverse adults operate includes the general factor of occupational discrimination. Any time you are different from a dominant culture or just simply any other culture, discrimination is a potential social outcome (Allport, 1954). African Americans, Asian Americans, Hispanic Americans, Native Americans, gay men and lesbian women, older people, people with (dis)abilities, and other cultural groups continue to experience job discrimination along with other forms of discrimination. Even with the passage of national employment antidiscrimination laws, such laws only provide remedies for the most heinous discriminatory behaviors. At the individual worker level, daily discrimination continues to be a part of the work lives of many Americans.

It is also important to note that not all cultural groups are protected classes under such laws. While race, ethnicity, gender, age, (dis)ability, religion, political affiliation, and other statuses are named in many such laws, sexual orientation remains unprotected in federal legislation. The failure to pass laws such as the Employment Non-discrimination Act (ENDA) by the U.S. Congress attests to the lack of acceptance of the needs of gay men and lesbian women in the workplace. Many national corporations, states, and cities are, however, including sexual orientation in their nondiscrimination personnel policies, and so this too is changing (Human Rights Campaign, 2003).

Furthermore, professional associations in mental health have developed general guidelines for working with culturally diverse individuals. Such guidelines are not focused specifically on career issues, but they are designed to address the general issues that mental health professionals encounter in providing services to culturally diverse individuals. The Association for Multicultural Counseling and Development (a division of the American Counseling Association) was the first to develop general multicultural counseling competencies (Sue, Arredondo, & McDavis, 1992). Other associations followed. The Association for Gay, Lesbian and Bisexual Issues in Counseling (a division of the American Counseling Association) developed special competencies that counseling professionals must have in providing services to sexual minorities (Terndrup, Ritter, Barret, Logan, & Mate, 1997). The American Psychological Association (APA) followed with its "Guidelines for Psychotherapy With Lesbian, Gay, and Bisexual Clients" (APA, 2000) and "Guidelines on Multicultural Education, Training, Research, Practice, and Organizational Change for Psychologists" (APA, 2003).

COUNSELOR SELF-PREPARATION

The first step for career counselors who want to work with culturally diverse adults is to take a personal inventory of the ways that their often subtle or unconscious biases may influence the career counseling process. Bias toward a particular culture will affect interventions that the individual career counselor chooses to use as well as how that intervention is used.

Even well-meaning counselors can sometimes cause harm. For example, Pope (1992) used the example of how heterosexually oriented counselors may have the idea that, if they can help a young man become more masculine in his behaviors, he can change his sexual orientation and will not have to deal with all of the problems that being gay might bring for him. Such counselors are simply trying to help, but these interventions are not research based and, although they may seem

intuitively appropriate to some counselors, there is no research literature that suggests (a) that training in gender-appropriate behavior is a determinant of sexual orientation or (b) that a same-sex sexual orientation is subject to change any more than an opposite-sex orientation is (LeVay, 1996).

Living in communities that routinely discriminate against culturally diverse individuals, it is virtually impossible, however, to avoid internalizing negative stereotypes or attitudes about "other" cultures. Misinformation or misunderstanding will quickly be evident to clients from these "other" cultures and may cause them to seek help elsewhere or not get help at all. Counselors, however, must be familiar with the various cultures of their communities so they are credible and congruent in their attitudes. Attending workshops, reading the literature, and participating in the diverse cultures in your community are effective ways to acquire knowledge about those cultures. Former clients and friends who come from culturally diverse groups will be an invaluable source of information.

In particular, career counselors who work with culturally diverse adults must understand the process of developing a cultural identity as this is a critical component in successful career counseling (Ponterotto & Park-Taylor, 2007). Many different cultural identity models have been suggested, including African American (Cross, 1991; Jackson, 1990), women/feminist (Downing & Roush, 1985), gay/lesbian (Cass, 1979), and Asian American (Sue & Sue, 1990). It is not the focus of this chapter to differentiate these models, but the stages that are described in each are similar but nuanced to respond to the contextual differences that each face in the development of their own identity. Generally, they follow similar stages as identified by Jackson (1990):

Stage 0: Naïveté: the individual has no awareness of self as African American.

Stage 1: Acceptance: accepts and conforms to White social, cultural, and institutional standards.

Stage 2: Resistance and naming: the person is dedicated toward rejection of White social, cultural, and institutional standards.

Stage 3: Redefinition and reflection: the individual attempts to develop uniquely Black values, goals, structures, and traditions; immerses self in Black culture; Black pride begins to develop.

Stage 4: Multiperspective internalization: a sense of inner security develops and the person can own and accept those aspects of dominant culture that are seen as healthy and can stand against those things that are not such as racism, sexism, homophobia, and other forms of oppression.

The process of cultural identity development is critical in the lives of culturally diverse adults, and career counselors need to be aware of their clients' stage of cultural identity development as well as their other development issues to provide effective career counseling (Fassinger, 1995; Prince, 1995). Counselors must also be aware of their own culture and cultural identity development as unawareness can have disastrous effects on career counseling outcomes.

Bowman (1995) provided an example of what might happen even when both the counselor and client were African American:

African American career counselors in the conformity stage (Stage 1) may not perceive certain occupations to be open to, or appropriate for, African Americans, so they may subtly dissuade clients from certain career paths. Clients in racial identity stages that are incongruent with the career counselor's stage . . . may be less likely to pay heed to the counselor's suggestions or recommendations. (p. 140)

Furthermore, issues of multiple identity are complex and challenging. Martinez and Sullivan (1998) examined the complexity of identity development in African American gay men and lesbian women. They identified three specific issues as adding the most complexity and as differentiating their identity development from most African American and gay/lesbian identity development models: racial prejudice, limited acceptance by the African American community, and a lack of integration into the larger, White gay community.

Career counselors must also become knowledgeable and aware of the special issues of a culture. For example, a variety of communication styles are in use in different cultures—some more direct, some more indirect (Leong & Gim-Chung, 1995). For example, the Chinese and individuals from other Asian cultures place more emphasis on indirect forms of communication, in what

is termed a *high-context message.* Such a message is anchored in the physical context where less reliance is placed on the explicit message content, extensively relying instead on the nonverbal behaviors. Meaning and understanding are, therefore, found more in what is unspoken. In this more emotion-based, person-oriented approach that is characteristic of high-context cultures, this leads to strong interpersonal bonds between individuals, creating a tendency to allow for considerable bending of individual interests for the sake of the relationship. For career counselors from a low-context culture who are communicating with high-context clients, the counselor needs to be aware of this, as the very fundamental basis for their communication may be in opposition. While the client may be uncomfortable with the explicitness of the conversation and miss key points, the counselor, on the other hand, may not be able to fully understand the client and counsel effectively.

For example, a Chinese client seeking career counseling might come into the office of a counselor and say quite gently, "I have been thinking about my results on the Strong Interest Inventory and wondered if we could over them one more time. If we do not have time, I understand." The counselor (from a low-context communicating culture) could easily misunderstand this request and dismiss it as the client had communicated this in a way that placed the request in a low priority ("if we do not have time, I understand"). The reality of the request for the client could be quite different and of high importance, but it was spoken with deference to the counselor as an authority figure. The request could come from a variety of sources, including that the client had shown the results to skeptical family members who questioned this method of obtaining data, the client may not be a native English speaker and had not understood what was being said when the original inventory interpretation was provided, and many others. In such situations, it is the responsibility of counselors to, as we say, use their "third" ear to read between the lines, to use their intuition and all their powers of observation, to use their knowledge of such a client's culture to develop alternate hypotheses for such a request and explore with the client the actual question and the genesis of that question, and finally to try to understand and honor the communication style of their clients so that clients can get their actual needs met. It is a simple request, but it is rich with opportunities to deepen the understanding and relationship between client and counselor.

Finally, counselors who cannot be affirmative in their attitudes toward any cultural group are ethically required to refer the client to a career counselor who has experience with that culture. The National Career Development Association, American Counseling Association, and American Psychological Association have well-defined ethical codes that offer guidance for individuals who work with cultural issues as well as career issues (American Counseling Association, 2005; American Psychological Association, 2002; National Career Development Association, 1994).

CLIENT-FOCUSED INTERVENTIONS

Client-focused interventions are career counseling interventions that are designed to be implemented at the individual or family level. Many career counseling recommendations have appeared in the published literature. Some are generally appropriate (with no special parenthetical identification), while others are culture specific (identified in parentheses as generally appropriate for collectivist cultures or as specifically appropriate for an identified culture): address occupational discrimination issues directly; identify the level of acculturation into the dominant culture (collectivist); identify the level of occupational knowledge the client has; involve the family in the career counseling process (collectivist); help people cope with the consequences of their decisions (if they go against the wishes of their support system) (collectivist); evaluate English-language proficiency for purposes of both testing and job search (non-native English speakers); provide assertiveness and communication training; use group career counseling for individuals from collectivist cultures; explore, especially with more traditional Hispanic females, a wide variety of careers and make particular efforts to increase their awareness of nontraditional careers; normalize the client's anxiety of not having a clear idea of what career to pursue and help the client understand the various stages of career development (Asian and Pacific Islander); explore issues of gender and the encouragement to strive for high-status and high-income careers along with expectations to maintain traditional gender

roles as wife and mother (Asian); train clients in asking and responding to informational interview and job interview questions such as "Are you married?" and "How many children do you have?" and "What is your religion?" and others (especially gay, lesbian, bisexual, and transgender); offer special programming to meet the career development needs of these diverse adults, including special programming on (a) résumé writing (what to include and what to not include) and (b) job interviewing; and for ethnic and racial minorities for whom English is not their first language, a more specific issue is the role of English-language proficiency in limiting career choices and as a factor in the actual process of career counseling. Some of the most important issues are addressed in more detail in the sections that follow.

Discrimination

Discrimination against individuals on the basis of their race, ethnic origin, gender, disability, religion, political affiliation, or sexual orientation is a fact of life in U.S. society. Professional career counselors who fail to recognize this and do not assist their clients in coping with this reality do a disservice to their clients.

Issues of dual and multiple discrimination also must be addressed when providing career counseling services. For example, lesbian women face at least two virulent forms of discrimination in U.S. society—sexism and heterosexism. If they are a member of an ethnic or racial minority, older, gay or lesbian, and physically challenged, they face daunting barriers to achieving their career goals. Bowman (1995), identifying the potential individual outcomes of such discrimination, found that past experience (direct or vicarious) with discrimination may result in anxiety about one's options and lowered self-esteem, including loss of hope, foreclosed horizons, and a tendency to set one's sights lower than necessary.

Openly addressing these issues and preparing clients to cope with the more overt manifestations of racism, sexism, heterosexism, ableism, ageism, and other forms of discrimination is an important and primary role of the career counselor. As simple as it may seem, talking openly with clients about issues of employment discrimination is very important. Even if clients are not the first to broach the subject, the issues ought to be discussed so that the client is aware of the career counselor's sensitivity and knowledge in this area. When these issues are openly and fully discussed, such discussions lead to improved decision making.

Group Career Counseling

Group career counseling has a strong appeal to many racial and ethnic minority clients (Bowman, 1995; Pope, 1999; Shea, Ma, & Yeh, 2007). Several characteristics of group-oriented or collectivist cultures—primacy of group survival over individual survival, interdependency, connectedness—make them especially suited to group career counseling techniques. For example, Asian clients' preferences for a more directive and authoritarian style of leadership, along with structured situations and practical solutions (Yu & Gregg, 1993), strongly coincide with the characteristics of career counseling groups in general.

R. C. Y. Chung and Okazaki (1991) noted the primary way that most people in "non-Western" countries receive psychological help is through systems of informal groups, composed of individuals who have chosen to be a part of the group (Blustein, 1982). Examples of informal groups are peer groups, book discussion groups, self-help groups, religious groups, and school groups.

Banawi and Stockton (1993) noted the role of groups in Islamic societies, including Indonesia, Malaysia, and parts of the Philippines. In these Islamic countries, there is an inherent group orientation that allows group counseling to "be seen as an optimal setting and a way for Muslims to experience personal growth" (p. 152). Salvador, Omizo, and Kim (1997) specifically recommended the use of group counseling, peer counseling, and family interventions as important when working with clients from the Philippines because of the special attributes of Filipino culture, which include *amor propio* (love of self), *pakikisama* (group solidarity), *kapwa* (recognition of shared identity), and *compadrazgo* (extending the family with godparents), to name a few.

Although ethnic and racial minority clients tend to underuse formal mental health services in general, career counseling is one type of counseling for which these individuals are especially likely to seek assistance and may even actually overuse these services (Lee & Mixson, 1995). In these cultures, seeking assistance for career issues does not have the same social taboo associated with seeking help for depression, for example.

Role of the Family

The role of the family, defined as broad and extended, is exceptionally important in the provision of career counseling services to individuals from collectivist cultures (Bowman, 1995; Flores, Navarro, & Ojeda, 2006; Pope, Cheng, & Leong, 1998; Rivera et al., 2007). In almost all important decisions in a person's life, both family and community are involved, whether it is getting married or choosing a career. Such issues, although moderated by increased levels of acculturation into the dominant U.S. culture, remain important to consider in providing career counseling services to individuals from collectivist cultures.

Similarly, career decisions for such clients are also rarely made without both family and community consultation. When clients first present for career counseling, it is important that counselors assess how much involvement of both extended family and community is needed by the clients in their decision-making process. This assessment of family influence should take into account such factors as the level of modernity of the family, the birth order of clients in their family of origin, clients' income in relation to the socioeconomic status of their family, and clients' educational level, occupational status, and age.

Where family members can be involved with the process, all or selected family and community members could attend each of the group sessions or may choose to only attend selected sessions. Prior to family attendance, it is especially important for the career counselor to discuss with the client the roles of each of his or her family and community members and to identify who are the most important persons in the group decision-making process. These persons will need the most information and most deference when the client is ready to choose an occupation (Pope, 1999).

One way to help the client identify the decision makers is through a family genogram. Sueyoshi, Rivera, and Ponterotto (2001) described how the use of a family genogram may be a helpful and culturally appropriate technique in career counseling with culturally diverse adults. This genogram was developed as part of the Career-in-Culture Interview, a 23-item semistructured interview protocol for use in multicultural career counseling (Ponterotto, Rivera, & Sueyoshi, 2000).

Dual-Career Couples

Another important intervention is providing career counseling with dual-career couples. The issue of dual-career couples has been explored more in the sexual minority career development literature than in the ethnic and racial minority literature, where the focus there has been more on the special role of the family in career decisions.

Most important is to work with both individuals in a relationship on dual-career couple issues (Pope, 1995a). The issues are important ones especially for the male couple or female couple with no experience and only few "out" dual-career couple role models. Two other special issues identified in the literature involved differences in socioeconomic status between the partners and spouse relocation.

Hetherington, Hillerbrand, and Etringer (1989) highlighted the issues facing same-sex dual-career couples—how to present the relationship, how to introduce one's partner, whether to openly acknowledge the love relationship, and how to deal with social events. Dual-career couple issues might also include geographic location, lifestyle that one partner would want to maintain while employed, problems that one partner's job may cause for a partner who may not want to be as open about this orientation, when to tell people at work, and how to handle situations that may arise at work for which the partner must be involved.

Career Interest Testing

Another aspect of providing career counseling to culturally diverse adults are the special procedures that have been recommended for using psychological tests with individuals from the various cultural communities. Career counselors need to know what special procedures are required to get accurate results or to make accurate interpretations. Because the use of career interest inventories, other personality tests, and card sorts are all important interventions in the repertoire of career counselors, how these items are used with culturally diverse adults is an important issue.

Some researchers have reported problems in the development of career interest inventories that might affect use with culturally diverse adults. Carter and

Swanson (1990) found problems with the development of the Strong Interest Inventory (1984 version). They reported that the validity studies used small samples that included few individuals from diverse ethnic and racial groups and that those who were included from such groups were usually male. They questioned the validity of that version of the Strong with culturally diverse adults. Later, in the 1994 renorming of the Strong, those issues were directly addressed and were reported prominently in the new technical manual (Harmon, Hansen, Borgen, & Hammer, 1994). Hartung et al. (1998) addressed these issues across a number of cultural groups and provided examples of how to use these inventories appropriately.

Fouad (1993) discussed the issues of bias in the construction of career interest inventories, including linguistic differences as well as the problems with functional and conceptual equivalence across vocational instruments.

Swanson (1992) studied the structure of vocational interests for African American college students and found that, for the most part, they were similar to White college students. In fact, cross-cultural studies of national *occupational* samples have found surprisingly few major differences between the criterion samples from one country to another (Harmon et al., 1994).

Some differences in the career interest patterns of various cultural groups in the United States have been identified in the literature. Knowledge of these differences is important for career counselors who are using such inventories with culturally diverse adults. Leong has written extensively on these issues with Asian American clients (e.g., Leong & Gupta, 2007; Leong & Leung, 1994).

Leong, Kao, and Lee (2004) studied Chinese Americans with a European American comparison group. Significant ethnic differences in career interests were found. The Chinese Americans' highest career interest was enterprising, whereas the highest for European Americans was social.

Y. B. Chung and Harmon (1994) used the Self-Directed Search (SDS) and compared gay and heterosexual men of equivalent age, socioeconomic background, ethnicity, student status, and education and reported that gay men scored higher on Artistic and Social scales of the SDS and lower on the Realistic and Investigative scales. They concluded that gay men's aspirations were less traditional for men, yet their aspirations were not lower in status than those of the heterosexual men.

These tools of the career counselor can be misused if not used cautiously and knowledgeably. For example, Pope (1992) identified and analyzed the use and misuse of specific subscales on five major psychological inventories used in career counseling and personnel selection (Strong Interest Inventory, Myers-Briggs Type Indicator, Edwards Personal Preference Schedule, California Psychological Inventory, and Minnesota Multiphasic Personality Inventory). Using a case study methodology, Pope wove into the cases technical and psychometric data to illustrate how psychological tests have been misused with gay and lesbian clients. He identified the following issues: fear of identification/ exposure of sexual orientation especially in the highly sensitive personnel selection area, bias and prejudice (heterosexism) of the counselor, appropriate interpretation based on identification of client response set, issues of sex role and "sexual orientation" stereotyping (male feeling types and female thinking types), and generally the appropriate interpretation of psychological tests with a gay male or lesbian client. Later, Y. B. Chung (2003) provided a broad overview of the professional and ethical issues in using psychological tests with gay men and lesbian women that specifically addressed many of these issues.

Another special career counseling intervention discussed in the professional literature is bibliotherapy. Bibliotherapy is an intervention in which clients read materials that directly address the specific issues relevant to their culture. Such materials might include biographies and autobiographies of individuals from their cultural community that include information on their career journey. Bibliographies containing the references for such materials should be developed and distributed by the career counselor in a particular locale.

Role of Internalized Oppression

Helping clients overcome internalized negative stereotypes or internalized oppression is another task of the career counselor (Bowman, 1995; Y. B. Chung & Harmon, 1994; Morgan & Brown, 1991; Pope, 1992).

It is important for the professional career counselor to understand the concept of internalized oppression as this may affect the client's life and occupational choices. Oppression oppresses even the mentally healthy and well-adjusted people in cultural minorities. Societal messages repeated over and over again about "evil, sick, lazy, over-sexed, stupid, etc." people may be believed and accepted at some conscious or unconscious level, and these messages permeate the U.S. popular culture.

Internalized oppression, when it occurs, cannot be overcome easily. It is important that career counselors understand and appreciate the effect that these messages can and do have on all cultural minorities in the United States. When the client is a sexual minority, a gender minority, and a racial/ethnic minority, these issues are intensified (Keeton, 2002). Culturally appropriate self-esteem interventions (e.g., positive self-talk; reframing; forgiveness) can be used here to overcome these internalized negative stereotypes.

"Coming Out" or Disclosing Cultural Membership

One special issue regarding clients for whom their cultural membership is not obvious (gay/lesbian/ bisexual/transgender, multiple race/ethnicity, political affiliation, religion, some (dis)abilities, and others) is the issue of whether to disclose one's culture to others. In the sexual minority counseling literature, this is termed *coming out* and has been central for gay men and lesbian women who are seeking career counseling (Pope, 1995a). Even if unstated, it is important for the counselor who knows the cultural membership to recommend this topic for discussion as part of the career counseling process. Career counselors can provide clients with opportunities for behavioral rehearsals directed toward developing and training strategies for informing others. The first step in this process—"coming out" to self—is many times followed by "coming out" to family and friends. The final step in this process for many is "coming out" in the workplace.

Anderson, Croteau, Chung, and DiStefano (2001) reported on the initial development of the Workplace Sexual Identity Management Measure (WSIMM). Psychometric properties of the WSIMM were examined for a sample of 172 student affairs professionals. The authors reported that the WSIMM successfully assessed a continuum of strategies for coming out in the workplace. Such measures as this are important to aid lesbian and gay workers in assessing their work environment and exploring appropriate strategies for sexual orientation disclosure.

Special attention also must be paid to the issue of "coming out" in families from cultures that do not readily accept same-sex sexual orientations. "There is not much qualitative difference between Asian and United States cultures in terms of traditional attitudes toward homosexuality, but the intensity of heterosexism and homophobia is much stronger in Asian cultures than in U.S. culture" (Y. B. Chung & Katayama, 1998, p. 22). The strategies that are used in more collectivist cultures (such as Asian) are different from those employed in more individualist cultures (such as the United States; Pope & Chung, 2000).

Wooden, Kawasaki, and Mayeda (1983) addressed the issue of sexual identity development (coming out to self) in a sample of Japanese men and found that, although almost all of the sample had come out to their friends, only about half had disclosed their sexual orientation to their families. These issues must be addressed when providing career counseling to lesbian women or gay men from such cultures, and strategies must be revised accordingly.

Other authors have similarly addressed these issues for African Americans (Martinez & Sullivan, 1998; McLean, Marini, & Pope, 2003), Hispanic Americans (Merighi & Grimes, 2000), and Native Americans (Piedmont, 1996).

PROGRAM-FOCUSED INTERVENTIONS

Program-focused interventions include interventions that are programmatic in scope and can be implemented in an agency or institution. All of the recommended interventions in this area have one commonality: Each tries to create more options for the culturally diverse adult making a career decision. Even with such clients who need more focus in their decision making, the procedures identified here are important ones to precede the decision-making stage of career counseling as they may suggest options that the client may not have explored. The interventions recommended here for career counseling include support and encourage role models; provide information on national networks of professionals and community people such as the Society for Indian Psychologists (Native American psychologists, allied with the American Psychological Association), Black Pages (directory of African American businesses and services in Saint Louis, Missouri), and the Golden Gate Business Association (gay/lesbian Chamber of Commerce in San Francisco); share information on existing local culturally focused community resources; offer special programming such as talks by professionals from specific cultures; arrange career shadowing opportunities with other culturally appropriate professionals; facilitate externships or cooperative education placements in business that are owned or operated by individuals from that culture; and establish mentoring programs.

Other recommendations include having the career counselor publish a list of individuals from that particular culture who would be available for informational interviews with clients and offer special programming to meet the career development needs of the specific cultural group, such as a job fair or support group that is focused on or composed of members of that specific culture group. Programmatic interventions in the workplace could include mentoring programs, diversity workshops, and culturally affirmative policies such as nondiscrimination policies and domestic partners benefits.

Occupational role model and networking interventions are very important for special populations that historically have been limited in their occupational choices by some type of societal stereotyping. Chinese have been stereotyped as computer programmers, research scientists, and owners of restaurants or laundries. Filipinos are supposed to work as nurses or maids. Lesbian women have been stereotyped as truck drivers, athletes, mechanics, and other occupations traditionally held by males. These very narrow stereotypes serve as "safe" occupations, in which these culturally diverse adults may feel more accepted, more able to truly be themselves; however, these occupations can also limit these individuals' occupational choices. For some individuals, however, they are seen as the only possible choices.

At the programmatic level, one simple way to get the word out that you are supportive of the struggles of culturally diverse adults who are seeking career counseling is by creating a supportive atmosphere in your office. It can be as simple as having a selection of culturally appropriate books on your bookshelf, along with your other professional literature. This will help some clients realize that you are prepared to work with individuals from diverse cultures. Placing such literature in the office waiting room will send a very overt signal that the career counselor is culturally affirming. Popular magazines and newspapers focused on various cultural communities send obvious signals to all clients and may help clients in general gain more information about their culturally diverse coworkers.

ADVOCACY OR SOCIAL ACTION INTERVENTIONS

Advocacy or social action interventions include interventions that are focused on the external, social environment of the client. Positive social advocacy for our culturally diverse clients could include lobbying for the inclusion of their cultural group in the nondiscrimination policies of local employers or picketing a speech made by an ex-gay who claims to have become a happy, fully functioning heterosexual. Some clients will need basic information on their cultural community as well as the facts on employment, housing, and other discrimination.

Such interventions could include counselors knowing and providing client information on the geographic location and the size of the cultural communities in their area, information on the employment policies and Equal Employment Opportunity (EEO) statements of local businesses, and information on local and federal antidiscrimination laws (assistance on clients avoiding arrest, assistance to clients about constructing affirming work environments, and working to change employer-related statements or policies that discriminate).

Career counselors working with any special culture group must be affirming of that group going beyond the "do no harm" admonition to encompass a positive advocacy for their clients and their rights. Examples of such a positive advocacy include working to change employer-related statements or policies that discriminate, working toward changing the laws that criminalize certain sexual acts between two consenting adults, changing housing laws that do not allow two

"unrelated" persons to live together, or working to stop police harassment and entrapment. Such laws are often used to prevent a person or family from renting a house or apartment or to deny employment to teachers, counselors, police officers, and other professionals.

Even if some laws are rescinded, people who have had such laws used against them are subject to continued problems because certain kinds of violations may remain on computerized police records for years. A professional who faces a background investigation as a routine part of employment may freeze due to fear that exposure of such a police record will lead to renewed public humiliation. Clients may decide to take the risk that previous histories may not be discovered or to not continue to pursue a particular job. Whatever the course of action selected, the career counselor can expect the client to experience significant anxiety and anger that this injustice may continue to be a limitation. While not routine, situations like this may lead some clients to choose to remain in unsatisfying or limited careers. Counselors have an opportunity to lobby law enforcement officials to stop entrapments as well as the unequal enforcement of laws. Career counselors must take an active advocacy approach to working with all cultural minorities.

SUMMARY

This chapter is composed of specific interventions directed at career counselors themselves, at individual career counseling activities, at career counseling programs within institutions, and at advocacy or social/community action. Providing effective and culturally appropriate career counseling services for culturally diverse adults is not an easy task. It is fraught with personal and social issues, including internalized oppression and employment discrimination and multiple cultural identities and much more. The career counselor who directly addresses these issues will find the path smoother and rewards greater for their clients who are seeking help with their career issues.

REFERENCES

Allport, G. W. (1954). *The nature of prejudice.* Cambridge, MA: Addison-Wesley.
American Counseling Association. (2005). *ACA code of ethics.* Alexandria, VA: Author.

American Psychological Association (APA). (2000). Guidelines for psychotherapy with lesbian, gay, and bisexual clients. *American Psychologist, 55,* 1440–1451.

American Psychological Association (APA). (2002). Ethical principles of psychologists and code of conduct. *American Psychologist, 57,* 1060–1073.

American Psychological Association (APA). (2003). Guidelines on multicultural education, training, research, practice, and organizational change for psychologists. *American Psychologist, 58,* 377–402.

Anderson, M. Z., Croteau, J. M., Chung, Y. B., & DiStefano, T. M. (2001). Developing an assessment of sexual identity management for lesbian and gay workers. *Journal of Career Assessment, 9,* 243–260.

Arbona, C. (1990). Career counseling research and Hispanics: A review of the literature. *The Counseling Psychologist, 18,* 300–323.

Banawi, R., & Stockton, R. (1993). Islamic values relevant to group work, with practical applications for the group leader. *Journal for Specialists in Group Work, 18,* 151–160.

Betz, N. E., & Fitzgerald, L. F. (1987). *The career psychology of women.* San Diego: Academic Press.

Blustein, D. L. (1982). Using informal groups in cross-cultural counseling. *Journal for Specialists in Group Work, 7,* 260–265.

Bowman, S. L. (1993). Career intervention strategies for ethnic minorities. *Career Development Quarterly, 42,* 14–25.

Bowman, S. L. (1995). Career intervention strategies and assessment issues for African Americans. In F. T. L. Leong (Ed.), *Career development and vocational behavior of racial and ethnic minorities* (pp. 137–164). Mahwah, NJ: Lawrence Erlbaum.

Carter, R. T., & Swanson, J. L. (1990). The validity of the Strong Interest Inventory with Black Americans: A review of the literature. *Journal of Vocational Behavior, 36,* 195–209.

Cass, V. (1979). Homosexual identity formation: A theoretical model. *Journal of Homosexuality, 4,* 219–235.

Chung, R. C. Y., & Okazaki, S. (1991). Counseling Americans of Southeast Asian descent. In C. C. Lee & B. L. Richardson (Eds.), *Multicultural issues in counseling* (pp. 107–126). Alexandria, VA: American Counseling Association.

Chung, Y. B. (2003). Ethical and professional issues in career assessment with lesbian, gay, and bisexual persons. *Journal of Career Assessment, 11,* 96–112.

Chung, Y. B., & Harmon, L. W. (1994). The career interests and aspirations of gay men: How sex-role orientation is related. *Journal of Vocational Behavior, 45,* 223–239.

Chung, Y. B., & Katayama, M. (1998). Ethnic and sexual identity development of Asian-American lesbian and gay adolescents. *Professional School Counseling, 1*(3), 21–25.

Cross, W. E. (1991). *Shades of black: Diversity in African American identity.* Philadelphia: Temple University Press.

Croteau, J. M., & Bieschke, K. J. (Eds.). (1996). The vocational issues of lesbian women and gay men [Special issue]. *Journal of Vocational Behavior, 48,* 119–255.

Croteau, J. M., & Thiel, M. J. (1993). Integrating sexual orientation in career counseling: Acting to end a form of the personal-career dichotomy. *Career Development Quarterly, 42,* 174–179.

Diamant, L. (Ed.). (1993). *Homosexual issues in the workplace.* Washington, DC: Taylor & Francis.

Downing, N. E., & Roush, K. L. (1985). From passive acceptance to active commitment: A model of feminist identity development of women. *The Counseling Psychologist, 13,* 59–72.

Fassinger, R. E. (1995). From invisibility to integration: Lesbian identity in the workplace. *Career Development Quarterly, 44,* 148–167.

Flores, L. Y., Berkel, L. A., Nilsson, J. E., Ojeda, L., Jordan, S. E., Lynn, G. I., et al. (2006). Racial/ethnic minority vocational research: A content and trend analysis across 36 years. *Career Development Quarterly, 55,* 2–21.

Flores, L. Y., Navarro, R. L., & Ojeda, L. (2006). Career counseling with Latinas. In W. Bruce Walsh & M. J. Heppner (Eds.), *Handbook of career counseling for women* (2nd ed., pp. 271–313). Mahwah, NJ: Lawrence Erlbaum.

Fouad, N. A. (1993). Cross-cultural vocational assessment. *Career Development Quarterly, 42,* 4–13.

Gainor, K. A., & Forrest, L. (1991). African American women's self-concept: Implications for career decisions and career counseling. *Career Development Quarterly, 39,* 263–272.

Gelberg, S., & Chojnacki, J. T. (1996). *Career and life planning with gay, lesbian, and bisexual persons.* Alexandria, VA: American Counseling Association.

Harmon, L. W., Hansen, J. C., Borgen, F. H., & Hammer, A. L. (1994). *Strong Interest Inventory: Applications and technical guide.* Palo Alto, CA: CPP.

Hartung, P. J., Vandiver, B. J., Leong, F. T. L., Pope, M., Niles, S. G., & Farrow, B. (1998). Appraising cultural identity in Career-Development Assessment and Counseling. *Career Development Quarterly, 46,* 276–293.

Hetherington, C., Hillerbrand, E., & Etringer, B. (1989). Career counseling with gay men: Issues and recommendations for research. *Journal of Counseling & Development, 67,* 452–454.

Hoyt, K. B. (1989). The career status of women and minority persons. *Career Development Quarterly, 37,* 202–212.

Human Rights Campaign. (2003). *The state of the workplace for lesbian, gay, bisexual, and transgender Americans—2003*. Retrieved January 15, 2004, from www.hrc.org

Jackson, B. W. (1990, April). *Building a multicultural school*. Paper presented to the Amherst Regional School System, Amherst, MA.

Juntunen, C. L., Barraclough, D. J., Broneck, C. L., Seibel, G. A., Winrow, S. A., & Morin, P. M. (2001). American Indian perspectives on the career journey. *Journal of Counseling Psychology, 48*, 274–285.

Keeton, M. D. (2002). Perceptions of career-related barriers among gay, lesbian, and bisexual individuals. *Dissertation Abstracts International, 63*(2-B), 1075. (Transaction Periodicals Consortium, Rutgers University)

Koegel, H. M., Donin, I., Ponterotto, J. G., & Spitz, S. (1995). Multicultural career development: A methodological critique of 8 years of research in three leading career journals. *Journal of Employment Counseling, 32*, 50–63.

Lee, W. M. L., & Mixson, R. M. (1995). Asian and Caucasian client perceptions of the effectiveness of counseling. *Journal of Multicultural Counseling and Development, 23*, 48–56.

Leong, F. T. L. (1985). Career development of Asian Americans. *Journal of College Student Personnel, 26*, 539–546.

Leong, F. T. L. (Ed.). (1995). *Career development and vocational behavior of racial and ethnic minorities*. Mahwah, NJ: Lawrence Erlbaum.

Leong, F. T. L., & Brown, M. (1995). Theoretical issues in cross-cultural career development: Cultural validity and cultural specificity. In W. B. Walsh & S. H. Osipow (Eds.), *Handbook of vocational psychology* (2nd ed., pp. 143–180). Hillsdale, NJ: Lawrence Erlbaum.

Leong, F. T. L., & Gim-Chung, R. H. (1995). Career assessment and intervention with Asian Americans. In F. T. L. Leong (Ed.), *Career development and vocational behavior of racial and ethnic minorities* (pp. 193–226). Mahwah, NJ: Lawrence Erlbaum.

Leong, F. T. L., & Gupta, A. (2007). Career development and vocational behaviors of Asian Americans. In F. T. L. Leong, A. Ebreo, L. Kinoshita, A. Inman, & L. H. Yang (Eds.), *Handbook of Asian American psychology* (2nd ed., pp. 159–178). Thousand Oaks, CA: Sage.

Leong, F. T. L., Kao, E. M.-C., & Lee, S.-H. (2004). The relationship between family dynamics and career interests among Chinese Americans and European Americans. *Journal of Career Assessment, 12*, 65–84.

Leong, F. T. L., & Leung, S. A. (1994). Career assessment with Asian-Americans. *Journal of Career Assessment, 2*, 240–257.

Leong, F. T. L., & Pope, M. (Eds.). (2002). Challenges for career counseling in Asia [Special section]. *Career Development Quarterly, 50*, 209–284.

LeVay, S. (1996). *Queer science: The use and abuse of research into homosexuality*. Cambridge: MIT Press.

Loveland, J. M., Buboltz, W. C., Schwartz, J., & Gibson, G. (2006). From 1994–2003: Implications and trends for practitioners and researchers from a decade of research. *Career Development Quarterly, 54*, 256–264.

Martin, W. E. (1991). Career development and American Indians living on reservations: Cross-cultural factors to consider. *Career Development Quarterly, 39*, 273–283.

Martinez, D. G., & Sullivan, S. C. (1998). African American gay men and lesbians: Examining the complexity of gay identity development. *Journal of Human Behavior in the Social Environment, 1*, 243–264.

McLean, R., Marini, I., & Pope, M. (2003). Racial identity and relationship satisfaction in African American gay men. *The Family Journal, 11*, 13–22.

Merighi, J. R., & Grimes, M. D. (2000). Coming out to families in a multicultural context. *Families in Society, 81*, 32–41.

Morgan, K. S., & Brown, L. S. (1991). Lesbian career development, work behavior, and vocational counseling. *The Counseling Psychologist, 19*, 273–291.

National Career Development Association. (1994). Code of ethics and standards of practice (rev. 1991). In D. W. Engels (Ed.), *The professional practice of career counseling and consultation: A resource document* (2nd ed., pp. 26–33). Tulsa, OK: Author.

Orzek, A. M. (1992). Career counseling for the gay and lesbian community. In S. Dworkin & F. Gutierrez (Eds.), *Counseling gay men & lesbians: Journey to the end of the rainbow* (pp. 23–34). Alexandria, VA: American Counseling Association.

Parsons, F. (1909). *Choosing a vocation*. Boston: Houghton Mifflin.

Phillips, S. D., Strohner, D. C., Berthaume, B. L. J., & O'Leary, J. (1983). Career development of special populations: A framework for research. *Journal of Vocational Behavior, 22*, 12–27.

Piedmont, O. (1996). The veils of Arjuna: Androgyny in gay spirituality, east and west. *Dissertation Abstracts International, 57*(6-B), 4076. (UMI No. AAM9633907)

Ponterotto, J. G., & Park-Taylor, J. (2007). Racial and ethnic identity theory, measurement, and research in counseling psychology: Present status and future directions. *Journal of Counseling Psychology, 54*, 282–294.

Ponterotto, J. G., Rivera, L., & Sueyoshi, L. A. (2000). The Career-in-Culture Interview: A semi-structured protocol for the cross-cultural intake interview. *Career Development Quarterly, 49,* 85–96.

Pope, M. (1992). Bias in the interpretation of psychological tests. In S. Dworkin & F. Gutierrez (Eds.), *Counseling gay men & lesbians: Journey to the end of the rainbow* (pp. 277–292). Alexandria, VA: American Counseling Association.

Pope, M. (1995a). Career interventions for gay and lesbian clients: A synopsis of practice knowledge and research needs. *Career Development Quarterly, 44,* 191–203.

Pope, M. (Ed.). (1995b). Gay/lesbian career development [Special section]. *Career Development Quarterly, 44,* 146–203.

Pope, M. (1995c). The "salad bowl" is big enough for us all: An argument for the inclusion of lesbians and gays in any definition of multiculturalism. *Journal of Counseling & Development, 73,* 301–304.

Pope, M. (1999). Applications of group career counseling techniques in Asian cultures. *Journal for Multicultural Counseling and Development, 27,* 18–30.

Pope, M., Barret, B., Szymanski, D. M, Chung, Y. B., Singaravelu, H., McLean, R., et al. (2004). Culturally appropriate career counseling with gay and lesbian clients. *Career Development Quarterly, 53,* 158–177.

Pope, M., Cheng, W. D., & Leong, F. T. L. (1998). The case of Chou: The inextricability of career to personal/social issues. *Journal of Career Development, 25,* 53–64.

Pope, M., & Chung, Y. B. (2000). From bakla to tongzhi: Counseling and psychotherapy issues for gay and lesbian Asian and Pacific Islander Americans. In D. S. Sandhu (Ed.), *Asian and Pacific Islander Americans: Issues and concerns for counseling and psychotherapy* (pp. 283–300). Commack, NY: Nova Science Publishers.

Prince, J. P. (1995). Influences on the career development of gay men. *Career Development Quarterly, 44,* 168–177.

Rivera, L. M., Chen, E. C., Flores, L. Y., Blumberg, F., & Ponterotto, J. G. (2007). The effects of perceived barriers, role models, and acculturation on the career self-efficacy and career considerations of Hispanic women. *Career Development Quarterly, 56,* 47–61.

Salvador, D. S., Omizo, M. M., & Kim, B. S. K. (1997). Bayanihan: Providing effective counseling strategies with children of Filipino ancestry. *Journal of Multicultural Counseling and Development, 25,* 201–209.

Shea, M., Ma, P. W. W., & Yeh, C. J. (2007). Development of a culturally specific career exploration group for urban Chinese immigrant youth. *Career Development Quarterly, 56,* 62–73.

Sue, D. W., Arredondo, P., & McDavis, R. J (1992). Multicultural counseling competencies and standards: A call to the profession. *Journal of Multicultural Counseling and Development, 20,* 64–88.

Sue, D. W., & Sue, S. (1990). *Counseling the culturally different* (2nd ed.). New York: John Wiley.

Sueyoshi, L. A., Rivera, L., & Ponterotto, J. G. (2001). The family genogram as a tool in multicultural career counseling. In J. G. Ponterotto, J. M. Casas, L. A. Suzuki, & C. Alexander (Eds.), *Handbook of multicultural counseling* (2nd ed., pp. 655–671). Thousand Oaks, CA: Sage.

Swanson, J. L. (1992). The structure of vocational interests for African-American college students. *Journal of Vocational Behavior, 40,* 144–157.

Terndrup, A., Ritter, K., Barret, B., Logan, C., & Mate, R. (1997). *Competencies in counseling gay, lesbian, bisexual, and transgendered clients.* Retrieved January 15, 2004, from http://www.aglbic.org/competencies.html

Wooden, W. S., Kawasaki, S., & Mayeda, R. (1983). Lifestyles and identity maintenance among gay Japanese-American males. *Alternative Lifestyles, 5,* 236–243.

Young, R. A., Marshall, S. K., & Valach, L. (2007). Making career theories more culturally sensitive: Implications for counseling. *Career Development Quarterly, 56,* 4–18.

Yu, A., & Gregg, C. H. (1993). Asians in groups: More than a matter of cultural awareness. *Journal for Specialists in Group Work, 18,* 86–93.

57

Designing Career Development Strategies for Older Adults From Diverse Racial and Ethnic Backgrounds

V. SCOTT SOLBERG AND JUDITH M. ETTINGER

This chapter focuses on how to design effective career development strategies for older adults from diverse racial and ethnic backgrounds who do not have the option of retiring but instead need to continue working to provide for basic needs. The counseling literature has addressed issues related to supporting the retirement process (Richardson, 2003; Sterns & Subich, 2005; Tinsley & Bigler, 2002) and making effective later life transitions (Gibson & Brown, 1992; Schlossberg, 2004). However, as a direct result of unequal distributions in wealth and retirement assets, many older adults from diverse racial and ethnic backgrounds will need to keep working and will be unable to pursue leisure and other avocational activities often associated with retirement. A study by the U.S. Federal Reserve clearly describes the inequality in wealth distributions in the United States (Aizcorbe, Kennickell, & Moore, 2003). They found that the median net worth

among White Americans grew over $30,000 from $86,200 in 1992 to $120,900 in 2001 (see Figure 57.1). During this same period, non-White Americans' median net worth grew less than $3,000 from $14,800 to $17,100. This reflects a median difference in wealth of over $100,000. Comparison of wealth by type of median assets also shows a stark contrast between White and non-White Americans (see Figure 57.2; Aizcorbe et al., 2003). Most notable differences in median assets were found for the comparative value of bonds, mutual funds, and retirement accounts. The median value for bond assets among adults from White racial and ethnic groups was $50,000 compared to $7,600 for adults from nonwhite racial ethnic groups. The differences among these groups were $22,500 for median value of mutual funds and $25,000 for median value of retirement accounts. By using the "median" as the estimator, it is understood that half of the sample is above and

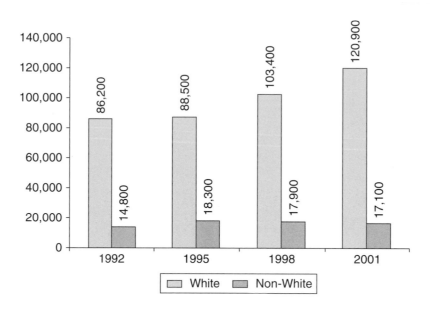

Figure 57.1   Median Net Wealth

Source: Aizcorbe, Kennickell, and Moore (2003).

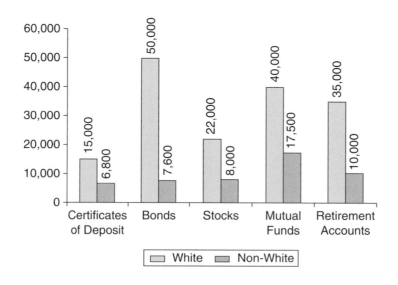

Figure 57.2   2001 Median Value of Assets

Source: Aizcorbe, Kennickell, and Moore (2003).

half below. Therefore, it can be assumed that a number of older adults from diverse racial and ethnic backgrounds have accumulated wealth and assets to support themselves in retirement. What can be inferred from the U.S. Federal Reserve study is that in order for a large number of older adults from racial and ethnic backgrounds to make effective later life transitions, they cannot choose to retire but must continue working to provide for basic housing, healthcare, and food needs.

Social Justice Perspective. The chapter incorporates a social justice perspective described in Prilleltensky's (1997) seminal work on describing an emancipatory communitarianism approach to service delivery that was later expanded in the context of career development by Blustein, McWhirter, and Perry (2005). Traditional career development strategies focus on helping the individual gain self-awareness of interests, skills, and values and then engage in effective decision-making strategies related to the range of specific careers and occupations to pursue that are consistent with the pattern of interests, skills, and values. These strategies often assume that the challenges associated with making later life career transitions are due in large part to the individual not possessing enough self-awareness and/or not engaging in effective career decision making. Alternatively, emancipatory communitarianism reconstructs the challenges a person experiences in making effective career and occupational transitions as a relational problem and places equal responsibility for making effective transitions on the individual and the societal context. Baltes (1997) argues, for example, that optimal development among older adults is seriously diminished when society fails to provide optimal developmental opportunities to help older adults continue developing the skills needed to actualize their goals. One central tenet from emancipatory communitarianism (see also developmental contextualism [Lerner, 2002] and the ecological model [Bronfenbrenner, 1979]) is that the challenges experienced by individuals, including older adults from diverse racial and ethnic backgrounds, are not a product of causes located within the individual (e.g., personality traits) but result from interacting in contexts that fail to support his or her optimal development. The primary thesis of this chapter is that in order for older adults from diverse racial and ethnic backgrounds to make effective later life transitions, they must be linked to new career development opportunities that support their optimal personal, occupational, and career development (Solberg, Soresi, Nota, Howard, & Ferrari, 2007).

Integration of Development and Person-Environment Fit Theories. This chapter prescribes a career development strategy that integrates two often opposing traditions of career theory: life span, life-space (Super, 1990), and person-environment fit models (Dawis, 2005; Spokane & Cruza-Guet, 2005). Drawing from Super's (1990) life span, life-space theory, we argue that career service delivery methods for older adults must facilitate and emphasize self-exploration and career exploration. While job placement will be a critical need for many older adults, engaging in self and career exploration is expected to generate avenues for continued development. Drawing from the theory of work adjustment (TWA; Dawis, 1995), it is expected that self and career exploration for older adults should evaluate qualities of the work environment as much as the content of the work being conducted. Drawing from Holland's RIASEC model (Spokane & Cruza-Guet, 2005), we propose that self and career exploration can be facilitated using assessment strategies that allow the individual to learn about the range of current and emerging occupational opportunities. From a developmental perspective, the intent of the assessment strategies is to facilitate deeper exploration, not simply to match the individual to "suitable" occupations.

Cultural Awareness of the Helping Professional. Prior to working with older adults from diverse backgrounds, it is imperative that the helping professional has established a level of personal awareness and understanding of how the social context affects development, especially context factors related to oppression (Freire, 1970) and White privilege (Hays & Chang, 2003). For individuals from White racial-ethnic backgrounds, it is assumed that the helping professional has achieved what Helms (1995) refers to as the pseudo-independence worldview and immersion/emersion worldview orientation. For individuals who themselves are from diverse racial-ethnic backgrounds, it is assumed that the helping professional has entered what Atkinson, Morten, and Sue (1998) refer to as the dissonance and appreciation worldview. From these two respective worldviews, individuals are ready to actively question majority-held views on rugged individualism and theoretical models that inherently blame the victim for their own oppression. Most notably, the helping professional is assumed to have achieved a level of "critical consciousness" (Quintana & Segura-Herrera, 2003) whereby he or she has begun to become aware of the unconscious and internalized assumptions one holds that legitimize oppression and the differential outcomes often experienced between individuals from White racial and ethnic backgrounds as compared to individuals from diverse racial and ethnic backgrounds. Applied to the context of career development, these perspectives share a common understanding that (a) economic sufficiency is an issue of personal and community power, (b) empowerment begins with creating a counseling context that allows the individual to define the range of challenges he or she experiences, and (c) growth occurs throughout the life span and occurs within learning contexts that provide culturally responsive support and opportunities for developing self-determined skills.

Case Examples. Three case examples will be used to explore ways to design effective career development strategies to support older adults from racial and ethnic backgrounds. The purpose of these brief case examples is to identify examples of how one might design culturally responsive career development strategies.

Donald is a 62-year-old African American and a salesman who has worked at a furniture store for the past 15 years. Before that, he worked as a cashier at the local department store that closed. He will be able to collect Social Security in a few years but realizes that his Social Security check will barely cover his rent. The store owners have been very generous in providing health insurance to their employees and a matched contribution savings program. Once Donald leaves the store, those benefits will end. He feels as though he has worked hard all his life, but in the end, he doesn't have much to show for it. The store owners have told the employees that with the new mall opening across town, they are planning to close the business.

Thomas is a 59-year-old Native American who fought in Vietnam. Since leaving the military, he has lived in many different communities. Many would probably think of him as homeless and unemployed, but he always seems to survive by staying with family members, friends, and sometimes living on the street. He left the military over 30 years ago and since then has worked mostly with temporary agencies working on construction sites, worked at a security agency, helped some friends who owned an auto repair shop, and was a roofer in a number of cities. He never stayed in one place very long, though, and has minimal financial support from the military. He has worn out his welcome with relatives and friends, so his future looks precarious. He is a wanderer in terms of his living circumstances, relationships, and a career. He does take a course now and again at the community college and frequents the career center to help him find employment.

Alicia is a 60-year-old Latina. She was married for 26 years when her husband died unexpectedly. Up until then, she ran a small daycare business out of her house and was very involved in volunteer work at the local high school. While she was volunteering, she discovered that she really liked helping the students work on their college applications, helping them to get organized and finding a school that was right for them. She thought she might become certified as a college counselor, but her husband's death put an end to those plans. She realizes she only has a small pension from her husband and his Social Security payment to live on. She knows that the pension isn't enough but can't figure out how to manage her finances in a way to make ends meet. A year ago, she injured her back, and the chronic pain has forced her to end her daycare business.

SELF AND CAREER EXPLORATION STRATEGIES

Van Esbroeck and his colleagues (Van Esbroeck, Tibos, & Zaman, 2005) outline a number of interrelated "activities" that facilitate the self and career exploration processes needed to help older adults make informed career-related choices. These activities include sensitization, self-exploration, environment exploration, exploration between self and environment, specification, and decision. It is assumed that these activities influence one another and are continually engaged in throughout the life span.

Sensitization

Sensitization involves awareness that a problematic situation exists in which decisions need to be made. For older adults, the problem could be one of needing additional income to support growing medical costs or property tax payments, needing income for basic needs, wanting to remain connected to others in the community, or needing to use one's skills in a meaningful way. Sensitization involves becoming aware of the career development activities that the individual should consider, challenges associated with those activities, and the consequences of making choices (or of not making a choice). Important challenges that are likely to surface include development of work-readiness skills, job search skills, and access to occupations that offer livable wages and health insurance. For both Donald and Alicia, the problematic situation is income related. Both will be relying on Social Security and are concerned they will not have access to quality health care. For Donald and Alicia, the sensitization process can begin with helping to identify the range of transferable skills they have accumulated. For Donald, sales should involve a number of interpersonal skills, and if part of his salary was based on commissions, then he is familiar with more entrepreneurial-based skills. An owner of her own day care facility, it can be assumed that Alicia possesses a number of transferable skills that could support her future career development. Certainly, her aspirations of being a helping professional could be discussed in more detail.

For a helping professional, the case of Thomas may seem the most critical because he has not maintained steady employment, may not have a stable living situation, and it is not clear whether he perceives a problem. Until recently, he has been able to find employment and housing, but it is possible that other cultural, mental health, and/or interpersonal issues could be contributing to the employment history. As a Native American and war veteran, cultural identity could be quite complex. For example, in addition to fighting a war for a country that destroyed his culture, many Vietnam veterans were not well received or supported upon

their return. Moreover, the concept of "work" for many Native Americans is a method of providing a tax base to maintain a country that is the source of their oppression.

Self-Exploration

Self-exploration activities relate to collecting and examining information about one's skills, interests, values, and aspirations. We strongly encourage beginning the self-exploration process using career development strategies, such as the ones described below, that allow the help provider to connect to the history and cultural background of the individual.

Career Style Interview. The narrative interview approach described by Savickas (2005) is a central tool in his career construction theory. Traditional person-environment fit models often provide a nomothetic approach to measuring the person's personality traits and matching those traits to occupations (Chartrand, Strong, & Weitzman, 1995). Alternatively, career construction theory provides an idiographic analysis of the individual's vocational self-concept and focuses on discovering how the self-concept is being expressed in one's personal and work roles. Using a narrative interview strategy enables the individual to maintain a degree of power by constructing a meaningful story about work and life from his or her own history and experience. "In chronicling the recursive interplay between self and society, career stories explain why individuals make the choices that they do and the private meaning that guides these choices" (Savickas, 2005, p. 58). Many older adults from diverse racial and ethnic backgrounds experienced tremendous societal change across their lifetime. In addition to changes in technology, many were victims of racial segregation, witnessed volatile uprisings during the civil rights movement, and were left jobless beginning in the 1970s when the manufacturing industry began its move to overseas locations. Using a narrative approach allows the helping professional to create the opportunity for the individual to express a life theme that encompasses the types of "preoccupations" that are worked on by the individual through chosen occupations.

Savickas's (2005) Career Style Interview consists of six questions. According to Hartung and Taber (2008), the description of what one admires in one's role models when growing up is felt to relate to the central life theme or problem. Preferred magazines, books, or television shows are felt to relate to the preferred environments, while the major characters point to challenges to which individuals may identify. Leisure activities are felt to relate to how individuals express themselves and their interests. Favorite sayings or mottos are felt to encapsulate a possible title for their life story. School or academic subjects are felt to indicate the types of work environments they may enjoy. And earliest memories are felt to point to a central problem they may spend their lifetime attempting to overcome.

From a social justice perspective, the Career Style Interview can be expected to solicit culturally rich information from which to construct a career story and identify meaningful themes. As with any technique, being responsive to culturally rich information demands that the helping professional accurately "hear" and interpret the relevant information. For the case of Thomas, the narrative interview strategy would allow him to identify themes and meaning about his life that are likely to explain his way of being in the world. The helping professional cannot know the particular experiences Thomas has had in relation to being Native American and a war veteran. Growing up on a reservation is quite different than growing up in an urban environment because Native Americans on reservations are able to connect to rituals and rights of passage that many urban Natives are unable to experience. It is not possible to make assumptions about serving in Vietnam because not all war veteran experiences were the same. According to Savickas (2005), by "telling career stories about their work experiences, individuals selectively highlight particular experiences to produce a narrative truth by which they live" (p. 43). For Thomas, the narrative interview allows him a degree of self-determination in the interview process by deciding what information is shared. However, one key factor is the degree to which the helping professional is culturally aware enough to effectively work with Thomas in constructing a meaningful story that represents Thomas's perspective and is not skewed by the helping professional's stereotypes or personal experiences.

In working with older adults, it would also be helpful to expand the interview process to incorporate the

individual's vocational and avocational history more directly. While Savickas's (2005) narrative interview asks about school and academic subjects, for older adults, an alternative may be to add a question about their favorite work and out-of-work experiences. Drawing from the TWA (Dawis, 2005), the essential ideas regarding satisfaction and satisfactoriness can serve as an important avenue of inquiry with older workers. According to TWA, individuals are satisfied when they receive feedback and support from the work context that they value as important. Alternatively, satisfactoriness emerges when the work context is satisfied with the skills and performance of the individual in relation to the occupational skill requirements. Asking about the individual's favorite work and out-of-work experiences can provide insight into the types of feedback and support the individual may desire as well as the salience of job skill performance as a condition for selecting an occupation. Anecdotal evidence invokes a strong sense that the affective qualities associated with the work environment—meeting the social and growth needs of individuals—creates a context for increased satisfaction to emerge, which can then lead to improved work performance (Yokoyama & Michelli, 2004). And for some individuals, being valued for a specific skill set may serve as the primary motivation for working; rewards could range from appreciation to financial incentives. The narrative inquiry method allows individuals to describe the quality work environment in ways that ensure that sociocultural and historical events that may have affected their career development become apparent. By incorporating these themes into the career story, the goal is for self-awareness as well as awareness about the types of work and work environment individuals may be interested in pursuing in this next phase of their lives.

For Alicia, her self-employment as a day care provider may reflect a number of satisfying qualities that would help her think about future job possibilities and may help her become aware of reasons for wanting to become a college counselor. For Donald, the narrative process may allow him to become aware of the satisfactoriness of the occupation—what it was about the reward structure and how the environment responded to him that kept him working in sales. Certainly, it is possible that the job was the only one available at the time and that it was neither satisfying nor rewarding. In such a case, exploring Donald's avocational experiences—leisure activities—may provide better information about what he may enjoy in an occupation and what need he has with regard to the work environment.

Use of Verb Descriptions. Another self-exploration strategy is to provide the individual with a list of verbs (J. M. Ettinger, personal communication, April 2008). Verbs can be gathered by the helping professional and presented in a list format. Sample verbs include *achieved, awarded, coached, designed, encouraged, estimated, improved, investigated, revised, solved, succeeded, translated,* and *upgraded.* The activity involves having the individual select the five that are deemed most meaningful to him or her. Then, from the five, the individual selects three. The individual is then prompted to share the nature of the three verbs and experiences that make the verbs meaningful to him or her. This strategy provides another way of constructing a narrative about the individual's life and career in a manner that provides him or her with the power to determine what is shared and at what level of depth the sharing occurs.

Incorporating Genograms. Ponterotto, Rivera, and Sueyoshi (2000) have also introduced a "career-in-culture" semistructured interview to incorporate more directly culturally relevant information. In addition to adding direct questions about one's cultural and ethnic background, they suggest using a genogram to generate a narrative history of the individual and identify recurring family themes. Genograms offer an opportunity for the helping professional to gain a deep understanding of family themes and cultural beliefs that may be passed on for generations (Hardy & Laszloffy, 1995; Howe, 1990). In working with older adults from diverse racial and ethnic backgrounds, using a genogram strategy could provide a richer context for understanding entry into the United States. While some may have ancestors who entered the country by choice, others may have entered as slaves or refugees or were colonized. These different entry points may affect one's orientation to work. While jobs offering livable wages may provide work motivation for some, for others, working for a "White" boss may invoke more negative feelings and attitudes. In all three cases, a genogram can help identify patterns of issues and challenges that families have re-created across generations. Particularly important is the experience of race and racism in the individual's history. While factory jobs were associated with many African Americans moving to the northern cities, many also may have fled to avoid the dangers and overt segregation occurring in the South. Exploring the genogram can also facilitate exploration of the individual's current racial identity by exploring what is similar in beliefs passed through the generations.

Environment Exploration

Environment exploration activities involve surveying career, occupation, and educational options that are available; collecting information about these options; and assessing this information in ways that allow the individual to critically examine the options. Traditionally, career and occupational options are generated as a result of completing a career interests–type instrument. Holland's (1997) RIASEC model has served as the standard from which to organize careers and occupations. "R" refers to Realistic dispositions, which often involve working outdoors, with one's hands, and adventure. "I" refers to Investigative dispositions, which involve finding out the answers to questions, scientific inquiry, and use of logical analysis. "A" refers to Artistic dispositions, which involve creativity and self-expression. "S" refers to Social dispositions, which involve helping others and interpersonal-related work activities. "E" refers to Enterprising dispositions, which involve sales and marketing ideas and products. "C" refers to Conventional dispositions, which involve working within set procedures and rules. Once an individual completes an interest inventory, careers and occupations are provided for the individual to explore and learn more about. According to Solberg et al. (2007), these traditional methods assume that individual differences and occupations are relatively stable. This was true during the Industrial Revolution era in which the older adults grew up, but the current era is better conceived as one of "high modernity" (Giddens, 1991). The characteristic quality of a high-modernity era is the level of technology being used and the amount and speed of information. The result is a rapidly changing world of work.

According to Solberg et al. (2007), career exploration "should focus on helping individuals catalogue the degree to which they possess a range of skills and interests and help them in mapping out the occupational opportunities that will allow them to continue their personal, vocational, and avocational development" (p. 11). Moreover, they argue that

> rather than using assessment as a method for cataloguing personality, the goal should be to provide information to an individual in ways that lead to self-discovery. Rather than providing an "answer" with regard to a personality profile or likely occupational fit, assessment should result in the individual asking "questions." In response to the age of high modernity and our new understanding regarding plasticity in human development, we believe assessment would more effectively serve youth and adults when it actively creates thought-provoking questions that lead to self-reflection and awareness. (p. 15)

From this perspective, career development strategies become "fit for modern times" when they support exploration as a process of self-discovery rather than attempting to match person-type patterns to career and occupational options.

A number of online career information systems provide ways for career assessment strategies to facilitate career exploration (e.g., O*NET, WISCareers). The Center on Education and Work, for example, offers an online system called WISCareers (cew.wisc.edu) that provides access to career assessments, résumé and cover letter writing tools, transferable skills, and job search engines to locate employment. These systems support the helping professional by offering access to a range of career resources that are organized and stored for the older adult in an electronic portfolio. The Wisconsin Careers online system offers career interests, skills, and values inventories. Once completed, the career interests and skills inventories immediately provide a report with links to occupations that are consistent with the pattern of results. Once the individual selects an occupation, the system automatically connects the individual to tremendous amounts of information about the occupation, including access to learning about training and education opportunities, job openings, and contact information. Rather than focusing on matching interests and skills to occupations, the online system uses this information to promote deeper exploration and discovery. From a social justice perspective, using online career information systems expands the range of potential career opportunities rather than providing a fixed amount or number. Online systems such as the ones offered through Wisconsin Careers operate as a learning context that encourages an active engagement in the career exploration process by providing a number of career options and immediate links to any information or questions an individual may have about the occupation such as educational requirements, local job opportunities, entry level skills, and so on.

For Donald and Alicia, using online career information systems will allow them to assess their respective transferable skills and identify a range of occupations they can explore that use those skills. Given their respective job histories, there is likely to be a profile of interests and transferable skills that relate to a wide range of occupations that they have not considered. By using the online information system to explore those occupations, they can learn more about the occupation, entry skills, educational opportunities, and potential jobs in their area. For Thomas, it is difficult to know what the interest assessment will uncover. To the extent that this pattern reflects no interest in work, a career assessment is likely to generate a flat profile.

Exploration Between Self and Environment

Once career opportunities have been identified, it is important for the helping professional to explore the degree to which the individual possesses the skills and knowledge needed to enter a desirable occupation, learning opportunities that are available to develop those skills and knowledge, and what it is about the occupations that are found to be interesting. It is important for the individual to determine how much education and training he or she would like to pursue. For Alicia, her desire to be a college counselor will demand going back to school. Permission and encouragement from a helping professional may be all that is needed to help her make a decision to apply to college. If the college environment is what Alicia is most attracted to, then a 2-year college degree or a certificate program offered in a 4-year college/university could allow her to work in a college environment and provide livable wages and health benefits but without the debt that is likely to be incurred in seeking a professional degree.

Continuing to Develop 21st-Century Work Skills. Entering today's world of work and obtaining jobs with livable wages demands at least a high school diploma and 2 years of postsecondary training. During the 1950s and 1960s, the plethora of manufacturing occupations allowed one to drop out of high school, gain an entry position, and increase one's income based on increased skill acquisition. Today's world of work demands higher literacy, technology, and interpersonal skills. Gewertz (2007) argues that soft skills are more in demand than ever before. The 21st Century Skills (Partnership for 21st Century Skills, 2007) initiative focuses on identifying the range of skills needed to remain an active and competitive employee. These skill areas include lifelong learning and self-direction, critical thinking and problem solving, computer and technology skills, reading and writing skills, and teamwork and collaboration skills. There are a number of avenues for older adults to develop these skills. Two-year technical colleges provide a range of options from adult high schools to technical degrees that lead directly to occupation opportunities. Online courses and training that are designed to teach specific skills are available as well. High schools often provide evening courses on special topics and community organizations often provide specific vocational development opportunities as well. The helping professional can facilitate this process by helping older adults identify the skill areas that they need and start by linking them to professional development and training opportunities. For older adults who are looking for part-time employment, the helping professional may want to encourage volunteer work opportunities that maximize the use of current skills and offer opportunities to apply those skills in different ways.

For Donald and Alicia, it is important to evaluate the range of 21st-century skills they may possess. Unless they developed the skills outside work, it is not likely that they have kept pace with the technology developments. Using word processing, data management, spreadsheets, and multimedia applications is desirable across the occupational spectrum. Access to technology and high-speed Internet access is a consideration in this regard as well. And access to training and technology is generally available through one's community in community college settings, nonprofit community organizations focused on workforce development, and evening classes through community recreation organizations. For Thomas, his many "short-term" and "entry-level" jobs indicate that he may need to address a range of 21st-century skill areas. He does appear to possess good survival skills, but surviving is not the same as flourishing.

Lifelong learning and continuous professional development involve an entrepreneurial attitude. In the past, it was assumed that the employer would provide a job with security and offer training needed to perform the duties effectively. Currently, employees need to evaluate jobs as opportunities to develop new skills and expand their résumé. Expanding one's skills provides for the ability of the older adult to adapt to changing work conditions as well as be able to take advantage of new job opportunities.

Incorporating the Support of Federally Supported One-Stop Job Centers. The U.S. Department of Labor's Employment and Training Administration provides funding for one-stop career centers around the country. The centers offer a comprehensive range of services designed to help individuals find employment (Career One Stop, www.careeronestop.org or servicelocator.org). By bringing together the training and employment resources into one location, individuals have access to both career development and job placement support. Job centers provide in-person and online access to services. For individuals in rural communities especially, linking online to a job center can provide the range of support services they may need to locate employment in their region or other parts of the country. Donald and Alicia could both benefit from one-stop career center resources. In addition to offering personal career counseling and access to career assessments, the resources include any number of job-seeking support services, including finding employment opportunities, preparing résumés and cover letters, and practicing for job interviews. For ideas regarding additional online career resources for working with older adults, see Kirk and Belovics (2005).

Specification

Framing the Career Development Process as a Career Transition. Specification refers to the ability to analyze information about self and one's career, occupational, and educational selections to begin narrowing down one's options. Baltes (1997) has found in longitudinal studies that transitions for older adults are more effective (e.g., health and well-being) when the adults are actively engaged in setting goals, optimizing opportunities to actualize those goals, and compensate by engaging in backup plans when faced with challenging circumstances. Drawing from Schlossberg's (1989) transition theory, individuals with a high SOC (for Selection, Optimization, Compensation) profile would be expected to make better life transitions because they have a history of being engaged in addressing difficult life changes, optimizing opportunities for support and development, and being actively engaged in strategizing to maximize positive outcomes by successfully achieving an initial or backup goal.

Self-determination theory (Deci & Ryan, 1985) also has important applications to understanding how to support individuals in making effective career transitions (Howard, Solberg, Kantamneni, & Smothers, 2008; Solberg, Howard, Blustein, & Close, 2002). From self-determination theory, individuals become engaged in performing career search activities or work activities because they are perceived as enjoyable and meaningful when the activities occur within a relational environment in which individuals feel connected and a sense of belonging.

The ability to manage life transitions is also due in part to how adaptable one is to change. Individuals who feel confidence in performing career search activities, for example, report engaging in more career search activity, have a clearer idea of what they wish to pursue, and report needing less additional information to make a career decision (Solberg, Good, Fischer, Brown, & Nord, 1995). Resilience (Masten, 2001) refers to individuals who feel able to manage their behavior when faced with challenging circumstances, such as a career transition. In addition to career search

self-efficacy (Solberg, 1998), other resilience characteristics that can be learned within effective career development strategies include social support, availability of resources and support, and stress and health management skills (Solberg et al., 1998).

Donald and Alicia could be expected to experience the career process as a major life transition. Both need to change occupations that they both have been relatively stable in for a number of years. It would be important to help each of them identify goals and to identify culturally responsive learning environments that will help them develop the skills needed to optimize the likelihood of achieving those goals. Depending on Donald's academic background, linking him to 2-year technical college settings could provide opportunities for developing skills and opportunities for finding both formal and informal sources of support. For Alicia, higher education could provide her with the training degree needed to pursue a college personnel degree, and with the addition of updating her computer skills, she may already possess a number of skills that could make her marketable within a high school or a number of business settings. Resilience related to self-efficacy is expected to increase in response to the helping professional's use of encouragement and support and the mastery and vicarious experiences he or she will receive as the result of engaging in new learning opportunities.

Framing the Career Development Process as Improving Level of Functioning. The International Classification of Functioning, Disability, and Health (ICF; World Health Organization [WHO], 2001) also serves as an important strategy for helping professionals to organize the range of services needed to support older adults in making career transitions (Soresi, Nota, Ferrari, & Solberg, 2008). According to the ICF, career development for older adults is predicated upon the individual's functioning characteristics and the resources available to support the individual. The ICF emphasizes three assessment areas: (a) level of functioning with regard to an individual's physical functioning, the types of activities he or she is involved with, and how much an individual participates in various activities; (b) identification of any disability or limitations that affect the individual's ability to participate in specific activities; and (c) other indicators of health and well-being, educational attainment, and work history. What makes the ICF valuable is its salient message that positive transitions, including career transitions, occur as a shared responsibility of the individual possessing the skills, interests, and abilities as well as the environment offering developmental opportunities and resources to support accessibility. In working with older adults to make effective career transitions, the ICF can serve as an important assessment tool for broadening the intake interview to include health status and access to health care, as well as expand a range of issues that fall under the category of "loss of functioning." The ICF not only helps to assess for these areas but also encourages the helping professional to link the individuals to the support systems needed to facilitate continued development and manage loss of functioning in a manner that provides the older adult with expanded choice and opportunity.

From a social justice perspective, specification processes are optimal when the helping professional supports the individual to engage in self-determined goals and aspirations, receive the resources needed to continue developing requisite skills, and help identify backup plans to manage loss or other experiences that may block him or her from achieving the initial goals. The transitions theory and ICF further prescribe the helping professional to link the older adult to multiple resources within the local or virtual community such as online career information systems and/or one-stop career centers. For older adults from diverse racial and ethnic backgrounds, it is also important for the helping professional to explore available resources to determine the cultural responsiveness of the offerings and services provided. In some communities, there may be a need to work with the available resources in encouraging and/or offering professional development to improve the level of cultural awareness. Links to culturally responsive online resources will also facilitate the older adults' ability to access quality information if culturally responsive direct service delivery is not available.

Alicia and Thomas would both benefit by the inclusion of the ICF to help design an optimal career development strategy. For Alicia, her chronic pain needs to be incorporated into thinking about what accommodations she needs within a training and/or work environment. For Thomas, the issues appear more complex,

and a more thorough ICF evaluation may provide a wider range of understanding regarding health, mental health, and other aspects of functioning that may contribute to his moving from job to job and his housing instability. Furthermore, as specific issues become apparent, the helping professional should consider incorporating support services from the Veterans Administration for further assessment and treatment planning.

Decision

Decision refers to establishing priorities, ranking preferences, developing decision-making skills, and establishing plans for pursuing one's preferred career, occupational, and educational options. This process involves movement and change and can be facilitated by the creation of a formal action plan that describes (a) occupational goals and aspirations, (b) skills needed to perform the occupation, (c) resources to develop the necessary skills, (d) job search strategies to be used, and (e) likely challenges to be experienced. In setting occupational goals, at least three should be considered, but more than five may be too many to focus the career planning process. The reason for at least three is that the individual should have backup plans if one occupation is not available or if employment is needed immediately and it will take longer to secure the most desirable occupation. The action plan should identify the skills needed to successfully enter the identified occupation(s). While the individual may possess some skills, in all likelihood, additional skills will be needed. The action plan should identify the resources needed to achieve those goals. Resources include identifying live and online education and training opportunities, connecting with one-stop job center programs, and/or using online career information systems. The plan should describe the purpose of each resource as well as contact information. The plan should outline the job search strategies that will be employed. Informational interviews are one powerful tool for engaging in the job search process, but the individual also needs to develop cover letters, résumés, and connect to job listings. Many online career information systems (e.g., WISCareers) provide features that help the individual design cover letters and résumés with little need for knowledge or skills in information processing. As well, these systems link the individual directly to employers to whom the cover letter and résumé can be e-mailed. The plan should also address challenges the client may face. These challenges may be due to working with individuals who are not sensitive to cultural differences or due to the individual's functioning or past history that may need to be disclosed in job interview situations. For individuals with disabilities, the helping professional can provide opportunities to practice how to address accessibility needs and to disclose the disability in appropriate ways (National Collaborative on Workforce and Disability for Youth, 2005; U.S. Department of Labor, 2005).

Since 1 in 26 Latino men and 1 in 15 Black men are estimated to be in prison (PEW Center on the States, 2008), it is likely that helping professionals working with older male adults from diverse racial and ethnic backgrounds will encounter a number of adults who have been incarcerated. In working with adults who have significant gaps in work history, the helping professional should encourage the use of functional and/or a combination of functional and chronological résumé styles. Helping professionals should also role-play ways to discuss an individual's past in interview settings and seek out resources and employers who are more disposed to hiring individuals who may have a criminal background (Ettinger, 2007).

Summary

We believe that to design optimal career development strategies for older adults from diverse racial and ethnic backgrounds, culturally aware helping professionals must incorporate a social justice perspective. As culturally aware helping professionals, we believe that three important awareness indicators include an understanding that economic sufficiency is an issue of personal and community power, empowerment for an individual is predicated on or by his or her ability to define the range of challenges he or she experiences, and career and personal development occurs throughout the life span when culturally responsive learning opportunities are provided. With regard to Sensitivity activities, we argued that gaining access to occupations that offer livable wages and access to health insurance is often determined by the degree to which an individual possesses a range of work-readiness and job search

skills. With regard to Self-Exploration, we argued for using narrative, genogram, and verb preferences strategies because each of them allows the individual to construct a career story in his or her own words. These strategies allow the individual to maintain control and power over the discourse, and with the support of a culturally aware helping professional, it is possible to construct a career and personal story that addresses the themes that are generated. For Exploration between Self and Environment, we argued that optimal career development strategies need to incorporate learning opportunities that facilitate acquisition of the 21st-century skills and provide access to one-stop job centers. For Specification, we argued for framing the experience as a career transition and encourage the use of the ICF as a tool for targeting which levels of functioning may need support and attention. For Decision, we discussed the importance of linking the individual to culturally responsive resources that will support him or her in the job search process.

We also believe that helping professionals should prescribe to a career theory framework that incorporates developmental and person-environment fit strategies. For Self-Exploration, we discussed how the narrative approach can integrate developmental and TWA frameworks by asking more specifically about the qualities of the individual's past vocational and avocational environments. For Environment Exploration, we argued that using Holland's (1997) RIASEC model is optimal when it is used as a starting point for continued self and occupational exploration as opposed to using the RIASEC profile as a prescription that links personality traits to congruent occupations.

PRACTICE STRATEGIES

The remainder of the chapter addresses four strategies that we believe will support the helping professional optimize career development strategies for older adults from diverse racial-ethnic backgrounds.

Incorporating Career Development Facilitators

Many helping professionals have focused on mental health areas because fee-for-service demands a DSM code, and many originally chose to become a helping professional to focus specifically on providing mental health–related services. Mental health and career counseling, while separate domains, do overlap such that operating in one area does have implications for the other (Krumboltz, 1993). For example, depression is estimated to cost over $40 billion per year as a result of loss of workplace productivity (Greenberg, Leong, Birnbaum, & Robinson, 2003). And losing one's job can also create significant mental health challenges depending on the manner in which the individual defines the job loss experience and frames his or her ability to manage the loss (Moore, Grunberg, Greenberg, & Sikora, 2007). Supporting older adults in making career transitions, however, demands a level of expertise that traditional mental health providers may not possess. Therefore, it is strongly recommended that when creating a professional practice that caters to older adults, the helping professional should either gain certification to be a career development facilitator (CDF) or employ a certified CDF as part of his or her practice. The CDF training is sponsored by the National Career Development Association and involves 120 hours of training. The CDF training program (Harris-Bowlsbey, Suddarth, & Reile, 2005) addresses a range of topics that include cultural sensitivity, career assessment, information gathering for career planning, use of computer systems in career work, and job-seeking and employability skills. CDF individuals may or may not possess a professional counseling degree but do have the skills needed to supplement one's practice. As a helping professional, becoming certified as a CDF will allow for direct integration of career development resources into the counseling context.

Infusing Effective Curriculum Ingredients Into Career Development Strategies

Howard et al. (2008) identified nine curriculum ingredients that increase the effectiveness of career development strategies. The ingredients were drawn from three sources: meta-analysis of career interventions conducted by Brown and Ryan Krane (2000), as well as empirically supported ingredients identified in social cognitive theory (Bandura, 1986, 1997) and self-determination theory (Deci & Ryan, 1985). Together,

these ingredients include use of written exercises, individualized interpretations and feedback, world of work information, modeling experiences, building support networks, mastery experiences, verbal persuasion, anxiety management, and creating stronger relational bonds between the individual, authority figures, and work-peers. Career development strategies that incorporate these ingredients are expected to increase career search self-efficacy (Solberg, 1998) and more effectively support the individual in becoming more engaged in the career search process and in developing new skills.

Using Psychoeducational Groups

Traditionally, mental health practice professionals can often rely on third-party payments to maintain a viable practice. Although many mental health conditions affect or are affected by career-related concerns, a number of individuals are likely to be seeking career counseling support, not mental health counseling. We encourage the establishment of psychoeducational groups as a preferred method of service delivery because it not only provides for a financially viable practice, but the support element is likely to prove more efficacious than offering individual support alone. Certainly, elements of the group program may incorporate individual work when conducting, for example, the narrative intake interview and providing individualized interpretations of career instruments. However, a large amount of the information can be conducted by designing a step-by-step process that allows the group members to learn about effective career exploration and job search strategies.

Community Outreach

Another consideration is the location of conducting the career practice. Often, helping professionals may not have access to large numbers of older adults from diverse racial-ethnic backgrounds or may not have space to conduct group sessions. Many communities offer adult recreation programs and use local high schools or community centers to conduct the activities. Connecting with these groups provides marketing exposure and accessible facilities. Local community groups may also be able to find funding to support the career development efforts. By working with the organizations, the helping professional can support efforts to solicit local foundations or other available funding sources. Often these funds are only available to nonprofit organizations, which then would hire or retain the services of the helping professional.

REFERENCES

Aizcorbe, A. M., Kennickell, A. B., & Moore, K. B. (2003, January). Recent changes in U.S. family finances: Evidence from the 1998 and 2001 Survey of consumer finances. *Federal Reserve Bulletin, Board of Governors of the Federal Reserve System (U.S.),* pp. 1–32.

Atkinson, D. R., Morten, G., & Sue, D. W. (1998). *Counseling American minorities* (5th ed.). Boston: McGraw-Hill.

Baltes, P. B. (1997). On the incomplete architecture of human ontogeny: Selection, optimization, and compensation as foundation of developmental theory. *American Psychologist, 52,* 366–380.

Bandura, A. (1986). *Social foundations of thought and action: A social cognitive theory.* Englewood Cliffs, NJ: Prentice Hall.

Bandura, A. (1997). *Self-efficacy: The exercise of control.* New York: Freeman.

Blustein, D. L., McWhirter, E. H., & Perry, J. C. (2005). An emancipatory communitarian approach to vocational development: Theory, research, and practice. *The Counseling Psychologist, 33,* 141–179.

Bronfenbrenner, U. (1979). *The ecology of human development.* Cambridge, MA: Harvard University Press.

Brown, S. D., & Ryan Krane, N. (2000). Four (or five) sessions and a cloud of dust: Old assumptions and new observations about career counseling. In S. D. Brown & R. W. Lent (Eds.), *Handbook of counseling psychology* (3rd ed., pp. 740–766). New York: John Wiley.

Chartrand, J. M., Strong, S. R., & Weitzman, L. M. (1995). The interactional perspective in vocational psychology: Paradigms, theories, and research practices. In B. W. Walsh & S. H. Osipow (Eds.), *Handbook of vocational psychology: Theory, research, and practice* (2nd ed., pp. 35–66). Hillsdale, NJ: Lawrence Erlbaum.

Dawis, R. V. (2005). The Minnesota Theory of Work Adjustment. In S. D. Brown & R. W. Lent (Eds.), *Career development and counseling: Putting theory and research to work* (pp. 3–23). Hoboken, NJ: John Wiley.

Deci, E. L., & Ryan, R. M. (1985). *Intrinsic motivation and self-determination in human development.* New York: Plenum.

Ettinger, J. (2007, October 1). Career counseling for individuals with a criminal history. *Counseling and Human Development.*

Freire, P. (1970). *Pedagogy of the oppressed.* New York: Herder & Herder.

Gewertz, C. (2007). 'Soft skills' in big demand. *Education Week, 40,* 25–27.

Gibson, J., & Brown, S. D. (1992). Counseling adults for life transitions. In S. D. Brown & R. W. Lent (Eds.), *Handbook of counseling psychology* (pp. 285–313). New York: John Wiley.

Giddens, A. (1991). *Modernity and self-identity: Self and society in the late modern age.* Stanford, CA: Stanford University Press.

Greenberg, P. E., Leong, S. A., Birnbaum, H. G., & Robinson, R. L. (2003). The economic burden of depression with painful symptoms. *Journal of Clinical Psychiatry, 64,* 17–23.

Hardy, K. V., & Laszloffy, T. A. (1995). The cultural genogram. *Journal of Marital and Family Therapy, 3,* 227–237.

Harris-Bowlsbey, J., Suddarth, B. H., & Reile, D. M. (2005). *Facilitating career development: Instructor manual.* Broken Arrow, OK: National Career Development Association.

Hartung, P. J., & Taber, B. J. (2008). Career construction and subjective well-being. *Journal of Career Assessment, 16,* 75–85.

Hays, D. G., & Chang, C. Y. (2003). White privilege, oppression, and racial identity development: Implications for supervision. *Counselor Education and Supervision, 43,* 134–145.

Helms, J. E. (1995). An update of Helm's White and people of color racial identity models. In J. G. Ponterotto, J. M. Casas, L. A. Suzuki, & C. M. Alexander (Eds.), *Handbook of multicultural counseling* (pp. 181–198). Thousand Oaks, CA: Sage.

Holland, J. (1997). *Making vocational choices: A theory of vocational personalities and work environments* (3rd ed.). Odessa, FL: Psychological Assessment Resources.

Howard, K. A. S., Solberg, V. S. H., Kantamneni, N., & Smothers, M. K. (2008). Designing culturally responsive school counseling career development programming for youth. In H. Coleman & C. Yeh (Eds.), *Handbook of school counseling* (pp. 269–289). Mahwah, NJ: Lawrence Erlbaum.

Howe, K. G. (1990). Daughters discover their mothers through biographies and genograms. *Women and Therapy, 9,* 31–40.

Kirk, J. J., & Belovics, R. (2005). Recommendations and resources for counseling older workers. *Journal of Employment Counseling, 42,* 50–57.

Krumboltz, J. D. (1993). Integrating career and personal counseling. *Career Development Quarterly, 42,* 143–148.

Lerner, R. M. (2002). *Concepts and theories of human development*. Mahwah, NJ: Lawrence Erlbaum.

Masten, A. S. (2001). Ordinary magic: Resilience processes in development. *American Psychologist, 56,* 227–238.

Moore, S., Grunberg, L., Greenberg, E., & Sikora, P. (2007). Type of job loss and its impact on decision control, mastery, and depression: Comparison of employee and company-stated reasons. *Current Psychology, 26,* 71–85.

National Collaborative on Workforce and Disability for Youth. (2005). *The 411 on Disability Disclosure Workbook*. Washington, DC: Institute for Educational Leadership.

Partnership for 21st Century Skills. (2007). *Beyond the three R's: Voter attitudes toward 21st Century Skills*. Retrieved May 2008 from http://www.21stcenturyskills .org/documents/P21_pollreport_singlepg.pdf

PEW Center on the States. (2008). *One in 100: Behind bars in America 2008*. The PEW Charitable Trusts. Retrieved May 2008 from http://www.pewcenteronthestates.org/ uploadedFiles/8015PCTS_Prison08_FINAL_2–1–1_ FORWEB.pdf

Ponterotto, J. G., Rivera, L., & Sueyoshi, L. A. (2000). The career-in-culture interview: A semi-structured protocol for the cross-cultural intake interview. *Career Development Quarterly, 49,* 85–96.

Prilleltensky, I. (1997). Values, assumptions, and practices: Assessing the moral implications of psychological discourse and action. *American Psychologist, 52,* 517–535.

Quintana, S. M., & Segura-Herrera, T. A. (2003). Developmental transformations of self and identity in the context of oppression. *Self and Identity, 2,* 269–285.

Richardson, V. E. (1993). *Retirement counseling: A handbook for geriatric practitioners*. New York: Springer.

Savickas, M. L. (2005). The theory and practice of career construction. In S. D. Brown & R. W. Lent (Eds.), *Career development and counseling: Putting theory and research to work* (pp. 42–70). Hoboken, NJ: John Wiley.

Schlossberg, N. K. (1989). *Overwhelmed: Coping with life's ups and downs*. Lexington, KY: Lexington Press.

Schlossberg, N. K. (2004). *Retire smart retire happy: Finding your true path in life*. Washington, DC: American Psychological Association.

Solberg, V. S. (1998). Assessing career search self-efficacy: Construct evidence and developmental antecedents. *Journal of Career Assessment, 6,* 181–193.

Solberg, V. S., Good, G. E., Fischer, A. R., Brown, S. E., & Nord, D. (1995). Relative effects of career search self-efficacy and human agency upon career development. *Journal of Counseling Psychology, 42,* 448–455.

Solberg, V. S., Gusavac, N., Hamann, T., Felch, J., Johnson, J., Lamborn, S., et al. (1998). The Adaptive Success Identity Plan (ASIP): A career intervention for college students. *Career Development Quarterly, 47,* 48–95.

Solberg, V. S., Howard, K. A., Blustein, D. L., & Close, W. (2002). Career development in the schools: Connecting school-to-work-to-life. *The Counseling Psychologist, 30,* 705–725.

Solberg, V. S. H., Soresi, S., Nota, L., Howard, K. A. S., & Ferrari, L. (2007). On the shoulders of giants: Making vocational psychology fit for modern times. In S. Soresi (Ed.), *Orientamento alle scelte: Rassegne, ricerche, strumenti ed applicazioni* (pp. 9–16). Florence, Italy: Giunti-Organizzazioni Speciali.

Soresi, S., Nota, L., Ferrari, L., & Solberg, V. S. (2008). Career guidance for persons with disabilities. In R. Van Esbroeck & J. Athanasou (Eds.), *International handbook of career guidance*. Brussels, Belgium: Springer.

Spokane, A. R., & Cruza-Guet, M. C. (2005). Holland's theory of vocational personalities in work environments. In S. D. Brown & R. W. Lent (Eds.), *Career development and counseling: Putting theory and research to work*. (pp. 24–41). Hoboken, NJ: John Wiley.

Sterns, H. L., & Subich, L. M. (2005). Counseling for retirement. In S. D. Brown & R. W. Lent (Eds.), *Career development and counseling: Putting theory and research to work* (pp. 506–521). Hoboken, NJ: John Wiley.

Super, D. E. (1990). A life-span, life-space to approach to career development. In D. Brown & L. Brooke (Eds.), *Career choice and development: Applying contemporary theories to practice* (2nd ed., pp. 197–261). San Francisco: Jossey-Bass.

Tinsley, D. J., & Bigler, M. (2002). Facilitating transitions in retirement. In C. J. Juntunen & D. R. Atkinson (Eds.), *Counseling across the lifespan: Prevention and treatment* (pp. 375–397). Thousand Oaks, CA: Sage.

U.S. Department of Labor, Department of Disability Employment Policy. (2005, August). *Interviewing essentials: Strategies for creating a positive impression*. www.dol.gov/odep/pubs/interviewing111507.htm

Van Esbroeck, R., Tibos, K., & Zaman, M. (2005). A dynamic model of career choice development. *International Journal for Educational and Vocational Guidance, 5,* 5–18.

World Health Organization. (2001). *International classification of functioning, disability and health (ICF)*. Geneva, Switzerland: Author.

Yokoyama, J., & Michelli, J. (2004). *When fish fly: Lessons for creating a vital and energized workplace from the world famous Pike Place Fish Market*. New York: Hyperion.

Author Index

Subject Index

About the Editors

Charlene Alexander is the director of the School Counseling program at Ball State University; she is also the past president of the Indiana School Counselor Association. Dr. Alexander's research interests are in the areas of multicultural counseling, school counseling, and international psychology. Dr. Alexander serves on the advisory board for the National Office of School Counselor Advocacy and the Education Trust's Transforming School Counseling Board. She has developed study-abroad counseling programs in Trinidad, West Indies, and St. Lucia.

J. Manuel Casas is currently a professor in the Department of Counseling, Clinical, and School Psychology at the University of California, Santa Barbara. He has published extensively on sociocultural and psychological factors that negatively affect ethnic minority populations. His work gives special attention to the resiliency factors that can help Hispanic families successfully lead sound and healthy lives. His expertise in this area has enabled him to serve as an advisor and consultant to various agencies and organizations both within and outside the United States.

Joseph G. Ponterotto is currently Professor of Counseling Psychology and the coordinator of the Mental Health Counseling Program at Fordham University's Graduate School of Education in New York City. His primary teaching and research interests are in the areas of multicultural counseling, research design, psychological testing and assessment, and career development. He is the author of a number of articles and books on topics related to multicultural counseling practice and research.

Lisa Suzuki is an associate professor in the Department of Applied Psychology at New York University. She is the co-editor with Dr. Ponterotto of the *Handbook of Multicultural Assessment,* now in its third edition. Her main research interests have been in the areas of multicultural assessment, training, and qualitative research methods. She is currently one of the associate editors of *The Counseling Psychologist.*

About the Contributors

Muninder K. Ahluwalia is currently associate professor and internship coordinator of the counseling programs at Montclair State University in New Jersey. Her primary teaching and research interests are in the areas of multicultural counseling, intersecting identities, assessment, and methodological issues in qualitative research. She serves on the executive board of the Asian American Psychological Association and the editorial board of *Training and Education in Professional Psychology*.

Laura Alarcón is a recent graduate from the Counseling Department at San Francisco State University with an emphasis in college and career counseling. Her primary research interests are in the area of transition to adulthood as it relates to career development. In recognition of her academic achievements and future education goals, she received the prestigious Merage American Dream fellowship in 2004 and the Graduate Equity Fellowship in 2008.

Heather Cunha Amato currently treats clients in her private practice in Manhattan. With adults, she specializes in trauma work, eating disorders, matters of infertility, and terminal diseases, and with children, she has specialized training in work with those who were abused and those in foster care. Dr. Cunha Amato also supervises extern-level students at the Psychological Services Institute of Fordham University and continues to pursue her research interests in the area of recurrent miscarriage.

Ryan Androsiglio recently received his PhD in counseling psychology from Fordham University and completed his internship at the Baruch College Counseling Center. Baruch was recognized as having the most diverse student body in the country. His professional interests include multicultural counseling, LGBT advocacy, college student development, and mindfulness-based cognitive psychotherapy. He is also co-author of a book chapter on multicultural competencies and conducted his dissertation research on workplace climate and burnout among gay men.

Patricia Arredondo has dedicated her academic career to four areas in psychology and counseling: immigrants' transitions and change and identity development, multicultural competencies and guidelines, Latina/o psychology, and organizational diversity management. Her publications and international presentations in the broad-based, multicultural psychology arena have led to numerous distinctions. She was named a *Living Legend* by the American Counseling Association in 2005 and received an honorary degree of Humane Letters from the University of San Diego in 1998—recognition for her extensive contributions to multicultural scholarship.

Germine H. Awad, PhD, is an assistant professor in the Human Development and Culture Program in the Department of Educational Psychology at the University of Texas at Austin. Her research interests include prejudicial attitudes toward minorities and immigrants, ethnic identity, racial identity, acculturation (with a focus on Arab and African Americans), affirmative action attitudes, and multicultural research methodology. She teaches courses in research methodology, statistics, psychology of women, and psychology of race and racism.

Carolyn G. Barcus, who is a member of the Blackfeet Tribe of northern Montana, retired in September 2008 after 23 years as a faculty member in the Psychology Department at Utah State University. She continues to direct the American Indian Support Project, and to mentor and support ethnic minority graduate students in the psychology PhD programs, to teach part-time, and to carry on her private practice. She also plans to raise Mountain Walking horses, and to continue her ride to Canada.

Angela R. Bethea, PhD, is a psychologist at Georgia Regional Hospital/Atlanta (GRH/A). Prior to arriving at GRH/A in 2008, she completed a 3-year clinical and research postdoctoral fellowship in Clinical Health and Addictions Psychology at St. Luke's-Roosevelt Hospital Center, Columbia University College of Physicians and Surgeons, New York. Her research interests are in racial and cultural identity development among Black ethnic groups in the United States, smoking cessation among African American women, the treatment of substance use disorders among individuals with chronic medical illness, and the quality of substance abuse training in counseling psychology programs.

Denise H. Bike is currently a doctoral student in counseling psychology at the University of Missouri–Columbia. Her primary research interests are in the areas of multicultural counseling and well-being, specifically (a) the intersection of social class, race, gender, and health, and (b) psychotherapist and trainee development and self-care. She has published and presented research on psychotherapist self-care and multiculturalism.

Rosie Phillips Bingham is currently Vice President for Student Affairs and professor in the Department of Counseling, Educational Psychology and Research in the College of Education at the University of Memphis. Her primary practical and scholarly interests are in the power of inclusion, multicultural psychology, and ethics. She is actively involved in the American Psychological Association, where she is serving a term on the board of directors through 2011.

Alan W. Burkard is an associate professor of counseling psychology and director of the School Counseling program at Marquette University in Milwaukee, WI.

His primary teaching and research interests are in multicultural counseling and supervision, cultural relations in schools, and school counseling program evaluation and evidence-based practice.

John J. Cecero, a Jesuit priest and clinical psychologist, is an associate professor in the Department of Psychology at Fordham University. He is also Rector of the Jesuit Community and Director of the Center for Spirituality and Mental Health at Fordham. His primary teaching and research interests are in personality assessment and the role of spirituality in mental health. He published *Praying Through Lifetraps: A Psycho-Spiritual Approach to Freedom* (Resurrection Press, 2002).

Mark H. Chae is Associate Professor of Rehabilitation Counseling at the University of Medicine and Dentistry of New Jersey. He received his PhD in counseling psychology from Seton Hall University. His research interests include Asian racial and ethnic identity development, multicultural issues in counseling, and the psychology of men and masculinity. He serves on the editorial boards of *Journal of Counseling & Development, Journal of Multicultural Counseling and Development,* and *Counseling & Values Journal.* He is co-editor of the forthcoming book *Culturally Responsive Counseling With Asian American Men.*

Eric C. Chen is Associate Professor of Counseling Psychology in the Graduate School of Education at Fordham University. Born and raised in Taiwan, he received his PhD from Arizona State University. His research interests and publications have encompassed topics of clinical supervision, group counseling, multicultural counseling and social justice, and career choice and development of immigrant youth. He is an associate editor of *Group Dynamic: Theory, Research, and Practice.*

Brian Cho recently graduated (Class of 2008) from the University of California, Santa Barbara, with a major in psychology and a minor in education and applied psychology. Brian's primary reason for majoring in psychology was to increase his understanding of the sociocultural and psychological factors that affect the human condition. He hopes to use such understanding to help those individuals who tend to be ignored by our society.

SooJean Choi-Misailidis is a clinical psychologist. Her primary interests are in the areas of mixed-race identity, indigenous communities, culturally relevant interventions, and women's wellness. She is currently clinical assistant professor at the University of Hawai'i.

Kevin O. Cokley, PhD, is an Associate Professor of Counseling Psychology at the University of Texas at Austin. Dr. Cokley's research can be broadly categorized in the area of African American psychology, with specific research interests in the construction of racial and ethnic identities, and understanding the psychological factors that affect African American student achievement. He is the editor-in-chief of the *Journal of Black Psychology* and the recipient of the 2008 "10 Rising Stars of the Academy" award by Diverse Issues in Higher Education.

William R. Concepcion is a practitioner and affiliate faculty in the psychology department at the University of Hawai'i, Hilo campus. His clinical, teaching, and research interests include Asian/Pacific Islander American mental health, racial identity, acculturation, culturally sensitive training and supervision, working with immigrant populations, and observing the psychological impact of racism on people of color. He has also published articles and book chapters in these areas. He is a past Fellow of the APA Minority Fellowship Program.

Katherine D. Daly is currently a doctoral candidate in the Counseling Psychology program at the University of Florida and Director of Research Training and Intervention on the Behavioral Medicine Research Team. Her research interests include culturally sensitive health care, the intersection between physical and mental health and health promotion/prevention in health care.

Michael D'Andrea is a professor at the University of Hawaii and the Executive Director of the National Institute for Multicultural Competence. His scholarly work, which includes the publication of six books and more than 200 book chapters, journal articles, research publications, and other scholarly works, has affected the fields of counseling and psychology in many ways. Dr. D'Andrea is the 2009–2010 President of the Counselors for Social Justice association. He is nationally respected for his social justice advocacy in general and his efforts to eradicate racism in the United States in particular.

Thu A. Dang is currently a doctoral student in counseling psychology at Washington State University in Pullman, Washington. Her primary areas of interest include multicultural research and counseling, specifically the effects of racism and microaggressions and the counseling of minority Americans. She earned her master's degree in mental health counseling from Boston College in Chestnut Hill, Massachusetts.

Judy Daniels is a professor at the University of Hawaii and long-time social justice and peace advocate in the fields of counseling and psychology. Her scholarly accomplishments include the publication of three books and more than 75 book chapters, journal articles, research publications, and other professional works. She is the 2010–2011 President of the Counselors for Social Justice association and the recipient of numerous professional awards, including the American Counseling Association's (ACA) Fellow Award and the prestigious ACA Wrenn Award. Dr. Daniels is nationally respected for her efforts to eradicate various forms of racism in the United States.

Andrea L. Dixon is currently an Associate Professor of Counselor Education and coordinator of the School Counseling Program at the University of Florida. Her primary teaching and research interests are in the areas of multicultural counseling with racial/ethnic diverse individuals and American Indian concerns, adolescents, mattering and meaning making, school counseling, and school counselor education. She is the author of a number of articles and book chapters on topics regarding the concerns of racial/ethnic minority concerns.

Diane Dodge is currently Executive Director of Seven Tepees Youth Program, a nonprofit organization in San Francisco. She spearheaded the College Career Program collaboration between Seven Tepees, San Francisco State University Masters of Career Counseling, the San Francisco Unified School District, and the Morrison and Foerster Foundation that currently serves 1,000 high school students each year. Previously, she had founded the Y-Scholars Program, a collaboration between the Berkeley YMCA, the University California at Berkeley, and the Berkeley Unified School District that has graduated more than 500 first-generation college students in its first 8 years. She has served as a teacher and administrator in secondary schools for more than 17 years. Her primary interest is creating model programs across institutions that promote higher education, youth development, and cultural identity for minority students.

Eduardo Duran has been instrumental in developing and implementing clinics that are culturally responsive to Native American and Indigenous People. His work has focused on bringing Native theory and practice into the modern therapeutic practice arena. The work continues to evolve through the integration of traditional Native healing methods with Western practices. He presently works as a consultant and does private practice.

Lisa M. Edwards is an assistant professor in the Department of Counseling and Educational Psychology at Marquette University. Her current research focuses on strengths among racial and ethnic minorities in the United States, with an emphasis on the role of cultural resources on Latina/o adolescents' well-being. Dr. Edwards currently teaches graduate courses in multicultural counseling, assessment, and group counseling, and she is a licensed psychologist in the state of Wisconsin.

Judith M. Ettinger is a senior staff member at the Center on Education and Work at the University of Wisconsin–Madison. She has been working in the field of career development for the past 30+ years. Currently, she is an instructor and Master Trainer for the Global Career Development Facilitator Training program and has been involved in that program since its inception. She is also a trainer for the National Institute of Corrections and one of the co-authors of the National Career Development Guidelines.

Michelle Fine is Distinguished Professor of Psychology, Urban Education and Women's Studies at the Graduate Center and founding faculty for the Participatory Action Research Collective at the Graduate Center, City University of New York. She has written numerous books, articles, and chapters on social (in)justice, urban education, mass incarceration, critical youth engagement, and participatory action research methods.

Pamela F. Foley is an associate professor at Seton Hall University, serving both on the faculty of the counseling psychology PhD program and as director of the MA programs in counseling and school counseling. She teaches courses in statistics, counseling assessment, and vocational psychology. She is also a licensed psychologist, maintaining a practice with nursing home residents. Her research interests are in workplace and career issues, multicultural issues including religion, and the intersections between these areas.

Nadya A. Fouad, PhD, is a professor training director of the Counseling Psychology program at the University of Wisconsin–Milwaukee. She was the recipient in 2003 of the John Holland Award for Outstanding Achievement in Career and Personality Research. She is the editor of *The Counseling Psychologist.* She serves on the editorial boards of the *Journal of Vocational Behavior* and the *Journal of Career Assessment.* She has published articles and chapters on cross-cultural vocational assessment, career development of women and racial/ethnic minorities, and interest measurement.

Mary A. Fukuyama received her PhD from Washington State University in 1981 and has worked at the University of Florida Counseling Center for the past 27 years as a counseling psychologist, supervisor, and trainer. She is an active member of the University of Florida's Center for Spirituality and Health, and her research interests include a qualitative study on multicultural expressions of spirituality. She has published numerous articles and books related to multicultural counseling.

Enedina García-Vázquez is currently Associate Dean/Deputy Director of the Physical Science Laboratory. She is a professor of school psychology and is the chair of the National Association of School Psychologists Program Approval Board. She also serves on the executive council of the Trainers of School Psychologists and holds the editorship of its primary refereed publication, the *Trainers' Forum.* She is the author of a number of articles on academic issues, school violence, and acculturation.

Lawrence H. Gerstein is Professor, Director of the Doctoral Program in Counseling Psychology, and

Director of the Center for Peace and Conflict Studies at Ball State University. He is co-editor of the *Handbook for Social Justice in Counseling Psychology: Leadership, Vision, and Action* and the *International Handbook of Cross-Cultural Counseling: Cultural Assumptions and Practices Worldwide*. Dr. Gerstein is an American Psychological Association Fellow, Co-Editor of *The Counseling Psychologist* International Forum, and President of the International Tibet Independence Movement. He has published extensively on international and social justice issues.

Younnjung Gong is an assistant professor in the Department of Education at Gyungin National University of Education in South Korea. She received her doctorate in counseling psychology from Purdue University. Her primary teaching and research interests include career development and vocational behaviors, counseling ethics, counselor supervision, multicultural counseling, and mental health counseling. She is the author of a number of articles on topics related to career counseling, ethical issues, and multicultural issues.

Timothy Gordon, MS, is a doctoral candidate in the Department of Counseling Psychology and Guidance Services at Ball State University. His clinical and research interests include racial, ethnic, and sexual minority issues in therapy; working with sexual assault survivors; men's issues; substance abuse treatment; social justice issues; and the inclusion of mindfulness techniques in clinical practice. For his dissertation, Mr. Gordon is researching the potential relationship between client sexual orientation and gender role in regard to therapists' potentially heterosexist judgment errors and the extent to which therapist heterosexual identity development can predict the overall level of heterosexist judgment error displayed.

George V. Gushue, PhD, is Associate Professor of Psychology and Education in the Department of Counseling and Clinical Psychology at Teachers College, Columbia University. In addition to interests in group and family functioning, his research examines the role of social cognition in two areas of multicultural counseling psychology: clinical assessment and high school career development.

Rebecca Hansen, MA, is a doctoral candidate in the Department of Counseling Psychology and Guidance Services at Ball State University in Muncie, Indiana. Her research interests include a variety of multicultural topics such as international issues, acculturation, cross-cultural awareness and global-mindedness, LGBT issues, and social justice issues. She enjoys working with the college student population and will be completing her predoctoral internship at the University of Missouri–Columbia Counseling Center during the 2009–2010 academic year. She plans to continue working with the university population focusing on diversity issues upon completion of her doctoral program.

Jeni Hart is an associate professor of higher education in the Department of Educational Leadership and Policy Analysis at the University of Missouri. Her teaching interests focus on diversity issues in higher education, student affairs administration, and college teaching. Her research focuses on gender and feminism in academe and campus climate issues. She has authored articles and book chapters on topics related to faculty activism and on the experiences of underrepresented populations in higher education.

Charlayne C. Hayling is a doctoral candidate in counseling psychology at Lehigh University, where she received her master's degree in counseling and human services. She has a strong commitment to children and adolescents of color, with an emphasis on African American youth. Her research interests related to this population include the role of ecology in the outcomes of youth with emotional and behavioral concerns, the racial socialization of black youth, intervention and prevention development, and multicultural competence.

Keith C. Herman is currently Associate Professor in the Counseling Psychology Program at the University of Missouri–Columbia. Dr. Herman is also Co-Director of the Missouri Prevention Center, an organization developed to design, implement, and evaluate research interventions geared toward reducing the societal prevalence of youth depression and aggression. His research interests are in the areas of developmental psychopathology and school mental health, the prevention and treatment of childhood depression, and parenting and family interventions.

Jason R. Holmwood received his BA in psychology from Houghton College, an MS in education from Alfred University, and an MA in counseling from Seton Hall University. He is currently a counselor and faculty member at Middlesex County College in New Jersey, where he provides short-term personal counseling, crisis intervention, and disability services to students. He is interested in motivation, multicultural counseling, religion and spirituality, trauma, and veterans' adjustment to college.

Casey A. Holtz is a doctoral candidate in counseling psychology at Marquette University in Milwaukee, WI. His primary research and clinical interests are in behavior disorders in children and adolescents, parenting, school consultation, and the improvement of services for disadvantaged populations.

John Huang, PhD, is currently a staff psychologist at the VA Healthcare System in Long Beach, CA. His areas of clinical specialization include diversity issues, meditation/relaxation, and PTSD. His scholarly interests include diversity as well as Buddhism, Christianity, Hinduism, and Native American spirituality. He has published a number of articles in the area of diversity and mental health.

Allen E. Ivey is Distinguished University Professor (Emeritus), University of Massachusetts, Amherst, and Courtesy Professor, University of South Florida, Tampa. His areas of interest have included serving as a counseling center director, intensive study of the interview via microskills and video, multicultural studies (since 1966), the integrative developmental counseling and therapy, and current work on the implications of neuroscience for the helping process. He is the author or co-author of more than 40 books that have been translated into 20 languages.

Margo A. Jackson, PhD, is associate professor and past training director, Counseling Psychology, Division of Psychological and Educational Services, Graduate School of Education at Fordham University. She is currently President-Elect of the national Council of Counseling Psychology Training Programs. Her clinical, research, and teaching interests and publications are in multicultural career counseling and psychotherapy training and supervision, and her focus is on

examining methods to assess and constructively address hidden biases of counselors and educators.

Neeta Kantamneni, MS, is a doctoral student in the counseling psychology program in the Department of Educational Psychology at the University of Wisconsin–Milwaukee. She graduated from the University of Wisconsin–Madison with a master's degree in counseling. Her research interests include investigating the role of context in vocational development, Asian American career development, women's career development, and multicultural counseling and competencies.

Merle A. Keitel is currently Professor of Counseling Psychology at Fordham University's Graduate School of Education in New York City. Her primary teaching responsibilities are in the areas of individual counseling and psychotherapy, counseling theory and process, and professional ethics. She is the author of a book and numerous book chapters and articles on topics related to women's issues and health psychology and presents on these topics regularly at national professional conferences.

Taleb S. Khairallah is a doctoral student in counseling psychology at the University of Missouri. He is a Licensed Professional Counselor who has provided services to diverse populations in various clinical settings. He has been involved in community organizations, advocacy and lobbying, and training on multicultural issues. His primary teaching and research interests are in the areas of multicultural competencies and counseling, gender, substance abuse treatment and prevention, and diversity in higher education.

Doris Kirkpatrick, MA, is a doctoral student in the counseling psychology program at Ball State University. She is specializing in multicultural issues and peace psychology and has as a focus social justice applications of psychology. She is currently completing her predoctoral internship at Ball State University Student Counseling Center. Her clinical training focuses on multicultural counseling, women's issues, and feminist therapy.

Eric L. Kohatsu is an associate professor in the Department of Psychology at California State University, Los Angeles, and the director of the Center for

Cross-Cultural Research. His research and clinical interests are in racial identity; racism and prejudice; alternative healing approaches; cross-cultural counseling; cross-cultural research training; and Asian American, African American, and Latino mental health. He has published articles and book chapters in these areas. He is a past Fellow of the APA Minority Fellowship Program.

Kwong-Liem Karl Kwan is a faculty member in the Department of Counseling at San Francisco State University. He is involved in various aspects of counselor training and supervision. His scholarship focuses on assessment and identity development within multicultural environments. He is the co-editor of the International Forum of *The Counseling Psychologist* and serves on the editorial board of *Psychological Assessment* (USA), *Journal of Counseling Psychology* (USA), *Asian Journal of Counseling* (Hong Kong), and *Educational Psychology Bulletin* (Taiwan).

Christopher Larres is a graduate student in the EdM program in the Counseling Psychology Program at Rutgers University. He earned his BA in 2007 from the Psychology Honors Program at William Paterson University. His research interests include multicultural counseling, acculturation and ethnic identity, and vocational psychology. He has presented research at several conferences, including the Annual Teachers College Winter Roundtable on Cross-Cultural Psychology and the annual meeting of the American Psychological Association.

Robert W. Lent is a professor of counseling psychology in the Department of Counseling and Personnel Services, University of Maryland. His research interests include applications of social cognitive theory to academic and career behavior; counselor development, training, and supervision; and psychological health. He is co-editor of the *Handbook of Counseling Psychology* (1st through 4th editions) and *Career Development and Counseling: Putting Theory and Research to Work.*

Cesar A. Leon is currently a PhD candidate in the counseling psychology program at Fordham University's Graduate School of Education. His primary research, clinical, and professional interests focus on developing psychological resilience among culturally diverse individuals in underprivileged urban communities. He is the recipient of a doctoral fellowship from the American Psychological Association's Minority Fellowship Program, which recognized his dedication to advancing multicultural issues in psychology.

Heather Z. Lyons is currently an associate professor at Loyola College in Maryland. Her teaching interests include counseling theories and skills, organizational psychology, and multicultural psychology. She has published and presented research on culture and work adjustment, training issues in multicultural psychology, and qualitative research. She sits on the editorial boards of the *Journal of Counseling Psychology* and the *Journal of Black Psychology*. She is a licensed psychologist with a private practice in Towson, MD.

Soumya Madabhushi is currently a doctoral student of counseling psychology at the University of Nebraska–Lincoln. She is from India and has lived in the United States for 7 years. Her professional interests are in the areas of multicultural counseling and the various dynamics of violence and victimization. She ultimately hopes to work in the field of peace psychology and conduct research in the areas of war, peace, and building supportive communities.

Michael Maestas is Director of Counseling and Psychological Services at the University of Kansas and a licensed psychologist. He received his doctorate from the University of Nebraska–Lincoln. Along with campus mental health [ADD] and administration, his teaching and professional interests focus on psychopathology, clinical interviewing, and assessment in personality and intellectual and neuropsychological functioning. He has contributed scholarly articles in the areas of acculturation, ethnic identity, and assessment of U.S. non-White populations.

Geraldine Mapel is a doctoral student at New York University, where she investigates the relational factors integral to the process of meaning-making and personal growth following traumatic experience. In her clinical work with individuals in recovery from substance abuse disorders, at St. Luke's-Roosevelt Hospital, helping clients heal from histories of interpersonal trauma is often integral to the therapeutic treatment.

Merranda Marin is currently a clinical psychologist at the El Paso VA Health Care System in El Paso, TX, where she is the lead of the Post Traumatic Stress Disorder Clinical Team. She also teaches courses on an adjunct basis in the Department of Counseling and Educational Psychology at New Mexico State University. Primary research interests are in the areas of resilience, multicultural counseling, and evidence-based treatments for PTSD.

Michael J. Martinez is a doctoral student in counseling psychology at Marquette University in Milwaukee, WI. His primary research interests include multicultural issues in schools, student race relations, and bullying.

Laurie D. McCubbin is an associate professor in the Department of Educational Leadership and Counseling Psychology at Washington State University. Her research focuses on positive adaptation and well-being among indigenous peoples, cultural identity development and families, and multicultural counseling. She is the Past-Chair for the Section on Ethnic and Racial Diversity (SERD) for the Society of Counseling Psychology. She also serves as the Associate Director of the Stress, Coping and Resilience Project: Individuals, Families and Communities in collaboration with the University of Hawai'i at Manoa.

Brenda X. Mejía, MA, is a doctoral candidate in the counseling psychology program at Teachers College, Columbia University. Her research interests include acculturation, ethnic identity, career development, and multicultural counseling, particularly as these issues relate to Latino populations.

Matthew J. Miller, PhD, is an assistant professor in counseling psychology at the University of Maryland–College Park. He conducts research that examines the multiple ways in which race, ethnicity, and culture affect behavior across a number of life domains for Asian Americans. Dr. Miller is currently on the editorial board of the *Journal of Counseling Psychology* and is on the board of directors of the Asian American Psychological Association.

Marie L. Miville, PhD, is an Associate Professor of Psychology and Education at Teachers College, Columbia University. Professor Miville has published on multicultural topics, including Latina/o mental health, universal-diverse orientation, and the interrelations of diverse dimensions of identity. More recent work focuses on cross-cultural understandings of gender and gender roles and the development of an integrative training model based on diversity practice guidelines. She is a Fellow of the American Psychological Association.

Susan L. Morrow is currently Professor of Counseling Psychology in the Educational Psychology Department at the University of Utah. Her primary teaching and research interests lie in qualitative research methodology and the broad scope of social justice, specifically, issues of feminism, multicultural counseling, gender, sexual orientation, and race/ethnicity. She works to integrate her activism and scholarship with the goal of social change.

Vicky Ng is a doctoral candidate in counseling psychology at Fordham University and currently completing her APA Internship at the Fifth Avenue Center for Counseling and Psychotherapy. Prior to her internship, she was employed as a vocational rehabilitation counselor for the state of New York. Her primary research interests include multicultural counseling, disability issues, and career development theories. She has co-authored several articles and collaborated on presentations related to LGBT psychology, acculturation, and career theories.

Michael O'Heron, MA, is a doctoral candidate in the Department of Counseling Psychology and Guidance Services at Ball State University (BSU). His research interests include sexual minority issues in mental health; lesbian, gay, and bisexual (LGB) counseling competencies; sexual identity development; social justice issues; and clients' attitudes toward counseling services. For his dissertation, he is researching attitudinal and behavioral predictors of LGB-affirmative counseling self-efficacy beliefs. He was recently awarded a grant from the BSU Diversity Policy Institute for conducting LGB affirmative research in counseling psychology.

Rhoda Olkin, PhD, is a Distinguished Professor in clinical psychology at the California School of Professional Psychology at Alliant International University,

San Francisco, and the Executive Director of the Institute on Disability and Health Psychology at CSPP. She is the author of *What Psychotherapists Should Know About Disability* and the DVD "Disability-Affirmative Therapy: A Beginner's Guide."

Amado M. Padilla received his PhD in experimental psychology from the University of New Mexico. He is Professor and Chairman of the Program in Psychological Studies in Education at Stanford University. A Fellow of the American Psychological Association, he has published extensively on numerous topics, including psychological assessment, ethnic identity, acculturation, second-language learning, and resiliency of immigrant students. He is the founding editor of the *Hispanic Journal of Behavioral Sciences*.

Thomas A. Parham is Assistant Vice Chancellor for Counseling and Health Services at the University of California, Irvine. He is a Past President of the Association of Black Psychologists and the Association for Multicultural Counseling and Development. Among his many awards is his election to the title of Distinguished Psychologist by the Association of Black Psychologists in 1998; the APA Dalmus Taylor Award for Leadership, Scholarship, and Advising in 1999; the American Psychological Association Society of Counseling Psychology Award for Lifetime Achievement in Mentoring in 2007; and the James M. Jones Lifetime Achievement Award from The APA Minority Fellowship Program in 2008.

Yong S. Park is a doctoral candidate in the Counseling/Clinical/School Psychology Program at UC Santa Barbara. He is currently completing his predoctoral internship at UC San Diego's Counseling and Psychology Services. His clinical interests include Asian American mental health and family issues, career and vocational counseling, and cross-cultural communication. His theoretical orientation includes an integration of cognitive-behavioral, interpersonal, and client-centered approaches. He is also actively involved in the Student Division of the Asian American Psychological Association.

Jennie Park-Taylor is an assistant professor of counseling psychology in the Department of Psychological and Educational Services at Fordham University. Her

clinical training focused on providing mental health services to immigrant children and their families through traditional and collaborative community efforts, and thus she approaches clinical practice from a systemic perspective. Her research has focused on examining the acculturation and ethnic and national identity of immigrant and first-generation youth and young adults.

Jennifer Teramoto Pedrotti is an associate professor in the Department of Psychology and Child Development at California Polytechnic State University, San Luis Obispo. Her research focuses on the intersection of multicultural topics and positive constructs, such as well-being in multiracial individuals, and the positive impacts of multicultural courses on undergraduate and graduate students. She currently teaches courses in multicultural psychology, positive psychology, clinical and counseling psychology, and research methods.

Patricia Perez is currently a psychologist at the Seven Generations Child and Family Counseling Program of United American Indian Involvement, Inc. She works with the diverse American Indian community living throughout Los Angeles County. Her primary clinical and research interests are in multicultural counseling. She has co-authored several articles and chapters related to this topic, particularly pertaining to the Latino population. She is a past Fellow of the APA Minority Fellowship Program.

Alex L. Pieterse is an assistant professor in the Counseling Psychology program at the State University of New York at Albany. His research interests focus on psychological aspects of racism, self-awareness development, and the influence of race and culture in counselor training. He teaches courses on counseling skills and psychological assessment and is currently serving on the editorial boards of *Measurement and Evaluation in Counseling and Development* and the *Journal of Multicultural Counseling and Development*.

Vicki L. Plano Clark is Director of the Office of Qualitative and Mixed Methods Research and a Research Associate Professor in the Quantitative, Qualitative, and Psychometric Methods (QQPM) program at the University of Nebraska–Lincoln. She teaches research methods courses, including foundations of research, qualitative research, and mixed methods research. Her writings focus on methodological discussions about mixed methods research, as well as empirical studies using this approach, in the areas of counseling psychology, education, and family research.

Mark Pope is professor and chair of the Division of Counseling and Family Therapy at the University of Missouri–Saint Louis. He is past-president of the American Counseling Association, the National Career Development Association, and the Association for Lesbian, Gay, Bisexual, and Transgender Issues in Counseling; past-editor of *The Career Development Quarterly;* and a Master Career Counselor. He is also an elder of the Saint Francis River Band of Cherokees.

Tarrell Awe Agahe Portman is currently an associate professor of counselor education and the coordinator of the School Counseling and Counselor Education and Supervision Programs at the University of Iowa. She serves as the Director of the Office of Graduate Ethnic Inclusion (OGEI) in The Graduate College. Her primary teaching and research interests are in the areas of American Indian counseling issues, qualitative research development and design, and school counselor training and transition from theory to practice.

Gina Prendes-Lintel Furr is currently a doctoral student in counseling psychology at the University of Oregon, as well as the therapy and outreach graduate teaching fellow at the University Counseling and Testing Center. Her primary interests are in the areas of multiculturalism and social justice, immigrants and refugees, and trauma. She also volunteers clinical and research time at a local agency in Eugene, Oregon, dedicated to providing services to refugee survivors of torture.

Maria Prendes-Lintel has worked with refugees and immigrants in various capacities since 1977. She received her bachelor's and master's degrees in social work in 1977. She completed her doctorate in Counseling/Psychology at the University of Nebraska–Lincoln in 1996. Dr. Prendes-Lintel has presented internationally, nationally, regionally, and locally on working with multicultural populations, immigrants and refugee needs, the psychosocial/physiological impact of stress, working with interpreters, treatment of immigrant/refugee trauma and torture, depression,

and areas related to behavioral health and multicultural populations. She is the founder and Director of FIRST Project, Inc. (For Immigrants and Refugees Surviving Torture), which opened its doors in 2000. Dr. Prendes-Lintel is also the president of a private practice, The Wellness Center, P.C. A native of Cuba, Dr. Prendes-Lintel is one of 14,200 children who came to the United States as unaccompanied minors in the undercover operation called Pedro Pan.

Tina Q. Richardson is currently an associate professor and training director of the Counseling Psychology Program in the College of Education at Lehigh University, Bethlehem, PA. She directs an international university partnership program between Lehigh and the University of Liberia that promotes behavioral health, reconciliation, and recovery from war in Liberia. Dr. Richardson serves as a member of the board for Women's Ventures International, an organization for women's economic development in Ghana, and the Pennsylvania Regional Community Policing Institute. She also serves as Secretary for APA's Division 17: Society of Counseling Psychologists and editorial board member for *The Counseling Psychologist.* Additionally, she has been awarded a 2009–2010 American Council on Education Fellowship.

Lourdes M. Rivera is Assistant Professor of Counselor Education in the Department of Educational and Community Programs at Queens College of the City University of New York. Her research interests are in the area of multicultural counseling and career development, particularly as it relates to diverse populations. She teaches courses in counseling techniques, counseling theories, multicultural counseling, and career development. Her PhD in counseling psychology is from Fordham University at Lincoln Center.

Marlon Rollins is currently employed as the Coordinator of Counseling Services at the Indiana Academy, a residential high school for gifted and talented students. He is completing his doctorate in educational psychology with a cognate in counseling psychology at Ball State University. He is a Nationally Certified Counselor and Licensed Mental Health Counselor. He also received his ordination in ministry as an elder in the Church of God in Christ in 2000. Mr. Rollins is committed to developing programs that promote diversity and raise awareness about equity and equality through education and outreach.

Elizabeth Sellers, MA, is a doctoral candidate in the Department of Counseling Psychology and Guidance Services at Ball State University. Her research interests include Third Culture Kids, international adjustment issues, social justice issues, and college students. For her dissertation, Elizabeth is researching the experiences and issues of living in a different culture prior to age 18 and the subsequent experiences and issues of returning to the original culture.

Lewis Z. Schlosser, PhD, ABPP, is an Associate Professor at Seton Hall University, where he serves as a core faculty member and practicum coordinator for the counseling psychology PhD program. He teaches courses on psychological assessment, psychopathology, and religion and spirituality in counseling and psychotherapy. His research interests include student-faculty relationships and multicultural counseling. His work in the multicultural area focuses on American Jews, Christian privilege, and intergroup relations. He was the recipient of the 2008 Early Career Mentoring Award from Division 17's Section on Ethnic and Racial Diversity.

Daniel T. Sciarra, PhD, LCMHC, NCC, is Professor of Counselor Education at Hofstra University. Fluently bilingual in Spanish, he works with Latino children, adolescents, and families. In addition to numerous articles and book chapters on the subject of multicultural counseling, Dr. Sciarra is the author of three books, *Multiculturalism in Counseling* (Peacock, 1999), *School Counseling: Foundations and Contemporary Issues* (Brooks/Cole, 2004), and *Children and Adolescents With Emotional and Behavioral Disorders* (Allyn & Bacon, 2010). A former school counselor with the New York City Board of Education, he holds a doctorate in counseling psychology from Fordham University, a master's degree in counseling from Boston College, and a bachelor's degree in English education from Fairfield University. He is a licensed psychologist, licensed clinical mental health counselor (LCMHC), and a national certified counselor (NCC). His research interests include multicultural counseling, racial identity development, and the role of the school counselor

in the promotion of academic achievement and educational attainment among students of color.

Hung-Bin Sheu is currently Assistant Professor of Counseling/Counseling Psychology at Arizona State University. He received his PhD in counseling psychology from the University of Maryland in 2007. His research and teaching interests are in the areas of multicultural counseling and training as well as subjective well-being and career development of racial/ethnic minorities. He has published articles and delivered conference presentations on topics related to the above areas.

Ellen L. Short is currently an assistant professor at Long Island University in the Department of Human Development and Leadership, Counseling Programs. She received her MA in counseling psychology from Northwestern University and her PhD in counseling psychology from New York University. Her areas of specialization in teaching, scholarly research, and publishing are group dynamics focusing on race, ethnicity, gender, and culture; HIV substance abuse and high-risk behaviors among heterosexual populations (dissertation); and multicultural assessment of intelligence tests. She is co-author of *Racial and Cultural Dynamics in Group and Organizational Life: Crossing Boundaries* (Sage, 2010).

Timothy B. Smith is a Professor of Counseling Psychology at Brigham Young University in Provo, Utah. He is the recipient of APA Division 45's Emerging Professional Award and is the former editor of the *Journal of College Counseling*. His areas of research include multicultural psychology, spirituality/religion and well-being, and relational approaches to counseling. He engages in community service and has served as a Bishop in the Church of Jesus Christ of Latter-Day Saints.

Erin Snyder is currently a Staff Psychologist, Outreach Coordinator, and Sexual Assault Liaison at Texas Tech University Student Counseling Center. She received her doctorate in counseling psychology from Ball State University in 2008. She also holds a master's degree in counseling and a bachelor's degree in psychology and religious studies from Indiana University–Bloomington. Social justice continues to be a passion of hers, and she is eternally grateful for the training she received as a part of the Stop Hate campaign at Ball State University.

Jason R. Soble is a doctoral candidate in the Counseling Psychology program at the University of Illinois at Urbana-Champaign. He has conducted research that examines White university students' racial attitude change. His primary clinical interests are in the areas of multiculturally appropriate psychological testing and assessment, as well as the study and treatment of severe and persistent mental illness among veterans.

V. Scott Solberg, PhD, is currently Associate Director of Research and the Director of Wisconsin Careers within The Center for Education and Work at the University of Wisconsin–Madison. Dr. Solberg's published research focuses on career and workforce readiness and designing school curricula for supporting at-risk school populations. He is author of *Success Highways*, a resiliency skills program for helping at-risk middle and high school students develop 21st-century skills.

Lisa B. Spanierman is an associate professor in the Department of Educational Psychology and 2008–2009 Distinguished Scholar in the College of Education at the University of Illinois. Dr. Spanierman's research program focuses on the psychological investigation of Whiteness, and her recent publications on the psychosocial costs of racism to White individuals appear in the *Journal of Counseling Psychology, The Counseling Psychologist,* and *Cultural Diversity and Ethnic Minority Psychology.*

Ellyn Poltrock Stein received her BA in psychology from Cornell University and her PhD in counseling psychology from Seton Hall University. She completed her doctoral internship at the Veterans Affairs New Jersey Healthcare System and is currently completing a postdoctoral fellowship in palliative care at James J. Peters VA Medical Center, Bronx, NY. Her interests include health psychology, psycho-oncology, trauma, grief and bereavement, and religion and spirituality.

Richard M. Suinn is Emeritus Professor/Head, Psychology Department, Colorado State University, past president of the American Psychological Association, and past president of the Association of Behavioral and Cognitive Therapies. He has served as a team psychologist for Olympians and mayor of Ft. Collins, Colorado. He is internationally known for books and articles on behavior therapy, stress management, ethnic minority issues, and sport psychology, including *Anxiety Management Training,* Suinn-Lew Asian Self-Identity Acculturation scale (SL-ASIA), and Mathematics Anxiety Rating Scale.

Erica Tennenbaum is currently treating clients at a private practice in New York City. She treats adults with a range of psychological illnesses. Dr. Tennenbaum specializes in clients with HIV/AIDS, issues of infertility, and/or trauma, as well as Dialectical Behavioral Therapy (DBT). Her primary research interests are in the areas of women's health, infertility, and multicultural counseling.

Rebecca L. Toporek is an associate professor in the Department of Counseling at San Francisco State University. Her interests include social justice advocacy, multicultural training, systemic interventions in discrimination, and career and college counseling. She was a coeditor for the *Handbook for Social Justice in Counseling Psychology; Handbook of Multicultural Competencies; ACA Advocacy Competencies: A Social Justice Framework for Counselors;* and, currently, the *Journal for Social Action in Counseling and Psychology.* She is involved in community partnerships in San Francisco and New Orleans.

Joseph E. Trimble is a Distinguished University Professor and Professor of Psychology at Western Washington University. He has generated more than 130 publications on cross-cultural and ethnic topics in psychology, including 17 books. He has received numerous excellence in teaching and research awards for his work in the field of ethnic and cultural psychology, including the Janet E. Helms Award for Mentoring and Scholarship in Professional Psychology from Teachers College, Columbia University; the Distinguished Elder Award from the National Multicultural Conference and Summit; and the Henry Tomes Award for Distinguished Contributions to the Advancement of Ethnic Minority Psychology; and the Distinguished International Lifetime Achievement Award from the University of Toronto's Ontario Institute for Studies in Education.

Felicia Tripp recently graduated from the master's degree counseling program at San Francisco State University. Her areas of specialization are college and career counseling, and her research interests are in the areas of multicultural counseling, education, and training. This is her first published article on multicultural counseling practice and research.

Carolyn M. Tucker is currently a Professor of Psychology, Professor of Community Health and Family Medicine, and a Research Foundation Professor at the University of Florida. She was recently appointed as the Richard and Thelma O. C. Barney Term Professor of Health Disparities in the College of Medicine. Dr. Tucker's passion is conducting community participatory research aimed at developing and testing "customized" culturally sensitive health care and health promotion assessments and interventions for use in modifying and reducing obesity and related physical and mental problems among racial/ethnic minority and low-income families.

Melba J. T. Vasquez, PhD, is in independent practice in Austin, Texas. She is co-author, with Ken Pope, of *Ethics in Psychotherapy & Counseling: A Practical Guide*. She served as a member of the APA Board of Directors, and as president of the Texas Psychological Association, of APA Divisions 35 (Society of Psychology of Women) and 17 (Society of Counseling Psychology). She is a Fellow of the APA and a Diplomate of the American Board of Professional Psychology.

Luis A. Vázquez is Associate Dean of the Graduate School and Endowed Chair at New Mexico State University. He is a professor of counseling psychology and Chair-elect of the Board for the Advancement of Psychology in the Public Interest. Dr. Vázquez is a consultant and diversity trainer for KMA working with Fortune 500 companies. He is the author of a number of articles and chapters related to multicultural issues, training videos, curriculum development, and acculturation.

Allison B. Ventura is a doctoral candidate in counseling psychology in the Department of Psychological and Educational Services at Fordham University. She earned her MEd and EdS degrees in school counseling from the University of Florida. Her doctoral research has focused on investigating the psychosocial concerns of immigrants and of multiethnic youth living in urban areas. Her dissertation will examine academic barriers and supports perceived by urban Hispanic middle school youth.

Sherry C. Wang is a doctoral student in the counseling psychology program at the University of Nebraska–Lincoln. Her research and clinical interests focus on immigrant and refugee mental health and the barriers to help-seeking attitudes and behaviors. Her interest in research design stems from her goal to develop culturally sensitive research methodologies for working with diverse cultural groups.

Joseph L. White is currently Professor Emeritus of Psychology and Psychiatry at the University of California, Irvine. Dr. White received his PhD in clinical psychology from Michigan State University in 1961 and is the author of several papers and five books. In addition to his teaching and research, Dr. White has been a practicing psychologist and consultant. He has served as a supervising psychologist and staff affiliate psychologist to five hospitals and three clinical practices in southern California. He has worked as a consultant with school districts, universities, private organizations, drug prevention programs, and government agencies. Dr. White was appointed to the California State Psychology Licensing Board by Governor Edmund G. Brown, Jr., and served as chairman for 3 years. He is currently a member of the Board of Trustees of The Menninger Foundation in Houston, Texas.

Claudette Williamson-Taylor is currently a doctoral candidate in counseling psychology at Lehigh University in Bethlehem, PA. Her primary interests are cultural influences on identity development and health outcomes, women's issues, and grief and loss. Her clinical and work experiences include interagency collaboration, mental health presentations, and crisis intervention. She has a wealth of experience conducting research and impact evaluations on youth and families in nonprofit organizations and academic institutions.

Leo Wilton, PhD, is an associate professor in the Departments of Human Development and Africana Studies at the State University of New York at

Binghamton. Dr. Wilton specializes in the areas of health disparities (HIV and AIDS), community-based research and evaluation, and Black psychological development and mental health. His scholarly research on the AIDS epidemic focuses on the intersectionality of race, gender, sexuality, and social class, particularly as related to the experiences of Black gay and bisexual men. Dr. Wilton is a lifetime member of the Association of Black Psychologists.

Roger L. Worthington is the Assistant Deputy Chancellor and Chief Diversity Officer at the University of Missouri, where he is also professor in the Department of Educational, School and Counseling Psychology. He has served on the editorial boards of *The Counseling Psychologist*, the *Journal of Counseling Psychology*, and the *Journal of Diversity in Higher Education*. His research interests include diversity issues in higher education; multicultural psychology; sexual identity; lesbian, gay, and bisexual issues; and scale development.

Gloria Wong was deeply moved by a powerful key note speech given by Dr. Rosie Bingham in 2007 about the importance of counselors and research alike addressing the experiences of people of color. Currently, Gloria is in a PhD program at UC Davis working with Stanley Sue and Nolan Zane on Asian American disparities research. She is interested in examining the Asian American experience, specifically the effects of racial and cultural images regarding Asian American perceived sexuality.

Christine J. Yeh is Professor of Counseling Psychology at the University of San Francisco. Her primary research interests are in the areas of immigrant cultural adjustment, cultural identities, indigenous healing, and school and community-based interventions for ethnic minority youth. She is the co-editor of the *Handbook of School Counseling* and is the author of several articles on topics related to Asian American and Asian immigrant cultural identity, values, mental health, and coping.

Mira Zaharopoulos is currently a doctoral student in counseling psychology at Fordham University's Graduate School of Education in New York City. She received her BA in psychology and English from the University of California, Los Angeles. Her present research interests are in the areas of empathy, the therapeutic relationship, multicultural counseling, and career development, and she is an adjunct career counselor at Kingsborough Community College.

Noreen K. Zaman received her PhD in Counseling Psychology from New York University. She completed her internship at the University of California, Berkeley and post-doctoral training at the University of Pittsburgh. She is the 2007 recipient of the Diversity Dissertation Scholarship from the American Psychological Association for her research on discrimination, psychological distress, and identity in Muslim Americans post-9/11. Her professional interests include university mental health, diversity training, South Asian and Muslim American mental health, and intersecting identities.

Stefanía Ægisdóttir is a native of Iceland and Associate Professor in the Department of Counseling Psychology and Guidance Services at Ball State University. Her primary teaching interests are research methodology, assessment, program development and evaluation, and clinical training. She has written about cross-cultural research methods, attitudes and expectations about counseling, clinical judgment, and international and cross-cultural issues in counseling research and training. She is a co-editor of the *International Handbook of Cross-Cultural Counseling: Cultural Assumptions and Practices Worldwide*.

Supporting researchers for more than 40 years

Research methods have always been at the core of SAGE's publishing program. Founder Sara Miller McCune published SAGE's first methods book, *Public Policy Evaluation*, in 1970. Soon after, she launched the *Quantitative Applications in the Social Sciences* series—affectionately known as the "little green books."

Always at the forefront of developing and supporting new approaches in methods, SAGE published early groundbreaking texts and journals in the fields of qualitative methods and evaluation.

Today, more than 40 years and two million little green books later, SAGE continues to push the boundaries with a growing list of more than 1,200 research methods books, journals, and reference works across the social, behavioral, and health sciences. Its imprints—Pine Forge Press, home of innovative textbooks in sociology, and Corwin, publisher of PreK–12 resources for teachers and administrators—broaden SAGE's range of offerings in methods. SAGE further extended its impact in 2008 when it acquired CQ Press and its best-selling and highly respected political science research methods list.

From qualitative, quantitative, and mixed methods to evaluation, SAGE is the essential resource for academics and practitioners looking for the latest methods by leading scholars.

For more information, visit **www.sagepub.com**.